The European Heritage in Economics and the Social Sciences

Series Editor:
Jürgen Georg Backhaus

For further volumes:
http://www.springer.com/series/5902

Editor
Prof. Dr. Jürgen Georg Backhaus
University of Erfurt
Krupp Chair in Public Finance and Fiscal Sociology
Nordhäuser Str. 63
99089 Erfurt Thüringen
Germany
juergen.backhaus@uni-erfurt.de

ISBN 978-1-4419-8335-0   e-ISBN 978-1-4419-8336-7
DOI 10.1007/978-1-4419-8336-7
Springer New York Dordrecht Heidelberg London

Library of Congress Control Number: 2011934677

Printed on acid-free paper

Springer is part of Springer Science+Business Media (www.springer.com)

Preface

Avant Propos

A further reason for studying the history of economic thought was provided by Pareto in the lead article of the "Giornale di Economisti" of 1918 (Volume 28; pages 1–18) under the title "Experimental Economics".[1] In as much as economic theories also have an extrinsic value, that is, they lead people to act as informed by the theory, such as in economic policy or public finance, the theory becomes a subject for economic investigation itself. The distinction between the intrinsic aspect and the extrinsic aspect of a theory is crucial for this argument. The intrinsic aspect of a theory refers to its logical consistence and, as such, has no further repercussions. As far as the intrinsic aspects are concerned, theoretical knowledge is actually cumulative. On the other hand, the extrinsic aspect of an economic theory will become a "derivation" (in Pareto's terminology) in that it serves as the rationalization of human activity. In Pareto's sociology, human action is determined by residues, innate traits that determine human behaviour, and derivations. Derivations are more or less logical theories or world views that guide people's behaviour. To the extent that economic theory can also guide human behaviour, economic theory becomes a social fact or construct that is itself subject to economic analysis. As we experiment with different economic theories to guide economic policy in general and fiscal policy in particular, the history of economic thought can actually be practised as experimental economics in documenting the impact different economic theories have on economic behaviour. Of course, this experimental kind of history of economic thought becomes the more relevant the more similar the situations are in which different economic theories are applied.

---

[1]The following account is based on Michael McLure, The Paretian School and Italian Fiscal Sociology. London, Palgrave 2007.

Contents

Contributors

Jürgen G. Backhaus University of Erfurt, Nordhäuser Street 63 99089, Erfurt, Germany
juergen.backhaus@uni-erfurt.de

Christos P. Baloglou Hellenic Telecommunications Organization, S.A. Messenias 14 & Gr. Lamprakis, 143 42 Nea Philadelphia, S.A. Athens, Greece
cbaloglou@ote.gr

Earl Beach Charles Beach, Department of Economics, John Deutsch Institute, Kingston, ON, Canada
beachc@qed.econ.queensu.ca

Royall Brandis University of Illinois at Urbana, Champaign, IL, USA

Lluis Argemí d'Abadal University of Barcelona, Diagonal, 690, 08034, Barcelona, Spain
argemi@eco.ub.es

Jan van Daal Triangle, University of Lyon-2,
Lyon, France
jan.van.daal@orange.fr

Hans Frambach Department of Economics, Schumpeter School of Business & Economics, University of Wuppertal, Gaußstraße 20, 42097 Wuppertal, Germany
frambach@wiwi.uni-wuppertal.de

Reginald Hansen Luxemburger Straße 426, 50937 Cologne, Germany

Arnold Heertje Laegieskampweg 17, 1412 ER, Naarden, The Netherlands
joab@simplex.nl

J.A. Hans Maks Euroregional Centre of Economics (Eurocom), Maastricht University, Maastricht, The Netherlands
h.maks@algec.unimaas.nl

Gerrit Meijer Department of Economics, Maastricht University, Larixlaan 3,
1231 BL Loosdrecht, The Netherlands
g.meijer@hetnet.nl

Karl Milford Department of Economics, University of Vienna,
Vienna, Austria
karl.milford@univie.ac.at

Michael R. Montgomery, PhD School of Economics, University of Maine,
5774 Stevens Hall, Orono, ME 04469, USA
michael.montgomery@umit.maine.edu

Elke Muchlinski Institute of Economic Policy and Economic History,
Freie Universität Berlin, Boltzmannstraße 20, 14195 Berlin, Germany
elke.muchlinski@fu-berlin.de

Helge Peukert Faculty of the Sciences of the State/Economics,
Law and Social Science, Nordhäuser Str. 63, 99089 Erfurt, Germany
helge.peukert@uni-erfurt.de

Karl-Heinz Schmidt Department of Economics, University Paderborn,
Warburger Street. 100, 33098 Paderborn, Germany
karl_schmidt@notes.uni-paderborn.de

Peter R. Senn 1121 Hinman Avenue, Evanston, IL 60202, USA

Yuichi Shionoya Hitotsubashi University, Kunitachi,
Tokyo 186-8601, Japan,
y.shionoya@blue.ocn.ne.jp

Andrew S. Skinner Adam Smith Professor Emeritus in the University
of Glasgow's Department of Political Economy, Glen House, Cardross,
Dunbartonshire G82 5ES, UK
a.s.skinner@socsci.gla.ac.uk

Hans-Joachim Stadermann Berlin School of Economics and Law,
Hochschule für Wirtschaft und Recht Berlin, Badensche Straße 50–51,
10825 Berlin, Germany
stadermann@aol.com

Otto Steiger Institut für Konjunktur- und Strukturforschung (IKSF),
FB 7 – Wirtschaftswissenschaften, Universität Bremen, Postfach 33 04 40,
28334 Bremen, Germany
osteiger@uni-bremen.de

Richard E. Wagner Department of Economics, George Mason University,
Fairfax, VA 22030, USA
rwagner@gmu.edu

Chapter 1
Introduction

Jürgen G. Backhaus

History of Economic Thought, what for? Joseph Schumpeter has noted: "Older authors and older views acquire ... an importance ... [when] the methods of the economic research worker are undergoing a revolutionary change."[1] In a time of economic crisis, a reflection of the roots of economic theory and methods prevents us from following the wrong path. Leland Yeager has outlined the responsibility of the historian of economic thought as follows:

"It is probably more true of economics than of the natural sciences that earlier discoveries are in danger of being forgotten; maintaining a cumulative growth of knowledge is more difficult. In the natural sciences, discoveries get embodied not only into further advances in pure knowledge but also into technology, many of whose users have a profit and loss incentive to get things straight. The practitioners of economic technology are largely politicians and political appointees with rather different incentives. In economics, consequently, we need scholars who specialize in keeping us aware and able to recognize earlier contributions – and earlier fallacies – when they surface as supposedly new ideas. By exerting a needed discipline, specialists in the history of thought can contribute to the cumulative character of economics."[2]

The Austrian process of time-consuming roundabout production, where the results get better over time, is hopefully true with respect to this book. The book grew out of lectures started on behalf of the graduate students at Maastricht University,[3] where I taught until the fall of the year 2000. The work has an encyclopedic

---

[1] Joseph A. Schumpeter, "Some Questions of Principle," unpublished introduction to his *History of Economic Analysis*, 1948/1949, p. 4 (I owe this reference to Professor Loring Allen, who found this manuscript in Schumpeter's estate at Harvard University.).

[2] Leland Yeager (1981), "Clark Warburton 1896–1979." *History of Political Economy* 13 (2), pp. 279–284, p. 283.

[3] dr. Peter Berends, still of Maastricht University, was my trusted partner in this.

J.G. Backhaus (✉)
University of Erfurt, Faculty of the Sciences of State, Nordhäuser Street 63 99089,
Erfurt, Germany
e-mail: juergen.backhaus@uni-erfurt.de

J.G. Backhaus (ed.), *Handbook of the History of Economic Thought*,
The European Heritage in Economics and the Social Sciences,
DOI 10.1007/978-1-4419-8336-7_1, © Springer Science+Business Media, LLC 2012

character which is why we completed the lectures at Erfurt University, where I have been since then.

In principle, there are at least four ways to answer the question "History of Economic Thought – what for?" One may first speculate about possible uses and purposes of the history of economic thought as revealed in the practice of teaching the subject matter; employ methods of literary interpretation in surveying earlier attempts along similar lines in order to amicably urge others to follow the guidelines of a program thus derived. This is the approach characteristic of the largest part of the substantial body of literature discussing the purposes of doctrinal history.

Second, we can consult the published record and determine what difference the use of historical analysis makes in published research. This will yield but a distorted picture. In many European universities, the emphasis on publishing research is much slighter than in their North American counterparts. Scholars like the late Piero Sraffa often command respect primarily for their contributions to the oral tradition. While the oral tradition has always remained important,[4] publishing research has become more important in European academe over the last few years, but was almost accidental before.[5]

Third, one could analyze survey data. While the problems associated with this method are generally recognized, this often proves to be the only feasible method.

Fourth, an analysis of the course titles of the history of economic thought classes taught will reveal a great deal about their contents. While in America, course titles tend to be standardized and are unlikely to vary with the instructor who happens to teach the course, this is most likely not so in the German, Austrian, and Swiss university. The curriculum guidelines tend to be more general, and each chair is generally responsible for the development of an area of research and instruction in a particular subdiscipline of economics. Hence, the course titles (and contents) are the work of the professor who offers the course and who tries to announce precisely what the course is going to be about.

The literature analysis revealed the following purposes commonly claimed for the history of economic thought instruction.[6] Table 1.1 lists purposes, an exemplary bibliographical source, and a category to which the purpose has been assigned in order to make the empirical task more manageable.

It should be obvious that this list of purposes, as long as it is, cannot possibly be said to be fully complete. There may be as many different purposes as there are

---

[4]Compare, e.g., Wilhelm Röpke's discussion in: "Trends in German Business Cycle Policy," *Economic Journal*, vol. XLIII, no. 171, (1933), pp. 427–441.

[5]The notion of "publish or perish" is still not descriptive of life in most European universities. Publication may often be prompted by a particular festive occasion, as when a colleague is to be honored with a *Festschrift*.

[6]These results (slightly updated) are based on and excerpted from Jürgen Backhaus, "Theoriegeschichte – wozu?: Eine theoretische und empirische Untersuchung." *Studien zur Entwicklung der ökonomischen Theorie* III, H. Scherf, ed. Berlin: Duncker & Humblot 1983 (Schriften des Vereins für Socialpolitik, N.V. 115 III). Compare also Jürgen Backhaus (1986): "History of Economic Thought – What For? Empirical Observations from German Universities," *The History of Economics Society Bulletin*, VII/2, pp. 60–66.

Table 1.1 Purposes

To learn		
The intellectual heritage and a critical posture in dealing with texts	Samuels (1974)	Introductory course
Principles of economics	Breit and Ransom (1982)	Principles
From the classical works that have withstood the test of time	Stigler (1969)	Advanced undergraduate
From the masters	Walker (1983)	Advanced
Economics as a history of economists	Recktenwald (1965)	Introduction
To receive new insights for current research	Schumpeter (1954)	Graduate research
To understand the "filiation of ideas," what succeeds, and how, and why	Schumpeter (1954)	Graduate research
Guidance when the science undergoes revolutionary change	Schumpeter (1948/1949)	Graduate research
Epistemological argument	Schumpeter (1954)	Research
Study of the competition of ideas	Stigler and Friedland (1979)	Research
Over time		
Across cultures		
Between schools		
Concerning cyclical developments	Neumark (1975)	Research
With respect to different factor markets	Perlman and McCann (2000)	Research
Preserving the stock of economic knowledge	Yeager (1981)	Research

historians of economic thought, and likely even more, since some resourceful writers such as Schumpeter (1954) managed to give several good reasons, without adhering to any one of them, while pursuing still different purposes. In order to reduce this complexity, in our empirical study[7] groups or categories of purposes have been formed, which in turn we tried to identify by appropriately grouping the course titles. The result of this effort is shown in the following table. It shows how many courses could be attributed to each category of purpose. In interpreting this result, one should note that in general only advanced students will be enrolled in courses studying special problems or subdisciplines of economics (Table 1.2).

It is probably not an overstatement to say that historians of economic thought have many different purposes in mind when they teach the subject.

It came as a great surprise when we learned that the extent of instruction in the history of economic thought of post WWII German universities is impressive

---

[7] Compare Backhaus, *op. cit.*, (1983). The purposes for offering courses in the history of economic thought at German, several Swiss and Austrian Universities have empirically been identified for the post WWII period until March 1980. Such a long time span was possible by making our survey comparable to an earlier study undertaken before the university reforms in 1960. Compare Bruno Schultz (1960), "Die Geschichte der Volkswirtschaftslehre im Lehrbetrieb deutscher Universitäten und einiges zur Problematik." In: Otto Stammer, Karl C. Thalheim (eds.), *Festgabe für Friedrich Bülow zum 70. Geburtstag.* Duncker & Humblot, pp. 343–362.

Table 1.2 Purposes and course titles

Category	Number of courses
General	191
Periods in the history of thought	72
The history of thought of subdisciplines	57
Focus on particular economists	31
Special problems	17
Other	8

Table 1.3 Ranking of economists

In German course titles	In Anglo-American journals
Marx	Smith
Schumpeter	Keynes
List	Ricardo
Smith	Malthus
Keynes	Marshall
Müller	Walras
Fichte, Petty, Ricardo	Knight, Veblen
	Fisher
	Schumpeter, Cournot, Quesnay
	Wicksell, J. B. Clark
	Pareto

and largely underestimated. Of the 54 universities surveyed, 27 offer instruction in the history of economics, while 13 do not. It is likely that of the remaining quarter, or 14 universities, more are involved in instruction in the subject than that are not.

These data even correct the earlier study by Schultz (1960). The reason for the differences is straightforward. Schulz had only consulted the university bulletins, while we had co-operated with each university on a case-by-case basis and therefore had received information not contained in the bulletins. This method yielded a substantial correspondence which proved helpful in assigning the courses to categories. The correspondence revealed more information about the purposes of the lectures than can be mentioned in this introduction.

It is interesting to note some cultural differences[8] between our survey results and Anglo-American findings. Apart from the obvious differences in the organization of courses, which turn on the chair system, cultural differences show up most pointedly when the course emphasis is on major figures in the history of economic thought. Table 1.3 shows a ranking of economists most often mentioned in course

---

[8] Werner W. Pommerehne, Friedrich Schneider, Guy Gilbert and Bruno S. Frey (1984), "Concordia discors: Or: What do economists think?" *Theory and Decision* 16.3, pp. 251–308. This cultural difference also shows up in the difference between the German and the English edition of Recktenwald's collection of biographical essays of major economists.

Table 1.4 Rankings of second research area

General economic theory	131
Economic history	45
Economic systems	33
General economics	31
Domestic monetary theory, etc.	13
Economic growth, etc.	10
Industrial organization, etc.	9
Economic education	6
Domestic fiscal policy, public finance	6
Not available	6

titles and, for purposes of comparison, a ranking drawn from a publications analysis undertaken by Stigler and Friedland (1979) and de Marchi and Lodewijks (1983).

In the period under consideration, the first place in German course titles takes Marx.[9] He does not figure in de Marchi and Lodewijk's (1983) study, since they consider Marx and Marxism as a subject area. If the numbers attributed to this subject area were attributed to the man, he would rank first in the American sample, too. Rudolph (1984), in the preface to his important study on Rodbertus,[10] lists the following reasons that justify research in the history of thought from a Marxist point of view: (1) to counter attempts at falsifying the historical record, undertaken by the enemies of progress (p. 7); (2) to uncover, preserve, and continue the progressive elements in our intellectual heritage (p. 7); (3) to make a contribution to the proto-history of sources and elements which Marx and Engels used for their revolutionary doctrine of scientific socialism (p. 9); and (4) Marxist social theory has reached a level of modernity and differentiation which requires new studies using refined methods of historical research (p. 11), for instance, the use of "the high art of citation" in which "Marx was a master." (p. 13)

As I have mentioned earlier, this study cannot be duplicated for the United States. However, it is readily apparent that research in the history of economic thought is undertaken by American and European scholars alike for reasons other than *l'art pour l'art*. This shows up when we look at the combination of research areas most often noted by historians of economic thought according to the AEA Handbook (1981). If the marginal products of research in the history of thought were invariant with the variation of secondary research areas, a stochastic distribution should be expected. Our count, however, is shown in Table 1.4.

Again, this result is only indicative of some interesting patterns along which historical research of economics proceeds. The selection of authors made in this book is complete as far as the Anglo-American approach is concerned, but adds the continental European perspective.

---

[9] East German universities were excluded from the survey.

[10] Rudolph, Günther (1984), "*Karl Rodbertus (1805–1875) und die Grundrententheorie: Politische Ökonomie aus dem deutschen Vormärz.*" Berlin: Akademie (Akademie der Wissenschaften der DDR – Schriften des Zentralinstitutes für Wirtschaftswissenschaften Nr. 21).

References

Backhaus J (1983) "Theoriegeschichte – wozu? Eine theoretische und empirische Untersuchung." *Studien zur Entwicklung der ökonomischen Theorie* III, H. Scherf, ed. Berlin: Duncker & Humblot (Schriften des Vereins für Socialpolitik, N.V. 115 III)

Backhaus J (1986) History of economic thought – what for? Empirical observations from German Universities. Hist Econ Soc Bull VII/2:60–66

Breit W, Ransom R (1982) The academic scribblers. The Dryden Press, Chicago

de Marchi N and Lodewijks J (1983) HOPE and the Journal Literature in the History of Economic Thought. Hist Polit Econ 15(3):321–343

Neumark F (1975) Zyklen in der Geschichte ökonomischer Ideen. Kyklos 29(2):257–258

Perlman M, McCann C (2000) The pillars of economic understanding: factors and markets. The University of Michigan Press, Ann Arbor

Pommerehne WW, Schneider F, Gilbert G, Frey BS (1984) Concordia discors or: what do economists think? Theory Decis 16(3):251–308

Recktenwald HC (1965) Lebensbilder großer Nationalökonomen. Kiepenheuer & Witsch, Köln

Röpke W (1933) Trends in German business cycle policy. Econ J XLIII/171:427–441

Rudolph G (1984) Karl Rodbertus (1805–1875) und die Grundrententheorie: Politische Ökonomie aus dem deutschen Vormärz. Akademie, Berlin (Akademie der Wissenschaften der DDR – Schriften des Zentralinstitutes für Wirtschaftswissenschaften Nr. 21)

Samuels W (1974) History of economic thought as intellectual history. Hist Polit Econ 6:305–322

Schultz B (1960) Die Geschichte der Volkswirtschaftslehre im Lehrbetrieb deutscher Universitäten und einiges zur Problematik. In: Stammer O, Thalheim KC (eds) Festgabe für Friedrich Bülow zum 70. Duncker & Humblot, Geburtstag, pp 343–362

Schumpeter JA (1948/1949) Some questions of principle. Unpublished introduction to his History of Economic Analysis

Schumpeter JA (1954) History of economic analysis. Oxford University Press, New York

Stigler G (1969) Does economics have a useful past? Hist Polit Econ 1(2):217–230

Stigler G (1979) Does economics have a useful past? Hist Polit Econ 1(2):217–230

Stigler G, Friedland C (1979) The pattern of citation practices in economics. Hist Polit Econ II(1):1–20

Walker D (1983) Biography and the study of the history of economic thought. Res Hist Econ Thought Methodol 1:41–59

Yeager L (1981) Clark Warburton 1896–1979. Hist Polit Econ 13(2):279–284

Chapter 2
The Tradition of Economic Thought in the Mediterranean World from the Ancient Classical Times Through the Hellenistic Times Until the Byzantine Times and Arab-Islamic World

Christos P. Baloglou

Cicero

Xenophon

C.P. Baloglou (✉)
Hellenic Telecommunications Organization,
S.A. Messenias 14 & Gr. Lamprakis, 143 42 Nea Philadelphia, Athens, Greece
e-mail: cbaloglou@ote.gr

J.G. Backhaus (ed.), *Handbook of the History of Economic Thought*,
The European Heritage in Economics and the Social Sciences,
DOI 10.1007/978-1-4419-8336-7_2, © Springer Science+Business Media, LLC 2012

Aristotle

Socrates

Introduction

Since modern economics is generally considered to have begun with the publication of Adam Smith's *An Inquiry into the Nature and Causes of the Wealth of Nations* in 1776, a survey and investigation of pre-Smithian economic thought requires some justification. Such an effort must offer both historical and methodological support for its contribution to the study of the history of modern economics.

Most of the histories of economics that give attention to the pre-Smithian background ignore the economic thought of Hellenistic and Byzantine Times, as well as Islamic economic ideas, although the Mediterranean crucible was the parent of the Renaissance, while Muslim learning in the Spanish universities was a major source of light for non-Mediterranean Europe. Another motivation, and a bit more fundamental, has to do with the "gap" in the evolution of economic thought alleged by Joseph Schumpeter (1883–1950) in his classic, *History of Economic Analysis* (1954): "The Eastern Empire survived the Western for another 1,000 years, kept going by the most interesting and most successful bureaucracy the world has ever seen. Many of the men who shaped policies in the offices of the Byzantine emperors were of the intellectual cream of their times. They dealt with a host of legal, monetary, commercial, agrarian and fiscal problems. We cannot help feeling that they must have philosophized about them. If they did, however, the results have been lost.

No piece of reasoning that would have to be mentioned here has been preserved. So far as our subject is concerned we may safely leap over 500 years to the epoch of St. Thomas Aquinas (1225–1274), whose *Summa Theologica* is in the history of thought what the southwestern spire of the Cathedral of Chartres is in the history of architecture."[1] Schumpeter classified several pre-Latin-European scholastic centuries as "blank," suggesting that nothing of relevance to economics, or for that matter to any other intellectual endeavor, was said or written anywhere else. Such a claim of "discontinuity" is patently untenable. A substantial body of contemporary social thought, including economics, is traceable to Hellenistic, Arab-Islamic, and Byzantine "giants."

Our purpose of this essay is to explore and present the continuity of the economic thought in the Mediterranean World from the Classical Times until the Byzantine and Arab-Islamic world. In order to facilitate the reader's appreciation and comprehension of this long period, the essay will open with an introductory section describing the significance of the Greek economic thought compared to the ideas of the other people lived in Mediterranean era. Following upon this general introduction, the essay deals with the economic thought and writings of the Classical Period in Greece (see section "The Classical Greek Economic Thought").

The economic thought during the Hellenistic period (323–31 BC) has not been studied extensively. Histories of economic thought, when they refer to ancient thought, usually pass directly from Aristotle or his immediate successors to medieval economic Aristotelianism. It would seem that ancient economic thought, having reached its zenith in Aristotle's *Politics*, disappeared, only to reappear as a catalyst for the reflections of medieval commentators. However, we show that several Hellenistic schools do refer to economic problems (see section "Economic Thought in Hellenistic Times").

The Roman writers do belong in the tradition of the European intellectual life. Economic premises and content of Roman law evolved into the commercial law of the Middle Ages and matured into the Law Merchant adopted into the Common Law system of England on a case-by-case basis, primarily under the aegis of Lord Mansfield, Chief Justice of the Court of King's Bench, 1756–1788 (see section "The Roman Heritage").[2]

The economic ideas of the Roman philosophers, and particularly of Plato and Aristotle against usury and wealth, influenced the Christian Fathers of the East, who belong to the Mediterranean tradition. Their aim is broadly to reflect upon the first- and second-generation Church literature to provide assistance in dealing with the new and baffling range of problems with which the Church of their day was confronted. Of considerable importance among the issues which the Fathers faced was the problem of the unequal distribution of wealth and similar related economic issues.[3] They reflected heavily in their works the ideas of the classical Greek philosophers.

---

[1] Schumpeter (1954 [1994], pp. 73–74).
[2] Lowry (1973, 1987b, p. 5).
[3] Karayiannis and Drakopoulos-Dodd (1998, p. 164).

Another central issue of the Byzantine History was that the scholars did get occupy of the social and economic problems of the State. The ideology of these scholars remained constantly in the patterns of the "Kaiserreden" (speeches to Emperors), which were written systematically in the fourteenth and fifteenth century (see section "The Byzantine Economic Thought: An Overview").[4]

While the influence of Islamic science and mathematics on European developments has been widely accepted, there has been a grudging resistance to investigate cultural influences; the troubadour and "courtly love" tradition is a case in point. We tend to forget that the court of Frederick II in the "Two Sicilies" in the twelfth century held open house for Muslim, Christian, and Jewish scholars. Also, there was the sustained Spanish bridge between North Africa and Europe that maintained cultural interaction through the Middle Ages when many scholastic doctors read Arabic.[5] The main characteristic of the Islamic economic thought is that the Greek and Iranian heritages figure most prominently in its literary tradition (see section "Arab-Islamic Economic Thought").

The Classical Greek Economic Thought

About 5,000 years ago, the Mediterranean region became the cradle of a number of civilizations. Egypt, Mesopotamia, Syria, and Persia figure in the history books as creative incubators of our cultural heritage. Their palace and temple complexes were of an unparalleled grandeur and arouse our awe even today. Their civilizations had relatively developed economies, with surplus production efficiently mobilized and redistributed for the administrative and religious establishment. Their scribal schools produced a great number of manuals with detailed instructions for the running of the complex system. But, in their compact worldview, there was no space for an autonomous body of political thought and still less for one of economic thought.[6]

Classical Greece made a quantum leap in the humanization of arts and philosophy. Its rationalism came as a challenge to the mythical worldview and to the religious legends and liturgies. Aristotle states that very precisely and appropriately by the following sentence: "οι Έλληνες δια το φεύγειν την άγνοιαν εφιλοσόφησαν [...] δια το ειδέναι το επίστασθαι εδίωκον και ου χρήσεώς τινος ένεκα" (*Metaphysics* A 983 b11).

The Greek rhetoricians and scholars were also the first to write extensively on problems of practical philosophy like ethics, politics, and economics. This is proved

---

[4] van Dieten (1979, pp. 5–6, not. 16).

[5] Lowry (1996, pp. 707–708).

[6] Baeck (1997, p. 146). It is evident that we meet descriptions of economic life and matters in Zoroaster's law-book and in the Codex Hammurabi. Cf. Kautz (1860, pp. 90–91). In the Talmudic tradition, the ethical aspect of the labor has been praised. Cf. Ohrenstein and Gordon (1991, pp. 275–287). For an overview of the economic ideas of the population round the Mediterranean, see Spengler (1980, pp. 16–38) and Baloglou and Peukert (1996, pp. 19–21).

by the works entitled "On wealth (peri ploutou)" and "On household economics (peri oikonomias)." In the post-Socratic demarcation of disciplines, ethics was the study of personal and interindividual behavior; politics was the discourse on the ordering of the public sphere; and the term *oikonomia* referred to the material organization of the household and of the estate, and to supplementary discourses on the financial affairs of the city-state (polis-state) administration. Greek economic thought formed an integral but subordinated part of the two major disciplines, ethics and politics. The discourse of the organization of the Oikos and the economic ordering of the polis was not conceived to be an independent analytical sphere of thought.[7]

Homo Oeconomicus: Oikonomia as an Art Efficiency

The word "Oikonomia" comes from "Oikos" and "nemein." The root of the verb "νέμειν (nemein)" is nem (νεμ-) and the verb "nemein" which very frequently appears in Homer means "to deal out, to dispense." From the same root derive the words νομή, νομεύς (a flock by the herdman), and νέμεσις (retribution, i.e., the distribution of what is due). This interpretation comes from Homer's description of the Cyclops, who were herdmen (νομείς) (Homer, *Odyssey*, ix, 105–115). According to J.J. Rousseau (1712–1778), the second word means decreeing of rules legislation: "The word economy comes from οίκος, house, and from νόμος, law, and denotes ordinarily nothing but the wise and legitimate government of the house for the common benefit of the whole family. The meaning of the term has later been extended to the government of the great family which is the state."[8] This term means Household Management – the ordering, administration, and care of domestic affairs within a household; husbandry which implies thrift, orderly arrangement, and frugality, and is, in a word, "economical." Here, in the primary sense of the root, oikonomos (οἰκονόμος) means house manager, housekeeper, or house steward; oikonomein (οικονομειν) means "to manage a household" or "do household duties," and oikonomia (οικονομία) refers to the task or art or science of household management.[9] According to Aristotle, the second word has the meaning of arrangement, and consequently, their harmonization for their better result (Aristotle, *Politics* I 10, 1258 a21–26).

The epic "Works and Days" seems to have been built around the central issue of economic thought: the fundamental fact of human need (*Works and Days*, 42ff). It follows the implications of that primordial fact into all its ramifications in the life of a Greek peasant. The problem, Hesiod teaches his brother, is to be solved not by means that nowadays would be labeled as "political" by force and fraud, bribery, and willful appropriation, but by incessant work in fair competition, by moderation, honesty and knowledge of how and when to do the things required in the course of seasons (*Works and Days*, 107–108), how to adjust wants to the resources available

---

[7] Baeck (1994, pp. 47–49).

[8] Rousseau (1755, pp. 337–349 [1977, p. 22]).

[9] Reumann (1979, p. 571).

and *On the Superintendant* (*peri tou epitropou*) (Diog. Laert. VI 15). It has been supported[22] that he influenced Xenophon in writing his "Oeconomicus."

By analyzing the proper economic actions, activities, pursuits, and responsibilities of the head of the Oikos, Xenophon developed interesting ideas "framed in terms of the individual decision-maker."[23] Xenophon uses as an example of good organization, management, administration, and control that exercised by the queen-bee. He mentions that the leader of the Oikos (kyrios) must organize and control the work done by his douloi and laborers and then distribute among them a part of the product as the queen bee does (*Oeconomicus* VII 32–34). He sets forth the Socratic idea that if you can find the man with a ruling soul, the *archic* man, you had better put him in control and trust his wisdom rather than the counsels of many.

After dealing with the content and scope of "oikonomia," Xenophon emphasized that every social agent acts as an entrepreneur-manager or as an administrator of the Oikos and is interested in the preservation and augmentation of the possessions of his Oikos: "the business of a good oikonomos (kalos kagathos) is to manage his own estate well" (*Oeconomicus* I 2). The master, however, may as the Xenophontic Socrates observes, entrust another man with the business of managing his Oikos. This seems to introduce another way of being an "Oikonomos," but one thoroughly familiar to an Athenian of that epoch, for Critoboulos instantly agrees "Yes of course; and he would get a good salary if, after taking on an estate (ousia), by showing a balance (periousia)" (*Oeconomicus* I 4).[24] Evidently, this delegated function has a narrower scope than that of the householder-master (despotes). It is related to payments and receipts and seems akin to moneymaking, for success is measured by the attainment of a "surplus" (periousia). This does not necessarily imply a capitalistic style of economic organization, but it shows how fluid the boundary between farming in sustenance and for profit had become and it talks of chrematistics and economy,[25] as if they were neighbors rather than opposites – in contrast to Aristotle from whom the two modes of economic life are divided by a chasm.

It would have been a serious omission not to mention that the worship of God by members of "Oikos" is a part of "oikonomia" (*Oeconomicus* V 19, 20). That particular characteristic of the Ancient Greek Oikos distinguishes is from the modern one.

Many examples can be cited of the Greeks' concern for the efficient management of both material and human resources. Xenophon's *Banquet* is an anecdotal account

---

[22] Vogel (1895, p. 38), Hodermann (1896, p. 11; 1899, ch. 1), Roscalla (1990, pp. 207–216), and Baloglou and Peukert (1996, pp. 49–53).

[23] Lowry (1987a, p. 147).

[24] Karayiannis (1992, p. 77) and Houmanidis (1993, p. 87).

[25] As Lowry (1987c, p. 12) comments: "The Greek art of oikonomia, a formal, administrative art directed toward the minimization of costs and the maximization of returns, had as its prime aim the efficient management of resources for the achievement of desired objectives. It was an administrative, not a market approach, to economic phenomena." See also Lowry (1998, p. 79).

of the "good conversation" associated with the leisurely eating and drinking and subsequent entertainment that accompanied the formal dinner. But Socrates' remarks to the Syracusan impresario who provided the dancing girls and acrobats for the entertainment were not about their skill or grace, but about the "economics" of entertainment. "I am considering," he said, "how it might be possible for this lad of yours and this maid to exert as little effort as may be, and at the same time give us the greatest amount of pleasure in watching them-this being your purpose, I am sure" (*Banquet* VII 1–5).

In his effort to interpret the term "oikonomia," Xenophon describes extensively the three kinds of relationships between the members of the Oikos:

1. The relationship between husband and wife: gamike (*Oeconomicus* VII 3, 5, 7, 8, 22–23, 36).
2. The relationship between father/mother and children: teknopoietike (*Oeconomicus* VII 21, 24).
3. The relationship between the head of household (kyrios) and domestic slaves (douloi) (*Cyropaedia* B II 26; *Oeconomicus* XIII 11–12; XXI 9; IV 9).

The description of the occupations in the Oikos and the relations between its members states precisely the content of the term "oikonomia." Xenophon will influence Aristotle, and the latter will analyze the meaning of the term "oikonomia."

The Oikos in the Aristoteleian Tradition

The objective of politics is to specify the rhythm of common political life in such a frame that would enable the man who lives in Politeia to enjoy happiness (eudaimonia) respective to his nature. Politics is projected against the other assisting "sciences, arts," such as strategike, oikonomike, and rhetorike (Aristotle, *Nicomachean Ethics* I 2, 1094 a25–94 b7). This happens because man is an inadequate part of the political whole and is unable to sustain his existence and achieve his perfection. Aristotle believes that the political community ontologically has absolute priority over any person or social formation: "Thus also the polis is prior in nature to the Oikos and to each of us individually. For the whole must necessarily be prior to the part" (*Politics* I 2, 1253 a19–21). According to the ancient political thought, as Aristotle expresses it, man is primarily a "political animal (zoon politikon)" (*Politics* I 2, 1253 a3–4; *Nicomachean Ethics* I 7, 1097 b11; 9, 1169 b18–19).

Apart from this dimension, man as a member of a "politeia which is called the life of a statesman (politicos), a man who is occupied in public affairs" (Plutarch, *Moralia* 826D), he has another dimension as a member of the Oikos. That is why the Stageirite calls him "economic animal": "For man is not only a political but also a house-holding animal (oikonomikon zoon), and does not, like the other animals, couple occasionally and with any chance female or male, but man is in a special way not a solitary but a gregarious animal, associating with the persons with whom he has a natural kinship" (Aristotle, *Eudemeian Ethics* VIII 10, 1242 a22–26).

This characterization introduced by Aristotle has not been mentioned by the most authors[26]; it is, however, of primal importance for the understanding of the parts of the Oikos.

Aristotle recognizes the three relationships in the Oikos:

1. Master and doulos-oiketes (household slave): despotike
2. Man and wife: gamike
3. Father and children: teknopoietike

These three relationships and the existence of a budget consist of the "economic institution" (oikonomikon syntagma).[27]

The Oikos is the part of the whole, of the Polis, and the relationships of the members of the Oikos are reflected in the forms of government (Aristotle, *Politics* I 13, 1260 b13–15; Idem, *Eudemeian Ethics* VIII 9, 1241 b27–29). Therefore, the relationship of the man and wife corresponds to the aristocracy (*Eudemeian Ethics* VIII 9, 1241 b27–32), the relationship of the father and children to kingship (*Politics* I 12, 1259 b11–12), and the relationship of the children corresponds to democracy (politeia) (*Eudemeian Ethics* VIII 9, 1241 b30–31). The relationship between master and doulos-oiketes consists of an object of the so-called, "despotic justice," which differs from the justice that regulates the relations of the members of the Polis and from the justice that rules the relationships of the citizens of an oligarchic or tyrannic government (*Nicomachean Ethics* V 10, 1134 b11–16; *Great Ethics* I 33, 1194 b18–20).

It is worth to note that Hegel presents in the Third Part of his work *Philosophie des Rechtes* the tripartite division Familie, Bürgeliche Gesellschaft, Staat, in a distinct manner as we believe, corresponding to the aristoteleian tripartite distinction: Oikos, Kome, Polis. Such division characterizes deeply the trends of the sociology of the nineteenth century, this tripartite Hegelian theory of society.[28]

Aristotle tells the reader that each relationship has a naturally ruling and ruled part – even the procreative relationships are informed by subjuration. Accordingly, the only unsubjurated part, one which Aristotle separates from the other three, is the fourth part of the Oikos, the art of acquisition (ktetike). Its concern is not with subjuration, but with acquisition or accumulation.[29]

Aristotle proceeds to a discussion of the kinds of acquisition and the ways of life from which they follow. He selects the word "chrematistic" to convey his meaning of the natural art of acquisition. According to several commentators of the *Politics*, the word while inexact, "often means money and is always suggestive of it."[30]

---

[26] For an exception, see Kousis (1951, pp. 2–3) and Koslowski (1979a, pp. 62–63). Cf. also Koslowski (1979b).

[27] Rose (1863, p. 181, Fr. XXXIII).

[28] Despotopoulos (1998, p. 96).

[29] Brown (1982, pp. 17–172).

[30] Newman, vol. I (1887, p. 187) and Polanyi (1968, p. 92): "Chrematistike was deliberately employed by Aristotle in the literal sense of providing for the necessaries of life, instead of its usual meaning of 'money-making.'" See Barker (1946, p. 27). See an extensive analysis in Egner (1985, ch. 1).

At this point, we should mention something that gets usually disregarded by most of the authors. The term "chrematistike" is found originally in Plato: "Nor, it seems, do we get any advantage from all other knowledge (episteme), whether of money-making (chrematistike) or medicine or any other that knows how to make things, without knowing how to use the thing made" (Plato, *Euthydemus* 289A). This term denotes this "episteme" (science) that relieves people from poverty; in other words, "it teaches them how to get money" (Plato, *Gorgias* 477 E10–11; 478 B1–2). It is not without worth to note that Plato places chrematistics parallel to medicine [cf. Plato, *Euthydemus* 289A; idem, *Politeia* 357 c5–12; idem, *Gorgias* 452a2, e5–8, 477 e7–9]. This emphasizes the fact that both "chrematistics" and "medicine" are "arts" (sciences), which have as target the support of the traditional goods: the external goods (wealth), the body (health). This widely accepted view of the parallel setting of medicine and chrematistics is adopted also by Aristotle (*Politics* I 9, 1258 a11–15; 10, 1258 a28–30; idem, *Eudemeian Ethics* I 7, 1217 a36–39; *Nicomachean Ethics* III 5, 1112 b4–5).

Simultaneously, in the dialog *Sophist* the kinds of "chrematistike" are explored. The acquisition (ktetike techne) is contrasted in "poietike" and subdivided in the division of hunting and of exchange, the latter in two sorts, the one by gift, the other by sale. The exchange by sale is divided into two parts, calling the part which sells a man's own productions the selling of one's own (autourgon autopoliken), and the other, which exchanges the works of others, exchange (allotria erga metavallomenen metavletiken), which is subdivided in "kapelike" (part of exchange which is carried on in the city) and "emporia" (exchanges goods from city to city) (Plato, *Sophist* 219 b, 223c–224d). These activities have a different moral evaluation: it is better to construct (poietike) rather than to acquire (ktetike); better to gain from nature than from transactions with others; better to offer than participate in the market. The method of working, the objectives, and the tools are the criteria for a classification which later in the work forms the basis for the treatment of the sophist (Plato, *Sophist* 219a-d).[31]

Aristotle, obviously influenced by Plato's analysis, distinguishes the three kinds of acquisition.

The first kind – "one kind of acquisition therefore in the order of nature is a part of the household art (oikonomike)" (*Politics* I 11, 1256 b27) – is the acquisition from nature of products fit for food (*Politics* I 11, 1258 a37), which is to be added as simple barter of these things for one another, which is the good metabletike. Similar to this kind of acquisition is the "wealth-getting in the most proper sense (oikeiotate chrematistike) (the household branch of wealth-getting)" (*Politics* I 11, 1258 b20) – whose branches are agriculture – corn-growing and fruit-farming – bee-keeping, and breeding of the other creatures finned and feathered (*Politics* I 11, 1258 b18–22).[32]

---

[31] Hoven van den (1996, p. 101).

[32] Susemihl and Hicks (1894, p. 171 and 210). Maffi (1979, p. 165) against Polanyi's thesis; Pellegrin (1982, pp. 638–644), Venturi (1983, pp. 59–62), Schefold (1989, p. 43), and Schütrumpf (1991, pp. 300–301).

The second kind is trade in general, kapelike, synonym with metabletike in the narrower sense or chrematistics in the narrower sense (*Politics* I 9, 1256 b40–41), in which Aristotle thinks men get their profit not of nature, but out of one another and so unnaturally (*Politics* I 10, 1258 b1–2: "for it is not in accordance with nature, but involves, men's taking things from one another.")

The third kind is, like the first, the acquisition from nature of useful products, but the products are not edible. Aristotle calls this kind "between" the latter and the one placed first, since it possesses an element both of natural wealth-getting and of the sort that employs exchange; it deals with all the commodities that are obtained from the earth and from those fruitless, but useful things that come from the earth (*Politics* I 11, 1258 b28–31).

The wealth which is the object of the second kind, consisting of money (*Politics* I 1257 b5–40), is unnatural as contrasted with the "wealth by nature" (ploutos kata physin) of the first kind (*Politics* I 1257 b19–20), and the commodities which form the wealth of the third kind are clearly more like the unnatural wealth. To them one might also apply what is said of money: "[…] yet is absurd that wealth should be of such a kind that a man may be well supplied with it and yet die of hunger" (*Politics* I 8, 1257 b15–16). Furthermore, the first kind of acquisition is more natural than the third in the sense that "natural" is opposed to "artificial" rather than to "unnatural."[33]

We have to emphasize the ethical evaluation of the "chrematistike." Aristotle does not condemn "chrematistics" as long as it does not go beyond the natural limits of acquisition of goods (*Politics* I 9, 1257 b31ff). For this reason, he calls it "oikonomike chrematistike."

Aristotle's ideas on "chrematistics" and wealth reflect a tradition in the Greek thought which is found in the Lyric poets, such Sappho, Solon, Theognis, and in classical tragedy (Sophocles, *Antigone* 312).[34] He makes clear that this search for profit (kerdos) is not denounced with respect to any specific method of earning wealth, but to the general hoarding of wealth (Sophocles, *Antigone*, 312). The expression "argyros kakon nomisma" (295–296), used by Creon, shows the ethical aversion of the excessive wealth by the ancient Greek thought. It is not accidental that Marx[35] does use the same expression, who describes the love for gold and the thirst of money, two phenomena which are produced with money.

Aristotle's dinstinction between "necessary" and "unnecessary" exchange and his dictum in the *Politics* (I 1257 a15–20) that "retail trade is not naturally a part of the art of acquisition" have been widely interpreted as a moralistic rejection of all commercial activity. M.I. Finley (1912–1986), for example, finds "not a trace" of economic analysis in *Politics* and maintains that in this work Aristotle does not "ever consider the rules or mechanics of commercial exchange."[36] On the contrary, he says, "his insistence on the unnaturalness of commercial gain rules out the possibility of such a discussion."

---

[33] Meikle (1995).

[34] Meyer (1892, p. 110), Stern (1921, p. 6), and Schefold (1997, p. 128).

[35] Marx (1867 [1962], p. 146).

[36] Finley (1970, p. 18).

Aristotle's theory of association in *Politics* is based upon mutual need satisfaction. Exchange, Aristotle says, arises from the fact that "some men [have] more, and others less, than suffices for their needs" (*Politics* I 1257a). Exchange, however, is not a natural use of goods produced for consumption. Where barter, the exchange of commodities for commodities (C-C′), occurs, goods move directly from the producer to the consumer, and Aristotle considered this form of exchange a natural or "necessary" form of acquisition because he says, it is "subject to definite bounds."

Aristotle viewed exchange with money used as an intermediary (C-M-C′) as "necessary" when its ultimate purpose is to acquire items for consumption, because the desire for goods is then still subject to the natural limit of diminishing utility.[37] He classified retail trade, where money is used to purchase commodities to sell in order to acquire more money (M-C-M) as an "unnecessary" form of exchange. Its objective, he says, is not the satisfaction of need, but the acquisition of money which has no use in and of itself and is therefore not subject to a natural limit of desire, as he illustrates with the Midas legend (*Politics* I 9 1257 b14–15). Further, this form of acquisition has "no limit to the end it seeks." It "turns on the power of currency" and is thus unrelated to the satisfaction of needs. The "extreme example" of "unnecessary" or "lower" form of exchange, and a still greater perversion of the exchange process, Aristotle says, is usury, for it attempts to "breed" money – "currency, the son of currency." Usury "makes a profit from currency itself (M-M′-M″) instead of making it from the process which currency was meant to serve" (*Politics* I 10, 1258 b5–9).

From the Economics of the Oikos to the Economics of the Polis

Sophists, who brought about a new movement of intellectuals in the middle of the fifth century BC in Athens, taught how to be virtuous. The knowledge which Protagoras claims to teach the youth "consists of good judgement (euboulia) in his own affairs (peri ton oikeion), which shall enable him to order his own house (ten heautou oikian dioikein), as well as teach him how to gain influence in the affairs of the polis (ta tes poleus), in speech and action" (Plato, *Protagoras* 318E5–319A2). A similar formula occurs in Aristophanes' *Frogs* (405 BC), where Euripides in his great agon with Aeschylus boasts, in a Sophist's manner, of having helped the Athenians "to manage all their household better than before (tas oikias dioikein)" (*Frogs*, vv. 975ff), by teaching them to ask the "why" and "how" and "what" of even the smallest things. Both phrases are formed by reduplication and may, to a modern reader, sound somewhat clumsy.[38]

---

[37] The only goods which Aristotle exempts from diminishing utility are "goods of the soul," physic goods. "The greater the amount of each of the goods of the soul," he says, "the greater is its utility" (Aristotle, *Politics* 1323b). Cf. Lowry (1987c, p. 19).

[38] Radermacher (1921, pp. 284–286) and Spahn (1984, p. 315).

One can see clearly the subsequence of economic issues and problems of the Oikos and the Polis, in the dialog between Socrates and Nicomachides, as described by Xenophon[39]: "I mean that, whatever a man controls, if he knows what he wants and can get it he will be a good controller, whether he controls a chorus, an Oikos, a Polis or an army." "Really Socrates," cried Nicomachides, "I should never have thought to hear you say that a good businessman (oikonomos) would make a good general" (Xenophon, *Memorabilia* III IV, 6–7).

The view of Socrates that the difference between the Oikos and the Polis lies in their size, only whereas they are similar to Nature and their parts, gets crystallized in the following passage from the same dialog between Socrates and Nicomachides, where Xenophon presents "the best lecture to a contemporary Minister of Finance," according to A.M. Andreades (1876–1935)[40]:

> Don't look down on businessmen (oikonomikoi andres), Nicomachides. For the management of private concerns differs only in point of number from that of public affairs. In other respects they are much alike, and particularly in this, that neither can be carried on without men, and the men employed in private and public transactions are the same. For those who take charge of public affairs employ just the same men when they attend to their own (hoi ta edia oikonomountes); and those who understand how to employ them are successful directors of public and private concerns, and those who do not, fail in both (Xenophon, *Memorabilia* III IV, 12).

Plato was also of the opinion that "there is not much difference between a large household organization and a small-sized polis" and that "one science covers all these several spheres," whether it is called "royal science, political science, or science of household management" (Plato, *Statesman* (*Politicus*) 259 b-e). These ideas of Xenophon and Plato are refuted by Aristotle in the *Politics* (I 1, 1252 a13–16).[41]

A characteristically Xenophontean passage dealing with this generalization of the administrative process gives us a persuasive view of this practical art ancient as well as modern times. After the dialog between Socrates and Nicomachides in "Memorabilia," Xenophon points out that the factor common to both is the human element. "They are much alike" he says, in that "neither can be carried out without men" and those "who understand how to employ them are successful directors of public and private concerns, and those who do not, fail in both."[42]

In Xenophon already, oikonomikos sometimes suggests being skilled or adept at finance, and this element in the idea grew in the popular Greek understanding of the concept (Xenophon, *Agesilaus* 10,$_1$): "I therefore praise Agesilaus with regard to such qualities. These are not, as it were, characteristic of the type of man who, if he should find a treasure, would be more wealthy, but in no sense wiser in business acumen."

---

[39] There are also other examples in the classical tragedy which seem quite interesting, because of the connection between the issue of managing the Oikos effectively and managing of the Polis. Cf. Euripides, *Electra* 386 ff.

[40] Andreades (1992, p. 250, not. 3).

[41] Schütrumpf (1991, pp. 175–176).

[42] See Strauss (1970, p. 87) for a discussion of this passage.

Aristotle had called someone managing the funds of a polis carefully "a steward of the polis (τις διοικῶν οικονόμος)" (Aristotle, *Politics* V 9, 1314 b8).[43]

The ancient recognition of the primary role of the human element in the successful organization of affairs is a facet we tend to ignore when we approach the ancient world from our modern market-oriented perspective.[44] They emphasized the importance of the human variable, of one's personal effectiveness in achieving a successful outcome in any venture. From this anthropocentric point of view, improving human skill in the management of an enterprise meant nothing less than increasing the efficiency of production. In ancient Greece, the maximization of the human factor was considered as important as that of any other resource.[45]

Apart, however, from the skillful administrative control over men, the Ancient Greeks provided the fact that the ruler has to have an interest in the public finances. From the conversations of Socrates reported by Xenophon in his *Memorabilia*, we learn that the finances of the polis of Athens were a subject with which young men looking forward to political careers might well be expected to acquaint themselves (Xenophon, *Memorabilia* III VI).

Management of public finance and administration of the Polis have extensively preoccupied Aristotle. In his letter to Alexander he adopts the term "oikonomein" to denote the management of the Polis finances. (I. Stobaeus, *Anthologium*) (henceforth Stob. I 36 p. $43_{,15}$–$46_{,2}$) In *Rhetoric*, he mentions that among the subjects concerning which public men should be informed is that of the public revenues. Both the sources and the amount of the receipts should be known, in order that nothing may be omitted and any branch that is insufficient may be increased. In addition to this, expenditures should be studied so that unnecessary items may be eliminated; because people become wealthier not only by adding to what they have, but also by cutting down their outlay (Aristotle, *Rhetoric* I 4, 1359 b21–23). A similar discussion is found in the *Rhetoric for Alexander* (II 2, 1423 a21–26 and XXXVIII 20, 1446 b31–36).

It is also worth noting that Demosthenes (fourth century BC) writes about the public finance. In his speech *On Crown*, he enumerates a politician's activities in the financial sector (Demosthenes, *On Crown* 309). In the *Third* and *Fourth Philippics* (IV 31–34, 35–37, 42–45, 68–69), the author makes particular proposals of a financial character which provided the essentials of a plan of finance.[46] It is worth to note that in the period between 338 BC (Battle of Chaironeia) and 323 (Death of Alexander) – where the orator Lycurg[47] was the Minister of Public Finance

---

[43] Reuman (1980, p. 377).

[44] Lowry (1987a, p. 57, 1987c, 1995, 1998).

[45] Trever (1916, p. 9) evidently had this point in mind when he observed that "Aristotle struck the keynote in Greek economic thought in stating that the primary interest of economy is human beings rather than inanimate property." In a conversation between Cyrus and his father in the *Cyropaedia* (I VI 20–21), we are presented with the clearest kind of analysis of successful administrative control over men.

[46] Cf. Bullock (1939, pp. 156–159).

[47] Conomis (1970).

of the Athenian Democracy – specific proposals of financial policy were provided by Aristotle,[48] Hypereides[49], and the aforementioned Demosthenes. Their target was a redistribution of wealth inside the polis between the citizens: the best proposal was to advise the rich to contribute money in order to cultivate the poor land or give capital to the poor people to develop enterprises (Aristotle, *Politics*, VI 5, 1360 a36–40).[50] However, while the advice on the surface was to favor the commons, it was really a prudent suggestion to the wealthier citizens, appealing to the selfish interest to avoid by this method the danger of a discontented proletariat (Aristotle, *Politics* VI 5, 1320 a36).

These proposals which set up on the idea that the richer citizens should help the poor is a common point in the Ancient Greek Thought. It is to underline that long before the Athenian philosophers and writers, the Pythagorean Archytas of Taras (governed 367–361 BC), not only the philosopher-scientist and technician,[51] but also a skillful political leader both in war and in peace provided in his work *Περί μαθημάτων (On lessons)* the fact that the wealthier citizens should help the poorer; by this method, the stasis and homonoia will be avoided, concord will come in the polis (Stob. IV 1, 139 H).[52]

The programme of economic and social policy, which is provided by the aforementioned authors, is included in the field of the policy of the redistribution of income which has been adopted by Welfare Economics.[53] The main difference between the proposal of the Ancients and the contemporary procedure lies in the intervention of the State in recent times, whereas in the Classical Times the richer people would play the role of the State.[54]

In the latter part of the nineteenth century, when histories of economic thought began to be numerous, various writers discovered that what they called the science of economics was late in its development, and that in Ancient Times the prevalence of household industry, the low esteem in which manual labor was held, the slight growth of commerce, the lack of statistical data, and various other circumstances brought it about that materials were not provided for the scientific study of economics and finance.[55]

---

[48] Aristotle, *Politics* VI 5, 1319 b33–1320 b18. For a comparison between Aristotle's proposals and Xenophon's program in *Poroi,* cf. Schütrumpf (1982, pp. 45–52, esp. pp. 51–52) and Baloglou (1998d).

[49] Hypereides, *For Euxenippos*, col. XXIII 1–13, col. XXXIX 16–26 (edit. by Jensen 1916).

[50] This advice is based on Isocrates' account of the ways of the rich in Athens in the days of Solon and Cleisthenes. Isocrates, *Areopagiticus* 32. Cf. Newman (1887, vol. IV, p. 535).

[51] Cardini (1962, p. 262), quoted by Mattei (1995, pp. 72–74).

[52] Archytas' proposal is set up on justice. The existence of justice will bring the welfare in the Oikos and in Polis. Iamblichus, *De Vita Pythagorica*, cap. XXX, 169.

[53] Psalidopoulos (1997, pp. 15–16) and Baloglou (2001a).

[54] Baloglou (1998d, pp. 50–55).

[55] For example, see Ingram (1888 [1967], pp. 5, 8) and Eisenhart (1891, pp. 2–3).

Concerning the above argument, we would like to say that at any time prior to the twentieth century such proposals would have been universally recognized as a logical and consistent plan of public finance, its parts well-balanced and nicely articulated with a view to securing the desirable financial result by uniting all classes of citizens in support of it.

The evidence that was mentioned establishes a way of thinking that overcomes the narrow boundaries of the Oikos and is not characterized by a simplistic empiricism.[56] Furthermore, we have to consider that the achievement of all the measures which have been proposed by the several programmes will lead in welfare of the citizens, which must be the target of each policy-maker. This economic and social policy would satisfy Wilhelm Roscher's (1817–1894) statement: "Die hellenische Volkswirthschaftlehre hat niemals den grossen Fehler begangen, ueber dem Reichthume die Menschen zu vergessen, und ueber der Vermehrung der Menschenzahl, den Wohlstand der Einzelnen gering zu achten."[57]

This literature provides that the term "oikonomia" does no longer have a lexicographic identity and has been transferred to the Economics of the Polis.

Economic Thought in Hellenistic Times

The economic thought during the Hellenistic Period – which includes the three centuries between Alexander and Augustus (323–31 BC) – has not been studied extensively. We show that several Hellenistic schools do refer to economic problems.[58] We add that several post-Aristotelian texts on the topic of oikonomike survive from the Hellenistic period: Xenocrates of Chalcedon (394–314), the Director of the Academy after Speusipp's death, wrote two treatises entitled *Oikonomikos* (Diog. Laert. IV 12) and *On Oikos* (Cicero, *De legibus* I 21, 55). From the view survived informations,[59] we conclude that the work *Oikonomikos* continues the hesiodean tradition concerning Oikos.[60] Other works from this period are the three

---

[56] Engels (1988, pp. 90–134) for an evaluation of the proposals in the Lycurgean era.

[57] Roscher (1861, p. 7).

[58] Glaser (1865, p. 313) expressed the view that we do not find any interesting economic topics during this period. Other works, though not extensively, are dealing with the economic thought in the Hellenistic period, such as Bonar (1896, ch. III), Trever (1916, pp. 125–145), Stephanidis (1948, pp. 172–181), Tozzi (1955, pp. 246–286, 1961, pp. 209–242), and Spiegel (1971, pp. 34–39) on the Cynics, Stoics and Epicureans (on p. 672 an interpretative bibliography); Baloglou and Constantinidis (1993, pp. 163–177), Baloglou (1995, ch. 11). The interesting paper by Natali (1995) is dealing with the term "oikonomia" in the Hellenistic period.

In recent studies, Baloglou (1998a, 1998c, 1999a, 2002a, 2004a) I dealt with the economic philosophy of the Early Stoics and Cynics. For the economic philosophy of the Cynic Crates of Thebes, see Baloglou (2000b).

[59] Heinze (1892, Fr. 92, 94, 98).

[60] Hodermann (1896, pp. 17–18) and Maniatis and Baloglou (1994, p. 52).

books of *Oeconomica*,[61] written by the member of the Peripatetic School, the treatise *Peri Oikonomias* written by the Epicurean Philodemus of Gadara,[62] the Οικονομικός (*Oikonomikos*) of the Neopythagorean Bryson (Stob. V 28, 15 p. 680, 7–681, 14), and Callicratidas (Stob. V 28, 16, p. 681, 15–688, 8: Callicratidas, *Peri oikon eudaimonias* (*On the Wealth of Households*)). Aside from the works entitled *Oikonomikos*, Diogenes Laertius informs us that several authors wrote works, entitled περί πλούτου (On wealth).[63] From a later age, in Roman Times, there are the *Oikonomikos* of Dio of Prusa[64] and the *Oikonomikos* of Hierocles (Stob. V 28, 21 p. 696, 21–699, 15).[65] Plutarch deals also with economic ideas in his *Conjuralia moralia*, which even though it does not bear the name *Oikonomikos* yet, is similar in content to them.[66] In his essay "Peri philoploutias" (*De cupiditate divitiarum* 3, 524 D), he moralizes on the folly of inordinate desire for wealth, in the Stoic vein.

The New Meaning of the Term "Oikonomia"

The Hellenistic authors use the term "oikonomia" in the first place to designate household management; (1) in the most traditional sense, *oikonomia* means control of the household's internal areas, which was left to the wife, as opposed to the external areas and political activity which was considered the man's affairs (Theophrastus, *Fragmenta*, ed. Winner, Fr.112,152,158; Theophrastus, *Characteres*, Foreword 16; XI). Furthermore, (2) the term implies, in general, the man's management of his property, as master of the house (*Oeconomica* II, I), or (3) the philosopher's management of his own possessions.[67]

The Hellenistic authors use the term *oikonomia* meaning in a figurative sense, any environment in which the capacity to manage a complex structure – big or small – well, can be applied with success.[68] The Greek historian Polybius, a distinguished figure of Roman Times, frequently uses the term *oikonomia* to specify the good organization of any kind of army equipment, such as supplies, sentries, and encampents [Polybius, *Histories* I 61, 8; III 32, 9; III 33, 9; III 100, 7; IV 65, 11; X 40, 2; VI 12, 5; VI 31, 10; VI 35, 11; X 16, 2; X 25, 2]. Another use of the term signifies

---

[61] Susemihl (1887) and Groningen and Wartelle (1968).

[62] Jensen (1907) and Hodermann (1896, pp. 37–40) for a summary statement of his teaching (Maniatis and Baloglou 1994).

[63] Cf. Diog. Laert. IV 4: Speusippus; Diog. Laert. IV II: Xenocrates; Diog. Laert. V 22: Aristotle; Diog. Laert. V 47: Theophrastus; Diog. Laert. VI 80: Diogenes; Diog. Laert. VII 167: the Stoic Dionysius; Diog. Laert. VII 178: the Stoic Sphairos; Diog. Laert. X 24: the Epicurean Metrodorus.

[64] Arnim (1992, p. 309: Appendix II).

[65] Baloglou (1992).

[66] See Hodermann (1896, p. 43) and Trever (1916 p. 127).

[67] Natali (1995, p. 97).

[68] Descat (1988, p. 107).

the division of spoils [Polybius, *Histories* II 2, 9; IV 86, 4; V 16, 5; X 17, 6; XX 9, 5]. Elsewhere, *oikonomia* refers to the general handling of political affairs in a polis or region, of alliances, of religious festivals [Polybius, *Histories*, I 4, 3; I 8, 3; IV 26, 7; IV 67, 9; V 39, 6; V 40, 4; VI 26, 5; XIII 3, 8; XXII 12, 8; XXXII 7, 5; XXVII 1, 11; XXXVIII 11, 5].

In other cases, the term *oikonomia* is actually used to mean the organized handling of wealth in the Polis, and therefore, takes on a meaning closer to the modern concept of "political economy." There is some evidence in Strabo and Polybius. The geographer Strabo of Pontos, when speaking of Egypt, says a good *oikonomia* generates business (Strabo, *Geographica* XVII 1 13). When he speaks about the administration of the Persian empire, he says "that in Susa each one of the kings built for himself on the acropolis a separate habitation, treasure-houses, and storage places for what tributes they each exacted, as memorials of his administration (hypomnemata tes oikonomias)" (*Geographica* XV 3 21). The same context of oikonomia, as in Strabo, we find in Polybius (*Histories* V 50, 5; X 1, 5; XVI 21, 44; XXIII 14, 5). It is also worth noting that many of these texts refer to Egypt, whose administration was compared to that of a huge Oikos, as M. Rostovtzeff says: "The king therefore ran the state in the same way as a simple Macedonian or Greek had run his own domestic affairs."[69] This is why king's administrators in the districts, regions, and subordinate territories were called *oikonomoi*.[70]

In Dionysius of Halicarnassus (middle of the first century BC) the term "politike oikonomia" means a public civil administration as opposed to the handling of military operations, and in particular, the management of trials and the resolution of controversies (Dionysius of Halicarnassus, *The Roman Antiquities*, XI 19, 5: "But since Cornelius endeavoured to show that his motion is impracticable, pointing out that the intervening period devoted to matters of civil administration (politikais oikonomiais) would be a long one...").

It is characteristically, too, as far as we know, has not been mentioned by the authors yet, that the several schools of the Hellenistic Age did occupy with economic issue – such as the distinction between "oikonomike" and "chrematistike" – and left a tradition which has been continued in the Arab-Islamic World and in the Renaissance.

Lyceum (Peripatos)

Two Aristoteleians of the late fourth and early third centuries deserve some notice. The first was Demetrius of Phalerum, a pupil of Aristotle who governed Athens for the Macedonian Cassander from 317 to 307, and who sought to translate into law

---

[69] Rostovtzeff (1941, vol. I, pp. 278, 352).

[70] Landvogt (1908).

many of Aristotle's ideas. Expelled from Athens by another Demetrius – "the Besieger" – he ultimately made his way to Egypt, where he might have inspired the foundation of the Museum at Alexandria, by Ptolemy I, to serve as a center of learned research, and where he is also recorded to have been the head keeper of the library, – the greatest library in Antiquity, – that rose by the side of the Museum (Diod. Sic. XVIII 74, 2; Diog. Laert. V 75). The other Aristotelian, a contemporary of Demetrius of Phalerum, was Dichaearchus of Messana, a pupil of Aristotle. He was a polymath in the style of his master, and his writings were many and various. In his treatise "Tripolitikos," he developed the perception that the best constitution is the mixture of the three known – monarchy, aristocracy, and democracy.[71] In his work *History of Greece,* there was a history of the degeneration of Greek civilization from the primitive ideal. He divided the history of human civilization into seasons, influenced by Hesiod's *Works and Days*. It is said to have begun with a study of the primitive life of man in the time of Cronus; to have gone on to a description of the culture of the East and its influence on Greece; and to have ended with an account of Greek cultural life as it stood in his time.[72] He introduced the idea that the introduction of private property was the cause for the arising of hate and strife among the citizens,[73] an idea which has been adopted by the Cynics and later by J.J. Rousseau (1712–1778) in his work *Discours sur l' origine et les dondements de l' inegalité parmi les hommes*.[74]

The Work *Oeconomica*

The *Oeconomica* consists of three books. The first book of *Oeconomica* consists of six chapters. Most of the material is an imitation of Aristotle's *Politics* and Xenophon's *Oeconomicus*; we find few new ideas.

In the first chapter, it is said that politics is the government of the many and that the family community is structured like a monarchic government (*Oeconomica* A I, 1343a 3–4). This idea is found in Aristotle's *Politics* (I 7, 1255 b19–20) too. The author considers that the family (Oikos) is by nature prior to the Polis (*Oeconomica* A I 1343 a14–15). The most distinctive point about the doctrine of the first book is its separation of economics (oikonomike) from politics (politike) as a special science (*Oeconomica* A I, 1343 a14, 15–18).

The author agrees with Aristotle, however, that it is the function of economics, both to acquire and to use, though without Aristotle's specific limitations upon acquisition (*Oeconomica* A I, 1343 a7–9; however, II 1343 a25 implies the limitation of occupations attendant on our goods and chattels, "those come first which are natural").

---

[71] Wehrli (1967, pp. 28–29, Fr. 67–72). This idea may have been, at any rate indirectly, parent of the ideas of the mixed constitution expounded afterwards by Polybius and Cicero. Cf. Barker (1956, pp. 49–50) and Aalders (1968, pp. 78–81).

[72] Wehrli (1967, pp. 22–25, Fr. 47–49).

[73] Varro, *Rerum rustic*. II 1, 3 in Wehrli (1967, p. 22, Fr. 48).

[74] Cf. Pöhlmann (1925, vol. I, p. 88, n. 1).

The author describes extensively the four occupations for a good head of the household (οικονόμος): acquiring, guarding, using, and arranging in proper order (*Oeconomica* A VI, 1344 b22–27). This idea is influenced by Xenophon's *Oeconomicus* (VIII 31, 40 and VII 10).

Agriculture is especially eulogized by the author, in the spirit of Xenophon and Aristotle. It is the primary means of natural acquisition, the others being mining and allied arts whose source of wealth is the land. It is the most just acquisition, since it is not gained from other men, either by trade, hired labor, or war (A II 1343 b 25–30), and it contributes most to many strength (A II 1343 b2–7). Retail trade and the banausic arts, on the other hand, are both contrary to nature (*Oeconomica* A II, 1343 a28–30), since they render the body weak and inefficient (*Oeconomica* A II, 1343 b3).

The second book consists of two parts. The first part (I) is purely theoretical.[75] The author devotes his attention to the question of acquisition relevant to the poleis and kings and makes an interesting classification: There are four forms of economy – royal, provincial, political, and private. The author researches the kinds of revenue of each kind of economy (*Oeconomica* B I 1345 b20–22; 1345 b28–31; 1346 a5–8; 1346 a10–13). For all four kinds of economy, the most important single rule is to keep expenditure within the limits set by revenue (*Oeconomica* B I, 1346 a16).

The distinction between these economies and their connection with the kind of government for the three kinds demonstrates originality of the author and a remarkable fact in the development of the economic thought of the Hellenes. The kind of government played a decisive role and described the economic structure of the polis.

The passage 1345 b12–14 is famous, because we find here the first appearance of the modern term 'political economy (politike oikonomia)'. The author characterizes with this term the revenues of a democratic polis. Andreas M. Andreades (1876–1935), who has been influenced by this work, saw in it the birth of modern *Financial Science*.[76]

Another characteristic feature of this part of the book is that the author deals with the significance of prediction for financial purposes (*Oeconomica* B I 1346 a21–25). This is an idea which we meet in *Rhetorica* (I 4, 1359 b24–28) and in *Rhetorica on Alexander* (II 33–35, 1425 b24–25, b24–28).[77]

The second part of this second book (B II) is empirical and is clearly Hellenistic in character. It contains a collection of Strategemata,[78] "anecdotes,"[79] anecdotal references,[80] by which various rulers and governments filled their treasures. These references deal with financial and monetary means, or others like city planning reforms.[81]

---

[75] See for instance Wilcken (1901, p. 187), Andreades (1915, p. 27), and Kousis (1951, p. 69).

[76] Andreades (1930).

[77] The relation and connection of these three works have been pointed out. Cf. Riezler (1907, pp. 37–43), Schlegel (1909, pp. 6–7), and Ruggini (1966, pp. 207–208). Cf. also Klever (1986).

[78] Papalexandris (1969, p. 12).

[79] Wilcken (1901, p. 187), Andreades (1915, p. 27), and Armstrong (1935, p. 323).

[80] Lowry (1979, p. 68).

[81] Like Hippias' reforms: *Oeconomica* B II 4, 1347 d4–8. See Sterghiopoulos (1944 [1948]).

The author of the second part seems to have taken for granted the Cynic theory that money need have no intrinsic value, at least for local purposes. Coinage of iron (*Oeconomica* B II 16, 1348 d17–34), tin (*Oeconomica* B II 20, 1349 d33–37), bronze (*Oeconomica* B II 23, 1350 d23–30), and the arbitrary stamping of drachmas with double value (*Oeconomica* B II 20, 1349 d28–34) are all offered apparently as a proper means of escape from financial difficulty. Like Aristotle, he accepted monopoly as shrewd and legitimate principle of finance.[82]

The third book has survived in two Latin translations and has the title "Νόμοι ανδρός και γαμετής." It is of later origin and is of no economic interest. According to Laurenti,[83] this book contains a little that is Peripatetic and is closer to the Neopythagorean writings.[84]

The Reception of the Work *Oeconomica* by the Authors of Middle Ages and Renaissance

The work *Oeconomica* was a significant part of the European intellectual corpus, studied as relevant to current problems by rulers as well as by ordinary men of affairs.

First of all, we have to mention that "Oeconomica" had a great acceptance in the Medieval Arab-Islamic World. There exists a translation of the first book entitled *Timar maqalat Arista fi tadbir al-manzil* (*Extrait of the Treatise of Aristotle's on Administration of the Household*) written by the philosopher and medicine man Abu-l-Farag Abdallah Ibn al-Tayyid (died in 1043), who lived in Bagdad.[85]

In the thirteenth century, the study of practical philosophy and of moral theology took a radical turn, a more theoretical foundation with the invasion of Aristotle's Ethics. The work of the Stagirite reached the Latin West in the company of Ibn Rushd's theoretical reworkings. Its intellectual impact provoked a break in the Latin translation.

The work *Oeconomica* was translated and commented along with the other two Aristoteleian works, the *Nicomachean Ethics* and *Politics*.

The work *Oeconomica* was translated by distinguished authors in West, like the Bishop of Lisieux Nicolaus Oresmius or Oresme (1320–1382), who translated and commented the work for King Charles V of France between 1370 and 1380.[86]

A remarkable event of the reception and diffusion of the work in the West was the translation and commentary by the Italian humanist Leonardo Bruni (1370–1444).

---

[82] *Oeconomica* B II 3, 1346 b24–25 on the citizens of Byzantium, who "the right of changing money sold to a single band...." Cf. Groningen (1925, pp. 211–222) and Newskaja (1955, pp. 54–56).

[83] Laurenti (1968, pp. 137–157).

[84] Nails (1989, pp. 291–297) and Natali (1995, pp. 52–56).

[85] Jackson (1982–1983, p. 155) and Zonta (1996, p. 550).

[86] Brunner (1949), Goldbrunner (1968, pp. 210–212), and Soudek (1968, p. 71). Cf. Menut (1940) for Oresme's French translations with commentary.

Bruni's translation of the work was the most widely read Renaissance translation of this work.[87] Bruni dedicated his translation of the work to Cosimo de Medici,[88] a man of wealth and culture who could afford to practice virtue and, as Bruni assured him, who could manage his riches in a praiseworthy fashion and enlarge them with honesty. To make the reading of the book easier for Cosimo, Bruni added to his version "an explanation of the more obscure passages."[89]

If the influence of Bruni's translation was responsible for a marked increase in the popularity of Aristotle's moral writings, this depended on a direct appeal to the aristocracy, a public which had hitherto shown little interest in complex ethical systems. Such men, who represented aristocracy, demanded neither a mere collection of "sententiae," nor a systematic philosophy; instead they looked for a practical handbook on how to best run their affairs. These requirements could, indeed, be met by Aristotle's moral writings. Bruni attempted to provide a polished version which would elevate the reader by force of language. He simplified Aristotle's system for the benefit of his patron: "Ethics," he claimed, caught the moral basis for action, "Politics" the principles of good government, and "Economics" the means of acquiring the wealth without which no prince may achieve greatness[90] – a model which was to provide material for many subsequent handbooks on the right government of princes.

Bruni's translation and commentary influenced the Italian humanists who wrote treatises on the household economy. In fact, three fifteenth-century Venetian humanists, Giovanni Caldiera (1400–1474), Francesco Barbaro (1390–1454), and Ermolao Barbaro (1453–1493), his grandson, provided in their treatises[91] – influenced by the Aristotelian works and *Oeconomica* – the best rules for the governance of the Oikos and the city.

Leon Battista Alberti's (1404–1472) dialog *Trattato del governo della famiglia*[92] – three books written between 1433 and 1434, and a fourth written in 1440[93] – was one of the most kindly disposed to the new economic spirit, which has been provided by Bruni. In the historical transition, as experienced by the Italian Humanism, Alberti was a prestigious and leading rhetorician who advocated the efficient use of one's time in economic activities. He praised these as creative endeavors. With Xenophon's *Oeconomicus* and *Oeconomica* as a model, Alberti's dialog offered a penetrating analysis of the value conflict between the traditional mould and the modern business spirit. Alberti's message is well-balanced: enjoy the things of this world without being tied to them.[94]

---

[87] Soudek (1958, p. 260, 1976) and Jackson (1992, 1995).

[88] Martines (1963, pp. 326–327) and Jackson (1992, pp. 236–237).

[89] Baron (1928, pp. 121, 8–10).

[90] Baron (1928, p. 120).

[91] G. Galdiera, *De oeconomia* (1463); Fr. Barbaro, *De re uxoria* (1415), a work dedicated to Lorenzo de Medici; E. Barbaro, *De coelibatu* (1471–1472). Cf. King (1976, pp. 22–48).

[92] Alberti (1994), cf. Bürgin (1993, p. 212).

[93] Furlan (1994, pp. 438–439).

[94] Burckhardt (1860 [1997], pp. 275–276). Ponte (1971, pp. 306–308, quoted by Goldbrunner 1975, pp. 114–115; Baeck 1997).

The *Oeconomica* had also a considerable resonance among the Cameralists.[95] It is of great importance that A. de Montchrétien (1575–1621), who used the term "political economy" in his work *Traité d' économie politique* (1615), and Louis de Mayerne Turquet (1550–1618), who introduced first this term 4 years earlier than Montchrétien in his book *La Monarchie aristodemocratique et le gouvernement compose et mesle des trois formes des legitimes republiques* (1611),[96] seem to support their ideas and arguments in the same tradition which goes back to Aristotle and the *Oeconomica*.[97]

The use of the term "political economy" will rise again in the texts of the Cameralists. Cameralism, basically an economic doctrine, discussed in the so-called police science (Polizeywissenschaft) the public law aspects of an orderly commonwealth, including jurisdiction, taxation but also sanitation, poor laws, and the like, typically in some kind of interconnected treatment.[98] The procedure of analyzing the methods of rising the revenues for the "camerae" of the monarchs seems to have similarities with the second book of *Oeconomica*.

The work *Oeconomica* – except from its popularity and significance in Medieval Times and Renaissance – is therefore important in that it explains very simply and effectively two ideas fundamental in Antiquity. The agrarian economy and country life are considered superior since they respond to the ideal of self-sufficiency, while trade not only makes a person dependent on others, but allows him to get rich only at the expense of others (according to the canon which belongs to the simple reproduction economy). These two ideas were so deeply rooted in Antiquity that, through humanistic culture, they influenced modern thinking and they were often to be repeated up to the late 1700s.[99]

The Economic Philosophy of Epicureans

Epicurus (341–270) was born in Samos by Athenian colonists, migrated to Athens after the expulsion of the colony, studied philosophy, and set up his own school in about 307/6.[100]

The central tenet of the Epicurean school was that in order to achieve happiness (eudaimonia) it is necessary to avoid trouble; the highest pleasure is the "absence of disturbance" (ataraxia). Epicurus' elegantly expressed letter to Menoikeus, preserved by Diogenes Laertius (X 121–135), gives a good idea of this. Epicurus taught that psychic value is unlimited (cf. Aristotle, *Politics* Book VII) and that the wise are

---

[95] Brunner (1949, pp. 237–280, 300–312, 1952).

[96] It was King (1948, pp. 230–231) who discovered Turquet's work. Cf. Bürgin (1993, p. 212).

[97] Andreades (1933, pp. 81–82). Cf. also Baloglou (1999b, pp. 34–35).

[98] Backhaus (1989, pp. 7–8, 1999, p. 12).

[99] Perrotta (2000, p. 118).

[100] Theodorides (1957).

contented with things easy to acquire (Diog. Laert. X 130; 144, 146). Real wealth is only gained by limitation of wants, and he who is not satisfied with little will not be satisfied at all (*Kyriai Doxai* XXIX). "Self-sufficiency is the greatest wealth," says Clement of Alexandreia (*Stromateis*, VI 2, 42, 18) for Epicurus' teaching. It is not increase of possessions but limitation of desires that makes one truly rich.[101]

In accord with his teaching, he seems to have lived very simply.[102] However, he did not go the extreme of the Cynics, but taught that the wise will have a care to gain property, and not live as beggars (Diog. Laert. X 119). Many subsequent sources insist on the fact that the wise Epicurean should neither marry nor have children. But his did not forbid the wise man from exercising his own particular *oikonomia*, probably in common with other men of wisdom.[103] In fact, Epicurus confirmed that one should laugh, philosophize, and *oikonomein* all together, with cheerful and unpersuasive management of one's own property.[104]

Epicuraenism gained advocates in Rome, especially among writers and intellectuals. Lucretius (ca. 94–55 BC), at the end of the fifth book of his *De rerum Natura* (v. 925–1457), which was written about the middle of the first century BC,[105] draws a picture of the development of human society, which is unique in Latin literature for its insight and originality. It is partly based on the ideas and teaching of Epicurus.

Among Epicurus' disciples was Metrodorus the Athenian (330–277) who wrote a treatise entitled Περί πλούτου (Peri ploutou, On Wealth) (cf. *Diog. Laert.* X 24).[106] He explains that tranquility cannot be achieved if we back away from all difficulties. Admittedly, many things such as wealth produce some pain when they are present, but torment us more when they are not. In fact, the greedy man seeks opportunities to get rich and he specializes in this art; the wise man, on the other hand, is satisfied if he knows how to acquire and to preserve what he needs.[107] It might be possible that this work influenced Philodemus, who cited Metrodorus' treatise (Philodemus, *Peri oikonomias* Col. XII 10).

Philodemus

Philodemus' of Gadara (110–40 BC) book *On Household-economics*[108] consists of three parts. In the first part (col. I–VII), Philodemus gives us an extended discussion, almost a line-by-line critical commentary of Xenophon's *Oikonomikos*.

---

[101] Usener (1887, p. 302 Fr. 473; p. 303, Fr. 476).

[102] Trever (1916, p. 130) and Shipley (2000, p. 183).

[103] Natali (1995, pp. 109–110).

[104] Barker (1956, pp. 179–180).

[105] Barker (1956, p. 173, 181). For the description of his theory of the development of the Society. See Lovejoy and Boas, George 1973.

[106] Sudhaus (1906).

[107] Perrotta (2003, p. 208).

[108] For the text of the work see Jensen (1907). For a systematic description of all editions and translations of this work see Baloglou and Maniatis (1994, pp. 139–140).

In the second part (col. VII–IX), he offers also a critical commentary of the first book of *Oeconomica*, which he attributes to Theophrastus (col. VII 6). In the third and last part of his work (col. XII–XXXVIII), Philodemus adds a whole section with economic and ethical instructions to the wise Epicurean.

Philodemus outlined precisely the area of his operation and the thematic parameters of his discussion: he does not intend to speak of right methods about organizing life at home, but only of the attitude one should have regarding wealth, dividing this problem into three points:

Acquisition
Maintenance
Acquisition suitable for the philosopher.[109]

In this way, compared to the four specific areas of oikonomia which Aristotle separated out, Philodemus eliminates the section on social, affectionate, and hierarchical relationships within the household and restricts the "economic" discussion to the simple point of wealth.

> 'I shall therefore discuss not', writes Philodemus, 'how one should rightly live in the house but how one should behave regarding the acquisition and preservation of wealth (chrematon kteseos te kai phylakes), points which specifically concern administration and the administrator (ten oikonomian kai ton oikonomikon), without in any way opposing those who would put other points under the above headings; and also the acquisition of goods most suited' to the philosopher, and not just to any citizen' (Col. XII 10).

The restriction laid down by Philodemus is not exactly a redefinition of the field of oikonomia.[110] He says that he does not want to change the scope of the study when he admits that others could put other points under the same headings (Col. XII, 12–15). He indicated, as far as economic practice is concerned, that he wishes to limit himself to examination of a point of direct interest to the philosopher and does not wish to take care of the question of internal family relations.

The question is important methodologically, given that the need to determine the theoretical field of a possible Epicurean art or science of "Economics" has been perceived.[111] The scope of Philodemus' idea is to indicate the principle of an "aristos bios" (Col. XIII). Therefore, he gives advice for the determination of the real measurement of the philosopher's wealth, of the determination of the ploutou metron, and this is something he deals with in another work: "There is a measurement of wealth for the philosopher, which I have illustrated according to our leaders in the book 'On wealth,' so as to show what the art of economics (oikonomiken) consists of with regards to its acquisition and preservation" (Col. XII 10).

Philodemus declares that it is legitimate for an Epicurean to write on points of Economics and he cites the examples of Metrodorus (Col. XII; XXI; XXVII) and Epicharmus (Col. XXIV 24), who insists, according to Philodemus, on the prediction

---

[109] Hartung (1857, p. 7), Baloglou and Maniatis (1994, p. 125), and Natali (1995, p. 110).
[110] This is apparently Schoemann's (1839) view.
[111] Natali (1995, p. 111).

of economic affairs (Col. XXV 24). From this point of view, Philodemus' treatise is very important, because it gives information about the Epicurean economic thought.[112]

In the section where Philodemus gives positive rules, he suggests that one should not concentrate too much on household management, overlooking external social relationships – it is the opposite of what Xenophon (*Oeconomicus* XI) advises; he talks, instead, about concerning oneself with affability, generosity towards friends, and attentiveness to one's most hard-up friends, even to the extent of remembering them in one's will (Col. XXII; XXIII; XXVII).

Stoic Economic Thought

The Stoics gave to the ancient world, during the whole of the six centuries which lie between Alexander of Macedonia and the Emperor Constantine I, the system of philosophy, of ethics, and of religion, which was generally current among thinking men. The fact that "the philosophy of the Hellenistic world was the Stoa and all else was secondary,"[113] and that the Hellenistic world transmitted this philosophy to the Romans of the later Republic and the early Empire, with modifications to suit their genius, proves the significance of this philosophical school.

Stoics write explicitly of political matters. Zeno's principal political work was entitled *Politeia*. Cleanthes wrote a treatise entitled *Politikos* (*Statesman*) (Diog. Laert. VII 175), Sphaerus wrote on the Spartan constitution, *Politeia Lakonike* (Diog. Laert. VII 178); Persaeus, Cleanthes, and Sphaerus wrote treatises on monarchy and kingship (SVF I 435 (Persaeus), 481 (Cleanthes), and 620 (Sphaerus)). These treatises belong to the "mirror of princes" literature,[114] which will be found later in Byzantine and Arab-Islamic thought.

The Stoics support the view that man is "naturally a political animal" (Stob. II, VII, 5^{b1}, p. 59, 6) and that "Polis is the most perfect society," which has been founded for the establishment of self-sufficiency (Stob. II, VII, 26, p. 150, 4–6).

The Stoics also recognized another dimension of man, as a member of the Oikos, the "economic animal" (zoon oikonomikon) according to the Aristotelian terminology (*Eudemeian Ethics*, VIII 10, 1242a 22–23).The Stoics claim that the establishment of the Oikos is the "first politeia" (Stob. II, VII, 26, p. 148, 5) and the Oikos constitutes the "beginning of the Polis" (Stob. II, VII, 26, p. 148, 7). They recognized the three relationships in the Oikos like Aristotle.

From this point of view, Oikos is a small Polis, while Oikonomia is a "narrowed" Politeia; Polis, in contrast, is a great Oikos (SVF II 80). This is a clear statement of a microeconomic concept. The wise man is not only a citizen of the Polis where he lives, but he is a citizen of the Megalopolis of the universe, the cosmos, which follows a single administration and law (SVF III 79).

---

[112] Baloglou and Maniatis (1994, p. 130).

[113] Tarn (1930, p. 325).

[114] Habicht (1958, pp. 1–16) and Chroust (1965, p. 173).

The wise man, on the basis of his superior doctrine, is the best economist. In Arius Didymus' Stoic anthology, the features of the wise man are described: "He sc. (the wise man) is fortunate, happy, blessed, rich, pious, a friend of divinity, worthy of distinction, and of being a king, a general, a politician kai oikonomikos (housekeeper) kai chrematisticos" (Stob. II, VII, 11^g, p. 100, 2). As far as the qualities of oikonomikos and chrematistikos are concerned, Stoics appear to have considered with attention what was implied by the use of these adjectives (Stob. II, VII, 11^d, p. 95, 9–23). In Arius Didymus' anthology cited by Stobaeus (II, VII, 11^m, pp. 109, 10–110, 8 = SVF III 686), we find that the wise man can gain from teaching. We view a different context of chrematistics than the Stoics which also differs from Aristotle's ideas.

The Stoics studied the phenomenon of value when they discussed the ethical subject of indifference. The value of things concerning which we should be indifferent depends on the possibility of their right use (SVF II 240; III 117, 122, 123, 135). Among the meanings of value, there is in fact one tied to trade and to the market: that which is given in return for a good, when it has been valued by an expert, for example a load of wheat of barley for a mule (Diog. Laert. VII 105). We will recall that in Stobaeus the position of Diogenes of Babylon is cited – he construed dokimaston not as the valued object, but as the expert who values it; and that in Cicero (*De officiis* II 50–55), the dispute between Diogenes of Babylon and Antipater of Tarsus on behavior in trade is cited:

> In deciding cases of this kind [sc. expediency vs. moral rectitude in business relations] Diogenes of Babylon, a great and highly esteemed Stoic, consistently holds on view; his pupil Antipater, a most profound scholar, holds another. According to Antipater, all the facts should be disclosed, that the buyer may not be uniformed of any detail that the seller knows; according to Diogenes of Babylon the seller should declare any defects in his wares, in so far as such a source is prescribed by the common law of the land; but for the rest, since he has goods to sell, he may try to sell then to the possible advantage, provided he is guilty of no misrepresentation. 'I have improved my stock', Diogenes' merchant will say: 'I have offered it for sale; I sell it at price no higher than my competitors- perhaps even lower, when the market is overstocked. Who is wronged?' – 'What say you?', comes Antipater's argument on the other side; 'it is duty to consider the interest of your fellow-men and to serve society…'

The above passage seems the Stoic conception on trade. It is interesting to note that there is a similarity to Aristotle's position. Like Aristotle – who had dealt with the problem of the market, not in the area of economics (*Politics* I, ch. 8–11), but in the context of his study of the kinds of justice – the Stoics had occupied this subject in the context of justice.[115]

Later Stoic Influences on the Field of Economics

It is evident that the economic doctrines of the Early Stoics reappear later in the Roman Times. A stoic influence can be seen in some of Philo's of Alexandreia (30 BC to AD 45) texts on oikonomia. In his treatise *De Iosepho*, which is also

---

[115] Baloglou (2002a).

entitled *The Statesman*, he presents a view of "the Statesman" as in the nature of an arbitrator, and thus like Solon of Athens: however powerful the people may be, the statesman must give no more than its due, just as Solon had done in his day and for its generation.[116] Philo in dealing with the period Joseph spent as a steward (epitropos) in Egypt holds this was beneficial for the future statesman (politician, politicos), who must first be trained and practiced in household management (ta kata oikonomian); for, he goes on, evidently quoting Chrysippus, "a household is a polis compressed into small dimensions, and household management (oikonomia) is a sort of epitome of state government, just as a polis is also a great house (ὡς καὶ πόλις μὲν οἶκος μέγας), and state management is a public household management of sorts. From these facts it is quite clear that the same man is both adept at household management (oikonomikon) and equipped for state administration, even though the magnitude and size of the objects under consideration differ" (Arnim 1963, SVF III 80, $_{13-16}$, Fr. 323). Similarly, again following Chrysippus, he writes that household management is "a special instance of stratecraft on a small scale, since stratecraft and household management (oikonomia) are related virtues which, it would not be amiss to show, are, as, it were, interchangeable, both because stratecraft is household management in the state, and because household management is stratecraft in the home" (Philo, *Problems and Solutions of the books of Genesis* 4. 164, SVF III 160, $_{8-11}$). This passage, as Reumann[117] has pointed out, preserved in Armenian, is found in older Latin translations. In spite, therefore, of the old distinction about size, "oikonomia" and "politeia" are related so that one can speak of household and state management as "the offspring of the same virtue, as equals in species yet unequals in magnitude, as house and state (ut domus et civitas)." (Philo, *De animalibus adv. Alexandrum* in Arnim 1963, SVF II, 209, $_{26-28}$). And thus the way was open for applying "oikonomia" to the care, administration, and management of larger units in human society than an estate.[118] Joseph has been trained in the household of Potiphar, before he became Pharaoh's minister; that is an allegory of the truth that the future politician must first be trained and practiced in household management (oikonomia). This idea closely recalls Plato's *Politicus* (Statesman), in which the distinction between household administration and civil administration is based solely on the different size of the two communities and not on their different natures.

Musonius Rufus (ca. 30–100 AD), Epictetus' teacher, speaks in his treatise *Whether Marriage is an Impediment to the Philosopher* (Stob. IV 22, 20, p. 497, $_{19}$– 501, $_{29}$) directly of the philosopher and asks for what reason marriage should be useful for the common man, but not for the philosopher: the philosopher is no worse than other men; indeed, he is better and juster than them, a guide and master of natural activities like marriage (Stob. IV 22, 20 p. 498, $_{2-15}$ and p. 501, $_{13-16}$). Furthermore, Musonius supports in his diatribe entitled *The Means of Acquiring Goods Most Suited to the Philosopher* (Hense 124, $_{17}$ - 125, $_{11}$) the view that the form of livelihood

---

[116] Barker (1956, p. 157). See also Schofield (1991, ch. 1).

[117] Reumann (1980, p. 370, n. 6).

[118] Reumann (1980, p. 370).

and acquisition of goods preferable to all is "philosophein and georgein," to till the soil and to philosophize. To live in the fields is more manly than to sit in the city like sophists, and it is more the mark of a free man to procure necessary items alone than to receive them from others (Stob. IV 15ª 18, p. 381,$_{10-15}$). The discourse then continues outlining a kind of agricultural commune, in which the disciples should be worked hard under the master's command and, as a reward, receive the master's philosophical wisdom. All this is controversially aimed at the "sophists," encouraging young people not to follow a master who teaches in the polis and not to stay to listen in a school (Stob. IV 15ª 18, p. 382,$_{12-13}$). It is clear enough that the argument was turned against views similar to those of Epicurus, Philodemus, and Chrysippus.

Another theme that occurs in connection with praise of the rural life is the contrast between life in the country and life in the town, when the former is seen in a positive light and the latter in a negative. This theme is also to be found in Musonius. In addition to excessive luxury, idleness, illhealth, and wickedness, he associates the city with the – in his eyes – inferior sophists.

We observe similar ideas by Dio of Prusa, also known as Chrysostom (c. 40–120 AD)[119] who lived in the period of the "Second Sophistic." Among the 80 orations which have been survived, the seventh oration, the "Euboicus," is the best of them, as a document illustrative of the social conditions and ideas current in the Greek world about AD 100, and especially the part of the oration which deals with urban conditions and the reform of urban life.[120]

Dio praises the simple life in the country. A simple life is possible in the city too, but a life in the country is still to be preferred. The simple life does eventually lead to inner freedom (see Or. 7, § 11, § 66, § 103); and as we can see in other works, Dio believes that the person who is free is also good and in possession of arête (see Or. 15, § 32; Or. 6, § 34).

Dio believes that it is easier for the poor to lead a good life in the country than in the city. This is why later in the treatise (Or. 7, § 107) he plays with the idea of, if need be, actually forcing the poor to settle in the country as farmers. He accordingly proceeds to ask what decent urban occupations can be found, to prevent the poor from being compelled, by the pressure of unemployment, to betake themselves to some low and degrading sort of trade (Or. 7, § 109). Unfortunately, he gives no clear or positive answer to the question. He confines himself to suggesting (1) what is the general nature of a decent urban occupation, and (2) what are the low and degrading forms of employment which ought not to be allowed in a city.

---

[119] It is always difficult to know in which philosophical school Dio should be placed. He is considered a Cynic by Paquet (1975), Blumentritt (1979), Schmitt (1972), Long (1974), and Dudley (1937, pp. 148–157). Barker (1956, p. 295), Jones (1978), and Moles (1978) regard him a both a Cynic and a Stoic. They are of the opinion that Dio was especially attracted to Cynicism during his exile (AD 82), but he rejected it during the last years of his life. Moles (1978) regards Dio as a person who throughout his life was a Cynic, a Stoic, and a Sophist. Jones (1978) finally prefers to see Dio as a Stoic. Brunt (1973, pp. 210–211) and Hoven van den (1996, p. 27) consider Dio to be a Stoic.

[120] Barker (1956, pp. 295–296), Triantaphyllopoulos and Triantaphyllopoulos (1974, pp. 34–40), and Triantaphyllopoulos (1994, p. 12).

It is worth noting that Dio's eulogy of the country life fits in the tradition of, for example, Xenophon's *Oeconomicus* and Cato's *De agricultura*. For, like these two writers, Dio believes the hard life of the country breeds physically strong men who are able to defend their towns (Or. 7, § 49).[121] Dio goes further than the aforementioned authors, whereas he wants to convince his listeners that virtue is compatible with poverty, and that poverty is superior to wealth. Poverty in this context should be understood as the state of having to work for a living so that, for Dio, virtue is automatically compatible with labor (Or. 7, § 112–113). Out of ethical and pedagogic convictions, Dio exhorted people to work. From this point of view, it is not improper to support that one aim of Dio's "Euboicus" was to obtain public support for the so-called "poor policy" of the emperor Trajan among others.[122]

After reading the conclusion that it is not practicable to resettle all the poor people from the city in the country, Dio goes on to list which city occupations could be practiced by these poor people in order to live in what he believes is the proper way (Or. 7, 109).

What we must finally conclude is that the speech preaches the Stoic ideal of the simple life with important component parts, such as self-sufficiency and dignifying tool. It should be noted that, certainly with reference to the last point, Dio takes an exceptional view for his time.

The important representative of the Middle Stoa, Panaetius of Rhodes (185–110 B.C.) – an aristocrat by birth and friend of Scipio Aemilianus – seems to have a preference for agriculture. We gather from Cicero's *De officiis* (I 151) that Panaetius, – together with Cicero – is of the opinion that "there is no kind of gainful employment that is better, more fruitful, more pleasant and more worthy of a free man than agriculture." His hommage to agriculture actually concerns only the landowner and the hard-working farmer, just like Xenophon's. So, on this point, Panaetius cannot be compared with his two fellow Stoics, Musonius and Dio, of a later period, who in addition to praising agriculture in general, extol the diligent labor of the farmer and consider him virtuous for it.

The Neopythagoreans

A whole series of economic texts, surviving in Stobaeus, belongs to the tradition of texts written by the Neopythagoreans. These include Bryson, *Oeconomicus* (Stob. V 28, 15 pp. 680,$_7$–681,$_{14}$); Callicratidas, *Peri oikou eudaimonias* (=On household

---

[121] Compare Xenophon, *Oeconomicus* IV 24 – V 17. Cato, *De agricultura*, preface; Livy VIII 20, 4. Brunt (1973, p. 213) remarks correctly with reference to Dio's comment that farmers make such good soldiers: "He does not feel the irrelevance of this ancient platitude to the normal conditions of a Greek city under the Roman peace, nor (if he was speaking at Rome) to those which obtained in the capital itself or throughout Italy; under Trajan the whole peninsula now furnished few legionaries." Cf. Garnsey (1980, p. 37) who believes that the emergence and promotion of the myth of the peasant patriarch came just at a time when the process of peasant displacement and the concentration of estates in the hands of the rich was spending up.

[122] Jones (1978, p. 60) and Grassl (1982, pp. 149–152).

happiness) (Stob. V 28, 16 pp. 681,$_{15}$–688, $_8$); Perictione, *Peri gynaikos sophrosynas* (Stob. IV 23, 61 and 61ª, pp. 588, $_{17}$–593, $_{11}$). Among epistolary collections, there are letters attributed to Pythagorean women, which make reference to points about oikonomia.[123]

The surviving fragment of Bryson's *Oeconomicus* consists of two parts (Stob. V 28, 15 pp. 680, $_8$–681, $_3$ and pp. 681 $_{,4–14}$). He dealt with specific issues of which we can give an overview: (a) The nature of economics (Stob. IV 28, 15 p. 680, $_{10–16}$). (b) The right methods of acquiring goods; the definition of wealth and economic welfare; agriculture and trade (Stob. IV 28, 15 p. 680, $_{15–18}$). (c) Relationships with slaves; types of slaves (douleia); the legitimacy of douleia (Stob. IV 28, 15 p. 681 $_{,4–14}$).

In the first part, he gives a catalog of vocations (Stob. V 28, 15 p. 680, 13–681, 2), similar to that of Xenophon (*Oecomonicus* I 1–4) and *Oeconomica* (A II, 1343a 26–27).[124]

In the Arabic text of Bryson's treatise, we find a strange theory about the fixity of professions: he maintains that, since there is a need in a polis for all crafts, it is praiseworthy to remain within one's own class (Plessner, 216, $_{12}$–217, $_{14}$) without desire to improve oneself by taking a superior craft. Otherwise, in time, everybody would be doing the same job and civilization would vanish (Plessner, 221, $_{29–31}$). This idea seems to be original, we are not able to say if this idea was connected with the economic conditions of the Roman Empire, or if it reflected Arab concepts.

In the second part of Stobaeus' fragment (V 28, 15 p. 681, $_{3–15}$), Bryson adds an anthropological study of the different kinds of slavery, isolating the psycho-physical characteristics in relation to the different duties assigned to them in the Oikos; while the author of *Oeconomica* (A V 1344 a23–44 b21), like Xenophon, distinguishes between two types of douloi according to their function (workmen and superinten-dents), Bryson distinguishes three kinds: firstly according to origins – by law, by lack of control, by nature (V 28, 15 p. 681, $_{5–8}$) – secondly according to their duties – domestic, personal, outdoor workers (V 28, 15 p. 681, $_{10–13}$). It seems to be a new approach in the slave theory of the Ancient Hellenes, while Aristotle distinguishes two kinds of douloi, by law and by nature (Aristotle, *Politics* I 6, 1255a 5: doulos by law; I 4, 1254b 15; 1254b 19; III 6, 1278b 33: doulos by nature).

A particularly interesting text is the first chapter of Bryson's *Oeconomicus*, which survives in an Arabic translation and is devoted to the subject of money. This chapter[125] consists of a practical section[126] dedicated to the problems of acquiring money, the conversation of one's estate, and the correct manner of expenditure; but before these instructions, Bryson put forward an anthropological theory of trade and money, based on medical considerations.[127] It is perhaps because of these elements that this work is attributed to Galen in some manuscripts of the partial Latin translation.

---

[123] All these texts have been edited by Thesleff (1965). For a philological analysis of the survived fragments see Wilhelm (1915).

[124] Baloglou and Constantinidis (1996, p. 49).

[125] Plessner (1928, pp. 218–219).

[126] Plessner (1928, p. 218, 16–219, 20).

[127] Natali (1995, p. 105).

Money arises out of difficulties in trade. The necessity of transactions creates a lot of needs; and it is difficult to know what exact quantity of each good one has to give to match another quantity of another commodity and we have tried to find something which corresponds to all the goods of any specific value. Then the need for money arose.[128] Money was invented as a method of circulation and as a measure of value, to use Marx's terms. In virtue of its existence and by equating a little of its kind with a great amount of other things, gold and silver were used to permit people to dispense with the inconvenience and trouble of transporting provisions to remote places.[129]

The aristocratic ideology of the ethical superiority of wealth gained by the cultivation of land and of the disrepute attached to commercial activity, already expressed in Xenophon (*Oeconomicus* IV–VI), in Aristotle (*Rhetoric* II 4, 1381 a21–24) and in *Oeconomica* (Book I, ch. II), turned up in Bryson's treatise.

Bryson's treatise became very famous and exercised an influence on the Arab-Islamic economic thought, as we'll show below.

Callicratidas' study entitled *Peri oikou eudaimonias* (*On Household Happiness*) is addressed to a despotes, as commonly understood. The term "oikodespotes" is used in the essay for the first time (Stob. V 28, 16 p. 682, $_{25}$). He considers that the family community consists both of people and of property (Stob. V 28, 16 p. 681, $_{14-15}$). He affirms that the family is a harmonious community of different elements, which tends towards the good of the head of the family and towards unanimity, the homophrosyna (Stob. V 28, 16 p. 682, $_{26-27}$).

Callicratidas compares the different kinds of family relationships to the different constitutions of the Polis in a very similar way to Aristotle (cf. *Politics*, I § 12; *Nicomachean Ethics* VIII 12, 1160 b22; 1161 a9). Then he analyzes the three relationships in the Oikos; the despotic, the superintendentic, and the politician (Stob. V 28, 17 p. 684, 17–18).

It is worth noting that Callicratidas compares the organization of the Polis and the Oikos with the organization of the world (cosmos) (Stob. V 28, 17 p. 685, $_{12-13}$). The view is a new one and is, in my opinion, influenced by the organization of the kingdoms (empires) in the Hellenistic World. This approach, which has not been explored yet, will be found later in the Stoic doctrines of the Roman times.

Wealth and Labor in the Cynic Sect

The essence of the Cynic state is the virtue of the self-sufficient individual, a state certainly attainable in practice. This state involves rejection of the polis and all its institutions – and so the Cynic idea of self-sufficiency, where the individual lives in the polis (Aristotle, *Nicomachean Ethics* I 9, 1099 a33ff; *Eudemeian Ethics* 12, 1244 b1ff; *Great Ethics* II 15, 1213 a24ff) – except those that have immediate practical utility. The minimalist Cynic requirements for subsistence mean that the

---

[128] Plessner (1928, p. 219).

[129] Plessner (1928, p. 219, 21–33).

Cynic can support himself by begging and "living of the land." The self-sufficient Cynic recognizes actual kinship with other Cynics. Hence, he may freely choose to have relations with fellow-Cynics. If children result, a Cynic community will come into being.[130]

Did Cynics have anything to say about "the means of production?" Not, it seems, very much, but there are Cynics, or Cynic-influenced, texts which endorse humble occupations[131] and we may perhaps get some idea of what a universal Cynic state would look like from the famous "Golden Age fragment" of Diogenes of Oenonanda: "then truly the live of the gods will pass to men. For everything will be full of justice and mutual love, and there will come to be no need of fortifications or laws and all the things which we contrive on account of one another. As for the necessaries derived from agriculture, since we shall have no [slaves at that time] (for indeed) [we ourselves shall plough] and dig and tend [the plants] and [divert] rivers and watch over [the crops], we shall (...)."[132]

The characteristic feature of the Cynic theory lies in the fact that they expressed a radical asceticism. Their founder Antisthenes (ca. 445-after 366), one of Socrates' pupils, boasts of his wealth because – he says – wealth and poverty are not in men's houses, but in their souls (Xenophon, *Symposium* IV 34). Wealth without virtue was not only worthless, but a fruitful source of evil (Xenophon, *Symposium* IV 35–36), the lover of money could be neither virtuous or free.[133] In utter antithesis to Aristotle (*Politics* I 1, 1253 a1–4), he declared polis life and civilization to be the source of all injustice, luxury, and corruption.

According to Diogenes of Sinope (412–323), "wealth without virtue is worse than poverty" (Stob. IV 31 p. 766, $_{12-13}$), and "virtue cannot dwell either in a wealthy state or in a wealthy house" (Stob. IV 29 p. 708, $_{9-12}$). Poverty accords better with virtue and is so the real cause of suffering (Stob. IV 32 p. 806, 17–807, 2). In his fifteenth letter he refers to love of money as the cause of all evil. According to Dio of Prusa (Or. 6, § 25), Diogenes said that people gathered in the towns in order to be free from injustice. But in the cities, they did the worst things, as if they had gathered with that aim. That would have been the reason of the punishment of Prometheus by Zeus, for the distribution of fire was the origin and cause of effeminacy and luxury (Dio of Prusa, Or. 8, 285R-286R).[134]

He wrote a treatise entitled *Politeia* in which he seems to have advocated fiat money to take the place of the hated gold and silver (Athenaeus, *Deipnosophistai* 159c) and to prevent the extensive accumulation of movable wealth. In this natural community, there is an absence of "chrematistics," because there is no place in the institution of private properties and in the exchanges relations (SVF I 590; Onesicritus in FGrH 134F 24 (20)).[135]

---

[130] Moles (1995, pp. 141–142, 1996, p. 111). For an overview of the cynic doctrines. See Branham and Goulet-Caze (1996, pp. 1–27).

[131] Hock (1976, pp. 41–53)=Billerbeck (1991, pp. 259–271).

[132] Smith (1993, F 56) and Diogenes of Oenoanda (1998, p. 90).

[133] Trever (1975, p. 131) and Eleutheropoulos (1930, p. 57).

[134] Cf. Bayonas (1970, p. 49).

[135] See Aalders (1975, p. 57) and Ferguson (1975, pp. 91–97).

Crates of Thebes (ca. 368/65–288/85 BC), a wealthy landowner, and therefore at the opposite end of the social spectrum from a poor exile like Diogenes, gives away his possessions exclaiming that in this way he is freeing himself (Diog. Laert. VI 86). If Diogenes is regarded as the embodiment of self-sufficiency (autarkeia), Crates may stand for that of philanthropy, variously symbolized in the conceptions of the Cynic as the Watchdog, as Doctor, or as Scout, working in the interests of humanity. He denounced everything which tended to limit or restrict freedom, viz., the care of property, pleasure seeking, patriotism, friendship, and love, and it was the greatest wish that he might be able to emancipate himself from dependence of food as he had done from other ties (Athenaeus, *Deipnosophistai* 10 422c; Diog. Laert. VI 90). Simplicity and Good Judgement must replace Luxury and Extravagance. But asceticism, and even philosophy, are not ends in themselves. They are means to the supreme end, which is of course *eudaimonia* (happiness), or what was synonymous to the Cynic, *apatheia*. Through asceticism and "philosophy," we may come to the "island of Pera," the Cynic paradise where the natural life of Cynics has been realized (Diog. Laert. VI 85).

Teles of Megara (fl. ca. 235 BC), a teacher and moralist, maintains that the possession of money is not free from want. The poor, not the wealthy, has pleasure because he can attain to contemplative life; while the wealthy is effeminate, because he does not need to work.[136]

The description of the Golden Age of Hesiod finds an imitator in the personality of Onesicritus of Astypalea, "one of Diogenes' distinguished pupils," according to Diogenes Laertius (VI 84). A great admirer of Diogenes, he later joined the expedition of Alexander, in which he played a not unimportant part, being the pilot of the King's ship, and chief navigating officer under Nearchus in the famous voyage through the Persian Gulf.[137]

The most interesting fragment of Onesicritus is probably his account of the Indian sages. We have two versions, the condensed one of Plutarch (*Alexander* 65) and the fuller one of Strabo (*Geographica* XV 1, 63–65), where Onesicritus' own language has sometimes been preserved. It is interesting to see how he represented a sect of Indian fakirs as so many Cynics, holding beliefs about a vanished Golden Age. Cynic is the way in which he writes of the simple virtue of savage races. In the description of the land of Mousicanus, Onesicritus provided the simple and healthful life of the citizens "despite the fact that their country offers abundance of every commodity [...]. They use neither gold nor silver, although mines exist in their country. Instead of slaves they use the young men in their prime [...]. They cultivate no science except that of medicine..."

Few figures in the Hellenistic world were more impressively versatile than Cercidas of Megalopolis (ca. 290–217),[138] who combined the roles of statesman

---

[136] Trever (1975, pp. 138–139).

[137] Brown (1949, pp. 1–23).

[138] Goulet-Caze and Lopez (1994, p. 271). It is not an exaggeration, we believe, if we compare Cercidas with Solon, who combined in his time the art of the poem and philosopher with that of the statesman.

(Polybius, *Histories* II 48,$_{3-41}$; 50–53; Aelian, *Varia Historia* XIII 20), military commander – he was the commander of the 1,000 Megalopolitan exiles, who faught on the Achaean side against Cleomenes of Sparta at Sellasia (222 BC) (Polybius, *Histories* II 65,$_{3-4}$), poet, and Cynic philosopher (Diog. Laert. VI 76–77). The paradox and "provocative" of his poem is that a citizen of one of the cities of the conservative Achaean League should have been so radical an exponent of the idea of social justice. The explanation could be, that Cercidas as a Cynic thinker, and as such an egalitarian, may have been attracted by Cleomenes' III of Sparta social reforms (cf. Plutarch, *Cleomenes*) to achieve some system of social justice.[139] After the destruction of the city in the course of a war with Sparta, and when plans for rebuilding it were being mooted, a proposal was made (which led to disputes) that one third of the estates of the land-owing class should be divided among new owners. Cercidas emphasized in his poem the great contrast between wealth and poverty.

Cercidas dissatisfied with the existing order exhorted his wealth friends to meet the threat of social revolution by healing the sick and giving to the poor. So, he emphasized the fact that

for sharing - with – others is a divinity, and Nemesis is still present on earth.[140]

"Nemesis" is a word which in its original sense means a proper distribution of shares. He is warning the ruling class to be generous and help the poor before they are overwhelmed. Cercidas' poem reflected the one expression of philanthropy in literature.[141] The poem is a call to the party of reform not to wait for the vegance of Heaven to strike the rich, but to act themselves under the inspiration of new triad of deities, Paean and Sharing, and Nemesis.[142]

The characteristic feature of the Cynic behavior is that the Cynics did have been respected by their contemporaries.[143] They influenced the Early Christian Fathers.[144] There are several elements in the behavior of the Cynics that remind us of extremist Christian movements. The search for suffering and mortification recall eastern monasticism of the first centuries after Christ. The missionary character of their preaching, the obsession with poverty and the practice of begging recall the pauperist movements of the twelfth to thirteenth centuries, and in particular, the Franciscans.

---

[139] It is worth noting that Cleomenes' reforms, which had a great success, led to an attack by Cercidas (Baloglou 2004a).

[140] López-Gruces (1995, p. 251, Vv. 31–32).

[141] Tarn (1930, p. 102).

[142] Dudley (1937 [1973], pp. 78–79).

[143] For instance the comic Menander, who was Theophrastus' disciple (Diog. Laert. V 36–37). See Tsekourakis (1977, pp. 384–399).

[144] For example by Gregor of Nazianz, who emphasized and annotated Cercidas' thought. See Gregor of Nazianz "De virtute," *PG* XXXVII (1862) col. 723. Cf. Asmus (1894 [1991]).

Utopias

The conquests of Alexander had broadened the vision of the Hellenes, so that they no longer thought in terms of the typical circumscribed Hippodamean polis of classical times, but rather in terms of world-state. Contact with distant peoples had led to a renewal of curiosity. A new kind of literature appeared, to so-called "Staatsroman."[145] Quite reputable historians and geographers might incorporate fictitious Utopias in otherwise sober works. There are two opposite tendencies in Greek speculation about the remote past, one of which thought of early society as rude and uncivilized, while the other looked back to a Golden Age. The Golden Age view is older, according to Rohde, finding support in later days in Plato, Dicaearchus, and ultimately in the Stoics. This has as a corollary the early Greek belief that at the edges of the earth there still existed a righteous and wholesome society.[146] The advance of geographical knowledge brought with it the names of other divinely happy people besides the Hyperboreans of Homer and Pindar. The Scythians in the far north are credited with all the virtues, as are the Indians in the Far East, and also the Ethiopians and the "Silk People" of India. Not only do these people live in a state of idyllic bliss, but they also enjoy a far longer life than ordinary men.[147]

We consider Theopompus' (380–300) *Meropian Land* (Aelian, *Varia Historia* III 18 = FGrH B II 115 F75), Hecataeus' *Aigyptiaca* (FGrH A III 264, F 7–14), Euhemerus' (c. 340–260) *Sacred Chronicle* (*Hiera Anagraphe*) (Diodorus Siculus, *Bibliotheca Historike* V 41–46)[148] and Iambulus' *Sun State* (Diod. Sic. II 55, $_1$–60, $_3$).

Hecataeus' work "On the Egyptians" is perhaps the best example of a complete ethnographic and historical description of a particular people and served as a model for many later writers. After a visit to Egypt – in the period 320–315[149] – he describes the kingdom of Pharaohs. He describes the ideal state,[150] which extends through administration, social organization, justice, marriage, education, health, religious customs, and burial practices. In a constitutional monarchy,[151] Hecataeus provides the ideal of King Euergetes (Benefactor), the "King Philanthrop,"[152] which is a characteristic feature of the Kings in Hellenistic Times. The King is the guarantee of justice and concord between the citizens[153] and is surrounded by highborn sons of

---

[145] Rohde (1893), Cf. also Rohde (1914 [1974]).

[146] Rohde (1914, p. 203).

[147] Rohde (1914, p. 203) and Brown (1949, p. 61).

[148] All the existing material concerning Euhemerus' life and work has been collected by Winiarczyk (ed.) (1991).

[149] Murray (1970, pp. 143–144).

[150] Pöhlmann (1925, p. 291) points out "eine Idealschilderung des alten Pharaonenstaates."

[151] Jacoby (1912, col. 2763) and Murray (1970, p. 159).

[152] Tarn (1930, pp. 50–51) and Murray (1970, p. 160).

[153] Steinwerter (1946 [1947]).

priests to serve him (Diod. Sic. I 70, $_2$). The whole population is divided in three "syntagmata," as Diodorus refers to: Shepherds, Farmers, and Craftsmen (Diod. Sic. I 74,$_{12}$). The social division of labor is mainly regarded as a matter of justice, which is essential for preserving the smooth function of the social life. The people were free from green for gain, civic strife, and all the ills that follow it. The ideal was not the greatest increase of wealth, but the development of the citizens to the highest social ideal (Diod. Sic. I 6, 93; 4).

Euhemerus of Messene describes in his work "Hiera Anagraphe" – written during Cassander's reign as King of Macedonians (306/5-297) – the ruler cult of Hellenistic times; with his explanations about the origins of the gods, he wants to show how a king may obtain divine worship by his greatful subjects.[154] This procedure reflected Alexander's Successors practice and expectations and, of course, Cassander's himself. In that case, the "Hiera Anagraphe" would partly be a "Fürstenspiegel (mirror of princes)," an issue which we will meet again and again in the Arab-Islamic and Byzantine World.

Here labor was held in high esteem. The social division of labor is the characteristic sign of the society of the Island. The population is divided in "three merides," as Diodorus calls them. The first "meris" composed of the priests, to whom the artisans are assigned; the second comprising the farmers; and the third consisting of the soldiers, with whom the shepherds are associated (Diod. Sic. V 45, 3–4). In this tripartite division of the population, Euhemerus follows a similar tradition which is known to the political theorists of the Classical Times and of Hellenistic Age (Plato, *Politeia* III 415 a–b; Plato, *Critias* 112b. Isocrates, *Bousiris* 15. Hecataeus, Aegyptiaca, in: Diodorus Siculus, *Historical Library* I 74,$_1$; Strabo, *Geographica* XVII 1,$_3$). All land and other means of production were common, except the house and garden (Diod. Sic.V 45, 5; 46, 1). The land was not worked collectively, but farmers and herdsmen alike brought their products to a common storehouse for common consumption (Diod. Sic. V 45,$_4$). The distribution is made by the priests. They give prizes for those farmers and shepherds who have produced outstandingly good results (Diod. Sic. V 45,$_4$). By this procedure is introduced the institution of the incentives in the productive process, which is absolutely necessary for the production of commodities in the best quality achievable. The process of production and distribution of the goods leads to the conclusion that there is no place for currency, and one would suppose that Euhemerus, like Zeno the Stoic and unlike Diogenes the Cynic, did away with it.

Iambulus (third century) described in his *Sun Polis* a sort of paradise of sun worshipers at the equator. Here the trees never fail of ripe fruit, and citizens never lose their strength and beauty. The citizens lived together in associations ("kata syggeneias kai systemata") of 400 members each (Diod. Sic. II 57,$_1$). There was collective ownership of all the means of production, and the communism extended also to the family (Diod. Sic. II 58,$_1$). The absence of slaves creates the necessity of the obliged labor by the adults. The time of labor is not very long, because the most products are

---

[154] Thus Dörrie (1967, col. 415) and Panagopoulos (1992–1993, p. 160).

given by the nature without cultivation. In the long time of leisure, they are occupied with the music and fine arts, especially with astronomy (Diod. Sic. II 57,$_3$). The recognition of the annoyance created by the uniform daily labor conducts in the degree of the alternation in the occupation of the productive work (Diod. Sic. II 59,$_6$). There is no elite; in principle, this society is completely egalitarian,[155] an idea for which an idealized Sparta may have been the model.[156] The existence of concord among the citizens is a characteristic feature of the "Sun State." The friendship and concord are recognized as the two stones in the Stoic city of the "wisemen" and the Cynic thought; both features declare in Iambulus' work, but in the political romancy in general, the presupposition of the internal stability of the city. Connected with the internal stability of the "Sun State" is the organization of labor. And it is really interesting indeed that the organization of labor in "Sun State" does not seem to have any equal historical preceding. The rotation in labor during the productive process constitutes Iambulus' originality. Thus, Iambulus recognizes the negative attitudes of the division of labor. He took it from Aristotle, who had met the idea somewhere and had criticized it (Aristotle, *Politics* II 2, 1261 a36–37).[157]

This idea of the "World-State," where all the citizens live in concord without differences, is presented by Zeno. It is the new idea propagated by various authors, like Arrian (*Histories* VII 11, 8 and 9) and Eratosthenes (Strabo, *Geographica* I 4,$_9$ (C. 66); Plutarch, *De Alexandri Fortuna aut Virtute* 329 B) and had been formed by Alexander who was the first to think of something which may be called the unity of mankind or a human brotherhood.[158] The concord and friendship are the characteristic features of Zenos' *Politeia*. Zeno did not concern himself with the size or geographical area of his ideal polis. Judging from the surviving reports, it could be a single city (Athenaeus, *Deipnosophistai* XII 561c), including several separate towns (Diog. Laert. VIII 33).[159] Zeno proposes that all citizens are to wear the same clothing and there shall be no artificial modesty (Diog. Laert. VII 33, 131). He also proposes the abolition of assemblies, temples, law-courts, and gymnasia (Diog. Laert. VII 33). The law-courts are not needed in a state guided by goodness and love. The gymnasia were rejected because they were concerned with bodily welfare, which is irrelevant to the true happiness of the wise.[160] There is no need for buying and

---

[155] Mossé (1969, p. 303). Kytzler (1973, p. 67), however, contends that there is a certain hierarchical order because men "have" the wives in common (Diod. Sic. II 58, 1), because women are not considered apt to rule their group, and because there is the authority that is always exercised by the oldest man in the group. It should, however, be noted that for ancient conceptions egality is very great in Iambulus and that only the modern mind can trace here some remnants of hierarchical structures.

[156] Mossé (1969, p. 304) and Huys (1996, p. 49).

[157] For a recent analysis of Iambulus' economic thought, see Baloglou (2000a, pp. 19–31). A full bibliography is given at pp. 21–22, not. 3; cf. Baloglou (2000c, pp. 159–172).

[158] Tarn (1939, p. 41, 1948) and Baldry (1965, pp. 113–115).

[159] Chroust (1965, p. 177).

[160] Baldry (1959, p. 11). Zeno is rejecting institutions which Plato had allowed in the *Laws*: temples (VI 771 a-7; 778 c4), law-courts (VI 766 d5; 778 d2), and gymnasia (VI 778d). Cf. Baloglou (1998c, pp. 27–28).

selling or commercial trading and, hence, no need for money in a Polis where the principles of friendship, concord, and mutual affection governs the whole community.

The ideal community where friendship and concord exist describes Megasthenes, who visited the court of Sandrakottos (Chandragupta) at about 300 BC as ambassador of Seleucus I several times (Strabo, *Geographica* XV (C. 724); Plutarch, *Alexander* 62).[161] According to Megasthenes, slavery was nonexistent in the whole of India (Diog. Sic. II 39, $_5$). He idealizes India, when he describes it as an extremely fertile country, in which scarcity of food is unknown (Diod. Sic. II 36 and II 40, 4), and when he eulogizes Indian institutions.

Another explorer, Agatharchidas of Knidos (Strabo, *Geographica* XIV 2, 15), describes the exchange of products. He explained the way use and scarcity were taken into account in determining exchange value by peoples in a region abounding in gold, as follows:

> They exchange gold for three times as much bronze, and for iron they give twice as much gold, while silver is worth ten times than gold is. Their method of fixing value is based on abundance and scarcity. In these things the whole life of men considers not so much the nature of the thing as the necessity of its use

> (Agatharchidas, *De mari rubro*, Ch. 49, in: FGrH II 86 F 19).

It is interesting to note that the German jurist and philosopher Samuel Pufendorf (1632–1694) mentioned Agatharchidas' description and explanation in his chapter on value and price.[162]

The Roman Heritage

The Greek culture which was brought to the Scipionic circle, about the middle of the second century BC, by three Greek visitors – the Stoic Diogenes of Babylon, Critolaus, and the Sceptical philosopher Carneades (Cicero, *Tusculan Disputations* IV 5; Plutarch *Cato* 22) – was a leaven and a stimulus to the germination of Latin thought.[163] But it may also be said that the triumphant movement of Roman legions and Roman government into the Eastern Mediterranean, after the defeat of the Seleucid King at Magnesia in 190 and that of King Perseus of Macedonia at Pydna in 168, gave Rome a new self-consciousness and a fresh power of self-expression which were the natural and inherent consequences of her political advance.[164] In these conditions, a Latin literature flowered; beginning with Plautus, and continued by Ennius and Terence during the first half of the second century BC, it achieved its great glories in the next century with Cicero, Lucretius, and Virgil. Greek had not,

---

[161] Muller (1878, vol. II, Liber IV, pp. 397–430).

[162] Pudendorf (1759 [1967], Liber V, ch. I, § VI, p. 675).

[163] Long ((1974) [1990], p. 172).

[164] Barker (1956, pp. 167–168).

of course, disappeared entirely during the Latin centuries. The 40 books of the *Historical Library* of Diodorus Siculus (ca. 60–30 BC), and the voluminous philosophical writings of Philo Iudaeus (in the first half of the first century AD), are testimonies to its survival.

There is an agreement between many authors that there is a small contribution of the Romans[165] to the evolution of economic thought; Roman economic ideas may be gathered from three main sources: (1) the few writers on agriculture (de re rustica); (2) the jurists and writers on legal matters; and (3) the philosophers, especially Cicero and Seneca.

The Roman Agricultural Economists

The best known writers on agriculture were Pliny, Cato, Varro, Columella, and Palladius. They were primarily interested in improving the agricultural methods and reforming land ownership and holdings. They produce semitechnical treatises on rural economy, dealing with the production of special goods, such as wine, oil, etc., the raising of different grain crops, and grazing. Then, in the introduction or some concluding book, general principles of private economy were added.

Marcus Porcius Cato (234–149 BC) wrote a work entitled *De agri cultura*, where he praised small farms and denounced the large ones.[166] Marcus Terentius Varro (116–27 BC) was trying to advise in his work *De re rustica, libri tres* (37 BC) both large and small landholders on what crops should be grown and on stockbreeding. He advocated a "back to the land" movement as a means of counteracting the increasing poverty of the masses and the certain impoverishment of the state. He also complained that land was being given over to olive and wine production, whereas the production of grains, especially wheat, was rapidly declining.[167]

L. Junius Moderatus Columella was the more significant of the "scriptores de re rustica;" he lived during the middle of the first century AD and was born in Spain. He was like Xenophon a landholder and farmer and he described his knowledge on agriculture in his famous work *Rei rusticae, libri duodecim*. He devoted most of the work to wine and olive growing, livestock, bees, and gardens, but neglected emphasizing grain crops. He praised small farms and denounced the large ones.[168]

---

[165] Cf. Sismondi (1819, p. 10), Ingram (1888, p. 19) who denied for a contribution of the Romans to the evolution of economic thought. For a different view which does refer to the contribution of the Romans, see Barbieri (1958, pp. 72–73, 1964, pp. 893–926) and Tozzi (1961).

[166] Kautz (1860, pp. 162–164) and Stephanidis (1948, vol. I, pp. 190–192).

[167] Riecke (1861), Kautz (1860, pp. 164–165), Stephanidis (1948, vol. I, pp. 192–193); Cf. also Harrison (1913).

[168] Kautz (1860, pp. 165–166), Gertrud (1926), and Stephanidis (1948, pp. 194–195).

The Economic Element in the Roman Law

The Roman Empire as a political entity passed away centuries ago, but Roman Law through its influence still remains a world force. Roman Law was developed by an evolutionary process over several centuries. From the founding of Rome (753 BC) to the death of Justinian (AD 565), more than 13 centuries elapsed.

The Twelve Tables (codified in 450 BC) mark the real beginning of Roman Law. The Roman jurists considered them the foundation of all law. In style, they were brief, terse, and imperative. They were a collection of legal principles covering the general outlines of the law, engraved on metal tablets and set up in the Forum.

The Roman jurists analyzed facts and produced principles that were not only normative, but also, by implication at least, explanatory. They created a juristic logic that proved to be applicable to a wide variety of social patterns – indeed to any social pattern that recognizes private property and "capitalistic" commerce.[169] They gave definitions – for example, of price, money, of purchase and sale, of the various kinds of loans (mutuum and commodatum), and of the two types of deposits (regulare and irregulare) – which provided starting points for later analysis.[170]

The Roman jurists formulate numerous economic concepts, which later in the Middle Ages would form the basis for the analysis of the new mercantile economy. These concepts had the great advantage of being free from the values and prejudices opposed to wealth-getting, commerce, and investment, which permeated the rest of ancient literature. They therefore reflected real economic phenomena.[171]

Worthy of mention is the fact that Roman jurists had a good appreciation of money. Juridical texts and literary sources demonstrate that Romans were not unaware of the interdependence between the availability of precious metal or money on the one hand, and price levels, as well as rates of interest, on the other. In a well-known passage from the jurist Paulus (first part of the third century BC) (cf. *Dig.* XVIII, 1, I), it is stated that the act of buying and selling springs from exchange; that originally men bartered useless things for useful things; that owning to the difficulties attendant upon the direct exchange of goods, a material was agreed upon to facilitate bartering. An official material was then to be established by the relevant authorities.[172] From Julius Paulus' remarks (echoed in Pliny *Naturalis Historia* XXXIII 6–7) spring a number of interesting questions, such as an allusion to "quantitas" – in the phrase "usum dominiumque non tam ex substantia praebet, quam ex quantitae" (is connected (sc. this material) the right to use and to own not so much

---

[169] It is worth to note, and still unknown, that the Romans quoted as an authority Theophrastus, Aristotle's pupil and successor in Lyceum, who wrote περί συμβολαίων (Cicero, *De finibus* V 4; Dig. 1, 3, 6=Dig. 5, 4, 3 Paulus on legislators). A precious fragment on sale, perhaps however inaccurately transmitted, has survived. Cf. Pringsheim (1950, pp. 134–142).

[170] Salin (1963, pp. 160–161) and Schumpeter (1954, pp. 69–70). For the economic concept in the Roman Law see von Scheel (1866, pp. 324–344), Bruder (1876, pp. 631–659), and Oertmann (1891).

[171] Perrotta (2003, p. 212).

[172] Vivenza (1998, pp. 292–293).

on account of its substance as on account on its quantity) – which economists[173] have interpreted as being a forerunner of the quantitative theory of money and as reflecting a preference on the Roman's part for the theory of money as merchandise rather than that of money as a sign. However, other scholars feel that the notion of "quantitas" in this passage is simply an allusion to the content of metal.[174]

What Paulus means and says is that the mediation of the right to use and to own by the instrumentality of money in the first place is expressed by the quantity of money and not by the substance of money, i.e., not by a certain amount of weight, as was originally done.[175]

In the earlier periods of Roman history, the law appears on the whole to have opposed interest-taking. The "Laws of the Twelve Tables," according to Tacitus (AD 55–117), set a maximum legal rate of "fenus unciarium," which most scholars belief to mean 1/12 part of the capital.[176] In 347 BC, this rate was reduced to "fenus semi-unciarium" (Tacitus, *Annals* VI, 16; Livy, *Ab Urbe Conditia* 7, 16); before in 342 BC, a "Lex Genucia" prohibited the taking of interest on loans at all (Tacitus, *Annals* VI, 16, 2; Livy, *Ab Urbe Conditia* 7, 42, 1). We do not know how long this prohibition lasted, but the "Lex Sempronia" of 193 BC attests again to the existence of a maximum legal rate; before 88 BC, the "Lex Unciaria" introduced the legal rate of "centesima usura" (12%). The Fathers of the Church will support their usury arguments referring to Roman Law.[177]

The Economic Thought of the Philosophers

The influence of the Stoic ideas is evidently on the two significant Roman philosophers, Cicero and Seneca.

Cicero (106–43 BC) was at once an orator, a man of affairs, and a voluminous writer on philosophy. His philosophical writings belong to the end of his life (52–43 BC), and especially to the troubled period after 45 BC – when the world was rent by political strife and armed conflict. Although Cicero's model incorporates the Stoic disdain for greed and for uncontrolled passions, it is actually closer to the moderate teaching of Epicurus.

Cicero's Stoicism is tempered by some considerations taken from Aristotle. For instance, the praise of parsimony as a source of income; or the praise of generosity, accompanied by a criticism of extravagance (Cicero, *Paradoxes* VI; Idem, *De officiis* II xv–xvii). He contrasts those who waste money on parties, shows, and donations for

---

[173] See e.g., Marget (1938 [1966], vol. I, p. 9), Heckscher (1935, vol. II p. 225), Kemmerer (1907, p. 2) and Wicksell (1936, p. 8).

[174] Nicolet (1984, p. 107) and Vivenza (1998, p. 293).

[175] Monroe (1923, p. 11) and Hegeland (1951, pp. 12–13).

[176] De Martino (1991, p. 169) and Maloney (1971, pp. 93–94).

[177] Haney (1949, p. 76) and Moser (1997a, pp. 7–8).

masses with the money spent by certain *aediles*, or civil magistrates, on walls, gates, and aqueducts.[178] However, Cicero also repeats more recent and more tolerant ideas; he thinks that large-scale commerce, unlike the retail trade, "is not so despicable," in that it brings goods from all over the world and provides work for so many people.[179]

Cicero belongs to those authors who supported the idea that the only honorable industry is agriculture. It is worth noting that he translated Xenophon's *Oeconomicus* into Latin. He wrote that "of all means of acquiring gain, nothing is better than agriculture, nothing more productive, nothing more pleasant, nothing more worthy of a man of liberal mind" (Cicero, *De officiis* I 42, 151). We would like to underline that this argument influenced sixteenth century culture. Cicero also repeats the Greek argument, the disdain for manual work, which is wretched; and for retail traders, he says, "they can never succeed unless they lie most abominably" (Cicero, *De officiis* I 42, 151). On the contrary, "commerce if large and rich, importing much from all quarters, and making extensive sales without fraud, it is not so very discreditable" (Cicero *De officiis* I 42, 151). In this context, there is a direct relationship with Plato's similar ideas (Plato, *Laws* XI 915d, 918d, 919d). Cicero provided the idea that the types of work to condemn more than any other are those that serve for sensual pleasures, from chefs and pastrycooks to perfumers, dancers, and jugglers of all kinds. Instead, respect should go to the liberal professions, which require intelligence and are useful (Cicero, *De Officiis* I 42, 151).[180] This reference on architecture and medicine does remind us a similar argument provided by Aristotle (*Nicomachean Ethics* I 1, 1094a). In the 1500s, these ideas frequently recur; they are certainly inspired, or at least supported, by the reading of Cicero.[181]

Though there was a feeling of disfavor among the upper classes, at least, toward the crafts and small-scale commerce, and the quietism in thought just noted, the Romans were notably careful in business relations and matters of account. Many instances might be cited of their accurate and cautious manner of recording both public and private transactions. Moreover, there is evidence that credit institutions similar to the check and promissory note were known and used, while Cicero requested Curius to honor Tiro's draft for any amount and asked Atticus to ascertain if he could get exchange in Athens (Cicero, *Epistula ad Fam.* XVI iv, 2; XI I, 2; XII xxiv, 1). While of little direct significance as to economic thought, these facts would indicate that the Romans must have had concrete ideas about economic relationships.

Cicero also reports in an approving tone the argument put forward by Hecaton of Rhodes, scholar of Panaetius, that it is the wise man's duty to improve his patrimony by legitimate means, not only for his own advantage, but also for that of his children and relations. In fact, "the means and affluence of each individually constitute the riches of the state" (Cicero *De Officiis* I viii 16; III xvi, 139). What is more, it seems

---

[178] Haney (1949, pp. 78–79).

[179] On the moderate attitude of Cicero toward riches see Tozzi (1961, pp. 55–56, 289–308) and Perrotta (2003, p. 211).

[180] For comments on *De Officiis* see Schefold (2001, pp. 5–32) and Vivenza (2001, pp. 97–138).

[181] Hammond (1951, pp. 81–83) and Barker (1956, pp. 185–186).

that Cicero hints at a fundamental modern principle that only Enlightenment thinkers really used: the relative nature of the concept of superfluous and the consequent rejection of Aristotle's dinstinction between natural and unnatural needs. According to Baeck,[182] the notion of superfluous applies to different things according to the time, place, and status of the person. What is considered luxury in a peripheral province can be a normal income in Rome.[183]

Seneca, the younger (Cordova 5. BC-Rome AD 65) son of the elder Seneca the Rhetor, was a rhetorician who cultivated a mannered style, wedded that style to a profession of Stoic philosophy, and attempted also, besides being stylist and a Stoic, to pursue the career of a politician.

Seneca elaborates, in difference to Cicero, of the fateful idea of a primitive state of society, a "Golden Age," which was followed by the era of the origin of the conventional institutions of society, as a remedy for the evils which brought this age to an end. This was a very significant doctrine – it appeared in Dichearchus' work – for it was taken up by the Christian Fathers and had considerable vogue all through the early Middle Ages.[184] In the "Second Epistotle" to his friend Lucilius, Seneca sets forth his theory of the primitive condition of society in the Golden Age of pristine innocence. In this period of primordial felicity, mankind lived without coercive authority, gladly obeying the wise, and without distinctions of property or caste. His explanation of the course of events which brought about the transition from this primitive stage to modern society is strikingly like that given by Rousseau in his *Discourse on the Origin of Inequality Among Men*. A similarity exists also to Dichaearchus' theory. The people became dissatisfied with the common ownership, and the resulting lust after wealth and authority rendered necessary the institution of political authority to curb the lusts of man.

In the nineteenth of his letters to Lucilius, which is a "Protrepticus" or exhortation to philosophy, Seneca deals with the argument of Posidonius of Apamea that philosophy was the inventor of the arts of civilization. He argues that it was mother-wit and chance, and not philosophy, which found out useful inventions, and in this he is at one with Lucretius (*De Rerum Natura* Vv 1448–1457); but he claims for philosophy the discovery of true wisdom – wisdom in the sense of an understanding of nature and human life and a grasp of ultimate truth.

It is worth noting and of great interest that the comparison of the philosopher and the artisan, which is existed in Bernand Mandeville's *Fable of the Bees* (1714)[185] and in Adam Smith's, *Wealth of Nations* (1776),[186] is also founded in Seneca's ninetienth letter. Seneca (*Epistles* XC, 24–25) mentions the specific inventions in the productive process of ships, and both men – Mandeville[187] and Seneca – comment the rudder in

---

[182] Baeck (1997, p. 159).

[183] Mase-Dari (1901) and Eliopoulos (1973, pp. 146–170).

[184] Barnes (1924, pp. 57–58).

[185] Mandenville (1924, vol. 2, p. 145).

[186] Smith (1937, p. 11).

[187] Mandenville (1924, vol. 2, pp. 143–144).

some detail. As Foley has pointed out,[188] the parallels are much closer between Smith and Seneca, since Seneca concentrates chiefly on two devices, grain mills and weaving (Seneca, *Epistles* XC 20 (weaving); 21–23 (grain mills)). Smith's discussion of grain mills in the Early Draft is quite detailed,[189] and in the first chapter of the "Wealth of Nations," he refers several times to the arts which cluster around cloth production, including weaving.[190] Seneca also discusses the plow (*Epistles* XC 21), to which Smith refers several times,[191] and the provision of windows in houses, which Smith repeats in the laborer's coat passage.[192] In the "Lectures of Jurisprudence," Smith mentions mining and writing, which also figure in Seneca.[193] Seneca repeats all the ideas of the canon against the increase in consumption.[194]

It is worth noting and it has not been mentioned by the economic historians yet, as far as we know, that C. Julius Caesar (100–44 BC) gives a full description of the division of labor by the construction of a bridge (Caesar, *De bello Gallico*, III 17, 1–10).

The above analysis would like to show that the works of Roman philosophers were read, studied by scholars of a later day in Europe, whose veneration for them gave them a weight which we can hardly realize. Moreover, the relative development in economic thought of the early moderns was not great, and their economics and ethics were not untangled. Thus, it is that this seeming commonplace of Cicero's or that of Seneca's had much greater influence that was warranted by its intrinsic economic worth, and greater than it could have with ourselves.[195] The writings of the Romans constitute a continuity of the history of economic thought, although they did not directly develop economic theory.

The Byzantine Economic Thought: An Overview

The Eastern Christian Fathers

In the second half of the fourth century AD, the Eastern Christian Fathers developed some interesting economic ideas and suggestions, scattered throughout their religious texts, the majority of which focused on solving the problem of the extreme

---

[188] Foley (1974, p. 223).

[189] Scott (1937, pp. 336–338).

[190] Smith (1937, pp. 5–6, § 11–12).

[191] Smith in the "Early Draft," in Scott (1937, p. 336).

[192] Seneca, *Epistles* XC 25 with Smith (1937, p. 336).

[193] Seneca, *Epistles* XC 11–13 (mining) and XC 25 (shorthand writing) with Smith (1978, p. 160).

[194] Perrotta (2003, pp. 212–213).

[195] Another example which does prove this continuity in economic thought is Fr. Hutcheson's acknowledgement to Cicero on the description of the social division of labor. Indeed, Francis Hutcheson (1694–1747) does repeat in his *System of Moral Philosophy*, vol. I, London (1755, p. 290), Cicero's passage in *De officiis* II, chaps. 3–5.

maldistribution of wealth.[196] The Fathers considered the only vital concern of man to be life after death. The personal path to salvation involved a disciplined and austere pattern of behavior on this earth. The Christian, however, lived in a setting of civil government and specific social institutions. Like other men, he needed in some manner to acquire the necessities of earthly life. The Fathers accepted the social and political institutions of their time as facts, substantially as unchangeable facts. They commanded the faithful to obey the civil authorities except where such obedience would involve a clear breach of divine law. Where such conflict of obligations did arise, the Fathers taught passive resistance, if necessary to the point of deliberate martyrdom. On the other hand, the Fathers never expressly recommended and often strongly warned against active participation by Christians in official life, military activities, or judicial functions, largely because such occupations often involved participation in pagan rites and ceremonials.[197]

The early Christian ideal was influenced by the doctrines of the Cynics. The Fathers maintained that in the beginnings of human society, all things were held and used in common. They were influenced by the Greek and Roman doctrines of the primitive Golden Age, and at times, assimilated it with the biblical myth of the Garden of Eden, perhaps in order to have a more convenient basis for social theorizing than the biblical model of a single pair living in the Garden of Eden.[198]

The assessment of the nature of the Economic Problem by the Early Christian Fathers and the Cappadoceans shows little affinity with that of the "Pentateuch" and the Johannine writings. Rather, interpreting the Scriptures with minds heavily conditioned by Hellenistic philosophy, they adopt a minimalist-retreatist position on economic activity that is similar to the outlook of their Cynic and Stoic contemporaries. Justin (c. 110–165) (Justin, *Defence* I XIV 2) and to a greater extent Clement of Alexandreia (c. 150–215) are significant exceptions to this general tendency which was to help stifle movement towards systematic economic analysis in Europe for many centuries.[199]

Under this aspect and in the frame of the Christian Ethics, the Christian Fathers of the East will deal with the following issues[200]:

(a) Wealth and poverty: The main economic concern of the Fathers was the moral consequences and implications of the existence side by side of rich and needy

---

[196] Katsos (1983, pp. 182–184). Karayiannis (1994, p. 39).

[197] Viner (1978, p. 13).

[198] Boas (1948, pp. 15–53) for the combination in the Patristic period of pagan "golden age" and biblical "Garden of Eden" ideas.

[199] Gordon (1975, pp. 91–92).

[200] The literature on the ethico-economic ideas of the Eastern Christian Fathers is extremely large. Bougatsos 1 (1980, 1988[2]) offers in his three-volume work a collection of those passages from the works of the Fathers which provide a social character. For an overview of the economic ideas of the Eastern Fathers, see Stephanidis (1948, pp. 248–279), Thurn (1961), Reumann (1961, pp. 370–379), Chrestou (1973, vol. III, pp. 291–297), Spentzas (1984, pp. 193–201), Houmanidis (1990, pp. 194–201), Baeck (1996, pp. 538–540), and Karayiannis and Drakopoulou-Dodd (1998). On the meaning of "oikonomia" in the patristic thought, see the two dissertations by Lillge (1955) and Thurn (1961).

poor. With the exception of Theodoretus (393–466), they never attached any religious value to private property as an institution or merit for any kind to it except in so far as there was no available substitute. They deplored the fact that, under private property, luxurious living and extreme poverty could exist side by side. They questioned or denied the possibility of acquiring great riches without resort to evil practices or without inheritance from persons who had resorted to them. They advised all Christians to avoid seeking riches, to avoid attaching value to them other than as reserve for almsgiving, and to beware of the propensity of the possession of riches to foster luxurious living, pride, and arrogance and distract attention from religious duties. As an ideal to keep in mind, if not to pursue actively, they pointed to the fully common use of possessions which they believed to have prevailed in the early days of mankind and among the first Christians.

Their main interest was in redistributing the general wealth and income of a community through almsgiving. Whether through lack of interest or of economic insight, they gave no attention to the possibility of finding a remedy for extreme poverty in measures or behavior which would augment community wealth and income. Above all, they refrained from recommending any action involving compulsion to relieve poverty or modify in any way the existing social structure. Any program of economic "reform" they may have entertained was restricted to advocacy of self-restraint in the pursuit of riches, just behavior in business, and generous but voluntary almsgiving to the needy poor.

(b) Theodoret: the transgressive legislation of economic inequalities.

Theodoretus of Kyrus (393–466), in a "Discourse on Providence" (PG 83, 652A-656B) written about 435, presents an elaborate defense of the existing economic society, without any reference to its being a necessary consequence of the Fall of man. God had given different functions to different men, each according to his nature, and had so arranged things that each was serviceable to the community. If riches were equally distributed, no one would be willing to do humble tasks for others. Either each would do everything needed for himself, or mankind would lack necessaries. But without specialization of occupations, there would be lack of skill. Inequality, therefore, is a mode of social organization which yields to the poor as to the rich a more agreeable life, since it is the mode by which all satisfy their needs by mutually supplying each other with what is lacking to them.

The service which the rich render to the poor is that of providing a market for their products. Theodoretus admits that most of the rich live unjustly, but claims that the existence of some rich people who managed their riches with justice and honesty, who had not exploited the sufferings of the poor to increase their own wealth, and who had given the needy poor a share of their opulence sufficed to limit condemnation to the unjust rich.

This seems to be a substantially different approach to the question of rich vs. poor than that of the other Fathers.[201]

(c) Work: The retreatism of the majority of the Fathers of the East is illustrated vividly by their treatment of the role of work in human existence. Given their Cynical or Stoic predispositions, the passages of the Book of Genesis in which work is portrayed as an activity commanded by God posed important problems. This command they endeavored to explain away by positing that "it is through idleness that man learned all evil."

In Basil's so-called *Corpus ascetism,* the *Regulae fusius tractatae* (*the longer rules*) and the *Regulae brevius tractatae* (*the shorter rules*) are of special importance. There is a set of 203 questions concerning the monastic life and answered by Basil.[202] In *Regulae fusius tractatae* 37, 1 Basil summarizes his views on work. He writes, "Our lord Jesus Christ does not just say 'someone' or 'somebody,' but 'the labourer is worthy of his food' (Matt. 10, 10). Likewise, the apostle instructs us to work and to make things with our own hands to give to the needy. Clearly one should work diligently. We may not believe that the importance attached to piety is an excuse for laziness and idle hands; rather, work offers an opportunity for struggle, for great effort, for patience in hard times, so that we can also say 'in labour and travail, in watchings often, in hunger and thirst' (*II Cor.* 11, 27)." The main purpose of labor was charity (Basil, *Reg. fus. tr.* 7, 1–4 and 35, 1–3). Work is a social duty with a socio-ethical meaning (Basil, *Reg. fus.* tr. 42).[203] He analyzed the content of many occupations, which would not disturb the peace and quiet of the monastery, but he shows his preference for farming (Basil, *Reg. fus. tr.* 38, in *PG* 31, cols 1016–1017).[204] St. Chrysostom also prefers the agriculture (*PG* 61, col. 87).[205]

(d) Usury:[206] If one considers the conformity between the Classical Graeco-Roman philosophy and the Old Testament in attitude towards lending at interest, it is somewhat surprising that usury was not an issue at all in the Christian writings of the first century AD. The New Testament, which contains the oldest surviving documents of Christianity almost contemporary with Philo, has nothing to say about usury. Lending at interest is mentioned only once, namely in the "Parable of Talents" (Matth. 25: 14–30; Lk 19: 11–27). If this passage contains a judgement about usury at all, it seems to be an approval, since the "Lord" punishes his servant for not having brought the money to the bankers to gain some interest

[201] Viner (1978, pp. 18–20), Gotsis (1997, pp. 30–32), and Baloglou (2003a, pp. 77–80).

[202] Hoven van den (1996, pp. 139–140).

[203] Savramis (1965, p. 28).

[204] Stephanidis (1948, p. 260), Drack (1960, pp. 412–413), and Savramis (1965, pp. 29–32).

[205] Stephanidis (1948, pp. 278–279).

[206] The literature on the ideas of the Eastern Christian Fathers concerning usury is extensively large. It seems to be an issue which has been covered until today. See, e.g., Maloney (1973, pp. 241–265), Gordon (1982, pp. 421–424), Bianchi (1983, pp. 321–342, 1984, pp. 136–153), Siems (1992), Osborn (1993, pp. 368–380), Kompos (1996, pp. 155–164), Gotsis (1997, pp. 40–41), Moser (1997a, b), and Schefold (2000a, pp. 149–151).

(Matth. 25: 27; Lk 19:23). But is not only the authors of the New Testament who show no interest in the usury law, the same is true for all other early Christian fathers, the Apostolic Fathers and the Apologists.

The issue of usury made its first appearance in Christian literature in Clement's of Alexandreia *Paedagogus* (AD 197). Its three books represent an instruction for new converts on Christian conduct in daily matters. Concerning the "just man" Clement quotes Ezekiel: "His money he will not give on usury, and will not take interest." "These words," Clement concludes, "contain a description of the conduct of Christians, a notable exhortation to the blessed life, which is the reward of a life of goodness-everlasting life" (Clement, *Paedagogus* I 10). Clement therefore regards the interest prohibition of "the Law" as still binding on Christians. The subject of usury is taken up again some years later in the second book of his major work *Stromateis*. Here he makes on several occasions copious use of Philo's *De virtutibus*. His arguments follow very closely Philo's words (*De Virt.* 82–83).

After the Church Fathers had clarified that the Old Testament interest prohibition was also valid for Christians, ecclesiastical legislation was soon to follow. In 306 AD, the provincial Counsil of Elvira, though only concerning Spain, stated for the first time a canonical prohibition of usury and in a degree of clarity and severity which was to remain unsupposed during the following centuries. Canon 20 prohibited the practice of usury to all clerics and laymen under penalty of excommunication. In 314 AD, the first Council of Arles representing all of the Western Church forbade in canon 13 usury only to clerics, but still under the penalty of excommunication. Finally, in 325 AD, the first general Council of Nicaea (and therefore valid for the entire Church) prohibited in its canon 17 the taking of interest, but (1) only to clerics und (2) only under the penalty of removal from office.

The Cappadocean Fathers brought the Aristotelian strain of argumentation through the Alexandrian tradition back into the Christian teaching on usury.

Descending from a wealthy aristocratic family, both Basil and Gregory of Nazianzus received a thorough education in Classical literature, rhetoric, and philosophy at different locations. What is new in the usury controversy is that they not only refer to the subject of interest-taking, but indeed devote entire writings to the matter. But since they were in close contact with each other and since the usury treatments of both the Gregorys were strongly dependent on Basil's work, we can consider them together as a group. First of all, they also used the scriptual argument which they enlarged: In his second *Homily* on Ps. 14, Basil quotes Ex 22:25, Dt 23:19, Jer 9:6, Ps 54:12, and Mt 5:42, the last three passages dealing in general with oppression, fraud, and charity. The clarity and forthright nature of the Old Testament texts in regard to the issue of usury can be seen by Gregory of Nyssa's statement in his *Contra Usurarios* (*PG* vol. 46). The creditor is asked as to how he will defend his employment of usury on the day of his final judgement: "You had the law, the prophets, the precepts of the gospel. You heard them all together crying out with one voice for charity and humanity." The motive-argument receives a comprehensive treatment. The usurer seeks money from the poor, and he takes advantage of the misfortunes of the wretched. However, there is a new argument, taken from the statements of the "Lord" in the Parable of Talents, that points into a new direction. As there should be no return on "idle" money, the "idle" creditor should not receive a wage: The usurer is, according to Basil, "gathering where he had not sowed and reaping where he had not strawed," and Gregory of Nazianzus adds "farming, not the land but the necessity of the needy" (*Oration* 16, 18). Citing Lk 6:35, Basil finally appeals to the rich to lend their money "that lies idle with them." Bringing forward the effect-argument, he gives a lively description of the sleepless nights and sorrows of the borrower over his debt. But he also deals with an objection against the effect-argument: "But many," he lets the money-lender say, "grow rich from loans," to whom he answers: "But many," he lets the money-lender say, "grow rich from loans," to whom he answers: "But more, I think, fasten themselves to halters. You see those who have become rich, but you do not count those who have been strangled." Gregory of Nyssa adds in his sixth *Homilia in Ecclesiasten*: "if there were not such a great multitude of usurers, there would not be such a crowd of poor people." But more original is their treatment of the nature-argument. On the one hand, they take up the Aristotelian line of thought again by explicitly playing with the work *tokos*. Basil devotes quite some effort to this subject. Referring to the fertility of hares he states: "By its nature, money is indeed fruitless. Nevertheless, through the industry of greedy individuals it surpasses all living things in productivity." He then explains that interest is called *tokos*, either because it bears evil of because of the travail it brings to the borrower. Compound interest in particular, he continues, is an "evil offspring of evil parents" like a "brood of vipers," because like vipers destroying the womb, usury is "born to destroy the houses" of the debtors. Interest is a "unnatural animal" since everything "natural" stops growing once it reaches its natural size, only the "money of the greedy" grow without any limits. Gregory of Nyssa remarks in his *Contra Usurarios* that usury is against nature since copper and gold, "things that cannot usually bring forth fruit, do not seek to have offspring." In his *Homilia IV in Ecclesiasten,* he calls usury "an evil union unknown to nature." But in addition to the sterility-version of the nature-argument, he also refers to the equality-version, since here he calls the usurer a thief who takes from the lender what does not belong to him.

(e) Slavery:[207] Slavery was, in the time of the Fathers, as it was to continue to be until the nineteenth century, a respectable private-property institution. If a few brief expressions of disapproval be disregarded, the Fathers accepted it as such; and it would be difficult to show from their writings that they were more hostile to slavery than to private property in general.

Some philosophers, both Greek and Roman, with the notable exceptions of Plato and Aristotle, condemned slavery in principle as inhumane, or as contrary to natural

---

[207] Wilks (1962, pp. 533–542), Ste Croix (1975, pp. 1–38), Viner (1978, pp. 18–22), Kontoulis (1993, pp. 119–378), and Nikolaou (1996, pp. 476–478).

law, but carried on no crusade against it. Such defense of slavery as can be found in the writings of the Fathers rested primarily on the proposition that slavery was a punishment for sin and to some extent a remedy for it. This was a novel argument for slavery, unavailable to the pagan Greeks and Romans. It did not mean, however, that the Fathers had adopted and provided a religious support of the Aristotelian view that slaves were by nature an inferior species of man, from whom the dignity of human personality could justly be withheld. On the contrary, the Fathers insisted that slavery was a merely material condition not affecting the spiritual quality of the slave. Many slaves, they said, were better men than their masters. Before God all men were equal. The only real slavery was the slavery to sin and subjection to the evil passions; the virtuous slave had more true freedom that the sinful master. Of itself, slavery in the objective sense was morally neutral; it was good or bad according to the disposition of the souls submitted to this trial. Aristotle and Plato accepted this was a more favorable view of the ethical quality of slavery as an institution than prevailed in the writings of the pagan philosophers. St. Basil, in apparently his only substantial treatment of slavery, begins with a denial that any man is a slave by nature, but continues with what seems to be an unqualified acceptance of slavery, as being in accord with wordly practice or in the interest of the slaves themselves in cases where they are by nature inferior to their masters.

Later Byzantine Authors

The Byzantine Thought and Literature has not shown a tradition of economic thought, similar to that of the West, and specific contributions which would make up a creative renovation or a systematic elaboration of the economic ideas and doctrines of the writers of the Classical Antiquity. From this point of view, a gap seems to be present in the historical evolution of the economic doctrines and theories, which cannot be covered only by the economic ideas of the Fathers or by the estimation of the Byzantine writers and scholars which are rather rare to find according to the nature or the causes of specific economic developments.[208] Moreover, these ideas are functioning as empirical observations of the economic phenomena or as dutiful suggestions of intervention in the function of the economic process.

Nevertheless, certain suggestions within a theoretical scope do appear, which could be classified within the province of the jurisdiction of more specific abstractions, having a more explanatory value, an issue which declares that the byzantine problematic, despite the absence of appearance of systematic economic theories, did not resign from introspecting the functions of economic phenomena as manifestations of such reality, which determines the private target and sets the boundaries for the possible selections of collective action.[209]

---

[208] Gotsis (1997, pp. 15–50, 53).
[209] Gotsis (1997, pp. 53–54).

It is obvious that, in the Byzantine World, the request for a more comprehensive research approach to the sphere of economic phenomena cannot take a specific form. The main part of the economic studies in Byzantium is expressed through legal texts and relevant provisions which do not reach a conclusion by means of treatises or other independent works: the cause of this phenomenon should be interpreted by taking account of institutional particularities, such as the structure of the Byzantine bureaucracy and its relation to the intellectuals, the ordering of the priorities of the authors.[210] It is worth noting at this point that the Byzantines have not put forward any political or philosophical theories to organize in a systematic way the prevalent opinions about the Emperor and the State.[211] On the contrary, the West was prolific in ideas and theories referring to the concept of the empire. This conflict is due to the different way of dealing with problems; the West was dominated by the horror of death and total destruction, a fact unknown to the East.[212]

As far as we know, a general overview of the subject matter about which we are concerned is not available. We would like, at this point, to refer to some interesting references to texts and authors, which prove an economic character and have not been systematically recognized yet.

In Byzantine Empire, three elements had a strong impact: Christianity, the Roman legal tradition, and the ancient Greek philosophical tradition. There people grappled with the issues both in terms of theoretical discourse and in practice.

The concept of social justice was deeply embedded in Byzantine society, where justice carried both the general meaning of equality and the specific meaning of the protection of the weaker members of society. At the same time, the principle of free negotiation was also present; through the centuries, one can see a development in the emphasis that was given to each of these two principles.[213] Until the middle of the tenth century, the state's concern was focused on the protection of the weak. Through the instruments of legal justice and legislation, the state intervened in the economic process, for example, in the matter of the formation of prices. The concept of the "just price" was a powerful one and the discussion revolved around one of its components, the just profit, more specifically the just profit of the merchant. The state set limits on interest rates, as well as on profit rates.[214]

In the second half of the eleventh century and during the next 100 years, Byzantine intellectuals engaged in the systematic study of the works of Aristotle, whose statements on justice in exchange have been scrutinized and commented upon by vast members of scholars and thinkers, providing the basis for the science of political economy. The Byzantines, and especially Michael of Ephesos, as Professor Angelike Laiou (1941–2008)[215] has emphasized, were the first to study and reflect upon the

---

[210] Hunger (1994, vol. III, p. 316) and Gotsis (1997, p. 58).

[211] Beck (1970, pp. 379–380) and Karayannopoulos (1992, pp. 13–14).

[212] Bryce (1904, pp. 342–344).

[213] Laiou (1999, p. 128).

[214] Laiou (1999, p. 129).

[215] Laiou (1999, pp. 118–124, 129).

fundamental problems of the formation of value, as well as upon the question of money and its function in the economy. Michael of Ephesos saw the economic process as a complex and dynamic problem. He sketched the elements of a concept of supply and demand, without developing it fully. His commentaries on the "Nicomachean Ethics" became the foundation stone for the subsequent analyses by the great scholastics of Western Europe.

The existence of a systematic collection of 20 volumes entitled Γεωπονικά (Agriculture), of which is identified the Emperor as author Constantine VII Porphyrogenitus, written during the years 944–959, contains technical issues concerning farming. The author gives also advices of an economic character.[216] He supports the view that the State is organized in three different and discrete levels: the army, the church, and agriculture (Γεωπονικά p. 2, 6–7).[217]

Observations on the Role of the Market and Price-Mechanism

Michael Psellus (1018–1081) wrote a *Life of Saint Auxentius*,[218] who lived in the fifth century, but the ideas which he is describing reflect the reality of the eleventh century, and indeed, Psellus' personal experience. Auxentius once walked along the Battopoleion – it should be an industrial district of Constantinople – and saw craftsmen in tears since they had been forced to close their shops under the duress of the moment (perhaps καιρός απραγίας means even more precisely "the shortage of employment") (*PG* 114, col. 1384A).[219] Auxentius went to succor one of the craftsmen: having changed his appearance, he proposed, to the craftsman's surprise, to run the shop for 3 days for a mere pittance – three follies a day; and in 3 days he managed to make "this shop" flourish. Psellus transforms the episode from a story of limited, individual help to one owner of a single shop, into a fact of broad economic significance. Instead of running a single ergasterion, Psellus' Auxentius improved the whole market situation in Constantinople. He realized that the merchants in the capital were doing poorly, that the workshops were in bad condition due to the general predicament, and that trade (=pragma) was on the verge of catastrophe and industry (Vtechne) could barely continue; the wares, says Psellus, were abundant while the population was unable to acquire goods, for prices were soaring. Auxentius gave support to the artisanal industry. How did he accomplish his difficult task? He changed the minds of citizens by convincing them to buy goods for the price demanded. Thus the city recovered, the merchants could breathe more easily, and Auxentius' theory (=philosophema) became the basis of a sound economy. Psellus concludes: where the plans of the emperor were inefficient, Auxentius'

---

[216] Lemerle (1981, p. 264).

[217] Hunger (1994, vol. III, pp. 88–89).

[218] The text has been published by Ioannou (1971, pp. 64–132).

[219] Kazhdan (1983, pp. 549–550).

virtue helped.[220] It is interesting to note that Psellus presented his holy man as a man of broad economic thought, and this is quite compatible with his self-image.[221]

Patriarch Athanassius I (ca. 1235-ca. 1315, tenure of office 1289–1293, 1303–1309) reveals in his letters to the Emperor Andronicus II. Palaiologos (1282–1328) specific hints of economic character for the recovery of the Byzantine economy. He organized a committee for the control of supply and the prices of the cereals in Constantinople.[222]

It is worth noting that Tzetzes expresses the view that the labor as an objective cost determines the price of the product (Tzetzes, *Epistulae* ed. P.A.M Leone, 81.16–82.2, Leipzig 1972, 121–122).

The *Strategicon* (or officer's manual) of Kekaumenos, an officer in the imperial service during the eleventh century – written between 1070 and 1081 – contains maxims and rules for the conduct of civil officials (Part 1), rules backed by examples and instances, for the conduct of a military officer (Part 2), suggests principles of conduct in private and domestic life (Part 3), and deals with the behavior which is proper in times of sedition and civil strife.[223] The third part (pp. 36–64) is concerned with the conduct of private life, oikonomia, and with the moral rules and maxims of ordinary behavior. It contains remarks on borrowing and lending, on agriculture, and on tax-farming. The author suggests that one should avoid changing one's occupation and maintaining rather a specific occupation, not because there are any legal restrictions, but because he recognizes that the continuous change of an occupation is in economic terms neither efficient nor profitable.[224]

The "Mirror for Princes" Tradition

In the East, where an absence of a political philosophy can be noted which would produce an economic thought, one could notice the existence of nonformulated thoughts and ideas which aim either at praising the emperor on the occasion of an anniversary, or at advising and teaching him, in order to compose the ideal form of the ruler. These are the *Mirror for Princes* (speculum principiis),[225] such as that found in *The Exposition of Heads of Advice and Counsel* addressed by Agapetus, a deacon of the Church of St. Sophia, to Justinian I (PG vol. 86, cols 1164–1185),[226] and as it began in this genre, so it continued in it for nearly a 1,000 years.

---

[220] Ioannou (1971, pp. 74, 11–22).

[221] Kazhdan (1983, p. 550).

[222] Laiou-Thomadakis (1972, Appendix).

[223] Wassiliewsky and Jernstedt (1896) and Barker (1957, pp. 120–125).

[224] Kekaumenos, *Strategicon* § 20, 22, edit. Tsougkarakis (1996, pp. 82–84).

[225] It is interesting to note, at by some way surprisingly, that the term appears in twelfth century by Gottfried von Viterbo (ca. 1125–1192), *Speculum regum* (1180/83). Cf. Hadot (1972, col. 556).

[226] Barker (1957, pp. 54–63). The text by Riedinger (1995, pp. 25–77). For a German translation see Blum (1981, pp. 59–80). Cf. Henry (1967, pp. 281–308), Sevčenko (1978, pp. 3–44), and Letsios (1985, pp. 172–210).

This literature which begins with the speeches of Isocrates[227] in Classical Antiquity reaches its peak in the Hellenistic Times; the Stoics wrote treatises "on Kingship" and the authors of this period describe the ideal king as the personification of the law itself.[228] The king is a model and example for all men, and all look to him and imitate his ways. The king disposes of the four virtues: courage, justice, temperance, and wisdom. This ideal, the King is Animate Law, has been later adopted by Themistius (317-385/90) in several speeches (Themistius, *or. 5*, 64b; *or. 16*, 212d; *or. 19*, 228a, ed. Schenkl and Downey 1965). He also declares the duties of the King and emphasizes the financial problems of the State, which the King has to solve.[229]

Q. Skinner[230] supports the view that the form of the mirror-for-princes-handbook had been used since the Middle Ages. According to Y. Essid,[231] the "mirror for princes" literature originated in Persia perhaps as early as the eighth century and suggests how "the art of government" had become the "object of great interest among Muslim writers." The approach drew inspiration from the oikonomia literature and analogized the management of the household to the management of the Kingdom.[232] As Hadot[233] had demonstrated, this tradition began in Classical Antiquity.

As an indicative example of the doctrine that the King is a copy of God is the "Letter of Aristeas," which is written during the reign of Ptolemy II Philadelphos of Egypt (285/3-246).[234] Synesius (ca. 373-414) adopts in his treatise "On Kingship" (*PG*, vol. 66, cols 1053-1108), addressed to Emperor Arcadius (AD 399), the ideals and the doctrines of the Hellenistic Tradition and invests them with the virtues of a christian ruler: "use in this way the goods which lie ready to your hand, I beg you," said Synesius; "it is only in this way that you can use them well. Let families, cities, peoples, nations, and continents enjoy the blessings of the wise care and royal providence which God, who has set Himself as the pattern to be followed by the realm of intelligible things, has given to you as an image of His providence, wishing things here below to be ordered in imitation of the world above" (PG vol. 66, col. 1054D-1055A).

Sometimes an emperor himself would write a manual of advice to his son: Basilius I is said to have addressed two such manuals to his son Leo the Wise (*PG* vol. 107, cols XXI-LVI)[235]; and Manuel II (r. 1391-1425), in the last days of the Empire, similarly bequeathed to his son John VIII (r. 1425-1448) a manual or

---

[227] Isocrates, *or. 2 ad Nicoclem; or. 9 Euagoras*. There belong also Xenophon's works *Cyropaedia, Agesilaos, Hieron* to this tradition.

[228] This ideal of the "Nomos empsychos" has been adopted by the Neopythagoreans Sthenidas, Diotogenes and Ekphantos. Cf. Steinwerter (1946, pp. 250–268) and Aalders (1968, pp. 315–329).

[229] Jones (1997, pp. 149–152) and Engels (1999, p. 138).

[230] Skinner (1988, pp. 423–424).

[231] Essid (1987, pp. 77–102).

[232] Cf. Moss (1996, p. 540) who adopted Essid's view.

[233] Hadot (1972, cols. 555–632).

[234] Bickermann (1976, pp. 109–136), Hadot (1972, cols. 587–588), and Tcherikover (1958, pp. 59–85). For a summary of Tcherikover's analysis, see Fouyas (1995, pp. 167–183).

[235] Blum (1981, pp. 39–41).

testament under the style of *Councels on the Education of a Prince* (PG vol. 156, cols 320–384).[236] More often a scholar – a monk or a bishop –wrote a treatise "on Kingship" or some form of eulogy of an emperor mixed with ethico-political advice, and works of this order became increasingly frequent as the Empire became progressively weaker. The interesting element of these treatises or manuals is that their authors wanted to draw the attention of the Emperor to the financial difficulties of the State as well. On the other hand, they would try to encourage him to protect the poorer citizens. They proposed that he should take measures for a better redistribution of the income, the final target being the happiness of the State. The archbishop Theophylact of Boulgaria (+1107/8) wrote an *Institutio Regia* (PG vol. 126, cols 253–285), in 1088, for Constantine, the son of Michael VII[237]; the monk and scholar Nicephorus Blemmydes (1197–1272) wrote a work entitled *Andrias Basilikos* (= the Statue of a King) (*PG* vol. 142, cols 657–674) for his pupil Theodore Lascaris II, and emperor who ruled in Nicaea during the Latin occupation of Constantinople.[238] Thomas Magister (?1275-1350/51), a monk who lived for some time in Thessalonica, followed the example of Isocrates and wrote two parallel addresses or orations, the first entitled *peri basileias* (*De Regis Officiis*) (*PG* vol. 145, cols 448–496), addressed to the Emperor Andronicus II (r. 1282–1328), and the second *peri politeias* (*De Subditorum Officiis*) (*PG*. Vol. 145, cols. 496–548), where he describes the duties of the citizens of Empire.[239] Magister recognizes the value of arts and crafts, and the obligation incumbent upon all ordinary citizens to follow an occupation and employ their faculties in production (Th. Magister, *Peri politeias*, PG 145, col. 500). He also recognizes the duty of the citizen to practice the arts of war, as well as the arts of peace, and to qualify himself by training and some form of military service to play his part in the militia which the State needs for its defense. (Th. Magister, *Peri politeias*, PG 145, col. 505).

The Occupation of the Intellectuals and Scholars of the Post-Byzantine Period with Economic Matters and Their Financial Proposals

The period of the two or three last centuries of the Byzantine Empire, which is directly connected with the name of Palaiologoi, is justified by the fact of the simultaneous appearance of a politically, economically, and socially shrunk and weakened state on the one hand and of a significant cultural production which had its influence on and left indelibly its spiritual presence in the Western Renaissance

---

[236] Blum (1981, pp. 54–55).

[237] Blum (1981, pp. 81–98).

[238] Barker (1957, pp. 151–198).

[239] Blum (1981, pp. 99–193). For an evaluation of the two treatises, which have also an ethico-economic character, see Baloglou (1999c, pp. 61–68).

on the other hand. This period, known as Post-Byzantine Period or the "Last Byzantine Renaissance," as Sir Steven Runciman (1903–2000) called it,[240] begins from the capture of Constantinople by the Greeks (15.VIII. 1261) and ends to the capture of the "Vassileusa" – as it is called – by the Ottomans (29. V. 1453) and is characterized by several economic and political events.[241]

In strange contrast with the political and economic decline, the intellectual life of Byzantium never shone so brilliantly as in those two sad centuries. It was an age of eager and erudite philosophers, culminating in its later years in the most original of all Byzantine thinkers, George Gemistos-Plethon. At no other epoch was Byzantine society so highly educated and so deeply interested in things of the intellect and the spirit.[242]

Another phenomenon of this period, which we have to mention, is the influence on the West. In both centuries, the connection with the Latin West grew closer: not only did Byzantine art influence the early painters of Italy, but Byzantine scholarship also began to move to the West and kindle the fire of the Italian Renaissance.[243] From the fourteenth century onwards, the Byzantine scholars were carrying their books and their scholarship to Italy. An example of this influence was the establishment of the Platonic Academy of Florence by Cosino de Medici who was inspired by Plethon, who visited Italy and was honored there.[244] An additional element that characterized the scholars of the period under discussion was the return to the classical patterns, especially to Ancient Sparta and Athens; they derived their arguments from Classical Greece for a provision of their ideas.[245] They often used the word "Hellene" to describe themselves. The use of this word was not an originality of this period, but from the fourteenth century onward, a general use of the term[246] was observed.

The intellectuals and scholars of these two centuries did know the problems of the State and tried to provide consistent and systematic solutions. They were influenced by the Classical Patterns, but also by the texts of the Early Christian Fathers.[247]

Thomas Magister (?1275-1350/51), Georgios Gemistos-Plethon (?1355-26. VI.1453), and Bessarion (1403–1472) did occupy with the financial problems and recognized the heavy taxes as the evil of all problems. Magister suggested that extra taxation without a specific reason should not be imposed because it revolted citizens and perpetuated social injustice (Thomas Magister, *Peri basileias*, PG 165 (1865),

---

[240] Runciman (1970).

[241] Baloglou (1998b, pp. 406–413) and the mentioned literature.

[242] Runciman (1970, pp. 1–2).

[243] Barker (1957, p. 49).

[244] Gill (1964), Kristeller (1974, vol. I, pp. 50–68, 225–226, 252–257, 1976, vol. II, pp. 101–114, 270) (on the Platonic Academy). Fouyas (1994, pp. 315–372).

[245] Pantazopoulos (1979, pp. 130–138).

[246] Runciman (1952, pp. 27–31) and van Dieten (1964, pp. 273–299).

[247] It is evident by Cabasilas' and Magister's proposals who do refer to Plato, Solon, and the Cappadoceans. See Baloglou (1996, 1999c, pp. 61–68).

col. 480A). For this reason, he pleaded to the Emperor to rearrange the system of tax collection and not sell them (Magister, *Peri basileias* PG 165 (1865), col. 480 C). As a consequence of a good and right tax policy, there came the correct handling of public money. The Emperor himself should show interest and improve the situation.

Under these circumstances, the State will be able to get armed regularly and be ready in case of war. "These who practice arts and crafts," wrote Magister, "should be of good repute on other grounds also [as well as on the ground of their skill]. They should not be half-servants of the State: their citizenship should not be limited to the works of peace; they should also have in their minds a spirit of gallantry and readiness for war" (Th. Magister, *Peri politeias*, PG 165 (1865) col. 545D; engl. transl. by Barker (1957) p. 171–173). Magister's main concern was that all alike –the working class of artisans as well as the rich and leisured– should have access to a liberal education which would be a training of character as well as of intelligence and would enable all to fulfill "the whole duty of a Christian man" [Thomas Magister, *Peri politeias*, PG 165 (1865) col. 548B; engl. transl. by Barker 1957, p. 171–173].[248]

Georgios Gemistos-Plethon, as a "theoretical philosopher of Neoplatonism,"[249] as a hellenocentric and progressive philosopher,[250] and as the main factor of the Neoplatonism in West,[251] analyzed in two treatises entitled *Advice to the Despot Theodore Concerning the Affairs of Peloponnese* (*PG* vol. 160, cols. 841–866)[252], presented in 1416, and *Georgios Gemistos to Manuel Palaeologus Concerned the Affairs of the Peloponnese* (*PG* vol. 160, cols 821–840),[253] presented in 1418 – which belong to a long tradition of the "mirror for princes"[254], a specific program which would reform the socioeconomic and military structure of the Peloponnese aiming at the best confronting of the Turkish threat, which ultimately was to sweep away the Byzantine Empire in the decade after Plethon's death. The central theme of these reforms is the mobilization of all socioeconomic and political factors in order to create a centralized, self-sufficient, and defensible territory.

Plethon considered monarchy to be the best-suited system of government. He claimed that monarchy is "the safest and most beneficial" (Lampros 1930, p. 199). For Plethon, the monarch would be surrounded by a council: the number of advisors must certainly be restricted, yet it must be sufficient, the members being of moderate financial status and having an excellent education (Lampros 1930, pp. 188–119). However, he was well aware of the various human weakness of the statesman and of his civil advisors. Thus, he stressed that the selection of civil servants and advisors must be based mainly upon their special knowledge and their nonself-interested

---

[248] Cf. Baloglou (1999c, p. 67).

[249] Masai (1956, p. 87).

[250] Bargeliotes (1989, pp. 30–31).

[251] Bargeliotes (1993, p. 104).

[252] Lampros (1930, vol. IV, pp. 113–135). For an English translation of this memorandum see Baloglou (2003b, pp. 26–35). For a German translation with commentary see Blum (1988, pp. 151–172).

[253] Lampros (1926, vol. III, pp. 246–265). For an English translation of this memorandum see Baloglou (2003b, pp. 36–42). For a German translation with commentary see Blum (1988, pp. 151–172).

[254] Blum (1981, pp. 30–59), Baloglou (2002c, pp. 110–114), and Triantare-Mara (2002).

behavior. Also, he suggested (Lampros 1930, p. 119) that all civil servants should be chosen by using objective criteria, namely that of meritocracy, and claimed that their corruption should be severely punished.

The successful application of the division of labor, which will contribute both to the improvement of the politeia and the achievement of happiness (Lampros 1930, vol. IV, p. 132, 7–12), the tripartite division of the population (Lampros 1930, vol. IV, p. 119, 23–120, 5), the abolishment of the many taxes and the establishment of an unique tax (Lampros 1930, vol. IV, p. 122, 18) – his reformed taxation system based upon four principles of taxation, so he became an ideological predecessor of the main principles of taxation developed later in eighteenth century literature, primarily by Adam Smith[255] and by considering agricultural income as the basis of taxation, he thus became a forerunner of the relevant Physiocratic theory[256] – the property reform (Lampros 1926, vol. III, p. 260, 1–18), and the control of imports and exports (Lampros 1926, vol. III, p. 263, 3–264, 12. Lampros 1930, vol. IV, p. 264, 11–16) constitute the main content of Gemistos's proposals.[257] Plethon's economic recommendations were based on the presupposition that the Peloponnese, a rich producer of raw materials, could be rendered economically self-sufficient. Plethon argued that the main function of government is the protection of individuals' property rights and peoples' freedom. Thus, it seems that he regarded sovereignty as a kind of "social contract" – a theory more fully explicated during the seventeenth century by Thomas Hobbes and John Locke.[258]

Cardinal Bessarion, Gemistos' disciple, proposed in his letter to Despot Constantine – the last emperor of Byzantium (r. 6.I. 1449–29. V. 1453) – written in April 1444,[259] a specific reform program: The discretion of the population of the Despotate of Mistra in tax-payers and not soldiers, and in non-tax-payers and soldiers (Lampros 1930, vol. IV, p. 35, 9–12), the reorganization of army (Lampros 1930, vol. IV, p. 36, 10–12), the control of imports and exports through selective duties (Lampros 1930, vol. IV, p. 41, 22–29), the connection of production and techno-logical education, and the recognition of the economic significance of education (Lampros 1930, vol. IV, p. 44, 1–14) are inclusive of Bessarion's main ideas.[260]

As we can conclude from this brief reference to the contribution of the Byzantine scholars, the intellectuals of the Late Byzantine Times were indeed occupied with applied economic facts; they did not seem to have any theoretical approximation in issues, like value, price, wage; we have, however, to include their contribution in the evolution of the Medieval Economic Thought.

---

[255] Spentzas (1964, pp. 122–123) and Baloglou (2001b, ch. 3).

[256] Spentzas (1964, pp. 114–115, 135, 139) and Baloglou (2001b, ch. 2).

[257] For an evaluation of Gemistos' economic ideas and their evolution in the History of Economic Thought, see Spentzas (1996), Baloglou (1998e, 2002b, pp. 12–19), and Karayiannis (2003).

[258] Spiegel (1991, p. 691).

[259] Lampros (1906, pp. 12–50, 1930, vol. IV, pp. 32–45) and Mohler (1942, pp. 439–449).

[260] For an evaluation of Bessarion's economic ideas see Baloglou (1991/92) and Mavromatis (1994, pp. 41–50).

Arab-Islamic Economic Thought

The first of the three major categories of medieval Muslim economic literature is the formal letter of advice for ruling an empire known as the "mirror for princes" literature. This literary tradition is usually framed as advice by a father of a savant to a young prince or heir-apparent and dates back to ancient Egyptian times and to Isocrates' Speeches. One of its famous modern expressions is Erasmus' advice to the expected heir to the throne, Charles V of Spain. This literature covers tax policy and personnel management for the absolute ruler, whose power is measured by the wealth and prosperity of his empire and the support and dependability of his military and commercial population. The Arabs assimilated much of this literature from the Iranian culture.[261] These treatises emphasized the importance of never taxing the peasantry or merchants so heavily as to discourage or adversely affect commerce or production. They reflected a sophisticated administrative tradition concerned with delegation and separation of power, the appropriate role of the *wazir* or prime minister, and the effective judging of personality and assignment of duties. Some of these tracts reported formally commissioned studies of the causes of price fluctuations.[262] As the best example is Abou Youssef Yakoub's (731–798) work entitled *Kitab al Kharaj* (*Manual on Land-Tax*), which was composed to answer questions put to him by the caliph Harum Al-Rashid. Yakoub analyzes there the following topics: (a) Type of taxation-fixed amount vs. proportional rate; (b) tax collection and administration; and (c) public financing of rural development projects.

The second genre of economically relevant literature encompassed the *hisba* manuals which provide a detailed description of the functions of the *muhtasib*, the municipal market manager. Such extensive treatments of supervisory duties are reminiscent of the functions of the Roman sensors and *aediles* and the Greek market regulators (*agoranomoi* and *metronomoi*). The principles and practices in these manuals revealed in the context of the economic and cultural traditions of medieval Muslim society. We cannot ignore, however, the fact that the concern over *talaqqi* – the practice of merchants meeting incoming caravans and telling them that the market is down, so as to buy up their merchandise cheaply – is nothing more or less than forestalling, which was made illegal in medieval English markets along with cornering and regrating. A clear elaboration of the relation of price to supply and demand is presented in the literature as a basis for identifying the conditions under which the market requires intervention and when it is self-regulating. The best representative of this category is Taqi al-Din Ahmad bin Abd al-Halim, known as Ibn Taimiyah (1263–1328). In his work entitled *The Hisba in Islam,* he discusses the economic role and functions of the state quite thoroughly. Promotion of socioeconomic justice being the supreme goal, the state must secure a balance between private interests and public pursuits. He argues the state must work toward such goals as the eradication of poverty, amelioration of gross income and wealth inequalities, regulation of

---

[261] Hosseini (1998, p. 655, n. 3).

[262] Essid (1987, pp. 83–84).

markets to minimize the adverse effects of market failures, and planning to provide the necessary socioeconomic infrastructure, just and enforcement of the laws. He discussed certain circumstances which might of the laws. He discussed certain circumstances which might warrant price regulation and controls – specifically when there are national emergencies.[263] According to him, prices reflect market conditions and price increases which result from a scarcity of goods or an excess in demand that are caused by God. Since scarcity, which is the reason for rising prices, is within the domain of God, he argued it would be unfair to penalize the merchant by setting arbitrary prices. On the other hand, monopolization, the action of creating an artificial scarcity in order to sell at a higher price, is by its nature an authoritarian fixing of price and against the welfare of the community.[264]

The third category of Muslim economic literature deals with the economics of the household, the Greek *Oikos*. The Muslim writers depended heavily upon the Neopythagorean Bryson for guidance in this field.[265] Bryson's work[266] is extensively quoted and commented upon in Arabic, but has been generally ignored by classicists. In Mediterranean societies, the extended family in agriculture or in stock-raising was the backbone of the economy. This functioning unit of production and consumption took care of the primary needs of its members and provided surpluses that fed the 10–20% of the population in the military, political, and economic superstructure. In a sense, this literature provides a microadministrative parallel to the "mirror of princes" material. This phase of Arabic thought reflects the direct Greek influence most strongly and focuses on the fundamental agricultural and familiar aspects of Mediterranean and Near Eastern society. The Muslim philosophers introduced as the Greek concept of *oikonomia* the term *falasifa*, and *oikonomia* (*tadbir*) would be used to designate management of the household (tadbir al-manzil), administration of government (tadbir al-mudum), and government of God on earth (tadbir al-alam).[267]

A line of Muslim authors, such as Farabi (873–950) with his work *Aphorisms of the Statesman*, Ibn Sina (Avicenna, 980–1037) with his *Tadbir Manzel* (*Household Management*), Abu Hamid Al-Ghazali (Algazel, 1058–1111) with his *Ihya Ulum al*-Deen,[268] Nasir Tusi (1201–1274), and Asaad Dawwani (1427–1501), copied and elaborated in more or less detail the lost text of the Neopythagorean Bryson. Some of them used nearly the whole text, while others copied long passages, sometimes modifying them to bring the text into line with Arabic social reality or with its ideological principles. The vicissitudes of Bryson's treatise demonstrate, in the realm of economic ideas, the inhospitable climate in Islam for the Greek heritage. In the first place, Bryson's work did not give rise to new or original analysis.

---

[263] Essid (1995, pp. 155–157), Ghazanfar (2000, pp. 16–17), and Ghazanfar (ed.) (2003, pp. 53–71).

[264] Essid (1987, p. 82). See Kuran (1987, pp. 103–114).

[265] Essid (1992, pp. 40–41) and Baloglou and Constantinidis (1996, pp. 46–55).

[266] See Plessner (1928). Cf. Bouyges (1931, pp. 259–260).

[267] Essid (1995).

[268] He identifies as part of one's calling three reasons why one must pursue economic activities: (a) self-sufficiency, (b) the well-being of one's family and (c) assisting others in need. Anything less would be religiously "blameworthy." Cf. Ghanzafar and Islahi (1990, p. 384) and Ghazanfar (ed.) (2003, pp. 381–403).

Second, his work was intended to explain the science of administration and production within an economic unit, the Oikos, but his ideas were redirected by the falasifa to support their own political theories. Beginning as a treatise on household management, it was used as a reference for political economy. The Muslim authors, by stressing the authoritarian structure of the household unit to reinforce their political ideas, missed the opportunity to use Bryson's work to enlarge their analytical perspective on the economy. The reason for this is to be found in the fact that, up to that time, political, ethical, and theological ideas in Islam had centered upon the community of believers and not on the Oikos. In the non-Arabic Muslim world of Persia, however, Bryson's work fitted into a long tradition of wisdom literature dealing with practical daily life which was free of the authority of Arabic jurisprudence (fiqh) and receptive to anything of Greek origin.[269]

One characteristic example of an influence of the Greek thought on the Arabic Muslim world is Farabi's work. Drawing in the principles of the administration and governance of the family household (tadbir) to develop a theory of the state, he emphasized the similarities between personal rule in the household and that of the ruler of the state. In this context, he followed Plato's analysis in *Politicus* (Statesman). Following Aristotle (*Politics*, Book I), he analyzes in his *Aphorisms of the Statesman* the four relations in the family household: husband and wife, master and slave, parents and children, and owner and property. He who is asked to rule, arrange, and manage all of the parts is the master of the household. He is called ruler and his duties are like those of the ruler of the city. After Farabi, the Arab-Islamic authors continued to follow the tradition of Plato's and Aristotle's works. This is evident in Ibn Sina's and Miskawayh's work.[270]

This tradition of the Arab-Islamic economic thought found its peak in Ibn Khaldun's work. He was both a distinguished jurist trained in traditional Islamic beliefs and a man of action closely involved with the powerful men of that time.

Ibn Khaldun's Economic Thought

Ibn Khaldun's (1132–1406) *Muqaddimah* (3 vols., transl. from Arabic by Franz Rosenthal, 1958)[271] is mainly a book of history. However, he elaborates a theory of production, a theory of value, a theory of distribution, and a theory of cycles, which constitutes the framework for his history.[272]

---

[269] Essid (1987, pp. 84–86).

[270] Cf. Baloglou (2004b).

[271] I also used the Greek translation of Issawi's work entitled *An Arab Philosophy of History. Selections from the Prolegomena of Ibn Khaldun of Tunis (1332–1406)* (London 1955), Athens: Kalvos, 1980 and the German translation in Schefold (2000b, pp. 103–164).

[272] For an evaluation and presentation of Ibn Khaldun's economic thought see Bousquet (1955) quoted in Houmanidis (1980, p. 443, not. 6), Bousquet (1957, pp. 6–23), Spengler (1964), Andic (1965), Boulakia (1971), Haddad (1977), Essid (1987, pp. 89–92), Baeck (1990, 1994, 1996, 1997, pp. 3–19), Schefold (2000b, pp. 5–20), and Essid (2000, pp. 55–88).

The whole presentation of the Muslim economic thought satisfies Spengler's statement –and he was one of the first economist, who did analyze Khaldun's thought that "the knowledge of economic behavior in some Islamic circles was very great indeed, and one must turn to the writings of those with access to this knowledge and experience if one would know the actual state of Muslim economic knowledge."[273]

According to Ibn Khaldun, two different kinds of social milieu have character-ized human development, the "umran al-badouri (nomad civilization)" and the "umran al-hadhari (urban civilization)." The difference between the two is based upon their ma'ah, a synthesizing concept into which is woven both the means of subsistence and the relationships between man and man, and man and nature. The social group is made possible by the productive activities which provide man's sub-sistence: farming, animal breeding, hunting and fishing, fabricating goods, and exchanging products, all of which are encompassed by *ma'achu*. This conception of ma'ach is central to Ibn Khaldun's philosophy and comprehends the qualitative and quantitative differences between a natural economy oriented toward the accumula-tion of unnecessary goods, the eager pursuit of profit, and a propensity for luxury. This dichotomy is reminiscent of Aristotle's distinction between *oikonomia*, the sci-ence of the acquisition of wealth oriented toward the good of the community, and *chrematistics*, the science of the unlimited accumulation of profit. But whereas Aristotle's conception is static, Ibn Khaldun's is a dynamic one. Aristotle pictured a family unit in an ideal agrarian society, whereas Ibn Khaldun's view encompassed the totality of human society in its historical development. On the one hand, Ibn Khaldun dealt with the art of managing the production and distribution of wealth, while, on the other, he developed a realistic analysis of the successive phases in the growth of human society. One can therefore understand why he had little regard for the science of tadbir or oikonomia as a branch of practical philosophy, preferring instead his science of society which had a historical dimension. When he drew on juridical science or treatises on social relations, it was solely for the purpose of vali-dating historical data or investigating the nature of society.[274]

Ibn Khaldun has been called a pioneer economist and a pioneer social scien-tist[275]; for in his economics we find, among others, the emphasis upon production as the source of wealth (Ibn Khaldun, *The Muqaddimah*, transl. by Franz Rosenthal, vol. 2, pp. 272–274); an extensive analysis and description of the division of labor (I. Khaldun, *The Muqaddimah*, vol. 2, p. 250); the beginnings of the labor theory of value (I. Khaldun, *The Muqaddimah*, vol. 2, p. 289: "The profit human beings make is the value realized from their labour"); an analysis of supply and demand in deter-mining prices (I. Khaldun, *The Muqaddimah*, vol. 2, p. 240); the view that precious metals, like gold and silver, are mere metals – but not a source of wealth – which are to be valued because of the relative stability in their prices and because of their

---

[273] Spengler (1964, p. 269).

[274] Essid (1987, pp. 90–93).

[275] To give a few examples, see Andic (1965, pp. 23–24), Boulakia (1971, pp. 117–118), and Haddad (1977, pp. 195–196).

appropriateness as a medium of exchange and as storage of value (I. Khaldun, *The Muqaddimah*, vol. 2, p. 274)[276]; and the argument that the more civilized the society, the greater the importance of services (I. Khaldun, *The Muqaddimah*, vol. 2, pp. 125–126). He is a pioneer in the sense that he found a new path, and far surpassed his contemporaries, but he is not a pioneer in the western sense of the term, for he had no followers, formed no school, and exercised no strong influence in his own time or in the generation immediately succeeding him.[277]

The state for Ibn Khaldun is an institution required by the nature of civilization and human existence. It is also an important factor of production. By its spending, it promotes production, and by its taxation, it discourages production. For Ibn Khaldun, the spending side of public finance is extremely important. On the one hand, some of the expenditures are necessary to economic activity. Without an infrastructure set by the state, it is impossible to have a large population. Without political stability and order, the producers have no incentive to produce. They are afraid of losing their savings and their profits because of disorders and wars (I. Khaldun, *The Muqaddimah*, vol. 2, p. 201).

On the other hand, the government performs a function on the demand side of the market. By its demand, it promotes production: "The only reason for the wealth of the cities is that the government is near them and pours its money into them, like the water of a river that makes green everything around it, and fertilizes the soil adjacent to it, while in the distance everything remains dry" (I. Khaldun, *The Muqaddimah*, vol. 2, p. 251). If the government stops spending, a crisis must occur: "Thus, when the ruler and his entourage stop spending, business slumps and commercial profits decline because of the shortage of capital" (I. Khaldun, *The Muqadimmah*, vol. 2, p. 92).

The money spent by the government comes from the subjects through taxation. The government can increase its expenditures only if it increases its taxes, but too high a fiscal pressure discourages people from working. Consequently, there is a fiscal cycle. The government levies small taxes and the subjects have high profits. They are encouraged to work. But the needs of the government as well as the fiscal pressure increase. The profit of the producers and the merchants decreases, and they lose their will to produce. Production decreases. But the government cannot reduce its spending and its taxes. Consequently, the fiscal pressure increases. Finally, the government is obliged to nationalize enterprises, because producers have no profit incentives to run them. Then, because of its financial resources, the government exercises an effect of domination on the market and eliminates the other producers, who cannot compete with it. Profit decreases, fiscal revenue decreases, and the government becomes poorer and is obliged to nationalize more enterprises. The productive people leave the country, and the civilization collapses (I. Khaldun, *The Muqaddimah*, vol. 2, p. 80, 81, 83–85). Consequently, for Ibn Khaldun, there is a

---

[276] I. Khaldun, *The Muquaddimah*, vol. 2, p. 274: "God created the two mineral 'stones', gold and silver, as the measure of value for all capital accumulations. Gold and silver are what the inhabitants of the world, by preference, consider treasure and property to consist of."

[277] Andic (1965, p. 24).

fiscal optimum but also an irreversible mechanism which forces the government to spend more and to levy more taxes, bringing about production cycles.[278]

His approach to the taxation problem will be similar to the corresponding of Georgios Gemistos-Plethon, who also recognized that heavy taxes discourage people from working.[279]

Ibn Khaldun discovered a great number of fundamental economic notions a few centuries before their official births. However, there is a tendency in the West not to take into account the share of oriental thought in the history of modern social, political, and economic thought, because of the enthusiasm to emphasize its European origins. This gives rise to underestimation of some of the real founders of the subject.

Conclusions

The Mediterranean area is self-sufficient even as regard the economic thought of the people who live in the area. The ancient Greeks, who first introduced the term "oikonomia" and determined its content, brought forward critical economic matters, such as value, the labor distribution, the internal division of labor, the just distribution of wealth, the private property, the money and its functions, and proposed detailed studies. The Greeks did not create an autonomous Economic Science, nor did they aim at doing so.

The expansion of the Hellenes to the East, as Alexander did, and the cosmopolitan character of that expansion created new manners and customs in the eastern part of the Mediterranean Sea, which as a consequence influenced extensively the economic thought as well. Works of specific economic content and problematic will be published. It is indicative that the representative work of this Age, the "Oeconomica," will become famous and will exercise a significant influence on the Scholars of the Renaissance and to the Cameralists.

The patristic thought of the Eastern Fathers focused on the problem of the right distribution of wealth. For that reason, their thought was not in favor of interest profits, in pursuance of the Greek view on the matter. Byzantium, which created political theology rather than political philosophy, does not seem to have created such prerequisities that would favor the development of an independent economic science. On the other hand, Byzance did not aim to do so, and such economic problems that appeared during the Middle Ages in the West did not appear.

In respect to the Arab world, the ancient Greek Philosophy did help in that it contributed to the elaboration of their doctrines when comparing their religious beliefs to those of the Christian World. The internal relevance of the Islamic World to the Ancient Greek Philosophy can be further proved when one notices that, through studying the Greek philosophy, the Arabs were led to such mysticism as

---

[278] Boulakia (1971, p. 1117).

[279] For a comparison between the economic thought of these scholars see Baloglou (2002b).

prevailed in the Byzantine World. The Islamic way of thinking as regard the problematic of "Oikos" and its relevance to the "Politeia" is quite evident.

The Mediterranean Sea, where most of the civilizations were born, was the basis of development of such conditions that permitted people to deal with the economic phenomena, which the modern economic thought deals with even in our time.

Appendix

This table shows the relation of the authors who lived in the Mediterranean and the evolution of their works.

Year	Name	Works
ca. 700 BC	Hesiod	Works and days (Hesiod)
638 BC	*Solon	
ca. 600 BC	*Semonides of Keos	
594/3 BC		Seisachtheia (Solon)
559 BC	Solon+	
470/460 BC	*Democritus	
469 BC	*Socrates	
450 BC	*Antisthenes	
436 BC	*Isocrates	
430 BC	*Xenophon	
428/7 BC	*Plato	
415 BC	*Diogenes the Cynic	
399 BC	Socrates+	
393–91 BC		Trapezitikos (Isocrates)
390 BC	Democritus+	
384 BC	*Aristotle	
	*Xenocrates	
380 BC	*Theopomp	Politeia (Plato)
		Oikonomikos (Xenophon)
		Panegyricus (Isocrates)
372 BC	*Theophrastus	
370 BC	Antisthenes+	
355 BC	Xenophon+	Poroi (Xenophon)
		On Peace (Isocrates)
354 BC		Areopagiticus (Isocrates)
348 BC	Plato+	Nomoi (Plato)
341	*Epicurus	
338 BC	Isocrates+	
335/323 BC		Politics; Nicomachean
		Ethics (Aristotle)
334	*Zeno of Citium	
323 BC	Aristotle+	

(continued)

(continued)

Year	Name	Works
	Diogenes the Cynic+	
314 BC	Xenocrates+	
314/01 BC		Politeia (Zeno)
300 BC	Theopomp+	
290/80 BC		Hiera Anagraphe (Euhemerus)
287 BC	Theophrastus+	
281 BC	*Chryssipus	Kyriai Doxai (Epicurus)
270/69 BC	Epicurus+	
264 BC	Zeno of Citium+	
250 BC		Cercidas of Megalopolis; his plea for social justice
234 BC	*Cato	
233 BC	Cleanthes+	
208 BC	Chryssipus+	
Third century BC		Sun State (Iambulus)
154 BC		De agricultura (Cato)
149 BC	Cato+	
116 BC	*Varro	
110 BC	*Philodemus	
106 BC	*Cicero	
94 BC	*Lucretius	
60–55 BC		Peri oikonomias (Philodemus)
56 BC		De Rerum Natura (Lucretius)
55 BC	Lucretius+	
ca. 54–51 BC		De re publica (Cicero)
44 BC		De officiis (Cicero)
43 BC	Cicero+	
40 BC	Philodemus+	
37 BC		Rerum rusticarum libri III (Varro)
30 BC	*Philo Iudaeus	
27 BC	Varro+	
ca. 5 BC	*Seneca	
23–24 AD	*Gaius Plinius the Older	
ca. 35 AD		Beginning of the missionary work of St. Paul, which lasted for the 30 years down to his death about 64 AD; composition of his Epistles during these years
40 AD	*Dio of Chrysostom	
45 AD	Philo Iudaeus+	
50 AD	*Plutarch	
58/59 AD		De vita beata (Seneca)
65 AD	Seneca+	
77		Historia naturalis (Gaius Plinius the Older)
79	Gaius Plinius the Older+	
98–104		Four discourses
		On Kingship (Dio of Chrysostom)

(continued)

(continued)

Year	Name	Works
100		Euboean oration (Dio of Chrysostom)
End of the first beginning of the second century AD	Epictetus	
112	Dio of Chrysostom+	
120	Plutarch+	
121	*Marcus Aurelius	
ca. 125	*Maximus of Tyros	
150	*Clement of Alexandreia	
ca. 150–185		Dialexeis (Maximus of Tyros)
ca. 172–180		Ta eis heauton (Marcus Aurelius)
180	Marcus Aurelius+	
185	*Origenes	
195	Maximus of Tyros+	
ca. 190–200		On the Salvation of the Rich Man (Clement of Alexandreia)
217	Clement of Alexandreia+	
ca. 220–230		Peri Archon (On the Principles) (Origenes)
ca. 246–248		Kata Kelsu (Against Celsus) (Origenes)
253/4	Origenes+	
317	*Themistius	
330	*Basileios	
ca. 335	*Gregorius of Nyssa	
354	*Augustinus	
364		Speech on Kingship (Themistius)
373	*Synesius of Cyrene	
Before 379		Ascetica; Hexaemeron (Basileios)
379	*Basileios+	
ca. 380–383		Kata Eunomiu (Gregorius of Nyssa)
385		Logos katechetikos ho megas (Gregorius of Nyssa)
385/90	Themistius+	
394	Gregorius of Nyssa+	On Kingship (Synesius of Cyrene)
ca. 400		Confessiones (Augustinus)
ca. 413–426		De civitate Dei (Augustinus)
414	Synesius of Cyrene+	
430	Augustinus+	
ca. 530		Ekthesis Kephalaion parainetikon...pros basilea (Agapetus Diakonus)
570	*Isidor of Sevilla	
ca. 625–636		Etymologiarum sive originum libri XX (Isidor of Sevilla)
636	Isidor of Sevilla+	
675	*Johannes of Damascus	
731	*Abu Youssef Ya'coub	
ca. 742–749		Pege gnoseos (Joh. of Damaskus)

(continued)

Year	Name	Works
749	Johannes of Damaskus+	
780		Kitab-al-Kharaj (Book of Taxation) (Ya'coub)
798	Ya'coub+	
800	Al-Kindi	
ca. 845/850	*Isaac ben Salomon Israeli	
873	*Al-Farabi (Alfarabius)	
Before 873		Fi'l-'aql (Al-Kindi)
873	Al-Kindi+	
940/950		Kitabal-Hudud war-rusum (Israeli)
940–950	Isaac ben Salomon Israeli+	
ca. 941–950		Mabadi' ara'ahl ad-madina al fadila (Al-Farabi)
950	Al-Farabi+	
980	*Ibn Sina (Avicenna)	
1018	*Michael Psellus	
Before 1037		Tabbir Manzel (Household Management) (Avicenna)
1037	Avicenna+	
1058	*Abu Hamid Al-Ghazali (Algazel)	
1078	Michael Psellus+	
1079	*Abaelardus	
1070–1081		Strategicon (Kekaumenos)
1080–1090		Ihya Ulum al-Deen (Algazel)
1095	*Petrus Lombardus	
1100		Instituto Regia (Theophylact archbishop of Bulgaria)
1111	Al-Ghazali+	
1118–1140		Dialectica; Ethica seu liber dictus scito te ipsum, Sic et non (Abaelardus)
1126	*Ibn Rushd (Averroes)	
1142	Abaelardus+	
ca. 1150/52		Libri quattuor sententiarum (Petrus Lombardus)
1160	Petrus Lombardus+	
1180		Tahafut-at-tahafut (Averroes)
1197	*N. Blemmydes	
1198	Averroes+	
1201	*Nasir Tusi	
1206/07	*Albertus Magnus	
1221	*Bonaventura	
1225	*Thomas Aquinas	
1254		Adrias Basilikos (N. Blemmydes)
1263	*Ibn Taymiyya	
1266	*Duns Scotus	
1267–1273		Summa Theologiae (Thomas Aquinas)
1270–1280		Summa Theologiae (Albertus Magnus)

(continued)

(continued)

Year	Name	Works
1272	Nikephorus Blemmydes+	
1273		Collationes in hexaemeron (Bonaventura)
1274	Nasir Tusi+	
	Thomas Aquinas+	
	Bonaventura+	
1275	*Thomas Magister	
1280	Albertus Magnus+	
1285	*Wilhelm von Occam	
ca. 1300		Quastiones subtilissimae super libros Metaphysicorum Aristotelis (Duns Scotus)
ca. 1300–1308		Ordinatio (Duns Scotus)
		The Hisba in Islam (Ibn Taymiyya)
1308	Duns Scotus+	
ca. 1317–1324		Scriptum in librum primum sententiarum, Summa totius logicae (Wilhelm von Occam)
1320	*Wyclif	
ca. 1320–1325	*Nicolaus Oresmius	
1324–1328		Peri basileias (De Regis Officiis) (Th. Magister) Peri politeias (Th. Magister) (De Subditorum Officiis)
1328	Ibn Taymiyya+	
1332	*Ibn Khaldun	
1349	Wilhelm von Occam+	
1350	Thomas Magister+	
1355?	*Georgios Gemistos-Plethon	
1370	*Leonardo Bruni	Tactatus de origine, natura, jure et mutationibus monetarum; Aristotelis Politica et Oeconomica; Decem libri ethicorum Aristotelis (Oresmius)
1376/77		De civili dominio (Wyclif)
1377		Muqaddimah (I. Khaldun)
1377–1382		Kitab al-'Ibar (I. Khaldun)
1382	N. Oresmius+	
1384	Wyclif+	
1396	*Georgius of Trapezus	
1401	*Nicolaus of Kues	
1403	*Bessarion	
1404	*Leon Battista Alberti	
1406	Ibn Khaldun+	
1416		Advice to despot of the Peloponnese Theodor II (Gemistos)
1418		To Manuel Palaeologus, on affairs in the Peloponnese (Gemistos)
1420/21		Commentaries on "Oeconomica" (L. Bruni)
1438/39		On the Laws (Gemistos)

(continued)

(continued)

Year	Name	Works
1440		De docta ignorantia (N. of Kues)
1440–1444		De coniecturis (N. of Kues)
1442–1444		Trattato del governo della famiglia (Alberti)
1444	Leonardo Bruni+	Letter to Constantine, Despot of Peloponnese (Bessarion)
1452	Georgios Gemistos-Plethon+	
1455		Comparationes philosophorum Aristotelis et Platonis (Georgius of Trapezus)
1464	Nicolaus of Kues+	
1466/69	*Erasmus of Rotterdam	
1460	*Machiavelli	
1472	Leon Battista Alberti+ Bessarion+	

References

Aalders GJD (1968) Nomos Empsychos. In: Steinmetz P (ed) Politeia und Res Publica. Palingenesia IV, Wiesbaden, pp 315–329

Aalders GJD (1975) Political thought in Hellenistic times. A. Hakkert, Amsterdam

Alberti LB (1994) I libri della Famiglia. A cura di Ruggiero Romano e Alberto Tenenti. Nuova edizione a cura di Francesco Furlan. G. Einaudi, Torino

Andic S (1965) A fourteenth century sociology of public finance. Public Finance 20(1–2):20–44

Andreades AM (1915) Περί των δημοσιονομικών θεωριών του Αριστοτέλους και της Σχολής αυτού, ιδία δε περί του Β' βιβλίου των Οικονομικών [= On Aristotle's financial theories and his school, especially on the II. Book of Oeconomica]. Επιστημονική Επετηρίς Πανεπιστημίου Αθηνών 11:25–144

Andreades AM (1930) La premiere apparition de la science des finances (Un chapitre de l' Économique d' Aristote), Economia Politica Contemporanea. Saggi di Economia e Finanza in onore del Prof. Camilo Supino, vol II, Padova, pp 289–297

Andreades AM (1933) A history of Greek public finance. Revised and enlarged edition [trans: Brown CN]. Introduction by Ch. J. Bullock. Harvard University Press, Cambridge

Andreades AM (1992) Ιστορία της Ελληνικής Δημοσίας Οικονομίας [= History of Greek public finance]. A reprinted edition of 1928 with an Introduction by C. Baloglou. Preface by A. Angelopoulos. Papadimas, Athens

Armstrong CG (trans) (1935) Oeconomica, Loeb classical library. Harvard University Press, London

Arnim J (1992) Dionis Prusaensis (Chrysostomi) quae extant Omnia. Teubner, Berolini (repr.)

Asmus R (1894) Gregorius von Nazianz und sein Verhältnis zum Kynismus. Theologische Studien und Kritikern 67:314–339 [repr. in Margarethe B (ed) (1991) Die Kyniker in der modernen Forschung. Aufsätze mit Einführung und Bibliographie. Gruner, Amsterdam, pp 185–206]

Backhaus J (1989) Die Finanzierung des Wohlfahrtsstaats. Eine kleine Ortsbestimmung an Hand der Theoriegeschichte, Maastricht

Backhaus J (1999) Constitutional causes for techno leadership: Why Europe? METEOR Universiteit Maastricht. Faculty of Economics and Business Administration. Working Paper WP/99/007

Baeck L (1990) La pensée économique de l'Islam classique. Storia del pensiero economico 19:3–19

Baeck L (1994) The Mediterranean tradition in economic thought. Routledge, New York [Routledge history of economic thought series, vol 5, 1994]

Baeck L (1996) Il pensiero economico cristiano dall' Anticita al Basso Medioevo (Pieroni R). In: Castronovo V (ed.) Storia dell' economia mondiale. Laterza, Roma-Bari, pp 531–554 [1996]

Baeck L (1997) Greek economic thought. Initiators of a Mediterranean tradition. In: Price BB (ed.) Ancient economic thought. Routledge, London, pp 146–171 [Routledge studies in the history of economics, vol 13, 1997]

Baldry HC (1959) Zeno's ideal state. J Hellenic Studies 79:3–15

Baldry HC (1965) The unity of mankind in Greek thought. Cambridge University Press, Cambridge

Baloglou C (1990) Ο Δημόκριτος για τον πλούτο, τη φτώχεια και την ευημερία [= Democritus on wealth, poverty and welfare]. Θρακικά Χρονικά 44(December):61–71

Baloglou C (1991/1992) Προτάσεις οικονομικής και κοινωνικής πολιτικής από τον Βησσαρίωνα (summary in German) [= Bessarion's proposals on social and economic policy]. Βυζαντινός Δόμος 5/6:47–68 [1993]

Baloglou C (1992) Αι οικονομικαί αντιλήψεις των στωϊκών Ιεροκλέους και Μουσωνίου Ρούφου (summary in German) [= The economic ideas of the Stoics Hierocles and Musonius Rufus]. ΠΛΑΤΩΝ 44:122–134 [1993]

Baloglou C (1995) Η οικονομική σκέψη των Αρχαίων Ελλήνων [= The economic thought of the Ancient Greeks]. Foreword by Kyrkos BA. Historical and Cultural Society of Chalkidike, Thessalonike

Baloglou C (1996) Η οικονομική σκέψη του Νικολάου Καβάσιλα [= Nicolas Cabasilas' economic thought], Βυζαντιακά 16:191–214

Baloglou C (1998a) Hellenistic economic thought. In: Todd Lowry S, Gordon B (eds.) Ancient and medieval economic ideas and concepts of social justice. Brill, Leiden, pp 105–146

Baloglou C (1998b) Economic thought in the last Byzantine period. In: Todd Lowry S, Gordon B (eds.) Ancient and medieval economic ideas and concepts of social justice. Brill, Leiden, pp 405–438

Baloglou C (1998c) The economic thought of the early stoics. In: Demopoulos G, Korliras P, Prodromidis K (eds.) Essays in economic analysis. Festschrift in honor of professor R. Theocharis. Sideris, Athens, pp 18–36

Baloglou C (1998d) Το πρόγραμμα δημοσιονομικής και κοινωνικής πολιτικής του Αριστοτέλη (Συμβολή στην οικονομική σκέψη και πρακτική των μέσων του 4ου π. Χ. αιώνα) [= Aristotle's program of financial and social policy (A contribution on the economic thought and practice of the middle of the 4th century B.C.)]. Eleftheri Skepsis, Athens

Baloglou C (1998e) Georgios Gemistos-Plethon:ökonomisches Denken in der spätbyzantinischen Geisteswelt. Foreword by Schefold B, Historical Publications St. D. Basilopoulos, Athens [Historical Monographs 19]

Baloglou C (1999a) Η οικονομική φιλοσοφία των Κυνικών (= The economic philosophy of the cynics). Mésogeios-Mediterrannée 4:132–146

Baloglou C (1999b) The influence of the work "Oeconomica" on the formation of economic thought and policy in the middle ages and in the Renaissance. In: Koutras D (ed.) Aristotle's political philosophy and its influence. II. International congress of Aristotelian philosophy, Athens, pp 23–26

Baloglou C (1999c) Thomas Magistros' Vorschläge zur Wirtschafts-und Sozialpolitik. Byzantinoslavica LX(1):60–70

Baloglou C (2000a) Η κοινωνική και οικονομική οργάνωση της 'Πολιτείας του Ηλίου' του Ιαμβούλου [= The social and economic organization of Iambulus' "Sun State"]. In: Proceedings of the 20th panhellenic historical congress, Thessalonike, pp 19–31

Baloglou C (2000b) Die ökonomische Philosophie des Kynikers Krates von Theben, III. International Congress of Boeotian Studies. Annals of the Society of Boeotian Studies, vol III, Athens, pp 258–270

Baloglou C (2000c) The social and economic organization of Iambulus' "Sun State." SKEPSIS XI:159–172

Baloglou C (2001a) Aristotle and welfare economics. ΦΙΛΟΣΟΦΙΑ 31:237–244

Baloglou C (2001b) Πληθώνεια Οικονομικά Μελετήματα. Eleftheri Skepsis, Athens

Baloglou C (2002a) Economics and chrematistics in the economic thought of the stoic philosophy. Hist Econ Ideas X/3:85–101

Baloglou C (2002b) The economic thought of Ibn Khaldoun and Georgios Gemistos Plethon: some comparative parallels and links. Medioevo Greco 2:1–20

Baloglou C (2002c) Γεωργίου Γεμιστού Πλήθωνος περί των Πελοποννησιακών Πραγμάτων [= Georgios Gemistos Plethon on the Peloponnesian Affairs]. Eleftheri Skepsis, Athens

Baloglou C (2003a) Theodoretus of Cyrrhus' economic thought. Orthodoxes Forum 17(1):77–80

Baloglou C (2003b) George Finlay and Georgios Gemistos Plethon. New evidence from Finlay's records. Medioevo Greco 3:23–42

Baloglou C (2004a) Cleomenes' III politico-economic reforms in Sparta (235–222 B.C.) and Cercidas' economic thought. In: Barens I, Caspari V, Schefold B (eds.) Political events and economic ideas. Ed. Elgar, Aldershot, pp 187–205

Baloglou C (2004b) Schumpeter's "Gap," medieval Islamic and Byzantine thought. J Orient Afr Studies 12:231–241

Baloglou C, Constantinidis A (1993), Die Wirtschaft in der Gedankenwelt der alten Griechen. Peter Lang, Frankfurt-Bern

Baloglou C, Constantinidis A (1996) The treatise "Oeconomicus" of the Neopythagorean Bryson and its influence on the Arab-Islamic economic thought. J Orient Afr Studies 7:46–55

Baloglou C, Maniatis E (1994) Φιλοδήμου, Περί Οικονομίας [Text, translation and commentary]. Eleftheri Skepsis, Athens

Baloglou C, Peukert H (1996) Zum antiken ökonomischen Denken der Griechen (800–31 v.u.Z) Eine kommentierte Bibliographie, 2nd edn. Metropolis, Marburg

Barbieri G (1958) Fonti per la storia delle dottrine economiche dall' Antichita alla prima scolastica. Marzorati, Milano

Barbieri G (1964) Le dottrine economiche nell' Antichita Classica. In: Padovani A (ed.) Grande Antologia Filosofia, vol II. Marzorati, Milano, pp 823–925

Bargeliotes L (1989) Ο ελληνοκεντρισμός και οι κοινωνικο-πολιτικές ιδέες του Πλήθωνος [= Hellenocentricism and Plethon's sociopolitical ideas]. Athens, edition of the author

Bargeliotes L (1993) Η αντιπαράθεσις νεωτερικής επιστήμης και συντηρητισμού στον Βόρειο Ελληνισμό [= The juxtaposing of innovative science and conservatism in Northern Hellenism]. Παρνασσός 35:101–126

Barker E (1946) The politics of Aristotle. Translated with an Introduction, notes and appendices. Clarendon Press, Oxford [repr. 1970]

Barker E (1956) From Alexander to Constantine. Passages and documents illustrating the history of social and political ideas 336 B.C.-A.D. 337. Clarendon Press, Oxford

Barker E (1957) Social and political thought in Byzantium. From Justinian I to the last Palaeologus. Passages from Byzantine writers and documents. Clarendon Press, Oxford

Barnes HE (1924) Theories of the origin of the state in classical political philosophy. Monist 34:15–62

Baron H (1928) Leonardo Bruni-Aretino. Humanistisch-Philosophische Schriften mit einer Chronologie seiner Werke und Briefe, Leipzig

Bayonas AC (1970) Η πολιτική θεωρία των Κυνικών [= The political theory of the cynics]. Papazissis, Athens

Beck H-G (1970) Res Publica Romana. Vom Staatsdenken der Byzantiner. Sitzungsberichte der Bayerischen Akademie der Wissenschaften, Phil.-Historische Klasse, vol II, München

Bianchi E (1983) In tema d' usura' Canoni Conciliari e legislazione imperiale del IV secolo. Athenaeum 61:321–342

Bianchi E (1984) In tema d' usura' Canoni Conciliari e legislazione imperiale del IV secolo. Athenaeum 62:136–153

Bickermann E (1976) Studies in Jewish and Christian history. E.J. Brill, Leiden

Billerbeck M (ed.) (1991) Die Kyniker in der modernen Forschung. Aufsätze mit Einführung und Bibliographie. Gruner, Amsterdam

Blum W (1981) Byzantinische Fürstenspiegel. Agapetos, Theophylakt von Ochrid, Thomas Magister. A. Hiersemann, Stuttgart [Bibliothek der Griechischen Literatur 14]

Blum W (1988) Georgios Gemistos-Plethon. Politik, Philosophie und Rhetorik im spätbyzantinischen Reich (1355–1452). A. Hiersemann, Stuttgart [Bibliothek der Griechischen Literatur 25]

Blumentritt M (1979) Zur Gesellschaftskritik Dions von Prusa', Wissenschaftliche Zeitschrift der Universität Halle-Wittenberg. Ges Sprachwissenschaftliche Reihe 28:41–51

Boas G (1948) Essays in primitivism and related ideas in the middle ages. John Hopkins Press, Baltimore

Bonar J (1896) Philosophy and political economy in some of their historical relations. Macmillan, London [repr. Kelley A, New York, 1966]

Bougatsos N (1980) [1988] Η Κοινωνική Διδασκαλία των Ελλήνων Πατέρων [= The social teaching of the Greek Fathers], 3 vols, 2nd edn. Eptalophos, Athens

Boulakia JDC (1971) Ibn Khaldun: a fourteenth-century economist. J Pol Econ 79:1105–1118

Bousquet G-H (1955) Un Precursore Arabo di Lord Keynes: Ibn Khaldun. Econ Storia 2:200–210

Bousquet G-H (1957) L' Économie Politique non Européano-chrétienne. L' exemple d' al- Dimashqi. Revue d' Histoire Économique et Sociale XLV:6–23

Bouyges M (1931) Review: M. Plessner, Der OIKONOMIKOC des Neupythagoreers "Bryson" und sein Einfluss auf die islamische Wissenschaft. Gnomon 7:256–260

Branham BR, Goulet-Caze M-O (1996) Introduction. In: Branham BR, Goulet-Caze M-O (eds.) The cynics. The cynic movement in antiquity and its legacy. University of California Press, Berkeley, pp 1–27

Brown TS (1949) Onesicritus. a study in Hellenistic historiography. University of California Press, Berkeley [1974]

Brown WR (1982) Aristotle's art of acquisition and the conquest of nature. Interpretation 10:159–195

Bruder (1876) Zur ökonomischen Charakteristik des römischen Rechtes. Zeitschrift für die gesamte Staatswissenschaft 32:631–659

Brunner O (1949) Johann Joachim Bechers Entwurf einer "Oeconomia ruralis et domestica". Sitzungsberichte Österr Akad Wissenschaf 226:85–91

Brunner O (1952) Die alteuropaeische "Oekonomik". Z Nationalökon 13(1):115–139

Brunner O (1968) Das "ganze Haus" und die alteuropäische "Ökonomik." in O. Brunner, Neue Wege der Verfassungs-und Sozialgeschichte, Wien, pp 103–127

Brunt PA (1973) Aspects of the social thought of Dio Chrysostom and of the Stoics. In: Proceedings of the Cambridge philological society, vol 19, pp 9–34 [repr. in Brunt PA (1993) Studies in Greek history and thought. Clarendon Press, Oxford, pp 210–244]

Bryce J (1904) The holly roman empire. Macmillan, London

Bullock CJ (1939) Politics, finance and consequences. A study of the relations between politics and finance in the ancient world with special reference to the consequences of sound and unsound policies. Cambridge University Press, Cambridge

Burckhardt J (1860) Die Kultur der Renaissance in Italien (Greek trans: Topale M). Nefeli, Athens [1997]

Bürgin A (1993) Zur Soziogenese der Politischen Ökonomie. Metropolis, Marburg

Cardini MT (1962) Pitagorici. Testimonianze e Frammenti, vol II, Roma

Chrestou P (1973) Οικονόμοι Θεού. Αξιολόγησις του πλούτου υπό του Μεγάλου Βασιλείου [= God's oikonomoi. Basil's the great evaluation of wealth]. Μελέται προς τιμήν Στρατή Γ. Ανδρεάδη [Studies in honour of Stratis G. Andreades], vol. III, Athens, pp 291–297

Chroust A-H (1965) The ideal polity of the early stoics: Zeno's politics. Rev Politics 27:173–183

Conomis N (1970) Lycurgus in Leocratem cum ceteris Lycurgi oratoris fragmentis. Teubner, Lipsiae

de Martino F (1991) Wirtschaftsgeschichte des alten Rom, 2nd edn. C. Beck, München

Descat R (1988) Aux origines de l' oikonomia grecque. Quad Urbinati Cultura Classica 28:103–119

Despotopoulos C (1991) Philosophy of history in ancient Greece. Academy of Athens. Research Center for Greek Philosophy, Athens

Despotopoulos C (1997) Συμβολή στην Φιλοσοφία της Εργασίας [= Contribution to the philosophy of labour]. Papazissis, Athens
Despotopoulos C (1998) Μελετήματα Φιλολογίας και Φιλοσοφίας [= Studies on philology and philosophy]. Hellenika Grammata, Athens
Diehl E (1949) Anthologia Lyrica Graeca. Teubner, Lipsiae
Diogenes of Oenoanda (1998) Οι πολύτιμες πέτρες της φιλοσοφίας. Η μεγάλη επιγραφή στα Οινόανδα. Introduction by Chr. Theodorides. Thyrathen, Thessalonike
Dörrie H (1967) Euhemeros. Der kleine Pauly, II, cols. 414–415
Drack B (1960) Beschauliches und tätiges Leben im Mönchtum nach der Lehre Basilius des Grossen. Freiburg Z Philos Theol 7(297–309):391–414
Dudley DR (1937) A history of cynicism from Diogenes to the sixth century A.D. London [repr. Olms, Hildesheim, 1973]
Egner E (1985) Der Verlust der älteren Ökonomik. Seine Hintergründe und Wirkungen. Duncker & Humblot, Berlin
Eisenhart H (1891) Geschichte der Nationalökonomik, 2nd edn. Fischer, Jena
Eleutheropoulos C (1930) Οικονομία και Φιλοσοφία [= Economy and philosophy]. Thessalonike
Eliopoulos C (1973) Αι περί εργασίας ως οικονομικού παράγοντος αντιλήψεις του Κικέρωνος [= Cicero's ideas on labour as economic factor]. Μελέται προς τιμήν Στρατή Γ. Ανδρεάδη [Studies in honour of Stratis G. Andreades], vol III, Athens, pp 139–180
Engels J (1988) Anmerkungen zum "Ökonomischen Denken" im 4. Jahrhundert v. Chr. und zur wirtschaftlichen Entwicklung des Lykurgischen Athen. Münsterische Beit Antiken Hand 7(1):90–134
Engels J (1999) Rezension: H. Leppin und W. Portmann, Themistios. Staatsreden. Übersetzung, Einführung und Erläuterungen, Stuttgart 1998. Byzantinische Z 92(1):137–140
Essid Y (1987) Islamic economic thought. In: Todd Lowry S (ed.) Pre-classical economic thought. From the Greeks to the Scottish enlightenment. Kluwer, Boston, pp 77–102
Essid Y (1992) Greek economic thought in the Islamic milieu: Bryson and Dimashqi. In: Todd Lowry S (ed.) Perspectives on the history of economic thought, vol. vii: perspectives on the administrative tradition: from antiquity to the twentieth century, Worcester, pp 39–44
Essid Y (1995) A critique of the origins of Islamic economic thought. E.J. Brill, Leiden
Essid Y (2000) Ibn Khaldun und die wirtschaftlichen Vorstellungen im Islam. In: Schefold B, Daiber H, Essid Y, Hottinger A, Ibn Khaldun's, Muqqadima'. Vademecum zu dem Klassiker des arabischen Wirtschaftsdenkens. Wirtschaft und Finanzen, Düssledorf, pp 55–88
Ferguson J (1975) Utopias of the classical world. Thames & Hudson, London
Finley MI (1970) Aristotle and economic analysis. Past Present 47:4–25
Foley V (1974) The division of labour in Plato and Smith. Hist Polit Econ 6:220–242
Fouyas M (1994) Έλληνες και Λατίνοι. Η εκκλησιαστική αντιπαράθεσις Ελλήνων και Λατίνων από της εποχής του Μεγάλου Φωτίου μέχρι της Συνόδου της Φλωρεντίας [The ecclesiastical diversification of the Greeks and the Latins from the time of St. Photius to the Council of Florence 858–1439], 2nd edn. Apostoliki Diakonia, Athens
Fouyas M (1995) Η Ελληνιστική Ιουδαϊκή Παράδοση [= The Hellenistic Jewish tradition]. Livanis, Athens
Furlan F (1994) Nota al testo. In: Alberti LB (ed.) I libri della Famiglia. G. Einaudi, Torino, pp 429–478
Garnsey P (1980) Non-slave labour in the Roman world. In: Garnsey P (ed.) Non-slave labour in the Greco-Roman World. Cambridge University Press, Cambridge, pp 34–37
Gertrud C (1926) Die Agrarlehre Columellas. Vierteljahrsschrift für Sozial – und Wirtschaftsgeschichte
Ghanzafar SM (2000) Public sector economics in medieval economic thought: contributions of selected Arab-Islamic scholastics. In: IV annual conference of the European society for the history of economic thought, Graz, 24–27 Feb 2000 [= Ghazanfar SM (ed.) (2003) Medieval Islamic economic thought. Filling the "Great Gap" in European economics. Foreword by Todd Lowry S. Routledge, New York, pp 381–403]

Ghazanfar SM (ed.) (2003) Medieval Islamic economic thought. Filling the "Great Gap" in European economics. Foreword by Todd Lowry. S. Routledge, London

Ghanzafar SM, Azim Islahi A (1990) Economic thought of an Arab scholastic: Abu Hamid al-Ghazali (A.H. 450–505/A.D. 1058–1111). Hist Polit Econ 22(2):381–403 [= Ghazanfar SM (ed.) (2003) Medieval Islamic economic thought. Filling the "Great Gap" in European economics. Foreword by Todd Lowry. S. Routledge, London, pp 53–71]

Gill JC (1964) Personalities of the Council of Florence and other essays. B. Blackwell, Oxford

Glaser JC (1865) Die Wirthschaftslehre der Griechen. Jahrb Gesellsch Staatswissenschaften 4:289–313

Goldbrunner H (1968) Durandus de Alvernia, Nicolaus von Oresme und Leonardo Bruni. Zu den Übersetzungen der pseudo-aristotelischen Ökonomik. Archiv Kulturgeschichte 50: 200–239

Goldbrunner H (1975) Leonardo Brunis Kommentar zu seiner Übersetzung der Pseudo-Aristotelischen Ökonomik: Ein humanistischer Kommentar. In: Buck A, Herding O (eds.) Der Kommentar in der Renaissance, Boppard a. Rhein, pp 99–118

Gordon B (1975) Economic analysis before Adam Smith: from Hesiod to Lessius. Barnes & Noble, New York

Gordon B (1982) Lending at interest: some Jewish, Greek and Christian approaches, 800 BC-AD 100. Hist Polit Econ 14(3):406–426

Gotsis G (1997) Προβλήματα οικονομικής και πολιτικής ηθικής στην πατερική και βυζαντινή σκέψη. Εισαγωγικά Μελετήματα [Problems of economic and political ethics in the byzantine-patristic thought]. Sakkoulas, Athens

Goulet-Caze M-O, Lopez Cruces JL (1994) Cercidas de Megalopolis (c 83). In: Goulet R (ed.) Dictionnaire Philosophique d' Antiquité, 2, Paris, pp 269–281

Grassl H (1982) Sozialökonomische Vorstellungen in der kaiserzeitlichen griechischen Literatur (1–3 Jht. n. Chr.). Wiesbaden [Historia Einzelschriften 41]

Groningen BA, Wartelle A (1968) Aristote, Économique. Texte etabli par B.A. Groningen et A. Wartelle. Traduit et annoté par A. Wartelle. Les Belles Lettres, Paris

Habicht C (1958) Die herrschende Gesellschaft in den hellenistischen Monarchien. Vierteljahr Sozial Wirtschaftsgeschichte 25:1–16

Haddad L (1977) A fourteenth-century theory of economic growth and development. Kyklos 30(2):195–213

Hadot P (1972) Fürstenspiegel. Reallexikon für Antike und Christentum, vol VIII. Hiersemann, Stuttgart, cols 555–632

Hammond M (1951) City-state and world state in Greek and Roman political theory until Augustus. Biblo and Tannen, New York

Haney L (1949) History of economic thought, 4th edn. Macmillan, New York

Harrison F (1913) Roman farm management in the treatises of Cato and Varro. Macmillan, New York

Hartung JA (1857) Philodem's Abhandlungen über die Haushaltung und über den Hochmuth und Theophrast's Haushaltung und Charakterbilder, Leipzig

Heckscher EF (1935) Mercantilism [trans: Shapiro M], vol II. MacMillan, London

Hegeland H (1951) The quantity theory of money. A critical study of its historical development and interpretation and a restatement. Götenborg

Heinze R (1892) Xenokrates. Darstellung der Lehre and Sammlung der Fragmente. Teubner, Leipzig [repr. Olms, Hildensheim, 1965]

Henry P (1967) A mirror for Justinian: the Ecthesis of Agapetus Diaconus. Greek Roman Byzantine Studies 8:281–308

Hock RF (1976) Simon the shoemaker as an ideal cynic. Greek, Roman and Byzantine studies 17:41–53 [repr. in Billerbeck M (ed.) (1991) Die Kyniker in der modernen Forschung. Gruner, Amsterdam, pp 259–271]

Hodermann M (1896) Quaestionum oeconomicarum specimen. Berolini

Hodermann M (1899) Xenophons Wirtschaftslehre unter dem Gesichtspuntke sozialer Tagesfragen betrachtet, Wernigerode

Horn HJ (1985) Oikonomia. Zur Adaptation eines griechischen Gedankens durch das spätantike Christentum. In: Stammler T (ed.) Okonomie. Sprachliche und literarische Aspekte eines 2000 Jahre alten Begriffs, Tubingen, pp 51–58

Hosseini H (1998) Seeking the roots of Adam Smith's division of labor in medieval Persia. Hist Polit Econ 30(4):653–681

Houmanidis L (1980) Οικονομική Ιστορία και η Εξέλιξις των Οικονομικών Θεωριών, vol. I [= Economic history and the evolution of economic theories]. Papazissis, Athens

Houmanidis L (1990) Οικονομική Ιστορία της Ελλάδος [= Economic history of Greece], vol I. Papazissis, Athens

Houmanidis L (1993) Xenophon's economic ideas. Arch Econ Hist 2:79–102

Hoven van den B (1996) Work in ancient and medieval thought. J.C. Gieben, Amsterdam [Dutch monographs on ancient history and archaeology XIV]

Hunger H (1994) Βυζαντινή Λογοτεχνία. Η λόγια κοσμική γραμματεία των Βυζαντινών, Greek transl., vol III, Athens

Huys M (1996) The Spartan practice of selective infanticide and its parallels in Ancient Utopian tradition. Ancient Soc 27:47–74

Ingram JK (1888) [1967] A history of political economy. MacMillan, New York. New and enlarged edition with a supplementary chapter by W.A. Scott and an Introduction by R. Ely, A. Kelley, New York

Ioannou PP (1971) Demonologie populaire-demonologie critique au XI siecle. La vie inedite de S. Auxence par M. Psellus, Wiesbaden

Jackson G (1982–1983) Sulla fortuna dell' Economico Pseudo-Aristotelico o di Teofrasto fino al XIV secolo. Annali dell' Istituto Universitario Orientale di Napoli. Sezione Filologico-Letteraria 4–5:141–183

Jackson G (1992) Leonardo Bruni e l' Economico teofrasteo o pseudo-aristotelico. Miscallanea di studi in onore di Armando Salvatore, Napoli, pp 223–256

Jackson G (1995) La diffusione dell' Economico Teofrasteo o Pseudo-Aristotelico nel Quattrocento. Annali dell' Istituto Universitario Orientale di Napoli, Sezione Filologico – Letteraria 17:295–328

Jacoby F (1912) Hekataios von Abdera (4). Realencyclopädie für die Klassische Altertumswissenschaft, VII (2), cols. 2750–2769

Jensen J (1907) Philodemi περί οικονομίας qui dicitur libellus. Teubner, Lipsiae

Jensen J (1916) Hyperides, Orationes. Teubner, Lipsiae [repr. Stutgardiae, 1963]

Jones CP (1978) The Roman world of Dio Chrysostom. Cambridge University Press, Cambridge

Jones CP (1997) Themistios and the speech "To the King". Classical Philology 92:149–152

Kakridis J (1962) Zum Weiberjambos des Semonides. Wiener Humanistische Blätter 5:3–10

Karayannopoulos J (1992) Η πολιτική θεωρία των Βυζαντινών [= The political theory of the Byzantines]. Vanias, Thessalonike

Karayiannis A (1988) Democritus on ethics and economics. Rivista Internazionale di Scienze Economiche e Commerciali 35(4):369–391

Karayiannis A (1992) Enterpreunership in classical Greek literature. South Afr J Econ 60(1):67–93

Karayiannis A (1994) The Eastern Christian fathers (A.D. 350–400) on the redistribution of wealth. Hist Polit Econ 26(1):39–67

Karayiannis AD (2003) Georgios Plethon-Gemistos on economic policy. In: Benakis L, Baloglou C (eds.) Proceedings of the international conference: Plethon and his time (Mistras, 26–29 June 2002), Athens, Mistra, 2003

Karayiannis A, Drakopoulos-Dodd S (1998) The Greek Christian fathers. In: Todd Lowry S, Gordon B (eds.) Ancient and medieval economic ideas and concepts of social justice. E.J. Brill, Leiden, pp 163–208

Katsos G (1983) Αναδρομή στο πνεύμα των Αρχαίων Ελλήνων και των πρώτων χριστιανών για την επίλυση του προβλήματος της δίκαιης κατανομής του εισοδήματος και του πλούτου γενικότερα [= A flashback to the spirit of the ancient Greeks and the Early Christians for the solution of the problem of just distribution of income and wealth]. Επιστημονική Επετηρίς Σχολής Νομικών και Οικονομικών Επιστημών Αριστοτελείου Πανεπιστημίου Θεσσαλονίκης, pp 169–187

Kautz J (1860) Die geschichtliche Entwicklung der National-Oekonomik und ihrer Literatur, Wien [repr. Scientia, Aalen, 1970]

Kazhdan A (1983) Hagiographical notes. Byzantion 53:538–558 [reprinted in Kazhdan A (1993) Authors and texts in Byzantium. Variorum, Aldershot, No III]

Kemmerer E (1907) Money and prices. Henry Holt, New York

King E (1948) The origin of the term "political economy". J Modern Hist 20:230–231

King ML (1976) Caldiera and the Barbaros on marriage and the family: humanist reflections of Venetian realities. J Medieval Renaissance Studies 6:19–50

Klever WNA (1986) Archeologie van de economie. De economiesche theorie in de Griekse oudheid. Markant, Nijmegen

Kock T (1880–1888) Comicorum Atticorum Fragmenta, 3 vols. Teubner, Leipzig

Kompos A (1996) Αι περί τόκου αντιλήψεις της Κλασσικής ελληνικής γραμματείας και η περί τούτου διδασκαλία της Αγίας Γραφής και εκκλησιαστικών συγγραφέων [= The conception on usury of the classical Greek grammar and the teaching of the Holly Bible and the ecclesiastical authors]. Τιμητικόν Αφιέρωμα εις τον Μητροπολίτην Καισαριανής, Βύρωνος και Υμηττού Γεώργιον, Athens, pp 133–164

Kontoulis G (1993) Zum Problem der Sklaverei (δουλεία) bei den kappadokischen Kirchenvätern und Johannes Chrysostomos, Bonn [Habelts Dissertationsdrucke: Reihe Alte Geschichte 38]

Koslowski P (1979a) Haus und Geld: Zur aristotelischen Unterscheidung von Politik, Ökonomik und Chrematistik. Philosophisches Jahrbuch 86:60–83

Koslowski P (1979b) Zum Verhältnis von Polis und Oikos bei Aristoteles. Politik und Ökonomie bei Aristoteles, München

Kousis D (1951) Αριστοτέλους Οικονομικά [= Aristotle's economics], Athens

Kristeller PO (1974) Humanismus und Renaissance, transl. in German by Renate Schweyen-Ott, vol I. W. Fink, München

Kristeller PO (1976) Humanismus und renaissance, vol II. W. Fink, München

Kuran T (1987) Continuity and change in Islamic economic thought. In: Todd Lowry S (ed.) Pre-classical economic thought. From the Greeks to the Scottish enlightenment. Kluwer, Boston, pp 103–114

Kytzler B (1973) Utopisches Denken und Handeln in der klassischen Antike. In: Villgrader R, Krey F (eds.) Der Utopische Roman. Wissenschaftliche Buchgesellschaft, Darmstadt, pp 45–68

Laiou-Thomadakis A (1972) Constantinople and the latins: the foreign policy of Andronicus II 1282–1328. Harvard University Press, Harvard

Laiou A (1999) Social justice: exchange and prosperity in Byzantium (in Greek with a summary in English). Πρακτικά της Ακαδημίας Αθηνών 74(B):102–130

Lampros S (1906) Υπόμνημα του Καρδιναλίου Βησσαρίωνος εις Κωνσταντίνον τον Παλαιολόγον [= Cardinal Bessarion's memorandum to Constantine Palaiologos]. Νέος Ελληνομνήμων 3:12–50

Lampros S (1926) [1972] Παλαιολόγεια και Πελοποννησιακά [= Palaiologeia and Peloponnesiaka], vol III. Athens [reprinted Gregoriadis, Athens]

Lampros S (1930) [1972] Παλαιολόγεια και Πελοποννησιακά, vol IV. Athens [reprinted Gregoriadis, Athens]

Landvogt P (1908) Epigraphische Untersuchungen über den οικονόμος (Ein Beitrag zum hellenistischen Beamtenwesen). Diss, Strasburg

Laurenti R (1968) Studi sull' Economico attribuito ad Aristotele. Marzorati, Milano

Lemerle P (1981) Ο πρώτος Βυζαντινός ουμανισμός [= The first byzantine humanism]. Cultural Foundation of National Bank of Greece, Athens

Letsios D (1985) Η "Εκθεση κεφαλαίων Παραινετικών" του Διακόνου Αγαπητού. Μία σύνοψη της ιδεολογίας της Εποχής του Ιουστινιανού για το αυτοκρατορικό αξίωμα. Δωδώνη 14(1):172–210

Lillge O (1955) Das patristische Wort οικονομία, seine Geschichte und seine Bedeutung bis auf Origenes, Erlangen

Long AA (1974) [1990] Hellenistic philosophy. Stoics, Epicureans, Sceptics. London. Gr. transl. Athens

C.P. Baloglou

López-Gruces JL (1995) Les meliambes de Cercidas de Megalopolis. Politique et tradition litté-
raire. Hakkert, Amsterdam
Lovejoy AO, Boas George (1973) Primitivism and related ideas in antiquity. With supplementary
essays by Albright WF, Dumont PE. Octagon Books, New York
Lowry ST (1973) Lord Mansfield and the law merchant: law and economics in the eighteenth
century. J Econ Issues 7:606–621
Lowry ST (1979) Recent literature on ancient Greek economic thought. J Econ Literature
27:65–86
Lowry ST (1987a) The archaeology of economic ideas: the classical Greek tradition. Duke
University Press, Durham
Lowry ST (1987b) Introduction. In: Todd Lowry S (ed.) Pre-classical economic thought. From the
Greeks to the Scottish enlightenment. Kluwer Academic Publishers, Boston, pp 1–6
Lowry ST (1987c) The Greek heritage in economic thought. In: Todd Lowry S (ed.) Pre-classical
economic thought. From the Greeks to the Scottish enlightenment. Kluwer Academic
Publishers, Boston, pp 7–28
Lowry ST (1995) The Ancient Greek administrative tradition and human capital. Arch Econ Hist
6(1):7–18
Lowry ST (1996) Review: Yassine Essid, A critique of the origins of Islamic economic thought
(1995). Hist Polit Econ 28(4):707–709
Lowry ST (1998) Xenophons ökonomisches Denken über "Oikonomikos" hinaus. In: Todd Lowry S,
Schefold B, Schefold K, Schmitt A (eds.) Xenophons "Oikonomikos." Vademecum zu einem
Klassiker der Haushaltsökonomie. Wirtschaft und Finanzen, Düsseldorf, pp 77–93
Maffi A (1979) Circolazione monetaria e modelli di scambio da Esiodo ad Aristotele. Ann Istituto
Italiano Numismatica 26:181–185
Maloney RP (1971) Usury in Greek, Roman and Rabbinic thought. Traditio 27:79–109
Maloney RP (1973) The teaching of the fathers on Usury: an historical study on the development
of christian thinking. Virgiliae Christianae 27:241–265
Mandenville B (1924) The fable of the bees or private vices, Public Benefits (1714), edited by
Kaye, London
Maniatis E, Baloglou C (1994) Φιλόδημος, Περί Οικονομίας [= Philodemus, on economy]. Greek
transl. by Maniatis E. Introduction and Commentary by C. Baloglou. Eleftheri Skepsis, Athens
Marget AW (1938) The theory of prices, vol I. Macmillan, New York [repr. 1967]
Martines L (1963) The social world of the florentine humanists 1390–1460. Princeton university
Press, Princeton
Marx K (1867) Das Kapital, vol I. in Marx-Engels-Werke, vol 23. Dietz, Berlin, 1962
Masai F (1956) Plethon et le platonisme de Mistra. Les Belles Lettres, Paris
Mase-Dari EMT (1901) Cicerone e le sue idee economiche e sociali, Torino
Mattei J-F (1995) Pythagore et les pythagororiciens. Les Belles Lettres, Paris. Greek transl.
Zacharopoulos, Athens
Mavromatis L (1994) Ο Καρδινάλιος Βησσαρίων και ο εκσυγχρονισμός της Πελοποννήσου
[= Cardinal Bessarion and the modernization of Peloponnes]. In: Moschonas N (ed.) Σύμμεικτα 9².
Μνήμη Δ. Ζακυθηνού [= Mélanges Dion. A. Zakythinos], vol II, Athens, pp 41–50
Meikle S (1995) Aristotle's economic thought. Clarendon Press, Oxford
Menut AD (1940) Oresme Maistre Nicole, Le Livre de Ethiques. Stechert, New York
Meyer E (1892) Zur älteren griechischen Geschichte. Niemeyer, Halle
Mohler L (1942) Kardinal Bessarion als Theologe, Humanist und Staatsmann, vol 2. Paderborn
Moles JL (1978) The career and conversion of Dio Chrysostom. J Hellenic Studies 98:79–100
Moles JL (1995) The cynics and politics. In: Laks A, Schofield M (eds.) Justice and generosity.
Studies in Hellenistic social and political philosophy. Cambridge University Press, Cambridge,
pp 129–158
Moles JL (1996) Cynic cosmopolitanism. In: Bracht Branham R, Goulet-Caze M-O (eds.) The cynics.
The cynic movement in antiquity and its legacy. University of California Press, London,
pp 105–120

Monroe AE (1923) Monetary theory before Adam Smith. Cambridge University Press, Cambridge [Harvard economic studies, vol XXV]

Moser T (1997a) The idea of Usury in patristic literature. In: Annual European conference on the history of economics, Athens, 17–19 April 1997

Moser T (1997b) Die patristische Zinslehre und ihre Ursprünge. Vom Zinsgebot zum Wucherverbot. H. Schellenberg, Winterthur

Moss L (1996) Platonic deception as a theme in the history of economic thought: the administration of social order. Hist Polit Econ 28:533–557

Mossé C (1969) Les utopies égalitaires a l' époque hellenistique. Revue Historique CCXLI Avril–Juin:297–308

Muller C (1878) Fragmenta Historicorum Graecorum, tome I–V. Parisiis

Murray O (1970) Hecataeus of Abdera and Pharaonic Kingship. J Egypt Archaeol 56:141–171

Nails D (1989) The Pythagorean women philosophers: ethics of the household. In: Boudouris K (ed.) Ionian philosophy. Ionia, Athens, pp 291–297

Natali C (1995) Oikonomia in Hellenistic political thought. In: Laks A, Schofield M (eds.) From justice to generosity. Cambridge University Press, Cambridge, pp 95–128

Newman WL (1887) The politics of Aristotle, with an introduction, two prefatory essays and notes critical and explanatory, vols I–IV. Oxford University Press, Oxford [repr. 1973]

Newskaja WP (1955) Byzanz in der klassischen und hellenistischen Epoche. Koehler und Amelang, Leipzig

Nicolet C (1984) Pline, Paul et la theorie de la monnaie. Athenaeum 72:105–135

Nikolaou T (1996) Rezension: G. Kontoulis, Zum Problem der Sklaverei (δουλεία) bei den kappadokischen Kirchenvätern und Johannes Chrysostomus, Bonn 1993. Byzantinische Z 89(2):476–478

Oertmann P (1891) Die Volkswirtschaftslehre des Corpus Juris Civilis. Diss, Leipzig

Ohrenstein RA, Gordon B (1991) Quantitative dimensions of human capital analysis in the Talmudic tradition. Festschrift in Honour of L. Th. Houmanidis, Piraeus, pp 275–287

Osborn E (1993) Theology and economy in Gregor the theologician. In: Brennecke HC, Grasmuck EL, Markschies C (eds.) Logos. Festschrift für Luise Abramowski zum 8 Juli 1993. De Gruyter, New York, pp 361–383

Panagopoulos A (1992–1993) Ευήμερος ο Μεσσήνιος και η κοινωνική ουτοπία της Ιεράς Αναγραφής του [= Euhemerus of Messene and the social utopia of his Hiera Anagraphe]. Πρακτικά Δ' Διεθνούς Συνεδρίου Πελοποννησιακών Σπουδών [Proceedings of the IV international congress of Peloponnesian studies], vol II, Corinth, Athens, 9–16 Sep 1990, pp 159–165

Pantazopoulos N (1979) Ρωμαϊκόν δίκαιον, εν διαλεκτική συναρτήσει προς το Ελληνικόν [= Roman Law, in dialectical function to the Greek], vol III. Sakkoula, Thessalonike

Papalexandris GF (1969) Τα οικονομικά στρατηγήματα της Αρχαιότητος [= The economic strategemata of Antiquity]. Εθνική Ανασυγκρότησις 219(January):12–14

Paquet L (1975) Les Cyniques grecs. Fragments et temoignages, Ottawa

Pellegrin P (1982) Monnaie et chrematistique. Remarques sur le mouvement et le contenu de deux textes d' Aristote a l' occasion d' un livre recent. Rev Philos de la France et de l' etranger 172:631–644

Perrotta C (2000) Wealth and poverty in the Hellenistic and Roman culture. European Society for the History of Economic Thought. Book of abstracts, Graz, p 118

Perrotta C (2003) The legacy of the past: ancient economic thought on wealth and development. Eur J Hist Econ Thought 10(2):177–219

Plessner M (1928) Der OIKONOMIKOC des Neupythagoreers Bryson und sein Einfluss auf die islamische Wissenschaft. C. Winter, Heidelberg (Orient und Antike 5)

Polanyi K (1968) Aristotle discovers the economy. In: Dalton G (ed.) Primitive, archaic and modern economies. Doubleday, New York, pp 78–115

Ponte G (1971) Etica ed economia nel terzo libro "della famiglia" de Leon Battista Alberti. In: Molho A, Tedeschi JA (eds.) Renaissance studies in honour of Hans Baron, Firenze, pp 285–309

Pringsheim F (1950) The Greek law of sale. Weimar, Böhlau

Psalidopoulos M (1997) Οικονομικές Θεωρίες και Κοινωνική Πολιτική [= Economic theories and social policy]. Aiolos, Athens

Pudendorf S (1759) De iure naturae et gentium. Leipzig und Frankfurt [repr. Minerva, Frankfurt, 1967]

Radermacher L (1921) Aristophanes' "Frösche." Einleitung, Text. Kommentar, Wien

Reumann JHP (1961) Οικονομία as "Ethical accommodation" in the fathers and its Pagan background. Stud Patristica 3(1):370–379

Reumann JHP (1979) The use of *oikonomia* and related terms in Greek sources to about A.D. 100. [Ekklesiastikos Pharos] 61:563–603

Reumann JHP (1980) The use of *oikonomia* and related terms in Greek sources to about A.D. 100. Church and Theology 1:368–430

Riecke A (1861) Marcus Terentio Varro, der römische Landwirth. Eine Schilderung der römischen Landwirthschaft zur Zeit des Julius Caesar, Stuttgart

Riedinger R (1995) Agapetos Diakonos. Der Fürstenspiegel für Kaiser Iustinianos. Athens: Εταιρεία Φίλων του Λαού- Κέντρον Ερεύνης Βυζαντίου 4

Riezler K (1907) Über Finanzen und Monopole im alten Griechenland. Norddeutsche Buchdrückerei und Verlagsanstalt, Berlin

Rohde E (1893) Zum griechischen Roman. Rheinisches Museum für Klassische Philologie 48:110–140

Rohde E (1914) Der griechische Roman und seine Vorläufer, 3rd edn. Leipzig [repr. Darmstadt, 1974]

Roscalla F (1990) Influssi antistenici nell' Economico di Senofonte. Prometheus 16:207–216

Roscher W (1861) Ansichten der Volkswirthschaft aus dem geschichtlichen Standpunkte. Leipzig und Heidelberg, Winter [reprinted with a companion volume by Streissler E, Baltzarek F, Milford K, Rosner P, Wirtschaft und Finanzen, Düsseldorf, 1993]

Rose V (1863) Aristoteles Pseudepigraphus. Teubner, Lipsiae

Rostovtzeff M (1941) The social and economic history of the Hellenistic world, 3 vols. Oxford University Press, Oxford [repr. Clarendon Press, Oxford, 1998]

Rousseau JJ (1755) Economie ou Oeconomie (Morale et Politique). In: Diderot Det d' Alembert J, Le R (eds.) Encyclopédie au Dictionnaire raisonné des Sciences, des Arts et des Métiers, vol V, Paris, pp 337–349. Quoted from the French-German edition entitled, Rousseau JJ (1977) Politische Ökonomie. Edit. and transl by Schneider HP, Schneider-Pachaly B. Klostermann, Frankfurt, pp 22–113

Ruggini GL (1966) Eforo nello Pseudo-Aristotele, Oec. II?. Atheneaum XLIV(III–IV):199–237

Runciman S (1952) Byzantine and Hellene in the fourteenth century. Επιστημονική Επετηρίς Σχολής Νομικών και Οικονομικών Επιστημών Αριστοτελείου Πανεπιστημίου Θεσσαλονίκης, 6 [volume for the 600th anniversary of C. Armenopoulos], Thessaloniki, pp 27–31

Runciman SS (1970) The last Byzantine renaissance. University Press, Cambridge

Salin E (1963) Kapitalbegriff und Kapitallehre von der Antike zu den Physiokraten. In: Salin E (ed.) Lynkeus. Mohr, Tübingen, pp 153–181

Savramis D (1965) "Ora et labora" bei Basilios dem Grossen. Mitt Jahrbuch 2:22–37

Schefold B (1989) Platon und Aristoteles. In: Starbatty J (ed.) Klassiker des ökonomischen Denkens, vol I. C.H. Beck, München, pp 19–55

Schefold B (1992) Spiegelungen des antiken Wirtschaftsdenkens in der griechischen Dichtung. In: Schefold B (ed.) Studien zur Entwicklung der ökonomischen Theorie XI. Die Darstellung der Wirtschaft und der Wirtschaftswissenschaften in der Belletristik. Dunker & Humblot, Berlin, pp 13–89

Schefold B (1997) Reflections of ancient economic thought in Greek poetry. In: Price BB (ed.) Ancient economic thought. Routledge, London, pp 99–145

Schefold B (2000a) Review: Th. Moser, Die patristische Zinslehre und ihre Ursprünge. Vom Zinsgebot zum Wucherverbot (1997). Eur J Hist Econ Thought 7(2):149–151

Schefold B (2000b) Aufstieg und Niedergang in der Wirtschaftsentwicklung Ibn Khalduns soziökonomische Synthese. In: Schefold B, Daiber H, Essid Y, Hottinger A, Ibn Khaldun's, Muqqadima. Vademecum zu dem Klassiker des arabischen Wirtschaftsdenkens. Wirtschaft und Finanzen, Düsseldorf, pp 5–20

Schefold B (2001) Von den Pflichten. In: Kloft H, Rüegg W, Schefold B, Vivenza G, Tullius M. Ciceros "De officiis." Vademecum zu einem Klassiker des römischen Denkens über Staat und Wirtschaft. Wirtschaft und Finanzen, Düsseldorf, pp 5–32

Schenkl H, Downey G (eds.) (1965) Themistii Orationes quae supersunt. Teubner, Lipsiae

Schlegel O (1909) Beitraege zur Untersuchung über die Quellen und die Glaubwürdigkeit der Beispielsammlung in den Pseudo-Aristotelischen Oeconomica. Diss, Berlin

Schmitt WO (1972) Aspekte des Humanismus und der Humanität in der Literatur der Kaiserzeit und der Spätantike. Wissenschaftliche Zeitschrift der Friedrich-Schiller Universität Jena, Gesellschafts– und Sprachwissenschaftliche Reihe, 21, 881–904

Schoemann GF (1839) Observationum in Theophrasti Oeconomicum et Philodemi Librum IX de virtutibus et vitiis, Gryphiswaldiae

Schofield M (1991) The Stoic idea of the city. Cambridge University Press, Cambridge

Schumpeter JA (1954) History of economic analysis. Allen & Unwin, London [reprinted with an Introduction by Perlman M. Routledge, London, 1994]

Schütrumpf E (1982) Xenophon. Vorschläge zur Beschaffung von Geldmitteln oder über die Einkünfte. Wissenschaftliche Buchgesellschaft, Darmstadt

Schütrumpf E (1991) Aristoteles Politik. Buch I. Über die Hausverwaltung und die Herrschaft des Herrn über Sklaven. Übersetzt und erläutert von E. Schütrumpf. Akademie Verlag, Berlin [Aristoteles Werke in deutscher Übersetzung, Bd. 9¹]

Scott WR (1937) Adam Smith as student and professor. Jackson, Sons &Co, Glasgow

Sevčenko I (1961) The Decline of Byzantium seen through the eyes of its intellectuals. Dumbarton Oaks Papers 15:167–186

Sevčenko I (1978) Agapetus, East and West: the Face of a Byzantine "Mirror for Princes". Rev Étud Sud-Est Europeennes 16:3–44

Sevčenko I (1981) Society and intellectual life in late Byzantium [London: Variorum Reprints, No II]

Shipley G (2000) The Greek World after Alexander 323–30 B.C. Routledge, London

Siems H (1992) Handel und Wucher im Spiegel frühmittelalterlicher Rechtsquellen. Hahn, Hannover [Monumenta Germaniae Historiae 35]

Simonde de Sismondi J-C-L (1819) Nouveaux Principes d' Économie Politique, ou de la Richesse, Paris

Skinner Q (1988) Political philosophy. In: Schmitt CB, Skinner Q (eds.) The Cambridge history of renaissance philosophy. Cambridge University Press, New York

Smith A (1776) An inquiry into the nature and causes of the wealth of nations, London. Edited with an Introduction, notes, marginal summary and an enlarged index by Ed. Cannan. The Modern Library, New York, 1937

Smith A (1978) Lectures on Jurisprudence. In: Meek RL, Raphael DD, Stein PG (eds.) Clarendon Press, Oxford (repr. 1987)

Smith MF (1993) Diogenes of Oenoanda: the Epicurean inscription. Bibliopolis, Napoli

Soudek J (1958) The genesis and tradition of Leonardo Bruni's annotated Latin version of the (pseudo-) Aristotelian economics. Scriptorium 12:260–268

Soudek J (1968) Leonardo Bruni and his public: a statistical and interpretative study of his annotated latin version of the (pseudo-) Aristotelian "economics". Stud Medieval Renaissance History 5:51–136

Soudek J (1976) A fifteenth-century humanistic bestseller: the manuscript diffusion of Leonardo Bruni's annotated latin version of the (pseudo-) aristotelian economics. In: Mahoney P (ed.) Philosophy and humanism. Renaissance essays in honor of Paul Oskar Kristeller. Brill, Leiden, pp 129–143

Spahn P (1984) Die Anfänge der antiken Ökonomik. Chiron 14:301–323

Spengler JJ (1964) Economic thought of Islam: Ibn Khaldun. Contemp Stud Soc Hist 6(3):268–306

Spengler JJ (1980) Origins of economic thought and justice. Southern Illinois University Press, Feffer and Simons. London, Amsterdam

Spentzas S (1964) Αι οικονομικαί και δημοσιονομικαί απόψεις του Γεωργίου Γεμιστού Πλήθωνος [= Georgios Gemistos-Plethon's economic and financial conceptions]. Athens

Spentzas S (1984) Η δημοσιονομική διερεύνησις του Βυζαντινού Κράτους [= The financial examination of the Byzantine State], 2nd edn. Papazissis, Athens

Spentzas S (1996) Αι οικονομικαί και δημοσιονομικαί απόψεις του Γεωργίου Γεμιστού-Πλήθωνος [= Georgios Gemistos-Plethon's economic and financial conceptions], Preface by Woodhouse CM. Kardamitsa, Athens

Spiegel HW (1971) The growth of economic thought. Duke University Press, Durham

Spiegel HW (1991) The growth of economic thought, 3rd edn. Duke University Press, Durham

Ste Croix G (1975) Early christian attitudes to property and slavery. In: Baker D (ed.) Church, society and politics. Blackwell, Oxford, pp 1–38

Steinwerter A (1946) ΝΟΜΟΣ ΕΜΨΥΧΟΣ. Zur Geschichte einer politischen Theorie. Anzeiger der Akademie der Wissenschaften in Wien (Phil.-Hist. Klasse) 83:250–268

Stephanidis D (1948) Η Κοινωνική Οικονομική εν τη ιστορική της Εξελίξει [= The social economy in its historical evolution], vol I. Athens

Sterghiopoulos C (1944) [1948] Μία αρχαία πολεοδομική διάταξις [= An ancient city planning order]. Πρακτικά Ακαδημίας Αθηνών 19:181–190

Strauss L (1970) Xenophon's socratic discourse: an interpretation of the Oeconomicus. Cornell University Press, Ithaca

Sudhaus S (1906) Eine erhaltene Abhandlung des Metrodor. Hermes 21:45–58

Susemihl F (1887) Aristotelis quae feruntur Oeconomica. Teubner, Lipsiae

Susemihl F, Hicks RD (1894) The politics of Aristotle. A revised text with introduction, analysis and commentary, Books I–V, London

Tarn WW (1930) Hellenistic civilization, 2nd edn. Ed. Arnold & Co, London

Tarn WW (1939) Alexander, cynics and stoics. Amer J Philol 60:41–70

Tarn WW (1948) Alexander the Great. II: sources and studies. University Press, Cambridge

Tcherikover V (1958) The ideology of the letter of Aristeas. Harvard Theol Rev LI(2):59–85

Theodorides C (1957) Επίκουρος. Η αληθινή όψη του αρχαίου Κόσμου [= Epicurus. The true view of the Ancient world]. Hestia, Athens

Thesleff H (1965) The pythagorean texts of the Hellenistic period. Abo [Acta Academiae Aboensis ser A, vol 30]

Thurn H (1961) Οικονομία. Von der frühbyzantinischen Zeit bis zum Bilderstreite. Semasiologische Untersuchung einer Wortfamilie, München

Tozzi G (1955) Economisti Greci, Sienna

Tozzi G (1961) Economisti Greci e Romani. Fertrinelli, Milano

Trever AA (1916) A history of Greek economic thought. Dissertation, Chicago [repr. Porcupine Press, Philadelphia, 1975]

Triantaphyllopoulos ND (1994) Δίωνος Χρυστοστόμου, Ευβοϊκός ή Κυνηγός [= Dion Chrysostom's, Euboicus or Hunter]. Stigme, Athens

Triantaphyllopoulos ND, Triantaphyllopoulos DD (1974) Ο "Ευβοϊκός" του Δίωνα Χρυσοστόμου [= Dion Chrysostom's "Euboicus"]. Αρχείον Ευβοϊκών Μελετών 20:33–73

Triantare-Mara S (2002) Οι πολιτικές αντιλήψεις των Βυζαντινών διανοητών από τον 10° έως τον 13ον μ.Χ. αιώνα. Herodotos, Thessalonike

Tsekourakis D (1977) Κυνικά στοιχεία στις κωμωδίες του Μενάνδρου [= Cynic elements in Menander's comodies]. Επιστημονική Επετηρίς Φιλοσοφικής Σχολής Αριστοτελείου Πανεπιστημίου Θεσσαλονίκης 16:377–399

Tsougkarakis D (1996) Kekaumenos, Strategicon. introduction – translation – commentary, 3rd edn. Kanakes, Athens

Usener E (1887) Epicurea, Freiburg

van Dieten J-L (1964) Βάρβαροι, Έλληνες und Ρωμαίοι bei den letzten byzantinischen Geschichtsschreibern. Actes du XIIe Congres International d' Études Byzantines, vol II, Belgrade, pp 273–299 van Dieten J-L (1979) Politische Ideologie und Niedergang im Byzanz der Palaiologen. Z Hist Forsch 6:1–35

van Groningen BA (1925) De rebus Byzantiorum ([Arist.] Oec. II p. 1346 b13–26). Mnemosyne 53:211–222

Venturi MF (1983) Aristotele e la crematistica. La storia di un problema e le sue fonti, Firenze

Viner J (1978) Religious thought and economic society. Hist Polit Econ 10(1):9–192

Vivenza G (1998) Roman thought on economics and justice. In: Todd Lowry S, Gordon B (eds.) Ancient and medieval economic ideas and concepts of social justice. E.J. Brill, New York, pp 269–331

Vivenza G (2001) Cicero und die traditionelle Wirtschaftsmoral in der Antike in Kloft H, Rüegg W, Schefold B, Vivenza G, Tullius M Ciceros "De officiis." Vademecum zu einem Klassiker des römischen Denkens über Staat und Wirtschaft. Wirtschaft und Finanzen, Düsseldorf, pp 97–138

Vlastos G (1945) Ethics and physics in Democritus. Philos Rev 54:578–592

Vogel G (1895) Die Ökonomik des Xenophon. Eine Vorarbeit für eine Geschichte der griechischen Ökonomik, Diss. Erlangen

von Pöhlmann R (1925) Geschichte der sozialen Frage und des Sozialismus in der antiken Welt, 3rd edn. C.H. Beck, München

von Scheel H (1866) Die wirtschaflichen Grundbegriffe im Corpus Juris Civilis Justinians. Jahrb Nationalökon Statistik 6:324–344

von Stern E (1921) Sozialwirtschaftliche Bewegungen und Theorien in der Antike. Niemeyer, Halle

Wassiliewsky B, Jernstedt V (1896) Cecaumeni Strategicon et Incerti Scriptoris de Officiis Regiis Libellus, St. Petersburg

Wehrli F (1967) Die Schule des Aristoteles, Part 1, 2nd edn. Schwabe, Basel

Wicksell K (1936) Interest and prices (trans: Kahn RF). Macmillan, London

Wilcken U (1901) Zu den Pseudo-Aristotelischen Oeconomica. Hermes 36:187–200

Wilhelm F (1915) Die Oeconomica der Neupythagoreer Bryson, Kallicratidas, Periktione, Phintys. Rheinisches Museum 70:161–233

Wilks MJ (1962) The problem of private ownership in patristic thought. Stud Patristica 6:533–542

Winiarczyk M (ed.) (1991) Euhemerus Messenius Reliquiae. Teubner, Stutgardiae et Lipsiae

Zonta M (1996) La traditione ebraica degli scritti economici Greci. Athenaeum 84(2):549–554

Chapter 3
Mercantilism

Helge Peukert

Introduction

In a narrow sense mercantilism describes the pattern of economic policy of the European states in the times of absolutism.[1] In a broader sense it means (a) an epoch of economic history, (b) an economic doctrine, and (c) a general pattern of economic policy (Schefold 1997, p. 163). It stretches over the seventeenth and eighteenth century, especially in England, but also in France (Colbert [1661–1683]) where it was definitely superseded by the physiocratic movement in the middle of the eighteenth century and declined already after the death of Louis XIV in 1715. To describe the epoch of mercantilism as stretching from the late Middle Ages in the fourteenth to the rise of liberalism in the eighteenth century (Heckscher 1932) seems too broad. In Germany, mercantilism began in 1668 with J.J. Bechers' *Politischen Discurs*. In England, mercantilism first appeared in Misselden's critique of the bullionist Malynes (1586–1641) after 1623 (see also Mun's long critique in 1911, Chap. 14). A. Smith's *Wealth of Nations*, first published in 1776, included an ardent critique of mercantilism and announced the ascendance of the capitalist entrepreneur and the supremacy of production over trade and the suspicion against the paternalistic state in liberalism. J. Steuart's *An inquiry into the principles of political economy*, first published in 1767, is the most remarkable and consistent but also the last major theoretical contribution of mercantilist thought.

Mercantilism reflects the problems of the seventeenth and eighteenth centuries: the strong gold imports to Europe, the quantitative increase and geographical enlargement of trade with the colonies, the war of 30 years and the ensuing contractive

---

[1]Blaich (1988, p. 35); see the earlier contributions by Cannan (1929), Johnson (1937), Eckert (1949), Minchinton (1969), and the more recent collection of articles in Blaug (1991a, b).

H. Peukert (✉)
Faculty of the Sciences of the State/Economics, Law and Social Science,
Nordhäuser Str. 63, 99089 Erfurt, Germany
e-mail: helge.peukert@uni-erfurt.de

J.G. Backhaus (ed.), *Handbook of the History of Economic Thought*,
The European Heritage in Economics and the Social Sciences,
DOI 10.1007/978-1-4419-8336-7_3, © Springer Science+Business Media, LLC 2012

consequences on population and production, the demands by merchants and traders for more support and/or liberty by the sovereign, the scientific revolution, the birth of a national economy, and the ascendancy of individual self-interest and an autonomous goal-oriented means-ends-rationality as an impact of the Renaissance and the Reformation (Schmidt 1994, pp. 38–39). Society at large was seen more and more as a common commercial company.

"One of the main factors in this transformation process was the flow of gold from the Americas. The prices in Europe tripled from 1500 to 1650. The social consequences were enormous. On the one hand, there was a gradual impoverishment of those classes, aristocrats and clerical, who lived on incomes which, being fixed by custom, adjusted extremely slowly to the fall in the value of money. On the other hand, there was an unprecedented enrichment of the mercantile class, who lived on 'profits upon alienation' … the identification of the interests of one particular social class, the merchant class, with those of the collectivity, was extremely important" (Screpanti and Zamagni 1995, pp. 19 and 26). The expansion of trade promoted the figure of the merchant-manufacturer. "Already by the end of the sixteenth century the craft model of production, where the craftsman was the owner of his tools and workshop and worked as a small independent businessman, had begun to be replaced, in the export sector, by a system of working at home, the 'putting-out' system" (Screpanti and Zamagni 1995, p. 19).

The aforementioned materialistic basic attitude which also characterizes mercantilism was very modern. In the endeavour to promote growth in non-industrialized countries, it was less modern and may serve as a positive prescription for developmental strategies of the NICs or as a horrible example of the so-called neo-mercantilism (protectionism and intensive state interventions especially what foreign trade is concerned).

From a free-market background neo-mercantilism must be rejected, but especially before the Asian crisis the dynamic and active intervening state in some Asian countries like South Korea has been seen by many as an alternative model of successful development in recent times. Another view of neo-mercantilism (Niehans 1945) stresses the *raison d'état* as the main element which leads to the principle of the increase of power, *étatisme*, a hostile trade policy and finally the willingness to start a war; mercantilism is then an essential driving force for the breakdown of the interwar economies and societies and a constitutive element of the Italian and German totalitarian systems after 1933 (see Raab 1932 as an example). J. Robinson (1966) argued that neo-mercantilism began after 1914 but that mercantilist thought can also be identified in the economic policies after 1945.[2]

In fact, the theoretical contributions of original early mercantilism never reached the unity of later economic theories like for example the classics or physiocracy.

---

[2] See the interpretation of the American Export Enhancement Program as a mercantilist approach to the US farm trade policy in Libby (1992), and for the mercantilist character of EU industrial policy Feldmann (1994); for the international context Pfaller (1986) and Strange (1985), for the developmental debate Lange (1995), on early mercantilist policy Schaefer (1993); see also Phillips (1992), Schweizer (1996), and Wolf (1995).

Mercantilism neither comprised an elaborate and unified theory nor was an easily identifiable movement of economic policy. Therefore, some scholars have concluded that "mercantilism was not a logical system. It may even plausibly be argued that, unlike scholasticism, the much vaunted mercantile system was not a system at all" (DeRoover 1955, p. 185). Blaug states "(t)hey had neither agreed principles nor common analytical tools" (1997, p. 10). In our view[3] it is nevertheless justified to speak of mercantilism as a separate and identifiable paradigm which is evidently visible in debates and dialogues with common assumptions and questions because at least some of their authors formulated insights and hypotheses on economic interdependencies and gave characteristic prescriptions for practical policy from a *staatswissenschaftlichen* background. The long-run aim was to increase the productive potential of countries so that it is correct to identify mercantilism as a doctrine of economic thought which is not only a doctrine of the past but also an interpretable pattern for recent practical economic policies.[4]

Main Economic Assumptions, Ideas, and Economic Policy Proposals of Mercantilism

In the following we will give an overview on mercantilism which is broadly in accordance with the basic assertions in the textbooks on economic history and on the history of economic thought (see, e.g. Bürgin 1961 and Saitzew 1941). Later we will see in how far this general picture of mercantilism is justified, or not.

Mercantilism views the economy from the perspective of an active state and its sovereign *and* forms the viewpoint of merchant capitalists. The essential assumption of mercantilism is an economy with unemployed resources. An increase of demand leads to the use of idle productive capital, land, or workers and increases GDP with no necessary effect on the price level. An increase of the money supply or its velocity – at that time in the form of precious metals – can induce growth with no inflationary side effects. Often, growth was not seen as conducive for higher consumption levels and general welfare per head (A. Smith's argument), but higher levels of employment and output were often seen as functional to make the country independent of the import of manufactured goods and strengthen the (military) power of the sovereign. But power and plenty were usually regarded as distinct aims, each valuable for its own sake (Viner 1996).[5] The opposite, a decrease in the velocity of money and the piling up of metals as a treasure (hoarding, which was a

---

[3] For the early debate see Coleman (1969), and the overview in Blaich (1973, pp. 1–10, and the literature on pp. 30–31).

[4] See also Salin (1944, pp. 55–74); on functional finance ideas in mercantilism see Schulz (1987, Chap. 5).

[5] For us, it is an open question in how far the link between a growth perspective and the independence view is typical for most mercantilists.

real and important phenomenon at the time) and the contractive consequences were also taken into consideration.[6] Money should therefore always be in circulation even if it is spent for luxury goods by the rich. But these goods should consequently not be imported.[7]

Besides money and employment, some mercantilists put great emphasis on the theorem of an active balance of trade (see the sympathetic reconstruction in Chipman 1993). In the literature (even by A. Smith, as we will see) the view of the mercantilists is sometimes confused with the approach of the bullionists or monetarists, a group of economists in the fifteenth and sixteenth century who held the view that the sum of precious metals (coins and bullion) in the country is the indicator of economic well-being and wealth. Every economic transaction which was accompanied by an outflow of money was thus considered detrimental. (Consequently applied by all nations, this necessarily leads to autarky.) The ideal is a passively held large hoarded treasure.

The first important debate where mercantilist ideas had been developed was Misselden's critique[8] of Malynes' view that the main causes of a disequilibrium in the balance of trade are due to changes in the exchange rate. If the exchange rate is higher than the metal parity, an outflow of precious metals takes place which will diminish the amount of money in circulation in the home country. The reduced prices worsen the terms of trade, the trade deficit increases. All this only happened as a consequence of more or less illegal monetary manipulations according to Malynes' *A treatise of the canker of England's Commonwealth* (London, 1603). By contrast, Misselden developed the idea that the deficit or surplus of the balance of trade lets the rate of exchange vary, so that the state should not be concerned with the exchange rate but fight the deficit by encouraging exports (see his *The circle of commerce*, London, 1623).

Like his precursor Misselden, the English mercantilist T. Mun (1571–1641, see below) also had a slightly different starting point in this respect (for the economic background of his time see Hinton 1991). In his view the overall result of the trans-actions of foreign trade should be taken into consideration. Wealth is measured as the amount of profits which can be gained by the active investment of money capital. A passive balance of trade with one country (e.g. India) may be due to the import of raw materials. This makes possible the production of manufactured goods. They may be sold with high profit and value-added to other countries (e.g. products of the textile industry can be sold to the Dutch). The overall result is a higher active balance of trade compared with the situation without the import of the raw materials from India (we will leave out here his inclusion of the capital balance). The practical economic policy conclusions are to prevent the import of finished goods. The import

---

[6] For example by the most important German mercantilists J.J. Becher [1635–1682] and J.H.G. Justi [1717–1771].

[7] A summary of the practical realization of these and the following principles in different European countries is given in Blaich (1973, pp. 112–199).

[8] [1608–1654]. He was a deputy-governor of the Merchant Adventurers' Company.

of raw materials and the export of finished goods should be encouraged. The raw materials of the country itself should not at all be exported. The instruments to enforce these prescriptions were manifold: the fixing of import quotas, simple prohibition and high tariffs (as we saw, the reasons were *not* primarily optimal tariff or infant industry arguments); further the granting of production and trading monopolies, the payment of subsidies, tax privileges, etc. (see for the interpretation of their view of international trade Rima 1993).

Also more specific political means and even a trade war have not been out of the spectrum of conceivable measures. This has to do with a (often more implicit) zero-sum assumption: a gain of one country is necessarily the loss of another country. Mercantilists were nationalists, their concern was not the wealth of nations (but remember also A. Smith's positive attitude vis-à-vis the navigation act) but only the wealth of their nation. The riches of the earth (raw materials and precious metals) are constant so that the wealth of nations depends on the distribution of the riches which are definitely limited in quantity. It has often been pointed out that this viewpoint – which is in exact opposition to the classical view of the positive-sum game of international trade – was not the expression of unreasonable pessimism but due to the facts of the competitive nation-building process and the background of a more static and pre-industrial economic structure without major technical progress, so that the limited natural endowments played a major role.

Besides foreign trade, the mercantilists also analysed the intranational economic situation and they formulated proposals to enhance economic performance. One aspect was their opting for a low wage level. If a positive balance of trade, that is, the role of exports of finished goods, is a key issue and the importance of productive capital is low (as it was, e.g. in the textile industry), low wages are important for the international competitiveness of the products of a nation's industry. The most natural way to hold wages down and increase production is to actively support the growth of the population by making emigration difficult and supporting immigration, early marriage, etc. (for the drastic measures see Nussbaumer 1991, pp. 31–33). Another target was the fight against a non-commercial mentality of the labour classes (leisure attitude and a back bending supply curve for labour). Therefore, the state fought against the blue Mondays, the many religious and other holidays, but also against the poor laws and charitable institutions to force people to work. They established compulsory work institutions like workhouses against the work dodgers. Another component was to improve human capital by the establishing of a rudimentary educational system with a practical orientation and efforts to improve the infrastructure (roads, canals, etc.).

A lot of other subjects have been treated by the mercantilists. An important question was how to increase the wealth of the sovereign without impeding the growth of the economy. This led to first reflections on the principles of taxation in the eighteenth century (this was also a topic for the German cameralists like J. Sonnenfels [1733–1817], see the reprint 1994). Justi formulated some principles of the limits of taxation, for example the principle that the substance of property and wealth should not be taxed away, the principle of equality (the taxes should be in proportion to the property of the taxpayer), and non-movable goods and property should be taxed (capital flight of the movable capital), accompanied by a personal tax for those who do not own movable capital (according to the principle of the ability to afford).

First Example: T. Mun's England's Treasure by Forraign Trade (1664)

The tract, which was probably written in 1630, is dedicated by Mun's son – who published the pamphlet – to the duke of Southampton (see the introduction by R. Biach in Mun 1911, pp. 7–98). The aim of the book is to take care of the treasure and income of the duke, as the title and the subtitle "The Ballance of our forraign trade is the rule of our treasure" indicate (for the economic situation of England in Mun's time see Conquest 1996, and Blitz 1991). The text is 100 pages long and has 21 chapters. In the preface to his son, the aim of the tract is defined to show the tasks and obligations for a good citizen who should love his country. The protection and enlargement of the state depends on the provisioning of the sovereign with gold. The provisioning of the country with gold is the duty of the merchants (1911, p. 105). The first chapter enumerates the qualities of an able merchant: he must have knowledge of the quality of products, of weights, calculation, writing, foreign languages, etc. He is the custodian of the (money) capital of the entire kingdom and the benefit of the merchant should be in accordance with the common good. The ideal merchant accumulates capital and pursues a decent style of living. We see that Mun already held the ideal of the thrifty, rich, and diligent bourgeois. A good merchant always tries to increase property and wealth and never engages in conspicuous consumption (1911, p. 110). The chapter shows the bias in favour of the merchants, the pretended fact of the usual interlocking of private and public interests. The book also contains practical policy for the merchant class: everything good is brought about by the "enigma of trade" (1911, p. 109), the influence and opinions of the merchants should not be neglected.

In the following, the book has a rather unsystematic starting point in Chap 2. He states right at the beginning that foreign trade is the only way to increase the possession of precious metals. The principle should be that in every year the exports exceed the imports (1911, p. 110). Mun only states this equation, he does not argue why the inflow of metals should be the major concern of economic policy. The wealth of England depends on the precious metals and they depend on an active trade balance. Consequently, Chap. 3 discusses the means and ways to increase the exports and how to reduce the consumption of imports. The cultivation of fallow land could reduce the import of raw materials. It could also be forbidden to import luxury goods. Luxury goods produced in the country may also employ the poor and encourage production (1911, p. 176). The export should be concentrated on goods with an inelastic foreign demand (1911, pp. 112–113).

We can already find a rudimentary theory of value in Mun. Value depends on rarity and utility, profit originates from trade as the difference between the selling and the buying price. Referring to Barbon who more explicitly theorized on value,

Screpanti and Zamagni summarize: "First, the natural value of goods is simply represented by their market price. Second, the forces of supply and demand determine the market price. Finally, the use value is the main factor on which the market price depends. The conditions of supply play a role only in the sense that, given the demand, the price tends to rise when the supply is insufficient and vice versa" (1995, p. 34). The goods should be shipped by the nation's own ships, so that freight and insurance costs would accrue to the nation itself. The consumption of foreign goods should be highly taxed. The exports of manufactured goods should be exported without any tariffs, so that many unemployed could find work.

Mun asserts that where the population is plenty and the crafts are excellent, trade develops and the country will become rich (1911, p. 120). We see here a combination of two separate aspects which are brought together in Mun's thought: the idea of the richness in precious metals as an indicator of wealth (exchange-surplus concept) and the idea of an increase of output and production by the enlargement of the labour force and productive investments (productivity concept). More important for Mun is the exchange-surplus aspect because in Chap. 4 he reiterates that an export of money to buy raw materials which are then manufactured and exported is the best way to increase the net inflow of gold (1911, pp. 121ff.).

But Mun also transcends the active balance of trade idea. He gives two further reasons for the export of gold (1911, pp. 125–126). One reason is that increased goods exports and gold imports would necessarily and constantly increase the price level. This is the basic implication of the quantity theory of money, foreshadowed by Bodin (1530–1596). Later mercantilists also accepted the quantity theory. But as a reaction to the long period of depression in and after the second half of the seventeenth century – which depended in their (correct) view on the reduced inflow of gold and silver from the Americas – deflation and not inflation was their concern. Consequently, they held the view that money stimulates trade in an economy with idle resources. This influences the level of transactions and not (primarily) the price level.

But he also holds that the constant increase of money is detrimental for society at large because it ultimately increases the price of the export goods so that the exports must diminish. Therefore, the gold surplus must always be reinvested abroad. We see that Hume's criticism of mercantilism in his *Political Discourses* in 1752 (existence of the price-specie-flow mechanism) had already been known more than 100 years earlier by the first notable mercantilist. Compare this fact with Blaug's statement that "(t)he mercantilists did not take account of Hume's self-regulating specie-flow mechanism" (1997, p. 19, compare p. 13 on Mun; see also Blaug's naive introduction in Blaug 1991b).

Mun combines this insight with the idea that a progressive movement of production/wealth/exchange/imports and exports does only work if there exists a certain mutual balance also between countries. The export of (indispensable) goods and the demand of the foreign country for the imported goods must balance. Buying and selling must take place in both countries. Rhetorically, he asks if we keep the gold in the confines of the home country, will the foreign countries be motivated and able to increase their demand of our finished goods? His answer is a definitive no

(1911, p. 125); he later also mentions the problem of retaliation (1911, p. 176). In these passages, Mun evidently foreshadows Smith's view of the beneficial mutual benefits of (increasing) international trade and the division of labour.[9] "Since hence here trade does not thrive by itself and certainly not if you hold back bullion right back into the empire, here as you see as our ware has been continually well priced, and hence supply and demand find its wonderful equilibrium" (1911, p. 125; J. Backhaus' translation). Mun even debunks the view that only gold is real wealth. Instead, he states that a person who owns a stock of goods can change it into gold if it pleases him. People who own goods need no gold. For Mun it is not an evident fact that gold is the vital power of trade because trade can also exist without gold. He gives the example of Italy where exchange of merchants is mediated by credit, bills of exchange, and promissory notes. In an earlier tract he stated already that "industry to increase, and frugality to maintain, are the true watchmen of a kingdom's treasury" (1968, p. 2).[10]

In Mun, four different ideas intermingle, the idea of a dynamic productive enhancement, the merchant idea of profit upon (foreign) alienation, the idea of an active trade balance, and the idea of mutually beneficial international trade (and division of labour). These ideas are not all compatible with each other, especially the active trade balance and the mutual international trade idea. This can be understood as the intermingling of more modern trade conditions with the resound of bullionism, combined with the search for a class compromise between the absolutist sovereign and the ascending merchant class. Mun's own self- or class interest as a member of the board of directors of the East-Indian Company since 1615 is especially evident in his defence of the company's activities (see Mun 1968, first published 1621). The British company was founded in 1600, the Dutch as the major rival in 1602.[11] The strategic aspect is also obvious in Chap. 5 where he argues that the land owners should have an interest in intensive foreign trade because an inflow of gold and greater demand for land by the merchants guarantees higher prices for their land (1911, pp. 129–131).

Chapter 6 of Mun's book discusses the special situation of Spain (1911, pp. 131–135). It came as a great surprise to the contemporaries that in the seventeenth century Spain with its massive metal imports impoverished and even had to use copper as money, whereas the Dutch as a small country with no important natural endowments and gold and silver production prospered, they had no gold and silver shortage, but a low interest rate and a strong fleet and military position. This paradox caused many writers of the time to think about the more or less hidden causes for power and prosperity. Chapter 6 highlights the historical background which explains

---

[9] It is not surprising that Heckscher saw a certain contradiction in the mercantilist's writings in this respect (1932, II, p. 291).

[10] Compare this with Blaug's statement that "(m)oney was falsely equated with capital … almost all mercantilist writers entertained the illusion that money is somehow *nervus rerum*" (1997, p. 11).

[11] For the broad historical background see Koehn (1994), a theoretical model is offered by Irwin (1991).

the time-bound combination of the different mercantilist basic ideas mentioned above. As mentioned, Spain had a shortage of gold in the country which depressed commerce in Spain, which was also often engaged in wars (a fact which Mun strongly criticizes, wars are detrimental to everybody in his view). Foreign countries like England only got metals and money by means of an export surplus (for the economic logic of this constellation see Dales 1991). In Chap. 8 Mun explains that gold is the general international measure of value and that manipulations of the gold content have only negative side effects. In Chap. 15 he defends interest for loans as beneficial for an exchange economy (1911, p. 174).

Chapter 16 deals with the delicate question of the sovereign's share of the economic product which should not oppress or discriminate against the subjects (1911, p. 177). Mun tries to harmonize, and he states that high taxes are no great burden for the citizens because the price for labour will rise accordingly. The income of the sovereign is usually also spent in favour of the community. But a wise prince will let the citizens become rich and satisfied so that they will love the prince, and support the kingdom in times of danger. Therefore, he should only impose moderate taxes (1911, p. 181) which are enough to build up a reserve for emergencies. The prince should also not be too wealthy because this makes him imprudent (1911, p. 183). The best form of government is elucidated absolutism with a parliament where the nobles and the people can utter their opinions but where the prince can take the final decisions in the interest of all (1911, p. 184). At the end he warns that wealth and power make a people lazy and depraved, poverty and modest living conditions keep them energetic (1911, p. 193). Finally, he restates that an active balance of trade is an honourable trade which assures a high income for the king, elegant activities for the merchant, an education for the crafts, a satisfaction of all needs, a progress for the land owners, a protective belt for the empire, a source for material wealth, and a great help in times of war (1911, p. 210).

The Theoretical Deep Structure of the Mercantile Approach

To understand the theoretical deep structure of the mercantile literature, we have to make an abstraction from the special topics under discussion and move to the basics of how the economy can be analysed. Following Rutherford (1996), economic analysis and theorizing faces "some *general* problems inherent in any attempt to deal with institutions" (1996, p. IX). The problems can be formulated as trade-offs between five complementary but dichotomous research strategies and perspectives: formalism vs. anti-formalism, individualism vs. holism, rationality vs. rule following, evolution vs. design, and efficiency vs. reform. A more formal-mathematical proceeding for example has analytical rigor, but there is a trade-off between rigor and relevance (see the discussion in Wehner 1995). The dichotomies mean in detail: "i. The role of formal theoretical modelling as opposed to less formal methods, including historical and 'literary' approaches. ii. The emphasis to be placed on individual behaviour leading to social institutions as opposed to the effect of social institutions in moulding individual behaviour. iii. The validity of rationalist explanations as opposed to those that place limits on the applicability of rationalist conceptions. iv. The extent to which institutions are the result of spontaneous or invisible-hand processes as opposed to deliberate design. v. The basis on which normative judgements can be made, and the appropriate role of government intervention in the economy" (Rutherford 1996, p. 174).

We can ask now in how far the mercantilist literature deviates from the present mainstream of (neoclassical) economics. (Let us note that the decision to argue or analyse from the left or right side of the five dichotomous horns is not equivalent to the theoretical/non-theoretical distinction.) On the one hand, neoclassical economics and for example new institutionalism emphasize more formalist techniques, that individuals create institutions, rational action, spontaneous processes, individualistic normative criteria, and a limited role for the government. By contrast and as a first approximation, mercantilists and for example old institutionalists on the other hand stress non-formal techniques, institutions which mould individuals, habits and social norms, collective choice, and social normative criteria and a larger role for the government. But this distinction is in a certain sense not really a correct approximation. A closer analysis shows a more complex picture. This has to do with the fact that in real economic life phenomena which are typical for one or the other dichotomous horn are apparent; their relative importance may also change in history (compare, e.g. the spontaneous introduction of the German cigarette currency after World War II and the following establishment of the D-Mark by deliberate design as two examples for one of the aforementioned dichotomies). There can also be no doubt that individual behaviour shapes social institutions – and the other way round. A complex and sufficient analysis of "reality" needs both perspectives as complementary. Both research programs have implicit reversed shortcomings, for example the right-side strategy has to assume some supra-individual actors ("the nation", "the state"), while the left-side-strategy stresses a more or less "reductionist version of individualism" (Rutherford 1996, p. 178).

To these dichotomies we could also add the distinctions of general and historical approaches, purely economic or more political economics, a more static or dynamic analysis, more or less classical theories of value or theories of the productive forces (List), and the view of the economy as a mechanic exchange machinery or as an organic unity (see, e.g. the methodological remarks in Salin 1944).

If we have a look at the mercantile literature in total we can observe a leaning to the right side of the dichotomies as already mentioned. But the more interesting fact is that many contributions are in a certain middle position, taking up one horn and the other in the same pamphlet or book. For example, the mercantile literature does not only use historical and empirical material. As we also saw, Mun did not develop formal formulae but (implicitly) he used the quantity theory of money (with a dynamic twist, see Dreissig 1939, and Tautscher 1942) and Hume's specie-flow mechanism. Social institutions mould individual behaviour and the rules of the state are not disputable but on the other hand Mun's ideal and starting point is the autonomous, self-conscious and self-interested individual. Citizens should orient their behaviour in accordance with the rules of the country and they should be committed to them, on the other hand goal-oriented behaviour and rational maximization are the major rules for the merchant. On the one hand, the economy should work in the interest of society and especially the prince. He has also to set the value premises and intervene into the economy. On the other hand the mercantilists saw in the economy a relatively independent force which evolves naturally (this is particularly evident in Steuart, see below). Often, the only values seem to be a crude power Darwinism and economic materialism, and Mun reminds the prince not to interfere too strongly into the economic sphere with regulations and taxation. The human being rarely has any other value commitments except his self-interest. But the mercantilists also thought that profit upon alienation would only accrue if some regulatory restriction of free competition occurs (see below).

We can explain this intermediate position in two ways. First, mercantilism can be interpreted as the expression of an intermediate historical phenomenon, that is, societies in which the policy still has supremacy and an emergent capitalism with a differentiated autonomous economy or market sphere. Second, mercantilism can be interpreted as an impressive methodological example which more or less successfully integrates research programs or orientation which are usually only applied in separate approaches which are therefore necessarily one-sided. The importance of the mercantilist literature today lies naturally on this second aspect.

The Debate on Mercantilism

The term mercantilism was made popular by A. Smith who devoted more than one fourth of his *Wealth of Nations* (1976, first published in 1776) to the history of economic thought in book four on the systems of political economy. There, he shortly describes physiocracy and concentrates on a fundamental critique of mercantilism. For Smith, political economy has two objects: "first, to provide a plentiful revenue or subsistence for the people … and secondly, to supply the state … with a revenue sufficient for the public purposes" (1976, book 4, Chap. 1, p. 449). He underlines that "(c)onsumption is the sole end and purpose of all production; and the interest of the producer ought to be attended to, only so far as it may be necessary for promoting that of the consumer" (1976, 4, 8, p. 179). For Smith, the pretended harmony of interests of all social strata in mercantile policy is mere ideology. One of the most interesting aspects in Smith's discussion is the interlocking of ideas, policies, and special interests. He leaves no doubt that "(i)t cannot be very difficult to determine who have been the contrivers of this whole mercantile system; not the consumers, we may believe … but the producers, whose interest has been so carefully attended to; and among this latter class our merchants and manufacturers have been by far the principal architects" (1976, 4, 8, p. 180). In our short analysis of Mun, we came to a conclusion which was close to Smith's.

After the definition of political economy and the final function of the economy, Smith starts with his reflections on mercantile principles. First was the idea that wealth consists in money (1976, 4, 1, p. 450). We saw that this was in fact always one of Mun's main presumptions. Smith first explains it with the layman's view that what holds for a person (a man is rich who has a lot of money) also holds for nations. In his view it is more correct to say that the accumulation of consumption goods defines wealth. He cites Mun's book as the example which became fundamental to the practical policy of all commercial countries, including England (1976, 4, 1, p. 456). Smith sees Mun's main message in the thesis that home trade "was considered as subsidiary only to foreign trade", but that in fact it is "the most important of all, the trade in which an equal capital affords the greatest revenue, and creates the greatest employment to the people of the country" (1976, 4, 1, p. 456).

He does not doubt that a country that has no mines must import gold and silver by foreign trade, but the problem will be solved as easily as the problem of the import of wine because "no commodities regulate themselves more easily or more exactly according to this effectual demand than gold and silver.... When the quantity of gold and silver imported into any country exceeds the effectual demand, no vigilance of government can prevent their exportation.... If, on the contrary, in any particular country their quantity fell short of the effectual demand, so as to raise their price above that of the neighbouring countries, the government would have no occasion to take any pains to import them" (1976, 4, 1, p. 457). If an import would not be possible, barter exchange, credit and a pure paper standard are conceivable. Precious metals are not important as a store of wealth, they primarily have to function as a medium to facilitate exchange. They do not indicate wealth. "Money, no doubt, makes always a part of the national capital; but it has already been shown that it generally makes but a small part" (1976, 4, 1, p. 459) besides real capital in the form of machines, (durable) consumption goods, etc. For a successful war it is not important to have gold reserves but a high annual produce of the domestic industry to purchase consumable goods and war material from foreign countries (1976, 4, 1, p. 462). An increase in foreign precious metals did not make Europe richer because it decreased the money value of gold and silver (1976, 4, 1, p. 469). For all these reasons, "(b)y advantage or gain, I understand, not the increase of the quantity of gold and silver, but that of the exchangeable value of the annual produce of the land and labour of the country, or the increase of the annual revenue of its inhabitants" (1976, 4, 3, p. 515). Smith's statements are mostly convincing. They show real weaknesses of the mercantile doctrine as far as we know it yet. His critique is sometimes polemical like the whole *Wealth*, but it is never really unfair or unreasonable.

In the next chapter he deals with restraints upon the importation from foreign countries of goods which can also be produced at home. Without doubt the monopoly for the home-market often gives great encouragement to that particular species of industry. "But whether it tends either to increase the general industry of the society, or to give it the most advantageous direction, is not, perhaps, altogether so evident", because "(t)he general industry of the society never can exceed what the capital of the society can employ" (1976, 4, 2, p. 475). The decision what to produce "every individual, it is evident, can, in his local situation, judge much better than any statesman or lawgiver can do for him", and if a "foreign country can supply us with a commodity cheaper than we ourselves can make it, better buy it of them with some part of the produce of our own industry" (1976, 4, 2, pp. 478–479; in this context the metaphor of the invisible hand is mentioned). Why are these measures nevertheless supported? "Merchants and manufacturers are the people who derive the greatest advantage from this monopoly of the home-market" (1976, 4, 2, p. 480). But Smith is not dogmatic, he argues that the navigation act is necessary for political reasons, retaliation may be necessary, a humane transition from former monopolized industries to free trade seems warranted, etc.

In Chap. 3 he discusses the restraints of the importation of goods from those countries with which the balance is supposed to be disadvantageous. Smith gives numerous examples of these restraints in the practical economic policy of his time. In his view their application only leads to hate among nations and a generalized beggar-my-neighbour attitude. Instead, the best customers of the nation's products are the rich countries (1976, 4, 3, p. 518). As we saw this was already an argument which was raised – not without contradiction – in Mun. The "spirit of monopoly" is supposed to be only in the natural interest of some merchants and traders. In the following chapters, he shows that drawbacks and bounties make no sense economically. It follows a long chapter on colonies[12] in which he castigates the mercantilist exploitation of the colonies by England, for example "she imposes an absolute prohibition upon the erection of steel furnaces and slit-mills in any of her American plantations" (1976, 4, 7, p. 95). For Smith, to "prohibit a great people, however, from making all that they can of every part of their own produce … is a manifest violation of the most sacred rights of mankind" (1976, 4, 7, p. 95). The colonies should be autonomous.

In the Marxist tradition, Smith's class analysis – that the merchants and manufacturers in general are the profiteers – has been refined. In a chapter on capital accumulation and mercantilism, Dobb[13] interprets the mercantile system as state-regulated exploitation by trade in the age of primitive accumulation. He states "while it is doubtless true that bodies like the Merchant Adventurers and the Elizabethan trading companies in their pioneering days brought an expanding market for English manufactures, it was their restrictive aspect – the stress on privilege and the exclusion of interlopers – that came into prominence towards the end of the sixteenth … century. Their limitation on the number of those engaging in the trade and their emphasis on favourable terms of trade at the expense of its volume increasingly acted as fetters on the further progress on industrial investment and brought them into opposition with those whose fortunes were linked with the expansion of industry…. For example, as cloth manufacture developed, the clothiers, while advocating a prohibition on wool export, had an interest in the development of cloth export" (Dobb 1947, pp. 193 and 211). We saw this conflict already existing in Mun. It can be argued that Smith did not mention this conflict because he was on the side of the middle bourgeoisie against the upper bourgeoisie which was concerned with the export market. But there were also common interests of the entire capitalist

---

[12] See the balanced view by Harper (1942).

[13] (1947, pp. 177–220), see also Fusfeld (1975, pp. 24–31).

stratum like low wages, an expanding supply of raw materials, differential protection for the (nascent) home industries (import tariffs), low import tariffs for foreign raw materials, etc.

The stronger the home country's own industry became the more liberal were the mercantilists. This started with Mun who substituted the particular-balance view by the general-balance view of the bullion-export, and continued with the strong free trade tendencies of late seventeenth century mercantile writers like North, Davenant, and Child. They reflected the critique that the regime of monopolies not only shifted profits to a privileged circle but that it profoundly limited expansion and growth in general. They clearly demonstrate paradox of the process of mercantile rationalization: that the support of merchants and entrepreneurs and the changes in the economic, social and cultural sphere to stabilize the absolutist system by increased taxes finally undermined the existing absolutist order[14] and lead logically to liberalism (see the interesting analysis of Helmer 1986). Some authors strongly underline that liberalism is more an extension of the former and that mercantilists had rather profound theoretical insights. "The idea of demand and supply as schedules is in Berkeley's *Queries*; cross-elasticity is in Child; utility in Barbon; the usefulness of capital markets in Malynes and Misselden; the idea that consumption is or should be the object of all effort is in Defoe, Tucker, and Postlethwayt..." (Grampp 1995, p. 6; see also Grampp 1991).

Dobb sees in the contradiction between the surplus idea of the trade balance and the idea of a mutual growth perspective a more general antagonism which was already obvious in Mun. "In order to expand, in order to find room for ever new accumulations of capital, industry requires a continuous expansion of the market (and in the last analysis of consumption). Yet in order to preserve or to enhance the profitability of capital that is already invested, resort is has from time to time to measures of monopolistic restriction, the effect of which is to put the market in fetters and to cramp the possibilities of fresh expansion" (Dobb 1947, p. 219).

Dobb also highlights a special feature of mercantilism and an implicit assumption of neoclassical economics. In times of mercantilism, the productivity of labour was low, the number of labourers employed by a single capitalist not very numerous, so that a profit could hardly emerge from production. For the mercantilists and in distinction to present day supply- and demand-schedules, surplus was conceived as depending on conscious regulation to produce it, that is, "their belief in economic regulation as the essential condition for the emergence of any profit from trade – for the maintenance of a profit-margin between the price in the market of purchase and the price in the market of sale.... Without regulation to limit numbers and protect the price-margin between what the merchant bought and what he sold, merchant capital might enjoy spasmodic windfalls but could have no enduring source of income" (Dobb 1947, pp. 199–200). Supply and demand conditions are institutional products, profit is the result of political pressure to influence them (Dobb 1947, p. 210).

---

[14] Regimentation of economic activities, elements of planning in economic policy, superiority of the political sphere, etc.

Dobb points out that a large part of the confusion in mercantilism, for example between the terms of trade and the balance of trade, is due to the ideological character of the literature to cloud reality and suppose an identity between special and general interests (of the state). In later writings, "(t)o the bullion-fetish they continued to pay at least lip service" (Dobb 1947, p. 214).

A completely different and definitely positive view of mercantilism has been given by the members of the historical school, notably Schmoller and Sombart. In contrast to Smith who deals with mercantilism as an economic doctrine they see it as a general pattern of economic policy so that they arrive at completely opposite results. Schmoller concentrates on the "connection between economic life and the essential, controlling organs of social and political life, – the dependence of the main economic institutions of any period upon the nature of the political body" (1967, p. 2, first published in German in 1884). Phases of economic development should be distinguished according to their controlling organs: the tribe, the village or mark, the district, the state, or even a federation of states. Schmoller had an ever enlarging political units or organs in mind.

For Schmoller the essence of the mercantile system does not lie in some doctrine on money, or on the balance of trade, but consists in the fight against the nobility, the towns, the corporations and provinces, and the struggle for uniform measures and coinage, a system of uniform credit laws and administration. All these were preconditions for the new division of labour and prosperity. "Questions of political power were at issue.... What was at stake was the creation of real political economies as unified organisms, the centre of which should be, not merely a state policy reaching out in all directions, but rather the living heartbeat of a united sentiment. Only he who thus conceives of mercantilism will understand it; in its innermost kernel it is nothing but state making ... state making and national-economy making at the same time" (1967, p. 50). Gömmel (1998) has shown that in former Germany (and not only in Prussia which was Schmoller's main example) the economic policy in the seventeenth century was obviously transformed into an integrated mercantile strategy, including for example an active population, trade and tariff policies.[15] M. Weber had shown that already in the larger early modern merchant and craft towns we can observe a mercantile town policy (Weber 1976, pp. 792ff.).

In his monumental book on modern capitalism, Sombart (1987, pp. 924–942) deals with the rationale of a mercantile national economic system in Chap. 56 of the second volume. Sombart remarks that his own theory of early capitalism was written in a mercantile spirit, so that his account of mercantilism has a very positive orientation. All thought in this tradition starts with the concentration on the common interest, especially the interest of the state and his power and independence (1987, pp. 924–925). Power means the living energy and number of its inhabitants and not some external characteristics like the extension of territory. The economy is not understood as the free play of anonymous forces but as a functional

---

[15] See also the studies by Skopp (1990), Rothermund (1978), Hosfeld-Guber (1985), and Henning (1991, pp. 758–783).

interplay of an economic organ to which regulation of the state is as important as individual self-determination (1987, p. 928).

In the centre of the mercantile economic doctrine, to which Sombart Mun, Davenant, List, Child, Petty, Locke, Becker, Justi, Forbonnais and others belong, stands the notion of productivity, that is, the total capabilities of the economy are seen as a living organism (1987, p. 930). The origins of the riches are first the production of goods in the country itself, depending on the increase of the population, the work of lazy people, children and women, the increase of the work day, etc. For Sombart, the practical relevance and structure of capitalism have been better understood by the mercantilists then by the physiocrats or the Smithians (1987, p. 937). They understood the promotion of a capitalist spirit and the increase of the entrepreneurs, the necessary amount of economic objects like the increase of the working class, the need of a sufficient and increasing capital reserve in the form of money as necessary conditions of capitalism. They always took into consideration the distribution of the goods produced, and they had an understanding of the legal and administrative preconditions of the capitalist development (1987, pp. 938–939). They never confounded money with wealth but they purported a dynamic theory of causality: the increase of money increases demand, production, and consumption and for most countries the only means to increase the amount of precious metals was to have a positive balance of payments (1987, p. 941). Like Schmoller he draws a very positive picture of mercantilism which neglects the self-contradictory and weak points we discovered for example in Mun's work.

In exact opposition to Schmoller and Sombart, Ekelund and Tollison (1981 and their marginal revisions in 1997) give an alternative interpretation of the special interest hypothesis. They ask why France and Spain did not experience an industrial revolution comparable to that in England. In a neoinstitutional vein, they interpret mercantilism as a rent-seeking phenomenon in the property rights and Buchanan's and Tullock's public choice tradition.[16] After the rise of centralized monarchies, the opportunity arose for the monarchs to raise revenue by selling monopoly rights. The difference between the economic potentials of the three countries compared results from the fall of power of the monarchy in England, and the move to a representative government. For the authors mercantilism was not a macro instrument for nation building as it was for Schmoller. These objectives were only rationalizations of rent-seekers. It "is a process through which rent seeking alters property rights systems in socially inefficient manners reducing exchange, efficiency and economic welfare" (1997, p. 385, in italics). In their model a supply side (the state) and a demand side (merchants, etc.) lead to an equilibrium for monopoly rights with detrimental results for society at large. "To the extent that resources are spent to capture monopoly rents in such ways as lobbying, bribery, and related activities, these resources are basically wasted (create no value) from a social point of view" (1981, p. 19).

The difference to Smith is first that their analysis is based on individual-choice behaviour and not on classes. In their model – which shares the normative bias for

---

[16] See also the respective but not at all convincing interpretation of communism by Anderson and Boettke (1997).

the consumer with Smith – the state is not the victim of the rent-seekers (as in Smith), but "the state may be pictured as a unified, revenue-seeking leviathan, where fiscal needs (defence, court expenses, and so forth) prompted the sale of protective legislation" (1981, p. 24). The authors present an interesting application of the rent-seeking approach to the phenomenon of mercantilism. They surely grasp an aspect of real historical development. That the state gave monopoly rights and received a rent is obvious, also that merchants tried to get the monopoly rights for extra profit and that resources were wasted for lobbying.

On the other hand their empirical-historical basis is very weak. The interesting aspects of the mercantilist literature is not that they were also motivated by interests and ideology but that they contained an analytical surplus which is of real interest for scientific discourse. Further, the authors do not say that "the state" (a collectivist term?) uses the revenue for luxury or consumption but that it uses the revenue for its fiscal needs, for example for the law system, defence, etc. If we understand rent-seeking this way, it is hard to see a difference to the mercantilist literature which states that the state needs revenue for exactly these tasks. If the authors reject or neglect the state-building motives and expenditure exigencies mentioned by Schmoller, they are one-sided because all major European states undertook developmental strategies to produce a market economy and tried to establish an adequate legal and institutional environment. But if they accept this as a major motive to finance state activities, then the distinctiveness of their hypothesis evaporates. They also do not deal with the different logic of a short- or long-run perspective, that is, Mun's Laffer curve type of argument that moderate taxes in the present (and we may add: limited allocation of monopoly rights) support growth and consequently higher tax revenues in the future. They only conceive non-elucidated short-run rent-seeking politicians.

Still the most extensive study of mercantilism is E. Heckscher's book on mercantilism.[17] Not convinced of the secondary literature (see his discussion in II, pp. 239–242), he defines mercantilism as a phase in the history of economic policy between the Middle Ages and modern liberalism which has the state as subject and object in the centre of concern, especially the external power of the state and its conditions (I, pp. 1–6). For Heckscher, himself a convinced liberal, the active balance of trade and the concern for money are secondary aspects of mercantilist thought. Mercantilism also comprises theoretical elements and is akin to popular economic thinking. For Heckscher (like Schmoller) the most important element is the unifying aspiration of the strong state which in fact only became an established fact much later in the nineteenth century. With this emphasis he fundamentally deviates from Smith who saw the interests of the merchant class as the driving force behind mercantilist policies. On 450 pages he describes the historical background, in particular the overcoming of the particularism of the Middle Ages what tariffs, the regulation of industry and the crafts, and foreign exchange in England and France are concerned.

The second element of mercantilism is of Heckscher's the concept of a system of power (Cunningham). On only 40 pages he describes two ways to pursue the interests

---

[17] (1932), first published in Sweden in 1931, see also Heckscher's reply to his critiques in Heckscher (1991).

of the state in an international competitive environment: special measures like the English navigation act or the concern for the general flowering of the economy. In the latter case, the state profits by higher taxes. The third constitutive element which is explained on 100 pages is mercantilism as a system of protection (e.g. export subsidies). Fourth comes the specific mercantile view of money which is analysed on further 80 pages. In the third and fourth building block of mercantilism, Heckscher identifies many theoretical mistakes. We may ask if he does not go too far in his conclusions, for example when he states that the fixation on power relations leads to a total neglect of the absolute amount of traded goods and the utility for the citizens but that they were only concerned with the relative superiority over foreign countries (II, p. 291). As we saw in Mun, this interpretation is at least exaggerated.

From today's perspective, the most interesting and lasting part of Heckscher's book may be the 50 pages of part five on mercantilism as a view of society (II, pp. 245ff.). Heckscher convincingly argues that – compared with the worldview of the Middle Ages and nineteenth century's conservative-romantic orientations – liberalism and mercantilism are very close as a general social doctrine. The economic doctrine of mercantilism was old-fashioned, but both thought in terms of natural rights and both supported the freedom in the confines of the national border. They rejected enterprises run by the state. They had an economic-materialist moral minimum view, interest for loans was not seen as problematic, and luxury consumption is evaluated from a purely economic functional and not ethical standpoint. Humans are weak, self-interested and more or less greedy, production is an end in itself, society is seen in a rationalist way and both share the opinion of social causality, that is, that the natural drift of economic development cannot be changed drastically by law and political design.

In Heckscher's view liberalism had a more humane orientation and anthropology of man[18] and rejected enforced labour; Smith thought that humans find fulfilment in work, etc. A second difference is the liberalist conviction that the free play of market forces has an innate rationality, the mercantilist does not believe so and opts for regulation and intervention (II, p. 295). But we saw that even Mun opted for moderate taxes and limited interventions of the prince into the economy even in times of absolutism. Heckscher points out that mercantilism had two sides, a liberal one and the more stronger interventionist opposite; both were in constant conflict with each other and he views liberalism as the executor of mercantilism in the social realm which overcame the mercantilist antiquated view of the economy.

In his ambiguous description of mercantilism Schumpeter (1965, pp. 423–472) comes to the opposite conclusion. If Smith and his disciples had improved the mercantile doctrine instead of rejecting it, we would have had a more rich and realistic theory of international economic relations today (1965, p. 472).

In his *General Theory*, Keynes devoted a part of Chap. 23 to positive notes on mercantilism (1976, pp. 333–353, see also Steele 1998, and Hahn 1957). For him, mercantilism was a precursor of his theory to some degree. He criticizes the negative

---

[18] For example regarding greediness, see Moss (1987) on the mercantilist Mandeville.

opinion of the classical free trade school, also obvious in Smith's *Wealth of Nations*, which saw in mercantilism little more than nonsense. He wants to show that there is an element of scientific truth in it. He asks in how far it is advantageous from a national perspective to be preoccupied with the domestic rate of interest and the balance of foreign trade (1976, p. 335). He shares with Smith the interpretive focus of the main elements of mercantilism. "At a time when the authorities had no direct control over the domestic rate of interest or the other inducements to home investment, measures to increase the favourable balance of trade were the only *direct* means at their disposal for increasing foreign investment; and at the same time, the effect of a favourable balance of trade on the influx of the precious metals was their only *indirect* means of reducing the domestic rate of interest and so increasing the inducement to home investment" (1976, p. 336).

Keynes is aware of the fact that an immoderate practical policy can lead to a senseless international competition for a favourable balance of trade and that the advantages of the international division of labour should not be forgotten. His claim is to show that the theoretical foundations of the laissez-faire doctrine, that a domestic interest rate consistent with full employment is unproblematic, are wrong and have been questioned by the mercantilists who "never supposed that there was a self-adjusting tendency by which the rate of interest would be established at the appropriate level" (1976, p. 341; we will leave out his remarks on the terms of trade and the fear for goods). Without solving the problems they raised theoretically, they testified intellectual realism and grasped the fact that the propensity to save is usually stronger than the inducement to invest (1976, pp. 347–348). Keynes positive view is a possible interpretation of some mercantilist remarks, for example on interest rates. But it may be doubted that for example Mun's main concern was structural under-investment in the Keynesian sense.[19]

In a recent work, Magnusson (1994) argues like Grampp that "Smith's greatest achievement was to melt all this together … it is ironic that he to such a great extent relied upon the previous work of seventeenth-century thinkers which we commonly recognize as 'mercantilists'" (1994, p. 2). He also shares a modernist interpretation and speaks of a real mercantilist revolution. It was characterized by an explicit discussion of how wealth was created and distributed; a Baconian scientific program with an empirical basis and logical argumentation (see, e.g. Petty 1992, and Wallace 1992), a materialist interpretation of man and society, and the view that "the economy must be perceived as a system" (1994, p. 11).

At least for Mun we saw that this fourfold classification is a little bit overdrawn. But if we take G. Berkeley's *The Querist* (1992, first published in 1735) we see the essential development of mercantilist thought and we may ask if Smith was fair to choose Mun as the main representative. The importance of Berkeley lies in the sphere of an economic and social vision, less in the delineation of some specific economic theorem(s). His main supposition is that labour is the true

---

[19] On the further development of the discussion on mercantilism as a doctrine in the history of economic thought see Coats (1996), Rashid (1991), and Magnusson (1994, Chap. 2).

source of wealth (Query 4). The aim of all states should be to encourage industry in its members (Qu. 3). The active balance of trade and the accumulation of specie are no subject for him. Money is only useful in so far as it "stirreth up Industry, enabling Men mutually to participate the Fruits of each others Labour" (Qu. 5). The division of labour with mutual benefits, the growth of industry is the problem he raises. He holds Marshall's later theory of the dialectics between wants and activities (Qu. 20), and the determination of price according to supply and demand (Qu. 24). He does not hold a subsistence (wage) approach of the working people. A people who had provided themselves with the necessaries of life would "soon extend their Industry to new Arts and new Branches of Commerce" (Qu. 68). A first objective should be the abolition of the dirt, famine, and nakedness of the bulk of the people (Qu. 23).

He never argues for special interests or the granting of monopolies, and states that the aim should be the well-being of the whole (Qu. 137). He absolutely rejects the bullion-fetishism in asking "whether the true Idea of Money, as such, be not altogether that of a Ticket or Counter" (Qu. 23, see also Qu.s 34, 35, 37 and 49). The only virtue of gold and silver is to set people at work (Qu. 32). If money is needed for transactions, money substitutes (like bills of exchange) will easily be found and used (Qu. 34). A massive inflow of gold and silver may even be detrimental to industrial development, for example for psychological reasons (Qu. 45). Trade, foreign or domestic, is in truth only the expression of the home commerce and industry (Qu. 38).

The policies of the state – for which he gives many examples (public work for criminals, bettering houses for young gentlemen, see Qu.s 57–59) – are summarized in the following question: "Whether if human Labour be the true source of Wealth, it doth not follow that Idleness should of all things be discourag'd in a wise State"? (Qu. 44). The state has an active role to play. Like a man who builds a house in the first place provides a plan, the public should not act without an end, a view, a plan (Qu. 53). Berkeley is in the materialist tradition of human anthropology: man is driven by interest, imitation, and passions. But he asks, if this insight "would be a good Argument against the use of Reason in public Affairs"? (Qu. 312). In principle, Smith and Berkeley raise the same critical arguments against Mun as the supposed typical representative of mercantilism. But Berkeley's tract was published some 30 years before the *Wealth of Nations*. His contribution shows that mercantilist thought liberated itself from the special interest perspective (no monopolies for the merchants and manufacturers, or high taxes for the sovereign are claimed), the prejudices of bullionism, and some self-contradictions which were partially evident in Mun (compare this with Blaug's negative statement on Berkeley in 1997, p. 22).

On the other hand the change in thinking in the economic field should also not be exaggerated. If we take J. Cary's *A discourse on trade* (1992, a reprint of the 1745 edition), the pamphlet of a Bristol merchant, as an example we see that he also proposes work houses for the poor and beggars. Further, he proposes a national soundly organized public credit system to reduce risk (he uses transaction cost arguments) which in turn would lower interest rates. But we also find the old bullionist and active balance of trade scheme in his thought. He meticulously describes international trade empirically and we also find free trade arguments (1992, p. 3). But he nevertheless proposes to establish a committee of trade to control and actively change by decree the flow of precious metals and goods, because mainly the East-Indian trade "exports our Bullion, spends little of our Product or Manufactures, and brings in Commodities perfectly manufactured, which hinder the Consumption of our own" (1992, p. 43).

Second Example: J. Steuart's An Inquiry into the Principles of Political Economy (1767)

To fully grasp the mercantilist revolution just mentioned with the Magnusson characteristics of an explicit discussion of how wealth was created and distributed, a Baconian scientific program, a materialist general interpretation, and the economy as a system view, let us analyse briefly the main aspects of Steuart's (1992) work. It is one of the last and the most systematic accounts of mercantilist thinking, written 130 years after Mun's treatise, developed on more than 1,500 pages. The book is the last defence of mercantilism, the foundations of English free-trade economics had already been laid for example by Hume in his *Political discourses* in 1752. Steuart (1712–1780) belonged to an influential Scottish noble family; he was trained as a lawyer and lived between 1745 and 1763 in exile because he supported the Stuarts. His work never received great recognition and Smith almost completely dismissed him. But Schumpeter holds him in high esteem (see 1965, p. 235).

The book has the subtitle "an essay on the science of domestic policy in free nations"; it underlines Steuart's pragmatic self-understanding. In the preface he states that the basis of his deliberations is not a logical system. "I was engaged to compile the observations I had carefully made, in the course of my travels, reading and experience" (I, pp. IV–V). Steuart follows an inductive comparative system's approach, and he strongly criticizes armchair theorizing. "The wit I here mention, is not that acquired in the closet" (I, p. 159). Citing Bacon (I, p. IV), he favours a systematized inductive method which rejects in principle generalizations in theory and practical policy and not only as a transitory phase (compare Schmoller). It is an interesting question to ask if and in how far his methodology depends on his mercantilist vision. Repeatedly, he thinks about "the habit of running into what the French call *Systemes*. These are no more than a chain of contingent consequence, drawn from a few fundamental maxims, adopted, perhaps, rashly. Such systems are mere conceits; they mislead the understanding, and efface the path of truth. An induction is formed, from whence a conclusion, called a principle, is drawn; but this is no sooner done, than the author extends its influence far beyond the limits of the ideas present to his understanding, when he made his deduction" (I, p. VII). Not surprisingly, empirical and historical facts and developments are broadly presented. "I pretend to form no system" (I, p. 5).

The first of the three books deals with population and agriculture and contains his elementary mercantilist vision. Economy is the art of providing for all the wants with prudence and frugality. He first describes the division of labour between the sovereign and the economic agents and their motives. He recapitulates "the governor must restrain, but the steward must lead, and, by direct motives of self-interest, gently conduct free and independent men to concur in certain schemes ultimately calculated for their own proper benefit. The object is, to provide food, other necessaries and employment, not only for those who actually exist, but also for those who are to be brought into existence. This is accomplished, by engaging every one of the society to contribute to the services of others, in proportion only as he is to reap a benefit from reciprocal services" (I, p. 149). Steuart – like Smith whose *Wealth* was published 9 years later – has a dynamic perspective, the increase of production and population is his concern. The market is a differentiated sphere in which self-interested individuals act (his anthropology also includes expediency, duty, and passion, see I, p. 6). He assumes that they conform to the laws and are not opportunists seeking with Williamson's guile (I, p. 165).

Unlike Smith, Steuart strongly stresses that the statesman has to establish a legal, motivational, and institutional framework so that the interplay of the economic agents works "as if" an invisible hand were in operation. His leading decisions are not restrictions of free enterprise, but a continuous precondition. In the first book we hardly find a word in Steuart about an active balance of trade, bullion-fetishism, profits by monopoly guarantees, etc.

Instead, he consequently follows a labour theory of value and societal development. "The earth's spontaneous fruits being of a determined quantity, never can feed above a determined number. Labour is a method of augmenting the productions of nature, and in proportion to the augmentation, numbers may increase" (I, p. 150). In book one, he clearly distinguishes the hunter and gatherer mode of subsistence and the system of agriculture and puts them in an evolutionary perspective.

No general blueprint can be formulated for the wise statesman (the sole individual who is not motivated by personal self-interest, see I, p. 162f.?). In the long Chap. 2, he explains that different people and nations have different spirits, i.e. "a set of received opinions relative to three objectives: morals, government, and manners" (I, p. 8). Because people do not only vary with regard to their mentalities, the consequence is clear. "If one considers the variety in the distribution of property, subordination of classes, genius of people, proceeding from the variety of forms of government, laws and manners, one may conclude that the political oeconomy in each must necessarily be different, and that principles, however universally true, may become quite ineffectual in practice" (I, p. 3). The statesman who is the impartial representative of the common interest above the classes should not support the specific spirit of a nation or culture, but has to "model the minds of his subjects so as to induce them, from the allurement of private interest, to concur in the execution of his plan" (I, p. 3). The plan may be hidden to the citizens if they are not advanced enough to understand it. He also considers the active planning of the birth rate in different social strata (I, Chap. 12). Slavery is justified as an early inducement to bring people to work (I, Chap. 7). But the patriarchal sovereign is not independent, because in a natural contract perspective he states that "a general tacit contract, from which reciprocal and proportional services result universally," exists (I, Chap. 83).

An elucidated statesman cannot act against the natural drift towards freedom and progress, but he can encourage and socially cushion and balance the consequences of change, for example when a rapid introduction of new machinery takes place. Steuart takes the Pareto principle as a concern for practical policy very serious, especially what unemployment is concerned. "The introduction of machines can, I think, in no other way prove hurtful by making people idle, than by the suddenness of it … I constantly suppose a statesman at the head of government, systematically conducting every part of it, so as to prevent the vicissitudes of … innovations from hurting any interest within the commonwealth" (I, p. 120; he also considers an ideal situation of economic reproduction and want satisfaction where no new machines are needed any more).

Steuart sees a close but not necessary connection between the increase of the population, economic prosperity, the orientations to work hard and innovate, and the need for sophisticated consumption. "We have supposed a country capable of improvement, a laborious people, a taste of refinement and luxury in the rich, an ambition to become so, and an application to labour and ingenuity in the lower classes" (I, p. 34).

These are the main ideas and concepts of book one. We have omitted all empirical and practical considerations which make up half of the text. The subjects of book two are trade and industry, the latter defined in a dynamic-innovative way as "the application to ingenious labour" (I, p. 166, in italics). A major stress is put on the demand side. The need to pay for goods is one thing and the ability to pay another thing so that a sufficient level and equilibrium between supply and demand may not but the possibility of unemployment may exist. Steuart develops an interesting three-stage growth approach which starts with the expenditure of the wealthy as the origin of demand in the first phase. "The increase in production stimulates the introduction of machinery in industry and productive improvements in agriculture, thus prompting an increase in labour productivity.… The second growth stage is reached when the country is able to produce a surplus for export. At this point luxury should give way to thrift. Growth would be sustained by the trade surplus. The third phase occurs when the country is no longer able to maintain a permanent surplus of its balance of trade. At this point, growth should return to being sustained by internal demand, and luxury could again play its role as a stimulus" (Screpanti and Zamagni 1995, p. 54). The short summary shows that Steuart is far away from the simplistic active balance of trade doctrine.

One of the most interesting and ignored parts in the secondary literature is his "value theory" or his theory of supply and demand. Human needs lead to demand and have short- or long-run effects, "the nature of a *gradual* increase of demand, is to encourage industry, by augmenting the supply; that of a *sudden* increase, is to make prices rise" (II, p. 59). Demand may be simple or compound (the latter means that competition exists between demanders), it may be great or small (depending on the quantity demanded), and it may be high or low ("high when the competition among the *buyers* is great; low, when the competition among the *sellers* is great", I, p. 174). He also discusses elastic (luxury goods) and inelastic demand (necessaries). In Chap. 3 he explains exchange in the traditional neoclassical way. "When wants are multiplied, bartering becomes (for obvious reasons) more difficult; upon this money is introduced" (I, p. 177).

In Chap. 4 we find his value theory. The price of goods is composed of the "real value of the commodity, and the profit upon alienation" (I, p. 181). The real value is the adding-up of first the average working hours to produce a good, second the workman's subsistence and necessary expenses, and third the value of the input materials. The price can never be lower as the real value, but thanks to profit it may be higher. "This will ever be in proportion to demand, and therefore will fluctuate according to circumstances" (I, p. 183). Despite a lack of final rigor, we do not see an essential difference to Smith's adding-up approach or even to Marshall's scissors. He describes the price setting with the following auction metaphor: "(T)o make a kind of auction, by first bringing down the prices to the level of the highest bidders, and so to descend by degrees, in proportion as demand sinks" (I, p. 195).

Industry and trade flower if the balance is perfect (translated in the German edition as equilibrium, see Steuart 1913, p. 271), i.e. the real value plus a normal profit ("a positive moderate profit", I, p. 220, in italics) determine prices. This is the case in "double competition", which prevents the excessive rise of prices and prevents their excessive fall. It means that competition "takes place on both sides of the contract" (I, p. 196). This form of competition takes place in most operations of trade. But, Steuart adds, we can also imagine the realistic case that no competition takes place on the demand or the supply side but collusive behaviour prevails (this is also possible in the formal market structure of full competition understood as many sellers and buyers). Profit depends on the relative degree of competition on both sides.

To assure the (perfect) balance of double competition is the great task of the statesman. The balance can be overturned in four ways, supply (Steuart's "work") increases or diminishes and demand remains constant, or demand in/decreases and supply remains constant. "If demand diminishes, and work remains the same … either those who furnish the work will enter into competition, in which case they will hurt each other, and prices will fall below the reasonable standard of the even balance; or they will not enter into competition, and then, prices continuing as formerly, the whole demand will be supplied, and the remainder of the work will lie upon hand" (I, p. 218). But does not the market mechanism work and restore equilibrium? "Whether, by this fall of prices, demand will not be increased? That is to say, Will not the whole of the goods be sold off? I answer That this may, or may not, be the effect of the fall, according to circumstances: it is a contingent consequence of the simple, but not the effect of the double competition: the distress of the workmen is a certain and unavoidable consequence of the first" (I, p. 220).

The necessity for intervention results if the imbalance continues and as a result, "by such profits subsisting for a long time, they insensibly become *consolidated*, or, as it were, transformed into the intrinsic value of the goods" (I, p. 221) because the average living conditions of the classes were a constituent part of the real value. In normal circumstances, profit fluctuates according to the demand conditions and cannot become a real value element, but this "happy state cannot be supported but by the care of the statesman" (I, p. 223).

In the following he discusses the economic competition of national economies in trade. He is moderately mercantilist when he sees it as a symptom of decline when a country is furnished from abroad with manufactures which were formerly made at home (I, p. 279). In Chap. 16 he gives as the natural reason for trade the Heckscher–Ohlin theorem and adds that all natural resources should be manufactured in the country. In Chap. 18 he discusses means to support export. But he concentrates on thriftiness, the reduction of luxury consumption, the introduction of more productive machinery, etc. and much less on price manipulations like subsidies which are often misused (I, p. 391).

We have to stop here (see the summary of book two in II, pp. 57–95). Book five deals with taxes in a profound and politically neutral way (III, 266ff., see the summary on pp. 421ff.). Book three and four, almost half of the total book, deal with money and credit. Here Steuart rejects the quantity theory of money and states that the central variable is the velocity of circulation (hoarding). Changes in relation to the needs of trade and the money supply are always adequate and can be controlled by economic agents through the velocity of money. Prices depend on real factors (level of output, costs, and competition). Compared with Mun, Steuart's considerations are a path-breaking progress. He is the only one in his century who tried to develop a monetary theory on an antimetallistic basis which sees money as a pragmatic symbol by decree, absolutely independent of gold or silver. In Schumpeter's view he is one of the most interesting monetary theorists[20] of his time but he made so many mistakes that his work did not become influential (1963, p. 376).

Conclusion

In our overview we understood mercantilism as an epoch of economic history, as an economic doctrine, and as a general pattern of economic policy. We described the historical circumstances and problems which led to a mercantilist thought in Germany, France, and England. We mentioned the most important representatives and the intellectual followers (physiocracy and liberalism). Mercantilism is understood as an autonomous paradigm in the history of economic thought and we rejected the sometimes unjust criticisms of mercantilism in the (recent) secondary literature.

We dealt with the main economic assumptions, ideas, and economic policy proposals as they are delineated in the more sophisticated textbook descriptions in part two and took also into consideration the ideological and interest bias of some mercantilist writers. Referring to the five Rutherford distinctions, we saw the interesting deep structure of mercantilism which is located between the horns of his dichotomies.

---

[20] See also his *Principles of money applied to the present state of the coin of Bengal* (1772).

We saw that a considerable progress in thinking about the economy was achieved from the early debate between Misselden and Malynes, the following contradictions in Mun, the productivist queries of Berkeley, and finally the most advanced in version of Steuart. He developed at least a rudimentary theory of value, time, and space depending on political policy proposals, a supply and demand scheme, and empirical research strategy (which resembles the inductivist inclinations of some representatives of the later German historical school), and an active interventionist role of the wise statesman (the enforcement of double competition).

In part five we saw the surprising variety of possible interpretations of mercantilism. A. Smith's ardent criticism grasps some weak points of early mercantilism but he did not attack the strongest version, Steuart's *Inquiry*. The Marxist analysis of Dobb refines the class and interest-based approach of Smith which is also not incompatible with Ekelund's and Tollison's rent-seeking interpretation which was deciphered as a little bit too one-sided.

The more positive accounts were evident in Schmoller, Sombart, to a certain degree Heckscher, and Keynes. They state the nation-building function of mercantilism or identify (Keynes) some good reasons to pursue an elucidated version of an active balance of trade (e.g. a money inflow and as a consequence a lower interest rate). We agreed with Magnusson that in its strongest version the mercantilist revolution consisted in the explicit discussion of how wealth was created and distributed, a Baconian scientific research program, a materialist interpretation of man and society, and the view of the economy as a system. Seen in this light the transition from mercantilism to liberalism (from Steuart to Smith) is perceived as more gradual and less fundamental or qualitative.

If we include in our strong basic definition of mercantilism a forward-looking interventionism of the (wise?) state(sman), mercantilist thought may serve as a counterweight against the present denigration of the influence of the state and the view that the more the markets are deregulated and the state disappears the better society fares in total. The neo-mercantilist message (see the comparison by Feldmann 1995) could be that for example the provisioning of public goods (especially education and infrastructure) is of overall importance for the citizens of developed countries to secure a high income level and an adequate lifestyle in times of global competition.

References

Anderson GM, Boettke PJ (1997) Soviet venality: a rent-seeking model of the communist state. Public Choice 93:37–53

Anderson JE, Neary JP (1999) The mercantilist index of trade policy. NBER Working Paper, no. 6870, Cambridge Mass

Berkeley G (1735, 1992) The Querist. Routledge, London

Blaich F (1973) Die Epoche des Merkantilismus. Wiesbaden

Blaich F (1988) Merkantilismus, Kameralismus, Physiokratie, In: Issing O (ed) Geschichte der Nationalökonomie. 2nd ed. Munich: Vahlen, pp 35–48

Blaug M (ed) (1991a) The early mercantilists. Edward Elgar, Aldershot

Blaug M (ed) (1991b) The later mercantilists. Edward Elgar, Aldershot

Blaug M (1997) Economic theory in retrospect, 5th edn. Cambridge University Press, Cambridge

Blitz RC (1967, 1991) Mercantilist policies and the pattern of world trade, 1500–1750. In: Blaug M (ed) The early mercantilists. Edward Elgar, Aldershot, pp. 147–163

Bürgin A (1961) Merkantilismus. In: Beckerath E et al (eds) Handwörterbuch der Sozialwissenschaften, vol 7. Tübingen, pp 308–317

Cannan E (1929) A review of economic theory. P.S. King & Sons, London

Cary J (1992) A discourse on trade. Routledge, London

Chipman J (1993) A theory of mercantilism. In: Rima IH (ed) The political economy of global restructuring, vol 2. Edward Elgar, Aldershot, pp 41–76

Coats AWB (1992, 1996) Mercantilism: economic ideas, history, policy. In: Irwin DA (ed) Trade in the pre-modern era, 1400–1700. Edward Elgar, Cheltenham, pp 351–369

Coleman DC (ed) (1969) Revisions in mercantilism. Methuen (publisher), London

Conquest R (1985, 1996) The state and commercial expansion: England in the years 1642–1688. In: Irwin DA (ed) Trade in the pre-modern era, 1400–1700. Edward Elgar, Cheltenham, pp 332–349

Dales JH (1955, 1991) The discoveries and mercantilism: an essay in history and theory. In: Blaug M (ed) The early mercantilists. Edward Elgar, Aldershot, pp 86–98

DeRoover R (1955) Scholastic economics: survival and lasting influence from the sixteenth century to Adam Smith. Q J Econ 69:165–187

Dobb M (1947) Studies in the development of capitalism. Routledge, London

Dreissig W (1939) Die Geld- und Kreditlehre des deutschen Merkantilismus. Berlin

Eckert G (1949) Der Merkantilismus. Braunschweig

Ekelund RB, Tollison RD (1981) Mercantilism as a rent-seeking society. Texas

Ekelund RB, Tollison RD (1997) On neoinstitutional theory and preclassical economies: mercantilism revisited. Eur J Hist Econ Thought 4:375–399

Feldmann H (1994) Der merkantilistische Charakter der EG-Industriepolitik. In: Vitzhum WG (ed) Europäische und internationale Wirtschaftsordnung aus der Sicht der Bundesrepublik Deutschland. Baden-Baden, pp 137–152

Feldmann H (1995) Wie merkantilistisch ist die Theorie strategischer Handelspolitik. Jahrbücher für Nationalökonomie und Statistik 212(13):522–536

Fusfeld DR (1975) Geschichte und Aktualität ökonomischer Theorien. Frankfurt

Gömmel R (1998) Die Entwicklung der Wirtschaft im Zeitalter des Merkantilismus 1620–1800. Munich

Grampp WD (1952, 1991) The liberal elements in English mercantilism. In: Blaug M (ed) The later mercantilists. Edward Elgar, Aldershot, pp 116–152

Grampp WD (1995) An appreciation of mercantilism. In: Rima IH (ed) Classical tradition in economic thought, vol 11. Edward Elgar, Aldershot, pp 1–16

Hahn LA (1957) Merkantilismus und Keynesianismus. In: Beckerath E et al (ed) Wirtschaftsfragen der freien Welt. Knapp, Frankfurt, pp 140–150

Harper LA (1942) Mercantilism and the American revolution. Can Hist Rev 23:1–15

Heckscher E (1932) Der Merkantilismus. Jena

Heckscher E (1936, 1991) Revisions in economic history: mercantilism. In: Blaug M (ed) The later mercantilists. Edward Elgar, Aldershot, Knapp, pp 37–47

Helmer H-J (1986) Merkantilismus und Kapitalismus im modernen Rationalisierungsprozeß. Frankfurt

Henning F-W (1991) Handbuch der Wirtschafts- und Sozialgeschichte Deutschlands, vol 1. Paderborn

Hinton RWK (1955, 1991) The mercantile system in the time of Thomas Mun. In: Blaug M (ed) The early mercantilists. Edward Elgar, Aldershot, pp 72–85

Hosfeld-Guber J (1985) Der Merkantilismusbegriff und die Rolle des absolutistischen Staates im vorindustriellen Preußen. München

Irwin DA (1991) Mercantilism as strategic trade policy: the Anglo-Dutch rivalry for the East-India trade. J Polit Econ 99:1296–1314

Johnson EA (1937) Predecessors of Adam Smith. King, New York

Keynes JM (1936, 1976) The general theory of employment, interest and money. MacMillan, London

Koehn NF (1994) The power of commerce. Cornell University Press, Ithaca

Lange T (1995) Colberts Urenkel: Über das Fortwirken merkantilistischer und imperialistischer Topoi in der entwicklungspolitischen Debatte. In: Andersen U et al (eds) Politik und Wirtschaft am Ende des 20. Jahrhunderts, Opladen, pp 203–216

Libby RT (1992) Protecting markets: U.S. policy and the world grain trade. Cornell University Press, Ithaca

Magnusson L (1994) Mercantilism: the shaping of an economic language. Routledge, London

Minchinton WE (ed) (1969) Mercantilism: system or expediency? Lexington (Mass.): Heath, Lexington

Moss LS (1987) The subjectivist mercantilism of Bernard Mandeville. Int J Soc Econ 14:167–185

Mun T (1621, 1968) A discourse of trade from England unto the East Indies. In: East Indian trade, no editor. Farborough, pp B1–B58

Mun T (1664, 1911) Englands Schatz durch den Aussenhandel (Englands treasure by forraign trade). Vienna

Niehans J (1945) Der Gedanke der Autarkie im Merkantilismus von einst und im Neomerkantilismus von gestern. Zürich

Nussbaumer J (1991) Zum Bevölkerungsproblem in der ökonomischen Dogmengeschichte. In: Fickl S (ed) Bevölkerungsentwicklung und öffentliche Haushalte. Frankfurt, pp 31–50

Petty W (1992) Several essays in political arithmetick. Routledge, London

Pfaller A (ed) (1986) Der Kampf um den Wohlstand von morgen: Internationaler Strukturwandel und neuer Merkantilismus. Bonn

Phillips PWB (1992) Whether free trade or fair trade, corporate mercantilism rules the day. Challenge 35:57–59

Raab A (1932) Staatspolitik und Sozialökonomie bis zum Beginn des Merkantilismus. Vienna

Rashid S (1980, 1991) Economists, economic historians and mercantilism. In: Blaug M (ed) The later mercantilists. Edward Elgar, Aldershot, pp 343–356

Rima IH (1993) Neomercantilism: what does it tell us about the political economy of international trade? In: Rima IH (ed) The political economy of global restructuring, vol 2. Edward Elgar, Aldershot, pp 27–40

Robinson J (1966) The new mercantilism. Cambridge University Press, Cambridge

Rothermund D (1978) Europa und Asien im Zeitalter des Merkantilismus. Darmstadt

Rutherford M (1996) Institutions in economics. Cambridge University Press, Cambridge

Saitzew M (1941) Der Merkantilismus. In: Schweizerische Gesellschaft für Statistik und Volkswirtschaft (ed) Schweizerische Wirtschaftsfragen, Festgabe für F. Mangold. Basel, pp 234–256

Salin E (1944) Geschichte der Volkswirtschaftslehre, 3rd ed. Bern

Schaefer KC (1993) Die merkantilistische Wirtschaftspolitik. In: Tilly RH (ed) Geschichte der Wirtschaftspolitik. Munich, pp 8–33

Schefold B (1997) Grundzüge und Hauptautoren merkantilistischer Theorie. Zeitschrift für Agrargeschichte und Agrarsoziologie 45:163–180

Schmidt K-H (1994) Merkantilismus, Kameralismus, Physiokratie. In: Issing O (ed) Geschichte der Nationalökonomie, 3rd ed. Munich, pp 37–62

Schmoller G (1884, 1967) The mercantile system and its historical significance. New York

Schulz F (1987) Zur Dogmengeschichte der funktionalen Finanzwirtschaftslehre. Berlin

Schumpeter JA (1965) Geschichte der ökonomischen Analyse, vol 1. Göttingen

Schweizer P (1996) The growth of economic espionage. Foreign Aff 75:9–14

Screpanti E, Zamagni S (1995) An outline of the history of economic thought. Clarendon Press, Oxford

Skopp HR (1990) Theorie und Praxis der Staatsverschuldung im Merkantilismus erläutert am Beispiel Kurbayerns. Marburg

Smith A (1776, 1976) The wealth of nations. In: Cannan E (ed) Methuen, Chicago

Sombart W (1916, 1987) Der moderne Kapitalismus, vol 2. Das europäische Wirtschaftsleben im Zeitalter des Frühkapitalismus. Munich

Sonnenfels J (1994) Aufklärung als Sozialpolitik: Ausgewählte Schriften aus den Jahren 1764–1798. Vienna

Steele GR (1998) Mercantilism, classical economics and Keynes' *General Theory*. Am J Econ Sociol 57:485–498

Steuart J (1767 (reprint of the 1770 edition), 1992) An inquiry into the principles of political oeconomy. Routledge, London

Steuart J (1767, 1913) Untersuchung über die Grundsätze der Volkswirtschaftslehre, translation by A. John, 3 vols. Fischer, Jena

Strange S (1985) Protectionism and world politics. Int Organ 39:233–259

Tautscher A (1942) Die dynamische Kredittheorie der deutschen Merkantilisten, Weltwirtschaftliches Archiv, 56/II, 143–167

Viner J (1948, 1996) Power versus plenty as objectives of foreign policy in the seventeenth and eighteenth centuries. In: Irwin DA (ed) Trade in the pre-modern era, 1400–1700. Edward Elgar, Cheltenham, pp 303–331

Wallace R (1992) A dissertation on the number of mankind. Routledge, London

Weber M (1976) Wirtschaft und Gesellschaft, 5th ed. Tübingen

Wehner B (1995) Die Logik der Politik und das Elend der Ökonomie. Darmstadt

Wolf M (1995) Cooperation or conflict? The European Union in a liberal global economy. Int Aff 71:325–337

Chapter 4
The Cameralists: Fertile Sources for a New Science of Public Finance

Richard E. Wagner

Introduction

The cameralist writers emerged after 1500, primarily in the German-speaking lands, and stayed on the scene until the middle of the nineteenth century. While I devote some effort to characterizing some of the works and themes of the cameralists, I devote most of this chapter to an examination of the contemporary relevance of a cameralist orientation for scholarship in public finance. To place such stress upon contemporary relevance is not to ignore the vast differences between their times and ours, but is only to affirm that there are some enduring themes within the cameralist orientation that could prove interesting and fruitful for contemporary scholarship in public finance.

The cameralists emerged around 1500, and were mostly located in the German-speaking lands. By the time they had disappeared in the middle of the nineteenth century, they had amassed a collective bibliography of more than 14,000 items, according to Magdalene Humpert (1937). To someone raised on contemporary economic theory, the cameralists would surely seem highly irrelevant. Among other things, they were oriented toward practice and not toward the refinement of theoretical schemata. Principles were present, to be sure, and these were brought to bear on various matters of substantive practice. The driving interest of the cameralists, however, lay in their ability to operate more effectively in a substantive manner, and not on the development of theoretical argument.

Schumpeter (1954, pp. 143–208) described the cameralists well when he referred to them as "Consultant Administrators." They were both consultants and administrators. They were consultants to the various kings, princes, and other royal personages who ruled throughout those lands. Indeed, the term cameralist derives from

R.E. Wagner (✉)
Department of Economics, George Mason University, Fairfax, VA 22030, USA
e-mail: rwagner@gmu.edu

J.G. Backhaus (ed.), *Handbook of the History of Economic Thought,*
The European Heritage in Economics and the Social Sciences,
DOI 10.1007/978-1-4419-8336-7_4, © Springer Science+Business Media, LLC 2012

camera or kammer, and refers to the room or chamber where the councellors to the king or prince gathered to do their work. The cameralists were not, however, anything like contemporary academic consultants. They were real-world administrators as well. They were engaged in such activities as managing mines or glass works. Many of the cameralists also held academic posts. The first chairs of cameral science were established in 1727, in Halle and Frankfurt on the Oder, and by the end of the eighteenth century 23 such chairs had been established (Backhaus 1993).

The cameralists were partly economists, partly political scientists, partly public administrators, and partly lawyers. They approached their subject matter in a manner that used all of these talents and capacities. My first recollection of cameralism dates to the spring of 1970. The occasion was the arrival of the March 1970 issue of the *Journal of Economic Literature*. There, Richard Goode had an article where he compared the treatment of public finance in two different social science encyclopedias, written a generation apart. One of these was the *International Encyclopedia of the Social Sciences*, which was published in 1968. The other was the *Encyclopedia of the Social Sciences*, which was published in 1930. While Goode duly noted the theoretical advances that had occurred in economics between 1930 and 1968, he also lamented the narrowing of the subject matter of public finance.[1] Goode concluded his lamentation on the state of public finance by asserting that "a sophisticated and unified treatment of the economic, political, legal, and administrative elements of public finance is needed. Unification would represent a return to a tradition as old as that of the cameralists, but for modern readers sophistication can be attained only by rethinking old problems and using new techniques. There is much to be done and work for a variety of talents" (p. 34).

My subsequent reading convinced me that Goode was correct, and that a postcameralist orientation offers an expanded and more interesting agenda for public finance.[2] In claiming that a return to the cameralist tradition would offer much of value to contemporary public finance, a distinction should perhaps be made between direct and indirect sources of value. By a direct source, I mean instances where cameralist formulations can be brought directly to bear on contemporary issues in public finance. I think there is very little of this in the cameralist formulations. By an indirect source, I mean the orientation, attitude, or point of view toward the subject matter of public finance that the cameralists held. The cameralist orientation can, I think, be very fruitfully carried forward into contemporary public finance, and is capable of generating what could very well be called a postcameralist public finance. I think the cameralist orientation has much to contribute to contemporary public finance, particularly in its ability to point the way toward a more integrated treatment of fiscal phenomena that are now often accorded separate treatment within

---

[1] Goode's lament was voiced brilliantly some years later in a different context by Leijonhufvud (1996), who said that "recent developments in macroeconomics remind him of the movies coming out of Hollywood: there isn't much to the plots anymore, but the special effects are spectacular."

[2] A valuable textbook by Blankart (1991, Ch. 2) presents cameralism as the source for the approach to public finance associated with such authors as Sax, Wicksell, Lindahl, and various turn-of-the-century Italian scholars.

faculties of economics, politics, administration, and law.[3] Before I examine some elements of a postcameralist public finance, I shall provide a short description of some of the cameralist writings and teachings.

The Setting for Cameralism

Cameralism has often been described as a Germanic version of mercantalism, though I have also seen it described as a Germanic version of physiocracy. These descriptions perhaps illustrate a form of heuristic for guessing, through assimilating something unfamiliar to something familiar. Mercantilism and physiocracy are clearly discussed much more fully in histories of economics than is cameralism. It is perhaps understandable that someone unfamiliar with cameralism who came across cameralistic observations about the importance of agriculture would treat cameralism as a form of physiocracy. It is similarly understandable that a similar person coming across a cameralistic discourse on the importance of stimulating internal manufacturing, so as to reduce the import of finished goods, would treat cameralism as a form of mercantalism.

It is, of course, common and often reasonable to classify something new with reference to what is already familiar. This leads to cameralism often being treated as a form of mercantilism and sometimes as a form of physiocracy. While cameralism does have points of contract with physiocracy and mercantilism, some of which have just been noted, it is nonetheless neither of these, but rather is something else entirely.[4] To be sure, cameralism and mercantilism both originated within authoritarian political regimes, and they represented efforts to give good counsel to the heads of those regimes, in light of an unchallenged presumption that those regimes are to continue indefinitely. From here, however, the differences dominate the similarities.

Most importantly, the cameralists and mercantilists differed in the international setting within which their regimes were located. Mercantilism arose among big players on the international stage. The English, the French, the Spanish, and the Dutch, the primary nations with which mercantilism is associated, were not price takers on the international scene. The ability of these powers to reach throughout the world to influence events and terms of trade provided the background for mercantilist thought and practice. The stress upon taxation and the prevalence of rent-seeking and other forms of venality were products of the big-player standing of the mercantile empires.

There were no such powers within the cameralist lands. Austria, probably the premier power early in the cameralist period, could not play with the mercantile powers. The Peace of Westphalia in 1648 recognized more than 300 independent units of governance within the cameralist lands, and there were even more before then.

---

[3] Related territory is addressed in Backhaus and Wagner (1987).

[4] For valuable, general surveys of cameralism, see Dittrich (1974) and Small (1909). Shorter and more focused, but also highly valuable is Tribe (1984, 1995, Ch. 2).

Cameralism arose under conditions of high political fragmentation. The cameralist lands were necessarily insignificant price takers on the international scene. A cameralist land faced a totally different setting than the mercantile regimes faced. There was no concern within the cameralist lands about influencing terms of trade, about the use of colonies as instruments of policy, and about one's relative standing among the preponderant powers. All of these concerns were foreclosed by circumstance to those who ruled within the cameralist lands. The focal point of cameralist concern was on survival of the regime. Survival, in turn, required a military capacity. It also required economic development, which in turn required the acquisition of improved technologies, the improvement of human capital within the population, the creation of new enterprises, and the growth of population.

This concern about development took place within regimes that were both absolutist and severely constrained. The prince was the ruler of his lands. He did not have to worry about surviving periodic elections, and he could hope to pass his principality along to his eldest son. His ability to do this, however, varied directly with the extent of economic progress within his land. A prince whose land was supporting a growing population of energetic and enterprising subjects would both be wealthier and face better survival prospects than a prince of a land where the population was stagnant or declining, and whose subjects were dull and lethargic. Furthermore, population was mobile in fact, even if it was mostly tied to the land at law through feudal restrictions. Distances between lands were typically short. A peasant who traveled to a new land was not likely to be returned. The rulers of the cameralist lands faced a competitive labor market. Indeed, the cameralist lands represented a kind of competitive industry among localized governments, much as Tiebout (1956) tried to characterize some 300 years later.

The Cameralist Analytical Framework

It may be stretching matters a bit to refer to a cameralist "analytical framework." A reference to "orientation" or "perspective" might be more circumspect. The cameralists proceeded much more by the statement and elaboration of practical maxims than through the construction and logical manipulation of analytical models. For instance, the cameralists generally favored growing populations, but did not articulate any model that characterized the impact of population growth upon cameralist objectives. It is most likely that the cameralist writers simply embraced an empirical belief that a growing population would be beneficial in their states, particularly in terms of the conditions that obtained at that time throughout the cameralist lands. The devastation wrought by plague and war would have provided the cameralists with a strong orientation or predisposition toward population growth, even in the absence of any systematic framework that linked population to some cameralist objective. It is also possible, however, to read some inchoate notion of increasing returns into the cameralist support for growing population. There are numerous claims that a growing population provides a particular stimulus to production that otherwise would be lacking. It would be easy enough to read such references as precursory versions of increasing returns that result from the increasingly fine division of labor that population growth makes possible.

The absence of a highly systematic approach makes it difficult sometimes to determine whether differences among particular cameralists are truly substantive or rather represent simply different ways of asserting the same thing. Take, for instance, the goals of cameralist policy. Population growth is supported as a means for advancing a desired end. But what is the end that cameralist policy seeks to promote? Compare, in this respect, two of the premier late cameralists, Johan Heinrich Gottlob von Justi and Joseph Sonnenfels. Justi (1782) asserted that the primary goal of cameral policy should be the happiness of the state and its subjects. In this, one could well imagine applause coming from Jeremy Bentham. Justi did not, however, engage in any effort at weighting utilities across rulers and subjects. Rather, he asserted that in a well-conducted state, one governed by cameralist principles, the happiness of all would rise and fall together.

Sonnenfels (1787) argued that it was not happiness that was the proper objective of cameralist policy, but an expanding population. A happy population would be an incidental and automatic by-product of a growing population. As a matter of empirical conduct at the time, the programs of Justi and Sonnenfels were indistinguishable. In this case, the distinction that Sonnenfels drew with respect to Justi may have represented an effort at product differentiation. Despite a possible empirical-historical congruence, the two programs might diverge in general. Neither author, however, provided a systematic framework of hypothesized relationships that would make possible any definitive statement.

To be sure, I think that simple regime-perpetuation, and not some notion of happiness for state and subject, is the best way of characterizing the prime objective of cameralist policy. The cameralists went through a lot of mental gymnastics to explain that all such pleasant-sounding platitudes as the promotion of happiness for state and subjects were invariably being promoted by the existing regime. The cameralists were not a highly critical bunch, and in this attitude they probably displayed a good deal of practical realism. They accepted the legitimacy of their regimes, and pursued their professional work within a means-end framework. The end to be attained, or sought after, by the state was the ruler's business. The cameralists were there to offer expert advice on the acquisition of revenues and their subsequent expenditure. In the next section I shall focus on the revenue side of the cameralist analytical framework. I shall give only cursory attention to the expenditure side, for otherwise I would not have enough space left to address some of the possible elements of a postcameralist public finance.

Cameralist Revenues

When one regime gives way to another, residues from the previous regime typically remain in place. By the 1880s, the cameralist period was but a historical memory, and it is probably reasonable to date its end with the Napoleonic wars. Yet one of the notable features of the cameralist regimes could still be detected in the fiscal

Table 4.1 Income from state farms as percentage of total state income

State	State farm income/total state income (%)
Noncameralist states	
France	1.5
Netherlands	1.9
Denmark	2.9
England	3.0
Italy	3.0
Russia	3.6
Greece	3.6
Austria-Hungary	3.9
Switzerland	4.1
Cameralist states	
Baden	7.1
Saxony	9.7
Württemberg	13.2
Prussia	16.4
Bavaria	17.3

Source: Backhaus and Wagner (1987)

Table 4.2 State enterprise revenue as percentage of total state revenue

State	Enterprise revenue/total state revenue (%)
Saxony	59.5
Prussia	56.8
Württemberg	47.7
Bavaria	30.7

Source: Backhaus and Wagner (1987)

data. This is the particularly heavy use made of revenues from state lands and enterprises as a means of financing state activities. Table 4.1 summarizes data presented at various places in Backhaus and Wagner (1987). This Table pertains to various dates in the late nineteenth century, and shows state income from agricultural enterprises as a percentage of total state income. Revenues from agricultural enterprises comprised generally between 2 and 4% of total state revenues in the noncameralist lands. By contrast, net revenues from farm enterprises were some 5–10 times more significant in the former cameralist states.

The cameralist emphasis on enterprise revenues did not stop with agriculture. Enterprise revenues of all forms played a substantial role in state finance in the former cameralist lands. Table 4.2, also from Backhaus and Wagner (1987), shows the importance of all state enterprises as a source of state revenue for 1896–1898, two generations or so after the end of the cameralist period. In the four large states shown there, enterprise revenues ranged between 30 and 60% of total state revenues.

This heavy use of net revenues from state enterprises to finance state activities was the central feature of the revenue side of cameralist public finance. By contrast, enterprise revenues occupied a minor position in state finance in the non-cameralist lands. To be sure, even this minor position was strikingly at variance with the position as objects of subsidy that state enterprises came to occupy in the twentieth century. I recall my astonishment as a graduate student when I came across Adam Smith's statement in the *Wealth of Nations* that "the post office ... affords in almost all countries a very considerable revenue to the sovereign" (p. 682). The American post office at the time was doing no such thing, but was receiving large subsidies from the treasury, as were most state enterprises. In earlier times, though, state enterprises often served as modest sources of revenue, when I was a student save in the former cameralist lands where state enterprises were significant sources of revenue.

Cameralist public finance treated state lands and enterprises as principal sources of revenue, and most certainly not as objects of subsidy. If one were to construct a model of the cameralist vision of the state, it would look like a model of a business firm. The state's lands were potential sources of revenue. Forests could be harvested, game could be caught, and mines could be built and worked. The ruler would also sponsor an assortment of commercial enterprises, including such things as the operation of a glassworks or a brewery. Taxes occupied a secondary position as a source of revenue. Taxes were a last resort option for public finance, and not the first source of revenue.

The cameralists' general predisposition against taxation as an instrument of public finance reflects the orientation that the state acts as a participant within the economic order. Individuals had their property and the state had its property. The state should be able to use its property to generate the revenues required to finance its activities. Or at least those enterprise revenues should support the major portion of state activity. Some of the cameralists argued that taxes should be earmarked for the support of the military, while all activities concerned with internal development should be financed from the prince's net commercial revenues. In any case, the state contains many business enterprises within its boundaries, and with the state itself being one of those enterprises. The state's enterprises are to be the primary source of revenue for the state. It was understood that the state would have significant expenses associated with its activities. These expenses, however, were not to become drains upon the private means of subjects. They were to be met from the lands and enterprises that constituted the state's property.

It was perhaps out of a recognition of the realities of power that there was no absolute prohibition on taxation. Rather there were various statements that taxes should be limited and low, for otherwise they would bring harm to the state and its subjects. It is instructive to compare the approach to taxation taken by Johann Heinrich Gottlob von Justi and Adam Smith, particularly with respect to the limits placed on the use of the power to tax. Smith, of course, is one of the premier figures of classical liberalism, and it is hardly surprising that his maxims of taxation are widely thought to serve as strong limits on the power to tax. Smith's four maxims of taxation have been stated repeatedly in public finance texts since he first articulated them in 1776. These are as follows:

1. Taxes should be levied in proportion to property.
2. Taxes should be certain and not arbitrary.
3. A tax should be convenient to pay.
4. A tax should be economical to administer, for both the taxpayer and the state.

Justi (1771, pp. 549–565) similarly articulates maxims for taxation, though these maxims, unlike Smith's, have not been carried forward in the public finance literature. What is surely most notable about Justi's maxims is that they go well beyond Smith in limiting the power to tax. While the precise arrangement of Justi's maxims differs from Smith's, Justi's maxims cover all of the territory covered by Smith's maxims, and then goes well beyond Smith in limiting the power to tax. Like Smith, Justi holds that a tax should be levied in proportion to property, that it should be certain and not arbitrary, that it should be convenient to pay, and that it should be economical to administer.

Justi, however, does not stop there. He offers two maxims that have no counterpart in Smith. One of these is that a tax should never deprive a taxpayer of necessaries or cause him to reduce his capital to pay the tax. A second maxim of Justi's that is not found in Smith is a requirement that a tax should neither harm the welfare of taxpayers nor violate their civil liberties.

To the extent the principles articulated by Justi and Smith were put into substantive practice, Justi would place far stronger limits on the use of taxation than would Smith. The comparison of Justi and Smith, however, does not stop here. Smith regarded taxation as the primary source of public financing, and thought ideally that it should be the sole source of public finance. For instance, Smith preceded his presentation of tax maxims with an argument that the state should eliminate its property and the revenues derived there from. In sharp contrast, Justi preceded his discussion of tax maxims with a discussion of why taxation should be a last resort or secondary means of public finance. Indeed, Justi argued that ideally the state would not tax at all.

This difference between Justi and Smith reflects one of the important orienting principles of the cameralists, namely, that the state acts as a participant within the society and its economic order. The cameralist advice on the use of state budgets and other policy instruments to promote the happiness of the state and its subjects took place within a presumption that the state itself was located inside the economic order and not outside it. The state is but another participant within the economic order of a society. Civil society and the state are nonseparable and co-emergent. This treatment of the state in relation to civil society contrasts sharply with various contemporary constructions where state and society are treated as autonomous and independent from each other. In this alternative construction, the state intervenes into civil society and its processes. This distinction between the state as participating within the economic order and the state as intervening into the economic order has numerous implications and ramifications, one of which concerns the generation of state revenues. The cameralist ideal, recognizing that practice rarely if ever conforms to ideals, was the state as a peaceful and productive participant within the economic order. The Smithian ideal was the state as a violent force for intervention into the economic order. It is perhaps no wonder that Schumpeter (1954, p. 172) described Justi as "A. Smith … with the nonsense left out."

In their 1980 book on the *Power to Tax*, Geoffrey Brennan and James Buchanan construed the state as a revenue-maximizing beast, a leviathan (Brennan and Buchanan 1980). While the leviathan of the Bible lived in the sea, it is easy enough to imagine it as living on the land. Smith's maxims for taxation are a recipe for living with the leviathan by doing such things as clipping the beast's nails and filing its teeth. A beast it will always be, and the objective of tax maxims should be to limit the damage caused by the beast. Justi's maxims for taxation, in conjunction with his preference for enterprise revenues over taxation, represent a contrary intellectual orientation that would seek to domesticate the beast.

Revenues, of course, are only one side of the fiscal account. The cameralists also devoted much effort to the expenditure side. Much of that discussion had a kind of capital-theoretic quality to it, where programs of expenditure today would generate increased revenues tomorrow. A great deal of the cameralist emphasis was placed on what is now called human capital, though it would not be appropriate to import too much of a conceptual framework into the cameralist works. A good deal of this emphasis stemmed from the concern with population. A growing population was desirable, to be sure, but that population in turn had to possess useful skills and talents, to be healthy, and to possess an industrious attitude. While the cameralists devoted a good deal of attention to such kinds of topics, they did not employ anything remotely resembling contemporary models or techniques. Still, a great deal of the cameralist discussion concerned the contribution of various expenditure programs to the well-being of the state and its subjects.

A Cameralist Orientation Toward Contemporary Public Finance

My primary thesis is that cameralism contains an orientation toward public finance as a field of academic scholarship that offers a wider and more varied analytical agenda than can be found within the bulk of public finance today, just as Richard Goode asserted in 1970. I should like to complete my remarks on the cameralists by exploring some aspects of what could be called a postcameralist public finance.

Cameralistic public finance is a choice-theoretic approach to public finance. The phenomena of public finance, state revenues and expenditures, arise out of a ruler's optimizing choices. It is quite different in modern democratic regimes. The phenomena of public finance do not arise from someone's optimizing choice, but rather arise through interaction among the many participants within the fiscal process. This interactive or catallactic approach to public finance leads often to quite different implications for public finance than the choice-theoretic approach (Wagner 1997). The dominant portion of contemporary public finance has maintained the choice-theoretic orientation toward public finance, as if fiscal phenomena are still generated through the same processes that were in place in mercantalistic and cameralistic times. This astonishing situation was noted in 1896 by Wicksell (1958, p. 82), when he complained that the theory of public finance "seems to have retained the assumptions of its infancy, in the seventeenth and eighteenth centuries, when absolute power ruled almost all Europe."

A choice-theoretic approach to public finance was suitable in cameralist and mercantilist times. A cameralist ruler could reasonably be described as seeking to use his fiscal means to promote his dynastic ends. For the cameralists it was historically accurate to ascribe the phenomena of public finance to the choices of the rulers. The state's revenues depended on the ruler's choices about how to operate his mines and how to farm his lands. The extent to which state expenditures were directed to projects that might increase future productivity was likewise objects of choice for the ruler. Suppose two kingdoms were observed to undertake different expenditure programs. In the first kingdom expenditures were heavily oriented toward such investments as draining swamps and building roads that would be likely to increase future production. The budget in the second kingdom, however, did little about swamps and roads, and instead spent lavishly on amusements for the king and his court. It would be reasonable in this case to compare the budgetary choice of the two kingdoms, and to say that the first king had a lower time preference, or was otherwise more far-sighted than the second king. To the extent it is possible to make inferences about preferences from the observation of choices with respect to private choices, it would be possible to do the same thing with respect to state choices within the cameralist setting. To be sure, the conduct of cameralist rulers was relatively civilized, and nothing like the experience with dictators in the twentieth century. The conceptual construction of a benevolent despot perhaps finds historical validation in the cameralist period. That does not, however, render empirically valid the use of constructions based on benevolent despots in public finance today.

Whether budgets in a democratic regime were tilted toward amusements or capital projects would not be a source of information about some person's preferences. Budgets emerge out of interactions among participants, and those interactions are governed and shaped by a variety of procedural rules.[5] The people who participate in a market make various choices, but it makes no sense to speak of the market itself as making choices. The market simply registers and reflects the choices and interactions among the participants. It is the same with budgetary outcomes within a democracy. Furthermore, the same set of people can generate quite different budgetary outcomes, depending on the institutional framework within which the budgetary process proceeds. In this respect, there is an indefinite number of particular budgetary processes that can be imagined, and it is conceivable that a wide variety of budgetary outcomes could be generated, if the experiment were performed of having the same people engage in successive interactions across differing institutional frameworks.

This consideration suggests immediately that a postcameralist public finance would place particular importance and significance on the institutional framework

---

[5] For a nice effort to pursue such an approach, see Kraan (1996).

within which budgets emerge. This institutional focus, moreover, would exist on two distinct conceptual levels. One level takes as given some particular institutional framework, or compares different institutional frameworks. In any case, the analysis at this level would take institutional frameworks as given data, and rest content with exploring how those frameworks guide and govern the interaction among participants into the generation of budgetary outcomes. The other level would recognize that people also generate and modify institutional frameworks as they go along, and would seek to give an account of the generation and dissipation of institutional frameworks.

The cameralists were clearly agents for their royal principals. Principals who were unhappy with their cameralist agents would dismiss them, and could well imprison them for malfeasance. Justi, for instance, died while imprisoned for alleged financial mismanagement. While modern democracies are quite different from the cameralist absolutisms, such categories as principal, agent, and property are present now just as they were then. The cameralists spoke of subjects. We now speak of citizens. It is the citizens who are the principals in a democracy. The head of state was the principal in cameralist times, but is now the agent. The same relationship of agency exists in modern democracies as existed in cameralist times, only the substantive character of that relationship is different in many respects.

All agency relationships raise questions of how strongly the agent will promote the desires of the principals.[6] This question has been examined in quite good measure in respect to business corporations. The basic thrust of that literature is that the existence of a market for ownership shares is the pivotal institutional feature in both (1) homogenizing the interests of shareholders (principals) and (2) inducing principles to promote the interests of principals. Governments face the same formal problems of agency that business corporations face. Indeed, there are many modern examples of business corporations that provide government-like services, and in a way that resemble the cameralist states.

Shopping centers, apartment complexes, and hotels all provide state-like services in a cameralist-like setting.[7] What these organizations do is offer forms of tie-in sales, where private and public services are offered as a package. Apartments and hotels offer rooms to residents. The rental price, however, also finances the provision of an array of public services. Hotels will have subways that run vertically. Hotels usually sweep their streets daily. Hotels and apartment complexes typically provide a variety of parks and playgrounds. Walt Disney World in Florida offers the

---

[6] They also raise questions of whether principals share some common standard for appraising agent performance. Without agreement among principles, it is dubious to speak of agency costs and related notions. It must suffice to say here that the degree of agreement among principles can be influenced by institutional arrangements. Market arrangements based on private property generally facilitate agreement among principals. Some democratic arrangements may operate in a similar manner, where others appear not to do so.

[7] This point is made in striking fashion by MacCallum (1970). For an extension of this outlook to cities, see Foldvary (1994).

same kind of arrangement, only it covers 45 square miles of territory. All topics relating to property and agency within the conduct of government would fit naturally within a postcameralist orientation toward public finance.

A great deal of contemporary public finance operates with a form of illusory concreteness. An effort is made to treat a theoretical construction as if it were something that can be observed in reality. For instance, the condition that price equals marginal cost is a theoretical construction. The treatment of this construction or condition as a pricing rule for state enterprises to follow is an example of illusory concreteness.[8] It treats this condition as something that is directly observable independently of who is doing the observing. The so-called Ramsey tax rule is another illustration of illusory concreteness. There, tax rates are supposed to vary inversely with demand elasticity. It would be difficult enough to try actually to tax people according to their weight or height, but at least these magnitudes that are directly accessible. Taxing people according to their demand elasticities is a nice theoretical exercise that does not even remotely fit the most elementary requirement of transparency that any genuine rule must surely possess.

The cameralists did not succumb to illusory concreteness. They were too firmly grounded in reality for that. Any theoretical construction obviously must involve abstraction, and the abstraction must in turn be servicable for the task at hand. Statements about marginal cost pricing and Ramsay taxes have their places in general equilibirum theorizing, but they are not constructions that resolve or facilitate the issues of state administration at which they appear to be directed. Their concreteness is illusory. From the perspective of today, we would call the cameralists multidisciplinary, with the primary disciplines being economics, politics, law, and public administration.

What is the relationship between public finance and these four disciplines? In the choice-theoretic approach to public finance, whose chief turn-of-the-century inspiration would be Edgeworth, public finance would be a proper subset of economics.[9] Just as there is a *Journal of Economic Theory*, so there would be a *Journal of Public Economic Theory* to cover that subset of economic theory that dealt with the state. Public finance would look like economic theory, only it would have a specialized subset of subject matter. In this respect, it would be no different from, say, agricultural economics or housing economics. These are also specialized subsets of economics that are, nonetheless, not anything other than economics. In sharp contrast, a postcameralist public finance would most surely not be a proper subset of economic theory. Suppose you were to draw a Venn diagram with intersecting circles denoting such fields of study as economics, politics, sociology, public administration, and law. Postcameralist public finance would cut through all of those fields, and in its own right would be a genuinely multidisciplinary field of study.

---

[8] See, for instance, the essays collected in Buchanan and Thirlby (1973).

[9] The chief turn-of-the-century inspiration for postcameralist public finance would be Wicksell.

References

Backhaus JG (1993) The German economic tradition: from cameralism to the Verein für Socialpolitik, Manuscript. University of Maastricht, Maastricht

Backhaus JG, Wagner RE (1987) The cameralists: a public choice perspective. Public Choice 53(1):3–20

Blankart CB (1991) Öffentlichen Finanzen in der Demokratie. Franz Vahlen, München

Brennan G, Buchanan JM (1980) The power to tax: analytical foundations of a fiscal constitution. Cambridge University Press, Cambridge

Buchanan JM, Thirlby GF (eds) (1973) LSE essays on cost. Weidenfeld and Nicolson, London

Dittrich E (1974) Die deutschen und österreichischen Kameralisten. Wissenschaftliche Buchgessellschaft, Darmstadt

Foldvary F (1994) Public goods and private communities. Edward Elgar, Hants

Goode R (1970) Public finance in the international encyclopedia of the social sciences: a review article. J Econ Lit 8(1):27–34

Humpert M (1937) Bibliographie der Kameralwissenschaften. Karl Schroeder Verlag, Köln

Justi, Johann Heinrich Gottlob von (1969a), Grundsätze der Policeywissenschaft, Frankfurt a. M.: Sauer & Auvermannn KG. [Reprint from the third edition of 1782.]

Justi, Johann Heinrich Gottlob von (1969b), Natur und Wesen der Staaten, Darmstadt: Scientia Verlag Aalen. [Reprint from 1771 edition.]

Kraan D-J (1996) Budgetary decisions: a public choice approach. Cambridge University Press, Cambridge

Leijonhufvud A (1996) Three items for the macroeconomic agenda, manuscript. University of Trento, Trento

MacCallum SH (1970) The art of community. Institute for Humane Studies, Menlo Park

Schumpeter JA (1954) History of economic analysis. Oxford University Press, New York

Seckendorff, Veit Ludwig von (1976), Der Teutscher Fürsten Staat, Glashütten im Taunus: Detlev Auvermann KG, with a Forward by Ludwig Fertig. [Reprint from the 1665 edition.]

Small A (1909) The cameralists: the pioneers of German social polity. Burt Franklin, New York

Sonnenfels JV (1787) Grundsätze der Policey, Handlung und Finanzwissenschaft. Strobel, München

Tiebout CM (1956) A pure theory of local expenditures. J Polit Econ 64(5):416–424

Tribe K (1984) Cameralism and the science of government. J Mod Hist 56(2):263–284

Tribe K (1995) Strategies of economic order: German Economic Discourse: 1750–1950. Cambridge University Press, Cambridge

Wagner RE (1997) Choice, exchange, and public finance. Am Econ Rev Proc 87:160–163

Wicksell K (1958) A new principle of just taxation. In: Musgrave RA, Peacock AT (eds) Classics in the theory of public finance. Macmillan, London, pp 72–118

Chapter 5
The Physiocrats

Lluis Argemí d'Abadal

Introduction

The physiocrats, a group of economists whose period of greatest activity was between 1756 and 1774, the year of the death of François Quesnay, master of the group, had a short life as a school. The birth of the school can be traced to the meeting of the two founders, François Quesnay and the Marquis de Mirabeau, in July 1757. But 2 years before, in 1755, an event of the greatest importance had taken place: the publishing, some 25 years after its writing, of the masterwork of Richard Cantillon *Essai sur la nature du commerce en général*. Cantillon's work has been defined as the first complete treatise on political economy, but it also contributed to the birth of physiocracy, the first school. So our history must begin with this contribution.

The Founders and the Disciples

Cantillon had numerous followers, not only because his work was well written, concise and convincing, but also because it had circulated informally for several years after its author's death. Others were thus able to plagiarize, adapt or translate it.[1] Versions of works originally written in other languages were regularly published

---

[1] In the eighteenth century plagiarism was not condemned as it is today. It was possible to quote other authors at length, without mentioning the source, and without a sense of transgressing the norms. Like Pierre Menard, Borges' "author" of the Quijote, they wanted to say the same thing, so they used the same words.

L.A. d'Abadal (✉)
University of Barcelona, Diagonal, 690, 08034 Barcelona, Spain
e-mail: argemi@eco.ub.es

J.G. Backhaus (ed.), *Handbook of the History of Economic Thought*,
The European Heritage in Economics and the Social Sciences,
DOI 10.1007/978-1-4419-8336-7_5, © Springer Science+Business Media, LLC 2012

throughout Europe, and particularly in France. It was a way of introducing foreign innovations.[2] In the case of Cantillon, however, the fact that the work had not been published meant that its translators/adaptors could plagiarize it blatantly; perhaps the best known of these plagiarists/adaptors and the most honest, since he acknowledged the fact in his introduction to his work, was Victor Riquetti, Marquis de Mirabeau (1715–1789), a great aristocrat from Provence, and father of the famous orator of the first phase of the French Revolution. In 1756 the elder Mirabeau wrote a work that would make him famous, *L'ami des hommes ou Traité sur la population*, in which he examined an old mercantilist theme, the relation between population and wealth, using new instruments, some of which he had borrowed from Cantillon. For "L'Ami des Hommes" – as Mirabeau became known after the success of the work – the wealth of a kingdom depended on the numbers of its inhabitants, a populationist idea which preserved the mercantilist tradition. The success of this work sparked a new fashion; after Mirabeau, "amis" of the country, of children, of women, of workers, of farmers, and a host of others were all published. Mirabeau was now famous. People flocked to see him, from the most humble who came out into the street as he passed by, to the very richest who invited him to their elegant salons.

Mirabeau's reputation came to the notice of François Quesnay (1694–1774), court physician (though not to the King) and *protégé* of Madame de Pompadour, the King's lover. Quesnay was keen to make Mirabeau's acquaintance. At their meeting in July 1757 the physiocratic school was born, after a long discussion that allowed Quesnay to convince Mirabeau.

François Quesnay was born into a family of small landowners from Meré, near Versailles.[2] He had received little formal education since he had many brothers and sisters, and he learnt to read late, by reading *Agriculture et maison rustique* (1506), a Renaissance classic on agriculture by Charles Estienne and Charles Liebault. The authors were both Parisian doctors, and the main objective of their work was to encourage self-sufficiency among peasant families, and to describe the medical properties of certain plants. This combination of agriculture and medicine was to mark Quesnay's future; he studied to become a surgeon, and studied agriculture as an amateur. He became a surgeon of repute and participated in the debates that would lead to the unification of the two professions, medicine and surgery. His speciality was the circulation of blood, and he wrote treatises on bleeding and gangrene, but more than his contributions to medical theory it was his discretion that won him many admirers.

The reputation he acquired in his profession won him valuable protectors, and finally took him to Versailles as physician to Madame de Pompadour, who was keen to shield him from the machinations of the court. It was there that Quesnay's career as an agriculturalist and economist began. His first friends were responsible for the country's agriculture, but his position of influence meant that many people sought

---

[2] A biography of Quesnay can be found in François Quesnay (1958), by Jacqueline Hecht. Hecht's book contains all Quesnay's known works at that time, and my references to the originals are taken from it.

his favour in their relations with the King. Voltaire asked him to intervene in the Calas affair; Diderot, d'Alembert and many other Enlightenment figures also enlisted his support. Soon a weekly gathering was organized in his rooms at the palace, and was attended regularly by Buffon, Helvétius, Condillac and the other philosophers. It was at one of these gatherings that he met Mirabeau. Mirabeau had published *L'ami des hommes*, but Quesnay by then had published two articles on themes of agricultural economy in the Encyclopédie, "Fermiers" and "Grains" (1756), having ousted Forbonnais, one of the last mercantilists, as main contributor to the work on economic matters. Although this was the extent of his involvement in the Encyclopédie, Quesnay wrote two more articles, "Hommes" and "Impôts" (1756), which were not published but were both referred to in other publications.

In their discussion, Quesnay and Mirabeau defended different positions. For Quesnay, population was not the cause of wealth but a dependent variable which reacted to other stimuli. Though he believed some of Mirabeau's arguments were correct, Quesnay thought that the aristocrat put the cart before the horse. At their famous meeting in July 1757, Mirabeau saw the light: the school was born, with a master and a doctrine, though in this case the disciple was also a key member of the institution.

Quesnay and Mirabeau formed a distinctive combination. They represent the two prototypes of the Enlightenment: Quesnay, the bourgeois, moderate rather than radical, who advocates change but is suspicious of social movements and trusts more in the King or despot to implement it; Mirabeau, the nobleman, keen to restore the prominence of the aristocracy – a position it has lost as a result of its own irresponsibility – a patrician who believes that to regain its influence the aristocracy must as a class be prepared to support the State, even economically, and to carry out the necessary reforms: change of a kind, but only to preserve the status quo. Symbolically, perhaps, Mirabeau died on July 13th, 1789, the day before the storming of the Bastille and the start of the French Revolution. This combination was the cause of the ambiguity of the physiocrats political position (and, in part, of the Enlightenment as a whole).

Once the nucleus of the school-sect was created, the real work began. It took three forms: the recruitment of followers, the establishment of alliances with other groups and the spreading of the doctrine. The physiocrats were highly successful in all three areas, because they realized that their objectives should be practical above all: their theories had not only to win over new supporters, but had to be applicable in practice. Therefore, they sought alliances with influential functionaries whose ideas coincided with theirs. Among their new disciples were figures such as Dupont de Nemours (the founder of the great chemical company in the United States), who ran the journals that published the schools articles; Mercier de la Rivière, the former governor of Martinique; and Patullo, an Irish agricultural expert and author of treatises on the new agriculture, all three well known in their respective fields. Other authors such as Abeille, Le Trosne and Baudeau also joined the school.

Quesnay and Mirabeau established contacts with the functionaries who served under Bertin, in charge of agricultural policy, and Gournay, the great defender of liberalism and author of the maxim "laissez faire, laissez passer". Among Bertin's disciples were the great agronomists, and among Gournay's was a figure as important as Turgot, later to be comptroller general (a post similar to minister of finance, and, in certain cases depending on the personality, similar to prime minister).

The creation of a group of this kind, which owed the name physiocrat to Dupont, was not a new phenomenon. A number of functionaries such as Bertin and Gournay had created groups of collaborators, and were competing for posts of responsibility. In addition, intellectuals had begun to organize themselves in specific disciplines in order to enlighten the country. Among these were the philosophers of the Encyclopédie, the group of Diderot and d'Alembert. Dupont was keen to maintain a certain distance from the philosophers, and saw the physiocrats knowledge as distinct: all embracing, but referring in particular to the social sciences. Nonetheless, the members of the school called themselves "economistes", and were sometimes known as philosopher-economists. So they were a school, but they were something more besides: they were the proponents of what they saw as a new science. And this fact attracted hatred and opposition. But, to a large extent, the origin of this opprobrium lay elsewhere. The physiocrats internal organization was more akin to that of a sect or a pressure group than to a scientific school[3]; indeed, they were a school not because they had a common vision inside an established discipline, but because they believed that they had invented a new science, which they termed economic philosophy or physiocracy, a science with a language that they alone understood and accepted, and with its own methods. The physiocrats opponents had to fight with physiocratic arms to argue with them, and even almost in the physiocrats own publications. In short the physiocrats behaviour was sectarian, and they were attacked on this account. And their advocacy was a sectarian one: whenever one of them was criticized, the others rallied to his defence.[4] Dupont, particularly, was capable of censoring the critical articles that appeared in the journals he controlled, especially the *Ephémérides du citoyen*. For these reasons the physiocrats were branded as sectarian, the possessors of knowledge of an outlandish science, with a cryptic language and incomprehensible methods.

They also acted to an extent as a lobby, party or pressure group. Their aim was to influence economic policy, and to this end they placed particular emphasis on obtaining posts of responsibility. They sought influence at court, where Quesnay's position was invaluable; indeed, even the creators of the *Encyclopédie* turned to them for help to maintain their publication. In this third function of political lobby the physiocrats most notable success was the appointment of Turgot as comptroller general, though it cannot be ascribed directly to their influence. But before this, they had to contend with a number of specific problems and an intellectual atmosphere that left its mark on them.

---

[3] The use of the term sect is standard. Weulersse (1968) uses the term party, and others, as Schumpeter (1954), prefer school.

[4] This statement by Le Trosne will serve as an example: "Sans se concerter, sans se connaître, ils se sont trouvés parfaitement d'accord dans leur principes et leur logique, aucun d'eux n'a desavoué ses compagnons d'armes, et n'a rien avancé qui ne soit avoué de tous": a perfect definition of a sect.

France in the Eighteenth Century

During the eighteenth century, the social and economic situation of France had deteriorated with respect to Britain. After the Edict of Nantes, which brought to an end the wars of religion of the previous century, and the adoption of an agrarian policy by the ministers of the first Bourbon, Henri IV, especially Sully, the country had enjoyed a certain prosperity. But the repeal of the Edict of Nantes, the exodus of many Calvinists and the loss of human capital that this entailed, and the adoption of an industrialist policy by Louis XIV's minister Colbert eventually created a sensation of crisis. On the death of Louis XIV, the country was exhausted. The enemies within were the splendours of the court, the advent of industrialism and intolerance, and the new vogue was the Rousseauesque return to nature. Voltaire celebrated the fact that at last the French were tired of the theatre and were now interested in wheat. Henri IV and his minister Sully, the agrarian, were venerated, and Colbert, the industrialist, and indirectly Louis XIV, were rebuked.

To this state of latent crisis, the 6 years war added new problems as France and Britain fought for hegemony in the New Continent. This war aggravated the problems of the French treasury, already under great pressure, as was commonly the case under the *Ancien Régime*. The treasury's problems were among the first that engaged the physiocrats and merely bore out the desperate situation of the French economy. It was against this background that the physiocrats developed their theories. In the final analysis, their objective was reformist, and their starting point the description of the problems afflicting the French monarchy.

The absolutist state was at its height. Its functioning depended on government officials, but of course, also on a good king. If Henri IV was remembered as a wise ruler, Louis XIV now receives posthumous criticism. His son, Louis XV, was less successful than his predecessors, according to the physiocrats unwritten opinions. But the main problem was the lack of confidence of intellectuals and government officials in the future king, Louis XVI. Though he was to show some astuteness in nominating Turgot as comptroller general, the events were soon to justify the functionaries concern.

At the cultural level, the most important fact was that the cultural renaissance of the previous century had not had an empirical component, as it had in Britain. It was based on rationalism, and this dependence conditioned the methodology available to the French scholars. In Locke's empiricism, nature was like pencil writing on the blank page of knowledge, but in rationalism, the human mind was already in possession of all the components of this knowledge, and all that was required to reveal it was introspection and reasoning.

Jansenism was another key element in the intellectual life of eighteenth-century France. The Jansenists were condemned by the Church but they exerted a powerful influence over many intellectuals. Disputes over Catholic dogma apart, they could be seen as Catholic Calvinists, given to an individualistic vision of the modern world and receptive to the economic practices that were developing at the time.

This situation had led high-ranking government officials to consider proposals for reform, though not before carrying out meticulous descriptions of the causes of crisis, many of which were linked to the nature of the Absolutist state itself. Among these authors Boisguilbert and Vauban stand out. Boisguilbert's conception of an economy governed by natural laws and his vision of the economic interdependence of the different social classes led him to liberalism. He was a philo-Jansenist, and his vision of economic activity was at odds with the predominant view of the time. Vauban, for his part, advocated fiscal reform and the creation of a single tax on income rather than on wealth or consumption.

Slightly later, as said before, Richard Cantillon, an expert in the economies of France and Britain, wrote his *Essai sur la Nature du commerce en général*. The work was not published until 1755, but it circulated freely beforehand and quickly became famous. It was the first compendium of the science that was to be known as political economy, and offered a vision of the economy as a world that could be described by means of theoretical laws. Boisguilbert, Vauban and Cantillon planted the seeds of the physiocrats theories.

But the prevailing vision of the economy at the time was quite different. Authors such as François Veron de Forbonnais and Galiani were the physiocrats main opponents. Forbonnais was a representative of late mercantilism, with certain liberal touches, in step with the economists who held sway in the rest of Europe: James Steuart in Britain; Justi and the Cameralists in Germany, then at the height of their influence; Genovesi, who was highly influential in Italy; and Campomanes in Spain. The pragmatic Galiani, difficult to classify in any one school, was an acute critic of the physiocrats. It was probably due to him (and to the other authors we have mentioned) that the dogmatic excesses of the physiocrats were abandoned in favour of an eclectic but practical vision of the problems of the economy.

The Works of the Physiocrats

There is no one book that contains all the ideas of physiocrat theory, though Mirabeau's Philosophie Rurale and others come close. The analysis should be based on in the works of Quesnay, who was averse to writing great tracts, but who wrote many short articles on specific subjects. Mirabeau, Dupont, Mercier and Patullo expanded on the themes that Quesnay examined, and in some cases their analyses are useful. The figure below lists these articles and publications of Quesnay, and elaborations on his ideas by other authors (Table 5.1).

The nucleus of physiocrat theory is to be found in these books and articles. Apart from the entries in the Encyclopédie ("Evidence", "Fermiers" and "Grains" mentioned above, plus "Hommes" and "Impôts" which were not published), we should mention Quesnay's articles on political theory, "Droit naturel", "Analyse du Gouvernement des Incas du Pérou" and "Despotisme de la Chine". The economic principles established in these articles were developed by Quesnay and Mirabeau in a series of publications, the most important of which are the different *Tableaux Economiques* published as a single work (containing the maxims that appeared in the article "Grains", though with slight additions), or included in longer works such as Mirabeau's *Philosophie rurale* of 1763.

Table 5.1 Physiocratic works

Work	Year	Short title	Related concept	Other references
Method				
Encyclopédie	1756	Evidence	Method	
(Encyclopédie) unpublished	1756	Fonctions de l'Âme	Method	Aspects de la psychologie (1760)
		Functions of the soul		Aspects of psychology
Politics				
Journal d'agriculture	1765	Droit Naturel	Ordre naturel	Traité de la monarchie (1757) unpublished
		Natural right	Natural order	Treatise on monarchy
Éphémérides	1767	Incas du Perou	Despotisme legal	L'Ordre naturel et essentiel des societés politiques
		Incas of Perú	Legal despotism	The natural and essential order of political societies
Éphémérides	1767	Despotisme de la Chine	Despotisme legal	
		Despotism of China	Legal despotism	
Agriculture				
Encyclopédie	1756	Fermiers	Grande et petite culture	Traité sur l'amelioration des terres (Patullo 1774)
		Farmers	Great and small agriculture (Avances)	Improvement of lands
			Capital	
Encyclopédie	1757	Grains	Produit net	Maximes generales (1774)
		Grains	Net product	General maxims
			Impôt unique	
			Single tax	

(continued)

Table 5.1 (continued)

Work	Year	Short title	Related concept	Other references
Economy				
(Encyclopédie) Unpublished	1757	Hommes Men	Population theory Bon prix Good price	Ameéíoration des terres (Patullo 1774) Improvement of land L'Ami des hommes Friend of humanity
(Encyclopédie) Unpublished	1757	Impôts Taxes	Tax analysis	Theorie de l'impôt Theory of tax
(Encyclopédie) Unpublished	1757	Interêt de l'argent Money interest	Limitation interest rate	Interêt de l'argent (Journal de l'agriculture 1766) Money interest
Tableau Economique Tableau Économique	1758–1760	Tableau Économique Economic picture	Economic interdependence Circular flow	L'Ami des Hommes Friend of humanity Philosophie Rurale Rural philosophy
Journal de l'agricultur	1766	Problème Économique	Tableau analysis (Bon prix)	
Physiocratie (Dupont, 1767) Physiocracy	1767	2° Problème Économique	Tableau analysis (*Impôt unique*)	
Journal de l'agriculture	1766	Analyse de la formule du Tableau	Simplification Tableau	

As can be seen, Quesnay's interests evolved over time, and we can classify chronologically his articles in five groups, or subjects. The only variation is in the themes referring to politics, which we place in the second group due to their methodology even though they were developed later, almost at the same time as the *Tableau Economique*. The doctrine as a whole can be summarized as in Table 5.2.

The first row presents the theoretical concepts that the physiocrats used. Evidence "a certainty so clear that the spirit cannot reject it", was the source of knowledge. Evidence suggested that in nature, both physical and social, there existed a natural order. Part of this order was that agriculture alone was productive and created wealth: but only large-scale agriculture (*grande culture*) with access to avances, stock of capital. The wealth created by agriculture they called *produit net* – net product or net revenue – which vitalized the economy by circulating or exchanging between sectors. These exchanges were represented in the *Tableau Economique*.

But each theoretical concept could produce a policy. The physiocrats advocated an educational system that would stress what to them was evident; a political system in accordance with the natural order, based on the despotism of the positive laws, provided these laws had been laid down by an enlightened despot well advised as to the character of the natural order; an agrarian change or reform that would impose in France an agricultural system like the English one, *grande culture*; and the *impôt unique*, a single tax, as Vauban had proposed, on produit net alone. Finally, they advocated the generalization of a system of liberty that would favour free individual action and thus allow the spread of the *produit net* to all sectors and establish a *bon prix* for grain – a price that was remunerative for producers, as Boisguilbert had proposed.

So first, the physiocrats were not only economists; their economics were integrated in a much wider body of social science. This broad sweep would be lost once the physiocrats had disappeared and compartmentalization set in. Second, the physiocrats were profoundly marked by their times. They appeared in the arena of ideas to deal with the problems of the moment, the debates that engaged the France of the eighteenth century (shown in the second row of the figure). But to intervene in the country's affairs it did not suffice to propose alternative political measures that might palliate the crisis; they had to seek out the theoretical justifications of their proposals, something which their opponents were unable to do.

The Theory of the Physiocrats

The various tenets of physiocratic theory require individual analysis. With the concept of *evidence*, Quesnay developed a theory of knowledge. The concept originated in Malebranche, and arose from radical Cartesian principles. For Descartes, knowledge was implicit in the brain, and reasoning was all that was required to reveal it. Malebranche radicalized this position, allowing that this knowledge could be evident,

Table 5.2 Physiocratic theories

	Method	Politics	Agriculture	Production	Circulation reproduction
Theory	Evidence	Natural order	Agriculture the only productive sector (*Avances*)	Produit net (Bon prix) (Prix fondamental)	Tableau Economique
Economic policy	Education	Legal despotism	Agrarian reform (Grande et petite culture)	Impôt unique	Trade freedom
Conceptual terminology	Avances	Grande culture	Produit net	Bon prix	Impôt unique
	Capitals	Capitalist extensive agriculture	Net product or surplus	High price remunerative	Single tax
				Prix fondamental	
				Cost of production	

but Quesnay suggested that the senses should aid in this perception, adopting some of Condillac's sensualist ideas.[5] So, to some extent, empiricism entered their method.

As a result of this method, it was evident that society was clearly governed by a natural order. It was this natural social order, analogous to the natural biological order that could be observed in the human body (at least by a doctor) that maintained the balance between its constituent parts, and the result of the natural laws that governed the functioning of the society and the economy. The political consequence of this natural order was a positive order that respected these natural laws. Rejecting Montesquieu's conception, after Quesnay the physiocrats defended legal despotism, a position that opened them to criticism in a world that was beginning to tire of full-blooded despotism. The idea of legal despotism was developed in the main by a disciple of Quesnay, Mercier de la Rivière; in his study the term denotes a despotism of laws rather than a despotism implemented by an individual. The positive laws, which corresponded to the natural laws, were to be applied despotically, and it was to be the laws that should govern. The task of the sovereign was merely to apply the natural laws with the aid of his counsellors, and the only partially autonomous power that the physiocrats admitted was the judiciary, a power that had to analyse whether the positive laws were in accordance with the natural order. And the principles that had to be maintained were Locke's: Liberty, property and security. Their motto was "Ex natura, ius, ordo et legis; ex homine, arbitrium, regimen et coertio".

The examples of despotism that Quesnay analysed were China and the Incas of Peru, which in certain aspects conformed to his idea of political order. Curiously, the Argentine national hero Manuel Belgrano, one of the few Hispanic physiocrats, drew on Quesnay's ideas during the struggle for independence of the Americas and proposed the reestablishment of the Inca monarchy as a political system for the continent.

In spite of the importance of Mercier's work on legal despotism, the two founders had specific ideas on the subject. The edition of the *Traité de la Monarchie* (1758) by Quesnay and Mirabeau[6] a work that they preferred not to publish reveals some of the contradictions they must have encountered in this theory. In the *Traité* they analyse the possible origin of the monarchy, and declare the primacy of the natural order over the ephemeral occupant of the throne. They appear to doubt the capacity of the monarch to achieve a true natural order, and to transform it into a positive order. But the positive law, the reflection of the natural law, was to serve as

---

[5] This sensualism is explained by Quesnay in these terms: "Les Sensations sont les motifs ou causes déterminantes de la raison et de la volonté décisive". The sensualist components may be seen in Steiner (1998) pp. 30 and ff.

[6] A session of the ESHET 1999 annual meeting was dedicated to this subject, with papers by, Eltis and Eltis (1999) and Cartelier (1999). The book, edited by Gino Longhitano, will be published shortly. A demonstration of Quesnay's "constitutional" vision that Eltis mentions can be seen in a conversation between Quesnay and the Dauphin, the future King Louis XVI, referred in Higgs (1968) p. 45. The *Traité* has seldom been studied before, an exception being Fox-Genovese (1976).

the framework for the monarchs activity: though they were against the division of powers, this political system recalls to an extent a constitutional monarchy in which no legislative body is required because the natural laws are the only ones that need be applied and established as a "constitution". Whether it was the character of the Dauphin, the future Louis XVI, that led them to advocate this limitation of the power of the monarch is a hypothesis that is still to be studied. In any case, the function of the enlightened counsel of the monarch is established more clearly to reveal the natural order.

This work was written at the same time as the *Tableau Economique*, and the two works should be seen as the two cornerstones the one political and the other economic of well-established societies, or, in the terms of the physiocrats, of the *Royaume Agricole*, the Agricultural Kingdom, as the ideal model for the country. The agricultural and economic components of the theory were to be found in other works. The *Tableau* is in a way the economic constitution of the Agricultural Kingdom, just as the monarchy with a positive legislation that observes the natural law is its political constitution. The *Maximes* added to the *Tableau* reinforce this impression. The two great conceptual pillars of physiocracy should therefore be analysed jointly.

In the articles on agricultural subjects the idea of agriculture as the sole productive area begins to emerge. "Fermiers" discusses the existence of two types of agriculture, *grande culture and petite culture*. *Grande culture*, mainly concentrated in the north of France, was the agriculture of the great tenant farmers using modern techniques (that is, horses, machinery and the three-field system) and with access to abundant capital; *petite culture*, on the other hand, was the agriculture of *métayers* (small sharecroppers), with few technical means, oxen in place of horses and a two-field system (crop-fallow rotation). The predominance of the latter type of agriculture in France, especially in the south, was at the root of the economic crisis, and this preponderance of *petite culture* and an irrational fiscal system plus the restrictions on freedom of trade were the cause of migration to the cities. Implicit in the physiocrats argument was the need to transform *petite culture* into *grande culture* whenever possible, in other words, to implement an agrarian reform similar to that effected by the enclosure movement in England.[7]

On the way, the physiocrats defined avances, capital necessary for production. They made a detailed description of the various types of capital necessary for the modernization and proper functioning of French agriculture: *souverains*, public capital for developing infrastructure; *fonciers*, for preparing land for crops; *primitives*, fixed capital for exploitation and *annuels*, circulating capital for annual production.

In the article "Grains", Quesnay calculated the profits that would be obtained from generalizing a system of grande culture and free trade, and by encouraging

---

[7] An apparent contradiction arises if we observe that the "modern" system, the three-field system, dates from Charlemagne's time, and became general in the twelfth to thirteenth centuries: it does not seem to be so modern. For an explanation, see Argemí (1994). A more general discussion in Mulliez (1975).

agriculture over trade or industry. In this article we find the idea of *bon prix* – the fair price – high enough to be remunerative, and which permits *produit net,*[8] the only surplus created by agricultural production. So, it included the idea of the unique productivity of agriculture.[9] The final part of the article contained a series of indications or maxims, which Quesnay would use in later works, especially in the *Tableau Economique*. These maxims formed the economic constitution of the ideal *Royaume Agricole*, or Agricultural Kingdom.

In a society like the France of the second half of the eighteenth century, the assertion that agriculture was the only productive sector appears accurate enough. First, agriculture represented the largest part of the economy and employed most of the population. In addition, when industry is relatively undeveloped and involves only a few small, independent craftsmen, there is a great temptation to confuse physical creation with economic creation. One grain produces several grains and a cow several calves, but the cloth of a shirt can produce nothing more than the shirt itself, and so there is no *produit net* or surplus. If this had been the only discovery of the physiocrats, they would hardly deserve credit as founders of a school, but behind their statements there lies something more: it has been called the land-theory of value, similar to the theory of Petty and, later, of Cantillon. The theory is based on a central idea that the origin and the measurement of the value of commodities are in terms of land (or in terms of grain, its product par excellence). The value of a commodity is thus calculated in terms of the amount of land necessary to produce it, or, considering an average yield in grain per unit of land, in terms of the amount of grain that the land produces.

The last articles written for the *Encyclopédie*, but not published at that time, contain few new ideas. The article "Hommes" looks again at the issue that had led to the formation of the school (wealth as a cause of population), including other concepts such as *prix fondamental*, fundamental price or production cost, *valeur vénale*, the market price and the need for free trade.[10] The difference between the *valeur vénale* and the *valeur* or *prix fondamental* is what constitutes the produit net or surplus, and so the former must be close to the bon prix to increase the surplus or *produit net.*[11] This article also includes the definition of manufacture as sterile, or more precisely of craftsmen as a sterile class, in consonance with the definition of agriculture as the only productive sector; this definition is developed more fully in subsequent works.[12]

The article "Impôts" presents a less radical position than is usually attributed to the physiocrats on the idea of the single tax, although in the final analysis it is this

---

[8] François Quesnay (1958), p. 462. According to Perrot (1992) its origin may be found in Duhamel (1750). vol V. p. 158.

[9] François Quesnay (1958). p. 472.

[10] For the relations between the different concepts of valeur and prix in Quesnay's works, see Vaggi (1987).

[11] François Quesnay (1958). p. 525 as an example.

[12] See François Quesnay (1958), *"Sur les travaux des artisans"* p. 885 and ff.

tax that has theoretical support (only net created wealth should be taxed). But this article contains a clear definition of a fundamental concept, *produit net*, the net product or net revenue corresponding to the idea of surplus: "the annual wealth that constitutes the income of the nation are the products which, once all expenditure is removed, form the profit obtained from the biens fonds (the land)".[13] In fact, this concept is the central point on which the whole of the physiocrats economic theory is founded; although it can be seen in embryo in earlier authors starting with Petty, it was the physiocrats who developed it in a more precise form. It is this concept that permits the proposal of a single tax imposed on it, and since in the physiocrats ideal situation the net product is paid by cultivators to the landowners in the form of rent, it is the landowners who will pay the tax, an idea none too attractive to the dominant classes of the times.

Finally, the article on interest merely considers the need to limit interest rates so that capital can be directed to productive activities and not to speculation, an idea at odds with Quesnay's liberalism, but consistent with his concept of production.

The *Tableau Economique*

The physiocrats great creation was the *Tableau Economique*. Its importance, according to Mirabeau, can be seen in this statement: "Trois grandes inventions principales ont fondé stablement les Societés, indépendamment de tant d'autres qui les ont ensuite dotées et decorées. Ces rois sont, 1¼ L'invention de l'écriture, qui seule donne a l'humanité le pouvoir de transmettre, sans altération, ses loix, ses pactes, ses annales, et ses découvertes. 2° Celle de la Monnaie, qui lie tous les rapports entre les Sociétés policés. La troisième enfin, qui est due à notre age, et donc nos neveux profiteront, est un dérivé des deux autres, et les complete également en perfectionnant leur objet: c'est la decouverte du Tableau Économique".

Prepared meticulously by Quesnay, it became the group's hallmark, so much so that Mirabeau compared its importance with that of the discoveries of money and printing. But its original zigzag form, as it became known, made it difficult to understand. It has been said that it was based on contemporary diagrams of blood circulation.[14]

A first interpretation of the *Tableau* is that of the different flows of expenditure generated by an initial income. This interpretation has a parallel in the one often used to explain the Keynesian multiplier. Each expenditure is an income for another class, which then spends in accordance with specified norms; this generates new incomes, and so forth.[15]

---

[13] François Quesnay (1958) p. 582.

[14] Foley (1973). The best descriptions may be found in Eltis (1975, 1996) and Herlitz (1996). The English picture is taken from Eltis (1975).

[15] This interpretation, perhaps the simplest, is taken from Tsuru (1942), but simplified.

The first models of the *Tableau* were based on a quantity of 400 pounds, a figure that increased to 2,000 pounds in later versions, and which in some of Quesnay's texts are referred to as *milliards* (thousands of millions). The variation in the quantity is probably an attempt to give an empirical presentation of the French economy of the time. In this regard, Schumpeter included the physiocrats in a chapter entitled "The econometricians and Turgot". We will use this example, assuming that it refers to 2,000 million pounds in the country as a whole. For the sake of simplicity, we will work with figures reduced to thousands, and ignore the use of money.

The starting point is the working capital of 2,000 pounds, the avances of the cultivators. In the productive process, these 2,000 pounds produce 5,000 pounds, but since 1,000 pounds are used to pay off the fixed capital (at a rate of 10%, which would mean that the capital invested, or the avances primitives, amounts to 10,000 pounds), the net reproduction, or the surplus, is 2,000 pounds. These 2,000 pounds, the net reproduction, are paid to the landowners in the form of 2,000 pounds of grain as rent for the land. Half of the sum is spent on manufactured goods produced by industry the previous year, and the landowners thus have 1,000 pounds at their disposal to spend on manufactured goods.

Annually, industry produces a gross total of 2,000 pounds of manufactured goods, and has only spent 1,000 pounds, in exchange for food with the landowners. It needs raw materials, and buys them from the cultivators with the other 1,000 pounds of manufactured goods. It thus exchanges 2,000 pounds of manufactured goods for 1,000 pounds of grain and 1,000 pounds of raw materials, with which it can begin the productive process of transforming 2,000 pounds in a particular form into 2,000 pounds in another form, without net creation of wealth.

Agriculture has produced 3,000 pounds of grain and 2,000 pounds of raw materials (e.g. linen, etc.); it has paid 2,000 in grain to the landowners and has sold 1,000 in the form of raw materials to industry, in exchange for manufactured goods (equipment), and can now begin the productive process with 3,000 pounds, 1,000 in the form of grain, 1,000 in the form of raw materials and 1,000 in the form of manufactured goods, which will generate 3,000 pounds of grain and 2,000 of raw materials (with a net creation of wealth). So, after the exchanges, the initial situation is "reproduced".

Even though the initial quantity (here 2,000 pounds) varied in the different editions of the *Tableau*, to make it consistent with the current situation, as we have said, there is one aspect that appears to be consistently inaccurate. The consumption of food by the three classes is assumed to be the same, 1,000 pounds; but the composition of the French population in the eighteenth century must have made this impossible. The small fraction of aristocrats might conceivably consume as much as the vast majority, who worked the land, if they bought sufficient quantities of luxury goods. But the small fraction of craftsmen could only consume the same quantity if they engaged in foreign trade, which might account for the volume, but would undermine the theory: foreign trade would be an indirect source of wealth, something that was alien to the physiocrats. This theoretical problem in the *Tableau* is one of the possible weak points of its analysis.[16]

---

[16] This fact was pointed out by Meek (1962), Chap. 2.

One of the most important consequences for economic policy of the *Tableau* in particular, and of physiocratic theory as a whole, is the idea of freedom, of economic liberalism.[17] Wealth had to circulate in the form and proportions described, and all types of interference were to be avoided. Additionally, if the composition of the expenditure of the various economic actors varied, the dynamic equilibrium reflected in the *Tableau* would be broken; economic circulation would be reduced, causing economic crisis.[18] So the landowners would have to spend not less than half of their income on agricultural products (be they necessary or superfluous) but excessive industrial luxury would decrease productive expenditure and reduce economic reproduction. Nonetheless, the idea of economic freedom, especially with respect to the trade in wheat, impregnates Quesnay's other works, from his first articles on agricultural themes, such as "Fermiers" and "Grains".

The writings of two of Quesnay's and Mirabeau's disciples also deserve mention. Dupont de Nemours wrote *De l'origine et progrès d'une science nouvelle* (1768a), and the articles "Catalogue des écrits composés suivant les principes de science économique" (1768b) and "Notice abrégé des différents écrits modernes qui ont concouru en France à former la science de l'économie politique" (1769) both published in the journal that he directed, *Ephémérides du Citoyen*, and the compilation of articles by Quesnay entitled *Physiocratie* (1768), where Dupont invented the term physiocracy. These writings form a first attempt to present a history of economic thought, evidently linked to what was for Dupont the highpoint of his own theory. We must add that Dupont included among their predecessors not only Boisguilbert, Vauban and Cantillon, but also Montesquieu and some agrarian writers such as Hèbert. And Quesnay included in his writings agronomists like LaSalle and Duhamel. Liberal agrarism and new agronomy are two other sources of physiocracy.

Mercier de la Rivière's *L'ordre naturel et essentiel des sociétés politiques* (1767) was a defence of the political theory, that is, of the concept of legal despotism, and it comes nearer than any other work to being a complete textbook of physiocracy. It was much valued by later authors such as Adam Smith. As is often the case with textbooks, however, much of the material it contained had been set forth by other authors in previous publications.

Interpretation and Evaluation of Physiocracy

We should begin with the interpretations that take into account the complete body of the physiocrats thought, both their theory and their policies, including their ideas on the political system. We will call them the doctrinal interpretations.

---

[17] As in some other concepts used in this article, the idea of liberalism appears elsewhere, but for the sake of consistency we ascribe it to the *Tableau*.

[18] The study of disequilibrium was made in the *Philosophie Rurale* (1764).

Some of these interpretations of physiocracy have paid excessive attention to the agricultural aspects of its proposals, and for this reason have described it as a rationalization of the feudal economic order.[19] But even for Marx, physiocracy was a system of agricultural capitalism, and, as such, the bourgeois reproduction of the feudal system.[20] But it was definitely capitalist, reflecting the new society that was evolving in the north of France.

Marx's ideas gave place to a second interpretation of physiocracy, an economic doctrine representative of the interests of a new social group, the new landowners capitalists, taking the place of the aristocrats, including even Quesnay, who bought an estate and tried to make it profitable.[21] But this new interpretation does not stress the essential fact, the capitalist nature of the exploitations that this group defended. This capitalist nature was the nucleus of the new society.

Additionally, the physiocrats were aware that this new society needed more than freedom in order to evolve and reach the level of dynamism that existed on the other side of the Channel. First, it required capital, an indispensable element for the type of production which the physiocrats considered ideal, large-scale agricultural production; and second, a system of free exchange between sectors. And though they were naive to believe that agriculture was the only sector that could produce surplus, this was because the conditions of capital flow and a social organization including capitalists and wage-earning labourers were beginning to emerge in the agricultural setting, and nowhere else. They erred in thinking that it was the conditions inherent in agriculture that created the surplus – and not the set of economic conditions which, in their model, were only to be found in agriculture.

In this regard, the physiocrats are the best representatives of a political economy of agrarian capitalism, as Petty and Cantillon had been before them.[22] The political economists between Petty and the physiocrats, and even reaching Smith, were a specific group whose main objective was an economy in which only agriculture had a modern form, and whose basic characteristics could be analysed through the study of this sector.

Another doctrinal interpretation, complementary to this one, sees physiocracy as a proposal of economic development based on agriculture.[23] In the eighteenth century there were a range of possible economic models: a commercial republic, along the lines of Venice in its heyday, and which had evolved in Holland in the seventeenth century; or a manufacturing nation, along the lines of England, once it had supplanted Holland as the leading trading nation. The Dutch model was the clearest example of a mercantilist policy; the English model was already shifting towards industry, and was progressing towards liberal ideas. The physiocrats economic policies aimed to create a distinct model. In France, a larger country than either England

---

[19] Beer (1939).

[20] Marx (1963) p. 50.

[21] Ware (1931).

[22] McNally (1988).

[23] Longhitano (1994).

or Holland, the importance of the agricultural sector favoured the *Royaume Agricole*, the Agricultural Kingdom, a proposal that differed from the Dutch and English models. In this context, their proposals for fiscal reforms acquired considerable importance, not only in their almost dogmatic defence of a single tax, but in the more sophisticated conceptions expressed in some of Quesnay's works. In fact, the key objective of the new science was the same as Adam Smith's, that is, to enrich both the people and the sovereign. Once the first objective had been achieved, the tax system was crucial to the success of the second. A rich, economically developed French state would be in a position to compete with Britain. The fiscal concerns of the physiocrats, that were among the first that spurred them to political and scientific debate, are proof of this idea. Incidentally, the three development models correspond to the "systems of political economy" analysed by Smith.

In a way, the physiocrats reproduced on French soil the English Augustean Debate of the Restoration, after the Revolution of 1688. The conflict between the defenders of a State based on the landowners, the Country Party and the defenders of foreign trade, the Court Party is to an extent reflected here, though the physiocrats position at court may make the comparison confusing.[24]

An evaluation of the science that the physiocrats developed is also important. In spite of inventing the new name physiocracy, their proposal included the term political economy, part of the new science of which Dupont spoke. This new science had a precise agenda of its own, and in the France of the eighteenth century it had to compete with other scientific approaches that studied the same phenomena. First was the mercantilist school, dominant at the time, championed by François Veron de Forbonnais, whom Quesnay replaced as writer on economic matters for the *Encyclopédie*. Forbonnais' science of trade was widely accepted throughout Europe, but it was replaced by the physiocrats political economy. After the disappearance of the physiocracy, the mercantilists would regain their position of prominence in France for a time, only to be swept away when Say introduced the ideas of Adam Smith.

Nonetheless, the physiocrats could not be said to have a conception of the economy such as those of contemporary agronomists and scientists. Though in eighteenth-century France an agronomist was considered a political economist concerned with the problems of agriculture,[25] and indeed scientists like Linnaeus wished to give a certain naturalist content to the science, the physiocrats proposals were far removed from these conceptions.[26]

The new science also had to compete with more purely empiricist approaches, along the lines of the English Political Arithmetic. Perhaps if Petty had published

---

[24] Pocock (1975), Chap. XIII.

[25] In his entry for "Agronomie", Rozier (1787) defined an *Agronome* as someone who wrote on subjects of political economy.

[26] Steiner (1998) studies the different definitions in the first chapter, p. 10 and ff. Of special interest are the definitions by Quesnay and Linnaeus; the two were new proposals in front of the mercantilist idea, and both relied on agriculture as the source of wealth.

the complement to his Political Anatomy, this work would have been close to the physiocratic approach. However, this arithmetical method had few practitioners in France. It was the physiocrats who brought the rationalist, abstract and theoretical approach to the science, an approach that finally won the day.

Besides the interpretation of the physiocrats economic thought or doctrine, and of their conception of political economy as a science, it is necessary also to interpret their economic analysis, or the scientific part of their thought. In the first place, the physiocrats scientific approach, like that of their predecessors, was based on a particular conception of the objectives of political economy. For them, political economy studied phenomena related to the creation of surplus, and the reproduction of the economic system on the basis of this surplus. Surplus and reproduction formed the basic concepts of their idea of political economy, and not scarcity and allocation, as in present microeconomics. This surplus-reproduction approach, characteristic of the classical school as defined by Marx, began with Petty and Boisguilbert, and ended with Sismondi and Jones, (and, we should add, with Marx as one of the last representatives of the classical school).[27] So, the physiocrats were the first to give form to this specific line of economic analysis.

A final interpretation, the standard one, would define the physiocrats as the first group to propose a liberal economic order, created spontaneously via the actions of self-interested men, and their proposal was made some time before this order was defined in its standard terms by Adam Smith's invisible hand. We should stress the precise formulation of the economic liberalism of physiocracy according to which the nascent capitalist society operated in accordance with the free play of individual interest: "The magic of a well-ordered society lies in the fact that each man works for others while believing that he is working for himself", said Mirabeau. But his liberalism was limited to the field of economics. Though some may claim correctly that this is more a doctrinal line than an analytical one, it must be mentioned because of the importance of liberal views on economic matters.

Some of the physiocrats instruments can also be interpreted in the light of modern theories. One modern interpretation of the *Tableau* is as an Input-Output Table.[28] Indeed, the inventor of Input-Output analysis, Leontiev, always described his work as a continuation of Quesnay. Although there are a number of technical difficulties involved in applying Leontiev's calculus to the present table, these difficulties can be surmounted by considering landowners not only as a productive sector that provides a very special service (i.e. allowing the land to be possessed by them), but as the final demanders. Doing so, and in confirmation of the physiocrats proposals, agriculture is clearly the only sector that creates wealth.[29]

With the Tableau and the idea that agriculture is the only productive area, there emerges a possible theoretical interpretation of some elements of physiocracy. As we have said, the physiocrats maintained what we might call the land-value theory.

---

[27] For this approach, see Cartelier (1976).

[28] See Phillips (1955).

[29] Maital (1972).

This theory could be reformulated with the instruments used by Sraffa, in a system of production of commodities by means of commodities, to show, as in the above case, the idea that agriculture is the only source of production. In this case, the value of a good is proportional to the amount of land necessary to produce it, either directly or in the form of land that produces food for the workers involved in the process.[30] Furthermore, this explanation gives a theoretical basis to the empirical *Tableau*, or Input-Output Table, thus linking the two above interpretations.

The Fate of Physiocracy

The physiocrats ideas on both economic theory and economic policy were soon forgotten. In the policy aspect, physiocratic measures were partially applied in areas of Baden, by the Margrave Karl Friedrich, a physiocrat, and in Tuscany, by the Archduke Pietro Leopoldo, a sympathizer. But largely physiocracy was seen as a "girl as beauteous as an angel, but unluckily a virgin".[31] Their methods were difficult to understand, for they were far ahead of their time; their proposals were conceptually radical; and the society around them was changing. They were treated with contempt, criticized and then ignored. So, the diffusion of their ideas was often partial and incomplete, and sometimes, only the reactionary interpretation of their despotism was accepted.[32] Liberal forms of late industrialist mercantilism and cameralism were now in the ascendancy, and very soon Adam Smith was to appear on the scene. But the contributions of the physiocrats endured, sometimes hidden behind other ideas. In the field of economic policy, Tocqueville, a leading conservative, clearly recognized the achievement of the physiocrats: that of having provided the basis for what would be the economic policy of the French Revolution. But Tocqueville was also aware of their ambiguous attitude to freedom: economic freedom, but political despotism. He classified them as "illiberal", a telling epithet coming from one who was hardly a supporter of the Revolution.[33]

But one way to assess their importance is to concentrate solely on the analytical aspects of their theory. In the theoretical field, their contributions can be evaluated fairly by comparison with the proposals of the scholar generally considered to be the father of our science, Adam Smith. Smith himself wrote a favourable critique of the works of Quesnay and his disciples, and to a certain extent, maintained partially some of their ideas (agriculture being more productive than the other sectors, for it created rent). But between them and Smith there was an intermediate step, which

---

[30] Gilibert (1977). For a fuller exposition see Candela, G. and Palazzi, M. "Presentazione", in Candela and Palazzi (1979).

[31] Argemí et al. (1995).

[32] Tocqueville (1973a, b). "Notes complémentaires".

[33] It is well known that Schumpeter said that of the four greatest economists of history, three were French: Walras was definitely one, and Turgot probably another.

was given by an ally of the physiocrats, a disciple of Gournay and probably one of Schumpeter's four greatest economists of all time – Turgot.[34] Merely for being the precursors of Turgot, and for having had direct and perhaps indirect influences on Smith, the physiocrats are assured of a position in the first rank of the history of political economy.

But the physiocrats did not take their place in the mainstream of the evolution of economic thought until well into the nineteenth century. With the compilation published by Daire,[35] the dimensions of their work could be evaluated; but this evaluation would have to wait until the middle of the nineteenth century when Marx[36] and other German authors such as Oncken[37] realized that the physiocrats proposals were among the milestones of the history of economic thought. Since then, economists have accepted physiocracy as one of the most important steps in our history. As we have seen, its legacy is still with us.

Summary

During the third quarter of the eighteenth century, economic debate in France was dominated by what can be considered the first structured school of thought in economic matters, the physiocrats. The term physiocracy, meaning rule or government of nature, reflects its members' interest in proposing a line of interpretation of the world that was complementary, but different, to the one obtained by the philosophers by means of philosophy. Its sphere was social science as a whole, not economics alone.

Physiocracy was defined by a precise conceptual model, created to allow its proponents to participate in the controversies on economic policies of the moment. The physiocrats defined themselves as such more by the almost sectarian defence of this theoretical and conceptual model, and of the language in which it was expressed, than by their proposals on policy questions.

In political matters, the term "Legal Despotism" was the physiocratic norm, but it admitted a range of interpretations: despotism based on law (that is to say, constitutionalism), or despotism protected by law (or despotism "tout court"). All the physiocrats agreed that, inside the framework of the *Ancien Régime,* it was only possible to implement the reforms they advocated from a position of power; consequently, it was to the positions of power that their advice and warnings were directed. Despotism had to be reformist, in spite of the difficulties involved in implementing reforms. At the same time, the physiocrats proposals had a liberal component, even though it was limited to the economic sphere.

---

[34] Lundberg (1964).

[35] Daire (1846).

[36] Marx (1963).

[37] Oncken (1888).

The core of the theoretical model included the following ideas: that agriculture was the only productive sector; the concept of *produit net*, its circulation through the *Tableau Economique* and, accordingly, the defence of a single tax and of free trade. But on the way, the physiocrats proposed a theory of value and advanced important economic concepts such as capital and economic interdependence. At the same time, the economic policy they proposed, the construction of a *Royaume Agricole*, can be seen as an alternative to the policies of the mercantile republics, or to those of the manufacturing nations (such as England) which they saw as nations of trade.

Physiocracy is one of the first attempts to build economic science, and as such is one of the ancestors of present day economics. Both the complete theory and some of the tools its advocates used can be interpreted in terms of modern economic theory, and some of the ideas they developed – the economic interdependence of sectors, the idea of a circular flow of income and the concept of capital – remain with us today.

Acknowledgement I must thank Michael Maudsley for his help with the English version

References

Argemí LL (1994) Quesnay, agronome. Paper presented at the Colloque François Quesnay. Versailles

Argemí L, Lluch E, Cardoso JL (1995) La diffusion de la physiocratie: quelques problèmes ouverts, in La diffusion internationale de la physiocratie (XVIII-XIX). Presses U. de Grenoble, Grenoble, pp 473–480

Beer M (1939) An inquiry into Physiocracy. Allen &Unwin, London

Candela G, Palazzi M (eds) (1979) Dibattito sulla fisiocrazia. Nuova Italia, Firenze

Cantillon R (1755) Essai sur la nature du commerce en géneral. Fletcher Gyles, London

Cartelier J (1976) Surproduit et Reproduction. PUG, Grenoble

Cartelier J (1991) L'economie politique de François Quesnay, ou l'utopie du Royaume Agricole, in F. Quesnay, Physiocratie, Paris: Flammarion. pp 9–64

Cartelier J (1999) The political foundations of Quesnay's Tableau Economique. Paper presented at the ESHET Annual Conference. Valencia

Daire E (ed) (1846) Physiocrates. Guillaumin, Paris

Duhamel de Monceau HL (1750) Traite de la culture des terres suivant les principes de Mns. Tull, anglais, Paris

Dupont de Nemours PS (1768) Catalogue des écrits composés suivant les principes de la science économique. Ephémérides du citoyen, T. II., pp 191–202

Dupont de Nemours PS (1768) De l'origin et des progrès d'une science nouvelle. Dessaint, Paris

Dupont de Nemours PS (1769) Notice abrégé des différents écrits modernes qui ont concouru en France à former la science de l'économie politique. Ephémérides du Citoyen, T. I., pp XI–LI; T. II., pp V–XLVIII; T. III., pp V–XXX; T. IV., pp III–XXIV; T.V., pp V–XLVII; T. VI., pp 5–52; T. VIII., pp 5–3.8. T. IX., pp 5–78

de Tocqueville A (1973a) Notes et Fragments Inédits sur la Revolution. Gallimard, Paris

de Tocqueville A (1973b) L'Ancien Régime et la Revolution. Gallimard, Paris

Einaudi L (1933) The physiocratic theory of taxation. In: Economic essays in honour of Gustav Cassel (ed.). Allen & Unwin, London, pp 129–142

Eltis W (1975) Quesnay: a reinterpretation. Oxf Econ Pap 27:167–200; 327–351

Eltis W (1984) The classical theory of economic growth. MacMillan, London

Eltis W (1996) The Grand Tableau of François Quesnay's economics. Eur J Hist Econ Thought 3:21–43

Eltis W, Eltis SM (1999) Quesnay's advocacy of Government by constitutional monarchy. Paper presented at the ESHET Annual Conference. Valencia

Estienne C, Charles L (1556) Agriculture et maison rustique. Jacques Du-Puys, Lyon

Foley E (1973) An origin of the Tableau Economique. Hist Polit Econ 5:121–150

Fox-Genovese E (1976) The origins of Physiocracy. Cornell University Press, Ithaca

Gilibert G (1977) Quesnay. Etas, Milano

Herlitz L (1996) From spending and reproduction to circuit flow and equilibrium: the two conceptions of Tableau Economique. Eur J Hist Econ Thought 3:1–20

Higgs H (1968) The physiocrats. Kelley, New York

Hoselitz B (1968) Agrarian capitalism, the natural order of things: François Quesnay. Kyklos 21:637–664

Kuczynski M, Meek RL (1972) Quesnay's *Tableau Economique*. MacMillan, London

François Quesnay et la Physiocratie (1958) Institut National D'études Démographiques (INED), Paris

Lluch E (ed) (1984) Máximas generales de François Quesnay. (Traducidas por Manuel Belgrano). ICH, Madrid

Lluch E, Argemí LL (1994) Physiocracy in Spain. Hist Polit Econ 26:613–627

Longhitano G (1994) Quesnay et les colbertistes: deux modèles de societé en conflit, paper presented at the Colloque François Quesnay, Versailles

Lowry ST (ed) (1987) Pre-classical economic thought. Kluwer, Boston

Lundberg IC (1964) Turgot's unknown translator. Martinus Nijhoff, The Hague

Maital S (1972) The Tableau Economique as a simple Leontiev model: an amendment. Q J Econ 86:504–507

Marx K (1963) Theories of surplus value. Progress Publishers, Moscow

McNally D (1988) Political economy and the rise of capitalism: a reinterpretation. University of California Press, Berkeley

Meek RL (1962) The economics of Physiocracy. Allen & Unwin, London

Meek RL (1968) Ideas, events and environment: the case of the French Physiocrats. In: Eagly RV (ed) Events, ideology and economic theory. Wayne State Uinversity Press, Detroit, pp 44–58

Mercier de La Rivière PP (1910) L'ordre naturell et essentiel des societés Politiques. Geuthen, Paris

Mirabeau, Victor Riquetti, Marquis de (1756) L'Ami des Hommes. A Avignon

Mirabeau, Victor Riquetti, Marquis de (1764) Philosophie rurale. Libraires Associés, Amsterdam

Mulliez J (1975) Du blé, mal nécessaire. Revue d'Histoire Moderne et Contemporaine 3–47

Oncken A (1888) Oeuvres économiques et philosophiques de F. Quesnay. Baer, Paris

Patullo H (1774) Discurso sobre el mejoramiento de los terrenos, Madrid: Real Compaa de Impresores y Libreros del Reino

Perelman M (1984) Classical political economy. Rowman, London

Perrot JC (1992) Une histoire intellectulle de l'Economie Politique. Ecole des Hautes Etudes Sociales, Paris

Phillips A (1955) The Tableau Economique as a simple Leontiev model. Q J Econ 69:137–144

Pocock JGA (1975) The Machiavellan moment. Princeton University Press, Princeton, pp 13–14

Schumpeter J (1954) History of economic analysis. Oxford University Press, New York

Soboul A, Lemarchand G, Fogel M (1977) Le siècle des lumières. PUF, Paris

Steiner Ph (1998) La science nouvele de l'économie politique. PUF, Paris

Tribe K (1988) Governing the economy. Cambridge University Press, Cambridge

Tsuru T (1942) On reproduction schemes. In: Sweezy P (ed) The theory of capitalist development. Monthly Review Press, New York, pp 365–367

Vaggi G (1987) The economics of François Quesnay. MacMillan, London

Ware N (1931) The Physiocrats: a study in economic rationalization. Am Econ Rev 21:607–619

Weulersse G (1968) Le mouvement physiocratique en France (de 1756 a 1770). Mouton, Paris

Chapter 6
Adam Smith: Theory and Policy

Andrew S. Skinner

Introduction

Adam Smith was appointed to the Chair of Logic in Glasgow University in 1751. He was translated to the Chair of Moral Philosophy in 1752 and held this post until he retired from academic life in 1764. During this period Smith took an active part in the administration of the University and also taught extensively, even by modern standards. On Mondays to Fridays he lectured to the public or graduating class from 7.30 to 8.30 A.M. and met the same class again at 11 o'clock in order to "examine" the students on the topics of the first address. He also lectured on the "private" class at 12 noon, 3 days a week.

According to John Millar, Smith's most distinguished student and later professor of public law, Smith devoted the bulk of his time in the private class to the delivery of a system of Rhetoric and Belles Lettres which was probably based upon the materials he had worked up when giving a private course in Edinburgh between 1748 and 1751. These lectures were concerned with such topics as the origin of language, style and above all with analysis of a variety of forms of discourse; in effect a general theory of the way in which we communicate ideas, including scientific ideas.

Smith's teaching from the Chair of Moral Philosophy fell into four parts. Again on the authority of John Millar, it is known that he lectured on natural theology, ethics, jurisprudence and economics in that order and in a style that confirms his debt to his old teacher, Francis Hutcheson. Millar also made it clear that the lectures on ethics formed the basis of the Theory of Moral Sentiments (TMS) (1759) and that the subjects covered in the last part of the course were further to be developed in the Wealth of Nations (WN) (1776).

A.S. Skinner (✉)
Adam Smith Professor Emeritus in the University of Glasgow's
Department of Political Economy, Glen House, Cardross, Dunbartonshire G82 5ES, UK
e-mail: a.s.skinner@socsci.gla.ac.uk

J.G. Backhaus (ed.), *Handbook of the History of Economic Thought*,   161
The European Heritage in Economics and the Social Sciences,
DOI 10.1007/978-1-4419-8336-7_6, © Springer Science+Business Media, LLC 2012

Adam Smith had a very definite research programme in mind from an early date; a fact which was made clear in the concluding passages of the first edition of the TMS. The point was also repeated in the advertisement to the sixth and last edition of the work (1790) where Smith indicated that the TMS and WN were two parts of a plan which he hoped to complete by giving "an account of the general principles of law and government, and of different revolutions which they had undergone in the different ages and periods of society".

Sadly, Smith did not live to complete his plan partly at least as a result of his appointment, in 1778, as Commissioner of Customs. But posterity has been fortunate as a result of the discoveries made by Edwin Cannan (1895) and John Lothian (1958) which brought to light two versions of Smith's lectures on jurisprudence as they were delivered in the sessions 1762–1763 and 1763–1764.

The three parts of Smith's great plan are highly systematic; each discloses a debt to contemporary scientific work especially in the fields of biology and Newtonian physics; all are interdependent.

The TMS, which builds upon the analyses of Hutcheson and David Hume (Winch 1978), is primarily concerned with the way in which we form moral judgements. It was also designed to explain the emergence, by natural as distinct from artificial means, of those barriers that control our self-regarding and un-social passions. The argument gives prominence to the emergence of general rules of conduct, based upon experience, which include the rules of law. The analysis also confirms that accepted standards of behaviour are related to environment and that they may vary in different societies at the same point in time and in a given society over time; a thesis which owed much to the persuasive influence of Montesquieu.

The lectures on jurisprudence on the other hand help to explain the emergence of government and its changing structure in terms of an analysis which features the use of four distinct types of socio-economic environment the celebrated stages of hunting, pasture, agriculture and commerce.

The ethics and Smith's historical treatment of jurisprudence were also closely linked with the economic analysis that was to follow. If Smith gave prominence to the role of self-interest in this context, auditors of his lecture course and readers of the TMS would be aware that the basic drive to better our condition was subject to a constant process of moral scrutiny. It would also be appreciated that economic aspirations had a social reference in the sense that it is chiefly from a regard "to the sentiments of mankind, that we pursue riches and avoid poverty" (TMS i.iii.2.1). Later in the book, the position was further clarified when Smith noted that we tend to approve the means as well as the ends of ambition. "Hence … the eminent esteem with which all men naturally regard a steady perseverance in the practice of frugality, industry and application" (TMS IV.2.8).

The lectures on jurisprudence helped Smith to specify the nature of the system of positive law, which might be expected in the stage of commerce and also throws some light on the form of government that might conform to it.

Finally, the treatment of jurisprudence is important because it helps to explain the origins of the modern economy and the emergence of an institutional structure (Rosenberg 1960) where all goods and services command a price. It is in this context that "Every man … lives by exchanging, or becomes in some measure a merchant" (WN l.iv.1); a position which leads to Smith's famous judgement that:

It is not from the benevolence of the butcher, the brewer, or the baker, that we expect our dinner, but from their regard to their own interest. We address ourselves, not to their humanity but to their self-love, and never talk to them of our own necessities but of their advantages. Nobody but a beggar chooses to depend chiefly upon the benevolence of his fellow citizens. Even the beggar does not depend upon it entirely (WN, l.ii.2).

The Workings of the "Invisible Hand"

As far as the purely economic analysis is concerned, it is sufficient to our present purpose to be reminded that in the WN the theory of price and allocation was developed in terms of a model which made due allowance to distinct factors of production (land, labour, capital) and for the appropriate forms of return (rent, wages, profit). This point, now so obvious, struck Smith as novel and permitted him to develop an analysis of the allocative mechanism that ran in terms of inter-related adjustments in both factor and commodity markets. The resulting version of general interdependence also allowed Smith to move from the discussion of "micro" to that of "macro" economic issues, and to develop a model of the "circular flow" which relies heavily on a distinction between fixed and circulating capital.

But these terms, which were applied to the activities of individual undertakers, were transformed in their meaning by their application to society at large. Working in terms of period analysis where all magnitudes are dated, Smith in effect represented the working of the economic process as a series of activities and transactions which linked the main socio-economic groups (proprietors, capitalists and wage-labour) and productive sectors. In Smith's terms, current purchases in effect withdrew consumption and investment goods from the circulating capital of society; goods which were in turn replaced and income re-generated by virtue of productive activity in a given time period over a series of such periods.

We should note in this context that Smith was greatly influenced by a specific model of the economy which he came across during a visit to Paris in 1766. The model was designed to explain the operation of an economic system treated as an organic system. It was first produced by Francois Quesnay, a medical doctor, and later developed by A.R.J. Turgot, Minister of Finance under Louis XVI (Meek 1962, 1973). The significance of the analogy of the circulation of the blood would not be lost on Smith – and not would the link with William Harvey, a distinguished member of the medical school of Padua.

Looked at from one point of view, the analysis taken as a whole provides one of the most dramatic examples of the doctrine of "unintended social outcomes" or the working of the "invisible hand". The individual undertaker (entrepreneur), seeking the most efficient allocation of resources, contributes to overall economic efficiency; the merchant's reaction to price signals helps to ensure that the allocation of resources accurately reflects the structure of consumer preferences; and the drive to better our condition contributes to economic growth. Looked at from another perspective, the work can be seen to have resulted in a great conceptual system linking together logically separate, yet inter-related, problems such as price, allocation, distribution, macro-statistics and macro-dynamics.

If such a theory enabled Smith to isolate the causes of economic growth, with the emphasis now on the supply side, it was also informed throughout by what Terence Hutchison has described as the "powerfully fascinating idea and assumption of beneficent self-adjustment and self-equilibration" (Hutchinson 1988, p. 268).

The argument is also buttressed by a series of judgements as to probable patterns of behaviour and actual trends of events. It was Smith's firm opinion, for example, that in a situation where there was tolerable security, "the sole use of money is to circulate consumable goods. By means of it, provisions, materials, and finished work are bought and sold, and distributed to their proper consumers" (WN, 11.iii.23). In the same way he contended that savings generated during any (annual) period would always be matched by investment (WN, 11.iii.18); a key assumption of the classical system which was to follow. In the case of Great Britain, Smith also pointed out that real wages had progressively increased during the eighteenth century, and that high wages were to be approved of as a contribution to productivity (WN, 1.vii.44). The tone is buoyant with regard to economic growth and this was duly reflected in the policy stance which Smith was to adopt.

Smith's prescription with regard to economic policy followed the direction of analysis just considered. He called on governments to minimise their "impertinent" obstructions to the pursuit of individuals. In particular, he recommended that the statutes of apprenticeship and the privileges of corporations should be repealed on the grounds that they adversely affect the working of the allocative mechanism. In the same chapter Smith pointed to the barriers of the deployment of labour generated by the Poor Laws and the Laws of Settlement (cf. WN, I.x.c;IV.ii 42). But there is also a moral dimension to the argument in the sense that all of the regulations so far reviewed constitute violations of natural liberty.

Smith objected to positions of privilege, such as monopoly powers, which he regarded as creatures of the civil law. The institution was again represented as impolitic and unjust; unjust in that a position of monopoly is a position of unfair advantage, and impolitic in that the prices of the goods so controlled are "upon every occasion the highest which can be got" (WN, 1.vii.27).

In this context we may usefully distinguish Smith's objection to monopoly in general from his criticism of one manifestation of it namely, the mercantile system, described as the "modern system" of policy, best understood, "in our own country and in our own times" (WN, IV.2). The system is represented as a coherent whole; as a set of policies based on regulation and therefore liable to that "general objection which may be made to all the different expedients of the mercantile system; the objection of forcing some part of the industry of the country into a channel less advantageous than that in which it would run of its own accord" (WN, V.v.a.24).

Professor Winch summarised Smith's advice to the Legislator (cf. Haakonssen 1981) in these terms:

> The system of natural liberty, should it ever come into existence, will produce a fairer distribution of income and fewer injustices in the form of infringements of natural liberties or rights such as those affecting choice of occupation, place of residence, and modes of employing capital and other types of property (1983, p. 529).

Functions of Government

Smith's view of the government, or rather the functions of government, was positive in other ways. Most obviously, he recognised that the state had an obligation to provide for defence since in the last analysis security is always more important than opulence. He also recognised the need to provide an adequate system of justice, both as a pre-condition of social order and as a basic pre-requisite for economic growth. Both of these essential services were designed to secure a stable environment – and so too were a number of economic policies.

In fact Smith was prepared to justify a wide range of policies, all of which have been carefully catalogued by Jacob Viner in his justifiably famous article on Adam Smith and Laisser-Faire Viner (1927). For example, he was prepared to justify the use of stamps on plate and linen as the most effectual guarantee of quality (WN, l.x.c.13), the compulsory regulation of mortgages (WN, V.ii.h.17), the legal enforcement of contracts (WN, l.ix.16) and government control of the coinage. In addition he defended the granting of temporary monopolies to mercantile groups on particular occasions, to the inventors of new machines and, not surprisingly, to the authors of new books (WN, V.i.e.30).

But four broad areas of intervention are of particular interest, in the sense that they involve issues of general principle. First, Smith advised governments that they were faced with taxes imposed by their competitors in trade retaliation could be in order especially such an action had the effect of ensuring the "repeal of the high duties or prohibitions complained of" (cf. Winch 1983, p. 509). Second, Smith advocated the use of taxation, not simply as a means of raising revenue, but as means of controlling certain activities, and of compensating for what would now be known as a detective telescopic faculty, i.e. a failure to perceive our long-run interest (cf. WN, V.ii.x.4; V.ii.k.50; V.ii.g.12).

Smith was also well aware, to take a third point, that the modern version of the "circular flow" depended on paper money and on credit (Zallio, 1990); in effect a system of "dual circulation" involving a complex of transactions linking producers and merchants, dealers and consumers (WN, 11.ii.88); transactions that would involve cash (at the level of household and credit) (at the level of the firm). It is in this context that Smith advocated control over the rate of interest, set in such a way as to ensure that "sober people are universally preferred, as borrowers, to prodigals and projectors" (WN, II.iv.15). He was also willing to regulate the small note issue in the interests of a stable banking system. To those who objected to this proposal, he replied that the interests of the community required it, and concluded that "the obligation of building party walls, in order to prevent the communication of fire, is a violation of natural liberty, exactly of the same kind with the regulations of the banking trade which are here proposed" (WN, 11.ii.94).

Although Smith's monetary analysis is not regarded as among the strongest of his contributions, it should be remembered that the witness of the collapse of the major banks in the 1770s was acutely aware of the problems generated by a sophisticated credit structure. It was in this context that Smith articulated a very general principle, namely, that "those exertions of the natural liberty of a few individuals, which might endanger the security of the whole society, are, and ought to be, restrained by the laws of all governments, of the most tree, as well as of the most despotical" (WN, il.ii.94).

Emphasis should be given finally to Smith's contention that a major responsibility of government must be the provision of certain public works and institutions for facilitating the commerce of the society which were "of such a nature, that the profit could never repay the expense to any individual or small number of individuals, and which it, therefore, cannot be expected that any individual or small number of individuals should erect or maintain" (WN, V.i.c.1). In short, he was concerned to point out that the state would have to organise services or public works, which the profits motive alone could not guarantee.

The examples of public works which Smith provided include such items as roads, bridges, canals and harbours – all thoroughly in keeping with the conditions of the time and with Smith's emphasis on the importance of transport as a contribution to the effective operation of the market and the process of economic growth. But although the list is short by modern standards, the discussion of what may be called the "principles of provision" is of interest for the emphasis which is given to situations where market forces alone will not generate services or facilities which are necessary to the economic well-being of the whole.

The theme is continued in Smith's treatment of another important service, namely education; a subject which was developed in the course of Smith's discussion of the social and psychological costs of economic growth; costs which he attributed to the division of labour. There are three applications. First, Smith suggested that economic development could lead to a decline in martial spirit; a problem which he likened to leprosy or any other loathsome disease – moving Jacob Viner to add public health to Smith's list of governmental functions (Viner 1927; Wood 1984, i. 162). In this connection Smith advocated a kind of military education akin perhaps to that of the territorial but not inconsistent with National Service.

Second, he drew attention to the problem of the relatively poor who lack the leisure, means and inclination to provide education for their children (WN, V.i.f.53). Smith's programme is limited but he did advocate the setting up of local schools of the Scottish model and suggest that the poor could be taught "the most essential parts of education ... to read, write and account" together with the "elementary parts of geometry and mechanics" (WN, V.i.f.54, 55). Smith was prepared to go so far as to infringe the natural liberty of the subject, where this is narrowly defined, in recommending that the "public can impose almost the whole body of the people the necessity of acquiring those most essential parts of education by obliging every man to undergo an examination or probation in them before he can obtain the freedom in any corporation, or be allowed to set up any trade either in a village or a town corporate" (WN, V.i.f.57).

Finally, Smith advocated training in the higher sciences, such as were taught in the universities and went so far as to suggest that government should act "by instituting some sort of probation even in the higher and more difficult sciences, to be undergone by every person before he was permitted to exercise any liberal profession, or before he could be received as a candidate for any honourable office or trust of profit" (WN, V.i.g.14). It will be noted that Smith did not regard education as a matter of choice but of compulsion.

Adam Smith on Equitable and Efficient Government

Smith not only identified the various services which the state was expected to provide but also gave a great deal of attention to the forms of organisation which would be needed to ensure and to induce efficient delivery thus returning the reader to the role of self-interest. For example, in the case of justice, treated as a public service, Smith contended that effective provision of so central a service depended crucially on a clear separation of the judicial from the executive power (WN, V.i.b.23).

But as Alan Peacock (1975) has pointed out, Smith's efficiency criteria are distinguished from this basic issue of organisation, the argument being, in effect, that the services provided by attorneys, clerks or judges should be paid for in such a way as to encourage productivity. Smith also ascribed the "present admirable constitution of the courts of justice in England" to the use of a system of court fees which had served to encourage competition between the courts of King's bench chancery, and exchequer (WN, V.i.b.20, 21). A further interesting and typical feature of the discussion is found in Smith's argument that although justice is a service to the whole community, nonetheless, the costs of handling specific causes should be borne by those who give occasion to, or benefit from them. He therefore concluded that the "expense of the administration of justice … may very properly be defrayed by the particular contribution of one or other, or both of those two different sets of persons, according as different occasions may require, that is, by fees of court" (WN, V.i.i.2), rather than by a charge on general funds.

The theme was continued in the discussion of public works where Smith suggested that the main problems to be addressed were those of equity and efficiency.

With regard to equity, Smith argued that public works such as highways, bridges and canals should be paid for by those who use them in proportion to the wear and tear occasioned. At the same time, he argued that the consumer who pays the charges generally gains more from the cheapness of carriage than he loses in the charges incurred (WN, V.i.d.4).

Smith also defended the principle of direct payment on the grounds of efficiency. Only by this means, he argued, would it be possible to ensure that services are provided where there is a recognisable need; only in this way would it be possible to avoid building roads through a desert for the sake of some private interest; or a great bridge "thrown over a river at a place where nobody passes, or merely to embellish the view from the windows of a neighbouring palace; things which sometimes happen, in countries where works of this kind are carried on by any other revenue than that which they themselves are capable of affording" (WN, Vi.d.i.6).

Smith also tirelessly emphasised the point, already noticed in the discussion of justice, namely, that in every trade and profession "the exertion of the greater part of those who exercise it, is always in proportion to the necessity they are under of making that exertion" (WN, V.i.f.4). On this ground, for example, he approved of the expedient used in France, whereby a construction engineer was made a present of tolls on a canal for which he had been responsible, thus ensuring that it was in his interest to keep the canal in good repair.

The "incentive" argument is eloquently developed in Smith's treatment of universities where he argued, notably in correspondence with William Cullen, an old friend and colleague, that degrees can be likened to the statutes of apprenticeship (Corr, 177) which offered no guarantee of quality, and protested against the idea of universities having a monopoly of higher education (Corr, 174) on the ground that this would inhibit private teachers, notably of medicine.

In particular Smith objected to a situation where professors enjoyed a stable and high income irrespective of competence or industry (WN, V.i.f.7): the Oxford, rather than the Glasgow model. In the same context, he argued in favour of free movement of students between teachers and institutions (WN, V.i.f.12, 13) as a means of inducing teachers to provide appropriate services. Smith concluded:

> The expense of the institutions for education and religious instruction is ... beneficial to the whole society, and may, therefore, without injustice, be defrayed by the general contribution of the whole society. This expense however, might perhaps with equal propriety, and even with some advantage, be defrayed altogether by those who receive the immediate benefit of such education and instruction, or by the voluntary contribution of those who think they have occasion for either the one of the other (WN, V.i.i.5).

While the modern reader has to make a considerable effort to understand Smith's intentions, students of his course in Glasgow and perhaps contemporary readers of his work would quite readily perceive that the different parts were important of themselves and also that they display a certain pattern of inter-dependence. As we have seen, the ethical argument indicates the manner in which general rules of conduct emerge, and postulates the need for a system of force-backed law, appropriately administered if social order is to be possible. The treatment of jurisprudence showed the manner in which government emerged and developed through time, and threw some light on the actual content of rules of behaviour, which are likely to prevail in the four different socio-economic states.

It would also be evident to Smith's students that the treatment of economics was based upon psychological judgements (such as the desire for status) which are only explained in the ethics, and that this branch of Smith's argument takes as given that particular socio-economic structure which is appropriate to the fourth economic stage, that of commerce. The lesson that he taught was that economic phenomena should not be seen in isolation.

Conclusion

The modern reader too will find much instruction in Smith's work, especially if the separate parts are seen, as Smith intended they should be seen, as making the parts a greater whole; an achievement which invites us to consider that economics, ethics and jurisprudence should be seen as the essential components of a system of social science.

There are further dimensions of Smith's thought which are also of continuing relevance and which reflect aspects of his teaching in jurisprudence and ethics, seen now from a different perspective.

It will be recalled that for Smith the fourth economic stage could be seen to be associated with a particular form of social and political structure which influences the outline of government and the context within which it must function.

Smith drew attention in this connection to the fact that modern government of the British type was a complex instrument; that politics was a competitive game with as its object the attainment of "the great prizes which sometimes come from the wheel of the great state lottery of British politics" (WN, IV, vii, c, 75). Smith added in a passage that reflects the psychological assumptions of the TMS (I, iii.2, "Of the origin of Ambition") that:

> Men desire to have some share in the management of public affairs chiefly on account of the importance which it gives them (WN, IV.vii.c.74).

This point leads on to another which was emphasised by Smith, namely that the same economic forces which had served to elevate the House of Commons to a superior degree of influence had also served to make it an important focal point for sectional interests – a development which could seriously affect the legislation which was passed and thus affect that extensive view of the common good which ought ideally to direct the activities of Parliament in fulfilling the functions of government outlined above.

If Smith was alive to the dangers of collective interests he also commented upon the "insolence of office" and warned against the man of system who "is apt to be very wise in his own conceit" and who "seems to imagine that he can arrange the different members of a great society with as much ease as the hand arranges the different pieces upon a chess board" (TMS, IV, ii.2.17).

At the same time, Smith noted that governments on the English model were likely to be particularly sensitive to public opinion – and as frequently constrained by it. Smith made much of the point and in a variety of ways. He noted, for example, that even if the British Government of the 1770s had thought it possible voluntarily to withdraw from the current conflict with America, it could not pursue this eminently rational course for fear of public discredit (Corr, 383).

Smith also gave a great deal of attention to the general problems presented by the confirmed habits and prejudices of a people and to the need to adjust legislation accordingly. For example, he likened the fear of engrossing and forestalling in discussing the corn trade "to the popular terrors and suspicions of witchcraft" (WN, IV.v.b.26), and described the law dealing with the exportation of wheat as one which "thought not the best in itself, is the best which the interests, prejudices, and temper of the Times would admit of" (WN, IV.v.b.53). The reference to the Wisdom of Solon in the context of the previous discussion finds an echo in the Moral Sentiments (VI.ii.2, 16).

We are reminded that governments as well as markets may have failings (cf. West 1976); failings which may reflect imperfect knowledge, and the problem of structure as well as the role of public opinion – ironically, one of the most important pillars of political freedom.

Smith recognised the point that in the modern state it is critically important that the citizen be vigilant, informed, above all else educated, in the broad sense of that term, if an adequate standard of moral and political behaviour is to be sustained. Or, as he put it:

> An instructed and intelligent people … are always more decent and orderly than an ignorant and stupid one. They feel themselves, each individually, more respectable, and more likely to obtain the respect of their lawful superiors. They are more disposed to examine, and more capable of seeing thought, the interested complaints of faction and sedition … in tree countries, where the safety of government depends very much on the favourable judgement which the people may form of its conduct, it must surely be of the highest importance that they should not be disposed to judge rashly or capriciously concerning it (WN, V.i.t.61).

The reference to the role of government reminds us that Smith regarded the study of political economy, in the old sense of that term, as a "branch of the science of a statesman or legislator;" of the contrast which he drew between the statesman and that "insidious and crafty animal" vulgarly called the politician and of his conviction that it was the duty of philosophers such as himself to encourage "the development of the public spirited attitudes of the legislator" (Winch 1983, p. 503). Professor Winch concluded that "the strategy of persuasion that lies behind the WN … provides the basis of Smith's case for bringing science to bear on the conduct of legislators" (op cit, p. 503; cf. Haakonssen 1981) and makes the point that "much of Smith's advice … depends on considerations that do not flow from economic reasoning alone" (op cit, p. 502).

"The argumentation of this chapter is drawn from A System of Social Science (OUP, 2nd ed., 1996)".

Works of Adam Smith

EPS   Essays on Philosophical Subjects, general editors D.D. Raphael and A.S. Skinner (OUP, 1980)
Corr   Correspondence, ed. E.C. Mossner and I.S. Ross (OUP, 1977)
TMS   The Theory of Moral Sentiments, ed. D.D. Raphael and A.L. Macfie (OUP, 1976)
LRBL   Lectures on Rhetoric and Belles Lettres, ed. J.C. Bryce (OUP, 1983)
WN   Wealth of Nations, ed. R.H. Campbell, A.S. Skinner and W.B. Todd (OUP, 1976)
Stewart   Dugald Stewart, Account of the Life and Writings of Adam Smith, included in EPS

References

Haakonssen K (1981) The Science of a Legislator: The Natural Jurisprudence of David Hume and Adam Smith. Cambridge: Cambridge University Press
Hutchinson T (1988) Before Adam Smith: the emergence of political economy, 1662–1776. Blackwell, Oxford

Meek RL (1962) The economics of physiocracy. Allen and Unwin, London
Meek RL (1973) Turgot on progress, sociology and economics. OUP, New York
Peacock AT (1975) The treatment of the principles of public finance in the wealth of nations. In: Skinner AS, Wilson T (eds) Essays on Adam Smith. OUP, Oxford
Rosenberg N (1960) Some institutional aspects of the wealth of nations. JPE iii:105–120, reprinted in Wood, 1984
Viner J (1927) Adam Smith and Laisser-Faire. JPE i:143–167, 35; reprinted in Wood JC (1984)
West EG (1976) Adam Smith's economics of politics. Hist Polit Econ 8(4):515– 539
Winch D (1978) Adam Smith's politics. OUP, Oxford
Winch D (1983) Science and the legislator. Econ J 93:501–529
Wood JC (1984) Adam Smith: critical assessments. Beckenham: Croom Helm
Zallio F (1990) Adam Smith's dual circulation framework. Royal Bank of Scotland Review 166

Chapter 7
Life and Work of David Ricardo (1772–1823)

Arnold Heertje

David Ricardo was born on April 18th, 1772 in London as the third child of Abraham Ricardo and Abigail Delvalle. Abraham lived until 1812, having been born in Amsterdam on March 11th, 1734. Abraham Ricardo was a stockbroker, just like his father Joseph Israel Ricardo (1699–1762). In the Spring of 1760, Abraham went to London as an agent for his father, and married there on April 30th, 1769. He was elected "Parnas", or warden, of the Portuguese Jewish Community of London in 1785, 1789, 1793, 1798 and 1802, and was also a very successful stockbroker for this Community. David Ricardo's grandfather, Joseph Israel Ricardo, had died in 1762 and was buried in Ouderkerk, the famous cemetery of the Portuguese Jewish Community, near Amsterdam. In 1721, he had married Hanna Abaz, a Christian lady who converted to Judaism (a "Gijoret"). In the municipal archives of Amsterdam, the father of Joseph Israel Ricardo is referred to as David Israel of Livorno. His brothers did not use the name Ricardo either, but just the name Israel, mostly "of Livorno". Often the profession of "coral maker" is mentioned in the archives, but perhaps coral trader is meant. It seems probable that the Ricardos had left Spain for Livorno around 1650.

When arriving in Amsterdam, the Ricardos became active members of the Portuguese Jewish Community. Abraham and most of his family gave financial support to the Talmud Tora and Ets Haim (Jewish religious educational establishments). But the Ricardos were not based entirely in Amsterdam. Apart from the Hague and London, they went to North and South America and Curaçao. For example, the son of David Hizkiau Ricardo (Abraham's brother) Mordechay Ricardo (1771–1842) went to Curaçao. There he became the protector of Simon Bolivar. Abraham's niece Rebecca was the mother of Isaac Da Costa, the Dutch poet (1798–1860).

Little is known about David Ricardo's youth. In 1824, *A Memoir of David Ricardo* appeared anonymously, in which it was said that his father wanted him to

A. Heertje (✉)
Em. Professor of Economics, University of Amsterdam,
Laegieskampweg 17 1412, ER Naarden, The Netherlands
e-mail: joab@heertje.nl

J.G. Backhaus (ed.), *Handbook of the History of Economic Thought*,
The European Heritage in Economics and the Social Sciences,
DOI 10.1007/978-1-4419-8336-7_7, © Springer Science+Business Media, LLC 2012

go into business, in particular in the stock exchange. We now know that this Memoir was written by his brother Moses. In it we learn that, to this end, Abraham sent his son David to Amsterdam from 1783 till 1785, where he stayed in the house of the widow of his uncle David Israel Ricardo Jr, where also his uncle Moses Israel Ricardo (1738-1800), registered as a Jewish trader, lived on the Nieuwe Keizersgracht (Heertje 2004, 2005). I assume that there he received general private lessons. After his return to London, he followed a normal school education "…till his father took him into business" (Memoir, Sraffa, VIII, page 3). From his 14th year, he helped his father on the stock exchange.

In a letter to her mother, dated November 14th, 1821, Maria Edgeworth wrote that Ricardo told her: "We were 15 children. My father gave me but little education. He thought reading, writing and arithmetic sufficient because he doomed me to be nothing but a man of business. He sent me at eleven to Amsterdam to learn Dutch, French, Spanish but I was so unhappy at being separated from my brothers and sisters and family that I learned nothing in 2 years but Dutch which I could not help learning" (Colvin 1971, page 266). Sraffa suggests that Ricardo was sent to the religious school of the Portuguese Jewish Community in Amsterdam, the Talmud Tora (Sraffa, X, page 210). However, I have come to the conclusion that this is not true. I did not find Ricardo's name in the list of pupils of the Talmud Tora. Moses, in his Memoir, does not refer to the Talmud Tora, and Ricardo did not mention to Maria Edgeworth that he had ever received a religious education. That his stay in Holland during 1783–1785 made a big impression on him follows from a letter written from Amsterdam to his eldest son Osman in 1822. "Although I had not been in this town for more than 30 years I had no difficulty in finding my way, alone, about those places which had formerly been familiar to me" (Sraffa 1955, page 208). This letter is part of a set of letters written to describe his tour on the continent with his wife and two daughters. His personal visits to Amsterdam in 1822 concern Portuguese Jews.

On December 20th, 1793, David Ricardo married Priscilla Ann Wilkinson, an English Quaker. This marriage led to a breach with his father and mother and the rest of his family. He left his father's firm and with the help of friends he established himself as stockbroker in the City of London. Within the space of only a few years, he managed to be far richer than his father. His prestige on the stock exchange was high. Around 1819, he retired from the financial world in London to live at his country house Gatcombe Park in Minchinhampton, which he acquired in 1814, and is now the house of Princess Anne.

From an intellectual point of view, Ricardo was in a certain sense a late flowering individual, although already in his youth he showed "a taste for abstract and general reasoning" (Sraffa 1955, page 4). He had no systematic education, and his natural gifts blossomed only after his financial activities and success. From his 25th year onwards, Ricardo's financial success enabled him to study mathematics, chemistry, geology and mineralogy. In 1808 he became a member of the Geological Society (Sraffa 1955, page 49). His inclination for the exact sciences changed direction when, almost by accident, he came across a copy of the *Wealth of Nations* in 1799 (McCulloch 1846, page XVII). As a result he then fell in love with economics, although it took another 10 years before he wrote, anonymously in the *Morning Chronicle,* an article on the "Price of Gold" (Sraffa 1955, page 30) which provoked many reactions. After this first article, he wrote several pamphlets, and eventually his magnum opus in 1817, *"On the Principles of Political Economy, and Taxation"* Ricardo 1817. In 1814, James Mill (1773–1836), father of the famous John Stuart Mill (1806–1873), had not only more or less forced Ricardo to begin writing his *Principles* but also urged him to take up a seat in Parliament (Sraffa 1955, page 138). At first, Ricardo was not inclined to act on either of Mill's suggestions on account of his innate modesty and apparent lack of eloquence, both orally and in writing. Nevertheless, in the Spring of 1819, Ricardo did become a Member of the House of Commons where he remained until his death in 1823. Once there, he aligned with neither the Whigs nor the Tories. Later, he was described as a "moderate oppositionist" and as somebody who "voted on the side of the people" (Sraffa 1955, page XIX). Ricardo made several speeches in Parliament, in particular on economic topics. Again and again, Ricardo defended the interests of the poor and in doing so revealed his social concerns.

His publications in the years 1809–1815 mainly dealt with monetary and financial topics. In these writings, Ricardo reacted to the problems of the day, and made use of his experience as a man of financial business. But, even in these contributions, he showed a high degree of independent thinking and originality. An interesting illustration of this was his proposal to substitute the gold standard for a gold bullion standard, which saves gold in relation to the quantity of bank notes. In his more theoretical publications after 1815, his sense for abstract reasoning and deduction came to the fore.

His book of 1817 illustrates the deductive method. The use of the word "suppose" is characteristic. Although Ricardo did not make use of mathematics himself, in a certain sense he laid down the foundations of the modern approach in economics, in particular the introduction of models in economic analysis. In Ricardo's hands economics is less a subject with absolute statements and becomes more relativistic. With a change in assumptions, the conclusions also change.

In our time economics has developed into a set of axiomatic systems. It is interesting to note that Ricardo was reproached for his use of the deductive method, which was criticized as being apractical and asocial. Both reproaches are unfounded and can be ascribed to an insufficient understanding of the axiomatic approach to study social relationships. Ricardo's method has the advantage of bringing into the open his assumptions and of making explicit the relationship between starting points and conclusions. This is the basis for the continuing improvement of the theory. Schumpeter referred to the habit of applying results of pure theory to the solution of practical problems as the *Ricardian Vice* (Schumpeter 1954, page 473). Moreover, his speeches in Parliament and his social behaviour only reflect his deep concern for the weak and the poor. His coolness as a theorist must be distinguished from his warmth as a person. His conclusion that wages will just cover the cost of living springs from his analysis of a decentralized economy in which the economic role of the state is modest. It does not imply that he considered the level of wages ideal.

This brings us to a very important aspect of Ricardo's position in economics. The fact is that the interpretation of his work is still under debate. On the one hand, we recognize the Sraffian, and on the other hand, the neo-classical interpretation of Ricardo. According to the neo-classical interpretation, Ricardo belongs to the

Classical School of Adam Smith, Thomas Robert Malthus and John Stuart Mill. As such, he is part of the harmony model in economics. In this model everybody aims at the maximization of individual welfare as consumer and producer, which leads to the best of all possible worlds. In modern economic theory, this is structured in terms of general equilibrium and Pareto-optimality. Political liberalism is based on it, and Ricardo was a liberal. He was neither dogmatic nor intolerant, knew how to separate personal feelings from business and preferred individual freedom to collective governance. He was a defender of free trade and in favour of small government (Hollander 1979, 1995).

At the same time, Ricardo's work opens the possibility to regard him as a forerunner of Marx, the founder of the conflict model in economics, i.e. the conflict between the proletariat and the capitalists. The following arguments play a role in this respect. In the hands of Karl Marx, Ricardo's labour theory of value became an absolute doctrine. Ricardo restricted his analysis of prices to the case of reproducible goods. Marx exploited this theory to make labour the source of value.

Ricardo also prepared the way for Karl Marx in another respect. While in the 1817 and 1819 editions of his *Principles*, Ricardo did not expect serious consequences, for the labourers of introducing machinery, he changed his mind on this issue in the third edition of this book in 1821. He added a new chapter "On Machinery", in which he explained that labourers may suffer from the introduction of machinery. Later, Marx quoted with approval Ricardo's famous phrase: "Machinery and labour are in constant competition" (Sraffa 1955, page 395). The essence of this is that technical change may cause a conflict between the proletariat and the capitalists. On the one hand the introduction of machinery raises the level of consumer goods, on the other hand its labour-saving character raises the level of unemployment. Again, in Marx's hands, a more or less incidental observation by Ricardo became the corner stone of his theory on the breakdown of capitalism (Cozzi and Marchionatti 2001).

Let me add a further note on Ricardo's distinction between reproducible and non-reproducible goods. Natural prices have to be distinguished from market prices in Ricardo's theory. Market prices are a short-run phenomenon. They are a result of demand and supply. The Sraffians put all the emphasis on Ricardo's long-run price theory. The neo-classical economists neglect the long-run approach in Ricardo, and refer to market prices and the market mechanism in Ricardo. As a member of the Classical School, Ricardo adhered to the notion of a one-way avenue of production to consumption. But, as a Sraffian, he would look at the economic process as a cyclical process, based on reproduction. He would be at ease with the title of Sraffa's book (Sraffa 1960): *Production of Commodities by Means of Commodities*. And even more so, Ricardo, Marx and Sraffa would be in full agreement.

While Ricardo put aside the case of non-reproducible goods, like paintings and historical monuments, as they are the exception rather than the rule, in our days these goods are becoming more and more relevant. From the point of view of price theory, there is still the problem of Ricardo's days. Nothing more can be said about such goods than what Ricardo himself already asserted in 1817 (Sraffa 1955, page 12), i.e. their value "varies with the varying wealth and inclinations of those who are desirous to possess them". In my view the distinction between reproducible and non-reproducible goods is a lasting contribution by David Ricardo to economic theory. The analysis of this distinction and its consequences for value and price theory is a challenge for present-day economic theory.

References

Colvin C (ed) (1971) Maria Edgeworth, Letters from England 1813–1844. Clarendon Press, Oxford

Cozzi T, Marchionatti R (eds) (2001) Piero Sraffa's political economy. Routledge, London

Heertje A (2004) The Dutch and Portuguese-Jewish background of David Rcardo, The European Journal of the History of Economic Thought, p. 281–294

Heertje A (2005) The Dutch and Portuguese-Jewish background of David Rcardo, The European Journal of the History of Economic Thought, p. 183

Hollander S (1979) The economics of David Ricardo. University of Toronto Press, London

Hollander S (1995) Ricardo – the new view, collected essays I. Routledge, London

McCulloch JR (ed) (1846) The works of David Ricardo, Esq-MP. John Murray, London

Ricardo D (1817) On the principles of political economy, and taxation. John Murray, London

Schumpeter JA (1954) History of economic analysis. Oxford University Press, New York

Sraffa P (ed) (1955) The works and correspondence of David Ricardo, I-XI. University Press, Cambridge

Sraffa P (1960) Production of commodities by means of commodities, prelude to a critique of economic theory. Cambridge University Press, Cambridge

Chapter 8
John Stuart Mill's Road to Leviathan: Early Life and Influences

Michael R. Montgomery

John Stuart Mill (1806–1873) was, during the middle third of the nineteenth century, the world's leading economist and also arguably the world's leading intellectual. Mill's collected works are massive, spanning not only economics but also philosophy, political science, psychology, and the entire range of social science (e.g. his *The Subjection of Women* is a founding feminist tract). Among major economists, only Adam Smith could conceivably be ranked with Mill in breadth of focus and power to integrate different fields of study into a powerful argument (David Hume conceivably outranks Mill in overall contribution to social science, but Hume is not usually considered to be a major economist).

The key to understanding Mill is that he is the only leading economist in the history of economics to explicitly advocate the principle of the subordination of economics to broader social science. To him, "economic truths," while of great importance, were trumped for policy purposes by societal context.[1] Despite Mill's deep respect for the internal logic of political economy and his insistence on its profound practical significance, no one did more than he to denigrate the notion that classical political economy was a suitable guide to social policy when unaided by the insights of broader social science (see, in particular, Bk. II, Chap. 4, of

---

[1] Wesley Mitchell writes that "[s]ocial philosophy is the larger, the controlling element in Mill's mind" (Mitchell 1967, 562). For example, the "iron laws" of Malthusian population theory were valid only on the assumption of an ignorant and culturally-bereft working class. By educating the masses, Mill thought, populations could be taught culture and self-discipline, controlling the sexual urge and defeating Malthusian "law." Further, Mill routinely rejected the materialism underlying economics as a basis for the broader social sciences, writing that "I regard any considerable increase in human happiness, through mere changes in outward circumstances, as hopeless…" (Mill 1969 [1833], 15).

M.R. Montgomery (✉)
School of Economics, University of Maine, 5774 Stevens Hall, Orono, ME 04469, USA
e-mail: Michael.montgomery@umit.maine.edu

J.G. Backhaus (ed.), *Handbook of the History of Economic Thought*,
The European Heritage in Economics and the Social Sciences,
DOI 10.1007/978-1-4419-8336-7_8, © Springer Science+Business Media, LLC 2012

Mill 1929 [1871], or of Mill 1965 [1871]), henceforth to be referenced as "*Principles*").[2] Accordingly, Mill often receives high praise from those who decry "economic imperialism" in social science, particularly with respect to public policy decisions. Mainstream historians of economic thought, by contrast, are more inclined to emphasize what they see as his relatively thin contributions to the development of technical economics (though it is widely acknowledged that he made important contributions).

While the scope and significance of Mill's technical additions to economic theory are still debated, few would deny that Mill's deepest influence falls in the areas of "heterodoxy" – the interplay between economics and broader social science. His *Principles of Political Economy*, while primarily a masterful summary of the field, was also shockingly heterodox (for its day) at numerous junctures. Whether for good or for ill, there is no doubt that Mill's text was one of the most influential books of the last two centuries. It was the supremely dominant introduction to economics from 1848 through the publication of Marshall's text in 1890, and Mill still was being widely-read during the Twentieth-Century's first decades. From 1848 through at least 1890, then, it is safe to say that most, if not nearly-all, English-speaking economists and policy-makers got their start in political economy through a thorough perusal of Mill's influential volume.

Mill exerted a powerful influence on progressive economists such as Richard T. Ely (founder of the American Economic Association) who were aggressively seeking rationales to expand the role of government power in economic affairs. In the last two books of the *Principles*, but especially in Book V, Mill argued passionately (if unknowingly) for just such an expansion of government authority in the economy – one that, while considered radical then, is mainstream today. This and the next article will argue that Mill's primary contribution to economics lies here, in his [historically] persuasive arguments favouring government-initiated nostrums for a wide range of perceived free-market failings.

Mill's remarkable reputation as an advocate for *laissez faire* was achieved through his many statements (in his *Principles*, in his *On Liberty*, and in many other sources) explaining and lauding free-market forces and individual freedom. To many, then, it comes as a bit of a shock to learn that Mill's overall verdict on free-market capitalism was far from enthusiastic (though there is some evidence that in his last years he was returning to a more pro-capitalistic viewpoint [see Mill 1967 [1879], 703–56]). In fact, Mill was among the first of the major figures who, while fully recognizing the numerous virtues in free-market forces, ultimately held that market forces also beget unacceptable drawbacks that, to be resolved, had to be addressed by government fiat. He was, accordingly, arguably a founder of the "Progressive" movement (he uses the term in a modern sense several times in

---

[2] The primary reference copy of the *Principles* consulted in this paper is Mill (1929 [1871]), the famous Ashley/Longmans edition providing complete information on Mill's revisions of the *Principles* as Mill took it through its various editions. For the reader's convenience, page numbers for the more accessible *Collected Works* edition are also provided (page references are first provided for the Ashley/Longmans edition, then for the *Collected Works* edition.

his *Autobiography*)[3] that swept the West in the late nineteenth and early twentieth centuries (and which is currently enjoying, at least in the U.S., an early-twenty-first century resurgence as well). A mixed economy in which the virtues of free-market capitalism would be tempered and guided by the enlightened hand of government authority is, therefore, the *logical* implication of Mill's system.

This article will argue that Mill himself failed to see the profoundly interventionist consequences of many of his "mildly interventionist" arguments. While Mill himself thought of such government intervention as exceptional – needed in relatively few and concrete instances – his arguments in Book V of the *Principles* are nothing less than an open-ended invitation for the government to assume a prominent, even dominant, role in the economy. In making his case (chiefly in Book V of the *Principles* and in *On Liberty*), Mill repeatedly displays a remarkable comfortableness with a type of government authority over economic affairs that Adam Smith likely thought he had dispelled once and for all in the *Wealth of Nations*. The government bureaucrat assumed in Book V of the *Principles* is honest, trustworthy, enlightened, and completely focussed on enhancing the general good of society – and Mill's great prestige as a free-market thinker gave others leave to think of government in this same way. That Mill had elsewhere shown a healthy skepticism of the government, government officials, and their typical motives did not appear to affect in the least his argument for greater government in the *Principles* and in *On Liberty*.

It is part of the mystery of Mill that ideas he emphasized in some parts of his work are not fully carried through in other parts where those ideas are clearly of vital importance. That essential contradiction, sometimes characterized as a "two Mills" hypothesis (e.g. Berns 1975), is substantially (but not fully) reconcilable via Mill's emphasis on the conditional nature of economic truths: Economic science must give way to broader social science. It not infrequently does so in the *Principles*, so that Mill often appears contradictory when in his own mind his position was consistent. It is often asserted that a thinker cannot be truly understood outside the context of his time and its influences – and with Mill, this is particularly so. A survey of his life and major influences is therefore useful.

Early Life[4]

Mill was born on May 20th, 1806 in London, to Harriet Burrow Mill and James Mill. His father James was a remarkable man in his own right, and his multi-volume *History of India* (begun in the year of John's birth) would soon catapult him into

---

[3] Mill (1981 [1873]). Henceforth references to Mill's autobiography will be cited in the text as "*Autobiography*".

[4] Primary sources for the rendition of Mill's early life are Mill's own autobiography ("The Autobiography of John Stuart Mill" [1981 [1873]]), Britton (1953) and Mitchell (1967). Mitchell's work was written during the first three decades of the twentieth century. The book is largely an assembly of his class notes and incomplete thoughts, but still a very thorough survey of the history of economic thought.

national prominence as a leading intellectual of the Benthamite school. JohnMill, in a sense, had two fathers: his biological one, and Jeremy Bentham, who indirectly (through his influence on James Mill) contributed much to the younger Mill's celebrated (notorious?) education at the hands of his father. Bentham and James Mill worked closely together during John Mill's childhood, and the famed utilitarian theorist was a frequent presence in the Mill household.[5] So were David Ricardo and numerous prominent leaders of the Benthamite school. Mill was raised at the feet of giants, and in due course, he himself became one.

The celebrated education of John Stuart Mill is the stuff of legends (Mill's own *Autobiography* is still the best source). Under the stern eye of his father, Mill began learning Ancient Greek at Age three, and by Age 15 he had mastered Greek, Latin, most of the works of Greek and Roman antiquity, mathematics through calculus, numerous classic Histories, and an immense volume of additional literature that passed the elder Mill's muster as sufficiently consistent with the Benthamite message he was determined to instil in his son. In the later years of his schooling, Mill studied philosophy (notably, Plato, whose consistent altruism he thoroughly absorbed), and political economy via Ricardo's *Principles* (Ricardo 2006 [1821]), *The Wealth of Nations* (Smith 1937 [1776]) and other works. The elder Mill needed routine walking for his health, and the young John would walk beside his father, notes of recent studies in hand, while the elder Mill would be quizzing, demanding, criticising (often and severely), praising little, correcting contemptuously, and above all always insisting upon greater effort and achievement from his beleaguered son than he was then giving (or, often, capable of giving, given John's age).

Writing much later, Mill expressed the view that his schooling at his father's hands had given him "an advantage of a quarter of a century over my contemporaries" (*Autobiography*, 33), and there is little doubt that such an intellectual advantage was indeed bestowed by his education. Also likely – and often speculated about – is that such an intense experience inflicted on one so young had damaging psychological effects. Mill's father gave him much discipline but little love (and in return, even late in life, Mill was unable to express any love for his father [*Autobiography*, 53]). His mother, a comparative cipher in the family, was of little help either in this regard. A modern psychologist would also point to his social stunting: He was kept from any normal contact with children his age through nearly the whole of his education. This supreme isolation, emotional separation, frequent criticism, and intense instruction likely made for a brilliant intellectual but an emotionally starved and psychologically unsettled child. In the opinion of many, these pressures would come home to roost in 1826 in the form of a much-discussed "mental crisis" (as Mitchell termed it (1967, 544); Mill referred to it as "a crisis in my mental history" [*Autobiography*, 137]). It was this breakdown or "mental crisis" that, to a remarkable extent, set Mill on the course he was to pursue through his most productive years.

---

[5] Apparently, Bentham's influence on John's education was, at least occasionally, more than indirect. Writing in her journal on April 9th, 1840, Caroline Fox records John's recollection that Bentham and James Mill "were very intimate, and *they* tried educational experiments on John!" (emphasis added) (Fox 1883, 106).

Mill emphasizes a visit to France he made at age fifteen, during which he mastered French and acquired life-long loves of mountains and French cultural sophistication (he also visited extensively on two occasions with J. B. Say[6]). He returned to England a year later and was soon granted his unofficial graduation from his father's schooling. He began to publish in his own right and continued work with Bentham and his father on various projects. Bentham, James Mill, and those in their circle were at work on various liberal projects considered outrageously radical for their day. Britton (1953, 9) describes them as:

> (1) the foundations of jurisprudence, and the reform of the law; (2) a theory of representative government based on utility, and the radical reform of Parliament; (3) the building of economics into a systematic body of knowledge, and the abolition of restraints on trade and labour; (4) a utilitarian doctrine of morality, and the reform and secularization of education. In all these undertakings, the rule to be applied was the principle of Utility, or the Greatest Happiness Principle.

Into this excitingly revolutionary intellectual movement, the young John Mill poured his entire heart and soul.[7] Mill also developed, for the first time, intellectual friends his own age. Britton (1953, 14–5) describes three significant examples. First, the Utilitarian society met routinely through about 1826, at which Mill exchanged views with other promising young Benthamite thinkers. Second, between 1825 and 1830, a reading group met mornings before work at George Grote's house, where the group studied Ricardo, James Mill's *The Analysis of the Human Mind*, the early psychologist David Hartley's *Observations on Man*, and other notable contributions to the knowledge of the day. They also studied German (which Mill learned at this time).

Finally, and arguably most significantly for his later development, Mill participated in a celebrated debating society which involved most of the leading young prodigies in London. Mill and his young Bethamite friends spent much time in formal and informal debate taking on, among others, the young Thomas Babington McCauley and his circle, as well as disciples of Samuel Taylor Coleridge (who in his day was not only celebrated as a poet but also as a profound essayist and philosopher). In 1823 he had also joined his father working at India House, where he would remain until it closed in 1856. Finally, he undertook the extremely challenging task of taking a huge heap of Bentham's papers on law totalling many thousands of pages, and turning them into a coherent manuscript. There were also various other writing projects. All these activities, pursued simultaneously, no doubt took their toll even on so prodigious a worker as Mill.

---

[6] These meetings with Say as a young man were arguably far from inconsequential. Schumpeter, for example, stresses Say's profound influence on Mill's system (Schumpeter 1954, 529).

[7] Upon first reading Bentham (e.g. Bentham 1970 [1779]), Mill had been thunderstruck by his rejection of all intrinsic-rights-based doctrines as foundations for legal systems. Here, thought Mill, was Reason at last applied without compromise to the problems of society. Bentham tossed aside such then-standard legal concepts as "rights of man," "social contract," "right reason," "law of nature," "moral sense," etc. These were mystical, metaphysical, essentially empty concepts. Bentham's principle of "the greatest happiness," Mill thought, "put an end to all this. The feeling rushed upon me, that all previous moralists were superseded, and that here indeed was the commencement of a new era in thought" (*Autobiography*, 67).

A "Mental Crisis"

Upon completion of Bentham's manuscript (at which he laboured intensively without pause for several years), Mill found that he had wound to a stop. He asked himself whether the goals he had elected to pursue in his life (the promotion of Benthamism and other liberal causes) would, if achieved, actually make him happy. The answer, to "hear" him tell it in the *Autobiography*, was a resounding "no!" The notion that all he had planned to do in his life would, it seemed, lead him only to a life of misery and despair was devastating to the young Mill. He found himself wholly unable to take pleasure anymore from the contemplation of great, noble, altruistic deeds. In fact, his very capacity to feel anything at all seemed lost. A crisis ensued, during which – while he was able to appear normal to family and friends – he in fact seriously contemplated suicide. Ultimately he instead tackled the problem of trying to understand and overcome his affliction.

Mill's great personal crisis peaked in 1826–1827 and continued in diminished form throughout the second half of the 1820s. He described it as "a crisis in my mental history" – that is, not a psychosis, but instead a clash between his feelings (or lack thereof) and his consciously-embraced convictions. It was also to a significant extent a *moral* crisis. Mill agonized over his inability to feel enthusiasm for a life of altruistic self-sacrifice. What was wrong with him? Where was the happiness that ought to have ensued from the prospect of charting a virtuous, reform-oriented, Benthamite course through life? Mill's conflict over what he "knew" was right and what he felt inside, caused him to intensively contemplate, over many months, what had gone wrong with his education and his beliefs to bring him to such a state. He ultimately reached several key conclusions that allowed him to emerge from his affliction, several of which revolutionized his intellectual life and beliefs.

First, he concluded that to worry about not being happy was actually to guarantee his unhappiness. Instead (he decided), just do the right things, and happiness would come. With that out of the way, he tackled his psychological state. *Why* was he unhappy? His education was supposed to have affixed the right feelings to the right actions (through a crude, mechanical kind of "conditioning" developed by the early behaviorist[8] David Hartley and embraced by his father). This had failed him, he concluded, because the practice of "analytical methods" – like those in which he had been intensively trained and at which he excelled – tended to fray, and ultimately sever, the links between right attitudes and happy emotions. Such methods, in fact, tended to heavily repress the emotions generally. This was, he decided, the explanation for his deadened emotional state as well as his baffling inability to call

---

[8] Technically Hartley was an "associationist" psychologist (Schumpeter 1954, 531), but it seems clear that, in his belief that purely external forces could thoroughly shape the psyche, Hartley was presaging the era of Skinner. Mitchell, for example, describes associationism as a doctrine that presumes "a person's mind is made up of associations among ideas, and it ought, therefore, be possible for the teacher or scientist, if he controlled the making of a mind, to make just as good a machine as the teacher or scientist is capable of" (Mitchell 1967, 540).

up properly enthusiastic feelings at the thought of achieving great, other-centred, deeds that helped society-at-large.

What, then, was happening to him? Thrashing about, looking for the answer, Mill picked up a copy of William Wordsworth's poetry. To his astonishment, he discovered that poetry and literature that lauded altruism in romantic terms – and especially the romantic poetry of Wordsworth – could not only soothe his soul, but actually restore both his capacity to feel strong emotion and his link of happy emotions to noble deeds.[9] After reading Wordsworth, Mill was able to slowly lift himself out of his mental crisis and back into the life he wanted. To John Mill, poetry quite literally saved his life.

The then-recent works of the Romantic poets had been conspicuously absent on James Mill's voluminous reading lists for his son. Now the younger Mill wove the absence of such works in his education into an elaborate theory, not just of what was ailing him, but also of what had been lacking in Bentham, in his father, in the entire Benthamite movement, and in society overall.

Bentham had famously stated that "all poetry is misrepresentation" (*Autobiography*, 115), and the Benthamites as a school were well known for their contempt for all forms of "sentimentalism."[10] Now Mill decided he had discovered that poetry – the deeply sentimental, perfect union of art and conceptualization – had the capacity to fully unify the intellectual and emotional sides of a human psyche (specifically, his own). There was, it appeared to him, a kind of technology of the soul, involving poetry (and the arts generally) as a counterweight to intense intellectual activity. It was not just that a properly-balanced mental state depended critically on a full appreciation of the role of poetry and the arts in one's life. An appreciation of poetry and the arts was essential to the building of a noble, virtuous, wise, and fully-aware *character*. To Mill, "character" meant the sum of one's beliefs, values, judgments, and actions. One's character determined, not only one's capacity to be honest, virtuous, altruistic, etc.; not just one's capacity to find emotional pleasure and enjoyment in such noble acts, but the actual ability to see the truth broadly in life – including in one's purely intellectual pursuits. Art was crucial in the making of the soul of one who could see Truth. He who failed to properly develop the artistic side of his character would invariably make serious mistakes of judgment and context, not only in day-to-day life, but also in purely intellectual life (see, e.g. Mill's critique of Bentham in Mill 1969 [1833], 88–100, especially 91–3; and 111–2).[11]

---

[9] In the extensive literature on Mill's discovery that Wordsworth's romantic poetry was a salve for his soul, it has apparently been missed that Wordsworth's "Tintern Abbey" is an explicitly altruistic work, that would thereby have likely spoken directly to Mill's problems as he then saw them.

[10] Mill however hastens to state that many Benthamites were "great readers of poetry" (*Autobiography*, 115). The crucial issue was the assessment of poetry's value. As he put it in discussing Roebuck (one of his Benthamite contemporaries), Roebuck "never could be made to see that these things have any value as aids in the formation of character" (*op. cit.*, 155).

[11] Mill speaks of a deficiency of Imagination in Bentham, and comments: "For want, indeed, of poetical culture, the images with which his fancy supplied him were seldom beautiful, but they were quaint and humorous…. The Imagination … is the power by which one human being enters into the mind and circumstances of another. This power constitutes the poet…" (Mill 1969 [1838], 91–2).

The "cultivation of character" – in an individual, a "class," or a nation – would become one of Mill's lifelong themes. To Mill, the development of a fully-formed noble character required deliberate training of one's emotional state just as much as it required the purely logical and ethical training he had received from his father (*Autobiography*, 147). The cultivation of art and especially poetry, therefore, were not mere leisurely activities: they were essential "balancing" elements desperately needed by a healthy psyche.

Mill's new doctrine of character did not cast either Bentham or even arguably his father in a particularly favourable light.[12] Mill saw Bentham as a great genius and believed that his utilitarianism had marked a profound advancement in social science. However, Bentham's crude utilitarian rationalism (as Mill now saw it) had made inadequate distinction between mean acts and noble acts. All that mattered to a consistent Benthamite was the pleasure gained by society from such acts, not their essential nature (Mill 1969 [1838], especially 95–6; 113; Mill 1969 [1861], 212).

Mill now saw such opinions as dangerously shallow. Noble acts helped build a noble character; base acts helped build a base character (Mill 1969 [1838], 98–100; 113). A virtuous, noble character, then, was a kind of broad capital asset that added to the public capital stock in numerous ways – among others, by setting a shining example from which others could learn and find inspiration. Bentham implicitly regarded the beneficial consequences of noble acts as little more than a 1-time flow – equivalent in ultimate effect to base acts that created the same amount of [more-or-less immediate]

---

[12] In the case of Bentham, we have as evidence Mill's rather savage portrayal of Bentham as a man of genius whose narrowness of experience and general lack of breadth led directly to what Mill thought of as very serious intellectual errors (see Mill 1969 [1833]; Mill 1969 [1838]). For the case of his father, the conclusion that James Mill's lack of sentimental expression constituted a serious flaw in character is more difficult to document. Mill is very protective of his father in his writings, but not so much so that another side of his view of his paternal relations cannot be observed. Based on a number of passages in the *Autobiography*, Mill clearly attributes his emotional starvation in his childhood as a core cause of his mental crisis, and this emotionally repressing environment, he recognizes, was chiefly due to his father's influence (see, e.g. *Autobiography*, 113–14). Further, one might quote from the *Autobiography's* first two chapters, among the many generous comments may be found quite a few criticisms of what he clearly thought of as unreasonable treatment at his father's hands during his education. One must also read Mill's many comments in the wake of his mental crisis about the weakness of mere reason without its complement, strong emotion (some of these quotes can be found in subsequent sections). Of the Benthamite movement's relation to poetry, Mill records the following (looking backward at his committed Benthamite period):

> as regards me (and the same thing might be said of my father), the correct statement would be, not that I disliked poetry, but that I was theoretically indifferent to it. I disliked any sentiments in poetry which I should have disliked in prose; and that included a great deal. And I was wholly blind to its place in human culture, as a means of educating the feelings. (*Autobiography*, 115).

It should also be noted that, as the leading disciple of Bentham, James Mill would be subject to many of the same criticisms that John Mill levelled at Bentham. Writing critically of the eighteenth century in his essay on Coleridge, John Mill writes of it: "There were few poets, and none of a high order; and philosophy fell mostly into the hands of men of a dry prosaic nature, who had not enough of the materials of human feeling in them to be able to imagine any of its more complex and mysterious manifestations…" (Mill 1969 [1840], 142). This criticism could be applied equally to Bentham or to James Mill.

pleasure. By contrast, Mill saw virtuous acts (and thoughts) as tiny inputs into the building of an accumulated stock of personal and societal capital – that is, "character." It was Romantic advocates of the "great man" theory like Wordsworth and Coleridge – not Bentham and his followers – who understood that it was great, noble men of character who truly determined (and ought to determine) the fate of societies – and, to a remarkable extent, also the *science* of societies.[13] Benthamism therefore needed to be fundamentally reformed to incorporate these vital insights.

Mill's doctrine of character also furnished him with the key to the puzzle of what had gone wrong with his education. He seems to have concluded that his father, while a virtuous and (in many ways) admirable man, nevertheless had a flaw of character which, through his teachings, he had passed on to his son (see discussions above). By failing to "cultivate" his emotional side, James Mill had over-emphasized his purely rational faculty at the expense of his emotions. His emotions had eventually become repressed, and his upbringing of John had, inevitably, reflected his emotional short-comings. He had taught John to be a kind of "reasoning machine,"[14] careless of emotion and the emotional needs that were so important as balances to the excesses of pure rationalism. In the younger Mill's opinion, the result of this imbalance had been his "mental crisis." This mental crisis, and his successful grappling with it, then became the basis for a wide-ranging re-evaluation of everything from the proper path to an individual's psychological "balance," to the need for a thorough making-over of society to properly reflect the preeminent significance of "character" – in determining the fates of individuals, entire societies, and [nearly] everything in-between.

"Character" as a Dominating Factor in Social Science

Mill's doctrine of "character" would heavily colour his future intellectual accomplishments. First, in Mill's mind the doctrine of character thoroughly dominated the insights of classical political economy. An example is Mill's treatment of Malthusian population theory. Malthusian theory held that the labouring classes – predominately

---

[13] See Lehman (1922); see also discussion of Coleridge below. Britton points out that, in Mill's essay on Coleridge, Bentham's science is derided as "the empiricism of one who has had little experience." By contrast: Coleridge "is placed on an equal with Bentham. The English empiricists are now shown to lack an adequate notion of society, and to have adopted a false *apriorism* in their science of government" (referring here to James Mill's famous essay "On Government," the skewering of which by Macauley had given John Mill great food for thought (Macauley 1829)). "The Coleridgeans (continues Britton) are the true successors of Bacon and Locke in this field; though their methodology may be wrong their methods are right" (Britton 1953, 32).

[14] In the *Autobiography* (111), Mill wrote: "I conceive that the description so often given of a Benthamite, as a mere reasoning machine, though extremely inapplicable to most of those who have been designated by that title, was during two or three years of my life not altogether untrue of me." After his new views caused him to seek out friendship among the Coleridgeans, Sterling told Mill "how he and others had looked upon me (from hearsay information), as a 'made' or manufactured man, having had a certain impress of opinion stamped on me which I could only reproduce…" (*op. cit.*, 163).

(in Mill's opinion) men of poorly-formed characters – could not control their basic sexual urges. Malthus and the orthodox Benthamites took men as they were and therefore predicted continuous problems with overpopulation in industrial societies. However, Mill's doctrine of character gave society, he thought, an escape from the Malthusian trap. Through enlightened education of the labouring classes, these men could be fundamentally changed. Character could be imparted unto these classes – one imagines them sitting together in a big circle and reading Wordsworth to each other, under the watchful eyes of the more cultivated – giving them the enlightenment (and self-discipline) to escape the Malthusian. (The rich landowners would "help" pay for this education via taxes on inheritances and legacies [*Principles*, Bk. II, Chap. 2; Bk. V, Chap. 2]).[15]

Secondly, the principle of rational self-interest that was at the core of classical political economy was just a conditional truth, a "merely provisional" (*Autobiography*, 241) feature of the state of mankind as-it-then-was at Mill's particular point in time. It was based (thought Mill) on the historically accurate, but ultimately arbitrary, assumption that the characters of men as they then were under capitalism – primitive, money-grubbing, base creatures unable to see beyond the crudest of pleasures (as Mill saw them; see, e.g. the several particularly caustic quotes to be found in *Principles*, Bk. IV, Chap. 6) – would remain forever the same. Again, proper education stressing the development of noble, other-centred, altruistic characters would alter the very human clay out of which future society would be built. A New Man would then emerge who was unwilling (nay, utterly unable) to act in any way that would enhance his individual well-being at the expense of broader society (*cf. Autobiography*, 237–41; Mill 1969 [1861], 227, 230–3).[16]

A society of such men would not need capitalism any longer in order to prosper. They would shed their outdated capitalistic values as a moth sheds its pupae, and

---

[15] In his general discussion of taxes, Mill wrote: "[T]he power of bequeathing is one of the privileges of property which are fit subjects for regulation on grounds of general expediency" (*Principles*, 809; 811). Mill suggested "as a possible mode of restraining the accumulation of large fortunes in the hands of those who do not earn them by exertion (e.g. the landed classes in particular), a limitation of the amount which any one person should be permitted to acquire by gift, bequest or inheritance ... I conceive that inheritances and legacies, exceeding a certain amount, are highly proper subjects for taxation: and that the revenue from them should be made as great as it can be made without giving rise to evasions.... The principle of ... levying a larger percentage on a larger sum, though its application to general taxation would in my opinion be objectionable, seems to me both just and expedient as applied to legacy and inheritance duties" (*ibid*; *ibid*). Further, all estates without an heir would automatically go into the state's coffers.

[16] "We looked forward to a time ... when it will no longer either be, or be thought to be, impossible for human beings to exert themselves strenuously in procuring benefits which are not to be exclusively their own, but to be shared with the society they belong to..." (*Autobiography*, 239).... "But the hindrance [in bringing about widespread other-centred behaviour] is not in the essential constitution of human nature. Interest in the common good is at present so weak a motive in the generality not because it can never be otherwise, but because the mind is not accustomed to dwell on it as it dwells from morning till night on things which tend only to personal advantage.... The deep-rooted selfishness which forms the general character of the existing state of society, is so deeply rooted, only because the whole course of existing institutions tends to foster it..." (*op. cit.*, 241).

emerge fully-formed in a new society of voluntarily-embraced socialism, joyously sacrificing themselves for the good of their neighbour. Capitalism would wither away and die, as individuals that had been carefully educated to have "virtuous" characters, adopted voluntary socialistic cooperatives based on noble brotherly love rather than the vicious selfishness of the profit motive (cf. *Principles*, 788–92; 790–4). Thus the truths of political economy (to the extent they were based on self-interested action) represented merely a temporary, barbaric stage of humanity's development, soon to be surpassed and overthrown by rational voluntary socialism.

Thirdly, as a direct corollary of the second insight, came the doctrine of the fundamental moral corruption of the capitalist, due to the diseased character that must inevitably be at the core of someone who makes his primary purpose the pursuit of mere material personal well-being. The capitalist, in fact, was twice damned in Mill's new framework: First, for the *method* of his pursuits (ignoring his emotional needs and over-emphasizing reason), and, second, for the *goal* of those pursuits (the self-centred scramble for mere material well-being). Mill's personal revolution of character caused him in his early writings to voice considerable suspicion and some contempt for the United States, where the crass materialists and their mercantilist principles held the most full sway over a society.[17] And he was positively caustic in his comments about English society. By contrast, Mill lauded the cultured and sophisticated character of French society, particularly the French peoples' comfortableness with the free expression of emotions (as compared to those stuffy English), and the great capacity of French intellectuals to conceive of, and proselytize for, an alternative society built on "other-centred" principles. In the years following his mental crisis, the young Mill would be routinely smitten with socialist French intellectuals, to whom he would look for many of his "Big Ideas."

Fourthly, England's "upper classes," whose material well-being (in Mill's opinion) was wholly unearned and, essentially, gathered at the expense of the rest of society, and whose self-declared mandate to rule Britannia flew in the face of the profound lack of character possessed by those born with the proverbial silver spoon in their mouths – were beneath contempt. They were corrupt and wholly undeserving of the disproportionate authority they claimed over English government and society. Mill "thought the predominance of the aristocratic classes, the noble and the rich, in the English Constitution, [was] an evil worth any struggle to get rid of … as the great demoralizing agency in the country" (*Autobiography*, 177, 179). Such people as a class merely made a mess of things and postponed the day of Reform when "The People" – appropriately educated and chastened by a proper vote-weighting scheme (discussed below) – would take power.

Fifthly, while democracy was well-and-good up to a point, the doctrine of character mandated that those of most noble character should have a disproportionately

---

[17] In the original 1848 edition of the *Principles* Book IV, Chap. 6, Mill had sneered at the U.S. as a land where, despite "very favourable circumstances … all that these advantages seem to have done for them is that the life of the whole of one sex is devoted to dollar-hunting, and of the other to breeding dollar hunters" (cf., *Principles*, Ashley Ed., 748[n]). Mill's suspicion of the U.S. seemed to diminish somewhat after 1860. He was especially impressed by the North's willingness to go to war with the South over slavery, and these comments were dropped from the Sixth (1865) and later editions.

powerful role in governing society.[18] Throughout his long life, Mill was fascinated by various voting schemes that were offered up as alternatives to pure, one-person-one-vote, democracy. In *Thoughts on Parliamentary Reform* (Mill 1977a, b [1859]), Mill proposed a voting scheme in which the more "cultivated" would receive multiple votes while the less "cultivated" would receive only a single vote. To Mill, those with the most "proved" education invariably were also those with the most "character" (thus, Mill's scheme featured "a plurality of votes, to be given, not to property, but to proved superiority of education" [*Autobiography*, 261]).[19] The undignified consequences of the cultured few being unduly inconvenienced by the voting power of the unwashed many would thereby be avoided in Mill's preferred State. We see, arguably, in such cultural elitism the lasting projection of Plato (whom both Mill and his father revered) and his "philosopher-kings." By contrast to its special treatment of the better-educated, Mill's voting system granted no special status to the self-educated, self-made businessman, thereby perpetuating the longstanding contempt in the West for the "character-challenged" capitalists of the merchant "class." The school of hard knocks, apparently, was not one to which Mill subscribed.

Sixthly, Mill gave special epistemological status to those whose characters were *intuitive* – those with poetical souls, like Wordsworth, Coleridge, and Thomas Carlyle, who just seemed, somehow, to *know* things.[20] For the rest of his life – but particularly in the years immediately following his mental crisis – Mill emphasized the power of those who could "know" directly through intuition. For example

---

[18] Mill, speaking for himself and his late wife, put the matter thusly: "We were now much less democrats than I had been, because so long as education continues to be so wretchedly imperfect, we dreaded the ignorance and especially the selfishness and brutality of the mass…" (*Autobiography*, 239). See also Mill's self-characterization of himself as an advocate of a tempered democracy late in the *Autobiography* (p. 288).

[19] Mill continues: "This recommended itself to me as a means of reconciling the irresistible claim of every man or woman to be consulted, and to be allowed a voice, in the regulation of affairs which vitally concern them, with the superiority of weight justly due to opinions grounded on superiority of knowledge." "Superiority of knowledge" would be assessed via "a systematic National Education by which the various grades of politically valuable acquirement may be accurately defined and authenticated." Regarding his proposal, Mill comments that "[a]s far as I have been able to observe, it has found favor with nobody." Those of this opinion, apparently, came to include Mill: in his next paragraph, he lauds the voting scheme advanced by Thomas Hare as "the greatest improvement of which the system of representative government is susceptible." (*Autobiography*, 261–62).

[20] This did not however mean that Mill was willing to be led in his economic theorizing by poets. Mill, who wrote of Coleridge that "[i]n political economy especially he writes like an arrant driveller…" (Mill 1969 [1840], 155) surely would not have gone that far. But it is no exaggeration to say that Mill regarded constant attention to "the cultivation of the feelings" (*Autobiography*, 157) through art and culture as a necessary condition for a social scientist to maintain the full, humanist context that alone (as Mill now thought) could lead to truly useful inquiry into society's proper values and behavior.

Thomas Carlyle, as a Being of intuition, had special status, and was not to be judged by the likes of Mill:

> I did not, however, deem myself a competent judge of Carlyle. I felt that he was a poet, and that I was not; and that as such, he not only saw many things long before me, which I could only when they were pointed out to me, hobble after and prove, but that it was highly probable he could see many things which were not visible to me even after they were pointed out. I knew that I could not see round him … and I never presumed to judge him with any definiteness, until he was interpreted to me by one greatly the superior of us both—who was more a poet than he, and more a thinker than I—whose own mind and nature included his and infinitely more. (*Autobiography*, 183)

This interpreter, "greatly the superior" of both Mill and Carlyle, was Harriet Taylor – Mill's future wife. Mill had made her acquaintance in 1830. At age 22, she already was "known as a very pretty woman with a quick wit and vivid manner" (Britton 1953, 23). There is little doubt that meeting her was the exclamation point on all that Mill believed he had learned in the wake of his mental crisis. Here was a person who understood, intuitively, all that he had reasoned out with such difficulty following his crisis, and more – a person with whom his mind and emotions were in near-perfect harmony. It was also Mill's first experience with any kind of romance. From the start of his relations with his future wife, Mill assumed a subordinate position with respect to many of her views and opinions. In a tellingly submissive phrase in the *Autobiography*, he writes of his good fortune at being admitted into her circle.

Harriet and John soon fell deeply in love,[21] a development which inevitably vexed the still-very-much-alive Mr. Taylor, whose collaboration with his wife included a young daughter (the marriage had been one of those arranged affairs that characterized the era). As a point of honour, the relationship between John and the already-spoken-for Harriet was to be (and by all accounts, was) merely spiritual, but this did not preclude their spending time together discussing, reasoning, intuitiving, and (to judge by their correspondence) longing for each other. Taylor, by all accounts a very good man, at first objected to and fought the "merely" spiritual relationship between his wife and another man, but eventually he became resigned to the situation and agreed to accept a diminished role in his wife's life. Obviously the relationship was satisfactory to no one except the rumour mill (at one point Carlyle wrote: "They are innocent says Charity, they are guilty says Scandal: then why in the name of wonder are they dying broken hearted?" Britton 1953, 24). Harriet and John wrote themselves and friends agonized letters over their plight, which seemed hopeless. The situation was solved, albeit tragically, by the death of John Taylor in 1849 (a death that both Harriet and John Mill deeply deplored, especially Harriet). In 1851, Mill and Harriet were wed. They would have only seven-and-a-half years together as man and wife.

Like Carlyle, Harriet Taylor had, in Mill's opinion, that special intuition which let her see at a glance truths that he himself could only arrive at through the plodding processes of mere book learning and formal reasoning. To Mill, she was a "woman of … penetrating and intuitive intelligence, and of an eminently meditative and

---

[21] This is judging by their early correspondence, captured in Hayek (1951).

poetic nature…" (*Autobiography*, 193), with "a heart which thoroughly identified itself with the feelings of others…" (*op. cit.*, 195). Mill wrote that she possessed *en masse* all of the admirable qualities which he previously had been glad to find singly in his friends and acquaintances. A greater intuitive Being thus succeeded Carlyle: "a person of the most eminent faculties, whose genius … continually struck out truths far in advance of me … the greater part of my mental growth consisted in the assimilation of those truths…" (*op. cit.*, 253).[22] Many of these "truths" were, it would seem, versions of the early socialism just-then beginning to emerge as the primary creed of the fashionable European intelligentsia. There is little doubt that Harriet, wielding such an influence over John, pushed him towards more explicitly socialist doctrines (however, neither Harriet nor John ever endorsed socialism of the Marxian type: their's was always a doctrine of society voluntarily converting to the allegedly superior socialist system).[23]

Despite Mill's glowing testimony to his wife's abilities in the *Autobiography*, history has failed to record any contemporary of Mill who shared his exceptionally high regard for her powers. Historians of economic thought also have seen little reason in her scanty writings to grant her such a lofty status.[24] Mill, however, showered his wife with superlatives and granted her nearly the equivalent of full co-author status in all his works between his publication of the *Logic* and his wife's death, particularly with respect to *On Liberty* (which he explicitly calls a joint work between them) and most of those sections in the *Principles* which he found most innovative (containing the heterodox insights of which he was particularly proud). It is far from clear that these attributions to Mrs. Taylor/Mill are unwarranted.

---

[22] An anomaly that requires resolution in Mill's acceptance of "intuition" is how it can be reconciled with his hardened rejection of the intuitionist theories of knowledge perpetrated by Kant and his followers. No more vehement opponent of such epistemological theories could be found than Mill. In his essay on Coleridge (a proponent of Kantian *apriorism*), Mill writes: "We see no ground for believing that anything can be the object of our knowledge except our experience" (1969 [1840], 128–29). The anomaly vanishes when we observe that, at least to the mature Mill, "intuition" was a special skill acquired from innate ability and experience, not from some innate source. In a letter late in life Mill writes: "I have long recognized as a fact that judgments really grounded on a long succession of small experiences mostly forgotten or perhaps never brought into very distinct consciousness, often grow into the likeness of intuitive perceptions" (Letter to William B. Carpenter, January 29th, 1872 (Mill 1972, p. 1868)). This was, however, not always Mill's view. As a young man, in a letter to Carlyle, Mill wrote: "I conceive that most of the highest truths are, to persons endowed by nature in certain ways which I think I could state, intuitive; that is, they need neither explanation nor proof, but if not known before are assented to as soon as stated" (Letter to Carlyle, July 5th, 1833 (Mill 1963, 163)). Shortly thereafter, it appears, Mill abandoned his notion of intuition as an inborn trait.

[23] It is due Harriet Taylor to relate Mill's own opinion of her influence: that she helped counter "a moment in my mental progress when I might easily have fallen into a tendency towards overgovernment, both social and political…" (*Autobiography*, 259). "[H]er practical turn of mind, and her almost unerring estimate of practical obstacles, repressed in me all tendencies that were really visionary. Her mind invested all ideas in a concrete shape … the weak point in any unworkable suggestion seldom escaped her" (*op. cit.*, 257).

[24] A reading of the considerable surviving correspondence between Mill and his future wife/wife makes it clear that she was highly intelligent and a fine writer.

Co-authorship relationships are not uncommon in which the spark is provided by one author and the grind-it-out work of putting the spark into tangible form is carried out by another author. To "hear" Mill tell it, this was precisely the professional relationship between himself and Harriet Taylor, with him playing the subordinate, grind-it-out role (Mill himself commented generally about co-authorship, pointing out that "the one who contributes least to the composition may contribute most to the thought" [*Autobiography*, 251]).

Harriet's strength (to say the least)[25] was not in technical economics, but rather in helping to provide, and pushing John to include, precisely those "heterodox" ideas which made the *Principles of Political Economy* in parts so deviant from the then-mainstream positions of political economy. Arguably, it was Harriet Taylor Mill, as much as or more than Mill himself, who was responsible for those sections of the *Principles* that (among other things) cleaved production from distribution, lauded socialist institutions over capitalist ones, prophesied a voluntarily-socialist "futurity of the labouring classes," and advocated that (as in Book V) increased activity of government was needed to counteract certain weaknesses of the capitalist system.[26] History abounds in cases where the spouse of a great figure exerted a disproportionate influence on that figure's work – even when the spouse's ability was only a smidgen of that of the great figure. With Harriet Taylor Mill we have a spouse of (at minimum) considerable ability, who, in a different era, would likely have had a successful academic career in her own right, and who was also a powerful, assertive, and even domineering personality in her relationship with John Mill. Such an individual could not fail to have considerable influence on the thinking of her husband and intellectual partner.

Reaction Against Bentham: Carlyle, the "Lake Poets," the Saint-Simonians and Comte

The manner in which Mill had emerged from his mental crisis convinced him that Benthamism, while still right in the main, nevertheless required a thorough reformation that fully incorporated the principles he had grasped in his crisis years. Bentham had died in 1832, his father in 1836. Mill had been reluctant to openly criticise Benthamism while his father was alive, although he had published an anonymous piece in 1833 that was at points sharply critical of Bentham and his movement. After his father's death,

---

[25] Writing about the *Political Economy* and Harriet's contribution to it, Mill wrote: "What was abstract and purely scientific was generally mine; the properly human element came from her" (*Autobiography*, 257).

[26] "For, on the one hand, she was much more courageous and far-sighted than without her I should have been, in anticipations of an order of things to come, in which many of the limited generalizations now so often confounded with universal principles will cease to be applicable. Those parts of my writings, and especially of the Political Economy, which contemplate possibilities in the future such as, when affirmed by Socialists, have in general been fiercely denied by political economists, would, but for her, either have been absent, or the suggestions would have been made much more timidly and in a more qualified form" (*Autobiography*, 257).

he began openly criticising and revising Benthamism in accordance with the insights he had gleaned during his "mental crisis" (cf. *Autobiography*, 213–4).

The primary literary vehicles[27] for this reformation were two lengthy pieces by Mill on Bentham's philosophy (in 1838) and Coleridge's (in 1840), whom Mill cast as the two leading thinkers of the age. On the surface, Mill was even-handed in the two essays, maintaining that these two famous figures, apparent antagonists in many ways, were in fact the bearers of complementary insights. Each had grasped essential truths that society needed, and each of them had a world-view that was incomplete without incorporating the insights of the other.

Despite the veneer of impartiality, it was Bentham who came in for the severe criticism – not only intellectually but, at points, personally – while Coleridge escaped mostly unscathed. Writing much later in his *Autobiography*, Mill recognized that in these two essays he had presented a moderately more favourable emphasis on the ideas of Coleridge vs. those of Bentham. He attributes it partly to his reaction against Bentham at this time, and partly due to the fact that he, writing for "Radicals and Liberals," needed to emphasize more those doctrines with which his audience was unfamiliar and likely to under-value without his guidance. Well – perhaps. But Mill's essay on Bentham contains an uncharacteristic ferocity that suggests a rejection of Bentham and his movement that is not only intellectual, but also deeply personal. There is a palpable tone of bitter protest against outrageous deception (even betrayal) in some of these passages (a tone that many who once gave one's life over to an intellectual "guru," only to then "outgrow" him/her, would recognize only too well). Mill later writes in the *Autobiography* of his excessive reaction against Bentham during these years. Throughout his long life, Mill never stopped thinking of himself as a Benthamite (albeit in a sense that he himself defined; *cf. Autobiography*, 221). It is doubtful, however, that the reformed Benthamism advocated by Mill would have been very recognizable to Bentham, or to his father.

The intellectual distance John Mill had travelled away from Bentham and his father is even more clearly revealed in his private correspondence. In an 1836 letter, Mill writes of his desire to use his ownership and editorship of the *London and Westminster Review* to promote "a utilitarianism which takes into account the whole of human nature not the ratiocinative faculty only ... which holds Feeling at least as valuable as thought, & poetry not only on a par with, but the necessary condition of, any true & comprehensive philosophy" (Mill 1963 [Letter to Edward Bulwer, November 23rd, 1836]).[28] These were shocking, even heretical, thoughts to an orthodox Benthamite, but they delighted elsewhere. Carlyle, reading Mill for the first time in this period, exclaimed approvingly "Here is a new mystic" (*Autobiography*, 181). The same element piquing Carlyle's interest generated, predictably, deep concern among Mill's former allies (a concern which with the

---

[27] See also Mill's *The Spirit of the Age* (1986 [1831]).

[28] It is due Mill to point out that he immediately continues this remark with the words: "I know I am writing very loosely & expressing myself very ill..." The message however easily bleeds through the perhaps poorly-chosen words.

passage of time would prove fully justified) over Mill's new views and the direction in which he was taking the English Liberal reform movement.

As editor, Mill routinely used the *Review* as a platform to advance his own "reformed" vision of Benthamism. Not only did his own articles, including those on Bentham and Coleridge, appear there, but he also published many pieces by Carlyle, John Sterling, and others "who were in sympathy with Progress as I understood it, even though I should lose by it the support of my former associates" (*Autobiography*, 215). Lose support by it he certainly did: his father's old friend Francis Place thought he was becoming "a German metaphysical mystic" (quoted in Britton 1953, 22). Sir John Bowring (a former editor of the *Review* who had also been Bentham's literary executor) characterized him as at bottom a philosopher who had "read Wordsworth, and that muddled him, and he has been in a strange confusion ever since, endeavouring to unite poetry and philosophy" (quoted in Britton 1953, 22). Harriet Grote (the wife of one of the Mill family's oldest friends) predicted as early as 1837 that the *Westminster Review* "would cease to be an engine of propagating sound and sane doctrines on Ethics and Politics under J. M." (quoted in Ashley 1929, x). Mill himself, writing in 1841, characterized himself as "having definitely withdrawn from the Benthamite school in which I was brought up and in which I can almost say I was born" (Ashley 1929, x–xi; quoted in Ashley, *ibid*).

The period from (roughly) 1828 through the early 1840s was when Mill's intellectual travels took him furthest from Benthamism and laissez-faire principles and closest to those Romantic, anti-Bentham, anti-capitalist thinkers whose influence was destined to separate Mill forever from the main trunk of social science that had been so carefully crafted by Bentham, Ricardo, and his own father. These included in England Carlyle and the "Lake Poets" (Wordsworth, and in particular Coleridge), thinkers in Germany such as Goethe, the French socialists of the Saint-Simonist school (founded by Claude Henri de Rouvroy, comte de Saint-Simon), and in particular the erstwhile Saint-Simonist, Auguste Comte.

Carlyle (who famously labelled political economy "the dismal science"), appealed to Mill by propounding "the coming of a new Idea, a new Faith – that men generally would acknowledge what the Poet, or Prophet, would discover" (Britton 1953, 29). This "new Idea" would engage and eventually overwhelm "the deficiencies of the present age" (*ibid*). Carlyle "condemned alike the English Empiricists and the French Enlightenment and poured bitter scorn on the mechanical philosophy of the Benthamites" (*ibid*). Mill was not so much enlightened by Carlyle's works as he was inspired by them: He wrote that "the good his writings did me, was not as philosophy to instruct, but as poetry to animate" (*Autobiography*, 183). Carlyle helped reinforce Mill's developing view that the "present age" was one of transition, and that its "truths" would not be those of that far-finer Age to come, in which Society's flaws would at long last be vanquished. Mill's anonymously-published *The Spirit of the Age* had so impressed Carlyle that he sought out Mill and made his acquaintance. A primary theme of this – Mill's first work expounding his "new modes of thought" – was that a sea-change was coming, one taking society away from "the anomalies and evils characteristic of the transition from a system of opinions which had worn out, to another only in the process of being formed" (*op. cit.*, 181). In his ability to poetically reinforce such a belief, Carlyle acted as a vital ally, and Mill in these years was "one of his most fervent admirers" (*ibid*). (Mill's continued insistence on the primacy of reason, and Carlyle's advancing mysticism, as well as the waxing influence of Harriet Taylor, by 1833 brought about a breach between the two men.)

Mill also read with enthusiasm the new doctrines coming out of Germany. Goethe in particular captured his interest, perhaps because Goethe was much like Mill himself, with one foot firmly planted in reason and classicism and the other placed on more ambitiously speculative notions. Goethe argued that "laws could not be created by pure rationalism, since geography and history shaped habits and patterns, … in sharp contrast to the prevailing Enlightenment view that reason was sufficient to create well-ordered societies and good laws…" (Wikipedia, *The Free Encyclopedia*, "John Wolfgang von Goethe"). Mill himself would come to believe fervently in the a-rational relativity of social "laws" – in the principle that the "truths" of one era or society were not necessarily those of future eras and societies (political economy being definitely included as an example of such conditional truths). Goethe argued further that "rational laws or fiats could not be imposed at all from a higher, transcendent, sphere" (*ibid*), an appealing idea to Mill, who was then aggressively weaning himself from rational, deductive, orthodox Benthamism. Goethe also "denied rationality's superiority as the sole interpretation of reality" (*ibid*), a position which Mill would not have accepted literally, but which captured poetically both his reaction against the excessive focus on rational processes in his education and his new concern with the overly-narrow construing of social science by (as he would come to call them) "the economists of the old school."

Wordsworth, and, especially, Coleridge, also exerted a profound influence on Mill in these years. Wordsworth's poetry, we have seen, had been instrumental in helping Mill emerge from his "mental crisis." Further, through their advocacy of a kind of "great man" theory of society, he and Coleridge also helped Mill clarify in his own mind his sharp differences with Benthamism. Bentham's utilitarianism recognized no special need for leaders, nor any special reason to believe leaders had any greater understanding than that of average men. Wordsworth and Coleridge, in sharp contrast, emphasized society's need for strong, enlightened men (and women) of character, who possessed the rare ability not just to make right decisions, but also to inspire those lesser lights who might otherwise lose their way. The superior character of such enlightened Beings led irresistibly to their having marked superiority in judgement and decision making. As Coleridge put it: "…the laws or principles of reason and the regulations of prudence or understanding can make contact only in the unifying mind of superior men" (quoted in Lehman 1922, 647). The "great man" theories of Wordsworth and Coleridge were instrumental inputs into Mill's critique of orthodox Benthamism. They also inspired his later profound distrust of one-man-one-vote democratic institutions.[29]

---

[29] Mill's exposure to Alexis de Tocqueville's *Democracy in America*, in which the author (in Mill's view) laid out the advantages and dangers of democracy in masterful fashion, also influenced significantly his receding from his former embrace of pure democratic institutions (cf., *Autobiography*, 199, 201).

Coleridge especially influenced Mill profoundly in this period, due not only to his writings but also to his ideas as-funnelled-to-Mill by Frederick Maurice and John Sterling, two talented disciples of Coleridge with whom Mill was in constant contact during the years of his change in views. With "[t]he influences of European, that is to say Continental, thought, and especially those of the reaction of the nineteenth century against the eighteenth" now "streaming in" upon him (*Autobiography*, 169), Mill found himself joining Coleridge's rejection of "the *let alone* doctrine, or the theory that governments can do no better than to do nothing..." (Mill 1969 [1840], 156). In particular Mill credits Coleridge for persuading him of the weakness of the case for applying private property principles to the ownership of land. Coleridge argued that land might properly be held by private citizens only as a de facto *trust* for the benefit of society as a whole. Mill agreed. "The land," Mill wrote, "the gift of nature, the source of subsistence to all, cannot be considered a subject of property in the same absolute sense in which men are deemed proprietors of that in which no one has any interests but themselves – that which they have actually called into existence by their own bodily exertion" (Mill 1969 [1840], 157).

Mill also was persuaded by Coleridgean methodological arguments that social science at his point in time could only be "a philosophy of history," not the theoretical and deductive science that Bentham and his father had envisioned. And to Mill, history had demonstrated conclusively a principle of which Benthamites seemed almost willfully blind: that an "essential condition of stability in political society, is a strong and active principle of cohesion among the members of the same community or state" (Mill 1969 [1840], 134–5). Society, Mill now thought, was quite a bit more than just a bunch of disjointed individuals. Mill now decided that the orthodox Benthamites and the "economists of the old school" had missed the vital fact that most people needed something – or perhaps, Someone – more than mere market forces to believe in. Such belief was, in fact (thought Mill), the glue that bound successful societies together (cf. *op. cit.*, 135). Coleridge had put forth the Church as the force in society that would play the binding-together role. Mill had no religious faith with which to embrace Coleridge's suggestion, but the broader principle itself gripped him. Now, in direct opposition to the views of Bentham and his father, Mill "found himself asserting the value, for human happiness, of an *orthodoxy*, supported by institutions capable of providing moral and intellectual leadership" (Britton 1953, 28).

But could such a valuable orthodoxy be generated in a secular form? Enter the French Saint-Simonians, who taught that there are "natural stages in social development," successive stages of societal change consisting of Ages of "settled ideas and practices and a settled order of government" followed by "Ages of Transition" (*ibid*). Mill felt himself to be living in such an "Age of Transition" – an era in which even the most settled principles of the present-day were subject to overthrow by the march of progressive ideas. In such an era, a "scientific" orthodoxy could replace the weakened theological framework, ushering in an era in which a "new settlement will rest, not on theology, not on a priori reasoning, but on 'positive' notions – on principles verified by observation in the manner of the physical sciences" (*ibid*). From the Saint-Simonians, Mill took a boundless faith in the potential power of observationally based (vs. merely deductive) social *science* to re-shape and reform society's institutions into Higher forms. Such positive institutions, in the firm-but-gentle hands of an intellectual elite, would guide society into those sunny uplands of socialist splendour about which he and his wife dreamed.

Mill was not too enamoured with the specifics of the socialistic scheme actually advocated by the Saint-Simonians.[30] He was less interested in the system itself than he was with the likelihood that Saint-Simonism would, in proportion to its success, help push civilization nearer to "an ideal of human society" (*ibid*), bringing to a close what he was coming to believe was a current era filled with social injustice. Here as well the Saint-Simonians caused Mill to "see":

> Their criticisms on the common doctrines of Liberalism seemed to me full of important truth; and it was partly by their writings that my eyes were opened to the very limited and temporary value of the old political economy, which assumes private property and inheritance as indefeasible facts, and freedom of production and exchange as the *dernier mot* [the last word] of social improvement. (*Autobiography*, 173, 175)

We see here, emerging out of Mill's intensive exposure to socialist writings and ideas, a utopian streak that would appear off-and-on, at odd moments, throughout his future writings. A new context for viewing society was being formed in Mill's mind. Political economy was an invaluable aid to policy in "the present age." Still, however valuable it was to that age, only a shallow-thinking "economist of the old school" would casually assume that such doctrine would be of any substantial value in the reformed Great Age to come. Mill's exposure to the Saint-Simonians taught him, "after some resistance … that some form of socialism might be the *ultimate* form of human society…" (Britton 1953, 27). The "Laws of Production" were fixed and intractable and would apply to any society, socialist or capitalist, but the laws of humanity – the laws of society (including the "Laws of Distribution") were not fixed. Henceforth, Mill felt himself justified in contemplating the "ultimate" form of human society as a separate quest from his investigations into how the economic laws of the *present* society actually worked. There would no longer be any reason to presume that the Grand Age to come would be constrained by the societal laws of the present age – including those "laws of economics" other than those purely technical ones pertaining to "production."

The continental thinker who influenced Mill most profoundly along these lines was Auguste Comte. Mill had first read Comte in 1828 along with a number of articles by other Saint-Simonians, and immediately marked Comte's piece as the most impressive. Comte subsequently differed with Saint-Simon and left the Saint-Simonian movement. Mill lost track of Comte for several years, but he resurfaced in 1838 as author of the first two volumes of his celebrated *Positive Philosophy*. Mill found its insights regarding the building of a "science of society" profound (calling it in one letter "very near the grandest work of this age" [quoted in Ashley 1929, xi]),

---

[30] Under the Saint-Simonian elite, "the labour and capital of society would be managed for the general account of the community every individual being required to take a share of labour either as thinker, teacher, artist, or producer, all being classed according to their capacity, and remunerated according to their works" (*Autobiography*, 175).

and he promptly initiated a lengthy correspondence between the two men (remarkably, they never met [*Autobiography*, 219]).

Mill took from Comte a grand vision of a comprehensive social science, which he labelled "sociology," that would be capable of explaining all social phenomena (within which the more-narrowly-premised fields such as political economy would fall into their proper place). As an former Saint-Simonian, Comte had his own version of "Stage Theory" – "three stages in every department of human knowledge: first, the theological, next the metaphysical, and lastly, the positive stage" – with the "positive stage," in which empirical science would become the captain of society, bringing in a new golden era of progress. This conception reads well until we recall that Comte's version of social science was in large part "scientific" socialism with a well-developed totalitarian bent (a conception that Mill would decisively reject when Comte published his plan for society [*Autobiography*, 221; see also, Mill 1969 [1865]]). At the time, however, Mill found Comte's scientific-seeming stage theory to be almost hypnotically compelling (cf. Ashley 1929, xi), particularly with respect to the building of an authentic science of society. As Mill himself put it in typically understated fashion, "This doctrine harmonized well with my existing notions, to which it seemed to give a scientific shape" (*Autobiography*, 173).

Comte's ambitious conception inspired Mill to attempt to develop a new science – which he named ethology – that he hoped would be worthy of Comte's vision. Ethology was to be a science of the formation of *character*, and, in combination with other related fields such as political economy, would be able to explain and perhaps predict the progress of an entire society. It would be an ambitious attempt to define societal "laws of motion" on the largest scale (Mill would likely have been transfixed by Asimov's *Foundation Trilogy* and its fictional development of "psycho-history" [e.g. Asimov 1951]). Mitchell describes Mill's quest for a general science of "ethology," a science which

> has not been developed but might be by a consistent thinker who set himself to do the job. This is the science which has to deal with the laws of the formation of individual character. One of Mill's deep-lying convictions about mankind was that the character of people in different countries and even to a considerable extent the character of people who lived in considerably separated periods in the same country, is considerably different. He thought that it should be feasible to study the conditions of greatest significance in forming the character of men, in a fashion which would go far toward explaining differences in character. The investigator then might account for the fact, for instance, that the British public had a certain character in economic transactions which Mill thought was appreciably different from that exhibited by the French, or Germans or other continentals. (Mitchell 1967, 589–90)

Thus Mill might have been thinking along the broad lines pioneered in the modern era by, say, Fukuyama (1995), who tries to explain differing levels of prosperity-enhancing social cooperation by reference to varying levels of "trust" in a society. One thinks also of the "social capital" movement, which has raised its flag in the border areas between sociology and economics (e.g. Putnam 2000). Mill had more than just a glimmer of such possibilities; e.g. from them stem his rejection (see quote above) of the notion of economics as a universally applicable social science equally valid in all societies regardless of time and place (a core premise of the doctrine of neoclassical theory). However, even after strenuous efforts, Mill was unable to make any substantial progress with "ethology" and abandoned his quest (though a brief discussion of it does appear in his *Logic*). Despite his failure, the conception of an over-arching unified theory of broad social science – one which recognized the importance of history and also was in touch with developments in the physical and biological sciences – never left him. It would later inspire his very broad-based approach to social science as seen (e.g.) in his *Principles*.

Comte's shining vision (to Mill) of a very broad "sociology" made, for a time, political economy pale by comparison in Mill's mind. Comte himself had seen only a provisional utility in the latter field, as it had helped to disrupt and discredit that "industrial policy of the *ancien regime*" (Ashley 1929, xiii) which, thought Comte, stood between civilization and further progress. However, having served that purpose, political economy ought now to assume its proper place as a thoroughly subordinate branch of Comte's broader scientific vision (indeed, its further development should await the culmination of that vision). Comte saw little remaining present purpose to political economy, which in his view wrongly propagated a narrow-minded rejection of useful government interventions in the economy while ceaselessly advocating "the sterile aphorism of absolute industrial liberty" (quoted in Ashley 1929, xiii). (Smith's *Wealth of Nations*, with its lofty breadth and canny observations of actual economic conditions, escaped Comte's censure, but the Ricardians had deviated disastrously from the path laid out by the Scottish Master.)

Fundamentally the difficulty Comte saw was with what he considered the excessively narrow foundational premises of political economy – premises like the automatic assumption of narrowly-focussed self-interest that divided political economy sharply and inappropriately from the other social sciences. Mill, in the midst of his reaction against Benthamism, responded enthusiastically to such arguments. The "interest-philosophy of the Bentham school," stated Mill in the *Logic*, was thoroughly unsatisfactory if one is trying to devise a general theory of government and its proper role in society (cf. Ashley 1929, xiii–xiv). For such a purpose, political economy was unsatisfactorily "founded on one comprehensive premise: namely, that men's actions are always determined by their interests" (*ibid*). When such narrow-minded "economists of the old school" succinctly summarized their theory of government with the slogan *laissez faire*!, they were being led by their narrow premises into blanking out essential features of the human condition that, if considered carefully and fully, would force upon them a far different policy conclusion:

> These philosophers would have applied and did apply their principles with innumerable allowances. But it is not allowances that are wanted. There is little chance of making due amends in the superstructure of a theory for the want of sufficient breadth in its foundations. It is unphilosophical to construct a science out of a few of the agencies by which the phenomena are determined, and leave the rest to the routine of practice or the sagacity of conjecture. (Mill, quoted in Ashley 1929, xiv)

When Comte suggested, however, that political economy as a field was fatally damaged by such critiques, Mill was quick to demur. The founding premises of political economy were appropriate for "one large class of social phenomena of which the immediate determining causes are principally those which act through the desire of wealth; and in which the psychological law mainly concerned is the familiar one that a greater gain is preferred to the smaller..." (Mill, quoted in Ashley 1929, xv). Mill was perfectly willing to defend the *existence* of a social science (economics) built on narrower premises: what he was unwilling to accept was such a science pretending that its premises were wide enough to support the entire superstructure of a proper social science.

The problem in Mill's mind, then, was not with political economy when applied in the proper manner to its appropriate subject manner (the quest for wealth and its consequences). The problems arose when political economy was applied to social problems where the narrowness of the "interest-philosophy" assumption was inappropriate for the object under study. In particular (thought Mill), the limiting scope of the orthodox political economist's premises prevented such an economist from seeing that, in the Enlightened Society That Is To Come, well-educated individuals of character would routinely resist the siren call of narrow self-interest in favour of the promotion of the larger interest of the group, potentially leading to a societal quality of life far higher than in the materialistic society. In such a society, even the sacrificer's life would be improved, since such a person of character would derive far more pleasure from knowing of the broad good he has done society, than he would have derived from narrowly-construed purely selfish and materialistic pleasures.

Such a "win–win" was precisely the kind of reasoning Mill and Harriet Taylor-Mill emphasized in painting an optimistic vision of a future for mankind as a voluntarily socialist society. From such speculations came their fondest hopes. Meanwhile, there was no reason in the current age to ignore the lessons of the best economic principles as put forth by the Ricardian school, the masters of the "interest-philosophy." The radically differing contexts separating the utopian future and the materialistic present explains how Mill could write a lengthy tome on classical political economy, over eighty percent of which consisted of quite orthodox insights based on the premise of individual self-interest narrowly construed, while at the same time inveighing against the role played by narrow self-interest in "the present state of society" and cherishing radical socialist visions for a future in which the "merely provisional" principles of political economy would be vanquished to the ash-bins of history.

The *Logic* and World Fame

Having seen Mill's focus in his early scholarly years on topics other than political economy, it is not surprising to find that Mill's "breakthrough book" was not on economics at all, but instead on philosophy and the methodology of science. Mill had been working on a comprehensive logic treatise through much of the 1830s and early 1840s. He published *A System of Logic: Ratiocinative and Inductive* in 1843 (Mill 1973 [1843]). The two-volume work was much broader in scope than the typical modern logic text, which tends to focus on deductive methods. Mill wanted to write a work successfully elucidating (and defending) *induction* as a potent method of acquiring knowledge. He wanted to defend a *tabula rasa* theory of knowledge with which to challenge the waxing Kantian intuitivism and Idealism. And, he wanted to talk sense about the methodology of the social sciences. He succeeded in doing all this and more.

The book was very well-received, and it made Mill's reputation as a first-class thinker. Mill's expression of surprise at the tome's success no doubt captures the sentiments of other authors who have had a triumph with a book of similar dryness: "How the book came to have, for a work of the kind, so much success, and what sort of persons compose the bulk of those who have bought, I will not venture to say read, it, I have never thoroughly understood" (*Autobiography*, 231). Mill cites "a revival of speculation" and the fortuitous arrival of complementary texts as factors. In his own view, a primary virtue of the work was its anti-Kantianism – its derivation of all knowledge directly from experience rather than from (as he saw it) some specious "intuition."

It seems likely, however, that Mill's accessible treatment in the book's latter sections of what we would today call the "scientific method also contributed" to the book's success. Here, at any rate, were proposed answers to important problems of inquiry. The *Logic's* focus on inductive methods, with its rules of proper generalization, fallacies of observation, etc., at any rate promised direct connection between scientific methods and the actual world – surely a vast relief for many facing an era of burgeoning Kantianism. Mill's "Theory of Inverse Deduction," by which hypotheses are examined by studying historical episodes and observing whether or not the hypothesis is contradicted by the episode, is an appealing notion that doubtless also drew contemporaries' attention. Finally, his Book VI on "The Logic of the Moral Sciences" addressed a topic then garnering more and more attention. But, overall, it was the book as a whole, with its majestic scope, and its blending of inductive and deductive methods, that likely gave it such influence over the nineteenth century. The book's stellar nineteenth-century reputation has not survived too well the twentieth, and Mill is today far better known for other works (most notably, *On Liberty* [Mill 1977a, b [1859]]). But in its day the *Logic* was regarded as a uniquely valuable contribution to scholarly knowledge. Writing early in the Twentieth century, Mitchell commented that the *Logic* "has an importance in the development of modern thought greater than that of his *Principles of Political Economy*" (Mitchell 1967, 557). We may gainfully close by relating the eminent British philosopher Karl Britton's tribute to the work's influence:

> The *Logic* has continued to influence philosophers as well as to guide the reflections of undergraduates. Jevons and Venn, Johnson and Keynes, based their work avowedly upon his, and the writings of the later Idealist logicians reveal a debt even where their authors fail to acknowledge it. (Britton 1953, 34)

The years from 1826 through 1843 were tumultuous ones for Mill. He stared down a frightening intellectual, moral, and personal crisis; he was swept to and fro by some of the most powerful intellectual currents of his era, and successfully weathered the storm, ultimately integrating it all with his early learning. He met Harriet Taylor, who would one day become not only his beloved wife, but also his full intellectual partner. He suffered tragic personal losses in his immediate family (the deaths of his father and his favourite younger brother). However, he soldiered through and developed a well-thought-through philosophy of life that would direct all his efforts in future years.

Through all his intellectual turmoil, Mill always visualized himself as one whose unique talent was seeing both sides of every debate – able to absorb vast amounts of material, pick apart the various threads, and present to third parties the lessons to be learned. Mill took as his own a phrase coined by Goethe – "many-sidedness" (*Autobiography*, 171). There were truths not to be lost in the older teachings of the eighteenth century he had been taught by his father and others. Vital insights were also being uncovered by the thinkers of the nineteenth century. But there was, Mill thought, no reason for either to eclipse the other. Too many times, advocates for the scholars of each century had been either unable, or unwilling, to see the truths of the other. The actual truth of the matter, thought Mill, was to be found only by incorporating the best thinking of both century's paradigms. Such, in any event, would be his own moderating approach as he entered into the period in which he wrote his most celebrated works.

References

Ashley WJ (1929) Introduction to Principles of political economy with some of their applications to social philosophy. In: John SM (ed) Longmans, Green and Co., London

Asimov I (1951) Foundation. Doubleday, Garden City

Bentham J (1970 [1789]) An introduction to the principles of morals and legislation. In: Burns JH (ed) The collected works of Jeremy Bentham, principles of legislation. University of London: The Athlone Press, London

Berns W (1975). "Two mills and liberty: [review of] on liberty and liberalism: the case of John Stuart Mill," by Gertrude Himmelfarb. Va Q Rev (Winter):127–131

Britton K (1953) John Stuart Mill. Penguin Books, Melbourne

Fox C (1883) Memories of old friends, being extracts from the journals and letters of Caroline Fox of Penjerrick, Cornwall, from 1835 to 1871. In: Horace NP (ed). Smith, Elder & Co., London

Fukuyama F (1995) Trust: the social virtues and the creation of prosperity. Simon & Schuster, New York

Hayek FA (1951) John Stuart Mill and Harriet Taylor: their friendship and subsequent marriage. University of Chicago Press, Chicago

Johann Wolfgang von Goethe, *Wikipedia, The Free Encyclopedia*, http://en.wikipedia.org/wiki/Johann Wolfgang von Goethe (accessed September 19, 2011)

Lehman BH (1922) The doctrine of leadership in the greater romantic poets. PMLA, Vol. XXXVI, pp. 60–78

Macauley TB (1829) Review of: Essays on Government, Jurisprudence, the Liberty of the Press, Prisons and Prison Discipline, Colonies, the Law of Nations, and Education," by James Mill. The Edinburgh Review, March/June 1829, XLIX, 159–189

Mill JS (1929 [1871]) Principles of political economy, with some of their applications to social philosophy. Longmans, Green and Co., London

Mill JS (1963) The earlier letters of John Stuart Mill 1812–1848 (collected works of John Stuart Mill, Volume XII). University of Toronto Press, Toronto

Mill JS (1965 [1871]) Principles of political economy, with some of their applications to social philosophy. In: Robson JM (ed). Collected works of John Stuart Mill, vol II, III. University of Toronto Press, Toronto

Mill JS (1967 [1879]) Chapters on socialism. In: Robson JM (ed). Collected works of John Stuart Mill, vol V. University of Toronto Press, Toronto, pp 703–756

Mill JS (1969 [1833]) Remarks on Bentham's philosophy. In: Robson JM (ed). Collected works of John Stuart Mill, vol X. University of Toronto Press, Toronto, pp 3–18

Mill JS (1969 [1838]) Bentham. In: Robson JM (ed). Collected works of John Stuart Mill, vol X. University of Toronto Press, Toronto, pp 75–116

Mill JS (1969 [1840]) Coleridge. In: Robson JM (ed). Collected works of John Stuart Mill, vol X. University of Toronto Press, Toronto, pp 117–164

Mill JS (1969 [1861]) Utilitarianism. In: Robson JM (ed). Collected works of John Stuart Mill, vol X. University of Toronto Press, Toronto, pp 203–260

Mill JS (1969 [1865]) Augustus Comte and positivism. In: Robson JM (ed). Collected works of John Stuart Mill, vol X. University of Toronto Press, Toronto, pp 261–368

Mill JS (1972) The later letters of John Stuart Mill, 1849–1873. In: Mineka FE, Dwight NL (eds). University of Toronto Press, Toronto

Mill JS (1973 [1843]) A system of logic ratiocinative and inductive, being a connected view of the principles of evidence and the methods of scientific investigation. In: Robson JM (ed). Collected works of John Stuart Mill, vol VII–VIII. University of Toronto Press, Toronto, pp 3–1243

Mill JS (1977a [1859]) Thoughts on parliamentary reform. In: Robson JM (ed). Collected works of John Stuart Mill, vol XIX. University of Toronto Press, Toronto, pp 311–340

Mill JS (1977b [1859]) On liberty. In: Robson JM (ed). Collected works of John Stuart Mill, vol XVIII. University of Toronto Press, Toronto, pp 213–310

Mill JS (1981 [1873]) Autobiography. In: Robson JM, Stillinger J (eds). Collected works of John Stuart Mill, vol I. University of Toronto Press, Toronto, pp 1–290

Mill JS (1986 [1831]) The spirit of the age. In: Robson JM, Robson AP (eds). Collected works of John Stuart Mill, vol XXII. University of Toronto Press, Toronto

Mitchell WC (1967) Types of economic theory: from mercantilism to institutionalism, vol I. Augustus M. Kelley, New York

Putnam RD (2000) Bowling alone: the collapse and revival of American community. Simon & Schuster, New York

Ricardo D (2006 [1821]) Principles of political economy and taxation. Cosimo Classics, New York

Schumpeter JA (1954) History of economic analysis. Oxford University Press, New York

Smith A (1937 [1776]) An inquiry into the nature and causes of the wealth of nations. The Modern Library, New York

Chapter 9
John Stuart Mill's Road to Leviathan II: The Principles of Political Economy

Michael R. Montgomery

The Principles of Political Economy

Following the success of the *Logic* (Mill 1973 [1843]), Mill turned again to political economy. In 1844, he took advantage of the *Logic's* success to arrange the publication of his *Essays on Some Unsettled Questions in Political Economy* (which had been written in 1829 and 1830) (Mill 1967 [1844]). Shortly thereafter, he began work on a project he had earlier conceived, while at work on the *Logic*, of writing "a special treatise on political economy, analogous to that of Adam Smith" (quoted in Ashley 1929, xvii; see Note 2, Chap. 8, for explanation of subsequent citations of the *Principle*). This would become the famous *Principles*, to be published in 1848. In combination with the *Logic*, the *Principles* cemented Mill's reputation as, arguably, the pre-eminent nineteenth-century thinker who wrote in the English language. As Mitchell puts it, the "*Logic* and the *Principles of Political Economy* together gave Mill a position in English life and thought such as no economist had enjoyed before him and such as no economist has enjoyed since his day in any country" (Mitchell 1967, 559) – a verdict that, with the possible exception of John Maynard Keynes, stands today.

The Principles, Its Scope and Reputation

The *Principles of Political Economy* was written far more rapidly than Mill's other major works. Mill struggled for over a decade with his *Logic* (Mill had particularly difficult troubles developing his theory of induction). By contrast, the

M.R. Montgomery (✉)
School of Economics, University of Maine, 5774 Stevens Hall, Orono, ME 04469, USA
e-mail: Michael.montgomery@umit.maine.edu

J.G. Backhaus (ed.), *Handbook of the History of Economic Thought*,
The European Heritage in Economics and the Social Sciences,
DOI 10.1007/978-1-4419-8336-7_9, © Springer Science+Business Media, LLC 2012

roughly thousand-page *Principles* was completed almost unimaginably rapidly in less than 2 years (during these 2 years, Mill also was working full-time at India House and further was deeply involved in peasant land-reform projects). Mill's remarkably rapid progress was due in no small part to his tightly constrained vision of the work's scope (at least for its more orthodox sections).[1] His primary objective was to take the works of his Classical predecessors and contemporaries and prepare a thoroughly up-to-date and readable rendition of the Classical school of political economy.[2] Mill was, of course, uniquely qualified to carry out such a project, and his efforts surely produced the "most mature statement of Classical theory" (Landreth 1976, 119), one with "an effect upon English thought second to none" (Haney 1968, 443). The clarity and high style of Mill's writing also often has been praised (though not always without a touch of irony: to Blaug (1985, 179), the book is not just easy to read, but is, "indeed … too readable [as] the argument flows along so smoothly that the reader is simply lulled into agreement".) Mill's "lucid exposition of Ricardian doctrine" (Landreth 1976, 132) helped to make his book among the most effective, and certainly the most influential, volume covering Political Economy in his day.[3]

Indeed, in some respects the very success of the book's summary of Classical doctrine has worked against its reputation. Mill the economist, write Ekelund and Hebert, is often wrongly denigrated as little more than "a sophisticated synthesizer of little theoretical originality" (1983, 152). This is in fact Wesley Mitchell's view (though he appreciates Mill's "beautifully articulated discussion") (1967, 565). To Haney (1968, 474–5), Mill "deserves recognition as a great expositor of social and economic doctrines", but his "name would hardly be mentioned" if the standard of judgment were how much new material he introduced into the body of economic theory. Others demur, finding not just significant improvements, but also notable theoretical innovations in Mill's rendition of classical theory. Blaug (1985, 220), Ekelund and Hebert (1983, 152–9), Landreth (1976, 146), and Sowell (2006, 146–7) see Mill's original contribution to orthodox theory as substantial, and Stigler (1965, 7) sees Mill as no less than "one of the most original economists in the history of the science".

However debated is the strength of Mill's orthodox contributions, there is broad agreement that the *Principles'* most notable innovations are in those "heterodox" sections where Mill steps outside the boundaries of classical political economy. We have seen in earlier sections how seriously Mill took the notion that political economy was built on premises too narrow to form an acceptable foundation for social science.

---

[1] Mitchell (1967, 559) accounts for the book's being written "at a high rate of speed only because Mill all his life had been thinking more or less about the problems with which the subject dealt, and because to him political economy was a pretty well finished product … it was a matter of arranging an ordered exposition of principles which had been formulated by his predecessors".

[2] Thus Mill's book was the first major appearance of a "Principles" book similar in intent to those we see today – it was, in fact, a kind of textbook, not meant to be a work of great originality and original achievement. In this mission it was spectacularly successful.

[3] The work went through seven editions plus a "Peoples' edition", the seventh (last) edition coming out in 1871, 2 years before Mill's death.

Political economy was "a branch of Social Philosophy, so interlinked with all the other branches, that its conclusions, even in its own peculiar province, are only true conditionally…" (*Autobiography*, 243). Mill thought that political economy, to be truly useful, needed disciplining by the insights of the other social sciences – a requirement often overlooked by lesser political economists who "knew nothing but political economy (and therefore knew that ill)" (*Autobiography*, 243). Such narrow-minded economists, blustering forth with errant policy pronouncements, merely furthered the agendas of those "numerous sentimental enemies of political economy, and its still more numerous interested enemies in sentimental guise" (*ibid*).[4] Mill's policy analysis, by contrast, would combat the damaging impact of these narrowly trained economists, helping "to disarm these enemies" (*Autobiography*, 244) of political economy by showing the field's power for good when used properly in conjunction with the other social sciences.[5]

Whatever we think of such a vision – and there are numerous "heterodox" scholars operating on the fringes of modern mainstream economics who would passionately embrace it (and many more orthodox modern economists who would promptly denounce it as the silliest drivel) – Mill's vision for his work led, without a doubt, to much of the most interesting (and controversial) material in his *Principles*. As Mitchell (1967, 562) points out, these parts of the *Principles* arguably are better described as Mill's applications of his and his wife's social philosophy to Political Economy, rather than the reverse.[6] Mill himself was of the opinion that his book's "applications to social philosophy" were of considerably more importance than its more orthodox parts:

> I confess that I regard the purely abstract investigations of political economy (beyond those elementary ones which are necessary for the correction of mischievous prejudices), as of very minor importance compared with the great practical questions which the progress of democracy and the spread of Socialist opinions are pressing on … (Letter to Karl Heinrich Rau, 1852, quoted in Mitchell 1967, 562)

Mill's and his wife's support for that capitalist system so admirably described in his *Principles* was, in fact, "merely provisional" – the best that could be done prior to the anticipated raising-up of the quality of mankind that the coming of widespread

---

[4] Mitchell writes of Mill's dissatisfaction with "the process of vulgarization through which political economy had gone in the generation after Ricardo, a vulgarization which adapted it to all sorts of partisan use, which made political economy in the hands of the well-to-do people a rationalization of their view of the proper treatment of the poor … a process that had made political economy, which professed to be a science, practically a weapon adapted to the uses of class warfare" (Mitchell 1967, 566).

[5] Mitchell (1967, 560) takes the contrasting view that Mill's interest in political economy's applications to social philosophy can be fully explained by that "keen interest in public welfare characteristic of the utilitarians in general and of Mill in particular". This view however seems difficult to defend in the face of Ashley's careful documentation of Mill's explicit linkage to Comte for his motivation in writing a text emphasizing applications to "social philosophy" (See Ashley 1929, x–xvii).

[6] Certainly this is not always so; as, for example, in Mill's survey of the consequences of the different incentive schemes facing various types of "peasant proprietors" (Book II, Chap. VI), where he masterfully analyzes the different economic consequences ensuing from differing institutional setups.

education for the poor and socialist institutions would inevitably produce. "Comes the revolution", thought he and his wife, and all that would be changed:

> The deep-rooted selfishness which forms the general character of the existing state of society, is so deeply rooted, only because the whole course of existing institutions tends to foster it … (*Autobiography*, 241)

Once selfish (i.e. capitalist) institutions could be replaced with their proper socialist substitutes, a New Man would arise filled with truly noble (i.e. altruistic) sentiments, and the world would change.[7] The breach between what works (capitalism) and what is moral (altruism) – a contradiction that had troubled Mill profoundly since at least the time of his "mental crisis" – would at last be closed. The New Man would be so made (through enlightened education) as to naturally produce prosperity in socialistic, not capitalistic, institutions.[8]

This utopian streak in Mill deserves more attention than it has received – not least as an open invitation to Karl Marx (who, of course, read Mill closely). In fact, it is the key to resolving most of the issues surrounding the claim that there are "two Mills" (e.g. Berns 1975).[9] Ironically, history's leading popularizer of classical

---

[7] Ashley writes: "Until the present social system should be fundamentally changed, Mill clearly regarded the Ricardian economics as so far applicable to existing conditions as to call for no substantial revision in method or conclusions" (Ashley 1929, xxiii).

[8] The *Principles* and the *Autobiography* are peppered with examples of Mill's faith in the development of a Higher Man who will replace mere Economic Man with a new one of altruistic sentiment; for example:

> When minds are coarse they require coarse stimuli, and let them have them. In the meantime, those who do not accept the current very early stage of human improvement as its ultimate type, may be excused for being comparatively indifferent to the kind of economical progress which excites the congratulations of ordinary politicians; the mere increase of production and accumulation. (*Principles*, 749; 754–55)

Or:

> The social problem of the future we considered to be, how to unite the greatest individual liberty of action, with a common ownership in the raw material of the globe, and an equal participation of all in the benefits of combined labour. …We saw clearly that to render any such social transformation either possible or desirable, an equivalent change of character must take place both in the uncultivated herd who now compose the labouring masses, and in the immense majority of their employers. Both these classes must learn by practice to labour and combine for generous, or at all events for public and social purposes, and not, as hitherto, solely for narrowly interested ones. (*Autobiography*, 239)

Such revelry is not entirely lacking today [2010] in the attitudes powering the behaviours of sundry "democratic" governments. Mill at times reads like a veritable John the Baptist heralding the imminent coming of that eternal Socialistic Saviour – "Higher" Man.

[9] Himmelfarb (according to Berns 1975) emphasizes the vast difference between "the Mill of *On Liberty*" and that "other" Mill "of the *Principles of Political Economy*, *Representative Government* (Mill 1973 [1861]), and the famous essay on Coleridge (Mill 1969 [1840]), among other works". It will be argued below, in contrast to Berns/Himmelfarb, that the "other" Mill is very much in evidence in these latter-mentioned works. Certainly it is true that there were two Mills – one named John and one named Harriet – but more than that it seems difficult to say.

economics looked longingly for the day when that economics would become obsolete. When at last a "higher" human being was created through successful socialist innovations, humankind could at last throw off its crippling self-centred institutions and begin a new life on a higher [collectivist] plane of a decidedly superior nature. The *Principles* taken as a whole, then – a book that might seem schizophrenic at first glance – is in fact luminously consistent with those broad themes that motivated Mill throughout his long life (and, further, arguably, the entire body of Mill's work exhibits a similar consistency). So long as there is capitalism, classical economics is an essential tool in crafting social policies yielding "the greatest good for the greatest number". Meanwhile let us work for better days. Thus there are not "two Mills" in the *Principles* – or, arguably, elsewhere. Rather there is one Mill thinking in two separate contexts, the sum of the thinking completely consistent with both Mill's roots in Benthamism and classical political economy as well as with the later "broadening of his perspective" at the hands of the socialist thinkers.

Organization of the Principles

Mill's organization of his *Principles* closely follows that of Say's *Treatise on Political Economy* and his father's *Elements of Political Economy*, with the notable exception that a section on "consumption" is omitted (although, of course, consumption is discussed throughout the work: e.g., the distinction between "productive" and "unproductive" consumption, comes early in Book I). Book I primarily concerns "production", Book II primarily "distribution" (including most of the discussion of socialism), and Book III (the longest) primarily value and "exchange". Book IV on the "Influence of the Progress of Society on Production and Distribution", marks an organizational departure where Mill introduces and elaborates his distinction in political economy between "statics" and "dynamics" (the core of which he took from Comte), discusses what we today refer to as "growth theory", and contemplates the likely future of the "labouring classes". Book V closes the work with a comprehensive discussion of government, its proper (and improper) functions, and its impact on the market system.[10]

Such an organization scheme contrasts sharply with that of Ricardo, who starts with Value theory in his Chap. 1 and then follows later with his theory of distribution.

---

[10] Both Say's *Treatise* (Say 1983 [1803]) and James Mill's *Elements* (James Mill 1844 [1821]) have a Book I on production and a Book II on distribution. Say's Book III is on Consumption, after which the book ends. James Mill's Book III is on exchange, and his Book IV is on consumption. Say discusses value at the start of Book II, Mill does so (like his son) at the start of his Book III. Ricardo (2006 [1821]), by contrast, begins his *Principles of Political Economy and Taxation* with a thorough discussion of his labour theory of value, then moves on to rent, wages, and other distribution topics, then to foreign trade and types of taxes, ending with a mixture of topics including his macroeconomic ones. Smith's *Wealth of Nations* (Smith 1937 [1776]) is organized substantially differently from all of the above and it is clear that J. S. Mill's inspiration from Smith did not extend to his scheme of organization.

It diverges also from what the marginalists later would do: Like Ricardo, they began with value theory and then used that theory to explain the distribution of the national product. Mill comes under criticism (e.g. Haney 1968, 475; Blaug 1985, 180) for failing to organize his book more like either his great predecessor or his farther-seeing marginalist successors. However, given Mill's cost-of-production value theory, one variant or another of which was at the time "state-of-the-art", value is anchored in production. Thus it is reasonable to begin with the fundamental concept of production, out of which in the Classical system value eventually emerges.

Mill himself attributes his placement of value theory fairly late in the book as an ordering derived from his fundamental separation of the "laws of production" from the "laws of distribution". The Laws of Production, he says, are independent of the questions of exchange, depending as they do only on physical (technological) truths. The question of value, then, pertains only to distribution, and even then political economy only has something to say here if pure exchange is governing the determination of prices. It is interesting that Mill's cherished distinction between production and distribution (discussed in greater detail below) is so fundamental to his system that it mandates, in Mill's mind, the postponement of the discussion of value to his third Book (a little-noticed explanation by the author of his own organizational decisions).

The Laws of Production and Distribution

Mill's famed distinction between production and distribution is so important to his framework that it requires immediate discussion before tackling his other contributions. Classical distributive doctrine was based on two pillars. First was the existence of diminishing returns to a fixed labour/capital mix across both the intensive and extensive margins of agriculture. Second was Malthusian population theory with its assertion that, in the "long run", the labouring population would adjust so that workers would earn precisely the subsistence wage (over shorter periods, labour's remuneration equalled the "wages fund", which petered out to the subsistence level in the steady state). With labour's share of national output thus determined, the remainder is split between landowners and capitalist-lenders.

Now consider the transition to the steady-state, starting from a period of "surplus" production. Imagine an economy growing (population increasing, technology increasing, land acreage fixed) and thus moving relentlessly towards the steady-state. To feed the growing population, land already under cultivation is more intensively farmed, while newly used raw land is (by assumption) less productive than land that already has been under cultivation (land being assumed to be brought under cultivation sequentially from most- to least-productive units). Since less-productive agricultural land has now been brought under cultivation, rent – "the excess of [a land-unit's] produce beyond what would be returned to the same capital if employed on the worst land in cultivation" (*Principles*, 425; 419) – rises for all the higher grades of land.

The percentage return from owning such land having risen, capital-funds flow out of manufacturing and into land until expected returns across the two industries are again equalized. Now imagine a population steadily growing toward its steady-state level, increasing the economy's demand for food, and forcing additional agricultural production on ever-less-productive units of land. Rents will continue to rise while manufacturing profits fall. And this path to the "steady state", in which profits will find their absolute minimum, is also marked by ever-declining economic circumstances for the labouring classes as the economy inexorably returns them to their long-run permanent state of economic subsistence. It was pictures like this that led Carlyle to label classical economics "the dismal science".

Having been raised [literally] with the Ricardian economics, Mill accepted its grim internal logic, but he was unhappy with how the pessimistic conclusions of the classical model predetermined the fate of the labouring classes. Policy conclusions based on classical principles already were being routinely put forth claiming that attempts to ameliorate the poor's conditions through "enlightened" social policy were doomed to failure by the "iron laws" of the classical system (Mitchell 1967, 566). Mill disagreed vehemently with these defeatist policy conclusions. Indeed, the revolution in his political thinking that followed his "mental crisis" in his early twenties had been largely about just such types of issues. Fears for a better future for mankind had been among the several main issues that had brought on his 1826 "crisis" in the first place (*Autobiography*, 149). Now, in crafting his own statement of political economy, Mill was determined to use what he had learned since 1826 to turn the essentially negative long-run message of classical political economy into a positive doctrine that held out hope for a better life for all of mankind – *especially* for the labouring classes, who were condemned by classical doctrine to lives of subsistence "in the long run".

Mill converted the long-run pessimism of the classical system to long-run optimism, through three suppositions. First, as was already generally acknowledged, in principle there was no necessity for population to outrun food supply so long as the labouring classes were willing to restrict the growth of their numbers through abstinence from sex and/or use of contraceptive techniques. The problem was in convincing them to do so. Mill had a life-long passion for this topic.

Second, the primary way in which the labouring classes could be induced to hold down their numbers and so stave off the Malthusian spectre was through an extensive and far-reaching process of education the likes of which a society had never before provided to its lowest classes. The labouring classes needed to be taught culture and through such teachings they would obtain that enlightened state of being that rejects the more "earthy" pleasures in favour of those of a "more elevated" nature. In particular, they would learn, as the Mills of the world already had learned, that a civilized being is distinguished primarily by that high altruistic bent that unfailingly places the needs of others before one's own needs.

Teaching this last, however, would truly require a thoroughgoing reform of society's self-oriented institutions, leading to the creation of a new culture where one's value was no longer determined by one's ability to "get on" through various sordid money-grubbing behaviours (see, e.g. Notes 16 and 17 in the previous chapter).

Instead one's personal success in the New Age would be measured (both by oneself and others) by one's capacity for self-enlightenment and, of course, by one's capacity to joyfully engage in a life of selfless service. This vision would dispatch the Malthusian spectre by transforming the labouring classes into poorer versions of the "more elevated" classes. So augmented by such culture and "higher understanding", the labouring classes would naturally choose to hold down their birth rates. They would, as newly enlightened beings, do so both for the good of themselves as well as that of others. This, Mill thought, was how to beat Malthus.[11]

However, these happy thoughts also confronted Mill with a serious obstacle – one prompting his third key supposition. A thoroughgoing [re-] education of the labouring classes as outlined earlier would not come cheap. Significant resources would have to be expended on the project, and, further, the considerable costs of reforming society's institutions also would have to be borne by someone. From where would the funds come to finance Mill's version of a "last, best hope for mankind"? Clearly, considerable monies from "unproductive" landlords and other owners of great inherited fortunes were in principle available for the taking in order to finance Mill's grand design – fortunes much of which he was prepared to see the government seize – through levies and restrictions on inheritances (*Principles*, Bk. II, Chap. 2) and through confiscation of income from the great landed estates (*Principles*, Bk. V, Chap. 2, Sctn. 5).

But here is where classical distribution doctrine stood in his way. According to classical theory, the distribution of society's production is fixed – determined by the immutable laws of the classical system. Natural law, said the classical economists, decreed that landlords would grow richer and workers (and capitalists) poorer as society headed for its preordained date with the "stationary state". Interference with the impersonal workings of the classical mechanism would only make things worse. Classical economists like Ricardo

> thought that any attack upon the security of property would make things immediately far worse for the bulk of mankind inasmuch as if property were not secure there would be no motive for the accumulation of capital; and if there were no capital in abundance there would not be the wherewithal to pay wages and cultivate land (Mitchell 1967, 568).

But [we might imagine Mill thinking] Ricardo was merely one of those narrowly focussed (albeit great) economists, lacking a grasp of broader social science and its higher-ranking role in policy. Ricardo had not lived in the era of promising socialist insights coming off the Continent as had Mill. He had not, therefore, grasped the way out of the Malthusian trap that Mill [thought he] had seen. He had not been given the chance to see that human nature itself could and must be changed. That vision of the future changed everything. Its realization required that classical distributive doctrine give way to a new era of government-led redistribution.

---

[11] Or, as Barber (1967, 104) phrases it, the state had an important role to play as a "'civilizer' – i.e. as the sponsor of improved educational facilities, as well as such cultural amenities as parks and museums. Elevation in popular tastes and aspirations, especially among members of the working class, was vital to the banishment of the Malthusian devil and to the exercise of human control over the distribution of income". Mill's case for public education based on such thinking will be discussed in detail when we reach the discussion of the *Principles*' Book V.

Mill used two arguments to break the chains with which classical distribution theory bounded social policy. First, the fixed distributive outcome that society obtained under *laissez faire* in the classical system, did not imply that other outcomes were not possible given that the principles of *laissez faire* were not permitted by society to operate fully. The economy might be usefully *conceived* as a mechanism, but it was *not* one. Neither was "society". Here, Mill saw a failure by economists to recognize these elementary facts – a failure which narrowed the focus of social science inappropriately. As Mill later put the matter in an 1869 letter to William Thornton, what now was needed instead was:

> what may be called the emancipation of political economy—its liberation from the kind of doctrines of the old school (now taken up by well-to-do people) which treat what they call commercial laws, demand and supply for instance, as if they were laws of inanimate matter, not amenable to the will of the human beings from whose feelings, interests, and principles of action they proceed. This is one of the queer mental confusions which will be wondered at by-and-by … (quoted in Mitchell 1967, 565).

That is, social policy should be "about people" (as some might say today), not about economics with its allegedly immutable laws of *laissez faire*. Political economy was the servant, not the master, of enlightened social policy. It was simply shallow-minded thinking to maintain that a lesser, derivative science (political economy) could spin a conceptual web (classical theory) that could bind higher-level science (social science generally) from taking needed steps to improve society. If, in order to finance these improvements, there needed to be a relaxation of certain longstanding "customs" regarding the property rights of [thoroughly "unproductive"] landlords and holders of large inherited fortunes, then so be it. Classical theory laid out the laws governing the production of valuable goods and services with great precision. It also laid out the distributive consequences of those laws under the working assumption of *laissez faire*. It did not, however, mean that those distributive consequences were logically necessary in the event of "enlightened" government intervention, and it certainly did not have anything at all to say about the desirability or undesirability of the *laissez faire* distributive solution. The laws of production were of natural design, but the "laws" of distribution were of human design – subject to societal control, and properly so. As Mill put the matter in a famous passage:

> The laws and conditions of the Production of Wealth partake of the character of physical truths. There is nothing optional or arbitrary in them. …It is not so with the Distribution of Wealth. That is a matter of human institutions solely. The things once there, mankind, individually or collectively, can do with them as they like. They can place them at the disposal of whomsoever they please, and on whatever terms. …The rules by which [the distribution of wealth] is determined are what the opinions and feelings of the ruling portion of the community make them, and are very different in different ages and countries; and might be still more different, if mankind so chose (*Principles*, 199–200; 199–200).

As Sowell (2006, 148) points out, Mill is aware that "production and distribution cannot be so independent of each other when the manner in which a given period's output is distributed affects the use of inputs – and therefore output – in subsequent periods". Only in the short term could distribution proceed independently of considerations of future production. Ultimately the consequences

> of the rules according to which wealth may be distributed … are as little arbitrary, and have
> as much the character of physical laws, as the laws of production. …Society can subject the
> distribution of wealth to whatever rules it thinks best: but what practical results will flow
> from the operation of those rules, must be discovered, like any other physical or mental
> truths, by observation and reasoning. (*Principles,* 200–201; 200)

And earlier in his preface where Mill first broaches this subject, he is careful to state that "though governments or nations have the power of deciding what institutions exist, they cannot arbitrarily determine how those institutions shall work" (*Principles,* 21; 21). Mill thus cannot be sensibly accused of proposing some kind of a naive split between production and distribution – he sees the connection between the two only too clearly. Clearly, certain types of redistributive schemes will come at the expense of lower output (which is not to say that Mill believed – as Classical theory seemed to imply – that *all* such schemes would do so).

Mill's celebrated distinction between production and distribution has played to decidedly mixed reviews. To Barber, Mill's distinction is "[p]erhaps the most significant of Mill's modifications in the orthodox classical tradition…" (Barber 1967, 99–100) in that it robbed classical distribution theory of its deterministic outcome as originally laid down by Malthus. Further, if economic growth were unaccompanied by a more "equitable" distribution of income, then now, under Mill's premises, something could be done about it. Mere economic progress, then, was not good-in-itself if it came at the cost of an "inequitable" distribution of income. Such a thorough tarnishing of the reputation of economic progress opened the way to Mill's favourable reinterpretation of the "steady-state" (*op. cit.,* 101–2). Landreth (1976, 133–5) similarly sees the production–distribution distinction as quite consequential, translating it into modern (post-marginalist-revolution) terms as "there is only a loose connection between the marginal productivity of the various factors and the personal distribution of income" (*op. cit.,* 135).

In sharp contrast, Sowell sees Mill's separation of production and distribution as "a distinction without a difference" (2006, 148) – "In the same sense in which society may distribute as it pleases and take the consequences, it may also produce as it pleases and take the consequences" (*ibid*). For example, society could [and does] decree that less efficient production techniques be used than are readily available. Likewise, Buchholz (1989, 103) deprecates Mill's "schizoid approach to production and distribution" – not only is distribution heavily dependent on production, but, in addition, production laws change over time.

In fact, the distinction between "consequential" and "schizoid" seems considerably determined by ideological perspective, with those leaning left pleased at the open door to meddling with market-based distributional outcomes, and those on the right worrying about the arguably excessive, and eminently mis-useable, power that government must soon acquire in such a society. Blaug (1985, 180) probably gets close to the heart of the matter when he says that while, speaking strictly, "the distinction between the two kinds of laws is untenable", it is arguably best interpreted as "an old-fashioned way of distinguishing between positive and normative economics, separating questions of 'what is' from 'what ought to be'".

The logical justification for Mill's celebrated distinction is, in the end, probably less important than its impact on the decades that followed it. Before Mill, classical distributive doctrine was a sturdy bulwark against the idea that government meddling with the distribution of income was a good thing. The classical doctrine, while wrong on the point that their argument irrefutably established the inadvisability of such meddling, still remained consistent with long-run capitalist stylized facts (a consistency more recognizable today than in Mill's time). Such stylized facts, at least in the opinion of pro-capitalist thinkers, include the notions that the productive tend, on an average, to earn higher incomes, and that there is a kind of rough justice on average in the outcomes achieved under the aegis of the free market (a rough justice in which Mill, not surprisingly, did not himself believe – see Mill (1973 [1861], 474), where he writes "accident has so much more to do than merit with enabling men to rise in the world"). Accordingly, the classical argument was a protector of the strong nineteenth-century trends towards greater economic freedom in the Western societies. This framework Mill now undermined. In its place, he supplied an open-ended rationale for government involvement in the distribution of society's income, without providing well-defined limits on how this power should be applied (as we will see, Book V of his *Principles* is remarkably forgiving of a wide range of government activities).

The clear result in the West has been the replacement of capitalism with a large, unwieldy, and hyper-expansionist welfare state, armed with an ever-broadening definition of "distribution" to fuel its widening assaults on capitalist institutions. Mill did not create this state of affairs explicitly, nor did he implicitly do so single-handedly. Likely he would see such a state as a serious threat to liberty (as it most certainly is). But the extraordinary influence of his *Principles* through the second half of the nineteenth century and well into the twentieth meant that his would be one of the most prominent influences in popularizing what was one – if not *the* – key building block of the modern Welfare State.

Mill's "Orthodox" Contributions in the Principles

Much of Mill's *Principles* consists of (often vastly improved) expositions of then-standard economic theory, where often Mill is synthesizing older ideas rather than presenting new ones. However, in the *Principles* Mill also breaks new ground in a number of significant ways.[12] It is convenient to separate these contributions into "orthodox" and "heterodox" ones. Orthodox contributions are those directly impacting the main line of economic thought, while heterodox contributions seek (in retrospect)

---

[12] This section focuses on Mill's primary orthodox contributions as judged by several leading works on the History of Economic Thought. For readers seeking a good comprehensive summary of the *Principles* focusing more on "what's in it", rather than what is predominately new, see Blaug's *Reader's Guide* to the book in (Blaug 1985).

to take economics away from its main stem. Thus, Mill's heterodox ideas, while often extremely influential, generally fall outside the realm of economic theory proper.

This section focuses on the most generally recognised of Mill's contributions. These fall in the areas of value theory proper, supply-and-demand analysis, international exchange ratios, the theory of joint supply, the theory of public goods, classical growth theory, and macroeconomics. It is convenient to begin with value theory not only because of the topic's significance, but also because Mill's exposition illustrates so well his ability to breathe new life into an old topic.

The Restatement of Classical Value Theory

In his Book III, Mill finally takes up the questions of value and value theory. Mill has been often criticized for failing to place his value theory at the start of his *Principles*, as did Ricardo and Adam Smith (e.g. Blaug 1985, 195).[13] Mill himself states his reasons for postponing his discussion of value at the start of Book III, Chap. 1 (it is peculiar that his own justification for his ordering has not received more attention). He regards the postponement of the treatment of value as being dictated by his distinction between the "Laws of Production" and the "Laws of Distribution". The Laws of Production, he says, are independent of the questions of exchange, depending as they do only on physical (technological) truths. The question of value, then, pertains only to distribution. Even then, political economy has the predominant say only if pure exchange governs the determination of prices. Since in reality custom is also quite important in determining prices, even this limited role for value theory must be discounted considerably (*Principles*, Bk. II, Chap. 4).

Mill is frankly critical of economists who seek to organize all of economics around "catallactics, or the science of exchanges" (*Principles*, 435; 455). Such economists commit "the error too common in political economy, of not distinguishing between necessities arising from the nature of things, and those created by social arrangements" (*op. cit.*, 436; 455) The mistake of over-emphasizing value theory, then, is but a species of the more general mis-steps by political economists of, on the one hand, classing "the merely temporary truths of their subject among its permanent and universal laws", and, on the other hand, mistaking "the permanent laws of Production … for temporary accidents arising from the existing constitution of society" (*Principles, ibid*; 455–6).

Mill's postponement of value theory based on his [in]famous cleavage of the laws of production and distribution, shows how fundamental to political economy he thought that his distinction was. Its thorough and complete grasping, in his view, mandated both a rethinking and a significant reorganization of political economy – even

---

[13] Notably, James Mill's *Elements of Political Economy* also begins with production, moves on to distribution and only then comes to exchange. James Mill's organizational scheme stems from his following goods through production to distribution to exchange and consumption, roughly the temporal order in which things occur in an initial production decision (*Elements of Political Economy*, 2–4).

to the point of downgrading a topic which, even then, was usually thought of as the starting point for the science. Mill's demotion of value theory compared with the treatment of earlier scholars does not mean that he was not impressed by its importance to pure theory. Once the context passed from the actual economy to a hypothetical pure market economy completely built around free exchange at market prices, Mill insisted that the "question of value is fundamental ... the smallest error on that subject infects with corresponding error all our other conclusions" (*Principles, ibid; ibid*). In this light, he proceeds with a discussion of the theory of value that closely tracks that of earlier thinkers, particularly Ricardo.

As is often the case with Mill, though the ideas he develops are not primarily his own, his presentation of those ideas sparkles. Take, for example, his discussion of the two conditions that are necessary if a good is to have value in exchange (*Principles*, Bk. III, Chap. 2). Anyone can simply state that such a good must have intrinsic value ("it must conduce to some purpose, satisfy some desire", [*op. cit.,* 442; 462]) and must be scarce ("there must also be some difficulty in its attainment" [*Principles, ibid; ibid*]). Mill in addition constructs a colourful and instructive example concerning a much-desired music box, owned by one of two passengers travelling into deep wilderness. The potential buyer will be there for many years, he will "part with before sunset" his fellow passenger and continue on to a post where no luxury can be purchased. Our passenger covets the music box (with its "magic with which at times it lulls [his] agitations of mind") and is "vehemently desirous to purchase it". But his fellow passenger and box-owner, aware of the box's value to his casual acquaintance, and even more fully aware that his acquaintance can acquire such a box only through him, will squeeze him to the absolute limit regardless of the irrelevant fact that such a box can be purchased cheaply back in London. As we might say today, the seller, with his absolute monopoly, will squeeze every last drop of consumer surplus out of the transaction. Cost-of-production is irrelevant to the price that will be needed to buy the box under these conditions – all that matters is how much the purchaser values the item. By contrast, in London, where such music boxes are routinely produced, our purchaser would find that it is the cost-of-production that governs the box's price, not his personal satisfaction from ownership. Consumer surplus [as we would say today] accruing to the buyer can be large in this circumstance. Mill's example nicely illustrates an important point: how both satisfaction and production costs contribute to the exchange process, even if it often appears otherwise due to the dominance of cost-of-production in setting the actual price. The example also illustrates how Mill had the essentials of the consumer surplus concept in hand, though not in a completely developed form.

Mill's core value theory closely follows Ricardo's lead in Mill's characteristic manner: which is, while claiming to be doing nothing but synthesizing and summarizing, he actually slips in changes that alter somewhat the doctrine he is addressing. A view often expressed is that Mill took Ricardo's labour theory of value and replaced it with his own cost-of-production value theory (e.g. Landreth 1976, 142–3). This is essentially correct, but, as Schumpeter (1954, 588–603) points out, the true relation between the two value theories is more complex.

Schumpeter defines value theory as an attempt at "indicating the factors that account for a thing's having exchange value or ... the factors that 'regulate' or 'govern' value" (*op. cit.*, 590). The first question to ask here is whether we are speaking of *absolute* value in some sense, or merely *relative* values. There is little doubt that both Ricardo and Mill defined the problem in the latter sense, focussing on rates of exchange between commodities in a way that failed to reveal, when an exchange ratio changed, which good had intrinsically gained or lost in value.[14] Ricardo, however, inspired by Adam Smith's Deer-and-Beaver example, also visualized a role for labour as both the source of value (in that the amount of labour "embodied" in goods determined their relative values under long run competitive conditions) and as a measure of value (in that if a standard labour unit could be defined, then all other market values could be measured in relation to that standard unit). However, Ricardo was forced to recognize quickly that abstinence, or waiting time, was also a component in a good's value, and that "waiting", unlike the other factors of production, could not be said to have an ultimate labour source. Therefore, a strict labour theory of value was incorrect. But he continued to see the labour theory as a useful close approximation to a correct value theory anyway, and therefore his analytical apparatus embraced concepts and methods that a strict application of logic would not.

Mill, while on the surface merely echoing Ricardo, in fact drove home the logic of the latter's argument in a way that made its limitations clear. The abstinence point was emphasized in Mill's volume, and presented in such a way as to definitely dispatch with Ricardo's labour theory (Mill's simultaneous pleading that the labour theory was "practically" correct fails to survive the force of his own arguments to the contrary). Mill also emphasized that not just quantity of labour but wages paid to labour also affect value. In his summary chapter, Mill sums up the conditions leading to one good's commanding a higher value as being one of the following:

> it requires for its production either a greater quantity of labour, or a kind of labour permanently paid at a higher rate; or that the capital, or part of the capital, which supports the labour, must be advanced for a longer period; or lastly, that the production is attended with some circumstance which requires to be compensated by a permanently higher rate of profit (*Principles*, 480; 498–99).

An expansion of value-sources to this extent is, of course, a *de facto* repudiation of the labour theory. In Book III, Chap. 5, Mill also amended Ricardo's pronouncement that rent is always not an element in cost-of-production (and thus not a contributor to value), upholding Ricardo's view "with qualifications which, if correctly stated and developed (which Mill did not do), amount to renouncing it ... and point toward the opportunity cost theory" (Schumpeter op. cit., 604).

In the process of laying out his cost-of-production-based value theory, Mill was naturally led to resolve what many saw as a fundamental contradiction between cost-based value theories and market-based theories (supply and demand). To Mill, there was no contradiction, at least for the case where a good could be reproduced

---

[14] Schumpeter (1954, 589) writes that "J. S. Mill only clinched prevailing practice when he emphasized that the term Value was, in economic theory, essentially relative and that it meant nothing but the exchange ratio between any two commodities or services".

indefinitely (within reason) at constant cost. Here, market gyrations were merely the froth on the sea's waves, while the underlying surface of the sea was given by cost-of-production (*Principles*, 453; 473). As Mill puts it at the end of his Bk. 3, Chap. 3:

> But in all things which admit of indefinite multiplication, demand and supply only determine the perturbations of value, during a period which cannot exceed the length of time necessary for altering the supply. While thus ruling the oscillations of value, they themselves obey a superior force, which makes value gravitate towards Cost of Production ... [D]emand and supply always rush to an equilibrium, but the condition of *stable* equilibrium is when things exchange for each other according to their cost of production ... (*op. cit.*, 456; 475–6).

Those interested in the history of the "perfect competition" paradigm will notice that many of the essentials of the model are already present in Mill's mid-century volume. Also worth mentioning is Mill's casual assumption that the forces of demand-and-supply combine to *quickly* bring about equilibrium.

Supply, Demand, Elasticity

Mill was the first prominent writer on economics to describe the forces of supply-and-demand in a way that is broadly consistent with the way in which we conceptualize these forces in the modern era however, (toiling in relative obscurity, Cournot had anticipated him by 10 years, even drawing supply-and-demand curves as we do today [Blaug 1985, 196]).[15] This is not, however, to say that classical terminology was the same: The classical economists typically used the terms "demand" and "supply" to denote what economists today would denote as "quantity demanded" and "quantity supplied" (e.g. *Principles*, 446; 466: "let us suppose that the demand at some particular time exceeds the supply, that is, there are persons ready to buy, at the market value, a greater quantity than is offered for sale".) Nonetheless, the main line of classical economists – at least Smith, Say, Malthus, Ricardo, and Mill – grasped that demand (and, in a short-run framework, supply also) was fundamentally a *schedule* that related price to units demanded (Sowell 1974, 105–7; Blaug 1985, 43).[16]

Both Smith and Ricardo had elected to analyze market forces within the context of a constant-cost industry assumption, thereby dictating a [long-run] horizontal supply curve fixed at the long-run average cost-of-production (e.g. Blaug 1985, 41, 113–4). It was left to long-run demand-side forces to determine the equilibrium quantity bought and sold at the price given by the horizontal supply curve. Smith supplemented

---

[15] Regarding supply-and-demand, Schumpeter (1954, 603) states that Mill "went much further than the majority of economists before him – always excepting Cournot – and may be said to have been the first to teach its essentials". Landreth (1976, 145) concludes that "it can be argued that our general understanding of the workings of supply and demand in allocating resources under competitive markets has not been fundamentally changed since Mill".

[16] "[T]he quantity demanded is not a fixed quantity, even at the same time and place; it varies according to the value; if the thing is cheap, there is usually a demand for more of it than when it is dear" (*Principles*, 446; 465–66). Sowell (1974, 107) attributes to Malthus the "earliest *schedule* concept of supply and demand", while Blaug (1985, 43) finds the gist of a schedule concept even earlier in *The Wealth of Nations* (Book I, Chap. 7).

his long-run theory with a short-run "market" theory of price-and-quantity determination in order to explain "temporary" deviations in price from the long-run value. In it, market price rises in response to shortages (and vice versa), as in the modern rendition of the theory (Blaug 1985, 42–3). Ricardo's understanding of the model is essentially that of Smith's – although, at least to Blaug, Ricardo's discussion "fosters the impression that cost of production is something separate and apart from demand and supply" (Blaug 1985, 113). The leaving of such an impression was probably inevitable in a restricted supply-and-demand framework where the truly meaningful (i.e. long run) part of the analysis was limited to the case where supply behaviour is completely beholden to the constant-costs assumption.

Mill's primary contribution was to release supply-and-demand with all its potential from the shackles of a constant-cost framework (*Principles*, Bk. III, Chap. 2). His analysis, while not employing graphical methods, still was noticeably more general and thorough than his predecessors. In essence, he presented three separate supply-and-demand frameworks, corresponding to the three main market-based industrial structures that he visualized. Mill recognized as the case of greatest importance, the Smith/Ricardo case of constant (average) costs. But he went on to recognize two additional cases. The second-most important was the case of agriculture and the "extractive" industries (e.g. mining), cases characterized by increasing long-run average costs as the scale of production increased. For these, an upward-sloping industry supply curve was the long-run result – and not merely as a transitional "market" phenomenon. Goods could be reproduced, but only at ever-increasing costs. Finally, Mill presented the case of goods in absolutely limited supply (e.g. old masters paintings), where long-run supply would be a vertical line due to the complete inability to increase the quantity of these types of goods (he did not consider the fact that supply could here be decreased by destruction, no doubt considering it irrelevant to his main point). While Mill did not employ graphical analysis in this discussion, it is easy to do so (e.g. Blaug 1985, 197; Landreth 1976; Wikipedia 2011 The Free Encyclopedia, "Johann Wolfgang von Goethe" 144). Mill's analysis seems surprisingly modern – perhaps because it was one of the primary sources Marshall utilized in crafting his own treatment, which presented supply-and-demand in full-fledged modern garb (Ekelund and Hebert 1983, 154).

The gap in understanding between Ricardo and Mill is greater than it appears at first glance. It is more than just that Ricardo concentrated on a special case while Mill got the more general result. To Ricardo, the long-run supply result is the crux of the matter and mere "market" moves away from that position were mere froth obscuring fundamental realities. In essence, "market" moves away from the long-run supply positions were of secondary, even trivial, importance – merely special short-run cases of a more general model dominated by the long-run industry supply curve. As Schumpeter aptly puts it, Ricardo conceptualizes "*as if determination of price by supply and demand were entirely different from, and incompatible with, determination of price by quantity of labour embodied*" (Schumpeter 1954, 592, italics in the original). Mill, by contrast, saw that constant costs were *not* the most general model. Accordingly, he conceptualized the matter in a manner far more like in the modern era: Supply-and-demand is the general model, and the constant-costs assumption is merely a special case of that more general model. This was a harder, more significant realization to achieve than can be seen outside its historical context, for classical economics conceived the supply-and-demand theory as the leading opponent of the classical labour theory of value (Ekelund and Hebert 1983, 138), making it even harder to see the greater generality of the former model. Here, Mill acts as a key transition figure between the Ricardian and Marshallian systems.

Mill's second significant achievement was to put to bed conceptualizations of the supply-demand tug-of-war that invoked the notion of a *ratio*. James Mill, for example, had written that "the quantity in which commodities exchange for one another depends on the *proportion* of supply to demand" (Mill 1844 [1821], 90). To John Mill, however, such phrases "fail to satisfy anyone who requires clear ideas, and a perfectly precise expression of them" (*Principles*, 446; 465). First, the ratio under discussion had different units in the numerator (a quantity) and in the denominator (a desire). Mill not only finds the ratio notion to be logically unsound, but also sees it as a source of what even then was understood as a circularity puzzle (price determines demand, but also demand determines price, etc.).

Mill then assaults the ratio interpretation of supply-and-demand head-on. If quantity demanded exceeds quantity supplied, then price must rise, but by how much? By the proportional size of the deficiency? For example, does a 10% gap between quantity demanded and quantity supplied imply that a 10% rise in price is needed? "By no means", says Mill: an article which "is a necessary of life" (*op. cit.*, 447; 466) may see a rise in price far beyond the percent given by the ratio, while, on the other hand, the demand for a good which is highly price-sensitive may see a price rise considerably less than the ratio. The ratio method thus offers little correlation or predictive power with respect to the actual adjustments in price needed to swing quantity demanded and quantity supplied into balance (what does correlate and predict, Mill perceives clearly, is the price *elasticity* of demand – though he of course does not have the term). Since the ratio method is conceptually unsound and fails to provide insight into price adjustment, it should be discarded. Instead of conceiving the problem in the terms of a ratio, "the proper mathematical analogy is that of an *equation* … the quantity demanded and the quantity supplied, will be made equal" by price adjustment (*op. cit.*, 448; 467).

International Exchange Ratios and Price Elasticity of Demand

Mill's understanding of the price elasticity of demand and its significant implications to market outcomes is made particularly clear later in Book III, Chap. 18, where he discusses the determination of international values.[17] Here, he describes the theory of reciprocal demand in international trade theory. Just as in regular supply-and-demand theory, equilibrium is where the total quantity of goods supplied equals the total quantity demanded. In international trade, where one country's exports are another's imports, this equilibrium is where the imports of one nation take off the market the

---

[17] Mill actually did much of this work in 1829 and 1830 (see his essay on Trade in his *Essays on Unsettled Questions in Political Economy*) (Mill 1967 [1844]). Mill's treatment there is arguably clearer than in the *Principles*.

whole of the goods another country wishes to export, and vice versa – that is, there is a *reciprocal demand* by one country for the other's exports. In the two-good and two-country case that Mill chiefly examines, relative price adjustment between the two goods continues until each country is induced to buy up the whole of the other's exportable goods with precisely the whole of its own goods produced for export.

Notable here by its absence is Ricardo's notion that cost-of-production governs the rate of exchange between goods. Why should cost-of-production not also fully explain terms-of-trade across borders; that is, why should there be any distinction drawn between international trade and domestic trade in political economy? Ricardo and other classical economists emphasized how a distinct theory of international values emerged out of the fact that factors of production (particularly capital) are unable to flow smoothly across borders the way they can do within a nation's borders. Mill pointed out that, under imperfect factor mobility across nations, there is no mechanism by which cost-of-production can directly control the prices at which foreign exchange occurs. How then are ratios of exchange determined? Since cost-of-production fails to provide guidance, the more basic theory of supply-and-demand must do so. Mill's distinct theory of international values, then, is that the "value of a thing in any place, depends on the cost of its acquisition in that place; which, in the case of an imported article, means the cost of production of the thing which is exported to pay for it" (*Principles*, 583; 595).

To Landreth (1976, 145), Mill's "analysis of the division of the gains from international trade among trading countries is probably Mill's most important and lasting contribution to technical economic theory". Schumpeter (1954, 605–15) also is impressed. The theory's details are now a standard part of international trade theory and, thanks to later work by Marshall and Edgeworth, have been concisely presented in graphical form (both Blaug 1985, 205 and Ekelund and Hebert 1983, 158 present the graphical version). Mill's verbal treatment is, however, notable for its very clear use and application of the price elasticity of demand concept in every sense but in using the name itself.

In laying out his theory, Mill faced the problem of finding the principle(s) that would explain which of two trading countries would gain the most from their trade. Ricardo had shown the conditions under which trade would occur, and the range (given by comparative advantage) within which the trading ratio would fall. At one extreme trading-ratio, one country would gain virtually all of the gains from trade; at the other, the other country would reap all the gains. What principle(s) determine where, in the range given by the two extreme ratio-values, the terms-of-trade would actually settle? Ricardo had "glibly assumed that the advantage would be halved" (Schumpeter 1954, 608), but Mill delved more deeply into the question.[18]

---

[18] In the original essay in the *Unsettled Questions*, Mill makes excuses for Ricardo on the grounds that Ricardo, "having a science to create" (page 4), had no time to trifle with second-order issues. Mill thus, in an oft-played role, assigns to himself the middling task of mopping up after Ricardo. In fact, as is usually the case while playing this humble role, Mill advances the state of understanding considerably of the topic at hand. Perhaps Mill's relative assessment of his contribution to the topic improved with time, for there is no hint of this self-effacing attitude in his discussion of it in the *Principles*.

Mill proceeds methodically, beginning with the pure statics of the problem. He sets up a two-country, two-commodity framework, where the given comparative advantage dictates that the original autarky be replaced by complete specialization by the two nations (England in broadcloth, Germany in linen). He shows how the equilibrium trading ratio will be where the entirety of Germany's linen production will exactly trade for the entirety of England's broadcloth production. He then moves on to comparative statics: supposing a decline in demand by England for German linen, can England alter the terms of exchange so as to improve their position relative to Germany? Mill concludes that indeed they can do so: England's "buyers' strike" will force Germany to offer more favourable terms of trade. Accordingly, the rate of exchange between the two commodities will move in favour of England, and more of the gains from trade will be distributed to England. Mill next introduces transportation costs ("cost of carriage") and shows that, if trade continues, transportation costs need not be shared equally among the trading nations (it "would depend on the play of international demand" (*Principles*, 589; 601)).

Mill becomes more specific regarding the splitting-up of the gains from trade in the next section where he extends his framework from two to three traded commodities. The country that "draws to itself the greatest advantage" from trade is "the country for whose productions there is in other countries the greatest demand, *and a demand the most susceptible of increase from additional cheapness*" (*op. cit.*, 591; 602, italics added). In his next section, where he postulates a cheapening in cost-of-production such that Germany's productivity in linen production increases markedly while England's remains unaltered, his use of elasticity becomes explicit (in everything but use of the word itself). "Linen", he says, "falls one-third in value in the German market, as compared with other commodities produced in Germany. Will it also fall one-third as compared with English cloth" (*op. cit.*, 594; 605), giving England the entire benefit of the improvement, or will England's gain be something less?

In deciding who gains and by how much from Germany's innovation, Mill breaks the problem down into three possibilities, defined by the inelastic, elastic, and unit-elastic cases (though, once again, he does not have the actual terms themselves). "The demand for linen in England … might be increased either in proportion to the cheapness, or in a greater proportion than the cheapness, or in a less proportion" (*Princples, ibid*; 606). In the case Mill regards as most common, the inelastic case, the demand in England for linen is inadequate to prevent total English expenditures on linen from falling despite rising unit demand. As a result, linen is even cheaper in England than in Germany, and Germany must offer less favourable trading terms to sell all of their linen. In this case, the non-innovating trading partner will out-gain the innovating country. The reverse holds in the case where demand is elastic, and the gains from the invention are shared equally in the unit elastic case.[19]

Mill goes on in later sections of the chapter to analyse the sense in which cost-of-production indirectly comes into play in determining terms of trade, a discussion in which elasticity continues to be prominently featured. At one point, as a simplifying

---

[19] Mill is aware of the possible inroads opened by his analysis for government-led manipulation of the terms of trade with other nations. He discusses the matter in Book V, Chapter 4 of the *Principles*.

assumption, Mill explicitly assumes what is today called the rectangular hyperbola demand curve (which features unit elasticity everywhere on it). Overall, in his discussion of international values and terms-of-trade adjustment, Mill advances the development of the elasticity concept well beyond where he had found it. His application of the concept to international exchange also was path-breaking. Schumpeter (1954, 609) is of the view that "[i]n this field Marshall did not do more than to polish and develop Mill's meaning". Landreth (1976, 146) states that no "major changes in the classical theory of international trade were made" until Ohlin and Keynes, early in the twentieth century.

Theory of Joint Supply

While there is often debate about how much of Mill's *Principles* is truly original, it is generally acknowledged that Mill's treatment of the problem of joint supply (or joint costs) was significant and new (cf. Blaug 1985, 198). Mill confronted the issue in his chapter on "Some Peculiar Cases of Value" (Bk. III, Chap. 16). As is now widely known, the problem pertains to the case of a single production process that by necessity generates two different products in fixed proportions (beef and hides, and coke and coal-gas are two of Mill's examples). Mill saw that the notion of profit maximization for each of the paired goods individually made no sense. It was the profit maximization of the entire production process that counted. As Mill put the matter: "Cost of production does not determine their prices, but the sum of their prices" (*Principles*, 570; 583).

Mill's treatment has the pedagogical benefit of using the identical method of approach that he had previously used in discussing supply-and-demand and international values. Again a case is found where cost-of-production does not provide the needed information; here, on how an equilibrium production of the two products is reached. Again, Mill falls back on the "more fundamental ... law of demand and supply" (*Principles, ibid*; *ibid*) to supply the insight that cost-of-production cannot. And again the problem is to find a price (or, in this case, prices) that will take the production of both goods in the joint process off the market.

It is not enough to maximize profits from production of Good A if the joint product Good B is not also contributing its maximum amount to joint profits. One must maximize profits over the whole of the joint process. Mill has a nice example using gas and coke. Gas is in demand and so a good equilibrium price is easily found for the whole of the gas production. However, to "force a market" for coke such that the whole of it is sold, coke's price must go very low – too low, in fact, to cover the costs of the entire manufacturing process. Under these circumstances, the price of gas is raised (note the assumption of market power) to cover the losses on coke, meaning there is a decrease in quantity demanded for gas. Gas prices rise and so do coke prices as their quantities diminish. At the end of this complicated adjustment process, says Mill, prices will settle where both markets are cleared and at prices that cover costs. "If there is any surplus or deficiency on either side ... the values and prices of the two things will so readjust themselves that both shall find a market" (*op. cit.*, 571; 584).

Mill's solution to the joint supply problem is still today's solution. In more modern terms, "the equilibrium price of each product must be such as to clear *its* market, *subject to the condition that the sum of the two prices equals their (average) joint costs*" (Ekelund and Hebert 1983, 155 [italics in the original]). Later, Marshall provided an elegant graphical treatment (see *ibid*). As Ekelund and Hebert (*op. cit.*, 156) point out, the joint supply problem has extensive applications, not just in manufacturing but in a wide range of circumstances (such as public-goods, and pollution). Mill's early solution to the problem of joint supply – achieved without any mathematical aid – is therefore quite a significant contribution to applied microeconomic theory.

Public Goods

Mill also breaks new ground in the *Principles* (Book V, Chap. 11, Section 15) by elucidating the concept of "public goods". Mill anticipated "the Italian writers on finance in the 1890s" (Blaug 1985, 218) by decades with his statement and lucid development of these concepts.[20] Mill lays out the difficulty with private supply, and the consequent argument for public subsidy/supply, of such goods in terms strikingly similar to the treatment of the topic found in modern Principles of Economics texts. "A voyage of geographical or scientific exploration", he says, "may be of great public value, yet no individual would derive any benefit from it which would repay the expense … and there is no mode of intercepting the benefit on its way to those who profit by it, in order to levy a toll for the remuneration of its authors" (*Principles*, 975; 968). As a second example, Mill cites lighthouses, which, he says, cannot be paid for via a levy at sea on those benefiting from the lighthouse "unless indemnified and rewarded from a compulsory levy made by the state" (*op. cit.*, 976; 968) – meaning that if private supply fails then government must step in and supply (or subsidize the supply of) such goods. Such enterprises are, therefore, generally left to governments to subsidize or undertake. As a third example, Mill mentions research into theoretical knowledge, which he recommends the government encourage through the [now-time-honoured] practice of creating university teaching posts that contain a research component. As is now generally understood, the primary potential problem with all such goods is that many people benefiting from such a good stand aside and wait for others to come forward and voluntarily fund the good. Such "free-riders" hope to enjoy the good's benefits without paying for the good. Thus, sufficient funds to finance the good cannot be accumulated since many of those who benefit will enjoy the good for free, paradoxically leading to the good not being supplied at all privately.

Mill's lighthouse example would later famously trigger the seminal paper by Ronald Coase (1974), which detailed how lighthouses routinely were privately built

---

[20] Mill however does not display a complete command of the public-goods concept, particularly as regards to its breadth. He treats the public good issue (discussed in Section 15) as separate from the incomplete coordination issue known today as the "who goes first" problem (discussed in Section 12). Modern public finance theory sees them as two varieties of the same prisoners' dilemma problem (cf. Buchanan 1967).

in the England of Mill's day. It is now widely held that Coase's argument refuted Mill's. However, Mill did not advocate public supply but rather *de facto* public funding of such goods, not through explicit funding but rather through laws empowering the private builders of lighthouses to collect fees from shipping (a sort of "tax-farmer" arrangement). This is more or less the model of supply that Coase demonstrates actually was in place to give incentive to private construction. Thus, despite Coase's critique, Mill's argument in the *Principles* remains sound.

It is somewhat surprising that Mill did not give more attention to the possibility of wholly private arrangements that might be able to do a creditable job of supplying public goods. Certainly, Mill saw no "coordination problems" implicit in the problem of creating and maintaining socialist workers' co-operatives (*Principles*, Bk. IV, Chap. 7, Sctn. 6). It would not have been unreasonable for him to ask why, if the problem of free-riding was so predominant in the supply of public goods; was it not then equally daunting in the creation and maintenance of such cooperatives? Such questions would, however, be left to future generations.

A Stepping-Stone to Modern Growth Theory

Mill's *Principles*, in the opening chapters of Book IV, conveys a rendition of the dynamics of economic growth that is a notable improvement from that of Ricardo and earlier thinkers. At times, the discussion seems almost modern. While, naturally, the approach is classical and therefore Malthusian, it hints strongly of the neoclassical growth theory that would be so influential in the second half of the twentieth century (and beyond).

Following a brief discussion of "statics" and "dynamics" at the start of Chap. 1, Mill launches quickly into one of the most profound and emphatic endorsements of the long-run benefits of capitalism that can be found anywhere in his works. The "civilized nations" have propelled themselves into an era marked by "perpetual, and so far as human foresight can extend, ... unlimited, growth of man's power over nature" (*Principles*, 696; 706). "Our knowledge of the properties and laws of physical objects shows no sign of approaching its ultimate boundaries", and moreover, "[t]his increasing physical knowledge is now, too, more rapidly than in any other period, converted, by practical ingenuity, into physical power" (*Principles, ibid; ibid*). In consequence, "it is impossible not to look forward to a vast multiplication and long succession of contrivances for economizing labour and increasing its produce..." (*Principles, ibid; ibid*).[21] These powerful trends are aided strongly by "a continual increase in security of person and property", not only against common thievery, but also "by institutions or by manners and opinion, [protecting] against arbitrary exercise of the power of government" (*op. cit.*, 697; 707). Further, "[t]axation, in all European countries, grows less arbitrary and oppressive, both in

---

[21] Interestingly, nowhere in this discussion does Mill state that it is capitalist institutions that have played a main role in creating this bounty, but this may be induced from other passages in the volume (e.g. Book I, Chap. 13, 189–90), and the "Peasant Proprietors" chapters explicitly linking favourable incentives to productive activity (Book II, Chaps. 6–9).

itself and in the manner of levying it" (*Principles, ibid; ibid*). International Trade (discussed in his next chapter) and the waning of warfare also plays a significant role, as does the growth of insurance. Mill emphasizes the promotion of prosperity given by enhanced security: "Industry and frugality cannot exist where there is not a preponderant probability that those who labour and spare will be permitted to enjoy" (*Principles, ibid; ibid*). Then, in a passage that reminds us that Hayek (1948 [1945]; 1972 [1944], Chap. 6) closely studied Mill:

> Experience has shown that a large proportion of the results of labour and abstinence may be taken away by fixed taxation, without impairing, and sometimes even with the effect of stimulating, the qualities from which a great production and an abundant capital take their rise. But those qualities are not proof against a high degree of uncertainty. The Government may carry off a part; but there must be assurance that it will not interfere, nor suffer anyone to interfere, with the remainder. (*Principles*, 697–8; 707)

These remarks largely anticipate the pro-capitalist positions which modern growth theory has, after a long and unproductive stint in the socialist-technocratic wilderness, come to advocate (cf., Hall and Papell 2005: Chap. 6 ["Growth and the World Economy"], which offers a concise introduction to this literature). Mill deserves great credit for anticipating such doctrines, and by so many decades.

Following an impressive defence of speculators in market systems, Mill next turns to the "nature and consequences" of the observed fact that "[a]ll the nations which we are accustomed to call civilized, increase gradually in production and population" (*Principles*, 696; 706) – or, as we might say today, *growth theory*. Mill's rendition of classical growth theory in Chap. 3 has arguably received less appreciation than it is due. True, Smith highlighted the topic of growth in the *Wealth of Nations*, while Ricardo followed with a tolerably complete treatment of the consequences of simultaneous and proportionate growth in capital and population. But in his Chap. 3, Mill lays his discussion out in remarkably similar fashion to how the Solow model (the foundation of modern neoclassical growth theory) is treated today – first he addresses the case where population alone is growing ("capital and the arts of production remaining stationary" [*Principles,* 710; 719]), then the case where capital alone is growing, then the Ricardian case where both population and capital are growing, and finally the case where progress in technology ("a sudden improvement made in the arts of production" [*op. cit.,* 715; 723]) occurs, in the absence of other changes. Mill's far more complete and systematic discussion advances the treatment of growth in the classical literature considerably, and, laid out as it is in modern fashion, it makes it easy to directly compare the workings and conclusions of classical growth theory in comparison with neoclassical growth theory. (A complete direct comparison is difficult, because of Classical growth theory's focus on the distribution of income, which has no real corresponding feature in neoclassical theory.)

Mill begins with a discussion of the effects of growth of population within Classical growth theory. Growth in the labour force in the absence of technological improvement or other offsetting factors lowers wages through greater competition for the same jobs. Workers suffer accordingly, and must cut back on consumption. However, since there are now more workers, Mill thinks that, in general, the demand for food will increase due to its inelasticity of demand. More food will be produced, and rents will rise due to diminishing returns to agriculture. Labourers lose from this process, while capitalists and particularly landlords gain. So far we see an argument that leads roughly where the neoclassical model leads in the event of an increased population *ceteris paribus*. There, the greater population leads to less capital-per-worker, accompanied by less growth and less well-being for the now-larger population (see, e.g. Jones 2002, Chap. 2).

So far, so good – different models reaching the same conclusions. But now the correlation ends jarringly in Mill's discussion of the consequences of an increase in capital in the Classical model. Mill uses "increase in capital" in a fixed-proportions / wages-fund way. An addition to capital only increases funds to support the sustenance of labour (e.g. capital is not conceived of as tools, machinery, etc.). Since each labourer needs a fixed amount of sustenance, and is already getting all he needs (by assumption), additional capital can do nothing to enhance the productive ability of labourers (this is in sharp contrast to the neoclassical approach which defines capital as complementary to labour and in variable proportions). Accordingly, all that additional capital can do is bid up the price of the fixed labour force. (Elsewhere, Mill even talks of how in a slow-growing country, introduction of machinery could badly hurt labour due to funds being taken out of the wages-fund to finance that machinery [*Principles*, 742; 749]). The additional capital therefore leads to no additional employment (he assumes there is little unused labour to be put to work), and its sole effect is to raise workers' wages and lower firms' profits. Output is unchanged. The additional capital in essence works as a kind of tax [!] on the hiring of labour by subsidizing additional competition for use of the fixed labour stock (this "tax" takes the form of a transfer from employers to workers and also landlords if – as Mill thinks likely – the demand for food increases). This bizarre argument builds in a profound pessimism about the ability of capital acquisition to increase output or contribute in any way to economic growth (again, here we are holding technology constant).

Mill's rendition of classical growth theory also is pessimistic about the ability of technological enhancements to improve the lot of the labouring classes – now for the familiar Malthusian reasons. It is not that Mill is unimpressed with the power of technological improvement to increase human well-being. As we have already seen, Book IV, Chap. 1 is dedicated to lauding past and likely future effects of technological improvement on society. It is, rather, that population growth among the labouring classes will quickly chew up any gains in living standards that briefly emerge (or, if he does not fully embrace this presumption in reality, at least he feels compelled to place it before the reader as a conservative measure).[22]

---

[22] Mill is not one for "trickle-down" theories: He speaks of how great progress can co-exist with a considerable underclass that gains little from progress at the higher income levels. "We must, therefore", he says, "in considering the effects of the progress of industry, admit as a supposition, however greatly we deprecate as a fact, an increase of population as long-continued, as indefinite, and possibly even as rapid, as the increase of production and accumulation" (*Principles*, 699; 709). Arguably, this passage should be interpreted as Mill denying that he believes in the Malthusian assumption he still feels compelled to make, but is coming to disbelieve. It would be interesting to see him explicitly step out of the Malthusian box and contemplate the consequences, but, at least in the analysis of Book IV, he never does, except – as usual – to propose ways of lowering birth rates.

In his analysis of the case of technological improvement, Mill's main line of discussion argues that improvements usually extend in their impact into the agricultural sector. Starting with this assumption, he then breaks his analysis into two parts; first, where the change is sudden and substantial, the second (much more common) where it is continuous and gradual. The first, "technology shock", case overwhelms the counterforce of labour-supply growth, pushing back the margin of land usage, lowering food prices and thereby lowering rents, and benefiting labour accordingly. Likely population growth will, however, eventually blunt these advantages, returning labour to its original state unless voluntary abstinence in fertility is followed (an abstinence which Mill sees as unlikely in the society in which he lived). Mill goes on to acknowledge that such declines in rents as predicted by the "technology shock" model in fact are not observed. This is because, in fact, technological change is slow and steady, not discrete. Accordingly population is constantly putting pressure on whatever gains technology offers society. These conclusions, again, are in sharp disagreement with those of neoclassical growth theorists, who, free to contemplate technological improvement in a non-Malthusian economy, are able to unleash the full power of technological progress as an unbridled benefit for mankind. Mill, never able to shake his fear of population growth, could not find his way to such a conclusion. Malthusian theory simply imposed unshakeable constraints on one's ability to fully see the power of technological change to improve the lot of humankind. Still, the potential of growth-enhancing forces is nicely highlighted by Mill in these chapters.

Commonsense Thoughts on Taxation, Government and Welfare (Bk. V, Chaps. 2–6; 8–11)

While many of the ideas presented can be found in earlier works, Mill's thorough treatment of public finance is a nice early contribution to the field. He begins by repeating Adam Smith's four dictums regarding appropriate taxes. Rates paid by citizens should be "proportionate to their respective abilities". Tax liabilities should be "certain, and not arbitrary". Taxes should be levied when it is easiest for the citizen to pay them. And (using modern terminology), a tax should impose as small burden (deadweight loss) as is consistent with other objectives of the tax. These are serviceable maxims which even today's copiously enlightened legislators might usefully find time to contemplate. Mill regards all but the first of these principles as self-explanatory. As for the first, he launches straightaway into a discussion of "equality" in taxation that touches nicely on most of the core concepts of modern taxation theory. Pursuit of equality of taxation, says Mill, means achieving equality of sacrifice – a principle that would seem to imply progressive taxation (the millionaire parts easily with $100, while the pauper is devastated by the loss).[23] Certainly

---

[23] "As, in a case of voluntary subscription for a purpose in which all are interested, all are thought to have done their part fairly when each has contributed according to his means, that is, has made an equal sacrifice for the common object; in like manner should this be the principle of compulsory contributions…" (*Principles*, 805; 808).

he favoured progressivity in taxing bequests and inheritances (*Principles*, 809; 811). For income taxes Mill favoured proportionality despite his approval of the principal of progressivity, due to disincentives to "saving the earnings of honest exertions" (*op. cit.*, 808; 811). He would combine this with an exemption for income below a certain amount. Mill was alive to the negative impact on economic activity of progressivity in income taxes, though he saw no such problems with the taxation of (what he saw as) idle fortunes (*op. cit.*, 808–9; 810–11). He also thought that, by taxing "luxuries" at a higher rate than necessities, society could indirectly impose some progressivity with respect to income without the heavy work-disincentives of a direct income tax.

Mill touches on many of the concepts of modern tax policy in his general discussion. Should taxes be imposed according to the benefits one receives from government protection of one's property? No, government's mandate is far broader than just protecting property, so this argument fails. Should the tax rate on "the profits of trade" (a profits tax or capital-gains tax) be at a lower rate than "incomes derived from interest or rent"? (*op. cit.*, 810; 813). Yes, such "life incomes", at least in comparison to the "perpetual incomes" flung off by land, are both shorter in duration and far more precarious, so that fairness in taxation should lead to their being taxed at a lower rate (by implication, the same argument would seem to apply to wage income). Interestingly, Mill does not advance any output-enhancement arguments for a lower tax on "profits from trade". Mill also fully treats direct, indirect, and miscellaneous taxes in these chapters (although the consistent malthusianism characterizing the analysis limits these sections' interest to the modern reader). He is an early advocate of what we today would call a consumption tax. Setting aside tax cheating, "the proper mode of assessing an income tax would be to tax only the part of income devoted to expenditure, exempting that which is saved" [*op. cit.*, 813; 815]. Also notable in this section is his discussion of the distortions caused by the curiosum known as the "window-tax", which was a house-tax "of a bad kind, operating as a tax on light, and a cause of deformity in building..." (*op. cit.*, 835; 837).

Mill supplies useful warnings against the dangers of excessive taxation. "Taxation should not encroach upon the amount of the national capital", he says, and, in particular, he is at pains to warn his reader that "[o]ver-taxation, carried to a sufficient extent, is quite capable of ruining the most industrious community, especially when it is in any degree arbitrary..." (*op. cit.*, 821; 822). Here, Mill implicitly recognises the core principles of both the Laffer Curve (with his concern about the output effects of "over-taxation") and Hayekian "rules vs. discretion" doctrine (the view that even high taxes can be tolerated so long as their burden is known to calculating agents [cf. Hayek 1972 [1944]]). Advocates of free-market principles however should have their celebration quickly. Mill closes the chapter paradoxically by arguing that, while taxes on "legacies and inheritances" are taxes on capital (a type of tax which, a page earlier, he had condemned), this should not prevent them being taxed anyway. The amount raised by such a tax "is but a small fraction of the annual increase of capital in such a country" (*Principles.*, 822; 823). He might also have mentioned the vast good he thought such revenues could do in the hands of wise and enlightened government officials (e.g. *Principles*, 741; 748).

Mill devotes the last hundred pages of the *Principles* to the question of the proper tasks of, and limits to, government action. Government's role as the protector of "person and property" (*op. cit.*, 881; 880) is essential to economic progress. Mill emphasizes how high taxes, if known and predictable, can be fairly well-tolerated by an economy. That having been said, high taxes alone can cause much damage to prosperity. Similarly, poorly administered justice, due not only to bad law but also poorly organized legal institutions that make legal recourse difficult and/or expensive to obtain, is a serious potential "tax" on society's productive members. Mill discusses inheritance law, contract law (including legal partnerships and incorporations), and insolvency law. Regarding contract law, he sees clearly the advantages of limited liability incorporation – then a relatively new innovation – in an industrial economy where the accumulation of "large capitals" is immeasurably aided by such legal protections. He is however not blind to the accompanying risks; specifically, the moral hazard problem of managers of such firms misusing their responsibilities for personal gain (*Principles*, 901; 898–9), and he discusses the disadvantages of such arrangements more thoroughly in Bk. V, Chap. 11, Sctn 11. Finally, Mill turns to insolvency (bankruptcy) law, which must be helpful to the indigent but not so well-crafted as to "protect idleness or prodigality" (*op. cit.*, 888; 886).

Mill's Chap. 10 identifies government interventions which economic theory condemns. Mill gives what are now considered to be the standard arguments against protectionism, usury laws, price ceilings in general, government-sponsored monopolies, and suppression of labour's right to organize. Government suppression of free thought is also condemned as "fatal to all prosperity" (*op. cit.*, 940; 935). Society, Mill thinks, has seen the last of these fallacious interventions: "The false theories of political economy which have done so much mischief in times past, are entirely discredited…" (*op. cit.*, 916; 913). Alas, all of them and more have dominated policy discussions in the bulk of the twentieth (and now, twenty-first) centuries, due in no small part to Mill's own progressive ideas, which have been used by others to justify far broader interventions than Mill himself would have advocated.

Turning now to Mill's treatment of welfare, the reader will find Mill writing in a fashion very reminiscent of the modern approach to welfare often espoused by conservative thinkers. Yes, "the claim to help ... created by destitution, is one of the strongest which can exist", and "the relief of so extreme an exigency" should be made "as certain to those who require it as by any arrangements of society it can be made" (*Principles*, 967; 960). But assistance must be given in a carefully measured quantity, lest people be made too dependent on the dole, to the disadvantage of society. Assistance should not be given to the extent that the recipient is as well off as his neighbour who has achieved success where the recipient has failed. Mill speaks of "many highly pauperized districts in more recent times, which have been dispauperized by adopting strict rules of poor-law administration, to the great and permanent benefit of the whole labouring class" (*op. cit.*, 968; 961–2). Further, on no account should those on the dole be given the right to vote themselves additional benefits. "Those who pay no taxes, disposing by their votes of other people's money, have every motive to be lavish, and none to economize" (Mill 1973 [1861], 471). Mill also advocates a complementary relationship between the public dole and private charity.

The state should not be in the business of distinguishing between the worthy and unworthy: its policies must be governed by a mandate to "act by general rules" (*op. cit.*, 969; 962). The state's role is to provide a small stipend to all who are needy, without trying to "discriminate between the deserving and the undeserving indigent" (*Principles, ibid*; *ibid*). The givers of public relief have no role to play as "inquisitors" (*Principles, ibid*; *ibid*). It should be the business of private charity to make those distinctions, and so determine who is worthy of additional support. In this way a "tyrannical" (*Principles, ibid*; *ibid*) welfare agency is prevented from coming into existence.

Mill's Macroeconomic Contributions

Mill's *Principles*, as a comprehensive summary of political economy, naturally contained a treatment of Classical "macroeconomics". It was, of course, built around Say's Law, which famously held that "the very act of production *guaranteed* that an equivalent amount of consuming power would be created" (Montgomery 2006). So long as Say's Law stood, underconsumptionist theories of underemployment were easily vanquished. The equivalency between production and consumption stated by Say's Law, however, was only true by definition in a barter economy. How did things stand in a monetary economy, where purchasing power could vanish into storage vaults, holes in the ground, and other such "sinks" of unspent value?

Classical economists saw clearly that equivalency between production and consumption was clear-cut so long as hoarding of purchasing power – i.e. of money – was ruled out. Early classical thinkers accordingly went to great lengths to "establish" the non-existence of hoarding. Their first thrust was to emphasize that money is valuable only as a facilitator of purchasing, thus implying (but not really demonstrating) that all (or nearly all) money would be constantly spent, not held. In his famous essay on Money in the *Principles* (Bk. III, Chap. 7), Mill himself held that money was only "a machine for doing quickly and commodiously, what would be done, though less quickly and commodiously, without it…" (*Principles*, 488; 506). Say had been more explicit in denying a store-of-value role to money, stating that the money "you will have received on the sale of your own products, and given in the purchase of those of other people, will *the next moment* execute the same between other contracting parties…" (1983 [1803], 13, emphasis added). Likewise Adam Smith argued that "[w]hat is annually saved is as regularly consumed as what is annually spent, and *nearly* in the same time too; but it is consumed by a different set of people" (Smith 1937 [1776], 321, emphasis added). The glib "nearly" was in fact a tacit admission that the time element was critical to the argument. As Blaug put it, "[t]he operative proposition hidden away in Smith's phraseology is that saving is tantamount to investment because 'hoarding', the building up of monetary holdings, is regarded as an exceptional occurrence" (Blaug 1985, 55–6).

The problem in all this for Classical theory was the implausibility of the claim that money was not a store of value. If money *were* hoarded, then it would be difficult to argue that there was no essential difference between a purely barter and a money economy. Writing in the late 1820s, a young Mill therefore sought to dismiss this difficulty.[24] Mill quickly ceded the point that money could act as a store of value, and that, therefore, there was no logical reason why purchasing power could not retire temporarily into idle cash balances. In fact, part of the value of money was that it allowed the moment of purchase to be separated from the moment when the money gained is used to acquire a new good. Therefore:

> The buying and selling being now separated, it may very well occur, that there may be, at some given time, a very general inclination to sell with as little delay as possible, accompanied with an equally general inclination to defer all purchases as long as possible (Mill 1967 [1844], 276).

Mill went on to describe a commercial "crisis" as a period of time where just such an episode would likely occur, during which money

> was in request, and all other commodities were in comparative disrepute. In extreme cases, money is collected in masses, and hoarded; in the milder cases, people merely defer parting with their money, or coming under any new engagements to part with it. But the result is, that all commodities fall in price, or become unsaleable. (*op. cit., 277*)

Thus a symptom (not a cause) of the crisis is the *excess demand for money* – the mirror image of the excess supply of goods that characterizes the crisis. But Mill argues that such a situation "can only be temporary, ... since those who have sold without buying will certainly buy at last..." (*ibid*). Mill is convinced (as were other Classical economists) that the crisis period is short and so such an excess demand for money / excess supply of goods also will last only for a short time. Such short-term disruptions, he says, bear no resemblance to the chronic demand deficiencies alleged by underconsumptionists like Malthus. Thus, the short-term disruption caused by a crisis offers no support to those who see the economy suffering from a chronic insufficiency of total demand.

One significant achievement Mill accomplished by this line of reasoning is to free the Classical framework from the restrictive assumption that money be used only as a medium of exchange, not also as a store of value. But this freedom came at a cost. The older line based on the premise that money was not a store of value established a strict equivalency between a barter economy and a monetary economy; in both, Say's law strictly guaranteed full employment. By broadening the classical view to include routinely storable money, and thereby eliminating an unpalatable assumption, Mill in one sense increased the plausibility of that view. However, his more general argument also weakened the case for money's neutrality. In "the long run", money was still neutral (hoarded money would eventually be spent), and Say's Law still guaranteed full employment (accordingly, Mill ended his essay with a brusque, incisive rejection of the underconsumptionist argument). But now there was a time period of a "short" but unspecified length (the "crisis") during which money's store-of-value function was vital in bringing about a period during which "all commodities fall in price, or are unsaleable" (*ibid*).

---

[24] "On the Influence of Consumption on Production", in his *Essays in Some Unsettled Questions in Political Economy* (Mill 1967 [1844]).

Mill's identification in the *Unsettled Questions* of a way in which demand for goods-in-general could for a time be deficient due to the unique role played by money in the economy, thus marks one of the beginnings of the transition from the Classical to the modern "macro-view". It is even, arguably, the start of mainstream macroeconomic theory.[25] Mill identified the key aspect of modern business cycle theory – that deviations from full employment are self-correcting but occur for reasons that are *not* essentially microeconomic in nature (they affect all sectors more-or-less equally).

This was an idea quite distinct from standard classical reasoning. Earlier classical discussions of aggregate economic difficulties predominately involved circumstances where problems in individual commodity markets were large enough to exert a significant aggregate impact – as in cases where "production is not excessive, but merely ill-assorted" (*Principles*, 559; 573), such as in Ricardo's "sudden changes in the channels of trade" argument (Ricardo 2006 [1821], Chap. 19). To the pre-Mill classical economists, aggregate economics issues were just the outcome of the issues of all the individual industries – a problem of microeconomics writ large. The notion that something might occur that would push more or less uniformly downward on demand for goods-in-general plays little role in Classical thinking.[26]

Mill's macroeconomic theorizing was of a milder sort than modern aggregate-demand based theories. Mill made no argument based on the notion of an *exogenous* decline in purchasing power due to an excess demand for money. He saw hoarding-type behaviour instead as an endogenous response to the circumstances of the crisis itself. The recovery from the crisis, and the elimination of the excess demand for money, occurred in tandem, with the recovery leading the way. Nonetheless, it was the existence of routinely storable money that allowed the crisis to develop in the manner it did – no "excess supply of goods" (as we would say today) could occur otherwise. The mirror-image of Mill's excess supply of goods is his excess demand for money. Perhaps the duration of the crisis – maybe even its cause – is due to the disequilibrium in the supply of, and demand for, money in the crisis period. Down this road lies monetary disequilibrium theory, pioneered by David Hume (1970 [1752], 37) in the context of a change in the money supply. Mill, arguably without intending to do so, raised the possibility of a monetary disequilibrium stemming from an "under-supply of money" (*Principles*, 561; 574), occurring not in Hume's context of an exogenous reduction in the money supply, but rather under circumstances where a sudden crisis-induced increase in demand for money causes the normal quantity of money to correspond to a state of excessive demand for money. This was

---

[25] Hume had earlier perceived that periods of money inflow corresponded to periods where "industry has encreased" (1970 [1752], 37) and vice versa (*op. cit.*, 40). Moreover, Hume had seen that "there is always an interval before matters be adjusted to their new situation…" (*ibid*). But he had dealt only with cases of change in money supply, and Hume's essay aggressively denies that money is anything but a medium-of-exchange and a unit-of-account.

[26] There are some exceptions. For example, Ricardo (2006 [1821], Chap. 21, 205–6) traces out the bare bones of a money-driven cycle based on confusion of real and nominal effects. But Ricardo discusses these within the context of a single representative merchant, and does not go on to draw out any economy-wide implications from these insights. Moreover, he places no special emphasis on these passages – they are merely ruminations in the midst of other loosely related ruminations.

a substantive break from previous classical arguments, but it was a clear antecedent of twentieth-century monetary theory; in particular, monetarism in its several forms.

The National Debt (Book V, Chap. 7)

In the midst of a general discussion in Book V on taxes, Mill addresses the National Debt, a topic we would today be more inclined to place under macroeconomics. Chapter 7, which discusses the National Debt and issues pertaining to it, is notable for its anticipation of many of the themes that would later animate the modern discussion of the topic. Suppose the government of a country must undertake a vast new expenditure – does it matter whether it is financed via taxes or public borrowing? Yes, says Mill. Assuming deficit finance under strict classical conditions, all funds borrowed by the government would otherwise have been used to enhance the wages fund, paying the wages of labour. Therefore, wages will be lower, and the revenues borrowed have been taken from labour just as surely as if they had all been taxed away instead. From this perspective, it makes no difference whether the new public spending is financed by a tax this year or borrowing followed by a drawn-out payment, except that society is worse off in the latter case due to the lengthy liability incurred by the public sector (Mill attributes this argument to Chalmers [*Principles* Bk 1, Chap. 5, Sctn. 8], rather than Ricardo), and except for the not inconsiderable costs of running the tax system itself ("expense, vexation, disturbance of the channels of industry, and other mischiefs over and above the mere payment of the money…" [*Principles*, 876; 876]).[27]

Mill does not stop there however but looks for exceptions to the principle asserted. If the borrowed funds would not otherwise have been used productively (unproductive expenditure), or if the funds are to be borrowed from abroad rather than out of the domestic wages fund, or if they consist of domestic funds to be lent elsewhere, or if (due to the approach of the stationary state) capital is suffering from returns so low as to be near Mill's "practical minimum", in all these cases, says Mill, the government may borrow funds without encroaching upon the employment of the labouring classes in the country. The test of which scenario occurs depends on whether or not the government borrowing raises the rate of interest in the country (thus here is an early version of the "crowding out" discussion that so motivated the US discussion of public finance in the 1980s, and is likely to come to the fore again given the explosion of public debt by the West in the early twenty-first century).

Mill believes that in principle, given a national debt, a nation should pay the debt off. However, somewhat surprisingly for someone who is so alive to the costs of deficit finance, Mill – in a touch that anticipates Milton Friedman – ranks the elimination of the most unpleasant taxes ahead of deficit reduction. Even with this accomplished, he ranks, ahead of paying off the debt, experimentation along the Laffer curve (as we would put it today) to find the lowest rate that collects whatever

---

[27] Mill has no patience with the "we owe it to ourselves" principle which is often advanced when discussing public borrowing of purely domestic funds. His simple retort is that the "transfer, however, being compulsory, is a serious evil" (*Principles*, 876; 876).

is the needed revenue. From this point on he would apply "surplus revenue" to eliminating the debt. Mill's healthy respect for the inconvenience, cost, and assault on liberty of many forms of taxation, even in the face of a significant national debt, is deserving of attention from those who fixate on their government's debt even to the extent of advocating much higher taxes to "manage" it.

Mill's Survey of Classical Macroeconomics

While many of his topics are of only historical interest today, Mill's survey of the macroeconomics of his era remains masterful – and, often, far from irrelevant to modern topics. His chapter on money (Book III, Chap. 7) is still the classic state-ment of the principle of money's neutrality. He follows this up with a tolerably complete description of the quantity theory of money (or, at least, of the equation of exchange) in Chap. 8. Chapter 9 addresses a crucial topic both for a commodity standard and for advocates of a cost-of-production theory of value – the value of money's dependence on its cost-of-production (he sees, not surprisingly, a close connection). His Chap. 10 nicely elucidates the peculiarities of a double-standard in a monetary system. Chapters 11 and 12 discuss at length the question of the role of credit in a monetary system. The *Principles* did much to popularize the so-called "banking school" of money and credit, as opposed to the "currency school" (the latter being widely regarded as an early version of monetarism). Credit does affect prices, says Mill, and "in whatever shape given", regardless of "whether it gives rise to any transferable instruments capable of passing into circulation or not" (*Principles*, 524; 538–9). Chapter 13 addresses questions concerning an incontrovertible paper currency. Mill focuses on the transfers of wealth implicit in the introduction of fiat money into a hard-money system, pointing out along the way the problem of money-illusion, the several costs of inflation, how inflation should be viewed as a kind of tax, and the redistribution of wealth among creditors and debtors implicit in the inflation brought on by paper money. Chapter 14 is his famous "Of Excess of Supply", the substance of which was discussed earlier. Chapter 15, "Of a Measure of Value", is notable as an early discussion of price indices – a discussion somewhat complicated by the intrusion of the labour theory of value into the treatment. Other macroeconomic topics appear, off and on, throughout the *Principles* (classical growth theory, for example, discussed in detail previously, appears in Book IV, and the macroeconomic role of capital is treated in Book I).

Mill's "Heterodox" Contributions in the Principles

In the opinion of the Mills, by far the most significant sections of the *Principles* were those that "pushed" political economy in directions very far-flung from its standard paths. Orthodox classical political economy's questions, thought Mill, were "of very minor importance compared with the great practical questions which

the progress of democracy and the spread of Socialist opinions are pressing on..."
(Letter to Karl Heinrich Rau, 1852 quoted in Mitchell 1967, 562). A major purpose
for writing the book was to rescue political economy from its reputation as the "dismal science" – as a field not really in touch with the new "insights" in broader social
science, and one ever-pronouncing pessimistic conclusions about the long-run
future of mankind (particularly the future of the "labouring classes").

One of Mill's most important heterodox ideas – discussed earlier – is the separation of the laws of production and the laws of distribution. Another idea quite foreign to classical theory, also discussed earlier, is the notion that government, acting
in the name of the people, ought to confiscate considerable amounts of the "bequests"
and "legacies" of the wealthy (Book II, Chap. 2), thereby striking a blow for equality while at the same time liberating vital funds which might then be put to use in
educating the labouring classes and carrying out other public works.

A third brief example of an important "heterodox" idea by Mill frames an issue
that would be a constant source of tension between mainstream economists and
more heterodox economists stemming from Mill's day through our own. This is
Mill's discussion in the *Principles* (Book II, Chap. 4) on the topic "Of Competition
and Custom". Here, Mill severely tries to draw lines of demarcation restricting the
laws of economics proper to what he saw as their correct usage. Political economists, he points out, "are apt to express themselves as if they thought that competition does, in all cases, whatever it can be shown to be the tendency of competition
to do" (*Principles*, 242; 239). Partly this is because only by invoking the power of
competition can economics actually make logically scientific deductions and predictions about market outcomes. But, to Mill, it is of the upmost importance in
social science to reject the view that "competition exercises in fact this unlimited
sway" (*Principles, ibid; ibid*). Many other forces – notably, custom – strive with
competition in the real world to impact the behaviour of decision-makers. Mill goes
on to describe many examples in numerous contexts, all designed to wean the budding economist of an over-emphasis on mere competitive forces when seeking to
understand or predict human economic behaviour. "To escape error, we ought",
maintains Mill, "in applying the conclusions of political economy to the actual
affairs of life, to consider not only what will happen supposing the maximum of
competition, but [also] how far the result will be affected if competition falls short
of the maximum" (*op. cit.*, 248; 244). One may induce from his argument that Mill
would have looked-on aghast at the excesses of deduction that characterize some of
the high points of neoclassical theory, and that he would be enthusiastic about some
of the intellectual trends that have supplanted (or at least, supplemented) that theory,
such as "behavioural economics".

The Dynamic Tendency of Profits to a Minimum

Like all the Classical economists, Mill believed in a living, breathing stationary
state that was utterly inevitable given the premises of classical theory – premises
that classical economics regarded as accurate descriptions of the actual society in

which they lived. Increases in capital beyond some limit crowd in upon the limited supply of land, raising rents and also raising either wages or population. Either event inevitably brings about a fall in the return on capital to its absolute minimum (thus also lowering the savings rate to its minimum sustainable level). Resource constraints – population growth plus the inevitable increases in food costs due to sharp limits to agricultural productivity – thus bring about minimum profits and eventually cause progress to grind to a halt. Mill asserts that "the rate of profit is habitually within … a hand's breadth of the minimum, and the country therefore on the very verge of the stationary state" (*op. cit.*, 731; 738).[28] Technological gains can just barely keep the economy ahead of the stationary state for a time, but cannot do so forever. The relentless pressure of population and food costs on the economy must sooner or later bring on the stationary state.[29]

In his depiction of the path to the stationary state, Mill is at pains to disavow the view that "there would be great difficulty in finding remunerative employment every year for so much new capital", leading to a "general glut" (*Principles*, 732; 739). Such is not the case, he says: All the new capital would find a market, but at the cost of "a rapid reduction of the rate of profit" (*Principles, ibid*; 740). Mill is delighted by such a prospect, which, he argues, "greatly weakens … the force of the economical argument against the expenditure of public money for really valuable, even though industriously unproductive, purposes" (op. cit., 741; 747).

Given sufficiently low profit rates for private investment, public investment can be justified as superior to low-return private investment, and the older economists' concerns about the consequent waste of society's capital at the hands of government fall to the ground (*Principles, ibid*; 748). Indeed, to Mill the truth is precisely the reverse of conventional classical wisdom as the economy approaches the stationary state. It is then in the private sector, where capital becomes very cheap as minimum profit margins are approached, that unacceptably low returns are earned. Mill's view is that much higher non-market returns are there-for-the-picking for society in the long-underappreciated, funds-starved public sector. Mill thus reveals one reason why he, alone among classical economists, welcomed the stationary state. The looming stationary state, in which "the rate of profit is habitually within … a hand's breadth of the minimum" (*Principles,* 731; 738) furnished Mill with additional

---

[28] Mill catalogues forces that might somewhat ameliorate the minimum-profits principle. One of his more interesting counter-forces in the light of recent world events [2008–2009] is "the waste of capital in periods of over-trading and rash speculation, and in the commercial revulsions by which such times are always followed" [*Principles,* 734; 741]. Others are technological improvements, international trade, and "the perpetual overflow of capital into colonies or foreign countries…" (op. cit., 735–9; 742–5). A few pages further on, Mill remarks casually that "[t]he railway gambling of 1844 and 1845 probably saved this country from a depression of profits and interest…" (op. cit., 743; 750).

[29] Mill offers little argument for why it might be that technological improvement cannot be fast enough to stave off the arrival of the minimum-profit, stationary state. Instead, the proposition is presented as, more or less, an article of faith (no doubt he was encouraged in this approach by the broad consensus among classical thinkers that there was a real, inevitable such state in the economy's future).

grounds (in a utilitarian sense) for his program to tax inheritances and legacies of the wealthy and to transfer formerly private wealth over to the public sector in order to fund "any great object of justice or philanthropic policy…" (*Principles*, 741; 748).

Since Mill wrote those words, many a "great object" of this nature, and more than a few not so great, have been brought to fruition by government power (and not all of them in a low-profit environment either). Once Mill throws open the door to government confiscation of a portion of private wealth for "public benefit", it is, of course, difficult to confine it solely to the circumstances that Mill himself imagined. Thus Mill's argument, while doubtless offered with good intentions, certainly provided powerful ammunition to those who longed for Big State solutions to public policy issues.

Reinterpretation of the Stationary State

Classical economists generally supported the notion that a no-growth "stationary state" was the inevitable end-point of societal economic activity. The Malthusian spectre could not be indefinitely postponed. Where Mill mainly differs from earlier Classical thinkers is in his highly favourable assessment of the stationary state. Standard classical theory held that, in a developed "old" country like England, economic growth was a necessary condition for economic well-being (*Principles*, 747; 752–3). This assumption, argues Mill, is in error. Continuing economic growth is only valuable in those societies which have as yet incompletely experienced "the progress of civilization" (*op. cit.*, 748; 754). In the old, developed countries, the "irresistible necessity that the stream of human industry should finally spread itself out into an apparently stagnant sea" (*op. cit.*, 746; 752) is not a prospect to be feared, but one to be welcomed – even relished. The great advantage Mill sees in the stationary state is that it would reign in capitalism. In one astonishing sortie after another, Mill savages the self-centred materialism that is the driving force of capitalism, and aggressively advocates the well-managed stationary state as being that condition where mankind could, at long last, be freed from its vicious, soul-numbing selfishness.

The only essential problem with the stationary state is that posed by population growth. But Mill thought that the stationary state, with its limits on employment prospects, might well bring about a condition in which "prudence and public opinion might in some measure be relied on for restricting the coming generation within the numbers necessary for replacing the present" (*op. cit.*, 748; 753). With the practicality of the stationary state established in this way, Mill is free to wax eloquent on its many advantages compared with capitalism:

> I cannot, therefore, regard the stationary state of capital and wealth with the unaffected aversion so generally manifested towards it by the political economists of the old school. I am inclined to believe that it would be, on the whole, a very considerable improvement on our present condition. I confess I am not charmed with the ideal of life held out by those who think that the normal state of human beings is that of struggling to get on; that the trampling, crushing, elbowing, and treading on each other's heels, which form the existing

type of social life, are the most desirable lot of human kind, or anything but the disagreeable symptoms of one of the phases of industrial progress. It may be a necessary stage in the progress of civilization … [and] it is not necessarily destructive of the higher aspirations and the heroic virtues; as America, in her great civil war, has proved to the world…. But it is not a kind of social perfection which philanthropists to come will feel any very eager desire to assist in realizing. (*Principles, ibid*; 753–4).

Here Mill plays the long-suffering Comteian-stage-theorist, patiently enduring the present for the sake of that Higher Stage Of Civilization which is surely to come. Mill's ideal society, realizable (he thinks) in the stationary state, is one within which, "while no one is poor, no one desires to be richer, nor has any reason to fear being thrust back by the efforts of others to push themselves forward" (*Principles*, 749; 754). If such crude levelling sentiments strike us today as "so very twentieth (and now, it would seem, twenty-first) century", we must remember how influential Mill's tome was through the early years of the 1900s. These types of "fine sentiments", however, often travel hand-in-hand with an eye-popping elitism, as Mill is quick to show us:

That the energies of mankind should be kept in employment by the struggle for riches, as they were formerly by the struggle of war, until the better minds succeed in educating the others into better things, is undoubtedly more desirable than that they should rust and stagnate. While minds are coarse they require coarse stimuli, and let them have them. In the mean time, those who do not accept the present very early stage of human improvement as its ultimate type, may be excused for being comparatively indifferent to the kind of economical progress which excites the congratulations of ordinary politicians; the mere increase of production and accumulation. …I know not why it should be matter of congratulation that persons who are already richer than any one needs to be, should have doubled their means of consuming things which give little or no pleasure except as representative of wealth; or that numbers of individuals should pass over, every year, from the middle classes into a richer class, or from the class of the occupied rich to that of the unoccupied (*Principles, ibid*; 754–5).

It is remarkable how many hoary assumptions and illicit conclusions Mill is able to stuff into this single paragraph. There is first the assumption that the minds of those who yearn for war are motivated by the same things as those who yearn for profit (as if Watt and Napoleon had the same aspirations). Then there is the notion that the "better minds" whom Mill lauds are themselves above an interest in profit – a notion confounded by the behaviour of virtually all of history's elites.[30] Next is the assumption that these elites are able and willing to educate the masses through selfless service, despite (typically) their knowing almost nothing about them, their daily lives, or their values. Then we are to assume that such self-sacrifice is self-evidently the acme of morality (never mind that the sacrificer in history usually wins his laurels by sacrificing *others*, not himself, on the alter of altruistic sentiment, and never mind either that the many industrial inventions then-sparking an unprecedented

---

[30] That Mill himself is quite aware of this historical tendency is made clear in the very next chapter, where he writes, in answer to those, like Carlyle, who would see the higher classes "protect and guide" (that is, control) the lower classes. Mill writes: "All privileged and powerful classes, as such, have used their power in the interest of their own selfishness, and have indulged their self-importance in despising, and not in lovingly caring for, those who were, in their estimation, degraded, by being under the necessity of working for their benefit" (*Principles*, 754; 759).

revolution in living standards in England were not achieved in the name of self-sacrifice.) Then there is the downgrading of "the mere increase of production", which is, in fact, the cause of the aforementioned revolution in living standards (in a later paragraph, Mill asserts, without evidence, his view that the many capitalist innovations have failed to help the poor). Next, there is Mill's notion that someone – perhaps, one of his "better minds" – is able to determine how rich "any one needs to be". This same person also is, marvellously, able to pierce the poisonous veil of materialism and see how pathetically tiny is the personal pleasure Burgher X can gain from a doubling of his means of consumption. Finally, there is the supposition that those who seek to bring new inventions to market seeking profit are truly only interested in doing so, so that they may raise their "class" status (a caddish slander of inventors and a profound twisting of their history). All this is from a scholar who is usually perceived as highly logical and friendly to capitalism. In fact, it is never more clear than in his chapter on the stationary state that Mill despised capitalism (or at least the incentives underlying it). In his eyes it was a moral outrage: the worst existing system except for all of the others that were then possible, to be replaced with an "enlightened socialism" at the earliest appropriate moment.

Mill closes his stationary-state chapter with several of his favourite themes: that in the developed economies a "better distribution" is a far more pressing issue than additional production or innovation; that sharp limits on bequests and inheritances are needed to assure the less-fortunate that there are "no enormous fortunes;" and, perhaps most shockingly, that enough of the necessary technological innovations for comfortable life already have been invented (meaning that if Mill had had his way, airplanes, automobiles, air conditioning, the microchip, the modern medicines that would almost certainly have saved his beloved wife's life, and countless other things invented since the 1870s would never have existed). Thoroughly unbowed by such considerations, Mill waxes eloquent on the perils of the pro-growth mind-set, maintaining that:

> [i]f the earth must lose that great portion of its pleasantness which it owes to things that the unlimited increase of wealth and population would extirpate from it, for the mere purpose of enabling it to support a larger, but not a better or a happier population, I sincerely hope, for the sake of posterity, that they will be content to be stationary, long before necessity compels them to it. (*op. cit.*, 750–751; 756)

Not surprisingly, given this type of passage, Mill has in recent years been adopted as a sort of pioneering mascot by the "sustainable development" movement (see, e.g. Dietz 2008),[31] an adoption that testifies, again, to the extraordinary influence Mill's ideas have had on the twentieth and early twenty-first centuries. In the case of the

---

[31] An even more emphatic passage occurs early in Book V when Mill debunks the idea that the main function of the law is to protect the producer's private property rights to what he has produced. Mill demurs, citing public environmental goods: "But is there nothing recognized as property except what has been produced? Is there not the earth itself, its forests and waters, and all other natural riches, above and below the surface? These are the inheritance of the human race, and there must be relations for the common enjoyment of it. What rights, and under what conditions, a person shall be allowed to exercise over any portion of this common inheritance cannot be left undecided" (*Principles*, 797; 801). A more succinct statement of the socialist premises of the modern environmental movement could hardly be found anywhere.

sustainable development movement, however, the alleged association is questionable at best. True, the Mill of the *Principles* questioned whether "all the mechanical inventions yet made have lightened the day's toil of any human being" (*Principles*, 751; 756), but by the time of his preliminary draft on socialism (Mill 1967 [1879]), Mill had changed his view, and in that work he strongly pointed to recent progress of the labouring classes. (Mill's profound critique of socialist doctrine in that work can still be read today with great benefit to anyone enamoured with the socialist siren call.) These late developments raise the legitimate question of whether, had Mill lived, he would have again revised his *Principles* to reflect these changes in his views. We can never know, but, certainly, Mill's thoughts as expressed in his unfinished fragment on socialism are difficult to fully reconcile with his much more [in]famous position condemning dynamic capitalism in his stationary-state chapter.

Looking backward at Mill's stationary-state chapter through the eyes of modern economics, it is easy to be harsh with Mill for his haughty contempt for economic growth, his castigation of the morality of capitalist institutions, his refusal to see mankind for what it is rather than what he wishes it to be, and his too-hasty, undocumented bald assertion in the *Principles* that capitalist innovation had not helped the labouring classes. However, we should not drop the full context of what Mill (and most classical economists) believed. Classical economics taught that, ultimately, economic growth could not stave off the stationary state and a resulting life of misery for the labouring classes. Mill, to his credit, was determined to uncover a better future for mankind – thus his attempt to overturn conventional wisdom regarding the stationary state. If capitalism could not save the bulk of mankind from eternal misery, then perhaps another, radically different social system might be able to do so.

Mill was not naive about the incentive structure implicit in socialism, but his utopian streak, fanned by Comte's and Saint-Simon's "stage of development" theories, encouraged him to believe that the man of the future would – with the crucial aid of well-chosen government policies – be purged of his acquisitive imperatives. *Homo Futurus* would be a "noble", happy altruist to the very core of his being. With all the wreckage of the twentieth century to learn from (and, it would appear, many more learning opportunities to be forthcoming in the twenty-first), it is easy now for the reader educated in market processes to be contemptuous of such socialist dreams. But in Mill's day those dreams were yet to be tried-and-found-wanting, while capitalism's promise seemed destroyed by Malthusian population theory. Mill's utopian voluntary socialism, naive as it seems today, can be forgiven him in a way that modern coercive socialists, with all the wreckage of failed socialist experiment after failed socialist experiment to contemplate, cannot and should not be forgiven.

Mill's astonishing chapter on the stationary state has received remarkably little critical analysis. Few commentators even bother to note the profound difficulties that must be caused for a capitalist system by such views if they are widely held. Commentators who might be expected to be critical, typically confine themselves simply to reporting what Mill said (if they discuss the chapter at all). Commentators more on the Left tend to pass by the actual substance of Mill's thoughts and instead focus on how Mill's "heart is in the right place" and on how his strongly expressed sentiments helped power the rise of the modern welfare state.

What is not to be doubted is that Mill's stationary-state chapter is among the clearest indications of Mill's contempt for capitalism as a social system. Mill refused to significantly amend these opinions through all the many editions of the *Principles*. That he failed to do so speaks volumes as to his comfortableness with these sentiments not just in the 1840s, but also through the remainder of his life.[32]

"Futurity" of the Labouring Classes

Mill's final chapter of Book IV (Chap. 7) was considered by him to be one of the most important (if not *the* most important) chapter in the entire volume.[33] Here, he lays out his views on the likely development of relationships in subsequent decades between labour and capitalism. Mill attributes this chapter – at 43 pages, one of the volume's longest – to the influence of Harriet Taylor-Mill, who "pointed out the need of such a chapter, and the extreme imperfection of the book without it…" (*Autobiography*, 255).

The Mills are convinced that the longstanding relations between the classes based on a patronizing and protecting upper class and a subservient, grateful labouring class are finished, both in England and in the more advanced Continental nations. Mill sees a bright future for the poor in the developing new system. As the working classes become more educated and as they become more mobile due to improvements in transportation (*Principles*, 756; 762), it will prove impossible to prevent them from assuming a prominent place in determining the development of society. Thus, the future of society depends greatly on whether the labouring classes "can be made rational beings" (*op. cit.*, 757; 763) and are willing and able to support appropriate societal policies. Mill is convinced that the labouring classes will rise to this challenge – both the men *and* the women. He sees the opening of the workplace to women as not only ethically essential, but also an effective bastion against overpopulation. The demand for children will fall (*op. cit.*, 760; 765–6) as the call of the workplace makes caring for children a substitute for work, rather than the complement to work that it is on, say, a family farm. Through such reasoning Mill glimpses the key insight of what today is often called the "Demographic Transition", and traces out the path through which societies actually would escape the Malthusian trap.

Mill next turns to those changes then-going-on in labour markets which he sees as holding promise for labour in the future. Regarding the relationship between employer and employee, he is a sharp-eyed witness to the early development of complex, sophisticated relationships between employer and employee like those we see in our times, and he is enthusiastic about their prospects to improve labourers' lives. The straightforward short-term labour-for-hire model, where neither hirer nor

---

[32] There is, however, another intriguing possible explanation. If these were passages written not by Mill but by his wife, then Mill for personal reasons would have been extremely reluctant to remove, or even alter, the words of his "almost infallible counsellor" (*Autobiography*, 261).

[33] He wrote in the *Autobiography*: "The chapter of the Political Economy which has had a greater influence on opinion than all the rest, that on 'the Probable Future of the Labouring Classes'…"

hiree has an incentive to cultivate the good will of the other, is seen by Mill as a fading paradigm, increasingly to be replaced with incentive schemes that create incentive compatibility between labour and capital. Mill is at his sharpest in explaining the moral-hazard difficulty and in giving enlightening illustrations of how the labour market is productively evolving towards bonus systems and profit-sharing systems, to the benefit of all involved in the business. He explains clearly how the problem of moral hazard (malfeasance by employees) is reduced by reserving to workers a share of profits as well as wages. He also explains how the absence of limited liability laws had previously prevented workers from receiving a portion of the profits without also accepting prohibitively severe losses should the firm not do well. Due to then-recent legal reforms, he predicts (correctly) a dramatic increase in such profit-sharing arrangements in the future. Here is Mill explaining the paths by which capitalist incentives can encourage the evolution of institutions that favour both business-owner and labourer alike. (He did not, apparently, think to re-evaluate his ferocious attack on capitalist incentives from his previous chapter in the context of these favourable developments brought on by the very capitalist incentives he had previously decried.)

Despite Mill's strong praise for the newly evolving relationship between employer and employee, his main enthusiasm is reserved for those institutions then-developing that featured labourers forming cooperative enterprises and competing directly with orthodox capitalism. Here, thought and hoped the Mills, was the future – the beginnings of a peaceful, voluntary evolution towards a socialism operating as a significant force in the workplace.[34] Mill is impressed by the high level of intellectual activity portrayed by the working men in the best cooperative ventures. "Piecework" was originally excluded from cooperatives, but over time it became clear that the moral-hazard problems stemming from the alternative of a fixed remuneration were too daunting to be tolerated (*Principles*, 779–80; 782–3). The cooperatives thus learned to "apportion all further remuneration according to the work done" (*op. cit.*, 780; 782). Mill also lauds the social welfare role played by several of the cooperatives, in that they: set aside a portion of profits to care for the sick and disabled (*op. cit.*, 781; 783–4); allocate remaining capital in the case of the cooperative's break-up "entire to some work of beneficence or of public utility" rather than dividing it among themselves; and have a rule which "is adhered to, that the exercise of power shall never be an occasion for profit" (*Principles*, *ibid*; 784). Thus, by taking workmen out of the capitalist model and into a non-profit cooperative one, workmen are made remarkably better off, writes Mill.

As is his wont, Mill waxes rhapsodic over the favourable consequences of the cooperative model to the workingman, which, "by placing the labourers, as a mass,

---

[34] Some appreciation of the Mills' enthusiasm for the cooperative model can be gleaned from the following: "…[T]he relation of masters and workpeople will be gradually superseded by partnership, in one of two forms: in some cases, association of the labourers with the capitalist; in others, *and perhaps finally in all*, association of labourers among themselves" (*Principles*, 764; 769 [emphasis added]).

in a relation to their work which would make it their principle and their interest – at present it is neither – to do the utmost, instead of the least possible, in exchange for their remuneration" (*Principles*, 789; 792). However, this material benefit accruing from the cooperative framework

> is as nothing compared with the moral revolution in society that would accompany it: the healing of the standing feud between capital and labour; the transformation of human life, from a conflict of classes struggling for opposite interests, to a friendly rivalry in the pursuit of a good common to all; the elevation of the dignity of labour... (*op. cit.*, 789–90; 792)

Such romantic reveries show that, while Mill flirts with the notion that an evolution of capitalist institutions will improve the lot of the labouring classes, it is in non-profit models where he finds his true hope and love. Mill's enthusiasm for the cooperative model is tempered, however, by his concern that the non-profit "socialist" co-operatives are increasingly choosing to adopt practices more like those of orthodox capitalism (establishing different classes of labourers and the like). Such impure cooperatives, thinks Mill, cannot succeed against "individual management", with its deeply committed owner-manager, whose firm accordingly "has great advantages over every description of collective management" (*Principles*, 790; 792). Despite these problems, Mill is optimistic that cooperative societies of labourers will prosper and eventually compete effectively against capitalist firms. He even ventures the conclusion that once such societies have "sufficiently multiplied", their appeal to the working man will bring forth a situation where "both private capitalists and associations will gradually find it necessary to make the entire body of labourers participants in profits" (*op. cit.*, 791; 793).

Thus, though Mill wrongly tags not-for-profit cooperatives as the wave of the future, he nevertheless correctly predicts the primary method by which capitalist firms would become more favourably disposed towards their employees – through profit-sharing institutions based on common ownership of shares in corporations. Mill however remains convinced that, ultimately, non-profit cooperatives, with their greater empathy towards the working man, will so displace capitalist firms that "the existing accumulations of capital might honestly, and by a kind of spontaneous process, become in the end the joint property of all who participate in their productive employment ... a transformation which, thus effected ... would be the nearest approach to social justice..." (*Principles*, 791–2; 793–4). Such a transformation (though not of the type – and not from the direction – Mill was expecting) would in fact occur in the twentieth century: the rise of the modern, publicly owned corporation, with considerable ownership by the firm's employees. Thus was Mill able to glimpse the future without ever fully grasping it in its essentials. Mill was simply unwilling to consider seriously that capitalist, not socialist, institutions, would triumph in the struggle to shape the new economic order of the century to come.

Lest his readers think that he has tilted too far towards the writings of the socialist thinkers, Mill closes Book IV with a ringing endorsement of market-based competitive forces (Chap. 7, Section 7). "[E]ven in the present state of society and industry", concludes Mill, "every restriction of [competition] is an evil, and every extension of it, even if for the time injuriously affecting some class of labourers, is always an ultimate good" (*Principles, ibid*; 795). With such moderating thoughts Mill closes his chapter (and his Book IV).

A Proposed Tax on "Unearned" Income from Land

Mill's discussion of tax policy in his Book V is on the whole reasonable and non-controversial (see Section "Commonsense Thoughts on Taxation, Government and Welfare (Bk. V, Chaps. 2–6; 8–11)"). But Mill is always capable, at a moment's notice, of swerving into heterodoxy mode. And so it is that, there in the midst of an eminently sensible discussion of orthodox tax policy and public finance, we suddenly stumble across Mill's remarkable proposition that the "future increase [in rents] arising from the mere action of natural causes" (*op. cit.*, 824; 826) accruing to land (especially to the English landed estates) should be entirely taxed away (Bk. V, Chap. 2, Sections 5 and 6). Due to "the ordinary progress of society" (*op. cit.*, 818; 819), such returns, says Mill, are "a kind of income which constantly tends to increase, without any exertion or sacrifice on the part of the owners; those owners constituting a class in the community, whom the natural course of things progressively enriches, consistently with complete passiveness on their own part" (*op. cit.*, 817; 819). The landed classes "grow richer, as it were in their sleep, without working, risking, or economizing" (*op. cit.*, 818; 819–20), often due to nothing more than their being born into one of the great landowning families. Accordingly, "it would be no violation of the principles on which private property is grounded, if the state should appropriate this increase of wealth, or part of it, as it arises" (*Principles, ibid;* 819).[35]

These propositions, which Mill seems to see as more or less self-evident, are in fact not entirely beyond reasonable criticism. First, we note the extraordinary notion that one has no right to the fruits of one's own property unless one engages in "working, risking, or economizing". If this is so, then the case for confiscation can hardly be confined to the revenues of the landed estates. After all, *all* durable goods, once safely in place and working, have as part of their return an element that is in some sense automatic and received without [further] effort. We may also question Mill's premise that owners of large tracts of land are growing "richer, as it were in their sleep, without working, risking or economizing". Even the most quiescent of landed "robber barons" must at least recognise the opportunity-cost principle which forces him to contemplate alternative uses of his land. Often such land, particularly if near cities or towns, can be sold to developers for vast fortunes (as in New York City during the early nineteenth-century). True, the English institutions of primogeniture and entails often heavily repressed such land sales (though not completely). However, if one is talking about land speculation in general and not the special case of the English estates, then there is something to be said for

---

[35] Mill is aware of the difficulty of separating this automatic component of rent with the rest of it which may well be connected to the "skill and expenditures on the part of the proprietor" (*Principles, ibid*; 820). He proposes that a "rough estimate" of the gain can be gleaned by the gain in value over a specified time period of "all the land in the country" (*Principles, ibid; ibid*).

the argument that the choice of which large tract of land to buy (e.g. whether you have accurately anticipated development patterns in your area) might involve some skill and not mere good fortune (in a later passage Mill makes clear that he also finds such gains objectionable).[36] All these are fairly straightforward objections (especially if, as is clear in the *Principles*, Mill is making a *general* statement about landed estates and their owners, rather than an England-centred one). Here then, one might reasonably wonder whether Mill's venomous sentiments toward the landed classes have not conspired successfully to get the better of him.

Regardless of the virtue (or lack thereof) in Mill's argument, one cannot doubt its deleterious impact on the century to come. Due to the extraordinarily wide circulation and influence of the *Principles*, doubtless Mill's discussion was instrumental in inspiring many of the "land reform" movements that percolated busily throughout the late nineteenth and (in particular) twentieth centuries, working everywhere to the detriment of the bedrock principle of inviolate property rights that modern growth theory has identified as being essential to a nation's emergence from poverty (cf. Hall and Papell 2005, Chap. 6). While Mill himself might have been reluctant to pass from the confiscation of mere rents to the seizure and re-allocation of the land itself, others, inspired by his example, would be bolder. Inevitably, such confiscatory "reforms" would acquire a political tint, with populist politicians using the cry of "land reform!" as a means to assault political enemies.

And this is not all of the influence of Mill's argument in this example of the Law of Unintended Political and Intellectual Consequences. Mill's picture of a landed class, merely sitting about with mouths wide-open waiting for the unearned manna-from-heaven to drop onto their tongues, was picked up wholesale by Karl Marx, who simply replaced Mill's bloodsucking landlords with Marx's bloodsucking capitalists. Mill, who by most accounts was wholly unaware of Karl Marx toiling away in the libraries of London on *Das Kapital*, nonetheless was therefore (in one of history's nicer ironies) likely to have been a vital inspiration to Marx's development of the doctrine of the exploitation of the *proletariat* by the *bourgeoisie*.

An Expanded Role of, and Scope for, Government (Bk. V, Chap. 1)

Mill dedicates the fifth book of his volume to a systematic exploration of government's role – for good and for ill – in the economy. In this he follows Adam Smith,

---

[36] He writes of the exceptional cases, like that of the favourite situations in large towns, "[where] the predominant element in the rent of the house is the ground-rent, and among the very few kinds of income which are fit subjects for peculiar taxation, these ground-rents hold the principal place, being the most gigantic example extant of enormous accessions of riches acquired rapidly, and in many cases unexpectedly, by a few families, from the mere accident of their possessing certain tracts of land, without their having themselves aided in the acquisition by the smallest exertion, outlay, or risk" (*op. cit.* 834; 835). Earlier, in Book IV, Chap. 2, Mill had written a passionate defence of the role played by speculators in society. Apparently, Mill would exclude land speculation from his earlier endorsement of speculation in general.

although Mill's scope is broader. The initial foray in Chap. 1 is devoted mainly to demonstrating the difficulties in setting "appropriate" limits to government activity. Mill accosts those who would try to confine government activity merely to "affording protection against force and fraud…" (*Principles*, 796; 800). Mill is dismissive of (as he clearly sees it) such naive notions. After all, if government can and should protect citizens against "force and fraud", then why not also against other evils? For example, how much freedom to enter into "private" contracts should society allow its citizens? Is a "private contract" under which one becomes the slave of another person acceptable? Mill thinks not – but then, if one private contract is intolerable, does this not open up them all to similar questions?

Indeed, Mill soon informs us that government's duties "consist of all the good, and all the immunity from evil, which the existence of government can be made either directly or indirectly to bestow" (*op. cit.*, 804–5; 807) – an expansive definition to say the least, and one that calls to mind the very big governments of modern times.[37] Mill's ideal government would seek "the true idea of distributive justice, which consists in … redressing the inequalities and wrongs of nature" (*op. cit.*, 805; 808). Such Rawlsian[38] notions shred the classical idea of liberalism and replace it with the modern version whereby government, far from merely protecting against "force and fraud", assumes the role of protecting and nurturing "your tired, your poor, your huddled masses yearning to be…" – governed?? It is hard indeed to associate these discussions by Mill with the principled defender of individual liberty of popular lore. Those who wonder how the term "liberal" could have been twisted from a term denoting *laissez faire* to one denoting explicitly socialist policies, could do worse in seeking their explanation than to peruse Book V, Chap. 1 of Mill's *Principles*.

Digression: Mill as a Mild "Constitutionalist"

While Mill's enthusiasm for government (working in what he sees as its proper context) is clear, his views about how government should be constrained are less so. Reading three of Mill's primary political works (Book V of the *Principles*, *On Liberty* (Mill 1977a, b [1859]), and *Considerations on Representative Government* (Mill 1973 [1861]), it is easy to conclude that, when push comes to shove, Mill sees virtually no effective (or even desirable) limit to "the interference of government by any universal rule, save the simple and vague one, that it should never be admitted but when the case of expediency is strong" (*Principles*, 800; 804). There are grounds

---

[37] In an 1829 letter to Gustave D'Eichthal, Mill also states this expansive definition of government, writing: "Government exists for all purposes whatever that are for man's good: and the highest & most important of these purposes is the improvement of man himself as a moral and intelligent being…" Letter of October 8th, 1829 (Mill 1963 [Vol. XII], 34–8 [Letter 27]). This shows that an expansive view of government coloured his perspective from his early years.

[38] See Rawls (1999 [1971]). The appearance here of Rawls is ironic, since Rawls was a strong opponent of utilitarianism in the sense Mill defined the term. See, for example, "John Rawls", in the *Internet Encyclopaedia of Philosophy*, www.iep.utm.edu/rawls.html.

for such an interpretation, though doubtless it is an exaggerated one (see further). In the three works referenced earlier – particularly in *Representative Government* – Mill often writes as if a proper education for the labouring classes, combined with special voting rules designed to both enhance and temper democratic forces, are nearly all the protection society needs from the extraordinary power of government.[39] Put the proper knowledge and voting procedures into place, Mill seems in these passages to say, and otherwise-unfettered democratic processes will make all well. Even the discussion in *On Liberty*, which is often interpreted as a passionate paean to the widest range of freedom of choice for the individual, is focussed on *why*, not how, the individual's freedom of decision should be left unfettered.

Even more telling than what Mill chooses to discuss is what he does not discuss. Mill seems to have little interest in the possibility that a *written* constitution could offer a stronger bulwark against the encroachment of government into what should be the private sphere. The notion of an explicit written-down American-style "Bill of Rights" is not something he finds interesting enough to discuss in these works either. The American strategy of trying to bind government tightly with specific, written restrictions was one for which he occasionally revealed considerable enthusiasm – but not to the point where he was willing to put such constraints forward as an essential part of keeping government in line. Mill speaks highly of federalism and the independent US Supreme Court as valuable innovations (cf. 1973 [1861], Chap. 17). However, regarding the American concept of "inalienable" individual rights, Mill, as a utilitarian, was bound to reject any such notion, whether given to man by God or by man's essential nature (Mill is willing to see some such rights *assigned* by the government as part of his unwritten constitution).

Mill read Tocqueville closely and also corresponded with him. He took great interest in the American experiment in constitutional government. However, his enthusiasm did not extend to any endorsement of American constitutionalism vs. the British version (an unwritten constitution consisting of all the laws of the land). Mill instead offers up what some might call a strange scheme proposed by Thomas Hare (1859), aimed at achieving "perfection in representation" (Mill 1973 [1861], 453). Hare's plan would allow citizens to vote for anyone they wished anywhere in the nation, so

---

[39] "The first element of good government, therefore, being the virtue and intelligence of the human beings composing the community, the most important point of excellence which any form of government can possess is to promote the virtue and intelligence of the people themselves" (Mill 1973 [1861], 390). After raising this point, Mill turns immediately to the "machinery" of good government, which consists, not in explicit restrictions on government power, but rather in there being clear rules of appointment and succession, etc. to which government is subject (*op. cit.*, 391–2). Later, great attention is given to Thomas Hare's voting scheme, which Hare (and Mill) believed would create a high "degree of perfection in representation" (*op. cit.*, 453 ff). An emphasis on a new vote-weighting system is consistent with the views of one who thinks the main problem is getting the "right people" into office, rather than setting up constraints that would constrain the *wrong* people should *they* somehow get in. Earlier, Mill himself suggested his own scheme in *Thoughts of Parliamentary Reform* (Mill 1977a, b [1859]) where he proposed special voting rules that would give extra weight to the votes of those "more qualified" (in practice, those with more formal education) to judge on political matters.

that any candidate who surpassed a particular vote total would be elected with no regard to geographical location of voters (*op. cit.*, Chap. 7). (Hare wanted to give minorities more opportunities to elect one of their own by concentrating their combined voting power on a relatively few seats.) The details of the plan are less interesting than is the fact that Mill gives great and sustained attention to it – which is indicative of his strong attraction to innovations in voting rules as the key to solving democracy's weaknesses. Mill looked as much, or even more, to the tweaking of voting systems as the key to democracy than he did to hard constitutional constraints.

All that having been said, Mill was not without appreciation for innovations that constrained government action. Mill is a mild *constitutionalist* in the sense that he endorses only those government actions that are allowed by a nation's laws. In a letter to Peter Alfred Taylor, he writes:

> I think it would be a fatal notion to get abroad among the people of a democratic country that laws or constitutions may be stepped over instead of being altered; in other words that an object immediately desirable may be grasped directly in a particular case without the salutary previous process of considering whether the principle acted on is one which the nation would bear to adopt as a rule for *general* guidance" (Letter to Peter Alfred Taylor, May 28th, 1869; Mill 1972, 1607).

Crucially, however, the power of the legislature to make laws in the public interest is to be limited by little save (he hopes) "when the case of expediency is strong" (*Principles*, 800; 804). Mill also shows little concern for the likelihood that existing laws may be interpreted by the executive in ways that violate their original spirit – interpretations that can amount to a *de facto* repudiation of constitutional government. He seems to think that properly structured democratic voting schemes, and a well-educated labouring class, would keep such shenanigans under control.

As a further bastion against unlimited Big State power, Mill has considerable appreciation for the notion that there should be a balance of power within a government. In Chap. 5 of his *Representative Government*, he emphasizes how any of the three powers in nineteenth-century British Government (the Crown, the Lords, and the Commons) could frustrate the will of the other two – though the Commons, representatives of the predominant popular will, clearly has (and should have, he thought) the upper hand. He also appreciates the balance of power achieved by the American constitution. Mill lauds especially the US Supreme Court, which, as final authority on legal disputes in federal court, acts as an independent check on government power. He also lauds the existence of the House of Representatives as a body directly elected by the people and representing them, with the Senate – in the Constitution's original form – being indirectly elected by state legislatures and so directly representing states' interests instead of the popular will. Mill also comments favourably on State "nullification" of national law as a potentially significant check on the powers of the American national government.

All of these are significant constraints on Big State power, and Mill, had he wished, could have chosen to advocate a radical proposal that emphasized the inclusion of these checks and balances as an *essential* part of any well-crafted constitution. He did not choose to do so, but instead discussed these matters almost incidentally, outside the context of his general recommendations for how government should be constituted. Mill may well have believed in the usefulness of these checks on government power, but he did not insist on them. He saw quite clearly the problem posed by special interests seizing power in the legislature, and he worried often about the potentially tyrannical nature of majority rule (particularly in *On Liberty*). Still, the somewhat paradoxical impression Mill leaves in his three primary works on government is of one who is not, when push really comes to shove, too terribly concerned about such government power *per se*. Even in *On Liberty*, he is more concerned with the prospect of power of all kinds (i.e. including social pressures by private citizens) being directed against unusual individuals than he is focussed specifically on the dangers of brute government force and the need to reign those dangers in. That is, he does not there draw a sharp distinction between the evils of public and private power.

In fact, Mill seems quite willing there to contemplate the use of coercive government power to reign in the majority's interferences with individual dissenters. He does not seem to see any marked danger in such a course. A properly educated voting population, voting under well-chosen voting rules, will cause the right people to be voted into power (see, e.g. his discussion in Mill 1973 [1861], 390, where "the virtue and intelligence of the human beings composing the community" is lightly taken as an accomplished fact for the bulk of the discussion). Unfettered democratic rule will restrain self-interest in the long run. This conclusion conveniently frees Mill's more utopian side to again rise to the fore in his discussions of government (most notably in Book V of the *Principles*, particularly in his last chapter – see discussion given further – where he recommends various government interventions in the economy).

By this route, the "classical liberal" Mill who is concerned with checks and balances seems to be replaced – when it matters most – with the Mill who is optimistic about the pure motives and benevolent intentions of those making up the government (as were his own motives while serving his short stint in Parliament near the end of his life). The problem of Buchanan and Tullock (1962), concisely expressed by the philosopher Karl Britton as: "Does not any government in fact consist of a group of men, and have not these men private interests of their own?" (Britton 1953, p. 89), often seems far from Mill's mind in his core political passages. Such absent-mindedness is even more strongly in evidence in those suggestions for government interventions that close his *Principles*. Of course Mill believes that private interests matter in a representative government. But in his core political writings, Mill steps over the problem – one which an Adam Smith might well have placed at the very center of his approach to government. Accordingly, in his assessment of and prescriptions for government, Mill often seems to be writing for a society of angels rather than for one of men. In this attitude, he calls to mind the modern [American] "liberal", who is generally trusting of ["other-centred"] government and suspicious of ["self-centred"] business.

Mill is, naturally, not unaware of the difficulties posed to Good Government by corrupt politicians and their accompanying hosts of unelected (but far from disinterested) officials. Still, he often gives the impression that a proper education for the labouring classes, combined with wisely chosen voting rules, will fix all that and put the right kind of people into power – modern Platonic "philosopher – kings", enlightened rulers all, who will understand the felicific calculus in the manner of, well, Mill, and act accordingly. If such sentiments seem naive today, we must remember that Mill is writing at a time when democratic institutions are still relatively young and not yet fully formed. It was easy then to believe that the main cause of depravity was ignorance. We may easily look back from the high ground of an extra century-and-a-half of experience with democratic institutions, and smirk our lips. But Mill was there at (or near) the founding of those institutions, trying to glimpse their futures and their consequences for their societies' evolutions. Omniscience cannot reasonably be expected of any man, no matter how powerful his intellect.

On the other hand, it would also be a mistake to give Mill a complete "pass" for his democratic utopianism. Either Adam Smith or David Hume (or, for that matter, his own father) could have pointed Mill towards a less utopian, more hard-headed prognostication of the likely relationship between humankind and democratic institutions. Mill however preferred to look primarily to the Continent for his Big Ideas (from where the charm of French sophistication had beckoned to him since adolescence). Anyway, such quintessentially Anglo-Saxon paths as those of Smith and Hume did not meander towards Mill's preferred future of spontaneously evolving socialist societies. The Mills were deeply committed to the vision of a "kinder, gentler" collectivist future for mankind. Other visions offered only capitalism and Malthusian misery (as the Mills might have put it). Better to grasp the larger hope.

It is interesting to compare Mill and Adam Smith on the relation between self-interested behaviour and good government. Mill states flatly that:

> Whenever the general disposition of the people is such that each individual regards those only of his interests which are selfish, and does not dwell on, or concern himself for, his share of the general interest, in such a state of things good government is impossible. (Mill 1973 [1861], 390)

Smith's "invisible hand" principle, by contrast, promotes a basic harmony between self-interested behaviour and benefits to society that also extends to society's broader interests.

> By pursuing his own interest he frequently promotes that of the society more effectually than when he really intends to promote it. I have never known much good done by those who affected to trade for the public good (Smith 1937 [1776], 423) (emphasis added).

Mill doubtless would claim that Smith was mainly describing the workings of market forces, and would offer his thorough agreement within that context. But more generally, Smith is also expressing comfortableness with the workings of private interest in society. True, Smith elsewhere in *The Wealth of Nations* penned the famous comment, much-quoted by anti-marketeers, "People of the same trade seldom meet together, even for merriement and diversion, but the conversation ends in a conspiracy against the public..." (*op. cit.*, 128). What is generally forgotten, however, is that Smith's comment comes in the midst of a section entitled "Inequalities occasioned *by the Policy of Europe*" (emphasis added). Smith is elucidating on how *government* actions help make such conspiracies possible, and how *market forces* are the cure to such conspiracies ("In a free trade an effectual combination cannot be established but by the unanimous consent of every single trader, and it cannot last longer than every single trader continues of the same mind" [*op. cit.*, 129]). That is, Smith's comment is in reference to *government failure*, not *market failure*. Mill sees the bogeyman of "interests which are selfish" behind every tree, wreaking havoc on the best-laid plans of predominately virtuous government officials. Smith sees as the key problem, inappropriate government actions that unleash those private interests on an unsuspecting population (that is, such interests become toxic only when supported by government policy).

To Smith, private interest, properly admonished by market forces, is predominately a force for good in society. To Mill, private interest *can* be beneficial, but not unambiguously so unless government too plays its proper role (one of tempering those "private interests", either directly through land reform or through preventing the accumulation of "excessive" fortunes, or indirectly through proper education of the masses, or through other means that occur to far-sighted, virtuous, benevolent government officers.) This comparison between Smith and Mill is interesting in that it shows how far Mill, at least in the main line of his government musings, strays from what was (until Mill) the Classical tradition in politics and political economy.

Building Leviathan: Mill's Mushrooming Role for Government Intervention

Book V, Chap. 11 of the *Principles*, entitled "Of the Grounds and Limits of the *Laisser-Faire* or Non-Interference Principle", closes out the book. It is one of the longest, and most consequential, chapters of the entire volume. Mill begins the discussion with passionate proclamations in favour of free-market forces. The ideological battle between interventionists and free-marketeers does not "admit of any universal solution" (*op. cit.*, 941–2; 937). But "under whatever political institutions we live, there is a circle around every individual human being which no government … ought to be permitted to overstep…" (*op. cit.*, 943; 938). "*Laisser-faire*, in short, should be the general practice: every departure from it, unless required by some great good, is a certain evil" (*op. cit.*, 950; 945).

Those thinking that these lofty sentiments surely must foretell a strong closing chapter advocating limited government and creative free-market-based solutions to society's problems, alas, do not yet know their man. A pointed hint of what is to come is provided by Mill's early bifurcation of government interventions into two kinds of action. Mill has little use for "authoritative" interference – government that forbids and demands. But he is enthusiastic about what we might call a "kinder, gentler" second type of government intervention that,

> leaving individuals free to use their own means of pursuing any object of general interest, the government, not meddling with them, but not trusting the object solely to their care, establishes, side by side with their arrangements, an agency of its own for a like purpose (*Principles*, 942; 937).

Thus, there could be (to use a term recently [2009–2010] bandied about in the US) a "public option", where government provides education, or banking services, or health care, or other such things (perhaps *very many* other such things, a cynic might here interject), without involving itself in the private-sector's activities in these areas.[40] In contrast to his view of "authoritarian" government, Mill thinks that the second, "public option", type of intervention is quite benign, except for the compulsory taxes that must be paid to support the parallel institutions that are set up "side by side" next to the private sector's offerings. With this second option, "there is no infringement of liberty, no irksome or degrading restraint", and so "[o]ne of the principal objections to government interference is then absent" (*op. cit.*, 944; 939).

Here Mill, arguably, reveals a certain naivete. Even if (setting aside the taxes) all this is true, so long as governments play by the rules that Mill lays out, what if they choose not to do so? How long before "side by side" public institutions, once they become thoroughly entrenched, grow jealous of their free-market rivals and seek their destruction and replacement with "proper", public institutions? We have learned much about such dynamics since Mill's day. While Mill cannot be held accountable for the future, he might have shown more insight into the ultimate likely consequences of such an incentive system. The notion of these public agencies – established with the explicit charter of looking after the general populace in some specific context – standing aside and smiling indulgently while their private-sector competition (as it might be said) "fails to live up to its moral obligations to serve the public" (and, purely coincidentally, injures the public agency's financial interests as well), is a notion that may well elicit a chuckle from a modern reader. One may not wave a red flag at a bull and then disclaim the resulting charge.

The Limits to Government

With Mill now having identified and advocated a mega-concept of government intervention which rationalizes a potentially vast expansion of public-sector involvement in the economy, it is high time for him to reassure his reader of his free-market *bona fides*. Accordingly, he unsparingly states downsides of Big Government. Repeating his earlier assertions, he argues that "authoritarian" government is dangerous and to be tolerated only in small amounts (Section 2). He points out how growing government throws out its tentacles from its new power bases, acquiring ever-greater direct and indirect influence (Section 3) – including power over minorities of opinion that he finds especially disconcerting (and which would later preoccupy him in *On Liberty*). And the machinery of government is easily overburdened, so that its additional responsibilities come at the cost of weighting down the entire mechanism (Section 4).

---

[40] "It is one thing to provide schools or colleges, and another to require that no person shall act as an instructor of youth without a government licence. There might be a national bank, or a government manufactory, without any monopoly against private banks and manufactories. There might be a post-office, without penalties against the conveyance of letters by other means. …There may be public hospitals, without any restriction on private medical or surgical practice" (*Principles*, 942; 937).

In addition, most things are simply done worse by governments than by self-interested individuals who "understand their own business and their own interests better…" (*op. cit.*, 947; 942) (Section 5). In the vast majority of cases, government action is unlikely to accomplish tasks remotely as well as would the private sector if given those same tasks. (Mill does not say whether the private sector referred to is orthodox capitalism or voluntary cooperative socialism, or both, but previous chapters do not suggest that Mill is talking here only of capitalist institutions.) Mill's fifth objection to "government agency" (Section 6) is his favourite. A wise government will encourage the people "to manage as many as possible of their joint concerns by voluntary co-operation; since this discussion and management of collective interests is the great school of that public spirit, and the great source of that intelligence of public affairs, which are always regarded as the distinctive character of the public of free countries" (*Principles*, 949; 944).

Mill's Broad Case for Government Intervention

Having established his limited-government credentials (or, at least, so it would seem), Mill at last turns, in the remaining two-thirds of the chapter, to his main undertaking. This is a laying-out of perceived weaknesses in the market system, and suggestions for the role that a wise, benevolent government might play in countering those weaknesses. In this endeavour, arguably, he manages to undo all (or more than all) of the pro-market principles he so carefully laid out earlier in the chapter.

All Mill's advocacy of an expanded role for government pertains to circumstances where (as Mill sees it) a decision-maker cannot adequately protect his own legitimate interests. Either individuals (predominately consumers) are unqualified to properly understand their own interests, or else individuals do understand, but are unable to coordinate effectively enough with others to achieve these interests. By merely alleging one or the other of these two broad classes of market failure, Mill carves out a vast potential role for government to act as protector of an inadequately informed, or inadequately empowered, populace. The resulting critique of laissez-faire and recommendations for ameliorating policy was destined to make a massive contribution to the empowerment of the West's public sectors and the corresponding diminishment in authority of its private ones.

The Argument from the Premise of Public Ignorance: "Culture" and Education

Mill begins with circumstances where decision-makers have meaningfully incomplete information about the decisions they must make (Section 8). Consumers are poor judges of matters with which they do not deal routinely. Accordingly, the "presumption in favour of the market does not apply in this case" (*Principles*, 953; 947), and "intervention by the authorized representatives of the collective interest of the state" (*Principles, ibid*; *ibid*) is therefore necessary.

Since "[t]he uncultivated cannot be competent judges of cultivation" (*Principles, ibid*; *ibid*), education, and culture generally, will be systematically under-consumed by the Great Unwashed, who are to be presumed wholly ignorant of such subtleties.

Parents failing to provide their children with a basic education "commit a double breach of duty, towards the children themselves, and towards the members of the community generally, who are all liable to suffer seriously from the consequences of ignorance and want of education in their fellow-citizens" (*Principles*, 954; 948). In his push for compulsory public education, Mill thereby promotes what soon would become two of the more mischievous and prominent arguments for government intervention. First is that government at key points knows the citizen's business better than the citizen himself. Second, daunting "spillover effects" make what looks at first glance to be a purely private matter into one in which society has a vital overriding interest. (When one recalls the era's many successful apprentice educations, its high number of low-skilled jobs requiring little other than on-the-job education, and its many self-educated success stories who went on to found whole new industries – and when one contemplates the horror of public education in the West today – it becomes a bit less clear that Mill was self-evidently right to advocate a compulsory and universal public education.)

Let us also note Mill's casual, unexamined assumption that [alleged] poor handling of education by parents implies that government will do better with the job. But if a market test is not to be applied to the viability of an education scheme, then from where will a substitute discipline to that supplied by market forces come? Presumably, supremely cultured, wise, benevolent, and other-spirited government officials are to be invoked as the problem's solution. Anyway, it is not for the "uncultivated" to question the wisdom of such "character-laden" experts. Taken seriously, this line of argument quickly turns education into the permanent plaything of government officials – who now and then would turn out to be not quite so altruistically benevolent as Mill was so eager to presume.[41]

Mill likely would have indignantly rejected the notion that he was advocating the establishment of government dominance of "elementary education". He would point with vigour to passages where he decries the creation of any government education monopoly (e.g. p. 956; 950). His "public option" schools would merely compete "side by side" with those of the private sector, keeping the latter honest. But on the same page, Mill calls the general quality of private education "never good except

---

[41]In fact, Mill seems to have been an early supporter of what is today the Civil Service. He emphasized:

> the distinction between the function of making laws, for which a numerous popular assembly is radically unfit, and that of getting good laws made ... and the consequent need of a Legislative Commission, as a permanent part of the constitution of a free country; consisting of a small number of highly trained political minds, on whom ... the task of making [a law] should be devolved: Parliament retaining the power of passing or rejecting the bill when drawn up, but not of altering it otherwise than by sending proposed amendments to be dealt with by the Commission (*Autobiography*, 265).

Despite the fig leaf of a legislature able to finally accept or reject a bill, it is still just to say that if this does not describe a system of rule by "wise, enlightened, experts", then it is difficult to imagine what does.

by some rare accident, and generally so bad as to be little more than nominal" (*op. cit.*, 956; 950). How then is it that giving the schools – and thus, indirectly, poorer citizens – an education subsidy (as Mill suggests *op. cit.*, 956; 949) will make these citizens better judges of the schools' comparative worth? And how long before the public authorities begin to bitterly (and strategically) complain about public funds being "wasted" on inferior private schools? These are the inevitable questions that inevitably bring such a school system under the domineering hand of government authority. Only a vast naivete about the nature of government can account for such a line of argument.

Mill's case for public education also sets a deep, ominous precedent for other policy areas. The argument would seem to justify public intervention in any "cultural" issue which impacts (or can be strategically claimed to impact) the labouring classes. There is hardly anything remotely "cultural" that governments do in the early twenty-first century that cannot potentially be rationalized by some version of Mill's argument. For the interventionist, Mill's position is a treasure-trove of "abatements and exceptions" (*op. cit.*, 953; 947) to the notion that consumers might be trusted to be in control of their own [cultural] lives.

The public would be treated to many such demonstrations in the 150 years after Mill wrote. Mill tried to stress the exceptional and limited nature of his arguments for government intervention. However, there would be simply no way to enforce such a viewpoint on those seeking new venues for government activity. Mill thought he was making a limited argument about culture and education. In reality, he was creating one of the most sweeping rationales ever conceived for government's expansion.

Mill might have brought a more critical eye to his examination of the "abatements and exceptions" to market principles. Instead, his casual assumption of broad public-sector integrity and competence suggest an astonishing naivete regarding the long-term internal workings of government institutions and the rent-seekers who seek to control them. It is the more astonishing because, in his fragment on Socialism, and even elsewhere in the *Principles* (e.g. 790–1; 792–3), he demonstrates considerable understanding of the flawed incentives that drive the decisions of such institutions. His highly influential argument advocating the concentration of greater power in such institutions would cost the West dearly in ensuing decades.

The Argument from Public Ignorance: Mental Incompetence, "Irrevocable" Decisions (Sections 9–10)

Mill's second argument for government intervention (Section 9) involves protecting the temporarily incompetent (children), the mentally incompetent, and – remarkably for his era – domestic animals. Women need no special protection other than equality before the law and in their treatment by society. In Section 10, Mill takes aim at "irrevocable" decisions like voluntary slavery, indentured servitude, and unbreakable marriage contracts. In general, "the law should be extremely jealous of such engagements" (*op. cit.*, 960; 954).

The Argument from Public Ignorance: "Delegated Agency" (Section 11)

Mill's next exception to laissez-faire concerns the proper relations between the State and the private corporation, which was then just beginning its rise to prominence in business affairs. Shareholders, thinks Mill, will have little success in reigning in their wayward managers. By contrast, government employees typically will be the better-supervised, due to "the greater publicity and more active discussion and comment, to be expected in free countries with regard to affairs in which the general government takes part" (*op. cit.*, 961; 954). Thus, publicly delegated agency will consistently outperform privately delegated agency due to the superior monitoring capacity of a democratic populace.

Perusing this argument, the reader may not be able to resist contemplating what type of wondrous Beings will fill the voting booths of these democratic societies. Evidently, Mill foresees a public filled with passionate civic idealism, eager to sacrifice themselves by putting societal welfare ahead of their own interests at every turn. Why citizens should be so focussed on public affairs when it is their private affairs that matter most to them, is a question that, one suspects, might have occurred to a David Hume or an Adam Smith – but not, apparently, to John Stuart Mill. Mill also does not notice the objection (oft-commented-upon since Mill's day) that no single voter can have any impact on any issue through becoming well-informed and voting his conscience, since any one vote cast (which equals any one voter's opinion) is trivial to the election's outcome. By contrast, individual stockholders, through their ability to control many shares of stock, can exert considerable influence on management's behaviour.

Here, with Mill's firm condemnation of corporations based on [what would one day be called] Galbraithian economic reasoning, the discussion might well have ended. However, in a sudden plot twist worthy of Victor Hugo, Mill now trumps his own economic argument in favour of one based on that favourite construction of his – a broader societal perspective. The previous verdict in favour of government management is to be vacated for one endorsing corporate management, despite the latter's perceived economic inferiority (albeit with some "reasonable" [*op. cit.*, 960; 956] regulation of corporations and of natural monopolies). This is on the strength of his earlier arguments about the broader societal advantages of a vigorous, engaged, and private citizenry.

Thus, on a purely economic level, corporate management is roundly condemned, while on a broader, societal level, such management is warmly embraced (on grounds quite divorced from the question of management's competence). Rarely does Mill-The-Political-Economist part company so firmly with Mill-The-Broad-Social-Scientist. Practically, however, the damage to private agency is done. Mill's broad-based case for private agency was forgotten: his seminal critique of the corporate structure was not. His argument amounted in practice to an open invitation for aggressive regulation of the new corporate structures and even, where politically possible, their replacement with nationalized industries. Mill's economic conclusions were crystal-clear: corporate governance causes serious problems, and only government intervention can correct them. Thus, Mill issues another invitation for government to massively extend its authority (and, often, near-hegemony) over what would become the dominant type of business structure in the West.[42]

Incomplete Coordination: The "Who-Goes-First" and Public-Goods Problems (Sections 12 and 15)

Mill next turns to circumstances where collective goods, the provision of which requires the co-operation of many separate individuals, are arguably under-produced by market forces due to the "who goes first"? problem (a problem to which he "requests particular attention" [*Principles*, 963; 956]). He postulates workers who wish to reduce the length of their workday by an hour a day without lowering their hourly pay. They could all agree that such a lowering is beneficial; yet, any one worker could gain by defecting from the agreement and working the tenth hour. If one such worker gains from defection, then eventually many will, and the agreement will break down. Mill suggests what is needed is a State enforcement of a to not work more than nine hours – essential if labour is to be able to coordinate so as to reap these gains. (He sees, naturally – as do legions of modern enthusiasts – many similar cases where useful coordination among decision-makers might be frustrated by these types of perverse incentives.)

By gratuitously presuming that all workers have voluntarily agreed to the contract, Mill avoids *explicit* advocacy of the State coercing labourers into accepting the contract (*Principles*, 963; 956–7). The State merely holds the workers to their freely given pledge. But what if some workers refuse to sign the agreement (if not existing workers, then perhaps future ones)? Without State coercion, Mill thinks, an initial minority of defectors would increase until the agreement collapses.

Here Mill halts his discussion – and he surely does so too early. For, to take this line is to admit that, in the real world where defectors exist, reaping the gains of the agreement requires government's coercion of non-cooperating labourers.[43] Thus, Mill's "voluntary" agreement among workers must, in practice, morph into some kind of a coercive system. Perhaps State coercion would be tempered by some need for a super-majority of labourers before the State gets involved (one might hope so). Or perhaps the State, "knowing" that labour needs its "help" to solve its coordination problem, would simply cut out the middlemen and directly impose the "necessary" coercion itself. History is not silent as to which path would be predominately taken. Down this route, arguably, lies that labyrinth of modern labour law so conscientiously and thoroughly applied by Western governments in the modern era.

---

[42] Surely here we also find one of the points of origin of the myth of the soulless, out-of-control corporate power, answering to no one but itself and its almighty god, Profit.

[43] Mill is not necessarily advocating the idea of lowering labour's work-day – though he is clearly sympathetic. He is merely using the case to illustrate the coordination problem and the argument for a government role that emerges from that problem.

Turning now to Mill's discussion of public goods (see Section "Public Goods", above),[44] it is interesting to note how quickly Mill presumes that his argument for government subsidy/supply of public goods is definitive. One might have expected, for example, that Mill would have contemplated circumstances under which voluntary private cooperation could have been successful in supplying such goods. The modern literature on the "private supply of public goods" shows how groups of private decision-makers often manage to overcome their coordination problems (by, e.g. supplying public goods through various stratagems such as "tying arrangements" which link the supply of a public good to another, private, good that can be withheld until payment is rendered). However, there is *no* such speculation – *no* such attempt to reign in what would become one of government intervention's most successful arguments – to be found in Mill's discussion.

Why did Mill present (by omission) such a pessimistic view of the private sector's ability to supply public goods? Certainly there was no such pessimism about group-coordination of productive activity in his lengthy discussion in Book IV, Chap. 7 covering workers' cooperative ventures. There Mill expresses great optimism about the ability of such voluntary *non-profit* cooperation to overcome the disincentives to cooperate that are summed up in modern economics as "prisoner's dilemma problems". (He does, however, express some reservations [*Principles*, 790; 792].) How are these happy thoughts to be reconciled with the professed insurmountable difficulties that for-profit group activity encounters when trying to profitably supply public goods? An argument deriding private supply of public goods on "who goes first"? grounds is at least as applicable to private non-profit cooperative ventures generally.

In any event, Mill's ruminations on coordination failure helped craft yet another extremely broad set of arguments for use by those who, whether for altruistic good or opportunistic ill, were looking for persuasive rationalizations to grow government. While Mill did not see these arguments as anything more than occasional exceptions to the rule of market principles, history would reserve for them a different role. Arguably, the broad conception of market failure defined by the public-goods and the "who goes first"? arguments has been more successful at advancing government agency than any other single rationalization, due to its great breadth of plausible (if not always justifiable) application. With a little effort, virtually any argument favouring an additional role for government in the economy can be attractively dressed-up in public good "who goes first"? garb. As a result, few arguments have been more often heard emanating from petitioners in the Great Halls of political authority.

---

[44] The reader should first notice in this argument what Mill does not: that the difficulty with supplying public goods is similar in nature to that of the "who goes first" problem. In both cases, the problem is that many people benefiting from such a good stand aside and wait for others to come forward and voluntarily fund the good. Thus, sufficient funds to finance the good cannot be accumulated since many of those who benefit will enjoy the good for free, paradoxically leading to the good not being supplied at all privately. The workers trying to organize for a lower work-week in the "who goes first" problem face precisely the same difficulty as the citizens trying to organize to privately supply a public good. Coordination difficulties are at the heart of the issues impeding the supply of collective goods in general.

Incomplete Coordination: External Effects (Sections 12 and 14)

Always the Malthusian, Mill saw a pressing societal need to reduce population in England. Therefore, he advocated financial support for colonization of other regions as one of the crucial areas in which government's role is justified. On the surface these arguments are of only historical interest to the modern reader. In discussing colonization, however, Mill manages to assert yet another very broad-ranging role for government agency – that of combatting the bad consequences stemming from "external effects".

Mill was a strong supporter of the Wakefield system of colonization, under which colonial governments would shape development by keeping land prices artificially high. Such a regime would discourage newly arrived colonists from buying land immediately upon arrival and becoming farmers, when the colony needed them more urgently as common labourers (*Principles*, 965; 958) (note the rejection of the notion that free labour markets might be able to bring about the right supply of labourers). It would also prevent too-much concentration of land ownership in a few hands.

Unfettered market forces could not prevent inappropriate land ownership patterns due to yet another "who goes first"? problem. Each colonist individually is unwilling to "go first" by restricting himself to small acreage while others purchase large acreage (*op. cit.,* 967; 958). Like lemmings, immigrants would simply buy up as much land as they could afford, due to "the instinct (as it may almost be called) of appropriation…" (*Principles, ibid*; *ibid*) (note the rejection of market forces as determining the demand for land, in favour of "instinct"). It takes a large proportion of colonists working together to reap the gains, and such coordination cannot be achieved without central control.

Mill therefore endorses Wakefield's stratagem of using artificially high land prices to retard ownership of large tracts of land. Intervention is needed to reap the otherwise-unrealizable societal gains arising from a "proper" pattern of land ownership. Later in Section 14, Mill describes a second advantage of such a centrally planned policy: that it "keeps the settlers within reach of each other for purposes of co-operation, [and] arranges a numerous body of them within easy distance of each centre of foreign commerce and non-agricultural industry…" (*op. cit.,* 973; 965). (Note the assumption that the settlers themselves are not competent to assess such matters unaided; similar considerations today make up much of the "smart" part of the "smart growth" movement.)

These are early arguments for, quite simply, a massive introduction of government control into the land markets of colonies. However, those enamoured with gains such as these will also favour policies that [can be argued to] reap similar gains in the "home country". The genie is out of the bottle, and, once out, there is no argument that restricts its busy-bodied "reform" of every conceivable aspect of land markets merely to the colonies.

Just how broad is the mandate is made clear when Mill caustically answers those who object to the Wakefield plan on free-market grounds. The objectors had the temerity to argue that "when things are left to themselves, land is appropriated and occupied by the spontaneous choice of individuals, in the quantities and at the times most advantageous to each person, and therefore to the community generally..." (*op. cit.*, 965; 959) – a straightforward free-market position. Wakefield's plan was criticized by these objectors as "the self-conceited notion of the legislator" (*Principles, ibid*; *ibid*) who thinks he knows people's good better than these people know it themselves. To Mill, the flawed logic of those criticizing Wakefield's argument is exactly analogous to the argument that, because it is in the interest of society as a whole that people do not rob and steal, there will be no theft, and that, therefore, there need be no police. Clearly, criminals can gain individually even as their actions injure society overall, and so police are necessary for the defence of society. The same, thinks Mill, holds true when society takes measures to prevent individual selfishness from creating land-use patterns that are inconsistent with society's broader needs. Mill does not observe that such arguments have, quite literally, unimaginably vast potential application. For example: All the land-use planning and regulation that has developed since Mill's day – from the earliest zoning acts through modern "smart growth" initiatives – arguably are implicit in his modest-sounding advocacy of the Wakefield plan.

The Argument from Public Ignorance: Charity and Welfare Programs (Section 13)

Mill draws a fundamental distinction between circumstances where people are looking directly after their own interests, vs. the case where they are seeking to be charitable by aiding those whom they do not know (or do not know well). Mill denies that individuals will necessarily do a good job with their own money when they are using those monies to promote the interests of the poor. Charity in private hands, he thinks, is likely to be handled only "uncertainly and casually" (*op. cit.*, 967; 960). Therefore, some role for government – at least as a significant supplement to private charity – seems necessary to Mill. There should be "systematic arrangements, in which society acts through its organ, the state" (*Principles, ibid*; *ibid*) (The specifics of Mill's welfare proposals are treated above [cf. Section "Public Goods"].)

We must pause briefly here to note that, in his discussion of private charity, Mill introduces yet another innocuous-sounding assumption that would not fail to have vast and fundamental consequences to the workings of Western democracy. The notion that individuals are indifferent-to-poor judges of how they can act to help others raises the question of whether they are acceptably good judges of their relations with their fellow human beings. Humans are skilled (on Mill's premises) at "looking out for Number 1", but at what costs to others? If humans cannot be trusted to make wise decisions about their charitable donations, can they be trusted to adequately retain a suitably charitable manner in their day-to-day dealings with their fellow men? Mill himself seems to think not: In *On Liberty*, he advocates, not just "protection ... against the tyranny of the magistrate", but "protection also against the tyranny of the prevailing opinion and feeling..." (Mill 1977a, b [1859], 220). "There is a limit", states Mill, "to the legitimate interference of collective opinion with individual independence ..." (*ibid*). *On Liberty* is, in fact, very heavily focussed on

Mill's notion that wide deviations among human beings are essential to create a wide enough base to support a vigorous, healthy, and active society. Accordingly, reasonable divergence from the social norm should not only be tolerated, but celebrated. Thus Mill's notion is arguably one of the founding-stones of the modern "diversity movement". It is not hard to see why, among all Mill's many works, it is *On Liberty* that appeals most palatably to the modern self-styled sophisticate's taste.

Mill is careful not to explicitly advocate the use of government force against those who illegitimately interfere with "individual independence". It is difficult though to see any practical consequences flowing from this apparent proscription. Mill also holds that "[a]s soon as any one part of a person's conduct affects prejudicially the interests of others, society has jurisdiction over it, and the question whether the general welfare will or will not be promoted by interfering with it, becomes open to discussion" (Mill 1977a, b [1859], 276). *Who* is to engage in such "interfering" if not the State? This remarkably broad criterion for intervention gives tremendous potential discretion to the government regulator looking to "protect" those of divergent views from those who would discriminate against them. The mandate for government to act is precisely as large as the ability of government and its allied activists to persuade "society" that someone is being unfairly treated in some particular social setting. Mill, therefore (in a twist he would not find amusing), arguably is one of the founders of the modern taste for "speech codes", laws preventing landlords from renting to those they prefer, the vast array of discrimination law, and the "economic rights" industry generally. If it is not also a dismal legacy, then at least it is an ironic one, given his deep desire for toleration in society of others' preferences.[45]

Later Life of Mill

Shortly after Mill's completion of the *Principles*, in 1849, John Taylor died of cancer, his grieving wife at his bedside (Hayek 1951, 161–2). In April, 1851, Mill and Harriet Taylor were at last united as man and wife (before the marriage, due to the lack of rights granted to women in the marriage contract of his day, Mill wrote out "a solemn statement of his disapproval of the whole character of the marriage relation as constituted by law" [Britton 1953, 36]).[46] During the rigid Victorian process leading up to the marriage, Mill felt that his sisters and mother had not accorded Harriet Taylor, and the marriage, the proper amount of respect. The result was that – despite agonized attempts by his family to repair the breach (see Hayek 1951, Chap. 8) – Mill cut off virtually all contact with his family for the remainder of his life.

---

[45] Some concluding thoughts about the last section of Mill's closing *Principles* chapter are provided in Section "Mill's Legacy" below.

[46] The statement can be found in Mill (1984 [1851]), 97–100.

During the seven-and-a-half years of his marriage, Mill (in intellectual partnership with his wife) wrote *On Liberty* (explicitly labelled a joint work between them), and "shaped his own views on *The Subjection of Women*" (Britton 1953, 37). Mill's conception of feminism was in many ways quite modern; for example, from his earliest exposure to Harriet, he had contemptuously rejected the Victorian view that there are "essential differences between the best masculine characters and the best feminine characters" (*ibid*). Instead, women with the highest "feminine" qualities also had the highest "masculine" qualities (*ibid*).[47] Many of Mill's remaining years would be spent addressing causes connected to the liberation of women from their chattel-like status in Victorian society.

For the great bulk of his busiest intellectual years, Mill also had worked in London at the India House, making policy on the governance of the British Empire's greatest colony. In 1856 he was appointed "Examiner of India Correspondence", the second-highest post in the India House. He held the office only 2 years. In 1858 the company failed to get their charter renewed and Mill, rather than join the newly constituted India Council, resigned from the service (his pension making him financially secure for life). He had worked there for 33 years, a period of time during which he wrote nearly all of his greatest works (see *Autobiography*, 247–8). Mill always believed that his busy schedule at India House was complementary with his intellectual work. He would no doubt have embraced Churchill's saying that "a change is as good as a rest". Mill also expressed gratitude for how the experience had taught him from early adulthood how to compromise and get the best he could in a group decision-making setting (Schumpeter and Sowell, on the other hand, flag the India House activities as likely adversely impacting the quality of Mill's primary life's work [*cf.* Sowell 2006, 152–4]).

During the early 1850s Mill also "suffered a first attack of the family disease" (tuberculosis) (*Autobiography*, 247), and to recover his health took an extended trip alone through Italy, Sicily, and Greece in the winter and spring of 1854–1855 (leaving behind fascinating letters to Harriet describing all aspects of these areas at the time, including Mill's impressions of the ruins of Ancient Greece's [see Hayek 1951, Chaps. 10–11]).[48] In November 1858, just before the final joint editing of *On Liberty* was to begin, Harriet Taylor-Mill died of tuberculosis at Avignon, France. She was buried in the Avignon cemetery. Mill quickly bought a small cottage in Avignon "as near as possible to the place where she is buried" (*Autobiography*, 251), where he lived during most of the year (given Mill's own tuberculosis, some move to a warmer climate was in any case essential to his own health). He was comforted, and aided in his work by his [step]-daughter Helen Taylor, who remained constantly by his side until his death. Helen Taylor assumed a

---

[47] This was, interestingly, too much even for Britton, who, writing at mid-twentieth century, could not resist recording his disapproval: "Mill held that a philosophy is to be judged by its conception of human nature: and it is somewhat disconcerting to find that his own conception suffered from this eccentric limitation" (Britton 1953, 37–8).

[48] Mill's wife was too ill to accompany him on such a long and arduous trip.

professional interaction with Mill not unlike that which Harriet Taylor had with him, and Mill praised her with superlatives not unlike those which he had rained down upon Harriet Taylor. As had been the case with Harriet, some documents (apparently, only letters, though some for newspaper publication) signed by Mill were in fact written by Helen (*Autobiography*, 286–7).

Mill's three primary achievements in the last decade of his life were his writing of the monolithic *Examination of William Hamilton's Philosophy* (Mill 1979 [1865]) – a lengthy critique of the ideas of England's leading Kantian, the writing of *The Subjection of Women* (1984) [1869], and Mill's surprising stint in Parliament from 1865 through 1868. Approached about running by leading citizens of Westminster (then a working-class district), Mill made make it clear that he had principles and that they would not be compromised. He would not help fund his own campaign, he would not give time if elected to "local interests", and he would not canvass. He was free with his own opinions, including his support of women's suffrage. Moreover, Mill had written in his *Parliamentary Reform* that the working classes (i.e. his would-be constituents!) were quite dishonest but at least were ashamed of their dishonesty. Challenged on this statement at a public meeting, Mill proudly acknowledged authorship, at which point his working-class audience burst into applause (*Autobiography*, 274). He was elected to Parliament and served while there many of the causes for which he had fought all his life.

It might appear from this story that, as a public servant, Mill begat yet another miracle to add to his uncanny literary achievements – that he proved that honesty pays in politics and that good-people-being-good easily get elected when they simply look exclusively after the public good as Mill himself always did his best to do. Those drawn to such a conclusion, though, ought first to consult the denouement. Mill lost his second election three years later due precisely to his extraordinary honesty and principled behaviour, which created too many opportunities for his opportunistic political competitors. Even during his time in Parliament, Mill had chosen not to support popular causes merely to court popularity among his fellow Liberals (he had supported mainly causes of little interest to many of his party and even some unpopular causes). During his re-election campaign, Mill also chose to financially support a man whom he saw as a superb candidate but who was very open about his lack of religious faith. As a result, Mill was painted with the same [accurate] brush. As Mill himself put it, in his support of a deserving candidate,

> I did what would have been highly imprudent if I had been at liberty to consider only the interests of my own reelection; and, as might be expected, the utmost possible use, both fair and unfair, was made of this act of mine to stir up the electors of Westminster against me. To these various causes, combined with an unscrupulous use of the usual pecuniary and other influences on the side of my Tory competitor, while none were used on my side, it is to be ascribed that I failed at my second election after having succeeded in the first (*Autobiography*, 289–90).

Such principled behaviour is highly laudable, but not that out of which successful political careers are made. No better argument can be found in favour of those who would sharply restrict the political power of elected politicians and their sundry bureaucratic proxies. Mill himself might have learned from his own experience, and if so, he might have altered or recanted some of his many policy recommendations (discussed previously at numerous points) the success of which hinged on politicians having the same politically suicidal commitment to principled behaviour in office that he himself had exhibited. There was, however, no evidence that he did so.

After failing in his re-election bid, Mill (who after his defeat received several offers of safe seats) instead chose to return to private life at Avignon. In his last years he worked on a book on Socialism, several chapters of which were published in his lifetime (other fragments of the work were published posthumously). The work in its incomplete form is notable for what might be termed a step back from his earlier pronounced optimism over likely future socialist developments. Instead, arguably, there is a notably greater emphasis on the virtues of market forces. It is interesting, but futile, to speculate on what might have been had Mill lived to complete this work (would he, e.g. have become aware of, and challenged, the budding Marxist movement?).[49]

Mill spent most of the remainder of his days quietly at Avignon, with his [step] daughter Helen, working on correspondence and on his uncompleted draft on socialism. On one of his trips to England, he christened his godson, the infant Bertrand Russell, who in the next century would go on himself to a distinguished intellectual career. While at home, Mill doubtlessly also lingered in his greenhouses where he pursued his botanical studies – a lifelong hobby. Mill died, at Avignon, in May 1873, "the victim of a local fever" (Britton 1953, 44). At his direction, he is buried in the same grave as his wife.

Mill's Legacy

What has been Mill's influence in economics? Mill wrote only two books on political economy.[50] First came his *Unsettled Questions* which he wrote as a young man, and then the *Principles*, predominately a textbook rather than an original work of theory – one which, for better or for worse, was the dominant "voice" of economics from 1848 through at least 1900 (with gradually moderating influence over the first 2 decades of the twentieth century). Mill's interpretation of Classical economics quickly became the standard interpretation, universally learned by nearly all who studied political economy (other texts of Mill's day tended to "piggyback" on his [cf. Schumpeter 1954, 533]). Mill's book ultimately was supplanted by Marshall's *Principles* (Marshall 1988 [1920]), first published in 1890. But Marshall's book is

---

[49] Schumpeter suggests that Mill's preliminary fragments on socialism are "perhaps more misleading than helpful", since the work's critiques were merely "exploratory sketches", and since, doubtless, the book would have included "a positive complement that might have reversed the impression the reader of these sketches is likely to get" (Schumpeter 1954, 532).

[50] Of course, he also wrote a number of articles on economic topics.

heavily indebted to Mill's (with the most notable exception being value theory), while [the microeconomic portions of] modern texts in turn have been written largely in Marshall's shadow. Mill's contribution as an expositor of economic principles is thus, through effects both direct and reflective, considerable.

As to the contribution of Mill and his *Principles* to economic doctrine, it is convenient to follow the main line of the paper and divide these into "orthodox" and "heterodox" contributions. Mill's theoretical achievements in orthodox economics are not the earth-shaking ones of a Smith (pioneering of modern economics), a Ricardo (theory of comparative advantage / rent), or a Jevons/Walras/Menger (subjective value theory), but nonetheless they are substantive and significant. Mill's cost-of-production value theory did not survive, but his restatement and reshaping of supply-and-demand analysis, and his explanation of elasticity (though lacking the term itself), closely anticipates modern treatments. He made indisputably original contributions in international finance, in joint production processes, in the theory of public goods, in what is today called growth theory (despite the handicap of his malthusian doctrine), and in laying out the skeleton of the perfect competition model with, arguably, greater precision than his great predecessors.[51] His macroeconomic analysis clarified the causes and limitations of economic "crises" and explained their origins in a way that clearly paved the way for monetary disequilibrium theory in all its forms (in addition, some of his macroeconomic statements in the *Unsettled Questions* essay on consumption and production clearly anticipate Keynesian arguments).

We should add to this the many classic statements of core free-market economics that are to be found in his *Principles*: the succinct, and very modern, critique of several common government interventions in Book V, Chap. 10, a powerful defence of unfettered competition at the end of Book IV, his undisguised enthusiasm for the entrepreneurial creativity of his "peasant proprietors" in Book II, his still-classic statement of the neutrality of money in Book III, and other arguments that pepper the *Principles*, all come to mind, among others. Mill was, then, in terms of his orthodox contributions, in many respects more than just an original economic theorist. He was also a good shepherd of the intellectual tradition established by Hume, Smith, Say, Ricardo, and his own father in orthodox political economy.

Mill's orthodox legacy, however, includes a darker side. The smothering influence of the *Principles*, not to mention that of Mill himself, almost certainly postponed the marginalist revolution. Jevons wrote bitterly of how Mill's "noxious influence of authority" (Jevons 1957 [1871], 275–7) delayed the arrival of subjectivist value theory. It was Mill who famously wrote (in one of the most-cited belly flops in intellectual history): "Happily there is nothing in the laws of value which remains for the present or any future writer to clear up; the theory of the subject is complete" (*Principles* 436; 456). Mill never budged from this position, and the

---

[51] By contrast, says Mitchell, Mill's "remarks on monopoly are of an exceedingly vague, and, from the modern viewpoint, unsatisfactory character" (Mitchell 1967, 581).

towering prestige of his text definitely repressed the breakthrough of new insights in this area. In another example, Mill's thorough and open-ended analysis in the *Unsettled Questions* of the complexities of Say's Law with storable money was trimmed down and replaced in the *Principles* with a discussion that was much less obviously a deviation from the main line of classical macroeconomic analysis. Sowell argues that Mill was also excessively protective of "the conceptual peculiarities of the Ricardian system and its assumptions..." (Sowell 2006, 153), contributing thereby to the ossification of economic theory around Malthusianism, input-based value theory, and a narrow rendering of Say's Law as the final word in aggregate speculations. Mill's work thereby repressed "contributions of other schools of thought that operated within different frameworks and with different assumptions" (*ibid*). Mill was sure of his subject, and at times it caused him to reject too quickly ideas that conflicted with Ricardian wisdom.

Turning now to Mill's substantial impact on heterodox economic theory: Here, Mill and the nature of his influence has been noticed (and generally, if not always explicitly, lauded) by numerous authorities. Wesley Mitchell's endorsement is perhaps the most trumpeting, appearing in the very title of his chapter on Mill ("John Stuart Mill and the *Humanization* of Classical Economics"). Mitchell writes of Mill's "wonderful later chapters" (Mitchell 1967, 570), and directs the reader's attention especially to the voluntarist socialist vision in the "Probable Futurity of the Labouring Classes" (Book IV, Chap. 7). To Barber, it is more Mill's anti-materialist values – so thoroughly on display in Mill's stationary-state chapter – that are worthy of emphasis. He highlights Mill's "challenge to an implicit value premise that had run through the whole of classical writing: that uninterrupted economic expansion was a goal of such obvious importance that it required no justification" (Barber 1967, 101–2). Echoing Barber, Landreth underlines Mill's hope for "...a new, better society no longer oriented toward strictly materialistic pursuits" (Landreth 1976, 141). Landreth is impressed also by Mill's attempt "to combine the hardheadedness of classical liberalism with the humanism of social reform to bring about a society and economy less concerned with the business of business and more concerned with the art of individual improvement and self-fulfilment" (Landreth 1976, 150). Further, Mill, "[m]uch more than Smith and Ricardo ... recognized that the working of market forces did not necessarily bring about a harmonious economic and social order..." (*op. cit.*, 140).

Other authors might well be cited on these and other points. But the upshot of it all is fairly clear, and it has little to do with economics. Mill is being lauded as a great spiritual apostle of altruism and anti-materialism – a man raised to glorify capitalism and laissez-faire but who one day woke up, turned on his intellectual captors, and chose instead heroically to advocate "people over profits", egalitarianism over individualism, "self-fulfilment" over "mere" material gain, and enlightened government intervention over the "unjust distribution" of the market system. Mill is, above all else, a great *story*: the tale of his "turning" is the account of one of the greatest triumphs in the entire history of the Left. It is natural to lavish praise upon those whose personal story validates one's own strivings, and one may forgive the occasional [free-market] apostasy of one whose heart is, in the end, so utterly "in the right place". Such was Mill, and such is the source of the power of his legend to advocates of "democratic socialism" everywhere.[52, 53]

Mill, of course, did not advocate [voluntarist] socialism in the "here and now". Instead, he endorsed it as the ultimate future system of humankind, toward which an "enlightened" future [world?] citizenry would naturally evolve over time. "Properly educated" humans would sooner or later voluntarily reject once and for all the contradiction between altruism and capitalism. Society (and economic prosperity) would at last be built on proper, altruistic foundations. Capitalism was both a moral and a practical dead end anyway: "We're all headed for the stationary state" and this single society-wide market failure was in itself sufficient to mark capitalism's apparent ability to create material progress as, ultimately, a false promise. Better to live within the confines of a permanent stationary state (or something like it) rather than fight the inevitable. We must have "sustainable" economic policies. It takes a village! … Save the Earth!… Social Justice Now! etc. (Those who find Mill's heterodox ideas dry, dull, old, and irrelevant, have just not been reading the newspapers.)

The Mill of the *Principles* is often perceived as being comfortably distant from these more apocalyptic visions. Despite Mill's hopes for the distant future, his vision for his here-and-now was decidedly free-market oriented. And, to be sure, the bulk of the book is Mill's best rendering of the generally *laissez faire* beliefs of the classical school. Anyone, even today, can read Mill and come away with understanding of free-market principles and why these principles promote economic prosperity – an understanding that then can be directly applied to the modern era. That the book can still speak to our own times and troubles are one of its most impressive characteristics.

Against that background, the *Principles'* heterodox suggestions for the improvement of the economy and the society of which it is a part, aided and abetted by Mill's separation of the laws of production from those of distribution, seem almost soothingly modest. Of course, bequests and legacies should be regulated to prevent "excessive" concentrations of wealth among the "upper classes" (Book II, Chap. 2).

---

[52] Revolutionary socialists despised Mill. Mill's arguments, says Schumpeter, "were gall and wormwood not only to Marxists but to all socialists who base their argument on the thesis of inevitably increasing misery and for whom the revolution is an essential article of faith" (Schumpeter 1954, 532).

[53] There is, however, an important difference between Mill's vision and that of his twentieth- (and twenty-first-) century admirers on the Left. Mill thought that Malthusian forces and the inevitable stationary state closed off the possibility of market economies expanding indefinitely to ever-greater wealth and material success. He did not imagine market societies a century-and-a-half after his death in which, in very many respects, people really did not have material worries in the sense that they had them a century earlier. His admirers today, still lauding his socialist stance, have watched precisely such an explosion of material well-being occur wherever capitalist institutions have been given even moderately free reign. Is it the *distribution* of wealth, or the average *standard of living*, that matters in the end? If the latter, then history gives a poor grade to those who would seek some version of Mill's democratic socialism in the early twenty-first century.

Certainly, "unearned" income from the great landed estates, from which the elite "grow richer, as it were in their sleep, without working, risking, or economizing" (*Principles*, 818; 819–20), should be appropriated and applied to the greater "public good" (Book. V, Chap. 2).

And also of course – as Mill explains in his final chapter on "limitations" to non-interventionism – while recognising that free-market principles must always be the rule, there must also be proper public action to combat the negative impact of the exceptions to the rule. Naturally, education of the masses should be in the hands of a cultured elite rather than parents themselves; after all, "[t]he uncultivated cannot be competent judges of cultivation" (*op. cit.*, 953; 947) (*Principles*, Book V, Chap. 11, Sctn. 8). Doubtless, the rise of "delegated agency" in the form of limited-liability corporations has its advantages, but the democratic processes that monitor public agency (i.e. elections) are indubitably more effective at reigning in public corruption than are the corresponding private monitoring processes seeking to control corporate corruption, so that, at the end of the day, on economic grounds, large nationalized firms are preferred to large corporate firms, and the remaining private corporations require constant close scrutiny by [wise, benevolent] government (Book V, Chap. 11, Sctn. 11). And obviously, private agents seeking to create various types of "public goods" are often, due to "who goes first"? problems, clearly incapable of effectively organizing themselves into appropriate bodies for pursuing their objectives, so that government involvement (and, if need be, government coercion) is required to allow these deserving individuals to reap these gains (Book V, Chap. 11, Sctns. 12, 15).

Manifestly, colonial governments (and home governments too) have a crucial role to play in controlling and containing land markets, by making sure colonists do not buy too much land or live too far from each other, so that the colony might reap full gains from cooperation and the benefits of "smart growth" might be fully garnered (Book V, Chap. 11, Sctn. 14). And self-evidently, those who give charity to others will be more cavalier about their actions than they would be if spending their own money on themselves, so that government-granted charity (and regulation of private charity, one may presume) will always be needed (Book V, Chap. 11, Sctn. 13). In fact (judging from certain passages in *On Liberty*), government also is needed to ensure that a sufficiently "charitable" attitude is displayed by "mainstream" citizens towards the deviant behaviours of their fellow citizens.

After penning these "exceptions" to his market principles, Mill rested, and surely he did so too soon, if he truly wished societies based on free-market principles to survive intact instead of being evolved into some form of Big State collectivism. Mill himself, just after triumphantly completing his litany of "exceptions" to market principles, admits candidly that "the intervention of government cannot always practically stop short at the limit which defines the cases intrinsically suitable for it" (*Principles*, 978; 970). What shall constrain these "exceptions" to market principles? Mill envisioned them as insignificant little fiefdoms within a vast domain of *laissez faire*. But what is to prevent them, once solidly entrenched and sure of themselves, from mushrooming outwards, extending their dominions of control over successively more and more areas once reserved for free market forces, until *laissez faire* is effectively overthrown and government power reigns supreme throughout the society's economic sector?

Will the public educator, armed with government power, stand by indefinitely as "side-by-side" private schools compete with the bureaucrat-blessed public schools? With Mill's firm assertion of the economic superiority of public agency over private agency, how long will the public sector tolerate unfettered private agency – or, perhaps, *any* private agency? With more and more legislators and lobbyists strategically twisting their personal agendas into some version of the "who goes first"?/ public-good coordination problem, how long before such problems will be "found" behind every tree, and how long until government takes it upon itself to address these problems with its powers of "persuasion"? How long before charges of "unstable" patterns of land usage (either in colonies, or in the home country) beget widespread regulation and control of *all* land, in the name of "economic efficiency"? How long before "proper" charitable behaviour, towards both the poor and those who are "diverse", are first suggested, then strongly recommended, then mandated by the one-time little fiefdoms now grown strong and supreme?

It is not that Mill did not discover legitimate issues. He did: imperfect knowledge by private decision-makers and its consequences, public goods and the "who goes first"? coordination problems, externalities (in land use and elsewhere), corporate vs. private governance – all these are fundamental issues of our time, and one of the earliest major figures to fully appreciate their potential significance to the argument for or against *laissez faire*, was John Stuart Mill. The problem is not with the arguments themselves; rather, it is with how those arguments, inevitably, are strategically used in democratic societies by those seeking various types of privileges from the public sector. Once such "exceptions" to market principles are enshrined, all who seek their bread from government power know that, if they can only figure out a way to present their petition in the guise of one of these pre-approved templates for government intervention, then their chances of success rise dramatically. A rent-seeker, like water, seeks the path of least resistance. Mill provided one – in fact, he provided several.

Mill erred tragically in another way when he foisted his "exceptions" to *laissez faire* upon society without at the same contemplating whether there were ways in which free-market institutions might not themselves prove capable of overcoming the various problems to which he pointed. Mill thought hard about voluntary coordination on the part of firms organized around the socialist principle, and he reported on these firms glowingly and in detail in Book IV, Chap. 7. Why then was he unwilling to contemplate the possibility of free-market cooperation in the face of his "exceptions", aided by market incentives in subtle ways? Had he done so, he might have anticipated the "private supply of public goods" literature by over a century. Since we know private citizens solve coordination problems, and we know also that they can do so in a market context, it would have been a natural progression for Mill to explore such a line of thought. But Mill, apparently satisfied with the qualified indictment of capitalist institutions he had found, chose instead to end his inquiry at the point where he identified an "exception" (what we today call a "market failure"). By ending his inquiry at that point, he encouraged others to conclude that demonstrating a "market failure" is more or less the same as demonstrating a need for government intervention. Such a bias, now deeply imbedded in economic policy, is one that can now only be escaped gradually, if at all.

But perhaps the most serious mistake Mill made (if he really was trying to protect his vision of a dominant private sector with a few government-influenced "exceptions" to market principles) was in his failure to see the manner in which real-world political competition plays out among those who rent-seek. Imagine a society-sponsored game where everyone must jump over a bar in order to win a coveted prize. Assuming the bar is not set too high, there will be a lot of people winning prizes (and thus a lot of expensive prize-giving by society). Now change the game: the height of everyone's jump is recorded, and only the three highest jumpers win a prize. The number of winners is now strictly limited; regardless of how many others finish close to the top three, they get nothing. If society is paying for the prizes, then society spends a lot less money in the second game than in the first. If each "winner" increases government's power at the expense of the free market, then society is going to lose its economic freedom a lot faster in the first game than in the second.

Democratic-government rent-seeking works on the same principle as the first variety of our game. You have a "pitch". You bring it before the political authorities. If the pitch is judged good enough, you get society's money to make your pitch a reality. There is no strong limit on how many people get to win; everyone whose pitch is "reasonable" gets "over the bar" ("reasonable" in practice coming to include things like, what are your political connections? etc.) The only constraints are how much money there is to give away and how subtle are the tongues of the petitioners. Now compare that to the rules of the second game: there are only three winners, no matter what. Society's tight budget thereby limits the losses suffered in the "rent-seeking game". But this is precisely what does *not* happen in the real-world relationship between a petitioner and his government.

Mill introduced a number of very broad rationales for bigger government into a society whose government plays the first variety of our game. Very many proposals are therefore accepted (virtually all of them expanding government authority at the expense of the principle of *laissez faire*). The game has no end, and no ultimate limits to the winnings it dishes out – it is simply a question of budgets and how many acceptable proposals come across the authorities' desks. Recall that such winnings are directly correlated with the loss of economic freedom. Mill failed to see that, if his "exceptions" were not to have the ultimate effect of crowding out free enterprise, then it was crucial that society play some version of the second variety of our game. In this way, society would no longer be held hostage to the persuasiveness of the rent-seekers and the gullibility of the fund-givers. Such issues, however, did not seem to occur to Mill; or, if they did, then Mill imagined that wise, honest, integrity-filled elected officials would, in essence, force upon society the second game, when in fact it was far more likely that the kind of officials able to reach and hold power would very much prefer to play the first variety of the game (more happy petitioners, more people owe you favours, more goodies for you down the pipe).

By all contemporary accounts, Mill was a thoroughly honest man; in fact, he is probably one of the most honest and decent men who ever lived. As such, he himself would never have used a legitimate economic issue to make an illegitimate argument for some kind of government intervention that benefited him personally. But Mill, a man of great honesty and principle, had a tendency to, too often, attribute similar honesty and principle to others. Mill did not see the problem of good government as had the Framers of the American constitution (see Section "Digression: Mill as a Mild 'Constitutionalist'", above). He did not see, as one of the key challenges of government, the creation of a system of checks and balances that would make it difficult for those who sought prosperity through government power to succeed. He did not see good government in terms of creating a system that frustrates those who seek to use government power as just another weapon to harness in pursuing their narrow self-interest.

Mill, instead, to a significant degree, saw the key problem of government as that of crafting voting systems and rules that would give democracy full and fair play – rules that differed from one-person-one-vote in ways that he thought preserved the due influence of the better-educated (his own scheme) and otherwise-disenfranchised minorities (Thomas Hare's scheme). The framers of the American constitution tried to combat the problem of evil in government by imagining evil in power and creating a system of government that would sharply limit the power and authority of that evil. Mill, by contrast, seems to have imagined a perfect voting system that would not have allowed the evil to ever win office. Arguably, the Framers were wiser.[54]

Mill's Road to Leviathan

There is little doubt that Mill thought of himself as a true friend of liberty and liberalism. And in many respects there is no doubt that he was. His passionate defence in *On Liberty* of diversity of thought and of dissident actors in society, his pioneering advocacy of equality among the sexes and his abhorrence of the institution of slavery (Mill 1984 [1850, 1851, 1869]), his powerful defence of economic competition (*Principles*, Book IV, Chap. 7, Sctn. 7), his thoughtful advocacy of sound money and free-market macroeconomic forces (Book III, Chaps. 7, 13 and 14), his paean to the material progress achieved by the rapidly developing Western economies due in large part to market forces (Bk. IV, Chap. 1), his undisguised enthusiasm for the entrepreneurial creativity of Europe's "peasant proprietors" (Bk. II, Chaps. 6 and 7), his thorough exposure of numerous interventionist fallacies many of which still dog economic policy today (Bk. V, Chap. 10), and his other free-market positions expressed in the *Principles* and many places elsewhere – all these and much more testify to Mill's considerable classical liberal values. His longstanding flirtations with alternative socialist schemes notwithstanding, he never

---

[54] The framers had no defence against the willful misinterpretation of their words by activist scholars and judges who saw those words (correctly) as bulwarks against the type of society *they* preferred.

reached the point where he repudiated market principles, *in practice*. He thought capitalism had an important place in the world of his day, and for some time to come. He (and his wife) hoped that the world of tomorrow would learn to live without it, but the path to that future was voluntarist and evolutionary, not authoritarian and revolutionary.

Mill embraced the capitalist present in large part because he thought it would ultimately stimulate society's evolution into the much-hoped-for socialist utopia of the future. Thus was Mill the great advocate *and* the great critic of capitalism. Mill was also the great theoretical compromiser, proud of his ability to take apparently antagonistic doctrines, separate out the good and the bad from each, and then combine these into a synthesis that captured the strongest points of them both. He writes: "...I had always a humble opinion of my own powers as an original thinker, except in abstract science ... but thought myself much superior to most of my contemporaries in willingness and ability to learn from everybody..." (*Autobiography*, 251–2). Such open-mindedness is in very many respects laudable, but it also carries within it the significant risks that one may be tempted to try to synthesize opposing systems into amalgamations that are unstable and unsound.

Mill summarized his and his wife's aspirations for the democratic societies as follows: "The social problem of the future we considered to be, how to unite the greatest individual liberty of action, with a common ownership in the raw material of the globe, and an equal participation of all in the benefits of combined labour" (*Autobiography*, 239). How is an "individual liberty of action" to be amalgamated with "a common ownership in the raw material of the globe"? Mill and his wife thought that such a mixture would be brought into being by the voluntary decisions of millions of individuals who, once educated into becoming beings of "character", would each voluntarily seek out socialist modes of economic and societal organization – thus allowing a squaring of the circle captured in the question several lines above.

While no one can forecast the future, to date either the education or else its impact has failed to bring about those core changes in human nature and values for which the Mills hoped and strived. Humankind remains, at the core, what it always has been – self-interested, materialistic, greedy for individual joys and pleasures, happy to be charitable on its own terms (but not so much on terms defined for them by others), focussed on self and family rather than on "the greater good", on occasion even spiritual and capable of looking up to something bigger than itself. In their quest to improve their lives, humans remain practical, calculating, and generally opposed to the notion that one – or one's government – is one's brother's keeper. At the core, there seems little difference between the preferences of the most "cultivated" and the most lowly. One drinks a fine Chablis and talks about the fine arts (or, increasingly these days, of goings-on in political capitals); the other swills a beer and talks about the local sports franchise. Adam Smith would look at humankind in the early twenty-first century and would have said, "what else"? Mill, by contrast, would probably be appalled.

The Mills failed in their attempt to bring voluntary socialism into the nineteenth century. But they may very well have helped greatly in bringing *in*voluntary socialism into the twentieth and now, twenty-first centuries. The moral case for socialism that Mill felt and advocated so passionately, arguably inspired many to believe that utopia was "just around the corner" – if only sufficient coercion could be added to passion, forcing "change". As is not uncommonly the case, the voluntarist passion of the dreamer was turned, by his successors, into the coercive orders and 5-year-plans of the apparatchik.

Mill's influential attempts to alter the economic policies of his day for the better have arguably also failed to build a better society. Certainly, versions of many of his social policies have been adopted, with some good effects (though what might have grown up in their place without them through private cooperation remains an interesting, but little-discussed, topic). Perusing the major democratic nations late in the first decade of the twenty-first century, it is hard for the student of Mill not to see Mill's quest for "social justice" as one of several forces powering much of the noxious gain in government influence that can be seen in the day's news. What would Mill likely think of this particular trend?

If we could bring Mill into the present, no doubt he would, most of all, be astounded at the astonishing material progress the world has achieved in the long era now [it appears] ending of relatively unfettered capitalism. He would probably notice next the declining trend of free market economics' influence (most notably in the United States) and the corresponding upward trend in government power. The opinions of various commentators on the Left notwithstanding, he would likely deplore everywhere the rise of government fiat to levels far above anything he would ever have recommended (after, of course, first verifying that there was no sign on the horizon of the long-hoped-for convergence of the world into a voluntarist socialist nirvana).

Mill would no doubt pronounce humankind not yet ready for voluntary socialism, and he would no doubt be right (as he would probably be equally right if returning at any time well into the distant future). Mill would likely also wonder how the world's economies ever came to backtrack into what he would see as the kind of blatant mercantilism he no doubt thought was dispatched long ago by Adam Smith. Learning how some of his ideas and suggestions probably helped bring about the marked decline he observed in free-market institutions, and the corresponding rise in government ones, he would no doubt want very badly to do whatever he could to set things once again onto a proper path.

Alas, too late!

References

Ashley WJ (1929) Introduction to principles of political economy with some of their applications to social philosophy. In: John SM (ed) Longmans, Green and Co., London

Barber WJ (1967) A history of economic thought. Penguin Books, New York

Berns W (1975) "Two mills and liberty: [Review of] on liberty and liberalism: the case of John Stuart Mill," by Gertrude Himmelfarb. Va Q Rev 27–131

Blaug M (1985) Economic theory in retrospect, 4th edn. Cambridge University Press, London

Britton K (1953) John Stuart Mill. Penguin Books, Melbourne

Buchanan J (1967) Cooperation and conflict in public-goods interaction. West Econ J 5:109–121

Buchanan J, Tullock G (1962) The calculus of consent: logical foundations of constitutional democracy. University of Michigan Press, Ann Arbor

Buchholz TG (1989) New ideas from dead economists: an introduction to modern economic thought. Plume (Penguin Putnam), New York

Coase RH (1974) The lighthouse in economics. J Law Econ 17(2):357–376

Dietz R (2008). "The Relationship Between Economic Growth and Biodiversity Conservation: Historical Review of the Ecological Economics Perspective." Paper presented at the annual meeting of the International Congress for Conservation Biology. http://www.allacademic.com/meta/p244412_index.html. (accessed on July 10, 2008)

Ekelund R, Hebert R (1983) A history of economic theory and method. McGraw-Hill, New York

Hall RE, Papell DH (2005) Macroeconomics: economic growth, fluctuations, and policy, 6th edn. W. W. Norton & Company, New York

Haney LH (1968) History of economic thought: a critical account of the origin and development of the economic theories of the leading thinkers in the leading nations, 4th edn. The MacMillan Company, New York

Hare T (1859) The election of representatives, parliament and municipal. Longmans, Green, Reader and Dyer, London

Hayek FA (1948 [1945]) The use of knowledge in society. In: Hayek FA (ed) Individualism and economic order. The University of Chicago Press, Chicago

Hayek FA (1951) John Stuart Mill and Harriet Taylor: their friendship and subsequent marriage. University of Chicago Press, Chicago

Hayek FA (1972 [1944]) The road to serfdom. University of Chicago Press, Chicago

Hume D (1970 [1752]) Of money. In: Eugene R (ed) David Hume: writings on economics. University of Wisconsin Press, Madison

Internet Encyclopedia of Philosophy contributors, "Rawls, John," Internet Encyclopedia of Philosophy, www.iep.utm.edu/rawls.html (accessed September 19, 2011)

Jevons WS (1957 [1871]) The theory of political economy. Kelley and Millman, New York

Jones CI (2002) Introduction to economic growth, 2nd edn. W. W. Norton, New York

Landreth H (1976) History of economic theory: scope, method, and content. Houghton Mifflin, Boston

Marshall A (1988 [1920]) Principles of economics, 8th edn. MacMillan Press, London

Mill J (1844 [1821]) Elements of political economy, 3rd edn. Henry G. Bohn, London

Mill JS (1929 [1871]) Principles of political economy, with some of their applications to social philosophy. Longmans, Green and Co, London

Mill JS (1963) The earlier letters of John Stuart Mill 1812–1848 (collected works of John Stuart Mill, vol XII). University of Toronto Press, Toronto

Mill JS (1965 [1871]) Principles of political economy, with some of their applications to social philosophy. In Collected Works of John Stuart Mill, vols. II, III. University of Toronto Press, Toronto

Mill JS (1967 [1844]) Essays on some unsettled questions in political economy. In Collected Works of John Stuart Mill, vol IV. University of Toronto Press, Toronto, pp 229–340

Mill JS (1967 [1879]) Chapters on socialism. In Collected Works of John Stuart Mill, vol V. University of Toronto Press, Toronto, pp 703–756

Mill JS (1972) The later letters of John Stuart Mill 1849 to 1873 (collected works of John Stuart Mill, vol XVII). University of Toronto Press, Toronto

Mill JS (1973 [1843]) A system of logic ratiocinative and inductive, being a connected view of the principles of evidence and the methods of scientific investigation. In Collected Works of John Stuart Mill, vols VII–VIII. University of Toronto Press, Toronto, pp 3–1243

Mill JS (1973 [1861]) Considerations on representative government. In Collected Works of John Stuart Mill, vol XIX. University of Toronto Press, Toronto, pp 371–562

Mill JS (1977a [1859]) Thoughts on parliamentary reform. In Collected Works of John Stuart Mill, vol XIX. University of Toronto Press, Toronto, pp 311–340

Mill JS (1977b [1859]) On liberty. In Collected Works of John Stuart Mill, vol XVIII. University of Toronto Press, Toronto, pp 213–310

Mill JS (1979 [1865]) An examination of William Hamilton's philosophy and of the principal philosophical questions discussed in his writings. In Collected Works of John Stuart Mill, vol IX. University of Toronto Press, Toronto

Mill JS (1984 [1850]) The Negro question. In Collected Works of John Stuart Mill, vol XXI. University of Toronto Press, Toronto, pp 85–96

Mill JS (1984 [1851]) Statement of marriage. In Collected Works of John Stuart Mill, vol XXI. University of Toronto Press, Toronto, pp 97–100

Mill JS (1984 [1869]) The subjection of women. In Collected Works of John Stuart Mill, vol XXI. University of Toronto Press, Toronto, pp 259–340

Mitchell WC (1967) Types of economic theory: from mercantilism to institutionalism, vol I. Augustus M. Kelley, New York

Montgomery MR (2006) The genesis of an idea: classical macroeconomics and the birth of monetary disequilibrium theory. Money and markets: essays in honor of Leland B. Yeager. Routledge, London

Rawls J (1999 [1971]) A theory of justice. Revised edition. Harvard University Press, Cambridge

Ricardo D (2006 [1821]) Principles of political economy and taxation. Cosimo Classics, New York

Say JB (1983 [1803]) Of the demand or market for products. In: Hazlitt H (ed) The critics of Keynesian economics. University Press, Lanham. First published in English in A Treatise on Political Economy, 1832. Originally Published in 1803 in Traite d'Economie Politique

Schumpeter JA (1954) History of economic analysis. Oxford University Press, New York

Smith A (1937 [1776]) An inquiry into the nature and causes of the wealth of nations. The Modern Library, New York

Sowell T (1974) Classical economics reconsidered. Princeton University Press, Princeton

Sowell T (2006) On classical economics. Yale University Press, New Haven

Stigler G (1965) Essays on the history of economics. University of Chicago Press, Chicago

Wikipedia contributors, "Johann Wolfang von Goethe," Wikipedia, The Free Encyclopedia, http://en.wikipedia.org/wiki/Johann_Wolfgang_von_Goethe (accessed September 19, 2011)

Chapter 10
Jeremy Bentham (1748–1832)

Christos P. Baloglou

Jeremy Bentham

Introduction

The English moral philosopher, jurist, social reformer, political economist, and founding father of modern utilitarianism, Jeremy Bentham, casts a long shadow over the development of modern jurisprudence and the social sciences. Both defenders

C.P. Baloglou (✉)
Hellenic Telecommunications Organization, S.A.
Messenias 14 & Gr. Lamprakis, 143 42 Nea Philadelphia, Attikis, Greece
e-mail: cbaloglou@ote.gr

J.G. Backhaus (ed.), *Handbook of the History of Economic Thought*,
The European Heritage in Economics and the Social Sciences,
DOI 10.1007/978-1-4419-8336-7_10, © Springer Science+Business Media, LLC 2012

and critics of legal primitivism, public administration, and modern welfare economics credit Bentham's influence in the development of these fields of inquiry.[1]

Born in London on the February 15th, 1748 as the son of the lawyer Jeremiah Bentham and Alicia Grove, Bentham[2] was a strangely precocious and a morbidly sensitive child, when it was decided in 1755 to send him to Westminster. He learned the catechism by heart and was good in Greek and Latin verses, which he composed for his companions as well as himself. He had also the rarer accomplishment, acquired from his early tutor, of writing more easily in French than English. Some of his writings were originally composed in French. He was, according to Bowring, elected to one of the King's scholarships when between nine and ten, but as "ill-usage was apprehended" the appointment was declined.[3] In 1760, his father took him to Oxford and entered him as a commoner at Queen's College. He came into residence in the following October, when only 12 years old. As schoolboy, he continued his schoolboy course. He wrote Latin verses, and one of his experiments, an ode upon the death of George II, was sent to Johnson, who called it "a very pretty performance for a young man". He also had to go through the form of disputation in the schools. Queen's College had some reputation at this time for teaching logic.[4] Bentham was set to read Watt's "*Logic*" (1725), Sanderson's "*Compendium artis Logicae*" (1615) and Rowning's compendious "*System of Natural Philosophy*" (1735–1742). Some traces of these studies remained in his mind.[5]

In 1763, Bentham took his B.A. degree and returned to his home. He returned to Oxford in December 1763 to hear Blackstone's lectures. In 1758, William Blackstone (1723–1780), barrister of the Inner Temple and fellow of All Souls, was appointed as the first Vinerian Professor of English Law at Oxford. Between 1765 and 1769, he published the first of many editions of the work which was to make his name perhaps more celebrated than that of any other English jurist. The "*Commentaries on the Laws of England*", based on Blackstone's Oxford lectures, rapidly established an unrivalled reputation and authority. In 1770, the author (an M.P. since 1761 and solicitor-general to the Queen since 1763) declined the post of solicitor-general in North's administration, but accepted knighthood and became a justice in the court of Common Pleas. This office he filled for the remaining 10 years of his life.[6]

Bentham attended the last courses given by Blackstone before his resignation of the Vinerian chair. Bentham has been influenced by Blackstone's matter and manner and it seems to have impressed him in the writing of the "*Commentaries*". It is clear from his own early manuscripts that the direction of Bentham's own thought at the outset of his career owed much to his critical but constant reading and re-reading of Blackstone.

---

[1] Kelly 1987 p. 156.

[2] The main authority for Bentham's life is Bowring's 1838–1843 account in the two last volumes of the "*Works*". See also Stephen 1900 [1968] vol. I, Chap. V; Atkinson 1905[1969]. See also the interesting articles by Kelly 1987 pp. 156–161. Mack IESS, vol. I, pp. 55–58. Pins 2006.

[3] Bowring, 1843, vol. X, p. 38.

[4] Bowring, vol. VIII, pp. 113, 217.

[5] Stephen 1900[1968], vol. I, p. 173.

[6] Burns and Hart 1977 p. xix.

Bentham, after leaving Oxford, took chambers in Lincoln's Inn. He visited Paris in 1770, but made few acquaintances, though he was already regarded as a "philosopher". In 1778, he was in correspondence with d' Alembert, the abbé Morellet, and other philanthropic philosophers, but it does not appear at what time this connection began.[7] He translated Voltaire's "*Taureu-Blanc*" – a story which used to "convulse him with laughter". His first publication was s defence of Lord Mansfield in 1770 against attacks arising out of the prosecution of Woodfall for publishing Junius's letter to the king. This defence, contained in two letters, signed Irenaeus was published in the *Gazetteer*.[8] At this time, Bentham says that his was "truly a miserable life".[9] Yet he was getting to work upon his grand project. He tells his father on October 1st, 1776 that he is writing his "*Critical Elements of Jurisprudence*", the book of which a part was afterwards published as the "*Introduction to the Principles of Morals and Legislation*".[10] In the same year, he published his first important work, the "*Fragment on Government*". The year was in many ways memorable.

The Declaration of Independence marked the opening of a new political era. Adam Smith's "*Wealth of Nations*" and Ed. Gibbon's "*Decline and Fall*" formed landmarks in speculation and in history; and Bentham's volume, though it made no such impression, announced a serious attempt to apply scientific methods to problems of legislation.

A turning point on Bentham's life was his absence from England during the years 1785–1788. His brother Samuel (1757–1831), whose education he had partly superintended,[11] had been apprenticed to a shipwright at Woolwich, and in 1780, had gone to Russia in search of employment. Three years later, he was sent by Prince Potemkin to superintend a great industrial establishment at Kritchev on a tributary of the Dnieper. There he was to be "Jack-of-all-trades – building ships, like Harlequin, of odds and ends – a rope-maker, a sail-maker, a distiller, brewer, malster, tenner, glass-man, glass-grinder, potter, hemp-spinner, smith, and coppersmith".[12] He was, that is, to transplant a fragment of ready-made Western civilization into Russia. Bentham left England in August 1785 and stayed some time at Constantinople, where he met Maria James (1770–1836), the wife successively of W. Reveley and John Gisborne, and the friend of Shelley. Thence he travelled by land to Kritchev and settled with his brother at the neighbouring estate of Zabobras. Bentham was interested in his brother's occupations and mechanical inventions and at the same time keeping up his own intellectual labours. The most remarkable result was the "*Defence of Usury*", written in the beginning of 1787. At the beginning of February 1788, he reached London, travelled through Poland, Germany, and Holland. He lived until his death in London writing and propagating his ideas.

---

[7] Bowring, 1843, vol. X, pp. 87–88, 193–194.

[8] Stephen 1900[1968] vol. I, p. 180.

[9] Bowring, 1843, vol. X, p. 84.

[10] Bowring, 1843, vol. X, p. 77.

[11] Bowring, 1843, vol. X, p. 77.

[12] Bowring, 1843, vol. X, p. 147.

Bentham met in 1788 the Swiss pastor and author Pierre Étienne Lois Dumont, who studied enthusiastically Bentham's work.[13] Dumont, born at Geneva in 1759, had become a Protestant minister; he was afterwards tutor to Shelbrune's son, and in 1788, visited Paris with Romilly and made acquaintance with Mirabeau. Romilly showed Dumont some of Bentham's papers written in French. Dumont offered to rewrite and to superintend their publication. Dumont became Bentham's most devoted disciple and laboured unweariedly upon the translation and condensation of his master's treatise. After long and tedious labours and multiplied communications between the master and the disciple, Dumont in the spring of 1802 brought out his "*Traités de legislation civile et pénale*". The book was partly a translation from Bentham's published and unpublished works – Bentham had himself written some of his papers in French, and partly a statement of the pith of the new doctrine in Dumont's own language. It had the great merit of putting Bentham's meaning vigorously and compactly, and free from many of the digressions, minute discussions of minor points and arguments requiring a special knowledge of English law, which had impeded the popularity of Bentham's previous works.[14]

Bentham's mind was attracted to various other schemes by the disciples who came to sit at his feet, and professed, with more or less sincerity, to regard him as a Solon. Foreigners had been resorting to him from all parts of the world and gave him hopes of new fields for codifying. As early as 1808, he had been visited at Barrow Green by the strange adventurer, politician, lawyer, and filibuster, Aaron Burr, famous for the duel in which he killed Alexander Hamilton and now framing wild schemes for an empire in Mexico. Burr's conversation suggested to Bentham a singular scheme for emigrating to Mexico. He applied seriously for introductions to Lord Holland, who had passed some time in Spain, and to Holland's friend, Jovellanos (1749–1812), a member of the Spanish Junta, who had written treatises upon legislation (1785), of which Bentham approved.[15] The dream of Mexico was succeeded by a dream of Venezuela. General Miranda spent some years in England and had become well known to James Mill. He was now about to start upon an unfortunate expedition to Venezuela, his native country. He took with him a draft of a law for the freedom of the press, which Bentham drew up, and he proposed that when his new state was founded, Bentham should be its legislator.[16] Miranda was betrayed to the Spanish government in 1812 and died (1816) in the hands of the Inquisition. Bolivar, who was also in London in 1810 and took some notice of Joseph Lancaster, applied in flattering terms to Bentham. Long afterwards, when dictator of Columbia, he forbade the use of Bentham's works in the schools, to which, however, the privilege of reading him was restored, and let us hope, duly valued, in 1835.[17] Santander, another South America hero, was also a disciple and

---

[13] Kitromilides 1998 pp. 144–145; Bowring, 1843, vol. X, p. 186.
[14] Stephen 1900[1968] vol. I, pp. 207–208. Kitromilides 1998 pp. 144–145. Guidi 2009 p. 375.
[15] Bowring, 1843, vol. X, p. 443, 448.
[16] Bowring, 1843, vol. X, pp. 457–458; Stephen 1900[1968] vol. I, p. 220.
[17] Bowring, 1843, vol. XI, pp. 553–54, 565.

encouraged the study of Bentham. Bentham says in 1830 that 40,000 copies of Dumont's *"Traités"* had been sold in Paris for the South American trade.[18] In the United States, he had many disciples of a more creditable kind than Burr. He appealed in 1811 to Madison, then President, for permission to construct a "Pannomion" or complete body of law, for the use of United States and urged his claims both upon Madison and the Governor of Pennsylvania in 1817, when peace had been restored. He had many conversations upon this project with John Quincy Adams, who was then American minister in England.[19] This, of course, came to nothing, but an eminent American disciple, Edward Livingston (1764–1836), between 1820 and 1830 prepared codes for the State of Louisiana and warmly acknowledged his obligations to Bentham.[20] In 1830, Bentham also acknowledged a notice of his labours, probably resulting from this, which had been made in one of General Jackson's presidential messages.[21]

In 1820 and 1821, Bentham was consulted by the Constitutional party in Spain and Portugal and wrote elaborate tracts for their enlightenment. Bentham even endeavoured in 1822–1823 to administer some sound advice to the government of Tripolis, but his suggestions for "remedies against misrule" seem never to have been communicated.[22] In 1823 and 1824, he was a member of the Greek Committee; he corresponded with Alexander Mavrocordatos, Theodore Negris, Adamantios Corais in Paris and Odysseus Androutsos.[23] He begged Parr to turn some of his admonitions into "Parrian" Greek for the benefit of the moderns.[24] Blanquière and Stanhope, two ardent members of the committee, were disciples; and Stanhope carried with him to Greece Bentham's *"Table of the Springs of Action"*, with which he tried to indoctrinate Byron. Bentham's disciples hoped to establish the teacher's ideas and reforms in the New State, and for this reason, Bentham commented the "Provisory Constitution of Epidaurus" and he proposed Corais to translate his works into Greek. There has been published the two-volume edition of the Dumont's edition into Greek by G. Athanassiou: vol. I: On the legislation of private and penial, Aegina 1834; vol. II: On the legislation of the rights and the criminal laws, Athens 1842 [= On legislation private and penal; vol. II: On legislation on duties and criminal laws].

The last years of his life brought Bentham into closer connection with more remarkable men. It was at Hendon, with George Grote (1794–1871), the historian of Greece, who had been introduced to his guest by Ricardo. In 1825, he visited Paris to consult some physicians. He was received with the respect which the French can always pay to intellectual eminence.[25] All the lawyers in a court of justice rose to receive him, and

---

[18] Bowring, vol. XI, p. 53.

[19] Bentham's letter to Adams in Bowring, 1843, vol. X, p. 554.

[20] Bowring, vol. XI, p. 23.

[21] Bowring, vol. XI, p. 40.

[22] Bowring, vol. VIII, pp. 555–600.

[23] Kitromilides 1998, p. 145.

[24] Kitromilides 1984, vol. II, pp. 285–308.

[25] Bowring, 1843, vol. X, p. 551.

he was placed at the president's right hand.[26] In the early part of February 1832, less than 4 months before his death, Bentham received a renowned statesman, Talleyrand. On the May 18th, 1832, he had his last bit of his lifelong labour, upon the "Constitutional Code". The great reform agitation was reaching the land of promise, but Bentham was to die in the wilderness. Bentham still able to write and capable of sustained thought, calmly awaited death, which took place on the June 6th, 1832.

It is worth to note that Bentham directed that his body should be dissected. This injunction was obeyed. The skeleton, covered with the clothes he commonly wore, and supporting a waxen effigy of his head, is carefully preserved in the Anatomical Museum of University College, London. Across one knee rests his favourite stick, "Dapple", and at the foot of the figure lies the skull, with the white hairs of the old man still clinging to its surface.[27]

> 'He never knew prosperity and adversity, passion
> nor satiety', wrote John Mill: 'he never had even the
> experience which sickness gives; he lived from child-
> hood to the age of eighty-five in boyish health. He knew
> no dejection, no heaviness of heart. He never felt life
> a sore and weary burthen. He was a boy to the last'.[28]

The Works of Bentham

Bentham translated in 1744 Voltaire's "*Taureau Blanc*". He told his father on October 1st, 1776 that he was writing his "Critical Elements of Jurisprudence", the book of which a part was afterwards published as the "*Introduction to the Principles of Morals and Legislation*".[29] In the same year, he published his first important work, the "*Fragment on Government*".

In the beginning of 1787, when Bentham was in Russia, near his brother, he wrote the "*Defence of Usury*". Bentham appended to it a respectful letter to Adam Smith, who had supported the laws against usury inconsistently with his own general principles. It is worth to note that Smith defended the State intervention by the legal determination of interest in the "*Wealth of Nations*".[30] Later he was the defender of the idea of the absolute freedom by the composition of the interest, probably influenced by Bentham's work, if we believe a conversation which took place in 1789 between Smith and Bentham's friend, who referred to a letter of G. Wilson, a close friend of Bentham to him.[31]

Bentham's major work entitled "*Introduction to the Principles of Morals and Legislation*" appeared in 1789. The preface apologized for imperfections due to the

---

[26] Stephen 1900[1968] vol. I, p. 229; Atkinson 1905[1969] p. 206.

[27] Richardson and Hurwitz 1987, pp. 195–198; Harris 2005, pp. 38–42.

[28] Mill 1833, in Parekh, ed., 1974, pp. 2–5.

[29] Bowring, 1843, vol. X, p. 77. Cf. Guidi 2002.

[30] Smith 1776[1937], Book II, Chap. II.

[31] Rae 1895 p. 423; Gide et Rist 1930, vol. I, p. 122, not. (1).

plan of his work. The book, he explained, laid down the principles of all his future labours and was to stand to him in the relation of a treatise upon pure mathematics to a treatise upon the applied sciences. He indicated ten separate departments of legislation, each of which would require a treatise in order to the complete execution of his scheme.

An interesting work, written by Bentham, which belongs to the Utopias, is the "Panopticon". The "*Panopticon*", as defined by its inventor to Brissot, was a "mill for grinding rogues honest, and idle men industrious".[32] It was suggested by a plan designed by his brother in Russia for a large house to be occupied by workmen and to be so arranged that they could be under constant inspection. Bentham was working on the old lines of philanthropic reform. He had long been interested in the schemes of prison reform, to which Howard's labours had given the impetus. Blackstone, with the help of William Eden, afterwards Lord Auckland, had prepared the "Hard Labour Bill", which Bentham had carefully criticised in 1778. The measure was passed in 1779 and provided for the management of convicts, who were becoming troublesome, as transportation to America had ceased to be possible. The project to construct new prisons in the country was allowed to drop. Bentham hoped to solve the problem with his "*Panopticon*". He printed an account of it in 1791.[33] He wrote to his old antagonist, George III, describing it, together with another invention of Samuel's for enabling armies to cross rivers, which might be more to his Majesty's taste.[34] After delays, suspicious in the eyes of Bentham, an act of parliament was obtained in 1794 to adopt his schemes. The "Panopticon Correspondence", in the eleventh volume of Bentham's "*Works*", gives fragments from a "history of the war between Jeremy Bentham and George III", written by Bentham in 1830–1831, and selections from a voluminous correspondence.[35]

Economic Writings

All of Bentham's economic writings are concerned with extending the realm of individual initiative in commerce, trade and industry as a means of increasing social welfare. Despite this unity of purpose, these writings fall into two broad categories. First, there are those which advocate the theory of economic liberalism, such as "*Defense of Usury*", "*Emancipate Your Colonies*",[36] "*Manual of Political Economy*",[37] "*Institute of Political Economy*"[38] and "*Observations on the Restrictive*

---

[32]Bowring, 1843, vol. X, p. 226.

[33]Stephen 1900[1968] vol. I, p. 201.

[34]Bowring, 1843, vol. X, p. 260.

[35]Stephen 1900[1968] vol. I, p. 202, n.2. For a detailed analysis of the function of Panopticon see Brunon-Ernst 2007. Cf. Guidi 2004 pp. 405–431, Sigot 2009 pp. 380–384.

[36]Bentham 1793a in Bowring [1838–1843], vol. 4.

[37]Bentham 1793b in Stark, ed., 1952–1954, vol. 2.

[38]Bentham 1801–1804 in Stark, ed., 1952–1954, vol. 3.

and Prohibitory Commercial System".[39] All of these works call for the restriction of government action in the realm of commerce, trade and industry because such action is self-defeating or detrimental to overall social welfare. Bentham considered these works as contributions to the science of political economy as they draw out specific implications from the basic principles of economic liberalism that he inferred from his utilitarian science of legislation. They develop specific policy proposals designed to implement the principles of economic liberalism in the face of mercantilist policies still being pursued by government, such as the subsidy or protection of various trades, monopolistic trading relations with colonies and the funding of government activities through public debt.

The second category of writings on the art of political economy is concerned with developing alternative policies which serve social welfare but which do not violate the principles of economic liberalism. A work such as *"Supply without Burthen; or Escheat vice Taxation"*[40] advocates the replacement of direct taxation as a means of financing government, and others such as *"Abstract or Compressed View of a Tract Intituled Circulating Annuities"*[41] develop schemes for repaying the national debt without resource to direct taxation or further borrowing. Also falling under the category of the art of political economy are works such as *"The True Alarm"*[42] and *"Defense of a Maximum"*,[43] which developed as attempts to resolve theoretical difficulties that arose from some of his practical proposals, and it is here that Bentham comes close to pre-empting developments in modern macroeconomic theory.[44] In *"The True Alarm"*, Bentham challenges Adam Smith's and David Ricardo's arguments against the utility theory of value which led them to posit a labour or production theory of value. Similarly in the *"Annuity Note Plan"*,[45] Bentham advocated monetary expansion as a means of securing full employment, and in this he used a number of ideas such as hoarding which bear striking resemblance to Keynesian concepts such as private over-saving. When Bentham came to write *"The True Alarm"*, he nevertheless exhibited a strikingly modern awareness of the inflationary dangers of monetary expansion as a means of addressing problems of underemployed resources. He failed, however, to develop these insights adequately in theoretical works and it was left to later generations to develop them. In Bentham's own time, it was Smith and Ricardo who set the agenda for economic debate, and consequently Bentham's ideas and his utilitarian version of economic liberalism were overshadowed by the Smithian and Ricardian orthodoxy. Indeed, one reason why "The True Alarm" was not published was because Etienne Dumont,

---

[39] Bentham 1821 [1995].

[40] Bentham 1795 in Stark, ed., 1952–1954, vol. 1.

[41] Bentham 1801a in Stark, ed., 1952–1954, vol. 2.

[42] Bentham 1801b in Stark, ed., 1952–1954, vol.3.

[43] Bentham 1801c in Stark, ed., 1952–1954, vol. 3.

[44] Kelly 1987 p. 161.

[45] Bentham 1801d in Stark, ed., 1952–1954, vol. 2.

Bentham's Genevan editor, sought the advice of James Mill and David Ricardo and both advised against its publication. Though Ricardo's long commentary still exists, the original Bentham manuscript has been lost; all we have is Dumont's translation.[46]

Bentham's Economic Thought

In a letter to John Stuart Mill written in 1841, Auguste Comte expressed the conviction that Bentham must be regarded as "the main origin of what is called political economy".[47] This may sound a very odd and amazing assertion, as most books on the history of economic thought do not so much as mention Bentham's name.[48] Yet there is a great deal of truth in Comte's statement, and Bentham himself would have heartily approved of it. "I was the spiritual father of Mill" said Bentham, "and Mill was the spiritual father of Ricardo, so that Ricardo was my spiritual grandson".[49]

It was not Bentham's technical economics but his utilitarianism that exerted the greater stimulation on the thought of his time, and it was through the notions embedded in his utilitarianism that he affected the future development of economics. Here he broke new paths leading away from laissez-faire, and here he also, by making utility a central concept in his plea for reform, significantly expanded an area of speculation that was to become a great concern of later generations of economists.[50] Bentham had become the revered head of the "philosophical radicals",[51] a movement which promoted inside and outside of the British public administration issues of social policies into the praxis.[52]

Bentham's method may be shortly described as the method of detail; of treating wholes by separating them into their parts, abstractions by resolving them into Things, classes and generalities by distinguishing them into the individuals of which they are made up; and breaking every question into pieces before attempting to solve it.[53]

This section gives an account on Bentham's thought in utility theory, his proposals for social policy and state intervention and property.

---

[46]Kelly 1987 p. 161.
[47]Lettres d' Auguste Comte à John Stuart Mill 1877, p. 4.
[48]Stark 1941 p. 60–61. Stark 1946 p. 583.
[49]Bowring 1843, vol. X, p. 498.
[50]Spiegel 1983 p. 341.
[51]So the title of Halévy's book; Halévy 1928.
[52]Psalidopoulos 1997 p. 68.
[53]Mill 1838, in Parekh, ed., 1974, pp. 2–5.

The Utility Theory

Bentham is usually regarded as the father of utilitarianism. Although Francis Hutcheson (1694–1746) and David Hume (1711–1776) had ideas similar to Bentham's, Bentham used the word "utilitarian" for the first time and developed the idea systematically in "*An Introduction to the Principles of Morals and Legislation*" published in 1789. Bentham's major aim in this publication was a reform of the British penal code, which was still based on the medieval idea that criminals should be punished for punishment's sake. Bentham argued that the penalty should be determined so as to maximize the utility or happiness of society. He states, "all punishment in itself is evil".[54] In his humanist approach, Bentham was a part of the philosophy of the European Enlightenment.[55]

Bentham starts his book with the remark: "Nature has placed mankind under the governance of two sovereign matters, pain and pleasure. It is for them alone to point out what we ought to do, as well as to determine what we shall do".[56] The same idea had been espoused by Democritus (460–390 B.C.).[57] These two concepts provide the basis for Bentham's theory of value and his theory of motivation. The sole efficient cause of action is the desire for pleasure and the avoidance of pain. Pleasures can take as many forms as possible actions, and Bentham does not assume simple uniformity of human nature such that all humans desire the same objects of pleasure, nor does he assume that all objects of pleasure are easily substitutable.[58]

Bentham teaches, pleasure and pain appear and act as definite magnitudes: "To a certain person, considered by himself", he says,[59] " the value of a pleasure or pain, considered by itself, will be greater or less, according to the four following circumstances: (1) Its intensity. (2) Its duration. (3) Its certainty or uncertainty. (4) Its propinquity or remoteness". Present feelings, therefore, have two dimensions:

> The magnitude of a pleasure is composed
> of its intensity and its duration: to obtain it,
> supposing its intensity represented by a
> certain number of degrees, you multiply that
> number by number expressive of the moments
> or atoms of time contained in its duration. Suppose
> two pleasures at the same degree of intensity – give
> to the second twice the duration of the first, the
> second is twice as great as the first.[60]

This is a solid basis, on which it is well possible "to apply arithmetical calculations to the elements of happiness":

---

[54] Bentham 1789[1970] p. 158.

[55] Amemiya 2007 p. 158.

[56] Bentham 1789[1970] p. 11.

[57] Karayiannis 1988.

[58] Kelly 1987 p. 157.

[59] Bowring vol. I, p. 16.

[60] Bowring vol. IV p. 540.

The quantity or degree of well-being experienced
during any given length of time is directly as
the magnitude (i.e., the intensity multiplied
by the duration) of the sum of the pleasures,
and inversely as the magnitude of the sum
of the pains experienced during that same length of time.[61]

Bentham described the doctrine of the dimensions of pleasure and pain as an "application of arithmetic to questions of utility".[62]

Bentham set out his "felicific calculus", which is supposed to provide a way of measuring the quantity of pleasure derived from an action or object. Bentham used certain language that suggests the possibility of a "political arithmetic", but he was acutely aware of the difficulties of providing any common metric for measuring the intensity or quantity of a psychological state.

The second half of the two sovereign passages from "*The Introduction to the Principles of Morals and Legislation*" identifies pleasure and pain as the basis for a utilitarian account of value; actions have value or can be described as good insofar as they produce pleasure and minimize pain and bad insofar as they produce pain and minimize pleasure. Most strongly manifest is Bentham's subjectivism in his concept of value "Value is subserviency to well-being – Value is subserviency to use".[63] With these definitions, Bentham from the very beginning takes a course different from that of Smith and Ricardo.[64] He makes the traditional distinction between value-in-use and value-in-exchange, but it is the value-in-use which he regards as the more important:

Value may be distinguished into (1) General,
or say value in the way of exchange, and (2)
Special, or say idiosyncratical –value in the way
of use in his own individual instance…The value of
a thing in the way of exchange arises out of,
and depends altogether upon, and is proportioned
to its value in the way of use: - for no man would
five anything that had a value in the way of use in
exchange for anything that had no such value.[65]

Bentham's doctrine of the factors of production is worth noting. "For the development of industry", he says,[66] "the union of power and will is required". In another place, he makes a more elaborate distinction: he divides power in the wider sense of the word into knowledge, i.e. "power so far as it depends upon the mental condition of the party whose power is in question", and power in the narrower sense, which "depends upon the state and condition of external objects". "Power, knowledge, or intelligence, and inclination: where these requisites concur on the part of him on whom the production of the desirable effect in question depends, it is produced;

---

[61] Bowring vol. VIII p. 82.

[62] Bowring vol. IV p. 542.

[63] Bowring vol. III p. 36,39.

[64] Stark 1946 p. 599.

[65] Stark ed., vol. III p. 226.

[66] Stark ed., vol. I p. 310.

when any one of them is wanting, it is not produced".[67] Compared with Smith's doctrine of the factors of production, this conception is the purest subjectivism: not the objective categories land, labour and capital are distinguished, but subjective categories: the power of man over the forces of nature (in soil and capital goods), the knowledge how to use this power and the will to do it.

Bentham and the Marginal Utility

Jeremy Bentham rediscovered marginal utility. He discovered it as a by-product of his reform projects. His central proposition, the balancing of pain and pleasure or the felicific calculus, was already known to Thomas Hobbes, Maupertuis, C. Beccaria, Hartley and M. Helvetius.[68] The felicific calculus means: in the pursuit of pleasure man ought to watch that additional pleasure prevails over additional pain.[69] Marginal utility is an aspect of the pain and pleasure man ought to watch that additional pleasure prevails over additional pain. Marginal utility is an aspect of the pain and pleasure comparison. For striking a balance between these two emotions, Bentham splits up pain and pleasure into small parts. The division of pleasure reveals the law of diminishing utility: "…the quantity of happiness produced by a particle of wealth (each particle being of the same magnitude) will be less and less at every particle; the second will produce less than the first, the third less than the second and so on".[70]

Like D. Bernoulli (1700–1780), his forerunner, Bentham was also interested in the possibility of measuring utility.[71] Bentham attempted several times to measure utility. Interpersonal measuring, Bentham wrote, is needed for purposes of practical legislation, for spreading happiness throughout society, but "the particular sensibility of individuals" and "diversity of circumstances" hinder the construction of a suitable yardstick.[72] Inspite of these obstacles, Bentham searched for the unity of measuring. He gave the number one to the smallest utility which can be felt. "Such a degree of intensity is an every day's experience; according as any pleasures are perceived to be more and more intense, they may be represented by higher and higher numbers".[73]

Baumgardt published Bentham's paper in which the British philosopher measured utility in money.[74] Bentham is aware of the essential obstacle, the law of diminishing utility. "One guinea, suppose, gives a man one degree of pleasure;[…]

---

[67] Stark ed., vol. III p. 34.
[68] Halévy 1928 p. 33. Viner 1949 p. 365. Kauder 1965 p. 35. Baujard 2009 p. 440.
[69] Bentham 1789[1970] p.11. As Halévy 1928 p. 26 mentions, the pain-pleasure calculus is taken almost word for word from Helvetius.
[70] Bowring ed. 1843, vol. 3, Pannomial Fragments, Chap. IV, p. 229. See also Kraus 1902 p. 59.
[71] Stigler 1950 pp. 307ff.
[72] Stigler 1950 p. 309.
[73] Stigler 1950 p. 310.
[74] Baumgardt 1952 p. 554.

it is not true by any means that a million of guineas given to the same man at the same time would give him a million of such degrees of pleasure".[75] But the law of diminishing utility is only efficient if great changes in the amount of money occur. It does not work with relatively small increases and decreases of income. Bentham is of the opinion that the marginal utility of money falls very slowly. If we deal with small quantities, "the proportion between pleasure and pain" will be very near the relation between corresponding sums of money. For all practical purposes, money is capable of measuring pleasure.

Would it have helped better understanding of measuring if Bentham had published these subtle reflections? It is very doubtful.[76] Many economists of his time knew Bentham and no one saw that some of the theories of the great utilitarian can be applied in economics. David Ricardo, James Mill, and John Stuart Mill were Bentham's friends and devoted followers, but all three of them had their blind spot; it did not occur to them to apply the felicific calculus to economic value.[77]

Proposals on Social Policy

Bentham's reforms, which were grounded in his utilitarianism and which he tirelessly promoted during his long and active life, changed the face of nineteenth-century England. They covered a large variety of programmes stretching from parliamentary to prison reform and prepared the ground for the adoption of such important social inventions as the civil service and statistical fact-finding. Bentham was, first of all, a student of law. He considered as his foremost task the reform of the law and the development of a science of legislation. This science, in turn, he attempted to derive from the principle of utilitarianism, which in the version he gave to it makes the happiness, not of an individual but of society, the "summum bonum" or "highest good". "Nature", he wrote in a famous passage, "has placed mankind under the governance of two sovereign masters, 'pain' and 'pleasure'. It is for them alone to point out what we ought to do, as well as to determine what we shall do [...] They govern us in all we do".[78] Central to his thought is not the individual's happiness but the "principle of utility" or greatest happiness principle, which considers as the highest good the greatest happiness of the greatest number. To Bentham, it was the function of legislation and of the science treating of it to establish a system of punishments and rewards that would induce individuals to pursue actions leading to the greatest happiness of the greatest number.

---

[75] Baumgardt 1952 p. 559.

[76] Kauder 1965 p. 37.

[77] Stephen 1950, vol. 2 p. 7ff; Halévy 1928 p. 107.

[78] Bentham 1789[1970] p.11.

The maximum happiness principle did not commit him to laissez-faire, but rather to the recognition of a substantial range of legitimate activities of the government. As derived from and "immediately subordinate" to the maximum happiness principle, he listed four great objectives of public policy, which he ranked in the order of subsistence, security, abundance, and equality, and which, he pointed out, may be "sometimes in a state of rivalry".[79] When he elevated equality to an objective of economic policy, even though to one ranking last, he broke a path on which J. St. Mill, who developed new views about distribution, was to follow him.[80] When he, in spite of his opposition to a ceiling on the rate of interest,[81] proposed to place a similar ceiling on the price of corn,[82] he demonstrated his unwillingness to rely always and invariably on the forces of the market. When he suggested that the government take over the life insurance business, he stated the germ of the idea of social insurance.[83] He stressed monetary expansion as a means to full employment,[84] and his discussion of this problem shows his awareness of the relevance of hoarding, forced saving, the saving–investment relationship, the propensity to consume, and other matters which form the content of modern income and employment analysis.[85]

Bentham on Property

For Bentham, property was the offspring of desire, as basic to man as the exercise of his own will. The "logic of the will" which Bentham expounded over many years, contrasting it emphatically with Locke's logic of the understanding, was a logic of desire, of possession, and implicitly of property.[86]

"Necessity [or nature] begat property" would do nicely for Bentham. And there can be no doubt that he saw it as one of civil society's primary objectives to protect this child of necessity by protecting the socio-economic status – quo:

> ...where the distribution of property and
> power is concerned, to keep things in the pro-
> portion in which they actually are, ought to be,
> and in general is, the aim of the legislator. His
> great purpose is to preserve the total mass of
> expectations as far as is possible from all
> that may interfere with their course.[87]

---

[79] Spiegel 1983 p. 342.
[80] Landreth & Colander 1989 p. 143–144.
[81] Stark ed., 1952 vol. 1, pp. 129–207.
[82] Stark ed., 1952 vol. 3, p. 48.
[83] Psalidopoulos 1997. Englander 1998.
[84] Stark ed., 1952 vol. 2, p. 310.
[85] Spiegel 1983 p. 342.
[86] Long 1977 p. x, 25, 39–40.
[87] Stark ed., 1952 vol. 3, p. 198.

Bentham virtually identified property with human feelings – pleasure, security and expectation. He viewed the ideas of a revolutionary change in the distribution of property with "horror":

> A revolution in property! It is an idea big with
> horror, a horror which can not be felt in a stronger
> degree by any man than it is by me…it involves the
> idea of possessions disturbed, of expectations thwarted:
> of estates forcibly ravished from the living owners, of
> opulence reduced to beggary, of the fruits of industry
> made the prey of rapacity and dissipation- of the
> levelling of all distinctions, of the confusion of all
> order and the destruction of all security[88]

Bentham's manuscript fragments of the 1770s and 1780s reproduce faithfully the priorities established in Blackstone's treatment of the "rights of Englishmen".[89] An Englishman's fundamental rights are three: "personal security, personal liberty and private property".[90] Yet Bentham and Blackstone do hold divergent views on property and their divergence arises from a consideration clearly raised by Blackstone.

The basic function and importance of property in civil society having been established, he asserts, "The only question remaining is, how this property became actually vested…".[91] Bentham wished to clarify the language and procedure of the law in relation to property. The vesting of title, the forms of conveyance, these and other aspects on the law of real – "immovable" – property were the initial focus of his attention.[92]

In the 1770s and 1780s, Bentham attended primarily to the pursuit of theoretical niceties. The four major works of this period, the "*Fragment on Government*", the "*Comment on the Commentaries*", the "*Introduction to the Principles of Morals and Legislation*", and "*Of Laws in General*", showed an increasing abstraction and intricacy in his theoretical treatment of property as time passed. Around the year 1790, a change occurred. The French Revolution (1789) filled Bentham (and many others) with an unprecedented sense of urgency: practical proposals for the protection of order and well-being in English society had to be promulgated without delay. Before 1790, Bentham's continuing obsession had been with the requirements of scientific social theory. After 1790, he was immersed instead in the gathering of the hard facts of social life. "Political economy, finance, [and] the administration of justice" now occupied him. In the 1770s, he had seen the analysis of criminal law as his primary goal. In the late 1780s and the 1790s, he devoted immense energy to problems of a civil nature. By civil, he meant simply "distributive". His writings in the 1780s show a steady rise to prominence and final ascendancy in his mind of the concept of distributive law, specifically "private distributive" (civil) law and "public distributive" (constitutional) law.[93] His earlier interest in the classification of punishable offences

---

[88] Supply Without Burthen: Or Escheat Vice Taxation, in Stark ed., 1952 vol. 3, p. 318.

[89] Long 1979 p. 228.

[90] Jones ed., 1973 p. 62; I Comm.1.

[91] Jones, Selections, 124; II Comm.1.

[92] Long 1979 p. 228.

[93] Burns and Hart 1970.

against property is superseded by a preoccupation with the principles of distribution of both corporeal and incorporeal objects of property. Bentham the censorial jurist becomes Bentham the political economist.[94]

Reception: Influence

As have been mentioned above, three major economists of Bentham's time did know Bentham's theories, but they were not satisfied with his theory.

The majority of later economists did not pay any more attention to Bentham than his contemporaries did. William Stanley Jevons was an exception. It is very unlikely that H. H. Gossen knew the British hedonist. Neither Walras nor Menger had any contact with this discoverer of marginal utility.

The following unkind but apt characterization of Bentham was given by Karl Marx in his *Das Kapital*:[95]

> Bentham is a purely English phenomenon. Not even
> excepting our philosopher Christian Wolff, in no time
> and in no country has the most homespun common-
> place ever strutted about in so self-satisfied a way.
> The principle of utility was no discovery of Bentham.
> He simply reproduced in his dull way what Helvetius
> and other Frenchmen said with *esprit* in the 18th
> century. To know what is useful for a dog, one must
> study dog-nature. This nature itself is not to be
> deduced from the principle of utility. Applying this to
> men, he that would criticize all human acts,
> movements, relations, etc., by the principle of utility,
> must first deal with human nature in general, and
> then with human nature as modified in
> historical epoch. Bentham makes short work of it.
> With the driest naivete he takes the modern
> shopkeeper, especially the English shopkeeper,
> as the normal man. Whatever is useful to this
> queer normal man and to his world is absolutely useful.

John Stuart Mill (1806–1873) had a strong utilitarian bias because James Mill was a close friend of Bentham and was himself a staunch utilitarian. As he reached adulthood, he was disillusioned by Bentham and revolted against his father. In his essay entitled "*Remark on Bentham's philosophy*" published in 1833, Mill "firmly dismissed Bentham's claims to contribute anything of importance to ethical theory".[96] In his essay entitled "*Bentham*" published in 1838, Mill wrote

---

[94] Long 1979 p. 241.
[95] Marx 1867[1953] vol. I., p. 571.
[96] Scarre 1996 p. 88.

> Man is never recognized by him as a being
> capable of pursuing spiritual perfection as an end;
> of desiring, for its own sake, the conformity of his
> own character to his standard of excellence, without
> hope of good or fear of evil from other sources
> than his own consciousness.[97]

In the 1840s and 1850s, however, Mill softened his criticism of Bentham under the influence of the feminist Harriet Taylor, whom he married in 1851 after a friendship lasting 20 years. In the autobiography published in 1873, Mill wrote

> In this period (as it may be termed) of my mental
> progress, which now went hand in hand with hers,
> my opinions gained equally in breadth and depth,
> I understood more things, and those which I
> had understood before, I now understood more
> thoroughly… I had now completely turned back
> from what there had been of excess in my
> reaction against Benthanism.[98]

It was in these changed circumstances that Mill wrote *Utilitarianism*, published in 1861.

Bentham found little response in Germany, where hostility both to utilitarianism and to the rival natural-law philosophy stifled economic theorizing. There was only one contemporary philosopher of name in Germany who expressed admiration for Bentham, and him Hegel had expelled from his position at the University of Berlin. Even a "liberal" such as Goethe referred Bentham as a "highly radical fool".[99] A relative lack of response to Bentham was also in America.[100] The main factor was the more deeply entrenched natural-law philosophy.[101]

For the most known Bentham's theory, the greatest happiness principle, let us call Lord Lionel Robbins' (1898–1983) words:

> If we consider it, not as the ultimate solution
> to all problems of ethics and valuation…but
> rather as a working rule by which to judge
> legislative and administrative projects affecting
> large masses of people, it still seems to me better,
> more sensible, more humane, more agreeable
> to the moral conscience if you like, than any other
> I can think of[102]

---

[97] Mill 1838 in Parekh ed., 1974 pp. 1–40.

[98] Scarre 1996 p. 90–91; Amemiya 2007 p. 160.

[99] Baumgardt 1952 pp. 4ff.

[100] Palmer 1941 pp. 855–871.

[101] Spiegel 1983 p. 747.

[102] Robbins 1965 p. 12.

References

Amemiya T (2007) Economy and economics of ancient Greece. London: Rouledge [Routledge explorations in economic history 33]

Atkinson CM (1905)[1969] Jeremy Bentham. His life and work. Methuen (repr. New York: A. Kelley)

Baujard A (2009) A return to Bentham's *felicific calculus*: from moral welfarism to technical non-welfarism. Eur J Hist Econ Thought 16(3):431–453

Baumgardt D (1952) Bentham and the ethics of today, with Bentham manuscripts hitherto unpublished. Princeton University Press, Princeton

Bentham J (1789)[1970] An introduction to the principles of Morals and legislation. In: Burns JH, Hart HLA (eds). London: T. Payne & Son/University of London. The Athlone Press.

Bentham J (1793a) Emancipate your colonies. In: Bowring (ed) 1838–43, vol 4

Bentham J (1793b) Manual of political economy. In: Stark (ed) 1952, vol 2

Bentham J (1795) Supply without Burthen; or Escheat vice taxation. In: Stark (ed) 1952, vol I

Bentham J (1801–1804) Institute of Political Economy. In: Stark (ed) 1954, vol III

Bentham J (1801a) Abstract or compressed view of a tract intituled circulating annuities. In: Stark (ed) 1952, vol II

Bentham J (1801b) The true alarm. In: Stark (ed) 1954, vol III

Bentham J (1801c) Defence of a maximum. In: Stark (ed) 1954, vol III

Bentham J (1801d) Annuity note plan. In: Stark (ed) 1952, vol II

Bentham J (1821)[1995] Colonies, commerce and constitutional law. In: Schofield P (ed). Clarendon Press, Oxford

Bowring J (ed) (1838–1843)[1872] The works of Jeremy Bentham, vols I–XI. William Tait, Edinburgh [reprint New York: Russell & Russell, 1962]

Brunon-Ernst A (2007) Le panoptique des pauvres-Jeremy Bentham et la réforme de l' assistance en Angleterre. Presses de la Sorbonne Nouvelle, Paris

Burns JH, Hart HLA (1970) Introduction. In: Bentham J (ed) An introduction to the principles of Morals and legislation. University of London-The Athlone Press, London, pp xxxvii–xliii

Burns JH, Hart HLA (1977) Introduction. In: Bentham J (ed) A comment on the commentaries and a fragment on government. University of London-The Athlone Press, London, pp xix–li

Englander D (1998) Poverty and poor law reform in 19th century Britain, 1834–1914. Longmann, London

Gide R et Rist G (1930) Histoire des doctrines economiques [Greek trans: Patselis N, vol I]. Athens: Pyrsos

Guidi M (2002) Bentham's Economics of Legislation. J Public Finance Public Choice XX(2–3):165–189

Guidi M (2004) My own Utopia. The economics of Bentham's panopticon. Eur J Hist Econ Thought 11(3):405–431

Guidi M (2009) Review: Cyprian Blamires. The French Revolution and the Creation of Benthanism. Basingstoke: Palgrave Macmillan, 2008, pp xii+442. Eur J Hist Econ Thought 16(2):375–380

Halévy E (1928) The growth of philosophic radicalism [trans: Mary Morris]. Faber & Faber, London

Harris J (2005) O Jeremy Bentham kai to <Automoioma tou. He ekkentrike diatheke henos philosophou, Historika Themata 38:33–43

Jones G (ed) (1973) The sovereignty of the law: selections from Blackstone's Commentaries on the Laws of England. University of Toronto Press, Toronto

Karayiannis A (1988) Democritus on ethics and economics. Rivista Internazionale di Scienze Economiche e Commerciali XXXV(4–5):369–391

Kauder E (1965) A history of marginal utility theory. Princeton University Press, Princeton

Kelly P (1987) Bentham, Jeremy (1748–1832). In: Eatwell J, Milgate M, Newman P (eds) The New Palgrave: a dictionary of economics, vol 2. Macmillan, London, pp 156–161

Kitromilides P (1984) Jeremy Bentham and Adamantios Corais, In Proceedings of the Conference "Corais and Chios" (in Greek), vol. I. Athens, pp. 285–308

Kitromilides P (1998) Politikoi stochastes ton neon chronon. Biographikes and hermeneutikes prossegiseis, 3rd. edn. Poreia, Athens

Kraus O (1902) Zur Theorie des Wertes. Max Nieweyer, Halle

Landreth H, Colander D (1989) History of economic theory, 4th edn. Houghton Mifflin, Boston

Long DJ (1977) Bentham on liberty: Jeremy Bentham's idea of liberty in relation to his utilitarianism. University of Toronto Press, Toronto

Long DJ (1979) Bentham on property. In: Parel A, Flanagan TH (eds) Theories of property Aristotle to the present. Wilfrid Laurier University Press, Waterloo, pp 221–254

Mack MP (1937) Bentham Jeremy. In: Int Encyclopaedia Social Sci 1:55–58

Marx K (1867)[1953] Das Kapital. Kritik der politischen Ökonomie, vol I. Dietz Verlag, Berlin

Mill J St (1838) Bentham. In: Bhikhu Parekh (ed) Jeremy Bentham. Ten critical essays [1974]. Frank Cass, London, pp 1–40

Palmer PA (1941) Benthanism in England and America. Am Polit Sci Rev 35(50):855–871

Parekh B (ed) (1974) Jeremy Bentham. Ten critical essays. Frank Cass, London

Pins M (2006) Bentham Jeremy. In: Herz D, Weinberger V (eds) Lexikon ökonomischer Werke. Wirtschaft und Finanzen, Düsseldorf, pp 34–35

Psalidopoulos M (1997) Oikonomikes theories and koinonike politike. He bretannike prossegise. 2nd. edn. Aiolos, Athens

Rae J (1895) The life of Adam Smith. London

Richardson R, Hurwitz B (1987) Jeremy Bentham's self-image: an exemplary bequest for dissection. Br Med J 295:195–198

Robbins L (1965) Bentham in the twentieth century. University of London, Athlone Press, London

Scarre G (1996) Utilitarianism. Routledge, London

Sigot N (2009) Review: Anne Brunon-Ernst, Le panoptique des pauvres-Jeremy Bentham et la réforme de l' assistance en Angleterre. Paris: Presses de la Sorbonne Nouvelle, 2007, p 271. Eur J Hist Econ Thought 16(2):380–384

Smith A (1776)[1937] An inquiry into the nature and causes of the wealth of Nations. Edited, with an Introduction, Notes, Marginal Summary and an enlarged Index by Edwin Cannan. With an Introduction by Max Lerner. New York: The Modern Library

Spiegel HW (1983) The growth of economic thought, 2nd edn. Duke University Press, Durham

Stark W (1941) Liberty and equality or: Jeremy Bentham as an Economist. Econ J 51:56–79

Stark W (1946) Jeremy Bentham as an Economist. Econ J 56:583–608

Stark W (ed) (1952–1954) Jeremy Bentham's economic writings. Critical edition based on his printed works and unprinted manuscripts, vols 1–3. Allen & Unwin, London [vol I, 1952, p 412, 30s; vol II, 1952, p 458, 40s; vol III, 1954, p 600, 45s]

Stephen L (1900)[1968] The English Utilitarians, vol I: Jeremy Bentham. Duckworth, London [reprinted New York: A. Kelley]

Stigler G (1950) The development of utility theory. J Political Economy 58:373–396 [Spengler JJ, Allen WR (eds) (1960) Essays in economic thought: from Aristotle to Marshall. Rand McNally, Chicago, pp 606–655]

Viner J (1949) Bentham and John Stuart Mill. The Utilitarian Background. Am Econ Rev 39:360–382

Chapter 11
Johann Heinrich von Thünen: A Founder of Modern Economics

Hans Frambach

Biographical Sketch

Johann Heinrich von Thünen was born on June 24th, 1783 on his father's estate in Kanarienhausen, a small town in the region of Jever near the German North Sea coast.

In February 1802, after serving an apprenticeship in agriculture, he visited the agricultural college of Lucas Andreas Staudinger, a friend of the famous writer Klopstock, in Groß-Flottbeck near Hamburg. In Flottbeck, von Thünen became acquainted with the Baron von Voght, a rich nobleman and patron of Staudinger. As Gerhard Lüpkes, an excellent expert in Thünen-research, points out, the meeting with von Voght was of great impact on the development of von Thünens' social attitude. Baron von Voght did experiments with beggars on his estate in Flottbeck: instead of living on charity he gave the beggars the opportunity to work (Lüpkes 1992, pp. 9–10).

In 1802, von Thünen already started writing some literature concerning the shape of agriculture, taking into consideration transport costs from the locations of agricultural production to the centres of consumption, the cities (Engelhardt 1993a, p. 462; Passow 1901, pp. 36–38). Prompted by the writings of Albrecht von Thaer and his "Einleitung zur Kenntnis der englischen Landwirtschaft" (Introduction to English agriculture) in particular, von Thünen enrolled in a course at von Thaer's Institute of Agriculture in Celle in Summer 1803. Although von Thaer was criticized by von Thünen in some fundamental points, he called von Thaer his real teacher in agricultural science (von Bismarck 1933, p. 16; Petersen 1944, p. 4). In October 1803, he registered at the University of Göttingen to study until the summer semester 1804. At this place, he had some experiences and meetings with people and works shaping his liberal and social ideas.

H. Frambach (✉)
Department of Economics, Schumpeter School of Business & Economics,
University of Wuppertal, Gaußstraße 20, 42097 Wuppertal, Germany
e-mail: frambach@wiwi.uni-wuppertal.de

J.G. Backhaus (ed.), *Handbook of the History of Economic Thought*,
The European Heritage in Economics and the Social Sciences,
DOI 10.1007/978-1-4419-8336-7_11, © Springer Science+Business Media, LLC 2012

From 1802 on, von Thünen wrote treatises and carried out calculations about agriculture. In 1810, he bought the estate Tellow, district Teterow, in Mecklenburg and lived there with his family until the end of his life. Between 1810 and 1820, he did a lot of experiments and calculations at Tellow and devoted himself to a very detailed accountancy.[1] The result of this meticulous venture provided the groundwork for his famous discoveries. The main result of these years of practical experience and theoretical research efforts was that, in 1826 von Thünen published his masterpiece in his major important work "The Isolated State" (only the first volume was published in 1826 containing among other things the location theory),[2] as Walter Braeuer (1951, pp. XXXIV–XXXVIII), the famous von Thünen researcher and editor of the "1966a-edition" of the "Isolated State", pointed out. Because of the new insights and the following success of the book, the philosophical faculty of the University of Rostock conferred the title of an honorary doctor on von Thünen in 1830. In the same year, the city of Teterow declared him a freeman. He declined a seat in the National Assembly of Frankfurt am Main (Frankfurter Nationalversammlung) in 1848 because of his bad state of health.

After finishing the second part of "The Isolated State" in 1850, which contains the wage, interest and capital theory, von Thünen died on September 22nd, 1850 at the age of 67 on his estate Tellow as a result of an apoplectic stroke (Schneider 1934, p. 7).

---

[1] For further reading concerning the "Tellow accountancy", see Eberhardt E.A. Gerhardt (1964), "Thünens Tellower Buchführung", 2 Vols., Meisenheim a. Glan.

[2] Original edition 1826: "Der isolierte Staat in Beziehung auf Landwirtschaft und Nationalökonomie", known as "The Isolated State", Part I (Hamburg, Perthes). A second revised and improved edition of this Part I appeared 1842 (facsimile edition, among others, in 1986 edited by Horst C. Recktenwald, Düsseldorf, Verlag Wirtschaft und Finanzen). Part II, section 1 "Der naturgemäße Arbeitslohn und dessen Verhältnis zum Zinsfuß und zur Landrente" appeared 1850 (Rostock). The second edition of Part I (1842) together with Part II/1 (1850) is known as the "real" second edition of "The Isolated State", the last edition personally supervised by the author. This second edition was newly edited by Heinrich Waentig in 1910 (1. Repr.), 1921 (2. Repr.), 1930 (3. Repr., Jena, Fischer), 1966 (4. Repr., Stuttgart, Fischer; in this paper referred as "von Thünen 1966a"), von Thünen (1990) (5. Repr., Aalen, Scientia). Section 2 of Part II and Part III "Grundsätze zur Bestimmung der Bodenrente, der vorteilhaftesten Umstriebszeit und des Wertes der Holzbestände von verschiedenem Alter für Kieferwaldungen" were published in 1863 (Rostock). The first time that all the three parts were published together in one book was in 1875, the so-called third edition of "The Isolated State" (Berlin: Wiegandt, Hempel & Parey; this third edition corresponds to the first complete edition). It contains 1276 pages und was prepared by Hermann Schumacher-Zarchlin, the Thünen-biographer, who had been instructed by von Thünen's family. This third edition was reprinted in 1966 (Darmstadt, Wissenschaftliche Buchgesellschaft), edited by Walter Braeuer and Eberhard E.A. Gerhardt (in this paper referred as "von Thünen 1966b"). A shortened English translation of extracts of "The Isolated State" was edited by Peter Hall (referred as von Thünen 1966c), and another translation of the text of the second part can be found 1960, in Bernard Dempsey's "The frontier wage; the economic organization of free agents. With the text of the second part of The isolated state by Johann Heinrich von Thunen" (Chicago, ILL, Loyola University Press, pp. 187–367). There is also a French translation of Part I, "Recherches sur l'influence que le prix des grains, la richesse du sol et les impôts exercent sur les systèmes de culture", by Jules Laverrière (Paris 1851), and of Part II, sections 1 and 2, "Le salaire naturel et son rapport au taux de l'intérêt", by Mathieu Wolkoff (Paris 1857).

Context in Theory and History

Facts to the Historical Background

After Prussias defeat against France in the battle of Jena and Auerstedt on October 14th, 1806, a time of humiliation began in the east and north of Germany. Prussia lost all its territories on the west side of the river Elbe, as a result of the peace terms fixed between France and Russia in Tilsit in 1807. After Napoleon's abdictation, Europe got reorganized following the old borders from before 1792; the relevant resolution was passed at the congress of Vienna in 1815. Parts of Saxony and wide areas of the upper-Rhine region were given to Prussia and it also took Habsburg's place as the direct neighbour and main enemy of France on the river Rhine. Prussia and Austria formed the main body of Central Europe.

In the individual states of Germany, nationalism became widespread and a unified, free and independent Germany was declared. However, these efforts of people vanished increasingly the more Prussia and Austria returned to absolutism, accompanied by censorship and political persecution. But at least it was a period of peace, and Germany entered into a phase which later was named the "Biedermeier period" characterized by attributes like pernickety, small-mindedness, well-ordered structures, thriftiness, liking for neatness and tidiness. But the appearances of peace and calm were deceptive and became interrupted by rebellious movements caused by an under-supply of food in the face of a rapid increase in population. Many individuals of the rural population found no work and moved to the cities, enhancing the number of slum inhabitants. Through reforms in agriculture, trade and taxes were intended to modernize the economy; they were too costly and so the tension between people and the Prussian official state came to a critical point.

Being afraid of a "French revolution on German soil" the Prussian government reinforced censorship and other devices of a police state. For an open revolt, the political and social unrest had only to be completed by an economic crisis – state crises had already taken place in 1813, 1817 and 1830, where problems in foreign affairs met economic under-supply – which was followed promptly in 1847/1848 by a severe famine and business crisis owing to a crop failure and a collapse in the consumer goods industry. On February 24th, 1848, King Louis Philippe was ousted from office in Paris and his throne was burnt on the place of the Bastille. In face of the political tensions in Germany, these occurances in Paris triggered off a wave of unrest and disturbances (Nipperdey 1998, p. 595). In Germany, on March 24th, 1848, the Schleswig-Holstein estates proclaimed their independency from Denmark and formed a provisional government; British warships demonstrated on the German North Sea coast; Russian armed forces marched to the border of East Prussia; there were revolts in Berlin, Munich and Vienna. On May 18th, 1848, 585 representatives of the German people met to form the German National Assembly in the Paulus-church, Frankfurt am Main. As already mentioned, von Thünen declined a seat in this National Assembly for reasons of health.

In those times, nearly half of the estates changed their proprietors (from the 1820s till 1850; by the 1870s it was more than two thirds; Nipperdey (1998), p. 162) von Thünen extended his property to a model-estate.

Theoretical Context

There are many theoretical influences which had an impact on von Thünen's thinking and writings. First of all, von Thünen can be perceived as a *classical economist,* who was strongly influenced by the works of Adam Smith. von Thünen was introduced to Smith's writings through the lectures he took at Georg Sartorius Freiherr von Waltershausen in Göttingen. Sartorius von Waltershausen held a chair for constitutional economics and politics (Staatswissenschaften und Politik) and stood completely in the tradition of Adam Smith in his economic writings. Another important teacher of von Thünens' was Albrecht von Thaer (1752–1870) in Celle, the intellelectual ancestor and famous representative of agricultural sciences, an advocate of English classical economy who based some of his economic concepts on Smith. von Thünen was also familiar with other classical writers like David Ricardo (1772–1823) or Jean Baptiste Say (1767–1832). Of course, von Thünen knew the German members of classical economy Friedrich Julius Heinrich Reichsgraf von Soden (1754–1831), Ludwig Heinrich von Jakob (1759–1827), Karl Heinrich Rau (1792–1870), Friedrich Benedikt Wilhelm von Hermann (1795–1868) and Hans Karl Emil von Mangoldt (1824–1868) who were, in essence, shaped by Smith, but had not managed to add their own original ideas to classical economy. The fundamental classical idea that the action of each individual increases both the individual's utility and the welfare of the whole, was shared by all of these authors.

Although von Thünen absorbed the writings of especially the French and English classical economists, he also adopted a critical position to these. von Thünen criticizes Smith, for example, in equating the interests of capital with the profit of an entrepreneur, in the insufficient treatment of the connection of wages and interest rates, and in the unsatisfying estimation of the nature of the right and natural wage (von Thünen 1966a, pp. 459–62, 478–80). von Thaer was criticized by von Thünen's empirical agricultural studies in showing that under certain conditions, the three-course system can be of economic advantage over the crop-rotation system (von Thünen 1966a, pp. 362–6). Above all, von Thünen showed that the market prices of agricultural products were independent of the cultivation form. He also argued against Ricardo and other classical economists in justifying wages on subsistence level. Like Thomas Malthus, von Thünen warned against unrestrained increase in population, but at the same time he saw hope for a solution in a better school education and the curbing of the human passions (causes which, by the way, prevent making economics absolute) (Engelhardt 1993a, pp. 465–6; von Thünen 1966a, pp. 441–4).

Liberalism, in its version of classical economy, rigorously trusts in the autonomous and independent acting of individuals, whereas the role of society and government is secondary. von Thünen differed strictly on this point. Since his apprenticeship in farming he had been involved in the "social question" and this in a practical *and* theoretical sense. In dealing with the social question, he could not deny the influences of German education and the spirit of the age. As theoretical background information we have to recognize the distinction of two main philosophical schools of thought within the continental countries, decisive for the further development of economics: On the one hand, the direction thinking that the economic life of a society follows some kind of natural law. Following this line, individuals are governed by egoism as the only relevant motive for their economic activities. The economic representative is classical economics based on the doctrine of natural law, especially the Scottish moral philosophy. On the other hand, we find the opinion that economy is not only guided through egoistically motivated individuals. Far from it, laws which base human action solely on egoism are evaluated as one-sided and wrong. This direction corresponds to the *romantic-ethical school of economics* coming out of the ethics of Immanuel Kant (1724–1804) and its successors, the (German) idealistic philosophy with representatives such as Johann Gottlieb Fichte (1762–1814) and Georg Friedrich Wilhelm Hegel (1770–1831), followed by economists like Adam Müller (1779–1854), Franz von Baader (1765–1841), and Friedrich List (1789–1846).

The romantic–ethical direction stresses the importance of cultural and moral aspects, even for economic life. von Thünen undoubtedly combined both directions and took up a position somewhere in between, and in this respect we can follow Hesse (1933, p. 172) in pointing out that von Thünen was neither a romanticist nor a rationalist, he was rather of the opinion that people reach freedom if they renounce following their own egoistic interests and pursue the welfare of society. People have to set voluntary limitations to come to deeper insights of their higher fate. The restriction of egoism as a kind of a benevolent egoism is a frequently emerging idea in von Thünen's "Isolated State" (von Thünen 1966a, pp. 193 (1966c, p. 119), 252, 435–50, 471–2, 513; 1966b, [Part II, sec. 2] pp. 1–14). Of course, the influence of the reading of Kant in particular is undeniable. Kant's "Critique of Pure Reason" (Kritik der reinen Vernunft), studied by von Thünen during his time in Göttingen, have had a lasting impact on his thinking (Lüpkes 1992, p. 13). von Thünen's idea of such benevolent egoism appeared in the several social actions he put into practice at Tellow, to support people to act frankly and liberally. For this, he made many attempts to bring people to be diligent, sparing, and to help them to help themselves.

In von Thünen's thinking, we discern the optimistic metaphor of Gottfried Wilhelm Leibniz's (1646–1716) "prästabilierter" harmony as used by Adam Smith combined with Kant's categorical imperative: The interests of the individual are associated with the welfare of the whole. The single individual suffers because of the incorrect action of others. Therefore, it is of great importance for each individual and the society as a whole to come to an understanding of what is right and honest (von Thünen 1966b, [Part II, sec. 2] p. 8).

The happiness of one person is combined with the happiness of all, and for that reason it turns to one's life's work:

> to develop and study the own strength in contributing to the enlightening and delight of the others.

By sacrificing one's subjective interest for the interest of mankind the miraculously resulting increase in welfare will lead to a beneficial reciprocal effect on the individual, and there is no need for another moral principle than this:

> Behave in the way, which will be of benefit for you if all the others would behave in exactly the same way, and be willing to sacrifice in the performance of this principle even when the others disobey.

> (von Thünen 1966b, [Part II, sec 2] p. 13 [transl. H.F.; indents as in the original])[3]

A third direction of influence can be recognized in von Thünen's engagement in the thinking and writings of socialists. Because of the aggravating social situation of workers and rural population, socialist ideas became more and more widespread. Simonde de Sismondi (1773–1842) played a special role. Coming from classical economy and the economics of Adam Smith in particular, Sismondi developed a class theory containing the thesis that competition does not lead to harmony but to the concentration of industrial power. The French movement of cooperative socialism reached its peak. Charles Fourier (1772–1837) developed the idea of the "phalanstères", of the productive-cooperatives, and of the "right of labour". Fourier's pupils Victor Considérant (1808–1893) and Louis Blanc (1811–1882) continued his ideas. Blanc, incidentally, was the founder of a socialist party in France and also member of the revolutionary government of 1848. Another socialist determining the character of socialist contemporary thinking in the first half of nineteenth century was Pierre Joseph Proudhon (1809–1865). In the competition principle, he saw the causes of all the societal conflicts and contradictions. Proudhon wanted to stop the exploitation of the workers and to improve their material situation.

The improvement of workers' material conditions as an aim of theoretical and practical activities was shared by von Thünen as well. In addition to that, von Thünen considered it a moral commitment of the rich to relieve the poverty and hardship of the poor (von Thünen 1966a, p. 578). Since his youth von Thünen was interested in such problems and the central question of "The Isolated State" is to ask for a law under which the return of labour is distributed between workers, capitalists, and landowners (von Thünen 1966a, e.g. p. 435). The appearance of "Der Sozialismus und Kommunismus des heutigen Frankreichs" in 1842 had a lasting influence on von Thünen's social convictions. This influential book by Lorenz von Stein (1815–1890) led von Thünen to do an intensive examination of the so-called "social question",

---

[3]Das Glück des Einzelnen ist also an das Glück Aller geknüpft, und dadurch wird es zur Aufgabe des Lebens:

> an der Aufklärung und Beglückung Anderer seine eigenen Kräfte zu entwickeln und auszubilden. Indem der Mensch sein persönliches Interesse dem Interesse der Menschheit zum Opfer bringt, fällt durch eine wunderbare Verkettung die Erhöhung des Wohls der Gesammtheit wohlthätig auf ihn zurück, und er bedarf keines anderen Moralprincips als dieses:

> Thue das, was dir, wenn alle Anderen ebenso handeln, zum Heil gereichen würde, und bringe willig die Opfer, die dies Princip fordert, wenn Andere dasselbe nicht befolgen.

> (von Thünen 1966b, [Part II, sec. 2] p. 13; indents as in the original)

the misery and poverty of many of the working people (Vleugels 1941, p. 344).[4] von Thünen had active correspondence about political ideas and problems of farming with Karl Rodbertus-Jagetzow (1805–1875), who was a pomeranian landowner, temporarily Prussian minister for education and cultural affairs, and alongside Wilhelm Weitling (1808–1871) and Ferdinand Lasalle (1825–1864) the most famous German utopian socialist. Rodbertus drew up the thesis that the relative part of the returns which the worker is entitled to, the wage rate, decreases with increasing returns. As a result of this and because of the compulsion to accept every wage rate, the worker will only receive the subsistence level.

To be sure, von Thünen was neither a socialist nor an utopian dreamer. He was a pragmatist, sympathetic towards socialist ideas and ideals, conceiving them as an expression of a rather respectable conviction than plans suitable to be brought into action in real life (von Thünen 1951, pp. 205–13; 1966a, pp. 577–8, 582–4).

Another scientific direction having an impact on von Thünen has to be mentioned: the German variant of mercantilism, the cameralistic sciences ("Kameralismus"). Especially the economic historians Hoffmann (1950), Henning (1972) and Pruns (1995) are concerned with some aspects reconciling cameralistic sciences with von Thünens approach (for a survey, see Engelhardt 1999, pp. 104–9). von Thünen took a look at the thinking of mercantilism probably at Johann Beckmann, a professor for agricultural sciences and "Kameralistik" in Göttingen.

Even though representatives of cameralistic sciences are not to be found in von Thünen's writings, some overlappings of a general methodological kind are remarkable: Neither cameralistic scientists nor von Thünen raised the development of theories excessively; scientific discoveries come out of experience. Agreement with von Thünen can also be seen in the registration of statistical data the way, for example, Wilhelm von Schröder (1640–1688) claimed in 1686 in his book "Fürstliche Schatz- und Rentenkammer". Georg Heinrich Zincke (1692–1769), known as the founder of business management, emphasized in his "Grundriß einer Einleitung in die Kameralwissenschaften" (1742) the problem of profitability for accountancy, a topic which also was of great importance to von Thünen. Further on, a parallel can be drawn between von Thünen and Johann Heinrich Gottlob von Justi (1720–1771). They both made statements on the problem of the arrangements of agricultural production under consideration of distances and transport costs. von Justi mainly pursued the supply of the town and the formation of prices, whereas it was the profitability of agricultural production under the viewpoint of profit maximization and also the application of mathematic tools that mattered to von Thünen (Hoffmann 1950, pp. 32–22). Finally, von Thünen was fully aware of the time he lived in. This includes the awareness of states, the economic policy of which had already passed through the period of late mercantilism. Even until the mid-nineteenth century, many European states and in particular Mecklenburg were influenced by traces of absolutist and mercantilist principles (Pruns 1995, p. 205).

---

[4] Von Thünen about von Stein's book: "I hardly know another book which I have read with a greater interest and from which I have learnt more than from this one". [Ich kenne fast kein Buch, das ich mit solchem Interesse gelesen, und aus dem ich soviel gelernt hätte, wie aus diesem.] (Schumacher-Zarchlin 1883, p. 219).

Summary of Main Contributions

In the field of economics, two salient points have to be especially mentioned, which are irrevocably intertwined with the name of Johann Heinrich von Thünen: the "Thünen-rings" and the wage and capital theory, including the famous natural wage formula and the application of differential calculus to economics.

The "Thünen Rings"

Von Thünen starts unfolding the assumptions of his model: Only one town situated in the centre of a fertile plain with no navigable river or canal to transport goods. At a great distance from this "central-city", the isolated state, the plain ends in an uncultivated wilderness. All the manufactured articles are produced only in this centre and the urban population is provided with food by the agricultural production occurring in the non-urban part of the plain. Ore mines and salt works are assumed to be situated right next to the central city (von Thünen 1966c, p. 7). In microeconomics and the location theory especially these assumptions are described as homogeneity of land, which means uniform fertility and uniform transport plain, uniform production costs, infinite elasticity of demand, a single market centre at which all crops are sold and to which they must be transported, the yield per acre of a certain crop depends on its demand price at the market, the production costs, the distance, respectively, the transport costs between market and place of cultivation (Stevens 1995, p. 17).

The general question is, what form of agricultural production will have the best results under these conditions, and especially, what is the impact on efficiently driven agriculture, when changing the distance to the centre (von Thünen 1966c, p. 8)? von Thünen explains that around the central town, agricultural production will take place in the form of concentric rings.[5] Close to the city, crops will be grown which are very expensive to transport, which are highly perishable or – taking the high price of land near the town into account – which can be cultivated very intensively, that is, cost-saving. That means, within the first ring, "the market will be preempted by crops that are capable of achieving the greatest reductions in total costs per unit of output as a result of intensive cultivation, and which therefore produce the highest ground rent by virtue of their particular location" (Blaug 1996, p. 598). Within the most distant ring, cattle breeding is dominant because here, far away from the central town, the cultivation of crops like rye, even when using the three-course system, will be too costly under consideration of the transport costs. Thus, von Thünen derives the general rule that with increasing distance from the central town (movement to the remote rings),

---

[5] In "The Isolated State" six rings are expounded (square brackets indicate Peter Hall's translation, see glossary, pp. xlix–liv): (1) the central city, called as "free economy" with horticulture and dairying [free cash cropping], (2) forestry, (3) advanced crop rotation sytem, perhaps best described as intensive arable rotation [crop alternation system], von Thünen (1966c), (4) a less advanced crop rotation system including pastoral farming [improved system], (5) three-field system, (6) cattle breeding [stock farming]; beyond the margin of cultivation is a wilderness inhabited only by hunters.

the intensity of agricultural production declines, which means a movement from different forms of the crop rotation system[6] to the three-course system to cattle breeding (von Thünen 1966c, e.g. pp. 157–8).

To be sure, out of the isolated state model and under certain conditions, every agricultural production method has its own advantages which makes it impossible to say that von Thünen has favoured the crop rotation system in general, on the contrary, he neglected von Thaer's general principle of the absolute superiority of the English crop rotation system over the three-field system by his "proof of the relative excellence of agricultural production systems" (Nachweis der relativen Vorzüglichkeit der Wirtschaftssysteme) (Hesse 1933, p. 173).

However, back to the isolated state and considering the transport costs as the decisive variable determining the value, the price, of an agricultural product, von Thünen states that transport costs will increase with greater distance from the central town and for that reason the product value will decrease (von Thünen 1966c, pp. 24, 31).[7] Following the fundamental principle that higher transport costs can be offset by lower rents (Morrill and Symons 1977, p. 218), the impact of a change in the price of grain in the form of agricultural production can be expressed in terms of land rent (the land rent equals the income from the sale of a product minus the costs of planting, cultivating, bringing in harvest (von Thünen 1966a, e.g. pp. 36, 41–3 (1966c, pp. 27–30)).[8] Starting with a high price of grain, its reduction will cause a fall in the land rent, and from a certain point the crop alternation system with a high intensity, for example, an eleven- or seven-period rotation, becomes unprofitable and has to be substituted by an alternation system of perhaps seven or six periods. Another change of production form – to the three-field system – takes place as the result of an additional price reduction. If the price of grain falls further, a level will be reached where even the three-course

---

[6] Von Thünen discussed the crop rotation system, or more exactly speaking: the improved English system of crop rotation, in many variations, from a six-period to the twelve-period alternation system. In comparison to the three-course system von Thünen favoured the seven-period alternation system, containing the rotation of cereal crops, root crops and short grasses (von Thünen 1966a, pp. 169–75). The three-course system was most widespread in Mecklenburg. In October, rye and wheat were planted, in the following year the winter grain was brought to harvest and the land was ploughed. Then oats and barley were cultivated and brought to harvest in August. From this time the land lay fallow until the next June. In the advancing nineteenth century the "Holstein paddock system", a special variant of the crop rotation system, was often to be seen in Mecklenburg. The number of rotations in the crop rotation system depends on an economy's size and the quality of land. For example, the eleven-period alternation system: (1) fallow land (fertilized), (2) winter grain, (3) summer grain, (4) winter grain, (5) summer grain, (6) winter grain (fertilized), (7–11) pastureland (Honcamp 1933, pp. 66–9).

[7] "The essence of von Thünen's complaint against Ricardo, in modern language, is that Ricardo developed his theory of rent in terms of an undifferentiated agricultural product. Von Thünen's great achievement was to point out that transport costs were the cause, and the rents the consequence, of important differentiations of agricultural, dairy, and forest production, according to distance from the market" (Clark 1967, pp. 370–1).

[8] In other words and referring to Ricardo: "the land rent is the amount of money the land-owner receives for using the original and indestructible forces of his land" (von Thünen 1966a, p. 28; transl. H.F.). Referring to the translation in Peter Hall's edition: "Rent is that portion of the produce of the earth, which is paid the landlord for the use of the original and indestructible powers of the soil". (von Thünen 1966c, p. 22).

system is too expensive. And thus we come to a price level too high to use the land for grain production (von Thünen 1966c, pp. 226–7). As a general result, it can be summarized that the form of agricultural production depends on the product prices and on the production costs (including the transport costs).

Holding the price of grain constant, the transportation costs (or, depending on the model, the price of labour or capital) are very low within the first ring and extremely high in the remotest ring; conversely, the land rent is maximum in the first ring and converging to zero at the outermost frontier of the isolated state (because costs are too high to transport the grain to the city and thus no sale and no income can be achived: the land rent is zero).

With regard to its practical application, many of the discoveries von Thünen made have become outdated as a result of secular change. The fundamental concept of the "Thünen-rings" has lost its practical meaning for agriculture. His theory of locality for urban areas, for example, can hardly be taken into account in contemporary economics (Stamer 1995, p. 50). Forestry, the second of the rings, is of no interest because the demand for firewood has vanished and the yields of wood remained on a comparatively low level (p. 53). The three-course system has absolutely no importance for modern agriculture after the use of fertilizers, and contemporary systems of crop rotation are completely different from those of von Thünen's days (pp. 54–5).

Wage and Capital Theory

Von Thünens theory is perceived as one of general equilibrium (Samuelson 1983, p. 1482) because after Cournot, von Thünen was the first who realized the interdependency of all economic variables and the necessity of its representation in a system of equations (Schumpeter 1967, p. 467). He also developed marginal productivity theory explaining the relationship between capital and labour, rents and wages. Capital is described as dead and as incapable of producing anything without the forces of labour; but on the other hand, it is impossible to provide people with clothes, food, tools, etc. without using capital. Consequently, "the product of labour p is (defined as; H.F.) the joint product of capital and labour" (von Thünen 1966a, 584).[9] The central question is: How can the contribution of every single factor to the joint production be evaluated (varying labour while capital and land is kept constant; varying capital while keeping the other factors constant)? von Thünen answers using the instruments of differential calculus:

> The significance of capital we have measured by the increase in the product of the labor of a man which results from an increase in the capital with which he works. Here labor is a constant, capital a varying magnitude.
>
> When, on the other hand, we consider capital as remaining constant and the number of workers as varying, we realize in a large business that the significance of labor and the share of labor in the product are determined by the increase in the product which results from the addition of another laborer.

---

[9]"The capital is the product of labour" (von Thünen 1966a, p. 591).

(von Thünen 1966a, p. 584, cit. from Samuelson 1983, p. 1469, who refers to an transl.
in Paul H. Douglas, 1934, Theory of wages, New York: Macmillan)

By the way, Paul Samuelson states that if von Thünen had only written these lines
he "would merit first-rank name in the annals of economic theory" (Samuelson
1983, p. 1469).

Von Thünen (1966a, pp. 544–52) goes on deriving his famous formula of natural
wage rate. I am following Schumpeter's often cited short-version interpretion
(Schumpeter 1967, p. 467) deviating only in some aspects:

Considering only one period

p	Denotes the labour product of the workers (dollar value of the national net product)
w	Wage sum workers receive (total pay roll); $w=a+y$, a is that part of the wage sum the workers need for consumption. In a broad interpretation, it corresponds to a subsistence wage at a rate where labour will be rewarded in accordance with its marginal productivity. y denotes that part of the wage sum exceeding the subsistence level $(y=w-a)$. Assuming that production costs are only represented by the wages, y can be interpreted as the amount being invested in the period assuming that a is constant
$p-w$	Total profit of employing the workers
$(p-w)/w$	Profit rate (or interest rate)

It follows that the investment of $(w-a)$ will bear $(p-w)/w$ interest. Maximizing the
investments of the period means to maximize $(w-a)(p-w)/w$ referring to w. The first
order condition is fulfilled when

$$w = \sqrt{ap},$$

this is the famous von Thünen formula of "natural wage" (e.g. von Thünen 1966a,
p. 596; 1966c, pp. 251–3).[10]

The formula expresses the identity of the natural wage rate to the geometric
mean of subsistence level (a) and the product of labour (p). In accordance with the
formula, the worker does not receive the full amount of his labour product, but a part
which exceeds the subsistence level in any case.[11] Because the natural wage rate (w)
exceeds the subsistence level (a) in the same way as the product of labour (p) exceeds
the wage (w),[12] von Thünen interpreted the wage rate (w) as natural and just, and
concluded that studying this question of natural wage intensively, one is lead

---

[10]The term "natural wage" or "natural wage rate" should not be confused with the same term of
classical economists. Natural wage in classical economy corresponds roughly to von Thünen's part
of the wage rate the worker needs for consumption, the subsistence level (a).

[11]$\sqrt{ap} > a$, accepting that only $p > a$ is of economic sense. If we consider only the worker (and not his
family) and perceiving the subsistence level (a) as the marginal product of labour, the formula shows the
natural wage rate as the geometric mean of marginal product (a) and average product of labour (p).

[12]$w > a \Leftrightarrow p > w$ ($w = \sqrt{ap} \Leftrightarrow p = w^2/a$; $w^2/a > w \Leftrightarrow w > a$).

"directly to the question about human fate" (von Thünen 1966a, p. 583). Therefore, the natural wage rate should not only follow the interplay of supply and demand, or the subsistence level, but should be taken as the expression of "free self-determination" of workers. von Thünen could not agree to calling the bare means of subsistence natural wage. It seemed inconceivable to him to explain wages solely upon Ricardo's thesis of subsistence level (Moore 1992b, p. 35; Winkel 1983, p. 554). He spoke of a degrading situation of the worker and rejected the determination of natural wage at the subsistence level as a result of competition (von Thünen 1966a, pp. 435–7, 450, 522–3, 582–3).

A wage rate below $\sqrt{ap}$ is regarded as unjust to the workers, and a rate above as unjust to the capital owners (von Thünen 1966a, pp. 594–6 (1966c, p. 252); Diehl and Mombert 1911a, pp. 2–3). In this respect, von Thünen contradicted classical wage theory which assumed wages were a result of demand and supply. He considered competition between demand and supply of labour nothing more than a manifestation of a real situation, a certain wage rate, but not as an explanation (von Thünen 1966a, pp. 435–6). Even beyond the marginal productivity theory of the following neoclassical economics, von Thünen stated a realization of joining the interests of capital owners and workers when paying wages in accordance with the natural wage formula. In doing so the workers automatically receive a share of the labour product, and in so far it agrees with Moore (1992b, p. 35), that the "The fundamental idea in the formula $\sqrt{ap}$ is that wages must vary with the product".

More generally, von Thünen differed from classical economic theory in some fundamental points (although sharing many of its essential features such as, for instance, Ricardo's theory of land rent).[13] The characteristic features of the classical theory of natural wages can be summarized as "(1) labour was treated throughout as a mere commodity; (2) natural wages were defined without reference to equity, the operation of natural law being the main fact considered; (3) natural wages were defined without reference to the product of labour. The requirements of the labourer as limited by his surroundings were regarded as determining his natural earnings" (Moore 1992a, pp. 2–3). "He was profoundly convinced of the evils resulting for the labouring class in consequence of the prevailing theory" (p. 3).

The formula is subject to strict assumptions, for example, p and a being treated as constants, but about which von Thünen was aware. Because of these assumptions, he was criticized by Samuelson speaking of "Thünen's major felony ... a crime against normative economics, and against the positivistic economics of competitive behaviour under laissez faire. He compounded this felony by a major misdemeanour, which is a crime against logic" (Samuelson 1983, p. 1483). Already Roscher

---

[13]Taking the stock rent into account, von Thünen's rent theory is much more complete than Ricardo's explanation. Furthermore, Ricardo deduces conclusion from axioms without examining its meaning in reality. von Thünen, on the other hand, underpins his assumptions and discoveries by self-collected data (Winkel 1983, p. 550).

criticized the payment arising from a strict relationship between a and p (Roscher 1874a, pp. 382–3, fn. 10; 1874b, pp. 895–7). Schumpeter was much more generous, asserting that von Thünen's unrealistic assumptions should not be taken as reason to declare his argument as wrong (Schumpeter 1967, pp. 467–8). Taking all the imperfections into account, the explanations about natural wages show many social features.

However, von Thünen's formula of natural wage gave scientific circles cause for extensive and sometimes excessive discussions (see, e.g. Engelhardt 1993b, pp. 27–28; Moore 1992b), and von Thünen himself was so convinced about the formula that it was engraved on his tombstone.

Salient Points Covering the Whole Range of Contributions

Most generally von Thünen's contributions may be best classified following Asmus Petersen (1944), the most important von Thünen researcher of the twentieth century (Folkers 1951, p. 74), into technical, economic and social achievements. For our purpose, distinction in more detail seems advantageous, including, for example, a short section concerning the contribution to business administration.

Contribution to Economic Method

It must be mentioned that perhaps the most fundamental scientific principle of von Thünen's thinking was that experience and theory have to go hand-in-hand absolutely: "...our German scholars consider the study of sciences only for its own purpose not being interested in its application" (von Thünen, letter to Prof. Röper, from 25.2.1841, cit. from Schumacher-Zarchlin 1883, p. 209). von Thünen broke new ground in methodology, introducing partial analysis into economic theory. He analysed the impact of a certain variable keeping all other factors constant and this with regard to both the impact on one firm and on the firms in total. Thus, von Thünen is a forerunner of partial analysis, more exactly speaking: using the ceteris paribus condition, he applied partial analysis as an instrument of economic theory (e.g. von Thünen 1966a, p. 586). Furthermore, von Thünen formulated the principle of marginal analysis and he anticipated fundamental parts of the following marginal productivity theory. For example, using comparative static analysis, von Thünen gave insights into the allocation process between quantities and prices of outputs and inputs and how they are influenced by technological advances or the change of, for instance, taxes and fees. The determination of differential rent in dependency of "marginal land" (rent differs with the distance of the location of production to the market), the determination of the wage rate following the marginal productivity of the last employed worker, of the capital rent depending on the last invested unit of capital, etc. are discoveries which preceded the state of knowledge in economic theory of the time by a long way (Diehl and Mombert 1911b, pp. 12–3; Winkel 1983, pp. 550–1).

Analogous to the mathematically abstract way of thinking of modern economists, he supports the "abstract-isolated method", a kind of fusion between inductive and deductive method, which is intended to filter-out the essence, the main structures, from the complexity of the real world's economic relationships, but always beginning from an empirically founded data base (Hesse 1933, p. 179). The famous representative of the *German historical school*, Wilhelm Roscher, called von Thünen the first German economist of an "exact" trend in German economics (Roscher 1874a, p. 881), applying mathematics and abstract-deductive method as instruments of economic theory (pp. 882–6). von Thünen (1966c, e.g. p. 175) was fully conscious about the fact that this method is accompanied by a loss of many facts of reality and thus, he never was subjected to the fallacy that his isolated state becomes a reality. He also realized the "deterrent effect" on the reader of "Isolated State", begging him to keep going, even when the assumptions of the model deviate strongly from reality. Such assumptions are necessary to explain the effects of certain variables which themselves are unclear in reality because of their dependency of many other variables (von Thünen 1966c, pp. 3–4).

von Thünen was one of the first economists who understood the quantitative character of economic theory and introduced mathematics as an instrumental aid for economic analysis ("...the application of mathematics must be allowed, where truth is impossible to find without it" [von Thünen 1966a, 569]); furthermore, he tested his theoretically derived results on the basis of self-collected data and thus he can be perceived as an early precursor of econometrics (von Böventer 1985, p. 9; Krelle 1987, p. 5). The application of marginal analysis, especially for the determination of the amount of wages and the amount of the rate of interest under conditions of competition is to be seen as an outstanding contribution to the introduction of marginal analysis as a fundamental instrument of modern economic theory (Schneider 1934, p. 10). But behind von Thünen's thinking there always stood one general question: What is the law which *naturally* determines the distribution of the return of labour between workers, capitalists and landowners? (von Thünen 1966a, p. 435 (1966c, p. 248)).

Contribution to Wage and Capital Theory

Von Thünen began his reflections on the price of labour, stating it as a problem that wages are only of very small amount in relation to the incomes of capital and land. The main reason is that the owners of capital and land appropriate the greatest parts of the value produced by the labourers. Taking this into consideration, von Thünen tried to find a law about the natural, that means, just or equitable distribution of the products of labour between workers, capitalists and land owners. Thus, distribution is both an economic problem and a problem of categories as ethics, morality and duty. von Thünen complained about classical economists' explanation of wages, which is based solely on the principle of competition, or the forces of demand and supply. von Thünen referred to $\sqrt{ap}$ as the fundamental contribution to distribution and participation. The natural wage rate exceeds the subsistence wage rate and increases with the product of labour. Consequently, the worker participates in the changing/augmenting value of his own labour product.

Taking into account von Thünen's doubts about the rigorousity of the intransigent laws of the market, he nevertheless was one of the most important and brilliant theoreticians who himself introduced marginal productivity theory to economics. He stated very clearly the distribution of the product of the factor production between workers and capital owners, following the laws of the marginal productivity of the factors (von Thünen 1966a, pp. 594–6 (1966c, p. 252)), coming straight to results which John Bates Clark described almost 50 years later. von Thünen anticipated the idea of general equilibrium as a paradigm and as an approach paving the way for a theoretical solution to economic problems using mathematical method even in the sense of analyzing interdependency of economic factors (Engelhardt 1953, p. 150; Krelle 1987, p. 5).

Social Contribution

The formula of natural wage can be understood as an ethical demand. von Thünen was conscious that the fate of millions of individuals depends on the question of determining wages. In Part II, sec. 1, § 2, "About the lot of workers. A dream of serious content" (Über das Los der Arbeiter. Ein Traum ernsten Inhalts) of "Isolated State" (von Thünen 1966a, pp. 440–7), he quoted the increase in the level of education and culture, and the creation and expansion of people's consciousness as the main factors for augmenting the wage level to improve the living conditions of people. He was impressed with a totally humanitarian attitude, advocating the perfecting of mankind and the development of the individual to a free, moral and responsible personality as the primary goal. Education and material welfare formed the basic conditions to reach this goal. Opposing forces were the inadequate payment of workers and they contemptuously held discussion of the wage question (Engelhardt 1993b, pp. 53–55; von Thünen, letter to Christian von Buttel, 11. Juli 1843, cit. from Schumacher-Zarchlin 1883, p. 219; Winkel 1983, pp. 554–5).

During von Thünen's lifetime, the "social question" took on huge dimensions and despite reducing it to a question of wage-level à la classical economist, von Thünen treaded a path more complex. In addition to his version of natural wage theory, he embedded his insights into a comprehensive humanitarian world view. In other words, reducing von Thünen's answer to the social question to his explanations about natural wage, does not go far enough. Economics and social policy are interrelated. von Thünen did not pursue the science of l'art pour l'art, he tried to mediate decision logic with empirical and historical theory. Two thoughts have to be taken into account (von Thünen 1966a, p. 583): (1) the rigorously demanded economic acting in "Isolated State", Part I, becomes relativized in Part II. In the latter part, we find a lot of critical assertions against economic theory. von Thünen turned away from a position which made economics absolute. For example, he declared the training of attitude, mental powers etc. as a value fin itself; (2) for von Thünen the question of what the natural wage is had a deeper meaning: In his opinion, the intensive study of this question must lead undoubtedly to the question of individual destiny.

Von Thünen absolutely refused to accept a conception of man characterized by egoism in the sense of classical economics and he claimed to tame egotistical interests (von Thünen 1966a, pp. 435–40, 513). Following the ideas to which he was introduced by baron von Voght, von Thünen tried to curb poverty by means of "productive care": Instead of living in charity he offered work to unemployed people. His social commitment to those affected by poverty, unemployment, or those expelled from their homeland can be observed by his dedication for 30 Büdner-families in the area of Tellow (Engelhardt 1993b, p. 60; (1999, p. 111), Schumacher-Zarchlin 1883, pp. 124–5).

From the position of an agricultural holding's owner, von Thünen drafted a kind of a single-firm-social policy, an idea which can absolutely be understood as a forerunner of social market economy. (Engelhardt 1999, p. 114) For example, he introduced the "Tellow profit sharing model", a measure for 21 families in Tellow to create wealth by participation of employees in savings and share-ownership schemes. On April 15th, 1848, von Thünen introduced the profit-sharing principle at Tellow estate with retroactive effect from 1 Juli 1847, based on research done on his formula and on experiences in profit-sharing with the governor since 1836 (Petersen 1944, p. 18). It was the purpose of the "Tellow social model" to come to an advantageous solution for all persons pursuing the business management objectives of organization and rationalization.

Great progress was made in paying the costs of illness (a precursor of health insurance) and implementing models of wealth participation to make provision for estate employees' old age. In 49 years of practising a share contract, von Thünen was in a position to put 3,354.30 marks as capital fund at the disposal of every participant, and this until the year 1896, which means until 46 years after his death. The contractual partners were von Thünen on the one hand, and on the other hand agricultural workers and/or their families, other villagers of Tellow such as the shepherd and the teacher.

In the first change of his will in 1845, von Thünen tried to avoid the sale of the estate by his sons after his death. He wished to increase the welfare and the morality of the estate employees. Each worker's potential existing capital was treated as an irredeemable savings deposit until his 60th year, paying 4% interest (Engelhardt 1999, pp. 114–5).

We also have to consider different kinds of payment. Beside time–work rate and share payment, which were absolutely customary in von Thünen's time, he also introduced piecework payment and bonus payment (Braeuer 1951, p.LV). By establishing these rewarding systems, von Thünen believed in joining the interests of the workers to the increase in production. These ideas coincided with socialist views, but von Thünen never went so far as to demand the transfer of property and assets to common property. In particular, he rejected suggestions to transfer property on estate accomadation to day labourers or their settlement at the manor as boarders in small units. (von Thünen 1966a, 596–602). The lecture of von Stein's "Socialism and Communism" (1842) in particular led von Thünen to make extended studies regarding his wage formula. He took the socialist matter seriously without being a socialist. Education and enlightenment of people were his proposed solutions to improve material situation.

Contribution to Business Administration

Besides being a theoretical economist, von Thünen was a theoretical and practical business manager preferring model-supported decision making and practising scientific bookkeeping. If we recognize modern economic study of firm's reference numbers and comparism of indices of firm's economic performance as a task of accountancy, von Thünen has to be realized as a person who did so successfully (Engelhardt 1983, pp. 582–3). He marked the state of development in management, in internal accountancy as well as in cost and performance accounting with respect to its application to agriculture (Jahnke 1995, pp. 79–82; Zeddies 1995, p. 190); one could call him the "founder of agricultural business management" (Hesse 1933, p. 174).

A principle target of von Thünen's, later called "Tellow bookkeeping," was the achievement of scientific knowledge (Aereboe 1933, p. 195). He took great efforts to obtain information about the "yields and costs of every fruit and act" as a prerequisite for cost and performance-accounting serving as the basis for calculations and entrepreneurial decision making. For example, von Thünen put a lot of time and energy into estimating the efforts and costs of a day labourer doing different activities, of a team of horses, a team of oxen, the wear and tear of tools, agricultural implements, maintenance of facilities, amortization of draught animals, etc. He meticulously collected such diverse data down to the last detail. He arranged and analysed such information, and derived his scientific discoveries from it. (Jahnke 1995, pp. 180–2). This is of great importance for modern agricultural holdings in particular, because in most cases the employees do not have the required knowledge about how to estimate such "yields and costs" with the necessary selectivity, and what perhaps is more important – in view of the pressure of costs in agricultural firms it is too expensive to employ workers with the relevant skills (most of the firms are organized as a family business).

Even on a more abstract level modern agricultural theory of business management which perceives the firm as a system can learn from von Thünen that (1) the processes in a firm have always to be integrated into the context of a system as a whole, taking into account several aims and restrictions on time, energy and costs, (2) the organization of a company always has to be flexible with reference to the structural conditions of a firm's environment, (3) provision with relevant information about the current situation of a firm as a system must be permanently available, and

(4) the most important property is that of structural efficiency, which means to keep firm's viability on a high level (Krüger 1995, p. 189).

von Thünen developed many practical instructions for managing an agricultural holding and came to fundamental insights into microeconomic principles and macroeconomic processes. The "Isolated State" can be perceived as an "econometric work in the best sense: theoretically underpined, provided with extensive empirical data, [and] of mathematical precision" (van Suntum 1989, p. 211; transl. H.F.).

Contribution to Spatial Economics

"The history of location theory begins with the publication of *The Isolated State* by Johann Heinrich von Thünen in 1826", the "'father' of the economics of space" (Blaug 1996, p. 597 [emphasis as in the orig]), or the founder of location theory. In the introduction to Part II of "Isolated State" von Thünen stresses the spatial representation of the influence of the corn price on farming as the starting point for the isolated state (1966c, pp. 226–7). That means, distances from the location of production to the place of selling, the market, can be understood as transport costs which, transformed into categories of prices and price structures, lead to different levels of production, intensity of cultivation and also to certain ways of using the land considered to be an homogeneous expanse. From these considerations, he came to the famous "Thünen-rings" which contributed to his good reputation and served to secure his important position within the History of Economic Thought. The "Thünen-rings" show very obviously the interrelation between good prices and the use of production factors (von Böventer 1985, pp. 12–3).

Contribution to Agriculture

Von Thünen experimented on methods of cultivating different arable crops and on methods of how to use (natural) fertilizers, he tried to change the condition of the soil putting mud on dry meadows, sand and marl on bog soil, experimented with crossing in sheep breeding (Braeuer 1951, pp.LIV-LVIII; see also, Schumacher-Zarchlin 1883, pp. 122–3, 125). Concerning the introduction and improvements of agricultural machines and implements into Mecklenburg's agriculture, von Thünen published seven articles in the "Neue Annales der Mecklenburgischen Landwirtschafts-Gesellschaft". He dealt with the improvement of the hook and/or its substitution for the plough. At Tellow, he tested and compared different kinds of ploughs and commended the Mecklenburg hook against the ploughs of Small and Baley even accepting some disadvantages of this "farm implement, only for digging" (Petersen 1944, pp. 13–4). In 1834, von Thünen invented the hook-plough which was named after him. The Thünen-hook-plough made topsoil as well as the normal Mecklenburg plough and was easier to pull; furthermore, it enabled the farmer to make a deeper furrow (at Tellow the topsoil was deepened from 4.5 to 6–7 in.). The hook-plough also came into operation at Tellow's neighbouring estates. In the end, the hook-plough (as other inventions of von Thünen) had become outdated as a result of the technical development of the plough (Petersen 1944, p. 14).

Contribution from the Point of View of Modern Theory

Von Thünen is regarded as one of the greatest economists. Among other scientists Edwin von Böventer called him the greatest of all the German economists and one of the greatest among all nations (von Böventer 1985, pp. 17); Wilhelm Krelle speaks of one of the greatest of the economic disciplines who we have to thank for brillant inventions (Krelle 1987, p. 5); Paul Samuelson placed him "in the Pantheon with Léon Walras, John Stuart Mill, and of Adam Smith" (Samuelson 1983, p. 1482) and "as one of the great microeconomists of all time" (p. 1487, fn.14). In 1941, Erich Schneider pointed out that nothing really new had been added to the pioneering work of von Thünen, Launhardt and Alfred Weber in spacial economics (Schneider 1941, p. 727). Schneider recognized von Thünen as "one of the great pioneers" (Schneider 1934, p. 8), as a "master of theoretical methods of work" (p. 9), and as "the ingenious creator of the instrument of marginal analysis" (p. 10), whose ideas had become either general knowledge or were anticipated in a relevance which was fully understood by a few economists 200 years later (p. 11). Mark Blaug called von Thünen "the true founder of marginal analysis in the nineteenth century" (Blaug 1996, 306).

Undisputably, von Thünen "is the founder of the location theory and pioneered the use of the concept of marginal productivity" (Negishi 1989, p. 24), those theories for which he is most likely to be remembered today (Staley and Charles 1989, p. 134). He also made important contributions to the origins of quantitative empirical economic research and econometrics. Many current models of modern location theory are unequivocally combined with the name von Thünen in their fundamental structures. The so-called "von Thünen economy", which means that locations differ only in terms of accessibility and land is homogeneous in quality, is an assumption often used in modern models of location theory (e.g. Arnott and Stiglitz 1979, p. 488; Bauer and Hummelsheim 1995, p. 82; Stevens 1995, p. 17). For instance, there are advantages to using von Thünen's theory through progamming models.[14] von Thünen introduced transportation costs as a relevant quantity of economic decision making and explained their significance for economic pricing. Because transportation costs are an essential component of transaction costs, von Thünen's achievements in

---

[14]"First, it has an immediate and obvious dualism between location patern and location rent. Second, both the spatial ordering of crops and existence of nonzero production for any crop are problems which implicitly involve inequalities. Finally, the extension of the theory to elastic demand, variations in transport rates, and nonuniform land fertility is relatively easy by programming methods but extremely difficult otherwise" (Stevens 1995, p. 17).

this field can be realized as a contribution to New Institutional Economics and *transaction cost economics*, in particular.

Although von Thünen's achievements in practical agricultural economy have no meaning for contemporary agriculture, his discoveries in agricultural business administration and in the agricultural holding as a system are of remarkable importance. But nothing diminishes the discoveries in the theories of land rent, the marginal productivity theory, the application of partial analysis and the anticipation of theory of general equilibrium – they were pathbreaking.

In face of the outstanding theoretical achievements in the field of economics, von Thünen was far from being a one-sided theoretician working in his ivory tower without any sense of reality. He took in everything going on around him and realized the social problems in particular. He explained the conflict of interest between capital owners and workers by attempts of entrepreneurs to force down the wages on the substistence level to reduce worker's share of their product to a minimum but he recognized, on the other hand, the compulsion of the laws of the market. von Thünen saw the best measure against the dissatisfaction of workers and the best protection against poverty and hardship in educating people and in linking the wage rate to the magnitude of the labour product, of course at natural wage rate level (von Thünen 1966a, pp. 598–601). To be sure, in contrast to the view of classical economists, von Thünen's natural wage rate lies above subsistence level and produces "a joint interest in augmenting the production" between capital owners and workers (p. 597). Clearly, one can have great doubts in the deviation of natural wage formula and von Thünen's exaggerated hopes concerning its social implications, but the idea which gives rise to the formula is commendable and pioneering. Although deviating from the strict course of marginal productivity theory with the natural wage formula, von Thünen combines economic interests with moral and ethical claims.

May be, as Wilhelm Krelle (1987, p. 7) points out, von Thünen could not imagine the enormous increases in marginal products during the centuries which provided a material situation far beyond poverty to most of the workers. Undoubtedly, at that time the productivity level was low and a working social security system did not exist. It is also true that a productivity level is an important prerequisite for sufficient economic wealth to a certain degree; but can productivity be the answer to everything? Even today where productivity rates are comparatively high in the developed countries, poverty is a serious problem not to mention the poverty in the poorer countries. Can economic problems solely be solved by increasing productivity, and what pre-conditions have to be fulfilled so that productivity can increase anyway? All these questions are questions concerning economic theory. For example, collective bargaining: As we know, productivity increase is only one relevant factor within the finding process of a wage rate between employers and employees, factors such as economic power, strategic competence, institutional backing, threatening power, etc. are of great importance as well. Furthermore, factors such as the cultural level of a society, the political and institutional stability should not be disregarded.

It is questionable to accuse von Thünen of being wrong in studying the thesis of natural wages in such an extensive and intensive manner as he himself did, and not only this, he discussed socialist ideas as well. Paul Samuelson criticized von Thünen, asking from today's view "How did so deep and subtle a mind get mired in the doctrine of the natural wage"? (Samuelson 1983, p. 1487). One has to take such a statement as an expression of the biased interpretation of modern economic theory rather than a weakness in von Thünen's logical consistency and rigorous theoretical argumentation. Even today's marginal productivity theory has trouble with combining aspects of economy and justice. von Thünen was fully aware of fundamental principles of economic theory. He realized that "the product of the worker last employed corresponds to his wage" (von Thünen 1966a, pp. 569, 572, 576 (1966c, pp. 254, 256)), and that for one and the same work only one wage has to be paid (p. 577; assumption of homogeneity of labour) but von Thünen was far from accepting these relations as true economic laws referring to a moral commitment of the rich (p. 578), the duties and responsibility of the state, the presence of religion and laws of humanity (p. 580). With such an attitude von Thünen showed a forward-looking idea which probably will be rejected by most of the contemporary representatives of economic theory, but which none the less is important: The understanding of dialectics to audit both sides of the coin, the awareness of the conflicting nature of things, and enduring to the conflict between economy and society. von Thünen is a great classical economist who taught us that moral, morality, ethics, thoughtfulnes, responsibility etc. have to be perceived as essential parts of economic action.

Undoubtedley, von Thünen is one of the most original founders of Political Economy. Primarily known as the founder of location theory and a researcher who paved the way for the theories of land rent and wages, his ideas of social treatment of workers became famous as well. Hardly any other economist can be found who succeeded in connecting economic modelling and economic experience as much as von Thünen. Because von Thünen's economic thinking and modelling was strongly influenced by a distinct social outlook and his experiences as a gentleman farmer, his scientific discoveries are more than ever important for a critical understanding of contemporary economics. Empirical foundation of economic modelling, applicability of economic abstraction, always combined with a social attitude and humanitarian way of thinking, are features which can be studied outstandingly in the person and the researcher Johann Heinrich von Thünen.

References

Aereboe F (1933) Die Bedeutung Johann Heinrich von Thünens für die landwirtschaftliche Betriebswissenschaft, in Wilhelm Seedorf and Hans-Jürgen Seraphim (eds), Joh. Heinr. von Thünen zum 150. Geburtstag. Versuch der Würdigung einer Forscherpersönlichkeit, Rostock: Carl Hinstorff, pp 193–196

Arnott RJ, Stiglitz JE (1979) Aggregate land rents, expenditure on public goods, and optimal city size. Q J Econ XCIII(4):471–500

Bauer S, Hummelsheim S (1995) Überlegungen zur Nutzung des ländlichen Raums aus heutiger Sicht, in Hans Stamer and Günther Fratzscher (eds), Johann Heinrich von Thünen. Seine Erkenntnisse aus wissenschaftlicher Sicht (1783–1850), Berichte über Landwirtschaft, Zeitschrift für Agrarpolitik und Landwirtschaft, Neue Folge, Bd. 210 Sonderheft, Münster-Hiltrup: Landwirtschaftsverlag, pp 66–83

Blaug M (1996) Economic theory in retrospect. Cambridge University Press, Cambridge

Braeuer W (1951) 'Thünens Leben und Werk', in Johann Heinrich von Thünen, Ausgewählte Texte, selected and commented by Walter Braeuer, series: Die grossen Sozialökonomen, vol.

VII, edited by Hans G. Schachtschabel and Berthold Fresow, Meisenheim a. Glan: Anton Hain, pp IX–LXII

Clark C (1967) Von Thünen's isolated state. Oxf Econ Pap New Ser 21:370–377

Diehl K, Mombert P (1911a) Introduction to Ausgewählte Lesestücke zum Studium der politischen Ökonomie, vol. 2: Der Arbeitslohn, Karlsruhe: G. Braunsche Hofdruckerei, pp 1–21

Diehl K, Mombert P (1911b) Introduction to Ausgewählte Lesestücke zum Studium der politischen Ökonomie, vol. 3: Von der Grundrente, Karlsruhe: G. Braunsche Hofdruckerei, pp 1–20

Engelhardt WW (1953) 'Die Theorien der Produktion, des Preises und der Verteilung bei J. H. von Thünen. Analyse seines Werkes unter verändertem Blickpunkt', Schmollers Jahrbuch für Gesetzgebung, Verwaltung und Volkswirtschaft, 73(I):129–160

Engelhardt WW (1983) Zum Situations- und Problembezug von Entscheidungsmodellen bei Johann Heinrich von Thünen. Zeitschrift für Wirtschafts- und Sozialwissenschaften 103:561–588

Engelhardt WW (1993a) 'Johann Heinrich von Thünen (1783–1850) im Fremd- und Selbstbild. Zum Verständnis des Klassikers in der Gegenwart' [Johann Heinrich von Thünen (1783–1850) His Image and Self Image. Toward an Understanding of this Classical Economist in our Times], Jahrbücher für Nationalökonomie und Statistik, 211(5–6):459–476

Engelhardt WW (1993b) von Thünen und die soziale Frage, Regensburg: Transfer

Engelhardt WW (1999) 'Johann Heinrich von Thünen und die Sozialpolitik', in Hans-Peter Müller (ed), Sozialpolitik der Aufklärung. Johann Beckmann und die Folgen: Ansätze moderner Sozialpolitik im 18. Jahrhundert, Münster/New York: Waxmann, pp 100–117

Folkers JU (1951) 'Johann Heinrich von Thünen' (speech on the occasion of von Thünens 100. day of death at 22. September 1950 in Jever) in Gerhard Lüpkes (ed), Beiträge zur Thünen-Forschung. Eine Studie für National- und Agrarökonomen, Leer (Ostfriesland): Grundlagen und Praxis, pp 66–82

Henning FW (1972) 'Die große Stadt in verschiedenen Verhältnissen betrachtet (J.H.G. von Justi, 1764)', Zeitschrift für Agrargeschichte und Agrarsoziologie, 20:186–197

Hesse P (1933) 'Die Methode Johann Heinrich von Thünens in seinem "Isolierten Staat" und ihre Bedeutung für die landwirtschaftliche Betriebslehre', in Wilhelm Seedorf and Hans-Jürgen Seraphim (eds), Joh. Heinr. von Thünen zum 150. Geburtstag. Versuch der Würdigung einer Forscherpersönlichkeit, Rostock: Carl Hinstorff, pp 169–189

Hoffmann F (1950) Thünen im Blickfeld des deutschen Kameralismus. Weltwirtschaftliches Archiv 65:25–40

Honcamp F (1933) 'Die mecklenburgische Landwirtschaft unter besonderer Berücksichtigung der Zeit von Johann Heinrich von Thünen', in Wilhelm Seedorf and Hans-Jürgen Seraphim (eds), Joh. Heinr. von Thünen zum 150. Geburtstag. Versuch der Würdigung einer Forscherpersönlichkeit, Rostock: Carl Hinstorff, pp 63–78

Jahnke D (1995) 'Enfluß der Erkenntnisse von Thünens auf die Entwicklung der Kosten- und Leistungsrechnung landwirtschaftlicher Unternehmer', in Hans Stamer and Günther Fratzscher (eds), Johann Heinrich von Thünen. Seine Erkenntnisse aus wissenschaftlicher Sicht (1783–1850), Berichte über Landwirtschaft, Zeitschrift für Agrarpolitik und Landwirtschaft, Neue Folge, Bd. 210 Sonderheft, Münster-Hiltrup: Landwirtschaftsverlag, pp 179–185

Krelle W (1987) 'von Thünen-Vorlesung' [von Thünen-lecture]. Zeitschrift für Wirtschafts- und Sozialwissenschaften 107(1):5–28

Krüger H (1995) 'Thünens Beitrag zur Erforschung des Systemcharakters der Landwirtschaftsbetriebe', in Hans Stamer and Günther Fratzscher (eds), Johann Heinrich von Thünen. Seine Erkenntnisse aus wissenschaftlicher Sicht (1783–1850), Berichte über Landwirtschaft, Neue Folge, Bd. 210 Sonderheft, Münster-Hiltrup: Landwirtschaftsverlag, pp 186–189

Lüpkes G (1992) 'Aus den Jugendjahren von Johann Heinrich von Thünen' (speech to the local historical society of Jever, 12. November 1975) in Gerhard Lüpkes (ed), Beiträge zur Thünen-Forschung. Eine Studie für National- und Agrarökonomen, Leer (Ostfriesland): Grundlagen und Praxis, pp 1–16

Moore HL (1992a) Von Thünen's theory of natural wages, part I: the classical theory and von Thünens's formula. In: Mark B (ed) Johann Heinrich von Thünen (1783–1850), Augustin Cournot (1801–1877), Jules Dupuit (1804–1866), series: Pioneers in Economics, vol. 24,

Aldershot: Edward Elgar, pp 1–14 (Orig. publ. in Quarterly Journal of Economics, IX, April 1895, 291–304)

Moore HL (1992b) 'Von Thünen's Theory of Natural Wages, Part II: Criticisms of the formula: Natural Wages = $\sqrt{ap}$ ', in Mark Blaug (ed), Johann Heinrich von Thünen (1783–1850), Augustin Cournot (1801–1877), Jules Dupuit (1804–1866), series: Pioneers in Economics, vol. 24, Aldershot: Edward Elgar, pp 15–35 (Orig. publ. in Quarterly Journal of Economics, IX, July 1895, 388–408)

Morrill RL, Symons J (1977) Efficiency and equity aspects of optimum location. Geogr Anal IX(3):215–225

Negishi T (1989) History of economic theory. North-Holland (Elsevier Science Publ.), Amsterdam

Nipperdey T (1998) Deutsche Geschichte 1800–1866: Bürgerwelt und starker Staat, München, C. H. Beck

Norton W (1979) The relevance of von Thünen theory to historical and evolutionary analysis of agricultural land use. J Agric Econ 1(XXX):39–46

Passow R (1901) Die Methode der nationalökonomischen Forschungen Johann Heinrich von Thünens. Zeitschrift für die gesamte Staatswissenschaft 58:1–38

Petersen A (1944) Thünens Isolierter Staat. Die Landwirtschaft als Glied der Volkswirtschaft, Berlin: Paul Parey

Pruns H (1995) 'Der Isolierte Staat Heinrich von Thünens und die agrarpolitische Staatsrealität des 19. Jahrhunderts: Modell und Wirklichkeit', in Hans Stamer and Günther Fratzscher (eds), Johann Heinrich von Thünen. Seine Erkenntnisse aus wissenschaftlicher Sicht (1783–1850), Berichte über Landwirtschaft, Neue Folge, Bd. 210 Sonderheft, Münster-Hiltrup: Landwirtschaftsverlag, pp 204–322

Roscher W (1874a) System der Volkswirtschaft [Volkswirtschaft]. Ein Hand- und Lesebuch für Geschäftsmänner und Studierende, Stuttgart: Cotta

Roscher W (1874b) Geschichte der National-Oekonomik in Deutschland, Geschichte der Wissenschaften in Deutschland. Neuere Zeit, vol. 14, München: R. Oldenbourg

Samuelson PA (1983) Thünen at two hundred. J Econ Lit XXI:1468–1488

Schneider E (1934) Johann Heinrich von Thünen. Econometrica II:1–12

Schneider E (1941) Der Raum in der Wirtschaftstheorie. Jahrbücher für Nationalökonomie und Statistik 153:727–734

Schumacher-Zarchlin H (1883) Johann Heinrich von Thünen. Ein Forscherleben [von Thünen-biography], 2nd edition (Orig. 1868), Rostock/Ludwigslust: Carl Hinstorff

Schumpeter JA (1967) History of economic analysis, 6th printing. George Allen & Unwin, London

Staley, Charles E. (1989) A History of Economic Thought. From Aristotle to Arrow, Cambridge (Mass.): Basil Blackwell

Stamer H (1995) 'Die Thünenschen Kreise aus heutiger Sicht. Erkenntnisse für Politik und Wirtschaft', in Hans Stamer and Günther Fratzscher (eds), Johann Heinrich von Thünen. Seine Erkenntnisse aus wissenschaftlicher Sicht (1783–1850), Berichte über Landwirtschaft, Neue Folge, Bd. 210 Sonderheft, Münster-Hiltrup: Landwirtschaftsverlag, pp 48–58

Stevens BH (1995) Location theory and programming models: the von Thünen case. In: Melvin LG, George N (eds) The economics of location, vol I. Edward Elgar, Aldershot (Hants), pp 12–27

van Suntum U (1989) 'Johann Heinrich von Thünen (1783–1850)', in Joachim Starbatty (ed), Johann Heinrich von Thünen. Seine Erkenntnisse aus wissenschaftlicher Sicht, Klassiker des ökonomischen Denkens, I, München: C. H. Beck, pp 208–224

Vleugels W (1941) 'J. H. von Thünen als deutscher Sozialist', Jahrbücher für Nationalökonomie und Statistik, 153, 339–362

Von Böventer E (1985) Johann Heinrich von Thünen und die Entwicklung der Raumwirtschaftslehre, in Klaus Brake (ed), Johann Heinrich von Thünen und die Entwicklung der Raumstruktur-Theorie. Beiträge aus Anlaß der 200. Wiederkehr seines Geburtstages, Oldenburg: Heinz Holzberg, pp 9–18

Von Thünen JH (1951) Ausgewählte Texte, selected and commented by Walter Braeuer, series: Die grossen Sozialökonomen, vol. VII, edited by Hans G. Schachtschabel and Berthold Fresow, Meisenheim a. Glan: Anton Hain

Von Thünen JH (1966a) Der isolierte Staat in Beziehung auf Landwirtschaft und Nationalökonomie, 4th Repr. of the last edition personally supervised by the author (1842 resp. 1850), ed. and introduced by Heinrich Waentig (1st Repr. 1921), Stuttgart: G. Fischer

Von Thünen JH (1966b) Der isolierte Staat in Beziehung auf Landwirtschaft und Nationalökonomie, edited by Walter Braeuer and Eberhard E.A. Gerhardt, based of the edition of 1875 (prepared by Hermann Schumacher-Zarchlin), Darmstadt: Wissenschaftliche Buchgesellschaft

Von Thünen JH (1966c) Von Thünen's Isolated State. An English Edition of Der Isolierte Staat by Johann Heinrich von Thünen, edited and introduced by Peter Hall, translated by Carla M. Wartenberg, Oxford et al.: Pergamonn Press

Von Thünen JH (1990) Der isolierte Staat in Beziehung auf Landwirtschaft und Nationalökonomie, some unpublished writings enclosed, edited and commented by Hermann Lehmann and Lutz Werner, based on outlines of 1818/1819 and the editions of 1826 and 1842, Berlin: Akademie

Von Bismarck [née von Thünen], Olga (1933) Studien zur Geschichte der Familie von Thünen, in Wilhelm Seedorf and Hans-Jürgen Seraphim (eds), Joh. Heinr. von Thünen zum 150. Geburtstag. Versuch der Würdigung einer Forscherpersönlichkeit, Rostock: Carl Hinstorff, pp 9–36

Winkel H (1983) Johann Heinrich von Thünen und die Rezeption in der englischen Klassik. Zeitschrift für Wirtschafts- und Sozialwissenschaften 103:543–559

Zeddies J (1995) 'Schlußwort: Johann Heinrich von Thünen – seine Erkenntnisse aus wissenschaftlicher Sicht', in Hans Stamer and Günther Fratzscher (eds), Johann Heinrich von Thünen. Seine Erkenntnisse aus wissenschaftlicher Sicht (1783–1850), Berichte über Landwirtschaft, Zeitschrift für Agrarpolitik und Landwirtschaft, Neue Folge, Bd. 210 Sonderheft, Münster-Hiltrup: Landwirtschaftsverlag, pp 190–191

Chapter 12
The Legacy of Karl Marx

Helge Peukert

Introduction

> Marx the economist is alive and relevant today … Marx has been reassessed, revised,
> refuted and buried a thousand times but he refuses to be relegated to intellectual history. For
> better or for worse, his ideas have become part of the climate of opinion within which we
> all think … (I)t is a dull mind that fails to be inspired by Marx's heroic attempt to project a
> systematic general account of the 'laws of motion' of capitalism.
>
> (Blaug 1997, p. 215)

The citation of Blaug's book, written in the tradition of the Whiggish mainstream,[1]
hints at the fact that Marx is still a challenge after the breakdown of the communist
world at the end of the 1980s. Almost all modern sociological (for example Weber)
and economic approaches[2] are to a great extent a reaction to Marx' (and Engels')
theory and critique of capitalism as a system of exploitation. Who was this German
intellectual who had such an immense international impact on the history of thought
and policy? Born in Trier in 1818, he enrolled at the University of Bonn at 17 to
study law where he came under the influence of the radical Hegelian philosophy. He
continued to study art, history, and philosophy in Berlin and received his PhD in
Jena in 1841. In the same year, he married and went to Paris; in 1843 he met the son

---

[1] Like most present day authors, Blaug severely criticizes Marx' economic and social theory (for
example 1997, p. 274). In the following we will argue against this tide in the better historian of
economic thought tradition, that is, we will not criticize Marx' theory from the confines of another
"modern" system of economic thought and dominant public preconceptions. Instead, we will first
try to understand Marx from the background of his time, his intentions and theoretical allegations
and measure Marx according to the criteria of his own system.

[2] For example the marginal revolution, the Austrian and Historical school, and at least the early
general equilibrium and neo-classical theories.

H. Peukert (✉)
Faculty of the Sciences of the State/Economics, University of Erfurt,
Nordhäuser Str. 63, 99089 Erfurt, Germany
e-mail: helge.peukert@uni-erfurt.de

J.G. Backhaus (ed.), *Handbook of the History of Economic Thought*,
The European Heritage in Economics and the Social Sciences,
DOI 10.1007/978-1-4419-8336-7_12, © Springer Science+Business Media, LLC 2012

of a manufacturer, Frederick Engels, his long-time intellectual collaborator and financial supporter. Expelled from France in 1845, he went to Brussels where he joined the Communist League. With Engels he published the *Communist Manifesto* (1848) which again led to his expulsion. So he went to France and Germany, but he had to leave for London because he was expelled again. In contrast to Smith who was professor in Glasgow or D. Ricardo, who was a rich banker in London, Marx never had an academic post for his radical rhetoric. He lived most of his lifetime in virtual poverty and only temporarily earned some money, for example as a correspondent for the *New York Tribune*. In 1864, he co-founded the First International. He published the first volume of *Capital* in 1867.[3] In 1883, he died in London of lung disease and general ill health.

Marx was a full-time activist in the European movements for social change, inspired positively by the values of the French revolution and negatively by the miseries of his time, the great inequalities of wealth, poor health conditions, average incomes at the bare minimum of subsistence, child and women labour, bad housing conditions, high infant mortality, etc.[4] Whereas (neo)classical economists justify capitalism for its rate of growth, technical dynamism, and productive efficiencies, Marx concentrated on the massive human costs of capitalism.

It is obvious, that Marx' approach deviates substantially from mainstream (economic) theorizing: (1) His theory is mainly formulated in a non-formalist manner; (2) Against methodological individualism he sets holism with "classes"[5] and "society" as the central concepts; (3) Not (individual maximizing) rationality, but historically variant forms of (collective, traditional, habitual and ideologically based) rule following prevails; (4) Against the concept of the unavoidable and beneficial spontaneous evolution, he points out the oppressive logic of existing social and economic systems and the futurity of conscious human design; (5) He argues against the efficiency (market) point of view and is strongly in favour of social reform (or revolution).[6] It should be taken into consideration that Marx wrote before the real advent of the social sciences.

---

[3] The publication of the writings of Marx and Engels has not been finished yet; on the publication history of their works see Honneth (1999). There are two main series in German, the selected *Marx-Engels-Werke* (*MEW*) and the complete edition, the *Marx-Engels-Gesamtausgabe* (*MEGA*), both originally published in Russian. The excellent subject index is the best and easiest way to study what Marx and Engels themselves really said. The *Collected Works* of Marx and Engels, begun in 1975, based on MEGA, published by Lawrence and Wishart (London) and International Publishers (New York) were only partially as not available for us in Germany.

[4] See for example Engel's book on *Die Lage der arbeitenden Klassen in England* (MEW 2, pp. 228 ff.), first published in 1845. The criticism of the living and working conditions of that time are apparent in almost every sentence Marx and Engels wrote.

[5] See the orthodox reconstruction of Marx' class theory in Mauke (1971).

[6] These dichotomies are explained in detail in Rutherford (1996) who shows that these basic orientations are still in the background of more recent discussions between different schools in economics, for example between old and new institutionalism.

He explained the aforementioned dismal facts primarily with the existence of private property of the means of production which he rejected. He joined various organizations that tried to transform capitalism in Europe into a cooperative commonwealth of freethinkers without exploitation and under the democratic guidance of the associated workers as the (only) producers of (surplus) value. Those who produce goods and services should own them and decide what to do with them. The respective system was called "socialism" or "communism". It is not identical with the structure of the (former) so-called real existing socialist countries in Eastern Europe, China, etc.[7] In fact, the revolutions in Europe around 1848 did confirm their revolutionary hopes in so far as they brought feudalism to a definitive end. But instead of socialism, capitalism was established in Europe and Marx was in exile in Britain until the end of his life. Marx as the son of comfortable parents (his father was a middle-level German state bureaucrat[8] and his mother came from an educated Dutch family) paid a high price for his theoretical and practical political commitment. In exile, always at the brink of poverty (only three out of six children with his affectionate wife Jenny von Westphalen[9] survived) he studied in an exceptional furor economic, political, sociological, philosophical but also anthropological and for example historical literature for many hours in the British library, day in day out. From his days as a German university student,[10] Marx was an all-round man not only in the social sciences. There was no field of inquiry which got unnoticed by him, including the natural sciences and present-day pamphlet literature, journals, newspapers, etc. From his youth, he read and wrote literature.[11] (Shakespeare and the classical Greeks were his favourites.)

The ultimate driving force behind his monumental writings was a yearning for social justice,[12] including an outspoken deliberate value judgement.[13] Marx appreciated capitalism for its technological dynamism, development in human knowledge and also cultural creativity. In so far he was a radical modernist who even supported colonialism in India for its destruction of stubborn social structures

---

[7] In 1845, Marx and Engels already explained that socialism in one or some countries is an impossibility and could only end up in state capitalism with a new ruling class (see for example Djilas 1996), which lets the old state apparatus unchanged (MEW 3, pp. 34–36).

[8] See the critical and kind-hearted letters of the humanistic father to Marx (Ergänzungsband, pp. 616–640, in the following EB).

[9] See the letters from Jenny to Marx (EB, pp. 641–655) which express a lot of sorrow and love from an educated background.

[10] Marx major field was jurisprudence and minor in economics and philosophy.

[11] Examples for his romantic over-zealous poetics can be found in the EB (pp. 602–615).

[12] For a much more critical understanding of Marx' personal equation see the bibliography of for example Raddatz (1975); to get a glimpse of the complexity of Marx' personality compare Raddatz with Fromm (1961); see also McLellan (1973) and Berlin (1939). A fair and readable overview on the "angry giant's" live, time and ideas can be found in Heilbroner (1989, pp. 136 ff.).

[13] In Marx' view, the proponents of a dispassionate value-neutral attitude and analysis usually take the existing social structure for granted and legitimize it (un)consciously. This insight gave rise to Marx' ideology critiques, for example in the economic field in his "Theories on surplus value" (MEW 26).

(MEW 8, p. 133). But at the same time he was critical about the unequal distribution of wealth, the existence of the working poor and the reduction of the worker to perform primitive routines as the other side of free contracts and private property. Smith, the main representative of classical political economy, who was also the classical starting point for Marx' economic theory, had not really foreseen and included the negative aspects of capitalism in his evolutionary design. Marx wanted to liberate the potential of capitalism as a high-productivity economic system by removing its oppressive components. Marx tried to combine the German idealist-humanist background of his time in the intellectual sphere, most characteristically expressed in Hegel's idealist scheme of world history as the self-alienation and reconciliation of the world spirit, with a somewhat opposing reality in the economic sphere. In contradistinction to the intellectual atmosphere for example in Britain (dominated by a more down to earth economics and utilitarianism), an idealist-religious discussion context dominated the critical discourses in Germany at Marx' youth, for example in the circle of the left Hegelians and in the critique of religion by Feuerbach.

Marx' "materialism" must be understood from this background as a counterbalance against the prevalent voluntaristic idealism of his time which he held responsible for the 1848 defeat because a thorough analysis of capitalism as an economic system and its potential realistic transformation was missing. For Marx, most revolutionaries of his time neglected the importance of the production and distribution of surplus value within the economy. Therefore, Marx put this criterion in the centre of his analysis of social formations, distinguished by "classes", that is, contributors or receivers of surplus labour values. It was his basic intuition, that the specific modes of the appropriation of surplus deeply influence the movement of prices, income and wealth and even shape our constructs of mind (religion, ideological self-interpretations) and societal institutions (for example family, political system, etc.). A dialectical method applied to Marxism means to see Marx' thoughts always in relation to what he criticizes, to understand for example *Capital* (MEW 23–25) in the sense of the subtitle as a "critique of political economy" and his refutation of Hegel's philosophy[14] not only as a simple reversion from idealism to materialism but also as a pronounced counterweight to their one-sidedness.[15]

The link between Marx and the idealist–religious–humanist–anthropological nexus around the 1840s and the question, in how far Marx' works are one integrated corpus can be evaluated much better today[16] because essential contributions of Marx were published posthumously, for example Marx' *Critique of Hegel's Philosophy of Right* (first published in 1927) (MEW 1, pp. 201 ff.), *The German Ideology* (MEW 3, pp. 9 ff.) and the *Economic-Philosophical Manuscripts* (both first published in 1932) (Ergänzungsband, pp. 465 ff., in the following EB), and the *Grundrisse*

---

[14] See for example Autorenkollektiv (1973), and compare with for example Garaudy (1970).

[15] A more balanced discussion of Marx comes as part of the peace dividend after the end of the cold war.

[16] For the profound impact of Hegel and Feuerbach on Marx see for example Avineri (1971).

(1974, first published in 1939). Especially these writings show the inadequacy of a deterministic understanding of Marx' theory, with objective laws in history and a complete and unchanging world-outlook including nature.

This is not to deny some ambiguity in Marx (as may be found in the writings of most interesting social scientist). There are some passages in Marx' writings which are somewhat dogmatic (for example in his introduction to *The Critique of Political Economy*, see MEW 13, pp. 8–9), where Marx stipulates to have found the laws of motion in society, the insuperable evolution and the necessary phases of historical social formations, the absolute pauperization of the working class, and for example the rigid form of the basis-superstructure distinction. The dogmatic non-dialectical version is predominant in "Marxism-Leninism". This orthodox determinist interpretation was at least a perfect legitimization ideology in the former state socialist countries. The writings of Engels are somewhat in-between, at least his later writings like the *Dialectics of Nature* and his *Anti-Dühring* (both MEW 20) are leaning in the objectivist and non-dialectical direction. But it should also be mentioned that Engels edited the second and third volume of *Capital* and contributed the philosophical essay on *Ludwig Feuerbach and the End of Classical German Philosophy*, written in 1888 (MEW 21, 259 ff.) where he states that it was Marx who developed a materialistic social science concept and that his own contribution was more secondary (MEW 21, pp. 291–292, fn.).

In Marx' and Engels' works, five types of writings can be distinguished. The most important are their scientific contributions in the stricter sense like *Capital*. But even in these more abstract works, polemics and criticism are an integral part of the dialectical exercise. Next come the interpretations of important historical events such as the *coup d'état* in France, analyzed in Marx' *Eighteen Brumaire of Louis Bonaparte*, written in 1852 (MEW 8, pp. 118 ff.). A third category comprises more educational writings like *Wage, Price and Profit* (MEW 16, pp. 101 ff.), an introduction to *Capital*. Fourth are the hundreds of articles on recent political occurrences like elections in Germany.[17] Quite another, the fifth category is formed by the pamphlets where the mission of communism is argued for, like the *Communist Manifesto* (MEW 4, pp. 459 ff.) to support and explain the 1848 uprisings in Europe. Evidently, the pamphlets are more straightforward and exaggerated in the formulations. The interpretive comments on daily events are more tentative and preliminary as other more scientific contributions.[18]

In the following, we will first discuss Marx' critique of capitalist societies, his "materialist" approach and the fundamentals of his economic theory. We will then take neoclassical economics as it is usually presented in the textbooks as an example of his method of ideology critique. We will ask further how his vision of a good society looks like, and see in how far a critical discussion on Marxist lines takes place today and finally ask which relevancy Marx may have for us today despite all shortcomings of the Marxian approach.

---

[17] Marx and Engels (1969).

[18] This is no excuse of their historical short-term misinterpretations, often guided by the revolutionary hope that the proletarian revolution is just around the corner.

The Criticism of Capitalism and the *Praxis* Approach

Marx' central ideas, basic value commitments, and the roots of his philosophical–dialectical materialism can already be found in his final high-school examination texts. "Nature herself has determined the sphere of activity in which the animal should move … To man, too, the Deity gave a general aim, that of ennobling mankind and himself, but he left it to man to seek the means by which this aim can be achieved; he left it to him to choose the position in society most suited to him, from which he can best uplift himself and society … (O)ur relations in society have to some extent already begun to be established before we are in a position to determine them. Our physical constitution itself is often a threatening obstacle, and left no one scoff at its rights … Worth is that which most of all uplifts a man, which imparts a higher nobility to his actions and all his endeavours … But the chief guide which must direct us … is the welfare of mankind and our own perfection … (M)an's nature is so constituted that he can attain his own perfection only by working for the perfection, for the good, of his fellow men" (Marx 1975a, pp. 3–4 and 7–8, EB, pp. 591–594). It is surprising how exactly Marx delineates his research program as early as 1835. In another examination essay on religion, he states that people should liberate themselves from the bonds of superstition and try to perfect themselves and to achieve a harmonious moral attitude and supersede brute egotism (EB, p. 598).

In his doctoral dissertation on Epikur and Demokrit, written in 1840–1841, Marx tried to show against the prevailing scientific opinion that Epikur had a very different philosophy of nature compared with Demokrit, the materialist determinist. In Marx' view, Epikur was much superior to Demokrit in that he was a sceptical and non-dogmatic philosopher who did not try to develop an objective philosophy of nature. For Epikur, knowledge of nature had only the function to improve the ataraxy of human self-consciousness; against the principle of determination he put chance and accident, leaving room for human free choice which is influenced by human drives and desires and the so-being of the surrounding nature. The feeling of repulsion and dependency of something in us and out there leads to a dialectical insight of our relativity and relatedness and ends positively in a *Aufhebung* of the polar concepts and antinomy of human free will vs. objective determination (EB, pp. 257 ff.).

For Marx – and this is the genuine and simple materialist aspect of his thinking – the fundamental question confronting all human societies concerns what we must do to survive as living beings with an energy consuming body. To live, we must combine our intelligence and our energy (our work) with the basic "materials" of the world we find ourselves in, its water, soil and air. For Marx, nature is the organic body of man. We must work with what is at hand in order to make this today into tomorrow. The economic organization of society, or the "mode of production", is therefore for him the most powerful force in determining the structure of human society. Today this Marxian basic principle sounds more self-evident and insofar we can say that we are all more or less Marxists now. But at Marx' time even Feuerbach's critique of Hegel's idealism was only a theological one.

In his *Economic-Philosophical Manuscripts*, written in 1844, Marx develops an empirical–critical study of economics, including a critique of law, politics and morals. His starting point is the asymmetry of power and the antagonism between capital and not only labour but also society at large, which was already an important point in Smith's *Wealth of Nations*.[19] For Marx, it was a scandal that the existence of the worker is reduced to and treated as any other commodity in the market (EB, p. 471). The workers produce more and more riches but because they sell their labour power to the capitalists who own the means of production, make the decisions on the volume and composition of output and increase their bargaining position with the increase of their riches, the paradoxical fact results, that the more the workers produce, these products act like a strange external force against them. The workers are alienated from their product. They have not the feeling of being the associated producer of the riches. "Similarly, the division of labour makes him more and more one-sided and dependent, introducing competition from machines as well as from men ... (T)he worker has been reduced to a machine ... (T)he object that labour produces, its product, stands opposed to it as *something alien*, as a *power independent* of the producer ... (I)t is the *objectification* of labour" (Marx 1975a, pp. 286 and 324, EB, pp. 474 and 511). In these sentences, Marx develops his thesis of alienation, isolation, self-estrangement, powerlessness and the commodification of all processes in society as a result of the alienating effects of a money economy in which all things are measured in monetary terms and can be bought with money (music, poetry, sex,[20] etc.).

Like Smith, he sees a basic class antagonism between capital and labour (EB, p. 505), which has been forcefully described and generalized in the *Communist Manifesto*: "The history of all society up to now is the history of class struggles. Freeman and slave, patrician and plebeian, lord and serf, guild-master and journey-man, in short, oppressor and oppressed stood in continual conflict with one another, conducting on an unbroken, now hidden, now open struggle, a struggle that finished each time with a revolutionary transformation of society as a whole, or with the common ruin of the contending classes" (Marx 1996, pp. 1–2; MEW 4, p. 462). In distinction to Smith, Marx thought that this class antagonism must be superseded and that it is not an inevitable by-product of the division of labour as such which is outweighed by its advantages in terms of productivity gains in the interest of the final consumer. Marx thought that the antagonism is essentially due to the existence of private property. In his perspective, the early phase of the accumulation of capital is characterized by colonialism, plunder, piracy, the slave trade, enclosures, and other forms of exploitation and less by thrifty middle-class bourgeois who save and invest money.

Work and labour are constituent parts of man and his evolution as a conscious and civilized being. "The animal is immediately one with its life activity ... Man makes his life activity itself an object of his will and consciousness ... It is true that

---

[19] See for example Smith (1976, p. 277).

[20] See for example Marx' ironical but very true remarks in the EB (p. 564).

animals also produce. They build nests … But they produce only their own immediate needs …, while man freely confronts his own product … man also produces in accordance with the laws of beauty" (Marx 1975a, p. 329, EB, pp. 516–517). A constituent part of Marx' active or dialectical *praxis* materialism is his view that the modern class antagonism and the technological innovations due to the profit motive have a progressive and ameliorative function for the secular development of humanity because "movement inevitably triumphs over immobility, open and self-conscious baseness over hidden and unconscious baseness, *greed* over *self-indulgence*, the avowedly restless and versatile self-interest of *enlightenment* over the parochial, worldly-wise, artless lazy and deluded *self-interest of superstition*" (Marx 1975a, p. 340, EB, p. 528). The accumulation of capital realizes what the humanists dreamt of: the universality of human relationships, in capitalism couched as a Hegelian *List der Vernuft* (cunning of reason) by the globalization of production processes and the realization of the world market. "The need for a constantly expanding outlet for their products pursues the bourgeoisie over the whole world … In place of the old local and national self-sufficiency and isolation we have a universal commerce, a universal dependence of nations on one another. As in the production of material things, so also with intellectual production" (Marx 1996, pp. 4–5, MEW 4, pp. 465–466).

Communism is defined by Marx as the reintegration and self-realization of man, to transform social circumstances so that they can conform to man's nature. Communism is defined as realized naturalism and humanism (EB, p. 536), integrating man as a social and individual being. Marx' reasoning necessarily implies an anthropology. In his theses on Feuerbach, Marx states that man is the ensemble of his social relationships but this is not to say that any social formation is compatible with man's outfit. Marx' anthropology and vision of a good society has the three dimensions[21] of the true, the good and the beautiful. The first is that social life and economic reproduction should be organized and planned collectively and democratically. Marx comes very close to the ideal of undistorted discourse (Habermas 1985), that is, the ideal speech community in which all participants can influence the course of events and decisions with good arguments. Hierarchies, ideologies and ascribed privileges with respect to property rights do not count. Formal labour contracts with a residual claimant are incompatible with this ideal.

Marx' second ideal or dimension refers to the interaction among individuals beyond their communicative rationality in everyday life with their feelings, their hopes and fears, their dependence on a mortal body, etc. We should take our fellow-beings as rich, multidimensional, complex personalities in their unique totality, realized in friendship, love, thankfulness, sympathy, compassion and generosity. In capitalism, the basic social relationship is to see the fellow-being as a potential depersonalized customer who should pay as much as possible for the often-unnecessary goods we offer him (EB, p. 547). Marx criticizes here what Weber called banalization (*Versachlichung*) of interpersonal relationships in market or commercial societies.

---

[21] They have been elaborated more fully in for example Heller (1978, especially pp. 159 ff.).

"The reason for the impersonality of the market is its matter-of-factness, its orientation to the commodity and only to that. Where the market is allowed to follow its own autonomous tendencies, its participants do not look toward the persons of each other but only toward the commodity; there are no obligations of brotherliness ..., and none of those spontaneous human relations that are sustained by personal union" (Weber 1968, p. 636). Marx saw in this tendency a dehumanization of society which is often masked by the imposition of ideology or religion (for example the assumption of some spiritual being beyond the real life-world as a projection of self-alienation, see EB, p. 575).

The third dimension refers to the "duty" of self-perfection and ability to uncontaminated sensual pleasures, that is, the rich development of our capabilities, intellectual, sensual and otherwise. Therefore, Marx describes the communist utopia as the negation of the division of labour in which it is possible "to hunt in the morning, fish in the afternoon, rear cattle in the evening, criticize after dinner, just as I have a mind, without ever becoming hunter, fisherman, shepherd or critic" (Marx and Engels 1940, p. 22, MEW 3, p. 33). Later, in *Capital*, Marx explains realistically that the realm of freedom of self-expression begins where the realm of reproductive necessity ends (MEW 25, p. 828). But his consequence is not to give up his third ideal but to underline the importance of the productivity increases and technological progress to reduce the necessary work-hours to the possible minimum. This idea is contrary to the alleged Marxian productivity or growth mania. Marx points out that most people are reduced to some specific job or professional skills and that compensation takes place in the form of "mean, capricious, conceited, presumptuous" (Marx 1975a, p. 367, EB, p. 555) consumption and possession of goods.[22] Marx is concerned about "the sensuous appropriation of the human essence and human life ... [this] should not be understood only in the sense of direct, one-sided consumption, of possession, of having". Instead, non-possessive "human relations to the world - seeing, hearing, smelling, tasting, feeling, thinking, contemplating, sensing, wanting, acting, loving - in short, all the organs of his individuality" should be developed (Marx 1975a, p. 351, EB, p. 539). In capitalism, a different character ideal is warranted. "(Y)ou must not only be parsimonious in gratifying your immediate senses, such as eating, etc. You must also be chary of participating in affairs of general interest, showing sympathy and trust, etc., if you want to be economical and if you want to avoid being ruined by illusion" (Marx 1975a, p. 362, EB, p. 550).

Summarizing, we see that Marx tried to transcend the antinomy of idealism and materialism, that he saw basic antagonisms in all hitherto existing societies. He criticized capitalism and he had a pluralistic, three-dimensional anthropological ideal (some trade-offs between the realization of the ideals are conceivable). It should be noted that his critique of capitalism is absolutely independent of some hypotheses usually presented in combination with his ideas on commodification or alienation, notably the alleged law of absolute impoverishment, the law of the concentration of capital, etc. In the last part, we will ask in how far Marx' criticism

---

[22] Marx refers here to the distinction between the modes of having and being, see Fromm (1976).

is still relevant for today's globalizing capitalism and in how far Marx' communist credo was realist or not in the sense that a modern, complex, productive, world-wide economic system is conceivable without the bads exclusively ascribed by Marx to the existence of private property (and not for example from the division of labour, the extension of markets, the result of millions of exchange activities with unintended consequences).

We will not discuss the validity of Marx' description of historical formations or phases in detail because some major assumptions of Marx and Engels have proven to be very questionable. One problem is their stage theory where feudalism is antedated by slavery which is supposed to have been the dominant production system for example in classical Greece. It is said that slavery was the basis of the antique system of production (MEW 3, p. 23); today we know that slavery was much less important in antiquity than Marx and Engels stipulated.[23] It is also open to doubt if an Asian mode of production can be disentangled.[24] Theorists in the tradition of Marx are also sceptical if Marx is right in his description of the development of early capitalism where a phase with manufactures is followed by a phase with the factory system.[25] There is also disagreement among Marxists about the exact ways how the contradictions of an old system work out and let evolve a new system. For example, the transition from feudalism to capitalism and the accompanying contradictions can be explained by the inner contradictions of feudalism itself. But other Marxists stress the emergence of the money economy in mediaeval towns as the main driving force of changes.[26]

But leaving all differences aside, the canonical final version of the Marxist theory of history, economy and society was formulated by Marx in his Preface to the *Critique of Political Economy*, written in 1859, where he states that "(i)n the social production of their lives men enter into relations of production which correspond to a specific stage of development of their material productive forces. The totality of these relations of production forms the economic structure of society, the real basis from which rises a legal and political superstructure, and to which correspond specific forms of social consciousness. The mode of production of material life conditions the social, political and intellectual life-process generally" (Marx 1996, pp. 159–160, MEW 13, pp. 8–9).

Although this sounds more determinist than Marx' earlier formulations, he never gave the basis-superstructure model an ultimate mechanical interpretative twist in his later writings, leaving a certain ambiguity for his interpreters and different Marxist schools.[27] The basic intuition behind the basis-superstructure distinction

---

[23] Peukert (1994).

[24] Wittfogel (1957) and Dutschke (1974).

[25] *Capital*, vol. 1, Chap. 24. Sombart (1916, vol. 2, pp. 702 ff.) for example argued that historically it is more correct to say that manufactures and factories existed side by side from the inception and for a long time.

[26] Dobb (1967) and Sweezy (1957).

[27] An impressive, very critical but informed survey on the main Marxist schools and debates can be found in Kolakowski (1978–1979).

can hardly be doubted. For example, religious beliefs in hunter and gatherer societies stress the role of nature and people within it, which reflects the importance to survival of the natural environment. It is surprising how predictable elementary structural symbolic decisions are made in hunter-gatherer societies compared with those of agriculture (Vivelo 1978). He usually took into consideration the overdetermination[28] of all spheres and their relative autonomy, the role of historical accidents and the unevenness of structures, his favourite example being the difference between the low level of productivity and development of the productive forces in general in classical Greek antiquity on the one hand and their impressive and high-level philosophical and literary contributions which Marx admired and which are in some respects still the norm today[29] on the other hand (see also MEW 13, p. 640). Overdetermination means, that economic aspects of society influence the non-economic spheres, but the reverse holds true as well. So "society" is influenced by three non-economic forces, the natural (biological and chemical transformations), cultural (the construction of meaning by language, arts, music, religion, etc.) and the political (legislative, administrative and judicial control).

To characterize Marxism, it is more important to identify the conceptual space than to refer to the base-superstructure model: the central problematic was the appropriation of surplus value in industrial capitalism. It can be analyzed structurally or historically, and can be traced in the domains (?) of law, ecology, politics, money theory, etc. (Jameson 1996, pp. 19–21).

For Marx, a further dimension of alienation as an expression of private property, markets, money and the class structure in capitalism consists in – speaking terminology – specific, relative autonomous subsystems or value-spheres are differentiated (for example the state, the church) form the life world processes. They are directed by internal rules and normative behavioural codes of their own. In modern sociology, this relative autonomy is interpreted as a necessary development in the process of rationalization[30] and adaptive upgrading. For Marx, it is the expression of insulation against society due to power and class domination.[31] In so far the base-superstructure distinction is less an affirmative, general, positive scientific concept and more a critique of existing social structures. "Bourgeois" social scientists could accuse Marx of trying to eat the cake and have it, that is, – in the terminology of Tönnies (1991) – to ask for a highly developed *Gesellschaft*, and at the same time call for the supposed pleasant characteristics associated with small scale *Gemeinschaften*. They can argue that all modern attempts to combine *Gemeinschaft* and *Gesellschaft* (notably communism and national socialism) led to the greatest catastrophes of our closing century. On the other hand, it cannot be denied that Marx' alienation approach deals with real problems of estrangement in our society today, notwithstanding if they can be overcome or diminished or not.

---

[28] Althusser (1969).

[29] *Grundrisse* (1974/1857–1858, pp. 29–31).

[30] Weber (1968), Parsons (1966), and Luhmann (1998).

[31] See for example EB, p. 551, MEW 3, pp. 32–33.

The Driving Forces of Modern Societies[32] and the Labour Theory of Value[33]

Marx theoretical starting point in economics was the labour theory of value, developed by the classics, notably Smith and Ricardo (Smith held an ambiguous value theory[34]). According to Marx, the value of any good is determined by the amount of labour embodied in the productive process, measured in time; more complex, difficult or hard work can be measured as a multiple of the abstract unit "labour", defined as the average necessary social time to produce a unit of a specific output. This elementary so-called reduction problem had been analyzed only in passing by Marx. The exploitation of labour takes place in that the capitalists pay the workers only a subsistence wage even though the workers produced output that was worth much more than their wages. In contrast to Ricardo, Marx did not hold an absolute subsistence theory of wages, but a subsistence theory modified by the prevailing cultural standards and habits (of clothing, housing, etc.). This more realistic approach implies the problem of indeterminacy of the value determination (Burchardt 1997, pp. 141 ff.) because the exchange value of the commodity labour now depends on historical, moral and bargaining strength – that is, non-objective and in the strict sense non-economic – factors.

He also differed from Ricardo in that he made clear that the worker is paid the equivalent of his exchange value (*Tauschwert*, equivalent to the reproduction cost of the worker); the capitalist uses the use value of labour (*Gebrauchswert*) which may be much higher, if the worker for example produces his subsistence wage goods in 3 h but has to work 8 h. The exploitation is the difference between the three and the 8 h, between the use and the exchange value of labour. In fact, the regular employment contract in capitalism is incomplete in that it specifies the hours of labour but not the intensity or quality. Further, in the wage contract, workers are free agents in a legal sense but they more or less lack control over the working conditions and aims. It is also a fact, that "work" and not for example natural endowments are the basis of the wealth of nations and the national accounting systems actually split national income into the two broad categories of wage and profit incomes and for example in the US two third of the national income accrues to labour. In addition, the so-called analytical assessment of places of work (*analytische Arbeitsplatzbewertung*) tries to make qualitatively different exemptions of labour quantitatively comparable.

The difference between the value of labour and the wage rate is the surplus value (also defined as the excess of gross receipts over fixed and variable costs, see below)

---

[32] The explanation of the natural economic laws of capitalism was Marx' explicit aim in his preface to *Capital* (MEW 23, p. 15).

[33] For the discussion of the labour theory of value and other relevant topics of Marxian economics see King (1990).

[34] Smith also held a summing-up approach in which the three elements of income (labour, rent and profit) were added up; see Dobb (1973, Chap. 2).

which is the source of the capitalist's profits; also interest payments for capital borrowing are paid out of surplus value. For Marx, this is the exact dividing line in his definition of class between those who produce the surplus (the working class) and between those who get an income by appropriating the surplus (the capitalist class). Taking into consideration the fact that among these classes many divisions and different interest positions exist, and some people may belong to both classes (for example workers owning bonds or stocks), Marx nevertheless held that each class is a community united by common interests.

According to Marx, in the labour market an exchange of equivalents takes place. Surplus value is unpaid labour but it looks as if profit is paid for total capital outlays, and seems to come only into existence in the sphere of distribution (change of commodities into money). The worker stipulates that he is paid for 8 h work instead of three. In feudalism, exploitation is more evident because the landlord visibly takes away a percentage of the peasants annual product. Marx subsumed the aforementioned misconception under the heading of commodity fetishism. Marx' (and Ricardo's) labour theory of value implies that constant capital in the form of machinery and raw materials only transmit their values to the product and do not create additional value. They are produced by capitalists and they are sold to capitalists so that mark-ups cannot explain profits because one capitalist's income is another capitalist's outlay. Surplus value can be only increased by a lengthening of the workday or by raising the productivity of labour.

The question why competition does not erode any surplus in excess of labour cost has to do with the increasing organic composition of capital and the accompanying increase or at least reproduction of the industrial reserve army (unemployment). The organic composition is defined as the ratio between capital (machinery) and labour in the production process. Its increase means that firms are displacing workers with machines. In order for firms to compete in the market or to earn extra profits, they have to invest in new, sophisticated machinery. The resulting higher unemployment (downsizing) will keep wages down. But it also implies that the number of workers firms can exploit will decline. Thus a fall in the rate of profit will take place, defined as surplus value divided by constant (depreciation charges on fixed capital and inputs of raw materials) and variable (wages of production workers) capital. Although the rate of exploitation and the absolute amount of profits may increase, due to the higher organic composition, the rate of profit may fall because surplus value can only be generated out of labour, but the percentage of the variable capital decreases.

Capitalists dig their own graves because they not only produce the revolutionary reserve army of the unemployed, but they are also motivated to substitute capital for labour to earn higher profits. However, the higher degree of mechanization leads to a lower rate of profit. We note in passing that Marx assumed only a tendency of the falling rate because there exist some countervailing economic forces (MEW 25, Chap. 14). Marx' general message is that profits are not a necessary cost payment and that they will have no function in a nationalized economy. The capitalist profit system has distributive consequences in that it reduces the income of workers, leads to the concentration of economic power (as a consequence to fight the falling rate of profit), impedes the influence of workers and consumers on management decisions and endangers the maintenance of full employment by constantly reproducing the reserve army.

The essential function of Marx' economic theory is not to develop a new or better theory of the business cycle, a new monetary theory, or a better theory of the determination of relative or absolute single prices but to explain the economic long-run evolution in capitalist societies. Three further problems in Marx' exposition should be mentioned.[35] First, it is not really convincing that the fall in the rate of profit really takes place due to a changing organic composition because the capital-output ratios in Western manufacturing branches are sometimes rising and sometimes falling. This has to do with a fact neglected by Marx, that is, that capital-saving innovations may outweigh labour-saving innovations and that technical progress is not neutral in the sense that labour productivity rises as fast in the capital as in the consumer goods industries. The second critical remark refers to some of Marx' predictions like absolute or relative impoverishment, the extinction of the middle classes (see for example MEW 4, p. 469), the thesis of the increasing severity of the business cycles, the absolute increase in unemployment, the concentration of capital and elimination of small- and medium-size firms, the dramatic fall in the rate of profit, etc. All these elements are mentioned more than once and combine to form a dismal picture of capitalism. In the final section, we will think about the relevance of Marx' economic analysis, let us mention here that his picture of the dismal future of capitalism has proven to be wrong up till now.

A third elementary problem of Marx' analysis is the so-called transformation problem, dealing with the fact that relative prices cannot correspond to relative labour values if we do not assume arbitrarily that the capital–labour ratio is identical in every industry. Only if we make this assumption, it follows that the ratio of profits to wage charges is the same for every product and therefore commodity prices will differ only due to the fact that some employ more direct and indirect labour than others. The transformation problem arises because competition equalizes the rate of profit in all industries despite of the fact of different capital–labour ratios. This necessarily produces different rates of surplus value between industries. When there are different rates of surplus value, but only one rate of profit the problem arises how values are transformed into prices.

In the third volume of *Capital* (MEW 25, pp. 151 ff.), Marx explains that although values usually do not correspond to prices of production, the sum total of deviations of prices from values is equal to zero and total profits must equal total surplus value. He arrives at this conclusion by arguing that capitalists sell products at prices of production (which is the cost price, that is, outlays for fixed and variable capital) plus a uniform mark-up proportional to the total capital invested without regard to

---

[35] We will not discuss other important and controversial aspects of Marx' economic theory, for example his theory of absolute and differential rent and his schemes of reproduction; see for example Desai (1979).

the specific organic composition in different branches. The problem with Marx' solution is that it is not so easy simply to count the total direct and indirect labour embodied in commodities by looking because the input of indirect labour by the application of machines can only be counted as a value compounded over time at the ruling rate of profit.[36] The debate shows that we can solve the transformation problem mathematically but we get an indefinite number of solutions and the sum of the values can equal the sum of production prices or the sum of surplus value can equal the sum of profits but not both at the same time. Sraffa (1972) has shown that a theory of production prices can be developed without any reference to the labour theory of value (and that neoclassical theory has a comparable problem of logical inconsistency in that it tries to measure the value of capital without reference to the rate of profit).

Despite all this shortcomings and problems, Marx has shown how the transformation from money to commodities can be understood, how these split up in means of production and labour, how the production process transforms the inputs and how more and different commodities are sold and more money results and in how far this is a never-ending process because the motive for transactions is the constant increase of money and its transformation into capital. After Marx, a subjective value theory was developed with at least as much internal problems, so that the value theory was first dissipated in a superficial supply and demand frame and then totally abandoned.

Economics and Ideology: The Example of Neoclassical Vulgar Economics[37]

Mainly in *Capital* and *Theories on Surplus Value* (MEW 26), where Marx analyses mercantilism, physiocracy and the classics, he argues that mainstream economics became apologetic after the victory of capitalism around 1830. A major reproach was that mainstream economics commits what may be called the fallacy of misplaced reification. This means that the structure and analytical categories to describe capitalist societies are disembedded from their historical context; for example the laws of exchange in capitalism are taken as natural, eternal laws (*Grundrisse*, p. 579) and they are justified and legitimized by mainstream vulgar economists. "Vulgar economy actually does no more than interpret, systematise and defend in doctrinaire fashion the conception of the agents of bourgeois production who are

---

[36] We cannot elaborate this intricate problem further; see the review of the debate in Quaas (1992). The transformation problem has never been solved satisfactorily in the confines of a labour theory of value, but we do not know of any value theory without such central problems (for example how can we measure utility).

[37] See already the critical analysis of Myrdal (1953). The following remarks are based on Wolff and Resnick (1988) who analyze the neoclassical building blocks in detail. See also Roemer (1978).

entrapped in bourgeois production relations" (Marx and Engels 1998, p. 804, MEW 25, p. 825). Transaction cost analysis can be taken as an example because vertical integration and relaxed anti-trust laws are justified as economically reasonable[38] in the age of big corporations, and advertisement is rationalized as a means to reduce transaction costs. Vulgar economics also reproduces the dominant stereotype on human nature and reifies a specific logic of rational behaviour. Profit is rationalized by the idea of the residual claimant in team production, a tight prior equilibrium is assumed to celebrate the market. In the following part of the chapter, we will briefly demonstrate how the dominant neoclassical school looks like through Marx' lenses.[39]

Neoclassical theory puts owning, buying and selling, the sphere of distribution and exchange, in the centre of analysis. Goods and services are privately owned by individuals who seek to maximize their satisfaction by consuming goods and services (exchange increases use values). The theory is based on some assumptions concerning human nature, namely that humans as monads try to maximize their material self-interest by utilizing their owned resources and the available technology. Self-interest-maximizing individuals are the ultimate determining cause of economic activities and developments. The arena in which transactions occur is the market where individual private property owners meet voluntarily. They are free to sell and buy. Markets are the best institutions for economic organization.

In markets, every transaction is mutually beneficial, otherwise it would not take place. Ideally, market allocations lead to efficiency and optimality, so that the interference with law, custom and tradition is no good advice. Society is the collection of individuals in it and the aggregate effects of their wants and activities. Market capitalism and a profit-seeking society are efficient and best conform to human nature in that they best help to maximize overall wealth. The basic intuitions of neoclassical economics turn out to conform to the dominant ideology in the most developed capitalist society today which is the United States with private property and competitive markets as key institutions. The scientific value of neoclassical economics is – in a Marxist perspective – not the practical application to solve economic problems or to serve as a toolbox, but to legitimize the major class institutions and behavioural motivation codes and to constitute a cultural hegemony (Gramsci).

The question of what determines the values and prices of goods is answered with reference to markets where demand and supply (graphs) intersect. It is usually framed as a constrained-maximization problem, that is, individuals try to maximize pleasure under societal constraints. Individual wants and productive capabilities are the essentials that generate demand, supply, etc. The neoclassical chain of causality is by no means self-evident. There is for example a chain running from a change of tastes to a change in the supply of goods, but there is no causality running from a change in prices or incomes to an (endogenous) change in tastes or preferences. Other strong assumptions are made, mainly the ability of every individual to rank all

---

[38] See for example Williamson (1987).

[39] For this exercise we can take any modern mainstream textbook, for example Kreps (1990).

goods and services in a consistent manner now and in the future and that we always prefer more rather than less of any good (nonsatiation). Further, we try to take maximum advantage of our opportunities.

The supply of labour depends on our free will and our preference between real income and leisure, and the total labour hours demanded and the money wage rate are fixed in the labour market. Involuntary unemployment is impossible, a higher labour demand can be achieved by lower wage demands. The wage pays labour what it deserves according to its marginal productivity. This means that high incomes in a market economy depend on individual's preferences for work instead of leisure and on the relatively high objective marginal productivity of that labour. So the rich are rich for good reasons and the poor are poor for good reasons.

Interest on capital depends on capital's contribution to output, exactly like the real reward paid to labour depends on labour's contribution to output. This rules out the possibility that any owner may receive less or more then his resources added to produce the outputs. Each individual gets back from society what it contributed. In market economies fairness rules instead of exploitation. Everybody is free to become a profit receiver, it only depends on his ability and willingness to work and to forfeit consumption instead of saving. The existence of public goods, externalities and other market imperfections like the inability of human beings to foresee the future excluded, and well-shaped indifference curves assumed, neoclassical economics demonstrates with the two Pareto welfare criteria that maximum profits are consistent with and even necessary to achieve maximal happiness for individualized consumers.

For Marx, neoclassical economics would primarily reflect the dominant self-understanding of modern capitalist societies to justify for example why 10% of the population own 90% of all stocks in the United States. He would not have been surprised that some heroic assumptions are necessary to reach the adequate conclusions. In his perspective, the formalization of economics by mathematics has the function to disguise ideological content and let it look value-neutral and scientific. For its elementary ideological function, the practical inapplicability of neoclassical armchair economics is no impediment at all.

Marx' View of a Good Society

Marx and Engels did not exclude that a communist revolution will first take place in underdeveloped countries like Russia (MEW 19, pp. 243 and 296). But they thought that the countries with the most advanced capitalist structures and highest developed (European) civilizations would very probably undergo the communist revolution earlier. For example, in1848, they held that the democratic revolution in Germany is only the prelude to the ultimate revolution of the proletariat (MEW 4, p. 493). In general, their picture of the desired future society is very fragmentary. This has to do with Marx' opinion that the working class has "no ideals to realise, but to set free the elements of the new society with which old collapsing bourgeois society itself is pregnant" (Marx 1996, p. 188, MEW 17, p. 343). Marx also denied describing the new society in detail because he believed in open historical alternatives which should not be foreclosed; it was his epistemological premise that history is also essentially determined by specific conditions which cannot be predicted in advance. He also wanted to distinguish himself from the utopian socialists who depicted detailed fantasies.

But one constituent element of the new society Marx and Engels talked about is the abolition and transcendence of the state in the longer run (for example, Bakunin held that the volitional abolition of the state should be the first and foremost activity of the more conspirational movement of the anarchists). Their prime positive example was the Commune in Paris in 1871, which was doomed to fail because of its local character and middle-class bias, but it nevertheless foreshadowed some principles of the new society like the abolition of the police and army, the direct election and possibility of permanent dismissal of the public servants and representatives; their average worker salaries, etc. (MEW 17, p. 596). Marx was in favour of universal suffrage but he did not support a parliamentarian system because the (hypothetical) balance of powers would lead to the necessary alienation of the parliamentary legislative power from the decision-making executive power.

For Marx the transcendence of the state as a separate body was essential because the state no longer will be "a separate entity, beside and outside civil society; ... it is nothing more than the form of organization which the bourgeois necessarily adopt both for internal and external purposes, for the mutual guarantee of their property and interests" (Marx and Engels 1940, p. 59, MEW 3, p. 62). In Marx' view, society should call back the differentiated state organs. But in the transition period between capitalism and communism the so-called "revolutionary dictatorship of the proletariat" was held necessary (MEW 19, p. 28). Although Marx always expressed this phrase in writings which were not primarily planned to be published, this was undoubtedly a formulation which legitimized the authoritarian and totalitarian concepts of the role of the revolutionary party and the structure of state and society by Lenin and Stalin in the Soviet Union.[40]

Even if we grant that a social structure which resembled more a military camp than a free society was necessary due to external pressures (this was also Trotsky's argument for the military as a model for the society in transition), it cannot be denied that the brutal extinction of the wealthier peasants and the concentration camps of the Gulag (Solzenicyn 1974) could be legitimized by the phrase of the dictatorship and the change from dialectical materialism to a more dogmatic, masterminded total world-view.[41]

---

[40] In his detailed and fair analysis of Marx' thought, White shows in how far "the ground [for orthodox dialectical materialism in theory and praxis] had been prepared by Marx himself" (1996, p. 366). In Chap. 2, he highlights the romantic heritage in Marx which may explain much of his vision of society in the future.

[41] Take the following sentence of the *Communist Manifesto* as an example: "The law, morality, religion, are for him so many bourgeois prejudices that hide just as many bourgeois interests" (Marx 1996, p. 11, MEW 4, p. 472). It may also be mentioned that the dialectical method was conducive as a diabolic instrument to justify inhuman activities. Unfortunately, Marx never wrote his promised book on method.

But it may also be noticed that even Engels who is to a certain degree responsible for the dogmatic materialist version noticed in his critique of the party program of the social democrats that the democratic republic with universal suffrage is the specific form of the dictatorship (MEW 22, p. 235). On the other hand, in the *Communist Manifesto* the fight for democracy is described as follows: "The proletariat will use its political power to strip all capital from the bourgeoisie piece by piece, to centralise all instruments of production in the hands of the state, that is, the proletariat organised as ruling class ... Political power in its true sense is the organised power of one class for oppressing another" (Marx 1996, pp. 19–20, MEW 4, p. 481–482). This sounds exactly like the authoritarian absolutist state type socialism in Russia after 1918. In their program for the transition period, Marx and Engels proclaimed as practical immediate policies strong progressive taxes, the nationalization of credit and transport, the abolition of all rights of inheritance, the abolition of child labour and free education. In this context, it is remarkable that they also mention a general coercion for everybody to work and the implementation of "industrial armies", especially in agriculture (MEW 4, p. 481). Their sophisticated plan for action and legislation did not include the nationalization of industry as such. In their program of the communist party in Germany, they added that every German over 21 years should be eligible and elect the representative body of the democratic republic (MEW 5, pp. 3–5).

After the transition phase, all production will be in the hands of the "associated producers" (MEW 4, p. 482), and public power will loose its political character. In the first (socialist) phase, every worker gets a wage exactly equal to the product of his labour (plus the necessary deductions, see MEW 19, p. 20). The principle is "to each according to his work". This is unjust insofar as one worker has to invest more effort to produce the social average product, or he has a family to feed, etc. In the later phase, after the overcoming of the "birth-marks of the old society", in the higher phase of communism, "society can inscribe on its banner: from each according to his abilities, to each according to his needs" (Marx 1996, p. 215, MEW 19, p. 21). In this later phase, the state will be transformed from an institution superimposed on society to one which is subordinated to society (MEW 19, p. 27), as Marx reiterates further in his critique of the Gotha program of the social-democrats in 1875. He often criticized the reformism of social-democracy. One point of disagreement refers to the question evolution or revolution and the necessity of the use of physical power, because in Marx' view the working class has to fight for its right of emancipation on the battlefield (MEW 17, p. 433).

It should be noted, however, that he did not proclaim a "law" that the transition from capitalism to socialism could not be achieved without physical power and some violence, especially where the working-class power through universal suffrage in England and the use of the collectivist Mir in Russia as an institution capable of a direct socialist transformation are concerned. He stated for example that "it is possible that the struggle between the workers and the capitalists will be less terrible and less bloody than the struggle between the feudal lords and the bourgeoisie in England and France. Let us hope so" (MEW 16, p. 204). For Marx, joint stock companies are the negation and transformation of the capitalist mode of production and a partial socialization of investment which breaks out of the control of private property (see for example MEW 25, pp. 454–456). Engels seems to have adopted a wholly evolutionary orientation in his later years. In his remarks to the Erfurt program of the social-democrats, he sees the possibility of a peaceful evolution in democratic republics like France and the USA and monarchies like England (MEW 22, pp. 235–236). But it is interesting to note that he did not mention Germany. For Marx and Engels, the most important conditions of success were that the objective conditions were ripe for a basic transformation and that the consciousness of the involved population undergoes a revolutionary qualitative change.

But let us return to their description of communism. We can observe a strong eschatological tendency in Marx' description of communism which is at odds with his more open dialectical reasoning. This can be interpreted as a secularized experience of the Judeo-Christian tradition. This eschatological current is already obvious in his early writings.[42] We already mentioned that Marx hoped that the division of labour and its alienation would disappear in communism. The power of the economic forces of supply and demand will be annulled because of reasonable associative planning, in harmony with nature or at least as its master, with an affluence of goods and a reduced or least fixed working day,[43] working conditions which let human's capabilities flourish, and all this on a global scale (for example MEW 3, pp. 33–35, and MEW 25, p. 828).

Besides its vagueness, a central problem with Marx' vision is the utopian character and the hypothesis that the dimensions of alienation have only to do with the private ownership of the means of production and are not, as mentioned, to a certain degree necessary side-effects of the hierarchical organization of labour (not only) in factories and of industrialization and urbanization; and that they depend also on the simple fact that numbers matter. The larger the involved number of persons, the higher is necessarily the impotence of the single individual even if a democratic decision-making process is envisioned. The long-lasting debate on self-owned firms also shows that the incentive and control problems do not easily disappear. Nove (1995) has demonstrated how chaotic the planning process in Russia really was and the Austrian argument, that in the planning process elementary informations get necessarily lost because they are bound to space and time, cannot easily be dismissed. It is also questionable if policy failures and rent-seeking activities will simply vanish with the abolition of the central classes.

At the moment, it seems that human beings in large-scale societies do not identify with Aristotle's anthropological dictum of man as a *zoon politicon*, but very often come surprisingly close to the self-interested consumer of neoclassical theory with a high degree of disinterest in politics. We can also ask if the problem of power, defined here as the peaceful distribution of scarce resources by the institutional–legal

---

[42] See for example the passages on private property and communism in the *Economic-Philosophical Manuscripts* (EB, pp. 533 ff.).

[43] Marx was relatively sure that the increase in future wants could be compensated by technological innovations.

nexus will disappear with the abolition of classes. There are also many more cleavages between humans (local, race, national) which may nurture a qualified social identity but not a universal feeling of belonging and sameness. A prime example is the quick change of opinion and support of the German social-democracy to the credits to pay the costs of World War I in 1914 and the nationalist enthusiasm of the working class to go to war after the rhetoric of international solidarity within the frame of the second International. Marx and Engels seem to have underestimated the strong forces which impede the solidarity of people who are situated in the same living or class conditions and some deep-seated psychological-anthropological constants. It seems as if the Veblenian diagnosis of emulation and status rivalry[44] based on envy corresponds much more to the real behavioural traits of the present day and yesterday Johnes's than Marx' class-conscious revolutionaries who have nothing to lose but their (now more golden?) chains.

History shows that human beings "as men and women, as father and mother, that is, as holders of specific sexual and familial roles very often behave less rational and global, future minded and open to experiments … as Marx and Engels assumed and hoped. … [It] is conspicuous, that they [human beings] have acted and act more traditional, and oriented to the past, more emotional, irrational and aggressive, but also more servile … [It is a fact] that the dependent always turns against his master and exploiter. The frustration he experiences topples over the outsider or also in the oppression of the even more weak … History is full of examples where the aggression is directed against the foreigner and the national enemy, against the ideological or religious enemy, but also against neighbours, colleagues, and equals, but finally also against outsiders and 'outcasts' [in German] as ideal scapegoats. In so far they help to stabilize power relationships" (Flechtheim 1978, pp. 43–44, and 70; our translation).

As mentioned, we can also question if Marx did not want too much in that he disregarded trade-offs, for example between the social integrity of society and the full development of every individual on the one hand and a high standard of technical efficiency and productivity on the other hand. The latter may necessitate affective neutrality, patent monopoly rents and the dangers of unemployment and disappearance from the market to keep the system running at pace. We can also ask if it is not an illusion to demand a first centralized stage called socialism with the dictatorship of the proletariat and then assume that this is a good precondition for the disappearance of all power and the dissolution in the friendly global community of the associated producers in the second phase. It is hard to see how we can reconcile a rationally planned international socialist or communist economic system with millions of people in the loosely organized, non-hierarchical social community of the associated producers. There is a tension in Marx between his urge for economic planning on the one hand and his sympathy with a decentralized-democratic political polis like process on the other hand.

---

[44] See Veblen (1995) and Frank (1985).

As we saw, Marx was also against a parliamentarian division of powers in the tradition of Montesquieu. Today we know a little bit more about the problems of direct unmediated democracy. One problem of a Commune or council system is the high fragility of such a system. If a minority coordinates its voting behaviour it can easily happen that the minority enforces decisions which do not represent the will of the majority, like the Bolsheviks in 1918 in Russia. If there exists only one social political hierarchy pillar, the seduction of unlimited power is immense as the history of the former communist countries demonstrates; not the abolition of classes but the reproduction of an emerging new class nurtured by state power as in the former *German Democratic Republic* was the natural drift of history. In a certain sense, this proves Marx' assumptions on the role and importance of class interests, be this in feudalism, capitalism and we have to add: socialism.

We have learned all these lessons in the short twentieth century[45] and we march somewhat disillusioned into the next century. The utopian idealism and totalitarianism is overcome, but the question remains if our present disenchantment is the last word after overconfidence. Let us ask therefore in a more balanced mood in how far Marx could still be relevant today. What's left?

Conclusion: Recent Contributions and Relevance of Marxist Thought Today

One line of development of Marxist thought naturally depended on the Russian revolution in 1917 and the transition from the civil war to a superpower. Lenin (1870–1924) was the main theorist in this period. This more dogmatic-deterministic interpretation of Marx found its culmination in Stalin's (and in China in Mao Tse Tung's) writings. Besides the codification of dogmatic Marxism,[46] there were also relevant debates on how to organize the society and economy in a new socialist country, how should for example the financial, human and natural resources be invested and divided among consumption and investment, etc.[47]

Another debate took place in the confines and strategies of European social democracy. In Germany, it was a long way from voluntaristic Marxism under prohibition to Kautsky's and later Bernstein's revisionism,[48] to the Godesberger program in the 1950s and diverse third ways at present.

---

[45] See the "century report" by the realistically enlightened Marxist Hobsbawm (1995).

[46] As mentioned, the dogmatic aspect is already an undercurrent in Marx himself. It cannot be denied that dogmatic Marxism – besides the underdevelopment of Russia and the hostile environment after the revolution – is essentially responsible for the atrocities in the former communist countries. See Amalrik (1970) and Courtois (1998), the literary account by Köstler (1941), and the recent description of life under and after state communism by Bednarz (1998).

[47] See the reconstruction of the debates and practical policies pursued in Elleinstein (1975), for the mostly unknown internal communist but heterodox debates see Wolter (1976).

[48] As one of the examples for a further theoretical development see Hilderding (1947).

There was a strong influence of Marxism on the decolonization policies in the 1960s and 1970s in Asia, Africa, and Latin America where for example the peaceful socialist policy by Allende in Chile was suppressed by national and American military forces. The influence of Marxism on Christian thought was felt in for example South Africa and Roman Catholicism in South America (the theology of liberation by archbishop Camarra). Marxism influenced the student's uprisings in 1968 and the feminist, antiracism, the peace and the environmental movements.[49]

Out of these movements and the experience with the state communist countries (which amounted to at least one third of the world population in the 1970s and 1980s) developed what may be called intellectual Marxism which went beyond the classical critique of capitalism. It includes the reception of Freudian psychoanalysis,[50] the changing role of the state in capitalism,[51] the history of the worker's movement,[52] a critical analysis of law,[53] the critique of the commodity aesthetics and ideology in capitalism,[54] the reception of Marxism in critical American institutionalism in the tradition of Veblen and Commons,[55] etc.

One major strand of critical Marxism is the negative dialectics of the Frankfurt critical school, originally developed by Horkheimer and Adorno,[56] where all eschatological dreams have been abandoned. Their most relevant disciple today is Habermas who after the linguistic turn supplemented the Marxian concept of labour as an elementary category of human self-expression by the autonomous dimension of communicative interaction[57] which should not be distorted.

It is not possible to review critical-intellectual Marxism in detail here.[58] Instead, let us ask briefly if a reformulated Marxism should have a place in the universe of science and public discourse today. Paradoxically, with the demise of socialism and the rise of capitalism as the dominating universal and globalizing system,[59] the Marx' way of looking at economy and society from an economic interest and

---

[49] It is a fact that almost all leading members of the German green party who have official posts now are former members of diverse Marxist groups.

[50] Reich (1945) and Marcuse (1966).

[51] Offe (1996).

[52] Thompson (1997), Hobsbawm and to a certain degree the research of the French "Annales" school.

[53] Abendroth (1967).

[54] Haug (1993).

[55] Knoedler et al. (1999).

[56] Horkheimer and Adorno (1999); see also Jay (1996) and Demirovic (1999).

[57] Habermas (1985).

[58] See for example Castoriades (1997).

[59] We can briefly define globalization by the emergence of supertrader nations, the slicing up of the value chains and the internationalization of capital flows. For a comprehensive analysis see Axelrod (1995) and Dicken (1992).

contradiction of interests and exploitation/alienation paradigm[60] may play a role in emphasizing the global and never-ending character of capital accumulation and direct our attention to the price of its normless dynamism in the economic, political, social, cultural, ecological,[61] and anthropological dimensions.[62]

In the economic dimension, let us only briefly mention the constant reproduction of a rising international reserve army,[63] the problem of increasing inequality between nations[64] and in the confines of nations,[65] the dysfunctional aspects of speculation over enterprise and the public policy in favour not of Main but of Wall Street,[66] the feeling of many people to life in an unjust and irrational society where the increase of unemployment is greeted with an increase in stock prices. Further, an economic system in which the link between effort and reward became relatively loose (winner-takes-all problem). The increase of internationally operating few oligopolies in major branches of industry,[67] the increasing practice of firms to lengthen the work-day without a monetary compensation due to the dangers to become unemployed in the age of downsizing,[68] and the international discrepancy between supply and demand and the resulting overaccumulation of capital for example in the car industry, may be taken as negative examples of global capitalism today from a Marxian perspective.

In the political sphere, the more and more subordinate role of the state to short-run business interests and the state's inability to confiscate sufficient taxes due to the mobility of capital deserves critical recognition.[69] The subjugation of all life

---

[60] An account of globalism in a non-dogmatic Marxian perspective, emphasizing the economic, cultural, social and ecological limits of globalization is given by Altvater and Mahnkopf (1997); see also Hirst and Thompson (1996) with a Marxist bias. For a more general critical perspective see Mander and Goldsmith (1997). Bourdieu et al. (1998) offer many life histories on the negative impacts of globalization on individual destinies.

[61] On Marx' concept of nature see Schmidt (1993).

[62] The broad reception of books like the globalization trap by Martin and Schumann (1989) and Forrester's (1997) terror of the economy demonstrate that many people in Europe are very sceptical about the fundamental changes taking place.

[63] In Europe, unemployment is high and wage deterioration is not so strong. In the US unemployment is much lower but wages are stagnating or sinking.

[64] See the yearly *United Nations Development Reports*; in the three composite dimensions of income, health and education one third of all countries are falling behind, some of them also in absolute terms.

[65] Reich (1991) argues that a cleavage in income and living chances between the 20% working in the symbolic-analytical realm and the 80% performing routine activities will take place and lead to major social disruptions if not counterbalanced by public policy.

[66] See the intricate analysis of Henwood (1997), who shows how Marxist ideas can inspire research if applied in a non-dogmatic way.

[67] Like the car, oil, banking, and insurance industries, see the data collection by Sherman (1996).

[68] In for example Germany behind the official social market regulative institutions like collective agreements there is a silent revolution to erode classical labour contracts and insurance. Among these innovations, part time labour without insurance, fictitious working independence, the lengthening of the time of probation etc. become usual.

[69] See the profound essay by Narr and Schubert (1994) who argue that the reconciliation between freedom, solidarity and material well-being becomes more and more problematic.

processes to the profit motive and commodification, the dissolution of social bonds,[70] the downgrading or international McDonaldization of culture,[71] the visible shrinking of high culture (literature, theatres, cultural foreign self-presentation like the Goethe-Institutes in Germany), and the commercialization and banalization of the mass media (especially TV),[72] can be interpreted as the increase in the three dimensions of alienation worked out by Marx.[73] It is the final price of commercialized capitalism in which the logic of profit-maximization and commodification invades all spheres of society[74] and transforms the individual character[75] into what intellectual-critical Marxists in the Hegelian tradition called an unhappy consciousness.

All this is not to say that Marx' predictions of the future of capitalism were correct. He often thought that socialism is a simple necessity in the not too distant future, and that the class struggle will lead to revolution and not to an integration of the working class into the capitalist system. He underrated the innovative dynamism of capitalist innovations to counteract the presumed fall in the rate of profit. He thought that the population in the capitalist centre would continue to increase. He did not see the population explosion in the so-called underdeveloped countries and he did (and maybe could) not foresee the dramatic global degradation of the environment.

The most radical consequence of the present situation is drawn in a Marxist perspective by Sarkar (1999) who argues that humanity's basic choices are universal capitalism and ecological disaster or what he calls eco-socialism, characterized by the values of equality, co-operation and solidarity. For him, the former socialist countries (which primarily tried to catch up economically) and capitalism are variants of industrialism and "economism", that is, continuous growth is considered possible and desirable and material affluence is held necessary for a good life. An opinion, we also found in Marx. For Sarkar, socialism today is more a question of human relations and moral growth and less of economic development. Sarkar argues that today the human specie has to take care of its survival facing the degradation of nature and the biosphere. Therefore, a sustainable socialism has to be combined with a limit to growth paradigm. Presently, the forces of production are not developed

---

[70] See the critical report on the disappearance of the civil spirit in America due to the increase in the pursuit of egoistic material self-interest by Bellah et al. (1996).

[71] The dialectical relationship between a commercial world culture and reacting defensive fundamentalism is shown in Barber (1996).

[72] The influence and policies of the internationally operating dream factories in the entertainment sector are discussed in Barnet (1994).

[73] The (self-)alienating character of modern life and behaviour is for example demonstrated in Reheis (1996).

[74] In the debate on ethics this has been worked out by Walzer (1989).

[75] Sennett (1998) argues that a socially dysfunctional corrosion of character and not the ascent of the children of freedom (U. Beck) takes place in the modern, flexible, networking economies because what is good behaviour in the economy ("flexibility") turns out to be a catastrophe in social relationships ("unreliability"). This makes people unhappy and they try to play multiple roles as a behavioural response. But this provokes behavioural and motivational double standards Marx already castigated in his *Economic-Philosophical Manuscripts* 150 years ago.

enough but due to ecological restraints they are too developed. An ecological policy in capitalism is doomed to fail because Marx was right that capitalism is essentially combined with the accumulation and extension of capital and the motivational forces of greed, status emulation and profit.

Eco-socialism means first contraction of the level of production and then a low-level steady state economy with a policy of simplified needs, the ecological regulation by a world economic trade council, de-centralized production structures (also due to the increased prices for transportation), and labour-intensive technologies. A one-world perspective, the active creation of a new vision of global civilization which may include a non-theistic spirituality is warranted in Sarkar's view in which socialism means first of all a change in values. Practically it means the planned and ordered retreat of the overdeveloped forces of production, the contraction of the industrial economies, in terms of GDP, energy consumption, etc. per head in the developed countries and a stop of population growth in countries with a growing population. In contrast to Marx' vision which depended on the much lower development of the means of production at his time, this vision would entail the acceptance of a lower standard of living (but not necessarily of happiness) than today which can be better accepted if the sacrifices are borne proportionately, which means a policy of radical equality.

The eschatological component of Marx and his promise to ameliorate all dimensions of human life[76] which disregards some societal trade-offs are less apparent in Sarkar's reformulation. The problem we face today may be that if we are honest and accept what we all know about world-wide ecological degradation and the catastrophe ahead in the presence of the rapid development in the newly industrializing countries like China with billions of ambitious consumers we understand the possible urgency of Sarkar's position. On the other hand, we know today that the attempt to plan an economy on a large scale may lead to an ultra-authoritarian political system, in this case an eco-dictatorship.

References

Abendroth W (1967) Antagonistische Gesellschaft und politische Demokratie. Luchterhand, Neuwied
Althusser L (1969) For Marx. Allen Lane, London
Altvater E, Mahnkopf B (1997) Grenzen der Globalisierung. Westfälisches Dampfboot, Münster
Amalrik A (1970) Voyage involontaire en Sibérie. Gallimard, Paris
Autorenkollektiv (1973) Einführung in den dialektischen und historischen Materialismus. Verlag marxistische Blätter, Frankfurt
Avineri S (1968) The social and political thought of Karl Marx. Cambridge University Press, Cambridge
Axelrod RM (1995) Die Evolution der Kooperation. 3rd. edn. Munich Oldenbourg
Barber B (1996) Jihad vs. McWorld. New York Ballentine Books
Barnet RJ (1994) Global dreams. Simon and Schuster, New York

---

[76] The humanization of human relations, the de-differentiation of the subsystems, technological and GDP growth, etc.

Bednarz K (1998) Ballade vom Baikalsee: Begegnungen mit Menschen und Landschaften. Europa Verlag, München

Bellah RN et al (1996) Habits of the heart. University of California Press, Berkeley

Berlin I (1939) Karl Marx: his life and environment. Oxford University Press, Oxford

Blaug M (1997) Economic theory in retrospect, 5th edn. Cambridge University Press, Cambridge

Bourdieu P et al (1998) Das Elend der Welt, 2nd edn. Universitätsverlag Konstanz, Konstanz

Burchardt M (1997) Marxistische Wirtschaftstheorie. Oldenbourg, München

Castoriades C (1997) The Castoriades reader. In: Curtis DA (ed) Blackwell, Oxford

Courtois S (1998) Das Schwarzbuch des Kommunismus. Piper, Munich

Demirovic A (1999) Der nonkonformistische Intellektuelle: Die Entwicklung der Kritischen Theorie zur Frankfurter Schule. Suhrkamp, Frankfurt

Desai M (1979) Marxian economics. Basil Blackwell, Oxford

Dicken P (1992) Global shift. Chapman, London

Djilas M (1996) The new class: an analysis of the communist system. Unwin Books, London

Dobb MH (1967) Studies in the development of capitalism. International Publishers, New York

Dobb M (1973) Theories of value and distribution since Adam Smith. Cambridge University Press, Cambridge

Dutschke R (1974) Versuch, Lenin auf die Füße zu stellen. Wagenbach, Berlin

Elleinstein J (1975) L'U.R.S.S., 4 vols. Editions Sociales, Paris

Flechtheim OK (1978) Von Marx bis Kolakowski. Europäische Verlagsanstalt, Köln

Forrester V (1997) The economic horror. Continental Books, Glendale

Frank RH (1985) Choosing the right pond. Oxford University Press, Oxford

Fromm E (1961) Marx's concept of man. F. Ungar, New York

Fromm E (1976) To have or to be? Harper and Row, New York

Garaudy R (1970) Marxism in the twentieth century. Scribner, New York

Habermas J (1985) The theory of communicative action. Beacon Press, Boston

Haug WF (1993) Elemente einer Theorie des Ideologischen. Argument-Verlag, Hamburg

Heilbroner RL (1989) The worldly philosophers, 6th edn. Touchstone, New York

Heller A (1978) Philosophie des linken Radikalismus. VSA-Verlag, Hamburg

Henwood D (1997) Wall street. Verso, London

Hilderding R (1947) Das Finanzkapital. Dietz, Berlin

Hirst P, Thompson G (1996) Globalisation in question. Polity Press, Cambridge

Hobsbawm E (1995) Age of extremes. Joseph, London

Honneth A (1999) Aus der Werkstatt eines kritischen Gelehrten: Die Marx-Engels-Ausgabe wird im Akademie-Verlag fortgesetzt, Frankfurter Rundschau, 13 March 1999, p ZB 3

Horkheimer M, Adorno TW (1999) Dialectics of enlightenment. Verso, London

Jameson F (1996) Actually existing Marxism. In: Makdisi S et al (eds) Marxism beyond Marxism. Routledge, New York, pp 14–54

Jay M (1996) The dialectical imagination. University of California Press, Berkeley

King JE (ed) (1990) Marxian economics, 3 vols. Edward Elgar, Aldershot

Knoedler J et al (1999) Essays in political economy: an introduction to Marx, Veblen, Keynes. Bucknell, Mimeo

Kolakowski L (1978–1979) Die Hauptströmungen des Marxismus, 3 vols. Piper, Munich

Köstler A (1941) Darkness at noon. Cape, London

Kreps DM (1990) A course in microeconomic theory. Princeton University Press, Princeton

Luhmann N (1998) Observations on modernity. Stanford University Press, Stanford

Mander J, Goldsmith E (eds) (1997) The case against the global economy. San Francisco Sierra Club Books

Marcuse H (1966) One dimensional man. Beacon Press, Boston

Martin H-P, Schumann H (1989) Die Globalisierungsfalle. Rowohlt, Reinbek

Marx K, Engels F (1940) The German ideology, Parts I and III, The Marxist-Leninist Library. Western Printing Services, Bristol

Marx K (1974) Grundrisse. Dietz Verlag, Berlin

Marx K (1975a) Reflections of a young man on the choice of a profession. In: Marx K, Engels F
    (eds) Collected works, vol 1. International Publishers, New York, pp 3–9
Marx K (1996) Later political writings. In: Carver T (ed) Cambridge University Press,
    Cambridge
Marx K, Engels F (1969) Deutsche Geschichte im 19. In: Fetscher I (ed) Jahrhundert. Fischer,
    Frankurt
Marx K, Engels F (1974 ff.) Marx-Engels-Werke (MEW). Dietz Verlag, Berlin
Marx, K, Engels F (1998), "Capital," vol. 3, Karl Marx and Frederick Engels. Collected works,
    vol. 37. International Publishers, New York
Mauke M (1971) Die Klassentheorie von Marx und Engels. Europäische Verlagsanstalt,
    Frankfurt
McLellan D (1973) Karl Marx: his life and thought. McMillan, London
Myrdal G (1953) The political element in the development of economic theory. Routledge,
    London
Narr W-D, Schubert A (1994) Weltökonomie: Die Misere der Politik. Suhrkamp, Frankfurt
Nove A (1995) An economic history of the U.S.S.R. Penguin Viking, New York
Offe C (1996) Modernity and the state. Polity Press, Cambridge
Parsons T (1966) Societies. Prentice-Hall, Englewood Cliffs
Peukert H (1994) Das klassische griechische Wirtschaftssystem und der Wirtschaftsstil unter
    besonderer Berücksichtigung des Geld- und Bankwesens. Schriftenreihe des Forschungsprojekts
    Wirtschaftssysteme im historischen Vergleich, Frankfurt
Quaas F (1992) Das Transformationsproblem. Metropolis, Marburg
Raddatz FJ (1975) Karl Marx: Der Mensch und seine Lehre. Heyne, Munich
Reheis F (1996) Die Kreativität der Langsamkeit. Wissenschaftliche Buchgesellschaft, Darmstadt
Reich W (1945) Character analysis. Organe International Press, New York
Reich R (1991) The work of nations. Knopf, New York
Roemer JE (1978) Neoclassicism, Marxism, and collective action. J Econ Issues 12:147–161
Rutherford M (1996) Institutions in economics: the old and the new institutionalism. Camnbridge
    University Press, Cambridge
Sarkar S (1999) Eco-socialism or eco-capitalism. Zed Books, London
Schmidt A (1993) Der Begriff der Natur in der Lehre von Marx, 4th edn. Europäische Verlagsanstalt,
    Hamburg
Sennett R (1998) Der flexible Mensch. Berlin-Verlag, Berlin
Sherman HC (1996) Globalisierung: Transnationale Unternehmen auf dem Vormarsch. Ifo-
    Schnelldienst 49:3–13
Smith A (1976) The wealth of nations. University of Chicago Press, Chicago
Solzenicyn AI (1974) The Gulag archipelago. Harvill Press, London
Sombart W (1916, 1927) Der moderne Kapitalismus, 3 vols. Duncker and Humblot, Munich
Sraffa P (1972) Production of commodities by means of commodities. Cambridge University
    Press, Cambridge
Sweezy PM (1957) The transition from feudalism to capitalism. People's Book House, Patna
Thompson EP (1997) The romantics. Merlin Press, Suffolk
Tönnies F (1991) Gemeinschaft und Gesellschaft. Wissenschaftliche Buchgesellschaft,
    Darmstadt
Veblen TB (1995) The theory of the leisure class. Penguin Books, New York
Vivelo FR (1978) Cultural anthopology handbook. New York, McGraw-Hill
Walzer M (1989) Spheres of justice. Blackwell, Oxford
Weber M (1968) Economy and society. In: Roth G, Wittich C (eds), 2 vols. Bedminster Press, New
    York
Williamson O (1987) Antitrust economics. Blackwell, Oxford
Wittfogel KA (1957) Oriental despotism. Yale University Press, New Haven
Wolff RD, Resnick SA (1988) Economics: Marxian versus neoclassical. Johns Hopkins University
    Press, Baltimore
Wolter U (ed) (1976) Die linke opposition in der Sowjetunion, 3 vols. Olle und Wolter, Berlin

Chapter 13
Friedrich List's Striving for Economic Integration and Development

Karl-Heinz Schmidt

Introduction

Modern history of economic thought applies diverse methods of analysis and interpretation of historical data and economic works. The following contribution turns to Friedrich List (1789–1846), the multi-talented author of numerous writings on economic integration and development during the first half of the nineteenth century in Europe and the USA. This chapter contains five sections dealing with (1) biographical notes, (2) historical data and notes covering the context of the author's works in political economy, (3) a summary of List's major contributions, (4) a survey on present views of List's works and (5) an evaluation of List's contributions from the point of view of modern economic theory and political economy.

The biographical data and notes expose three phases of List's life and activities: in the Kingdom of Württemberg and other German states (up to 1825), in Pennsylvania and the USA (1825–1832), again in Germany and other European countries (1832–1846).

The historical data and notes concern the structure and reforms of public administration and public finance, and the indicators of economic development in Württemberg, Pennsylvania and Germany during the phases of List's life.

List's major contributions are summarized as to three main fields of his activities: (1) public administration, (2) economic development and (3) infrastructure policy, especially concerning education and transportation. The result is that there is more continuity in List's visions and writings than it was presumed.

This statement turns out to be valid also for the evaluation on the grounds of present views of List's writings and of modern economic theory and political economy. Mainly List's theory of productive powers, his arguments concerning educative

K.-H. Schmidt (✉)
Department of Economics, University Paderborn, Warburger Street 100,
33098 Paderborn, Germany
e-mail: Karl_Schmidt@notes.uni-paderborn.de

J.G. Backhaus (ed.), *Handbook of the History of Economic Thought,*
The European Heritage in Economics and the Social Sciences,
DOI 10.1007/978-1-4419-8336-7_13, © Springer Science+Business Media, LLC 2012

tariffs, his endeavours regarding innovations of new technologies and his contributions in the field of public administration and public finance are acknowledged.

Summarizing, List is understood as an author of the early nineteenth century who looked forward to the future of Europe and the USA even to a world-wide economic system and a "world-state". We should read his articles, pamphlets and books again in order "to go back to the roots" and to conclude from List's arguments and results on behalf of our future.

Biographical Notes on Friedrich List (1789–1846)

From the point of view of modern history of economic thought, it is interesting to learn how differently authors of diverse time periods, scientific origin, schools or methodologies have interpreted the biographical data of Friedrich List. This German clerk, bureaucrat, autodidact economist, professor, manager, politician and journalist lived during a pre-revolutionary time period (Brinkmann 1959, p 634). He was tremendously creative as to proposals for reforms of bureaucracies, politics and infrastructure, but as to the majority of his proposals and projects he failed, resigned, was opposed to the political institutions and even had to emigrate for several years of his life. He ended his life by suicide. But his numerous published works were discussed and translated world-wide. He became the most popular and well-known German author of political economy of the nineteenth century – apart from Karl Marx.

To enumerate the main important biographical data of Friedrich List, the following informations are listed (Henderson 1983, pp 1 ff; Häuser 1989, pp 227 ff; Seidenfus 1987, p 926): He was born in 1789 in the Swabian city of Reutlingen, located in the former Kingdom of Württemberg. His father was a well-known artisan and politician in that city, and the young Friedrich List entered his father's business after having quitted high school. But he disliked that job and started a career as a clerk in the small city of Blaubeuren. After exams, he worked in Ulm and Tübingen. Here, he participated in lectures at the University and practised self-instruction and private studies. After several exams he became a secretary and high-ranked bureaucrat – "Rechnungsrat" – of the public administration (1816). As long as liberal ideas were tolerated in Württemberg after the wars against Napoleon, List was allowed to expose his liberal ideas. He even was promoted to teach public administration ("Staatspraxis") as a professor at the University of Tübingen. But the political reaction by the conservative politician Metternich and his adherents brought List in a conflict with the political system. Moreover, he became involved in the foundation of an organization of tradesmen and manufacturers in Frankfurt, in a foreign country. This event was too much of a burden for the political system of Württemberg; to avoid further conflicts, List decided to quit his activities in the University of Tübingen (1819). Having returned to his native town of Reutlingen he was elected to act as a deputy in the Chamber of Württemberg. But again he failed, this time because of his provocative writings on public administration and on publicity of court proceedings. The Government immediately ordered his exclusion from the Chamber and his condemnation to 10 months of jail. List escaped. Since then his life was determined by unrest and trouble. He tried to live in France, in Switzerland and in the German state of Baden, but he was not allowed to stay. Therefore, he returned to Württemberg in order to ask the King to forgive him. But again he was put to jail (1825). Only under the condition of emigrating to the USA he was allowed to leave the prison (1825).

In America List settled for 5 years in Pennsylvania (1825–1830). Being always active, creative and flexible, he became a successful journalist, adviser of politicians, farmer and entrepreneur. As vice-president of the "Little Schuylkill Navigation Rail Road and Coal Company", he contributed to the development of one of the first American railroad networks. In Reading (PA) he founded a German-language newspaper, the "Adler;" it turned out to be an effective instrument of a movement for protective tariff policy. His creative ideas and proposals even influenced the concept and measures of American economic policy. On behalf of his reputation and influence, he was appointed to act as a consul in Hamburg (1830), but because of political opposition he could only start this career in Baden (1832) and Leipzig, Saxonia (1834).

Back in Germany, List became a moving force aiming at unification, reforms of tariff systems and acceleration of the development of roads and railroad networks. He worked on projects of German railroad companies and tracks, especially in Saxonia, but he could not get a long-term contract as a company manager. He failed again.

Therefore List left Germany again. He went to Paris (1837), there he wrote two essays, which he sent to the French Academy of Moral and Political Sciences, yet, without any success. But he developed the concept of these essays furthermore, and (early in 1840) he finished his book on the "National System of Political Economy". His publisher Cotta, Stuttgart and Tübingen, accepted and published it (List 1841, 1927–1936, 1971). The book was a great success, and List had in mind to write additional volumes. But neither in Württemberg nor in Bavaria or elsewhere he could get a long-term appointment. He refused the position of chief-editor of a new journal, the "Rheinische Zeitung", a job which then was offered to Karl Marx. List instead established a new journal by Cotta since 1843, when List moved to Augsburg. Here he published more than 600 articles. He had success and earned money rather continuously. But he failed again, because he fell into serious conflicts with his publisher, the younger Cotta.

List again preferred to travel and to advise bureaucrats and politicians. He travelled to Vienna, Preßburg and Budapest (1844), in order to advertise his ideas on a customs union and on railroad networks in Europe. He also tried to convince the states of Northern Germany, especially Hannover, Hamburg and Bremen, to enter the customs union. List therefore travelled to England in order to advertise his idea of educative tariffs (1846). But he came back to Germany without success. He decided to recover for a few weeks in Meran. Being underway, in Kufstein, Austria, he finished his last travel (November 30th, 1846), after having suffered from heavy pain in his head, depression and unrest. Edgar Salin, the former president of the List Society and author of famous books and articles on Political Economy, called List's life "the tragedy of a political visionary", a man who relied on the strength of the future, but who was broken by the strength of his present time (Salin 1960, p. 5 f).

Historical Data and Notes

List was born in 1789, the year of the French Revolution, and his life ended in 1846, 2 years prior to the German Revolution. During the first half of the nineteenth century he survived the wars against Napoleon, followed by the policies of restoration and reconstruction in Europe, the agricultural crises after 1815 and the social and economic effects of the industrialization lagging behind the technological changes and economic development of England since the 1820s (Häuser 1989, pp 227–230; Recktenwald (ed) 1989). List recognized that the Kingdom of Württemberg had to carry out reforms of the public administration, public policy, trade and industrial policy. The state had to bear high amounts of costs of adaptation to new conditions of production and trade.

The following historical data are important indicators of the structural disruptions, social conflicts and barriers of economic development in List's environment; herewith three levels of analysis have to be distinguished (Kiesewetter, Fremdling (eds) (1985):

(1) The regional level, especially the Kingdom of Württemberg, (2) the national level, especially the German states and (3) the international level, especially the USA, moreover the state of Pennsylvania.

Though the wars against Napoleon, the English continental barrier policy and the French continental system of trade barriers seem to have been less harmful as to the majority of the German states than these policies were evaluated by earlier studies, the Kingdom of Württemberg had to solve three main problems of economic development (Cipolla and Borchardt (1976–1980); vol. 4; pp 146 ff):

(1a) the pre-industrial population pressure, (1b) the crises of agricultural production, and (1c) the reorganization of trade policy and economic policy.

List's early analyses of the economic situation of the German states were based on three groups of causes: societal, internal economic and international economic causes. His diagnosis exposed the agricultural sector as the basic pillar of any industrial production system, but it also demonstrated a general economic depression. In order to push the economic development, List recommended a German trade system. It should apply two measures: abolishment of internal tariffs in Germany and the introduction of a general tariff level to be applied by the whole Federation of the German States. The latter, yet, should be applied only defensively, until all nations would practise free trade everywhere. These defensive and restricted tariffs were understood by List to practise three functions: external protection, internal protection and external self-defence of a country, the latter including his demand for a retaliatory measure.

The crises of the agricultural production strongly influenced the development of population. Bad harvest (1816/1817) and good harvest (1817 and later) brought about rough changes in corn prices. The population was pressed to the minimum of subsistence. Mortality and emigration were increased, birth-rates were decreased.

During the 1840s again agricultural crises and emigration of parts of the population characterized the economic development in Germany. At a growing extent social conflicts were exposed, but mainly because the industrialization process began to influence the manufacturing production in various German states, to some extent also in the Kingdom of Württemberg (Müssiggang 1968; Strösslin 1968).

The political changes and the instability of the economic development in Europe also influenced the political and economic development in the USA at the beginning of the nineteenth century. The expanding cotton production in the southern states and the decrease of manufacturing and industrial production in the Northeast brought about the first depression in the USA (Schafmeister 1995, p. 177). When List arrived in Pennsylvania, the country was involved in heavy structural changes and political reorganization. Consequently, List found environmental – political and economic – conditions, which may have been nearly familiar to him, as there was also a great need of adaptation in Pennsylvania, a problem well known to him from his home nation Germany.

List's Major Contributions to Political Economy

Friedrich List's contributions to political economy can be arranged in three groups, covering three different fields: (1) articles and pamphlets on public administration and public finance (2) economic development policy and (3) infrastructure policy, especially transportation, education and integration systems. His life-time includes three phases, the first and third of which he spent in Europe, mainly in German states, while during the second phase he worked in the USA. The topics of his contributions to political economy differed during those phases. The first phase – the time prior to his enforced emigration to the USA (1825) – starts with lectures on political economy and writings on public administration and public finance. The second phase – his stay in the USA (1825–1832) – is dominated by publications on economic development, especially on protective (educative) tariffs and customs unions and on railroads and additional transportation networks. The third phase – covering List's return to Europe and his diverse activities in diverse German states and neighbour countries (1832–1846) – is characterized by publications on economic integration, especially on industrialization and trade and on the development of railroads and transportation systems in Germany and Central Europe (Table 13.1).

Comparing the activities and publications which List carried out during these periods, it seems that there was much discontinuity in his life. In contrast to this

Table 13.1 Periods of F. List's lifetime and activities

1815–1825: first phase: List in Germany	
1815	"Sulzer Petition": List's ideas and proposals for a new Constitution of the Kingdom of Württemberg
1815–1819	Conflict concerning the legislation of a new Constitution of the Kingdom of Württemberg
1819	New legislation on public finance. List's criticism of public administration and public finance
1820	"Reutlinger Petition": demand for a fiscal budget plan, including the reduction of tax rates and public expenditures

(continued)

Table 13.1 (continued)

1816–1820	Articles and reports on the causes and effects of poverty, population and emigration to America; first chamber speech: "On Württemberg's Trade Policy" (13.12.1820), List Werke 1.2, p. 673
	Articles and pamphlets on Württemberg's trade policy and trade development
1819	First Petition to the German Federal Assembly (April 14th, 1819)
	To abolish the internal tariffs in Germany
	To introduce a general, defensive and restricted external tariff of all German States
1818–1819	Lectures on taxation and public administration and policy ("Polizeiwissenschaft")
1819/1820	Petitions, pamphlets and articles on the economic situation, the development of manufacturing production and trade and the trade policy in Germany; demand for a "German Trade System"
1820	Petition concerning the situation of trade and manufacturing in Germany (Petition to the Vienna Congress, February 15th, 1820): "Trade, manufacturing and agriculture of the Germans, the whole *productive power* of the nation, is fixed and weakened by tariffs … and restrictions…" (Werke, 1.2, 1820, p. 528)
1822–1825	Imprisonment, refuge to neighbouring states, return to Württemberg, arrest in the prison Hohen Asperg near Ludwigsburg/Stuttgart, release under the condition of emigration to the USA
1824	First contacts with railroads in England
1824	List proposed to build a railway track from the Black Forest to the lower areas
	In Le Havre (4/1825) List wrote in his notebook that a railway network should be developed, in order to connect Le Havre with the river Rhine in Southern Germany; the growth of trade and the decrease of transportation costs would be the effects; "Es lebe der Dampf" (4/1825)
1825–1832: second phase: List in the USA	
1827	Outlines of American Political Economy, in a series of letters … to Charles Ingersoll …, printed by Samuel Parker, Philadelphia
1829	Mitteilungen aus Nordamerika von Fr. List, hrsg. V. E. Weber und E.W. Arnoldi, Hamburg, Hoffmann + Campe
1829	Reports on the improvement of the Little Schuylkill, Reading, in: Madison Papers, vol 78, 1829
1832–1846: third phase: List in Europe	
1827	Das natürliche System der politischen Ökonomie, Pariser Preisschrift von 1837, Akademie-Verlag, Berlin (Ost), 1961
1837	Die Welt bewegt sich: Über die Auswirkungen der Dempfkraft und der neuen Transportmittel auf die Wirtschaft, das bürgerliche Leben, das soziale Gefüge und die Macht der Nationen, Pariser Preisschrift von 1837, hrsg. v. E. Wendler, Vandenhoeck & Ruprecht, Göttingen 1985
1841	Das nationale System der politischen Oekonomie, Erster Band, Der internationale Handel, die Handelspolitik und der deutsche Zollverein, J.G. Cotta'scher Verlag, Stuttgart und Tübingen, 1841, Neudruck, Sammlung socialwissenschaftlicher Meister, hrsg. v. H. Waentig, 5. Auflage, Jena 1928

hypothesis, yet, List's works may also be interpreted to point out continuity of the development of his ideas, concepts, demands and programmes. His central target during his whole life turns out to be the increase of welfare and wealth for the nation and for mankind, of course with differentiation of the medium-term and long-term targets and of the measures to be applied.

In his articles on public administration and public finance, List demanded more efficient methods of organization of the relations between the individuals and the state (Eisermann 1956, pp 111f). He complained about mismanagement of public administration and ineffective organization of the public finance system. His ideas and proposals were orientated to the increase of individual freedom and of cooperation of institutions up to the level of a world-wide state ("Weltstaat") (1818). The intensive relations between the individuals and the state should furthermore characterize the economic development of the nations. Therefore, he wrote down his definition of economics: "...die Lehre von den Naturgesetzen der Produktion materieller Güter durch Handel, Gewerbe und Ackerbau, von ihrer Verteilung und endlich von ihrer Konsumtion, welche Lehre nun als Richtschnur dienen muß, inwiefern die Einwirkung der Staatsgewalt für das wirtschaftliche Wohl des einzelnen, der Staaten und der Menschheit nützlich oder schädlich ist, also den Rechten des einzelnen, dem" Zweck des Staates und der Bestimmung der Menschheit entspricht oder nicht (List Werke 1.1, Enzyklopädie der Staatswissenschaften, 1823, p. 440; Schafmeister 1995, p. 281 f).

List's writings of the first phase concerned the Constitution of the State and the public administration, but by working on the reform of the Constitution and the public administration of the Kingdom of Württemberg, he became interested also in the problems of trade policy and economic policy. In his pamphlets and articles, he exposed two demands: (1) representation of the people by the Constitution and (2) the principle of publicity (Schafmeister 1995, p. 82).

List demanded that the state should be based on the freedom of the individual citizen. In his view the public power will follow from summing up all individual powers in order to realize the total welfare. But in order to make sure that the individual person can live in "rational freedom", independent corporations (Korporationen) and independent communities are needed, according to List's demands. The state primarily is to set up the general legislation and to make use of the power of individuals and communities, yet, without restricting the individual freedom too much. Second, the state has to leave the corporations in their field, to fulfil their targets based on specific statutes which must be coordinated with the legislation of the state. List obviously argued in favour of federalism. The basic element is the "rational freedom" of the individual citizen. He is understood to live as a member of his autonomous, self-administered community, where the individual is organized in corporations. They are orientated by statutes to the general legislation of the state.

Summarizing, List substantiated his vision of federalism by four arguments: (1) strong interest of the individual in the satisfaction of the individual preferences, (2) strong relations between the individual citizen and the state by close relations between the corporations, (3) increase of civil freedom by free corporations and (4) increase of productivity by increase of freedom of the citizens and corporations (Schafmeister 1995, p. 83 f).

The writings, in which List exposed his ideas and demands concerning the public ideas and demands concerning the public administration and public finance, are published in his Collected Works (von Beckerath E, Goeser K, Lenz F, Notz W, Salin E, Sommer A, Sch K.-H (eds) (1971): Friedrich List Schriften/Reden/Briefe, 10 volumes, reprint, Scientia Verlag Aalen, cited as: Werke 1–10). In his earlier articles he criticized the Government and the public administration on the grounds of his liberal views of public policy. He mainly commented on the reforms of the Constitution of the Kingdom of Württemberg (von Beckerath E et al (eds) (1971) Friedrich List (1816): Werke 1–10, reprint , Scientia Verlag Aalen, especially List (1816): Gedanken über die württembergische Staatsregierung, Werke 1, 87–148, 823–843; List (1816/1817): Kritik des Verfassungsentwurfs, Werke 1, 205–283, 863–900; List (1818): Die Staatskunde und Staatspraxis Württembergs im Grundriß, Werke 1, 284–307, 900–903). Apart from his statements and comments on the reforms of the Constitution and of the public administration on the grounds of personal experience and accumulated knowledge, List created a coherent system of aims, institutions and instruments of community economics (List (1816/1817): System der Gemeindewirtschaft, Werke 1, 149–204, 843–863). He furthermore commented on the functions and failures of the institutions of public administration, herewith developing basics of institutional economics (List (1818): Über die Verfassung und Verwaltung der Korporationen (Vorlesung), Werke 1, 308–316, 903–905); List (1817): Gutachten über die Errichtung einer staatswirtschaftlichen Fakultät, Werke 1, 341–352; 914–921; List (1817): Über die württembergische Verfassung, Werke 1, 353–434, 921–942; List (1823): Enzyklopädie der Staatswissenschaften, Werke 1, (435–445, 942–944). Further writings directly turned to the basic problems of the reforms of public finance (List (1820): Zur württembergischen Finanzreform (Kammerrede), Werke 1, 333–337, 909–911).

In these writings List insisted on two principles of his visions: (1) representation of the people and (2) publicity of the decisions of public administration and public finance. The latter he turned to in several articles and pamphlets concerning his demands for more efficient taxation, the decrease of public expenditures and the reform of the organization of public administration and decision-making in public finance (Schafmeister 1995, 85). In his expert evidence concerning the establishment of a special faculty of public economics (Staatswissenschaftliche Fakultät) at the University of Tübingen, List demanded a general scientific analysis of public administration and public finance at the university level (List (1817): Gutachten über die Errichtung einer staatswissenschaftlichen Fakultät, Werke 1, 341–352, 914–921).

List's basic concept of the state, public administration and public finance can be recognized from his writings on the system of community economics and on the public institutions and practice of public policy in the Kingdom of Württemberg (Klein 1974). His thoughts referring to the Government of Württemberg point out the relations of the constitution, the government and the public administration (List (1816): Gedanken über die württembergische Staatsregierung, Werke 1, 88–148). The author herewith develops economic principles of public legislation and public administration. He emphasizes the coordination of public offices and the hierarchy of the institutions of public administration. But instead of demanding general principles, List points out that differentiated arrangements are needed because of the diversity of the geographical location, the specialization of functions and the different strengths of the public servants (List (1816): Gedanken über die württembergische Staatsregierung, 96).

The community is characterized to be of the same "nature" as in the state as a whole. List argues that in the small unit all institutions are related to each other as in the large unit, on the state level. He explains the constitution of the community being composed by a basic constitution ("Grundverfassung") and a constitution of the local government, comparable to the state level. The basic constitution determines the purposes, the legal relations and the institutions of the community. The constitution of the local government concerns regulations of the processing of community policy and administration. List's definition of the community is based on the relations between the individual and the state: the community is a relation ordered by the state, referring to a number of citizens living in a certain district and considering their person and their property pursuing two purposes: first, to increase the individual welfare by cooperative activities as it would be possible without additional cooperation with other communities, and second, to consolidate the state and to enable a regular public administration of the state. Each community consists of two elements: the object, i.e. the property of the citizens located in the community district, and the subject, that is the relations of the persons and their individual rights. The purpose of the community is to be realized by three kinds of special purposes: (a) law and jurisdiction ("Rechtspflege"), (b) welfare and security ("Wohlfahrtspflege", "Polizei") and (c) maintenance and utilization of the community property (community economics, "Gemeindewirtschaft"). List explains the latter by distinction of a material part, regarding the principles, and a formal part, concerning the institutions and processing of public finance on the community level. The receipts of the community are composed of regular and accidental receipts, and the regular receipts are distinguished as being of a specific or a subsidiary kind. Interestingly, List deals with local taxes as receipts of a subsidiary kind. The principles as to which the private property is to be taxed in order to satisfy the preferences of the state are dealt with in a short paragraph only. Every person is to be taxed according to the personal wealth. List calls it "the theory of Wilhelm Tell" (List (1816/1817): System der Gemeindewirtschaft, Werke 1, 149–204, esp. 190). But List also argues in favour of indirect taxes – except tariffs. The method to be applied should be to leave a certain proportion of the total receipts of the indirect taxes to the communities (List (1816/1817), 192). This proposal is under discussion continuously.

Regarding List's further writings on public finance and public administration, it turns out that they are orientated to start from the empirical data and problems in the Kingdom of Württemberg, but that the author attempts to draw general conclusions as to the stabilization of the state and the economic development. Figure 13.1 exposes List's view of the political and economic problems in the Kingdom of Württemberg 1815–1825. Figure 13.2 shows his criticism of the public administration and public finance in Württemberg 1816–1821. So far the first group of List's writings are considered.

Political and Economic Problems in the Kingdom of Württemberg 1815 – 1825

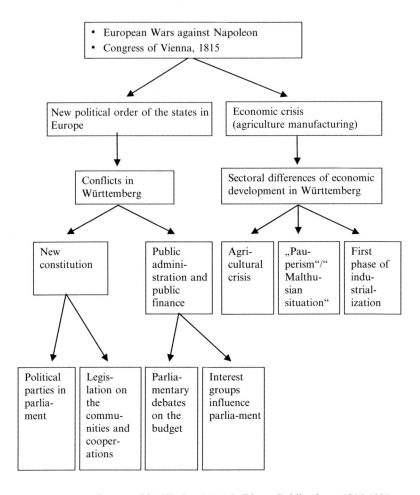

Fig. 13.1 Political and economic problems in the Kingdom of Württemberg 1815–1825. *Sources*: List Werke, 1.1, 1.2, Diverse Publications, 1816–1820

The second group of List's writings mainly concerns problems and proposals referring to the policy of economic development (Strösslin 1968; Tribe 1988a; Schumpeter 1965 vol I, p 619; Winkel 1977, pp 75 ff). Though these publications cover a variety of problems of economic integration and infrastructure investment, the hypothesis of continuity of List's ideas and visions in his writings turns out to be valid again.

In his early German writings of the first phase, List already pointed out that the state should increase the national welfare by public institutions, which should function as adequate means in order to strive for external security of the society and internal security in the country. List argued in favour of an externally independent state,

**List's Criticism of Public Administration
and Public Finance in Württemberg 1816 –1821**

Contra	Pro
Participation of interest groups in the administration of tax receipts	Safety considering interventions of the public power of the state into the administration of tax receipts; Public and corporative controls of tax administration
Centralisation of state property and public property	Separate administration of receipts from state property and public property
Increase of public expenditures	Decrease of taxes and public expenditures
Increase of public debt	Decrease of public debt
Inefficiency of public administration and public finance	Analysis of public finance, especially of tax receipts/national income

Sources: List Werke, 1.1, 1.2, Divers Publications, 1816-1820

Fig. 13.2 List's criticism of public administration and public finance in Wurttemberg 1861–1821. *Sources*: List Werke, 1.1, 1.2, Divers Publications, 1816–1820

disposing of public institutions which should be characterized by adequate opportunities of decision-making and implementation (List, Werke 1.1, Enzyklopädie der Staatswissenschaften, 1823, p. 440; Werke 1.2, Denkschrift: Die Handels- und Gewerbsverhältnisse Deutschlands betreffend, 1820, p. 528; Werke 1.2, Bittschrift an die Bundesversammlung, 1819, p. 494; Werke 1.1, Die Staatskunde und Staatspraxis Württembergs, 1818, p. 286 f).

His diverse articles, pamphlets and petitions of 1819/1820 show three lines of arguments: (1) the diagnosis of the economic situation, (2) the analysis of the causes of the economic situation and (3) the measures of economic policy. He distinguished societal, internal economic and external economic causes of the economic depression in Germany 1819/1820.

Concerning the internal and external economic causes, he considered the differences of the economic structure and development in the economic sectors: agriculture, manufacturing and trade. List proposed a "German trade system" exposing two demands: (1) abolition of all internal tariffs between the German states and (2) the introduction of a general external tariff rate as a measure of opposition, valid at all foreign borders of the German Federation (List, Werke, 1.2, Bittschrift an die Bundesversammlung, 1819, p. 493, 495). Herewith, List already applied the idea that the external tariff would be necessary in order to sustain the sectoral economic development, especially of manufacturing production and trade (Hoffman, Fikentscher 1988, pp 630 ff). Furthermore, he pointed out that external tariffs are apt to protect and by that to sustain the economic development of the German Federation (List, Werke, 1.2, 1819, p. 493). These tariffs should be valid for a restricted time period, and they should be of a defensive character only. By means of these tariffs, the German products should become more competitive in foreign markets, foreign competitors should be kept off the German markets and industrial companies of the German Federation countries should regain competitiveness in the internal markets. Then the economic development of the industrial sector would be stabilized and sustained. List therefore applied a sectoral analysis in his studies of the foreign trade and economic development (Pausch 1989 ; Pohl (ed) 1989; Pohl 1989 pp 648–660). The three functions of the defensive and restricted external tariffs – internal protection, external protection and external self-defence – turn out to be List's basic ideas, on which he founded his later visions of economic development policy in the USA and after his return to Germany. Surprisingly, List's ideas are often disregarded in the new economic literature on protectionism and economic development (Krugman (1990): Rethinking International Trade, 118 f; Broll and Gilroy (1994): Außenwirtschafts-theorie, 2. Auflage, Teil III, Handelspolitik, 175–221). As infant industry argument based on Alexander Hamilton's contributions, List's ideas, yet, are considered in the present discussion on tariffs under specific conditions of industry and trade (Krugman (1990), 113, 119).

In the USA List developed his arguments referring to protective tariffs and economic growth furthermore. These arguments were based on his "theory of productive resources". Though this terminology was often applied at List's time, he did not deliver a specific definition. Adam Smith had introduced the term "productive powers of labour" in the introduction of his "Wealth of Nations", and former German authors on Cameralism had used the term "industrial productive power" (von Soden F J H (1805–1824) Die Nazional-Oekonomie, 9 vols, especially vol. 4 (1810), Leipzig, p. 167). These authors already recognized that present expenditures may bring about an increase of future output, and that institutional factors like the legislation and education system also contribute to economic growth.

List at first applied the term "productive powers" in his "Outlines of American Political Economy" (1827), but only in his study on "The Natural System of Political Economy" (1837) he used the term "theory of productive powers" (Fabiunke 1961). The various examples which he mentioned – instead of a definition of that term – have become famous. In his "National System" List wrote: "The power to create riches is infinitely more important than the riches themselves". (List (1928): Das nationale System der politischen Ökonomie, 5. Auflage, Jena, p. 220).

Moreover the examples exposed his intention, to demonstrate, that the quantity and quality of productive resources are changed during the process of economic development, and that the common activities of men enforce the development and make the "productive powers" increase, the network of traffic and transportation included (Schmidt 1990, p. 86). Furthermore, List applied the "theory of productive powers" in order to explain the structural changes, which designate the economic development. He therefore combined the analysis of "productive powers" with his "stages of economic development" (Winkel 1977, pp 75 ff; Priddat 1988). Herewith he emphasized two departments of economic policy: (1) trade policy and (2) infrastructure policy, especially (a) education policy and (b) transportation networks and traffic policy. He always tried to point out new opportunities to develop and to apply

List's Phases of Political Economy considering the "German Trade System" (1819/1820)

	Sectoral analysis				
	Agriculture	Manu-facturing industry	Internal trade	External trade	Total society
Diagnosis of the economic situation	Agricultural crisis	Beginning of the industria-lization	Local/ regional trade	Restrictions	Economic crisis
Institutional analysis	Restrictions of individual freedom; inflexibility of bureaucracy; need of reforms				Institutional crisis
Exposition of lacks and deficits	Inflexibility of taxation and public expenditures; tariffs as barriers of interregional /national trade				Need of reforms
Announce-ment of targets	Steady growth of individual and national economic welfare				Public discussion
Analysis of instruments	Reforms of public administration and public finance; abolishment of national tariffs; general external tariffs				Establishing faculty of university
Pro-gramming and implemen-tation	"German Trade System"				Parliament and bureau-cracy
	Land reform	Tax reform	Reduction of internal tariffs and controls	General external tariff and control	
	Administrative reforms				
Evaluation	Analyses and report by expert committees, faculty of university, politicians				Reports, legislation

Sources: Backhaus, J., 1990, p. 103-113
                 List Werke, 1.1, 1.2
                 Schafmeister, K., 1995, p. 153

Fig. 13.3 List's phases of political economy considering the "German Trade System" (1819/1820). *Sources*: Backhaus (1990, p. 103–113); List Werke, 1.1, 1.2 Schafmeister (1995, p. 153)

new technologies – or in Schumpeter's terminology: new combinations of resources (Schumpeter 1914; 1965 vol I, pp 617 f).

List's target – to sustain the economic development – also made him demand for "protective" – more precisely – "educative"-tariffs, especially for the industrial sector. He distinguished phases of political economy and applied the sectoral analysis, considering agriculture, manufacturing industry, internal and external trade. The instruments of economic policy which he recommended, he designed as "German Trade System". Figure 13.3 exposes the measures to be programmed and implemented according to List's concept. In order to stabilize economic growth, he investigated the conditions of optimal allocation of resources, but he pointed out neither the existing nor the forthcoming distribution of incomes and wealth. Two reasons may be exposed: (1) the focus on the processing of economic growth and (2) the vision of long-term equilibrium or "harmony" of economic growth and income distribution. Later, during the 1840s, List returned to the consideration of changes of the income distribution and of the structure of manufacturing production. In diverse smaller articles he mentioned the poverty of workers in England. But the "social question" in his concept only had the meaning of an adaptation problem. He was deeply convinced that the workers would earn higher wages on behalf of the development of the "productive powers". In the long run also free trade would dominate.

On the other hand List must be interpreted as an expert of public administration and public finance. In this context, he had in mind that tariffs should be distinguished according to two different functions: (1) to finance public expenditures, for instance subsidies (Andel 1988; pp 504 f), and (2) to modify the allocation of productive resources, either to protect the national production system, or to develop and to educate the resources towards a higher level of productivity and social benefits.

Present Views on List's Works

After a long-term and intensive discussion of the reception of List's writings at least *five* different views can be distinguished presently: (1) List and the economic history of industrialization, (2) List and the present theory of public administration and bureaucracy, (3) List and the actual problems of public finance, (4) List and the present status of the theory of international economics and (5) List and the theory of economic development.

Ad (1): Relevant new contributions deal with the exploited materials of archives and museums in Germany and the USA, especially on quantitative data of tax receipts, public debt and public expenditures in Württemberg, Germany, Pennsylvania and the USA during the first half of the nineteenth century. The question is, if List had the correct empirical data at hand when he criticized the public policies in Germany and the USA.

Ad (2): List's criticism of the public administration and bureaucracy turns out to be highly relevant under consideration of the present problems of bureaucracy on the national, supranational and international level.

Ad (3): Actual problems of public finance like the increase of the quota of indirect taxes and of specific contributions – mainly for social security – can be analysed on the grounds of List's criticism of taxation, tariffs and public expenditures.

Ad (4): International economics may benefit from List's view of protective, better educative tariffs. Furthermore, his plea in favour of restricted educative tariffs as a means of development policy makes clear that international economics and economic development are closely interrelated.

Ad (5): The theory of economic development benefits from List's writings because of his broad view including institutional, economic and political perspectives.

List's Contributions and Modern Economic Theory and Political Economy

"Modern" is what is dealt with in articles published actually in academic journals, reviews and books. List's contributions to "modern" economic theory and political economy mainly refer to: (1) the theory of the state, bureaucracy, public administration and public finance, (2) the theory of international trade and (3) the theory of economic development. The majority of the academic publications of the 1990s deal with the tariff-problem, to a large extent focussing on the allocative and distributive effects of protective/educative tariffs. Consensus seems to be around concerning the long-term benefits of educative tariffs, if they are applied for a restricted time period, in innovative sectors of the economy and under the condition of abolishment of internal (national, regional) trade. Educative tariffs abolish themselves even in international perspectives, if the causes for their introduction are no more relevant, that is if the conditions of free trade, optimal allocation of resources and income distribution are fulfilled. Jürgen Backhaus has demonstrated that List should be understood as an author of economic policy and public finance (Backhaus 1990, p. 107), even as an expert of the theory of public administration (Backhaus 1990, p. 111). List aimed at free trade finally, but he demanded the application of "the principle of education of the nation for self-determination and self-employment" (Selbständigkeit). Protective tariffs should be allowed only for a restricted time period. They should substitute fiscal tariffs, which would restrict manufacturing and trade. Insofar the protective/educative tariff fits into List's concept of tax reform.

List's contributions to the modern economic theory of the state, bureaucracy, public administration and public finance are based on his experiences in his career as a bureaucrat, manager, politician and professor of public administration. An efficient bureaucracy was in List's view a precondition of a stable economic development. This perspective was exposed by J. Backhaus, too, but seldom it is pointed out in modern textbooks or articles on public administration and public finance.

More often to be found in textbooks and articles of journals and reviews are List's contributions to economic development, yet, mainly regarding the institutional and political framework instead of modelling the economic development. The relevant literature is registered to some extent in the later articles and books on List (Schafmeister 1995; Besters 1990; Schefold 1990; Starbatty 1989).

References

Andel N (1988) Art. Subventionen, in: Handwörterbuch der Wirtschaftswissenschaft (HdWW), vol 7, ungekürzte Studienausgabe, Gustav Fischer u.a., pp 491–510

Backhaus J G (1990) Die politische Ökonomie der Schutzzolltheorie, in: Schefold B (ed) Studien zur Entwicklung der ökonomischen Theorie X, Duncker, & Humblot, Berlin, pp 103–113

Besters H (ed) (1990) 'Die Bedeutung Friedrich Lists in Vergangenheit und Gegenwart', Gespräche der List Gesellschaft e.V., N.F. Band 12, Baden-Baden: Nomos Verlagsgesellschaft

Brinkmann C (1959) Art. Friedrich List, in: Handwörterbuch der Sozialwissenschaften, vol 6, Göttingen, pp 633–635

Broll U, Gilroy BM (1994) Außenwirtschaftstheorie, 2nd edn. Oldenbourg, Munich-Vienna

Cipolla C, Borchardt K (eds) (1976–1980) Europäische Wirtschaftsgeschichte, vols 1–5, Stuttgart, New York

Eisermann G (1956) Die Grundlagen des Historismus in der deutschen Nationalökonomie. Ferdinand Enke, Stuttgart

Fabiunke G (1961) Das Natürliche System der Politischen Ökonomie, Ökonomische Studientexte, vol 2, Berlin

Fulda FC (1816) Grundsätze der ökonomisch-politischen oder Kameralwissenschaften, Tübingen, 2nd ed, 1820

Fulda FC (1827) Handbuch der Finanzwissenschaft. von C.F. Osiander, Tübingen

Gehrig H (1956) Friedrich List und Deutschlands politisch-ökonomische Theorie, Leipzig

Häuser K (1989) Friedrich List (1789–1846). In: Starbatty J (ed) Klassiker des ökonomischen Denkens I. Munich, C.H. Beck, pp 225–244

Häuser K, Lachmann W, Scherf H (1989) Vademecum zu einem schöpferischen Klassiker mit tragischem Schicksal, Handelsblatt-Bibliothek, Klassiker der Nationalökonomie. Wirtschaft und Finanzen, Düsseldorf

Henderson WO (1983) Friedrich List. Economist and Visionary 1789–1846. London, Frank Cass

Hoffmann L, Fikentscher WR (1988) Art. Zölle I: Theorie und Politik, in: Handwörterbuch der Wirtschaftswissenschaft (HdWW), vol 9, ungekürzte Studienausgabe, Gustav Fischer u.a., pp 630–647

Kiesewetter H, Fremdling R (eds) (1985) Staat, Region und Industrialisierung. Scripta Mercaturae, Ostfildern

Klein E (1974) Geschichte der öffentlichen Finanzen in Deutschland 1500–1870, Wiesbaden

Krugman PR (1990) Rethinking International Trade. The MIT Press, Cambridge Mass

Lifschitz F (1914) Die historische Schule der Wirtschaftswissenschaft, Bern

List F (1841) Das nationale System der politischen Ökonomie, Stuttgart, new edition with introduction by H. Waentig (1928), 5th ed, Jena: von Gustav Fischer

List F (1927–1936) Schriften, Reden, Briefe, edited by E. von Beckerath et al, 10 vols, Berlin, zitiert als: Werke 1–10

List F (1971) Outlines of American Political Economy (The American System). In: Notz W (ed) Friedrich List, Grundlinien einer Politischen Ökonomie und andere Beiträge der amerikanischen Zeit 1825–1832. Neudruck, Aalen

Müssiggang A (1968) Die soziale Frage in der historischen Schule der deutschen Nationalökonomie, Tübingen

Ott AE, Winkel H (1985) Geschichte der theoretischen Volkswirtschaftslehre. Vandenhoeck & Ruprecht, Göttingen

Pausch A (1989) Friedrich List als Steuerfachmann und Zollpolitiker, Heidelberg: C.F. Müller, Wirtschaft & Steuern (Dr. Peter Deubner)

Pohl H (ed) (1987) Die Auswirkungen von Zöllen und anderen Handelshemmnissen auf Wirtschaft und Gesellschaft vom Mittelalter bis zur Gegenwart. Steiner, Stuttgart

Pohl H (1988) Art. Zölle II: Geschichte, in: Handwörterbuch der Wirtschaftswissenschaft (HdWW), vol 9, ungekürzte Studienausgabe, Gustav Fischer u.a., pp 648–660

Priddat BP (1988) "Produktive Kraft, sittliche Ordnung und geistige Macht", in: Priddat BP (ed), Denkstile der deutschen Nationalökonomie im 18. und 19. Jahrhundert, Beiträge zur Geschichte der deutschsprachigen Ökonomie, vol 13, Marburg: Metropolis

Raymond D (1820) Thoughts on political economy, Baltimore, 2nd ed (1823), the elements of political economy, 2 vols. Baltimore, Fielding Lucas

Recktenwald HC (ed) (1989) Vademecum, Kommentar zur Faksimile-Ausgabe der 1841 erschienenen Erstausgabe von Friedrich List: Das nationale System der politischen Ökonomie. Wirtschaft und Finanzen, Düsseldorf

Riha Th (1985) German political economy: the history of an alternative economics. Int J Soc Econ 12:1–5

Roscher W (1874) Geschichte der National-Oekonomik in Deutschland. R. Oldenbourg, Munich

Rose K (1964) Theorie der Außenwirtschaft. Franz Vahlen, Berlin and Frankfurt am Main

Rosen HS (1988) Public finance, 2nd edn. Irwin, Homewood

Salin E (1960) Friedrich List. Kerneuropa und die Freihandelszone, in: Recht und Staat in Geschichte und Gegenwart, Tübingen

Schafmeister K (1995) Entstehung und Entwicklung des Systems der Politischen Ökonomie bei Friedrich List, Beiträge zur südwestdeutschen Wirtschafts- und Sozialgeschichte, edited by Gert Kollmer and Harald Winkel, vol 18, St. Scripta Mercaturae, Katharinen

Schefold B (ed) (1990) Studien zur Entwicklung der ökonomischen Theorie X, Schriften des Vereins für Socialpolitik, vol 115/X. Duncker & Humblot, Berlin

Schmidt K-H (1990) Lists Theorie der produktiven Kräfte, in: Schefold B (ed) Studien zur Entwicklung der ökonomischen Theorie X, Duncker & Humblot, Berlin, pp 79–102

Schumpeter JA (1914) 'Epochen der Dogmen- und Methodengeschichte', in: Grundriß der Sozialökonomik, part I, Tübingen, pp 19–124

Schumpeter JA (1965) Geschichte der ökonomischen Analyse, vol I. Vandenhoeck & Ruprecht, Göttingen

Seidenfus H (1987) St.: List, in: Staatslexikon, edited by the Görres-Gesellschaft, 7th edition, vol 3, Freiburg-Basel-Vienna: Herder, pp 925–927

Sommer A (1926) 'Friedrich Lists Pariser Preisschrift von 1837', in Mitteilungen der Friedrich-List-Gesellschaft e.V., nr. 3, vol 30. November, pp 44–93

Starbatty J (ed) (1989) Klassiker des ökonomischen Denkens, vol. I, C H Beck, München, pp 225–244, 313, 314

Strösslin W (1968) Friedrich Lists Lehre von der wirtschaftlichen Entwicklung. Basel, Tübingen

Tribe K (1988a) Friedrich List and the critique of "Cosmopolitical Economy". Manchester School 56(1):17–36

Tribe K (1988b) Governing economy. The Reformation of German Economic Discourse 1750–1840. Cambridge

Tribe K (1995) Strategies of economic order. German economic discourse, 1750–1950. Cambridge, Tribe (1995) publisher unknown

von Eheberg K Th (1925) 'List, Friedrich' in: Handwörterbuch der Staatswissenschaften, 4th ed, vol VI, Jena, pp 361–364

Winkel H (1977) Die deutsche Nationalökonomie im 19. Jahrhundert. Wissenschaftliche Buchgesellschaft, Darmstadt

Chapter 14
The Entwickelung According to Gossen

Jan van Daal*

Introduction

Although many (young) economists are not familiar with the name of Hermann Heinrich Gossen (1810–1858), they all are acquainted with some versions of his first and second law. Gossen's first law states that the marginal utility of some enjoyment decreases while uninterruptedly continuing it. According to the most known version of the second law, an individual with a certain income will distribute this income over the various enjoyments such that for each of them the quotient of marginal utility and price is the same. In his only published work, *Entwickelung der Gesetze des menschlichen Verkehrs und der daraus fließenden Regeln für menschliches Handeln* (1854),[1] Gossen said it as follows (pp. 4–5 and 93–94):

*Centre Walras, Triangle, Université Lyon–2, France. An earlier version of this chapter appeared, in Dutch, in: G. van der Laan et al. (red.), *Econometrie in beweging. Bundel bij het afscheid van prof. dr. A.H.Q.M. Merkies*, Vrije Universiteit, Amsterdam, 1997, pp. 63-78. This Festschrift was presented to Nol Merkies at the occasion of his 65th birthday and retirement as professor of econometrics. I thank him for his consent to use the Dutch version as a basis for an enlarged English version and for his many useful suggestions. Likewise, I thank Yukihiro Ikeda (Keio University, Tokio), Hans Maks (Maastricht) and Paola Tubaro (University of Greenwich) for their good comments.

[1] Translated into English under the title *The laws of human relations and the rules of human action derived therefrom,* by Rudolph Blitz, with an introductory essay by Nicholas Georgescu-Roegen, The MIT Press, Cambridge, 1983; the English translations of German citations are taken from this book.

J. van Daal (✉)
Triangle, Université Lyon-2, Lyon, France
e-mail: jan.van.daal@orange.fr

Die Größe eines und desselben Genusses nimmt, wenn wir mit Bereitung des Genusses ununterbrochen fortfahren, fortwährend ab, bis zuletzt Sättigung eintritt.[2]

and

Der Mensch erlangt also ein Größtes von Lebensgenuß, wenn er sein ganzes erarbeitetes Geld, *E*, der Art auf die verschiedene Genüsse vertheilt (…), daß bei jedem einzelnen Genuß das letzte darauf verwendete Geldatom den Gleich großen Genuß gewährt.[3]

Gossen's laws did not escape Occam's razor. The first evolved into the theorem that for utility maximisation under the condition of a budget constraint, the upper contour-sets should be (locally) convex.[4] In the more modern approaches, the second law has made place for the requirement that for such a utility maximisation, the first derivatives of the problem's Lagrangian should be zero (provided the utility functions are differentiable).

Reading work of pioneers of our science may be very instructive and often highly rewarding. The richness and profundity of the legacy of these explorers amaze everyone who reads them. Often they exhibit a wonderful "modernity", and always much tenacity. All these elements we find back in Gossen's work, the subject of this chapter. First, I shall present some facts of his life and his book. Then four sections concerning his positive theory follow, framed in three laws. His policy recommendations are briefly dealt with in the subsequent section. In the conclusion, I shall make some remarks on Gossen's quasi-religiosity and the seemingly evolutionary nature of his thought.

Gossen and His Book

On September 15th, 1878, Léon Walras received at his home address in Ouchy sous Lausanne a letter from his London friend William Stanley Jevons informing him that their Manchester colleague Robert Adamson recently bought a German book

which contains many of the chief points of our theory clearly reasoned out. It is by Hermann Heinrich Gossen and is entitled somewhat as follows — Entwickelung der Gesetze des menschlichen Verkehr (??).[5]

They were already in search of the book for a long time because 4 years earlier, Adamson had found in a textbook by the Austrian-Hungarian economist Julius

---

[2] The magnitude [intensity] of pleasure decreases continuously if we continue to satisfy one and the same enjoyment without interruption until satiety is ultimately reached (1983: 6). (See also note 13.) The expressions between square brackets have been inserted by the translator, just as in the subsequent quotations from Blitz's translation.

[3] Man obtains the maximum of life pleasure if he allocates all his earned money *E* between the various pleasures (…) in such a way that the last atom of money spent for each pleasure offers the same amount [intensity] of pleasure (1983: 108–109).

[4] One might call this the "law of increasing relative satiation" because it means that a person possessing a certain good and wanting to exchange some of it against one unit of another good while keeping his utility at the same level has to give up the more of the first good the more he initially possessed.

[5] Walras (1965), Letter 417. Walras kept all the letters he received and copies of all he sent out.

Kautz (1858–1860, vol. 1, p. 9) a brief but striking characterisation of the essence of Gossen's book, from which they concluded that it must be strikingly similar to Jevons's *Theory of Political Economy*. Jevons urged Adamson to look for the book, which was apparently not an easy task.[6]

Walras would not have been Walras if he had not immediately acted. He was both highly interested in the book and afraid to lose claims of originality. Where it took Adamson 4 years to get a copy of the book, Walras obtained one within some months, borrowed from the university library of Munich. Soon he was set at ease regarding the claims to cede. Gossen could only claim from Walras those things he already ceded to Jevons, some years before (Walras 1874, 1885). Jevons, indeed, immediately passed them on to Gossen, together with some other findings (in particular, Fig. 14.4 below; see the preface of the second edition (1879) of his *Theory*, Jevons 1957: xxxii–xxxix).

To obtain some knowledge about the person behind the book, Walras started an extensive correspondence. Via the Swiss embassy in Berlin, he came in touch with a professor of mathematics in the University of Bonn, Hermann Kortum (1836–1904), the only son of one of Gossen's two sisters. Kortum wrote to Walras that his uncle already died in 1858. Furthermore, on Walras's request, he promised to prepare a short biography for insertion into the translation into French of the book, meanwhile prepared by Walras.[7] The note indeed arrived in Lausanne some time later (Kortum 1881). It is practically the only source of information about Gossen's life.[8]

---

[6] In a first note, Kautz wrote (my translation) "Recently Fr. [sic] Gossen tried to present a veritable theory and philosophy of pleasure [des Genusses] (and even on a mathematical basis!) in his book *Entwickelung der Gesetze des menschlichen Verkehrs*, 1854 (pp. 1–45 ff.)." In a second note on the same page, "Gossen remarks (o.c. p. 2): that all individuals always try to maximise their pleasure and that this has been established in human nature by God himself as the eventual life purpose of Man." It is not amazing that this arose Jevons's curiosity. So it seems that Gossen has been saved from total neglect by Kautz's two remarks on the one hand, and, on the other, by the fact that Adamson was very well-read in German economic literature and happened to know Jevons's *Theory*. According to Jürg Niehans (1987), these footnotes and another equally scanty one in a book by F.A. Lange (1875) are the only references to Gossen before Jevons and Walras did justice to him. See also Kurz (2008 and 2009) and Ikeda (2000).

[7] This translation saw the light relatively recently (Gossen 1995). Further, there exist two Italian translations and an English one (Gossen 1950, 1975, 1983). There is also an abridged Japanese translation, dating from 1920.

[8] The original text of this note is lost. There are two French translations, both made by Walras, a "spontaneous" and a "revised" one. The latter can be found in Walras's *Études d'économie sociale* (1990: 473–482). The former has recently been unearthed (its existence was even unknown until then) and has been published along with the French translation of Gossen's book (1995: 41–58). In the spontaneous version, some less mild judgements about Gossen can be found. These have been replaced by euphemisms in the revised one (The word "lazy", for instance, became "a little indolent sometimes".).

Around 1900, some German scholars studied the texts written by Gossen for the examinations he had to pass for obtaining a higher rank. They also studied the official reports on him. However interesting, this did not yield much news in comparison to what can be found in Kortum's note. Unfortunately,

Gossen was born in 1810 in Düren, the Rheinland, Germany. He wanted to study mathematics, but his father wanted him to become a Prussian civil servant. Consequently, he studied cameralistics in Bonn, with a short interruption at the university of Berlin. The position of a civil servant was not his vocation. He worked successively in Cologne, Magdeburg and Erfurt, where he was often absent from office without valid reasons. His career neither brought him quick promotions, nor did it give pleasure to his superiors. Eventually, in 1847, after his father's death, the only thing he could do was to submit his resignation. After a short misadventure in the field of life insurance, he moved into the house of his two sisters in Cologne. There he worked on his book. He wrote under high pressure because his health was badly deteriorating. The book was published in 1854, at his own costs. It was for a good deal based on ideas already put forward in essays for his examinations. In 1858, the author died from tuberculosis, disappointed because his book had sold so very badly.

Right from the first sentence, it is evident that Gossen's orientation is utilitarian:

> Der Mensch wünscht sein Leben zu genießen und setzt seinen Lebenszweck darin, seinen Lebensgenuß auf die möglichste Höhe zu steigern.[9]

Alexander Gray, an English polyglot and one of the first authors of an English book on the history of economics with a long passage devoted to Gossen, stated that Gossen "out-Benthams Bentham" (Gray 1931: 337). This sounds funny (as many remarks in Gray's book), but it puts the reader on the wrong leg because there is no indication of a direct influence of Bentham upon Gossen.[10] A possible direct influence could rather be found in the French literature, well known at the time. A line of influence from or via Helvétius is conceivable if one takes account of the fact that Gossen paid much attention to egoism of Man.[11]

The utilitarian orientation of Gossen's book emerges even more clearly if one considers its first sentence together with the title: *Entwickelung der Gesetze des menschlichen Verkehrs und der daraus fließenden Regeln für menschliches Handeln.*[12] This clearly indicates that the book consists of two parts: a positive and a normative one. Such a partition is more or less standard in utilitarian writings by Bentham and his followers and most continental utilitarian authors. Often much emphasis is put upon the second, normative part. The questions to be answered in

---

all this material was lost during the two world wars. Then, or before these wars already, nearly all traces that could directly witness of Gossen's existence disappeared: his birthplace, his grave and his personal belongings, such as his violin, his notes for and fragments of a book on music and his texts on life insurance. See Georgecu-Roegen's essay in Gossen (1983): xxvii ff. Gossen's birth certificate, however, is still kept in the town hall of Düren; it has been reproduced in Gossen (1995), p. 39.

[9] Man wants to enjoy life and make it his goal to increase pleasures enjoyed throughout life to the highest possible level (1983: 3).

[10] At most an indirect influence; see "Introduction des éditeurs" in Gossen (1995), pp. 1–29.

[11] Claudius Hadrien Helvétius (1715–1771), French philosopher, atheist, is considered as a "materialist" believing that self-interest is one of Man's principal motives. Helvétius was a collaborator of the *Encyclopedie*. He emphasised the importance of education of Man.

[12] The title of the English translation is *The laws of human relations and the rules of human action derived therefrom.*

this literature are as follows: (1) What is the motivation of Man's behaviour? (2) How should society be organised and how should Man behave in this society? The answers are largely based on the following principles, which can be found in this literature: (1) During his lifetime, Man maximises his utility (or, if one should wish so, his happiness), which depends on "his pleasures and his pains". (2) Individual behaviour of Man must be based on good instruction and on adequate legislation. (3) The ultimate goal of Society is the maximisation of the total happiness of all people together. We find all these, somewhat incoherent, elements in Gossen's book.

The conception of utilitarianism as a broad system with a positive and a normative part is widely adhered to in economic circles. Alternatively, there exists also a vast body of literature according to which utilitarianism is considered solely as a big normative system. Remarkably, sharp pro and anti feelings go with this idea; see, for instance, Vergara 1995.

Man as an Isolated Individual

Gossen used geometrical tools to analyse Man's behaviour. The magnitude of pleasure ("die Größe des Genusses") an individual derives from a certain matter during a certain period is represented by the area of a triangle or part of a triangle. Gossen uses the expression "the magnitude of pleasure" here in a meaning we now express by the word "utility", which word I shall mainly use in this chapter. Gossen uses the same expression to indicate what we now call "marginal utility". From the context, however, it is always clear what he is talking about; he never makes a mistake.[13]

Gossen started with the analysis of the thing that is scarce to everybody, namely time. In his graphical analysis, he measured along the horizontal axis the time spent on enjoying some object (watching a picture, for instance); see Fig. 14.1 (Gossen 1854: 8 ff.; I use Gossen's notation). The intensity of pleasure (marginal utility we would say now) is measured along the vertical axis; according to the first law, it is a *decreasing* function of time spent. Measurements of utility do yet not exist, Gossen said, and so, for the time being, he supposed marginal utility to be a linear function of time (1854: 10). Total pleasure (utility) of spending time ad to the enjoyment in question is then equal to the area of the trapezium $adec$. The intensity of pleasure (marginal utility) at the moment d is represented by ed.

If Gossen's work were not totally neglected by the profession but received as a basic, generally accepted piece of theory, right from its publication, economists perhaps would have dealt differently with the notion of time as they actually did. True, the Austrians paid some attention to time, in particular Von Böhm Bawerk, but Jevons did not and Walras only did implicitly; after that, the subject felt into oblivion for a long period.

Gossen first applies the above idea to a situation in which some person has the choice between two pleasures and disposes only of a limited period E of time to

---

[13] At the concerning places in the English translation of the *Entwickelung*, Bliss always added the word "intensity", between square brackets. See, e.g. footnote 2, above. In editing Walras's translation of Gossen's book (Gossen 1995), we brought in similar insertions where necessary.

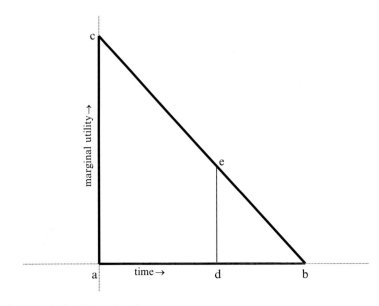

Fig. 14.1 Marginal utility at time *d*

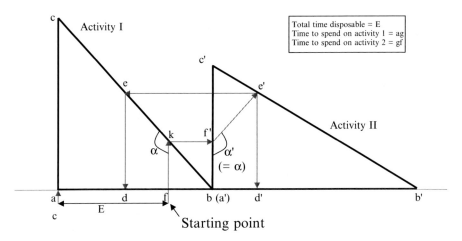

Fig. 14.2 Optimal allocation of time over two enjoyments (Gossen 1854, pp. 12–13)

spend on these pleasures. (One may think, e.g. of the case where one has to wait, say, 10 min in a room in which two Picasso's are exhibited.) This is illustrated in Fig. 14.2 (1854: 13). Let *abc* and *a'b'c'* be the person's "triangles of pleasure"[14] for the activities I and II.

---

[14] Freely adapted from Pareto's terminology (Pareto 1909: 170–171).

If our individual allocates his time optimally, the problem can be formulated as follows: Find two points d and d' on ab and $a'b'$ respectively such that $ad + a'd' = E$ and the sum of the areas of the two trapeziums $adec$ and $a'd'e'c'$ is as high as possible. This maximum will be obtained, as Gossen rightly asserts, if the last intensities, that is to say, the marginal utilities of both pleasures when the time E has been used up, are equal. In Gossen's words, E has to be split over the enjoyments "in einem solchen Verhältniß daß die Größe eines jeden Genusses in dem Augenblick in welchem seine Bereitung abgebrochen wird, bei allen noch die gleiche bleibt" (1854: 12).[15] In modern terms, marginal utilities should be equal. Apparently, Gossen assumed *intra*-personal cardinality of utility. The result is simply demonstrated, Gossen correctly says, by observing that any allocation of E deviating from the just mentioned one would yield a lower sum of the utilities.

For the case of two activities, Gossen presents (more or less between the lines of his pages 12 and 13) a method to construct the point d. In Fig. 14.2, the two triangles are placed with their bases on one and the same horizontal line such that the points a' and b coincide. Let f be the point on ab with $af = E$, the totality of disposable time. Obviously, it is advantageous to start with activity I. The vertical through f on ab cuts bc in k. The intensity fk is manifestly less than $a'c'$. This implies that it is not advantageous to spend all the time af on I; a quantity of pleasure measured by the surface of trapezium $acfk$ would be the result. How to determine the moment of passing from I to II? Let f' be the point on $a'c'$, with $a'f' = fk$. Let point e' on $b'c'$ be constructed such that $\angle a'f'e' = \angle fke$. The horizontal line through e' cuts bc in e. The vertical line through e' cuts $a'b'$ in d', the one through e cuts ab in d. Our individual obtains maximum pleasure if he spends time ad on the first activity and df on the second. His total pleasure is then measured by the sum of the surfaces of the two trapeziums $adec$ and $a'd'e'c'$. In this way, he gains a quantity of pleasure measured by the triangle $f'e'c'$ in comparison with the situation where he had spent all the time E on I. Obviously, a deviation from the optimal partition ad-df will always result in a decrease in total pleasure compared with the optimal situation: the loss in terms of pleasure (utility) would be greater than the gain.

The solution can also be constructed by means of Fig. 14.3. The curve $cc''b'$ in this figure is the result of horizontal addition of the graphs cb and $c'b'$ of Fig. 14.2. Point f on the horizontal axis has been chosen so that, again, the length of af is equal to the available time E. The vertical line through f cuts $cc''b'$ in g. The horizontal line through g intersects cb in e. The vertical from e intersects the time axis in d. For optimally allocating his time E over the two enjoyments, our individual should spend ad units of time to enjoyment I and $df = a'd'$ units to

---

[15] In such a manner that the magnitude [intensity] of each single pleasure at the moment when its enjoyment is broken off shall be the same for all pleasures (1983: 14).

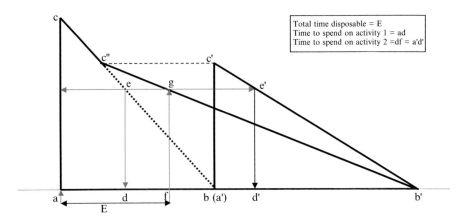

Fig. 14.3 Optimal allocation of time over two enjoyments (general method)

enjoyment II.[16] The advantage of this construction over the foregoing is that it can be generalised to an arbitrary number of goods. Gossen further argues that addition of a new one to the totality of enjoyments implies often an augmentation of the total amount of utility to be obtained by the individual (1854: 21). Because there is only one solution, both constructions are equivalent.

However, for enjoying, one needs more than only time. Generally, the origin of an enjoyment is to be found in goods. In Chap. 1 (1854: 24–27), one finds an analysis of the notion of a "good", resembling Menger's later one (1968 (1871): 7–10). Gossen only distinguished three categories of goods: (1) goods yielding utility on their own, (2) goods yielding utility only when combined with one or more other goods, and (3) goods that do not yield utility on their own, or in combination with other goods, but are used to produce other goods. Gossen asserts that his first law is applicable for all these goods.[17]

Goods can only be obtained by more or less considerable labour by the person who wants to benefit from them. Gossen analysed this in exactly the same way as Jevons (1957 [1871]: 173, Fig. 9) later did; see below, Fig. 14.4 (1854: 39, Fig. 17). On the horizontal axis of this figure, time spent on labour is measured. There are two

---

[16] Gossen's notation is confusing. Here, the symbol E indicates an interval of time; elsewhere in the book, it is used to indicate subsequently total work exerted, income and savings in the land-nationalisation plan. Throughout the whole book, he changes the meaning of certain symbols (see the alphabetical indexes in Gossen 1983, 1995). This detracts the reader from the otherwise well-organised, albeit a little diffuse and bizarre presentation. Each geometrical explication is followed by a "translation" into algebra, which, in its turn, is followed by one or more tables in which the matter is once more presented for certain numerical choices of the parameters of the problem in question (for those who know neither geometry, nor algebra).

[17] Here, he was walking on slippery ground. He considered the period in question as consisting of a large number of "atoms of time" and supposed that each atom of a good is consumed in exactly one atom of time. This "permitted" him to "generalise" figures such as Fig. 14.3 above. Fortunately, he did not go till the dead end of this dubious path of antiquated atomism and found a better basis for making goods comparable, namely labour time, as will be set out below.

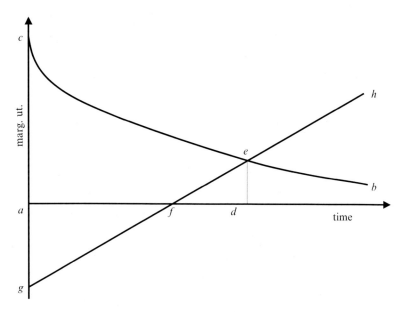

Fig. 14.4 Optimal labour time

graphs in the figure. One, *gh*, displays marginal "disutility of labour". Initially, this disutility may be negative since working is often experienced as agreeable if it is not lasting too long. From time *f* onwards, it becomes gradually more disagreeable. The second graph, *cb*, represents marginal utility of the goods produced. Until time *d*, the marginal utility of the goods produced exceeds the momentary discomfort of labour needed to produce them. The optimal labour time will then be *ad*. The area *cge* indicates total utility; this is the maximum utility to be obtained. With this analysis, Gossen is certainly the first economist who explained the supply of labour by means of utility maximisation. Jevons's approach, in his *Theory*, is similarly graphical and Walras expressed the very same ideas in mathematical formulae in his *Éléments*.

Gossen continued his investigations with the question "which factors determine the magnitude of the area of the triangle?". He judged talent for enjoying things, on one hand, and, on the other hand, ability to work as the two most important factors. Both factors can be enlarged by education in general and instruction in particular. Hence, Gossen's plea for good instruction, for boys as well as for girls, will not come as a surprise. Here, however, a problem arises, as we shall see below.[18]

Exchange

Each person living in isolation faces two contradictory prescriptions to increase total happiness. The first one is specialisation, which leads to greater productivity but a smaller number of goods, and the second is extension of the number of goods

---

[18] For a nice alternative presentation of Gossen's mathematics of utility and disutility, see Tubaro (2009).

available, which leads to a greater potential of happiness. The individual cannot simultaneously fulfil these two requirements on his own. This, Gossen explains, is why there was always exchange. Therefore, he goes on to analyse actions and inter-actions of two or more persons. It appears that Gossen was puzzled a little by this extension and confused the notions of maximum individual utility and maximum collective utility, as we shall see.

In exchange, each individual involved should benefit personally, Gossen pro-claims as a preliminary condition. He starts with the simple case of two exchangers, one possessing a quantity of a certain good and the other some of another good. Again, making use of geometrical tools, he makes clear that it may be advantageous to both persons to exchange a part of their good for some quantity of the other good (1854: 83).

The quite reasonable prerequisite that all exchangers should profit personally from an exchange is a too broad criterion for its unambiguous explanation. Therefore, Gossen needed a "workable" criterion whose application leads to a clear result. He found such a criterion, but, unfortunately, at the cost of the prerequisite, as we shall see. This criterion, to be fulfilled by a "correctly accomplished" exchange, is as follows: exchange should bring about the *highest total utility of all participating people together.* Here, he introduces without warning the notion of collective utility over and above individual utilities; apparently, he supposes utility to be cardinal. So he wonders (1854: 85):

> Wie ist der Tausch einzurichten, damit ein Größtes von Werth entsteht?[19]

Gossen's correct answer to this inappropriate, irrelevant question is (ibid.) as follows:

> Damit durch den Tausch ein Größtes von Werth entstehe, muß sich nach demselben jeder einzelnen Gegenstand unter alle Menschen so vertheilt finden, daß das letzte Atom, welches jedem von einen Gegenstande zufällt, bei ihm den gleich großen Genuß schafft, wie das letzte Atom desselben Gegenstandes bei einem jeden andern (1854: 85).[20]

The above-mentioned prerequisite would then automatically be fulfilled, Gossen believed wrongly. Walras was probably the first who disapproved of Gossen's utili-tarian rule.[21] According to Gossen's criterion, Walras argues, the final distribution of the goods only depends on the totals of the goods brought in and not on the partici-pants' individual quantities with which they enter into the exchange.[22] Such a maxi-mum, therefore, can never be the result of free exchange. It can only be enforced by some authority, because the rights of property of some of the participants may be infringed upon. Once the maximum of the sum of all individual utilities is attained,

---

[19] How is exchange to be arranged so that a maximum of [total] value will result (1983: 100)?

[20] In order that a maximum of [total] value be achieved through exchange, it is necessary that after its completion, each commodity be distributed among all individuals in such a way that the last atom of each commodity received by every individual will create for him the same pleasure as the last atom of the same commodity received by every other individual (ibid.).

[21] In his *Études d'économie sociale,* 1896: 209–212 (1990: 181–184; English translation: Walras (2010: 137–40), and in the second edition of *Éléments d'économie politique pure* (Walras 1988: 250–251). See, however, also Wicksell (1954): 19.

[22] 'Given that the individuals do not have all the same, linear utility function.

Walras argued, the ensuing individual amounts of utility do not necessarily coincide with maximum utility for each individual personally, given the quantity of goods with which he entered into the exchange. (In other words, the maximum of a sum is not the same as the sum of the maxima.) It may even be possible that somebody's utility will decrease in an exchange à la Gossen. This can be made clear by the following, somewhat extreme, example. Let there be a number of persons who all possess only a little of one of a number of goods and let there be one single person possessing all these goods in large quantities. If all these persons entered into an exchange where Gossen's criterion is applied, then, after the exchange, the latter individual would have less of everything than he possessed before. Nevertheless, the sum of all the individual utilities taken together would be considerably greater than before, because the poor people's high marginal utilities taken together will certainly exceed the rich man's marginal utilities, which are, because of Gossen's first law, considerably lower. It escaped Gossen that his criterion does not guarantee that all goods will be exchanged in fixed proportions against each other; in other words, Gossen does not notice that there are no exchange ratios (prices) equal for everybody. His rule may be a matter of course when friends have a party where people bring in dishes of food and bottles of beverages to put together and to be consumed freely,

> mais, enfin, la société n'est pas un pique-nique,

as Walras (1990: 184; 2010: 140) says. The eventual result of this "pick-nick" only depends on the totality of the goods brought in, not on the individual people's initial quantities. Walras summarises (1990: 181, italics in original; 2010: 138):

> Ce troc, aussi bien défini (…), est donc une opération par laquelle la satisfaction des besoins des (…) troqueurs pris ensemble est portée au maximum absolu et non plus relatif, aucun compte n'étant tenu des quantités de marchandises possédées, autrement dit, abstraction étant faite du droit de propriété de chaque troqueur sur sa marchandise. C'est un troc *communiste* : il n'aura lieu en toute certitude que par l'*autorité* de l'État, et il amènera l'*égalité* qui résulterait à la fois de l'égalité des besoins et celle des moyens de les satisfaire. Il s'opère sur le terrain de la *fraternité*.[23]

Gossen apparently was ignorant of all these subtleties and continued his story by remarking that in reality, people do not directly barter goods. In practice, it became usual to exchange all goods against some specific one acceptable to anybody, which therefore can be used to obtain other goods. This good, Gossen explained, is called money and the goods are exchanged for money in proportions fixed for everybody; most people buy goods by means of money earned by selling their labour force. In other words, there is a price system. How all this comes into being remains vague. This is not amazing if one considers his misconception of the notion of exchange.

---

[23] Hence, this exchange, however well defined (…), is an operation by which the satisfaction of (…) the exchangers taken together is brought to an absolute maximum and not to a relative one, because the quantities possessed of the commodities have not been taken into account. In other words, abstraction has been made of each exchanger's right of property on his merchandise. This is a *communist* exchange: it can certainly not take place otherwise than by the *authority* of the State and it will bring about the *equality* that results simultaneously from the equality of the needs and that of the means to satisfy them. It functions in the domain of the *fraternity* (See also Wicksell 1954: 19, Berthoud 1988, and Lallement 1988).

The maximisation problem discussed above (maximisation of total utility of all individuals together) should now be resolved for the more advanced situation, where money is the means of exchange. Now, Gossen makes another mistake, which, however, turns out fortunately.[24] He arrives at the untenable conclusion that the aforementioned maximum of social utility will be attained together with the simultaneous attainment of maximum lifetime utility of all individuals separately (1854: 93–94). From this it follows that, in Gossen's view, the solution of one of the two maximisation problems has been found, once the other has been solved. In the more general case, with money as a means of exchange, the problem of individual utility maximisation seems to be the simplest of the two. Its solution has been formulated in what would become known as Gossen's second law, repeated here because of its importance:

> Der Mensch erlangt also ein Größtes von Lebensgenuß, wenn er sein ganzes erarbeitetes Geld, E, der Art auf die verschiedene Genüsse vertheilt (…) das bei jedem einzelnen Genuß das letzte darauf verwendete Geldatom den Gleich großen Genuß gewährt.

In itself, this citation is a true assertion. Gossen's proved it, just as in the preceding section, by observing that any deviation from the prescription above will lead to a lower amount of utility. It is a necessary condition for individual utility maximisation given prices and income as, indeed, Gossen said in his own words, but it is not true that it has something to do with the maximisation of social utility, as is likewise his assertion. Hence, something went wrong in Gossen's reasoning.

Gossen used his algebra for illustrative purposes only and not as an analytical tool. If he only had written out his results in mathematical symbols, he would have detected his mistake. For the maximisation of the sum of all individual utilities together, the following relations should hold good:

$$r_{A1} = r_{A2} = \cdots = r_{AJ}$$
$$r_{B1} = r_{B2} = \cdots = r_{BJ}$$
$$\cdots$$
$$r_{M1} = r_{M2} = \cdots = r_{MJ}. \tag{14.1}$$

The symbol r_{A1} denotes the marginal utility of good (A) for individual 1 and so forth.

For the maximisation of all the individual utilities separately, the following relations should hold good:

$$r_{A1} / p_A = r_{B1} / p_B = \cdots r_{M1} / p_M$$
$$r_{A2} / p_A = r_{B2} / p_B = \cdots r_{M2} / p_M$$
$$\cdots$$
$$r_{AJ} / p_A = r_{BJ} / p_B = \cdots r_{MJ} / p_M. \tag{14.2}$$

The symbol p_A stands for the price of good (A) and so forth.

Gossen, too, would immediately have seen that the two conditions are not identical, irrespective of the fact that in (14.2) prices have been introduced. In (14.1), the

---

[24] See also Van Daal (1993, 1996).

equalities are per good over the individuals and in (14.2) per individual over the goods. Where (14.1) relates to an absolute maximum of all utilities added together, the solution of (14.2) would in general lead to a lower total of the individual utilities. Gossen's thesis that free exchange will lead to maximal collective utility is one of the first examples of a confusion that is lasting in theoretical economics until nowadays, particularly in welfare economics.

Anyway, for Gossen, the second law indicated how Man has to act in order to achieve maximum lifetime utility, given his personal endowments of mind and body and his material wealth, from all of which he has the fullest right to reap the fruits himself. So the problem of Gossen's dubious utilitarianism was solved automatically, since from this point onwards in the book (that is to say, the last 180 pages), the second law is the guiding principle. The law's formulation, however, changed thereby tacitly:

> Every individual will spend his income such that the (marginal) utility of the last "atom of money" spent on a certain good or service is the same as the (marginal) utility of the last atom of money spent on whatever other good or service and is also the same as the (marginal) disutility of the labour to obtain the last money atom of income.

Gossen was somewhat vague about the economic environment in which all this happens. Apparently, he took the economic parameters and in particular their determination for granted. It can be read from between the lines that he had in mind a situation of free competition where prices fall more or less out of the blue. Considering prices as given and acting according to the second law, the individuals maintain a situation of general economic equilibrium avant la lettre.

Gossen's stipulation that everybody involved in an exchange should personally benefit from that exchange does not make him a precursor of Pareto, whose criterion relates to a state, or rather a collection of individual positions: in a Pareto-optimal state, it is impossible to bring some individuals in a better position without harming others. Both Gossen's stipulation of maximum collective utility and his second law are prerequisites for exchange itself, although the first one is untenable if combined with a price system where every good has only one price.

Concluding, we can say that Gossen found "the right path" (i.e. the one beginning with his second law) only after having made two mistakes that cancelled each other in a fortunate way.

Habits

Now, an important question comes up, as Gossen noticed: How does all this work out in daily practice? In this connection, he points to a notable trait of mankind (1854: 127):

> Jeder Mensch, mag er welch immer einer Stande angehören, nimmt sich im Großen und Ganzen zur Einrichtung seines Lebens die Sitte zur Richtschnur, wie sie sich bei seinen Standesgenossen gebildet hat.[25]

---

[25] Every individual, regardless of his status, will, by and large, take custom, as it has developed among people of his own class, as a guideline in the conduct of his own affairs (1983: 150).

This does not mean considerable rigidity in Man's behaviour. However, there was, there is and there will always be a certain general pattern in a person's conduct, usually differing per social class. The patterns will change gradually because everybody has the right to deviate from custom, thereby taking care not to infringe upon others' rights or possessions, in order to test whether this will yield more pleasure. If so, he no longer submits to the prevailing custom and other people will follow him. Improved customs will result. Such improvements go hand in hand with increasing knowledge of the laws of nature and new insights with respect to production methods of goods and creation of new pleasures. For Gossen, the maturation of customs, i.e. the evolution of society, is a substantial consequence of human conduct. This conduct is guided by the laws concerning enjoyment and, more generally, the Man's life purpose. Here we see, indeed, Gossen as a very early herald of pieces of theory that are now known under names such as adaptive behaviour and learning processes.

Hence, Gossen's *main principle* that human happiness should be brought to its maximum will be achieved by the operation of three laws:

- The law of decreasing marginal utility (Gossen's first law).
- The law of balancing marginal utility (Gossen's second law).
- The law of taking custom as a starting point for deviating from "normal" behaviour.

The latter shall henceforth be indicated as "Gossen's third law"; see Jolink and Van Daal 1998.

Gossen's first law is not a law at all; it is a hypothesis. Gossen's second law is not a law either; it is rather a theorem, derived from the hypothesis that an individual maximises his utility under the restriction imposed by his income, or his budget. Gossen's third law (he himself speaks of a *moral law* (1854: 143)) is neither a law in the present sense of fact of nature, nor a legal law, but rather a rule of behaviour derived from observation. Notwithstanding the above terminological objections, I shall continue to speak of Gossen's three laws.

The Main Principle and the Three Laws: Synthesis

Gossen used his laws in the rest of his book, while dealing with practical problems and policy recommendations. Every individual apart must obtain maximum happiness by just following his own way in the egoistic sense mentioned above. Gossen meant by this, as I already said above, that everyone tries to spend his income such that the marginal utility of the last "atom of money" spent on whatever good or service is the same for all these goods and services and is equal to the marginal disutility of the labour by which he acquired that income (his second law, somewhat generalised). This second law is, indeed, necessary for optimally acquiring and spending income, but it is not the condition of maximum total utility, as has been set out above. Total utility can only be maximised if some people are willing to transfer for nothing some of their belongings to others, or are willing to accept less favourable exchange ratios (prices) than other people. This can never have been Gossen's design, and so it was fortunate that he (intuitively?) took the second law, in the formulation just above, as the guideline to be used further in his book.

The third law is helpful in the sense that the fact that most people follow customs has, as Gossen guesses, a stabilising effect on prices and other parameters that determine the economic framework within which the individuals have to try to find their way.

However, there is more.[26] As is well known from the literature on optimisation problems, there are often several, different optimal situations among which there is at least one *optimum optimorum*, with utility at its absolute maximum. If an individual started his optimisation procedure just from scratch, there would be a good chance that he missed the absolute maximum, and had to satisfy himself with a lower level of utility than possible in his situation. Here, the third law comes in. Taking customs as a starting point for his optimisation procedure, an individual who has somewhat more initiative, shrewdness and subtlety and has perceived some changes in the economic parameters or has some new ideas will more likely find the new global utility maximum. It may be expected, namely, that the establishment by trial and error of customs in the past has led to optimal behaviour, and so one may imagine that an individual who thinks that circumstances have changed and starts from custom as the point of departure to try to find a new optimum is restricting the domain of his maximisation problem in an efficient way. Therefore, there is a good chance that there will not be a multitude of maxima most of which are only local and therefore ineffectual. Of course, Gossen did not express this argument in precise terms, but it can be inferred in between the lines of the pertinent passages and in some statements, such as in the paragraph passing over from page 132 to page 133 of his book in which he says that it is the task of a teacher to help his student to find an "environment" in which the student may find "greatest total life pleasure" to be achieved by "means also available by the student". The teacher tries to achieve this by pointing to examples given by other people whose situation resembles the student's (future) situation.

Policy Recommendations: Removing Obstacles

Gossen concludes the first part, on positive theory, as follows (1854: 121):

> Die Menschheit kann ihren Wohlstand nur dadurch erhöhen, wenn es gelingt beim Einzelnen Menschen: (1) die absolute Größe der Genüsse, (2) die Arbeitskräfte und die Geschicklichkeit im Gebrauch derselben, (3) die Lebenskräfte zu steigern, und (4) den Rechtszustand zu befestigen (…).

---

[26] David Levy brought me upon the idea of this paragraph.

Hierauf, verbunden mit Wegräumung der Hindernisse, welche sich dem Einzelnen in den Weg stellen, den günstigsten Productionszweig zu ergreifen und sein Geld in freiesten Weise zu verwenden, ist darum einzig und allein das Augenmerk zu richten, um der Menschheit zur höchstmöglichen Glückseligkeit zu verhelfen.[27]

This can only be done by looking further into the world surrounding Man. Therefore, Gossen dealt extensively with the outer world of Mankind. First, he described a number of contemporaneous evils, which I will pass over in the present chapter. Then he concluded that there are still too many obstacles that prevent Man from acting according to the "laws of nature" as set out above. The rest of the book consists of a systematic, lengthy treatment of each of these obstacles and the reform schemes to take them away. The obstacles and the ensuing policy recommendations will now briefly pass the review.

The first obstacle (1854: 191–198) is formed by the fact that Man is born helpless without any skill. This has to be overcome by proper education, whereby no distinction should be made between girls and boys and where the children should be protected by the prohibition of child labour. Postponing entry into the labour market and spending the free time to education will enable a person to increase his lifetime, his lifetime production and, therefore, his and others' lifetime utility.

Second (1854: 198–228), where Man has specialised in the production of one or only a few products, he must be able to exchange his production for other goods, to be used for his own consumption.[28] However, there is nothing that is by itself the best means of exchange. Therefore, Gossen carefully devised and exposed a monetary system, with only metallic currency.

Third (1854: 228–238), people should freely and completely benefit from the fruits of their own labour because history testifies that freedom and private property, together with safety, have been most beneficial for the increase of human wealth. Therefore, there should be no protection, no entrance limiting institutions as guilds and examinations, and no subsidies. Everybody who wants to exist should create himself the means for his existence, but then he must be able to enter freely the profession that is most suited for him.

Fourth (1854: 239–249), in the same connection, Man should be able to obtain sufficient capital for his production. Therefore, Gossen proposed a (cooperative) credit system of which he presented all the details.

Fifth (1854: 250–273), in the same line, he required that Man should dispose of enough, appropriate land for exercising the profession he has chosen. This has led

---

[27] Humanity can increase its welfare only if the single individual succeeds (1) in increasing the absolute magnitude of pleasures, (2) in increasing the capacity for work and the efficiency in its use, (3) in increasing the vital forces [life expectancy] and (4) in strengthening law and order (…).

To help humanity attain the highest possible state of bliss, full attention must be paid to these matters. To achieve the goal, we must attempt to remove obstacles that confront the individual in the choice of the most promising field of production and in spending his money without any constraints (1983: 144).

[28] Gossen seems sometimes only to consider independently working labourers (1854: 121).

Gossen to a scheme for land reform that must eventually lead to a situation in which the State owns all the land, which will, then, be hired out competitively (procuring an income for the State which allows abolition of taxes).[29] Note that the last three points clearly indicate that Gossen already had a lucid conception of the notion of production factors and their subdivision into the three categories land, human capital and artificial capital.

Conclusion

In spite of his plea for State ownership of the land, the *Entwickelung* depicts a highly liberal scheme in which Man has his destiny in his own hands in a society evolving to a state of bliss (1854: 276):

> und so fehlt dann der Erde durchaus Nichts mehr zu einem vollendeten Paradiese.[30]

For Gossen, the point of convergence of this evolution was clear: an ideal situation on earth.

In the last page (1854: 277), he draws a parallel between, on one hand, the simple laws of nature that determine the forces that hold the physical world together and let it continually develop, and, on the other hand, how Man's *egoism* is

> die Kraft die den Fortschritt des Menschengeschlechts in Kunst und Wissenschaft in seinem materiellen und geistigen Wohl allein und unaufhaltsam bewirkt.[31]

In the last phrase of the book, Gossen seems to reveal himself frankly as the preacher-economist:

> Mensch, hast Du ganz und gar die Schönheit dieser Construction der Schöpfung erkannt, dann versinke in Anbetung vor dem Wesen, welches in seiner unbegreiflichen Weisheit, Macht und Güte durch ein anscheinend so unbedeutendes Mittel so Ungeheures, und für Dich so unberechenbar Gutes zu bewirken im Stande und geneigt war, und mache Dich dann der Wohlthaten, mit denen dieses Wesen Dich überschüttet hat, dadurch würdig, daß Du zu Deinem eigenen Wohle Deine Handlungen so einrichtet, daß jenes wünschenswertheste Resultat möglichst beschleunigt wird![32]

---

[29] Walras must have been very amazed when finding systematically worked out his own scheme for land reform, advanced from the beginning of his career onwards (1859; see Walras 1881). Jevons did not inform him on this point, because Adamson only translated some parts of the book.

[30] There is nothing further wanting in the world to make it a perfect paradise (1983: 298).

[31] The sole and irresistible force by which humanity may progress in the arts and science for both its material and intellectual welfare (1983: 299).

[32] Mankind, once you have recognised completely and entirely the beauty of this plan of the Creation, steep yourself in adoration of the Being, which in its incomprehensible wisdom, power, and goodness has been able, by means apparently so insignificant, to bring about on your behalf something so enormously incalculably beneficial. Make yourself worthy of all that this Being has showered upon you, organising your actions for your own benefit in such a manner that this most desirable result is brought about as quickly as possible! (1983: 299).

With this hollow phrase in adoration to a completely passive, if not absent Being, Gossen says, in fact, no more and no less than that it would be unwise to violate economic laws. Throughout the whole book, one can find passages in which Gossen refers to the Creator. At the same time, however, he makes clear that this Creator, once having achieved his creation, is now entirely passive, leaving it to Man (in truth to Gossen) to discover the rules that will lead him to happiness, and to apply these rules. Gossen's "religiosity" should, therefore, be taken *cum grano salis.*[33]

I believe one may safely conclude from the preceding account that Gossen, indeed, had a complete theory for describing and explaining human behaviour in all its economic aspects and that from this he deduced a detailed prescription for that behaviour. This means that it is unfair to consider him only as a precursor of later pioneers as Jevons, Menger and Walras. The main reason for the bad treatment Gossen has met with in the literature is the fact that only few writers have read his book from cover to cover; those writers' opinions were repeated by the rest of the writers on Gossen. The latter opinions concentrated mainly on his first two laws, on his "apostleship" and on the bizarre wording by means of which Gossen expressed himself. Indeed, he wrote in complete isolation without the help of colleagues or ghostwriters. The *Entwickelung* is, however, not that inaccessible as one tries to make us believe.

We have seen how Gossen envisaged a gradual change of human society as a consequence of a system of "laws of nature" in which customs and habits have found a place, thus suggesting a fascinating relation between these laws and evolution. The notion of evolution should thereby be comprehended in the special significance of a kind of mechanism leading society smoothly to the ideal situation. As so many other visionaries, Gossen did not present a clear, detailed description of that ideal. It may be inferred, however, from some passages and from between the lines of his book that what Gossen meant was a situation in which the afore-mentioned obstacles have been removed and where everybody, on the basis of the three laws above (the third one becoming more and more superfluous), will be allowed to provide for himself what he needs for meeting his wants, freely using his own capacities and property, in free competition with other individuals without infringing upon their rights, and where the role of the State will be restricted to guaranteeing this freedom. The State will own all the land and the individuals will freely compete for its use, which will lead to an optimal utilisation of the land; this will provide the State with an income and make taxation needless.

I think that the idea of such an evolution can be found already in the title of the book, in particular in the first word, *Entwickelung*. Walras translated it into "exposition" (Gossen 1995) and Bagiotti into "sviluppo" (Gossen 1950, 1975). Blitz evaded the problem by leaving the word out of the translation of the English title (Gossen 1983). Both Walras's and Bagiotti's translations seem to be correct since the German word is somewhat ambiguous: it may mean exposition, as Walras has understood, but it may also mean something as development, spread, growth or expansion, and this looks as to have been Bagiotti's interpretation. Understanding the word in the latter

---

[33] See also Steiner (2010), who went more deeply into this element of Gossen's work.

signification, I suggest, perhaps in line with Bagiotti, that Gossen indicated already in the title of his book that the "laws" governing human society should develop to those that form his system and that this entails progress of society to the ideal.

References

Berthoud A (1988) "Economie politique et morale chez Walras," *Économies et Sociétés*, Série *Oeconomia*, Histoire de la Pensée Economique, PE, n° 9, 3/1988: 65–93
Gossen HH (1854) *Entwickeling der Gesetze des menschlichen Verkehrs und der daraus fließenden Regeln für menschliches Handeln*, Braunschweig: Vieweg und Sohn. (Second edition: Prager, Berlin, 1889; Third edition (introduced by F.A. von Hayek): Prager, Berlin, 1927; Reprints of the first edition: Liberac, Amsterdam, 1967, and (W. Krelle and C. Recktenwald (ed)), Verlag Wirtschaft und Finanzen, Düsseldorf, 1987) (*Bibliographic note*: There is some confusion with respect to the exact title of Gossen's book. The title mentioned above can be found on the title page and the front cover of the first edition; the half-title (p. III), however, differs slightly: its first word is "Entwickeling". The second edition is in fact a sort of reedition of the first one in the sense that the unsold copies of the first edition have been given a new title page with a new date, a new half-title with "Entwickeling" instead of "Entwickeling", thus removing the inconsistency between the titles, and a short publisher's preamble motivating the publication of the new edition as a consequence of the increased interest in the book because of the work of Jevons and Walras. In the third edition the word "Entwickeling" has everywhere been changed into "Entwickeling", as it is spelled nowadays)
Gossen EE (1950) Sviluppo delle leggi del commercio umano, translated and introduced by Tullio Bagiotti, Padua: Cedam
Gossen HH (1975) Sviluppo delle leggi di comportimento umano e delle regolo d'azione che ne derivano, in Marginalisti matematici (Gossen, Launhardt, Auspitz, Lieben), revised translation and new introductions by Tullio Bagiotti, UTET, Turin 1975, pp 87–425
Gossen HH (1983) The laws of human relations and the rules of human action derived therefrom, translated by Rudolph Blitz, with an introductory essay by Nicholas Georgescu-Roegen. The MIT Press, Cambridge
Gossen HH (1995) Exposition des lois de l'échange et des règles de l'industrie qui s'en déduisent, translated (in 1879) by Léon Walras and Charles Secrétan, introduced and annotated by Jan van Daal, Albert Jolink, Jean-Pierre Potier and Jean-Michel Servet, under the auspices of the Centre Auguste et Léon Walras, Université Lumière Lyon-2 and the Tinbergen Instituut, Erasmus Universiteit Rotterdam. Economica, Paris
Gray A (1931) The development of economic doctrine. Longmans, Green and Co., London
Ikeda Y (2000) Hermann Heinrich Gossen: a Wirkungsgeschichte of an ignored Mathematical Economist. J Econ Stud 27:394–415
Jevons WS (1957 [1871]) The theory of political economy; reprint, 5th edn. Kelley, New York, 1965
Jolink A, van Daal J (1998) Gossen's laws. Hist Polit Econ 29:43–50
Kautz J (1858–1860) Theorie und Geschichte der National-Oeokonomie, 2 vols. Carl Gerold's Sohn, Vienna
Kortum KJH (1881) "Notice biographique sur H.H. Gossen", translated (from German) by Léon Walras, in Gossen 1995, pp 33–39
Kurz HD (2008) Hermann Heinrich Gossen, in Heinz D. Kurz (ed), Klassiker des ökonomischen Denkens, vol 1, Von Adam Smith to Alfred Marshall, Verlag C. H. Beck oHG, Munich
Kurz HD (2009) Wer war Hermann Heinrich Gossen (1810–1858), Namensgeber eines der Preise des Vereins für Socialpolitik? Schmollers Jahrbuch 209:1–28
Lallement J (1988) "Léon Walras et les idéaux de 1789," in G. Faccarello and Ph. Steiner (eds), La pensée économique pendant la révolution française, PUG, Grenoble, pp 609–618

Lange FA (1875) Die Arbeiterfrage. Ihre Bedeutung für Gegenwart und Zukunft, 3rd edn. Bleuler-Hausheer, Winterthur

Menger C (1968) Grundsätze der Volkswirtschaftslehre (1871). Band I of Gesammelte Werke, edited by F.A. von Hayek, J.C.B. Mohr (Paul Siebeck), Tübingen

Niehans J (1987) Gossen, Hermann Heinrich (1810-1858). In: Eatwell J, Milgate M, Newman P (eds) The New Palgrave, a Dictionary of Economics, vol 2. MacMillan, London, pp 550–4

Pareto V (1981[1909]) Manuel d'économie politique, volume VII of Vilfredo Pareto, Oeuvres complètes, edited by Giovanni Busino. Droz, Genève

Steiner P (2011) The creator, human conduct and the maximisation of utility in Gossen's economic theory. Eur J Hist Econ Thought 18(3):353–379

Tubaro P (2009) Les mathématiques du plaisir et de la peine: la théorie du choix individuel de Hermann Heinrich Gossen, in A. Alcouffe et C. Diebolt, 2009, La pensée économique allemande, Economica, Paris, 245–267

Van Daal J (1993) La deuxième loi de Gossen: Trouvaille heureuse. Revue d'Économie Politique 103:719–729

Van Daal J (1996) From Utilitarianism to hedonism: Gossen, Jevons and Walras. J Hist Econ Thought 17:271–286

Vergara F (1995) "Utilitarisme et hédonisme. Une critique d'Elie Halévy …et d'autres", Économies et Sociétés, Cahiers de l'ISMEA, Série Œconomia, PE n° 24, Octobre 1995, pp 31–60

Walras L (1874) "Principe d'une théorie mathématique de l'échange. Correspondance entre M. Jevons et M. Walras." Journal des économistes, tome 34, 3e série, n° 100:5–21 and n° 102:417–422

Walras L (1881) "Théorie mathématique du prix des terres et de leur rachat par l'Etat", Bulletin de la Société vaudoise des sciences naturelles, 2e série, vol 17, pp 189–284

Walras L (1885) Un économiste inconnu, H.H. Gossen. Journal des Économistes 30:68–90; 260–261 (Also in Gossen 1995: 41–58)

Walras L (1965) Correspondence of Léon Walras and related papers, 3 vols. Edited by William Jaffé, North-Holland Publishing Company, Amsterdam

Walras L (1988) Éléments d'économie politique pure, ou théorie de la richesse sociale, variorum edition of the editions of 1874, 1877, 1889, 1896, 1900 and 1926 (and of de edition of the Abrégé of 1938) augmented with a translation of the notes by W. Jaffé in Elements of pure economics (1954), prepared by Claude Mouchot, under the auspices of the Centre Auguste et Léon Walras, Université Lumière Lyon-2, volume VIII of Oeuvres économiques complètes d'Auguste et Léon Walras. Economica, Paris

Walras L (1990) Études d'économie sociale (Théorie de la répartition de la richesse sociale), prepared by Pierre Dockès, under the auspices of the Centre Auguste et Léon Walras, Université Lumière Lyon-2, volume IX of Oeuvres économiques complètes d'Auguste et Léon Walras, Economica, Paris. First edition 1896

Walras L (2010) Studies of Social Economics, English translation by Jan van Daal and Donald Walker of the second edition (1936) of Léon Walras, Études d'économie sociale (first edition 1896), augmented with an introduction and annotations, Abingdon/New York: Routledge

Wicksell K (1954) Value, Capital and Rent, translation (by SH Frowein) of Über Wert, Kapital und Rente (1893); reprint: Kelley, New York, 1970

Chapter 15
Gustav Schmoller as a Scientist of Political Economy

Reginald Hansen

Introduction, Controversial Opinions About Schmoller. Was He a Historian or an Economist?

Schmoller was during his lifetime and still is a most controversially disputed scientist. Supporters of socialistic opinions would blame him for having helped the antiquated capitalism to survive.[1] Adherents of liberalistic views accused him – and still do so – or present arguments and tools for blending a natural order of economy with obstructive and most troublesome interventions, delaying progress.[2] Many scholars of economic sciences picked up the accusations J.A. Schumpeter attributed to Schmoller's contributions when stating in 1913 that "the term theory became so outlawed, that it is today sometimes replaced by that of "intellectual reproduction" or "doctrine" in order not to revoke from the start a host of prejudices", so that "a reaction began to set in under Austrian and foreign influence against economics without thinking..."[3] And F.G. Lane in 1956 stated that "the high praise that Schumpeter bestowed on Schmoller in 1926 was primarily a tribute to the position which Schmoller, 9 years after his death then occupied within Germany".[4] In fact, Schumpeter had in the meantime given a positive review in 1926, which for all his

---

[1] As example, see Völkerling, F. (1959), Der deutsche Kathedersozialismus, Berlin, Diss. Halle-Wittenberg, p. 29, p. 63.

[2] See: Holzwarth, Fritz (1985), Ordnung der Wirtschaft durch Wettbewerb, Entwicklung der Ideen der Freiburger Schule, Stuttgart, p. 19 ff.

[3] Schumpeter, J.A. (1912), Economic Doctrines and Method, London, p. 12. Translated 1954. Schumpeter, J.A. (1954), History of Economic Analysis, New York, p. 84.

[4] Lane, F.C. (1956), "Some Heirs of Gustav von Schmoller", in, Lambie, J.T. (1956) (ed.), Architects and Craftsmen in History. In Honour of Abbot Payson Usher, Tübingen, p. 10, p. 22.

R. Hansen (✉)
Luxemburger Str 426, D-50937 Cologne, Germany
e-mail: dr.reghansen@t-online.de

J.G. Backhaus (ed.), *Handbook of the History of Economic Thought*,
The European Heritage in Economics and the Social Sciences,
DOI 10.1007/978-1-4419-8336-7_15, © Springer Science+Business Media, LLC 2012

life he never thought necessary to repeat. So from leading text books on the history of economic sciences, students of economics in Germany until to today learn the summarising verdict Schumpeter reflected in his *History of Economic Analysis* in 1954, that "economic theory as understood in England was in many places almost completely in abeyance for several decades…".[5] As a matter of fact, according to the very influential economist Erich Schneider, Schmoller even delayed progress of all economic science in Germany for more than 3 decades.[6] Sometimes the question was discussed: Was Schmoller an Economist or was he a Historian? Economists often preferred to classify him as a Historian and vice versa. For Historians, this was due to the shift of approach Schmoller had employed for his historical contributions as will be shown. Similar judgements were discussed among historians after Schmoller's death.

Also for politicians, questionable characteristics about Gustav Schmoller's activities were made public, even making him responsible for circumstances leading to World War I. The notorious German weekly magazine *Der Spiegel* in an article in 1964 put the name Gustav Schmoller in front of a list of politicians and scientists judged to be responsible for Germany's setting out for the disaster of 1914.[7] The magazine read by the majority of Germany's population for this opinion quoted the book *Griff nach der Weltmacht* (Grip to the world domination), which was written by Fritz Fischer in 1961, a professor for History at the University of Hamburg.[8] The interpretation of the events in this book was thoroughly in line with the re-education principles of the victorious allied nations prescribed to the German teaching authorities.[9] But this judgement was certainly thoroughly inconsistent with the spirit and the contexts of Schmoller's many contributions for which he often would ironically

---

[5] Schumpeter, J.A. (1954), History of Economic Analysis, p. 804.

[6] Schneider, E. (1970), 3.A Erführung in die Wirthschaftstheorie, IV. Teil, Ausgewählte Kapitel der Geschichte der Wirtschaftstheorie I. Bd., p. 295 und 325–328.

[7] Augstein, R. (1964), Article in: Der Spiegel, Heft 11, 1964, p. 47: see: Fischer F. (1961), Griff nach der Weltmacht, Die Kriegsschuld des Kaiserlichen Deutschland 1914/18, Düsseldorf, p. 18. See also the most negative review of Gustav Schmoller in German schoolbooks, such as: Anderson, P. (1971), "Gustav von Schmoller", in, Deutsche Historiker, 2. Bd., Göttingen, in: Wehler, H.U. (ed.) (1985), Das deutsche Kaiserreich in der Geschichte, Bd. 3, p. 39–65.

For re-education see: Mosberg, H. (1991), Re-education. Umerziehung und Lizenzpresse in Nachkriegsdeutschland, München (Diss. Kiel 1989). Therein: Report of a Conference on Germany after the War called by the Committee on Post War Planning representing the American Association on Mental Deficiency, American Branch of the International League Against Epilepsy, American Neurological Association, American Arthopsychiatric Association, American Psychiatric Association, American Society for research in Psychosomatic Problems and the National Commity for Mental Hygiene, inc. held at the College of Physicians and Surgeons, Columbia University, New York City, on April 29th and 30th and May 6th, 20th and 21st, and June 3rd and 4th 1944. See: long term plans, items 5 to 8, page 178.

[8] Fischer, F. (1961), Griff nach der Weltmacht. Die Kriegsschuld des Kaiserlichen Deutschland 1914/18, Düsseldorf, p. 18.

[9] See note nr. 7.

in Germany during his lifetime be called a mercantile-minded immigrant from Württemberg as a Prussian by option. So prejudices displaced historical truth.

Right at the beginning of this paper, I would like to state that except for the officially so-called Pflegeversicherung, that is the old-age care insurance, I know of no item of today's German Social Market Economy (Soziale Marktwirtschaft) that was not demanded as necessary or advisable by Gustav Schmoller in an article printed in the liberal periodical "Preußische Jahrbücher" in three continuations in 1864 and 1865.[10] The law to integrate all citizens in an obligatory old-age care insurance was not introduced until 1995.[11] It benefits all citizens and not the poor in distress only, to which Schmoller had devoted all measures of social policy he demanded. Redistribution of income on a large scale in Germany of today is a characteristic of a welfare state to which since 1957 the social state of Germany has gradually been transformed. The old-age care insurance is the best example for the change of the guiding principle of institutions for which Schmoller 40 years after his death cannot be made responsible. Schmoller refused redistributive measures producing contra-productive consequences and so endangering economic progress and stability of a free order of society.

How then could Schmoller disintegrate not only the scientific community of economists but also historians in Germany to such an extent and even lasting up to today for more than 80 years after his death?

Let me try to give some answers:

First of all, it seems reasonable to give a brief list of questions which will be dealt with in my paper more or less roughly:

1. Schmoller's personal background.
2. His education, school and university training and his professional interests after his graduation.
3. Reasons for Schmoller's continuous interest for Methodology of Social Sciences and the attention he paid to institutions. His interest for historical research.
4. Schmoller's efforts to achieve a suitable statistical equipment for scientific social research.
5. Schmoller's assessment of the economic circumstances in 1864. Before taking over a chair for statistics at Halle University, Schmoller specified his lifetime social research programme.
6. Schmoller continued his methodological interests and intensively criticised famous conservative historians after 1864.
7. The importance Schmoller attributed to institutions as instruments for technical and social progress to increase social wealth. Social policy as precondition for social balance and progress. The so-called social reform (Sozialreform) Schmoller recommended.

---

[10] Preußische Jahrbücher, 14. Band, Berlin 1864, p. 393-p. 424, p. 523-p. 547, 15. Bd., Berlin, 1865, p. 32-p. 63.

[11] Gesetz zur sozialen Absicherung des Risikos der Pflegebedürftigkeit (Pflege-Versicherungsgesetz-Pflege-VG) vom 26.5.94 in BGBL I 94, p. 1014.

8. Why was Schmoller's influence so enormous? His membership in the so-called Verein für Socialpolitik.

9. Schmoller as professor of political economy at Berlin University after 1881 next to his colleague Adolph Wagner. His editorship of famous periodicals. The controversy of methods in social sciences.

10. Schmoller's textbook outlining his life work of 1900 and 1904 in two volumes called *Grundriß der Volkswirtschaftslehre*.

11. The effects of Schmoller's engagement for social policy from his own viewpoint. Modern comments on the effects of the German social policy compared with the British developments of the same time period.

12. Enemies of Schmoller among industrial leaders, politicians and scientists, some of them seething with hatred in 1900.

13. The debate on value judgements after 1900 and Schmoller's commitment. The reasons for this heated debate.

In the following chapter, I will accentuate on the topics which so long nobody has bothered about and which when taken into account show a thoroughly different picture of Gustav Schmoller than what we are used to when reading textbooks and biographies.

Schmoller's Approach to Political Economy and the Debate on Value Judgements

In 1900, the first volume of Schmoller's textbook *Grundriß der Volkswirtschaftslehre* appeared on the market. Schmoller's fellow combatant in methodological matters Wilhelm Hasbach reviewed the book in a periodical comparing Schmoller's comprehensive outline with an event 125 years earlier, the appearance of Adam Smith's *Wealth of Nations*.[12] This comparison was felt as provocation by many of Schmoller's great many enemies. The conservative historian Georg von Below could no longer suppress his contempt for Schmoller and published an article seething with hatred consisting of eight continuations with hardly no arguments relevant to the point.[13] Von Below seemed so furious and outraged that he did not even mind and stop insulting the reviewer Hasbach in further supplements, which the editors, several professors in strong liaison to leaders of industry, printed with concealed satisfaction.[14]

---

[12] Hasbach, W. (1902), "Gustav Schmoller. Grundriß der allgemeinen Volkswirtschaftslehre", in, Jahrbücher für Nationalökonomie und Statistik, III Folge, 23. Bd., p. 387 ff. here p. 403.

[13] Below, G. von (1904), "Zur Würdigung der historischen Schule der Nationalökonomie", in, Wolf, J. (Hrsg.), Zeitschrift für Socialwissenschaft, VII Jahrgang, p. 145 ff., p. 221 ff., p. 304 ff., p. 367 ff., p. 451 ff., p. 654 ff., p. 710 ff., p. 787 ff.

[14] Hasbach, W. (1905), "Erklärung", in, Zeitschrift für Socialwissenschaft, VIII Jahrgang, p. 137 f.; Below, G. von (1905), "Erwiderung", in, dto, p. 139 f.; Hasbach, W. (1905), "Letter to the editor", dto., p. 267; Below, G. von (1905), "Erwiderung", dto., p. 267; For characterisation of the editors and their interests see: Lindenlaub, D. (1969), "Firmengeschichte und Sozialpolitik", in, Manegold, K.H. (1969) (Hrsg.), Wissenschaft und Technik, München, p. 273.

Three years earlier a well-to-do "saloon demagogue",[15] as he was nicknamed by friends, endowed with high rhetoric talents had written an article entitled "Ideale der Sozialpolitik", ideals of social policy,[16] which was an open challenge to Schmoller's political economy. In this paper, Sombart continuously accused Schmoller of directing his research on arbitrary personal priorities and so erecting his political economy voluntarily on unsystematic value judgements selected at random. Sombart emphasised that social science must perceive the blind and inexorable laws of historical development. Politicians and scientists wishing to make the world more reasonable are thereafter advised to take into account from the social scientist the knowledge of what is inevitably going to happen. And since this development is inevitable, it seemed for Sombart to be a scientific decision based on scientific foresight. It would be madness, so he believed, to attempt to resist. So for Sombart, and the same applied to the social scientists and historians of other political colours and therefore believing in other–in fact opposite, liberal–ends of history, Schmoller's recommendations for social policy were at random thoroughly arbitrary and missing any scientific justification. They blamed him not to perceive historical trends and tendencies and, therefore, to refuse to acknowledge inevitable necessities of development.

After Max Weber in 1904 had published an article demanding neutrality in economic sciences for the sake of scientific objectivity, stating that value judgements cannot be perceived by economic reasoning, the situation for those engaged in the discussion became most confusing.[17]

Shortly later, asked by the high court at Berlin to deliver an experts opinion in an action for slander, Sombart underlined that the recommendations for social policy of the members of the younger historical school were thoroughly erroneous and arbitrary. The very conservative judges preferred to listen to the oratorical tycoon Sombart rather than trying to understand the complicated and to the sophisticated arguments of Gustav Schmoller, continuously indicating that the complainant was an

---

[15] Schmoller, G. (1903), "Review of: W. Sombart (1902), Der moderne Kapitalismus", Leipzig, in, Jahrbuch für Gesetzgebung, Verwaltung und Volkswirtschaft im Deutschen Reich, N. 27 Jg. (1903), p. 292; for the following see also Schmoller's characterisation of Sombart in: "Karl Marx und Werner Sombart", in, Schmollers Jahrbuch für Gesetzgebung, Verwatlung und Volkswirtschaft im Deutschen Reiche, XXXIII Jg. (1909), p. 1235, here p. 1239.

[16] Sombart, W. (1897), "Ideale der Sozialpolitik", in, Archive für Soziale Gesetzgebung und Statistik, Berlin, 10. Bd., p. 1 ff. here especially p. 39 ff., p. 44; see also Sombart, W. (1900), Sozialismus und soziale Bewegung, p. 29, p. 32, p. 42, p. 97, p. 98, p. 99 etc. It is never mentioned, that Sombart had learnt from Schmoller to restrain from value judgements on personal priorities in science. See: Sombart, W. (1892), "Die neuen Handelsvertrage Deutschlands", in, Jahrbuch für Gesetzgebung Verwaltung und Volkswirtschaft im Deutschen Reich, 16. Jg., p. 549. Here he outlines duties of a scientist originated and often repeated by Schmoller.

[17] Weber, M. (1904), "Die Objektivität sozialwissenschaftlicher und sozialpolitischer Erkenntnis", in, Archiv für Sozialwissenschaft und Sozialpolitik, NF 1 Bd. (1904), p. 22 ff. For a modern interpretation of Webers article, see: Albert, H. (1966), "Theorie und Praxis. Max Weber und das Problem der Wertfreiheit und der Rationalität", in, Albert, H. und Topitsch, E. (Hrsg.) (1971), Werturteilsfreiheit, Darmstadt, p. 200 ff. Weber in 1904 very continuously criticised Schmoller's Methodology (p. 81) because he missed the scientific background of Schmoller. He had studied history and law. Weber never condemned the open selection of a field for scientific concern by a scientist. Herefore see: Albert, H. (1966), p. 205.

opportunist and by no means in line with the opinions of the members of the socialists of the chair, as the founders of the "Verein für Socialpolitik" were called.[18]

Sombart had so secured that for statements insulting a professional scientist being a member of the socialists of the chair for opportunistic and unscientific recommendations, nobody could anymore be brought to court and sued by action for slander.

These and many further procedures brought great confusion into the public discussion of Schmoller's engagement in social policy lasting up to today.

Did Schmoller's Contributions Miss Neutrality and Therefore Scientific Dignity?

Max Weber had condemned value judgements as essential elements of scientific statements because they could not be proved or better falsified by comparing them with reality. But Weber never refused open evaluations for selecting political ends to be achieved or for deciding of priorities for a selective research programme for pursuing political aims.[19] And exactly that was what Schmoller had done as we will see in 1864 even before starting his career as a teacher of statistics and political economy at the Halle University.

Furthermore, for the scientific opponents mentioned and the enemies of Schmoller, the interpretations of history by historical prophecy or dogmatically assumed trends or tendencies of development were the basis for all reasonable realistic political action. So most of their theoretical activities aimed at interpreting the past in order to predict the future. And they were convinced of their theory that society will necessarily change, but along a predetermined path that cannot be altered since it is predetermined by inexorable necessity. The desire for an increase of reason in social life – say by social policy measures – in this set of ideas can only be satisfied according to these scientists by studying and interpreting history in order to discover the laws of development. Activism can be justified only so long as it acquiesces in impending changes and helps them along.[20] Therefore, social policy can only do that much: it can shorten and lessen the birth pangs. This was the function Schmoller's opponents would assign to social scientists to fulfil, to act like a midwife as Adolph Wagner for himself claimed to be performing in 1887.[21]

---

[18] For information of the legal proceedings and the judical hearing see: Brentano, L. (1931), Mein Leben im Kampf um die soziale Entwicklung Deutschlands, Jena, p. 410 ff.; see also: Lindenlaub, D. (1965), Richtungskämpfe im Verein für Socialpolitik, Wiesbaden, p. 441 ff. and Hansen, R. (1968), "Der Methodenstreit in den Sozialwissenschaften zwischen Gustav Schmoller und Karl Menger. Seine wissenschaftshistorische und wissenschaftstheoretische Bedeutung", in, Beiträge zur Entwicklung der Wissenschaftstheorie im 19. Jahrhundert, Meisenheim, p. 156.

[19] See note 17.

[20] For this criticism see: Popper, K. (1957), The Poverty of Historicism, London, p. 51 and Popper, K. (1952), The Open Society and its Enemies, Vol. II, London, p. 135 ff.

[21] Wagner, A. (1887), "Finanzwissenschaft und Staatssozialismus", in: Zeitschrift für die gesamte Staatswissenschaft, 43. Jg., p. 121; see also: Popper, K. (1957), The Poverty of Historicism, p. 51.

But the conviction of a scientific and reasonable character of political recommendations in this system is of enormous importance. It rests on the decision to believe in holistic historical predictions or better in prophecy of social development of a fatalistic character. To speak of a universal law of this kind is misleading, since a hypothesis of this kind rather has the character of a particular singular or specific historical statement. Anyhow, it seems important to make explicit the hidden imperative or principle of conduct implied in this basic decision. It is "Adopt the moral system of the future!" And "That we should accept the morality of the future just because it is the future morality is surely a moral problem and cannot be solved as correct by proving reality".[22] It certainly is a value judgement though hidden behind rhetorical drugs.

In vain, Schmoller had since 1863 emphasised methodological research as most important.[23] And he was the only German scientist of Political Economy to do so and after taking over a chair at the Berlin University in 1881 periodically to give lectures on Methodology.[24] As Schmoller often mentioned, he believed it necessary to modernise social sciences, most parts of which he believed to still show a traditional metaphysical status.[25] Schmoller continuously refused to acknowledge historical laws of development, criticising Karl Marx, Adolph Wagner, Lugo Brentano, Werner Sombart, Karl Lamprecht and others, and he rejected the fatalistic character of such assumptions as evidentially false or in any case problematic. He claimed that universal statements can only be qualified as laws if they were provable or better if they can be falsified by observation of reality.[26] The so-called laws of historical development are not because they refer to an advancing singular process.

Schmoller until 1911 when he was 73 years old had never claimed his evaluations of social aims or research priorities as imparted by some mysterious revelation, perception or knowledge. He simply judged them as product of his personal moral intuition and devotion. But he also simultaneously mentioned concrete reasons for their importance and this especially for social measures regarding the further development of society. There can be no doubt that Schmoller convinced his listeners, among which were many scientific opponents. Obviously, there are great differences in between the historical reality of Gustav Schmoller's position as a scientist of political economy and the reports and commentaries of the discussions in which he was involved. This might be the consequence of the instance that nobody so far

---

[22] Popper, K. (1952), The Open Society and its Enemies, Vol. II, p. 205.

[23] See: Hansen, R. (1993), "Gustav Schmoller und die Sozialpolitik von heute", in, Backhaus, J. (Hrsg.) (1993), Schmoller und die Probleme von heute, Berlin, p. 112 and 113 and footnotes 8–10; see: Schmoller, G. (1911), "Volkswirtschaft, Volkswirtschaftslehre und –methode", in, Handwörterbuch der Staatswissenschaften, 3.A., 8. Bd., p. 497.

[24] According to the university calendar of the Berlin University, Schmoller delivered a course of lectures on methodology of social sciences in 1883, 1890 and 1896.

[25] Schmoller, G. (1881), "Über Zwecke und Ziele des Jahrbuches, vom Herausgeber", in: Jahrbuch für Gesetzgebung, Verwaltung und Volkswirtschaft im Deutschen Reich, NF.5.Jg., p. 3, S. 7.

[26] Schmoller, G. (1894), "Volkswirtschaft, Volkswirtschaftslehre und –methode", in, Handwörterbuch der Staatswissenschaften, 1.A. 6. Band, p. 555.

bothered vigorously to explore Schmoller's scientific background and the resulting methodological convictions. These were – as will be shown – thoroughly different to all of his colleagues, be they friends or opponents. There was only one exception and that was Wilhelm Hasbach mentioned in the beginning as fellow combatant.

The Scientific Background of Gustav Schmoller and His Efforts for a Modernised Methodology of Social Sciences. Schmoller's Method of Historical Research

Schmoller was born at Heilbronn in 1838. Here in Württemberg, his father was the administrator of the district treasury and director of the revenue office. Heilbronn at that time was a little town of approximately 18,000 inhabitants with a prospering industry and trading centre. When Schmoller was at the age of 4 years, his mother became disabled and died. And for this reason, from then on he spent most of his time in the household of his grandfather at Calw in the Black Forest (Schwarzwald) not far from Heilbronn.[27] This is of great importance because his grandfather and his great-grandfather, Carl Friedrich Gärtner and Joseph Gärtner, had been famous scientists.[28] Their home at Calw embodied the intellectual centre of the district, especially since they belonged to a rich and well-known trading family with contacts in all of Europe for the supply of linen manufactured in the villages of the Black Forest.

Gustav Schmoller later on occasionally reported that his ancestors were parsons, officers and scholars and that here at Calw in his youth, he had learnt how sound scientific research, disinterested for any personal benefits, was conducted. Great-grandfather and grandfather were learned and qualified physicians, chemists, pharmacists and biologists, engaged in scientific experimental research. Grandfather Carl Friedrich Gärtner had also studied chemistry and was a supporter of the shift of vision for theoretical explanation of natural proceedings, which had been originated by Antoine L. de Lavoisier.[29] Thomas S. Kuhn speaks of a scientific revolution caused by a "change of paradigm" created by the discoveries of Lavoisier bringing about a change of the frame for theoretical explanation from traditional alchemy to modern scientific chemistry.[30] The difference was the use of systematic experimental research measures, the new frame of scientific reasoning allowed for.

---

[27] Schmoller, G. (1918), "Meine Heilbronner Jugendjahre", in, Von schwäbischer Scholle. Kalender für schwäbische Literatur und Kunst, Bd. 7, p. 53, here p. 55; Schmoller, G. (1908), "Erwiderung", in, Reden und Aussprachen, gehalten am 24.6.1908 bei der Feier von Gustav Schmollers 70. Geburtstag. Als Handschrift gedruckt. p. 4 ff., here p. 48.

[28] Ascherson, J. (1878), "Gärtner, Karl Friedrich von", in, Allgemeine Deutsche Biographie, 28. Bd., p. 382; Creizenach, W. (1878), Allgemeine Deutsche Biographie, 8. Bd., Gärtner, J.G., p. 377.

[29] Graepel, P.H. (1978), Carl Friedrich von Gärtner (1772–1850), Familie-Leben–Werk. Ein Beitrag zur Geschichte der Sexualtheorie und der Bastarderzeugung im Pflanzenreich, Diss. Marburg, p. 80.

[30] Kuhn, Th. S. (1970), The Structure of Scientific Revolutions, (2nd ed.), p. 56, p. 126.

Carl Friedrich Gärtner had when growing old invested his large fortune in achieving knowledge of the reproduction of plants. Biology since Aristotle was believed to be the most important of natural sciences. According to the traditional doctrines still in line with the Aristotelian philosophy, the reproduction of plants had so long been a question of volume and quality of nourishment only. In 9,560 series of experiments, Gärtner examined this together with the basic hypothesis of the unchangeable steadiness of the species.

The result of Gärtner's 25 years of experimental endeavouring was the irrefutable evidence of the sexuality of plants.[31] And even more, Gärtner showed the possibility to change and alter the features and peculiarities of plants by controlled artificial pollination and this even so to suit human demands.[32] So the knowledge obtained in experiments for hybridisation could allow universal statements, laws of natural procedures, and these could be made use of for practical purposes. This possibility is not uncommon to us today but it was beyond thought during Gärtner's lifetime.

Science obtained by experimental research could now show a link between coercion by natural laws and artificial purposeful intervention by mankind. More still, Joseph and Friedrich Carl Gärtner were advocates of a gradually spreading scientific revolution. Scientists of a traditional attitude had taken evolution to be a steady goal-directed process.[33] The idea of man and of the contemporary flora and fauna and their evolutionary development was thought to have been present from the first creation of life, perhaps being the mind of God. The Gärtners, though many relatives being parsons, were not religious. The results of Gärtner's research led to an abolition of that assumed teleological kind of revolution.

Joseph and Carl Friedrich Gärtner were members of the leading European academies. Carl Friedrich Gärtner was honoured by, among many other awards, a prize from the royal Dutch Academy of Sciences in 1837.[34] Both were members of many scientific associations and well known for their contributions to science. So for instance, William Whewell reviewed Joseph Gärtner's *System of Plants* in his *History of the Inductive Sciences*, and Darwin quoted Carl Friedrich Gärtner for evidence of important topics in his book *On the Origin of Species* and held contact with him.[35]

---

[31] Graepel, P.H. (1978), Carl Friedrich von Gärtner (1772–1850), Familie-Leben–Werk. Ein Beitrag zur Geschichte der Sexualtheorie und der Bastarderzeugung im Pflanzenreich, Diss. Marburg, p. 244.

[32] Gärtner, C.F. (1849), Versuche und Beobachtungen über Bastard-Erzeugung im Pflanzenreich. Mit Hinweisungen auf ähnliche Erscheinungen im Tierreiche, Stuttgart, p. 663 ff.; see: Hansen, R. (1996), Die practischen Konzequenzen des Methodenstreits, Berlin, p. 190 ff.

[33] Kuhn, Th. S. (1970), The Structure of Scientific Revolutions, London, p. 171.

[34] Graepel, P.H. (1978), Carl Friedrich von Gärtner (1772–1850), Familie, Leben – Leben – Werk. Ein Beitrag zur Geschichte der Sexualtheorie und der Bastarderzeugung im Pflanzenreich, Diss. Marburg, p. 256.

[35] Graepel, P.H. (1978), Carl Friedrich von Gärtner (1772–1850), Familie, Leben – Leben – Werk. Ein Beitrag zur Geschichte der Sexualtheorie und der Bastarderzeugung im Pflanzenreich, Diss. Marburg, p. 335; Sachs, J. (1860), Geschichte der Botanik vom 16. Jahrhundert bis 1860, München, p. 474 ff., here p. 596; see: Hansen, R. (1993), "Gustav Schmoller und die Sozialpolitik von Heute", in, Backhaus, J. (1993), Gustav Schmoller und die Probleme von Heute, p. 112, note 8.

After passing school, Gustav Schmoller was trained and learned the problems connected with taxation and the financial and administrative practices and got early experiences of life by working in the office of his very strict and busy father before enrolling at the Tübingen University.

During his school days, Schmoller had like his ancestors been most interested in natural sciences, especially in mathematics and technology. At the University, he followed the same line of interests but additionally cared for studying law, history and philosophy and thereby neglected political economy.[36] Before passing the two examinations for becoming a civil servant in the administration of Württemberg, Schmoller took part in a competition preparing a historical report and expertise on the economical opinions prevailing during the reformation period.[37] Schmoller produced a long account exploring the relation of the contemporary individuals of different religious opinions and the economic consequences they caused in respect of production of necessary commodities, purchase, possession, use, prices and supply of indispensable terrestrial goods during the reformation period. For this treatise, Schmoller was awarded a prize and he took his doctorate degree.

In this long exploration, Schmoller already on the first three pages mentioned his, as he believed, most important discovery that the fundamental psychological assumptions of Adam Smith dealing with the behaviour of individuals do not allow for historical proof. As statements of universal character and as a theory of behaviour they were false, so Schmoller complained.[38] He, therefore, criticised Adam Smith here and later on continuously for assuming an unchangeable economic behaviour of individuals and not to realise and take into account the great differences when examining various countries, regions or places and this at alternating periods.[39] According to Schmoller's opinion, Smith's theoretical framework was therefore unqualified to explain the observable instances and proceedings of economic reality.

Schmoller's report then showed the economic results of the most controversial religious institutions during the reformation period. He underlined that in the end, the poor and weak were the victims of the complete loss of balance of society. For these conclusions as a result of an analysis, Schmoller needed a thoroughly different theoretical approach of his research compared with the usual access of historians to the data. Individual facts, appearances and events were of interest only or with priority in respect

---

[36] For any information on Schmoller's youth, education and university training, see: "Schmoller meine Heilbronner Jugendjahre …"as note nr. 27 and "Reden und Aussprachen …"likewise note nr. 27, and Graepel , P.H. (1978), Carl Friedrich von Gärtner … as note 29, p. 161 ff.

[37] Schmoller, G. (1860), "Zur Geschichte der nationalökonomischen Aussichten in Deutschland während der Reformationsperiode", in, Zeitschrift für die gesamte Staatswissenschaft, 16. Band, 1860, p. 461 ff.

[38] Schmoller, G. (1860), "Zur Geschichte der nationalökonomischen Aussichten in Deutschland während der Reformationsperiode", in, Zeitschrift für die gesamte Staatswissenschaft, 16. Band, 1860, p. 461–465.

[39] Schmoller, G. (1860), "Zur Geschichte der nationalökonomischen Aussichten in Deutschland während der Reformationsperiode", in, Zeitschrift für die gesamte Staatswissenschaft, 16. Band, 1860, p. 463.

of presenting, confirming or falsifying regularities of consequences affecting economic life. The causal consequences of interconnected elements in society showing regularities even though limited to regional or local districts and periods continuously raised his attention. And he endeavoured to furnish findings with statistical data.

Mankind is integrated in two worlds, Schmoller underlined as result of his research in his dissertation, the world of mind or spirit, genius, and the world of matter, and he is not only provided with a free will but also limited at the mercy of coercive natural laws which can be brought to light by scientific skill.[40] In this dissertation, Schmoller in 1860 treated the history of economic proceedings during the reformation period, that is, the sixteenth century, like working in a laboratory, guessing, assuming, comparing and refuting consequences in between religious movements altering institutions and data of economic life.

The different religious beliefs, so he assumed, caused very different social institutions, this term used in a broad sense. The historical items, according to Schmoller, could then be made use of like an artificial experiment designed for comparing proceedings in a similar social frame of a closed period, observing regular alterations of interest.

In such an investigation, institutions then could appear like physical instruments and could be evoked upon from a functional point of view. They could be seen as means to certain ends or even as convertible to the service of certain ends, as tools so to say.

This technological procedure means applying the experimental method to social sciences by historical research. Of course, any assumed generalisations or better laws or regularities are then confined to separately defined periods of similar cultural circumstances – bestimmter wirtschaftlicher Kulturzustand – as Schmoller 30 years later advised in his article on methodology.[41]

In conformity with this procedure in all scientific contributions, Schmoller through all his life continuously demanded what he would call "Detailuntersuchungen".[42] This he roughly defined as investigation of causal interconnections of elements of social reality restricted so not to lose precise control and easy to survey, therefore limited to a closed period. This is identical with what today Karl Popper calls "practical technological approach" and qualifies as a basis for "social engineering".[43]

Already the reviewer of Schmoller's disssertation, Wilhelm Roscher[44] in 1861 stated that the peculiar historical description or better examination of the reformation period by Schmoller was in fact a theoretical analysis of institutional changes of

[40] Schmoller, G. (1860), "Zur Geschichte der nationalökonomischen Aussichten in Deutschland während der Reformationsperiode", in, Zeitschrift für die gesamte Staatswissenschaft, 16. Band, 1860, p. 462.

[41] Schmoller, G. (1894), "Volkswirtschaft, Volkswirtschaftslehre und –methode", in, Handwörterbuch der Staatswissenschaften, 6. Band, p. 559.

[42] Schmoller, G. (1881), "Über Zweck und Ziele des Jahrbuches", in, Jahrbuch für Gesetzgebung, Verwaltung und …, 5. Jg., p. 7.

[43] Popper, K.R. (1952), The Poverty of Historicism, London, p. 42.

[44] Roscher, W. (1861), "Review of: Schmoller, Gustav, Zur Geschichte der nationalökonomischen Aussichten …", in, Liberarisches Centralblatt für Deutschland, 1861, p. 761.

property rights and the thereby inaugurated social consequences. Schmoller did not try to describe individual occurrences as was done in a competing treatise dealing with the same question written by a distinguished historian and learned philologist Dr. H. Wiskemann[45] as Roscher underlined, thereby mentioning that Schmoller was still a student. Unlike the historian Wiskemann, Schmoller was endeavouring to find causal interconnections in between important elements of economic life, regularities of importance so Roscher noticed.[46]

For this very reason, a shift of interest mentioned by Roscher in 1861, Schmoller was during his lifetime never accepted by the profession as a historian. Friedrich Meinecke, a famous German historian, announced after Schmoller's death that his many historical contributions during his lifetime spread the smell of a laboratory.[47] That was certainly a correct judgement since it corresponded to Schmoller's early intention. This makes it easier for us to understand Schmoller's critical remark in his review of Menger's "Untersuchungen" that he would be fired out of every laboratory.[48] Menger, like all scientists of political economy of the period discussed, was unaware of experimental research.

For Schmoller, all knowledge of reality including political economy had to be approved for by observation and he opposed John Stuart Mill in this respect whose treatise *On Liberty* he admired. But he denied Mill's dogmatic statement that experiments were not possible in all of social sciences.[49] The fact that Mill rested political economy on principles which he called "laws of human nature" obtained by introspection was rejected by Schmoller because they did not meet the essential necessity to be interpersonally provable. In this respect, Schmoller criticised Mill's contribution of methodology and followed William Whewell's *Philosophy of the Inductive Sciences* against whom John Stuart Mill in 1843 had written his book on *System of Logic*.[50] This he had done to justify the Ricardian deductive method for political economy because he was convinced of the impossibility of conducting experiments in social sciences.

Mill believed that the experimental method cannot be applied to social sciences because we cannot reproduce at will precisely similar experimental conditions.[51] But in

---

[45] Wiskemann, H. (1861), Darstellung der in Deutschland zur Zeit der Reformation herrschenden nationalökonomischen Aussichten, Leipzig.

[46] Roscher, W. (1861), "Review …", as note 44, p. 761.

[47] Meinecke, F. (1922), "Drei Generationen deutscher Gelehrtenpolitik", in, Historische Zeitschrift, Bd. 125, p. 251. See also: Oestreich, G. (1969), "Die Fachhistorie und die Anfange der sozialgeschichtlichen Forschung in Deutschland", in: Historische Zeitschrift, Bd. 208, p. 323.

[48] Schmoller, G. (1883), "Zur Methodologie der Staats- und Sozialwissenschaften", in, Jahrbuch für Gesetzgebung, Vewaltung und Volkswirtschaft im Deutschen Reich, 7. Jg., p. 979.

[49] Schmoller, G. (1894), "Volkswirtschaft, Volkswirtschaftslehre und –methode", in, Handwörterbuch der Staatswissenschaften, 6. Band, p. 539, p. 540, p. 42, p. 543, p. 546, p. 555, p. 557, see also p. 987.

[50] Mill, J. St. (1874), Selbstbiographie, Stuttgart, p. 132, p. 173.

[51] See: Mill, J. St. (1844), "On the Definition of Political Economy; And on the Method of Investigation Proper to it", in, Essays on Some Unsettled Questions of Political Economy, London, p. 120 ff., here p. 147; and: Mill, J. St. (1898), System of Logic, Ratiocinative and Inductive, Peoples Edition, London, Book VI, Chapter VII, § 2.

fact, experimental physicists know that often very dissimilar things may happen under what appears to be precisely similar conditions. The question what are to be described as "similar conditions" depends on the kind of experiment and can be answered only by using experiments. The argument that social experiments are fatally hampered by the variability of social conditions, and especially by the changes which are due to historical development, loses its force when examined. Experiments may lead us to unforeseen results. But it would be experiments which alone lead us to discover the change in social conditions. And experiments only can teach us that certain social conditions change with the historical period,[52] so Schmoller's answer could be read.

So after finishing his university studies, Schmoller intended to write an essay on the development of political economy from the philosophical systems of the eighteenth century and the thoroughly new methodological necessities of modern science at his lifetime.[53] Later on, Schmoller mentioned of feeling regret for not having invested more endeavour towards working on and answering pure methodological questions. But he admitted that this would have easily occupied his full attention for all his life.[54] He found satisfaction in his belief that he had devoted his life as scientist chiefly to the more pressing social problems of the time and mentioned that his contributions could never have been judged as sound if he had not worked hard for acquiring solid basic methodological convictions.

During all his life, Schmoller continuously followed up the discussion on methodology in sciences and after appointed chair holder at the Berlin University in 1881, he lectured methodology in cycles of every 6 years.[55]

Experimental knowledge only enables mankind to master and control nature, but nevertheless in conditional boundaries. This Schmoller had learnt from the scientific activities of his ancestors. Carl Friedrich Gärtner had shown how to produce useful fruits and plants by artificial pollination. Schmoller's dissertation made evident the importance of institutions for the economic development of a country. So for Schmoller, the question of formulation and alteration of institutions became to be of the greatest interest. Later on, he devoted himself to answer this question in an article which he altered, supplemented and improved 4 times before having it printed in 1881 in the periodical, the editorship of which he took over. Therein he linked the question of the origin of institutions with the idea of Justice in Political Economy, as he headlined the article. He later mentioned this article as of fundamental importance in all his contributions.[56] Since he evaluated this essay as of guiding importance,

---

[52] See: Popper, K.R. (1957), The Poverty of Historicism, London, p. 94.

[53] Hintze, O. (1919), "Gustav Schmoller. Ein Gedenkblatt (1919)", in, Soziologie und Geschichte, Göttingen, 1964, p. 523.

[54] Schmoller, G. (1912), "Volkswirtschaft, Volkswirtschaftslehre und –methode", in, Handwörterbuch der Staatswissenschaften, Band, 3.A., p. 497/8.

[55] See note 24.

[56] Schmoller, G. (1881), "Die Gerechtigkeit in der Volkswirtschaft", in, Jahrbuch für Gesetzgebung, Verwaltung und Volkswirtschaft im Deutschen Reich, p. 19 ff., translated: "The Idea of Justice in Political Economy", in, Annals of the American Academy of Political and Social Science, Vol. IV, 1894, p. 697.

he had it inserted as the first article after announcing his rousing programme as the new editor of the periodical *Jahrbücher für Gesetzgebung, Verwaltung und Volkswirtschaft im Deutschen Reich* in 1881.

The concept of institutions thereby was used by Schmoller in the broadest sense. A rough definition could read "The total of habits or behavioural patterns and moral norms, of customs and traditions and the law, all re-enforced by common behavioural standards in which a people conducts life".[57]

For Schmoller, economic institutions were a "product of human feelings and thought, of human actions , human customs and not to forget human law". And for Schmoller, they were "the core of all economic policy" as shall be shown.[58]

This certainly was controversial to Adam Smith to whom institutions had been just irritating, annoying and a nuisance to economy as Schmoller during his life often complained.

Immediately after passing his university examinations, Schmoller was asked to work in Württemberg's states industrial craft census of 1861. For this, Schmoller composed a final theoretical analysis and an evaluation of the economic situation. He further on showed great interest in improving the theoretical orientation of statistical inquiries. From functioning as an auxiliary science for history – the traditional governing principle was still relevant for Carl Menger and with exceptions for Adolph Wagner – to a most important aid for experimental historical research.[59] This necessity, to use statistics for more than just furnishing historical reports with economic data was 30 years later underlined in his article on methodology.[60]

Schmoller's Activities as a Chairholder for Statistics at Halle University. The Practical Significance of His Theoretical Approach to Political Economy

Before commencing his appointment as professor of statistics at Halle University simultaneously with preparing his lectures, Schmoller wrote an article on the most pressing problems of the time which demonstrated his programme as a teacher of statistics and economics and also demarcated his later lifetime field of research. His essay entitled "Die Arbeiterfrage", or, translated, problems of the labour force, was

---

[57] Schmoller, G. (1900), Grundriß der allgemeinen Volkswirtschaftslehre, S. 61/62; also: Schmoller, G. (1894), Justice in Political Economy, p. 718.

[58] Schmoller, G. (1884), "Review of Friedrich List: Das nationale System der politischen Ökonomie", in, Jahrbuch für Gesetzgebung, Verwaltung und Volkswirtschaft im Deutschen Reich, 8. Jg., p. 282.

[59] See: Hansen, R. (1993), "Gustav Schmoller und die Sozialpolitik von Heute", in, Backhaus, J. (1993), Schmoller und die Probleme von Heute, Berlin, p. 140 u. p. 141, notes 98–100.

[60] Schmoller, G. (1894), "Volkswirtschaft, Volkswirtschaftslehre und –methode", in, Handwörterbuch der Staatswissenschaften, 6. Band, p. 541 ff.

printed in the liberal periodical *Preußische Jahrbücher*, in 1864 and 1865 in three continuations.[61] It was of great influence and the recommendations therein after 1872 became the programme of the association called "Verein für Socialpolitik" for which he was among the founders.

In this article, Schmoller outlined the social problems caused by the contemporary proceeding transition from a traditional order of economics to an industrial society as consequence of the technical revolution which brought about most undesirable social problems accelerating since 1850. Traditional tools were replaced by machinery, handcraft by factories, professional division of labour multiplied efficiency, manpower was substituted by natural resources and even more. The resulting social problems were enormous.[62]

The rise of an industrial working class of proletarians, the growth of cities and flight of the population from the land seeking jobs, the replacement of old industrial centres and the sudden emergence of new ones, missing accommodations, large numbers of unemployed often on the run, breakdown and insolvencies of small crafts and the growing crowd of desolate poor raised questions pressing for adequate solutions. Additionally, the growing age of machinery created great social problems.

At that time, two recommendations promising improvement were openly debated. The calls for mankind to perceive ethical obligations and to change habits of conduct forwarded by F.A. Lange and E. Dühring, both philosophers and economists, were hardly discussed in the public. But adherents of economic liberalism, dogmatically believing in the doctrine of "laissez – fair" received great public interest. As a matter of fact, the ideas of Adam Smith had turned out to be of greatest help to the development of the thoroughly disordered Prussian economy after the occupation by Napoleon's troops.

The second advice controversially debated was advanced by the followers of Karl Marx, F. Lassalle and other socialists, demanding the abandonment of private property for all production equipment. The exponents of both these theories dogmatically believed in laws of development, inevitably leading to the political ends they thought somehow to be normal and desirable.[63]

Schmoller's recommendations for solving the social problems of the time were different. In the given situation, Schmoller saw a great opportunity for improving the wealth of all citizens by making use of the technical progress through increased utilisation of machinery.[64] But by his historical research for his dissertation, Schmoller had learnt that the society could lose its balance if the traditional institutions are unqualified to maintain appeasement. This danger he believed decisive.

For Schmoller, Adam Smith had drawn a picture of individuals living in a natural economic system of harmony, increasing the wealth of the community by just

---

[61] Schmoller, G. (1864/5), "Die Arbeiterfrage", in, Preußische Jahrbücher, 14. Bd., pp. 393 – 424, pp. 523 – 547 and 15. Band, pp. 32 – 63.

[62] Schmoller, G. (1864), "Die Arbeiterfrage", p. 394.

[63] Schmoller, G. (1864), "Die Arbeiterfrage", p. 413 ff.

[64] Schmoller, G. (1864), "Die Arbeiterfrage", p. 394 ff.

following their egoistic personal interests. In this draft, the clumsy interventions by statesmen in a sophisticated natural clockwork of a trading society instead of limiting their support on maintenance of peace and justice could only spoil an unproblematic optimal natural performance. But natural harmony for Schmoller was a utopian idea if there are no accepted institutions regulating the behaviour of individuals. And individuals are of very different abilities and temper. Waiting for a satisfying spontaneous order usually leads, as Schmoller underlined, to an exploitation of the poor by the well to be and mighty, and in the end to destruction of the balance of society and so endangers democracy to turn into plutocracy.[65]

The socialists on the opposite side believed in an inexorable law of development to the goal of a free society by the abandonment of private property of production equipment. Schmoller likewise saw no solution for the pending present problems of society in such measures. His later experimental historical research showed the fundamental basis of such statements regarded as universal hypothesis to be falsified.[66]

The experimental treatment of historical studies by comparing developments had shown Schmoller that the economic consequences of both political recommendations since resting on questionable utopian assumptions would lead society to lose balance. Technical progress instead of making possible increasing wealth for all citizens would end in a disaster of a revolution and this would favour the rich and mighty only.

As he had learnt from his historical investigations, for Schmoller, the key for protecting the balance of society rested in the harmonising consequences of the most important reform of institutions. To Schmoller, they were the core of all economic policies.[67] And as he later stated in his article on Justice in Political Economy which he announced as the most important foundation of all of his contributions to economics, they had to be in accordance with the leading convictions of justice by the public.[68]

Schmoller published his suggestions aiming at making technical progress a basis for increase of wealth for all citizens in articles in 1864 and 1865, implemented in 1870, 1872 and 1874. He then was fiercely attacked by a conservative historian, the teacher of Georg von Below, mentioned in the beginning of my paper, as a patron and supporter of socialism.[69] Schmoller immediately answered in a long article reasoning

---

[65] Schmoller, G. (1900), Grundriß der allgemeinen Volkswirtschaftslehre, p. 422.

[66] Such knowledge Schmoller achieved from historical research by treating the data like an experiment in a laboratory. For instance, in a review discussing the articles of James Rogers and Karl Lamprecht describing "Die soziale Entwicklung Deutschlands und Englands hauptsächlich auf dem platten Land des Mittelalters", Schmoller combined a result showing the main thesis of Karl Marx as a general law of development to be false. See: Schmoller, G. (1888), Jahrbuch für Gesetzgebung, Verwaltung und Volkswirtschaft im Deutschen Reich, 12. Jg., p. 203 ff., here p. 218.

[67] See note 58.

[68] Schmoller, G. (1894), "Justice in Political Economy", in, Annals of the American Academy, p. 4 and p. 14.

[69] Treitschke, H. von (1874), "Der Sozialismus und seine Gönner", in, Preußische Jahrbücher, 34. Band, pp. 67 – 110 und pp. 248 – 301.

his theoretical approach to Political Economy by including many methodological arguments supporting his recommendations.[70]

A typical governing principle in Schmoller's answer reads as follows:

> Sie haben sicher recht, daß wir nicht alles ordnen können, wie es menschlicher Weisheit gut dünkt, daß wir dem Zufall vieles anheim geben müssen. Aber was wir ihm entreissen können, das sollten wir auch. Denn dazu allein ward uns der Stempel des Geistes aufgedruckt. Wir sollten selbstbewußt und mit Absicht in die Naturordnung eingreifen, soweit wir irgend können. Jede Position, die wir dem Zufall abgewinnen ist ein Sieg menschlichen Kultur.[71]

My brief translation is:

> You surely are right assuming that we cannot regulate all procedures in conformity with the wisdom of mankind, that we often must trust in pure accidental chance. But what we can snatch and take over into our own responsibility that we should do. That is what we were gifted for with spirit and intellect. Self-confident we should purposeful intervene in the order nature provides at the best of our possibilities. That is what we were furnished for with mind and intellect.

So Schmoller in 1864 and 1865 and further on made suggestions on how to make possible for the entire society including proletarians, the labour force and the poor to participate in the advantages of the technical progress. The so-called natural order (Naturordnung), the Liberals believed to be the normal basis for Political Economy achieved by preventing any state intervention, Schmoller demanded to be modified into a cultural order (Lebensordnung) in which institutions safeguard necessities of life for every citizen.[72]

The list of recommendations Schmoller suggested must begin by mentioning his appeal to the emperor to devote himself to the protection of the weakest groups in society and the poor. The peace of society, Schmoller demanded, should be guarded by the two public representatives of the state, a neutral bureaucracy and a socially conscious sovereign (soziales Königtum) legitimised by history and capable of balancing judgement.[73]

And further, more institutions should be erected to improve the educational knowledge and the "standard of life" (cit.) of the labour class, to allow the establishment of trade unions and to provide an insurance system containing an accident insurance, an old-age insurance with an old-age pension scheme, an invalidity insurance,

---

[70] Schmoller, G. (1874/1875), "Über einige Grundfragen des Rechts und der Volkswirtschaft. Ein offenes Sendschreiben an Herrn Professor Dr. Heinrich von Treitschke", Halle, in, Jahrbücher für Nationalökonomie und Statistik, 23. Band, (1874), p. 225 ff. und 24. Bd. (1875), p. 84 ff.

[71] Schmoller, G. (1874), "Über einige Grundfragen des Rechts und der Volkswirtschaft. Ein offenes Sendschreiben an Herrn Professor Dr. Heinrich von Treitschke", Halle, in, Jahrbücher für Nationalökonomie und Statistik, 23. Band, (1874), p. 281/282.

[72] Schmoller, G. (1865), "Die Arbeiterfrage", p. 51; Schmoller wanted the "standard of life"(sic) of all citizens to be raised.

[73] Schmoller, G. (1874), Die soziale Frage und der preußische Staat, in Preußische Jahrbücher, 33. Bd., p. 323, here p. 342.

a health insurance and later on an unemployment insurance and further more to the support of labourers and the poor.[74]

Schmoller never suggested direct interventions into the price-building mechanisms of the markets. He was convinced of the importance of competition and liberalism as basic for economy. The suggested institutions should be the frame in which economic activities could be conveyed.[75]

In the beginning, I mentioned that the introduction of all those institutions we today regard as obvious and essential consistments of an adequate order of society in Western countries was demanded by Schmoller in his articles demarcating his further research programme as a chairholder for economic sciences in 1864 and 1865.

But these recommendations invited a storm of objections among dogmatic liberals and likewise socialists. Many teachers of Political Economy would soon call Schmoller and his followers "socialists of the chair" (Kathedersozialisten).[76] This was viewed as an adjective for a person under sentence, but after just 2 decades it obtained the sound of praise but to be debased again to a summary for an economist following unscientific oversized proceedings after 1900.

To reject misleading interpretations, Schmoller refused to allow the state to interfere in economic affairs more than was believed necessary. He wanted priority for competition and recommended to follow the principle of subsidiarity by interventions wherever possible. For this reason, he opposed his colleagues Adolph Wagner just as well as Lujo Brentano due to the fundamental differences in methodological respects.[77]

Schmoller was an undogmatic liberal since his youth. For this reason, he even voted for granting John Stuart Mill a doctorate degree *honoris causa* by his University of Halle in 1866.[78] Of course, it was the John Stuart Mill after 1849, the advocate of social policy, the author of *On Liberty* and husband of Mrs. Harriet Taylor, and not the author of methodical essays and the *Logic* whom he wanted to be honoured.

---

[74] The reorganisation of institutions and the foundation of new institutions recommended by Schmoller were not only intended for helping labourers and the poor. Schmoller's suggestions were directed at establishing a social reform consisting of many thoroughly new regulations. So Schmoller recommended an income tax reform and just as well a new patent law, an inheritance tax and the installation of saving banks for the middle classes and many more regulations which are obvious for today's citizens. A list containing the most of the different items demanded by Schmoller after 1864 can be found in: Hansen, R. (1993), (1993), "Gustav Schmoller und die Sozialpolitik von Heute", in, Backhaus, J. (Hrsg.) (1993), Schmoller und die Probleme von Heute, Berlin, p. 160. Schmoller's aim was to make the market system durable and reliable, to raise the efficiency of the economy and thereby to diminish class differences and so to improve the "standard of life".

[75] Schmoller rejected direct interventions into the price system. Competition showed keep being the guiding principle of the economy. See: Schmoller, G. (1864), "Die Arbeiterfrage", in, Preußische Jahrbücher, 14. Bd., p. 535 f.

[76] Conrad, Else (1906), Der Verein für Sozialpolitik und seine Wirksamkeit auf dem Gebiet der gewerblichen Arbeiterfrage, Jena. p. 37.

[77] For more information see: Hansen, R. (1993), "Gustav Schmoller und die Sozialpolitik von Heute", in, Backhaus, J. (Hrsg.) (1993), Schmoller und die Probleme von Heute, Berlin, p. 151 ff.

[78] Hansen, R. (1968), "Der Methodenstreit in den Sozialwissenschaften zwischen Gustav Schmoller und Carl Menger", Meisenheim, S.144, note 34; additionally: Suchier, W. (1953), Bibliographie der Universitätsschriften von Halle-Württemberg 1817–1885, Berlin, p. 687, Jurist. Fak. Nr., 145.

The "Verein für Socialpolitik" was founded in 1872 by suggestion of a journalist. Although not president before 1890, Schmoller convinced most of the members though often of thoroughly different, opposite political opinions of his theoretical concept. Schmoller's arguments were just convincing to everyone. This was due to the convincing theoretical basis of the measures recommended by Schmoller. And this was so even though Schmoller was opposed to Lujo Brentano, Adolph Wagner and many others and lacked the ability to generate enthusiasm, fascination or passionate feelings for his ideas and opinions by listeners in an audience. For this, he was far too sober and sound in his speech and his arguments as exchanged in discussions.

As a matter of fact, his opinions were taken over by the government as frame for social policy after 1880.

Later on after 1900, Schmoller could observe that his predictions turned out to be correct.

The "standard of life" as Schmoller in 1864 and 1865 had called his point of interest was raised in Germany at a higher rate than in any western industrial country. He showed this in statistical figures and noting the differences in his last published book without any comment, sober and typical for all his contributions.[79]

At the beginning of his university career, Schmoller had foreseen the great advantages for the wealth of mankind concealed in the technical progress of the beginning age of machinery in Germany. Treating historical research as a basis for sound knowledge, he had learnt the unavoidable necessity for adjusting and forming old and new institutions so to safeguard society against loss of balance by political revolutions. In an article of 1903, Schmoller reviewed the development of the age of machinery after installing appropriate institutions for social security of all citizens as a necessary path leading to the increase of wealth for all inhabitants.[80] The term wealth for him meant not only promotion of the production of commodities, but also included the gradual relief of hard work and even the easing of woman's daily troublesome kitchen annoyances as possible development.[81]

Schmoller foresaw this path leading to a society deriving benefit from technical progress and restricting freedom only as far as required regarding social security to the inhabitants.

After 1900, a younger generation of economists no longer judged the social policy Schmoller in 1864 had recommended as indispensable supporting pillars to this end. As described in the beginning of my paper, many of them denounced his interest for social policy as erroneous and arbitrary and even missing scientific neutrality. They did not appreciate the use Schmoller made of historical research by employing

---

[79] Schmoller, G. (1918), Die soziale Frage. Klassenbildung, Arbeiterfrage, Klassenkampf, Leipzig, p. 251 ff.

[80] Schmoller, G. (1903), Über das Maschinenzeitalter in seinem Zusammenhang mit dem Volkswohlstand und der sozialen Verfassung der Volkswirtschaft, J. Springer, Berlin; see also note 66.

[81] Schmoller, G. (1903), Über das Maschinenzeitalter in seinem Zusammenhang mit dem Volkswohlstand und der sozialen Verfassung der Volkswirtschaft, J. Springer, Berlin, p. 16.

history as a substitute for experiments. This judgement applied to liberal and also economists of a socialist mood. Brentano, Marx, Sombart and others like Mill, Comte and Buckle believed to be able to perceive laws of historical development and made this the basis of their scientific approach. This had been rejected by Schmoller.[82]

For the socialists in 1903, Karl Kautsky blamed Schmoller for having by his activities cemented the power of capitalists and owners of production plants, raising their profit and thereby worsening the position of the working force.[83]

Kautsky claimed that Schmoller's article on the consequences of the age of machinery (Über das Maschinenzeitalter) was misleading because he would not admit that only abandonment of property of all production equipment could lead mankind to appeasement and lessen the burdens of the many, and increase wealth and equal freedom for all citizens.[84]

Schmoller as a matter of fact had, so his contributions show, falsified the dogmatically assumed basic statement of the consequences of private property by historical evidence.[85] He had often condemned as arbitrary the fatalistic interpretation of laws of historical development of the socialists, and likewise the liberals concerning an assumed goal of history. But Schmoller's contributions had by this time obviously lost their convincing power.

In his *Outline* (Grundriß), published in 2 volumes in 1900 and 1904, Schmoller recollected the results of his most important investigations which were carried out in order to prepare a scientific basis for his target: securing a prosperous society through promotion of technical progress and adjusting institutions when necessary to sustain political balance. Adam Smith had not seen the problems of the technical revolution, so his contributions could give limited help to politicians only. He had also missed to see the importance of adjusting old and founding new appropriate institutions.

Schmoller's Interest for Methodology

I would like to add to supplement the picture of Schmoller: Schmoller did not only carefully watch the methodical discussion in books and articles on natural and moral sciences throughout his life. He also carefully took notice of the developments in Political Economy as a science. Most important, books edited during his lifetime

---

[82]See: Brentano, L. (1931), Mein Leben im Kampf und die soziale Entwicklung Deutschlands, München, p. 110; Sombart, W. (1902), Der moderne Kapitalismus, Leipzig, 1. Bd., p. XXVIII f; Schumpeter, J.A. (1893), Capitalism, Socialism and Democracy, London, 1943, p. 44. They all believed in laws of economic development to be treated by Mill's theoretical approach to history and blamed Schmoller for not following theoretical interests.

[83]See also: Völkerling, Fritz (1959), Der deutsche Katherdersozialismus, Berlin, p. 56 ff.; see: Kautsky, K. (1904), "Schmoller über den Fortschritt der Arbeiterklasse", in, Die Neue Zeit, Nr. 34, Jg. XXII, Band 2, p. 228 ff.

[84]Kautsky, K. (1904), "Schmoller über den Fortschritt der Arbeiterklasse", in, Die Neue Zeit, Nr. 34, Jg. XXII, Band 2, p. 240 f.

[85]Albrecht, G. (1922), "Zur Lehre von der Entstehung der sozialen Klassen", in, Jahrbücher für Nationalökonomie und Statistik, 3.F. Bd. 64, p. 273 ff.

were reviewed in his periodical *Jahrbuch für Gesetzgebung, Verwaltung und Volkswirtschaft im Deutschen Reich*. Many were introduced by himself.

In this *Outline* (Grundriß), he criticised the Benthamite Political Economy including Jevon's contributions correctly for the reason that introspection as the basis for utility theories provides information on personal emotions that are incompatible and not comparable interpersonally. As such, the information cannot be related to an unbiased, practically defined provable cardinal metric scale. This makes, as Schmoller often mentioned, speech of differences in values, pleasures, pains or utility or of diminishing marginal utility and of maximisation of utility thoroughly useless for a science of Political Economy.[86]

Schmoller tried to make use of the advantages that the most successful natural sciences had provided for mankind, thereby making use of the same methodology for the social sciences. He dismissed Mill's deductive methodology for social sciences. He believed that scientific knowledge needs to be provable by observation. Scientific statements must allow for making predictions and they must be proved before the statement is added to our knowledge of reality. So Schmoller believed in two sources of knowledge. Research starts with guesswork. Thereafter, false theories are sorted out by observation. Schmoller demanded this access to research to his goal in order to support the growth of wealth for all citizens.[87]

In 1981, Douglas S. North wrote a book entitled the *Structure and Change in Economic History* dealing with the developments and importance of economic institutions.[88] The following might be added since it is at present a custom to compare Schmoller and North. North in his book makes use of neo-classical characteristics of individual behaviour patterns and seems to assume harmonious development of institutional change. The difference to Schmoller's approach is the difference between experimental historical research and artificial models of reasoning which Schmoller watched with greatest suspicion. Therefore, he kept believing methodical research to be of high priority for Political Economy and underlined the necessity for proof of theories by observation. According to Schmoller, theories of practical significance must provide the possibility to make predictions provable by observation.

I personally believe that North stops his research where Schmoller carries on. Schmoller did not deliver guesswork only; he also delivered theoretical knowledge based on historical evidence. North seems to believe in a natural harmony set by nature in advance, an opinion Schmoller put in question for convincing reasons

---

[86] Schmoller, G. (1894), "Volkswirtschaft, Volkswirtschaftslehre und –methode", in, Handwörterbuch der Staatswissenschaften, 6. Bd., p. 550. Schmoller, G. (1900), Grundriß der allgemeinen Volkswirtschaftslehre, p. 23, p. 32, p. 71.

[87] Schmoller, G. (1894), "Volkswirtschaft, Volkswirtschaftslehre und –methode", in, Handwörterbuch der Staatswissenschaften, 6. Bd., p. 539, p. 542, p. 546, p. 555, p. 558, p. 559.

[88] North, D.C. (1981), Structure and Change in Economic History, New York, see especially chapter 12; See: Review: Borchardt, K. (1977), Der "Property-Rights-Ansatz" in der Wirtschaftsgeschichte – Zeichen für eine systematische Neuorientierung des Faches, in, Kocka, J. (1977), Theorien in der Praxis des Historikers. Forschungsbeispiele und ihre Diskussion, Göttingen, p. 140 ff. see: page 150 ff.

based on empirical evidence. Schmoller aimed at finding knowledge proved by observation.

I cannot comment here the great significance Joseph A. Schumpeter assigned to Schmoller for influencing Mitchel, Veblen and commons in respect to the importance of institutions in 1926 after he had judged the dispute on methods (Methodenstreit) between Schmoller and other colleagues including Menger in 1913 as thoroughly superfluous.

I would like to repeat the following:

Schmoller's recommendations for social policy were followed by the regulations of the German administration as social reform in 1881 and the years later.

After 1949, the regulations for social security were gradually carried too far. The guiding principles of Schmoller's recommendations were forgotten about. Schmoller should not be blamed for exaggerations after his death. I agree to the statement the historian Gregor Schöllgen shortly made:

Max Weber was the so long most overrated German scientist of the nineteenth century.[89] I would like to add: Gustav Schmoller has so long been the most underrated scientist of the nineteenth century.

References

Albert H (1966) Theorie und Praxis. Max Weber und das Problem der Wertfreiheit und der Rationalität, in, Albert H und Topitsch E (Hrsg) (1971), Werturteilsfreiheit, Darmstadt

Albrecht G (1922) Zur Lehre von der Entstehung der sozialen Klassen, in, Jahrbücher für Nationalökonomie und Statistik, 3.F. Bd. 64

Anderson P (1971) Gustav von Schmoller, in, Deutsche Historiker, 2. Bd., Göttingen, in: Wehler HU (ed) (1985) Das deutsche Kaiserreich in der Geschichte, Bd

Ascherson J (1878) Gärtner, Karl Friedrich von, in, Allgemeine Deutsche Biographie, 8. Bd., p 382

Augstein R (1964) Article in: Der Spiegel, Heft 11, 1964, p 47

Below GV (1904), Zur Würdigung der historischen Schule der Nationalökonomie, in, Wolf J (Hrsg) Zeitschrift für Socialwissenschaft, VII Jahrgang

Below GV (1905) Erwiderung, in, Zeitschrift für Socialwissenschaft, VIII Jahrgang

Below GV (1905) Erwiderung, Zeitschrift für Socialwissenschaft, VIII Jahrgang

Borchardt K (1977) Review: Der "Property-Rights-Ansatz" in der Wirtschaftsgeschichte – Zeichen für eine systematische Neuorientierung des Faches, in, Kocka J (1977) Theorien in der Praxis des Historikers. Forschungsbeispiele und ihre Diskussion, Göttingen

Brentano L (1931) Mein Leben im Kampf um die soziale Entwicklung Deutschlands. Jena

Brentano L (1931) Mein Leben im Kampf und die soziale Entwicklung Deutschlands. München

Conrad E (1906) Der Verein für Socialpolitik und seine Wirksamkeit auf dem Gebiet der gewerblichen Arbeiterfrage. Jena

Creizenach W (1878) Allgemeine Deutsche Biographie, 8. Bd., Gärtner, J.G

Fischer F (1961) Griff nach der Weltmacht, Die Kriegsschuld des Kaiserlichen Deutschland 1914/18. Düsseldorf

---

[89]Schöllgen, G. (1998), Max Weber, München, see: p. 162 ff.

Gärtner CF (1849) Versuche und Beobachtungen über Bastard-Erzeugung im Pflanzenreich. Mit Hinweisungen auf ähnliche Erscheinungen im Tierreiche. Stuttgart

Graepel PH (1978) Carl Friedrich von Gärtner (1772–1850), Familie, Leben – Leben – Werk. Ein Beitrag zur Geschichte der Sexualtheorie und der Bastarderzeugung im Pflanzenreich. Diss. Marburg

Hansen R (1968) Der Methodenstreit in den Sozialwissenschaften zwischen Gustav Schmoller und Karl Menger. Seine wissenschaftshistorische und wissenschaftstheoretische Bedeutung, in, Beiträge zur Entwicklung der Wissenschaftstheorie im 19. Jahrhundert. Meisenheim

Hansen R (1993) Gustav Schmoller und die Sozialpolitik von heute, in, Backhaus J (Hrsg) Schmoller und die Probleme von heute. Berlin

Hansen R (1996) Die practischen Konzequenzen des Methodenstreits. Berlin

Hasbach W (1902) Gustav Schmoller. Grundriß der allgemeinen Volkswirtschaftslehre, in, Jahrbücher für Nationalökonomie und Statistik, III Folge, 23. Bd

Hasbach W (1905) Erklärung, in, Zeitschrift für Socialwissenschaft, VIII Jahrgang

Hasbach W (1905) Letter to the editor, Zeitschrift für Socialwissenschaft, VIII Jahrgang

Hintze O (1919) Gustav Schmoller. Ein Gedenkblatt (1919), in, Soziologie und Geschichte. Göttingen, 1964

Holzwarth F (1985) Ordnung der Wirtschaft durch Wettbewerb, Entwicklung der Ideen der Freiburger Schule. Stuttgart

Kautsky K (1904) Schmoller über den Fortschritt der Arbeiterklasse, in, Die Neue Zeit, Nr. 34, Jg. XXII, Band 2

Kuhn Th S (1970) The structure of scientific revolutions. University of Chicago Press, London 1962

Lane FC (1956) Some Heirs of Gustav von Schmoller, in, Lambie JT (ed) Architects and Craftsmen in History. In Honour of Abbot Payson Usher, Tübingen

Lindenlaub D (1965) Richtungskämpfe im Verein für Socialpolitik. Wiesbaden

Lindenlaub D (1969) Firmengeschichte und Sozialpolitik, in, Manegold KH (Hrsg) Wissenschaft und Technik, München

Meinecke F (1922) Drei Generationen deutscher Gelehrtenpolitik, in, Historische Zeitschrift, Bd. 125

Mill JS (1844) On the definition of political economy; and on the method of investigation proper to it. In: Essays on some unsettled questions of political economy. Reprinted by the London School of Economics and Political Science (University of London) 1948, London

Mill JS (1874) Selbstbiographie. Stuttgart

Mill JS (1898) System of logic, ratiocinative and inductive. Peoples Edition, London, Book VI, Chapter VII, § 2

Mosberg H (1991) Re-education. Umerziehung und Lizenzprozesse in Nachkriegsdeutschland, München (Diss. Kiel 1989). Therein: Report of a Conference on Germany after the War called by the Committee on Post War Planning representing the American Association on Mental Deficiency, American Branch of the International League Against Epilepsy, American Neurological Association, American Arthopsychiatric Association, American Psychiatric Association, American Society for research in Psychosomatric Problems and the National Commity for Mental Hygiene, inc. held at the College of Physicians and Surgeons, Columbia University, New York City, on April 29th and 30th and May 6th, 20th and 21st, and June 3rd and 4th 1944. See: long term plans, items 5 to 8, p 178

North DC (1981) Structure and change in economic history. Oldenbourg Verlag München. New York

Oestreich G (1969) Die Fachhistorie und die Anfange der sozialgeschichtlichen Forschung in Deutschland, in: Historische Zeitschrift, Bd. 208

Popper K (1952) The open society and its enemies, vol II. Routledge and Kegan Paul, London 1945

Popper K (1957) The poverty of historicism. Routledge and Kegan Paul, London

Preußische Jahrbücher (1865) 14. Band, Berlin 1864, 15. Bd., Berlin

Roscher W (1861) Review of: Schmoller, Gustav, Zur Geschichte der nationalökonomischen Aussichten…, in, Liberarisches Centralblatt für Deutschland

Sachs J (1860) Geschichte der Botanik vom 16. Jahrhundert bis 1860. München

Schmoller G (1860) Zur Geschichte der nationalökonomischen Aussichten in Deutschland während der Reformationsperiode, in, Zeitschrift für die gesamte Staatswissenschaft, 16. Band

Schmoller G (1864/1865) Die Arbeiterfrage, in, Preußische Jahrbücher, 14. Bd., pp 393–424; 523–547; 15. Bd., pp 32–63

Schmoller G (1870) Zur Geschichte der deutschen Kleingewerbe im 19. Jahrhundert. Statistische und Nationalökonomische Untersuchungen. Halle

Schmoller G (1872) Arbeitseinstellung und Gewerksvereine, Referat auf der Eisenacher Versammlung vom 6. u. 7. Oktober über die soziale Frage. Jena

Schmoller G (1874) Die soziale Frage und der preußische Staat, in Preußische Jahrbücher, 33. Bd., pp 323–342

Schmoller G (1874/1875) Über einige Grundfragen des Rechts und der Volkswirtschaft. Ein offenes Sendschreiben an Herrn Professor Dr. Heinrich von Treitschke, Halle, in, Jahrbücher für Nationalökonomie und Statistik, 23. Band, (1874) und 24. Bd. (1875)

Schmoller G (1881) Die Gerechtigkeit in der Volkswirtschaft, in, Jahrbuch für Gesetzgebung, Verwaltung und Volkswirtschaft im Deutschen Reich, translated: "The Idea of Justice in Political Economy", in, Annals of the American Academy of Political and Social Science, vol IV, 1894

Schmoller G (1881) Über Zwecke und Ziele des Jahrbuches, vom Herausgeber, in: Jahrbuch für Gesetzgebung, Verwaltung und Volkswirtschaft im Deutschen Reich, NF.5.Jg

Schmoller G (1883) Zur Methodologie der Staats- und Sozialwissenschaften, in, Jahrbuch für Gesetzgebung, Vewaltung und Volkswirtschaft im Deutschen Reich, 7. Jg

Schmoller G (1884) Review of Friedrich List: Das nationale System der politischen Ökonomie, in, Jahrbuch für Gesetzgebung, Verwaltung und Volkswirtschaft im Deutschen Reich, 8. Jg

Schmoller G (1888) Jahrbuch für Gesetzgebung, Verwaltung und Volkswirtschaft im Deutschen Reich, 12. Jg

Schmoller G (1894) The idea of justice in political economy. In: Annals of the American Academy of Political and Social Science, March 1984, p. 697 et seq

Schmoller G (1894) Volkswirtschaft, Volkswirtschaftslehre und –methode, in, Handwörterbuch der Staatswissenschaften, 1.A. 6. Band

Schmoller G (1900) Grundriß der allgemeinen Volkswirtschaftslehre

Schmoller G (1903) Review of: W. Sombart (1902) Der moderne Kapitalismus, Leipzig, in, Jahrbuch für Gesetzgebung, Verwaltung und Volkswirtschaft im Deutschen Reich, N. 27 Jg

Schmoller G (1903b) Über das Maschinenzeitalter in seinem Zusammenhang mit dem Volkswohlstand und der sozialen Verfassung der Volkswirtschaft. J. Springer, Berlin

Schmoller G (1908) Erwiderung, in, Reden und Aussprachen, gehalten am 24.6.1908 bei der Feier von Gustav Schmollers 70. Geburtstag. Als Handschrift gedruckt

Schmoller G (1909) Karl Marx und Werner Sombart, in, Schmollers Jahrbuch für Gesetzgebung, Verwatlung und Volkswirtschaft im Deutschen Reiche, XXXIII Jg

Schmoller G (1911) Volkswirtschaft, Volkswirtschaftslehre und –methode, in, Handwörterbuch der Staatswissenschaften, 3.A., 8. Bd

Schmoller G (1912) Volkswirtschaft, Volkswirtschaftslehre und –methode, in, Handwörterbuch der Staatswissenschaften, Band, 3.A

Schmoller G (1918) Meine Heilbronner Jugendjahre, in, Von schwäbischer Scholle. Kalender für schwäbische Literatur und Kunst, Bd. 7

Schmoller G (1918) Die soziale Frage. Klassenbildung, Arbeiterfrage, Klassenkampf. Leipzig

Schneider E (1970) 3.A Erführung in die Wirthschaftstheorie, IV. Teil, Ausgewählte Kapitel der Geschichte der Wirtschaftstheorie, I. Bd

Schöllgen G (1998) Max Weber. München

Schumpeter JA (1893) Capitalism, socialism and democracy. George Allen and Unwin Ltd. London 1946

Schumpeter JA (1912) Economic doctrines and method. London. Translated 1954. University of Chicaco Press 1962

Schumpeter JA (1954) History of economic analysis. Oxford University Press, New York 1955

Sombart W (1892) Die neuen Handelsvertrage Deutschlands, in, Jahrbuch für Gesetzgebung Verwaltung und Volkswirtschaft im Deutschen Reich, 16. Jg
Sombart W (1897) Ideale der Sozialpolitik, in, Archive für Soziale Gesetzgebung und Statistik, Berlin, 10. Bd
Sombart W (1900) Sozialismus und soziale Bewegung
Sombart W (1902) Der moderne Kapitalismus, Leipzig, 1. Bd
Suchier W (1953) Bibliographie der Universitätsschriften von Halle-Württemberg 1817–1885. Berlin, Jurist. Fak. Nr., 145
Treitschke HV (1874) Der Sozialismus und seine Gönner, in, Preußische Jahrbücher, 34. Band, pp 67–110; 248–301
Völkerling F (1959) Der deutsche Kathedersozialismus. Diss. Halle-Wittenberg, Berlin
Wagner A (1887) Finanzwissenschaft und Staatssozialismus, in: Zeitschrift für die gesamte Staatswissenschaft, 43. Jg
Weber M (1904) Die Objektivität sozialwissenschaftlicher und sozialpolitischer Erkenntnis, in, Archiv für Sozialwissenschaft und Sozialpolitik, NF 1 Bd
Wiskemann H (1861) Darstellung der in Deutschland zur Zeit der Reformation herrschenden nationalökonomischen Ansichten. Leipzig

Chapter 16
The Empirical and Inductivist Economics of Professor Menger

Karl Milford

Biography

Carl Menger was born as Carl Menger von Wolfesgrün on February 23rd, 1840 in Neusandez on the fringes of the Austrian–Hungarian Empire. Today Neusandez is called Nowy Sacz and lies in Poland. He died as Professor Dr. Carl Menger briefly after his 81st birthday on February 26th, 1921 in Vienna, the former capital of the Austrian–Hungarian monarchy. After the Great War, Vienna became the capital of the young Austrian republic in which titles of nobility were generally abolished by law. The precise date of Menger's refusal to attach the title of nobility "von Wolfesgrün" to his name is not exactly known, but it certainly dates back long before the decline of the Austrian–Hungarian Empire in 1918 and the birth of the new Austrian republic. It rather seems that Menger's liberal but not libertarian political views had been responsible for this decision. The family of his father, Anton Menger, seems to have emigrated from the German Reich and eventually found a new home in Galicia, which then belonged to the Austrian–Hungarian monarchy. Anton Menger was a lawyer and in 1833 married Therese Gerzabek, the daughter of a relatively well-to-do business family. They had ten children of which many died in very young years as was quite common in those days. Apart from Carl, who was the third child, two of his brothers have to be mentioned here: Max, who was 2 years older than Carl, choose a political career and became a representative of a national liberal party, and later became a member of the Reichsrat, the parliament of the monarchy. Anton, who was about one and a half years younger than Carl became, like Carl, university professor at the University of Vienna. Yet, they not only belonged to the same university but also to the same faculty, i.e. to the faculty of law and political science (Juristische und Staatswissenschaftliche Fakultät). In contrast

K. Milford (✉)
Department of Economics, University of Vienna, Vienna, Austria
e-mail: karl.milford@univie.ac.at

J.G. Backhaus (ed.), *Handbook of the History of Economic Thought*,
The European Heritage in Economics and the Social Sciences,
DOI 10.1007/978-1-4419-8336-7_16, © Springer Science+Business Media, LLC 2012

to Carl, however, who was a professor for political economy, and who strongly supported liberal political views, Anton was a professor for civil law and rather defended social democratic positions (Boos 1986; Yagi 2006).

Not much is known about Menger's youth; and a biography of Menger, based on serious historical research is still lacking. However, it is well documented that in 1859 Menger started to study law at the University of Vienna, which he continued at the University of Prague from 1860 until 1863. Until the end of the twentieth century, the law curriculum included a substantial education in political economy and public finance since many law students later chose a career as civil servant. Thus Menger received an economic and public finance education in the course of his studies and thereby also may have become aware of the open problems which those areas of research faced at that time. However, it is most important to note that Menger received his economic education within different variations of a special tradition developed by German economists from the late eighteenth and early nineteenth century. This tradition became quite dominant at German and Austrian–Hungarian universities and only waned after Menger had entered the academic world and started to habilitate young scholars such as Wieser and Böhm-Bawerk, and established the so-called Austrian School of Economics.

The German tradition was inspired by two major elements: a theory of subjective evaluations as a basis for price theoretical explanations and the position of methodological inductivist essentialism. It was Menger who showed that this combination had to be discarded in order to develop a satisfactory explanation of exchange and prices and to provide a unified price theory. In 1867, Menger obtained a law doctorate from the University of Krakau and after having worked as journalist in Lemberg he became a secretary of the editorial staff (Redaktionssekretär) of the "Wiener Zeitung". The "Wiener Zeitung" was the official paper of the government and by becoming a Redaktionssekretär of the editorial staff, Menger simultaneously entered a career as civil servant. However, it also seems that this period marks the beginning of his detailed and critical studies of different economic treatises, particularly those of German authors, such as Rau (1826) and Hermann (1932). Menger's critical reading of their works triggered the development of his own positions and theories which he finally published in 1871 in his *"Grundsätze der Volkswirthschaftslehre"*, (Menger 1871) his first major work. With this work Menger obtained his "Habilitation" and "venia docendi" from the law faculty of the University of Vienna in 1872. In 1873, Menger was appointed to the position of "wirklicher" Ministerialsekretär in the Ministerratspräsidium. He now held a most prestigious position for a most promising and brilliant career in the imperial bureaucracy of the Austrian–Hungarian empire. However, Menger did not choose to pursue this career opportunity any further. He substituted this socially prestigious career for one which at that time carried much less prestige, i.e. that of a university professor. University professors in Austria at that time were permanent and irremovable civil servants and after having been appointed as an associate professor by the faculty of law, in the same year Menger entered an academic career.

In 1876, the imperial court appointed Menger to teach crown prince Rudolf political economy and statistics. However, he not only lectured the crown prince but also accompanied him on his educational journeys to a number of European countries. It seems that Menger's liberal political position influenced the crown prince to quite some extent. Rudolf and Menger, for instance, authored very critical contributions with respect to the role and importance of the Austrian nobility and published them anonymously in the "Wiener Zeitung". Menger also served as a responsible editor for the economic part of the so-called "Kronprinzenwerk", but it seems that his relations with the crown prince had ended in 1886. They had ended presumably because conservative members of the court took offence against Menger's liberal political views and his influence on the crown prince. For his activities as tutor to the crown prince, Menger was rewarded several imperial distinctions. In 1879, he became full professor and was called upon the chair for political economy by the faculty of law of the University of Vienna.

It is interesting to note that the reception of Menger's *Grundsätze* in the German speaking academic world was rather disappointing. In this work, Menger tries to develop a unified price theory on the basis of a combination of methodological individualism and a theory of subjective evaluations. Showing that the theory of subjective evaluations carries methodological import only if combined with methodological individualism, Menger develops the concepts of what in modern terms is called "marginal utility" and "equimarginal principle" in order to explain exchange and relative prices.

However, the reviews which appeared after the publication of Menger's work show that his basic ideas had not been grasped. Accordingly Menger set out to explain the importance and fruitfulness of a combination of methodological individualism and a theory of subjective evaluations for economic research in a volume which he primarily dedicated to the analyses of epistemological and methodological problems. This volume *Untersuchungen zur Methode der Socialwissenschaften und der Politischen Oekonomie insbesondere* (Menger 1883) was published in 1883 and provided a devastating critique of the Historical school's positions of methodological inductivist essentialism or methodological collectivism. In contrast to the *Grundsätze*, this work triggered fierce reactions among economists belonging to the so-called German Historical School of Economics such as Roscher or Schmoller. The *Untersuchungen* is Menger's second major work and the fierce debate following its publication came to be known as the "Methodenstreit". In the course of this controversy, Menger published three additional methodological contributions: in 1884, *Die Irrthümer des Historismus in der deutschen Nationalökonomie* (Menger 1884), a little booklet written in the form of letters to an unknown addressee, providing an answer to Schmollers critical review (Schmoller 1883) of the *Untersuchungen* (Menger 1883); in 1887 *Zur Kritik der Politischen Ökonomie* (Menger 1887); and in 1889 *Grundzüge einer Klassifikation der Wirtschaftswissenschaften* (Menger 1889). However, none of these methodological contributions match the quality of the *Untersuchungen*. Although the Methodenstreit continued to rage on for several more decades, Menger refused to participate in it any more. His followers and disciples such as Mises and Hayek, however, continued this debate until the second half of the twentieth century.

Already in 1887, Menger had returned to the study of economic problems. In 1888, he published a work on capital theory (Menger 1888) developing ideas which he had previously indicated in the *Grundsätze*. In this work, like in his previous analysis of value in the *Grundsätze* Menger aimed at showing that essentialist theories of capital have to be rejected since they require considerations regarding the origin of capital and not of economic problems. His theory explaining interest on capital emphasizes the command of capital goods and their utilization in certain time periods. But Menger not only contributed to the capital theory, he also contributed to the monetary theory. In 1892, he became a member of an imperial committee whose task consisted in providing answers to currency problems of the Austrian–Hungarian monarchy. After all, it seems that Menger's suggestions for reform were not accepted. But in 1892, perhaps due to the discussion in that committee, he published his famous article on money in the *Handwörterbuch der Staatswissenschaften* (Menger 1892). In this article, he considers metallistic and functional explanations of money but also discusses considerations relating to the quantity theory. However, his position in that context remains rather ambivalent. Apart from his activities in that committee, Menger also worked on tax problems and played a very active role in redesigning the law curriculum of the University of Vienna.

Since the early 1890s, Menger was awarded numerous academic honours and distinctions, and in 1900 he became member of the house of lords of the Austrian–Hungarian parliament, i.e. the Reichsrat. In 1903, he retired and became professor emeritus in order to work on the second edition of the *Grundsätze*, something which he had planned long ago. Unfortunately, he was unable to achieve this aim and the second edition of the *Grundsätze* appeared posthumously in 1923 after having been completed by his son, the brilliant mathematician Karl Menger. Menger had already died on February 26th, 1921 in Vienna, after having lived the inspiring academic life of a true scholar.

Menger's Critique of Methodological Inductivist Essentialism

In his *Grundsätze der Volkswirthschaftslehre,* Menger explains that his main object is developing a satisfactory explanation of exchange and relative prices. He emphasizes that the heterogeneity of the prevailing price theory is most unsatisfactory because it explains prices of factors and inputs and of final goods according to different principles. Instead Menger intends to develop

> …a price theory based upon reality and placing all phenomena (including interest, wages, ground rent, etc.) together under one unified view.

> (Menger, 1981, p. 49).

In order to solve this problem, he develops a special framework which consists of two major elements: methodological individualism and a theory of subjectivist evaluations. Methodological individualism is a methodological position regarding the structure of a satisfactory explanation in the theoretical social sciences. According to this position, satisfactory explanations in the theoretical social sciences explain social facts, processes, and institutions as an unintended result of the interplay of intended actions of individuals. In contrast to this methodological position, the theory of subjectivist evaluations is an empirical theory explaining the evaluative behaviour of individuals. According to this theory, individuals evaluate objects and actions as goods and services according to their subjective preferences only. Menger's analysis shows that the combination of methodological individualism and the theory of subjective evaluation is especially fruitful for economic analysis. In his view, this results from a particular relationship which exists between this methodological position and that empirical theory. Methodological individualism requires an explanation of the intended actions of individuals in order to explain social institutions as the unintended result of the interplay of individual actions. By explaining the evaluative behaviour of individuals on the basis of a theory of subjectivist evaluations, Menger provides such an explanation and thereby enhances the power of methodological individualism to its full effect. If methodological individualism is not combined with a satisfactory explanation of the evaluative behaviour of individuals it simply remains "blind" because the requirement of explaining social institutions as an unintended consequence of intended actions is without any consequences then. However, if the theory of subjectivist evaluations is not combined with methodological individualism, it simply remains a psychological theory which has no import for the theoretical social sciences; it becomes "empty".

However, by combining methodological individualism and the theory of subjective evaluations and by developing a unified price theory on that basis, Menger not only shows the special fruitfulness of that combination for economic analysis. He also shows that methodological individualism and the theory of subjective evaluations are incompatible with any essentialist approach in economics. Menger's investigations in the *Grundsätze* as well as in the *Untersuchungen* constitute a devastating critique of different essentialist positions, which according to Menger seriously impeded the progress of economics. According to him, essentialist doctrines come in three different forms: as a methodological position in the form of methodological inductivist essentialism; in a derivative form of that position as an organic explanation of social phenomena; and in the form of labour cost theoretical explanations of exchange and relative prices. In his view, the first two are defended by authors of the so-called German Historical School of economics, in particular by Roscher; and the third one for instance by A. Smith. In contrast to these essentialist doctrines, Menger intends to develop a nominalist and relational behavioural theory which explains the economic behaviour of individuals under different conditions. In his view, the tasks of economics is to explain

> Whether and under what conditions a thing is *useful* to me, whether and under what conditions it is a *good*, whether and under what conditions it is an *economic good*, whether and under what conditions it possesses *value* for me and how large the *measure* of this value is for me, whether and under what conditions an *economic exchange* of goods will take place between two economizing individuals, and the limits within which a *price* can be established if an exchange does occur. ... Economic theory is concerned ... with the *conditions* under which men engage in provident activity directed to the satisfaction of their needs.

> (Menger 1981, p. 46)

The first essentialist doctrine which Menger criticizes is methodological inductivist essentialism. This position holds that individualistic explanations of social institutions are unsatisfactory for principal methodological reasons. It emphasizes that methodological individualism violates fundamental methodological standards regarding the methodological characteristics of genuine scientific knowledge and explanations. These standards require that genuine scientific theories and explanations are verified or at least highly probabilified; they require that theories and explanations are proven true, absolutely or highly partially certain and that they are as a consequence, ultimate theories and explanations. This view, however, conflicts with the principles of methodological individualism because individualistic explanations of social processes and institutions seemingly trigger an infinite regress of explanations and do not provide ultimate ones. The cause of this seeming infinite regress is that individuals always act within a given socio-cultural and economic frame work, and that individualistic explanations of that framework always require the assumption of a previous one. Thus, in this view, there exists at least one social fact which cannot be explained on an individualistic basis for principal reasons. Accordingly, methodological individualism has to be discarded and substituted by an approach which conforms to the methodological standards of genuine science.

This approach is methodological inductivist essentialism. It results from two principal ideas: from a special version of Aristotelian essentialism as developed by German historism and the view that synthetic and empirical knowledge can only be obtained by the method of induction. According to the historists' version of essentialism, essences reside within objects, are real, and like seeds contain some potential characteristics that become observable in concrete historical situations. Being observable, essences can be uncovered, for instance by observing the historical development of objects or institutions. According to inductivism, genuine new synthetic or empirical knowledge can only be obtained through inductive inferences. Their content-enlarging and truth-preserving nature permits the drawing of inferences from "known" domains to "unknown" ones thus genuinely enlarging knowledge about the world. Since the conclusions of inductive premises are logically stronger than their premises, they provide genuine additions to knowledge, quite in contrast to deductive inferences which are analytical and capable only of unfolding what the premises already contain. As essences are uncovered by studying historical development, laws of historical development describing them can be obtained by inductive inferences; in this view, theoretical social science is theoretical history.

Menger criticizes this position in a version which Roscher develops in his *Leben, Werk und Zeitalter des Thukydides,* (Roscher 1842) in his *Grundriß zu Vorlesungen über die Staatswirthschaft* (Roscher 1843) and in his *Grundlagen der Volkswirthschaft* (Roscher 1886). This version is based on Ranke's essentialist doctrine of ideas and on some nineteenth century naïve inductivist views. Following Herder and Humboldt, Ranke's essentialist doctrine of ideas suggests that the Volksgeist or the essence of a people emanates in its concrete socio-cultural and economic institutions, traditions and in its language (Iggers 1997). A nation has its own customs and traditions thus creating its unique history and determining its presently existing social structures. Hence the Volksgeist, the essence or the nature of a people can be uncovered by studying the historical development of its socio-cultural, political and economic institutions.

Accordingly, Roscher opines that the task of the social sciences is to uncover laws of historical development on the basis of inductive procedures.

In his *Leben, Werk und Zeitalter des Thukydides,* he aims at clarifying the epistemological status of the social sciences and provides a naturalistic account of the methods of the social and natural sciences. These views are much inspired by Bacon's ideas. Like all inductivists, Roscher holds that genuine new scientific knowledge can be obtained by inductive procedures only. In order to explain these procedures, he introduces a passive psychology of knowledge. According to that theory, the human mind is a digestive system which processes the incoming flow of sense data obtained by sense organs. He explains that the results of intellectual activities are the products of this process. He links that passive psychology to a phylogenetic theory explaining the development of cognitive faculties and distinguishes four different stages according to the different intellectual products resulting in each stage. Intellectual products such as utterances and gestures characterize the first and most basic stage of this development process; the products of art and music characterize the second one; scientific theories the third one; and philosophical systems the fourth and highest stage. Whereas the analysis of the first two stages runs in psychological terms, the third one runs in sociological terms providing a "naturalistic" account of the methodology of the social sciences. In this account, Roscher simply translates his passive psychological theory into a description of scientific activities and distinguishes between "historical craftsmen" and "masters of history". Historical craftsmen have the task of collecting data and facts that constitute the empirical basis from which the masters of history infer social and historical laws by content-enlarging and truth-preserving inferences. Whereas historical craftsmen are capable only of collecting and perhaps of organizing data, the masters of history select the relevant data and facts and process them into theories by discovering regularities and similarities. This naturalistic description of social science methodology provides the simple Baconian inductivist picture of science according to which science starts from unprejudiced observations which form the basis for inferring absolutely certain and proven true theories by inductive methods.

Roscher's analysis encounters several difficulties. The most important one here is a demarcation problem. It results from his theory that all products of human intellectual activities like art, science and philosophy are an outcome of inductive procedures. In order to demarcate empirical science from other realms of human inquiry, he proposes a very rudimentary correspondence theory of truth. In contrast to science, philosophy and art have to meet different standards: philosophy for instance logical consistency and the products of art certain laws of aesthetical sentiment. Another difficulty here is the applicability of inductive methods in the social sciences. Like many other inductivists, Roscher as well believes that the possibility of repeated observations is a precondition for applying inductive methods. In his view, the natural sciences do not meet any difficulties here. Ontologically the natural universe is characterized by the so-called principle of the uniformity of nature which guarantees the possibility of repeated observations. In contrast, the ontological characteristic of the social universe is change and seemingly renders the making of repeated observations and the application of inductive methods impossible.

Nevertheless, Roscher opines that inductive methods are applicable in the social sciences. History provides a basis for making repeated observations and by comparing the historical development of nations, of institutions and of other holistic entities, social laws and laws of historical development can be induced (Milford 1995).

Menger criticizes Roscher's position of methodological inductivist essentialism with different arguments. By organizing the *Grundsätze* according to the requirements of methodological individualism, he rejects that position by way of his general analysis. This is shown by the chapter sequence of that book. In order to solve the problem of a unified price theory which explains exchange and relative prices as an unintended outcome of the interplay of individual intended actions, Menger starts his analysis by explaining individual intended actions. In the first three chapters, he provides a relational theory of the evaluating behaviour of individuals analyzing their behaviour under different conditions. The first chapter "The General Theory of the Good" scrutinizes the conditions that must exist in order that individuals evaluate objects and actions as goods and services. In the second chapter "Economy and Economic Goods", he proceeds by showing that observations such as the scarcity of goods basically result from the preferences and from the evaluating behaviour of humans under different conditions. In the third chapter "The Theory of Value", Menger provides a more precise explanation of the standards and the processes according to which individuals evaluate objects (actions) as goods (services). This theory provides the basis for explaining exchange and relative prices Chap. 4, "The Theory of Exchange" explains exchange and Chap. 5 "the Theory of Price" proceeds by explaining prices as an unintended result of the interplay of individual intended actions. Chapters 6 and 7 are degressions and clarifications; but Chap. 8 provides another example of explaining institutions along the lines of methodological individuals, i.e. money. But apart from organizing the *Grundsätze* along methodological principles which are incompatible with methodological inductivist essentialism, Menger also indicates that this position is based on a misunderstanding with respect to the application of inductive methods in the social sciences. Obviously having methodological inductivist essentialism in mind he writes that

> past attempts to carry over the peculiarities of the natural scientific method of investigation uncritically into economics have led to most serious methodological errors, and to idle play with external analogies between the phenomena of economics and those of nature.

(Menger 1981, p.47)

and he proceeds explaining that authors defending such positions although calling "… themselves disciples of Bacon … completely misunderstand the spirit of his method" (Menger 1981, p. 47).

Due to his primary aim of developing a satisfactory price theory, Menger refrains from providing a more elaborate critique of this version of essentialism in the *Grundsätze*. However, in the *Untersuchungen,* he launches a devastating attack on methodological inductivist essentialism. There he shows that this position rests on rather naïve views with respect to inductive methods and that they have to be rejected on logical and epistemological grounds. His first objection refers to the so called argument of the transcendence of first order. According to him, methodological inductivist essentialism attempts to avoid abstraction from a given empirical basis, that is, from the "immediate given". In this view, generalizations transcend experience and always carry the risk of failure not to arrive at absolutely certain conclusions which are proven true. And according to this view, the risk of developing false theories or concepts increases even more if it is assumed that the empirical basis of the social sciences, i.e. history, changes, as some representatives of the Historical school seem to believe. Menger points out that as a consequence the authors defending methodological inductivist essentialism basically sought to avoid all kinds of abstractions in the process of concept formation. However, he explains that this view has to be rejected on logical grounds. He emphasizes that even singular observational statements require universals in order to be able to describe observations and that even singular statements presuppose some kind of abstraction from the immediate given. Thus the research program of methodological inductivist essentialism as represented by many authors of the Historical school of economics has to be rejected because it cannot be carried out for logical reasons.

But according to Menger, the Historical schools' research program as defended by Roscher on the basis of methodological inductivist essentialism cannot be carried out even if the first order transcendence is conceded. In his view Roscher's version of methodological inductivist essentialism simply disregards the logical objection against the validity of content enlarging and truth preserving, i.e. inductive inferences. However, in order to be valid, inductive inferences have to be justified by some kind of principle of induction; if not, the possibility of an empirical and strictly universal social science cannot be shown. The idea of inferring strictly universal statements or theories which are empirical from an absolutely certain empirical basis by content enlarging and truth preserving inferences has then to be given up. Menger writes

> If the world of phenomena is considered in a strictly realistic way, then the laws of the latter signify merely the actual regularities, determined by way of observation, in the succession and in the coexistence of real phenomena which belong to certain empirical forms. A 'law' obtained from the above point of view can in truth only state in reality, regularly and without exception, phenomena belonging to the empirical form C have followed the concrete phenomena belonging to the empirical forms A and B or that they were observed coexistent with them. The conclusion that the phenomenon C follows the phenomena A and B *in general* (that is, in all cases, even those not observed!), or that the phenomena under discussion here are *in general* coexistent, transcends experience, the point of strict empiricism. From the standpoint of the above manner of consideration it is *not strictly* warranted.

(Menger 1985, p.57)

And he summarizes:

> The realistic orientation of theoretical research excludes in principle, rather, in all realms of the world of phenomena the possibility of arriving at strict (exact) theoretical knowledge.

(Menger 1985, p. 58)

Menger, however, shows that satisfactory theoretical explanations require statements or laws – or as he says strict or exact typical relations – which are strictly universal and empirical. Roscher's aim of uncovering laws of historical development by inductive procedures cannot be attained for principal logical reasons unless the problem of the validity of inductive inferences has been solved. However, since Roscher and other authors of the German Historical School simply disregard this logical and epistemological situation, their position is to be rejected. Moreover, on the basis of their position, the social sciences cannot be demarcated as empirical science and the problem of the epistemological status of the theoretical social sciences still awaits a satisfactory resolution.

According to Menger, the second form in which essentialism comes is the so-called organic view or "organic understanding of social phenomena". In his view, it is a derivative of methodological inductivist essentialism resulting, however, from unclear and dubious analogies of social systems and organism. He criticizes this position in the *Untersuchungen* where he contrasts it with methodological individualism. Both positions attempt to solve the problem of explaining human products which, however, are not the products of human design. Menger, however, emphasizes that the analogy of regarding social systems as organic wholes cannot help here. Methodological inductivist essentialism suggests of course a holistic analysis of institutions by investigating their historical development. But to assert that institutions as a whole or that society as a whole has developed organically in the course of history, simply amounts to saying that institutions have developed in history.

> The origin of a phenomenon is by no means explained by the assertion that it *was present from the very beginning* and that it *developed originally*.

> (Menger 1985, p. 149)

In Menger's view, however, the task of the theoretical social sciences is explaining the origin and the development of social institutions and not by assuming their existence. Satisfactory explanations of the origin and the development of social institutions or other "wholes" therefore have to be structural explanations; either in the form of explaining them as unintended consequences of the interplay of individual intended actions, or by explaining them as a result of an agreement of individuals. However, if social and economic institutions are explained as an agreement among individuals, i.e. as a product of human design, only psychological explanations are possible. In this case, explanations of social institutions will refer to the psychological motivations of individuals causing that agreement and not explain them as unintended results of the interplay of intended individual actions. Methodological inductivist essentialism implies psychologism in the social sciences and as a consequence the idea of a genuine theoretical social science is given up. The social sciences are then subdisciplines of psychology.

According to Menger, the labour cost theories explaining exchange and relative prices constitute a third form of essentialism in economics. Menger criticizes this version in the *Grundsätze* as well as in the *Untersuchungen*. In particular, his critique refers to positions held by A.Smith and provides one empirical and two methodological arguments. The empirical argument refers to the empirical falsity of an explanation of exchange on the basis of a theory of objective evaluations; the two methodological arguments launch an attack on essentialism in economics. The first one argues that labour and labour cost theories are basically essentialist theories and that the essentialist nature of those theories prevents reasonable explanations of exchange. In the second, Menger argues that the essentialist nature of labour theories triggers an unfruitful research programme in economics with unwanted and disastrous consequences for its progress.

Menger points out that Smith and other classical authors tried to explain exchange and relative prices on the basis of a theory of objective evaluations. According to that theory, individuals evaluate physical objects (human actions) as goods (services) on the basis of an objective standard, for instance time, commonly given to them. Time, for instance, measures the quantities of labour inputs required to produce commodities, and individuals therefore will exchange goods according to the labour quantities spent in their production. Menger reasons that according to their theory, individuals will be prepared to exchange equivalents only because in general nobody will be prepared to accept a smaller amount of labour in the form of products than was expended on the production of one's own goods. However, according to Menger this explanation of exchange is empirically false. It is falsified by simple observations, such as that exchange processes terminate and are irreversible.

He writes:

> If these goods had become equivalents in the objective sense of the term as a result of the transaction, or if they had already been equivalents before it took place, there is no reason why the two participants should not be willing to reverse the trade immediately. That experience tells us that in a case of this kind neither of the two would give his consent to such an arrangement.

(Menger, 1981, p. 193)

According to Menger, the hypothesis that individuals exchange equivalents is empirically false and cannot explain exchange. But instead of rejecting that hypothesis, the authors defending a theory of objective evaluations choose to maintain it and support it by introducing additional hypothesis. However, since the hypothesis that individuals exchange equivalents was to be maintained any explanations referring to different preferences of individuals had to be rejected. Menger opines that as a consequence, Smith sought to explain exchange by introducing an additional hypothesis about the psychological nature of man. According to this hypothesis, individuals are endowed with a special propensity to trade and barter. To this hypothesis, Menger, however, objects that it cannot explain exchange for principal reasons: to propose that individuals have a propensity to trade and barter means that in the process of exchange individuals satisfy a special need, namely that to trade and barter. But according to Menger this hypothesis has no explanatory power because it cannot explain the irreversibility as well as the termination of exchange processes. He states

> If trading were a pleasure in itself, hence an end in itself, and not frequently a laborious activity associated with danger and economic sacrifice, there would be no reason why men should not engage in trade…there would, in fact, be no reason why they should not trade back and forth an unlimited number of times. But everywhere in practical life, we can observe that economizing men carefully consider every exchange in advance and that a limit is finally reached beyond which two individuals will not continue to trade, at any given time

(Menger, 1981, pp 176,177)

According to Menger, the hypothesis that individuals exchange equivalents has several unacceptable consequences. It is empirically false; it requires authors to introduce ad hoc a psychological hypothesis, and by requiring that psychological hypothesis becomes incompatible to methodological individualism because by referring to psychological motivations socio-cultural and economic institutions are explained as an agreement, i.e. as an intended and not as an unintended result. In his view, the labour and the labour cost theoretical explanations of exchange trigger disastrous consequences for the progress of economics in general and are therefore unwanted. Taken by themselves, these arguments provide sufficient reasons to discard labour cost theoretical explanations of exchange right away.

However, Menger proceeds with this analysis and aims at showing that labour cost theoretical explanations of exchange are the result of a more fundamental approach to economics. In his view, they are the result of an essentialist approach which has to be rejected altogether if economics was to make any further progress. He explains that the labour cost theoretical explanations' unsuccessful attempts basically result from the essentialist nature of the theory of objective evaluations upon which these attempts rest. As mentioned previously, the Aristotelian version of essentialism asserts that essences reside within objects, are real, and contain potential characteristics to become observable in concrete situations. An essentialist theory of goods proposes a special characteristic or essence inherent in a physical object which through that essence transforms that physical object into a good thereby demarcating it from physical objects which are not goods. By analysing the causes that may have led to the development of a theory of objective evaluations and consequently to the idea that individuals exchange equivalents, Menger concludes that observations that individuals exchange goods at one observable price may have triggered the idea that individuals exchange equivalents. Labour theories explain that physical objects are goods only if they are products of labour, labour being the essence that transforms physical objects into goods. Observations of the fact that goods exchange at one observable price may therefore have been regarded as observable manifestation of an essence that makes goods to equivalents and economists accordingly sought to uncover that essence. Observables' prices may have been regarded as observable manifestations of an essence that makes goods equivalents, an essence which transforms them in to goods; and some authors, so Menger, regarded this essence to be labour. In his view, physical objects were regarded as values or goods because it was thought that they have that inherent property, characteristic or essence of being a labour product, which as such can be objectively measured. Menger writes

> But since prices are the only phenomena of that process that are directly perceptible, since their magnitudes can be measured exactly, and since daily living brings them unceasingly before our eyes, it was easy to commit the error of regarding the magnitude of price as the essential feature of an exchange, and as result of this mistake to commit the further error or regarding quantities of goods in an exchange process as equivalents. [And that]...writers in the field of price theory lost themselves in attempts to solve the problem of discovering the causes of an alleged *equality* between two quantities of goods.

(Menger, 1981, p. 192)

And Menger also emphasizes that Aristotle committed that error as well and regarded goods in exchange as equivalents. (Menger 1981, p. 305 appendix F)

However, Menger not only argues that labour and labour theoretical explanations are based on an essentialist approach. He also argues that this approach has to be seen in a more general context and not in this specific form only. According to him, this approach is of major importance for economics in general since it determines its basic research question and research programmes. By determining the basic research questions of economics, however, any kind of essentialist approach to economics is most important for the progress and the future development of that science. In Menger's view, however, any essentialist approach in economics has disastrous consequences for the progress of that discipline. Any attempt to uncover an essence of goods transforming physical objects into goods necessarily triggers most unfruitful questions and research traditions. In his view, the idea to uncover essences leads to questions regarding the origin of physical objects and not to research questions regarding the evaluating behaviour of individuals. But to analyze the origin of physical objects instead of the evaluating behaviour of individuals poses a false question of research.

Menger's Position of Methodological Inductivist Nominalism

Menger's criticism of essentialism shows that this approach is inadequate for the tasks of the theoretical social sciences. In its form as methodological inductivist essentialism, this approach has to be rejected for logical and epistemological reasons; its derivative, the organic understanding of social phenomena, cannot meet the task of providing satisfactory explanations of institutions because it assumes them; and the essentialist approach of explaining exchange and relative prices basically discards the idea of a theoretical social science by transforming it into a subdiscipline of psychology. In contrast, Menger aims at developing a nominalist and relational behavioural theory based on a combination of methodological individualism and a theory of subjective evaluations and which is based on experience.

However, although Menger is quite critical of the way in which methodological inductivist essentialism applies inductivism to the theoretical social sciences, he nevertheless shares the basic idea that the empirical sciences are characterized by inductive methods. Accordingly, he believes that the empirical sciences start from certain observations or rather from absolutely certain and proven statements describing observations or personal experiences; that on that basis specific general statements or laws are inferred by content-enlarging and truth-preserving inferences; and that these laws provide the bases for an explanation of complex situations, processes and facts. Menger opines that this is the method and procedure of any empirical science, i.e. of the natural sciences as well as of the social sciences, which he undoubtedly ranks among them. Discussing the methods of the social sciences in the preface of the *Grundsätze* he accordingly explains:

> In what follows we have endeavoured to reduce the complex phenomena of the human economy to the most simple elements which are accessible to certain observation, apply a measure to them which is adequate to their nature, and by sticking to it firmly to analyzing how the complex economic phenomena develop from these elements according to laws.

(Menger 1871, Vorrede, p. viii; my translation)

Thus, according to Menger, science starts with "certain observations" or rather with descriptions of observations which are proven true and absolutely certain. He suggests that by finding an adequate measure for them it is possible to establish regularities or laws between them. And that once having been inferred from that basis these laws provide the foundations for explanations of other complex situations, processes or facts. It seems that these views are much inspired by those regarding the methods of the natural sciences, as Mill describes them in his *Logic* (Mill 1843). Menger's description here transforms into the social sciences some principal nineteenth century ideas regarding the role and the importance of experiments as they also can be found in Mill's work. According to these views, experiments provide the possibility of certain observations, of measuring them by some adequate measure and of establishing regularities or laws on that basis. It is therefore not surprising that Menger opines that his description of the social science method pertains to the natural sciences as well. Referring to his description of the methods of the social sciences he writes

> This method of research attaining universal acceptance in the natural sciences led to very great results and on this account came mistakenly to be called the natural scientific method. It is in reality a method common to all fields of empirical knowledge and should properly be called the empirical method.

(Menger 1981, pp. 46–47)

In agreement with that method, Menger develops a price theory derived from certain and simple observations. Due to the requirements of methodological individualism and due to his non-essentialist approach, he starts his analysis by reviewing the conditions under which individuals evaluate objects and human actions as goods and services. He states them in the form of four typical initial conditions of a social situation in which individuals evaluate objects (actions) as goods (services) and justifies them by observations. Accordingly, it is derived from observation that individuals have needs and wants which they want to satisfy since their well-being depends on this. Observation or experience also shows that humans satisfy concrete wants with concrete quantities of goods; experience also shows that humans rank wants according to their importance with respect to kind and necessity; observation also shows that to a certain extent objects need to have the technical quality of satisfying specific wants; but they also show that in certain situations individuals mistakenly believe that they are capable of fulfilling wants and that nevertheless markets emerge. And observation or experience also shows that individuals must have command of the objects which they evaluate as goods. Menger also investigates under which conditions objects and actions expended in the process of the production of final goods (first order goods) are evaluated as goods or rather as inputs and services (higher order goods). Again, on the basis of observations, Menger discusses within this hierarchical conception of goods and services the importance of complementary relations among them and establishes different regularities here. He also discusses the importance of time processes and that of incorrect evaluations of situations with respect to economic decisions and emphasizes that the economic decisions taken in the presence are determined by the appraisal of future situations.

According to him, the presence does not determine the future but that precisely the opposite is the case. From the many possibilities existing in present social situations, the decisions taken with respect to the future determine the present actual historical situation; a view which is quite in contrast to what methodological essentialism would suggest. All this Menger infers from ample empirical evidence.

However, part of that empirical evidence is not provided in the first but in later chapters only. But the main result of Menger's analysis regarding the conditions under which individuals evaluate objects (actions) as goods (services) as well as the conditions under which they refrain from doing so is that any essentialist approach of explaining the evaluative behaviour of individuals has to be rejected. Whether individuals evaluate objects and actions as goods and services depends mainly on their opinions, knowledge, fantasies and appraisals. It is a human judgment and as a consequence Menger emphasizes that any essentialist notion of goods which regards the essence of a good to be inherent in that good is false. He writes

> [f]rom this it is evident that the goods-character is nothing inherent in goods and not a property of goods, but merely a relationship between certain things and men, the things obviously ceasing to be goods with the disappearance of this relationship.

> (Menger 1981, p 52, n 4)

Menger emphasizes this point several times in his analysis. For instance, after having discussed the concept of higher order goods, i.e. the complementary relation of inputs he states

> Again it is necessary that we guard ourselves. ... In the general discussion of goods-character I have already pointed out that goods-character is not a property inherent in the goods themselves ... the order of a good is nothing inherent in the good itself and still less a property of it.

> (Menger 1981, p. 58)

But according to Menger the inductive methodology of the empirical sciences not only requires that science starts with certain observations. It also requires to "apply a measure to them which is adequate to their nature" in order that laws or regularities can be established. In the first two chapters of the *Grundsätze* he basically explains the conditions under which individuals evaluate objects (actions) as goods (services). In the third chapter, "The Theory of Value", however, he attempts to find a "measure" which is adequate to observations regarding the evaluating behaviour of individuals. Based on experience, Menger emphasizes that the scarcity of goods originates in the individuals judgments, i.e. in the evaluating individual behaviour. Individuals attach value to goods according to the importance which they have for them in satisfying wants. Accordingly he emphasizes that like in the previous case of goods any essentialist notion of value has to be discarded. He writes

> Value is nothing inherent in goods, no property of them, nor an independent thing existing by itself. It is a judgment economizing men make about the importance of the goods at their disposal for the maintenance of their lives and well-being.

> (Menger 1981, p. 121)

The adequate measure Menger is looking for is a measure which measures the importance which individuals attach to goods in order to satisfy their wants. In modern terms, this is marginal utility and subsequently the equimarginal principle. Both ideas are formulated by Menger and systematically applied in order to explain exchange and relative prices. However, it is interesting to note that the terms in which Menger phrases these conceptions differ from those in modern text books to quite some extent. Modern text books usually provide a positive description or definition of marginal utility and derive the equimarginal principle as a result of an exercise in linear optimization. In contrast to these modern approaches, Menger bases both conceptions explaining the evaluative behaviour of individuals on experience and observation. This explains the particular way in which Menger describes these concepts. Whereas modern text books formulate the concept of "marginal utility" positive as an increase in utility given an increase in the consumption of a good by one unit under ceteris paribus conditions, Menger provides a negative formulation.

> [T]he value … to [a certain] person of any portion of the whole available quantity of the good is equal to the importance to him of the satisfactions of the least importance among those assured by the whole quantity and achieved with an equal portion.

> (Menger 1981, p. 132, original italics)

The reason for not having formulated this measure in positive but in negative terms is Menger's view that empirical sciences and hence also the social sciences are based on observation and experience. It is impossible to observe and to measure the increase of utility given an increase in the consumption of a good by one unit, ceteris paribus; but it is possible to observe that individuals satisfy concrete wants by consuming concrete quantities of goods and that they refrain from satisfying that concrete want which for them is the least important one if the quantity of a good is reduced by one unit. Accordingly, Menger also derives the equimarginal principle from observation

> If a good can be used for the satisfaction of several different kinds of needs, and if, with respect, with respect to each kind of need successive single acts of satisfaction have a diminishing importance according to the degree of completeness with which the need in question has already been satisfied, economizing men will first employ the quantities of the goods that are available to them to secure those acts of satisfaction, without regard to the kind of need, which have the highest importance for them. They will employ any remaining quantities to secure satisfactions of concrete needs that are next in importance, any further remainder to secure successively less important satisfactions. The end result of this procedure is that the most important of the satisfactions that cannot be achieved have the same importance for every kind need, and hence that all needs are being satisfied up to an equal degree of importance of the separate acts of satisfaction.

> (Menger 1981, p. 131)

Having stated those "certain observations" and that "adequate measure" which permit inferring the laws describing the evaluative behaviour of individuals under different conditions Menger proceeds to showing how these laws form the basis of satisfactory explanations of exchange and relative prices.

Menger's Solution of the Problem of Induction

There remains one important problem which according to Menger needs urgent resolution. His criticism of essentialism shows that only a nominalist and relational behavioural approach to economics based on observation and experience can provide satisfactory social and economic explanations. However, he is also aware that some representatives of historism and of the German Historical school of economics intended to improve economic theory by basing their analysis on observation and experience and by developing price theories on the basis of a theory of subjective evaluations. Accordingly he regards the German authors' attempts to explain prices on the basis of a theory of subjective evaluation as extraordinarily fruitful. However, he also believes that their combining these theories with the position of methodological inductivist essentialism explains why these attempts remained unsuccessful. Theories of subjective evaluations lose their methodological import if they are not combined with methodological individualism. If for whatever reasons the idea to explain social and economic institutions as unintended results of the interplay of individual intended actions is rejected, any theory of subjective evaluations remains a psychological theory. If the idea that prices are to be explained as unintended results of individual intended actions is discarded, theories of subjective evaluations explain the evaluating behaviour of individuals by referring to the factors determining their decisions only and have no methodological import for an attempt to explain prices as the unintended result of those decisions. In Menger's view, this explains why the German authors were incapable of providing a satisfactory explanation of exchange and of relative prices, although they based their theories on a theory of subjective evaluations and although some authors like for instance Schäffle (1981, p. 300) even formulated the idea of a marginal principle. Having lost the methodological import of a theory of subjective evaluations by rejecting methodological individualism and by defending methodological inductivist essentialism, the German authors were capable only of developing so-called reservational price theories and taxonomies of mainly psychological factors influencing individual decisions. And Menger also points that since these authors reject methodological individualism they had to introduce, like Smith, a psychological hypothesis in order to explain the coherence of social institutions. On the basis of their theory of subjective evaluations, the German authors suggest that individuals act egoistically and only according to their interests. However, once methodological individualism is rejected, the problem of explaining the coherence of social institutions is unresolved and needs resolution. According to Menger, the German authors sought to solve that problem by introducing a special Gemeinsinn, i.e. a special psychological hypothesis about the nature of humans. This Gemeinsinn checks the egoistic action of individuals and explains the coherence of social institutions in societies inhabited by egoistic individuals. Similar to the case of Smith, whose essentialist explanation of exchange forces him to introduce the psychological hypothesis of a propensity of humans to truck and barter, the German authors' essentialist approach in the form of methodological inductivist essentialism forces them to introduce a psychological hypothesis in order to explain social phenomena as well and develop so-called pragmatic explanations only.

> Adam Smith and his school have neglected to reduce the complicated phenomena of human economy … to the efforts of individual economies … They have neglected to teach us to understand them theoretically as a result of individual human intentions. Their endeavours have been aimed … subconsciously … at explaining them on the basis of [a] fiction [Menger refers here to the holistic fiction of a national economy as an entity acting like individuals]. On the other hand, the historical school of German economists follow this erroneous conception consciously. It is even inclined to see in it an incomparable deepening of our science.
>
> (Menger 1985, p. 196. Cf also Menger 1883, p. 237; partly my translation)

But Menger not only shows that methodological inductivist essentialism has to be rejected because the theory of subjective evaluations loses its methodological import if is combined with that position, his criticism of that position also shows that the inductivist views of the authors of the German Historical school need to be rejected on logical and on epistemological grounds. Yet Menger is an inductivist and defends the usual link of empirisim as an epistemological position and of induction as method of inferring strictly universal and empirical statements, or as Menger calls them strict or exact laws. However, Menger is well aware that his logical objection against the naïve inductivist view of the German authors renders the inference of strictly universal and empirical statements impossible. It triggers a conflict between the methodological requirements of strict universality and empirism defining empirical science. Yet in Menger's view, the statements or theories which the theoretical social sciences propose claim to be valid independent of time and error and are emprical: they are strictly universal and the foundation of their truth value is experience. The method of induction seemingly shows the possibility of fulfilling both requirements simultaneously, since it allows content-enlarging and truth-preserving inferences. Strictly universal statements or theories which are empirical transcend experience; but experience remains the foundation of their truth value if it is possible to reduce them logically to singular statements describing observations or personal experiences. However, Menger's own logical argument directed against the position of the German Historical School that past experience can for logical reasons only establish empirical statements which are only numerically but not strictly general seems to reject his inductivist and empirical position as well. If empirical statements are summaries of past observations only the methodological requirement of empirism is satisfied but the claim that they also are strictly universal has to be rejected.

The contrast of empirism, according to which the foundation of the truth value of singular and strictly universal statements is experience and of strict universality according to which the statements which theoretical science proposes are strictly universal and empirical is triggered by the logical objection to content-enlarging and truth-preserving inferences. This is the so-called problem of induction and since Menger threatens his own empirical and inductivist position by providing an argument against the validity of inductive inferences, he attempts to solve that problem.

And since by triggering the conflict of strict universality and empirism the problem of induction also renders the impossibility of demarcating empirical science from non-empirical science, Menger by trying to solve that problem also attempts to clarify the epistemological status of the theoretical social sciences, i.e. the problem of demarcation.

Menger attempts to solve the problems of induction and demarcation by introducing an induction principle. It is interesting to note that already in the opening paragraph of the first chapter of the *Grundsätze,* Menger presents such a principle in a form which Mill gave to it in his *Logic* (Mill 1843). This principle is the law of causation according to which every effect has a cause. According to Menger,

> All things are subject to the law of cause and effect. The great principle knows no exception, and we would search in vain in the realm of experience for an example to the contrary. Human progress has no tendency to cast it in doubt, but rather the effect of confirming it and of always further widening knowledge of the scope of its validity.

> (Menger 1981, p. 51)

However, due to the prime intentions which he pursues in the *Grundsätze,* Menger refrains from discussing this issue any further. Yet it is interesting to note that he obviously felt the necessity to justify his inductivist and empirical approach in the *Grundsätze* by providing such a principle. In contrast to the *Grundsätze,* the *Untersuchungen* provide a much more elaborated and detailed analysis of the problem of induction. There Menger shows that such a principle simply permits content-enlarging and truth-preserving inferences, and that if it can be shown that this principle is strictly universal, empirical and proven true a solution of the problems of induction and demarcation can be found within an inductivist framework.

Accordingly, Menger first introduces such an induction principle and then attempts to justify it by showing that his principle fulfils all the requirements which have to be met by any other induction principle as well. In order to transform the numerically general empirical laws into exact or strict laws Menger introduces the following induction principle:

> The only rule of cognition for the investigation of theoretical truth which as far as possible is verified beyond doubt not only by experience but simply by our laws of thinking, and which is of utmost fundamental importance for the exact orientation of research is the statement that *whatever was observed in even only one case must always put in an appearance again under exactly the same actual conditions*;

> (Menger 1985, p. 60 my translation)

Menger believes that this rule meets all the requirements necessary for a valid induction principle. It is a strictly universal and a synthetic statement because it asserts the existence of a regularity or law governing the world; and it is proven true because experience and our laws of thinking verify it beyond doubt. However, it is obvious that Menger cannot provide a correct justification of that principle by referring to experience and the laws of thinking. Basing an induction principle on further experience triggers an infinite regress of justifications because even additional experience cannot verify a strictly universal statement; and basing it on some kind of synthetic judgment apriori by saying, as Menger does, that the laws of thinking are valid by necessity also cannot help here because it is impossible to establish synthetic judgments which are apriori true. As a consequence, Menger distinguishes between two different epistemological positions or orientations of research: the empirical realistic orientation of theoretical research and the exact orientation of theoretical research. The empirical realistic orientation of research retains the principle of empirism that every empirical statement of science is decided by experience. However, due to the logical invalidity of inductive inferences Menger emphasizes that if the methodological requirement of empirism is retained that of strict universality has to be given up. Accordingly, the realistic orientation of theoretical research cannot establish strictly universal laws; yet, Menger is aware that if the methodological requirement of strict universality is retained that of empirism has to be rejected. Accordingly, he emphasizes that experience cannot be the foundation of the truth value of strict or exact laws and that the exact orientation of the theoretical orientation of research establishes laws which are not empirical. Albeit that the exact and the empirical orientation of theoretical research are logically incompatible, Menger believes in a pragmatic solution of the problem and proposes to apply both orientations of research in economics. However, his attempt to justify inductive inferences and to provide an epistemological justification of a social science that is theoretical and empirical fails (Milford 1990).

Evaluation of Menger's Contribution

Although Menger cannot find a correct epistemological justification for the theoretical social sciences, his methodological contributions are most important. Especially his attack on essentialism shows that there exist intrinsic reasons which explain the unsuccessful attempts of providing a satisfactory explanation of exchange and of relative prices. They also show that only by discarding all kinds of different essentialist notions progress in that field can be made. Only by discarding essentialism and by introducing methodological individualism instead, a theory of subjectivist evaluations receives its full methodological import and makes further progress in economics possible. This is perhaps the most important general message which the *Grundsätze* as well as the *Untersuchungen* contain. That it is really of decisive importance is seen that by combining methodological individualism and the theory of subjective evaluations Menger is able to apply the ideas of "marginal utility" and the "equimarginal principle" systematically for an explanation of exchange and relative prices and to improve price theory in general. His analysis shows that even if "marginal utility" is combined with methodological inductivist essentialism one cannot attain the aim of improving price theory. That Menger believes that his economic theory is based on experience and that the laws he proposes are inferred by content enlarging and truth preserving inferences is of lesser importance with respect to the progress of economics. But his belief is important insofar as it supports the idea that essentialist theories have to be substituted by nominalist and relational theories explaining the behaviour of individuals within an empirical theory.

In this context his analysis with respect to induction is indeed important though compared with the prevailing epistemology of his times not quite as original as for instance his economic analysis. By discussing the induction he shows that he is one of the very few authors to realize the importance of the problem of induction and its epistemological consequences. However, by failing to solve that problem he fails to demarcate the theoretical social sciences as empirical sciences from non-empirical sciences such as logic but also from pseudoscience. However, the consequences of not being able to demarcate empirical from non-empirical science has fatal consequences for the rationality of science. If the idea that experience is the foundation of the truth value of scientific theories is given up, the rationality of science is endangered. And Menger's logical objection against inductive inferences precisely shows that within an inductive framework experience is not the foundation of the truth value of economic theories. It is therefore most important to find an answer to Menger's logical objection. For if not "[t]he lunatic who believes that he is poached egg is to be condemned solely on the ground that he is in a minority, or rather – since we must not assume democracy – on the ground that the government does not agree with him" (Russell 1975; Roscher 1842, p. 646). – says Russell with respect to Hume who was one of the first authors to state that logical objection. Certainly Menger would not have welcomed such consequences.

References

Boos M (1986) Die Wissenschaftstheorie Carl Mengers. Böhlaus Nachf, Wien

Hermann FBW (1932) Staatswirthschaftliche Untersuchungen. München

Iggers G (1997) Deutsche Geschichtswissenschaft. Böhlau, Wien

Menger C (1871) Grundsätze der Volkswirthschaftslehre. In: Carl Menger, Gesammelte Werke, Bd. I, hrsg. von Friedrich A. von Hayek, J.C. B. Mohr (Paul Siebeck), Tübingen 1968

Menger C (1883) Untersuchungen über die Methode der Socialwissenschaften und der Politischen Oekonmie insbesondere, in: Carl Menger, Gesammelte Werke, Bd. II, hrsg. von Friedrich A. von Hayek, J.C. B. Mohr (Paul Siebeck), Tübingen 1969

Menger C (1884) Die Irrthümer des Historismus in der deutschen Nationalökonomie. In: Carl Menger, Gesammelte Werke, Bd. III, hrsg. von Friedrich A. von Hayek, J.C. B. Mohr (Paul Siebeck), Tübingen 1970, pp 1–98

Menger C (1887) Zur Kritik der Politischen Ökonomie, in: Carl Menger, Gesammelte Werke, Bd. III, hrsg. von Friedrich A. von Hayek, J.C. B. Mohr (Paul Siebeck), Tübingen 1970, pp 99–132

Menger C (1888) Zur Theorie des Kapitals, in: Carl Menger, Gesammelte Werke, Bd. III, hrsg. von Friedrich A. von Hayek, J.C. B. Mohr (Paul Siebeck), Tübingen 1970, pp 133–184

Menger C (1889) Grundzüge einer Klassifikation der Wirtschaftswissenschaften, in: Carl Menger, Gesammelte Werke, Bd. III, hrsg. von Friedrich A. von Hayek, J.C. B. Mohr (Paul Siebeck), Tübingen 1970, pp 185–218

Menger C (1892) 'Geld', in: *Carl Menger,Gesammelte Werke*, Bd. IV, hrsg. von Friedrich A. von Hayek, J.C. B. Mohr (Paul Siebeck), Tübingen 1970, pp 1–116

Menger C (1981) Principles of economics. New York University Press, New York; English translation of Menger 1871

Menger C (1985) Investigations into the method of the social sciences with special reference to economics. New York University Press, New York; English translation of Menger 1883

Milford K (1990) Menger's methodology. In: Carl Menger and his legacy in economics. History of political economy, annual supplement to volume 22. edited by Bruce J. Caldwell, Duke University Press, Durham and London 1990

Milford K (1995) Roscher's epistemological and methodological position. Journal of Economic Studies 22(3/4/5):26–52

Mill JS (1843) A system of logic. Rationcinative and inductive. In: Robson JM (ed) Collected works of John Stuart Mill, vol VII, VIII. University of Toronto Press, London 1974

Rau KH (1826) Grundsätze der Volkswirthschaftslehre. Winter, Heidelberg

Roscher W (1842) Leben Werk und Zeitalter des Thukydides. Vandenhoeck und Ruprecht, Göttingen

Roscher W (1843) Grundriß zu Vorlesungen über die Staatswirthschafskunst. Nach geschichtlicher Methode, Dieterich, Göttingen

Roscher W (1886) Grundlagen der Nationalökonomie. Cotta, Stuttgart

Russell B (1975) History of western philosophy. George Allen & Unwin LTD, London 1974

Schmoller G (1883) Zur Methodologie der Staats- und Sozialwissenschaften. In: Jahrbuch für Gesetzgebung, Verwaltung und Volkswirtschaft, 7. Jg., pp 975–994

Yagi K (2006) Anton Menger. In: Lexikon ökonomischer Werke, p 318, Hrsg. Herz, Dieter und Weinberger Veronika, Verlag Wirtschaft und Finanzen, Stuttgart

Chapter 17
Antoine Augustin Cournot

Christos P. Baloglou

Antoine Augustin Cournot

C.P. Baloglou (✉)
Hellenic Telecommunications Organization,
Messenias 14 & Gr. Lamprakis, 143 42 Nea Philadelphia, S.A., Attikis, Greece
e-mail: cbaloglou@ote.gr

J.G. Backhaus (ed.), *Handbook of the History of Economic Thought*,   437
The European Heritage in Economics and the Social Sciences,
DOI 10.1007/978-1-4419-8336-7_17, © Springer Science+Business Media, LLC 2012

Introduction

Antoine Augustin Cournot[1] was born on the August 28th, 1801 at Gray, in Haute-Saône, in France. The family background was essentially rural, but an uncle of his was a public notary. He exercised a considerable influence in Cournot. He wrote in his *Souvenirs* concerning his birth: "Pour mon propre compte, je suis redevable de mon apparition dans ce monde à la révolution de 18 brumaire. Quelque temps après ce grand événement, mon père, parvenu à la quarantaine, crut les choses assez rassises et la liberté de conscience assez assurée pour songer à prendre charge de femme et d' enfants. Cependant, comme je suis né en 1801, six mois avant le Concordat, j' ai encore été, à la manière des temps primitifs, baptisé en chambre par un prêtre qui se cachait ou qui était censé se casher, car, dans la réalité, on ne craignait plus l' application des lois révolutionaires."[2]

He received his early schooling in his native town and his first special discipline in mathematics at the Lycée at Besançon in 1820. He lists in his *Souvenirs* the work of Laplace *Essai philosophique sur les probabilités* and Cordorcet's *Essai sur l'application de l'analyse à la probabilité des décisions rendues à la pluralité des voix* among the books which he read at this time and influenced him. In 1821, he entered the École Normale at Paris, where he continued his mathematical studies. He entered to the school with Auguste Walras, who was destined to become notable economist in his own right apart from being the father of Léon Walras.[3]

His stay at the École Normale was short for it was closed in 1822 by the government because of the alleged republican feelings of its students and Cournot had to transfer to the Sorbonne from which he graduated in Mathematics in 1823. His teachers included Laplace, Lagrange, and Poisson, who befriended him and helped him considerably in his later career. His stay at Sorbonne was very fruitful for him: "Je n'avais rien à lire, rien à composer, rien trouver, rien à projeter, je n'avais qu'à écouter et à réfléchir: Ce temps a été le plus heureux de ma vie."[4]

He became Professor of Mathematics at Lyons in 1834 on the recommendation of Poisson. One year earlier he was engaged in the translation of two works, one in mechanics, and one on astronomy.[5] He held the chair in Lyons for only one year, for in 1835 he was appointed, again on the recommendation of Poisson, Rector of the Academy of Grenoble. In 1836, he was provisionally appointed to the post of the *Inspecteur Général des Études*, an appointment which became permanent in 1838, the year of his marriage and the publication of his first book, the *Recherches*

---

[1] The main source for Cournot's Biography is his *Souvenirs*, which were completed in 1859 but published in 1913 by Bottinelli. The main biographies of Cournot are contained in Moore (1905a, b, pp. 370, 521–543), Reichardt (1954), Moore (1991), Waffenschmidt (1991, pp. 57–69), Theocharis (1983).

[2] Quoted in Moore (1991, p. 19).

[3] Walras (1905) quoted in Theocharis (1983, p. 213).

[4] Moore (1991, p. 23).

[5] These were *Eléments de mécanique* de Kater et Lardner, which were *modified and completed* by Cournot (Paris 1842) and *Traité d'astronomie* de Herschel (Paris 1835). Both were translated from English.

sur les principes mathématiques de la théorie des richesses. He was made Knight of the Legion of Honour in 1838, and Officer in 1845. Parallel to the office of the Inspector-General, he held other educational offices during his career as an official, chiefly the membership of the "Commission des hautes études" and the presidency of the "Concours d' agrégation des mathématiques." He became Rector of the Academy at Dijon in 1854, but in 1862 retired from active teaching. The remaining years till his death on the March 30th, 1877 he spent in Paris engaged in philosophical meditation and writing.

The Works of Cournot[6]

Cournot was an economist, a philosopher and a mathematician. Among Cournot's mathematical writings mention can be made to his *Traité élémentaire de la théorie des fonctions et du calcul infinitésimal*, appeared in two volumes in 1841. This was followed in 1843 by the *Exposition de la théorie des chances et des probabilités* which is a systematic exposition of the calculus of probabilities and its application to statistics, and in 1847 by the *De l'origine et les limites de la correspondance entre l'algèbre et la géométrie.*

Cournot's philosophical works began to appear in 1851 when the *Essai sur les caractères de la critique philosophique* appeared.[7] This was followed by the *Traité de l'enchaînement des idées fondamentales dans les sciences te dans l'histoire* (1861) and the *Considérations sur la marche des idées et des évènements dans les temps modernes* (1872).[8] A last philosophical work entitled *Matérialisme, Vitalisme, Rationalisme: études sur l'emploi des données de la science en philosophie* appeared 2 years before his death in 1875.[9]

There are, however, his books in the field of Economics, which gave him fame and survive his name among future generations. Cournot started and finished his career as an author with an economic work. The *Recherches sur les principes mathématiques de la théorie des richesses* appeared in 1838[10] and the *Revue*

---

[6] It is interesting to note and emphasize that Martin (1998) gave a "complete" bibliography, concerning not only Cournot's complete works, including the various French and foreign editions, as well as the different studies published about his works, but also a comprehensive review of all the references to Cournot in the world literature. Altogether there are 1,478 references of articles or books, listed and classified under 17 thematic headings. Cf. the reviews by Vatin (1999, pp. 310–312) and Larson (1999, pp. 377–378).

[7] It was published in two volumes. A second edition appeared in 1912 and a third edition in one volume in 1922.

[8] It appeared in two volumes. A new edition in 1934.

[9] A new edition appeared in 1923.

[10] The English translation bears the title *Researchers into the Mathematical Principles of the Theory of Wealth* translated by N.T. Bacon 1897, with an Essay and a *Bibliography of Mathematical Economics* by I. Fisher, 1927, New York, A. Kelley 1971, an edition to which we refer to. There is also a German translation entitled, *Untersuchungen über die mathematischen Grundlagen der Theorie des Reichtums* translated by W.G. Waffenschmidt, Jena: G. Fischer, 1924.

Sommaire des doctrines économiques in 1877,[11] the year of his death. A third book entitled *Principes de la théorie des richesses*, which is essentially a repetition of the *Recherches* without the mathematics, appeared in 1863.[12]

The Background of the "Recherches"

It has been a matter of considerable interest among all those who ever wrote about Cournot's economic work how he, an accomplished mathematician, was included not simply to turn to the study of economics but actually to appear for the first time before the wider public as an author of an economic treatise. It is difficult, as we believe, to answer this question and give an exact answer. We would like to make some assumptions.

First of all, the relationship between Cournot's economic works and French literature in Political Economy requires a preliminary questioning about Cournot's own relationships with economics. Let us recall that Cournot devoted his first book entitled *Recherches sur les principes mathématiques de la théorie des richesses* (1838) and his last book *Revue sommaire des doctrines économiques* (1877) to economics. In the intermediate period, he published ten books on other matters, such as mathematics and philosophy, the only exception being his book *Principes de la théorie des richesses* (1863).

Second, in spite of certain features, Cournot's contribution to economic theory does not belong to any French school of economic thought whatever. In fact, the so called French school of mathematical economics, to which Cournot is classically related, seems to be a mythical reconstruction. There were French economists[13] who used the mathematical method before Cournot (1838), but there were almost the French engineer economists from the eighteenth century up to now, who were especially fertile during the nineteenth century. However, Cournot was not an engineer. On the other hand, Walras worked hard in order to promote in France mathematical economics after 1860. Cournot was still alive, but he never accepted to be enrolled in the Walrasian campaign.

Third, Cournot's study of economics was a side interest. But having read Smith, Ricardo, and Say, as he himself admits,[14] he must have found their analyses vague

---

[11] Reprinted by A. Kelley, New York 1968.

[12] Reprinted by Bizzarri, Rom 1969.

[13] There are C.-F.-J. d' Auxiron, *Principes de tout gouvernment* (1766), A.-N. Isnard, *Traité des Richesses*, London and Lausanne, 2 vols, 1781. L.F.G. de Cazaux, *Elémens d' économie privée et publique; Science de la valeur des choses et de la richesse des individus et des nations*, Paris – Toulouse, 1825. C. Courtois, *Mémoire sur différentes questions d' économie publique, relatives à l' établissement des voies de communication*, Paris, 1833. On Isnard's very rare book, see the excellent edition prepared by Van den Berg (2005, pp. 68–198). See Theocarakis' review in Theocarakis (2006). On Auxiron se Van den Berg and Dhesi (2004). On the French mathematical economists, see Theocharis (1961, pp. 66–69, 90–91). Theocharis (1988, pp. 265–273).

[14] Cournot (1938[1971], p. 4).

and confusing. He found that economic science was assuming "the dignity of a science of laws," and, as he was already influenced by A. Comte's ideas of a science of "social physics," the idea must have come to his mind that by developing the mathematical approach he could evolve a science of "economic physics." Cournot noted in the *Recherches* that of the previous attempts to apply mathematics to economics he had learned only the titles, except for one, Nicolas-François Canard's *Principes d' économie politique* (1801),[15] "a small work [...] crowned by the Institut."[16] Although he asserted that its principles "are so radically at fault," as Cournot underlined, "and the application of them is so erroneous" he later wrote that Canard's *Principes* was his point of departure, albeit a discouraging one. Cournot said that Canard's work embodied a false point of view and that works such as it would not incline economists like Jean-Baptiste Say and David Ricardo to use algebra.[17] Cournot may have been familiar with A. Walras, which had mathematical leanings. Lastly,[18] it has been proved that Canard's *Principes* had a direct influence on Cournot.

The Use of the Mathematical Method

The aim of the *Recherches* is not to develop a theory of wealth, but to apply the mathematical method to those parts of the theory, which Cournot thinks are susceptible to such a treatment. "I have not set out to make complete and dogmatic treatise on Political Economy. I have put aside questions to which mathematical cannot apply, and those which seem to me entirely cleared up already," he writes.[19]

Cournot can be considered as a direct product of a French mathematical tradition. It is well known that he was preferred pupil of Poisson. He honestly confessed in his *Souvenirs* that he was not a first-rate mathematician, in spite of Poisson's hopes, but he possessed an excellent training in mathematics and a vivid sympathy for ideas and theorization.

Cournot never denied the existence of a link between mathematics and the "science of wealth" even when the refrains from mathematics, but he defends his position at two different levels. In the *Principes*, he reproduced the analysis of the philosophical foundations of economics. Economics develop the opposite point of view from the law and jurisprudence on the same topic. While the laws are concerned by individual cases, the economists study phenomena determined by large numbers. If not Cournot's economics belong to the family of the mathematical sciences, because it is rooted in the ideas of numbers and measurement, in the *Recherches*, he explains the use of mathematics in economics. He held that the solution to the general questions of the theory of wealth depend "not on elementary

---

[15] For an evaluation of Canard's book in the history of economic thought, see Waffenschmidt (1958), Theocharis (1961, pp. 72–87), Tortajada (1990), Larson (1999, pp. 109–131).

[16] Cournot (1838[1971], p. 2).

[17] Cournot (1838[1971], p. 2.)

[18] Larson (1999, pp. 109–131).

[19] Cournot (1838[1971], p. 5).

algebra, but on that branch of analysis which comprises arbitrary functions, which are merely restricted to satisfying certain conditions."[20]

Thus, part of Cournot's dissatisfaction with the *Principes* must have been due to its use of a type of mathematics that he found inappropriate for economics.

Cournot's method is not aiming at finding directly numerical results; its aim is to ascertain what form of relation exists between two or more economic quantities and to apply there the theory of functions. Cournot underlined the fact that as only very simple conditions will be considered, "the first principles of the differential and integral calculus suffice for understanding this little treatise."[21] The determination of the relation may be vague but nonetheless the theory of functions will be applicable. Thus, the relation between quantity demanded and price may be presented by the function $D = F(p)$. It is sufficient to know some of its properties – in this case e.g., that it is decreasing and continuous – in order to find by means of analytical symbols "relations equally general which would have been difficult to discover without this help."[22]

This conception of the role of mathematics in economic theory struck, Cournot thought, at the roots of the argument of those authors, who although theorists of repute, mistakenly thought that "the use of symbols and formulas could only lead to numerical calculations, and as it was clearly perceived that the subject was not suited to such a numerical determination of values by means of theory alone, the conclusion was drawn that the mathematical apparatus, if not liable to lead to erroneous results, was at least idle and pedantic."[23]

Cournot was a mathematically sophisticated philosopher who, influenced by Fourier and his theory of heat, postulated that mathematical equations describing phenomenological entities were viable with any ontological commitments concerning the underlying phenomena.[24] Already in the preface to the *Recherches* he announced that in writing the book he had "put aside questions to which mathematical analysis cannot apply."[25] Further, the idea most authors had about the applicability of mathematical analysis to economics did not agree with Cournot's view:

> They imagined that the use of symbols and formulas
> could only lead to numerical calculations, and as it was
> clearly perceived that the subject was not suited to
> such a numerical determination of values by means of
> theory alone, the conclusion was drawn that the
> mathematical apparatus, if not liable to lead to
> erroneous results, was at least idle and pedantic.[26]

---

[20] Cournot (1838[1971], p. 4).
[21] Cournot (1838[1971], p. 4).
[22] Cournot (1838[1971], p. 5).
[23] Cournot (1838[1971], p. 3).
[24] Vázquez (1997, p. 126).
[25] Cournot (1838[1971], p. 5).
[26] Cournot (1838[1971], p. 3).

Cournot's Forerunners and His Originality

It was Frisi's originality who first used the calculus in 1772 to determine when price would become a maximum or a minimum.[27] T. R. Malthus made in 1814 certain suggestions, in which he called attention to the potential usefulness of differential calculus for economics and related sciences.[28] Ten years later Perronet Thompson, who like Malthus had excelled as a student of mathematics at Cambridge, employed the calculus in economic analysis. The problem that Thompson posed was to maximize the pain of a government that purchases goods and services with paper money, the issue of which is attended by rising prices. Thompson's article entitled "On the Instrument of Exchange" was the first response to Malthus's suggested employment of the calculus.[29] In 1815, a continental writer, the German Graf Georg von Buquoy, who stressed the managerial side of economics, advised farmers to maximize their net revenue by holding production at a level at which the first derivative disappears and the second becomes negative.[30] Later on, when new economic problems emerged with the operation of railroads, similar ideas were advanced. In 1839 Charles Ellet, a noted American railroad builder, applied calculus to determine an optimum tariff that would maximize profits.[31]

Cournot's book does put things in a new place. It is astonishingly modern, and it contains, for those who take the trouble of reading it, many discoveries.[32]

The Content of the "Recherches"

Entering upon the book itself, we find that it naturally falls under three parts. These are (a) the pure theory of price[33], (b) the theory of rates of exchange and international trade[34], and (c) his theory of Social Income.[35]

---

[27] On Frisi's notes to Verri's, *Meditazioni sulla Economia Politica*, Livorno 1772, see Theocharis (1961, pp. 27–34, 36–39), Luini (1996, pp. 127–147).

[28] Spiegel (1971, p. 507).

[29] Thompson (1824, pp. 171–205). On his contribution to mathematical economics, see Theocharis (1961, pp. 122–123).

[30] von Buquoy (1815[2005], p. 54). On this contribution see Theocharis (1961, pp. 112–113), Homberg (1971, pp. 61–62), Baloglou (1995, pp. 57–60), Bieri (1968, p. 138, n. 4) emphasized that v. Buquoy is Cournot's forerunner.

[31] Charles Ellet, *An Essay on the Laws of Trade in reference to the works of internal improvement in the United States* (1839). Cf. Theocharis (1993, pp. 21–40).

[32] Robbins (1998, p. 252).

[33] Cournot (1838[1971], pp. 7–116).

[34] Cournot (1838[1971], pp. 117–126).

[35] Cournot (1838[1971], pp. 127–171).

Value and Price

Chapter I[36] is devoted to defining wealth, the term Cournot uses in the sense of value in exchange. He carefully distinguishes this idea from "utility," with which he conceives the economist has no direct concern. What relations exist between wealth thus conceived and the welfare of the human race, Cournot regards as too difficult a problem to admit of present solution.

The second chapter entitled "Changes in Value, Absolute and Relative"[37] deals with the problem of value.

The very idea of value in exchange implies the necessity of comparison between two things; the idea of value is to fall into a logical contradiction. There can be absolute changes in one or both of the terms making up the ratio of value and these will affect the value of the ratio, but the idea of an absolute "change" in one of the terms of the ratio must be clearly distinguished from the idea of the ratio itself. "There are no absolute values" emphasized Cournot[38] "but there are movements of absolute rise and fall in values." Clinging to the physical analogy, Cournot cites the remarkable passage in Newton's *Principia*[39] in which an "absolute space" is supposed as a background for mechanical motion, distinct from the "relative space" made up of the system of moving points. He does despair of distinguished statistically absolute and relative changes, and observes that in case all commodities except one, such as gold or silver, preserve the same relative values; the probability to preserve the same relative value is greater that the one commodity has changed than that all the others have changed.[40]

The Law of Demand

The determination of price is the result of the play of the forces of supply and demand. Cournot believed that it was demand which played the essential part, "supply is the necessary counterpart of demand and consequently the accessory fact."[41] Cournot devotes a whole chapter, Chapter IV, entitled "Of the law of demand (De la loi du débit)"[42] to the discussion of demand, while his discussion of supply is hidden away as a discussion of costs in the chapter of Monopoly.

Cournot, though openly admitting that demand depends on utility, dispatched the embroiled classical discussions on the subject as ill-suited for the foundation of a scientific theory. Those ideas, he held, are by nature capable of neither enumeration

---

[36] Cournot (1838[1971], pp. 7–17).

[37] Cournot (1838[1971], pp. 18–28).

[38] Cournot (1838[1971], p. 24).

[39] Cournot (1838[1971], p. 20).

[40] Cournot (1838[1971], pp. 25–26).

[41] Roy (1933, p. 17).

[42] Cournot (1838[1971], pp. 44–55).

nor measurement, and it is therefore plain that no algebraic law can encompass the behavior of prices.[43]

Cournot assumes that the demand for a commodity, in the sense of the quantity of it annually consumed, varies with – is a "function" of – its price. This relation may be generally written as[44]

$$D = F(p), \tag{17.1}$$

where D indicates the demand of a commodity during a given period, a year,[45] in a given market,[46] and p the average price of the same commodity during the year. In this case he considers price as the independent variable, but later in the treatment of oligopoly he gives the form of the function as $p = F(D)$, when the quantity becomes the independent variable.[47] The relation between price and demand is delineated by the new familiar "demand curve" which Cournot was the first to introduce.[48] The character of this relation depends on "the kind of utility of the article, on the nature of the services it can procure, on the habits and customs of the people, on the average wealth, and on the scale on which wealth is distributed."[49]

Cournot makes another assumption, that of the continuity of the demand function, from which it follows that there may be a linear approximation to it within short ranges. "The wider the market extends," says Cournot, "and the more the combination of needs, of fortunes, or even of caprices, are varied among consumers, the closer the function $F(p)$ will come to varying with p in a continuous, manner. However, little may be the variation of p, there will be some consumers so placed that the slight rise or fall of the article will affect their consumptions, and will lead them to deprive themselves in some way or to reduce their manufacturing output, or to substitute something else for the article that has grown dearer."[50]

The demand curve is not only downward sloping and continuous; as the price in the function $F(p)$ has been taken to mean the average price during a year, the curve $F(p)$ is "in itself an average off all the curves which would represent this function at different times of the year."[51] The demand curve has in general the form and in the following Fig. 17.1.

The total revenue $pF(p)$ is maximized, when

$$\frac{\mathrm{d}pF(p)}{\mathrm{d}p} = 0, \tag{17.2}$$

---

[43] Cournot (1838[1971], pp. 10, 47). Cf. Vázquez (1997, pp. 126–127).

[44] Cournot (1838[1971], pp. 47–48).

[45] Cournot (1838[1971], p. 51).

[46] Cournot (1838[1971], pp. 51–52), note *Cournot's book (1971).

[47] Theocharis (1983, p. 138).

[48] Cournot (1838[1971], Fig. 1 of the Appendix).

[49] Cournot (1838[1971], p. 50).

[50] Cournot (1838[1971], p. 50).

[51] Cournot (1838[1971], p. 52).

Fig. 17.1 The demand curve

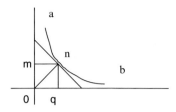

or by denoting by F' the differential coefficient of function F

$$F(p) + pF'(p) = 0. \tag{17.3}$$

The additional condition for maximization is[52]

$$2F'(p) + pF''(p) < 0. \tag{17.4}$$

The price oq which maximizes total revenue is found from Fig. 17.1 at such a point n on the curve anb, such as $on = nt$, where nt is the portion of the targent to the curve at the point n, which lies between n and the abscissa.[53]

In his discussion on the problem of maximization of the total revenue, Cournot further elaborate his concept of the elasticity of demand. For, he says, we would examine by statistical observation what happens to the total revenue $pD = pF(p)$, if there is a small change in price.

If the price becomes $p + \Delta p$, where Δp is a small fraction of p, the annual consumption would become $\Delta - \Delta D$. Then if[54]

$$\frac{\Delta D}{\Delta p} < \frac{D}{p}, \tag{17.5}$$

the increase in price will increase the total revenue $pF(p)$. The contrary would happen if

$$\frac{\Delta D}{\Delta p} > \frac{D}{p}, \tag{17.6}$$

when total revenue would decrease as a result of a rise in price and demand would be elastic.

It is, therefore, according to Cournot, of importance to know whether "the two values p and $p + \Delta p$ (assuming Δp to be a small fraction of p) fall above or below the value which makes the product under consideration a maximum."[55] Cournot suggests that "commercial statistics," as he says, should separate economically important commodities into two categories in accordance with their demand elasticity or, as he

[52] Cournot (1838[1971], pp. 53–54).

[53] Theocharis (1983, pp. 140–141).

[54] Cournot (1838[1971], pp. 53–54).

[55] Cournot (1838[1971], p. 54).

puts it, "according as their current prices are above or below the value which makes a maximum of $pF(p)$."[56] As Professor R.D. Theocharis had emphasized, "long before Marshall himself, he fully elaborated the concept of the Marshallian elasticity of demand."[57]

Cournot points out that $pF(p)$ might have several maxima and pass through minimum values between, depending on the shape of the demand curve. He proves that whenever $F''(p)$ is negative or when the curve $D = F(p)$ "turns its concave side to the axis of the abiscissas, it is impossible that there should be a minimum, not more than a maximum. In the contrary case, the existence of several maxima or minima is not proved to be impossible."[58] On this question Cournot thinks that in actual practice, it is improbable that the function $pF(p)$ will present such a problem "inside of the limits between which the value of p can vary."[59] The question therefore is always whether within the limits of the oscillation of p, "the function $pF(p)$ is increasing or decreasing for increasing values of p."[60]

Given the law of demand, Cournot first supposes a complete monopoly of the commodity in question, and shows what price will yield the maximum profit.

We have already seen that Cournot had given as the condition of maximizing revenue, where there are no costs:

$$\frac{\mathrm{d}pF(p)}{\mathrm{d}p} = 0, \tag{17.7}$$

which leads to

$$F(p) + pF'(p) = 0. \tag{17.7a}$$

If there does exist a monopoly, as in the case of the proprietor of a mineral spring with exclusive salutary properties,[61] he will seek to maximize his revenue by applying (17.7a) above which gives as the maximizing price

$$p = \frac{F(p)}{-F'(p)}, \tag{17.8}$$

and the total revenue of the monopolist is

$$pF(p) = \frac{F(p)^2}{-F'(p)}. \tag{17.9}$$

---

[56] Cournot (1838[1971], p. 54).

[57] Theocharis (1983, p. 142). It was worth to note that William Whewell (1794–1866) had used the concept of demand elasticity a little earlier than Cournot (Whewell 1829), but there is no indication that the latter was aware Whewell's contribution. Theocharis (1961, pp. 125–127), Rashid (1977).

[58] Cournot (1838[1971], p. 55).

[59] Cournot (1838[1971], p. 55).

[60] Cournot (1838[1971], p. 55).

[61] Cournot (1838[1971], p. 56).

Under monopoly, if there are costs, the net receipts to be maximized are[62]

$$pF(p) - \varphi(D), \tag{17.10}$$

and the maximizing condition is

$$\frac{dpD}{dp} - \frac{d\varphi(D)}{dp} = 0. \tag{17.11}$$

$$\frac{dpD}{dp} = \frac{d\varphi(D)}{dp}. \tag{17.11a}$$

The condition is the explicit formulation that the monopolist, the seller of a unique product, who is eager to maximize his net revenue, will charge a price at which marginal revenue equal marginal cost.

Cournot gives (17.11) in the form[63]

$$D + \frac{dD}{dp}\left(p - \frac{d\varphi(D)}{dD}\right) = 0. \tag{17.12}$$

Cournot denotes the change in cost in response to a change in quantity as $\varphi'(D) = d\varphi(D)/dD$. He uses the graphical representation to show how the monopoly price can be determined when there are costs.[64]

Cournot discusses further the effect of the monopoly price of a change in the various conditions of costs. He also discusses the effects of taxation on the price which is established under a monopoly.[65] These results depend on whether the tax is a fixed tax or direct levy proportional to the income of the seller (when there will be no effect on monopoly price or quantity) or whether the tax is a specific tax on the commodity (when there are repercussions as this means an additional cost to the producer).

The Theory of Oligopoly[66]

In passing from the study of perfect monopoly to that of perfect competition, Cournot considers also the intermediate case of a few, say, two, competitors. Cournot's treatment

---

[62] Cournot 1838[1971] p. 57.

[63] Cournot (1838[1971], p. 57).

[64] Cournot (1838[1971], Fig. 5).

[65] Cournot (1838[1971], Ch. VI, pp. 67–78).

[66] The first use of the term "oligopolium" is in Thomas More's *Utopia* (1516), where he had argued that an increase in the number of sheep might not lend to a fall in their price because, though there was not "monopolium," as the sheep did not belong to a single person, there was an "oligopolium" as the sheep belonged to a few rich people who could afford to wait until they got the desired price. For the authors who contributed to the theory of oligopoly prior to Cournot cf. Theocharis (1983, pp. 151–155).

of this difficult problem is "brilliant and suggestive."[67] The central supposition is that each individual will act on the assumption that his rival's output is constant, and will survive only to so regulate his own output as to secure the largest profits.

Cournot entitles his Chapter VII of the *Recherches*, in which he discusses the theory of oligopoly, "Of the competition of producers." He now imagines two owners of two springs' of which the quantities are identical, and which, on account of their similar positions, supply the same market in competition.[68] As a result of this assumption there is only one price. He now, defines the price p as a function of the quantity demanded, so that

$$p = F(D). \tag{17.13}$$

The total quantity of sales D will be

$$D = D_1 + D_2, \tag{17.14}$$

whether D_1 the sales from the spring (1) and D_2 the sales from the spring (2).

If neither of the producers has any costs, the net revenue of the first will be his sales at the current price, pD_1 and the net revenue of the second will be pD_2.

The net revenue of the first will be

$$pD_1 = D_1 f(D_1 + D_2), \tag{17.15}$$

and that of the second will be

$$pD_2 F(D_1 + D_2). \tag{17.16}$$

Cournot makes two assumptions, which have great importance for his analysis. The first is that there is no collusion between the sellers. "*Each of them independently*"underlines Cournot,[69] will seek to make this income as large as possible". This is essential, "for if they should come to an agreement as to obtain for each the greatest possible income, the results would be entirely different, and would not differ, so far as consumers are concerned, from these obtained in treating of a monopoly.[70] The second assumption seems to be of the most crucial importance, because it assumes that either of the sellers seeks to maximize his revenue by assuming that his rival's quantity will remain unchanged. That leads to the fact that "proprietor" (1) can have no direct influence on the determination of D_2 : all that he can do, when D_2 has been determined by proprietor (2), is to choose for the value which is best for him.[71] This assumption is followed by the next sentence where shows that Cournot did not exclude price adjustments: "This he will be able to accomplish by properly adjusting his price, except as proprietor (2), who, seeing himself forced to

---

[67] Fisher (1898, p. 126).

[68] Cournot (1838[1971], p. 79).

[69] Cournot (1838[1971], p. 79) (Italics by Cournot).

[70] Cournot (1838[1971], p. 80).

[71] Cournot (1838[1971], p. 80).

accept this price and this value of D, may adopt a new value for D_2, more favorable to his interest than the preceding one."[72]

The first seller's revenue will be a maximum, for constant D_2, when

$$\frac{d(D_1 p)}{dD_1} = p + D_1 f'(D) = 0, \tag{17.17}$$

which may be written as

$$f(D_1 + D_2) + D_1 f'(D_1 + D_2) = 0. \tag{17.17a}$$

The second seller's revenue will be a maximum, for constant D_1 when

$$\frac{d(D_2 p)}{dD_2} = p + D_2 f'(D) = 0, \tag{17.18}$$

which may be written as

$$f(D_1 + D_2) + D_2 f'(D_1 + D_2) = 0. \tag{17.18a}$$

Equations (17.17a) and (17.18a) form a system of equations,[73] the solution of which gives $D_1 = D_2$ as "ought to be the case, as the springs are supposed to be similar and similarly situated."[74]

The addition of (17.17a) and (17.18a) leads to

$$2f(D) + \left(D_1 + D_2\right) f'(D) = 2f(D) + D\frac{dp}{dD}$$

$$= 2p + D\frac{dp}{dD} = 0$$

Multiplying[75] this by dD / dp the result can become[76]

$$D + 2p\frac{dD}{dp} = 0.$$

Cournot uses also the graphical representation to solve this problem.[77]

---

[72] Cournot (1838[1971], p. 80).

[73] Cournot (1838[1971], p. 81).

[74] Cournot (1838[1971], p. 82).

[75] Theocharis (1983, p. 221, n. 164).

[76] Cournot (1838[1971], p. 82).

[77] Cournot (1838[1971], Fig. 2). Cf. Theocharis (1983, pp. 158–159), Magnan de Bornier (2001, pp. 168–171).

Further Extensions of the Theory of Oligopoly

Passing on the case of "unlimited competition,"[78] Cournot shows that the price is, in this case, equal to the "marginal cost of production." Cournot himself does not use this term nor is any other verbal description of the magnitude involved. He confines himself to mathematical symbolism.[79]

If we plot the relation between the product of each individual and his resulting marginal cost, we have a system of individual supply curves. These may be combined into a single general supply curve, which Cournot uses.[80] He shows that the intersection of this general supply curve with the general demand curve determines price. It is significant "of the slow growth of economic science that these graphic pictures of supply and demand, now in almost universal use in textbook and classroom" as I. Fisher emphatically wrote,[81] "were ignored or forgotten by Cournot's contemporaries, and were only restored in 1870, when independently obtained by Fleeming Jenkin." It is worth to note that the German economist Karl Heinrich Rau (1792–1870) came independently[82] to the same result as Cournot, 3 years later (1841).[83]

In the same chapter Cournot enunciates two other principles which have become classic; the first one is in regard to the law of diminishing returns,[84] and the second is that a tax on a commodity subject to "unlimited competition" will raise the price by an amount less than the tax itself.[85]

The Oligopoly of Complementary Goods

Cournot next considers the "mutual relations of producers"[86] or the connections between complementary materials, such as copper and zinc, which enter jointly into the production of a composite, such a brass.[87]

---

[78] Cournot (1838[1971], Ch. VII, pp. 90–98).

[79] Fisher (1898, p. 127).

[80] Cournot (1838[1971], Fig. 6).

[81] Fisher (1898, p. 127).

[82] Rau constructed the graphic representation of the law of demand and supply in 1841. Rau (1841a, p. 527), Rau (1841b, pp. 148–151). For the evidence that Rau came independently without Cournot's contribution to same result, see Baloglou (1995, pp. 160–167).

[83] Brandt (1968, pp. 90–91), Homberg (1971, pp. 97–100), Hennings (1979, pp. 1–14), Theocharis (1993, pp. 150–153), Baloglou (1995, Ch. 4), Vázquez (2002).

[84] Cournot (1838[1971], p. 91).

[85] Cournot (1838[1971], p. 93): *in all cases the rise in price will be less than the increase in cost* (Italics by Cournot).

[86] Cournot (1838[1971], Ch. IX, pp. 99–116).

[87] Cournot (1838[1971], p. 100).

Cournot assumes that there are two factors: (a) and (b), "which have no other use beyond that of being jointly consumed in the production of the composite commodity (ab)."[88] It is also assumed that there are no additional costs involved in the production of (ab), except for the reward of the two factors, which is paid to their owners. It is further assumed that the production of each factor costs nothing to its owner. Cournot assumes further that the two factors are used in the manufacture of the commodity in a fixed proportion $m_1 :: m_2 :$ "and $m_1 : m_2$ the proportion of copper to zinc in the brass," as Cournot says.[89]

This assumption leads to the equation

$$p = m_1 p_1 + m_2 p_2,$$

where p_1 is the factor of the price of the factor (a) and p_2 of the factor (b).

The quantity of the commodity demanded at price p is given by the demand function.

$$D = F(p) = F(m_1 p_1 + m_2 p_2).$$

If we suppose each of these to be handled by a monopolist, and "if we apply to the theory of the mutual relations of producers the same method of reasoning which served for analyzing the effects of competition,"[90] the condition of the maximization of the seller's revenue are

$$\frac{d(p_1 D_1)}{dp_1} = 0 \quad \text{and} \quad \frac{d(p_2 D_2)}{dp_2} = 0.$$

The development of these equation leads to the system.[91]

$$F(m_1 p_1 + m_2 p_2) + m_1 p_1 F(m_1 p_1 + m_2 p_2) = 0.$$

$$F(m_1 p_1 + m_2 p_2) + m_2 p_2 F(m_1 p_1 + m_2 p_2) = 0.$$

The solution of the above system gives as a result that the price of each will in equilibrium be such that the profits of the two sellers are equal

$$m_1 p_1 = m_2 p_2 = \frac{1}{2} p.$$

[88] Cournot (1838[1971], p. 99).
[89] Cournot (1838[1971], p. 100).
[90] Cournot (1838[1971], p. 100–101).
[91] Cournot (1838[1971], p. 101).

The equilibrium price of the first will be equal to

$$p_1 = \frac{p}{2m_1},$$

and the equilibrium price of the second seller will be

$$p_2 = \frac{p}{2m_2}.$$

The addition of the equations of the above system gives

$$F(p) + \frac{1}{2} pF'(p) = 0,$$

which leads to

$$\frac{1}{2} p = -\frac{F(p)}{F'(p)}.$$

"The composite commodity," writes "Cournot,"[92] "will always be made more expensive, by reason of separation of interests than by reason of the fusion of monopolies. An association of monopolists, working for their own interest, in this instance will also work for the interest of the consumers, which is exactly the opposite of what happens with competing producers." That is, in the case of complementary commodities, it is better for the consumer to be at the mercy of one of monopolist than two. A levy of a tax on one of the two component commodities will raise the price of that commodity and of the composite commodity, but will lower the price of the other component.[93]

The Theory of Social Income

The solution of the problem of price determination was affected by Cournot under ceteris paribus conditions, which included the condition that incomes remain unchanged. But Cournot felt that this was only an approximation and that the ideal thing would be "to take the entire system into consideration."[94] This, he estimates

---

[92] Cournot (1838[1971], p. 103).
[93] Cournot (1838[1971], pp. 112–116).
[94] Cournot (1838[1971], p. 127).

beyond the powers of mathematical analysis and he chooses to make another approximation and investigate how changes in prices of consumer's goods directly affect individual incomes and by implication the national income.[95]

Cournot defines social income[96] or national income[97] as "the sum total of individual incomes, of rents, of profits and of wages of every kind, in the whole extent of the national territory[98] and it includes 'the annual amount of the stipends by means of which individuals or the state sustain those classes of men which economic writers have characterized as unproductive, because the product of their labor is not anything or salable.'"[99]

Let us D denote the entire consumption of a "commodity for consumption" and p the price, "the product pD will express the sum to the extent of which this commodity co-operates in making up the social income."[100] If $p_0 D_0$ be the value of this product at one time, and $p_1 D_1$ at another, the difference between them, $p_0 D_0 - p_1 D_1$ expresses the diminution of social income. This diminution occurs in the incomes of the various persons contributing to the production of the commodity in question; and Cournot argues that the incomes of all other persons may be considered unchanged, for perturbations in the prices of other commodities are apt to occur as much in one direction as in the other.[101]

According to this reckoning, a dearth of a necessity of life may cause an increase of social income if the price rises faster than the quantity consumed falls. To overcome this difficulty, Cournot distinguishes between the "nominal" reduction of income $p_0 D_0 - p_1 D_1$ and a real reduction of income. He attempts to describe this real reduction of income without describing any "real income." The real reduction is found by taking into account the sacrifices that consumers of the commodity suffer in paying higher prices. Although it was already shown that the incomes of consumers, as a whole, may be considered as unchanged, still those who continue to buy after the price has risen have to pay the rise $p_1 - p_0$ on their purchase D, thus expending

$$(p_1 - p_0)D_1,$$

more income for precisely the same return. Hence they "are really in just the same situation as to fortune as if the commodity had not risen and their incomes had been diminished by $(p_1 - p_0)D_1$."[102] Adding this loss of income for consumers to the loss already shown for producers

[95] Theocharis (1983, p. 182).

[96] Cournot (1838[1971], p. 128).

[97] Cournot (1838[1971], p. 150).

[98] Cournot (1838[1971], p. 150).

[99] Cournot (1838[1971], p. 128).

[100] Cournot (1838[1971], p. 128).

[101] Cournot (1838[1971], pp. 129–132).

[102] Cournot (1838[1971], p. 134).

$$p_0 D_0 - p_1 D_1.$$

Cournot obtains

$$p_0 (D_0 - D_1),$$

as the total real loss.[103] He confesses, however, that, even with this amendment, he has not taken account of the loss to consumers who have ceased to buy the commodity because of the increased price, or of part of the loss to those who do buy, but buy less. He pleads in extenuation of this omission: "But this kind of damage cannot be estimated numerically [....]. Here comes in one of those relations of size which numbers can indicate, indeed, but cannot measure."[104] Edgeworth remarks at this point, that if Cournot had reached the conception of "consumers' rent," he would have seen that numbers can measures as well as indicate the damage in question.[105]

The Theory of International Trade

Cournot's contribution to the theory of international trade is elaborated in the last chapter of the *Recherches* entitled "Of the variations in the social income, resulting from the communication of markets."[106] The target of this chapter according to Cournot, is to prove "how commerce between two markets[....] causes the value of the social income to vary, as well in the importing as in the exporting market."[107] It is worth to note that, like in previous chapters, he again introduces losses and profits of the various involved agents.[108] Thus, Allais appears fully justified when he affirms: "Augustin Cournot should be credited with the merit of having introduced the concept of loss in economy (...) in 1838, i.e., 6 years before the first article of Dupuit, and of having approached the calculation of the first differential in simple cases."[109]

His analysis of the effects of international trade consists of three parts. In the first he develops a "highly ingenious,"[110] theory of foreign exchanges[111] the second deals with the effects of trade between markets, which were previously isolated, on

---

[103] Cournot (1838[1971], p. 134).
[104] Cournot (1838[1971], p. 134).
[105] Edgeworth (1898, p. 628). Cf. Fisher (1898, p. 132).
[106] Cournot (1838[1971], Ch. XII, pp. 150–171).
[107] Cournot (1838[1971], p. 150).
[108] Alcouffe (2002, p. 10).
[109] Allais (1981, p. 168), quoted in Alcouffe (2002, p. 10).
[110] Edgeworth (1925, p. 446).
[111] Cournot (1838[1971], pp. 151–155).

prices.[112] Finally, the third part seeks to apply Cournot's ideas about social income and its variations to the theory of international trade.[113]

It is this chapter that had had the most negative critiques. The first critique was made by Karl Heinrich Hagen (1785–1856), a professor of Political Science and Economics at the University of Königsberg, in a booklet entitled *Die Nothwendigkeit der Handelsfreiheit für das Nationaleinkommen, mathematisch nachgewiesen,*[114] the professed aim which was to demonstrate, through the use of mathematical analysis, the necessity for free trade. In its concluding part Hagen[115] acknowledged that he had been led to his demonstration through the study of Cournot's *Recherches* and discussed the latter's treatment of the effects of international trade on social income. With the aid of a very crude analysis of the relation between price, quantity demanded, and costs, Hagen was led to an "importation" and an "exportation" formula, which according to him would express the national income effects of international trade.[116] Cournot himself had already employed an approach similar to that used by Hagen in order to analyze the effects of international trade or national income, through its effects on prices and quantities produced or consumed, that, is on gross revenue.[117] One criticism leveled by Hagen against Cournot's treatment concerned the latter's use of gross revenue for measuring national income, without taking costs into account.[118] He also criticized the fact, that Cournot had failed to take into account in examining national income effects the fact that, when a branch reduced its activity, the funds previously employed by it would flow to other activities, and the contrary would happen when a branch expanded.[119]

Cournot himself attempted later in his *Principes*[120] to answer Hagen's criticism. He argued that through his "principle of compensation of demands" he had taken into account "in the appreciation of average results, of the transfer of funds withdrawn from the demand of article A, to the demand of articles E, F...."[121] But to the observation of Hagen that the increase in the production of a branch can come about only at the expense of other branches, he concedes that "there may be circumstances when an industry will not be able thus to develop except at the expense of another."[122]

---

[112] Cournot (1838[1971], pp. 155–160).

[113] Cournot (1838[1971], pp. 161–171). For an extensive analysis of Cournot's theory of international trade, see Theocharis (1983, pp. 185–194), Baloglou (1995, pp. 111–118).

[114] Hagen (1844). On Hagen's critique see Theocharis (1983, p. 196, 1990, p. 924), Baloglou (1995, pp. 128–129).

[115] Hagen (1844, pp. 30–32).

[116] Hagen (1844, pp. 11, 13). Cf. Theocharis (1993, pp. 170–172), Baloglou (1995, pp. 119–124).

[117] Cournot (1838[1971], pp. 150–171), Theocharis (1983, pp. 191–199).

[118] Hagen (1844, p. 31), Theocharis (1983, pp. 196, 231).

[119] Hagen (1844, p. 31).

[120] Cournot (1863[1981]).

[121] Cournot (1863, p. 212), quoted by Theocharis (1990, p. 924).

[122] Cournot (1863, p. 213).

The main criticism that could be leveled against Cournot's and Hagen's analysis[123] is that their discussion of the effects of international trade is carried in a partial equilibrium context.

Cournot in 1863

In 1863, 25 years after the publication of his *Recherches*, A. Cournot published his second economic work, the *Principes de la théorie des richesses*.[124] Deeply disappointed that his first work had not gained the recognition it deserved, he felt that what had gone wrong had been his use of the mathematical method. He declared in his work, that "I would like to see today whether I have erred basically in my ideas or only formally; and for this purpose I have again taken up my work of 1838 by correcting it, by developing it where the developments were missing, by completing it in those points which I had obtained from touching, and above all by absolutely stripping it of the algebraic apparatus which scares so much in these matters."[125]

Cournot considered that his *Principes* were his way of appealing against the sentence of non-appreciation imposed on his *Recherches*. "Since," he wrote,[126] "it has taken me 25 years to appeal against the first sentence, it goes without question that I do not intend, whatever may happen, to use another way of appeal. If I lose my case a second time, the only consolation left for me will be that the judgment, which condemns them, will be quashed 1 day in the interest of the law, that is, the truth."

It should be noted that, despite the above declaration of his intentions, 14 years later he published the nonmathematical *Revue Sommaire des Doctrines Économiques*,[127] which was his final attempt to reach the ever elusive goal of wider recognition.

Whereas, the *Recherches* did not provoke any reaction among the French circle of economists, the *Principes* were immediately commented by various authors, who did not share the same views on political economy: liberals such as Roger de Fontenay (1863), actuaries such as Chauveau (1864), and even the young Walras (1863).[128] Behind the *Principes,* their observations were mainly dedicated to the *Recherches*. Thanks to the *Principes*, Cournot's major economic work, the *Recherches* came to be recognized by several members of the French economic community a quarter of century after its publication. Unfortunately, however, this

---

[123] Theocharis (1983, pp. 138–139).

[124] Cournot (1863[1981]).

[125] Cournot (1863, p. II).

[126] Cournot (1863, p. II).

[127] Cournot (1877[1968]).

[128] All these reviews have been reprinted in Cournot (1982).

late interest of the *Recherches* was overcompensated by a lack of sympathy, rapidly transformed into a total loss of interest in the *Principes*. In his last publication, Cournot summarized the situation in the following skeptical words:

> Mais voyez mon guignon. Si je gagnais un peu tard sans m'en être
> mêlé mon procès de 1838, je perdais mon procès de 1863 si l'on
> voulait bien faire rétrospectivement quelque cas de mon algèbre,
> me prose (j'ai honte à le dire) n' obtenait pas chez le libraire un
> meilleur succès.[129]

According to a long and still dominant tradition, the *Principes* would be only a pale translation in words of the mathematical content of the *Recherches* for strategic considerations of communications. More recently, a careful reading of the *Principes* leads to an opposite appreciation: Cournot would have changed his ideas on economics from the *Recherches* to the *Principes*, in their substance as well as in their methods.[130]

It is worth to note that the *Principes* had been received by Léon Walras, who as a student had become acquantainted with Cournot's *Recherches*. Walras underlined Cournot's contribution to introduce the mathematical method and emphasized them.

In the Preface of the *Principes*, Cournot underlined the continuity between the *Principes* and the *Recherches*. Several chapters of the *Principes* concerning the Law of Demand (Chapter VI), Monopoly and Competition (Chapter VII, Book 1), the Communication of the Markets (Chapter IV, book II), and the Social Revenue (Chapter V, Book II), are directly derived from the *Recherches*. On the other hand, Book II of the *Principes* entirely devoted to a criticism of economic optimism is quite new. The main argument in favor of a discontinuity is provided by the many digressions extracted from the philosophical *Traité de l' enchaînement des idées fondamentales dans la science et dans l' histoire* incorporated by Cournot in the *Principes*. As, for example, Cournot made a distinction between an absolute and a relative Maximum (or Minimum) and contest the possibility of an optimum, because of our limited knowledge of the economic order. Such views, which do not appear in the *Recherches*, reutilize previous developments on the same topic in the *Traité de l'enchaînement des idées*. Going through philosophy Cournot offered an opportunity for new insights into economics.[131]

Fact that Cournot "linked with an attempt to apply mathematics to Political Economy, a serious and honourable attempt, the first and only one of its kind which has been made, and about which it is impossible for us not to say a word, because it is of interest to a high degree for the future of Political Economy." Referring to the *Principes*, Walras expressed his disappointment at the abandonment of the mathematical method. He felt that if Cournot had chosen the course "of renewing his economic principles in order to apply again to the mathematical analysis" there might at last result, "if not a complete and definitive theory of change and of social

---

[129] Cournot (1877, p. 111).

[130] Ménard (1978), Vatin (1998).

[131] Jaffé (1935) in Walker 1983 p. 18.

wealth, at least a new and precious chapter of pure political economy." Instead Cournot had rejected the original and fruitful mathematical element of his 1838 work, while he had retained and excessively developed its economic part.[132]

A second lengthy review of the *Principes* was published in 1864 by Roger de Fontenay (1809–1891), a graduate of the École Polytechnique and editor of F. Bastiat's works.

The reviewer started his essay by referring to Cournot's preface in the *Principes* where that author had explained why he had decided to present again the ideas of his original work of 1838 without the mathematical apparatus. Cournot had written in that preface that he had been wondering whether the failure of his *Recherches* had been due to basic errors in the ideas contained in that book or only in the form used. Fontenay expressed the opinion that the economic content in both of Cournot's books has not been quite up to the mark, as it was incomplete and sometimes wrong. Since he [sc. Cournot] has been able, as he says himself, to recast, correct, and even complete the first essay, said Fontenay, "by stripping it completely of the algebrical form, the ordinary economist appears to me to be entitled, up to a certain degree, to tell, him: Why have you amused yourself to talk to us in scary hieroglyphics, since you could present all this to us, and even better than this, in simple French prose and without algebra!"

According to de Fontenay, the algebraic process may either depart from precise and defines relations in order to arrive at numerical results and applications – this he calls the "triumphant" algebra; or, this process may involve the operation on vague formulas expressing relations, which are not reducible to numbers, in order to derive from them other theoretical forms and general laws – this he calls the "militant" algebra "of research, of progression and of theory." It was the second kind of algebra that Cournot chose to use in his Recherches by introducing functions of an indefinite nature and using the differential and integral calculus.

De Fontanay was a defender of the use of the mathematical method in economics. Algebraic analysis is a tool. It is "without doubt, the most powerful and the most extraordinary instrument of reasoning and investigation which the human genius has invented," and it was natural and absolutely justified for the able mathematicians to seek to apply their method to every science whose stage of development had reached a point where such application appeared feasible.

It is worth to note that de Fontanay recognized the disadvantages of the use of mathematics. First, there is the need of constantly seeking verification of the results obtained through this method. More important though is the limited scope and the uncertain nature of the results obtained. The application of the mathematical method requires right from the start the precise definition of all the initial data of the problem; it requires what we would today call the introduction of a model. This leads to the adoption of various devices, of subsidiary or simplifying assumptions etc. All these affect the result in such a way that in most cases the final conclusions reached are nothing else "but formulas which apply only to exceptional cases."

The most serious objection, according to de Fontanay, against the mathematical method is the fact that its very precision may be a serious handicap when it is applied

---

[132] Theocharis (1993, pp. 234–235).

to sciences which have not yet been fully developed. In order to use mathematical analysis in such cases and in view of the inadequacy of the available data, one may either decide to make arbitrary assumptions, which would lead to uncertain and faulty results; or one may use only evident and incontestable, but inadequate, data, in which ease his base would be so thin as to lead to insignificant or null results.

It was the time when the economic science had not been fully developed at the time of writing the *Recherches* that, according to de Fontenay, Cournot's introduction of the mathematical method, despite its merits, could not be successful. "A political economy is not yet a nature and made up science in any of its part and as it was infinitely less in 1838," commented de Fontanay, "we must not be surprised that despite all his talent as dialectician and algebraist, M. Cournot has only arrived at results which are very mediocre from the point of view of economic interest, and which are sometimes more than questionable, as far as exactitude is concerned."

The reviewer emphasized and underlined the merits of the work, although he objects the acceptance of the Ricardian doctrine and Cournot's treatment on international trade. According therefore to de Fontenay "the important and capital thing is … the attempt made to give to political economy a mathematical foundation," which, as he said, explains why he devoted the major part of his review to the work of 1838 and not to the *Principes* of 1863. As far as the *Principes* concerns, he observed that it is the *Recherches* deprived of the conciseness and generality of its mathematics; and the second, which is interwoven with the first, is a presentation of ideas fundamental in the sciences and in history. The reviewer mentioned that Cournot introduced in *Principes* the concept of "economic equivalents," in the sense that such equivalents produce the same amounts of product. De Fontenay criticized Cournot's views regarding the effects of the introduction of machinery on the employment of workers. He also criticized Cournot's thought in the *Principes* against the system of economic freedom and its efficacy to obtain the optimum results from the point of view of human happiness. He even accused Cournot of not believing in the principle of economic liberty and in the ability of the economic system to self-adjust satisfactorily, as that author rejected both the existence of an organic economic harmony and the possibility of a mechanical adjustment of economic interests.[133]

Conclusion

A. A. Cournot's *Recherches sur les Principes mathématiques de la théorie des richesses*, which appeared in 1838, is the first consistent and systematic application of mathematical analysis, not simply to a single problem but to a number of topics – and this differentiates that book from earlier contributions to mathematical economics.[134]

---

[133] This part is based on Theocharis' treatment. See Theocharis (1993, pp. 235–240).

[134] For a detailed analysis of the contributions of the authors to the mathematical economics prior to Cournot (1838), see Moret (1915, pp. 64–78), Weinberger (1930, pp. 36–42), Robertson (1949, pp. 523–536), Reichardt (1954, pp. 67–69), Bousquet (1958), Theocharis (1961). On the German authors prior Cournot see especially Homberg (1971), Baloglou (1995, pp. 29–53), Baloglou (2003, pp. 127–134), Vázquez (2006, pp. 533–541).

Cournot's book has the dual distinction of being the first economic treatise where, on the one hand, the calculus has been applied consistently and successfully throughout and, on the other hand, diagrams have been used extensively as an accepted form of exposition and analysis. The same can be said for Gossen's book.

Cournot is also the first author to put in clear mathematical terms the notion, that, ceteris paribus, the quantity demanded and the prices are functionally related; and to develop the concept of elasticity of demand long before Alfred Marshall. In discussing the conditions of supply, he introduces the idea of total and marginal cost and points out that under free competition the condition of equilibrium for the individual producer is the equalization of his price to his marginal cost.

Cournot determines, both analytically and graphically and under conditions of free competition, the static partial equilibrium of price, at the point where the total quantity demanded equals the total quantity supplied. He was the first to show that monopoly price would be fixed at the point where marginal cost equals marginal receipts and net revenue is a maximum. Cournot's approach to monopoly is very much alive today.

We have to underline that Cournot's contribution to the theory of oligopoly survives to the present day and it is truth, as R.D. Theocharis[135] has pointed out that "every author who has dealt with the problem of oligopoly price determination since the appearance of the *Recherches*, has not escaped the temptation to comment upon Cournot's solution, either critically or favourably."

References

Alcouffe A (2002) Cournot's international trade theory: between rejection and neglect. In: VI. Annual conference of the European Society for the history of economic thought (14–17 March 2002). Book of Abstracts, Rerthymnon, pp 10–11

Allais M (1981) La théorie générale des surplus. Paris Cahiers de l' I.S.M.É.A., n° 1 à 5, P.U.F., 1989, pp 18, 22, 161, 168, 191, 203–204, 229, 295, 297, 304, 325

Baloglou C (1995) Die Vertreter der mathematischen Nationalökonomie in Deutschland zwischen 1838 und 1871. Vorwort B. Priddat. Metropolis, Marburg

Baloglou C (2003) Researches in mathematical economics: the reception of Cournot's in Germany (1839–1871). Οργάνωση του Αθλητισμού 1(2):127–134

Bieri S (1968) Zur Stellung der frühen deutschen Finanzwissenschaft unter besonderer Berücksichtigung von Jakob, Sodenl, Lotz und Malchus, Zürich

Bousquet GH (1958) Histoire de l' économie mathématique jusqu' à Cournot. Metroeconomica X(III):121–135

Brandt K (1968) Die graphische Methode in der Nationalökonomie. In: Henn R (ed) Operations Research Verfahren, vol 5. Anton Hain, Meisenheim, pp 81–107

Cournot AA (1838) [1971] Researches into the mathematical principles of the theory of wealth (trans: Bacon N) (With an essay and a 'Bibliography of mathematical economics' by Fisher I). A. Kelley, New York

Cournot AA (1863) [1969] Principes de la théorie des richesses. Hachette, Paris [Bizzarri, Roma]

---

[135] Theocharis (1993 p. 19).

Cournot AA (1877) Revue sommaire des doctrines économiques. Hachette, Paris [A. Kelley, New York]

Cournot AA (1982) Revue sommaire des doctrines économiques. Vrin, Paris

Edgeworth FY (1898) The pure theory of international values. Econ J 4:606–638

Edgeworth FY (1925) Papers relating to political economy, vol II. Macmillan, London

Fisher I (1898) Cournot and mathematical economics. Q J Econ 12:119–138

Hagen KH (1844) Die Nothwendigkeit der Handelsfreiheit für das Nationaleinkommen, mathematisch nachgewiesen. Grafe und Unzer, Königsberg

Hennings KH (1979) Karl Heinrich Rau and the graphic representation of supply and demand. Diskussionspapier. Fachbereich Wirtschaftswissenschaften Universität Hannover. Serie C, Volkswirtschaftslehre, No 35

Herschel JF (1835) Traité d'astronomie, par Sir John F.W. Herschel, traduit de l' anglais et augmenté d' un chapitre sur l' application de la théorie des chances à la série des orbites des cométes par A.- A. Cournot, Paulin, Paris

Homberg G (1971) Die Vertreter der mathematischen Nationalökonomie im deutschsprachigen Raum vor dem Erscheinen des Cournotschen Werkes (1838). Diss., Freiburg

Jaffé W (1935) Unpublished papers and letters of Léon Walras. In: Walker DA (ed) William Jaffe's Essays on Walras. Cambridge University Press, Cambridge, 1983, pp 17–35

Kater H, Lardner D (1842) Éléments de mécanique par le capitaine Kater et le Dr Lardner, traduit de l' anglais, modifiés et complétés par A.- A. Cournot, Paulin, Paris

Larson B (1999) Canard on direct exchange and taxation: a perspective on Cournot. Hist Polit Econ 31(1):377–378, Spring

Luini L (1996) Scienze naturali e scienze sociali. Le chiose matematiche di Frisi a Verri e Lloyd. In: Curzio AQ (ed) Alle Origini del pensiero economico in Italia. Il Mulino, Milano, pp 127–146

Magnan de Bornier J (2001) Magnan de Bornier on Cournot-Bertrand: a rejoinder to Clarence Morrison. Hist Polit Econ 33(1):167–174, Spring

Martin T (1998) Bibliographie Cournotienne, in collaboration with Jean – Philippe Massonie. Annales Littéraires de l' Université de Franche-Comte. Les Belles Lettres, Besancon

Ménard C (1978) La formation d' une rationalité économique: A. A. Cournot. Flammarion, Paris

Moore HL (1905a) The personality of Antoine Augustin Cournot. Q J Econ 19:370–399

Moore HL (1905b) Antoine Augustin Cournot. Rev Métaphys Morale XIIIᵉ année 521–543, mai

Moore HL (1991) Antoine Augustin Cournot (1801–1877). In: Schefold B, Moore HL, Alcouffe A, Fraysse J, Waffenschmidt W (eds) Vademecum zu einem Klassiker der mathematischen Wirtschaftstheorie. Wirtschaft und Finanzen, Düsseldorf, pp 19–33

Moret J (1915) L' emploi des mathématiques en économie politique. G. Briard & E. Brière, Paris

Rashid S (1977) William Whewell and early mathematical economics. Manchester Sch Econ Soc Stud 45:381–391

Rau KH (1841a) Grundsätze der Volkswirthschaftslehre, 4th edn. C. Winter, Heidelberg

Rau KH (1841b) (Communications); Economie politique. 1er et 2nd Extraits. Bulletin de l' Académie des Sciences et Belles – Lettres à Bruxelles VIII(pt I):145–152

Reichardt H (1954) A. A. Cournot. Sein Beitrag zur exakten Wirtschaftswissenschaften. J. C. B. Mohr, Tübingen

Robbins L (1998) A history of economic thought. In: Medema SG, Samuels W (eds) The LSE lectures (Foreword by Baumol W). Princeton University Press, Princeton

Robertson RM (1949) Mathematical economics before Cournot. J Polit Econ LVII:523–536

Roy R (1933) Cournot et l' école mathématique. Econometrica 1:13–22

Spiegel HW (1971) The growth of economic thought. Duke University Press, Durham

Theocarakis N (2006) Review: Richard Van den Berg, at the origins of mathematical economics: the economics of A. N. Isnard (1748–1803). Routledge, London 2005. Hist Econ Ideas 14(2): 147–151

Theocharis RD (1961) Early developments in mathematical economics (Foreword Lord Robbins). Macmillan, London

Theocharis RD (1983) Early developments in mathematical economics (Foreword Lord Robbins), 2nd edn. Porcupine Press, Philadelphia

Theocharis RD (1988) C. Courtois: an early contributor to cost-benefit analysis. Hist Polit Econ 20:265–273

Theocharis RD (1990) A note on the lag in the recognition of Cournot's contribution to economic analysis. Can J Econ 23(4):923–933

Theocharis RD (1993) The development of mathematical economics. The years of transition: from Cournot to Jevons. Macmillan, London

Thompson ThP (1824) The instrument of exchange. Westminst Rev 1:171–205

Tortajada R (1990) Produit net et latitude: Nicolas-François Canard. In: Faccarello G, Steiner P (eds) La Pensée Économique pendant la Révolution Française. Presses Universitaires, Grenoble, pp 151–172

Van den Berg R (2005) At the origins of mathematical economics: the economics of A. N. Isnard (1748–1803). Routledge, London [Routledge Studies in the History of Economics, No 76]

Van den Berg R, Dhesi D (2004) The equilibrium is never perfect: The dynamic analysis of C.- F.- J. d' Auxiron. Hist Polit Econ 36(1):1–29, Spring

Vatin F (1998) Économie politique et économie naturelle chez Antoine – Augustin Cournot. Presses Universitaires de France, Paris

Vatin F (1999) Book review: Thierry Martin, Bibliographie Cournotienne (1998). Eur J Hist Econ Thought 6(2):310–312

Vázquez A (1997) The awareness of Cournot's Recherches among early British economists. Res Hist Econ Thought Meth 15:115–137

Vázquez A (2002) Karl Heinrich Rau y el diagrama marshaliano. Rev Hist Econ XX(1):109–139

Vázquez A (2006) Slonimsky's view on Antoine – Augustin Cournot. Eur J Hist Econ Thought 13(4):533–541

von Buquoy G (1815) Die Theorie der Nationalwirthschaft nach einem neuen Plane und nach mehrern eigenen Ansichten dargestellt. Breitkopf & Hartel, Leipzig [(2005) Nachdruck mit einer Einleitung herausgegeben von Christos Baloglou und Bertram Schefold. G. Olms, Hildesheim]

Waffenschmidt WG (1958) Einleitung. In: Canard NF (ed) Grundsätze der Staatswirtschaft [German trans]. Kohlhammer, Stuttgart, pp 1–58

Waffenschmidt W (1991) Cournot und sein Werk. In: Schefold B, Moore HL, Alcouffe A, Fraysse J, Waffenschmidt W (eds) Vademecum zu einem Klassiker der mathematischen Wirtschaftstheorie. Wirtschaft und Finanzen, Düsseldorf, pp 57–69

Walras L (1905) Cournot et l' économie mathématique. Gazette de Lausanne 13 July, rept. in L. Walras, Mélanges d' économic politique et sociale, vol. VII of OEuvres économiques complétes d' Auguste et Léon Walras. Economica, Paris, 1987, pp 461–466

Weinberger O (1930) Mathematische Volkswirtschaftslehre. Teubner, Leipzig und Berlin

Whewell W (1829) Mathematical exposition of some doctrines of political economy 1829. Cambridge Philos Transact 3(1830):191–229

Chapter 18
Léon Walras: What Cutes Know and What They Should Know

J.A. Hans Maks and Jan van Daal

The general idea among contemporary university-trained economists ("cutes") of what Léon Walras (1834–1910) has contributed to analytical economics may be summarised in modern notation as follows: Let a system of equations be given: $e(p) = 0$, where the symbol p denotes an n-dimensional vector of prices of goods brought to the market and e is a vector-valued function of the prices representing the n excess demands in the market for the goods. The equation expresses market equilibrium and the generally accepted view seems to be that there is a so-called auctioneer who takes care that such an equilibrium will occur. To that end, he, the auctioneer, announces an initial vector p' of prices. The people who bring the goods to the market in order to exchange (part of) them for other goods react on these initial prices by establishing certain quantities of goods demanded or supplied. The auctioneer aggregates all this into a vector $e(p')$ of excess demands. If this vector of excess demands is not a vector of zeroes only, then no trading takes place and the auctioneer announces another price vector p'' by increasing somehow in p' all prices of goods with a positive excess demand and by decreasing those with a negative excess demand. The function e has such properties that the new excess demand $e(p'')$ will be closer to zero than $e(p')$. If there would not yet be equilibrium at prices p'', the auctioneer announces other price vectors p''', p^{iv}, …, until eventually a vector p^* is obtained with $e(p^*) = 0$. Then trade will take place, at prices p^*. The process of groping from the arbitrary initial price vector p' to the equilibrium vector p^* is known as Walras's tâtonnement process. Below we shall see that there is much more to say on tâtonnement. Let us already now point out that Léon Walras himself never made use of the fiction auctioneer.

All standard mainstream textbooks deal with the essence of this system; sometimes, a word on production in Walras's work is added. The standard general perception is

J.A.H. Maks (✉)
School of Business and Economics, Department of Economics, Maastricht University,
P.O. Box 616, 6200 MD Maastricht, The Netherlands
e-mail: h.maks@maastrichtuniversity.nl

J.G. Backhaus (ed.), *Handbook of the History of Economic Thought*,
The European Heritage in Economics and the Social Sciences,
DOI 10.1007/978-1-4419-8336-7_18, © Springer Science+Business Media, LLC 2012

that he ignores, among other things, capital, savings and money and that any allusion to dynamics is lacking. A possible explanation for this situation might be the publication, in the fifties of the last century, of Gerard Debreu's *Theory of Value* (1959). In this influential book, and in preceding articles, general conditions for the existence of a (unique) general economic equilibrium are presented in an elegant and modern mathematical way. In fact, however, *Theory of Value* is restricted to a model with exchange and production only. Since then, textbooks confine themselves mainly to reproduce general economic equilibrium theory more or less rigorously in this narrow setting. In the last decades, however, there is a growing awareness that Walras contributed much more than is generally recognised and that the problems he was concerned with are still vital issues for contemporary economists. In this paper, we want to substantiate this.

In the next section, a short sketch of Walras's life will be presented. This small biography already makes the indefensibleness of the above narrow view apparent. Then outlines of his various contributions to the several domains of economic science follow: pure economics (§§ 3–7) and applied and social economics (§§ 8–11). Some secondary literature on Walras will pass the review in § 12. We end with a few concluding remarks (§ 13).

Some Biographic and Bibliographic Facts

Léon Walras was born in 1834 in Évreux (Normandy).[1] In about 1854, he went to Paris where he became a student at the École des Mines. Largely due to his father's influence, he was greatly interested in what was called the "Social Question", that is the misery of the poor, and the problem of how to alleviate their situation. This and his Bohemian temperament made him hardly fit for the mining business. The consequence was that he was a student only in name. It seems that as such he did not produce any papers. Instead, he felt a calling to become a man of letters. He thought this was the best way to put himself at the service of the Social Question. Indeed, by 1858 he had written a novel, entitled *Francis Sauveur* (with a long introduction on the Social Question), a short story and much more prose expressing his social ideas. The reaction of the public outside Walras's own circle was not, to put it mildly, encouraging, so that making a living out of these activities did not seem to be very hopeful.

The reaction of his father, the economist Antoine-Auguste Walras (1801–1866), an able literary man himself, was severe, but not altogether negative. On the one hand, Auguste judged his son unfit for literature: Léon should not go on. Accordingly, he stopped paying for his son's university training. On the other hand, however, he

---

[1] Walras's great-grandfather was born in Arcen in the Southern part of The Netherlands, under the name Andraeas Walravens and migrated to the South of France. His son became a kind of lower magistrate in the city of Montpellier. In between, the name was shortened into Walras. Because of the Dutch origin of the name, the s in Walras has to be pronounced (see Walras 1965, Letter 999).

respected Léon's aspiration to contribute to the solution of the Social Question. Therefore, he suggested that his son should set up a career as a publicist on economic matters. With his father's help, Léon found a job as a kind of junior editor of the *Journal des économistes*. Furthermore, and that was most substantial, Auguste put his library and his vast collection of unpublished writings at his son's disposal, after which the two started a comprehensive and broad correspondence on economic matters. This provided Léon with a large number of subjects and ideas.

For Léon Walras, twelve hard, laborious and studious years in Paris followed. From the very beginning, he was a prolific writer and moreover, he was active on many other fronts. During this period, he wrote more than 80 books, articles, brochures and other papers altogether (Walker 1987b). Nevertheless, it was difficult to earn a living. His employers were not always happy with the ideas expressed in his writings and so he was often obliged to look for another occupation. There were several failures and only a few successes. One of these successes, however, was decisive for the rest of his career. In 1860, he participated in a conference on taxation in Lausanne, where he attracted some attention. There he encountered a young Swiss lawyer, Louis Ruchonnet. They became friends and met several times afterwards. Ruchonnet's career developed successfully and by 1870, he had risen to the function of chief of the department of education of the Swiss Canton Vaud. In that quality, he was responsible for the reorganisation of the Académie de Lausanne and this led him to suggest that Léon Walras should apply for the new professorship of economics. Indeed, Walras was nominated, although he had no academic degrees and in spite of the fact that he did not make a secret of his interest in the Social Question, which made him simply a socialist in many people's eyes but not in his own. The run up to the professorship was, therefore, not a walkover. Three of the seven members of the Nomination Committee eventually considered his allegedly socialist ideas as insurmountable for the function. Some of the other members hesitated, too. Consequently, he was in first instance nominated for 1 year only, with the lowest possible majority of the committee. On December 16th, 1870, his 36th birthday, he started his lectures in Lausanne. Ruchonnet, however, stood squarely behind Walras. To people who know the working of the university system, then and now, it was therefore not very surprising that 1 year later Walras obtained his tenure. He lectured until 1892; then he retired because of serious health problems. He continued his research until about 1900 and died in 1910.

Léon Walras was a dutiful lecturer. He wrote out all his lessons in full (see Walras 1996). His oral presentation, however, does not seem to have been brilliant, to say the least. His political ideas did not gain him distinction, either. It is his research that has made him famous, especially on general economic equilibrium, as we shall see below. It should not be forgotten that the Social Question was thereby the leitmotiv.

Auguste Walras's main message to his son was that if one wants to raise people, and in particular those in misery, to more favourable conditions, then one must first study their economic circumstances. Léon apparently believed it was necessary, to devise a theoretical economic framework in which each person, or at least each family, is considered an individual entity because the happiness of every person counts. Walras did so in his pure theory. This part of his research is well known and his fame rests on it. It is set out in his *Éléments d'économie politique pure, ou théorie de la richesse sociale* (first edition, in two instalments, 1874–1877). In the *Éléments*, he presented his theory of the utility maximising consumer and that of general economic equilibrium under the regime of free competition, the former being the ferment to the latter. The book was to be the basis for his further work on applied and social economics. Walras's intention was to deal with these two topics in two other broad, systematic treatises.

As so many first-generation academic economists, Walras felt (and indeed was) obliged to provide an overall picture of the whole field. Starting with pure theory, however, he ran out of time (and his health deteriorated). So he did not succeed in completing the other treatises envisaged. Instead, he consolidated the bulk of his other research in two volumes, entitled *Études d'économie sociale* (Walras 1896) and *Études d'économie politique appliquée* (1898). Both volumes consist of papers already existing. In this form, they could not compete with the *Éléments d'économie politique pure* and, therefore, the latter book received more attention. The *four* editions of the *Éléments* and the two *Études* contain the essence of Walras's work.[2]

Free Competition and Laisser Faire

For Léon Walras, the basic economic phenomenon was exchange of scarce, useful goods between freely competing parties. Therefore, he saw as his basic task the explanation of ratios of exchange, i.e. prices. Consequently, neither the Robinson Crusoe economy, nor the two-goods-two-exchangers economy was an appropriate starting point for his analysis. His assumption of free competition may look, indeed, more reasonable if each good or service would be offered and demanded by at least two persons, in other words, a group. Free competition means, according to Walras, that demanders and suppliers of goods and services are free to engage in processes of higgling and haggling in the markets, which will equalise supply and demand of these goods and services, and that entrepreneurs are free to enter into or withdraw from all branches of industry to seek benefits or to evade losses. All these activities take place simultaneously and influence each other. Free competition, Walras says, is a self-regulating mechanism that brings about equilibrium in the markets at unique prices per good or service, and equality of selling prices to cost prices in all the branches of industry. Walras was interested, as we shall see, both in the final result of free competition, i.e. the equilibrium situation, and the process of bringing about

---

[2] After the first edition of the *Éléments*, three revised editions followed, in 1889, 1896 and 1900. Walras did not live to see in print the revisions he made after the fourth edition. These appeared in the posthumous, fifth edition of 1926. An English translation, by William Jaffé, of the latter edition appeared in 1954. From 1987 onwards, the "Centre Auguste et Léon Walras", Lyon, republished (with Economica, Paris) Léon Walras's complete works in nine volumes as part of the fourteen volumes of *AUGUSTE AND LÉON WALRAS, ŒUVRES ÉCONOMIQUES COMPLÈTES*, completed in 2005. See also the Walras bibliography in Walker 1987, where 239 titles are mentioned.

this equilibrium, i.e. what actually happens in the markets. Furthermore, he wanted to be able to study these two aspects of free competition separately.

The question rises: "Was Léon Walras a partisan of unlimited free competition?" The answer should be "No, absolutely not!" At the very first page of his very first analytical publication on the subject (a paper presented at a meeting of Parisian colleagues in 1873), Walras makes his position clear (see Walras 1874a, b, 1987: 262). He wants to study theoretically the phenomena of production and exchange of goods and services "under the regime of the most free competition, the most absolute *laisser faire, laisser passer*, abstraction made from any consideration of interest or justice". However, he continues: "I am absolutely not saying [that I am doing this] because free competition would be more useful or more equitable, but I only want to know what would happen".

Laisser faire, laisser passer, i.e. free competition under all circumstances, was the order of the day among "les économistes" at that time, whereas the "socialists" abhorred it. Both groups restricted themselves to slogan mongering, instead of underpinning their opinions with sound arguments. Here, Walras saw a task. He compared himself with a medical researcher who tries to learn everything about a certain drug, not because he wants it to be used under all circumstances, but in order to know, as a doctor, when to prescribe it and when not.[3] Therefore, Walras set out to find conditions for and consequences of free competition. This became the core of his pure theory. However, he was quite aware of the existence of alternatives and of the need to study their effects. Below, we shall sketch his analysis of monopoly and his remedy of its unwanted effects. But now we will turn to Walras' analysis of general economic equilibrium in a period.

General Economic Equilibrium in a Period: Temporary Equilibrium

To make things more comprehensible, Walras stylised the economic process as a sequence of periods of time where production and trade per period take place determined by the working of a carefully devised mathematical model. Walras wrote, as it were, a spectacle of economic activities approaching a situation of free competition as

---

[3] Walras expressed it as follows in a letter to W. Lexis du 17 mars 1883 (Walras 1965, letter 548):

(....) il m'a semblé que vous me considériez comme un partisan de la libre concurrence absolue (en raison de ce fait que j'étudie très attentivement et très minutieusement les effets de la libre concurrence). Quoi qu'il en soit, je tiens à vous faire savoir que, tout au contraire, c'est plutôt le désir de repousser les applications mal fondées et inintelligibles de la libre concurrence, faites par des économistes orthodoxes qui m'a conduit à l'étude de la libre concurrence en matière d'échange et de production. Un médecin qui aurait analysé dans le dernier détail les effets physiologiques d'une substance serait à la fois, par ce fait, très partisan de son emploi dans certains cas et très opposé à cet emploi dans certains autres cas. Telle est ma position (...).

accurately as possible. He did this for two reasons. First, he hoped to gain more insight into the working of the economic world of his time. Second, he hoped to obtain a theoretical basis for social reform. The analogy with a play or, if one wishes so, a drama, goes further. The "acts" are the periods and they consist of various scenes, as we shall see. The accessories, i.e. the stage properties, are the goods and services and their prices, including wages and the rate of interest. The actors are the people in the roles of consumers with their preferences of the period in question, producers with the technology of that period, capitalists with the stocks of that period and entrepreneurs.

At the outset of the period under consideration, both individual quantities of capital and the parameters of the model are given: technology in the form of the production coefficients and preferences of the consumers in the form of utility functions. Moreover, the composition and size of the population are considered as given. All these data are assumed to remain fixed during the period. Then the "play" starts with the first "act", i.e. the first period. There will be a break at its end, when the concerning period's equilibrium is reached. Endogenously determined quantities of newly constructed capital goods result to be used in the next period. Together with what remains of the existing capital goods and with the (possibly changed) exogenous variables, they form the initial conditions for the next period, the second act. A new equilibrium emerges and this goes on in subsequent periods. Apparently, capital endogenously transfers wealth from period to period.

Like his father, Walras made a distinction between consumption goods and capital goods, i.e. production factors. He thereby distinguished three types of capital: (1) land, (2) human capital and (3) capital proper (fixed capital: houses, machines, etc., and circulating capital: stocks of products and money).

During a period, the entrepreneurs hire capital of all three types, that is to say, they buy services of this capital and use it during the period in question. One of the entrepreneurs' tasks is to take care that services bought are transformed into consumption and capital goods proper. The price they pay for these capital services to the owners is used by the latter to buy consumption goods, from the entrepreneurs, or to save.

Accordingly, there are four types of agents: (1) landowners, (2) labourers, (3) capitalists and (4) entrepreneurs. One or more of these types may be united in one and the same person.

Walras clearly pointed out this in the competitive markets of his model simultaneously:

1. Demanders will bid higher prices in case of excess demand and suppliers will ask lower prices in case of excess supply; this will eventually, in equilibrium, reduce excess demand and supply in all markets of goods and services to zero.
2. If in a certain branch the cost price is higher than the selling price, entrepreneurs in this branch will leave it or will decrease their production, and if the cost price is lower than the selling price, the opposite will take place; this will make the cost price of each product equal to its selling price and bring equilibrium profit rates to zero.
3. Similarly, the use of capital services and the formation of new capital will be shifted by entrepreneurs and capital owners from one application to another, until eventually the ratios of the net revenue (after having taken account of wear and

tear) per unit of some capital good and the selling (= cost) price of it are the same for all capital goods; this will make the total amount of gross savings equal to the total value of newly produced capital, and all capital goods equally profitable.

4. This same ratio, finally, will be the equilibrium rate of interest that equalises total demand and supply in the money market.

These four points together describe a situation of economic equilibrium in the period considered in its most comprehensive form. They generate what a spectator sees in this "theatre of economic life". Walras presented them as separate "scenes" in his play, but in reality, they take place simultaneously, of course. They result from the mathematical model (to be dealt with in the next sections), which, as such, is invisible on the stage. It is, therefore, invisible on the stage that in the equilibrium situation, each individual's utility is at its maximum given the equilibrium prices. Furthermore, these prices are for each individual proportional to his marginal utilities. Walras reserved a special name for this marginal utility: *rareté*.

Approaching the Reality of Free Competition

Walras had a whole sequence of models from simple to highly complicated. Above, we were talking about the last one of this sequence, the most complicated and most complete model. We chose to start with presenting this one, because we wanted to start with the end since most students never come to it. With his chain of cumulative models of general economic equilibrium, Léon Walras was one of the first economists to make use, for pedagogical reasons, of the method of decreasing abstraction. In order to explain his ideas on economic equilibrium, he first devised, in Part II of the *Éléments*, a model dealing with a group of people possessing a quantity of some good (A) who want to exchange this, whether or not partly, for some quantity of good (B) owned by the people of a second group who, on their turn, want to exchange this against good (A). These exchanges take place, of course, under a regime of free competition. Adding up the individual demand curves, based on utility maximisation, Walras obtained aggregate demand functions for (A) and (B) and from these, he came to aggregate supply functions for (B) and (A) respectively. In equilibrium, there is equality of aggregate demand and supply. This was extended, in Part III of the *Éléments*, into a model of exchange of an arbitrary number of goods, the one we started with in the introduction.

Walras's next step (Part IV) was building his "model of production", in which only consumer goods are produced, by using services of land, human capital and capital goods proper (i.e. no circulating capital). Production is, as we know, characterised by fixed coefficients of production. All capital services are used up in either production of consumer goods, or in personal consumption (leisure, riding their own horses, living in their own houses, etc.). The model of production was enlarged in Part V to the "model of fixed-capital formation" in which production of capital goods proper was included. Finally, in Part VI, the model of capital formation was expanded into two models, one with circulating capital and fiat money

Fig. 18.1 Walras's equilibrium
models

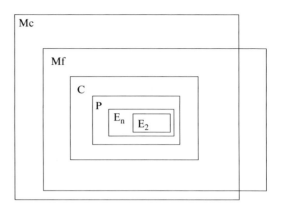

(e.g. paper money) and one with circulating capital and commodity-based money (gold, e.g.). All these models, except the last one were intended as pedagogical devices, to explain this last one, to be used for policy recommendations. For all Walras's models, modern proofs of the existence of a solution exist now (see § 7). Below, the models have been placed in a scheme that represents their hierarchy. E_2 indicates the model of exchange of two goods only, E_n the model of exchange of n goods only, **P** the latter extended with production of consumer goods, **C** denotes model **P** extended with formation of fixed capital, **Mf** signifies model **C** extended with circulating capital and fiduciary money and, finally, **Mc** stands for model **C** extended with circulating capital and commodity-based money (Fig. 18.1).[4]

We end this section with some considerations concerning the relevance of Walras's successive models for present-day economics. With his method of decreasing abstraction, Walras attempted to approach the reality of a situation of free competition. Note that equilibrium in a period is followed by equilibrium in the next period, equilibrium in the then next period, etc. As stated above, the subsequent equilibria may differ in initial conditions. Preferences may change and technology may improve exogenously, whereas stocks of capital goods will change endogenously. Walras assumed thereby that the equilibrium prices of the present period are expected to persist.[5] This implies that we have agents with highly myopic expectations: in a given period, future capital income is assumed to be constant over all periods to come. Changes in preferences, technology and available capital and its future income are not foreseen. Hence, the sequence-of-periods equilibria (or temporary equilibria) are not likely to be coordinated over time. So, we note that a general *inter-period* equilibrium is not implied by Walras' analysis. Agents are not assumed to have rational expectations in Muth's sense.[6]

---

[4] The hierarchy is not complete (see Van Daal 1994; Van Daal and Jolink 1993b, Chaps. 14–16).

[5] See Van Witteloostuijn and Maks (1988 and 1990).

[6] In the case of Walras, a non-econometric, or perhaps pre-econometric case, we mean with the expression "rationality in Muth's sense" that economic agents are (supposed to be) at least as clever as the economist who is modelising their behaviour concerning the formulation of expectations for the (near) future. See Muth (1960, 1961). Walras's agents seem to be much more stupid.

It is more and more acknowledged nowadays that Walras' analysis of free competition only offers a scope for a sequence of uncoordinated temporary equilibria.[7] This might play a role in the debates on free competition and economic progress.[8] One of the most serious failures of "free competition" is perhaps its apparent inability to coordinate events over time, which may substantially reduce free markets' capacity to generate steady decreases in scarcity or, in more familiar terms, to increase society's welfare. If the free markets would follow capricious animal spirits, serious damage may occur in terms of volatility, recessions and crises, and substantial losses might result.[9] Most important, fundamental economic debates are related to this question now and will be in the near future.

But this is not all. Walras takes a further step in approaching the reality of free competition. Probably, this is best demonstrated by the following quotations (*Éléments*, §322):

> Finally in order to come still more closely to reality, we must drop the hypothesis of an annual market period and adopt in its place the hypothesis of a continuous market. (…)
>
> Such is the continuous market, which is perpetually tending towards equilibrium without ever actually attaining it, because the market has no other way of approaching equilibrium except by groping, and, before the goal is reached, it has to renew its efforts and start over again, all the basic data of the problem, e.g. the initial quantities possessed, the utilities of goods and services, the technical coefficients, the excess of income over consumption, the working capital requirements, etc., having changed in the meantime. Viewed in this way the market is like a lake agitated by the wind, where the water is incessantly seeking its level without ever reaching it. But whereas there are days when the surface of the lake is almost smooth, there never is a day when the effective demand for products and services equals their effective supply and when the selling price of products equals the cost of productive services used in making them. The diversion of productive services from enterprises that are losing money to profitable enterprises takes place in several ways, the most important through credit operations, but at best these ways are slow. (…)
>
> For, just as a lake is, at times, stirred to its very depths by a storm, so also the market is sometimes thrown into violent confusion by crises, which are sudden and general disturbances of equilibrium. The more we know of the ideal conditions of equilibrium, the better we shall be able to control or prevent these crises.

It might be worthwhile to read and reread these quotations, realising that these lines have not been written by Keynes or a Keynesian economist, or by a neo-Austrian or an evolutionary economist, but by Walras, much more than one century ago.

---

[7] See Van Witteloostuijn and Maks (1988 and 1990), Mckenzie (1987): 503 and Van Daal and Jolink (1993b): 74.

[8] Walras defined this as follows (*Éléments*, § 327): "Progress (…) consists in a diminution of the *raretés* of the final products along with an increase in population". See also Lionel Robbins's seminal *An Essay on the nature & Significance of Economic Science* (Robbins 1932), where scarcity "means limitation in relation to demand" (p. 46). This book perhaps caused the breakthrough of the neo-classical (Walrasian) definition of economics: "Economics is the science which studies human behaviour as a relationship between ends and scarce means which have alternative uses" (p. 15.).

[9] See for similar wordings Keynes's *General Theory* (Keynes 1936, Chap. 13).

Systems of Equations and Existence of a Solution

Let us now concentrate on the systems of equations and their foundations. The solution of the equations of the most extended model yields the most general of the situations of economic equilibrium considered by Walras, as we have seen in section 4: prices, wages and the rate of interest at which markets clear (demand equals supply); further, they yield market-clearing quantities of all goods and services in the period in question. In underpinning these equations, Walras paid most of his attention to consumers' behaviour. In 1900, in a letter to Knut Wicksel, he wrote "[My theory] is the pursuit of *Grenznutzen* [marginal utility] in the last details of economic equilibrium". At the same occasion, he declared to leave further development of the production side (marginal productivity, for instance) to his successors.

Since the individual consumers own the capital goods, entrepreneurs can only provide themselves with capital services by renting land from landowners, by employing workers or by hiring capital. Of course, as we already said, combinations of two or more of the roles of landowner, worker, capitalist or entrepreneur in one person may exist.

Selling capital services procures the individual an income that permits him to buy consumption goods and capital services, and to repair or replace pieces of capital to keep his stock at the level of the period's beginning. The rest of this income is per definition net savings (negative, zero or positive). Walras assumed that positive net savings are used to buy newly produced capital proper in order to assure the savers in question a future income increase. Hence, *three kinds of variables* appear in the (additively separable) individual utility functions: firstly, quantities of the various consumption goods; secondly, quantities of the services of capital goods to be consumed by the individual himself and thirdly, the amount of expected additional future income.[10] From these utility functions, Walras derived individual demand and supply equations, by assuming that consumers maximise utility, given their income and the prices. One may consider these demand and supply functions as schedules from which a consumer can infer, at every price constellation, the quantities of the various goods and services that will yield him maximal utility at these prices. With these schedules in mind, as it were, he enters the markets. Aggregated, i.e. added up per good or service over all the individuals, these schedules enter into the model. We stress once more that Walras was aware that preferences (as described in the utility functions) might change from period to period.

The production side of the models is less developed. For simplicity's sake, Walras supposed *constant coefficients of production* in his formal models. So he assumed that for production of a unit of some product, fixed quantities of productive services

---

[10] By introducing present utility of the expectation of future additional income, Walras was able to bring himself "as close as possible to the dynamic point of view" in his formal models (Éléments, editions 4 and 5, §272). Here is meant "inter-period dynamics", in contradistinction to the "intra-period dynamics" of tâtonnement. It is again to be emphasised that the expected future income is based on a very simple myopic expectations scheme: agents assume that the equilibrium prices of the period considered will also hold in the future; see Maks and Van Wittteloostijn (1987, 1988, 2001).

are needed, irrespective of the level of production. It may be that at Walras's time, this was less arguable as it appears to be now. Anyway, the result is a set of relatively simple production functions. But, of course, he was aware that the coefficients of production, constant within a period, may change over the periods. Moreover, in his analysis of the conditions and consequences of economic progress, he emphasised the variability of the production coefficients. In Part VII of the *Éléments*, editions 4 and 5, lesson 36, § 326 (Walras 1988: 589), he set out how the production function in the regular flexible form of the textbooks can be introduced.[11] He concluded there the following:

1. Free competition brings the cost of production down to a minimum.
2. In a state of equilibrium, when cost of production and selling price are equal, the prices of the services are proportional to their marginal productivities, i.e. to the partial derivatives of the production function.

To the production functions (with the fixed production coefficients) and the (aggregated) demand and supply functions are added equations expressing the final result of free competition: market clearing for all goods and services, money included, equality of selling price and the cost price of each product, equality of the interest rate to the ratio of net revenue and the cost price of every capital good. To give an idea of the size of Walras's system in the version without money, let us suppose that there are ten types of consumption goods, three types of land, three types of human capital, three types of capital proper and four types of raw material. Then Walras's most comprehensive model consists of 88 equations, with 88 variables. Using the individual demand and supply equations, individual quantities demanded and supplied can be found. The latter quantities are amounts of goods and services that maximise the individual consumers' utility, given the equilibrium prices.

Now we turn shortly to the existence problem. Since the coherence of his theory depends on it, the existence of a solution of his systems of equations was most important for Léon Walras. In his days,[12] the method of counting equations and unknowns was widely used in pure mathematics and in economics, although one was aware that systems might be inconsistent and equations redundant. The equality of the number of the variables of the model to the number of independent equations was, therefore, important enough to Walras for meticulously counting equations and variables. Nevertheless, he dealt quite subtly with this question. As Jaffé rightfully observes in a translator's note (Walras 1954: 502), Walras does not belong to those economists who only count equations.[13] In the context of the exchange model (*Éléments*, §§ 65–68), Walras analyses the possibilities of having a unique solution, a multiplicity of solutions or no solution at all. This follows from an interesting

---

[11] While staying within the realm of constant returns to scale.

[12] And later; see Bowley (1924).

[13] Or (Schumpeter 1954: 1006): "Of all the unjust or even meaningless objections that have been levelled at Walras, perhaps the most unjust is that he believed that the existence question is answered as soon as we have counted 'equations' and 'unknowns' and found that they are equal in number".

figure in the *Éléments* (Plate I; Walras 1954: 110–111; 1988: 86) in which supply and demand intersect in three points. The point in the middle is an unstable equilibrium. The other two are locally stable.[14] In discussing the situation depicted in this figure, Walras firstly points out that the shape reveals the possibility of several, in this case three, equilibrium points. Then he goes on to explain that one of the intersection points is instable because (*Éléments*, § 67):

> [I]n this case, to the right of the point of equilibrium, the demand for the commodity in question is greater than its offer, which must lead to a rise in price, that is, to a movement farther and farther away from the point of equilibrium. And, in this same case, to the left of the point of equilibrium, the offer of the commodity in question is greater than the demand for it, which must lead to a fall in price, that is, to a movement once again away from the point of equilibrium.

He goes on explaining the nature of the other two equilibrium points. Both are locally stable. One is associated with a high quantity and a low price, the other with a small quantity and a high price. From these observations, one may safely conclude that Walras knows that counting (independent) variables and equations is neither sufficient nor necessary for the existence of a unique stable equilibrium. He even distinguishes stable and unstable equilibria, as we saw. He was also the first economist to associate an instable equilibrium with a backward bending supply curve and a more steeply falling demand curve (Jaffé, translator's note, 1954: 504).

Later, existence proofs meeting the most rigorous standards of modern advanced mathematics have been found.[15] This, however, is of such a technical nature that it is impossible to deal with it within the scope of this article. Having dealt with the existence of equilibrium in a period, the question rises how such equilibrium might be brought about, starting from the period's initial situation. Let us, therefore, pass to Walras's tâtonnement.

Tâtonnement

There is a great discrepancy between Walras's tâtonnement and what is called Walrasian tâtonnement in the literature. He devised it as a means "to establish that the theoretical solution and the solution of the market are identical" (*Éléments*, §124), but it has become one of the most misunderstood notions of his heritage. In devising the notion of tâtonnement, his intention was to show that the outcome of the equations of the model is, indeed, the same as the outcome of the market process in the period under consideration. The essence of the process of tâtonnement is that buyers will bid up prices in case of excess demand, sellers underbid in case of excess supply and entrepreneurs withdraw from the industries where they incur losses and enter those where benefits may be expected. In Donald Walker's (1996) book,

---

[14] See also Van Daal and Jolink (1993b), Fig. 4.5 (p. 26).

[15] See Van Daal (1998), where proofs are presented for all Walras's models.

it has been made clear that it is not some authority above the groups to determine prices (and quantities); the groups themselves do this. This means that there is no need for an auctioneer in Walras's models. Thus, the word "auctioneer" is absent in all Walras's writings. It is an invention by later authors, attempting to grasp and explain the working of Walras's models, in particular those from the fourth edition of the *Éléments* onwards. Tâtonnement, furthermore, is something that entirely takes place within a certain period and is connected with the existence and the nature of equilibrium in that period only. It has, therefore, nothing to do with the transition from equilibrium in a period to that in the next one (see below).

The idea of Walras's tâtonnement is as follows. For simplicity's sake, we restrict ourselves to the case of simple exchange, unaffected in all editions of the *Éléments*. As a matter of fact, this case is the only one that is generally known in some form or another to present-day economists. There are m goods to be exchanged, indicated by (A), (B), (C), (D)…; (A) is the numéraire. For the non-numéraire goods, there are $m-1$ excess demand equations; further, there is the budget equation. Hence, if there is zero demand for $m-1$ goods, then excess demand for the mth good is also zero. A vector p_1 of prices of the $m-1$ non-numéraire goods is cried at random (the price of (A) is equal to 1). These prices will in general not produce equality of demand and supply in all markets. Hence they are not equilibrium prices and trade will not take place. Starting from this vector p_1, Walras presented a procedure to find a second vector p_2 more close to the equilibrium prices. This was done in several steps. The first step was to replace the first price of p_1, the price of (B), by one that, together with the other prices of p_1, brings about market clearance for (B). By a mathematical argument, he made plausible that such a new price for (B) exists.[16] The second step was replacing the price of (C) by one that brings about equality of demand and supply in the market for (C), together with the changed price of (B) and the rest of the prices of p_1. This change will most probably disturb the equilibrium in the market for (B). Going on, a new vector p_2 of prices results. It will in general not bring about general equilibrium, because continuing the construction of p_2 will offset an equality just fulfilled. But Walras argued (or, rather, supposed) that these latter, so-called secondary effects might be expected to have a smaller impact on a price than the primary effect, i.e. the effect from the change of this price itself. Moreover, secondary effects do not all have the same signs and may, therefore, cancel more or less. So Walras concluded that p_2 lies nearer to the equilibrium price vector than p_1 in the sense that all excess demands for p_2 are closer to zero than those for p_1.

Similarly, starting from p_2, a vector p_3 of prices can be obtained that will bring the inequalities of demand and supply still nearer to equality, and so on. Hence, Walras concluded, there are prices that will bring to zero the excess demands of all the m goods. These prices – obeying the equations of the model – are the equilibrium prices and transactions may start. This process of tâtonnement, as Léon Walras baptised it from the first edition of the *Éléments* onwards, reflects reasonably well the phenomenon of outbidding and underbidding as it happens

---

[16] Walras supposed that demand and supply curves are so located and shaped that they intersect.

in well-organised markets. In the Bourse of Paris, for instance, transactions were only allowed if demand equals supply for all shares and bonds. See Walker 1997. The way in which this was brought about was Walras's inspiration for the reasoning above. It cannot be denied that Walras's idea of the primary and secondary effects is highly suggestive, but he did not work it out into a rigorous proof of the convergence of tâtonnement. Later generations of economist had to complete it in this respect.[17]

In the first three editions of the *Éléments*, Léon Walras developed very complicated tâtonnement processes for the other models of his sequence, those with production. In these cases, the initial situation was not a vector of prices only, as p_1 above, but a vector of prices of productive services together with quantities of products to be produced in first instance. In these first three editions of the *Éléments*, Walras admitted of *disequilibrium production*. The goods produced in disequilibrium were exchanged according to a tâtonnement process, as described above. The announced vector of prices and quantities is unlikely to generate a situation of general economic equilibrium, but Walras was able to derive from it a new situation closer to equilibrium. This situation was then used as a new initial situation to find a third situation still more close to equilibrium, and so on. The details are highly complicated, while the idea of primary and secondary effects is profusely applied. See Van Daal 2000. So, in first instance (i.e. in the first three editions of the *Éléments*), tâtonnement was really intended to reflect dynamics of daily economic life during a period. Consumers work, get money, buy goods and consume them; producers hire workers, buy raw materials and intermediate products, produce products and sell them; capitalists save and the money saved is invested in capital goods. Between all these things, there exists some order, and it is this what Walras tried to model by means of the tâtonnement in the first three editions of his *Éléments*.

From the fourth edition of the *Éléments* onwards, Walras removed disequilibrium production from his models because it might lead to inconsistencies.[18] Instead the agents respond now with written "pledges".[19] These pledges present actions that

---

[17] Indeed, later authors have elaborated on it, proving rigorously the convergence of the sequence p_1, $p_2, p_3, \ldots$ of prices to equilibrium prices. Allais (1943, vol. 2: 489 ff.) was the first to provide in this way a proof of the existence of equilibrium in the case of exchange only: he had to impose the condition of so-called gross substitutability. See also Morishima (1977), Chap. 2.

Nevertheless there is somewhat more to say. Walras assumes that his *rareté* functions only depend on the quantity of the own commodity and are always (dis)continuously decreasing in that quantity. This can be seen in all graphs depicting *rareté* curves, (*Éléments*, §§ 74–84). Hence, the *rareté* functions do not shift if the quantities of the other commodities change. Starting from this concept and assuming that the marginal utility elasticities of all commodities vary (on the average) in their normal range between 0 and −1, it can be proved that gross substitutability holds and that the prices p_1, p_2, p_3, … indeed converge to equilibrium prices (see Maks 2006).

[18] For that same reason, Walras had discarded from the outset the possibility of disequilibrium transactions in the case of exchange only.

[19] Walras's French word was "bon". Jaffé translated it as "ticket". We prefer the translation "pledge", proposed in Walker (1987a).

the agents would undertake in answer to the "crying" of prices and quantities and that should be binding if they generate equilibrium. Generally, this is not the case in first instance, and then these pledges give rise to new cries. The play of crying and pledging will continue until equilibrium prices are reached. Then production and exchange are permitted to take place according to the "equilibrium pledges".[20] As a consequence of this unhappy modification, however, Walras had to suppose in his models of the last two editions that the whole economic process of a period, in all its complexity, had to take place simultaneously and instantaneously. This means an enormous decrease of the degree of reality of the models.[21]

The way Walras amended tâtonnement in the fourth edition of the *Éléments* has reduced it, in fact, to a mathematical device for an alternative proof of the existence of equilibrium, no more, no less. Walras's original tâtonnement, of the editions 2 and 3, has become so unknown that it has been reinvented under the name *"non-tâtonnement"*, of all names.

We observed already that tâtonnement has nothing to do with inter-period dynamics. This latter kind of dynamics deals with the transition from a period to the next one, in particular what happens in a certain period may depend on what happened in preceding periods; see above, § 5. It is, however, in the context of *inter*-period dynamics that tâtonnement has sometimes been (mis)understood in the literature. Walras himself did not explicitly elaborate inter-period dynamics, though it was certainly in the back of his mind. He was rather dealing with what may be called *intra*-period dynamics, viz. his tâtonnement. Where the interpretation in the context of *inter*-period dynamics seems to be incorrect, it is not surprising that tâtonnement started an own life and evolved into a direction that, however interesting, does not have much to do with Walras's work itself. As it stands now, he would hardly have recognised it.[22] Alternatively, some authors went as far as associating tâtonnement with the problem of stability of equilibrium, which Walras had only taken up for the case of exchange of two goods; in fact, this is simply studying stability of tâtonnement itself, no more, no less.

Now we turn to Walras's applied economics. We start with monopoly.

---

[20] For a comprehensive and authoritative discussion of all tâtonnements and of Walras's way of trying to embed this in an institutional framework, we refer to Walker (1996). In particular, we refer once more to Walker's explanation of how the market agents can do without an auctioneer.

[21] At the same time, it means a complete change of what happens during a period. The models with production (i.e. all models after those of pure exchange) of the third edition describe quite other "events" during a period than those of the fourth.

Walker, too, considers the new tâtonnement as unfortunate. He appears to be a partisan of its predecessor. Personally, we think that both are problematic (see Van Daal 2000).

[22] The mechanism that transforms a price vector into the subsequent one differs in most modern textbooks from that invented by Walras himself. Walras's procedure works consecutively, price by price, and the process goes through a number of intermediate situations. In the textbooks, all prices change mostly instantaneously and simultaneously in one single non-stop flight from the initial value to the equilibrium prices (see Van Daal 2000).

Free Competition and Monopoly; Private and Public Goods

Walras drew some general principles from his equilibrium models that might be used in economic policy. A highly important conclusion in this respect was that free competition should be the rule, *provided that its conditions be fulfilled*. In a situation of equilibrium under free competition, each consumer obtains the highest possible utility, given the equilibrium prices. His income follows from them, because then there are only incomes from capital, i.e. from land, human capital and capital proper; there are no profits, or losses. Walras saw all this as highly attractive, and *he was of the opinion that the eventual state of the economy should resemble as most as possible a situation of free competition, at least in its outcome.*

Which are these conditions? Walras mentioned two necessary conditions: (1) the goods must be susceptible of private ownership, and (2) they must be produced by a large number of enterprises. The first condition means that public goods cannot belong to the realm of free competition. Hence, Walras paid a lot of attention to these goods in his social economics. In particular, he had to deal with the production of and the payment for them. The latter aspect brought him upon the subject of taxation. The second condition led Walras, in his applied economics, to investigate monopoly and negative effects of monopoly profit. Under what circumstances might monopoly be admitted and how should it, then, be regulated? There are three situations to be distinguished regarding the two conditions above:

1. Both conditions are fulfilled.
2. Condition (1) only is fulfilled.
3. None of the conditions is fulfilled.

We shall consecutively deal with these three situations.

In the first situation, free competition can do its work. This does not mean that things can be left to themselves. No *laisser faire* in this case. Instead, free competition implies active participation of the State. In his *Études d'économie politique appliquée* (further to be called *EPA*), Walras left no room for misunderstandings, when he says, for instance (Walras 1992: 426–427), the following:

> Saying free competition is absolutely not saying absence of all *State intervention*, as one will see. First, this intervention is necessary for establishing and maintaining free competition there where it is possible. Landowners, labourers and capitalists are inclined to establish monopoly of services. Entrepreneurs are inclined to establish monopoly of products. If such monopolies would be against public interest, then the State has to stop it in any case that it is not based on natural right. (…)
>
> (…) Nevertheless, let us repeat here that instituting and maintaining free competition in economics in a society is an undertaking of legislation, very complicated legislation, belonging to the State.

Thus, Walras advocated a kind of regulated free competition, a framework of rules in which the economic agents interact in relative freedom. These rules regard a wide variation of issues: minimum prices, mutual price agreements between the enterprises, advertising, product information and consumer credit.

In the second situation, there are private goods that cannot be produced by a great deal of relatively small enterprises. Walras's examples were water, gas and railway transport. All kind of price manipulations, as monopoly price fixing and price discrimination, should be subject of State intervention to ensure equality of the, single, selling price of each product to its cost price. Walras says it as follows (*EPA*, p. 268; 1992: 247–248; capitals and italics in original):

> Furthermore, the functioning of economic competition presupposes essentially "the possibility of a shift of entrepreneurs to enterprises who make profit and withdrawal from enterprises at loss". There are several reasons that may prevent that this shift will take place and that will turn an enterprise into monopoly. This may be the case from the beginning onwards as we have seen with respect to bringing of water or gas into a city, or the construction and exploitation of a railway between two cities. It may also occur after a certain time because of special features of the enterprise in question: for instance, in an industry where general costs are at the same time considerable and sensibly fixed. In both cases competition would not work. A few entrepreneurs disposing of huge amounts of capital would first kill the small ones. After that, they would contest till the extermination of all by one of them or by a coalition of two or three surviving firms until monopoly will occur anyhow. Monopoly procures maximum satisfaction of the needs only under the reservation of maximum benefit of the entrepreneur. Hence:
>
> — *In the interest of society and excluding exceptions founded on natural right, the* STATE *should undertake production at cost price of* SERVICES AND PRODUCTS OF PRIVATE INTEREST, NOT SUSCEPTIBLE TO INDEFINITE COMPETITION, *or it should concede this production, under a monopoly on its behalf, to the lowest bidder at an auction on the selling price.* [23]

As an example of an exception founded on natural right, Walras mentioned the case of an inventor of a new product or of a new production technique, beneficial to society. Such an inventor should be granted to benefit from his invention by permitting him to keep his secret for himself during a certain period.

In addition to the *economic monopolies* of the foregoing situation, there are also so-called *State monopolies*, in case of situation three. No individual appreciation of the goods and services in question through the notion of individual utility exists. Their wants are collective, public. One could think of defence, police, administration

---

[23] Presumably, Walras meant here that enterprises interested in producing and distributing, say, gas under monopoly in some city, meet in an auction to try to get the concession. This auction might be organised as follows. The interested parties are invited by the auctioneer to propose a price at which they will produce and supply the product. The price proposed by the first bidder will perhaps exceed the cost price of one or more of the parties. Then the auctioneer tries to solicit a lower selling price. Let us suppose that somebody makes such a bid, possibly still above one or more cost prices. A third selling price might then be proposed, and so forth. Under certain conditions, this process might converge to a bid equal to the cost price of the most efficiently producing party. Here, we cannot speak of a Dutch auction, where the auctioneer starts with a high, unacceptable price and then proposes prices gradually lower and lower and where the first participant who calls "mine" at a certain price is bound by it. In an "English auction", the auctioneer tries to solicit higher and higher bids from the participants, till nobody wants to make another bid. The highest bidder is then bound by his bid. Both systems are aimed at the achievement of a final price as high as possible. See, for instance, Vickrey (1961). The procedure indicated above in the case of Walras might perhaps be called an "inverse English auction".

of law, infrastructure and so on. The production of these goods can hardly be expected from the particular initiative. Walras suggested that the State should engage in their production (*ibid.*, capitals and italics in original):

> Individuals appreciate services and products of private interest and the State services and products of public interest. Individuals feel and measure wants for bread, meat, clothing, furniture; the State for troops, courts, schools, and roads. Since there is in general an indefinite number of consumers of services and products of private interest, there will, as a result, be an indefinite number of entrepreneurs, whereas there will be no entrepreneur for services or products of public interest, for there is in general only one single consumer. Who will think of something as constructing a stronghold or organising a university for selling it or renting it out to the State? Hence:
>
> — *In the interest of society, the* STATE *should undertake production of* SERVICES OR GOODS OF PUBLIC INTEREST THAT ARE NOT PRODUCED BY PARTICULAR INITIATIVE.

Ownership and Taxation

In the foregoing paragraph, we dealt with Walras's preoccupation with the right conditions for an abundant production of social wealth. However, how should this wealth be distributed among the members of the society? An important part of Walras's *Études d'économie sociale* (*EES*) deals with this problem of (just) distribution, which can be separated into the problems of ownership and taxation (*Éléments*, § 8; 1988: 31):

> [T]he theory of property and the theory of taxation are simply two aspects of one and the same theory of distribution of wealth in human society, the first representing this society as composed of separate individuals and the second representing it as a collectivity in the form of the State.

Walras's point of depart in dealing with the notion of property was that "the owner of a thing is the owner of the services of it (…) as well as of the [money] price of it" (*EES*, pp. 206–207; 1990: 178). Hence, property rights of products originate through exchange from those of the capital goods, land, personal capital and capital proper. The latter kind consists of products as well and should, therefore, be owned by those who have manufactured them. So the problem was reduced to ownership of land and personal faculties. Personal faculties clearly belong to the concerning individuals themselves. The times of slavery are past. Remains land. According to Walras, this belongs to all of us, not only to this generation but to all generations. Since all people have the same rights to pursue their destiny, they should all benefit equally from resources offered by nature to accomplish these destinies. Land, Walras argues, must therefore belong to the community, i.e. to the State. The State as owner of the land will be the owner of its services, and of the products obtained by these services. This provides it with an own income. In that (ideal) situation, taxes can be abolished. Rent received will enable the State to pay its expenses, and to pay back the former owners because rents will increase considerably, land becoming increasingly scarce in future. This increase, incidentally, belongs certainly to the community as a whole and not to the individuals who happen to be the owners of the land in question. For Walras, this was another reason for putting all the land in the State's hands.

Taxation, either on income, or on capital other than land, either direct or indirect, is unjust, says Walras, because it is a claim by the State on a thing it does not possess. Taxes, or subsidies as negative taxes, will always lead to some aberration from the pursuit of giving each economic agent what is rightly his. Wealth is the reward for labour and savings; poverty is the consequence of and penalty for idleness and prodigality (*EES*, p. 438; 1990: 404):

> Individual moral will have its natural sanction and the State may leave it to the individuals to ask freely to religion or philosophy the aid they need to endure hardships of nature or to overcome own weakness. Taxation will bar the way to that ideal.

Accordingly, the State might consider both a land tax and the expropriation of land. In the first case, the State would be, in fact, a kind of co-owner of the land. In the other case, a rightful repurchase of it must take place.

This repurchase takes a long period. The actual situation in Walras's time was one in which the land was privately owned, even though the French revolution could have changed this, as he contended. The question was how the State can obtain privately owned land. It should be prevented that a factual injustice be remedied by another injustice. The actual situation is not the present landowners' fault. Gossen, who claimed on similar grounds nationalisation of land, already dealt with the question.[24] He, too, pointed to the continually rising prices of land (services). Walras read Gossen's book (in fact, he rediscovered it, together with Jevons) in the seventies of the nineteenth century. In 1893 (Walras 1965, Letter 1172), he wrote:

> The point of tangency of moral economics with pure economics can be found in the law of the surplus value of the rent of land in a progressing society.

Blueprint of the Ideal

We saw that Léon Walras extensively dealt with monopoly and other market organisations, public goods, taxation and ownership, in particular State ownership of the land. It was always his intention to insert these elements in a comprehensive system, in which public goods would be produced by the State and this same State would be the demander of them. This may be inferred from the following citation (*EES*, p. 433; 1990: 400, emphasis added):

> The idea of want curves or utility curves of the products and services of public interest would be indispensable for *completing the mathematical theory of the economic equilibrium*.

---

[24] Gossen (1854), pp. 250–273; Chap. 23 of the English translation.

This same idea can also be found in many other places throughout the *EPA* and the *EES*. See, for instance, the passage in the last citation of § 8 above: "Individuals feel and measure wants for bread, meat, clothing, furniture; the State for troops, courts, schools, and roads".

As already indicated above, Walras paid so much attention to pure theory that he ran out of time and the synthesis was never achieved. Some time ago, an attempt has been made to fill this lack. A broad design for the economic framework of the ideal envisaged by Walras could be synthesised in what was called "*general* general economic equilibrium models".[25] In these models, the above elements have been inserted:

- All firms produce with fixed coefficients of production. This applies to production of both private goods (under free competition or (regulated) monopoly) and public goods.
- All goods are supplied at cost price, both under free competition and under monopoly.
- The State enters on the scene as an individual that plays a role that mathematically does not differ from that of an individual. The abolition of taxation combined with State ownership of land and the fiction of a social welfare function with quantities of public goods as variables has the effect that the State has a real budget constraint with rent as income and that it has a utility function just as all individual consumers.

Hence, the general economic equilibrium models can be fashioned such that they have the same mathematical structure as the models discussed in the *Éléments*. This is not amazing because, firstly, the assumption of constant returns to the scale of production, expressed in the assumption of fixed coefficients of production, is maintained and hence marginal costs and average costs will always coincide. Secondly, the demand side does not change formally. Consequently, regarding optimality, these extended models do not differ from the models exposed in the *Éléments*.

Walras believed that under these circumstances, people have more chance than in any other economic order to come to a situation of wealth by using their own abilities and their own gifts. This, we think, is Léon Walras's solution to the Social question.[26]

Digression on Money

In the ideal situation envisaged by Léon Walras, where misery belongs to the past, prices should not fluctuate unexpectedly, haphazardly. Therefore, he proposed a system of *global* price control. Any particular price should neither be controlled nor

---

[25] Van Daal and Jolink (1993a, b), pp. 120–126; see also Van Daal (1999).

[26] Albert Jolink (1991, 1996) perhaps was the first to present a complete view of Walras's oeuvre from an evolutionist standpoint with the Social Question as the continuous thread running through it.

prescribed, but measures should be taken such that the price system as a whole will "behave well". Therefore, Walras proposed his well-known project for reform of the monetary system. The essence of his proposal was that (1) gold should be the money commodity, with the same value both as money and as merchandise, (2) there should be silver money[27] to be brought into circulation or withdrawn in adequate quantities by the State in order to stabilise the price level. In addressing himself to the meeting of the Latin Union (Belgium, France, Greece, Italy and Switzerland; a first European monetary union), he said it as follows (*EPA*, p. 17; 1992: 16, italics added):

> The silver token should be minted by the State; it will only circulate within the country of its emission and will only be accepted for payments up to a certain amount. The quantity of token that may be issued by each of the States forming the Latin Union will be determined by international conventions. This should be done (…), as regards to the regulating token, *for assuring a regular variation of the value of money.* Every State of the Union will benefit of profits and will bear losses coupled with issue or retreat of its token.

In many papers, Walras went at length to explain this "open-market policy avant la lettre". He thereby introduced the ephemeral notion of the "economic tides", borrowed from Jevons. The monetary authorities should be well aware of the time of ebb and flood in the economic tides. Therefore, Léon Walras pleaded for better statistics. He gave thereby many practical hints and stressed some fundamental ideas. Highly important, he said, is the fact that the issue of banknotes can be part of the cause of instabilities. In his "Théorie mathématique du billet de banque" (*EPA*, pp. 339–375, dating from 1879; 1992: 311–342), he went at length in analysing the nature of banknotes and in exposing their disadvantages.

The economic tide as such is according to Walras a natural phenomenon that should not be influenced as such. It is the variation of the tide that must be managed, as is exemplified by Fig. 18.2 below (1992: 144). Without the introduction of the regulating token, the price level would have been represented by curve ABCDE. Introduction of silver token at the right moments would result in the curve ABCcD'dE'.

This process evolves in time and can easily be associated with an underlying sequence of Walras's temporary (or periods') equilibria uncoordinated over time. This lack of coordination is caused by the lack of foresight of Walras's economic agents. See also § 5 above.

Another issue of importance in this respect is formed by Walras's ideas on monometallism and bi-metallism. As often, here also he takes a middle position, which made him unpopular in all champs. The following citation makes this clear (Walras 1886, 1992: 138):

> The final result of this whole study is that the greatest possible stability of prices cannot be obtained by trying to find it [exclusively] in one or another of these four systems: gold-monometallism, silver-monometallism, bimetallism, regulating token, but by making an alternating use of all four of them. One should imagine the four systems as placed in the following order […]:
>
> Silver-monometallism — Bimetallism — Regulating token — Gold-monometallism.

---

[27] Or, rather, *silver token*, because its real value must be somewhat less than its nominal value.

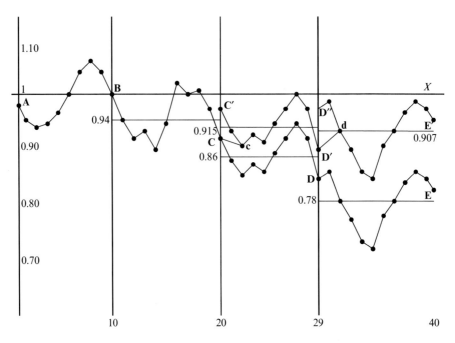

Fig. 18.2 Introduction of regulating token at time 20 and at time 29

Walras's Influence

The Period Before 1954

In reviewing Walras's reception in the literature, it makes sense to distinguish the periods before and after 1954. The most important reason for this separation is the publication in that year of Jaffé's translation of the *Éléments*. In the same year, both Schumpeter's *History of Economic Analysis* and Arrow and Debreu's seminal *Econometrica* article "Existence of equilibrium for a competitive economy" saw the light.

Before 1954, we can hardly speak of a substantial direct "interschool" influence of Walras. During Walras's career, Alfred Marshall (1842–1924) was undoubtedly the most important economist. His *Principles of Economics* was published from 1890 until 1920 in eight editions. In the first edition, in the last paragraph of a footnote in Appendix H, § 2, dealing with unstable equilibria, Marshall acknowledges Walras and himself as independent inventors of the theory of unstable equilibrium. In all later editions, this is omitted.

One would expect references to Walras's *Éléments* in book V of the *Principles*: "General Relations of Demand, Supply, and Value". Marshall is dealing here with topics clearly related to Walras's *Éléments*. But no word is spent on the *Éléments*. Marshall only refers 2 times to Walras's "Économie Politique Pure" if he addresses the question of how to define production factors as labour (note 1, p. 138, 8th ed.) and capital (note 1, p. 788, 8th ed.). Finally, he mentions Walras without any specification as one of the authors who criticise classical value theory (p. 821).[28] One would at least expect a comment by Marshall, as the "master of partial analysis", on Walras's critical attitude regarding this type of analysis; see *Éléments*, Appendix II, from the third edition onwards.

On the other side of the Atlantic Ocean, we focus upon John Bates Clark (1847–1938). In the preface (p. x) of his *Essentials of Economic Theory*,[29] Clark acknowledges the influence of authors like Irving Fisher, Friedrich von Wieser and Eugen von Böhm Bawerk, but nowhere in the book a reference to Walras can be found.

Leaving these two "champions" of the Anglo-Saxon marginalists, we return to the old continent, to "the" representative of the Austrians: Eugen von Böhm Bawerk (1851–1914). His chief work is *Kapital und Kapitalzins*, published in 1884. A revised and enlarged edition was published from 1909 until 1914. The unchanged fourth edition appeared in 1921. It contains 1384 pages in three volumes. Its main topic is also covered by Walras, mainly in part V of his *Éléments*. Altogether we can find eight references to Walras. Two relate to his definition of capital, one deals with his definition of labour, two further references acknowledge Walras's contribution to value theory, one classifies his capital theory as related to Menger's and, in a note, Von Böhm Bawerk agrees with Walras's opinion that the marginal utility principle also applies to altruistic actions. In the last reference (Vol. II, book 1: 458, note 1), Von Böhm Bawerk agrees with a conclusion of Walras's capital theory. But he adds that this conclusion is deduced from an essentially flawed theory, although with valuable details. This is not further elaborated. Remarkably, in his third edition, von Böhm Bawerk refers only to the first and second editions (Walras 1874a, b, 1889) of the *Éléments*, although the fourth one was available.

From these observations, the impression emerges that the spread of Walras's ideas into the direction of the "other schools of the marginal revolution" was not very substantial. This impression is corroborated in what perhaps still is by far the best "History of Economic Analysis": Joseph A. Schumpeter's, *History of Economic Analysis* (1954; see especially part IV, Chaps. 5 and 7).

Fortunately, there are exceptions. Indirect international influence originates from Italy with Enrico Barone (1859–1924) and Vilfredo Pareto (1848–1923). Firstly, it is not exaggerated to link the so called calculation debate to Walras, via Barone,[30] who asserts that for each economy, a central socialist plan can be calculated with the

---

[28] This meagre result is the more striking because Marshall has read the Éléments. The copy of the book in the Oxford University Library reveals Marshall's hand written notes (stopping at page 169).

[29] *E.g.* the unchanged 1924 edition; the book was first published in 1907.

[30] And others like, *e.g.* O. Lange. The original version of Barone's paper was published in 1908, in Italian. It became generally known after the publication of its English translation, "The Ministry of Production in a Collectivist State" in F.A. von Hayek (ed.), *Collectivist Economic Planning* (Barone 1935).

same outcome as a perfectly competitive equilibrium for that economy. Theoretically, the plan might be implemented by a central social agency. Barone obviously was inspired by the Walrasian systems of equations and without Walras's insights, those of Barone would have been impossible to develop.

The most important critical reaction on the calculation debate inspired by Barone's ideas came from Ludwig von Mises.[31] He emphasises that information about the basis on which the agents can decide and revise their demand and supply decisions only can be produced by the functioning of free markets. Without this, the necessary information about scarcities in the economy will not be revealed and, hence, will never become available to a central social agency. This implies that such an agency will never be able to calculate (in theory or in practice) the allocation corresponding to a perfectly competitive equilibrium.[32]

Next we should deal with Pareto, Walras's successor at the University of Lausanne. His most important contributions to economic science[33] are his generalisation of the extreme simple utility concept used by Walras, Jevons and Gossen, the notion of ordinality based upon Edgeworth's indifference apparatus and, of course, what nowadays is called the Paretian welfare criterion. It is obvious again that Paretian welfare economics was based upon the essence of the Walrasian equation systems and that its development would not have been very likely without Walras's perception.

Finally, it is inevitable to step outside the marginalist schools. In section seven, Chap. 7 (pp. 998–1020) of his *History of Economic Analysis*, Schumpeter reviews Walras's general equilibrium theory. This review, written in the last year (probably the last months) of Schumpeter's life, is a highly enlightening introduction to part I to VI of the last edition of the *Éléments*. For the first time, we see that the structure of the *Éléments* is exactly followed and exposed by a reviewer: exchange, production, capital and money. Unfortunately, Schumpeter does not pay attention to the parts devoted to growth, imperfect competition and taxes. Schumpeter takes much care in this exposition to point out the relations with Marshall expert John Maynard Keynes's *General Theory of Employment, Interest and Money* (1936); see page 999,[34]

---

[31] L. Von Mises, "Die Wirtschaftsrechnung im Sozialistischen Gemeinwesen" translated as "Economic Calcualation in the Socialistic Commonwealth" in F.A. von Hayek, ed., *Collectivist Economic Planning* (Von Mises 1935).

[32] Von Mises further developed his reputation as a critic of socialism. He published in 1932 his revised second edition of *Die Gemeinwirtschaft, Untersuchungen über den Sozialismus*. Since we know that Walras was advocating State ownership of the land, one might expect some reference in Von Mises's book to this idea. But in the whole book, one cannot find any reference to Walras. Even in discussing "Das Gemeineigentum an den Produktionsmitteln" (pp. 25 ff.), he does not refer to Walras.

[33] See *Manuel d'économie politique* (1981[1909]), translated from his *Manuale di economia politica* (1906).

[34] Here, Schumpeter emphasises that it is a misunderstanding to think that Walrasian micro-analysis is in need of a supplement by a Keynesian income or macro-analysis.

page 1001, note 7,[35] page 1013, note 38,[36] page 1017, note 49[37] and page 1023, note 65.[38] Dealing with monetary theory in Chap. 8, Schumpeter concludes (1954: 1082) that Walras's theory of money "simply did not exist for the overwhelming majority of economists", and he emphasises Lange's 1938 conclusion that the "Keynesian analysis of the *General Theory* (…) is but a special case of the genuinely general theory of Walras".

So, considering all the observations of Schumpeter's, one might want to know to what extent Keynes himself in his *General Theory* refers to Walras. In the whole book, there is precisely one reference to Walras, on page 177: Keynes classifies Walras as an economist in the "classical tradition" in one breath with Marshall, Cassel, Taussig and others who believe that "the rate of interest is the variable which brings [saving and investment] together".

To be fair, we should also check Keynes's reaction to Knut Wicksell (1851–1926). Apart from Walras's successor in Laussanne, Pareto, Wicksell is one of the few economists on whom Walras had a substantial influence in this period via his monetary theory. Walras wanted to maintain the separation of the real part of the economy from the part where the money interest and the money prices are determined, to be able to work with a kind of "quantity theory". Wicksell was probably the first to observe that, in this sense, money could not be neutral in the Walrasian model.[39] So one would expect Keynes to comment on Wicksell.[40] Keynes refers 2 times to Wicksell in his General Theory, but not very pertinently. First, he points out, without further specification, that the contemporary economists' neutral interest rate differs from Böhm Bawerk's and Wicksell's natural rate. The second reference is more relevant where he explains (pp. 242–243) that in his *Treatise on Money*, he attempted to clarify and to further develop Wicksell's natural rate theory, but that his *Treatise*'s intuition appears to be untenable in the light of his *General Theory*. He defines (1936: 243) the neutral interest rate of money in a situation of an output-employment equilibrium in which the output elasticity of employment is zero. But we do not see a discussion of Wicksell's or Walras's ideas about the (non)-neutrality of money.[41]

---

[35] Here, Schumpeter stresses that Walras was prepared to admit that capitalists lend money and not capital goods. He concludes that this observation is important to see the affinity between the Walrasian and Keynesian systems.

[36] In this note, Schumpeter warns us against making individual demand only dependent of the own price and income for pedagogical reasons. This deeply obscures Walras's approach and, in the end, it does not help the student to understand the relation between Keynesian and Walrasian economics.

[37] In this note, Schumpeter points out that it is not true that Walras neglected the influence of income, but Keynes neglected the influence of prices.

[38] Here, Schumpeter observes that the precautionary and the speculative motive for holding cash can be inserted in the Walrasian theory.

[39] See Wicksell's "Zur Zinstheorie" in *"Die Wirtschaftstheorie der Gegenwart"* ed. H Mayer, III, 1928 (Wicksell 1928).

[40] And on Pigou, who also adhered to non-neutrality of money in his *Theory of Unemployment* (Pigou 1933).

[41] Or to the related considerations in Pigou (1933).

When Keynes discusses the "quantity theory of money" (esp. pp. 304-4-306), he comes up with a number of equations that might or might not be compatible with Wicksell's work.[42] However, Keynes does not address this question at all.

From 1954 Onwards

In the year 1954, as mentioned above, three relevant publications appear. Firstly, we refer to Jaffé's translation of the last edition of the *Éléments*. The translation made this book accessible for a much wider audience, especially in the Anglo-Saxon world. Next, we point out the appearance of the already discussed *History of Economic Analysis* by Schumpeter. Here, we see probably for the first time an adequate appraisal of Walras's *Éléments* in a(n advanced) text book. To a certain extent, these publications can be seen as a fruitful basis for what since then happened with Walras's legacy.

Especially after the seventies of the previous century, we see[43] an increasing number of publications, substantiating that this legacy is much more than the simple static general equilibrium model reproduced in most micro-economic textbooks. We should like to memorise here especially the ongoing efforts of Donald Walker that resulted in the publication of two impressive volumes *The Legacy of Léon Walras* (2001) under his editorship. These volumes bundle a considerable part of the publications that appeared since the seventies and are preceded by a valuable introduction to which we readily refer. Nevertheless, still a minority among the economists fully appreciate Walras's legacy in its fundamental aspects as has been exposed above. This brings us to the third relevant publication in 1954.

In 1954, Econometrica publishes the article "Existence of equilibrium for a competitive economy" by Arrow and Debreu. They concentrate in this paper on the conditions of static equilibrium under perfect competition in the context of an economy with exchange and production. They do not focus upon capital, saving and money.[44] Nor do they acknowledge another essential feature: the context in which Walras develops his argument by introducing additional complexity in his subsequent models to analyse periodical or temporary equilibrium of a free market system.[45] In 1959, Debreu published his *Theory of Value* in which the same theory was set out once more. This booklet became most influential. Remarkably, almost every contemporary

---

[42] Probably because the Keynesian analysis neglects relative prices.

[43] Together with a substantial decrease in weight of Keynesian macro-economics.

[44] Pascal Bridel devoted his *Money and General Equilibrium Theory* (Bridel 1997) to this important part of Walras's oeuvre; see also Van Daal and Jolink (1993b), Chaps. 10–16.

[45] This is completely in line with the interpretation of Walras by Hicks (1934). Hicks claims to be the first to analyse a sequence of temporary equilibria (Hicks 1939). The previous sections have clarified that this claim is unjust.

micro-economics textbook contains a reproduction of what is presented as Walrasian general equilibrium theory that is much closer related to the Arrow and Debreu simplification than to the much richer original. This applies even to advanced textbooks as, e.g. Mass-Colell et al. 1995. This tendency in the textbooks explains to a large extent the poor state of "Walras knowledge" among what we have denoted as "cutes".

Concluding, we can say that on the one hand, we observe a growing awareness of the significance of Walras in all his ideas, as we have attempted to sketch in this contribution, especially from the seventies onwards.[46] This growing awareness inspires a rich research programme varying from the role of the entrepreneur in the imperfectly competitive process (towards and away from the moving temporary equilibrium and welfare properties of such a process), to the properties of sequences of uncoordinated temporary equilibria with agents acting with less than rational expectations.[47] On the other hand, we observe that the majority of cutes are still trained by the narrow Debreu approach as reproduced in most textbooks.

Conclusion

Léon Walras bequeathed to us three substantial, major books; nine smaller books and more than two hundred other publications; see Walker 1987a. Having gone through all this, we may say that his oeuvre forms a narrative on the subject of economic life that can be considered as a complete account in the sense that it deals with the functioning of practically all aspects of the economy as he saw it in his days. When one reads Walras's works, one understands soon that persuasion certainly was one of his aims. We hope to have made evident on what points he tried to convince his readers. This could raise the question whether it would be worthwhile to subject Walras's oeuvre, in particular its rhetoric, to an examination à la McCloskey.[48] A thorough analysis of Walras's writings from the viewpoint of rhetoric would certainly give us an answer to the question why there is and always has been such a considerable gap between, on the one hand, the part of his message that people caught and, on the other hand, the totality of this message. This analysis could very well be carried out by means of the six points of Donald McCloskey's 1994 book on persuasion. Where these points find their origin in rules for the structure of Greek discourses, Léon Walras, well versed in the classical languages, would

---

[46] See Walker (2001). This collection (65 articles in two volumes) is the third of its kind. Mark Blaug published a volume with 25 articles in 1992 and in 1993, John Cunningham Wood a three volume set of 68 papers. Further, the volume with 19 articles by William Jaffé on Walras, edited by Donald: Walker (1983), should be mentioned. Altogether, these bundles contain 148 different articles. Walker's two collections stand out because of excellent editorial work, especially the original introductions.

[47] See, e.g. the mentioned volumes of Walker (2001), but also Schinkel (2002).

[48] See MacCloskey (1985), 1994) and also Henderson (1995).

undoubtedly have approved of such an analysis. Till now, nobody had the courage to take such an enormous job upon him.

Another interesting point regarding Walras's work in its entirety as a narrative is the question how it has been structured and whether this structure is unique, typically Walras's, or rather similar to that to be found in the other great economists' texts. In a doctoral thesis, submitted in Évry (Fréjaville 2001), first results of a study in this line have been reported. After having studied and analysed the notion of a narrative in general (and of fairy tales in particular), the author of this thesis leads us to the economic narratives. In those that may be considered as complete, one can always distinguish the following five elements: (1) individual norms, (2) collective norms, (3) behaviour, (4) mechanism and (5) the State. In Walras's oeuvre, too, these elements are clearly present. We have seen how the individual consumers' and the individual entrepreneurs' norms (maximal utility and maximal profit) lead to their behaviour in the markets. This, in its turn, gives rise to a mechanism leading to equilibrium. The outcome of this equilibrium does not always correspond with collective norms (public goods and market forms) and, therefore, we need a State to redress this. Like Adam Smith, Léon Walras must be considered as an "invisible hand economist" in the sense that individuals are considered to be ignorant of the consequences of their behaviour on the collective level; they are even uninterested in such consequences. Of course, this does not apply to the State in its roles of market regulator, consumer of the public goods and owner of the land.

References

Allais M (1943) Traité d'économie politique pure, 2 vols. Imprimerie Nationale, Paris
Arrow KJ, Debreu G (1954) Existence of equilibrium for a competitive economy. Econometrica 22:265–290
Barone E (1935 [1908]) The ministry of production in a collectivist state. In: von Hayek FA (ed) Collectivist economic planning. Routledge, London
Blaug M (ed) (1992) Léon Walras (1834–1910). Edward Elgar Publishing, Aldershot
Bowley AL (1924) The mathematical groundwork of economics. Clarendon Press, Oxford
Bridel P (1997) Money an general equilibrium theory. Edward Elgar Publishing, Cheltenham
Cunningham Wood J (ed) (1993) Léon Walras, critical assessments. Routledge, London
Debreu G (1959) Theory of value. Wiley, New York
Fréjaville A (2001) Normes, comportement et mécanismes dans la littérature économique: L'exemple de Léon Walras, Doctoral thesis, University of Évry
Henderson W (1995) Economics as literature. Routledge, London
Hicks JR (1934) Léon Walras. Econometrica 2:338–348
Hicks JR (1939) Value and capital. Clarendon Press, Oxford
Jolink A (1991) Liberte, égalité, rareté, Doctoral dissertation, Erasmus Universiteit Rotterdam
Jolink A (1996) The evolutionist economics of Léon Walras. Routledge, London
Keynes JM (1936) The general theory of employment, interest and money. Macmillan, London
Maks JAH (2006) Gross substitutes, Walras' "rareté" and the stability of the middle class. In: Backhaus JG, Maks JAH (eds) From Walras to Pareto. Springer, New York
Marshal A (1920) Principles of economics, 8th edn. Macmillan & Co, London

Mass-Colell A, Whinston MD, Green JR (1995) Microeconomic theory. Oxford University Press, Oxford

McCloskey D (1985) The rhetoric of economics. University of Wisconsin Press, Madison

McCloskey D (1994) Knowledge and persuasion in economics. Cambridge University Press, Cambridge

McKenzie L (1987) General equilibrium. In: Eatwell J et al (eds) The New Palgrave, a dictionary of economics, vol 2. MacMillan, London, pp 498–512

Morishima M (1977) Walras' economics. Cambridge University Press, Cambridge

Muth JF (1960) Optimal properties of exponentially weighted forecasts. Journal of the Statistical Association of America 55:299–306

Muth JF (1961) Rational expectations and the theory of price movements. Econometrica 29:315–335

Pareto V (1981[1909]) Manuel d'économie politique, volume VII of Vilfredo Pareto, Oeuvres complètes, edited by Giovanni Busino. Droz, Genève

Pigou AC (1933) The theory of unemployment. MacMillan, London

Robbins L (1932) An essay on the nature &significance of economic science. MacMillan & Co, London

Schinkel MP (2002) Disequilibrium theory. Reflections towards a revival of learning, doctoral dissertation. University of Maastricht, Maastricht

Schumpeter JA (1954) History of economic analysis. George Allen & Unwin, London

Van Daal J (1994) De la nature de la monnaie dans les modèles monétaires de l'équilibre général économique de Léon Walras. Économies et Sociétés, Série Oeconomia, Histoire de la Pensée Économique, PÉ, no. 20–21:115–132

Van Daal J (1998) Léon Walras's general economic equilibrium models of capital formation: existence of a solution. Revue Économique 49(1998):1175–1198

Van Daal J (1999) Léon Walras et le capitalisme. Revue européenne des sciences sociales Tome XXXVII(116):83–99

Van Daal J, Jolink A (1993a) On Walras's 'general general equilibrium model.' In: Hebert RF (ed) Perspectives on the history of economic thought, vol IX. Edward Elgar Publishing Company, Aldershot, Ch. 9 (Reprinted in Walker DA (ed) The Legacy of Léon Walras, Edward Elgar Publishing Ltd, Cheltenham (UK), 2001, Vol II, pp 390–405

Van Daal J, Jolink A (1993b) The equilibrium economics of Léon Walras. Routledge, London

Van Dall J (2000) Les tâtonnements dans le modèle de la production chez Léon Walras. Bons à rien?', in : L'économie walrasienne, Actes du Colloque de l'Association Internationale Walras, 16 septembre 1999, Les Cahiers du CERAS (Reims), Hors-série n° 1, juin 2000, pp. 58–78

Van Witteloostuijn A, Maks JAH (1988) WALRAS: a Hicksian avant la lettre. Économie Appliquée 41:651–668

Van Witteloostuijn A, Maks JAH (1990) Walras on temporary equilibrium and dynamics. Hist Polit Econ 22:223–237

Von Mises L (1935 [1920]) Economic calculation in the socialistic commonwealth (translated). In: von Hayek FA (ed) Collectivist economic planning. Routledge, London

Walker DA (ed) (1983) William Jaffé's essays on Walras. Cambridge University Press, Cambridge

Walker DA (ed) (1987a) Walras's theory of Tatonnement. J Polit Econ 95(4):758–774

Walker DA (ed) (1987b) Bibliography of the writings of Léon Walras. Hist Polit Econ 19(4):667–702

Walker DA (ed) (1996) Walras's market models. Cambridge University Press, Cambridge

Walker DA (ed) (1997) The relation between the nineteenth century bourse and Léon Walras's model of an organized market. Paper presented before the History of Economics Society. Charleston

Walker DA (ed) (2001) The Legacy of Léon Walras. Edward Elgar Publishing Ltd, Cheltenham

Walras L (1874a) Principes d'une théorie mathématique de l'échange. Journal des économistes 34(100):5–21

Walras L (1874b) Éléments d'économie politique pure, ou théorie de la richesse sociale, first instalment, Lausanne: L.Corbaz; Paris: Guillaumin; Basel: H. Georg

Walras L (1877) Éléments d'économie politique pure, ou théorie de la richesse sociale, second instalment, Lausanne: L. Corbaz; Paris: Guillaumin; Basel: H. Georg

Walras L (1886) Théorie de la monnaie. Lausanne: Corbaz; Paris: L. Larose & Forcel; Rome: Loescher; Leipzig: Duncker & Humblot

Walras L (1889) Éléments d'économie politique pure, ou théorie de la richesse sociale, second edition, Lausanne: Rouge; Paris: Guillaumin; Leipzig: Von Dunker & Humblot

Walras L (1896) Éléments d'économie politique pure, ou théorie de la richesse sociale, 3rd edn. Lausanne: Rouge; Paris: F. Pichon; Leipzig: Von Dunker & Humblot

Walras L (1900) Éléments d'économie politique pure, ou théorie de la richesse sociale, 4th edn. Lausanne: Rouge; Paris: F. Pichon

Walras L (1926) Éléments d'économie politique pure, ou théorie de la richesse sociale, definitive edition, revised by the author, Paris: R. Pichon & R, Durand-Auzias; Lausanne: Rouge

Walras L (1954) Élements of pure economics, or the theory of social wealth, translated and annotated by W. Jaffé, Homewood, Ill: Irwin; London: Allen and Unwin

Walras L (1965) Correspondence of Léon Walras and related papers, 3 vols. Edited by William Jaffé. North-Holland Publishing Company, Amsterdam

Walras L (1987) Mélanges d'économie politique et sociale, edited by Jean-Pierre Potier and Claude Hébert, under the auspices of the Centre Auguste et Léon Walras, Lyon, Vol. VII of AUGUSTE ET LÉON WALRAS: ŒUVRES ÉCONOMIQUES COMPLÈTES. Économica, Paris

Walras L (1988) Éléments d'économie politique pure, ou théorie de la richesse sociale, variorum edition of the editions of 1874, 1877, 1889, 1896, 1900 and 1926 (and of the edition of the Abrégé de 1938) augmented by a translation of the notes of William Jaffé in Elements of pure economics (1954), edited by Claude Mouchot, under the auspices of the Centre Auguste et Léon Walras, Lyon, Vol. VIII of AUGUSTE ET LÉON WALRAS: ŒUVRES ÉCONOMIQUES COMPLÈTES. Économica, Paris

Walras L (1990) Études d'économie sociale: théorie de la répartition de la richesse sociale, edited by Pierre Dockès, under the auspices of the Centre Auguste et Léon Walras, Lyon, Vol. IX of *AUGUSTE ET LÉON WALRAS: ŒUVRES ÉCONOMIQUES COMPLÈTES.* Économica, Paris (First edition 1896, second edition 1938. English translation by Jan van Daal, titled /Studies of Applied Economics/, augmented with an introduction and annotations, two volumes, Abingdon/ New York: Routledge, 2005)

Walras L (1992) Études d'économie politique appliquée (Théorie de la production de la richesse sociale), edited by Jean-Pierre Potier, under the auspices of the Centre Auguste et Léon Walras, Lyon, Vol. X of *AUGUSTE ET LÉON WALRAS: ŒUVRES ÉCONOMIQUES COMPLÈTES.* Économica, Paris (First edition 1898, second edition 1938 English translation, titled /Studies of Social Economics/, by Jan van Daal and Donald Walker, augmented with an introduction and annotations, Abingdon/New York: Routledge, 2010)

Walras L (1996) Cours, edited by Pierre Dockès, Jean-Pierre Potier and Pascal Bridel, under the auspices of the Centre Auguste et Léon Walras, Lyon, Vol. XII of AUGUSTE ET LÉON WALRAS: ŒUVRES ÉCONOMIQUES COMPLÈTES. Économica, Paris

Wicksell K (1928) Zur Zinstheorie. In: Mayer H (ed) Die Wirtschaftstheorie der Gegenwart, vol III. Springer, Wien

Chapter 19
Alfred Marshall

Earl Beach[†]

Introduction

What I have to say about Alfred Marshall is very different from what you read in the literature, either in brief references or in longer biographical studies. My graduate work was done at Harvard in the 1930s, and I was enamoured with the mathematical approach to economic analysis. But in mid life I became interested in the employment effects of automation and devised a new approach, which seems to be more realistic than the abstract analyses that characterize current work. This approach got me into arguments with colleagues and rejections by editors. I had been teaching a course on the history of economic thought and re-examined the field. Marshall came into focus. I re-read his Principles, and some parts of the book many times. Marshall's economics is not understood in one reading.[1] His interest in realism is not being appreciated.

As a further introductory note I should like to say, also, that I am addressing myself to graduate students, as instructed, rather than to a more general professional audience. As a person who has slowly learned a great deal in a long life, my approach

---

[†] Deceased.

[1] Students who do look into Marshall's Principles read Book V and perhaps peek into the Mathematical Appendix. Marshall suggested that the heart of his theory lay in Book V, but that was for a particular reason. His success with the integration of supply and demand theory led to an emphasis on a balancing of forces. Marshall explains in terms of an equilibrium concept. As it turned out, this has been very unfortunate, as will be explained. The student, who is willing to make the effort, should read carefully the Prefaces, Book I and Appendix A. Other parts will be suggested below. He should read with more than the usual care because Marshall was very deliberate with his composition.

E. Beach (✉)
Charles Beach, Department of Economics, John Deutsch Institute, ON, Canada
e-mail: beachc@qed.econ.queensu.ca

J.G. Backhaus (ed.), *Handbook of the History of Economic Thought*, 495
The European Heritage in Economics and the Social Sciences,
DOI 10.1007/978-1-4419-8336-7_19, © Springer Science+Business Media, LLC 2012

is that of a perpetual student. A recently published book (Beach 1999) shows these later "down-to-earth" tendencies. It attempts to explain the causes and processes of economic development, in which Marshall plays a very important role.

A recent biographer describes him as a "soaring eagle". That description was a fitting evaluation a century ago, but few economists today would regard it as appropriate. This change in attitude by the profession is the result of a very different approach to economics that today is deemed suitable. The difference lies in less emphasis on realism in current analyses. Much importance is now given to abstractions, often expressed in models. The idea or the construction is considered to be significant. Its application is left to others. This divorce of theory and practice has produced rather poor results, at least in the minds of non-economists.

To Marshall, on the other hand, realism was essential. He wished to understand how economic events actually happened. He sought to appreciate the unfolding of the minutiae of economic life and sense their interrelations. He recognized that an equilibrium position is unrealistic in economics, although equilibrating forces are very realistic. Thus his general setting is that of non-equilibrium conditions, i.e. realistic dynamics.

This reverence for abstraction has been unfortunate for the profession, whose self-evaluation is not echoed by outsiders. Allyn Young warned us about the danger in 1928, over 70 years ago. I shall try to start a re-evaluation of this great man to the soaring status, of which Young himself would have approved.

Biography

Alfred Marshall was born in 1842 and grew up in London, England. His father was a cashier at the Bank of England, so that the family had no great wealth. Yet he had a good public school education with an academic record, which was good enough to allow him into Cambridge University.

His father wanted him to take up the ministry, but he wished to continue with his education, and financial help from an uncle allowed him to complete a Cambridge degree in mathematics. He paid back his uncle when he began to teach mathematics at the University. He took a very good degree, becoming second wrangler in mathematics, which means that he was second highest.

He had a continuing interest in the welfare of mankind and studied a number of fields before he came to economics, specifically John Stuart Mill's Principles of Political Economy, which had been published some 2 decades before, and was then widely read. He applied mathematics to testing the propositions he found in Mill's text. He must have found the results to his liking. He made economics his life's work.

During this period Marshall would usually spend a part of his holidays walking in the Swiss Alps. He would carry books in a packsack and occasionally sit and read. I have found this to be a useful habit in my own work. After a bit of serious reading, one should allow the mind to dwell upon the subject for a while rather than dash off to some other activity. Walking alone is a good way to allow the mind to continue to work on the material. Sometimes surprising thoughts occur.[2]

Marshall married one of his women students, Mary Paley,[3] and had to vacate his fellowship at the college. The couple moved to Bristol where he took on the leadership of Bristol College. The administrative work in a new university was not to his liking and the demands of the job were found to be burdensome. He developed an illness that bothered him the rest of his life. He resigned from his position at Bristol and enjoyed a year of recovery in Italy where he returned to writing economics.

He spent a year of study at Berlin, interested particularly in the German economic historians and philosophers. He had also made a trip of exploration to the United States. Later, he spent a great deal of time on government work, writing submissions, giving evidence or acting as commissioner (Groenwegen 1996). Clearly he felt that his understanding of economics required close observation of current economic activity and of the historical past. With mathematics as his basic study at the university, this is a very interesting and important development. Few economists have the ability to do such careful analysis and then make use of such a wide understanding of social reality. Even his vacation trips were scheduled to include visits to factories.[4]

He returned to Cambridge in 1882 to lecture on economics and in 1885 became the Professor of Political Economy, where he remained until he retired in 1908. He died in 1924 at the age of 81. He spent much time in revising his Principles, the eighth edition appeared in 1920. He published two more books. *Industry and Trade* is a substantial volume which some found more readable than the Principles. His last book, *Money Credit and Commerce* (Marshall 1923b), was mostly a collection of his many notes. He did not get around to writing a book on economic progress. This is unfortunate because it would have given him a basis for presenting his monetary theory, which had been carefully excluded from his Principles, as an essential ingredient in the process of development, as Schumpeter recognized. This could have established Marshall's claim to economic dynamics in a realistic context.

There has been some discussion of his teaching. His students were expected to read the Principles on their own. His lectures dwelt on current events, trying to get the students to think for themselves. Sometimes he might provoke them with ramblings. He gave much attention to students who would ask questions, having them

---

[2] Twice in my lifetime this technique has produced remarkable results. Walking through the stacks of Widener Library at Harvard as a graduate student, a thought came which became my doctoral dissertation. Later in life I was reading Ben Seligman's Most Notorious Victory, lamenting the loss of work to computers. As a respected economist, he should have offered a more balanced view of the goods and bads. As I walked to the university, I was suddenly taken by the thought of a formula that would offer such a solution. It has proven to be very useful.

[3] Mary Paley, of good family, was very helpful to Marshall. She was in the process of writing an introductory textbook in economics, which became a joint publication, and Marshall's first effort in the field. After Marshall's death she was for many years in charge of his papers, which became the Marshall Library at Cambridge.

[4] Adam Smith also was keenly interested in current business affairs.

to tea and lending them books for further reading. His method was successful in that many of his students went on to hold chairs at other universities in Britain. However, they showed limited understanding of his basic thought when attacks came from Sraffa and others.

Keynes wrote an excellent obituary for the *Economic Journal* (Keynes 1924), of which he was the editor at the time. Guillebaud has a shorter note (Marshall 1961) in his 1961 edition of Marshall's Principles. Groenwegen has recently given us a thorough study (Groenwegen 1995). Guillebaud quotes Homan (1928) who gives us an assessment of the man as he began his life of economic study:

> It is possible thus to see what manner of young man it was who ceased his mathematical lectures in 1868 and took up a new lectureship in the Moral Sciences, specially founded for him at St. John's College at the instance of the master, Dr. Bateson, where his weight listed the ship sharply to the side of political economy. A brilliant mathematician, a young philosopher carrying a somewhat undigested load of German metaphysics, Utilitarianism and Darwinism; a humanitarian with religious feelings but no creed, eager to lighten the burdens of mankind, but sobered by the barriers revealed to him by the Ricardian Political Economy – one sees the background of the man who was to be to his students sage and pastor as well as scientist; whose objective scientific approach was to give economics a renewed public standing; whose sympathy for social reform was to rout its enemies; whose high gifts were to be as zealously devoted to his intellectual mistress as any artist's to his muse.

Context

Marshall's Principles of Economics was published in 1890, which was, in time, about half way between the appearance of The Wealth of Nations in 1776 and the present day. Before Marshall there were Malthus (1798), Ricardo, John Stuart Mill and a number of lesser figures. Contemporaneous were Walras and Menger, who, with Marshall, were important contributors to the "marginal revolution". With them, the concept of the margin became a key concept in economic analysis. There has been some quarrelling about priorities, but we shall not be concerned. Marshall's mathematical background suggests that the concept was not new to him. Furthermore, he had been playing with such ideas for some years, and he was slow to publish because he wanted to avoid misunderstandings. He had good reason for such fears, as history has demonstrated.

A major contribution of his Principles was his solution to an old problem with his marrying of the concepts of supply and demand for the determination of value. For this he was widely proclaimed. In a sense he tried to marry economics with history, in economic analysis, but with very little acceptance by either historians or economists. This failure was about as spectacular as his earlier victory. The study of economics was becoming popular and an increasing demand developed for its professionalization, in which Marshall played a role. This trend brought a desire for increased precision and this, in turn, inspired a greater use of mathematics and abstraction.

Marshall was one of the leaders in this trend towards the increased use of mathematics, but he kept his mathematical skeletons hidden in his language. He felt that if the mathematics had been appropriately used, the results could be explained in ordinary language. For him, mathematics was an aid to his thought and not an end in itself.

Those who followed did not favour this careful approach. Sraffa's (1926) article attempted to "tidy up" Marshall's "imprecise" expressions. Samuelson's Foundations (1947) attempted to "reverse" this "dictum" of Marshall, suggesting that the mathematical solutions were taken to be "economics". Brems (1986) illustrates this Samuelsonian approach very well. He attempts to put into mathematical language the abstract concepts of leading economists. For Marshall, such formulations were but a beginning in understanding good economics.

Shortly before Samuelson began writing his dissertation at Harvard, Allyn Young expressed dissatisfaction with this trend to mathematical abstraction. He had moved from Harvard to London to replace Cannan (1893, 1917) who had made economic theory an important part of the London curriculum. Young must have been highly regarded for the Brits seek a foreigner to continue Cannan's work (1930). Of course, most other theorists in Britain were Marshall's products.

Young was soon asked to head the British Association. His presidential address was published as a lead article in the *Economic Journal* in 1928. In it he expressed misgivings about the direction that the works of leading economists was taking. Remember, Young was the person who reviewed the first edition of Pigou's (1928) great work and questioned its lack of realism. Here he expressed great appreciation of the work of Smith and Marshall.

Unfortunately he died shortly thereafter, apparently the victim of London's climate, and his message was forgotten. It did not gibe with the current trend. This message was a very important one. He expressed the fear that "the apparatus that economists were erecting ... would stand in the way of a clear view of the more general aspects ..." of the problem. Many examples are to be found in Beach (1999) showing that such fear was justified.

Even if Young had lived, he would have probably been unsuccessful in stemming the flow of mathematical abstraction. Like Marshall, his students did not appreciate his message. At Harvard he had been the supervisor of a dissertation by Chamberlin, which was to become a well-known text on imperfect competition. Chamberlin (1932) used static tools with dynamic pretensions. At London, Young supervised the work of Kaldor who, not long after, published an article (Kaldor 1932) in which the concept of equilibrium was central to his analysis of technological unemployment. Salter was later to point out that the equilibrium assumption had little place in the analysis of technological change (Salter 1960). Some years later Kaldor (1972) recanted on the concept of equilibrium, expressing appreciation of Young's (1928) article. These three references, Young, Salter and Kaldor, are not given their due in the economic literature.

In summary it may be claimed that Marshall marked the start of modern economic analysis and suggested paths of progress towards realistic analysis. Unfortunately the profession chose to march off in a very different direction, towards abstraction, and is now facing an unbelieving and critical public.

Another matter that should be considered is the idea that Marshall was unduly nationalistic. In Victorian England that is perhaps understandable, if not forgivable in an economist. However, the whole Marshallian context should be considered. Central to Marshall's thought, as to that of Adam Smith (1776, 1904), was the question of how did the country achieve its economic status, and where was it likely to be going in the years ahead. The Wealth of Nations appeared just as the Industrial Revolution was reaching a high level of activity, and Marshall was teaching in the great period of Victorian England, the great empire period. These things had happened in England. He wished an explanation.

An important part of his answer was entrepreneurship in the form of businessmen, those ceaselessly striving, calculating people of the modern world. The English learned some important things from the Dutch in the sixteenth and seventeenth centuries. Knowledge of accounting and banking came earlier from northern Italy. During the nineteenth century, Englishmen were spreading their expertise across Europe.[5] It is particularly interesting that Marshall sensed a strong trend to improvement in morality among able businessmen.[6]

Winch was critical of Marshall (1969, 32): "He … had what many would regard as an exaggerated regard for the 'captain of industry' as a character type … Marshall's anxiety to maintain these virtues, rather than any specific economic doctrine, was the chief factor underlying his attitude to questions of individualism and socialism". This interpretation is quite wrong. The "captain of industry" was the instrument of change and development, which made the industrial revolution happen. Moreover the activities of these captains were an integral part of his "doctrines". This misinterpretation by such a respected economic historian is surprising.

Parsons (1932, p. 335) was more biting than Winch:

> Englishmen have often ridiculed Hegel for supposing that the evolution of the Weltgeist had taken place solely for the purpose of producing the Prussian state of the early nineteenth century. And yet Marshall, good Englishman that he was, supposes that the whole process leads to the production of the English businessman and artisan of the latter part of the same century. With all due respect to these worthy gentlemen, does anyone really suppose that they alone will inherit the earth? I am not here concerned with disputing the validity or propriety of Marshall's ethical conviction of the supreme value of one type of character. What is important is whether such subjective ethical convictions should be allowed to color the whole prospect of the past and present tendencies of social development as it undoubtedly does in the case of Marshall. The complete disregard of most other things which it entails is a narrow-mindedness hardly compatible with the ideal of scientific objectivity … he cannot be interpreted otherwise than as taking a position of the highest importance on the fundamental question he professes to ignore …

---

[5] When I first went to McGill University in Montreal, Canada, in 1940, many of the top brass were British – the principal, the dean of the faculty of graduate studies, the registrar and the secretary of the Board of Governors. Shortly afterwards we acquired two more who soon became vice principals. During my stay these officials were replaced by Canadians – many of whom had received some part of their training in other countries. Canadians wanted to run things themselves.

[6] Marshall wrote (1890, 1920, p. 303): "It is strong proof of the marvelous growth in recent times of a spirit of honesty and uprightness in commercial matters, that the leading officers of great public companies yield as little as they do to the vast temptations to fraud which lie in their way …"

Parsons (1931) continues in his fashion, arguing that Marshall wrote poor sociology. Marshall could have replied as he did to Cunningham's accusation that his history was inadequate. He was trying to write economics, not sociology, and certain factors were of special importance. Thus it could be said that Parsons wrote poor economics; indeed his sociology, in a broad sense, could be questioned. However one judges Marshall's appraisal of English businessmen, their importance in the development of the industrial revolution must be recognized.

In Industry and Trade (1923a, pp. 172–5) Marshall discusses "national character". It may be noted, in passing, that a feeling that Marshall is being nationalistic has alienated many readers, yet as emphasized elsewhere in this book, differences in national character are crucial to the question at issue, economic development. The Teutons did approach matters differently from the Latins.

Parsons' tirade on Marshall contrasts with the good things he wrote about Weber in his Translator's Preface (Weber 1958). Apparently, here he does not seem to appreciate the similarities in their themes. In an earlier article Parsons (1932) he clearly recognizes this similarity but suggests that Weber's analysis was based on rationality whereas that of Marshall seems to be little more than sentiment. It is interesting to note that Marshall makes no reference to Weber, and Weber does not refer to Marshall, although he mentions Petty several times. Perhaps it should be mentioned here that Weber's (1930, 1976) great work was on Religion and the Rise of Capitalism in which the ideas and habits of the people played a major role in the Industrial Revolution.

Maloney (1985, p. 198, 9) criticizes Parson's treatment of Marshall's handling of evolutionary and ethical questions,[7] as did Matthews (1990, p. 40). Coase (1990, p. 164): "Given Marshall's 'religion of self respect' the long run interdependence and compatibility of economic, social, characterological and ethical changes seemed assured; and this constituted the basis of Marshall's belief in the superiority of late nineteenth-century British society by comparison with both its past, and the contemporary state of less developed nations".

Marshall's praise of the character of the participants in the industrial progress of the nation stands in contrast to Smith's tendency to emphasize the undesirable traits of businessmen. Marshall was more appreciative of the contributions of such people, despite their faults, and perhaps of the environmental factors shaping that behaviour.

Contributions

Marshall established economics as a major subject for university study and he laid out the structure of analysis and programmes for study and research. He established a high respect for the subject, and his students became professors at other British

---

[7]O'Brien wrote (1990, p. 140) that "economists may have cited [Parsons] a little too uncritically".

universities. Cambridge became the university of choice for those who wished to study economics and so Keynes had a receptive audience in the 1930s.

We may take notice of specific areas of interest to illustrate these statements. First, we note that he recognized the importance of history in the study of economics. He had spent some time in Berlin, interested particularly in the German economic historians, and from Schmoller (1884) he took the phrase "walking on two feet".[8] The early editions of his Principles had a good deal of historical material in the early pages. In later editions he relegated most of this material to an appendix in recognition of criticisms, though he defended his approach against Cunningham (Marshall 1898). He stated that he was not trying to write history like an historian, but seeking material that is needed in the building of good economic analysis.

The study of economic history has all but disappeared from graduate studies in the leading universities. Even the study of the history of economic thought is disappearing, which is most unfortunate, because the history of the treatment of Marshall after his death illustrates that this history is not a simple linear accumulation, as in the sciences, but subject to serious aberrations and detours (Loasby 1971).

The current rage for modelling has produced models that are ahistorical, or worse, anti-historical. A case in point is one produced by Samuelson (1978) on Adam Smith's theory of economic growth. Hollander published some well-considered criticisms 2 years later, but they had no effect on Samuelson's conviction that he had captured the essence of Smith. He even went so far as to state that the classical political economists, Ricardo (1821) and J.S. Mill, did not know much about the real world. It is interesting to note that the latter was a longtime secretary of the East India Company and the former had made himself wealthy at an early age on the London markets, and has a history of notable speeches in the House of Commons.

One of Samuelson's colleagues, Robert Solow, once suggested (Solow 1965) that economics was much like physics in that each had low-powered theory and high-powered theory. There was an important difference, however, in that young physicists worked on their low-powered theory before they progressed to more difficult work – and the result had been very gratifying in the progress made in the understanding of physics. In economics, he said, he would not trust his students with low-powered theory until they had proven their merit with high-powered theory. Thus, he used abstract, mathematical analysis as a sieve. That is, of course, an accepted way to test the fundamental intelligence of students. Marshall himself stated that mathematics was perhaps the best preparation for the study of economics. But I can think of a number of areas where other studies are also important, and the theory of economic development is one of them. Moreover, Marshall's interest in mathematics did not preclude his ability to appreciate the broader context, as it seems to have done in many others.

Let us turn now to another area to be considered, that of mathematics itself. I have long struggled with this subject. In 1957 I published a book on Economic Models in

---

[8] Marshall did a much better job of it than Schmoller who "was extremely hostile to the abstract axiomatic-deductive method …" (Hagemann and Trautwein 1999).

which I recommended the use of more mathematics in order to sharpen up the arguments. Since then I have been suggesting more care with its use. I had long forgotten Marshall's cautions in the use of mathematics until I turned to his work later in life. I was surprised to find in his work, not the "static analysis" so often proclaimed by the critics,[9] but an approach that offers a live, dynamic concept of the real world. His simple abstractions are for instruction. In order to understand, repeated readings are necessary. The Prefaces of his Principles are purported to explain this. A comparison of the first and the eighth are instructive. Of course, the critics claim that this is but a statement of unfulfilled hopes. That is not so.

Marshall is, perhaps, himself to blame for some of this misunderstanding because he stated that the heart of his theory lay in Book V where he presents his static analysis of a market. He wished to emphasize the importance of the concepts of equilibrium and equilibrating forces. Careful study of the Principles reveals that he has much to say about these equilibrating forces, but little is done with the static concept of an equilibrium position. On page 461 of the 1920 edition we read: "The theory of stable equilibrium … when pushed to its more … intricate logical consequences … slips away from the conditions of real life … The statical theory of equilibrium is only an introduction to economic studies; and it is barely even an introduction to the study of progress and development of industries which show a tendency to increasing return".

These points may be brought out by some relevant examples. Pigou's first and probably his most important work which became known as The Economics of Welfare first saw light in 1915 (Pigou 1920). It was Pigou's re-working of Marshall's Chap. 13 of Book V on Maximum Satisfaction. Marshall was very cautious. Pigou was ambitious. He used the static concepts of supply and demand to derive far-reaching conclusions.

In 1922 Sraffa expressed his dissatisfaction with Marshall's analysis and sought more precise answers. In the course of the article he started with Marshall's concept of "free competition", which is a dynamic concept of people entering and leaving the markets for their many different reasons. But as Sraffa's argument progressed, the concept gradually transformed into the concept of "perfect competition", a static concept implying uniformity of price. Sraffa's conclusion that the monopoly concept be given more prominence is based upon this static concept. The subsequent publications by Robinson (1933) and Chamberlin are based on such static concepts.

In 1928 Pigou again illustrated his misunderstanding of Marshall. He suggested that the concept of "representative firm" (Robbins 1928) be replaced by the concept of "equilibrium firm". The former is a dynamic concept, inserted to simplify the complications of a moving complex of firms growing and failing, making changes daily. The latter concept kills any hope of dynamic analysis. Pigou's next goof was his Theory of Employment during the early depression years. He attempted to analyze employment with the concept of elasticity. This is certainly a static concept, even though Hicks

---

[9] See for example Hutchison (1953, pp. 79, 80).

tried to generalize it to "elasticity of expectations", with limited success. It is notable that this book by Pigou was the one which was subjected to severe criticism by Keynes in his General Theory. Keynes put Marshall in with the "classical" economists, but he could not find much in Marshall to base his criticisms.

Perhaps an aside may be injected. It is ironic that Pigou was so central in the growing use of static concepts. He was, after all, Marshall's choice of a successor to his chair, much to the discomfort of Marshall's friend, the economic historian, Foxwell (Coats 1972). But to Marshall at that time it was important to find a theorist to continue the momentum, which he had established at Cambridge in the development of economic theory. Unfortunately, Pigou reduced economic theorizing to a static level and missed a great opportunity for continuing Marshall's realistic analysis. Clearly Pigou could not match Marshall's talents.

And so Marshall's analysis has been condemned widely for being static, whereas it is his successors who have developed static theory. When Harrod (1946) was writing his lectures on Economic Dynamics, he re-read Marshall and found "no trace" of the kind of dynamics he expected. By that time Harrod was thinking, like Hicks, that dynamics was to be found in macroeconomics.

We tend to read his Principles too quickly without really tasting it. After all he spent long hours in revising the book, with eight editions. We should savour his words carefully. He thought that it was preferable to meet the arguments of critics by perfecting his presentation. But it should be noted that his students could not stand up to Sraffa's arguments.

It is interesting that two of his students, Robertson (1930) and Shove (1930), were unable to counter Sraffa's arguments in the famous symposium. One of them, Shove (1933), soon thereafter showed his Marshallian spirit. His 1932 review of Hicks' Theory of Wages was important. He notes Hicks' invention of the "elasticity of substitution" as a "nice bit of theory" but that it was not suitable for the purpose of analyzing actual events, as Hicks intended. Hicks felt the criticism and attempted a revision. This turned out to be in macro terms which Hicks felt represented dynamics. Schumpeter was later to proclaim (Schumpeter 1954, p. 684) that Hicks' static theory of labour substitution stilled the long and bitter argument over the matter of "compensation" because "it left nothing to argue about". How wrong he was can be seen in the continuance of that dispute.

This section may be concluded with more emphasis on Marshall's sense of realism. Schumpeter (1934) felt that it was misplaced. Yet his forecasts stand up well relative to those of Schumpeter (1942), who worried in Capitalism, Socialism and Democracy that social forces would undermine capitalism. He was too much influenced by Marx's social dynamics. In that book, before he presents Marx's dynamics, he has a chapter on Marshall explaining his concept of Marshall's dynamics, which is, of course, quite false.

Schumpeter's (1941) fascination with Marxian ideas, reflected again in his Capitalism, Socialism and Democracy, stands in contrast to the great postwar surge of capitalist vigour. Schumpeter's evaluation contrasts with Marshall's evaluation of the fundamental weakness of a controlled economy (Marshall 1907) that has not received its share of recognition. Marshall had long been interested in general welfare.

He had associated with the labour movement and with socialism movements. He sympathized with the interests of these groups, but felt that their economic analysis was deficient. In this 1907 article he stated that if a system were based on altruism rather than the drive of personal gain, it would fail because the work would not be done and rules and regulations would increase so as to smother the economy. Thus he forecasted the downfall of the communist system 10 years before it began.

Other Great Economists

An appreciation of Marshall's achievements can be expressed by considering his work in relation to the work of other economists. The contrasts help to clarify some very important issues in which Marshall's reach towards realism is crucial. The list need not be long.

Adam Smith

Smith's great achievement was the idea of an economic system that has an independent existence. Driven by market forces in the hands of energetic and far-sighted individuals, it builds up and uses economic resources, continually improving technology, to provide an ever-expanding output. It asks government to provide social stability and a rule of law, but little more – indeed this new system was created largely despite laws, limitations and restrictions imposed by oppressive and self-serving governments. It created a truly middle class, transforming society. A money economy was created in Western Europe, which spread throughout the world.

Marshall followed Smith's pattern of a continually unfolding society, driven by market forces, in which changing technology was an important aspect. Thus he tried "to present a modern version of old doctrines with the aid of the new work, and with reference to the new problems, of our own age (1890, 1920)".

Karl Marx

There are more of Marxian concerns in the Principles that may be apparent. In the early pages Marshall states that religion and economics were the two great motivating forces of mankind. He considers not just how people offer work and consume goods, but how these activities affect the people, which was an important concern of Marx (1867).

Marshall did not give much attention, in his Principles, to Marx. He might have helped his students if he had considered Marx's dynamics more specifically. Perhaps he did not consider Marx's interpretation of economic growth, in terms of accumulation based on greed, to be sufficiently respectable. Or perhaps he had little sympathy for a Marxian world that was driven by psychological or philosophical forces, with a sense of certainty, and with little place for market forces with all their irregularity and unpredictability. Certainly Marx was interested in how a society developed, as was Marshall, and some comments on Marxian methods and ideas would have been helpful. After all, the Marxian ideas spread widely and became a powerful force; and they were being presented to the world at the time that Marshall was forming his. The contrasts in their approaches and in their results could hardly have been more emphatic. Marshall was above all realistic. Marx's forecasts may almost be considered surrealistic. The "withering away" of the socialist state is perhaps the most dramatic, contrasting with Marshall's forecast of the downfall of communism. Increasing alienation is debatable, with so many people liking their jobs, and the prospect of increasing choice and mobility in the future. There has been no great decline in the rate of profit – except, as competition has tended to limit monopolizing.

Joseph Schumpeter

The work for which he is to be remembered is his theory of economic development. He was much enamoured with Marx's dynamics, but he made substantial changes. Marx's grasping capitalist became Schumpeter's entrepreneur with very constructive implications. The simple reproduction became a circular flow; expanded reproduction became a great leap forward in economic expansion. He kept with Marx's pessimism, as seen in a later work, Capitalism, Socialism and Democracy, in contrast with Smith. His use of the concept of a macro equilibrium circular flow was confusing.

It has been claimed that Marshall's emphasis on continuity has handicapped him in respect to adjusting to a Schumpeterian expansion (Moss 1982). The latter suggested that simply adding mail coaches would not make a train. However, in order to encompass a larger scene we need to simply enlarge the scope of the discussion. In considering the market for the transportation of goods in a certain region, the movement from horse-drawn wagons to trains is but an incident, like opening a new canal. Marshall's concept of economic progress can handle small and large change, and it should be noted that a multitude of small changes make a large difference. Some of these changes come in depression times. Salter tells us (1960, p. 5) "… in fact, many experienced observers rate the cumulative effect of small unnoticed modifications and improvements as equally great as the more significant changes normally regarded as innovations …"

J.M. Keynes

J.M. Keynes' *General Theory* (1936) changed the landscape of economics towards macroeconomics. A new generation of economists grew up thinking that Keynesian economics was essentially the whole of economics and that micro theory was but a small sideshow.

Keynes had a strong sense of reality as shown in his evaluation of the peace settlement of the First World War. He later played an important role in post Second World War monetary and fiscal international arrangements. His path-breaking General Theory was essentially realistic, recognizing an aspect of economics that had been neglected, but it was a strange mixture of statics and dynamics, and not easily understood. It is notable that many interpretations, expressed in models, emphasized statics, losing much of Keynes' attempt to emphasize dynamics.

F.A. von Hayek

This Austrian economist is noted for his opposition to Keynes' ideas. He seems to have missed the significance of the use of macro variables, lost in the worries about macro controls (von Hayek 1949, 1954). He is notable for reaching beyond economics in the narrow sense. In his writing of the Road to Serfdom (von Hayek 1944, 1972), he seems to have been quite unaware of Marshall's 1907 article. Like his fellow compatriot, Schumpeter, he seems to have been out of sympathy with Marshall. It could be that these continentals felt strongly Marshall's supposed racial bias. Both of them could have benefited from a true understanding of Marshall's ideas, and we would all of us have been better off.

Paul A. Samuelson

Samuelson is a great star of modern times, and he epitomizes the modern trend to the elaboration of the apparatus of analysis. A key to his thought is that the essence of a problem may be captured in some precise mathematical formulation, in contrast to Marshall's thought that when that abstraction is captured, the student has just begun his studies of the real problem. Sometimes, Marshall thought, the abstraction can mislead, and in such a case it should be discarded. Whitaker (1975) tells us that Marshall had worked out, quite early, a mathematical model of growth, much like some of the modern ones, but he seems to have discarded it because there is no vestige of it in his Principles. It would have some descriptive value, but its analytical value is limited.

Samuelson has argued that exchange and distribution are but facets of the same thing (1978). Such an argument requires that the elements be in equilibrium and in real life this is not so. In Marshall's 1898 article there are quotes to be found that might be seen as supporting Samuelson's position. On p. 66 we read: "… I venture to adhere to the opinion that distribution and exchange are fundamentally the same problem, looked at from different points of view". This statement should be read in the light of the controversies that had taken place over the years, and to be taken as an attempt to relate these elements as he did in using the scissors to integrate supply and demand in the case of value theory.

An important implication of this difference in analysis is the place of the theory of value. To Samuelson, the theory of value is central to all economic theory, and other aspects are derivable from it. For Marshall, economic progress is the "high theme" and an understanding of the theory of value is an essential step along the road to understanding how economic progress takes place. The concept of equilibrium is a tool to be used with care in analyzing these questions.

Further examples of the difference between the Samuelson and Marshall methods may be seen in Kuenne (1967) and Frisch (1981). Of special interest is Samuelson's classical canonical model (1978) in which Smithian growth is said to reach a plateau. He finds enough in The Wealth of Nations to support his theory, and will not be dissuaded (1980) by Hollander's careful presentation (1980) of evidence to the contrary. Dorfman (1991, p. 575) states a version of the Smithian model, which is that of Samuelson. However, Smith himself casts doubt on this model when, in discussing "the profits of stock" in Book I Chap. 9 writes: "But this complement [of stock] may be much inferior to what, with other laws and institutions … might admit of. A country which neglects or despises foreign commerce …" He continues in this fashion for many more lines. It should be noted, also, that the very important opening pages of The Wealth of Nations gives no hint of such general limitations on growth.

It appears that Samuelson should be regarded as a theorist who is unwilling to stay long with the grubby details of life. He is, at heart, a simplifier. In a letter to Edgeworth (Pigou 1966, p. 437) Marshall wrote: "… the work of the economist is to 'disentangle the interwoven effects of complex causes'; and that for this, general reasoning is essential, and that a combination of the two sides of the work is ALONE economics PROPER. Economic theory is, in my opinion, as mischievous an imposter when it claims to be economics proper as is mere crude unanalyzed history". The careful statements of the last two chapters of the Principles may be contrasted with Samuelson's less useful conclusions. In these two chapters we find the results of Marshall's "composition", his combining abstract theory and observation. There is much here for those interested in economic progress, but it has been ignored by both economists and historians.

Assessment

It has been thought that Keynesian theory sealed Marshall's coffin. We have not fully realized how much good macroanalysis must be based on good microanalysis. Any medical scientist would certainly agree. Microanalysis has been left for technicians. It should be re-evaluated.

Marshallian economics has been called obsolete. For economists generally his theory has the reputation of being static, fuzzy and even bankrupt. Such descriptions are inappropriate. We should turn, rather to Young's forgotten 1928 presidential address, which expresses admiration for the two great founders of realistic economics, Smith and Marshall, and explains misgivings about the work of the technicians who were more concerned with the "apparatus" of analysis rather than its substance. We must ask once again: What is economics? What is needed for its analysis? To what extent does economics differ from the natural sciences, and how should our approach differ from theirs?

In recent years there has been a good deal of attention given to differences of method, but I do not think that these discussions will lead very far until an alternative can be offered to current approaches. It is being suggested here that such an alternative can be created on the basis of Marshall's carefully thought out ideas. We need, first of all, the concept of an active, dynamic market such as Smith suggested, with a mixture of exogenous and equilibrating forces, producing changes continually.

Such a market as a strong active force is not the allocating market of Robbins (1932), Vickers (1995), and others, but a creative force pushing change and progress. A fall in supply brings alternative supplies. An increase in supply pushes down prices and leads to increased use of the product. An increase in demand brings more supply, and a fall in demand puts pressure on producers to lower prices. Inducement to improve production and provide new products is continuing.

Such an active market is not found in the early chapters of Marshall's Book V, because he concentrated on explaining the concept of equilibrium and the equilibrating forces. Such explaining was probably wise a century ago.[10] A dynamic market is seen in the rest of the Principles where the equilibrium condition is little used, but equilibrating forces are ubiquitous. Students should read carefully the Prefaces, and especially the Preface to the last, the eighth edition. Then they should be sure to read the very first chapter of the book, where there will be found material that is seldom seen in modern textbooks.

In addition there is a need for an understanding of the process of creation of real capital. When Marshall decided not to discuss money and credit in his Principles, it became difficult for him to produce a model of the process of development. Schumpeter has filled this need, with his portrayal of the expansion periods in business cycle history. However, his portrayal was flawed in his attachment to equilibrium situations, his theory of interest and his emphasis on explosive leaps as the whole story. This part of the theory of economic development remains to be written definitively.

It was Marshall who put together the technical analysis that is needed in a more satisfactory statement of the process of development. That is not to say that his techniques need not be improved, but the basis has been laid[11] with the help of Smith's beginning.[12] Marshall did not think in terms of producing a "model" of economic development. He wished to explain the nature of economic reasoning, and economic progress was the "high theme".

---

[10] Cf. Jevons's use (1871, 1931) of A causes B, which causes C.

[11] Marshall's contributions include the concepts of representative firms and internal and external economies, which have a place in a Smithian dynamic world. The key role of the businessman is established.

[12] Smith's contributions include the concepts of an active market, technical improvement, and with continuing change, the need for social and political flexibility.

References

Beach EF (1982) Samuelsonian theory and the process of change. In: Feiwel G (ed) Samuelson and Neoclassical economics. Kluwer, Boston

Beach EF (1999) Progress and prosperity. Trafford, Victoria

Brems H (1986) Pioneering economic theory 1630–1980. John Hopkins, Baltimore

Cannan E (ed) (1893, 1917) A history of the theories of production and distribution. King, London

Cannan E (ed) (1930) A review of economic theory. King, London

Chamberlin EH (1932) The theory of monopolistic competition. Harvard University Press, Cambridge

Coase RH (1990) Alfred Marshall's family and ancestry. In: Tullberg RM (ed) Alfred Marshall in retrospect. Edward Elgar, Aldershot

Coats AW (1972) The appointment of Pigou as Marshall's successor: comment. J Law Econ 15(2):487–495

Cunningham W (1892) The perversion of economic history. Econ J 2(7):491–506

Frisch H (ed) (1981) Schumpeterian economics. Praeger, New York, NY

Frisch R (1936) On the notion of equilibrium and disequilibrium. Rev Econ Studies 3:100–105

Groenwegen P (1995) A soaring eagle: Alfred Marshall 1842–1924. Edward Elgar, Aldershot

Groenwegen P (ed) (1996) Official papers of Alfred Marshall, a supplement. Cambridge University Press, Cambridge

Hagemann H, Hans-Michael T (1999) Verein fuer Socialpolitik – the Association of German-speaking Economists. Royal Economic Society Newsletter, issue 107, October

Harrod RF (1946) Towards a dynamic economics. Macmillan, London

von Hayek FA (ed) (1944, 1972) The road to serfdom. University of Chicago Press, Chicago, IL

von Hayek FA (ed) (1949) Individualism and economic order. Routledge, London

von Hayek FA (ed) (1954) Capitalism and the historians. University of Chicago Press, Chicago, IL

Hicks JR (1932, 1963) Theory of wages. Macmillan, London

Hicks JR (1971) Reply to Professor Beach. Econ J 71(324):922–925

Hicks JR (1973) Capital and time. Clarendon, Oxford

Hicks JR (1982) Money, interest and wages. Harvard University Press, Cambridge, MA

Hollander S (1980) On Professor Samuelson's canonical model of political economy. J Econ Lit 18(2):559–574

Homan PT (1928) Contemporary economic thought. Harper, New York, NY

Hutchison TW (1953) A review of economic doctrines. Clarendon, Oxford

Stanley JW (1871, 1931) The theory of political economy. Macmillan, London

Kaldor N (1932) A case against technical progress? Economica 12:180–196

Kaldor N (1972) The irrelevance of equilibrium economics. Econ J 82(328):1237–1255

Keynes JM (1924) Alfred Marshall 1842–1924. Econ J 34(135):311–372; reprinted in Pigou AC (1925), Memorials of Alfred Marshall. Kelley, New York (1966)

Keynes JM (1936) 1973. The general theory of employment, interest, and money. Vol. 7 of The Collected Writings of John Maynard Keynes. Macmillan, London

Kuenne RE (1967) Monopolistic competition theory. Wiley, New York, NY

Landes DS (1998) The wealth and poverty of nations: why some are so rich and some are so poor. W.W. Norton, New York, NY

Loasby BJ (1971) Hypothesis and paradigm in the theory of the firm. Econ J 71(81):863–885

Maloney J (1985) Marshall, orthodoxy and the professionalisation of economics. Cambridge University Press, Cambridge

Maloney J (1990) Marshall and business. In: Tullberg RM (ed) Alfred Marshall in retrospect. Edward Elgar, Aldershot

Malthus TR (1798) An essay on the principle of population. Kelley, New York, NY (1967)

Marshall A (1890, 1920) Principles of economics. Macmillan, London

Marshall A (1892) A reply. Econ J 2(7):506–519

Marshall A (1898) Distribution and exchange. Econ J 8(20)37–59; reprinted in Guillebaud CW (ed) (1961) Marshall's principles of economics, vol 2. Cambridge University Press, Cambridge, pp 62–76

Marshall A (1907) The social possibilities of economic chivalry. Econ J 17(65):7–29, reprinted in Pigou AC (1925) Memorials of Alfred Marshall. Macmillan, London, reprinted by Kelley, New York, NY (1966)

Marshall A (1923a) Industry and trade. Macmillan, London

Marshall A (1923b) Money credit and commerce. Macmillan, London

Marshall A (1961) Principles of economics, 9th (variorum) edition with annotations by Guillebaud CW (ed), two volumes. Macmillan for the Royal Economic Society, London.

Marx K (1867) Capital, vol 1, original English translation by Moore S, Aveling E, revised from the 4th German edition by Untermann E (1906) Kerr, Chicago. Volumes II and III published in 1884, 1885, translated by Untermann E, Kerr, Chicago, IL (1909)

Moss L (1982) Biological theory and technological entrepreneurship in Marshall's writings. Eastern Econ J 8(1):3–13

O'Brien DP (1997) Marshall and his correspondence. Econ J 107(445):1859–1885

Parsons T (1931) Wants and activities in Marshall. Q J Econ 46:101–140

Parsons T (1932) Economics and sociology: Marshall in relation to the thought of his time. Q J Econ 46:316–347

Pigou AC (1920) The economics of welfare. Macmillan, London

Pigou AC (1925) Memorials of Alfred Marshall. Macmillan, London; reprinted by Kelley, New York, NY (1966)

Pigou AC (1928) Analysis of supply. Econ J 38(150):236–257

Pigou AC (1933) The theory of unemployment. Macmillan, London

Ricardo D (1821) Principles of political economy and taxation, Gonner ECK (ed) (1932) London: G. Bell

Robbins L (1928) The representative firm. Econ J 38(151):387–404

Robbins L (1930) On a certain ambiguity in the conception of stationary equilibrium. Econ J 40(158):194–214

Robbins L (1932) Essay on the nature and significance of economic science. New York University Press, New York, NY

Robertson DH (1930) Increasing returns and the representative firm. Econ J 40(1257):80–89

Robinson J (1933) The economics of imperfect competition. Macmillan, London

Salter WEG (1960) Productivity and technical change. Cambridge University Press, Cambridge

Samuelson PA (1947) Foundations of economic analysis. Harvard University Press, Cambridge

Samuelson PA (1967) The monopolistic revolution. In: Kuenne RE (ed) Monopolistic competition theory. Wiley, New York, NY

Samuelson PA (1978) The canonical model of classical political economy. J Econ Lit 16:1415–1434

Schmoller G (1884), The Mercantile system and its historical significance, reprinted by Kelley, New York, NY (1967)

Schumpeter JA (1934) The theory of economic development. Harvard University Press, Cambridge

Schumpeter JA (1941) Alfred Marshall's principles: a semi-centennial appraisal. Am Econ Rev 31(2):236–248

Schumpeter JA (1942) Capitalism, socialism and democracy. Harper, New York, NY

Schumpeter JA (1954) History of economic analysis. Oxford University Press, New York

Seligman B (1966) Most notorious victory. Free Press, New York, NY

Shove GF (1930) Increasing returns and the representative firm. Econ J 40(157):94–116

Shove GF (1933) Review of Hicks's theory of wages. Econ J 43(171)460–472, reprinted in Hicks JR (1966) Theory of wages. Macmillan, London

Smith A (1776, 1904), An inquiry into the nature and causes of the wealth of nations, reprinted by Oxford University Press, New York (1904)

Solow RM (1965) Capital theory and the rate of return. Rand McNally, Chicago, IL

Sombart W (1967) The quintessence of capitalism (translated by M. Fertig). Epstein, New York, NY

Sraffa P (1926) The laws of return under competitive conditions. Econ J 36(144):535–550
Vickers D (1995) The tyranny of the market. University of Michigan, Ann Arbor, MI
Weber M (1930, 1976) The Protestant ethic and the spirit of capitalism (translated by Talcott Parsons). Allen & Unwin, London
Weber M (1958) The Protestant Ethic and the Spirit of Capitalism, Scribner's Press, New York
Whitaker JK (1975) The early writings of Alfred Marshall 1867–1890, 2 vols. The Royal Economic Society, London
Winch D (1969) Economics and policy: a historical study. Hodder & Stoughton, New York, NY
Young A (1913) Pigou's wealth and welfare. Q J Econ 27:672–686
Young A (1928) Increasing returns and economic progress. Econ J 38(152):527–542

Chapter 20
Knut Wicksell and Contemporary Political Economy

Richard E. Wagner

Introduction

After briefly sketching the life and times of Knut Wicksell, three primary lines of contribution are examined to illustrate Wicksell's contemporary relevance. The first is Wicksell's treatment of capital and production in relation to the theory of marginal productivity. The second is Wicksell's contribution to monetary theory, economic stability, and coordinationist macroeconomics. The third is Wicksell's contribution to just taxation and the theory of public finance. While portions of each of these three examinations will be purely descriptive, considerable attention will also be given in each part to some contemporary themes that can plausibly be claimed to reflect a Wicksellian orientation.

Suppose someone were to compile a list of all economists whose published work spanned the nineteenth and twentieth centuries, and were then to ask contemporary economists to rank those earlier economists. I am positive that Knut Wicksell would appear in the top ten in that subsequent ranking. He would most likely make the top five, and would surely receive a good number of votes for number one. This strong reputation was achieved, moreover, by someone who turned to economics only around the age of 40, and who then pursued economics mostly on a part-time basis because journalism and social agitation were continually making claims on his time. I shall begin this presentation by sketching briefly Wicksell's life and work, after which I shall describe and examine the three areas of Wicksell's work that account for most of his scholarly reputation. These are his contributions to marginal productivity theory, his integration of capital and money to provide a framework for exploring macro fluctuations, and his theorizing about public finance and collective action.

I should perhaps note that it is not my intent here to engage in any effort at historical reconstruction. Rather, my intent is to undertake a form of contemporaneous

R.E. Wagner (✉)
Department of Economics, George Mason University, Fairfax, VA 22030, USA
e-mail: rwagner@gmu.edu

J.G. Backhaus (ed.), *Handbook of the History of Economic Thought,*
The European Heritage in Economics and the Social Sciences,
DOI 10.1007/978-1-4419-8336-7_20, © Springer Science+Business Media, LLC 2012

reflection upon some of the places where Wicksell's work speaks to contemporary issues in economic theory, thereby placing Wicksell within the "extended present," to use a term from Kenneth Boulding (1971). Let me give a brief illustration of the distinction I have in mind. David Davidson was a contemporary of Wicksell's who engaged in a substantial controversy with Wicksell over the conditions for monetary stability. Where Wicksell argued that stable prices would promote stability, Davidson argued that Wicksell's own framework required falling prices. An effort at historical construction would seek to bring the reader into the context of those debates, giving the reader a sense of watching the action unfold. My focus on contemporaneous reflection would seek only to explore whether Wicksell's formulations have any relevance for contemporary discussion.[1]

Knut Wicksell's Life and Work

The facts surrounding Knut Wicksell's life, while probably more interesting than those of most economists, can be relayed briefly. He entered this world in 1851, on the 20th of December. He departed nearly half-way through his 75th year, on the 3rd of May 1926. He was the youngest of five children, three of whom were girls. His mother died when he was six. When Knut was ten, his father brought a stepmother into the house. Five years later, Knut's father died.

Wicksell was always an outstanding student, and in 1869, he entered the University of Uppsala. He graduated in 1872, and then continued with advanced studies in mathematics and physics. In his early ears, Wicksell was religiously devout and participated regularly in Church services. In his 23rd year, in 1874, he experienced a crisis of faith, brought on by his belief that he could not reconcile the claims of religion and the requirements of science. Wicksell chose for science, and ejected the Church from the rest of his life. He did, however, receive a Christian burial, though this was his wife's doing.

Wicksell might have seemed poised on the verge of a scholarly career in 1874, but this didn't happen. A quarter of a century would pass before Wicksell would take a place within the academy. This quarter of a century was a period of energetic activity, mostly of a journalistic nature. While he continued his mathematical studies, he became increasingly interested in the neo-Malthusian orientation toward population questions. Wicksell became increasingly active in lecturing and writing on population, immigration, birth control, alcoholism, and a variety of related issues that so firmly established his standing as a social agitator that he became a subject for cartoonists. Wicksell's fervently radical nature did not wane as he aged. In his 57th year, for instance, he was convicted and imprisoned for 2 months for blasphemy.[2]

---

[1] For a contemporary statement of the issues that were joined in this debate, see George Selgin (1997).

[2] To be sure, Gardlund's (1958, 249–250) description of Wicksell's prison quarters creates an image of a minimun security, country club type of arrangement, where he could have his own furniture and food. He had to scrub the floor of his cell once a week, and other than that was able pretty much to read and write as he chose.

In late 1885, Wicksell went to London, sponsored by a grant from the Lorén Foundation. There, he studied such economists as Walras, Jevons, and Gossen, and developed an appreciation for the application of marginalist theory to economics. He continued his journalism, but thereafter his attention was drawn increasingly toward economics, which he continued to pursue by visiting a number of European universities.

In 1893, at age 41, Wicksell saw the publication of his first book-length contribution to economic theory. This was *Value, Capital, and Rent*, which quickly became a well-regarded statement of marginal utility, capital, and the structure of production. Despite the book's outstanding achievement, Wicksell recognized that the university authorities were not going to award him the doctorate for it. So he changed fields of study to fiscal law, and wrote a study on tax incidence that brought him the doctorate in 1895.[3]

While turning to the study of law and moving through the curriculum at twice the normal pace, Wicksell continued to pursue his economic investigations. He published a second classic-to-be, *Interest and Prices*, in 1898. This was a substantial statement on monetary theory, where Wicksell presented his alternative to the quantity theory of money and developed the distinction between the natural and the loan or market rate of interest that came quickly to occupy a prominent place in monetary theory. Despite possessing a publication record that would ensure him a secure place in anyone's Economics Hall of Fame, Wicksell still had no academic position, though he was now getting close. He finally received a docent position in Uppsala in 1899, and then took a temporary position in Lund in 1900. That position became permanent in 1901, the same year that the first volume of his *Lectures on Political Economy* was published. He stayed there until his retirement in 1916, when he returned to Stockholm.

Wicksell died 10 years later, and his wife, Anna Bugge, whom he married in Paris in 1889, died 2 years later. They had two sons: Sven, born in 1890, and Finn, born in 1893. Anna and Knut fell upon one of the most painful of life's possible experiences, when they had to bury one of their children. This they did in 1913, when Finn, a 19-year-old medical student at the time, did not survive his fall from a window. Sven, by contrast, lived to bury both of his parents, surviving his mother by 11 years.

Primary Analytical Contributions

While Wicksell's contributions to economic analysis are dispersed across more than 100 items, the central features of the contributions on which his reputation rests can be found in five books. Two of these have already been noted, *Value, Capital, and Rent* (1893) and *Interest and Prices* (1898). Refinements and extensions of the themes portrayed in those volumes were presented in his two volumes of *Lectures on Political Economy* (1901, 1906), with the first volume exploring value and distribution and the second volume exploring money. The fifth volume was Wicksell's contribution to public finance, *Finanztheoretische Untersuchungen* (1896).

---

[3] In what was normally a 4-year program of study, Wicksell completed all the requirements in 2 years.

This book contained three essays, the second of which made Wicksell a household word among public finance scholars after it was translated and published as "A New Principle of Just Taxation" in the *Classics in the Theory of Public Finance* (1958), edited by Richard Musgrave and Alan Peacock.

In the presentation and discussion of Wicksell's work that follows, I organize the material into three parts. First, I consider Wicksell's contribution to theories of capital, production, and marginal productivity. Wicksell followed Eugon Böhm-Bawerk (1884–89) in adopting an orientation that conceptualized production as a sequence of stages, where consumer goods at the bottom are supported by a structure of capital goods. Some of those capital goods are close in time to where they will yield consumer goods, while others are far away. What governs this structure of production, what might loosely be called the length of the production structure, is the rate of time preference held by people within the society in conjunction with the potential yield from new forms of capital goods. This Wicksell described in *Value, Capital, and Rent*, along with further examination in *Lectures on Political Economy, I.*

Second, I examine Wicksell's contribution to money, interest, and economic stability. In Wicksell's formulation, as well as in Böhm-Bawerk's, interest was not just one more price to take its place with all other market prices. Rather, interest infused itself throughout the entire network of prices. Indeed, the structure of production was what it was and not something else, because the rate of interest was what it was and not something else. For instance, a decline in interest that followed a fall in time preference would alter the entire structure of prices. This, in turn, would make the production of relatively higher order capital goods more profitable relative to lower order capital goods, which would bring about a change in the structure of production. Monetary changes could thus affect production relationships throughout a society, through changes in the market rate of interest. Wicksell's contributions on these matters are presented in *Interest and Prices* and *Lectures on Political Economy, II.*

Third, I examine Wicksell's contribution to public finance. His major book on public finance was published in 1896, *Finanztheoretische Untersuchungen*. The first of the books' three essays undertook an analysis of tax incidence while making use of Böhm-Bawerk's framework of a structure of production. This essay on tax incidence has been vastly overshadowed by his second essay on a new principle of just taxation. This essay asked what kind of institutional framework for parliamentary governance might make it possible for the state to act as a productive participant within the economic life of a society. Hardly anyone would dispute the statement that a government should expand its services so long as the value that is created exceeds the cost that people must bear through the value they must sacrifice to pay for those services. But how might this situation actually be achieved? The difficulty of the challenge has led many scholars to avoid it, either by refusing to examine government or by asserting that the appropriate budgetary magnitudes are tautologically those that governments establish. In contrast to those scholars, Wicksell approached the topic directly. He advanced an institutional framework for accomplishing this end, and in so doing showed how the Pareto principle could be made applicable to the state, which is something that Pareto did not think possible.[4]

Capital, Production, and Stationary States

A huge turn-of-the-century controversy developed among economists over the laws of return.[5] The marginal productivity theory of factor pricing held that the prices paid to inputs were equal to the values of their marginal products. All units of a like input receive the price received by the marginal input. This formulation brought the problem of adding up or product exhaustion to the foreground of analytical attention. Let total output be produced by the two inputs, labor and capital. Each unit of labor is priced at its marginal product, and so is each unit of capital. The total amount paid to labor is the product of the marginal product of labor and the amount of labor. Similarly, the total amount paid to capital is the product of the marginal product of capital and the amount of capital.

The problem of product exhaustion concerns whether the total amount paid to the inputs adds up to the total amount of product. Logically, there are three possibilities. One is where input payments are exactly equal to the total product. This would seem to be a happy situation, much like a clerk whose cash box balances at the end of a day. As with the case of the clerk, there are two situations that are not so conducive to a restful repose. One is over-exhaustion of the product. Not enough product is available for factors to be paid according to their marginal products. People will have to accept less than the values of their marginal products to cover the deficiency. The other unhappy situation is under-exhaustion. In this case, there is product left over after factors have been paid according to their marginal products. There is a surplus value for someone to capture or otherwise distribute.

The theorists of the time were attracted to the nice properties of exact exhaustion. A regime of free competition would seem more pleasant if it turned out that payments according to marginal productivity were to equal exactly the amount produced within the economy. A theorem from Euler showed that this would happen if output in a society were generated according to a production function that was linear and homogeneous. The aggregate production function acquired significance in economic discourse that it has never lost, despite its obviously fictive character. Where some authors were content to postulate linear homogeneity as an assumption and proceed, Wicksell took the argument further. Suppose exact exhaustion did not prevail. This would mean that some people were getting too much or too little, in comparison with their marginal products. Under free competition, this situation was

[4] On Wicksell and Pareto in this respect, see Hennipman (1982). More generally on the Pareto principle, see Backhaus (1980). For a general treatment of Wicksell's thought, see Uhr (1960).

[5] The various historical contributions are presented and assessed in George Stigler (1941).

not consistent with a stationary state. People would be repelled from situations where they were asked to take less than their marginal products. They would be attracted into situations where they could receive more than their marginal products. Hence, a stationary equilibrium will require product exhaustion. This does not require some production function to be linearly homogeneous, but only that an existing production function shares a point of tangency with such a function.

Product exhaustion under free competition was thought by many to be an important attribute of a social order based on free competition. Many of the turn-of-the-century economists participated in the controversy over marginal productivity ethics, as illustrated by a claim to the effect that justice resides in free competition and a linearly homogeneous production function. Such notables as Leon Walras, Vilfredo Pareto, and John Bates Clark argued that free competition was a process that maximized welfare within a society. If each trade improves the welfare of the traders, and if free competition is just a name for a gigantic network of such trades, it would seem tempting to advance such a claim.

Wicksell did not join those who advanced this claim. He rejected marginal productivity ethics on the grounds of what is now known as the second theorem of welfare economics. The first theorem reflects what was just stated, namely that free competition generates an allocation of resources where it is impossible to make one person better off without making someone else worse off. The second theorem states that there are an indefinite number of such competitive allocations, with one such allocation being transformable into another through an appropriate set of lump sum taxes and transfers. The second theorem makes any welfare evaluation of free competition contingent upon an evaluation of the initial starting points possessed by the various participants.

The tenacious hold of marginal productivity theory on the allegiance of economists is simultaneously troubling and instructive. It is troubling because of its readily apparent inadequacies. It is a totally logical construction that is disconnected from any movement of a society through time. To be sure, stationary state modeling commanded stronger allegiance among economists a century ago than it does now. Wicksell, for his part, seemed to think that a model of a stationary state was not too bad of an approximation. He thought that the nineteenth century was a period of rapid invention that was not likely to be repeated in the future. It is notable that marginal productivity theory has been subject to precious little effort at direct testing that would develop independent estimates of marginal productivity and check those observations against actual factor payments. To the contrary, their typical procedure is to take observed factor payments as a measure of marginal products.

At the same time, the experience with the survival of marginal productivity theory provides excellent instruction about the often-made point that it takes a theory, not a criticism, to displace a theory. While marginal productivity theory has no independent claim to scientific validity, it is an essential building block in the edifice of contemporary general equilibrium theory. Take away marginal productivity theory, and theories concerning factor markets and business firms loose their explanatory punch.

While Wicksell developed his analysis of marginal productivity within the framework of a stationary state, he also worked with the notion of a structure of production. Within a stationary state, however, a structure of production adds nothing but analytical clutter. Consider a simple process where wine is aged 8 years before it is consumed. In the stationary setting, wine that is 8 years old is replaced each year by new wine, with the older wine then consumed. A Böhm-Bawerkian or Wicksellian production function would state that $X = f(L,K,t)$, where L denotes labor input, K capital input, and t the passing of time.

In the stationary state, however, the incorporation of time adds complexity without changing anything else, and so, following the razor principle articulated by William of Ockham, time should be dropped from consideration. In the same year that new wine is laid down, wine that is 8 years old is consumed. The production of wine can be written more simply as $X = f(L,K)$. This ability to eliminate time from a structure of production, and to characterize the process of production as a circular flow instead, was articulated strongly by Joseph Schumpeter (1934) in his *Theory of Economic Development*. The economics of stationary states generated far greater analytical tractability with the mathematical techniques that economists were using, which may help to give some account for the popularity of stationary state economics throughout the twentieth century. To do this, of course, is to allow economics to be driven by its techniques rather than by its phenomena.[6]

A focus on a structure of production in place of a circular flow requires a vision of the economic process other than that of a stationary state. The methods that economists have used throughout most of the twentieth century, however, were more suitable for the examination of equilibrium stationary states. With the growing interest in evolutionary and other forms of non-equilibrium modeling that is now underway, I think it is quite likely that economists will come more fully to incorporate structural formulations of production into their models.[7]

Money, Interest, and a Coordinationist Macroeconomics

The structure of production within a society is governed by time preferences and the opportunities for the productive employment of capital. Consider such an elemental aspect of life as the ability to consume potable water. The supply of potable water that is available within a society can be expanded by the development of bottling facilities, the construction of reservoirs, and through research into such matters as the treatment and recycling of waste water and technologies for reducing evaporation. An expansion in bottling capacity will result pretty quickly in an increased availability of water. The construction of a reservoir will require a longer wait before increased water is available for consumption. The creation of a laboratory to

---

[6] Schumpeter, to be sure, did not take a stationary state seriously as a description of reality. Rather he had a modeling strategy were a stationary state was continually punctuated by episodes of entrepreneurial creativity.

[7] For one interesting effort to pursue non-equilibrium, as distinct from either equilibrium or disequilibrium, see Donald Katzner (1998).

conduct research into methods of treatment, and the technologies to implement those methods, will involve a still longer period before the fruits show up in an increased availability of water for current consumption. Research into evaporation may take even longer to yield increased supplies of potable water.

What governs the concrete structure of production within a society is the willingness of people to delay consumption, which is represented by time preference, in relation to the returns from doing so. A society whose members truly believed that the end of the world was at hand would construct neither laboratories nor reservoirs. Whether water might be bottled would depend on just what concrete duration "at hand" might refer to. In any case, lower rates of time preference within a society would correspond generally to a structure of production that included a larger number of projects whose contribution to consumption resided in the future.[8] Time preference would also play a part in governing such things as how many resources are placed into bottling and otherwise storing water, relative to resources placed into such activities as research into water purification or evaporation.

To this framework of a structure of production, Wicksell postulated the existence of two distinct rates of interest. One was the natural rate of interest. This is a purely analytical construct, as distinct from the interest rates that can be observed directly on the financial pages of newspapers. It is the rate of interest that would generate an equilibrium structure or pattern of production in light of time preferences and the returns from the creation of capital goods. As an exercise in comparative statics, a fall in the natural rate of interest would lead to a deepening of the structure of production, whereas a rise would lead to a more shallow structure of production.

The natural rate of interest is a kind of analytical foil that accepts the contemporary convention among economists that the real economy can be directly accessed independently of money-assisted inference. There is no room in this formulation for any recognition that money, like language, is a tool for reasoned thought. This construction leads to a general equilibrium theory of a barter economy, where money is introduced as an afterthought. The reality, of course, is that modern economic life would have been impossible without money, just as it would have been impossible without language. This formulation in terms of a general equilibrium of the real economy injects a massive fiction to attain analytical tractability, though the nature of this tradeoff is much clearer now than it was a century ago.[9]

The natural rate of interest is the imagined rate of interest that secures equilibrium within the structure of production, as this was modeled in the barter economy of general equilibrium theory. Within this equilibrium constellation of relationships,

---

[8] I think it is possible to acknowledge the general validity of this orientation toward a time structure of production without professing any ability actually to develop some measure of the average period of production within a society.

[9] Ulrich Witt (1997) explains that F. A. Hayek fell into the same trap in his neo-Wicksellian formulation of business cycle theory. He started from a model of general equilibrium, as that was the only option that was available at the time. This point of departure was, however, inconsistent with his work on the use of knowledge in society, particularly when put in the context of a process of continual development, which he came subsequently to pursue.

the market rate of interest on actual loans would equal the natural rate of interest. This equality was invoked as a necessary condition for equilibrium, just as product exhaustion was invoked as a necessary condition for equilibrium.

Anything that disturbed the equality between the natural and loan rates of interest would disturb the stationary equilibrium. Any divergence between the two rates would set in motion a process of expansion or contraction. Which would occur would depend on the direction of divergence. For instance, the invention of new technologies might increase the natural rate of interest. With a loan rate that now provided entrepreneurs with profitable borrowing opportunities that were not there prior to the invention of the new technologies, a capital expansion will take place, and will continue until the two rates are restored to equality once again. Wicksell's analytics in *Interest and Prices* were of real changes that led to changes in the structure of production.

Wicksell's work on capital and money helped to generate a new approach to the explanation of business cycles. Ludwig von Mises (1934) took the step in 1912, in his *Theory of Money and Credit*, of letting the divergence of interest rates start from an expansion in bank credit. In this case, what resulted was a change in the structure of production that was only temporary. Hayek (1932, 1935) extended this neo-Wicksellian approach to business cycles in *Monetary Theory and the Trade Cycle* and *Prices and Production*. Arising around the same time as this Austrian literature on business cycles was a Swedish literature that was developed by such scholars as Erik Lindahl, Gunnar Myrdal, and Erik Lundberg.

Both the Swedish and Austrian formulations of business cycle theory can be reasonably designated as neo-Wicksellian enterprises. After the 1976 Nobel Prize was awarded jointly to Myrdal and Hayek, I recall hearing and reading a number of commentaries to the effect that this was an award grounded in lunacy. The reasons for this alleged lunacy, however, were based on the political orientations of the mid-1970. Myrdal was a social democrat. Hayek was a liberal in the classic tradition, or what these days is called a libertarian in the US. In the 1930, however, Myrdal and Hayek shared a similar orientation toward economic instability. At base, instability was rooted in pricing problems due to the operation of money and credit that led to miscoordination in saving-investment relationships. Business cycles were conceptualized as products of miscoordination among market participants. Whereas we normally assert that market prices facilitate economic coordination, the neo-Wicksellian approach to cycles sought to explore how market prices might generate miscoordination.

In the business cycle literature in the 1930, the Austrian and Swedish contributions commanded strong professional respect. This can be seen clearly by consulting such treatises as Gottfried Haberler (1937) and Alec Macfie (1934). To be sure, these were not the only approaches that were discussed at that time. A version of monetarism, associated particularly strongly with Ralph Hawtry, also commanded professional respect. Twenty years later, the length of time that Rip van Winkle napped, the professional landscape had changed dramatically. The Austrian and Swedish approaches had disappeared from the analytical radar screens of economists. Monetarism was still present, and now the Keynesian formulations also had a mighty presence.

This sudden change in 20 years is surely somewhat of a mystery, at least if it is approached in terms of conventional notions about scientific procedure. Early in this century, people believed in Piltdown Man. But those beliefs quickly vanished in the face of massively disconfirming evidence that revealed the original story to have been a hoax. There is nothing about the Great Depression, however, that constitutes strong disconfirmation of the Austrian or Swedish formulations. There is nothing about the Great Depression that would reveal obviously superior explanatory powers for monetarist or Keynesian formulations than for the Swedish or Austrian formulations. And yet a description of the intellectual landscape written in the 1950 would differ dramatically from one written in the 1930.[10]

It could be argued that the Keynesian orientation incorporated the Austrian and Swedish orientations. After all, Keynes also located cycles as stemming from miscoordinations between saving and investment. This much is true. Yet there are also vast differences between the two orientations. The Keynesian orientation divorces the micro and macro realms, whereas the Austrian and Swedish orientations seek to weave them into a seamless garment. For instance, Erik Lindahl (1939, pp. 51–53) distinguished micro from macro very differently than is done now. Micro referred to individuals, whereas macro referred to all forms of interaction among individual units. In this Swedish-Austrian orientation, macro emerges out of micro interactions. One macro variable never acts directly upon another macro variable, for any such action is intermediated through micro relationships. To be sure, there are a number of signs of a growing awareness of bringing genuine coordination problems back into macro theory, a good illustration of which is Leijonhufvud (1981). I think there is a good chance that people describing the state of business cycle theory 20 years hence will refer once again to a neo-Wicksellian frame of reference, in one fashion or another.[11]

Just Taxation and the Theory of Public Finance

Two principle approaches to public finance can be identified today, and Knut Wicksell stands as the primary source of influence over one of those approaches. If those two approaches were to be identified in terms of economists who wrote a century ago, they could well be identified as the Edgeworthian and Wicksellian approaches. The Edgeworthian approach to public finance locates the state outside the economic process. The state is construed as an entity that intervenes into the economy to promote its purposes; however, these might be defined. Usually, these purposes are defined in terms of some notion of maximizing a social welfare function. In any case, and most significantly, the phenomena of public finance arise out of the choices of some maximizing entity and represent interventions into the economy to bring about different outcomes from what would otherwise have resulted.

---

[10] One such description that first appeared in 1952 is Robert Gordon (1961).

[11] I expand upon this belief in Wagner (1999).

The Wicksellian approach construes the state as a participant within the economic process. The state itself is a process or a framework of rules and procedures that governs human relationships. Fiscal phenomena do not result from the optimizing choices of some exogenous being, but rather emerge through interactions among participants within various fiscal and political processes. Those interactions, in turn, are shaped and constrained by a variety of conventions, institutions, and organizational rules. Fiscal phenomena, like market phenomena, are catallactical and not choice theoretic phenomena.[12] The size and extent of governmental activity, within the Wicksellian orientation, is to be explained with references to the same principles that are used to explain other features of economic activity within a society. The same categories of utility, cost, demand, supply, productivity, and the like are to be brought to bear upon the explanation of fiscal phenomena as are brought to bear on the explanation of market phenomena.

Wicksell's particular institutional interest was his effort to describe a network of institutional relationships that would make it possible for people in their capacities as taxpayers reasonably to say that their tax monies were directed as they wished. The ability for people to say this would locate government on the same plane as other economic participants. Wicksell assumed that through proportional representation it would be possible to select a parliament that would serve reasonably well as a miniature model of the Swedish population. If this parliament were then bound by a rule of unanimity, its decisions would conform closely to unanimity within the underlying population. The state would participate within the economic process on the same terms as other participants. Its size relative to that of other organizations in society would depend on the effectiveness of its officers in gaining acceptance for proposals in parliament, relative to the ability of other producers to gain favor from people.

Wicksell did not truly advocate a rule of unanimity. Rather he articulated a principle of unanimity, which he relaxed to a practical rule of approximate unanimity, which he illustrated by such notions as three-quarters and seven-eighths. Wicksell recognized that this shift to approximate unanimity involved the creation of a tradeoff. True unanimity would insure that people would not have to pay taxes for activities they were not willing to support. But it would also prove costly to any effort of trying truly to work out arrangements for collective support. Some modest movement away from unanimity might, Wicksell thought, be a reasonable compromise to expediency. James Buchanan and Gordon Tullock (1962) subsequently converted this compromise to expediency into a framework for constitutional analysis, and which can be traced through to the contemporary scholarship on public choice and constitutional economics.[13]

The Wicksellian tradeoff, as adumbrated by Buchanan and Tullock, shows some important affinities between constitutional theory and statistical decision theory. Within the framework of decision theory, there are two kinds of error. A proposition

---

[12] I should note that I am not using catallactical as a synonym for voluntary, but as an antonym for choice. Fiscal phenomena involve a mixture of exchange and duress, both of which I regard as catallactical, as distinct from choice-theoretic phenomena. See, for instance, Backhaus (1992) and Wagner (1997).

[13] For an examination of the relation between Wicksell, Buchanan and Tullock, and contemporary scholarship on public choice and constitutional economics, see Richard Wagner (1988).

can be called true when it is false, or it can be called false when it is true. The chance of making one type of error can be reduced by imposing more stringent requirements, but this necessarily brings with it an increased chance of making the other type of error. Perfection is not possible. Errors will be unavoidable, and all that can be controlled is the relative mixture of the two types of error.

What holds for decision theory holds for the conduct of the state as well. In the limit, a rule of complete unanimity will prevent the error of undertaking expenditure programs that are not judged to be worthwhile to taxpayers. Unanimity will also, however, lead to a failure to undertake some volume of programs that would have been worthwhile to taxpayers, only they became buried beneath the complexities and strategies of complex bargaining processes. A reduction in the degree of consent that is required to undertake collective action reduces the error of failing to undertake beneficial activities. At the same time, however, it necessarily increases the error of undertaking activities that were not worthwhile to taxpayers, as against being worthwhile only to subsets of taxpayers because the costs were placed on others.

The Present Value of the Wicksellian Legacy

With the passing of time, a scholar's influence must almost invariably wane. Even if the scholar is dealing with eternal conundrums, his influence will almost surely diminish as new scholars come to insert their efforts into the world. Some of this will be due to new formulations, and some will be due to the development of new technologies for thinking. In any case, a scholar's influence is a wasting asset. Very few old books in the libraries find readers, and this is as it must and should be.

While Wicksell is less influential than he was a century ago, he continues nonetheless to exert a notable influence over significant precincts within economic scholarship, even if that influence is not always be recognized by contemporary practitioners. This influence is surely most notable in public finance, particularly that portion associated with public choice and constitutional economics. This influence, of course, does not reside so much in the details of Wicksell's own analytical models as in his orientation toward his subject matter. Wicksell's influence likewise remains notable in matters concerning money and the macroeconomy. This influence, moreover, may well experience some expansion in coming years, if coordination comes to exert an increasing claim upon the attention of economists concerned with explaining general economic conditions.

References

Backhaus JG (1980) The Pareto principle. Analyse und Kritik 2(2):146–171
Backhaus JG (1992) The state as a club. J Publ Fin Publ Choice 10:3–16
von Böhm-Bawerk E (1959) Capital and interest, 3 vols. Libertarian, South Holland, IL [orig. ed. 1884–1889]

Boulding KE (1971) After Samuelson, who needs Adam Smith? Hist Polit Econ 3(Fall):225–237
Buchanan JM, Tullock G (1962) The calculus of consent. University of Michigan Press, Ann Arbor
Gardlund T (1958) The life of Knut Wicksell. Almqvist & Wiksell, Stockholm
Gordon RA (1961) Business fluctuations, 2nd edn. Harper & Row, New York [orig. ed. 1952]
Haberler G (1964) Prosperity and depression, 5th edn. Allen & Unwin, London [orig. ed. 1937]
Hayek FA (1935) Prices and production, 2nd edn. Routledge and Kegan Paul, London
Hayek FA (1932) Monetary theory and the trade cycle. Harcourt, Brace, New York
Hennipman P (1982) Wicksell and Pareto: their relationship in the theory of public finance. Hist of Polit Econ 14(1):37–64
Katzner DW (1998) Time, ignorance, and uncertainty in economic models. University of Michigan Press, Ann Arbor
Leijonhufvud A (1981) Information and coordination. Oxford University Press, New York
Lindahl E (1939) Studies in the theory of money and capital. Farrar & Rinehart, New York
Macfie A (1934) Theories of the trade cycle. Macmillan, London
von Mises L (1934) The theory of money and credit. Jonathan Cape, London [orig. ed 1912]
Schumpeter JA (1934) The theory of economic development. Harvard University Press, Cambridge
Selgin G (1997) Less than zero: the case for a falling price level in a growing economy. Institute of Economic Affairs, London
Stigler GJ (1941) Production and distribution theories. Macmillan, New York
Uhr CG (1960) Economic doctrines of Knut Wicksell. University of California Press, Berkeley
Wagner RE (1999) Austrian cycle theory: saving the wheat while discarding the chaff. Rev Austrian Econ 12:65–80
Wagner RE (1997) Choice, exchange, and public finance. Am Econ Rev, Proceedings 87:160–163
Wagner RE (1988) The calculus of consent: a Wicksellian retrospective. Publ Choice 56:153–66
Wicksell K (1954) Value, capital, and rent. Macmillan, London [orig. ed, 1893]
Wicksell K (1936) Interest and prices. Macmillan, London [orig. ed, 1898]
Wicksell K (1958) A new principle of just taxation. In: Musgrave RA, Peacock AT (eds) Classics in the theory of public finance. Macmillan, London, pp 72–118
Wicksell K (1896) Finanztheoretische Untersuchungen debst Darstellung und Kritik des Steuersystems Schwedens. Gustav Fischer, Jena
Wicksell K (1901, 1906) Lectures on political economy, 2 vols. Routledge & Kegan Paul, London
Witt U (1997) The Hayekian puzzle: spontaneous order and the business cycle. Scot J Polit Econ 44:44–58

Chapter 21
Werner Sombart

Helge Peukert

Introduction[1]

The "conception of capitalism as a historical formation with distinctive political and cultural as well as economic properties derives from the work of those relatively few economists interested in capitalism as a "stage" of social evolution. In addition to the seminal work of Marx and the literature that his work has inspired, the conception draws on the writings of Smith, Mill, Veblen, Schumpeter and a number of sociologists and historians, notably among them, Weber and Braudel. The majority of present-day economists do not use so broad a canvas, concentrating on capitalism as a market system, with the consequence of emphasizing its functional rather than its institutional or constitutive aspects" (Heilbroner 1988, p 350b).

His opus magnum, *Der moderne Kapitalismus* (1863–1941), also tries to analyse (the development of) capitalism as a historical phenomenon with distinctive political, cultural and economic properties (Sombart 1916–1927, 1987). The third volume of his modern capitalism was completed in 1927 and is often considered as the most comprehensive synthesis of the research of the historical school. As the last major representative of the youngest historical school, he stood in the tradition of "theoretical historicism … , a synthesis between historical empiricism and theoretical economics … Sombart's principal interest was in the great tendencies of capitalist evolution, including the evolution of its institutions in time" (Chaloupek 1999, pp 467, 470).

---

[1] Many thanks to J. Backhaus for discussions and translations and to H. Bruhns for discussions and a grant at the CNRS (Maison de l'homme) in Paris to write this paper.

H. Peukert (✉)
Faculty of Economics, Law and Social Science, University of Erfurt,
Westerwaldstrasse 38 a, 99089 Erfurt, Germany
e-mail: helge.peukert@uni-erfurt.de

J.G. Backhaus (ed.), *Handbook of the History of Economic Thought*,   527
The European Heritage in Economics and the Social Sciences,
DOI 10.1007/978-1-4419-8336-7_21, © Springer Science+Business Media, LLC 2012

Sombart is missing in Heilbroner's list and this is not surprising because his oeuvre is very often neglected, criticized and rejected.[2] There are several reasons for his bad personal and scientific reputation. One criticism is that he changed his basic orientation several times, especially his alleged switch from the support of social reform to a conservative cultural critique at the turn of the century.[3] Another point is his never-ending production of new hypotheses without delivering sufficient empirical support, especially what the emerging conditions of capitalism are concerned, often combined with the allegation of insufficient analytical rigour, e.g. compared with Weber (Lehmann 1996, Chap. 6). Others are wondering if he ever escaped being "only" an economic historian in the tradition of the historical school (Stölting 1986, pp 109–110; Schefold 1992, p 314).

A major point may also be his temporary support for national socialism, and in fact, there are absolutely no excuses for his irresponsible Bohemian flirtations.[4] A final and in our opinion very important aspect of the prevailing more or less open aversion against Sombart is the simple fact that Sombart – and this is a constant in all of his writings – opposed liberalism and capitalism[5] and many if not most social scientists today hold the opposite view (see his critical remark in 1987, II, p 1137). For all these reasons, Sombart's work is relatively neglected. No complete bibliography of his writings exists,[6] not even a selected version of his many essays is

---

[2] See for example from a Marxist-Leninist standpoint (Krause 1962; Pasemann 1985). But see also the more positive reviews and discussions in Brocke (1973), Schepansky (1979), Bobek (1979), Schmidt (1991), Grundmann and Stehr (1997), Glombowski (1998), and Backhaus (1996, 2000).

[3] See for example Harris (1942); Wayne (1950; Herf (1984, pp 130–151; Loader and Tilman (1995; Sieferle (1995, pp 74–105; Genett 1998). See also Mitzman's thesis 1987 and 1988 of Sombart's collapse into kitsch-Nietzscheanism or Nietzschean *Herrenmoral*, and völkisch sentimentalism. But compare the excellent study by Lebovics (1969, especially pp 49–78) who puts Sombart besides Salin, Spann, Fired et al. in the German context of social conservatism to rescue the middle classes. "Social conservatives were not crypto-Nazis; rather, the Nazis were vulgar social conservatives" (1969, p 10).

[4] For Sombart's attitude from a sociological background, see Rammstedt (1986, pp 55, 64, 74, 79, 95, 109–112). On the one hand, he underlines Sombart's euphoric support for national socialism in his letter to Plenge dated 24 September 1933 on p 79, fn. 60; on the other hand, he shows that in 1934 his enthusiasm already vanished and that after 1936 he openly criticized for example Freyer for his substitution of sociology into *Volkskunde* as bad metaphysics, see Rammstedt (1986, p 74, fn. 40). Against the common downplaying of the general *Gleichschaltung* of sociology after 1933, Rammstedt (1988 shows that the opposite is true. It should be mentioned that Sombart never adapted to national socialism in an opportunist way in his writings. For Sombart's extremely chauvinist position especially during the war, see Lenger (Lenger 1996, 1997a, b), and Lübbe (1963, pp 207–219).

[5] As we will see below, this is not to say that he was a "Marxist" or social democrat before 1900 which was his stigma at the time and may have coincided with his preference to *épater le bourgeois*. In fact, six nominations for professorship have been turned down by the grand duke of Baden mainly for this reason.

[6] See Brocke (1987, pp 435–443); Appel (1992, pp 275–284; Lenger (1994, pp 513–523); Backhaus (1996, pp 359–367); and the reviews by Chaloupek (1994a, b, 1995a, b). These contributions also demonstrate a growing interest in Sombart in the 1980s and 1990s, mainly what his biography and selected parts of his work are concerned. See also Blaug (1992).

published in a critical edition; his modern capitalism was not published in English. But Sombart is also considered as a founder of economic sociology (Reinhold et al. 1997, pp 15–17). He was also admired for his style of writing, his universal knowledge in the social sciences and humanities, his original and manifold hypotheses and his quality as a speaker.[7]

Taking this sceptical attitude as our starting point, we will first give a short overview of Sombart's life and discuss his first scientific contribution and ask if we can find some overarching continuing principles that are the basis of his further research.[8] We will also have to include his specific early version of socialism and follow his intellectual development regarding social reform. To fully grasp his endeavour, we will proceed by a backward induction and start with his anthropology (1938, the distribution had been limited by censorship) and sociology (1923 ff.). Third, we will study his methodology (1930). A central part will then be the analysis of his specific version of "theoretical historicism" in his modern capitalism: is his analysis analytically rigorous, is it only historical, what does "theoretical" mean for Sombart? We will further ask what his version of national socialism (1934) exactly is about and how he saw the future of capitalism at his time. Finally, we will ask if his analytical concept and his social and cultural critiques of capitalism are still relevant for social research today.

Sombart's Life and His First Study

Sombart was born in 1863 in Ermsleben in Prussia.[9] He studied political economy (Staatswissenschaften), history and philosophy at the universities of Berlin, Pisa and Rome. His dissertation, supervised by Schmoller, the heir of the younger historical school, was on tenancy and labour relations in the Roman campagna. His father Ludwig made a career and became a sugar industrialist who bought a manor to realize the agrarian ideal of inner colonization. He surely influenced Sombart in the choice of his Ph.D. thesis. He was a co-founder of the *Verein für Socialpolitik* and member of the *Reichstag*, whereas Werner became the Verein's president after 1932 and was engaged in communal policy in Breslau. W. Sombart was a later child and the atmosphere in his father's house was liberal and upper middle class. From 1888 to 1890, Werner was syndic at the Board of Trade in Bremen.

---

[7] His public lectures were so impressive that they were the subject of conversation even ten years later by the inmates of the Dachau concentration camp, see Rost (1999, p 88).

[8] For reasons of space, we will not discuss the comparative "Sombart-Weber-spirit of capitalism" debate, see for example Parsons (1928, 1929); Fechner (1929); Leich (1957); Kraft (1961); Fleischmann (1981); Bruhns (1985, 1987); Mitzman (1987, 1988); Rehberg (1989); Joas (1989); Töttö (1991); Fishman (1994); Tyrell (1994); and for a comparison and comment on Weber's thinking on Sombart in his protestant ethics see Lichtblau and Weiß (1993). We will also neglect the reception of Sombart in specific countries, for France see for example Bruhns and Haupt (1990).

[9] Sombart's life is described in the literature mentioned in fn. 4; see also N. Sombart (1984).

Since 1888, he was married with F. Genzmer who died in 1920. They had four daughters, but it was no happy marriage (especially after 1900); one great love was M. Briesemeister. In 1890, Sombart got the extraordinary professorship at Breslau University, thanks to Althoff. He had no habilitation and only the campagna book was published. In Breslau, he was professor, active citizen, communal politician and very engaged in active social policy. In 1900, he supported the formation of the *Internationale Vereinigung für gesetzlichen Arbeiterschutz* in Paris, and in 1903, he formulated the statues of the *Gesellschaft für soziale Reform*. He read Marx since 1890 and he carried out many factory visits with his students and made precise descriptions of the situation of the home-workers.

He lived in an elegant house in a residential suburb, and in 1909, bought a park and a villa in Oberschreiberhau (Riesengebirge) where he usually wrote in solitude from eleven at night until five in the morning. When he sold park and villa in 1919, the money value was reduced to zero, and some days later, the German inflation set in. Also due to his famous *Sozialismus und soziale Bewegung* (1896, nine editions by 1923), he only got an ordinary professorship at Berlin University in 1917. Already in 1906, he became professor at the new business school (Handelshochschule) in Berlin, but he was not authorized to teach at Berlin University. In 1922, he married his Romanian student C. Leon who was 30 years younger. They inhabited a villa in the Grunewald with an impressive library which was later sold to Osaka. He retired in 1933, but gave lectures until 1940. Sometimes he had to teach in the new auditorium and filled the 1,400 seats. In Berlin, he was also privy councillor (Geheimer Regierungsrat). Sombart had some key positions as president of the *Verein* since 1932, due to his activities in the *Soziale Reformgesellschaft*, as a co-editor of the *Archiv für Sozialwissenschaft und Sozialpolitik,* and as one of the most active and important members of the *Deutsche Gesellschaft für Soziologie.*[10]

Among Sombart's friends were O. Braun, O. Lang, F. Tönnies, M. Scheler, and C. Hauptmann. In more than one respect, he was a typical savant of Wilhelmian Germany: he had intensive contacts to artists. He was conservative. He acquired a broad humanist education. He was elitist, and privileged, and belonged to the upper class (at least until the end of World War I, his income was exceptionally high also thanks to the lecture fees and publication allowances). The contradictions of the mandarins of that period are especially pronounced in Sombart: he proclaimed not to believe in God, kings or morals and at the same time he praised the good old German customs. He was in principle a defender of civilized family life and at the same time he thought proper to need strong impulses and diversion in sexual matters from time to time. In Breslau, he was in favour of social egalitarian policy (e.g. public home-building); at the same time he was against public transport (a trolley line) in the street where he lived (noise). He was a supporter of social policy, but he never became member of the social democrats (SPD) and he was in favour of the military naval expansion program.

---

[10] See Käsler (1984), especially pp 35–37, 41–54, and 422–430.

Let us now have a closer look at Sombart's first relevant publication, his dissertation (1888) on tenancy and labour relations in the Roman campagna.[11] In our view, in 180 pages Sombart delineates in a nutshell his complete further research program in an applied manner. In the introduction, he states that the functions of his work are not only to get some insights in theoretical agriculture and the historical development of a specific economy in time and space, but also – and this was relevant for him for general economic theorizing, see 1888, p 6 – to extract some peculiar economic systems (his central notion of *Wirtschaftssystem* is mentioned twice, on pp 3, 6).[12] Further, he wanted to arrive at some practical-social policy conclusions, especially concerning the conflict between personal and social interests. The interests of the economical powerful may contradict the interest of the national/local economy (p 7).

Sombart tries to understand the Campagna organism in applying the synthesizing method of theoretical historicism. On the one hand, he draws a secular historical picture of the development of the campagna in the last centuries (pp 132–140). He further describes in detail the natural environment like climate, soil, etc. (pp 10–26), and the applied technical procedures in agriculture and cattle breeding and its changes like machine use and forest culture over time (pp 27–50). He uses all statistical, empirical, and historical material available (including government questionnaires, personal observations, interviews, etc., see p 85). His description becomes very concrete and illustrative and is written in a prosaic language. But he never looses the track of his analysis: to delineate a specific economic system, the "campagna organism."

This becomes most evident when he turns to the analysis of the social structure in terms of the property relations as the most relevant element. He analyses the change of the property distribution and its size (50% of the land is owned by 5% of the population) and develops a classification of classes (the aristocracy, the church, the bourgeois, the workers). The basic structure is that the landed non-functional aristocracy rents the land to the rich tenants in the cities. They rent little plots to the final little tenants. His classification is developed along the lines of a social interest group model, but it is not Marxist because Sombart includes, for example, the church as an interest group and he underlines the importance of little and capital-intensive great tenants and farmers which crosscuts class categories (see part three of the book). The different categories of workers (like wood-cutter, charcoal burner, herdsman, daily paid land hands, itinerant worker, etc.) and their living conditions are analysed along the lines of what he later called personal types (1930, p 243). He has a social-functional (not a natural rights) theory of property and therefore he always asks in how far concentrated property (e.g. land in the hands of the aristocracy which he severely attacked) is conducive in social, political, cultural or economic respects (he does not reject the private possession of the means of production in general).

---

[11] In the following, we will not deal with the background stories and the personal and biographical connotations of his works, but see the profound work of Lenger (1994).

[12] Sombart in fact established the notion of economic system as a scientific notion not only in Germany, see Ritter (1999, p 123).

His interpretative frame is a regional economy in dissolution: the disappearance of the common field system, the decrease of little peasants, the concentration of land ownership, the substitution of agriculture by farming, the increase of a proletariat and the decrease in real wages due to overcompetition are clear indicators for him that the working of free market mechanisms (which he castigates, see e.g. pp 80, 147–148) has social degenerative impacts and invokes an ill organism (p 93).

Sombart does not ask in how far free markets can be established and allocation or adaptive efficiency be enhanced to increase GDP by creating non-attenuated property rights (for an attenuated version see North 1996). His unit is not the self-interested individual, but the social groups and classes. He asks for the impacts for a cultural nation, not economic performance per se, but the social and cultural consequences of changing social structures are important for him. Sombart holds that, in rural areas, the familial peasant households and holdings are the regular and normal case and not the concentration of property and proletarianization as a natural result of free competition. He has no narrow concept of exploitation, but an idea of a decent life which includes an acceptable wage, comfortable and hygienic conditions, no overwork, social embeddedness (e.g. no long-term separation of families), existential security, and a cultural minimum level (books, etc.). Maybe the most important point is that human action should be autonomous and not heteronymous, that is, action under an extraneous will, for example, the worker in a factory (see 1930, p 225). As we will see in the next section, for Sombart this contradicts the anthropological constitution of man.

The increasing cattle breeding and proletarianization is in the interest of the powerful owners and great tenants. It will continue as the natural drift of unregulated competition. Therefore, Sombart asks for a straight reform by the state. It should act against this natural drift. His reflections are very modern when he discusses the impact of the world market (p 114), the existence of an excess population due to machinery, etc. They remind the reader of the problems of recent globalization and, for example, the non-regulated transformation in former socialist countries. For Sombart, the big mistake was to auction the immense property holdings of the church without qualification so that the economically more powerful became even more so (p 152). His proposition is to nationalize the big holdings (with recompense which will cost a lot of money, see p 162) and to redistribute it to little peasants in hereditary tenure (see Sombart 1888) to support a more healthy agricultural campagna organism. Positive state action is needed for social reform (pp 160 ff.) in an encompassing way to create a specific economic spirit (compare 1930, pp 206–207) with an orientation of non-pecuniary satisfaction according to need and economic structures of self-sufficiency; an organism with specific goals, motives and rules of behaviour (1930, p. 181). Sombart's early work already implies his later threefold differentiation of spirit, organization and technique and is a fine example of the approach of the historical school (summarized by Betz 1966). His value judgment is against an untamed capitalist spirit and social structure; it is oriented against what he called the embrace of capitalist civilization. The campagna study tries to offer an agrarian alternative. Sombart holds that his ideal is not against economic logic and efficiency in the long run, because the aristocracy chooses big tenants and they choose cattle breeding mainly for reasons of convenience, not maximum yield. It is in the interest of society at large to choose a decentralized but intensive mode of agricultural cultivation, instead of extensive stock farming to have a higher product to finance imports (see pp 114 ff.).[13]

On Human Nature and Social Action

Sombart's last book was on anthropology (1938).[14] It should constitute and be a first step towards a general theory of culture. In the literature, it was viewed as a more or less confuse compilation of diverse thoughts without a unifying idea, the product of a disillusioned old man. In our view, it is the key and heart core to understand his thinking. On 430 pages, he tries to substantiate his view that man's distinguishing characteristic and human substance is to have "spirit" (Geist, pp 17–21, not identical with the more narrow concept of mind). Spirit materializes in religion, the state, the family, the economy, language, moral and esthetical maxims and norms (pp 315, 417). Therefore, the social realm is constituted by culture as symbolic meaning systems (pp 68, 77). It makes humans free to act and gives them responsibility for their actions (p 288). But it also makes us a spiritually endangered species (p 52).[15]

With *Geist*, man falls out of the realm of nature, he is a creature *sui generis* (p 109) and in so far not part of nature (p 416). Sombart is arguing against the concepts of "animalism" where the notion and reality of spirit are lost. Animalism exists in the two versions of physical-chemical mechanical materialism and Darwinian organic biologism (pp 286–287). Both are aberrations (p 109) and expressions of the power of natural science thinking over modern man (p 93). There is always a close relationship between the image of man and scientific methods (p 109). Sombart strongly emphasizes the basic dichotomy between an "animalistic" and a "oministic" current (p 99).

But besides the basic dichotomy, his construction is much more complicated because he introduces the soul (*Seele*) as an expression of the biological organism which is the vital centre of the human person and expression of life (motivation,

---

[13] We cannot discuss the validity of Sombart's empirical hypotheses here. He states for example that Italy will never become an industrialized country 1888, p 114, and in one of the few critical reviews, Dietzel (1889) doubts that Sombart has proven the antagonism between private and social interests, or that the campagna is typical for Italy, further that he cannot empirically show the income disparity between capital and labour and the long-term superiority of farming compared with cattle breeding.

[14] Besides the necessarily dialectical way of reasoning the book contains in fact many departures from the main road; we will leave all these like his reflections on Goethe, his elitist threefold classification of mankind, see 1838, p 150, his meditations on merchants, heroes and saints and the undercover arguments against race theories, see 1938, pp 133, 137 ff., out here.

[15] It is interesting that he excludes technique. He argues that its function is always and in all culture spheres to relate means to pre-given ends, see 1938, p 82.

desire and reproduction). Both independent parts, *Seele* and *Geist*, constitute man and we have to choose between vital nature (*Seele*) and spirit (p 338). Animalistic concepts negate both (*Entseelung* and *Entgeistung*). Sombart's recommendation is not that *Geist* should substitute nature (*Seele*), because *Geist* in its purest form has the tendency of self-alienation in the form of schematising, bureaucratisation, hyperorganization, the elaboration of formal taxonomies, etc. (p 20), which may remind the reader of Simmel's distinction between *Geist* and form. Sombart distinguishes between pure *Geist* (with no material correlation like the sentence of Pythagoras), bounded *Geist* (which depends on a material substratum) and living *Geist* (embedded in a human life history, see p 79).

Seele may degenerate to, for example, pure mechanical drive satisfaction. Sombart leaves open if *Seele* has in principle the vital constructive element in itself or if it depends in this regard from the influx of *Geist*. The more *Geist* expands, the greater is the danger of the form deviation of *Geist*. This may also explain why Sombart's book looks disorganized: he does not give any clear formal ("scientific") definition of *Geist* and he does not say where it exactly comes from (god, the brain, etc.). Instead, he always cites literature, philosophy, and scientific literature in a cursory way and leaves the final answer open. In a certain sense, this is necessary because a formal-mechanical-logical definition of *Geist* would be an expression of its own self-alienation (Veblen: self-contamination). So the playful and essay character is the necessary *Geist* part of the reasoning. This is not to deny the problematic of many paradoxes in the book (see the fair criticisms in Vleugels' 1940, Wieses' 1940, and Klotter's 1988 reviews).

The book ends with the remark that human existence consists of a constant conflict of our spiritual essence and our natural conditions (p 432).[16] In his view, there is an optimum of the balanced spiritual and natural portions in human action. Untamed and non-functionalised nature is important for this balance because it represents and strengthens the vital and natural component in us out there. This harmonious balance is disturbed in modern capitalism with its economic rationalism. This leads Sombart to his culture and deep ecological critique (especially pp 324–339, compare Scaff 1988) which will be discussed later.

Scheler's influence consists in the assumption of a formal hierarchical realm and stratification of value spheres (from the pleasant/useful, the vital feelings/health, the beautiful, the true and the truthful, truth, up to the holy and their respective opposites, see Scheler 1966, p 122 ff.). The higher value sphere always has a natural preponderance over the lower ones. People always give meaning to their actions; they always have a subject of faith. The upheaval of values means that in modernity lower value spheres (e.g. the pleasant in utilitarianism) become more important than the higher ones or they are set as the Absolute (Allodi 1989, p 469).

Sombart places in front of his noo-sociology the basic principle that all social life, and man, is necessarily sociable and is (mediated by) *Geist*, that is, symbolic

---

[16] This view has surely to do with Sombart's position vis-à-vis his own erotic ambivalence (see Sombart 1930, p 220).

meaning transferred by language (1936, pp 23–24). He distinguishes his sociology from natural rights (Hobbes), historical (A. Smith), metahistorical (Spann), formal (Simmel), "German" (Freyer), and natural science concepts of sociology. The last concept is subdivided into physical (Pareto), biological (Spencer), and psychological (Giddens) approaches.[17] All social units are to be understood as *Geist* (spiritual forms) which he calls associations (*Verbände*).[18]

Sombart distinguishes genuine and not genuine associations (1956, p 29 ff., first published in 1930). In the latter category, a spiritual connection is missing, for example, in language communities, statistical and affective groups. Genuine associations are subdivided into ideal (family, state/nation, religion), final (purposive and structured organizations like firms), and intentional associations (the *Geist* must be in the consciousness of the actors, for example, interest groups without a permanent organization). The central notions in the three categories are ideas – goals – intentions. The purest social forms are ideal associations where a transcendental component dominates, whereas in the goal type individual interests and the rational nature prevail. In the family, as an example for ideal associations, the eternal meaning is the completion and reproduction of human partial forms of existence (man, woman, child).

Varieties of "Socialism"

But was not Sombart a Marxist at the beginning of his intellectual career? We do not think so and argue in the following that, behind his alleged Marxism lurk, there are the premises of the aforementioned anthropology and sociology.

Sombart's reputation as a Marxist rests on a positive article on Marx (1894). It is often contrasted with the fifth edition of *Sozialismus* (1905, pp 73–90) and later articles and books where Sombart raises criticism against the Marxist evolutionary hypotheses (the law of concentration, the law of the necessary breakdown of capitalism, the thesis of pauperisation, etc.). An analysis of the early texts shows that this change of mind did not take place. In the 1894 article, Sombart does not only criticize Engels for the bad arrangement of Capital III, but his discussion of the transformation problem is also peculiar. He does not say that it is solved, but that it is no real problem because "value" is only a concept of mind ("gedankliche Thatsache," p 574) and does not correspond to motives or real tendencies. He leaves open the quarrel between subjectivists and objectivists in economics at the end (p 594).

The contents of the first edition of his *Sozialismus* (1896, translated in 1898 by AP Attenburg into English) are surprising. The book, a compilation of lectures in Zurich,

---

[17] For his criticism (teleology, naturalism, etc.) of these concepts, see also the reconstruction by Allodi (…).

[18] In König's view (1983, p 49, 1987, p 267), this is a misnomer which simply means "group." For Sombart's highly sceptical assessment of sociology as a discipline in 1934, see Sombart in Käsler (1985, pp 98–101).

starts with the critique that Marx did not recognize the existence of communities like nations; not only social, also national differences exist. As in 1906, he describes the living conditions of the proletariat. Besides the material conditions, he stresses that all old ideals broke down, man is alone and looks for community in the socialist groupings. A general nervousness and the transformation of all living spheres make the workers sick (pp 7–10). He classifies the English, French and the German types of socialism which depend on their national mentalities. He stigmatizes the brutal egoism of the (British) trade unions (p 42).

The central aspect of the socialist movement is the creation of a new society, the establishing of a new ideal (p 3). Marx is a social philosopher; for Sombart, his theories are wrong in most points and can hardly be defended any more (pp 63–68)! The philosophy of historical necessity is wrong (p 71), but the intrinsic necessity of the socialist ideal is right; socialism needs a psychological foundation of history (p 72). Private property should not be abolished (p 81), the fight for social reform should be in the confines of law, and evolutionary reform. For the movement, religious and national values are necessary (pp 112–122). All "internationalism" notwithstanding, the socialist movement will support nationalism if a war looms; a precise prediction of the behaviour of the social-democratic parties in 1914 (p 118).

In our view a precise reading of the book shows that he already argues implicitly from the background of his later sociology and anthropology, ingrained with conservative, national and paternalistic elements which are a possible, but by no means necessary specification of his elementary metaphysics.

But Sombart never forgot social criticism. His book on the proletariat in 1906 gives an impressive picture of their deplorable situation in an encompassing way, warmly and forcibly formulated with much empathy and with the specific Sombart emphasis (already evident in 1896) on the loss of a fatherland, and a native place (*Heimat*), the loosening of family ties, the breakdown of the role of father and mother due to the working and living conditions, the permanent danger of unemployment and the lack of social security, the poor accommodations, and hygiene, the lack of education for the children, etc. In his booklet on Marx (Sombart 1909) he delineates the potential and elements of the method of *Verstehen* and the literary psychological analysis in Marx. These are precursory statements of his book on method (Sombart 1930).

In his *Grundlagen* (Sombart 1919) he defines the essence of socialism as practical-social rationalism with an anti-chrematistic tendency (p VII); the social emancipation of classes and the theory of social development are characterized as foreign or arbitrary elements (*Fremdkörper*, p VIII ff.) to socialism. In his voluminous book on proletarian socialism (Sombart 1924), he consequently defines power, reason and love as the primordial principles upon which societies can be based. Socialism is uniform rationalism – later explained by the self-alienation of *Geist* – as the unique principle of an ideal-rational society with political, social, intellectual, and moral equality (Sombart 1925, vol 1, part 1). It is an effect of the dissolution of the old orders and the abolition of god (*Entgottung*, p 116). Socialism means unitary rationalization which is incompatible with his anthropology mentioned earlier, less so with his sociology (socialism as an ideal association). Pfister (1927, especially pp 94, and 134–135) shows that the links between all of his works on modern capitalism and socialism are the dimensions of *Geist* and style, the axis idealism-naturalism and Scheler's rejection of the pleasant as the absolute normative basis.

The more socialism gave up the character of a movement with ideals and the more the mere formulation of material interests were placed into the foreground, the more Sombart rejected this movement. Sombart's work shows the full mastery of the literature on socialism. But besides some questionable comments, for example the negative remarks on the founders of socialism, it can be asked if his frame of reference is correct. As we have argued elsewhere (Peukert 2000b), pure Marxism indeed had the element of uniform reason, but at the same time romantic elements (abolition of the state, etc.) and the element of power (suppression of other classes). In an interesting review Briefs (1926, p 12) argues that socialism was not the prime mover of quantitative hedonism but simply the expression of the materialist-individualist spirit of the age.

His book on *German socialism* (1934) argues along the same lines as his other writings on socialism. It is only exceptional because Sombart expressly states to have a national socialist orientation (p XII) but at the same time he criticizes national socialist writers in general and is sure to find many enemies in the national socialist party (pp XIII, XV).[19] The book is in many parts very ambivalent: a leader is necessary but it may also be a leading group, blacks may "feel German," Sombart rejects race concepts but Jews should in principle not exert higher professional functions (pp 191–192). The economy should be planned but with private property of the means of production, etc. But the base line of the book is clear. He argues again against the 150 years old economic epoch and the primacy of the economy. His targets are population growth, agglomerations, the industrialization and decline of agriculture, the massification of culture, production and consumption, the destruction of nature, the ideals of newness, big – and quickness, etc. (part 1).

Socialism is defined as social normativism, the direction of behaviour by binding norms (part 2), proletarianism and Marxism is rejected (materialism, naturalism and evolutionism, see part 3), the German soul is revealed, and he proclaims the anti-capitalist and cultural nature of German socialism (p 120 ff.). The state is defined as an ideal association with a metaphysical rooting. Sincere and non-artificial local community life should be encouraged (238 ff.), etc. We will not discuss his relatively precise policy proposals here (see Werth 1996a, b).[20] We only wanted to show the continuity of Sombart's thought on socialism over almost 40 years.[21] It was embedded in his metaphysics (anthropology, noo-sociology). Let us see now in how far it influenced his thinking on method.

---

[19] The changing relationship to the national socialists is described in Brocke (1987, pp 50–57).

[20] Autarky, support of agriculture, car free zones of nature etc., which have been instantaneously criticized, and the compilation "Deutscher Sozialismus im Urteil der Presse," Berlin, 1935.

[21] We have to leave out Sombart's contributions to socialism in the US (1906, 1969), but see Foner (1984), and Tütsch (1988).

A Method Called Verstehen

In his most pronounced contribution to method, Sombart (1930) distinguished three
types of economic theories (in German the *richtende, ordnende* and *verstehende*
approach). They all consider themselves exclusive and universal. He rejects the first
orienting (*richtende*) type (Aristotle, the scholastics, Spann, Hegel but he also
includes the hedonist school and, for example A. Smith). It is normative and says
what should be, for example no chrematistics in the *polis*. For Sombart (like Weber),
science implies the principle of value neutrality because different norms can be
chosen. The *richtende* economics must be rejected because it cannot argue in favour
of one norm instead of another. It is interesting to see that Sombart explains the
emergence and existence of this approach by the overarching cultural value systems
and social structures of the time (e.g. in the Middle Ages). Does this suggest that a
meaning system produces the wrong intellectual superstructure?

The *ordnende* or ordering economics comprises mostly mainstream economics
(1930, Chap. 9), subdivided into the objectivists (Marx), subjectivists (Menger) and
the relationists (Walras). Despite all their disagreements, Sombart chooses again an
externalist history of thought, they belong to the same type. It emerged as a result of
mainly cultural but also structural changes in the last 500 years: the secularisation of
the life style, the decline of feudalism and its unitary culture, the disenchantment of
nature and society, etc. The aim of knowledge is now to control (natural) processes.
The scientist has emotional distance, a depersonalisation of knowledge generation
takes place. "The results of scientific inquiry have to be objective, separate from the
person who does the inquiry; in this sense they can be "proven," that is, impressed
upon an outsider" (1930, p 96).[22] The external ordering in quantitative terms is in the
centre, not the understanding of the substantial how and why of things and relations.
Sombart's catalogue coincides with McCloskey's ten commandments of modern
economics (1985). The greatest influence on economics exerted the ideal of the exact
natural sciences and their practical success since the eighteenth century. It should be
mentioned that his three basic types and his putting into boxes is all but self-evident:
Smith could also be found in the *ordnende* economics, some would put Schmoller in
the *verstehende* economics (henceforth VE), others Menger (see Leube 1994).

What is Sombart's criticism of this program? Some minor points are his unclear
notion of economic laws and the "quantification only" principle (p 130). But when
he introduces his favourite VE in Chap. 10, he makes the strong assertion that VE is
adequate to the subject matter which implies that *ordnende* economics is not (see
e.g. pp 140, 292). This is a general statement, he does not, for example, say that
classical economics was right at the time of liberal capitalism and is wrong in late
capitalism or that there is a division of labour between the approaches depending
on the respective scientific questions which constitute different objects of knowledge (for Amonn (1930), this would have been a more adequate line of reasoning).

---

[22] All German references are our translations.

He does also not explain the VE by an externalist culture approach as he did in his discussion of the *richtende* and *ordnende* economics. The ontological quality of his view is underlined by the fact that he rejects the typical heterodox criticisms of a lack of a national, social policy or ethical component or the allegations of atomism, chrematistics, statics, arm chair theorizing, etc. (140 ff.). The essential mistakes are the ten commandments of the natural science attitude (does this not imply atomism in the sense of decomposability of elements?). For Sombart, even Schmoller and Roscher went into the natural science trap (pp 154–155; in our view this is only partially correct, see Peukert 1998, Chap. 3) and into the aberrations of psychologism, historicism and teleology. The foundations for VE were therefore laid by historians (Vico, Droysen), philosophers (Dilthey, Rothacker), sociologists (Cooley) and some few economists (Gottl, Spann).

To introduce VE, he first explains the nature of economics and the economy. Economics deals with the need of subsistence (*Unterhaltsfürsorge*, p 173), the provisioning of material goods. Second, it is an empirical science (*Erfahrungswissenschaft*) in that it depends on reality in time and space. In our view, both do not exclude an approach according to Robbins' definition of the subject matter of economics. But third, it is a cultural science, "since body and soul find their purpose only in the spirit. They can be understood only by means of the spirit, they can become an object of "understanding" only in the context of the spirit" (p 175). For Sombart, this is the essential point (why not the other two?) so that Korsch (1930) castigates his idealism. It can also be argued that if we assume the motive structure of A. Smith's baker as given and the existence of markets and their mechanical price and quantity setting as near to the facts (as idealized in supply and demand diagrams), why should we care so much about motives and *Verstehen*?

Sombart chooses an ontological absolutist introduction of VE which does not convince us. One reason for this is his commitment to the principle of value neutrality (see Landmann's arguments 1930 why in a VE perspective value commitments can hardly be excluded in research (Landmann 1930)). In a certain sense, he accepts the *ordnende* economics' viewpoint only to say and describe "what really is." But if all knowledge depends on symbolic meaning structures, there is no simple answering "what really is." He could have said that he has a specific image of man (anthropology – *Geist*) and a specific understanding of "the social," formulated in his noo-sociology. It follows his interest to analyse which type of human being (Weber's *Menschentypus* in Hennis' interpretation) is drilled in different economic systems.

Sombart also introduces the concept of "system" in an absolutist way in Chap. 12. For him, "system" is a logical idea (Kant), a precondition of science and reason. The choice is again given by the nature of the subject, so we arrive naturally at the idea of the "economy" and the three parts of the "economic system": the economic spirit, the structural order and the technique (p 181). No reasonable scientific argument is possible without this correct *Gestaltidee*.[23] If we understand his system in the general

---

[23] See also the intriguing hermeneutical interpretation of Sombart's methodological ideas in Weippert (1953).

sense of systematic, it is to general, but if we accept his threefold classification and dichotomies, it is too specific because many other reasonable classificatory approaches (e.g. Spiethoff's) exist. They all depend on the researcher's predilections and questions, but none of them has an ontological dignity in our view.

Sombart next introduces "working ideas" as notions of reason (p 185 ff.), as-ifs for research like a static or dynamic, an organic or mechanic way of seeing things. He also includes in this epistemologically very constructivist part the ideas of an exchange economy or a national economy (*Volkswirtschaft*, a living entity, p 189). For Sombart, both ideas are valuable, depending on the economic system and the research question (p 181). He even includes the relative validity of opposite value theories like Marx vs. the marginalists in his functional argument. Having repudiated mainstream classical approaches in toto as *ordnende* economics in Chap. 9, he now puts his opinion in a context and accepts their relative validity.

But here Sombart falls in a certain relativist trap because he cannot hold both statements at the same time. The market/exchange models of his time implied that stability and welfare are brought about by the workings of the objective market mechanisms; the opposite view is that we need strong social institution building, otherwise society will collapse and welfare will decrease.[24] This was the quarrel between Schmoller and Menger and this was also Sombart's point against the Italian government in his campagna study. It is still the dividing line in the debate on globalization. It is not enough to say that an exchange paradigm is naturally only and partially good for capitalist exchange economies because we know that the exchange paradigm has – for good or bad reasons – been used for all types of economic structures (e.g. slavery as an implicit contract), even by the proponents of the historical school (Pearson 1997). We have the impression that Sombart shifts from an absolutist to a relativist view in a questionable way in Chap. 12.

Understanding (*Verstehen*) tries to grasp meaning, it asks "why" do people act this or that way. We can understand, because the objective *Geist* (e.g. the meaning of a modern firm) obeys the same laws as our personal subjective *Geist* (individual actions). He differentiates three types of understanding. *Sinnverstehen* (understanding of meaning) refers to the timeless and a-historical idea of the economy already mentioned with the parts, spirit, organization and technique. It is a priori. We already mentioned that others found different elementary categories and no methodological rule tells us how Sombart found the categories without historical studies. It is obvious that the dichotomies like traditionalism vs. rationalism, solidarism vs. individualism and satisfaction according to need vs. the principle of profit (*Bedarfsdeckungs –* vs. *Erwerbsprinzip*, see pp 206–207) are closely linked to the transition from the Middle Ages to modern capitalism. They are not transhistorical principles.

The second category is *Sachverstehen* (understanding of circumstances), real historical understanding, comprising first the understanding of goals (this is in fact the behavioural logic of mainstream economic man). It is followed by the understanding

---

[24] The problem here has to do with the fact that the *ordnende* economics implies what Sombart calls *Wesenserkenntnis*, a general interpretation of the world, even if it is only formulated in mathematical language, see Schams (1934).

of objective interrelations, for example, that if the corn harvest in the US perishes, the more will be produced in Argentina due to the expected price increase. With *Sachverstehen*, Sombart brings back in the basics of (neo)classical macro-economics (see e.g. Samuelson and Nordhaus 1989). It is not clear in how far his listing under *Sachverstehen* makes a methodological or substantial difference to mainstream economics. After having thrown out the mainstream theories and tool-boxes under the heading of *ordnende* economics firsthand, Sombart now brings back in the basics of mainstream economics (Schams 1930, pp 469–470) to present VE as all-inclusive. But at the same time, it becomes a less specific approach. It can even be stated that neoclassical economics is based on *Sachverstehen*, Sombart's economics more on *Sinnverstehen*, so that the basic opposition *ordnende* vs. VE simply vanishes.

The third category is *Stilverstehen* (understanding of style), for example, in how far the behaviour of economic agents is oriented at the spirit of capitalism. It is per-plexing to see that he negates the modern economy as a connection in style (*Stilzusammenhang*) because there exists no meaningful relationship of economic behaviour to an underlying meaningful style (p 217). If this is the case, we may ask if his construction of the spirit of an economic system as the primordial principle in *Sinnverstehen* is not obsolete in capitalism. This would be a nice argument for main-stream economists to be content with *Sachverstehen* in capitalism.

The last category is the understanding of individual motives, called *Seelen-verstehen*. All action has to be reduced to human intentional motives; the free will is a necessary assumption of VE (which has no developed logic, see p 235). The basic notions are understood in an essentialist manner. We understand "hammer" not by some categorical abstractions (made of wood), but by understanding its func-tion: to hammer. He distinguishes between heteronymous vs. autonomous, tradi-tional vs. rational and goal vs. value-oriented (p 225) action. But usually we are not interested in individual motives but in real average motives in typical constellations, exemplified in his analysis of the different types of bourgeois. The limits of this understanding are the unconscious, nature, the transcendental and mental illness.

Sombart's edifice becomes more and more complex and resembles the following of a maze where the arrangement of more and more VE elements gets out of hand and the general view is lost. Next, Sombart introduces the *Sinngesetze* (laws of mean-ing), that is, meaningful necessary relations. First are the mathematical laws of size like the quantity theory of money, the market law (the size of the markets determines the degree of specialization, see pp 254–255), etc. We see that Sombart once again tries to cannibalize elements of orthodox economics. Next come the structural laws of part and whole, for example, capitalism can only expand if the proletariat increases (p 257). Finally, we have the functional laws, the rational means-ends calculations where it is not so easy to see the difference to the aforementioned *Zweckverstehen*. They are rational schemes. They imply what Sombart calls fictional laws. The prime example is the classical law of supply and demand (p 261). His only criticism is that the classics thought this were natural laws, but they in fact depend on specific condi-tions. The noteworthy point is that Sombart accepts that abstract knowledge without reference to the attribution of natural values (*Bedeutungszuschreibungen*) generates interesting and relevant insights as an elementary step to understand the real world.

Next, he asks why uniform actions of many actors occur. His answer includes the common human nature, the same environment, rational behaviour in systemic constraints, imitation, climate, soil, etc. Here Sombart is on slippery ground because VE implies that human motives are the final bedrock where causal investigations have to stop, otherwise he himself would walk in diverse traps (like behaviourism). The last section of his book is the distinction between economic philosophy including ethics, economic science and economics as an art (*Kunstlehre*). There are many interesting and controversial aspects in this part; we will only mention his ambivalence towards mainstream theorizing and only focus on his example of the transfer problem (p 301). He argues that the quantitative theoretical mainstream scheme is not helpful because there are so many disturbing psychological, political and other elements in reality that the law like assumptions cannot really work out, so that the disturbing noise, the deviation from the scheme, is what VE is about. But this is a problematic argument because neither Keynes nor Ohlin doubted the noise and Sombart seems to accept the rational scheme (in fact there were diverse transfer problem theories) as a starting point. He seems to have no alternative frame of analysis except empirically realist investigations. This is not enough. Probably, Sombart's VE has a different fundamental task in the division of scientific research. Indeed, on the last pages he comes back to the proper field of VE, as part of the humanities, with strong ties to philosophy and culture; practical utility plays a minor role and the answering of the question of the cultural meaning and basic structure of the economy is in the centre.

As a result, we see that the problems in his book on method depend on two polar dichotomies which cannot be fulfilled at the same time: on the one hand the commitment to value neutrality (p 289) and to formulate an all-embracing economic approach vs. a very specific understanding of economics in the sense of VE, which depends on his image of man. On the other hand, we find the polarity between realism and constructivism in his book.[25] This is not to deny the legitimacy and possibility of a hermeneutical *verstehens* approach (Peukert 1998). Sombart's importance for VE is less in the methodological (ambiguities) but in the applied field, for example, his studies on the campagna or on modern capitalism.

Modern Capitalism[26]

Compared with the first, the second edition of modern capitalism (1916–1927) has worked up more empirical material, more influences which lead to capitalism have been considered and the distinction between historical and empirical parts is made

---

[25] We cannot review the intensive debate on Sombart's book, maybe the best review is still the short article by Löwe (1932).

[26] For a brief overview of the structure of modern capitalism, see Backhaus (1989, 1992). We will leave out the discussion of all publications around modern capitalism on the military, see Sombart (1913a), luxury consumption, see Sombart (1913b), the influence of the Jews, see Sombart (1911), etc. for reasons of space. These publications do not at all differ in orientation from the respective passages in modern capitalism. We even neglect Sombart's book on the bourgeois, see Sombart (1988), first published in 1913, a relatively disorganized but important precursor.

more clear (I, XIII).[27] But the basic approach is the same: a general history of the common economic (but also, social, cultural and political) development of European societies since the Carolingian times.[28] The method is distinctively historical-theoretical (I, XV), the exposition genetic-systematic. It is distinguished by normal historical research by the long time horizon (almost one thousand years, in fact a *longue durée*), the level of abstraction and inclusiveness (common properties of all European societies) and the ideal-type method of systemic analysis.[29]

The introduction deals with the now familiar essentials of the need of subsistence, the social character of work, the dimensions of the environment, the people and their culture, the concept of economic system and the three building blocks of spirit, technique and organization (I, 13–21). The subcategories of them are spelled out in the following way (see also 1930, pp 206–207, and 1927, pp 14–32): The difference in the dimension of the economic spirit between the Aristotelian principle of the satisfaction according to need and the principle of profit (*Bedarfs* – vs. *Erwerbsprinzip*) is related to the purpose of economic activity: the satisfaction of specific needs or as much money as possible. The second spiritual category deals with the subjective mode of the choice of the means of the activity: traditional vs. rational, that is, the means are used because they are historically usual or they are constantly and critically checked. The third category, individualist vs. solidary, deals with the relation among people. It is the orientation of pure self-interest vs. the inclusion of the interests of the larger community.

The second broad category, the form or organization of the economy, is first divided into bound vs. free rules. Bound means orientation at supra-individual norms, free means that only specific actions are forbidden, and what is not forbidden is allowed. The next category is private vs. public orientation, that is, is the economic structure based more on private or public enterprises (note: a private economy can also operate in a bound rule system). Democratic vs. aristocratic refers to the question if many people are decision makers or if most people are decision takers (e.g. in capitalism or medieval feudalism). The difference closed vs. dissolved concerns the question if the economic units perform all economic activities themselves or not. Next is the economy of satisfaction according to need vs. the market economy (*Bedarfsdeckungs* – vs. *Verkehrswirtschaft*); it refers to the objective constellation (not the subjective spirit), if goods are produced for the market or if the producing units are also the consuming units (e.g. in socialism or self-sufficient systems). The satisfaction according to need can also prevail in exchange systems (e.g. the crafts system). The last organizational category is individual vs. communal firms (in communal firms, the working process is divided among the workers).

---

[27] We cannot present and discuss the rich literature on modern capitalism in detail, but see the reviews in Brocke (1987, p 67 ff.), Appel (1992) and the contributions in Backhaus (1996).

[28] We cannot discuss the problem of continuity here, see Töttö (1996); for the opposite view, see for example Breuer (1996, p 234).

[29] This research program has survived for example in Braudel (1979).

Finally, the principles of technique can be based empirically (practical, personal, historical knowledge) or scientifically (systematic search for empirical rules and laws). Next comes the difference between stationary (techniques change only over long time horizons) vs. revolutionary (permanent change). Last, we have the difference between organic vs. non-organic, that is, the dependence on living organisms (plant, animal, humans) and their growth processes or not. If they do not, they can be mechanical if production and transport do not depend on humans or animals as means but on mechanisms or chemisms. The procedure can also be inorganic, if respective resources like coal, minerals, etc. or inorganic power like electricity are used. All in all, we arrive at three subdivisions of economic systems (spirit, organization, technique) and 12 polarities. One implication of Sombart's system is that it does not make sense to think about a general superiority of systems and their variables because the measuring rod depends on the spiritual orientation.[30] It also does not make sense to think about "welfare effects" or "efficiency" without specifying the system under consideration. Efficiency considerations beyond specific economic systems are meaningless for Sombart.

In principle, Sombart distinguished the following system types: the early self-sufficient types of (1) the tribal societies; and (2) the peasant village economy. To exemplify: In the village, economy dominates the principle of satisfaction according to need, traditionalism and solidarism; the technique is empirical, stationary and organic. Next we have the aristocratic self-sufficient types; (3) the *oikos* economy in ancient Greece and Rome; and (4) the manored farm (*Fronhof*) economy in the European Middle Ages. Sombart mentions (5) the craft system and (6) the socialist type. It is opposed to (7) capitalism (see the precise description of all types in Sombart 1927, pp 20–30).

The systematic aspect in Sombart is the emphasis on the dominant economic system in historical epochs and the thesis that history is composed of clearly identifiable distinguished systems (e.g. no one-way road to reduce transaction costs in history, no at best camouflage self-interested individuals all the time). Further and in agreement with his metaphysics, it is the "the basic message of this work is that a different economic spirit has dominated at different times, and that it is the spirit that seeks its adequate form and in this way creates economic organization" (I, p 25).

Pre-capitalist societies have the Aristotelian idea of nourishment (*Nahrungsidee*, I, p 34), a socially defined and limited standard of material living, the principle of the need of subsistence and the principle of the satisfaction according to need (*Bedarfsdeckungsprinzip*), embedded in moral and legal rules and customs (I, p 32). It dominates in all pre-capitalist societies and it is opposite for example to the spirit of capitalism (the profit principle). Another important feature is the behavioural traditionalism. The prior early medieval economic system in primitive and rural Europe is the system of self-sufficiency (*Eigenwirtschaft*, I, p 45 ff.) in the peasant village communities (democratic type) and on the manored farms (*Fronhöfe*, the

---

[30] We will not discuss Sombart's basic notions of production, consumption etc., see Sombart (1960), which seem not to be peculiar or important.

aristocratic type) which were based on politically different forms of feudal dependency (including slavery). Until the thirteenth century (I, p 87), both were oriented at the self-sufficient mode of production and the principle of satisfaction according to need, organized in a communitarian way in the case of the villages which distributed land collectively according to the principle of satisfaction according to need.

Sombart's historically rich and multifaceted analysis is far from self-evident: Did little villages and village solidarity among the peasants really prevail, did they not try to make money and accept a modest standard of living? Was trade absolutely underdeveloped? Did the landlords conform to the principle of satisfaction according to need (he mentions himself that they always wanted to have more means for ostentation, see I, pp 62–63)? F. Oppenheimer, a contemporary critic who doubted that the difference between the spirits[31] holds, argues that the profit principle was no goal in itself for the capitalists, but to increase luxury, security, power, etc. (see also Harnisch 1928). Conversely, also the medieval craftsman searched for the best increase of his money earnings. This may not be chrematistic because the motive could be security for the family, etc.

Sombart's essential line of reasoning is to highlight the contrast to capitalism as an epoch-making difference in a "primitivist" tradition,[32] that is, leaning on the left hand side of his dichotomies and trying to show like Polanyi (1977) that exchange is an historical but not an elementary category of economic behaviour which came up relatively late in economic history. So he explains that exchange activities began relatively late (between the tenth and thirteenth century) and were locally confined. In his absolutely unorthodox theory of the emergence of cities (I, Chap. 9, see the definition on p 128), he argues that the founders of the few little consumption cities were kings and landlords who could buy the necessary agricultural foodstuffs of the environing agricultural land and pay with taxes or feudal interest revenues. This contradicts all theories[33] which say that the city is the basis of trade, production and the new spirit of freedom and enterprise which undermines self-sufficiency and feudal bonds (see also Mackensen 1970; Schäfers et al. 1976; Berndt 1977). Chapter 11 explains that the cities were ruled by the idea of community and economic self-sufficiency and the principle of satisfaction according to need.

But the city saw the emergence of a new economic system or mode of production and economic idea: the craft system, that is, legally and economically independent,

---

[31] The spirit concept was itself a nebular concept for him, see 1929, pp 1135, 1149–1153; see also for example Weede (1990, p 35). Most of the following criticisms of Oppenheimer were shared by the professional historians who mostly discussed partial aspects of his work in a very critical way, among them Dopsch, Brentano, and Below, see for example Below (1920).

[32] In the debate on classical Greece, modernists (Meyer, Beloch, Pöhlmann) and primitivists (Bücher, Hasebroek, Bolkestein) were distinguished according to their view on the social, economic and historical modernity of the Greek *poleis*. Oppenheimer was also very critical about Sombart's primitivism, see for example 1929, pp 420, 824–827, 1075, 1094–1095, 1116–1117, 1142–1143, on Sombart's thesis of the solidary (Teutonic) peasant communities, see 1929, p 515. On Oppenheimer's critique of Sombart, see Kruse (1996).

[33] See for example Oppenheimer (1929, pp 818–819, 854–855, 1144–1147), also Nuglisch 1904.

traditionally acting craftsmen (see I, p 188 for the definition). They followed the principle of satisfaction according to need but in an exchange nexus. The craftsman produces for the market, but the idea of "craftsmanship" corresponds to the dominating principles in the peasant villages because the market is in every respect tamed and non-competitive by the solidary self-regulation of the guilds and cooperatives of the craftsmen (stable and fixed demand and prices). It is further oriented at traditional and non-profit principles and empirical-organic techniques. In the little craft shops, the *Seele* principle could live. The pride to create unique products in which the personality of the craftsman is incorporated was a safeguard against cold economic rationalization. Also the little traders lived and operated in a crafts-like environment (I, p 291). Sombart tries hard to substantiate this claim empirically against the many opposing views.

The second book deals with the historical foundations of modern capitalism. A completely new economic system and idea of the economy emerges (I, p 319 ff.). It is an exchange economy, with two major groups, those who own the means of production and those who do not. The principles of economic rationalism (vs. traditionalism) and the principle of profit (vs. *Bedarfsdeckung*) begin to work. The capitalist enterprise is characterized, and the functions of the entrepreneur are differentiated (organizing, trading, calculating, I, p 322 ff.). The essence of capitalism is the new spirit which came up from the deep underground of the European soul (I, pp 327–333). "It is the same spirit which creates the new state, the new religion, the new science, the new technique and in all this the new economic life. We know that it is a spirit which is secular and based in this world, a spirit which with enormous power can destroy natural formations, can destroy old bonds and old barriers; and with the same strength it can reconstruct new forms of life both ingenious and artistic functional forms. It is the same spirit which since the declining Middle Ages has pulled man out of his quiet organically grown forms of love and community and which has propelled them onto an orbit of the restless search for self-determination and individual gain" (I, p 327).

Not only Sombart's feelings about the new spirit are ambivalent, also this spirit itself has a polar orientation which distinguishes Sombart's from Weber's spirit concept. "It is the spirit of Dr. Faustus: the spirit of inner doubt and restlessness which has taken possession of the people … Shall we call it the quest for the sky that we see manifesting itself again and again. We can do this with a certain measure of truth because the goals have been pushed to the limit. All the natural standards of organic bonds have become wanting, restrictive and narrow … With this Faustian spirit a new spirit has found an alliance this is the spirit which grants economic life a certain order, a measure of numerical exactitude, which has come about by defining purposes in exact terms this is the spirit of the bourgeois … Where the entrepreneurial spirit wants to conquer and acquire the bourgeois spirit wants to create order and protect" (I, pp 327–329).

In the following, Sombart describes the modern state (I, p 334 ff.) and its policies (currency, and trade policy, etc.) and the reasonable aspects of a mercantilist policy for capitalist dynamic development (I, p 362 ff.). The next lengthy chapter traces the development of technique. A lot of inventions and discoveries were made until the eighteenth century, but the assumption of *Seele* in nature was an impediment. The new spirit, the Faustian will to knowledge, the desire for making money, research for the military, and the transition from the empirical-traditional to the scientific-rational mode of investigation changed the way of technical research and implementation. The findings and production of precious metals (I, p 513 ff.) is considered as a major and very important "accident." The inflow of species eased the establishment of capitalism and Sombart investigates the relationship between specie inflow, prices and production over the centuries. His ambiguous statements concerning the quantity theory of money are interesting and – as we saw – typical for him (I, pp 543–547).

In conformity with his primitivist position, he explains the first phase of the concentration of fortunes (not capital) as a precondition of early accumulation not by referring to merchants and trade, etc. (I, p 608 ff.), but to the increase of earnings of the land rents (I, p 619) and the earnings in the mining industry. The third important source was simple robbery, including the plundering of the later colonies (I, p 668 ff.), the reintroduction of slavery and the colonial exploitation (robbery of natural resources and general environmental degradation, see I, p 709).

He then turns to the demand side and analyses the demand shift in luxury goods (I, p 719 ff.). The next topic is the labour market, the oversupply and misery of the new proletariat (including a critique of Marx' historical view on the first phase of accumulation). He discusses the problem that the new spirit was missing because the proletarians were "natural," "lazy" people with a clear idea of the virtues of leisure. They also held a sufficiency standard for income, a *Bedarfsdeckungsprinzip* (I, p 807, compare E.P. Thompson), so that the mercantilist state was inventive to motivate them to work more (I, Chap. 54). The other side is the birth of the capitalist entrepreneurs, the class whose ingenuity is power and creative genius is the major force in the winds of change (I, p 836). As strongly as Sombart points out the situation of the *misérables* does, he emphasize the qualities and deeds of the emerging capitalist class. He distinguishes early merchant, conqueror and founder types (I, p 872 ff.) and identifies the social groups where they mainly come from: foreigners, Jews, heretics and chrematistic landlords (I, Chap. 57). But they also come from former little merchants and other categories of citizens (I, Chap. 58). The first volume ends with these ideal-type characterizations of types and descent groups of early entrepreneurs.

Volume two analyses early capitalism in Europe in which the old and the new spirit and organizational forms existed side by side. Different principles fight for supremacy; it is a period of transition dated from the fifteenth to the middle of eighteenth century. The first local beginnings can be found in the thirteenth century (Siena). The material driving forces are multifold: the emergence of nation states, the discovery of America, the religious persecutions, modern military systems (see the discussion in Wachtler 1985), the system of double accounting, etc. The general evolutionary path is from traditionalism to rationalism, from a static to a dynamic economy, from the organic to mechanical ways of human interaction (II, Chaps. 1–3).

In less then 40 pages, Sombart describes impressively the new spirit of early capitalism. It is a prime example of the *Verstehen* method in practice which Sombart handles masterly (II, pp 25–64). He contrasts the "romantic" element in which force intrudes and where the roles of merchant, pirate and adventurer are hard to distinguish (II, p 26). The overseas companies had the elements of medieval solidary communities and freebooting. The other part is the bourgeois, civilian aspect (*Bürgergeist*), including methodological, rational goal-oriented behaviour and an ideal of contract loyalty with religious, and philosophical roots. Commenting the debate on the just price, Sombart shows that the principle of honourable and honest acquisition was more important than maximum gains and cut-throat competition. "Even when conducting business, the individual would not get absorbed by the noise and ado of business affairs. He remained true to himself. He retained the dignity of an independent man who will not compromise his honour to personal gain. In trade and commerce, personal pride remained dominant" (II, p 62).

Sombart now comes to the organizational aspect of his classification. He discusses the mixed and transitory forms of firm organizations (like the single-event corporations) and then analyses the modern capitalist firm, that is, the division of the personal and the business, the rationalization of production, the rationale of making profit, etc. His main example for the tendencies of objectification and mechanization is the history of double entry bookkeeping since Pacioli. In Chap. 11, he delineates the capitalist organizational forms (e.g. general partnership). But also in these detailed historical and empirical descriptions, the emphasis is on cultural economics, for example when he shows that joint stock companies are alien to the spirit of early capitalism (II, p 162). After a short digression on state companies, he comes to the second main part of the book on the extension of the market due to population increases, and political and technical changes (Chap. 13). The new big armies and luxury demand are influences from the demand side (Chap. 14) which is in general less important than the changes on the supply side in Sombart's investigations.

He further describes the erratic-traditional modes of more or less subjective price setting, which depended on conventions, administrative influences and transport and informational obstacles. In a lengthy part (II, pp 229–418), he describes the technical improvements in transport, travelling, the mail system and publications. More and more the law of one price was effective as a result of the depersonalisation and mechanization of the price setting process by, for example, institutionalized auctions and stock exchanges (Chap. 15). The same tendency holds good for the distribution of commodities from door-to-door salesmen to established regular markets, organized chains of distribution (II, p 441), and the modes of payment (II, p 513 ff.).

The modern business cycle did not exist; there were many crises but no rhythm; the boom phase is missing due to the dependency on organic techniques and the lack of fixed capital. The crises are simple sales crises (Chap. 16). He then describes the mostly rural population. Agriculture remained self-sufficient and traditional between 800 and 1800; the trades in towns remained craft-oriented (II, pp 650–681). But changes took place in the crafts guild systems because the profit motive invaded the old system which degenerated and a class-like polarization between master and journeyman occurred. But Sombart adds: not before the nineteenth century (II, 692–693). Another major change refers to the new organizational forms of production, firms, manufactories, the putting out system and big industry (II, p 730 ff.; for the changes from *Seele* to *Geist* see, e.g. II, pp 783, 787). Later he discusses their advantages compared with the crafts system (mass production, uniformity and promptness of delivery, e.g. for the military, see II, pp 841–886). Against Marx, he argues that firms and manufactories went side by side for a long time and he describes their different types, the division of labour, the work process, and new techniques in specific branches. The craft system could also not adapt due to its particular spirit (II, p 887). After discussing locational aspects (immobilization and decentralization, see also II, pp 901–906), he comes to the slowly changing working conditions.

He defines the ideal-type scheme of the capitalist-worker relationship. The conditions are: "1. A pure capitalist entrepreneurship is confronted by wage earners without any property or any other means of subsistence; 2. on both sides there is a determined capitalist economic spirit: The profit principle and the principle of economic rationality are shared both by the entrepreneur and the wage labourer. This implies that on both sides there is a will and determination to organize the labour contract with the view to maximize a) profits and b) wages; … 3. the labour relationship rests on a free contract and is based on the strict contractual quit pro quo … The purposes that follow from this economic spirit can best be realized with: a) short term; b) money-based labour contracts; … 4. labour is being utilized without any regard to the personal circumstances of the labourer" (II, pp 811–812). From Sombart's point of view, the recent work contracts (short-term, outsourcing, etc.) and rationalized production processes of turbo-capitalism correspond with the ideal type of capitalism compared with the social market contracts (long-term, etc.) and socially regulated working conditions. He goes on to summarize the real social position of the workers, their mentality, the content of the contracts in early capitalism, the organization of labour in the factories, and child and women labour (II, p 813 ff.).[34]

He then turns to the economic macro process. The first part describes mercantilist theory as a reasonable concept for practical policy; against the static-mechanical exchange paradigm of the British (he could not suppress some awkward chauvinist remarks here) mercantilist theory is a dynamic-organic theory of production with active idealism – an original and informative digression on the history of economic thought (II, p 913 ff.). Next come the changes in international economic relations (II, p 943 ff.), trade balances, balances of payments etc. which are surveyed. Again he gives a primitivist account; only (and mainly consumption) goods in excess supply in the countries and almost no means of production are traded. The main part is colonial goods (II, pp 1029, and 1036). He further describes the new stratification of early capitalist societies, its old and new classes and the estates, including the new middle class and the new power of money (bourgeoisie) besides the old powers of kings and feudal lords (II, p 1085 ff.). The development of economic forces in early capitalism took place in the national dimension; this immensely increased the power

---

[34] See also his impressive handbook article in 1959 (Sombart 1931, 1959), first published in 1931, on the historically changing arrangements of the labour contract, where he masterly applies his historic-systematic ideal-type approach.

of the nation states (Chap. 65). Higher taxes were a natural result of higher national income as a result of higher productivity (for the reasons see II, p 1059), which nevertheless had been slowed down by wars, the influence of the church, psychological factors, and transport conditions, but not essentially by the traditional industrial code. This has surely to do with the fact that the existence of markets is not an essential feature for Sombart as a driving force for increased productivity because he holds the industrial and not the market paradigm (see Boltanski and Thévenot 1991).

Two aspects are salient at the end of the second book. The first is his summary statement on the beginning mechanization, depersonalisation, banalization, and contractualization of society in the tradition of his cultural economics (II, pp 1076–1084). The second is his emphasis on the fundamental ecological break at the end of early capitalism, which could have brought the new development to an early end: the overuse of wood as raw material, combustible and general organic source of energy since the early Middle Ages and its severe shortage since the sixteenth century which escalated in the eighteenth century (II, 1137 ff.; see also Sieferle 1982). Sombart's analysis testifies a high level of ecological consciousness long before a modest recognition of the natural restraints of capitalism has set in.

Four features are outstanding in Sombart's outline so far: first, the rich empirical details, second, the arrangement according to his threefold distinction, third, his emphasis of cultural economics ("rationalization")[35] and fourth, his primitivist bias.[36] The references for his investigation was scientific literature of all kinds, statistical investigations (but no regression analysis or econometrics), monographs, personal observations, statements of accounts, biographies, literature, laws and official declarations, travel reports, etc. (see, e.g. II, pp 421–435).

Volume three, which was first published in 1927, captures the phase of high capitalism from 1760 to 1914 when capitalism dominated all other partial economic systems. For him, it is a unique and strange historical episode. He thought that after World War I capitalism would never recover in full again (an assertion which may be doubted today). The driving force is the search for profit, for Sombart an uneconomic and in some sense irrational goal because it has nothing to do with the need of subsistence (*Unterhaltsfürsorge*) as such.[37] In the preface, he further mentions how much he owes to Marx (despite his book on proletarian socialism). But Marx lived in the early stages of capitalism so that it is no surprise that he made wrong predictions and that he was a cultural optimist. In Sombart's view, capitalism has produced nothing in the cultural sphere. Capitalism should be rejected today (III, p XXI).

---

[35] See his short discussion on method as *verstehende* sociology where the final causes are human motives in II, pp 844–845.

[36] He holds for example that there were no real commodity exchange markets before the ninenteenth century and no commodity drawn bills until the eighteenth century, see II, pp 499–500, and 525.

[37] "Through the pursuit of such an uneconomic goal as profit hundreds of millions of men … have been given a chance to life, culture has been restructured from the bottom to the top, empires have been founded and destroyed, the mystery world of technology has been created, the planet has been changed. And all this has happened only because a handful of people has been driven by the passion to make money" (III, p XIV).

Like Schumpeter (for a comparison see Chaloupek 1995) and against Marx, he stresses that not "capital" is the major driving force but human beings and their motives, in capitalism especially the entrepreneurs (Chap. 1). He describes the functional differentiation from the ownership of the means of production, and the different types (merchant, financial and the expert type). He stresses the democratization of their recruitment disentangles their motives (vanity, power, money, drive for activity, etc., but he also mentions the sense of responsibility, see III, p 36). He highlights the mixture of bourgeois rationality and calculation and the Faustian drive for infinity (III, pp 14–23). The spiritual difference to early capitalism lies in the disembeddedness and independence of religion, customs, family, etc. Now a spirit of progress, the dominance of the achievement values, love for the business (neglect of culture, etc.), and the profit motive take the lead (Buß 1995, pp 21–22).

In a very short part, he deals with the now much less powerful modern state, which comprises an ambiguous composition of liberal principles and political power aspects. The modern state is secular, individualist, and has to recognize the interests of capital (taxes). Germany has the bureaucratic-legal style (III, p 57). The general exterior policy is despite all liberal phraseology neo-mercantilism. Imperialism plays a role, but the origins are in the political sphere. The next Chap. 7 deals with the changes in the technical domain from a very general but impressive perspective, in which the Faustian motive and rational empirical research are combined with the disenchantment of nature as a precondition. Applying his basic dichotomies of technique, the fundamental change lies in the scientific and rational character, which substitutes the empirical and traditional mode. Discoveries are an essential component for economic growth. Modern man lives in a technical social atmosphere where everything technical is admired. Innovations and inventions are imposed, the final consumer is seen as a passive innovation taker (III, p 95).

Due to the inorganic nature of modern technical progress, emancipation from the boundaries of organic nature takes place. The coke procedure is a major precondition and basis of modern capitalism. We see that Sombart stresses once again culture economics, but at the same time does not neglect the material preconditions of change at all. In earlier times, man lived from the yearly income of sun energy. "And all of a sudden mankind had at ist disposal the energies of the sun as treasures in the interior of the earth which had been accumulated there over millions of years through radiation down from the sun. A wealth had been found which mankind was not able to consume through the inventions of modern technology … We now live in an age in which mankind can consume its wealth in energies and substances and can in this way show off an unheard of glitter and wealth. What we call high capitalism is easily explained in the sudden increase in the wealth of mankind … By braking the piggybank of earth and spending with both hands he succeeded in showing off an unheard of wealth" (III, pp 122, 272). Not efficient allocation and the markets are for Sombart the essential origin of wealth, but the exploitation of the earth, formulated in a neo-physiocratic and deep ecological way (compare Georgescu-Roegen 1971; on the importance of minerals and inorganic production techniques, and the extinction of species see, e.g. III, pp 263–268).

The second main part deals with the structure of capital, its different types, like money capital, the mobilization of the commodity world (increase in goods, transport, etc., which also depended on the state infrastructure), and the essential function of a rationalized credit system for an expanding economy. Modern credit increased the depersonalisation, denaturalisation and putting into details of (economic) live (*Dekonkretisierung*, see the list in III, p 222). All these aspects are discussed in a descriptive, taxonomic and empirical way (III, pp 127–303). Sombart does not include the early debates on capital theory and monetary theory, probably a weakness in his project to describe modern capitalism. It is at least an omission in the light of his book on method (1930) which argued that *verstehende* economics includes relevant laws and insights of *ordnende* economics.

He asks next where the labour force came from and distinguishes and criticizes naturalist, economic, and sociological hypotheses (see III, p 304 ff.). He stresses first the importance of forced labour (coloured slavery, III, p 325), second, the free excess population due to the dissolution of the old village communities and agrarian reform, and third, the simple increase of the population (III, p 354). He also describes the new personality and behavioural ideal of the man in town (III, p 348). Before discussing the internal and external distribution (III, p 470 ff.), he highlights the necessity and ways to socialize the workers into the new spirit (Chap. 26). "The new economic order needed such partial men bereft of their personality reduced to spirit happy and able to function as tiny wheels in a big and complicated clockwork" (III, p 424). Force, drill, the religious spirit (Weber), the educational force of machine work etc. are presented. This part which resembles the research of E.P. Thompson, Foucault and for example Bourdieu and their matrices of discipline shows that, for Sombart, cultural economics does not only mean the harmonious socialization and functioning of norms, but that culture also may have a power and force component.

It is surprising that Sombart calls the capacity of markets to regulate the economic activities by the price setting through supply and demand a wonder (III, p 519). Specific markets can be analysed according to the spirit, organization and technique scheme (III, p 527). Sombart mentions the laws of price: supply and demand determine prices, the price determines supply and demand, the purchasing power has an autonomous influence on prices (see also his description of the mechanical emergence of an average price at the stock exchange as an example for the rationalization of price setting, III, p 667). Also for the labour market, the price laws hold, but it is only "as-if," because labour is no commodity. On commodity markets, the price is determined by the production costs (III, p 529). "Artificial" intervention into the free markets can take place, for example, by the state (taxes, but also tariffs, patents, laws, market orders, social security, etc.), which influences the free actions of the market participants. It is remarkable that Sombart's "price theory" is less then elementary. He does not consider the "theoretical" literature at all (see also the missing literature in the part on competition, III, pp 551–553).

Second, he accepts the distinction between the free market as such into which intervention takes place. It would have been more natural to develop here a concept of markets as instituted processes in the tradition of old institutionalism (see, e.g. Hodgson 1988). It is a major weakness that Sombart never developed an alternative, institutional price and market theory.

He goes on to discuss the influences on markets by labour (trade unions) and capitalist institutions (e.g. cartels, which are later discussed as legitimate and economically beneficial, see pp 696–697). Later, he also deals with the protection against risk (e.g. insurance, Chap. 43). He distinguishes three forms of competition (Chap. 34): quality, surrogate and forced competition. Competition by quality (*Leistungskonkurrenz*) is acceptable, but it is an overvalued and secondary driving force of capitalism (III, p 558). Surrogate means advertisement which he strongly rejects because it fools the customer with wrong or arbitrary nonsense (III, p 559). This was often criticized as cultural elitism in Sombart. Forced competition means cut-throat competition to undermine competition and to establish monopolies. In a later chapter, he describes the rationalization of markets in the sense of greater uniformity and bigness and motivation (Chap. 36, and III, p 637 ff.) which also depended on better transport conditions (III, p 650). Speculation in the real and the monetary sphere has no productive function; it expresses the instinct for play (III, p 664). Later, he describes the joint stock companies (and their interdependent networks and the conglomeration of power in some few hands) as functionally and spiritually the best fit with high capitalism (III, pp 712–747, see also Chaps. 48–50). He also nicely describes the spirit of high capitalist competition (III, p 557).

Besides having discussed demand and forms of firms (Chaps. 31, 33, and 37), he delineates the emergence of the real, rhythmical, expansionary business cycle since 1825 (Chap. 35). The stabilization of cycles is first sign of capitalism becoming old (Chap. 45). Cyclical expansions are possible due to the inorganic production goods. Slumps are the result of the disproportion between the expansion in the organic and the limits of expansion in the non-organic production spheres.[38] His cultural economics is manifest in his depiction of the spirit of demand (restlessness, nervousness, need for constant change, e.g. in fashion), its uniformization and would-be elegance (III, pp 604–605, and 625–627). This corresponds with the depersonalisation and *Vergeistung* of transactions, dominated by "contractual forms in which the individual contracting partner enters into a system of objective conditions which rule the relationship from the very start a relationship which he can use for his personal ends like a mechanism … where there is no relationship between soul and soul but where the relationship is only realized through the mediation of an abstract legal concept" (III, p 657). *Geist* here only appears in the self-alienated version and is defined as follows. "The spirit is … immaterial what is not soul. Spirit leads its existence of its own without being alive. The soul is always tied to life, the soul of a being is tied to this being's life. The soul of a human being is bound to the life of this man. Spiritualization is then the process to move from the soul to the spirit, to isolate and make objective the processes of the soul, a sort of 'reification'" (III, p 895). The *Geist* component should reduce costs, render possible accountability, and better control of the work force (III, pp 925–926).

---

[38] See Backhaus (1987a, b, 1989), Lowe (1989), Krohn (1977, pp 58–65).

He rejects Marx's thesis of unilateral concentration; his empirical results show that concentration varies according to branches and depends on the optimal size of the firms (which hinges on production, distribution, and finance criteria, see III, p 517). In most branches (except agriculture), the average size increased but only in very few branches have some big corporations extinguished little and middle firms; mergers are often due to prestige activities of managers (III, p 881 ff.). He comes back to the tendency of the abstractification of principles and rules; one example for these tendencies is the introduction of business economics (III, pp 886 ff.).

In the last part, Sombart restates his aim to delineate the spiritual European background of the archetype of this wondrous greatest product of the civilized world called capitalism. It made possible, "to feed, cloth, and house a population which grew by the hundreds of millions also ultimately to give them jewellery and fashion and to amuse them every night" (III, p 952). We hear again his ambiguous attitude. He then asks how the older economic systems will fare. Self-sufficient economic structures still persist well, the crafts make half of the working population, but they changed and most craftsmen are little bourgeois entrepreneurs in 1927 (III, pp 957, 963).[39] The peasants are still holding a respectable margin of GDP, but their average living conditions are depressed and partially the achieving spirit creeps in (III, pp 969–971). The cooperative system, defined as an association of non-wealthy economic subjects to improve their economic situation and performance by large-scale enterprise (III, p 896), differs in strength in different countries and may have a great future, but it has a more modest present (II, p 998). The public and semi-public sector was strong at Sombart's time, but he thought that its future is open (III, p 999). The last Chap. 60 on the future will be discussed in the next paragraph.

Sombart's third volume had been expected with much interest. Many had been disappointed. There is no doubt that the book is less structured than the other two volumes and that sometimes a certain exhaustion can be felt. The spheres of law and politics are mostly missing. Sombart does not present an alternative theory of markets, competition and prices. It is nevertheless one of the most impressive contributions in the social sciences as far the broadness of the presentation, the application of his systems approach and his excellent application of cultural economics are concerned. Sombart was an applied methodological radical: he rejects pure theory in principle and *homo oeconomicus* as universal phenomena even on the level of ideal types (compare Weber). Not rational action but concepts of mind (spirit) are in the centre, historical-theoretical economics should substitute mainstream economics, evolution is not Darwinist or economically rational but governed by idiosyncratic mentalities (see for the pattern variables Gislain and Steiner 1995).

---

[39] Sombart changed his opinion on the future of the crafts system in the face of the empirical data. In for example (1919, p 279 ff., first published 1903), he thought that the crafts would more or less disappear.

Sombart on the Future and the Future of Sombart

We will concentrate on four texts to summarize Sombart's discussion of the future (Sombart 1916–1927, 1987, Chap. 60; 1928; 1932; 1934, p 160 ff.; see also Chaloupek 1996). In the last chapter of modern capitalism (1916–1927, 1987, Chap. 60), Sombart predicts the general persistence of the capitalist system and an adding of new and different economic systems, so that corporations, crafts, cooperatives, mixed public-private organizations, peasants, and other self-sufficient production systems exist side by side. Sombart thought that the capitalist elements would loose their preponderance. But there will be no shortage of energy and many mouths have to be fed.

Further, capitalism will be more regulated by the state, subdued to normative ideas, and it will become more quiet, less turbulent, adult. Big firms will become ponderous machines (III, pp 1012–1013). Non-capitalist economic system elements will increase which implies a planning economic element which supersedes the profit principle. For the human condition, he sees no great difference in a stabilized capitalism or a rationalized socialism. The difference is, if the economic systems in which the *Seele* element rules (self-sufficiency, farming, and handicraft) will have a chance in the future (III, pp 1016–1017).

Inner colonization and the increase of peasantry seem inevitable because the former colonies are or will become independent and so the cheap furnishing of foodstuff will end. His (wrong) estimate was that the peasantry would increase significantly as a share of the population and GDP. He holds that farming will never be totally rationalized (*vergeistet*).

In his paper for the meeting of the *Verein* in Zurich on the changes of capitalism, Sombart (1928) confirms the main points of his view: the emancipation of the developing countries, the necessary increase of agriculture, the intensification of regulation and rationalization, the decrease of entrepreneurship, and the pluralization of economic systems. His discussion is organized around the classification of changes in spirit, organization and technique, that is, the *Gestaltidee* (1930, pp 206–207) of economic systems we discussed above. We can only mention the main points here. He emphasizes that the developing countries in Asia and Africa will further advance, but that the West has not enough capital to invest because capital accumulation will decline. The reasons are a stagnant population in the developed countries, and the productivity of labour will decrease. He puts an emphasis on the concentration of capital and cartels (1928, p 248) and the dominance of finance capital. The worker will live like a public servant (fixed working hours, administered wages, etc., see p 251). For Sombart, capitalism becomes older; it is – since the war – in the season of fall; he calls it late capitalism.

The next text is about the future of capitalism presented in 1932. Now Sombart does not only ask how the future looks like, but how the future should be shaped actively, which is a problem of will (1932, 1987, p 394). He points out the plurality of systems, concentration, *Vergeistung*, administered prices by cartels and bargaining, etc. Then he proposes a planned economy, but not the abolition of private property. It should be uniform planning on the national level but with freedom, for example in the sphere of consumption, with a multitude of different economic systems and spheres and free competition. But also partial socialization is considered and other types of influence like subsidies, taxes, etc. (1932, 1987, p 409). He actively supports autarky in the sense of a strictly controlled and diminished foreign trade and some import substitution. Further, he asks for a partial return to an agrarian state (*Reagrarisierung*, 1932, 1987, pp 415–417). According to him, 40% of the population should work in the only partially mechanized farming sector. To realize this program of fundamental reform, all depends for Sombart on the spirit of the population to realize an alternative economic style (1932, 1987, p 418).

Practically, Sombart formulated a strategy against unemployment which had been added to the full employment plan of the *Studiengesellschaft für Geld – und Kreditwirtschaft* for the German chancellor of the *Reich* in August 1932 (see Backhaus 1989, pp 94–98). He supported bilateral trade relations and an immediate massive deficit-financed infrastructure employment program by the state. The money should be strictly reserved for investments in the augmentation of the productive capacities in the organic part of the economy (where Sombart typically assumed the bottleneck). He proposed the implementation of peasant villages and agricultural cooperatives, drainage, canals, a certain rationalization of agricultural production, for example the consolidation of farmland, etc.

Further, he supported smallholder do-it-yourself villages to further strengthen the self-sufficient mode of production. (He rejected, e.g. luxurious highway projects.) All these measures would absorb the unemployed, reduce the bottlenecks and re-energize economic activity. This or similar plans were not realized. When Hitler won the elections in 1934, the highway/rearmament/high tech variant was chosen. In 1939, the Germans were not living a peaceful life near to nature, but went to war.

Some points of Sombart's theoretical and practical ideas are repeated and specified in his *German socialism* (1934, p 244 ff.). Technical development should be tamed and controlled by a patent agency which decides according to the public interest. A simpler life style and the creation of peasant communities are his ideal. The opulence and sophistication of goods, too many cars, planes and noise are criticized. He pleads for a drastic reduction of the productive and transport superstructure of society and the creation of natural free areas where a simple and natural life is still possible. The strengthening of the middle class, the peasants, the self-sufficient producers and the craftsmen is proposed. A number of branches ripe for socialization are enumerated, e.g. the great banks and transport (1934, pp 300–301).

Sombart's prognosis of calm late capitalism has proven more or less wrong (especially in the last years). But we should note that, for Sombart, no objective laws exist, so everything depends finally on the free will of the economic actors. His prediction that regulation of capitalism will increase and that a plurality of economic systems will coexist side by side (craft system, capitalist firm, etc.) has some evidence.

In our view, Sombart's systems approach has still relevance. Countries in transition like China or Malaysia can be analysed in an encompassing way with his classification. In general, what we are missing today are interdisciplinary analyses which overcome the specialization of professions and disciplines. Another strong point in Sombart is his formulation of strong hypotheses like the book on the influence of the Jews on capitalism (1911). Even if he overstated his cases, they were the starting point of highly relevant debates and what Popper would have liked: strong theses with a high potential of falsification.

In our view, Sombart's primitivism is another strong point against the tide because today we can observe the opposite extreme: because we life in a capitalist society, its origins and behavioural codes are retrospectively assumed to have existed until the dawn of man and will persist forever. Sombart's assumption of clearly distinct systems and styles includes the possibility that there may never be an end of history and that we will see another major distinct system in the future (based again on the principle of satisfaction according to need?). His work is also a counterpoint against the economic tendency in modern economic history, not only in cliometrics, only to ask for the forces of growth and its impediments in a transaction costs and property rights framework. From that perspective, capitalism and non-attenuated private property are the yardstick of success and failure in a historical unilateral perspective in which world history converges to capitalism. For Sombart, capitalism was more a strange and exceptional surprise.

He also posits another image of man in his anthropology against the opportunist pleasure and pain utility maximizer, our beloved *homo oeconomicus*. A further point concerns his basic criticism of capitalist society, whereas today we have an almost uniform approval which sometimes seems to come close to ideological legitimization.

Another aspect worth mentioning is his ecological and energetic component (wood, coke and the exploitation of minerals), the plundering of nature as a precondition of capitalism. Today, we have the economics of the environment as a clearly separated and often highly formalized field of research. For Sombart, the ecological dimension has to be taken into consideration in *any* reflection of capitalist development. His critical remarks are truer than ever, the extinction of species increases, and the hothouse effect leads among other things to the melting of the arctic ice. The visible end of fossil energy (oil) is taken notice of in the oil producing countries (e.g. in the Emirates). Will solar energy be accompanied by a completely different economic style?

A certain principle of autarky is discussed in the debate on the EU where some support a certain economic closure to hold environmental and social standards and fight against social and environmental dumping and beggar-my-neighbour policies. Sombart's support of a stronger agrarian basis and a careful inner colonization could certainly find an open ear in the green back to nature movements.

Sombart's cultural criticism which has been mostly left out here seems to be relevant today.[40] There is an extensive and critical recent debate on the rationalization

---

[40] As mentioned above, in his book on German socialism he speaks of the age of economics in the last 150 years. He criticizes the primacy of the economy, the profit motive in most human interactions, the population increase, agglomerations, the mechanization and depersonalisation in production and everyday live, monotonous working conditions, the unification (of houses, furniture, fashion, etc.), the deterioration of religious faith and lack of a common ethos, the destruction and fictionalization of nature, the flooding of the world with commodities and motor vehicles, the dissolution of village communities and the disappearance of the cosy and restful personality instead of the nervous person with strong will and intellectual functions, the abolition of natural rhythms, the hurry up mentality and the ideals of meaningless bigness, quick and hasty movements, and the constant new (see Sombart 1934, Part 1). For the hurry up mentality and non-stop transmutations, see Garhammer (1999).

of all aspects of human life, including politics, in the social sciences (one example is the highly interesting McDonaldization debate, see Ritzer (1993, 1998), and for the critics Alfino et al. (1998), where hundreds of recent examples for rationalization are discussed). It surely grasps an element of modern life. If rationalization in the sense of Sombart is the unequivocal tendency in modern firms and business, relations may nevertheless be doubted. His emphasis on the unnatural loss of *Seele* which was an often neglected but existing component of human interaction in big organizations (state bureaucracies, firms, etc.) and the relative degeneration of *Gemeinschafts* structures in them in the last years due to rationalizations is one major distinguishing criterion in the definition of post-modernity in the highly original and creative approach of Galtung on the costs of modernization (1997, pp 43–92).

It can be argued that Sombart's negative vision of capitalism and the essence of it came genuinely to the fore only after the breakdown of the so-called socialist countries and in the process of the globalization of economies, that is, a certain income polarization in society, the inferiority of politics, the increasing abstractification of the money economy with joint stock speculation as the new pop culture, the decline of trust, the *Auto*-mobilization and commercialization in all parts of the world, the depersonalisation of the work process due to computers, the decline of natural rhythms and relaxation (Garhammer 1999), the reduction and subjugation of all human interactions to the individual revenue-maximizing principle, etc.

In a very interesting and informative book on global capitalism by Luttwak (1999), consultant and Senior fellow at the Center for Strategic and International Studies in Washington DC, we read: "(T)he logic of turbo-capitalism is that nothing should stand in the way of economic efficiency, neither obstructive government regulations nor traditional habits, neither entrenched interests nor feelings of solidarity for the less fortunate, neither arbitrary privileges nor the normal human desire for stability … The human consequences of turbo-capitalism are both liberating and profoundly disorienting. The loss of individual authenticity that Friedrich Nietzsche predicted is now upon us in full force. This process of depersonalisation is visibly complete in the modern television politician" (1999, pp 222, 224). Like Sennett, Bellah and others, Luttwak (who does not know Sombart)[41] meticulously describes how the "revenue-maximizing spectacle" intrudes all spheres of social life, the family, sports, medicine, and firms (for Germany see on a more journalist level Kurz 1999). All these authors conform with Marx and Sombart that capitalism is unique in history, that it is the fundamental shaping force in society and that it has non-acceptable social, political, cultural and ecological costs.

We arrive at the paradox that Sombart may be right because he was wrong. His diagnosis of the end of high capitalism and its further bastardisation after 1914, the low impact of technological improvements in the confines of the coke paradigm, the

---

[41] For the parallels in the critical perspective, see Mitzman (1973, p 6 ff.). The authors mentioned demonstrate that cultural criticism is not a strange extreme of old German conservatism and elitism. For Luttwak's remark on politicians, compare Sombart (1907).

necessary decrease of foreign trade and productivity, etc. were obviously wrong predictions in the longer run (but not what the available data of his time were concerned). But with the description of the pure logic of what he called capitalism and its consequences, including the cultural sphere, was he wrong?

A first step in a forward-looking direction and application of Sombart was presented by Boltanski and Chiapello (1999).[42] In the conscious tradition of Weber and Sombart, the book analyses the third ideological configuration of the capitalist spirit which emerged in the 1980. The empirical basis of their description is the hermeneutical comparison of some 60 books of the managerial literature in the 1990. The key element is what they call the metaphysics of the network pattern, including the positive judgment of adaptation, change, flexibility, teamwork, communication, creativity, etc. This necessitates a charming, autonomous flexible, communicative, opportunist and light (vis-à-vis passions and values) character and a permanent mental radar screening of the environment. Besides the social, their cultural critique formulates the personal and mental problems of the flexible networker, his anxiety to be disconnected (handymania), the exhaustion due to forced autonomy, the divide between flexible adaptation and the need for authenticity.

Therefore, Sombart's relevance today could lie in the application of his approach to an analysis of the third industrial revolution with the information techniques as the material basis, after the breakdown of capitalism, the acceleration of globalization and deregulation; an analysis including all of Sombart's dimensions (the new economics business cycle, the organization and restructuring of international firms, the empirical distribution of capital flows, the exhaustion of non-renewable resources, etc.) under the guidance of his spirit, organization, technique systems idea with the strong emphasis on changes of "spirit" as the ultimate driving force. This could be a starting point for further research in the Sombart tradition.

References

Alfino M et al (1988) McDonaldization revisited, London
Allodi L (1989) Die Analyse des modernen Menschen bei Max Scheler und Werner Sombart. Annali di Sociologia 5:458–493
Amonn A (1930) Die drei Nationalökonomien. Schmollers Jahrbuch 54:193
Appel M (1992) Werner Sombart – Historiker und Theoretiker des modernen Kapitalismus. Metropolis, Marburg
Backhaus JG (1987a) Werner Sombart's theory of the business cycle, Working paper 87–018. Limburg University, Maastricht, Faculty of Economics
Backhaus JG (1987b) Werner Sombarts Konjunkturtheorie, Research memorandum 87–036. Faculty of Economics, Limburg University, Maastricht
Backhaus JG (1989) Werner Sombarts Konjunkturtheorie. In: Schefold B (ed) Studien zur Entwicklung der ökonomischen Theorie VII, Berlin, pp 77–98

---

[42] See our review (Peukert 2000a, b).

Backhaus JG (1989b) Sombart's modern capitalism. In: Blaug M (ed) Gustav Schmoller (1838–1917) and Werner Sombart (1863–1941), Elgar reference collection series: Pioneers in Economics Series, vol 30. Elgar, Aldershot, pp 93–105

Backhaus JG (ed) (1996) Werner Sombart, 3 vols. Metropolis, Marburg

Backhaus JG (ed) (2000) Werner Sombart (1863–1941) – Klassiker der Sozialwissenschaften. Metropolis, Marburg

Below G (1920) Die Entstehung des modernen Kapitalismus. Probleme der Wirtschaftsgeschichte, Tübingen, pp 399–500

Berndt H (1977) Identität und Formwandel der Stadt. Die Alte Stadt 4:165–182

Betz HK (1966) Historicism, romanticism and Marxism in Sombart's work. Dissertation, University of Utah, Salt Lake City, UT

Blaug M (ed) (1992) Gustav Schmoller (1838–1917) and Werner Sombart (1863–1941), Elgar reference collection series: Pioneers in Economics Series, vol 30. Elgar, Aldershot, pp 93–105

Bobek H (1979) Rentenkapitalismus und Entwicklung im Iran. In: Interdisziplinäre Iran-Forschung: Beiträge aus Kulturgeographie, Ethnologie, Soziologie und Neuerer Geschichte; Beiträge des internationalen und interdisziplinären Symposiums Gegenwartsbezogene Iran-Forschung, Tübingen, 17–19 June 1977, pp 113–123

Boltanski L, Chiapello E (1999) Le nouvel esprit du capitalisme. Gallimard, Paris

Boltanski L, Thévenot L (1991) De la justification. Gallimard, Paris

Braudel F (1979) Civilisation matérielle, économie et capitalisme: XVe au XVIIe siècle, 3 vols. Armand Colin, Paris

Breuer S (1996) Von Tönnies zu Weber: Zur Frage einer 'deutschen Linie' der Soziologie. Berliner Journal für Soziologie 6:227–245

Briefs G (1926) Proletarischer Sozialismus [Review]. Schmollers Jahrbuch 50:1–27

Brocke B (1973) Werner Sombart. In: Wehler H-U (ed) Deutsche Historiker, Göttingen, pp 616–634

Brocke B (ed) (1987) Sombarts "Moderner Kapitalismus": Materialien zur Kritik und Rezeption, Munich

Bruhns H (1985) De Werner Sombart à Max Weber et Moses I. Finley: La typologie de la ville antique et la question de la ville de consommation. In: Leveau P (ed) L'origine des richesses dépensées dans la ville antique, Aix-en-Provence, pp 255–273

Bruhns H (1987) Economie et religion chez Werner Sombart et Max Weber. In: Groupe de la Recherche sur la Culture de Weimar (ed) L'éthique protestante de Max Weber et l'ésprit de la modernité, Paris, pp 95–120

Bruhns H, Haupt H-G (eds) (1990) Werner Sombart. Journée d'études franco-allemande au Centre de Recherches Historiques, Paris

Buß E (1995) Lehrbuch der Wirtschaftssoziologie, Berlin

Chaloupek G (1994a) The concept of maturity and the transformation of economic systems. Rev Polit Econ 6:430–440

Chaloupek G (1994b) Von Sombart zu Schmoller? [Review Appel 1993 and Backhaus (eds.) 1993]. Wirtschaft und Gesellschaft 20:314–321

Chaloupek G (1995a) Glanz und Ende der historischen Schule: Werner Sombart 1863–1941 [Review Lenger 1994]. Wirtschaft und Gesellschaft 21:352–359

Chaloupek G (1995b) Long-term economic perspectives compared: Joseph Schumpeter and Werner Sombart. Eur J Hist Econ Thought 2:127–149

Chaloupek G (1996) Werner Sombarts "Spätkapitalismus" und die langfristige Wirtschaftsentwicklung. Wirtschaft und Gesellschaft 22:385–400

Chaloupek G (1999) Werner Sombart (1863–1941). In: Backhaus JG (ed) The Elgar companion to law and economics. Edward Elgar, Cheltenham, pp 466–471

Dietzel H (1889) Sombart: Die römische Campagna [Review]. Archiv für soziale Gesetzgebung und Statistik 2:676–679

Fechner E (1929) Der Begriff des kapitalistischen Geistes bei Werner Sombart und Max Weber. Weltwirtschaftliches Archiv 30:194–211

Fishman A (1994) Religious socialism and economic success on the orthodox Kibbutz. JITE 150:763–768

Fleischmann E (1981) Max Weber, die Juden und das Ressentiment. In: Schluchter W (ed) Max Webers Studie über das antike Judentum. Mohr Siebeck, Frankfurt, pp 263–286

Foner E (1984) Why is there no socialism in the United States? Am J Soc Feminist Hist 17:57–80

Galtung J (1997) Der Preis der Modernisierung, Vienna

Garhammer M (1999) Wie Europäer ihre Zeit nutzen: Zeitstrukturen und Zeitkulturen im Zeichen der Globalisierung, Berlin

Genett T (1998) Comeback des ersten Starsoziologen? Reflexionen zu Werner Sombart. Berliner Debatte Initial 9:90–104

Georgescu-Roegen N (1971) The entropy law and the economic process. Harvard University Press, Cambridge, MA

Gislain J-J, Steiner P (1995) La sociologie économique, Paris

Glombowski J (1998) Werner Sombarts Theorie der Mode. In: Glombowski J (ed) Zur kontinentalen Geschichte des ökonomischen Denkens. Metropolis, Marburg, pp 67–114

Grundmann R, Stehr N (1997) Klima und Gesellschaft, soziologische Klassiker und Außenseiter: Über Weber, Durkheim, Simmel und Sombart. Soziale Welt 48:85–100

Harnisch L (1928) Darstellung und Kritik der Sombart'schen Auffassung vom Unternehmen und Unternehmertum als Kernpunkt seiner Stellung zu dem System des freien Wettbewerbs, Frankfurt

Harris A (1942, 1992) Sombart and German (National) Socialism. In: Blaug M (ed) Gustav Schmoller (1838–1917) and Werner Sombart (1863–1941), Elgar Reference Collection series: Pioneers in Economics series, vol 30. Edward Elgar, Aldershot, pp 41–71

Heilbroner R (1988) Capitalism. In: Eatwell J et al (eds) New Palgrave dictionary, vol 1. Macmillan, London, pp 347–353

Herf J (1984) Reactionary modernism. Cambridge University Press, Cambridge

Hodgson GM (1988) Economics and institutions. Polity Press, Cambridge

Joas H (1989) Die Klassiker der Soziologie und der Erste Weltkrieg. In: Joas H, Steiner H (eds) Machtpolitischer Realismus und pazifistische Utopie: Krieg und Frieden in der Geschichte der Sozialwissenschaften, Frankfurt, pp 179–210

Käsler D (1984) Die frühe deutsche Soziologie 1909 bis 1934 und ihre Entstehungsmilieus, Opladen

Käsler D (1985) Soziologische Abenteuer: Earle Edward Eubank besucht europäische Soziologen im Sommer 1934, Opladen

Klotter C (1988) Bausteine des Menschen: Werner Sombarts 'Versuch einer geisteswissenschaftlichen Anthropologie'. In: Jüttemann G (ed) Wegbereiter der Historischen Psychologie, Munich, pp 162–168

König R (1983) Die analytisch-praktische Doppelbedeutung des Gruppentheorems: Ein Blick in die Hintergründe. In: Neidhardt F (ed), Gruppensoziologie: Perspektiven und Materialien, Kölner Zeitschrift für Soziologie und Sozialpsychologie, Sonderheft 25, Opladen, pp 36–64

König R (1987) Soziologie in Berlin um 1930. In: König R (ed) Soziologie in Deutschland: Begründer, Verfechter, Verächter, Munich, pp 258–297

Korsch K (1930) Sombarts "verstehende Nationalökonomie". Archiv für die Geschichte des Sozialismus und der Arbeiterbewegung 15:436–448

Kraft J (1961) Das Verhältnis von Nationalökonomie und Soziologie bei Franz Oppenheimer, Werner Sombart, Max Weber und in der sozialwissenschaftlichen Systembildung des 19. Jahrhunderts, Göttingen

Krause W (1962) Werner Sombarts Weg vom Kathedersozialismus zum Faschismus, East-Berlin

Krohn CD (1977) Zur Krisendebatte der bürgerlichen Nationalökonomie in Deutschland während der Weltwirtschaftskrise 1929–1933. Gesellschaft, Beiträge zur Marxschen Theorie, Frankfurt, pp 51–88

Kruse V (1996) Entstehung und Entfaltung des modernen Kapitalismus: Zur historischen und allgemeinen Soziologie Franz Oppenheimers. In: Caspari V, Schefold B (eds) Franz Oppenheimer und Adolph Lowe, Marburg, pp 163–193

Kurz R (1999) Schwarzbuch Kapitalismus, Frankfurt

Landmann E (1930) Wissen und Werten. Schmollers Jahrbuch 54:95–111

Lebovics H (1969) Social conservatism and the middle classes in Germany, 1914–1933, Princeton

Lehmann H (1996) Max Webers "Protestantische Ethik", Göttingen

Leich HGR (1957) Die anthropologisch soziologische Methodik bei Karl Marx. Werner Sombart und Max Weber, Köln

Lenger F (1994) Werner Sombart (1863–1941): Eine Biographie, Munich

Lenger F (1996) Werner Sombart als Propagandist eines deutschen Krieges. In: Mommsen WJ et al (eds) Kultur und Krieg, Oldenbourg, pp 65–76

Lenger F (1997) Ethics and economics in the work of Werner Sombart. In: Koslowski P (ed) Methodology of the social sciences, ethics, and economics in the newer historical school, Berlin, pp 149–163

Lenger F (1997) Werner Sombart: Ein Sozialwissenschaftler zwischen Kaiserreich und nationalsozialistischer Diktatur. In: Altrichter H (ed) Persönlichkeit und Geschichte, Erlangen, pp 173–192

Leube KR (1994) Begreifen und Verstehen: Bemerkungen zur methodologischen Position der österreichischen Schule der Nationalökonomie innerhalb der Geisteswissenschaften in den 20er Jahren. In: Nörr KW et al (eds) Geisteswissenschaften zwischen Kaiserreich und Republik: Zur Entwicklung von Nationalökonomie, Rechtswissenschaft und Sozialwissenschaft im 20. Jahrhundert, Stuttgart, pp 361–337

Lichtblau K, Weiß J (eds) (1993) Max Weber: Die protestantische Ethik und der "Geist" des Kapitalismus, Bodenheim

Loader C, Tilman R (1995) Thorstein Veblen's analysis of German intellectualism: Institutionalism as a forecasting method. Am J Econ Sociol 54:339–355

Löwe A (1932) Über den Sinn und die Grenzen verstehender Nationalökonomie. Weltwirtschaftliches Archiv 36:149–162

Lowe A (1989) Konjunkturtheorie in Deutschland in den Zwanziger Jahren. In: Schefold B (ed) Studien zur Entwicklung der ökonomischen Theorie VIII, Berlin, pp 75–86

Lübbe H (1963) Politische Philosophie in Deutschland, Basel

Luttwak E (1999) Turbo capitalism. Orion, London

Mackensen R (1970) Verstädterung. In: Akademie für Raumforschung und Landesplanung (ed) Handwörterbuch der Raumforschung und Raumordnung, Hannover, pp 3589–3600

McCloskey DN (1985) The rhetoric of economics. University of Wisconsin Press, Madison

Mitzman A (1973) Sociology and estrangement: three sociologists of Imperial Germany, New York

Mitzman A (1987) Personal conflict and ideological options in Sombart and Weber. In: Mommsen WJ, Osterhammel J (eds) Max Weber and his contemporaries, London, pp 99–10

Mitzman A (1988) Persönlichkeitskonflikt und weltanschauliche Alternativen bei Werner Sombart und Max Weber. In: Mommsen, WJ, Schwentker W (eds), Max Weber und seine Zeitgenossen, Göttingen, pp 137–146

North DC (1996) Institutions, institutional change and economic performance. Cambridge University Press, Cambridge

Nuglisch A (1904) Zur Frage nach der Entstehung des modernen Kapitalismus. Jahrbücher für Nationalökonomie und Statistik 28:238–250

Oppenheimer F (1929) Abriss einer Sozial- und Wirtschaftsgeschichte Europas von der Völkerwanderung bis zur Gegenwart. Erste Abteilung, Jena

Parsons T (1928, 1929) Capitalism in recent German literature: Sombart and Weber. J Polit Econ 36, 641–661; 37, 31–51

Pasemann D (1985) Werner Sombarts Gesellschafts- und Geschichtserklärung. In: Küttler W (ed) Gesellschaftstheorie und geschichtswissenschaftliche Erklärung, Vaduz

Pearson H (1997) Origins of law and economics. Cambridge University Press, Cambridge

Peukert H (1998) Das Handlungsparadigma in der Nationalökonomie, Marburg

Peukert H (2000a) Boltanski L, Chiapello E: Le nouvel esprit du capitalisme [Review]. Economic Sociology: European Electronic Newsletter, 1, Part 2, 19–21 (http://www.siswo.uva.nl/ES)

Peukert H (2000b) Karl Marx, paper presented at Maastricht University. The Founders of modern economics: Maastricht lectures in poltical economy, Maastricht

Pfister B (1927) Werner Sombarts "Proletarischer Sozialismus" [Review]. Zeitschrift für die gesamte Staatswissenschaft 83:93–135

Polanyi K (1977) In: Pearson HW (ed) The livelihood of man. Academic, New York

Rammstedt O (1986) Deutsche Soziologie 1933–1945: Die Normalität einer Anpassung, Frankfurt

Rammstedt O (1988) Klassiker der Soziologie – was ist das eigentlich? Soziologische Revue 11:269–276

Rehberg K-S (1989) Das Bild des Judentums in der frühen deutschen Soziologie: 'Fremdheit' und 'Rationalität' als Typusmerkmale bei Werner Sombart, Max Weber und Georg Simmel. In: Wiehn ER et al (eds) Juden in der Soziologie, Konstanz, pp 127–172

Reinhold G et al (1997) Wirtschaftssoziologie, 2nd ed, Munich

Ritter UP (1999) Das Wirtschaftssystem. In: Helmedag F, Reuter N (eds) Der Wohlstand der Personen, Marburg, pp 121–151

Ritzer G (1993) The McDonaldisation of society. Newbury Park, Pine Forge

Ritzer G (1998) The McDonaldization thesis: explorations and extensions. Sage, London

Rost N (1999) Goethe in Dachau, Berlin

Samuelson PA, Nordhaus W (1989) Economics, 13th edn. McGraw-Hill, New York

Scaff LA (1988) Das Unbehagen im Weber-Kreis. In: Maier H et al (eds) Politik, Philosophie, Praxis: Festschrift für Wilhelm Hennis zum 65. Geburtstag, Stuttgart, pp 174–188

Schäfers B et al (1976) Zur Entwicklung der Stadt-, Gemeinde- und Regionalsoziologie in Deutschland: Ein Überblick nebst einer in Auswahl kommentierten Bibliographie. Soziologie 2:57–77

Schams E (1930) Die 'zweite' Nationalökonomie. Archiv für Sozialwissenschaft und Sozialpolitik 64:453–491

Schams E (1934) Wirtschaftslogik. Schmollers Jahrbuch 58:1–21

Schefold B (1992) Nationalökonomie als Geisteswissenschaft: Edgar Salins Konzept einer anschaulichen Theorie. List Forum für Wirtschafts- und Finanzpolitik 18:303–324

Scheler M (1966) Der Formalismus in der Ethik und die materiale Wertethik, Bern

Schepansky EW (1979) Ein Beispiel zur Sozialgeschichte des Fremden: Mennoniten in Hamburg und Altona zur Zeit des Merkantilismus. Hamburger Jahrbuch für Wirtschafts- und Gesellschaftspolitik 24:219–234

Schmidt K-H (1991) Zum 50. Todestag von Werner Sombart. Wirtschaftsdienst (Hamburg) 71:258–261

Sieferle RP (1982) Der unterirdische Wald, Munich

Sieferle RP (1995) Die konservative Revolution: Fünf biographische Skizzen (Paul Lensch, Werner Sombart, Oswald Spengler, Ernst Jünger, Hans Freyer), Frankfurt am Main

Sombart N (1984) Jugend in Berlin 1933–1943, Munich

Sombart W (1888) Die römische Campagna, Leipzig

Sombart W (1894) Zur Kritik des ökonomischen Systems von Karl Marx. Archiv für soziale Gesetzgebung und Statistik 7:555–594

Sombart W (1896) Sozialismus und soziale Bewegung im 19. Jahrhundert, Jena

Sombart W (1903, 1919) Die deutsche Volkswirtschaft im 19. Jahrhundert, 4th ed

Sombart W (1906, 1969) Warum gibt es in den Vereinigten Staaten keinen Sozialismus? Darmstadt

Sombart W (1907) Die Politik als Beruf, Morgen, 26 July, pp 195–199

Sombart W (1909) Das Lebenswerk von Karl Marx, Jena

Sombart W (1911) Die Juden und das Wirtschaftsleben. Leipzig

Sombart W (1913, 1988) Der Bourgeois, Reinbek

Sombart W (1913a) Krieg und Kapitalismus, Munich

Sombart W (1913b) Luxus und Kapitalismus, Munich

Sombart W (1916–1927, 1987) Der moderne Kapitalismus, 3 vols, Munich

Sombart W (1924) Der proletarische Sozialismus ("Marxismus") 2 vols, Jena

Sombart W (1925, 1927), Die Ordnung des Wirtschaftslebens, Berlin

Sombart W (1928) Die Wandlungen des Kapitalismus. Weltwirtschaftliches Archiv 28:243–256

Sombart W (1930) Die drei Nationalökonomien, Berlin

Sombart W (1931, 1959) Arbeiter. In: Vierkandt A (ed) Handwörterbuch der Soziologie, new edition, Stuttgart, pp 1–14

Sombart W (1932, 1987) Die Zukunft des Kapitalismus. In: Brocke B (ed) Sombarts "Moderner Kapitalismus", Munich, pp 394–418

Sombart W (1934) Deutscher Sozialismus, Berlin

Sombart W (1936) Soziologie, Berlin

Sombart W (1938) Vom Menschen, Berlin

Sombart W (1960) In: Chemnitz W (ed) Allgemeine Nationalökonomie Berlin. Duncker & Humblot, Berlin

Stölting E (1986) Akademische Soziologie in der Weimarer Republik, Berlin

Töttö P (1991) Werner Sombart, Tampere

Töttö P (1996) In search of the U-turn. In: Backhaus JG (ed) Werner Sombart (1863–1941): Social Scientist. Metropolis, Marburg, pp 227–239

Tütsch HE (1988) Das Fiasko des Sozialismus in den Vereinigten Staaten von Nordamerika – ein Sonderfall? In: Giger H, Linder W (eds) Sozialismus, Ende einer Illusion: Zerfallserscheinungen im Lichte der Wissenschaften, Cologne, pp 179–197

Tyrell H (1994) Protestantische Ethik – und kein Ende die Neuausgaben der 'Protestantischen Ethik'. Soziologische Revue 17:397–404

Vleugels W (1940) Auf dem Wege zur Lehre vom Menschen als wissenschaftlicher Grundlegung der Geisteswissenschaften [Review]. Jahrbücher für Nationalökonomie und Statistik 151:625–650

Wachtler G (1985) Militärsoziologie und Gesellschaftsstruktur. In: Hradil S (ed) Sozialstruktur im Umbruch: Karl Martin Bolte zum 60. Geburtstag, Opladen, pp 235–246

Wayne BW (1950) The neo-historismus of Werner Sombart, Chicago, IL. Dissertation, University of Chicago, Chicago, IL

Weede E (1990) Wirtschaft. Zur Soziologie der kapitalistischen Marktwirtschaft und der Demokratie, Tübingen, Staat und Gesellschaft

Weippert G (1953) Werner Sombarts Gestaltidee des Wirtschaftssystems, Göttingen

Werth CH (1996a) Sozialismus und Nation: Die deutsche Ideologiediskussion zwischen 1918 und 1945. Westdeutscher, Opladen

Werth CH (1996b) Werner Sombart und seine Idee vom Sozialismus. Orientierungen zur Wirtschafts- und Gesellschaftspolitik 70:60–64

Wiese L (1940) Das Problem einer Wissenschaft vom Menschen. Zeitschrift für öffentliches Recht 20:1–19

Chapter 22
The Scientific Contributions of Heinrich von Stackelberg

Peter R. Senn

Introduction

> I have no intention of neglecting any analytic work that has been done or is being done in 'totalitarian' countries, and the mere fact that such work is presented in the wrappings of a "totalitarian" philosophy *or even intended to serve and to implement it* (original italics) is no more reason for me to neglect it than my strong personal aversion to utilitarianism is a reason for neglecting the analytic work of Bentham.
>
> Joseph Alois Schumpeter (p. 1153)

Heinrich von Stackelberg (1905–1946) is an interesting person in the history of economic thought. From the time of his earliest work, he was recognized as a major contributor to the application of mathematics to important economic problems. The fact that he was a member of the National Socialist German Worker's Party (*National Sozialistische Deutsche Arbeiter Partei*, henceforth Nazi) has led to negative judgments, neglect, and misunderstanding of his work.

Writing about John Stuart Mill (1806–1873), George Joseph Stigler (1911–1992) expressed the viewpoint of this paper. "When we are told that we must study a man's life to understand what he really meant, we are being invited to abandon science" (p. 91). An individual's politics and his scientific output do not necessarily influence each other. There is no necessary relationship between a person's scientific work in economics and his politics.

With this understanding, we can agree with Stigler that "some elements of a man's milieu must be known to understand him" and turn now to some biographical information (p. 91).

P.R. Senn (✉)
1121 Hinman Avenue, Evanston, IL 60202, USA

J.G. Backhaus (ed.), *Handbook of the History of Economic Thought*,
The European Heritage in Economics and the Social Sciences,
DOI 10.1007/978-1-4419-8336-7_22, © Springer Science+Business Media, LLC 2012

Biographical Sketch[1]

Heinrich von Stackelberg was born in Kudinovo, Russia, to the Estonian branch of an old Baltic German noble family on October 31st, 1905. Shortly after the outbreak of the First World War, the family moved to their summer home in Yalta and stayed there until it was certain that Yalta would fall to the Communists.

By the time he was thirteen, he, and his family, had fled the Russian Communists twice, from Russia to Estonia and then to Upper Silesa. The family settled in Cologne in 1923. There, in 1924, at the age of 19, he obtained his high school diploma. He then entered the new University of Cologne. He received his first university degree in 1927 and his doctorate in 1930.

In 1919, when the family was still in Silesia and he was only fourteen, he joined an association of patriotic, aristocratic German youths (*Deutsche-Nationaler Jugendbund*). He enrolled later in another such organization in Cologne, the Club of Patriotic Youth (*Jungnationaler Bund*). This was one of many such associations of young Germans during the time of the Weimar Republic which today might be labelled "rightwing" but not Nazi. In 1930, he joined another group, the Baltic Brotherhood (*Baltische Bruderschaft*). It was largely composed of dispossessed Germans from Estonia and Latvia who were ardent Lutherans.

Stackelberg's political writings occurred during 1931–1933, when he was in his twenties. Jürg Niehans (p. 190) has him contributing six articles, James Konow says five (p. 148) to the *Voice of Patriotic Youth (Jungnationale Stimme)*, the organizational magazine of which he became editor in 1932. "Generally, he either shunned issues with little or no economic content, as with racial and church policy, or focused on their economic aspects as with military policy" (Konow, p. 149).

In December 1931, he joined the Nazi party.[2] In 1933, he became a member of one of the many branches of the *Schutz-Staffel* (honour guard or defence corps, henceforth SS), the elite paramilitary organization of the Nazi party.[3] The SS was a complex political and military organization made up of three separate and distinct branches, with related but different functions and goals. The General SS (Allgemeine-SS) was the main branch of this extremely complex organization. It served political and administrative roles. The SS-Deaths Head Organization

---

[1] This section relies heavily on a more complete account, Senn (1996a) from which some parts have been taken.

[2] Niehans has 1933 (p. 190). I have examined the Party documents.

[3] Konow (p. 148) has him attaining the rank of staff sergeant. He enlisted as a private in the reserves. Conversations with, and letters from Stackelberg's son, Hans-Heinrich Freiherr von Stackelberg, are the reason that some of the standard sources are questioned. All the references to Hans-Heinrich von Stackelberg are to personal communications from him as are those labelled "(Personal communication)".

Konow and Niehans give the standard German sources for information about Stackelberg's life. Senn has them for the English language. There are other places where a few paragraphs about him, mostly second hand, appear. For an example, see Heinz D. Kurz's review.

(SS-Totenkopfverbande) and, later, the Armed-SS (Waffen-SS) were the other two branches. The Armed-SS, formed in 1940, was the main fighting organization.

After the Nazi takeover in 1933, the *Voice of Patriotic Youth* was shut down along with all other non-Nazi youth organizations. This was part of the Nazi move toward centralization (*Gleichschaltung*) and control of German youth. After this Stackelberg stopped his political writings and began a dramatic change in his views about Hitler and the Nazis.

By 1931, he was lecturing at the University of Cologne. In 1934, his habilitation thesis, then a general requirement for admission to German professorates, *Market Forms and Equilibrium* (*Marktform und Gleichgewicht* henceforth *Market Forms*), was published. Already internationally recognized, in 1935 he joined the faculty of the University of Berlin. He was tenured in 1937 as a professor without a chair (*Extraordinarius*).

He met the Countess (Gräfin) Elisabeth (Elisabet) von Kanitz (born 1917) who was to become his wife, in the spring of 1936. Stackelberg was a devout and dedicated Lutheran who attended church regularly. He was married in 1936 in church over objections by the SS. By this time he was well on his way to rejection of Nazi ideas. As early as 1936 Stackelberg was discussing how to quit the Nazi party without harm coming to his family. Obviously, he decided it could not be done (Personal communication).

At the end of 1936, the Baltic Brotherhood, of which he was a member, was dissolved by the Nazis (Konow, p. 160). If the 1933 closing of the *Voice of Patriotic Youth* was the beginning of change in Stackelberg's view of the Nazis, the 1936 dissolution of his Baltic organization probably marked his complete estrangement from them. Important among the reasons for this estrangement was that he did not share the Nazi anti-Semitism.

His attitude toward Jews can be illustrated by the experience of the person who was probably the last Jewish academic to receive his Ph.D. in Germany before the Second World War. Arnold Horwell (formerly Horwitz), who was alive and living in England in late 1996, was Stackelberg's last Jewish Ph.D. candidate. In his report (*Seminar-Zeugnis*) evaluating the work Horwell did in the summer semester of 1936, Stackelberg speaks highly of him and awards Horwell the grade of "excellent" (*sehr gut* or magna cum laude). This was after the Nuremberg Laws of September 1935 which deprived Jews of many of their rights.

In February 1937, Horwell passed his oral examinations (*mündliche Prüfung*) cum laude. The University regulations at that time prohibited the granting of the degree he had earned. Constantin von Dietze (1891–1973) was the other economics professor sponsoring Horwell. In a successful petition to the administration of the University of Berlin, von Dietze states that Stackelberg supports the granting of the degree (Document on file). Thus, despite both the Nuremberg and university by-laws that prohibited it, Horwell got his degree. Ironically, it is very possible that Stackelberg's membership in the Nazi party played a role in getting Horwell his Ph.D. degree.

In 1940 he received calls to the economics departments at the German universities in occupied Prague and Strasbourg. He visited both places and turned them both down on the grounds that he did not like the nationalism he found (Personal communication from his son Hans-Heinrich Stackelberg). In 1941, he accepted a call to become a professor with a chair (*Ordinarius*) at Bonn.

Stackelberg was never promoted while a member of the SS. Soon after the outbreak of the Second World War, he was drafted into the army. It is worth noting that "after lengthy discussions with his father-in-law and friends he refused to follow a request to join the ranks of the Armed SS when he was drafted into the regular army at the beginning of World War II" (Personal communication).

Stackelberg passed the examinations qualifying him as an interpreter of Russian shortly before being drafted.[4] He served at least two tours of duty on the Eastern Front. Konow says two (p. 160). Niehans (p. 191) and Hans-Heinrich Stackelberg say "several".[5] His rank, for at least part of his army service, was that of a *Sonderführer* (special officer – equivalent to major) used for positions like those of interpreters. Stackelberg was also asked to do some economic studies of the occupied territories (Personal communication).

Stackelberg was released from the army in 1943. He was ill after his last tour of duty on the Russian front. In that same year, he participated in the first meeting in Freiburg, of the Freiburg Circle (Freiburger Kreis).[6] He was a founding member of this illegal and oppositional group which was based on the assumption that Germany would lose the war. The group set themselves the task of planning the economy of Germany after the war. Several members were executed in the aftermath of the failed coup against Hitler.

The Freiburg Circle was largely inspired by Walter Kurt Heinrich Eucken (1891–1950), but chaired by Erwin Emil von Beckerath (1889–1964), one of Stackelberg's teachers. Von Dietze was also a member. Eucken, von Beckerath, and several of the other members of the group became important figures in the economic changes that accompanied the German reconstruction after the Second World War.

Stackelberg was also a close friend of Ulrich von Hassell (1881–1944), the former German ambassador to Rome and one of the leaders of the resistance. Von Hassell was executed in the aftermath of the failed assassination attempt on Hitler. In his diary, he mentions Stackelberg and his wife in such friendly terms that it is easy to conclude that he considered Stackelberg to be with him in opposition to Hitler.[7]

Stackelberg was also a close friend of the Berlin economist, Jens Jessen (1896–1944). Like Stackelberg, Jessen shared some Nazi ideas down to about 1933. Some time after that, Jessen joined the underground movement against Nazism. Jessen was hanged "for his partnership in the Beck-Goerdeler plot to overthrow the Hitler regime" (Schmölders, p. 135). Many members of the resistance were early Nazis who began to resist as they saw the evil regime develop.

In the fall of 1943, Stackelberg went to the University of Madrid as a visiting professor in the Economics Department of the Institute for Political Studies. This move might well have saved his life. His relationships with his Spanish colleagues

---

[4] He also knew English, French, Italian, Spanish, ancient Greek and Latin (Konow, p. 147).

[5] Again, the standard sources about his military service are probably unreliable. Some have him serving on both the Eastern and Western fronts and wounded.

[6] Niehans says these meetings began about 1942 (p. 191).

[7] See von Hassell (pp. 323, 352, 363) for examples.

were cordial. His 3 years in Spain were very productive. His personal influence and his work left a significant mark on later economic policies in that country. There is a substantial literature in Spanish about him. *The Theory of the Market Economy* was first published in Spanish as *Principios de Teoría Económica*.

He remained in Spain for the rest of his life, teaching, writing, and revising his earlier work. He died on October 12th, 1946, after a long bout with Hodgkin's disease, shortly before his 41st birthday. He left his wife, two daughters, and a son, Hans-Heinrich, born on May 31st, 1945.

After the war, his widow was granted a pension by the German government – something not likely if he had been thought to be an active or important Nazi. In 1948, Stackelberg was posthumously denazified (Konow, p. 161). In early 1996, his widow and two daughters were living in Germany and his son was a German diplomat in New York.

The Theoretical and Historical Context of Stackelberg's Work

Because a person's scientific work appears one way to himself and his contemporaries another way in the evolution of a science, it is necessary to say something about the context in which he wrote. The least important of these was political but it is a sad commentary on the times that many who have written about Stackelberg have allowed their politics to influence their judgments about his economics.

This is despite the fact that attempts to link Stackelberg's politics with his economics have not been successful. Like most such efforts, they fail to recognize that the political and intellectual realms of a person's life can be, and often are, separate – and that both often change over time.

The most important contexts that influenced, and in some cases shaped, his work were the state of economic theory and mathematics. The state of economic theory was the most important of these.

Antoine Augustin Cournot (1801–1877) is generally given credit as the first economist to tackle the theoretical problems of monopolistic situations. From his time on, some of the greatest names in the history of economic thought worked on a variety of issues related to monopolies, the case of a single seller; duopolies, cases in which two sellers produced an identical product; and oligopolies, cases in which a few sellers produced identical products.

They were mainly concerned with how prices were determined, the roles of buyers and sellers, the workings of markets of various kinds, and the possibilities for and kinds of equilibrium that might result. Up to the late 1920s, despite several important suggestions, there was little agreement about the role of imperfect competition and how it worked in the economies of the time.

Then came the Great Depression. Prices fell, unemployment rose, businesses failed everywhere. Policies based on accepted theory did not work. There was little agreement about how prices were determined in such situations.

By 1933, as the Cambridge economist Joan Violet Robinson (1903–1983) put it, "A moment has been reached in the development of economic theory when certain definite problems require to be solved and many writers are at work upon them independently" (Preface, vi). Three path-breaking books brought new ways of thinking. Two appeared in the same year, 1933. They were by the American Edward Hastings Chamberlin (1899–1967), *The Theory of Monopolistic Competition,* and Robinson's, *The Economics of Imperfect Competition*. Stackelberg's book, Market Forms was published in 1934.

Roy Forbes Harrod (1900–1978), in his review of Chamberlin's book, pointed out that "It is recently come to be realized more and more clearly that the concepts of competition and monopoly do not cover the whole economic field, that there is an intermediate area of great importance, probably of greater importance than the areas of pure monopoly and pure competition, and that in order to analyse a phenomena belonging to this area, something more is required than the mere statement that it is intermediate" (p. 662).

All three books recognized the importance of the area between pure monopoly and pure competition although they dealt with it in different ways.

Robinson's mathematical apparatus was primarily that of geometry. There are 82 figures in the 352-page book. There was little use of the calculus. Both Chamberlin and Stackelberg employed more sophisticated mathematics.

The key point about the mathematical context was that the mathematics of the time was not powerful enough to resolve all of the problems the three authors recognized. The situations they described were too complex for the mathematics of the time. The development of many of their contributions was limited by the state of mathematics. None of them could have developed all of their ideas to their full potential.

Many concepts, as for example those of control and feedback from engineering, and practically all of game theory were not yet invented. Neither were many modern mathematical tools such as topology and linear programming. Until the advent of digital computers, many of the calculations required to solve their equations were excessively tedious.

In summary, the historical and theoretical context was that of the Great Depression and the widespread recognition that the existing conceptual framework of economists could not provide policy solutions. The mathematics of the time limited how far economists could go is solving the problems they recognized. The reason all three authors are enshrined in the history of economic thought is because they brought new ways of thinking about markets and how they worked.

Stackelberg's Main Contributions

It is hazardous to try to outguess history. Estimates of Stackelberg's most important contributions must vary with the interests of the historian and the time. My own view is that he will be most remembered for his contributions to the theory of monopolistic markets. The most important scientific contribution Stackelberg made was in his demonstration that in a majority of duopolistic and oligopolistic situations, most market prices were indeterminate, showing no tendency to reach an equilibrium position. Put another way, his main contribution was in the analysis of "unstable" market forms (imperfect or monopolistic competition) which did not fit the equilibrium conditions of earlier writers.

But he did much more. Wilhelm Krelle (born 1918) summarized his work as follows:

> Stackelberg was the most gifted theoretical economist in Germany during his time. His habilitation thesis Marktform und Gleichgewicht (1934) has had a lasting influence on price theory. "Stackelberg asymmetric duopoly" is known all over the world. His contributions to Austrian capital theory are the basis for all modern extensions of this theory. His textbook *Grundzüge der theoretischen Volkswirtschaftslehre* (1934) was the first "modern" introduction to economics in the sense that it is based on a coherent theory of household and firm behaviour. Moreover, Stackelberg contributed to several other fields: cost theory, exchange rate theory, saving theory and others. (vol. 4, p. 469)

All of the important histories of economic thought evaluate Stackelberg's work in slightly different ways. Karl Pribram's (1877–1973) *A History of Economic Reasoning* contains the best short summary of Stackelberg's contribution.

> In a remarkable study of duopolistic and other oligopolistic situations, Heinrich von Stackelberg elaborated the idea that in the majority of markets prices show no tendency to reach equilibrium positions, but remain indeterminate. He started from the simple case of two sellers competing in a market and discussed the alternatives confronting them, showing how the number of alternatives increased with the number of sellers striving for leadership in the market. He reduced the great variety of conditions of restricted competition to a limited number of types and paid special attention to oligopolist situations in which the market was divided among several sellers through product differentiation but was not closed to the entry of new firms. In his treatment of such cases, he assigned a particular market to each differentiated product, and argued that varying elasticities of demand for such products enabled each producer to adopt an active or a passive attitude not only with regard to the volume of output but also with regard to price. The main cases Stackelberg distinguished were oligopoly, monopoly, and limited monopoly of supply and demand, and bilateral monopoly. (pp. 445–446)

There are many other appraisals of his contributions. Wassily Leontief (1906–1999, Nobel prize 1973) gave *Market Forms* an extensive review in *The Journal of Political Economy* in 1936. After some preliminary general remarks, Leontief wrote, "In *Marktform und Gleichgewicht*, Heinrich von Stackelberg performed the difficult task of strictly deductive reformulation of the theory of monopolistic competition with much skill and elegance" (p. 554).

Among his fundamental insights were those about "leaders" and "followers" in the context of duopoly (two sellers) and oligopoly (a few sellers). He was concerned with understanding the kinds of behaviour that could lead to various kinds of equilibrium.[8] He developed mathematical and analytical techniques that enabled him to solve his problem under certain specified conditions.

---

[8] Krelle explains in another way, "The difficulty of oligopoly theory consists in the fact that the oligopolists are in a game theoretic situation which, in general, cannot be put into the form of a pure maximum problem. Stackelberg's seminal idea was that this can nevertheless be done if – in the case of a duopoly – one firm takes a "dependent" position (that is, takes the actual price or production of the other firm as given) and the other an "independent" one (that is, knows this behaviour and fixes its price or production accordingly so that it maximizes its profits or other utility indices)". "Since it is unclear which position the firms will take, Stackelberg considered the oligopoly as a market form without equilibrium" (p. 469).

There are many ways to assess Stackelberg's contributions. His place in the histories of economic thought is sure evidence of a contribution. But the interests and focus of historians vary widely. Louis Henry Haney (1882–1969), in his *History of Economic Thought*, points out that, "In addition to the purely quantitative profit principle, he introduces several elements in pricing. These include habits, tendencies to stability, agreements, and time lags. Stackelberg distinguishes and analyses various cases of duopoly and of joint demand" (p. 707).

Joseph Alois Schumpeter (1883–1950), in a chapter devoted to equilibrium analysis. (p. 7 in Part 4), mentions *Market Forms* as one of "several excellent critical histories" on the theory of monopoly (fn. 10, p. 976).

In summary, Stackelberg was one of the seminal thinkers in economics of the middle twentieth century. He was one of the trio who revolutionized the way economists thought about markets and how they work. Although he contributed to several parts of economics, his ideas have become indispensable for some of mathematical economics and game theory. His original work was both useful and of the kind on which those who followed him could, and did, build upon. His contributions pass the ultimate test for durability in the history of economic thought, the development of theory or concepts or techniques on which future generations are able to build.

Applications in Economics and Business Today

Because there is so much misunderstanding about the term "application," some explanation is required. An elementary requirement is the answer to the question, "What is being applied, an idea or a technique"? By an idea we mean a viewpoint or approach. By a technique we mean how something is done. The next question is, "To what is the idea or technique applied"?

The essence of the power of Stackelberg's ideas and techniques is that they are applicable to situations where people must act without necessarily knowing exactly what will happen as a result of those actions. This means that there are many possible applications.

Broadly speaking, applications of scientific techniques can be focused in two main areas. One is general or theoretical, the other is practical. General or theoretical applications are not necessarily aimed at specific situations found in the real world. Practical applications are. They look to provide guidance for politicians, bureaucrats, businessmen, and others who must deal with real issues. It is the later with which we are concerned.

Applications of Stackelberg's or anyone else's ideas face an intractable problem of transition. A person's ideas can only be said to be an application when they are actually used. Properly speaking, they must be put into practice by businesses or bureaucratic regulators or law by politicians, courts, and lawyers. Since the overwhelming bulk of would-be applications come from academics who do not have to deal with the complexities of any given reality, it is not often that an immediate, unchanged and direct application of an idea is found.

The situation is different for techniques or a body of knowledge about how to do things. Immediate, unchanged, and direct applications of techniques are often found. Stackelberg gave us both ideas and techniques.

There are now thousands of applications of Stackelberg's techniques and insights.[9] The place to look for the applications is in the citation indexes for periodical literature and dissertations as well as books. Documentation and the specific references for all those summarized here and many more are to be found in Senn 1996b. This section will, therefore, be devoted to a general discussion of the various kinds of applications.

A word of caution is needed about the enormous literature on applications. Because it is predominately mathematical, it sometimes does not even pretend to be based on any kind of existing economic institutions or reality. Authors of this kind of application evidently think that behaviours and institutions either fit, or could or should be changed to fit, their assumptions.

It is also important to notice that applications of Stackelberg's ideas are not limited to the social sciences and business. Applications are also to be found in mathematics, science, biology, engineering, and both economic history and the history of economic thought. Our interest is in the applications of his ideas in business and economics.

There is no ideal way to organize the applications of Stackelberg's ideas and techniques because the categories often overlap. I have chosen three main areas, applications for business, for industry and for policymakers such as judges, bureaucrats and politicians and a catchall, other.

Business Applications

There are many applications which look at how firms in a Cournot-Nash model behave under conditions of uncertainty in market demand with attention to risk factors. Applications have been developed to show what happens when oligopolists use different strategies. Using signalling game theory, a model has been built which demonstrates that a firm's decisions about the choice of sequencing provide additional information.

For the corporation, the profitability of forming independent rival divisions has been found practical under some circumstances. Although it is not legal in some jurisdictions, unilateral most-favoured-customer pricing will provide superior profits in some cases.

Labour economics has not been neglected. Several games with applications to labour economics on such topics as policy credibility and inflation in wage setting exist.

---

[9] It is necessary to distinguish between the applications Stackelberg made and those others have made. Stackelberg's applications are discussed above in connection with his contributions and below in connection with his policies.

Applications have also been made to just-in-time purchasing and the role of audit technology and the extension of audit procedures in strategic auditing.

Industry Applications

There has been found a relationship between entry deterrence and overexploitation of fishing grounds. Although Milton Friedman (born 1912) long ago showed that cartels are unstable, Stackelberg's techniques have added to our understanding of some problems of the dynamic inconsistency of oil prices. Dynamic demand, consumers' expectations and monopolistic resource extraction have been used to analyse OPEC pricing policies. Along these lines, the effects of tariffs and quotas in the face of international oligopoly have been analysed using Stackelberg techniques.

Many articles are concerned with games and their applications. There are studies, which demonstrate how economics affected game theory with special attention to industrial economics. Using a game-theoretic analysis of price-sustainable industry configurations in natural monopoly it has been demonstrated that the sustainable configuration is the unique Nash equilibrium, and the conditions under which it is also a Stackelberg equilibrium.

Applications for Policymakers

Some possible implications for antitrust policy have been drawn from comparisons of performance and welfare in three classical oligopoly models: Stackelberg leader, Cournot, and collusive monopoly.

There are also applications which show the influence of corporate and personal taxation on the optimal investment, financing, and dividend policies of a firm as a Stackelberg differential game. Several studies model the economic relations of government-private sector relations as a Stackelberg game. Nash and Stackelberg strategies and the conditions for operative intergenerational transfers have been studied.

There are many applications of Stackelberg's techniques in the field of monetary and fiscal policy. Applications include the macroeconomic consequences of the European monetary union, how fixed exchange rates and non-cooperative monetary policies might work, monetary policy choices among countries with different degrees of coordination, full, partial coordination and none, and the role of leadership in international monetary policy on exchange rates. Other policy applications include macroeconomic policy interaction under flexible exchange rates and a game approach to regional economic policy.

There are many other studies. Urban planners have used his approach in the study of the multi-centred city.

Other

The universality of Stackelberg's ideas is demonstrated by the fact that economists of every political hue use his ideas and techniques. There are models of capitalism using different assumptions, for example under worker's leadership. Several studies try to estimate the adjustments workers and governments must make when they have opposing interests. Regulatory enforcement and regulation by participation have been modelled as games.

The following list of topics show the wide variety of applications:

- Regulation and crime in hazardous waste disposal
- Renewable resources
- Large bilateral reductions in superpower nuclear weapons
- Consumer learning and brand loyalty when product quality is unknown
- The transition to nondepletable energy
- International migration
- Liability rules
- Interstate tax competition and locational efficiency
- Market structure, innovations, and welfare
- Altruism, fundraising, and the measurement of crowding out in economies with charitable giving
- Senatorial elections
- The United States nursing market
- Retirement decisions in dual career households

Many of Stackelberg's ideas have been analysed from the point of view of concepts developed after he died. One such application has been called "Stackelberg Rent-Seeking".

It is significant that the flexibility and power of Stackelberg's ideas fit many situations. It is certain that the possible applications have not been exhausted.

I have not found much explicit recognition of the political aspects of oligopolistic struggles, but perhaps that is asking too much in the present stage of our knowledge. If it could be done, it would help applied economists to make their advice more significant and more immediately useful.

I am sure that there are many other areas of business and economics that might benefit from Stackelberg's ideas. I was surprised to find no references to the strategies of war and defence and communications. My guess is that there are many applications in these fields which are not made public. It also seems to me that marketing and manufacturing, are under-represented.

Stackelberg's Contributions from the Point
of View of Modern Theory

From the point of view of modern theory, it turns out that Stackelberg did not and could not have developed all of his ideas to their full potential. The fruitfulness of some of his contributions, for example "leader" and "follower" in price setting, became apparent only after his death. I stress this because I do not find much in Stackelberg's work that is wrong or incorrect. The picture, rather, is one of careful theoretical constructions and brilliant insights into many important areas of economics.

Typical is his view about the role of the state with respect to markets. This has been misunderstood by all but a few of the historians of economic thought. Pribram says, for example, "He arrived at the conclusion that adequate stability of the economy should be undertaken by consistent price and production policies operated by the government" (p. 446).

The reason for the misunderstanding is that his later views as "a determined critic of every form of planned economy" were expressed in a mathematical paper that he read to the small resistance group in 1943. Eucken explains that "He had come to the conclusion that the competitive order is the only principle by which the economic problems of our time can be solved, but he drew a sharp distinction between the competitive order and a system of *laisser-faire*" (pp. 133–134).

Mark Blaug (born 1927) and Paul Sturges had it right when they wrote that his "Later work was on capital theory, and at the time of his death he was attempting a theory of the whole economic process. A stalwart opponent of central planning he worked out his criticism in an mathematical form" (p. 362).

Stackelberg was concerned with economic policy. There is no doubt that, as Eucken says, "he was fully aware of the importance of the task of elaborating a suitable legal framework for" the competitive order he envisioned. He hoped "to contribute to this task" (p. 134). In Spain, he made clear that "theory is able to guide practice". Juan Valarde Fuertes gives him credit for the "quantum leap" in Spanish economic policy which opened it up to greater roles for the market and a balanced budget (p. 138).

Jürgen G. Backhaus has the most complete discussion in English of Stackelberg's views about the relation of economic theory to policy and his preference for a decentralized market economy. Backhaus also describes Stackelberg's functional theory of economic policy instruments. "Stackelberg conceived of a very wide range and scope of economic policy, and his theory in this respect was designed to make these economic policies, whatever their goals, both effective and efficient (in terms of the resources involved)" (p. 145).

Today there is a broad consensus about the usefulness of a competitive order along with the necessity for governments to set limits to individual activities. Mainstream theory also embraces the viewpoint that economic policy instruments should result in the efficient use of available resources.

Stackelberg used mathematical and graphical techniques. He wanted to be precise about the specifications of the behaviours he studied. "Economic theory is a decidedly difficult study. This is not so much because of the complexity of its various propositions but because of the degree of abstraction necessary to master the tremendous multiplicity of economic phenomena and because of the peculiar interdependence of relations in the economic system which have neither beginning nor end and could be compared with the 'snake that bites its own tail'" (Preface to the first German edition of *The Theory of the Market Economy*, p. ix).

The conclusion of the Preface shows how he thought about the uses and limits of mathematics in economic theory.[10]

> All that mathematics can do is to produce *precise thinking* [original italics] even about "imprecise data", and that is certainly of some consequence. It is partly the fashion in our profession because of the great complexity of our subject matter to skip lightly over the difficulties and to take refuge in some all-embracing conception derived from imaginative but often unreliable speculation. This becomes entirely impossible if mathematics is used, for mathematics forces the theorist to impose the strictest discipline on his thoughts. But this self-discipline is the essence of economic thinking and with it economic theory stands or falls. (1952, preface to the first German edition, 1943, p. xiii)

This approach is entirely consistent with mainstream modern theory and practice.

His practice of mathematically specifying behaviours is another reason for the continuing development of his ideas. The number of possible behaviours in any situation is very large. The number of possible economic situations is probably close to infinite. Multiplying the number of possible behaviours by the number of possible economic situations must result in an enormous set of possibilities. Only a few thousand of these have been investigated.

The power of Stackelberg's conceptions when combined with game theory and modern mathematics gives ample room for many more applications. Modern theory has demonstrated the extraordinary utility and variety of uses to which Stackelberg's theoretical apparatus is applicable. New applications appear as this is recognized.

Because I have detailed many of them in my 1996 publication, I will only add two more recent. In 1996, Peter Oberender and Claudius Christl discussed the question, "Was Heinrich von Stackelberg only a pioneer in price theory"? Their answer was that he was much more.

Stefan Baumgärtner, in 1998, detailed, for the first time in English, "the remarkable contribution of Heinrich von Stackelberg to the theory of costs under joint production given in his Kostentheorie" (Abstract). This has led to joint product models in which institutional changes produce a public good but happens because narrow interest groups seek rents for themselves.

His contribution is in the tradition of microeconomics because it emphasizes the study of individual behaviour that must precede the study of aggregates. One of the reasons for the continuing development of his ideas is the growing recognition that this is a required sequence for sound economic analysis.

Modern economic theory has many components, for example, the role of mathematics in models. Looking backward, it is clear that Stackelberg would have insisted that the models should be constructed to fit the institutional, historical, political, and economic context.

---

[10] He often played the mathematics down as in *Marktform und Gleichgewicht* where most of the mathematics is in a *Mathematischer Anhang* [Mathematical Appendix], pp. 106–138.

The importance of Stackelberg's work was immediately and internationally recognized. The extraordinary utility and variety of uses to which Stackelberg's theoretical apparatus was applicable could only come later. The power of Stackelberg's conceptions needed to be combined with game theory and modern mathematics for their full realization.

The Faculty of Economics and Business Administration of Humboldt University in Berlin is absolutely right when it puts Stackelberg among its most prominent professors along with other great men who have a permanent place in the development of economics, Gustav von Schmoller (1838–1917), Werner Sombart (1863–1941), Adolf Wagner (1835–1917), and Max Weber (1864–1920) (http://www.wiwi. hu-berlin.de/fakultaet/geschichte.shtml).

Acknowledgments   Jürgen Backhaus, Ursula Backhaus, Wolfgang Drechsler, Merle Kingman, Gerrit Meijer, and Hans-Heinrich Freiherr von Stackelberg helped me with useful critiques for which I thank them. I am particularly obligated to Mary Stone Senn who, in addition to making many specialized computer searches, was helpful in countless other ways. Thanks also to Anita Lauterstein who did much of the typing. Any errors are my own.

References

Backhaus JG (1996) Stackelberg's concept of the post-war economic order. J Econ Stud 23(5/6):141–148

Baumgärtner S (1998) Heinrich Von Stackelberg's theory of joint production. Discussion Paper no. 265, Department of Economics, Interdisciplinary Institute of Environmental Economics, University of Heidelberg, Germany

Blaug M, Sturges P (eds) (1983) Who's who in economics: a biographical dictionary of major economists 1700–1981. Wheatsheaf Books Ltd., Brighton

Chamberlin EH (1933) The theory of monopolistic competition. Harvard University Press, Cambridge (Revised edition 1948)

Eatwell J, Murray M, Peter N (eds) (1987) The New Palgrave: a dictionary of economics, 4 vols. The Stockton Press, New York; a division of Grove's Dictionaries

Eucken W (1948) Obituary: Heinrich von Stackelberg. Econ J 58(229):132–134

Fuertes JV (1996) Stackelberg and his role in the change in spanish economic policy. J Econ Stud 23(5/6):128–140

Haney LH (1949) History of economic thought: a critical account of the origin and development of the economic theories of the leading thinkers in the leading nations, 4th enlarged edition. The Macmillan Company, New York (First edition 1911)

Harrod RF (1933) Review of Edward Hastings Chamberlin. The theory of monopolistic competition. Econ J XLII(172):661–666

Konow J (1994) The political economy of Heinrich von Stackelberg. Econ Inq 32(1):146–165

Krelle W (1987) Stackelberg, Heinrich von (1905–1946), vol 4. In: Eatwell J, Murray M, Peter N (eds) The New Palgrave: a dictionary of economics, 4 vols. The Stockton Press, New York, p 469; a division of Grove's Dictionaries

Kurz HD (1993) Review of Stackelberg's 'Gesammelte Wirtschaftswissenschaftliche Abhandlungen'. Eur J Hist Econ Thought 1(1):211–216

Leontief W (1936) Stackelberg on monopolistic competition. J Polit Econ 44(4):554–559

Niehans J (1992) Heinrich von Stackelberg: relinking German economics to the mainstream. J Hist Econ Thought 14(2):189–208

Oberender P, Claudius C (1966) Heinrich von Stackelberg: Nur ein Pionier der Preistheorie? in Jahrbücher für Nationalökonomie und Statistik, vol 215. pp 363–376 (I have not seen this article)

Pribram K (1983) A history of economic reasoning. The Johns Hopkins University Press, Baltimore

Robinson J (1933) The economics of imperfect competition. Macmillan and Co., Limited, London (The book was reprinted many times. I worked from the 1948 reprint)

Schmölders G (1948) Jens Jessen (1896–1944). Econ J 58(229):135–136

Schumpeter JA (1954) History of economic analysis, edited from manuscript by Elizabeth Boody Schumpeter. Oxford University Press, New York

Senn PR (1996a) A short sketch of Stackelberg's career. J Econ Stud 23(5/6):8–11

Senn PR (1996b) Heinrich von Stackelberg in the history of economic ideas. J Econ Stud 23(5/6):12–35

Stackelberg HV (1932a) Grundlagen einer reinen Kostentheorie. Zeitschrift für Nationalökonomie 3(333–367):552–590

Stackelberg HV (1932b) Grundlagen einer reinen Kostentheorie. Julius Springer, Vienna. Konow says this book was an expansion of the article above. (163) Backhaus suggests that it was probably the other way around (Jürgen Backhaus, letter to the author, September 1995)

Stackelberg HV (1952) The theory of the market economy, translated from the German and with an introduction by Alan T. Peacock. Oxford University Press, New York. This is a translation of Grundlagen der theoretischen Volkswirtschaftslehre (Foundations of Economic Theory). It has an interesting history. The first edition was entitled Grundzüge der theoretischen Nationalökonomie (Outlines of Economic Theory). It was almost entirely destroyed in an air raid on Stuttgart in 1943. Stackelberg revised and enlarged it during his time in Spain. It was published first in Spanish, as Principios de Teoría Económica, and then in German in 1948

Stigler GJ (1976) The scientific uses of scientific biography: with special reference to John Stuart Mill. In: The economist as preacher and other essays. The University of Chicago Press, Chicago, 1982

von Hassell U (1988) Die Hassell-Tagebücher 1938–1944: Aufzeichnungen vom Andern Deutschland, nach der Handschrift revidierte und erweiterte Ausgabe unter Mitarbeit von Klaus Peter Reiss herausgegeben von Friedrich Freiherr Hiller von Gaertringen. Siedler Verlag, Berlin

von Stackelberg H (1934) Marktform und Gleichgewicht. Julius Springer, Vienna

Chapter 23
Joseph Alois Schumpeter: The Economist of Rhetoric

Yuichi Shionoya

Schumpeter's Intellectual Field and *Habitus*

Pierre Bourdieu (1984), the French sociologist, conceptualizes various aspects of social life in terms of *fields*, which constitute the locus of struggle over a central stake called *capital*. Capital is a resource that yields a particular position, authority, power, and reward. An intellectual field is made up of agents who take various intellectual positions and compete with each other for cultural capital, i.e., the legitimacy of knowledge. The configuration of the intellectual field represents a distribution of power held by different theories and schools. Combined with the intellectual field is the concept of *habitus*, which refers to a set of dispositions, attitudes, and habits. Since *habitus* is not only a subjective mental state but also shared, to a certain extent, intersubjectively in a society, it represents a view of the world embedded within individual people. *Habitus* in an intellectual field makes a picture of the world as the research object of the various academic disciplines and at the same time is reproduced socially through research and educational institutions.

Schumpeter's professional achievements were the results of his behavior, and the intellectual habits and abilities that produced his behavior were to be found within his own person. At the same time, his mind-set was a creation of the intellectual field of his day and was understandable and transposable through communications among a certain group of individuals. This conception of intellectual habits or *habitus* will make it possible to appreciate Schumpeter's work from both subjective and objective points of view.

Schumpeter demonstrated a strong interest in the intellectual products of the past in a wide area of the social sciences, and constructed his positions by responding to the totality of challenges posed by the global intellectual fields of the time. He did

Y. Shionoya (✉)
Hitotsubashi University, Kunitachi, 3-34-8 Sakuragaoka, Tama, Tokyo 206-0013, Japan
e-mail: y.shionoya@blue.ocn.ne.jp

J.G. Backhaus (ed.), *Handbook of the History of Economic Thought*,
The European Heritage in Economics and the Social Sciences,
DOI 10.1007/978-1-4419-8336-7_23, © Springer Science+Business Media, LLC 2012

not want to belong to any single school of thought. Rather he was avid in his desire to examine all points of view and to absorb everything that was good in them. His erudition is well known, yet it was not a matter of taste but of resources for scientific work. For Schumpeter, the most relevant parts of the intellectual field were Neoclassicism, Marxism, and German Historicism. In terms of a broader intellectual tradition, he took both positivism and idealism seriously. Schumpeter could assimilate conflicting ideas, since, for him, they were not alternatives to be chosen for scientific specialization but materials to be integrated for intellectual innovation. Innovation meant a new combination. That was Schumpeter's *habitus*.

Schumpeter is regarded as one of the greatest economists of the twentieth century, ranking with John Maynard Keynes, who was born in the same year, 1883. As economists and sometimes as rivals, they were equally concerned with the instability of capitalism, such as inflation and deflation, business cycles, and unemployment, in the early 1900s. Neoclassical economics – the mainstream economics of the day – could not explain business cycles and unemployment because it addressed static equilibrium with full utilization of economic resources. To solve the problems of that period a new theory had to be constructed on a new basis. That was the challenge to economists.

In the face of that common challenge, the intellectual fields of Keynes and Schumpeter were quite different. For Keynes, the only relevant field was neoclassical economics, particularly Alfred Marshall's economics. Keynes criticized neoclassical full employment economics and developed a new paradigm of static macroeconomics, whereby the cause of business cycles was found in the changes of effective demand under fixed supply conditions. In contrast, Schumpeter tried to construct a dynamic theory of economic change, focusing on innovations on the supply side, in place of static theory. For him, depressions were essential and inevitable part of business cycles produced by the dynamism of entrepreneurial capitalism. Furthermore, Schumpeter worked to establish a vision of the evolution of a capitalist system against the background of the intellectual views of Marx and the German Historical School.

Schumpeter was a great admirer of Léon Walras, one of the founders of neoclassical economics. Since he believed in the scientific value of Walras's mathematical formulation of general equilibrium, he appraised the Lausanne School more highly than the Austrian and Cambridge Schools. Although Walrasian economics was his core conception of economics, Schumpeter's intellectual field was much wider because he absorbed a lot from the special German and Austrian intellectual climate. At the University of Vienna, he gained familiarity with Austro-Marxism through his friendship with future Marxist leaders such as Otto Bauer, Rudolf Hilferding, and Emil Lederer. As Böhm-Bawerk's provocative article "Zum Abschluss des Marxschen Systems" (1896) illustrates Marxism was not only a political movement but also a topic of serious academic debate at Vienna. Furthermore, the *Methodenstreit*, which started between Carl Menger and Gustav von Schmoller at the end of the nineteenth century, had posed grave philosophical and methodological questions to economists. Schumpeter was drawn to methodology by the controversy and contributed, in his first book, a positive solution based on instrumentalism, which can be compared to another solution by Max Weber in terms of the theory of ideal type.

In quite different directions, Keynes and Schumpeter struggled for a new theory to shed light on the great problems relating to the destiny of capitalism. The world responded favorably to Keynes, accepting his theory and proposals for public policy immediately and enthusiastically. Paul A. Samuelson described the impact of Keynes's *General Theory* as "the unexpected virulence of a disease first attacking and decimating an isolated tribe of south sea islanders" (1947, p. 146). The Keynesian Revolution prevailed so overwhelmingly that Schumpeter's long-term, wide-ranging perspective was long neglected.

An appraisal of Schumpeter's outlook began only recently: the founding of the International Joseph A. Schumpeter Society in 1986 and its *Journal of Evolutionary Economics* would symbolically attest to the resurrection of his thought in recent decades. Since the 1980s, probably with the centenary of Schumpeter's birth in 1983 as a turning point, the growing interest among economists in the long-tem development of capitalism has drawn attention to technological innovations, institutionalism, and evolutionism through a reappraisal of Schumpeter's work. His rich vision of the long-term and wider perspective has certainly given a stimulus to broadening the scope of economics.

A Biographical Sketch

There are several biographies on Schumpeter (Allen 1991, Swedberg 1991, März 1991, Stolper 1994, McCraw 2007). Joseph Alois Schumpeter was born in 1883 in Trest, a small Moravian town in the Austro-Hungarian Empire. (The Germans called it Triesch, but that name is no longer used and the town is now in the Czech Republic.) Schumpeter's father, a textile manufacturer, died when Joseph was 4 years old. Schumpeter was the only child and his mother was dedicated to her precocious son. Owing to her remarriage to a high-ranking army officer, Schumpeter was able to enter the high society of Vienna and be educated at the Theresianum, a hotbed of the Austrian aristocracy, and the University of Vienna. But for his father's early death and his mother's remarriage, Schumpeter probably would have lived in obscurity in the little-known town of Central Europe without getting in touch with, let alone leaving his mark on, the intellectual history of the world. Schumpeter, the economist, was the brainchild of the crucial moment.

There is no doubt about Schumpeter's natural gifts and herculean efforts, but at the same time he was a conceited and showy person. One of his biographers described him as possessing pretentious arrogance, a sense of self-importance and superiority, elaborate courtesy, and an omniscient attitude; he was elitist, a snob's snob, known for his conspicuity, ambition, and spats; he would wear an unusual vest or cravat, a bracelet, colored or two-toned shoes, and carry a silver-headed cane; he had flamboyant yet impeccable manners (Allen 1991, vol. 1, p. 55). To mystify people, Schumpeter sometimes spoke of his three ambitions in the youth: "I wanted to be the greatest lover in Vienna, the greatest horseman in Austria, and the greatest economist in the world, but I failed to achieve one of the three".

In 1901–1906, Schumpeter studied law, history, and economics at the University of Vienna and soon made his debut as an *enfant terrible* in the field of economic theory. At that time, Vienna was a center of economic studies, ranking with Cambridge and Stockholm; Carl Menger, the founder of the Austrian School of Economics, had just retired from the university. As the second generation of the Austrian School, Böhm-Bawerk and Friedrich von Wieser began their work and Schumpeter became their pupil.

Schumpeter's early trilogy – *Das Wesen und der Hauptinhalt der theoretischen Nationalökonomie* (1908), *Theorie der wirtschaftlichen Entwicklung* (1912), and *Epochen der Dogmen- und Methodengeschichte* (1914) – dealt with static economics, dynamic economics, and the history of economics, respectively, and established a system of basic theoretical economics. The first book explored the methodological foundation of neoclassical economics and, in my interpretation, adapted the methodology of Ernst Mach's instrumentalism to Walras's general equilibrium theory. The second volume represented a breakthrough in overcoming the limitations of economic statics; it presented a unique system of economic dynamics identifying the fundamental phenomenon of economic development with the innovations of entrepreneurs. Schumpeter won his immortal reputation with this single book. The third volume, although small, attempted an imaginative scenario based on a theoretical formulation: Schumpeter regarded the discovery of economic circulation by the Physiocrats as epochal in the history of economics; he then described the system of the Classical School and contrasted the Historical and Marginal Schools.

Schumpeter completed all three volumes by the age of thirty. Schumpeter was of the opinion that scholars achieve their truly original work in their twenties, which he called the "decade of sacred fertility". This applied to Schumpeter himself because his work in the second half of his career can be seen as an effort to bring his work in the first half to fruition.

There is an interpretation that Schumpeter started his career as a theoretical economist and then moved to economic sociology and historical studies in later life. I have doubts about this. In his curriculum vitae submitted to the University of Bonn in 1925, he wrote that while attending the Theresianum and the University of Vienna he developed sociological, philosophical, and historical interests, and after mastering mathematical economics he proceeded to the research field of Gustav von Schmoller (Shionoya 1997, p. 16). From the beginning of his academic life Schumpeter had a wide range of interests in history, sociology, and economic theory. He had already begun sociological studies in 1912, when he published his theoretical work on economic development. The focus of his sociological concern was a theory of social class that would serve as the crucial link between the concept of leadership in various areas of social life, on the one hand, and the overall concept of civilization and the *Zeitgeist*, on the other. As we shall see, this sociological link became the key to his thesis of failing capitalism. His sociological writings are collected in Schumpeter (1918, 1951b, 1953, 1987, 1991).

Schumpeter taught at the University of Czernowitz in 1909–1911 and at the University of Graz in 1911–1918. After World War I, he was Ministry of Finance in the Austrian coalition cabinet of the Social Democratic Party and the Christian Social Party for 7 months in 1919. He was against overall socialization of industry because he thought that the time was not ripe, but he did predict the eventual fall of capitalism. From 1925 to 1932 he was a professor at the University of Bonn. In 1932, Schumpeter emigrated to the United States to become a professor at Harvard University, where he remained until his death in 1950. Schumpeter's political writings in the interwar period are collected in Schumpeter (1985, 1992, 1993). His writings on economic theory in his European period are edited in Schumpeter (1952).

In his American period, Schumpeter wrote his later trilogy: *Business Cycles* (1939), *Capitalism, Socialism and Democracy* (1942), and *History of Economic Analysis* (1954a). Having developed the pure theories of statics and dynamics, his next tasks were, first, to analyze the historical process of capitalist economic development, and, second, to diagnose the future trend of the economic, social, and cultural system of capitalism.

The first task required the empirical identification of economic changes with entrepreneurial innovations that were accompanied by cyclical fluctuations. *Business Cycles*, in two massive volumes, with the grandiose subtitle "A Theoretical, Historical and Statistical Analysis of the Capitalist Process", was intended as an expansion and elaboration of the theory of economic development in a historical and statistical context, but it was unsuccessful because it was not equipped with sufficient theoretical and statistical tools to deal with historical complexities. In this connection, it is noted that Schumpeter's effort to develop a theory of money, which would be one of the pillars of his theory of innovations, became a failure. Unfinished manuscripts are published in Schumpeter (1970).

But this book included interesting vision of integrating theory and history by the use of the Kondratieff cycle. This long wave with a periodicity of 50 years provided Schumpeter with a framework for not only statistical analysis of technological paradigms but also historical research of sociological and institutional background. The latter research may be called a study of the *Zeitgeist*.

The second task was undertaken in *Capitalism, Socialism and Democracy,* where Schumpeter developed evolutionary economic sociology to address the interactions between economic and noneconomic areas with the intermediary of social class theory. Rejecting the view that capitalism would fall because of its economic failure, he presented his famous thesis that the very success of capitalism in economic terms would erode its social and moral foundations.

Finally, *History of Economic Analysis,* published posthumously, was really Schumpeter's *tour de force* and demonstrated that he was perhaps the last of the great polymaths. It was soon accepted as his most authoritative work. Half a century later, no other work on the history of economics had surpassed it in terms of scale and insight. His other writings on the history of economics are published in Schumpeter (1915, 1951a, 1954b, c).

Why was Schumpeter so interested in the history of economics? For him, the developments of economy and society, on the one hand, and the developments of thought and science, on the other, were two aspects of the same evolutionary process. As he was engaged in the history of economic development, so was he interested in the history of economic doctrines; these two areas of investigation constituted his approach to the evolution of the mind and society, which offered a substitute for Marx's economic interpretation of history concerning the relationship between the substructure and the superstructure of a society.

To identify Schumpeter's contributions to economics and to show how he approached the field, the section III presents my formulation of his overall scheme for a comprehensive sociology (or alternatively, a universal social science or a two-structure approach to the mind and society), which is little known to economists. Although Schumpeter's name has been exclusively connected with his theory of economic development and innovation in a capitalist economy, economic analysis was merely a part of his overall research program. I believe that this is the most significant gap in Schumpeter scholarship. Then, in section IV, I will set out the central ideas underlying his overall research program; the importance of these ideas is delineated in terms of his model of economic development, which has in fact been explored more fully than other parts of the scheme. Finally, in sections V-VII, I will illustrate how Schumpeter tackled the insurmountable tasks of constructing a universal social science with his mastery of rhetoric.

The Research Program for a Comprehensive Sociology

What style of science did Schumpeter plan and pursue through his lifelong academic activities? In an interview with the *Harvard Crimson* in the later stage of his life, Schumpeter called his long-standing research program a "comprehensive sociology" and observed: "Early in life I formed an idea of a rich and full life to include economics, politics, science, art, and love. All my failures are due to observance of this program and my success to neglect of it: concentration is necessary for success in any field" (Harvard Crimson 1944). Comprehensive sociology means the integration of the social sciences by treating separate social phenomena from the sociological perspective.

In his early work on the history of social thought, Schumpeter predicted the future direction of the social sciences to be their *Soziologisierung*, which can be understood to mean a comprehensive sociology (1915, p. 133). He expected an epoch similar to the eighteenth century, when the social sciences were dominated by the unifying principle of moral science or moral philosophy as the science of man. *Soziologisierung* of the social sciences for their reunification is the basic framework within which to understand Schumpeter's work.

In fact, he did not develop a comprehensive sociology, but rather two sociologies – economic sociology and the sociology of science – that may be interpreted as his strategic version of a comprehensive sociology. In this sense, I call the total body of Schumpeter's work a "two-structure approach to the mind and society" after his

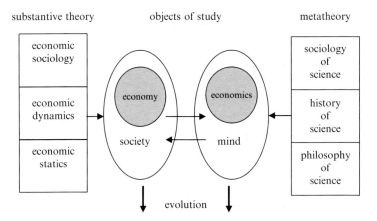

Fig. 23.1 Schumpeter's two-structure approach

discerning characterization of Giambattista Vico's work as "an evolutionary science of the mind and society" (1954a, p. 137).

By a "two-structure approach to the mind and society" I mean two systems each consisting of three layers (Shionoya 1997, pp. 260–265). The *system of substantive theory,* about the economy, consists of economic statics, economic dynamics, and economic sociology. The *system of metatheory,* about economics, includes the philosophy of science, the history of science, and the sociology of science. These two systems are parallel in viewing the economy, on the one hand, and economics, on the other, from the viewpoints of, first, static structure, second, dynamic development, and third, their activities in a social context.

If the two sets of thought are likened to buildings, we can envisage two intellectual buildings (Fig. 23.1) – one for society and one for the mind, or, more specifically, one for the economy and one for economics. They each have three stories, with their third floor linked by a passage representing what Schumpeter called "comprehensive sociology."

The System of Substantive Theory

Schumpeter's economic writings cover all three layers in the system of substantive theory. *Wesen* is concerned with economic statics, *Entwicklung* with economic dynamics, and *Capitalism, Socialism and Democracy* with economic sociology.

For Schumpeter, a general equilibrium in economic statics was not a fiction but the logic of an economy that formulates the consequences of the adaptive behavior of ordinary economic agents responding to their exogenously given circumstances. He regarded economic statics as the Magna Carta of economic theory in the sense that economics should be established as an exact and autonomous science on the basis of economic statics. Economic statics is applied to the process of circular flow, in which the economy repeats itself year after year, with its size and structure remaining constant under given conditions. According to Schumpeter, economic growth based on an increase in population and capital can also be explained by economic statics because these changes are exogenous.

By an analogy with economic equilibrium, he assumed the presence of static order in other areas of social life such as politics, science, art, and morality and explained static states by reference to the adaptive behavior of ordinary people. His unique view was that the dynamic phenomenon in the economic process is brought about by a destruction of the previous equilibrium by forces from within the economy, i.e., by the innovations of entrepreneurs. He also argued, using an analogy with economic dynamics, that such dynamic phenomena occur in other areas of social life, also by innovators' destruction of the existing order. If innovators succeed in introducing a new way of life to specific areas, the direction in which the general public will follow is set, and they become the leaders in these areas. Adaptive behavior is to statics what innovative behavior is to dynamics; just as a static state in any area is characterized by the average man following conventions and customs, so is a dynamic state marked by a leader who has enough energy and will, foresight and creativity to introduce innovations. The entrepreneur in the economic area is a special kind of leader.

The logic of economic sociology, the third branch in the system of theory, consists of an analysis of institutions that are exogenously given to economic theory and are lumped together to include all noneconomic factors. Schumpeter defined economic sociology as "a sort of generalized or typified or stylized economic history" (1954a, p. 20). It is the concept of an institutional framework that can generalize, typify, or stylize the complexities of economic history. In other words, economic sociology is the generalization, typification, and stylization of history by means of institutional analysis.

Economic sociology does not deal with the totality of interactions between all areas of social life, which Schumpeter termed "sociocultural development," but it summarizes the interactions between economic and noneconomic areas by focusing on the institutional factors that condition the purposes of economic activities. In this sense, economic sociology is an approximation of the study of sociocultural developments. Sociocultural development as a whole is the theme of what Schumpeter called a comprehensive sociology or a universal social science, and this was the ultimate goal of his scientific endeavors. The idea of a universal social science which would deal with the sociocultural development was presented in chapter 7 of the first edition of *Entwicklung*. This important chapter, however, was eliminated in the second edition of 1926 and the English translation of 1934.

Schumpeter found the source of economic sociology in the work of the historical and ethical method advocated by Schmoller for the German Historical School. In his important article "Gustav v. Schmoller und die Probleme von heute" (1926, reprinted in 1954b), Schumpeter regarded Schmoller's approach as the prototype of economic sociology and argued that economic sociology or institutional analysis of economic history would realize "reasoned history," i.e., the synthesis of theory and history. The foremost concept of economic sociology that Schumpeter found in the research program of the German Historical School was the integration of two viewpoints, the unity of social life and development – the idea of the endogenous evolution of society as a whole through interactions among the various areas of social life. Thus, Schumpeter developed a substantive solution to overcome the antagonism between theory and history in the *Methodenstreit,* in addition to the methodological solution to the various issues raised by the controversy.

The System of Metatheory

It is generally recognized that Schumpeter accomplished excellent work on the history of economics, but his system of metatheory, which comprises the history of economics as a part, is little known. I find in Schumpeter's writings a set of metatheories with three layers that can be regarded as the counterpart of his set of substantive theories on the economy. Metatheory is a theory about theory. Just as his economic studies contain three layers, i.e., economic statics, economic dynamics, and economic sociology, his studies on science have three parallel layers, i.e., statics of science, dynamics of science, and sociology of science. In the common usage, the first one is called the methodology of science (or the philosophy of science), which is concerned with the static structure and rules of science; the second, the history of science, which deals with the dynamic development of science; and the third, the sociology of science, which views scientific activities as social phenomena. It is natural that a strong structural parallelism exists between the systems of substantive theory and metatheory because the same methods of observation are applied to the two areas of social life, i.e., economy and science; the same methods will permit analysis of static equilibrium, dynamic development, and interactions with other social areas, respectively.

Schumpeter's methodology of science was developed in his first book, *Wesen.* Since his contribution to economics is considered to be in the realm of dynamic theory, his no-less-important work on static theory has not received the attention it deserves. Even the fact that this book is about methodology is not generally known. Schumpeter ingeniously applied to economics the instrumentalist methodology and phenomenalist epistemology developed at the end of nineteenth century by natural scientists such as Ernst Mach, Henri Poincaré, and Pierre Duhem. Instrumentalism is the view that theories are not descriptions but instruments for deriving useful results and are neither true nor false. Unlike the present-day narrow view of instrumentalism, useful results of theories, for Schumpeter, should be interpreted broadly to include not only the generation of predictions but also the classification, organization, and explanation of observable phenomena and guides for action. If theories are instruments in this sense, it is useless to ask whether they are true or false; it is only possible to ask whether they are useful for certain purposes. Therefore, the realism of assumptions in a corpus of theories does not matter.

The *Methodenstreit* was concerned with the explanatory primacy of historical vs. theoretical methods, or inductive vs. deductive methods. But this cannot be a genuine issue of debate because both methods are indispensable depending on the problems involved. The genuine issue was not methods but problems to be pursued. Whereas the Historical School focused on the economics of institutions and evolution, the Neoclassical School claimed the economics of utility and prices.

Schumpeter was much influenced by Mach's phenomenology, according to which science should not indulge in a metaphysical speculation that assumes the essence behind phenomena, and it should reject the notion of causality, which attributes phenomena to some ultimate cause. Mach argued that one should address only the functional relationship between elements that are found in the phenomenal world through sensual experiences. Walras's general equilibrium model conceptualizes the world in terms of the general interdependence between prices and quantities of goods and factors of production. Schumpeter discovered in Walras's theory the best case for the application of phenomenalism, and this is the reason why he admired Walras so much. The mathematical elegance of general equilibrium was irrelevant.

In constructing a scenario on the historical development of economics, Schumpeter applied the same patterns of thought as established between statics and dynamics of the economy. He introduced the concept of the "classical situation" as a device of periodization in history; defining it as "the achievement of substantial agreement after a long period of struggle and controversy – the consolidation of the fresh and original work which went before" (1954a, p. 51). Thomas Kuhn (1970) later termed the same situation the establishment of a "normal science." Once the classical situation is established, scientists are engaged in the production of potential scientific results under a new paradigm; this is compared with a stationary economy that is repeating itself on a fixed channel with a constant scale and structure.

Dynamic phenomena in science involve a scientific revolution and its aftermath; parallel to innovative entrepreneurs in the economy, innovators in science challenge traditional paradigms by introducing new ideas and new theories. The formation of schools in science is compared to the clustering of imitators who follow the innovators. Revolution and synthesis are the two moments in scientific development.

If we combine the results of Schumpeter's historical research on economic development in his *Business Cycles,* on the one hand, and the development of economics in his *History of Economic Analysis*, on the other, an interesting picture will emerge. According to the Kondratieff framework of long waves in economic activities, which Schumpeter used for historical investigation, the Industrial Revolution Kondratieff (1787–1843), the Bourgeois Kondratieff (1843–1898), and the Neomercantilist Kondratieff (1898–1950) are distinguished. Similar 50-year cycles are also evident in the chronology of the history of economics: the first classical situation was marked by the acceptance of Adam Smith's system of economic thought around 1790, the second by the maturity of classical economics at John Stuart Mill around 1848, and the third by the synthesis of neoclassical economics by Alfred Marshall and Knut Wicksell around 1890. Although Schumpeter did not explicitly mention a fourth period, by following his procedure we can probably define the fourth classical situation as the establishment of Keynesian economics around 1950. The long waves in the history of the economy and economics, which Schumpeter just suggested, present a stimulating methodological question concerning the evolutionary interrelationship between the mind and society.

Developments in science, according to Schumpeter, do not proceed in a linear fashion in which the past achievements are carried over to the future so that scientific knowledge grows cumulatively. Important creative ideas are sometimes left behind the mainstream that gains power by caprice and chance. Thus, developments in science are not a logical process but a proper subject of the sociology of science, the third branch of metathory. For Schumpeter, the subject of the sociology of science was twofold: schools and vision. The formation of schools is an important strategy in establishing the "classical situation."

Along with the concept of the "classical situation," which concerns the mechanism of revolution and ensuing synthesis, Schumpeter put forward another concept of the "filiation of scientific ideas," one that produces a theoretical reformulation of neglected ideas. Through discourses with past history, fragments left in the shadow of that history will revive as a vision to guide the formation of new theories. This form of filiation in history emerges from a combination of vision and theory that takes place over time.

Fundamental Ideas

To understand Schumpeter's overall framework of a universal social science, I will set out the fundamental ideas organizing that framework. There are three such ideas in Schumpeter's thought: (1) the dichotomy of statics and dynamics in terms of the type of man, (2) the evolutionary development of society through interactions between social areas, and (3) the notioin of institution as the synthesis of theory and history. Each of these ideas represents a response to the challenges to Neoclassicism, Marxism, and German Historicism, all of which are Schumpeter's intellectual fields. These responses are designed to organize the framework of a universal social science.

Insofar as society is seen as composed of individuals and their interactions, we must start with some conceptions of individuals. The conception of the agent as a rational utility maximizer based on fixed preferences has occupied a central place in mainstream neoclassical economic theory and is often labeled *homo oeconomicus* or economic man. Various criticisms have been raised of the notion of economic man: for example, holism against individualism, altruism against egoism, and irrationalism against rationalism. But, from the viewpoint of instrumentalist methodology, the realism of the assumptions should not matter; the conception of man should depend on what problems are to be addressed. Schumpeter's problem was to explore a new horizon of dynamic economics vis-à-vis static economics. For this purpose, he proposed to define the dynamic man in contradistinction to the static man in such a way that the dynamic man was innovative, whereas the static man was adaptive to given conditions. He called the static man "hedonistic" and the dynamic man "energetic." This is the most orthodox approach to methodological individualism in view of other dynamic approaches to saving-investment relations, monetary disturbances, period analysis, disequilibrium analysis, and expectations.

Schumpeter's idea of the dynamic man has some affinity with contemporary sociological thought such as the superman of Friedrich Nietzsche, the *élan vital* of Henri Bergson, the circulation of the elite of Vilfredo Pareto, the imitation of Jean Gabriel Tarde, the charisma of Max Weber, the law of a small number of Friedrich von Wieser, and the life philosophy of Ortega y Gaset. These examples are variants of human typology and Schumpeter was probably animated by them. But his originality was twofold: first, he applied the sociological dichotomy to the basic assumptions of the static vs. dynamic system by the rhetoric of *antithesis*, and second, he applied the dichotomy not only to economic area but also to all other areas by the rhetoric of *analogy*.

Schumpeter's second fundamental idea was the evolutionary development of society through interactions between various social areas. This was his response to the Marxian challenge of historical materialism, which viewed historical processes as unilateral relations from production processes as the substructure of society to political, social, and cultural processes as the superstructure of society through the pivotal position of the class structure of capital and labor. For Schumpeter, social class also occupied an important place in evolutionary development as a whole, but his conception of social class was not confined to the economic area but consisted of more open social dynamics derived from leadership formation in various social areas. Although he mentioned the notion of comprehensive sociocultural development, his actual work was confined to the two social areas; economic and noneconomic, the latter referring to a way of thinking, social values, and the *Zeitgeist*. This division of the two areas preserved the Marxian influence of the super- and substructure concepts. The basic idea of *Capitalism, Socialism and Democracy* is that capitalist economic development driven by the innovation of entrepreneurs will make the *Zeitgeist* of society anticapitalistic and this in turn will gradually create a social atmosphere in which it is more difficult for innovations to occur.

If it were possible to analyze comprehensive sociocultural developments comprising various social areas, more important results would be obtained from the Schumpeterian apparatus. Social class has the function of weighing and integrating various social areas, in which successful leaders ascend to the top of a society. In the past, such areas as economy, politics, religion, and the military played important social roles, according to which a hierarchy was established among the social classes of the various areas to create a social order. The determinant of the hierarchy is called "social value," meaning the aptitude for fulfilling socially necessary functions in a specific historical situation. *Social values*, which weigh and integrate social classes into a hierarchical system, and the *Zeitgeist*, which is the ideological expression of the hierarchy, characterize the nature of a society as a whole. It is possible that social values and the *Zeitgeist* will conflict: Schumpeter's famous thesis on the fall of capitalism is reduced to the argument that the social values demanded by capitalism and the *Zeitgeist* produced by capitalism may collide. This collision, in turn, is reduced to the antinomy between heroism and rationalism, each being derived from the definition of the dynamic and static man, respectively. If an analysis could be extended to specific interactions between major social areas such as the economic, political, religious, intellectual, and military spheres, one would address the prospect of changing social values and of shifting the locus of innovative human resources after the fall of capitalism or the system of economic dominance.

Now let us turn to the third basic idea of Schumpeter's research program: the notion that institution is intended to achieve the synthesis of theory and history. This was his response to the *Methodenstreit* between theory and history and opened a new frontier to the theoretical analysis of history. Schumpeter believed that history is much more important than theory because "the subject matter of economics is essentially a unique process in historic time" (1954a, p. 12.) The concept of institution is a means of generalizing historical events, but it is generally limited due to its historical relativeity. Thus, it can be conceived of as a compromise between the generality meant by theory and the individuality meant by history. Both economic sociology and the sociology of science, with their focus on the concept of institutions, lump together all factors exogenous to the proper areas of economy and science in a convenient grab bag of institutions.

It is the core proposition of institutional economics that institutions and individuals constitute an action-information loop. Institutions are social norms, consisting of laws, morality, and customs. Institutions offer information on normative rules to individuals, and actions of individuals, in turn, provide institutions with habitual behaviors. Schumpeter sometimes called the institutional totality simply the *Zeitgeist* that exists outside the economy. Therefore, the action-information loop between institutions and individuals presents another picture of the interactions between economic and noneconomic areas. Institutional economics and economic sociology provide complementary approaches to the goal of a comprehensive sociology.

Against the background of his three fundamental ideas, it will be realized that Schumpeter's theory of economic development marks only the midpoint in his journey. But, at the same time, it should be remembered that this theory contains a core of the whole scheme. So let us examine its structure. There are three key words. The first is *innovation*, the cause of economic development. Innovation covers the introduction of a new product, a new method of production, the opening of a new market, the acquisition of a new source of supply, and the reorganization of an existing industry. The second key word is *entrepreneur*, the subject of economic development or the agent of innovation. Because innovation requires foresight and originality, resolution and action, innovators are rare. If one succeeds in introducing a change, he can get entrepreneurial profits. The third element is *bank credit*, the means by which the entrepreneur accomplishes innovation. In economic statics, there is no room for the essential role of money to command economic resources.

Although the mechanisms of dynamics in major areas of social life – for example, economic, political, scientific, or religious – are naturally quite different from each other, the general nature of dynamism is essentially the same: there must be innovation, innovators, and an instrument. Given the developments in all areas of social life, the essence of the tasks of Schumpeter's universal social science is how to integrate them to understand the evolutionary patterns of society as a whole. This is the question for institutional economics and economic sociology to explore beyond the theory of economic development. Now we have come to the stage where we can see how Schumpeter addressed it. An analysis of the fundamental ideas in his universal social science from a different perspective is given in Shionoya (2004).

Intellectual Field and the Rhetoric of *Antithesis*

Twentieth-century economics was remarkably precise. In spite of that, or rather because of that, economics is unable to tackle the huge problem of social evolution. However sharp a razor may be, it is not fit for cutting trees; such work requires an axe. This is the challenge of agreement between problem and method. When Schumpeter presented a unique vision of the historical evolution of a capitalist society in terms of a comprehensive sociology or universal social science, he capitalized on rhetoric to articulate his ideas. No other methods were available. For Schumpeter, rhetoric played the role of the axe to cut a path through an unexplored field. In a field that is beyond existing theory, a vision of objects must be presented first. The history of science often shows that when an attractive vision is received, a clear theoretical formulation will follow sooner or later. In fact, Schumpeter's notion of "the filiation of scientific ideas" applies to the successful combination of early vision and later theory over time.

Although rhetoric is traditionally expelled from positivist logic and the philosophy of science, it has an important role to play in the context of discovery rather than in the context of justification of scientific thought. On the other hand, traditional rhetoric as the art of making speeches is engaged in the detailed classification of modifying phrases and sentences, but not in the formulation of tools for thinking and expressing visions. I am not so much concerned about a figure of speech as a figure of thought. Rhetoric as a figure of thought is an instrument for posing entirely new questions and for stimulating further exploration. In my view, the most important types of rhetoric as a figure of thought are *antithesis, metaphor*, and *paradox*. I will use them in analyzing Schumpeter's rhetoric.

The concept of *antithesis* sets out a binary relation A and B and emphasizes the contrast, opposition, and contraposition between them. Examples include subjective and objective, fact and value, theory and practice, and East and West. The aims of using antithesis are, first, to distinguish literally between the two; and second, to synthesize the two through the interplay of opposing polarities (for instance, the dialectic of Hegel and Marx). These two cases, presupposing the existence of two contraries, propose a distinction or synthesis between them. In contrast, there is a third aim: to create B against existing A on the supposition that one cannot get along with A alone. Because B does not yet exist in the proper shape of an idea or fact, it is required to appeal to rhetoric to persuade one of the necessity and significance of B in comparison to A. This is a function of creation.

Schumpeter encountered a wide intellectual field that involved plural antitheses between schools of thought, and he responded positively to all of them. Here I will discuss only two instances: (1) Schmoller and Menger and (2) Walras and Marx.

Schmoller and Menger

In Schumpeter's opinion, the *Methodenstreit* between Schmoller and Menger was a useless debate based on a false conception of antithesis between theory and history. In *Wesen,* he proposed a compromise based on the methodology of instrumentalism, according to which the theoretical or historical method should be chosen depending on the problems to be addressed. This solution separates theory and history, which is not argued on mere rhetoric but is based on methodology.

However, when Schumpeter introduced an economic sociology that went beyond economic statics and dynamics, he focused on the cooperation of theory and history, instead of their separation and differentiation, in order to deal with complex problems. In his 1926 article on Schmoller, Schumpeter provided an appraisal of Schmoller's historical and ethical economics and characterized it as economic sociology in which theory and history could be integrated (1926). Among several attempts to deal with the great problem of historical evolution, Schumpeter rejected a "single hypothesis of the Comte-Buckle-Marx kind" (1954a, p. 811) that reduces historical dynamism to the working of a single element, and he was quite sympathetic to Schmoller, whose main work he called a "comprehensive mosaic" (1954b, p. 165) compared with Marx's monolithic structure. With regard to Marx's attempt to integrate history and theory, Schumpeter's rhetoric asserted that it was not "technical" but "chemical" (1950, p. 44).

Walras and Marx

The antithesis of Walras and Marx means in a symbolic sense the antithesis of economic statics and dynamics. The aims of this rhetoric are twofold: to claim the need of dynamic economics beyond Walrasian statics and to declare the need of economic sociology beyond economic statics and dynamics. When Schumpeter explained his goal in the study of economic change in his preface to the Japanese edition of *Entwicklung*, he thought it is necessary to refer to two great names, Walras and Marx, meaning that his theory embraced both of their ideas (1951c, p. 159). Most commentators regarded it as one of Schumpeter's many paradoxes, asking how it was ever possible to believe in the thought of general equilibrium and that of falling capitalism at the same time. This criticism was brought about by Schumpeter's provocative rhetoric, but, I argue, it is based on the misunderstanding or ignorance of his system, which I have interpreted by the three-layer structure.

Schumpeter accepted Walras's theory because it – for the first time in the history of economics – clarified the mechanism of general economic equilibrium by which all economic variables are interdependently determined under given exogenous conditions, and because it described the functioning of markets as a real force moving toward equilibrium in spite of apparent disturbances so that the economic system could be regarded as stable. Walras's idea ensures scientific autonomy for economics. Schumpeter's dynamics must be constructed on the basis of the Walrasian economic logic and mechanism because, in Schumpeter's view, economic development is merely a destruction of equilibrium and does not possess dynamic equilibrium.

On the other hand, Schumpeter was also a great admirer of the Marxian view because it – for the first time in the history of economics – grasped the endogenous evolutionary process of the capitalist system in the context of the historical time, and because it presented a scenario of failing capitalism owing to its inherent contradictions. Although his reasoning is different from Marx's, Schumpeter shared the insight with Marx that capitalism does not continue to work forever like a perpetual motion machine. Although in *Entwicklung,* Schumpeter just described the operation of capitalism within the economic area, where there is no obstacle to the emergence of entrepreneurial innovation, he could reach the level of Marx's argument for declining capitalism only when he addressed the scope of economic sociology developed in *Capitalism,* integrating interactions between various social areas. Given Schumpeter's three-layer system of economic statics, economic dynamics, and economic sociology, there is nothing paradoxical in accepting the view of both Walras and Marx.

Intellectual Frontier and the Rhetoric of *Metaphor*

Among the various forms of rhetoric, the most often discussed is *metaphor*. When an object is to be described, metaphor uses a different term to stand in for that object to which it does not properly apply. (Example: "Henry is a lion.") Metaphor is a subcategory of a broader concept of analogy that also includes simile, allegory, metonymy, and synecdoche. In this case, it is only necessary to refer to simile and allegory. *Simile* is an explicit comparison of one thing with another; two things are expressed and in what respect they are compared is shown. (Example: "Henry is brave like a lion.") In contrast, in metaphor the similarity between the two things being compared ("bravery" in the example) remains implicit. The reason for keeping the similarity implicit in metaphor is not always intentional; rather, metaphor is used because the feature of an object is hard to express literally. Therefore, a comparison of two things in metaphor without describing a point of similarity will allow a wide range of different interpretations and imagination. The production of images through metaphor is important for the creation of vision and thought. When it is difficult to properly describe an object in question X, metaphor is used as an analogical inference and to acquire a cognition about X on the basis of information about well-known Y. The merit of metaphor is not in the substitution of Y for X where the feature of X and Y is already known, but in the discovery and construction of X on the presumption of a similarity between X and Y where the feature of X is unknown. Thus metaphor is creative and heuristic.

Whereas metaphor applies to isolated words, phrases, or sentences, *allegory* applies to a system or structure that is composed of a series of metaphors representing a certain point of view. When unknown X is supposed to have a structure, allegory based on known Y is a heuristic to discover the whole structure of X.

A creative role of rhetoric is found in science and thought, where a series of metaphors in the form of an allegory are structurally applied to a wide area, so that the totality of methods and structure in a developed discipline may be metaphorically applied to another discipline or field of thought. In this sense, metaphor provides a structural viewpoint to expand the frontier of an intellectual field. To view physics as a model of economics or to apply the theory of evolution to economics is a grand rhetoric of metaphor or allegory. Schumpeter took part in these efforts on various economic fronts including physics and economics, entrepreneur and leader, and biology and evolutionism.

Physics and Economics

A typical early case of metaphor in economics was the *tableau économique* of the physician François Quesnay, which was derived by depicting the circulation of blood in the human body. In the formative period of neoclassical economics, the dependence of economics on physics was wide ranging; the entire paradigm of neoclassical theory was a metaphor of physics. It was believed that economics could become a science by adopting the methodology of physics and by imitating the structure of physics, not simply by introducing mathematics.

Schumpeter's contribution in this direction was to establish a methodological foundation of neoclassical economics by applying the philosophy of science of contemporary physicists, especially Ernst Mach. Schumpeter found the possibility of metaphor between Mach's phenomenological physics and the general equilibrium model, both dealing with functional relations between objects based on sensory experience. Although he started with Austrian economics, he opposed essentialism and psychologism from the phenomenologist standpoint. At the same time, he accepted the role of the utility concept, which is not measurable, in the instrumentalist methodology.

It is interesting to note that Ernst Mach, in turn, depended on metaphor from economics. He is known for the idea of "economy of thought" to describe the world as economically as possible, without the need to know mere individual facts, and adapted the principle of economy to science. Viewed in this way, economy and science are analogically related by the principle of economic rationality. This fact might justify Schumpeter's development of his "two-structure approach to the mind and society." If economic rationality is the regulating principle for statics in the economy and science, the dynamic principle should be a passion for excellence of the dynamic man in both areas.

Entrepreneur and Leader

While Schumpeter was engaged in the reconstruction of statics, he resorted to metaphor from the developed science of physics. When he launched economic dynamics to explore a new frontier, he consistently used metaphor from sociological imagination. That was the idea of human typology. Alternatively, an analogy of dynamics in physical science was considered, but Schumpeter's mathematical ability did not make it worthwhile to pursue it. What was called leadership sociology distinguished between leader and follower, the elite and the masses. Schumpeter daringly imposed the dichotomy of human type on economics to explore metaphorical implications in the context of economic statics and dynamics. There was no usage of the two types of man in economics. Although the terms "entrepreneur" and "producer" appeared, they had no relevance to dynamic economy. Schumpeter called a leader in the economic area an "entrepreneur" and assigned him the role of carrying out innovations.

Schumpeter emphasized the endogenous nature of economic development in that innovations are the activities associated with the person of entrepreneur, thus metaphorically defined. Apparent dynamic phenomena such as an increase in population and capital, improvement of productive methods and organizations, and developments of desire are changes in given circumstances, to which the economy adapts passively through the behavior of the static type of man. Furthermore, apparent innovations are not necessarily regarded as dynamic in terms of the capitalistic spirit if they are carried out in an impersonal and bureaucratic manner.

Biology and Evolutionism

Anticipating the structure of economic sociology, Schumpeter resorted to zoological metaphor rather than physical metaphor. He rejected the common view that the distinction between statics and dynamics was introduced into economics from physics, claiming that it came from zoology. His zoological metaphor was that if a study of the organism of a dog is comparable to statics, research on how dogs have come to exist at all in terms of concepts such as selection, mutation, or evolution would be analogous to dynamics. Schumpeter's theory of economic development does not contain an image of biological or zoological evolution. Although it certainly deals with a dynamic process associated with innovation, the institutional framework of capitalism remains intact. The idea of biological or zoological evolution can be found in his work of economic sociology, *Capitalism, Socialism and Democracy*. This book analyzes the evolutionary process of capitalist economic society as a whole through the interactions between economic and noneconomic areas. If noneconomic areas are regarded as an environment of economic areas, one may catch a glimpse of a Darwinism that would identify economic evolution with changes in the noneconomic environment.

Intellectual Synthesis and the Rhetoric of *Paradox*

Paradox is a situation in which two inconsistent statements appear to be true or a statement alleges that they are both true. If one of the two statements is generally received as common sense, it is not necessarily stated and a paradox merely presents a heterodox view that is contrary to the standard opinion. A paradox sometimes engenders shocking effects, because one statement denies the other while each is based on different reasoning. In this case, the question arises, why can't one say that one of them is true or false? According to Aristotle, outside the world of apodeictics or logical reasoning where judgments of truth and falsity are possible, dialectics or the art of persuasion must be used and here is the case for the rhetoric of paradox.

An analysis of paradox requires identification of the contexts or dimensions in which each statement does hold an explication of why two conflicting statements are proposed. When we understand paradox not as the rhetoric of a mere figure or sophistry but as the rhetoric of thought, it is important to recognize two points: first, conflicting statements reveal a "gap in knowledge," and second, the rhetoric of paradox is interpreted as an attempt to provide the "coordination of knowledge." By a "gap in knowledge" I mean a situation of split knowledge surrounding us as a result of scientific specialization. We are confined to segmented dimensions and contexts of knowledge, so that we are little aware of the split. In these circumstances, an attempt to disclose a "gap in knowledge" works as the rhetoric of paradox, or more correctly, it works *only* as the rhetoric of paradox, because separate dimensions in which each statement is valid are logically incommensurable with each other, so that a relationship between two statements cannot be dealt with as philosophical knowledge but only as rhetorical knowledge.

The rhetoric of paradox demands the "coordination of knowledge." From ancient times, solutions to celebrated paradoxes, such as Achilles failing to overtake the tortoise and the flying arrow failing to fly, have been discussed as problems of logic, but Schumpeter's paradox is not concerned with formal logic but with the methodology of social analysis and requires a commensurate style of coordination. Let us examine three major examples: (1) the importance of statics, (2) creative destruction, and (3) decaying capitalism because of success.

The Importance of Statics

Schumpeter distinguished economic statics and dynamics and located them in the rhetoric of antithesis, as I discussed earlier in reference to Walras and Marx. He depended on the rhetoric of antithesis to emphasize the need for dynamics in contrast with statics, but when he stressed the importance of the logic of statics while arguing the essence of dynamics as the destruction of statics, he was looked upon as proposing a paradox. The paradox is formulated in this way: while the theory of economic statics applies only to a limited area of the economy (this is the reason why dynamics is required), it works universally throughout the economy (this is the reason why statics is not discarded); therefore, the core of the static theory should not be replaced by the dynamic theory. Straightforward recognition of both the limitations and universality of static is Schumpeter's paradox.

Schumpeter explains the universality of economic logic that is only formulated by statics: first, however abstract the equilibrium theory may be, it gives the essence of the economic logic; second, it describes the response mechanism of an economic system to changes in the data, whether exogenous or endogenous; third, the concept of equilibrium is indispensable as the standard of reference, whether for analytic or diagnostic purposes; and fourth, the primary relevance of the equilibrium concept depends on the tendency toward equilibrium in the real world.

According to Schumpeter, the essence of statics lies not in the stationary feature of the economy but in the nature of the social process involving the masses and of the economic process consisting of their adaptive behavior and the exogeneity of changes.

Creative Destruction

Schumpeter invented the paradoxical term "creative destruction" to indicate the functions of innovation. He emphasized the dynamic nature of capitalism and the central functioning of markets. The traditional economic theory conceptualizes market competition in the static sense that competition works to equalize demand and supply and achieve an equilibrium in light of given consumer preferences and industrial technology. Schumpeter's concept of creative destruction provided an antithetical view of competition. As a corollary of his conception of competition, the market power of commercial firms in the form of production restriction and price control in the process of innovation has acquired a new meaning.

As the term "creative destruction" is the oxymoron of creation and destruction, it appears to be a paradox. But what it means is to create the new and destroy the old, and the new and the old are not on the same dimension. Whereas creative destruction is literally a paradox, its meaning is clear if two different dimensions are identified. The view of the market process as the elimination of the old way of economic life, not as the achievement of a Paretian equilibrium, and the view of the dynamic efficiency of monopolistic firms are also corollaries of the conception of creative destruction and understandable in this wide perspective.

Decaying Capitalism Because of Success

In *Capitalism, Socialism and Democracy*, Schumpeter presented his famous thesis on the demise of capitalism in consequence of its success. This thesis appears to be paradoxical, but the trick of paradox is discovered by reference to the framework of Schumpeter's economic sociology, which discusses the relationship between economic and noneconomic areas. Observation of the economic area in isolation leads us to the dynamic picture of economic development and business cycles that works forever without disturbances from outside, but capitalism as a comprehensive civilization is confronted with changes in social, political, and cultural circumstances surrounding the economic area, that emerge as the result of economic success and affluence. The impact of outside forces on the economic area is sometimes negative to economic development.

Schumpeter's reasoning can be summarized as follows. First, as innovations are organized and automated, economic development becomes the task of experts in large organizations, and the function of entrepreneurs tends to become obsolete. Second, as rationalization proceeds, the precapitalist elements that supported the moral and disciplinary aspects of capitalism are destroyed. Third, the development of capitalism has created a political system of democracy that is interventionist in the interest of workers and an intellectual class that is hostile to capitalism. And fourth, the value scheme of capitalist society loses its hold, and there is an increased preference for equality, social security, government regulation, and leisure time.

This is not a deterministic argument that the demise of capitalism and the march to socialism are inevitable. Instead, Schumpeter merely pointed to trends that, if allowed to continue unabated, would result in a controlled economy. Schumpeter's method of analyzing the great problems of institutional transformation is more important than any conclusions derived from specific assumptions with regard to economic/noneconomic relationships.

In view of his three-layer structure of economic statics, dynamics, and economic sociology, what constitutes the paradox of failing capitalism is the gap between the isolated abstract economic world and the comprehensive society as a whole. This gap is the counterpart of another gap between economic statics and dynamics. Schumpeter's paradoxes urge us to establish coherent of statements in economic statics, economic dynamics, and economic sociology in the overall context of a comprehensive sociology.

Schumpeter's Rhetorical Gems

Although this text is concerned with the rhetoric of thought rather than the rhetoric of phrase, let me quote some of Schumpeter's literary gems:

"I wish to state right now that if, starting my work in economics afresh, I were told that I could study only one of the three [theory, statistics, and history] but could have my choice, it would be economic history that I should choose." (1954a, p. 12.)

"Unlike other economic systems, the capitalist system is geared to incessant economic change….Whereas a stationary feudal economy would still be a feudal economy, and a stationary socialist economy would still be an socialist economy, stationary capitalism is a contradiction in terms." (1951c, pp. 173–74)

"This process of Creative Destruction is the essential fact about capitalism. It is what capitalism consists in and what every capitalist concern has got to live in." (1950, p. 83.)

"What we are about to consider is that kind of change arising from within the system which so displaces its equilibrium point that the new one cannot be reached from the old one by infinitesimal steps. Add successively as many mail coaches as you please, you will never get a railway thereby." (1934, p. 64.)

"The entrepreneur is our man of action in the economic area. He is an economic leader, a real commander, not merely seeming to be commander like a static economic agent." (1912, p. 172.)

"The entrepreneur is the pioneer of a jejune way of thinking, of a utilitarian philosophy – the brain that was first able and had reason to reduce beefsteak and the ideal to a common denominator." (1926, p. 134.)

"There is no more of paradox in this than there is in saying that motorcars are traveling faster than they otherwise would because they are provided with brakes." (1950, p. 88.)

"The game [in capitalism] is not like roulette, it is more like poker." (1950, p. 73.)

"Capitalism and its civilization may be decaying, shading off into something else, or tottering toward a violent death. The writer personally thinks they are. But the world crisis does not prove it and has, in fact, nothing to do with it. It was not a symptom of a weakening or a failure of the system. If anything, it was a proof of the vigor of capitalist evolution to which it was – substantially – the temporary reaction." (1939, vol. 2, p. 908.)

"Capitalism creates a critical frame of mind which, after having destroyed the moral authority of so many other institutions, in the end turns against its own." (1950, p. 143.)

"The true pacemakers of socialism were not the intellectuals or agitators who preached it but the Vanderbilts, Carnegies and Rockefellers." (1950, p. 134.)

Conclusion

In this essay, I have emphasized that Schumpeter had a grand vision of a universal social science and that his writing is characterized by broad rhetorical knowledge as distinct from scientific knowledge. My intention is not to distinguish sharply between the two, but to see how they form a continuum in the spectrum because science itself is based on rhetoric. In his presidential address, "Science and Ideology" (1949), delivered at the annual meeting of the American Economic Association a year before his death, Schumpeter argued the important relationship between theory and vision. In my view, it is impossible to recognize the nature of Schumpeter's contributions to economics without paying attention to the rhetoric that was an instrument to express his imaginative vision.

In the eighteenth century, the social sciences maintained unity in the form of moral science. In contrast, in the twentieth century, logical positivism prevailed among most groups of scientists, and economics was dominated by Keynesianism, a useful doctrine for public policy, and by mathematical formalism, a sophisticated doctrine for a virtual world. With the fall of these two concepts, Schumpeter's idea of a universal social science at last seems to enjoy the opportunity to receive the examination and appraisal that it deserves. Although Schumpeter was out of step with the economic thought of his time, he may well have pioneered in creating the time to come.

Indeed, rhetorical thought might sometimes prove to be fallacious or mere political ideology. But, at the same time, rhetoric can serve as a hotbed that stimulates scientific research and eventually establishes scientific thought. Rhetoric might be common sense or prejudice, but it can be a novel idea that destroys conventional wisdom and stimulates new findings. Schumpeter's writing attests to the fact that rhetoric is the driving force of science.

In *The Picture of Dorian Gray*, Oscar Wilde wrote: "There is no such thing as a moral or an immoral book. Books are well written, or badly written. That is all" (Wilde 1985. p. 3). Analogically, it may be said that in the Schumpeterian perspective, "there is no such thing as a scientific or an unscientific book. Books are well written, or badly written. That is all." Writing well is nothing but good rhetoric. Schumpeter was the economist of good rhetoric.

References

Allen RL (1991) Opening doors: the life and work of Joseph Schumpeter, 2 vols. Transaction Publishers, New Brunswick

Böhm-Bawerk E. von (1896) Zum Abschluss des Marxschen Systems. In Staatswissenschaftliche Arbeiten, Festgabe fuer Karl Knies, edited by O. von Boenigk. Haering, Berlin

Bourdieu P (1984) Distinction: a social critique of the judgement of taste, translated by R. Nice. Harvard University Press, Cambridge

Harvard Crimson, Professor Schumpeter, Austrian minister, now teaching economic theory here. 11 April 1944

Kuhn T (1970) The structure of scientific revolutions, 2nd edn. University of Chicago Press, Chicago

März E (1991) Joseph Schumpeter: scholar, teacher and politician. Yale University Press, New Haven

McCraw TK (2007) Prophet of innovation: Joseph Schumpeter and creative destruction. Harvard University Press, Cambridge, MA

Samuelson PA (1947) The general theory (3). In: The new economics: Keynes' influence on theory and public policy, edited by S.E. Harris. Dennis Dobson, London

Schumpeter JA (1908) Das Wesen und der Hauptinhalt der theoretischen Nationalökonomie. Duncker & Humblot, Leipzig

Schumpeter JA (1912) Theorie der wirtschaftlichen Entwicklung, 2nd revised edn. 1926. Duncker & Humblot, Leipzig

Schumpeter JA (1914) Epochen der Dogmen- und Methodengeschichte. J.C.B. Mohr, Tübingen

Schumpeter JA (1915) Vergangenheit und Zukunft der Sozialwissenschaften. Duncker & Humblot, Leipzig

Schumpeter JA (1918) Die Krise des Steuerstaats. Leuschner & Lubensky, Graz und Leipzig

Schumpeter JA (1926) Gustav v. Schmoller und die Probleme von heute, Schmollers Jahrbuch. Reprinted in Schumpeter (1954b)

Schumpeter JA (1934) The theory of economic development: an inquiry into profits, capital, credit, interest, and the business cycle, translated by R. Opie. Harvard University Press, Cambridge

Schumpeter JA (1939) Business cycles: a theoretical, historical and statistical analysis of the capitalist process, 2 vols. McGraw-Hill, New York

Schumpeter JA (1942) Capitalism, socialism and democracy, Harper & Brothers, New York

Schumpeter JA (1949) Science and ideology. American Economic Review. Reprinted in Schumpeter (1951c)

Schumpeter JA (1950) Capitalism, socialism and democracy, 3rd edn. Harper & Brothers, New York

Schumpeter JA (1951a) Ten great economists, from Marx to Keynes. Oxford University Press, New York

Schumpeter JA (1951b) Imperialism and social classes, translated by H. Norden. Augustus M. Kelley, New York

Schumpeter JA (1951c) Preface to Japanese edition of Theorie der wirtschaftlichen Entwicklung 1937. In Essays of J.A. Schumpeter, edited by R.V. Clemence. Addison-Wesley Press, Cambridge

Schumpeter JA (1952) Aufsätze zur ökonomischen Theorie, edited by E. Schneider and A. Spiethoff. Tübingen, J.C.B. Mohr

Schumpeter JA (1953) Aufsätze zur Soziologie, edited by E. Schneider and A. Spiethoff. J.C.B. Mohr, Tübingen

Schumpeter JA (1954a) History of economic analysis. Oxford University Press, New York

Schumpeter JA (1954b) Dogmenhistorische und biographische Aufsätze, edited by E. Schneider and A. Spiethoff. J.C.B. Mohr, Tübingen

Schumpeter JA (1954c) Economic doctrine and method: an historical sketch, translated by R. Aris. George Allen & Unwin, London

Schumpeter JA (1970) Das Wesen des Geldes, edited by F.K. Mann, Vandenhoeck & Ruprecht, Göttingen

Schumpeter JA (1985) Aufsätze zur Wirtschaftspolitik, edited by W.F. Stolper and C. Seidl. J.C.B. Mohr, Tübingen

Schumpeter JA (1987) Beiträge zur Sozialökonomik, edited by S. Böhm. Böhlau, Vienna

Schumpeter JA (1991) The economics and sociology of capitalism, edited by R. Swedberg. Princeton University Press, Princeton

Schumpeter JA (1992) Politische Reden, edited by C. Seidl and W.F. Stolper. J.C.B. Mohr, Tübingen

Schumpeter JA (1993) Aufsätze zur Tagespolitik, edited by C. Seidl and W.F. Stolper. J.C.B. Mohr, Tübingen

Shionoya Y (1997) Schumpeter and the idea of social science: a metatheoretical study. Cambridge University Press, Cambridge

Shionoya Y (2004) Scope and method of Schumpeter's universal social science: economic sociology, instrumentalism, and rhetoric. Journal of the History of Economic Thought

Stolper W (1994) Joseph Alois Schumpeter: the public life of a private man. Princeton University Press, Princeton

Swedberg R (1991) Joseph A. Schumpeter: his life and work. Polity Press, Cambridge

Wilde O (1985) The picture of dorian gray (original 1891). Penguin Classics, London

Chapter 24
Against Rigid Rules – Keynes's View on Monetary Policy and Economic Theory

Elke Muchlinski*

Introduction

The focus of my paper is to explain why Keynes's economic theory is not compatible with rigid principles by sketching his view on "rules" in monetary policy and international monetary relations.[1] Any reference to formal aestheticism or rigidly defined rules seems to imply an inadequate interpretation of his work. Keynes's objections to formal aestheticism trace back to his view that economics is a moral science or soft science, respectively. Economic theory lacks fundamental presumptions which are indeed necessary to construct a hard science.

There is no controversy about this point: the terms *uncertainty, expectations and expectation-building, confidence* is the *core* of Keynes's economic analysis and also important to understand central banking and international monetary relations. I am, then, going to link Keynes's economic theory loosely to an academic discourse on the question if economic theory should become a hard science or a formal brilliantly designed theory.

Of course after more than seven decades since Keynes wrote his contributions, a link to the present debates should be as cautious as possible (see Moggridge 2002). Reading of any piece of Keynes's work is inevitably a subject of interpretation to the meaning of it (Rorty 1991).

*Elke Muchlinski, Economist, Visiting Professor, and Philosopher, has held teaching positions at the Free University of Berlin, the University of Halle (2010–2011), the University of Trier (2009) and the University of Hamburg (summer term 2008).

[1] I gave a first appraisal of the issue Keynes, rules and monetary policy: Muchlinski (2005, 2007b).

E. Muchlinski (✉)
Institute of Economic Policy and Economic History, Freie Universität Berlin,
Boltzmannstraße 20, 14195 Berlin, Germany
e-mail: elke.muchlinski@fu-berlin.de, http://www.fu-berlin.de/wiwiss/institute/
wirtschaftspolitik-geschichte/muchlinski

J.G. Backhaus (ed.), *Handbook of the History of Economic Thought*,
The European Heritage in Economics and the Social Sciences,
DOI 10.1007/978-1-4419-8336-7_24, © Springer Science+Business Media, LLC 2012

The paper starts in Part 1 with a short description of the "rules *versus* discretion" debate. Part 2 points to present debates. Part 3 refers to Keynes' work on monetary policy and international monetary relations, which does not reveal preferences for rigidly fixed rules of shaping international monetary system. Part 4 provides a brief discussion of the philosophical terms and meaning which are introduced in this paper. In Part 5, I explain why Keynes' concepts and economic theory go beyond views as outlined in Part 1. Finally, I will present my concluding thoughts in Part 6.

Notes on "Rules *versus* Discretion"

Historical lines of the debate on "rules *versus* discretion" document several re-constructions of the meaning of both the debate itself and the term "rule" and "discre-tion" (Issing 1996). The roots of the "rules versus discretion" debate trace back to an argument between advocates of the *Banking School* and *Currency School* (see Bordo and Eichengreen 2009). A modern interpretation of this controversy differentiates between those adherents favouring rigid rules on monetary policy and international monetary system, and those favouring discretionary monetary standards (Mishkin 2009; Orphanides and Wieland 2008; Issing 2011). *Rules* in international monetary relations are determined to mitigate exchange rate movements (gold standard, fixed exchange rates) and to avoid balance of payments imbalances (McKinnon 1993).

The trade-off between rules and discretion traces also back to Simon's work (1936). According to the quantity theory, Simons countered that the quantity of money cannot be constructed as a rigidly fixed quantity as adherents used to do. Simons argued that the quantity itself is fragile, because it is dependent on the velocity of money, which cannot be anticipated with certainty. Any coherent view, then must recognize that the market will respond not to the fixed nature of quantity but to the central bank policy, its perceived and understood decision-making and actions by the public (Muchlinski 2011a). There is no doubt that the interpretation and meaning of "rules versus discre-tion" has been changed throughout past decades. One standard interpretation differen-tiates between fixed, i.e., non-reactive rules, which define a path of instruments or targets without any reference to the observed situation and a non-fixed reactive rules, which implies the response reaction due to the observed situation. Whereas, the non-reactive rule focuses rigidly on the implementation of the rule itself, the reactive rule focuses on the announced target by using reactive methods of adaptability.

In New Classical Macroeconomic (NCM), for instance, the market is acquainted with modes of reactions; consequently reactive rules are defined as "feed-back rules". Rules in monetary policy are interpreted as a method to restrict discretionary decisions of central bankers and their supposed inclination to fool the public by an "inflation bias".[2] Blinder pointed out:

> In case of the modern incarnation of the rules versus discretion debate, based on time incon-sistency, I have argued that things are starkly different. In my view, the academic literature

---

[2] There is no space and time to discuss this point here (Blinder 1998; Muchlinski 2011a, b, 2005).

has focused on either the wrong problem or a non problem and has proposed a variety of solutions (excluding Rogoff's conservative central bankers) that make little sense in the real world (Blinder 1998, 50).

In modern theory of central banking, discretionary decisions are interpreted as decision based on perceived situations "unconstrained by rules of either kind" (Tobin 1983, 507). A common sense statement today is that central banking is not compatible with fixed rules (Blinder 1999, 2005). The central bank influences expectation-building by forward-looking decision making (Bernanke 2004). Changes in the overnight interest rate affect the decision making and actions of the agents. Therefore, the central bank needs to explain its own view on the current and future performance of the macroeconomic reality. Woodford (2005) pictured the central bank as a "manager of expectations", endowed with the power to set shape future conditions of interest rates in money markets. He, among other authors (Blinder et al. 2008; Issing 2005a), opposed to the mechanical analogy because "central banking is not like steering an oil tanker or even guiding a spacecraft" (2005a, 4). At this point, the constitutive role of language activities in central bank theory and practice can hardly be ignored. The guiding of expectations in the market cannot be separated from the use of language and communication (Muchlinski 2011a, c).

According to the Great Inflation in the United States, steering market expectations through setting the Federal Reserve funds rate was associated with a Keynesian strategy, whereas focusing on a rigidly fixed monetary supply or monetary growth rates, respectively, was seen as a Monetarist strategy (Lindsey et al. 2005). However, the Federal Reserve had neither intended to act upon nor could have acted upon the basis of a monetarist "k-percent-rule" (Muchlinski 2011a).

The monetary transmission channel is driven by changing expectations of the market participants. A central bank must be able to act flexibly but this does not imply acting without committing itself. Self-commitment is linked to transparency, independence, and accountability. Transparency implies understanding of what a central bank is, in fact, doing (Issing 1999). The central bank must be concentrated on this expectation-building process in order to influence its long lasting horizon and to "anchor inflation expectations at a level consistent with the mandate of maintaining price stability" (Issing 2009, 7).

Bernanke (2004) attributes great attention to the question of whether a fixed rule implies a higher effectiveness of monetary policy:

> The problem is that a number of contingencies to which policy might respond is effectively infinite (and, indeed, many are unforeseeable). While specifying a complete policy rule is infeasible, however, there is much that a central bank can do – both by its actions and its words – to improve the ability of financial markets to predict monetary policy actions. With respect to actions, the central bank should behave in as systematic and as understandable a way as possible, given the macroeconomic and financial environment. That is, although monetary policy cannot be made by a mechanical rule, policy can and should have "rule like" features. Obviously, the more systematic and the more consistent with a few basic principles the conduct of monetary policy becomes, the easier it will be for the public to understand and predict the Fed's behavior. (…). Words are also necessary.

The theoretical debates based on rigid premises which are not linked to the contemporary world have never reached the realm of central bank practice which focuses on the effectiveness of monetary policy in practice. All *numbers by painting* or *painting by numbers* (Vickers 1998) have to refer to contemporary word, i.e., the perceived world. Why, then, do we talk about fixed rules or a dichotomy "rules versus discretion"? Economic theory and modelling often try to make complex economic considerations compatible with a formal language approach or as simple as possible. "Simplicity gives them their political appeal and power" (Tobin 1983, 508).

On State-Contingent Rules *and* Discretion

I would like to turn briefly to research on the Keynes-White-Plan. Boughton stated, "Keynes articulated a (…) proposal for state-contingent policy rules published *in Lloyd's Bank Monthly Review*" (2002, 6).[3] What is a state-contingent rule? King explained: "The optimal strategy is a state-contingent rule, which allows flexibility in the response of policy to shocks while retaining a credible commitment to price stability" (1997, 94). Therefore, "state-contingent rule" is to be seen as a flexible response by the central bank to shocks without jeopardizing their goal of price stability.

I would like to give some additional information on this "state-contingent rule". In some models of monetary policy the "rational expectations hypothesis" is required for the sake of model consistency and as a constitutive element of monetary policy itself. In this model view, central bankers are configured as representative agents. The "state-contingent-rule", then, is based on the "rational expectations hypothesis", acted out by *representative agent* (Kirman 1992). The promise of the premise was to eliminate any reasons for a Lucas critique (Muchlinski 1999a). Blinder commented:

> The important thing is to make sure our models are congruent with the facts. Lucasians, it seems to me, reverse the sequence. They want to begin with fully articulated, tractable models and worry later about realism and descriptive accuracy. (…) The issue is how religiously we must adhere to frictionless neo-classical optimising principles until that glorious day arrives (1987, 135).

Within a monetarist framework for instance, the "k-percent-rule" represents the presumption of a rule-based decision-making process. A rule, then, is defined for the sake of simplicity and formal precision. For reasons outlined in this section, a compatibility of the "state-contingent rule" with Keynes' thinking on monetary policy or international monetary relations cannot be justified. Therefore, the dichotomy "rules *versus* discretion" depends on a paradigm in order to justify a construction like this.

Keynes' Economic Theory: A Brief Reconsideration

This part deals with examples of Keynes' contributions on monetary policy and international monetary relations. Why is Keynes' view of relevance? There is no "Keynes-rule" to be discovered like the "Taylor-rule". One reason is that Keynes

---

[3] October 1935, reprinted in C.W., XXI, 360–369.

recognized monetary policy and international monetary relations as a subject committed to a discretionary manner.

Monetary Policy and International Monetary Policy

The need to face each policy decision anew and to respond without formal constraints can be seen as constitutive to central banking. Focussing on rigidly fixed rules is an artificial way. Keynes criticized the artificial world in his article on the theory of interest rates:

> All these pretty, polite techniques, made for a well-panelled Board Room and a nicely regulated market, are liable to collapse (...). I accuse the classical economic theory of being itself one of these pretty, polite techniques which tries to deal with the present by abstracting from the fact that we know very little about the future (Keynes 1973–1989, C.W., XIII, 215).

The other way is on aiming to better understand the implication and goals of rules (Blinder et al. 2008). To the extent that monetary policy acts on the basis of defined rules, these rules cannot be interpreted as rigidly defined rules. These rules are to be interpreted as serving a method in steering public expectation-building and debates. Rules, then, serve as a coordinative mode within the process of decision making and communicative interaction.

Only in a mechanical analogy, the expectations of market participants are modelled as being driven by fixed rules. The effectiveness of monetary policy is not a consequence of a deductive reasoning based on the stimulus–reaction of a model world, based on rigidly defined premises.

The problem of acting strongly to markets is especially due to the non-synchronization of time. Whereas, the central banks action is realized in a particular time, the responses by market participants are realized with different time-lags. This non-synchronization of time fundamentally concerns the term structure of interest rates in different markets. The formation of the term structure of interest rates is due to "past experience and present expectations of *future* monetary policy, (which) is considered unsafe by representative opinion" (Keynes (1973–1989), C.W., Vol. VII, 203).[4] Keynes's emphasis on the lack of confidence and uncertainty is not compatible with the model of rational expectations hypothesis which maintains the certainty of future outcomes. His concepts express the precariousness and fragility of knowledge.[5]

Therefore, rigid or robotic rules, independent of the contemporaneous economic perceived situation are not adequate for monetary policy. Keynes pointed out to discretion rather than rigid rules or rigidly fixed parities:

> We can, and should, commit ourselves – (i) to maintain short-term stability within a certain range; (ii) not to resort to devaluation merely to obtain competitive advantages in foreign trade (...) But we must retain an ultimate discretion to do whatever is required to relieve

---

[4] Blinder discussed the determination of different time structure of interest rates (1998); similarly Keynes described monetary policy (Keynes (1973–1989), C.W., Vol. VII, 203).

[5] See for instance, Chapter 12 of the *General Theory of Employment, Interest and Money* (GT), (1936), C.W., VII.

either a sudden and severe or a gradual and continuing strain, without laying ourselves open to any kind of reproach.

With good faith and genuine collaboration between central banks rigidly fixed parities are not necessary for international trade; without such conditions they are not only danger-ous, but entirely unreliable. We shall get better collaboration if we do not put too a great strain upon it and allow to the collaborators an ultimate individual discretion (Keynes 1935, *The Future of Foreign Exchange*, C.W., XXI, 368).

Given this statement, one has to ask why, Keynes, then, refers to gold standard (see textual evidence in Keynes (1973–1989), XXI, 368) as the foundation of international monetary relations?[6]

I have assumed throughout that gold will remain the basis of international exchange, in the sense, that central banks will continue to hold their reserves in gold and to settle balances with other central banks by the shipment of gold. The only alternatives would be sterling or some kind of B.I.S. bank money; but neither of these is practicable today as the basis of a world system (ibid).[7]

The reference to gold is interpreted as an international standard which entails both cred-ibility and lack of feasibility. The lack of feasibility implies the impossibility of an empir-ical proof. It functions as an epistemological possibility. The reader may think on the concept of the "output gap" as a crucial part of the "Taylor rule" (see ECB 2001, 50).

In the paper, The *International Note Issue and the Gold Standard*, Keynes argued against external restrictions and in favour for discretion. At the same time, he voted for defining each currency in relation to gold as "qualified return to the gold stan-dard" (C.W., IX, 362). Is this a contradiction? Does this imply a rigidly fixed con-struction of international monetary system? Certainly not! Keynes wrote:

It may seem odd that I, who have lately described gold as 'a barbarous relic', should be discovered as an advocate of such a policy, at a time when the orthodox authorities of this country are laying down conditions for our return to gold which they must know to be impossible of fulfilment. It may be that, never having loved gold, I am not so subject to disillusion. But, mainly, it is because I believe that gold has received such a gruelling that conditions might now be laid down for its future management, which would not have been acceptable otherwise Keynes (1973–1989), C.W., IX, 62).

The return to gold standard was a pragmatic solution, not the acceptance of the "rules of the game" (C.W., XXI, 361). Keynes proposed a *de facto parity* as an alter-able parity according to economic circumstances, because it would "be desirable to maintain permanently some power of gradual adjustment between national and international conditions" (C.W., IX, 362). We find more textual evidence in the *Collected Writings* for this hesitance to define each currency in relation to gold as rigid rules based on index numbers. He also avoided any precise definition of a reasonable equilibrium of exchange rates (ibid). As a convention he proposed to coordinate the exchange rate movements.

A set of rates of exchange, which can be established without undue strain on either side and without large movements of gold (on a balance of transactions), will satisfy our condition

---

[6] We find more textual evidence given in: *The Means to Prosperity* (1933, 360), reprinted in Keynes (1973–1989) C.W., IX, 335–366.

[7] He distanced himself from the proposed sterling as international money later on.

> of equilibrium. (…) It will be sufficient if a set can be found which the various central banks can accept without serious anxiety for the time being, provided that there is no substantial change in the underlying conditions (C.W., XXI, 361–362).

In "A Tract on Monetary Reform" (1924) Keynes had explained that neither rigid rules nor faith in a stability of any metallic standard are reasonable methods to succeed. Interpreting his view I would like to add, pure theory is no way to get clarity if its premise are not linked to contemporary world. Pure theory which is constructed for the sake of simplicity or formal aestheticism is a blind concept. "The non-metallic standards, of which we have experience, have been anything rather than scientific experiments coolly carried out" (Keynes (1973–1989), C.W., Vol. IV, 170). This argument is of great importance. The alleged non-active rule of metallic standard "was becoming precarious by reason of its artificiality" – a long time before the war (1924, 171).

The "rules of the game" were a construction, as Keynes had already analyzed in his book *Indian Currency and Finance* (1913). The "rules of the games" were not applied to practice since it was perceived and interpreted as a promise (see Eichengreen 1995; Muchlinski 1999b).

Keynes countered that the problems of the post-war period – which of course were both a problem of adequate terms and concepts to identify and describe real economic problems – cannot be solved with a reliance on formal aestheticism.

> To suppose that there exists some smoothly functioning automatic mechanism of adjustment which preserves equilibrium if only we trust to methods of *laissez-faire* is a doctrinaire delusion which disregards the lessons of historical experience without having behind it the support of sound theory. (…). International currency *laissez-faire* was breaking down rapidly before the war. During the war it has disappeared completely (C.W., XXV, 21–22).

He was persistently reluctant to fill the gap of cognitive solutions with illusion. The track back to the sound theory of formal brilliantly designed premises was impossible and not even desirable. He, then, stepped into the realm of terminological and economic uncertainty for the sake of clarity.

Keynes also made his objections to the orthodox theory, which states that the Bank rate and credit contraction could be instrumented in order to readjust international imbalance by reducing the level of employment and the money wages and therefore to serve for an external equilibrium. He explained: "As a result of this better understanding of its *modus operandi*, I do not believe that it will ever be used again for this purpose" (C.W. XXI, 368).

Keynes focused on the interest rate as a means to reach internal goals. He did not speak in favour of rigidly fixed exchange rates since any central bank should manage the rate of interest instead of sacrificing this instrument to external balance. Furthermore, exchange rate movements should be stabilized in the short run within a certain target, whereas every country is compelled to avoid strategies like competitive devaluations (C.W., XXI, 368). There is no "invisible hand" which co-ordinates the countries' decisions with the result of an international equilibrium. This is also true for central bank policy in the light of modern theory:

> In the modern world of paper currency and bank credit there is no escape from a 'managed' currency, whether we wish it or not; convertibility into gold will not alter the fact that the value of gold itself depends on the policy of the Central Banks. (…) It would have been

absurd to regulate the bank rate by reference to a 'proportion' which had lost all it significance. (…) The bank rate is now employed, however incompletely and experimentally, to
regulate the expansion and deflation of credit in the interests of business stability and the
steadiness of prices (Keynes 1924, 172).

Keynes view on central banking is compatible with the modern view. One could be
inclined to argue his plans were not only beyond rigid rules, but also beyond the
trade off of rules *versus* discretion, because he did not explain his theory within
such a dichotomy or dual terms.

Shaping International Monetary Relations

I would like to turn closer to Keynes's view on *shaping the international monetary*
relations which was fundamentally based on a multilateral system.[8] Keynes had
changed his view on international mechanism of methods of adjustments several
times, but one dominant proposition can be manifested: He did not express a faith
in flexible exchange rates as a method of market clearing process. According to the
international monetary relations he proposed rules of adjustments always giving
attention to the contemporary situation of the country. This does not include a strategy of competitive devaluation of any individual country's preference.[9]

Moggridge sketched in his pioneering work, that Keynes had rejected rigid rules
of the White Plan because "such a surrender of sovereignty and such rigidity were
unacceptable to the British, who had pushed Keynes's own scheme in the direction
of greater discretion, and in the attempts at synthesis, which took the Stabilization
Fund as the basis for drafting, the matter of national initiative in initial exchange
rate setting was central" (Moggridge 1986, 68). I think his argument sheds light on
what is important, whereas Boughton argued from a different point of view.
Boughton (2002) wrote that Keynes lost all battles against White because he wanted
to defend the Empire, resisting multilateralism.

In my interpretation, a proposal which would have roughly injured the British
interests or any other country's interest could not have been the foundation for adapting
any international agreement. The different drafts "The Origin of the Clearing Union"
provides textual evidence on how Keynes tried to develop his plan of multilateralism.
Keynes also précised the term multilateralism: "That is fully international, being, based
on one general agreement and not on a multiplicity of bilateral arrangements" (Keynes
in Horsefield 1969, 21). To be brief on the framework of an International Clearing Union
(I.C.U.), which involves both the creditors and debtor countries: "A country is in credit

---

[8] Textual evidence is given in his drafts for an "International Clearing Union" (I.C.U.) reprinted in
Horsefield (1969), also in C.W. XXV, 21–33. For details, see Dostaler (1994, 2005), Moggridge
(1986, 1992) and Moggridge and Howson (1974).
[9] See his opinion to past strategies of the United Kingdom in *Means to Prosperity*, 1933
(Keynes (1973–1989), C.W., IX, 352).

or debit with the Currency Union as a whole. This means that the overdraft facilities, whilst a relief to some, are not a real burden to others" (C.W., XXV, 74–75). He gave examples why bilateral arrangements are to be judged with scepticism. One main objection to bilateral arrangements was that these are dependent on partial political reasons and could cause or worsen divergences between countries.[10] Neither the creditor nor the debtor country should be able to remain passive according to their balance of payments. This exactly is the *core* of his *multilateralism*. Keynes's proposal for discretionary methods of adjustments is documented in his drafts on the I.C.U. with clarity.[11]

Let me conclude: The I.C.U. was conceptualized as a method for dealing with international problems rather than avoiding them. Therefore Keynes linked his ideas, concepts and categories to the empirical world (see C.W., XXV, 77). This is the reason why Keynes defined the Bancor to gold, because he did not want to see the finance of the world economy depend on the US economy and US currency.

The adjustment mechanism Keynes had explained was beyond the *laissez-faire method*. Moreover, it was beyond the dichotomy of "rules *versus* discretion" because he attracted attention to the contemporary situation as a whole in which each country will possesses a temporary position. A change of an individual's position will also change the outcome of the whole, but not in an additive manner, because the whole is not simply the sum of its parts.[12] If one takes the whole as a changeable whole, rather than as a fixed entity, the investigation of its parts requires distinct methods and means of analysis. A whole is to be interpreted as based on organic interrelations and not as an linear addition of its components.

In brief, we have looked at some textual evidence of Keynes' work. The next point I would like to make is to introduce some methodological aspects.

Some Philosophical Considerations

For Keynes the need of shaping international monetary relations was linked to the need of developing new terms and concepts. It is not possible to explain economic problems in terms which exclude problems at all. The need of a new thinking required new categories and terms which step beyond the faith in illusionary concepts or rigidly designed propositions, proposed certainty and complete knowledge. Keynes used the term proposition in the meaning of judgment and persuasion (see Muchlinski 2003a). Therefore, a proposition is linked to contemporary world, to experience and expectations.

---

[10] See his drafts on I.C.U. (1941–1943) and the role of the Bancor mechanism reprinted in Horsefield (1969, Vol. III, 27). Keynes emphasized international responsibility; see also Keynes (C.W., XXV, 77–76).

[11] "Proposal for an International Clearing Union" (April 1943) collected by Horsefield (1969, Vols. I–III), reprinted in C.W., XXV; The synthesis of C.U. and S.F. and Keynes's objections are reprinted in C.W., XXV, 308–314.

[12] We find textual evidence in *Ethics in Relation to Conduct* (1904), see Muchlinski (1996).

It was Keynes's demand to leave elements which were constructed for the sake of formal elegance and determined by the orthodox theory in the past and to introduce a modern view of economic thinking. Orthodox theory is loosely equated with classical theory and neo-classical theory and their implicit premises and strictly defined assumptions. The core of it are the equilibrium theory, the assumption of rational optimal behaviour and the formal model approach to expectation-building, hence the axiomatic deduction as the predominant method.

Keynes, in contrast, demanded to make explicit what is implicit in the use of premises and claims. The predominance of deductive reasoning is a further inadequacy for economics as a social science. Keynes emphasized the relevance of inductive reasoning in economics. He stated: "It seems to me that economics is a branch of logic, a way of thinking. (…) Progress in economics consists almost entirely in a progressive improvement in the choice of models. (…) Economics is a science of thinking in terms of models joined to the art of choosing models which are relevant to the contemporary world" (C.W., XIV, 295–296, Letter to R.F. Harrod, 4 July 1938). Whereas, model building is the appropriate theoretical approach, deduction as the only way of reasoning should be judged with caution and supplemented by individual judgment and conventional judgment (Muchlinski 1999a, 2003a). This is the reason why some of his early manuscripts and *A Treatise on Probability* are of importance to understand the *turn of categories* he implemented (Muchlinski 2002, 2003b, 2007a).

I briefly describe some basis principle of ontological realism, traditional view on empiricism and constructivism in order to clarify the reasons why Keynes's economic thinking cannot be assign to views which are relevant for orthodoxy.

Corresponding to the historical lines of the philosophy of science, one can sketch some historical epochs (Chalmers 2006). The need to apply realist principles to economic theory has been proposed by some economists (Baert 1996). Contrary to idealism, realism includes an acceptance of an outside or ontological given world. It is hard to deny that certain objects, like stones, trees, houses do exist. But this does not imply, that economic circumstances or "facts" are part of the ontological given world.

To be brief: Ontology assumes that objects exist independently of one's perception or recognition. An ontological view maintains that A's exist independently of how one thinks or feels about them. More generally: A property or principle is ontological if it is a part of the very substance (itself). Therefore, the property or principle is inherent to the object. Kant as well as New-Kantian was opposed to ontology.

The question is, if ontological realism has any relevance for economic science. I would rise some scepticism because economic structures and objects are not already given. Economic facts are created or constructed facts. They are based on definitions and concepts in order to describe economic decisions and actions on markets. As Keynes explained economic decisions and actions are based on expectation-building in the light of uncertainty and conventional judgment or "average opinion" because "to a man in a state of ignorance" there is no "escape clause" (Muchlinski 2011b). Moreover, economic facts are not independently of one's perception or recognition. According to Keynes's work, I propose to interpret that his view is not based on ontological realism.

I turn now to the traditional view on empiricism. This branch of empiricism focused on the correspondence between truth and reality. Two basic hypotheses are to be mentioned: One maintains that there is no role for a priori principles. The second hypothesis states that any proposition about facts or events basically roots in experience. This proposition is either a description of experience or possesses a logical relation to this empirical description based on an inductive conclusion. Hume's view that experience is the accumulation of subjective experience caused the problem of justifying objective knowledge.[13]

This was the starting point for Kant's philosophy, a transcendental perspective. Kant asked in *Critique of Pure Reason* (CPR), *what is being*? He answered by linking the question to thinking and thought. Science, as he outlined with the *Copernican turn* "only express a relationship with the faculties of knowledge" (Kant Critique of Pure Reason (1781/1965), Part B 266). Knowledge is a result of an interaction of intuition and concept. In all of this, uncertainty still remains since intuition is just a prerequisite of knowledge, not a final point in justifying knowledge. Thinking is also linked with transcendental logic which implies that a real potency is reduced to *epistemological possibility*. There is no epistemological certainty in Kant's epistemology. His conception of being emphasizes the intelligibility of things, their relation to our perception and understanding, in which logic has an important place. An important conclusion of the Kantian philosophy is a different understanding of experience. Scientific methods do incorporate a non-observable systematic order independently of its supposed empiricist real order. That is to say, that any observation is to be seen as impregnated by theories. Consequently, the dualism of observation and theory broke down. The transcendental philosophy, say Kant's philosophy, works out the superior function of logic as embedded in language and *a priori principle*. Nevertheless, all theories must lead back to experience otherwise they would be called "empty" or "blind" concepts. Kant's critique of knowledge has taken the place of ontology and metaphysics. Let us turn briefly back to Kant's philosophy:

> We are in possession of certain modes of a priori knowledge. (…) In what follow therefore, we shall understand by a priori knowledge, not knowledge independent of all experience. (…) Thus we would say of a man who undermined the foundations of his house, that he might have known a priori that it would fall, that is, that he need not have waited for the experience of its actual falling (Kant Critique of Pure Reason (1781/1965), Part B 3).

Kant emphasized: "though all our knowledge begins with experience, it does not follow that it all arises out of experience" (Kant Critique of Pure Reason (1781/1965), Part B 1). Analogous to Kant, Keynes pointed out the limits of experience as a guide to decision. His criticism is addressed to the British empirical school:

> If our experience and our knowledge were complete, we should be beyond the need of the calculus of probability. And where our experience is incomplete, we cannot hope to derive from it judgements of probability without the aid either of intuition or of some further a

---

[13] For a discussion on Hume's view: Keynes (1921); for a discussion of how Keynes was concerned with Kant, Fitzgibbons (1998), Muchlinski (1998).

priori principle. Experience, as opposed to intuition, cannot possibly afford us a criterion by which to judge whether on given evidence the probabilities of two propositions are or are not equal (Keynes (1973–1989), C.W., Vol. VIII, 94).[14]

This transcendental approach of Kant emphasizes experience without neglecting its limitations (Parsons 1992). The quintessence of it all is that any object is given by perception. It excludes the possibility of identifying the perceived object with this object itself. For Kant, language is not only a medium of communication, but also a constituent element of knowledge. Whereas, the Kantian Philosophy is a transformation of metaphysics, the Analytical Philosophy – the later Ludwig Wittgenstein (his work since 1929) and Gilbert Ryle (1966) among others – in turn has taken the place of ontology. Wittgenstein and Ryle picked up on these ideas more precisely (Muchlinski 2011c).

Is there any link to Keynes work? His economic theory does not build upon traditional empiricism as introduced earlier. Keynes' theory of knowledge implies uncertainty and the unsurmountable fragility of knowledge. He objected to empiricism in *The Treatise on Probability*. He explained probability from an epistemological point of view. A probabilistic proposition contains the perceived fact by an individual and the *a priori principle*.

The next point, I would like to make deals with constructivism. Without going into greater details on the origins and developments of constructivism, constructivists maintain that scientific knowledge is a result of scientific work in progress or thinking. Consequently, facts are not revealed to scientists, but are constructed by them. Scientific knowledge therefore is constituted. Of course there are different interpretations among and about constructivists. Whatever the difference may be, one particular feature of constructivism can be identified: Science does not discover a determinate structure of reality. According to this interpretation, two possible conclusions can be made: One leads to the idea that any scientific process has to deal with social constructions for the sake of an understanding. The second interpretation is basically more pessimistic because it states that neither social facts nor the society can better be understood than the natural world. In its strong version, constructivism denies that any object refers to contemporary world since it follows the view of mind constructed reality. As a mind construction reality is nothing more than a notion or in the meaning of Kant, an empty concept.

Contrary to the version outlined in the previous paragraph a modified approach to constructivism shall briefly be introduced: It refers to truth as a matter of considerable importance.[15] However, truth, facts and events are bound by social constructions. Finally, truth is socially constructed. According to this view, economics is due to the interpretation, definitions, perceptions, and their acceptance by the *community*

---

[14] There is no systematic connection between "truth" and probability of a proposition as Keynes argued: "It has been pointed out already that no knowledge of probabilities, less in degree than certainty, helps us to know what conclusions are true, and that there is no direct relation between the truth of a proposition and its probability" (Keynes (1973–1989), C.W., Vol. VIII, 356); see Carabelli (1988), Davis (1994).

[15] Samuels provided a critical assessment of it (Samuels 1996).

of science. What follows from this? The consequences are first at all the refutation of the positivist view of science and its presumed idea of a homogeneous truth. Therefore, assumptions and concepts in economic theories i.e., liquidity preference or axiom of scarcity, the category of doubt and uncertainty, should be discussed within the social circumstances in which they have been established and not as ontologically given reality.

In brief, we have considered features of some lines of philosophy. Philosophical theory should be distinguished from scientific theory and its methods, for instance the economic theory. Scientific methods imply a non-observable systematic order which is not linked to a supposed real order, because of the importance of a priori principle.

I am now turning to Keynes's economic theory in order to explain why his view is compatible with the transcendental philosophy. Consequently, experience can explain to us what happened, but it cannot reveal to us what *will* happen.

A Closer Look at Keynes's Economic Theory from a Philosophical Point of View

Keynes's thinking provided the basis for his criticism of orthodoxy and model building in economics. He transformed orthodox categories such as rigour and complete knowledge into uncertainty and ignorance, expectations, state of confidence, degree of belief, etc. He characterized knowledge in *The General Theory* as "vague and scanty" (Keynes (1973–1989), C.W., Vol. VII, 148).

For Keynes, it is important to relate concepts or categories to the perceived world. This approach excludes that he was dedicated to realism in the meaning of ontological realism. Evidence for my hypothesis is provided by Keynes's work on the international monetary system. International monetary coordination should avoid a *fallacy of composition*. It relied on the very idea of individuals – or countries – must take responsibility for their own benefits regarding the consequences as a whole. Keynes explained the *fallacy of composition* that an individual's rationality does not necessarily imply a rationality of the whole – i.e., the entire economy or the global market – because the latter is not simply an addition of its parts.[16]

Against Rigidly Fixed Rules as Dry Bones

Where are the roots of his view that rigidly fixed rules independent of the contemporaneous economic that are not adequate for monetary policy and international monetary relations? The roots are to be found in his objection to the explicit and implicit premises of the classical theory (GT, xxi, 33, 192, 371; C.W. XIII, 488).[17]

---

[16] *Ethics in Relation to Conduct* (1904), *Egoism* (1906), Muchlinski (1996).
[17] See also Carabelli (1991).

His instrument of thought was logic, but not bivalent logic.[18] He did not criticize the empirical unacceptability of its conclusions or a logical inconsistency between premises and conclusion, but rather the implication of orthodox premises. As Keynes stated: "Granted this, all the rest follows" (GT, 1936, 21). The superstructure of classical theory was constructed in a careful way in order to achieve "logical consistency" (Keynes (1973–1989), C.W., Vol. VII, xxi). Keynes defined classical logic (i.e., Aristotelan logic) as *dry bones*. Therefore, he characterized the premises of neo-classical economic theory as *dry bones*.[19]

He objected to rigidly fixed rules which are designed for the sake of formal aestheticism or rigidity and which are to be interpreted as *dry bones*.[20] Keynes rejected (neo) classical assumptions because of its alleged universality in space and time. In his view an important criteria in determining a model's validity is its link to the *contemporary world*, that is, the *perceived world* (Keynes, C.W., XIV, 296). Therefore, the (neo) Classical theory is to be rejected because of its missing link to the contemporary world and its bivalent logic. In this meaning, he rejected constructivism.

The Situational Context or the Corpus of Knowledge

The philosophical roots of Keynes's view lead back to his theory of probability, which is of course a theory of knowledge (Keynes (1973–1989), C.W., Vol. VIII, 19). In *A Treatise on Probability*, (1921) he sketched the metaphor *corpus of knowledge* to explain why acquiring knowledge does not lead to certainty since the fragility of knowledge still remains (Keynes (1973–1989), C.W., Vol. VIII, 4). He transformed traditional notions by transforming traditional understanding of logic. He made the turning point in his position even more transparent:

> As soon as we have passed from the logic of implication and the categories of truth and falsehood to the logic of probability and the categories of knowledge, ignorance, and rational belief, we are paying attention to a new logical relation in which, although it is logical, we were not previously interested, and which cannot be explained or defined in terms of our previous notion (Keynes (1973–1989), C.W., Vol. VIII, 8).

Keynes emphasized inductive elements of reasoning. Induction is an element of outlining what probability means. The theory of probability refers to the implication

---

[18] Classical logic refers to Aristotelan logic or bivalent logic: "a *or* non-a". Keynes judged on basis of "fuzzy logic", which implies the abandonment of dualist concepts. One important principle of fuzzy logic is "multivalence", which implies the understanding of "a *and* non-a" (Kosko 1993).

[19] In Chapter 2 of the GT, Keynes outlined the implicit assumptions underlying the classical theory of employment, which all led back to a single central one: the assumption of independence from the level of output and employment (Keynes (1973–1989), C.W., Vol. VII, 21–22; GT, xxxii–xxxiii, 18; C.W. XIII, 278).

[20] *Should Economics Be Hard Science?* – Duménil and Lévy introduce four arguments against formal aestheticism in economic theory. They outline that the formalist approach to economic theory is only *one* possible method or language; "but this role is non-exclusive. The notion of a multiplicity of language in economics refers to a plurality of approaches" (Duménil and Lévy 1997, 276).

of induction. In contrast to deduction, induction bears no possibility to use the logical conception of Aristotle called *bivalent logic*.

> But it has been seldom apprehended clearly, either by these writers or by others, that the validity of every induction, strictly interpreted, depends, not on a matter of fact, but on the existence of a relation of probability. An inductive argument affirms, not that a certain matter of fact *is* so, but that *relative to certain evidence* there is a probability in its favour (Keynes (1973–1989), C.W., Vol. VIII, 345).

As we have seen, logic is part of Keynes's *theory of knowledge*, and lies beyond the classical conception of logic. We are able to link this consideration with the Wittgenstein's later work, Wittgenstein (Muchlinski 2011b). The citation given previously is important from the viewpoint of the *history of economic thought*. This transformation of concepts and categories documented the distance from the British Empirical School, as well as ontological realism and constructivism.

Keynes described probability as a logical relationship between two propositions: premise and conclusion (Keynes (1973–1989), C.W., Vol. VIII, 11). Not only two propositions, but the acquaintance which allows one to speak of probability (Keynes (1973–1989), C.W., Vol. VIII, 19). To say something upon a probability-relation implies receiving a representation of it, rather than the thing as it is supposed to be ontologically. He referred to *ignorance* (Keynes (1973–1989), C.W., Vol. VIII, 356). Therefore, the significance of probability depends on individual judgement under uncertainty in order to perceive the relation between propositions with a "rational degree of belief":

> The theory of probability is logical, therefore, because it is concerned with the degree of belief which it is *rational* to entertain in given conditions, and not merely with the actual beliefs of particular individuals, which may or may not be rational (Keynes (1973–1989), C.W., Vol. VIII, 4).[21]

He conceptualized the theory of probability as a theory of knowledge. This provided a certain framework which is paradigmatically found in his economic theory, for instance, state of confidence, liquidity-premium, expectation and conventional judgement.[22] Keynes' position can be described as a *realistic approach* insofar as one accepts a world outside of the individual. In his later work, Wittgenstein comes to the consideration that it is in language that expectation and fulfilment make contact (Muchlinski 2006). The realist approach should not be confused with the so called "critical" realism.[23] In Keynes's view, one finds also rationalist elements (O'Donnell 1989). He was opposed to idealism, i.e., he rejected empty concepts, and traditional empiricism, i.e., he emphasized the limits of experience and of the British Empirical School (Muchlinski 2002).

---

[21] Keynes explained the term *rational degree of belief* in Chapter 2 of the *Treatise on Probability* by reference to propositions and knowledge. "The highest degree of rational belief, which is termed *certain* rational belief, corresponds to *knowledge*" (Keynes (1973–1989), C.W., Vol. VIII, 10).

[22] See Bateman (1991) on induction in Keynes' thinking.

[23] Further investigation on "critical realism" is given by Baert (1996), Parsons (1992).

Transformation of Categories: Or the Roots of Uncertainty and Ignorance

The transformation of categories as outlined in the previous paragraph provides the methodological foundation that there is no sound theory of formal brilliantly designed and rigid premises to be found in his work. Keynes, then, stepped into the realm of terminological and economic uncertainty for the sake of clarity. Uncertainty is inevitably inherent concerning decisions, actions and choices. This is why all plans or drafts are to be interpreted as a chance to succeed or to fail.

In contrast, the criteria in classical theory are universality and rigour as the basis for certain knowledge, deduction and formal aestheticism. (Neo) Classical theory seeks to reduce uncertainty to the same epistemological status as certainty by using mathematical calculus (C.W., XIV, 1937, 213).[24] According to Keynes's argument, economy as a system contains aspects of irreversibility created by interactions among different people who are involved in pursuing their economic goals. He relied on conceptions of degree of credibility, degree of confidence, degree of rational belief, etc. In summary, Keynes economic theory goes beyond constructivism, ontological realism and empiricism since he defined economic theory as a social science based.

Concluding Thoughts

Keynes tried to balance his ideas for the new international monetary system with the contemporary and perceived situation. The debates on international monetary arrangement, to which Keynes' lent his influential voice, documented that his theoretical view is beyond constructivism, ontological realism and empiricism. He thereby revolutionized economic theory by integrating the categories of knowledge, ignorance, rational degree and precariousness. He abandoned constructivism because he rejected empty concepts as *dry bones*. He also left traditional empiricism and ontological realism behind him since he needed to develop and to discuss new categories as a priori principles. His view of economic theory encompasses fragility and precariousness of knowledge since he had already rejected Benthamine calculation. He viewed bivalent logic as inadequate for his purpose to find solutions to economic problems. What needed to be discussed is how this simplicity fits with perceived economic problems (Duménil and Lévy 1997; D'Autume and Cartelier 1997).

One crucial point is, although the nature of rules in models is a particular description, rules itself often are interpreted as normative guidelines without deeper reflection on the normative sense.[25] Moreover, they are taken as universal rules or universal laws.

---

[24] Hillard argued, Cartesian reductionism in classical theory was of no relevance to Keynes's thinking (Hillard 1992, 66).

[25] Caution is required as Edward Levi said: Economists, like jurists often argue by example, maintaining, for instance: "the controlling similarity between the present and prior case" (Levi 1948/1967, 7).

As Keynes said, "taken (it) for granted" all the rest follows. Rules or the dichotomy of "rules versus discretion" as introduced earlier are not given by the law of gravity. Economics and economic theory is neither guided by rigidly constructed terms nor by universal laws. On the contrary, terms, rules and laws need to be related to economic actions, perceptions, experiences and decisions. The often claimed relation to natural phenomena like the law of gravity is not convincing. Economic actions and decisions are not driven by universal power or hidden tendencies or mechanisms.[26]

Economic parameters like short-term and long-term interest rates and prices are to be understood as results of the decision-making process under uncertainty. Surprisingly or not, the community of science has not been successful in defining the term *rule*; no one has ever written down a satisfactory rule until now. "When formal elegance becomes an end – rather than a means to an end – for theoretical research, theory risks being of little help as a guide for practical decision making. The difficult quest for a model which can be trusted completely as a descriptive – let alone prescriptive – tool for economic policy is still only at its beginning" (Issing 2005b, 13).

Talking about monetary policy as constructed by a false dichotomy, i.e., "rules *versus* discretion", pretending credibility seems to be a contradiction. The effectiveness of monetary policy is not a result of a continuity of fooling the public about the goals, strategies, and forecasts made by central banks. One result of my contribution is that the famous dichotomy "rules *versus* discretion" is of no relevance to Keynes, because he had used the term "rules" not in the meaning of a formal brilliantly designed notion. He definitely made a distinction between non-rigidly-fixed rules *and* discretion.

References

Baert P (1996) Realist philosophy of the social sciences and economics: a critique. Cambridge Journal of Economics 20:513–522

Bateman B (1991) Das Maynard problem. Cambridge Journal of Economics 18:101–111

Bernanke BS (2004) The logic of monetary policy. Washington, DC. http://www.FederalReserve reserve.gov/boarddocs/speeches/2004/20041202/default.htm.Accessed date 15.12.2007

Blinder AS (1987) Keynes, Lucas, and scientific progress. The American Economic Review 77:130–136

Blinder AS (1998) Central banking in theory and practice. MIT Press, Cambridge

Blinder AS (1999) Central bank credibility: why do we care? How do we build it? NBER, Working Paper No. 7161. MIT Press, Cambridge

Blinder AS (2005) What have we learnt since October 1979? CEPS Working Paper No. 105. Princeton University Press, Princeton

---

[26] Conventions do play a particular role for the decision making process. "In practice we have tacitly agreed, as a rule, to fall back on what is, in truth, a *convention*" (Keynes (1973–1989), C.W., Vol. VII, 152; Muchlinski 1998).

Blinder AS, Ehrmann M, Fratzscher M, De Haan J, David JJ (2008) Central bank communication and monetary policy: a survey of theory and evidence. Journal of Economic Literature 46(4):910–945

Bordo M, Eichengreen B (2009) Bretton Woods and the great inflation. In: Bordo MD, Orphanides A (eds) The great inflation. University Press of Chicago, Chicago

Boughton JM (2002) Why White, not Keynes? Inventing the Postwar International Monetary System. IMF Working Paper, WP/02/52. Washington, DC. http://www.imf.org

Carabelli A (1988) On Keynes's method. Macmillan, London

Carabelli A (1991) The methodology of the critique of the classical theory: Keynes on organic interdependence. In: Bateman B, Davis JB (eds) Keynes and philosophy. Essays on the origin of Keynes's thought. Edward Elgar, London, pp 104–125

Chalmers AF (2006) What is this thing called science? Open University Press, Maidenhead

D'Autume A, Caterlier J (1997) Is economics becoming a hard science? Edward Elgar, Cheltenham

Davis JB (1994) Keynes's philosophical development. Cambridge University Press, Cambridge

Dostaler G (1994) Keynes et Bretton Woods. De l' Ordre des Nations à l' Ordre des Marchés. Bretton Woods, Cinquante ans Plus Tard. In: Interventions économicques. Pur uns Alternativ Sociale, No 26. Québec, pp. 53–78, Une collection développée en collaboration avec la Bibliothèque Paul Émile-Boulet de l' Université du Québec à Chicoutimi. http://bibliotheque. uqac.uquebec.ca/index.htm

Dostaler G (2005) Keynes et ses Combats. Albin Michel, Paris,

Duménil G, Lévy D (1997) Should economics be a hard science? In: D'Autume A, Cartelier J Edward Elgar, Cheltenham. pp 276–303

Eichengreen B (1995) Central bank cooperation and exchange rate commitments: the classical and the interwar goldstandards compared. Financial History Review 2:99–117

European Central Bank (2001) Issues related to Monetary policy rules. Monthly Report October, Frankfurt am Main, pp 37–50

Fitzgibbons A (1998) Against Keynes' recantation. Cahiers D'Économie Politique. Histoire de la Pensée et Théories 30–31(L'Harmattan):147–165

Hillard J (1992) Keynes, orthodoxy and uncertainty. In: Gerrard B, Hillard J (eds) The philosophy and economics of J. M. Keynes. Edward Elgar, London, pp 59–79

Horsefield KJ (1969) The International Monetary Fund 1945–1965. Twenty years of international monetary cooperation. Volume III: documents. International Monetary Fund, Washington, DC

Issing O (1996) Regeln versus Diskretion in der Geldpolitik. In: Bofinger P, Ketterer K-H (eds) Neuere Entwicklungen in der Geldtheorie und Geldpolitik. J. C. B. Mohr, Tübingen, pp 3–20

Issing O (1999) The eurosystem: transparent and accountable or 'Willem in Euroland'. Journal of Common Market Studies 37(3):503–519

Issing O (2005a) Communication, transparency, accountability: monetary policy in the twenty-first century. The Federal Reserve Bank of St Louis Review 87(pt 1):65–83

Issing O (2005b) Monetary policy in an uncharted territory. In: Issing O, Gaspar V et al (eds) Imperfect knowledge and monetary policy. The stone lectures in economics. Cambridge University Press, Cambridge, pp 12–76

Issing O (2009) In search of monetary stability: the evolution of monetary policy. BIS Working Paper No 273, Bank for International Settlements (BIS). http://www.bis.org

Issing O (2011) Lessons for monetary policy: what should the consensus be? IMF Working Paper WP/11/97, Research Department. http://www.imf.org

Kant I (1781/1965) Critique of Pure Reason. Translated by Norman Kemp Smith (unabridged ed.) New York: St. Martin's Press

Keynes JM (1904) Ethics in relation to conduct. Keynes Papers, MSS, King's College, Cambridge

Keynes JM (1906) Egoism. Keynes Papers, MSS, King's College, Cambridge

Keynes JM (1973–1989) The collected writings (C.W.) of Maynard Keynes, vols I–XXIX. In: Moggridge DE, Johnson E (eds). Macmillan, London

King M (1997) Changes in UK monetary policy: rules and discretion in practice. Journal of Monetary Economics 39:81–97

Kirman AP (1992) Whom or what does the representative individual represent? The Journal of Economic Perspectives 6(2):117–136

Kosko B (1993) Fuzzy thinking. Hyperion, New York

Levi E (1948/1967) An introduction to legal reasoning. University of Chicago Press, Chicago

Lindsey DE, Lindsey DE, Orphanides A, Rasche RH (2005) The reform of October 1979: how it happened and why. Federal Reserve Bank of St Louis Review 87(2, pt 2):187–235

McKinnon RI (1993) The rules of the game: international money in historical perspective. Journal of Economic Literature XXXI:1–44

Mishkin F (2009) Will monetary policy become more of a science? In: Bundesbank D (ed) Monetary policy over fifty years. Experiences and lessons. Routledge, London, pp 81–107

Moggridge DE (1986) Keynes and the international monetary system 1909–46. In: Cohen JS, Harcourt GC (eds) International monetary problems and supply-side-economics. Macmillan, London, pp 56–83

Moggridge DE (1992) Maynard Keynes. An economist's biography. Routledge, London

Moggridge DE (2002) Rescuing Keynes from the economists? The Skidelsky trilogy. Economic History of Economic Thought 9(1):111–123

Moggridge DE, Howson S (1974) Keynes on monetary policy, 1910–1946. Oxford Economic Papers, New Series 26:226–247

Muchlinski E (1996) Keynes als Philosoph. Duncker & Humblot, Berlin

Muchlinski E (1998) The philosophy of John Maynard Keynes. A reconsideration. Cahiers D'Économie Politique. Histoire de la Pensée et Théories 30–31(L'Harmattan):227–253

Muchlinski E (1999a) The lucas critique & lucasianism – considering the history of macroeconomics. Department of Economics, Freie Universität Berlin, Nr. 1999/1. http://129.3.2041/eps/mac/papers/0503/0503019.pdf

Muchlinski E (1999b) Macropolicy within a tripolar regime. Department of Economics, Freie Universität Berlin, Nr. 1999/2. http://www.fu-berlin.de/wiwiss/institute/wirtschaftspolitik-geschichte/muchlinski/forschung/macropolicy1999-2.pdf

Muchlinski E (2002) Transzendentaler Realismus oder Transformation der Kategorien? In: Bauer L, Hamberger K (eds) Epistemological perspectives on the social sciences. Springer, Wien, pp 215–234

Muchlinski E (2003a) Knowledge, knowledge sharing and convention in Keynes's thinking. In: Helmstädter E (ed) The economics of knowledge sharing. A new institutional approach. Edward Elgar, Cheltenham, pp 129–145

Muchlinski E (2003b) Épistémologie et probabilité chez Keynes. L' Actualité Économique Revue D'Analyse Économique 79(1–2) (HEC Montréal, Sociéte Canadienne de Science Économique):57–70

Muchlinski E (2005) Central bank transparency: reasons for creative ambiguity. In: Hölscher J, Tomann H (eds) Globalization of capital markets and monetary policy. Houndsmills B et al. Palgrave, Macmillan, Hampsphire, pp 130–147

Muchlinski E (2006) Was meint Wittgenstein mit 'In der Sprache wird alles ausgetragen'?, Logos Verlag, Berlin

Muchlinski E (2007a) Keynes' a treatise on probability. http://www.keynes-gesellschaft.de

Muchlinski E (2007b) Keynes against rigid rules. http://ideas.repec.org/p/wpa/wuwpma/0503018.html

Muchlinski E (2011a) Central banks and Coded Language. Risks and benefits. Palgrave Macmillan, Houndmills, Basingstoke, UK

Muchlinski E (2011b) Keynes' economic theory – judgment under uncertainty. In: Cate T (ed) Keynes' general theory seventy five years later. Edward Elgar, Cheltenham

Muchlinski E (2011c) Wissen, Sprache und Bedeutung in der Ökonomik. Studien zur Entwicklung der ökonomischen Theorie Bd. 15/Reihe XXVI-Wissen/The knowledge economy. Duncker & Humblot, Berlin, pp 83–102

O'Donnell RM (1989) Keynes: philosophy, economics and politics. The philosophical foundations of Keynes's thought and their influence on his economics and politics. Macmillan, London

Orphanides A, Wieland V (2008) Economic projections and rules of thumb for monetary policy. Fed Reserve Bank St. Louis Review July/August 2008 Vol. 90, No 4, pp 307–324

Parsons C (1992) The transcendental aesthetic. In: Guyer P (ed) The Cambridge companion to KANT. Cambridge University Press, Cambridge

Rorty R (1991) Inquiry as recontextualisation: an anti-dualist account of interpretation. In: Hiley DR, Bohmann JF, Shusterman R (eds) The interpretive turn. Philosophy, science, culture. Cornell University Press, Ithaca, pp 59–80

Ryle G (1966) The concept of mind. Hutchinson, London

Samuels WJ (1996) Postmodernism and economics: a middlebrow view. Journal of Economic Methodology 3(1):113–120

Simons HC (1936) Rules versus authorities in monetary policy. Journal of Political Economy 44:1–30

Tobin J (1983) Monetary policy: rules, targets, and shocks. Journal of Money, Credit, and Banking 15(4):506–518

Vickers J (1998) Inflation targeting in practice: the UK experience. In: Speech at the conference on implementation of price stability, CFS, Frankfurt/M, 11–12 Sept 1998

Woodford M (2005) Central bank communication and policy effectiveness. NBER Working Paper 11898, Cambridge, December 2005

Chapter 25
Keynes's "Long Struggle of Escape"

Royall Brandis

The impact on economics of John Maynard Keynes's *The General Theory of Employment, Interest, and Money* of 1936 has been so large as to make it difficult over 65 years later to reconstruct the professional economics stage onto which it entered. While scholarly attention to the work began in different institutions at different times after its publication, by 1950 it would have been difficult to find a college or university whose economics teaching or research programs were uninfluenced by *The General Theory*.

A personal note: I began my formal study of economics in 1937 in a college setting in which the received Marshallian view of theory (essentially microtheory) was undisturbed by Keynes's just-published *General Theory*. However, then-standard courses in "business cycles" and in "money and banking" were offered alongside a "value and distribution" microtheory course without any sense of inconsistency between the three areas. (Today's familiar categories of microeconomics and macroeconomics were unknown at the time. Indeed, these terms entered the English language only after World War II. For convenience, we use the terms even when referring to an earlier period.) It was only when I entered upon graduate study at Duke University in 1940 that I learned of *The General Theory*. Calvin B. Hoover, who chaired the Duke University economics department, was a personal friend of Keynes and, no doubt, was responsible for the early introduction of the book into the Duke graduate economics program.

The book's influence on public policy is equally a story of overwhelming success although its policy prescriptions were always politically controversial. No one in the history of economics has set out so consciously to make his ideas the ruling ones both with the profession and with policymakers and succeeded to the extent that Keynes did. Why and how did he do it?

R. Brandis (✉)
University of Illinois at Urbana, Champaign, IL, USA

J.G. Backhaus (ed.), *Handbook of the History of Economic Thought*,
The European Heritage in Economics and the Social Sciences,
DOI 10.1007/978-1-4419-8336-7_25, © Springer Science+Business Media, LLC 2012

Keynes's own explanation is well known. He said at the beginning: "I have called this book the [sic] *General Theory of Employment, Interest and Money,* placing the emphasis on the prefix *general.* The object of such a title is to contrast the character of my arguments and conclusions with those of the *classical* theory of the subject, upon which I was brought up...I shall argue that the postulates of the classical theory are applicable to a special case only and not to the general case..." (Keynes [1936] 1973a p. 3, emphasis in original).

In a footnote to the word "classical," Keynes said he meant it to include, among others, Alfred Marshall, Francis Edgeworth, and Arthur Pigou – the immediate past and then-present leaders of the English economics profession. Furthermore, Keynes said, this difference between his ideas and theirs went far beyond that of a mere argument among scholars, for "the characteristics of the special case assumed by the classical theory happen not to be those of the economic society in which we actually live, with the result that its teaching is misleading and disastrous if we attempt to apply it to the facts of experience." (Ibid).

Thus, both the dominant theory and its policy implications were wrong: the theory because it purported to be exhaustive when it only met a special case, the policy implications because they were for a theoretical world that had no counterpart in the real world. Now, in 1936, after a century of error by the best minds in the discipline, all was to be made clear. Later in *The General Theory*, Keynes did acknowledge a few predecessors, notably Malthus. Surely, this must be the supreme example of chutzpah in economics. If Keynes had not been a leading economist and an important figure in British public life, it is doubtful that many reviewers would have read further than chapter I before dismissing the work as that of a crank.

In fact, by 1936, not even classical microeconomics was encompassed entirely in Marshall's *Principles.* The year 1933 had seen the publication of Edward Chamberlin's *Monopolistic Competition* and Joan Robinson's *Imperfect Competition.* Macroeconomics had never pretended to be Marshallian or Ricardian even though the latter's macroeconomic view was said to have triumphed early in the nineteenth century over Malthus's ideas in their argument about "gluts." For a century before 1936, macroeconomics had been fully occupied with two broad questions: (1) the relationship between money and prices, especially the general price level, and (2) business cycles. In the latter area, major concerns were changes in total employment and in the economy's aggregate output.

Indeed, Keynes, himself, by 1936, was no stranger to either of these two macroeconomic areas. As long ago as 1913, he had authored a paper entitled, "How Far are Bankers Responsible for the Alternations of Crisis and Depression?" (Keynes [1913] Keynes 1973b, 13 pp. 2–14) Ralph Hawtrey authored a book (*Good and Bad Trade*) on the same subject in that same year. Hawtrey seems to have been working along lines similar to Keynes, but earlier than Keynes; however, he was not a member of the Cambridge School, and he does not seem to have taken the final steps that Keynes took in *The General Theory*.

Keynes's 1913 paper offered what Keynes hoped was a new theory of what caused business cycles. More recently, he had published in 1930 what he must have hoped was a definitive work on money – the two-volume A *Treatise on Money*.

By 1936, over twenty years after his first essay in business cycle theory, he still had not achieved a dominant place in that area of macroeconomics either. Yet, in the 1920s and early 1930s, he was constantly publishing pieces on macroeconomic policy. Many of these dealt with the effects of the business cycle – especially unemployment.

Business Cycle Theory in 1936

It will be useful to review the state of business cycle theory at the publication of *The General Theory*. In September 1930 (the same month Keynes's A *Treatise on Money* was published), the League of Nations commissioned Gottfried Haberler to do a study of business cycles (or "trade cycles" in British terminology). The study was to cover both theory and statistical testing of theory. The statistical work was interrupted by the onset of World War II and apparently never completed. The theoretical volume was divided into two sections: Part I, a survey of then-current theories of the business cycle, and Part II, an attempt by Haberler to synthesize these theories into a theory of the cycle. This volume, with the title, *Prosperity and Depression,* was first published as a League of Nations document in 1936. In one of those coincidences dear to the heart of a historian, the preface to a later (1939), public edition, tells us that the manuscript of the 1936 volume "was substantially completed" in December 1935. (Haberler [1936] 1939, viii) Keynes's Preface to *The General Theory* is dated 13 December 1935. Thus, we have, precisely dated, the last word on business cycle theory at the time of the completion of *The General Theory.*

Haberler's book first impresses the reader by its roll call of distinguished economists (mostly twentieth century) who had, by 1936, made contributions to business cycle theory. Among these were R. G. Hawtrey, F. A. Hayek, F. Machlup, L. Mises, L. Robbins, G. Cassel, J. Schumpeter, A. Aftalion, J. M. Clark, S. Kuznets, R. F. Harrod, W. C. Mitchell, D. H. Robertson, A. Hansen, F. W. Taussig, E. Lindahl, G. Myrdal, B. Ohlin, W. S. Jevons, H. L. Moore, and A. C. Pigou. Keynes is mentioned, but in a minor way – usually grouped with Hawtrey, Pigou, and Robertson; the reference is to his *Treatise on Money.*

Haberber's book is also notable for the fact that there is only one mention of Say's Law and that is in the citation of a title to an article by Hans Neisser. Even here, the reason for the citation is Neisser's cycle theory; there is no discussion of Say or Say's Law here or elsewhere in Haberler's book. Coming at this same question from Keynes's position, his chapter (22) in *The General Theory,* "Notes on the Trade Cycle," while clearly separating his new theory from then-current business cycle theories, is at the same time, very respectful of those theories. Again, there is no mention of Say's Law. What Keynes purports to do is to use his new theory to clear up questions raised, but not answered satisfactorily, by existing cycle theories. He says, "if we are right ... our theory must be capable of explaining the phenomena of the trade cycle." (Keynes [1936] 1973b p. 313).

From this, it seems fair to say that whatever may have been the status of Say's Law in 1936, business cycle theory had a life of its own. Indeed, one might argue that this had been true for 100 years past. Over that long period, virtually every notable name in economics had participated in the business cycle colloquy. The fact that the economic history of that 100 years had been characterized by recurring periods of prosperity and depression was undeniable although the quantity and quality of data concerning the phenomena were far less than what we have today.

What had resulted by 1936 from all of this effort was a multiplicity of theories, none of which (including Haberler's own attempted synthesis) had come to dominate the field. It was through this morass that Keynes sought a clear, but hitherto untrodden, path. To a considerable degree, Keynes's bold attack on Say's Law and classical theory may have been a smoke screen behind which he could construct a new approach to business cycle theory.

A few general statements can be made about the development of business cycle theories: First, they had always been dynamic theories. They began with a recognition of the fact of continual change in the overall economy. Further, they were historical theories. There was a basic assumption that whatever economic conditions are today, they are, at least in part, the result of the past history of the economy, especially the history of the recent past. Finally, almost all who worked on the problem were attracted (perhaps distracted) by the idea that there was a periodicity in terms of calendar time to the various aspects of the cycle.

Scientism no doubt played a part in this. Jevons, who was explicit in his belief that economics should be like physical science, thought he could tie business cycles to the periodic change in sunspots. His mechanism operated via changes in agricultural output (believed to be correlated to sunspot changes *via* the weather) which, in turn, sparked change throughout the economy. Jevons believed he could demonstrate statistically that the periodicity of the sunspots was the same as that of the business cycle. Thus, economics, or at least a key part of the subject, could attain the predictive power of astronomy. Jevons may have carried connection of the cycle to calendar time further than anyone else, but business cycle theorists generally were entranced by the possible periodicity of the cycle with respect to the calendar. This notion withered gradually and is marked by the shift from the use of the word "cycle" to that of "fluctuation." We should note that this emphasis on calendar time marked a clear separation from Marshallian microeconomics in which time, e.g., "the short-run," was measured in purely economic terms without regard to the calendar.

The broadest classification of the theories presented by Haberler was twofold: monetary and real. Under each category were theories emphasizing different aspects of the economy as well as mixed theories that attempted to incorporate factors from one category into a theory emphasizing the other. The causal focus from the monetary point of view was on the quantity of money and its velocity (transactions or income velocity). The general idea was that an increase in MV accompanied rising physical output and employment while a decrease was associated with the reverse effect. However, in a prescient footnote, Haberler added: "It is conceivable that the rise and fall of the volume of production might be accompanied by an opposite movement of prices." (Haberler [1936] 1939, 14, f.2) In general, writers on the monetary aspects stressed the familiar factors of bank credit conditions, interest rates, and price level changes. This led to consideration of central bank policy and to the "rules" of sound banking under the gold standard, this latter institution being largely moribund by 1936, but not expected to remain so.

The proponents of the real side as the prime mover in business cycles stressed either investment in physical capital and the Acceleration Principle or the failure of consumption to keep pace with rising output. Both the interest rate and entrepreneurial expectations were recognized as key factors in determining changes in the level of capital creation. Under-consumption business cycle theories faced directly the relationship of saving and investment. About the closest Haberler comes to Say's Law is at this point:" it is clear that the social function of saving is to release resources from the production of goods for immediate consumption for the production of producers' goods." (Haberler [1936] 1939, p. 125) However, this is followed shortly by the statement that while the "opponents [of under-consumption theories] have shown the theoretical *possibility* of a smooth absorption of savings in new investment, they have not shown its necessity." (Ibid, p. 126, emphasis in original) A special case of real causes of the cycle was variation in agricultural output. The relative decline of importance of agriculture in the advanced economies by 1936 had reduced interest in this approach. The role of Jevons in such special theories has already been mentioned.

In summary, by 1936 business cycle theory had reached a stage of sophistication at which all the theoretical problems attacked in *The General Theory* had been raised and various solutions proposed. However, there was no agreement as to the relative importance of any particular problem and no agreement as to its correct solution. Equally important was the inability to derive from the theories any agreed governmental policy to ameliorate the human suffering spawned by unemployment. The Great Depression of the 1930s had given this problem particular urgency.

Business Cycle Policy in 1936

Business cycle theoretical work was far more advanced in 1936 than were policy recommendations. The reasons for this are not hard to find. The fundamental approach of cycle theory did not treat any one phase of the cycle as normal and the other phases as abnormal and, thus, something to be modified or eliminated. It was the *cycle* that was normal. Of course, economists recognized the full-employment, prosperity phase of the cycle as much the happiest for the participants in the system, but attempting to reduce or eliminate the other phases or to extend the length of the prosperity phase meant interfering with the mechanism of the cycle – to many a dangerous procedure which might make matters worse.

If one believed, as some did, that the business cycle had the inexorability of some natural mechanism in the physical world, there was nothing to be done. One might as well talk of having a policy governing the acceleration due to gravity. Others thought something could be done, but only with great caution, for interference with the "natural" course of the cycle might only make things worse. There was no agreement among this latter group as to just what ought to be done.

A prevalent idea was that one might mitigate the worst features of the depression phase by damping down the best features of the prosperity phase, in other words, settling for less-than-full employment at all times to prevent larger scale unemployment part of the time. Again, there was no agreement on how this could be accomplished. Moreover, stability at something like a recession level was not a very happy solution. It would be like replacing periodic bouts of serious illness with a continuing malaise. Keynes, himself, was an advocate of no one policy. His predilection was to produce a situation-specific policy, but one point was clear: the social concern which Marshall, no doubt, had nurtured led Keynes to refuse to accept the notion that the laws of economics severely narrowed the options open for public action to relieve unemployment in recession or depression.

Another difficulty in the 1930s in trying to achieve a better, that is higher average level of operation of the economy was the minor responsibility for the performance of the economy often assigned to government in the industrialized nations. This was particularly true in the United States where the economic policy roles (if any) of the federal, state, and local governments were not clearly demarcated. It was the Roosevelt Administration's New Deal in 1933–1938 that laid the groundwork for acceptance of Keynesian-type policy proposals, not the other way round. Furthermore, the changes in the Federal Reserve Act, made in that same 1930s period, coupled with the virtual abandonment of the gold standard, meant that the bounds of monetary policy were vastly extended. Most importantly, the federal government was no longer restricted in its fiscal policy by the danger of gold outflows from the Treasury or the banking system. Thus, in the United States, the institutional foundation was laid for Keynesian economic policies before or contemporaneously with the arrival of *The General Theory* in 1936.

In Britain, where Keynes had a voice that was heard – if not always heeded – on economic policy, he had to deal with institutional and political arrangements different from those in the United States. Also, the British economy was much more sensitive to the international economic situation than was the U.S. economy of that day. By 1928, Keynes was advocating policies that indicate rather clearly that he reached "Keynesian" policy conclusions before he had constructed a theoretical base for them in *The General Theory*. As Moggridge put it in summarizing a mid-1928 article by Keynes on the British unemployment problem: "He advocated an expansion of public expenditure with a supportive, slightly expansionary, monetary policy" (Moggridge 1992, p. 461). Obviously, by 1928, Keynes was well along on his *A Treatise on Money,* but it was not to furnish the theoretical underpinning for these policy recommendations that one might have expected.

The Reception of *A Treatise on Money*

Although a congratulatory letter from J. A. Schumpeter upon the publication of the *Treatise* said, "I believe it will ever stand out as a landmark in its field" (quoted in, Keynes 1973 13 p. 201), the professional reception of the book generally was respectful, but more critical than Schumpeter's letter. Keynes, himself, was not really happy with the volumes although he had been seven years in the writing. The book appeared a year after the stock market crash in the United States, and that nation, as well as the rest of the industrialized world was already a fair way down the slope of recession that was to reach bottom in the U. S. in 1932–1933. The *Treatise* must, upon publication, have seemed vaguely out of date. Considering what the following decade was to bring in the Great Depression, it was certainly the case that policymakers would not find in the book the kind of answers that they had begun to seek ever more desperately.

In the other area important to Keynes – academic economics – he was equally disappointed. Two years after publication, it was clear that the profession was not according to the ideas of the *Treatise* more than cursory attention. As Haberler's treatment indicates, the *Treatise* made only a minor stir in the over-crowded field of business cycle theory. The book's emphasis on the role of money and the rate of interest in determining the overall level of economic activity looked more and more to have missed the point. When scholarly criticism of the *Treatise* began to be heard almost literally on Keynes's doorstep (with the "Cambridge Circus" of colleagues), Keynes gradually came to see the need to do more than just revise the *Treatise*. The result, of course, was *The General Theory*.

The Challenge Facing Keynes

The challenge Keynes faced in the mid-nineteen-thirties had three aspects. One was the current British economic situation and what had preceded it. For whatever reasons (Keynes would have said the terms under which Britain returned to the gold standard in 1924), the nation had not enjoyed the prosperity of the 1920s that much of the world, including the United States, had experienced. For Britain, the decade of the 1920s had been marked by unemployment of varying degrees of severity. The depression of the 1930s only made a bad situation worse. Through all of this Keynes had been frequently in the public eye, usually as a critic of the ruling economic policy and a proposer of policies of his own devising. He had had very little success in achieving adoption of such policies. After 1933, American economic policy did seem to be in step with his ideas, but that was largely coincidental; its basis was pragmatic, not a new theoretical orientation. Keynes met Roosevelt in 1934, but if Keynes offered economic policy advice on that occasion it must have passed Roosevelt by. After the meeting, Roosevelt told Frances Perkins, his Secretary of Labor, that Keynes was very charming, but Roosevelt couldn't understand what he was trying to tell him.

The second aspect had to do with the state of business cycle theory in the 1930s. The problem was not that there were no theories, but that there were far too many of them. As Haberler's book well demonstrates, there were so many different theories, each upheld by one or more leading economists, that still another theory – no matter how ingenious – stood little chance of acceptance by economists or of becoming the basis for public policy. In his early (1913) entry into this crowded arena, Keynes had said that he was offering, "a general explanation of fluctuations which is to some extent novel..." (Keynes [1913] 1973 13 p. 2) Keynes was never modest when it came to promoting his ideas. From the cycle theory point of view, the later (1930) *Treatise,* no matter how respectful its reception, could only be judged a failure – and failure was something Keynes had little stomach for.

The third aspect falls in the domain of the sociology of economics – treacherous terrain indeed. How *could* Keynes make the economics profession (and, in turn, the policymakers) listen to him? Harry Johnson's very perceptive essay on the 35th anniversary of *The General Theory* (Johnson [1971] 1978, especially pp. 188–189) listed five characteristics required for a revolutionary theory in economics: (1) it should attack the central tenet of orthodox theory (2) it should appear to be new, but retain as much as possible of the old ruling theory – here Johnson suggested the efficacy of giving old concepts new and confusing names (3) it should be difficult, but not too difficult to understand; this would lead seniors in the profession to try to dismiss it while hungry younger ones could learn it and use it to challenge their elders (4) it should offer a new methodology more attractive than what was then available and (5) it should offer an important empirical relationship -in Keynes's case the consumption function – to attract the quantitatively inclined. *The General Theory,* Johnson believed, satisfied all five characteristics.

Without denying any of the above, I would like to go back a step before Johnson's analysis to ask the question Keynes must have asked himself at some point between the publication of the *Treatise* and the conceptual beginning of *The General Theory:* How could he make the profession listen to him? Surely, not by entering the field of business cycle theory more directly than he had with the *Treatise.* That would require overcoming the Hydra that was the state of cycle theory in the 1930s. Unless the Hydra was overcome, there was little chance that Keynes's theory would be pronounced *the* theory of the cycle. Yet there would seem little point in starting again from orthodox monetary theory. He had gone that route more than once, most recently with the *Treatise.*

Three chapters of the *Treatise* were devoted to what Keynes called the "credit cycle." Unemployment is given some attention in this part of the work although prices and the interest rate are in the forefront. Haberler, in 1935, on the basis of the *Treatise,* classified Keynes as a monetary over-investment cycle theory advocate. We can note that nowhere in the *Treatise* is there a reference to J. B. Say, to Say's Law, or to T. R. Malthus. The walls of Keynes's prison appear to have been invisible ones.

We know from his preface to the Japanese edition of the *Treatise* that as late as April 1932, Keynes saw a need only for "extending and correcting the theoretical basis of my views." (Keynes [1930] 1973, p. xxvii) Indeed, in a summary chapter of the *Treatise,* he seems already to be well outside the stockade of Say's Law. He said, "The chapter [20] is...an essay in the internal mechanics of the price-wage-employment structure during the course of a cycle which represents a recovery in the volume of employment from a preceding slump which has reached an *equilib-rium* between prices and costs of production, but is still characterized by unem-ployment." (Keynes [1930] 1973 p.274, emphasis supplied) Yet, in *The General*

Theory, Keynes was going to state, "Say's law, that the aggregate demand price of output as a whole is equal to its supply price for all volumes of output, is equivalent to the proposition that there is no obstacle to full employment" (Keynes [1936] 1973 p. 26). It was this Law that Keynes argued blocked understanding of the unemployment problem as well as prevented adoption of policies to correct the problem. It is almost as though there were two different economists at work on the same problem.

Keynes's Response to the Challenge

Sometime after April 1932 (the date of the preface to the Japanese edition of the *Treatise*), Keynes must have concluded that he had to find an entirely new angle of attack on the ruling economics establishment if he were not to be merely one of a number of economists who were listened to more or less respectfully on business cycle problems. Since we will differ with it somewhat, let us first present the 1973 opinion of Donald Moggridge whose familiarity with Keynes's writings and activities during the 5-year period between the *Treatise* and *General Theory* is unsurpassed.

Moggridge, who edited the *Collected Writings* volume on the preparation of *The General Theory,* has this to say about why changes in aggregate output moved to center stage in Keynes's thinking: "Three outside influences seem to have been preeminent: the worldwide slump after 1929, which moved the English 'local difficulties' of 1922–1929 on to a wider stage, the general reception given to the *Treatise,* and discussions in Cambridge during 1930–31." (in Keynes 1973 v.13: p. 338) We should note that the Cambridge "discussions" amounted to a critical seminar on the *Treatise* by some of Keynes's younger colleagues. While scholarly and well meant, they may well have rankled Keynes. One participant, the young Joan Robinson, in 1933, would publish her *Imperfect Competition* to immediate acclaim and notice in the profession. This was hardly likely to improve Keynes's satisfaction with his own performance in the *Treatise.*

What can be said contra Moggridge? I do not find Moggridge's explanation persuasive in concentrating the origin of the revolutionary ideas of *The General Theory* in the period immediately following the publication of the *Treatise.* It ignores Keynes's important role as a public man in Britain as well as his personal history.

I wish to emphasize that I do not mean to disparage the technical work done by Keynes or the contributions of his colleagues in the early 1930s after the publication of the *Treatise.* All of this aspect of the development of *The General Theory* is beautifully laid out in Volume 13 of the *Collected Writings.* What I do mean to argue is that this is an incomplete explanation. It yields a picture of the genesis of *The General Theory* as being solely in theoretical questions, puzzles, professional criticisms and the responses which they elicited from Keynes. It presents a model of scholarly, scientific advance. It ignores the human motivations of a complex and proud man.

There is now another, carefully researched, and very different sociological evaluation of the activities of the same persons in the same period. This is an article by Nahid Aslanbeigui and Guy Oakes in the March 2002 issue of the *Journal of the History of Economic Thought.* The article is entitled, "The Theory Arsenal: The Cambridge Circus and the Origins of the Keynesian Revolution." I do not think the article contradicts what I have to say, but it is less accepting of the orthodox explanation than I am. Let me give a brief description of the argument of the piece. I begin with some quotations from the article.

"The Keynesian Revolution did not emerge complete and in glittering perfection from the text of *The General Theory,* like Minerva from the head of Zeus. The revolutionary consensus of 1936–1946 was not achieved on the basis of the intrinsic scientific merits of *The General Theory* or its inherent explanatory power" (p. 6).

"The Keynesian Revolution is best understood not as a book but a collection of intersecting social mechanisms: a complex of social interactions, negotiations, adjustments, and a host of contingencies that occurred between the publication of the *Treatise on Money* and Keynes's death" (p. 6).

"For the Keynes of *The General Theory,* a theoretical choice was a strategic choice. Theory became strategy. It follows that *The General Theory* cannot be understood on the basis of a philosophy of science committed to the idea of an epistemologically pure theory and a clear distinction between a theory and its uses" (p. 7).

The authors' argument is that, after the publication in 1930 of the *Treatise on Money,* a small group of Keynes's young colleagues at Cambridge (the now famous Cambridge Circus) formed what can only be called a conspiracy to replace "classicism," that is, the orthodoxy of the time, with a new approach. Keynes became the stategist of this movement. However, the young revolutionaries (as well as Keynes), were steeped in the Cambridge tradition of economic analysis which had been inherited from Alfred Marshall. This tradition was essentially a microeconomic one, but did have any connection to the macroeconomic area of money and prices. There was no identifiable Marshallian business cycle theory tradition. The authors do not examine this reliance on microeconomic theory as the base for constructing a new macroeconomic theory. I will, however, return to this point.

Austen Robinson, then virtually the only survivor of the between-the-wars group of Keynes's close Cambridge colleagues, speaking in 1983 at the Keynes Centenary Conference at King's College said that the present generation of economists did not grasp the fact that Keynes's first concern was policy – not theory.

As I have already indicated, the actual crystallization of Keynes's determination to write a revolutionary book must have come *after* the writing of the preface to the Japanese edition of the *Treatise* in April 1932. However, I would argue that the underlying motivating force had its inception in the period at the end of World War I.

Clearly, we are now moving into an area of analysis that economists – even historians of economic thought – usually seek to avoid. The idea of the economist as the dispassionate scientist is a very attractive one. Alas, it may not always be an accurate description, particularly when considering the work of a man like

Keynes. In 1919, Keynes published *The Economic Consequences of the Peace* (Keynes [1919] 1973) and, overnight, went from the position of a young professional economist with a promising academic/public career to the status of a best-selling author whose controversial reportage, analysis, and criticism of the Versailles Conference and Treaty were being discussed by intellectuals and policymakers worldwide as well as in his own country. Sudden fame is a very heady experience which no man comes through unaltered. One of the things that contributed to the controversy (and to the book's large sales) was Keynes's brash treatment of the major national leaders at the Versailles Treaty Conference. He was not only critical of their product, the Treaty, but limned their personalities and motivations in unflattering ways. It was, for Keynes, a very rewarding experience, professionally and financially.

A second, much quieter activity also made its contribution. At least as early as 1922, Keynes had begun reading each year a paper on Malthus to the undergraduate Political Economy Club at Cambridge. This was a charming piece having mostly to do with Malthus the man and with the *Essay on Population.* That Keynes would be interested in Malthus is no surprise. After all, both he and Malthus had India connections, Keynes spending two years as a civil servant in the India Office as well as lecturing and publishing a book on Indian finance (Keynes [1913] 1971a) while much of Malthus's career was spent on the faculty of the East India College. Perhaps even more to the point, both were young men when they published books that brought them wide public notice. Malthus was 32 when the *Essay* appeared; Keynes was 36 when *Economic Consequences* was published.

By 1933, when he was preparing the Malthus paper for publication in his *Essays* in *Biography,* (Keynes [1933] 1972) Keynes had added two sections to his paper – one on Malthus's macroeconomics, the other on the controversy between Malthus and Ricardo over "glut." Included in the addition was the memorable sentence: "If only Malthus, instead of Ricardo, had been the parent stem from which nineteenth-century economics proceeded, what a much wiser and richer place the world would be today!" (Ibid pp. 100–101) Also in 1933, the Ricardo-Malthus correspondence over "gluts" first became available in its entirety to Keynes. From this material to J. B. Say and Say's Law as the point at which the discipline took the wrong turn, would not have been a difficult path for Keynes to backtrack. And now he had the great names of the orthodox discipline arrayed against him: Ricardo, John Stuart Mill, Marshall, and Pigou. (Keynes [1936] 1973 pp.18–21) This, of course, paralleled the case of the *Economic Consequences of the Peace* with Keynes's treatment of the great figures of the Versailles Conference: Woodrow Wilson, Lloyd George, and Georges Clemenceau. Now it all came together and Keynes launched himself on his new project. No one date can be fixed for its beginning, but by December 1933 he had put down his first try at a Table of Contents for the new book (something Keynes always did very early in the composition process). Two years later, the book was finished and our world was never to be the same again.

Advance and Retreat

Was Keynes's "struggle for escape" a struggle to escape a prison largely of his own devising? I would argue that it was. Clearly, the impression he gave in *The General Theory* of a profession in thrall to a century-old idea (Say's Law) was not correct. After all, when Ricardo and Malthus were arguing about "gluts," industrialization and a monetary system that penetrated the entire economy were so new that the later notion of a business cycle could then only dimly be perceived. The notion that there was essentially no development of macroeconomic theory between Ricardo and Keynes will not stand up. Indeed, Keynes's own very respectful treatment of business cycle theories (and theorists) at the end of *The General Theory* (Keynes [1936] 1973 pp. 313–332) shows that he did not think the profession impotent in understanding, or even in generating, useful policy ideas to combat what all acknowledged in the 1930s to be a critical economic situation.

What was the case was that none of the policy recommendations to be derived from the business cycle or monetary theories of Keynes's day went far enough to satisfy the social consciousness of a product of Marshall's teaching and the Bloomsbury environment. The inevitability of the cycle meant the inevitability of less than full-employment much of the time, and Keynes would not accept that. Why try to be heard in an already over-crowded field when the end result would still be a disappointment? The concentration of monetary theory on prices rather than on output also led to a policy dead end.

However, when Keynes set out on his new path, those who came after him followed only part of the way. When Keynes rejected business cycle theory (by omission rather than overtly), he turned from its dynamic approach and took the static Marshallian microeconomic approach as his model. He sought to transfer the familiar Marshallian microeconomic concepts of demand, supply, equilibrium price, and equilibrium quantity from an individual market to the overall economy. He sensed that this approach brought with it new theoretical problems, and he made a start on trying to solve, or at least to define, them. To those who followed in his footsteps these problems appeared peripheral; they had no qualms about ignoring them.

These problems are important today not only because they expose fundamental difficulties in Keynes's theory but also because they underlie our inability to explain real-world conditions that fall outside Keynes's theory (despite his claim of the theory's generality). These problem areas are: (1) the relationship between microeconomics and macroeconomics and (2) the relationship between relative prices and the general price level. Obviously, problem 2 can be thought of as a subset of problem 1 and, to some extent, Keynes did think of it in that way.

Problem 1 was described by Keynes in a typical Keynesian turn of phrase. He said, "We have all of us become used to finding ourselves sometimes on the one side of the moon [microeconomics] and sometimes on the other [macroeconomics], without knowing what route or journey connects them, related, apparently, after the fashion of our waking and our dreaming lives" (Keynes [1936] 1973 p. 292). He rejected the disciplinary division of his day between "the theory of value and distribution" on the one hand and "the theory of money [or prices]" on the other. It was this division, Keynes argued, which was at the root of the confusion in economic theory. (Ibid pp. 292–293).

Keynes suggested several new bifurcations of economics without really settling on one as most appropriate. The one that is most familiar today was that between "the theory of the individual industry or firm" and "the theory of output and employment *as a whole.*" (Ibid p. 293, emphasis in original). By shifting the emphasis, if not the contents, in the micro/macro division, Keynes seems to have believed he had found a path between the two sides of the moon. However, it was by virtue of another division, namely, that "between the theory of stationary equilibrium and the theory of shifting equilibrium" that Keynes seems to have thought he had solved the problem (Ibid p. 293). In this schema, macrotheory ceased to be a theory of money and became incorporated into the theory of value and distribution although money still played a key role as "a subtle device for linking the present to the future" (Ibid p. 294). Keynes laid out no clear path between his "stationary equilibrium" and his "shifting equilibrium" models. We are still waiting for such a path although there is a large literature which purports to show the way. More precisely, we still have no logically consistent model that includes both microeconomics and macroeconomics. Consequently, we are often offered microeconomic policies as solutions to macroeconomic problems and, less often, the reverse. The theoretical ground for such policies is, to say the least, shaky.

The second problem, that of the general price level, Keynes spoke of as a measurement concept included in one of the "three perplexities which most impeded my progress in writing this book" (Ibid p. 37). He went on to say, "the well-known, but unavoidable element of vagueness which admittedly attends the concept of the general price level makes this term very unsatisfactory for the purposes of a causal analysis, which ought to be exact" (Ibid p. 39). It was to avoid this problem that Keynes introduced the notions of the labor unit and the wage unit. His audience quickly rejected those unfamiliar concepts.

The Nature of the Problem

At the heart of Marshallian microeconomics is the concept of the equilibrium price for a product. This price equates the quantity of product demanded with the quantity of product supplied in a market. The units of quantity are arbitrarily selected. It is only required that the same unit be used on both sides of the market. This equilibrium price is a *relative* price and therefore can be operationally defined. In an epistemological sense, therefore, it has meaning. Given the relative prices of any two products, the value of a unit of one in terms of units of the other is determinable.

What Keynes wanted to do was transfer this analytical device to the macroeconomic sphere, but he knew there was no way to add and average all the prices in an economy and thus arrive at *the* general price level at some moment in time. Similarly, he was aware that there was no unit of measurement which would serve to encompass all products and be summed to yield the economy's aggregate supply at that same moment in time.

Keynes's attempt to find a way out of his dilemma is laid out succinctly in Chap. 4 of *The General Theory*. He failed in this endeavor, but he knew there was a dilemma. Those who followed simply substituted *changes* in the price level for *the* general price level without comprehending that by doing this they were shifting from a Marshallian static theoretical basis to a dynamic one reminiscent of business cycle theory. Something similar occurred with the supply side concept.

When Alvin Hansen published his very influential A *Guide to Keynes* in 1953 (Hansen 1953), his treatment of Keynes on this point was cavalier: "Keynes's analysis could have proceeded quite as well had he adopted the price index as his deflator instead of his wage-unit ...Fundamentally the matter is of no great consequence. On balance Keynes's readers would probably have preferred constant-value dollars to constant wage-unit dollars" (Ibid p. 44). Hansen completely missed Keynes's point that there was a serious flaw in using the general price level (not the price index) as a measurement device. If Keynes's proffered solution to the problem was not an improvement (which it was not), that did not remove the original problem which concerned Keynes. Nevertheless, once the imprimatur of the acknowledged leader of American Keynes scholars was placed on this faulty interpretation, Keynes's "perplexity" was allowed to fade away.

Conclusion

We have long since become accustomed to having some economist publicly "explain" a rise in the price index by naming some item(s) in the index that rose in price more than the average increase for the relevant period. This view of things is thoroughly ecumenical – the political orientation of the then-current Administration or of the economist makes no difference. It is as if one explained the cause of a fever by reference to the behavior of the mercury in the thermometer. In the quieter arena of academia, we have become equally inured to the ubiquitous insertion of the letter "P" in macroeconomic equations or graphs to represent the general price level at a moment in time. Alas, the reality of the letter does not confer reality on the concept.

If this were just intellectual gymnastics practiced by academics, we might safely ignore it, but macroeconomic policy recommendations important to the well-being of all are expected of our profession.

We can have no more confidence in our policy recommendations than we have in the theory that underlies them. We badly need to strengthen our macrotheory base which today has an immense superstructure built on it. It is a curious twist in the history of economic thought that while Keynes was trumpeting his escape from classical theory, he was, in fact, quietly slipping the shackles of business cycle theory. At the same time, he was relying heavily on static Marshallian microtheory concepts to build his new dynamic theoretical model.

Sic itur ad astra.

References

Aslanbeigui N, Oakes G (2002) The theory arsenal: the Cambridge circus and the origins of the Keynesian revolution. J Hist Econ Thought 24(1):5–37

Haberler G (1939) Prosperity and depression. League of Nations, Geneva

Hansen AH (1953) A guide to Keynes. McGraw-Hill, New York

Hawtrey RF (1913) Good and Bad Trade. Longmans, London

Johnson ES, Johnson HG (1978) The shadow of Keynes. Basil Blackwell, Oxford

Keynes JM [1913] (1971a) Indian currency and finance. Vol. 1 of The Collected Writings of John Maynard Keynes. Macmillan, London

Keynes JM (1971b) A treatise on money, vols V and VI. Macmillan, London

Keynes JM (1972) Essays in biography, vol X. Macmillan, London

Keynes JM (1973) The general theory of employment, interest and money, vol VII. Macmillan, London

Keynes JM (1973) In: Moggridge D (ed) The general theory and after, Part I, vol XIII. Macmillan, London

Moggridge DE (1992) Maynard Keynes: an economist's biography. Routledge, New York

Chapter 26
John Maynard Keynes and the Theory of the Monetary Economy*

Hans-Joachim Stadermann and Otto Steiger

Introduction

Starting with an outline of the life and career of John Maynard Keynes, the paper focuses on his "Monetary Theory of Production" as a challenge to "the Classical School". As the title of the paper reveals, it analyses whether Keynes understood the conditions of the existing monetary economy.

The core of the paper consists of a critical assessment of Keynes's theories of money, of central banking, as well as of interest and employment. It demonstrates that, inspite of his promising distinctions between money of account and money proper as well as between individual and aggregate demand, there are severe flaws in Keynes's monetary analysis, especially: (1) the confusion of mutual clearing of debt titles with a substitution of money proper for debts, (2) the confusion of debt titles offered by a creditor with those offered by a debtor, (3) the confusion of an explanation of the rate of interest with the possibility of earning interest by giving up money, and, therefore, (4) badly established links between the rate of interest, money, and output.

These flaws explain why Keynes missed to correctly formulate the conditions of a monetary economy, especially with regard to the links between the rate of interest, good securities, and the creation of money. Unable to distinguish between debt titles bought by the central bank from creditors and titles bought by it from the Treasury, he eventually proposed "Government printing money" as the source

*Slightly revised and abridged version of Stadermann and Steiger, 2001, 283–321. Translation by Ariane Stadermann

H.-J. Stadermann (✉)
Berlin School of Economics and Law, Hochschule für Wirtschaft und Recht Berlin, Badensche Straße 50–51, 10825 Berlin, Germany
e-mail: stadermann@aol.com

of finance for current public expenditures. In the end, his insufficient monetary analysis contributes to his failure to overcome the orthodoxy of his time. In this, he resembles Marx and, therefore, Keynes can be called the Karl Marx of neoclassical economics.

An Outline of the Life and Career of John Maynard Keynes

John Maynard Keynes (1883–1946) is regarded as the greatest economist of the twentieth century. He was born in Cambridge as the only son of John Neville Keynes, economist and later registrar of Cambridge University.

Keynes was educated at Eton and studied mathematics (receiving a degree in 1905) as well as economics at King's College, Cambridge under Alfred Marshall and Arthur Pigou. He then entered the Civil Service, where he worked for the India Office. His first book in economics, *Indian Currency and Finance* (1913), grew out of this work.

In 1908, Keynes became lecturer in economics at Cambridge University, where in 1909 he submitted his dissertation *A Treatise on Probability* (published in revised form in 1921). Shortly after the outbreak of World War I, Keynes entered the Treasury, and by 1919 he was its principal representative at the Peace Conference at Versailles. His disagreement with the Peace Treaty led to his resignation and to his vehement denunciation of the treaty in *Economic Consequences of the Peace* (1919), which made him a world celebrity overnight.

In the wake of his success, Keynes resigned his lectureship at Cambridge and earned his living in the following two decades as a publicist on economic-political topics and from speculation on the stock market. At the same time, he became editor of *The Economic Journal* and also wrote a trilogy, with which he made fundamental contributions to monetary economics: *A Tract on Monetary Reform* (1923), *A Treatise on Money* (1930), and *The General Theory of Employment, Interest and Money* (1936). The latter publication paved the way for the new discipline of macroeconomics. Whether the book triggered a revolution in economic theory or not is still under discussion – also in this paper.

Between the two World Wars, Keynes was a leading figure in various British governmental bodies, amongst others, the famous Macmillan Committee (1929–1931). He also played a leading role in the negotiations with the United States government during World War II. In 1944, he became one of the architects of the Bretton Woods agreement, which established the International Monetary Fund and the World Bank.

Keynes also played a prominent role in the cultural and intellectual life of contemporary Britain. For many years, he was a member of the famous Bloomsbury Circle, and he was instrumental in establishing the Arts Council – interests which ranged far beyond the confines of economics.

Monetary Theory of Production as a Counter Argument to the Classical School

Just like Karl Marx aimed to overcome classical economics with his "critique of political economy" in the nineteenth century, Keynes also sought to bring down classical as well as neoclassical economics, which he both termed "the Classical School", in the first third of his century. He states that this school only dealt with "a special case", but cannot comply with the fundamentals of the economic system within which we live, "with the result that its teaching is misleading and disastrous if we attempt to apply it to the facts of experience" (Keynes 1936, 3).

Keynes's critique mainly argues against the *barter* or *real exchange economy* of the Classical School. He goes beyond the traditional argument of whether money is neutral or not and emphasises that money has to be regarded as an operational factor, which influences the economic motives and decisions of individuals. In his "Monetary Theory of Production" (Keynes 1933b), he specifically argues against Alfred Marshall's *Principles* (1890), where money is used as an important but ultimately neutral medium to determine the economy's barter exchange relations or the relative prices of goods. The Classical School define them as the decisive factors for economic activity. Instead, Keynes emphasises that statements about the barter economy are not necessarily transferable to the monetary economy. Despite this, he does not intend a total break from classical and neoclassical theory but aims to complete the barter theory the Classical School. Keynes interprets that school, as a specific case of his *General Theory* which only deals with the unusual state of full employment. A general theory of the economy should also analyse phenomena such as business cycles, crises, and unemployment in which money and interest are important factors (Keynes 1933b, 125).

In the *General Theory*, which indeed is also a theory of the rate of interest and money, one can – surprisingly – not find an analysis which really sheds light on the differences between barter and monetary economy. Keynes shows a non-elaborated theorem, which he believes to be capable of overcoming the false dichotomy of economic theory between value theory and monetary theory. Its central argument is that *"the importance of money essentially flows from its being a link between the present and the future."* But this only happens at the end of his theory of employment, developed in books I to IV of the *General Theory*, (Keynes 1936, 293).

The correct dichotomy, therefore, has to be stated as follows: the theory of value as a theory of relative prices in a barter economy works with given quantities of employment. All agents have stable expectations about the future. Consequently, no particular link is needed between the present and the future. The same is true with respect to a particular theory of money. However, money is necessary for a theory of the monetary economy within which macroeconomic variables, output and employment in particular, cannot be regarded as given. They need to be determined, because expectations are insecure and, consequently, changes in expectations about the future will trigger changes in decisions in the present. Therefore, the assumption of given employed resources cannot be sustained. The fact that expectations may change necessitates a medium to reduce the uncertainty resulting from this change. Such a medium is money as the most secure way of storing up value.[1]

Theory of Money

So what does Keynes consider to be money, and how does he explain its origin, and what does he think about its role in the economic process? In the *General Theory*, he only discusses the latter question. The quantity of money M can be created without any problems as "loanable funds" or "pool" by the banking system in the form of M_1 and M_2, depending on the demand of the public for transaction and speculation funds, L_1 and L_2, respectively (Chap. 15). Keynes is aware of the difference between non-interest-bearing money and interest-bearing claims on money. At the same time, however, he does not only consider central bank money to be part of the money supply – banknotes and credit balances at the central bank – but also demand deposits and time deposits up to three months at commercial banks (Keynes 1936, 167, fn. 1).

How the demand for cash, needed for current transactions of the economic agents, is to be fulfilled, is not considered by Keynes in Chap. 15. He is content with the general conclusion that the quantity M_1 changes independently from the rate of interest, i, and is directly associated with changes in aggregate income, Y. He is only interested in the creation of money for the purpose of speculation, M_2. Here the focus is on the rate of interest or the price of fixed-interest-bearing securities and, consequently, the variation of this part of the money supply by open market operations of the central bank. This relationship creates the opportunity for a monetary policy capable to regulate investment by the rate of interest. The benchmark for investment, however, is the long-term interest rate which is not determined directly by the money market. The central bank – limited to transactions on the money market – can only try to influence the rate of interest on the capital market. Therefore, according to Keynes, the central bank – instead of just buying and selling short-term securities – should also enter into long-term engagements with the aim of directly influencing the rate of interest in the capital market (Keynes 1936, 197). This unusual conclusion – unusual at least with regard to the state of the predominant theory of banking of that time – is derived from Keynes's analysis of money as *State money* in his *Treatise on Money*, which is heavily influenced by Georg Friedrich Knapp (1905).

---

[1] Keynes does not even ask how this insecurity could be overcome by the use of forward contracts.

Keynes starts the *Treatise* with a promising distinction between *money of account* and *money proper*, which is based on the works of James Steuart (1767, I, 526) and Ralph Hawtrey (1919, 2).[2] Similar to their approaches, Keynes regards money of account as the primary concept of the theory of money, as it directly stems from debts, and money proper can exist only in relation to a money of account.

"A money of account comes into existence along with debts which are contracts for deferred payment, and price lists, which are offers of contracts for sale or purchase. Such debt and price lists, whether they are recorded by word of mouth or by book entry on baked bricks or paper documents, can only be expressed in terms of a money of account."

"Money itself, namely that by delivery of which debt contracts and price contracts are *discharged*, and in the shape of which a store of general purchasing power is *held*, derives its character from its relationship to the money of account, since the debts and prices must first have been expressed in terms of the latter. Something, which is merely used as a convenient medium of exchange on the spot, may approach to being money, inasmuch as it may represent a means of holding general purchasing power. But if this is all, we have scarcely emerged from the stage of barter. Money proper in the full sense of the term can only exist in relation to a money of account" (Keynes 1930a, 3).

Furthermore, Keynes emphasises that money in any case has to be legal tender which, therefore, must be accepted as a means of dissolving debts, not just as a means of barter to enable the transaction of goods. At the same time, however, he always considers money proper as State money, whose quality and quantity is determined arbitrarily by government, which means that the latter can also change the money's quality over time.[3]

According to Keynes, this State money has existed as the only money in the crude form of monetary economy for millennia. A development in the monetary system only began in early modern times, when it was discovered that debts denominated in a money of account could be used as a substitute for money proper when winding up credit contracts. Keynes calls these titles "bank money" and emphasises that they must not be confused with money proper. The discovery of bank money led to a revolution in the monetary system, as soon as the State in the 18th century declared its own debt titles as legal tender. "The state may then use its chartalist prerogative to declare debt itself is an acceptable discharge of a liability" (Keynes 1930a, 5). He refers to the French Revolution and – without mentioning it explicitly–to

---

[2] See also Hawtrey's (1930, 545) remarks that debts are not defined by money, but that "money must be defined in terms of debts". Neither Steuart nor Hawtrey are acknowledged by Keynes.

[3] Keynes's notion of State money is slightly misleading, as is it not bound to the existence of genuine states. In a historic discourse about the development of money, he shows that State money had already existed in early societies as commodity money, where authorities are supposed to have determined what quantity of certain goods (such as cereals or goats) had to be the standard unit used as money of account in loan contracts (Keynes, 1930a, 10–12).

the revolutionary authorities' issue of *assignats*.[4] The missing properties of money in such State paper notes had been demonstrated correctly by James Steuart (1767, I, 131 f.) and Jean-Baptiste Say (1803, 283).[5] However, seemingly unimpressed by their findings, Keynes (1930a, 6; emphasis added) maintains that such notes are money. "A particular kind of bank money is then transformed into money proper – a species of money proper which we may call *representative money*. When, however, what was merely a debt has become money proper, it has changed its character and should no longer be reckoned as a debt, since it is of the essence of a debt to be enforceable in terms of something other than itself."[6]

In this, Keynes makes a serious mistake, which up until now has not been corrected in the literature about money. He confuses the mutual netting of claims, which make the use of money redundant, with the substitution of money for claims, which he wrongly calls bank *money*. Within banking operations, this netting of liabilities is generally feasible without any problems: a creditor's claims for money can be netted off with claims for money against third parties instead of payment, i.e. instead of a transfer of money. However, the liability does *not* substitute *money* in this case but a clearing of liabilities is simply substituted for the *payment* of money. This may at first sight seem like splitting hairs, but the distinction is an important one. Its omission in Keynes's work makes the distinction between genuine money and State notes, brought into circulation at a forced rate, impossible. The same flaw occurs in his discussion of "bank money", where he misinterprets various kinds of claims. "Bank money" does not just include bills of exchange and cheques, with which the public can bring mutual claims or claims

---

[4] In the case of the *assignats* that from 1789 onwards were issued for disowned church possessions of land, royal domains and the land possessions of emigrants, the necessary securities did not exist. They lacked the opportunity to safely enforce them. It was lacking because they could only be transferred into private *property* from the *possession* of the State through a competing public. At the same time, it was predetermined that, as soon as there was a desire to redeem these titles, the competition would not cease to exist until the price of the land had risen toward infinity and the value of the *assignats* had fallen to zero.

The original *assignats* issued at sight at the *Caisse de l'Extraordinaire* were never paid at all. They were received in payment for the national domains bought by competing individuals. However, as has been admirably shown by Jean-Baptiste Say, their nominal value could never give any determinate value to the *assignats*, because the value of the former increased exactly in proportion as that of the latter declined. The Treasury did not bother about this, because the rise in the price of its domains enabled it to cash a greater amount of *assignats* and re-issue new ones for its expenditures, without enlarging the quantity of the *assignats*. The Treasury was not aware that, notwithstanding these advantages, the rise in the price of the domains meant a rapid devaluation of the *assignats*. "The error was discovered in the end, when it was impossible any longer to purchase the most trifling article with any sum of *assignats*, whatever might be its amount. The next measure was to issue *mandats*, that is to say, papers purporting to be an order for the absolute transfer of the specific portion of the national domains expressed in the *mandat*: but, besides that it was then too late, the operation was infamously executed" (Say 1803, 283).

[5] See more detailed Stadermann and Steiger (2011 p XXX). On Say confer also fn. 4 above.

[6] Most interestingly, Keynes's idea of "representative money" has its renaissance in the Post Keynesian theory of money, especially by Randall Wray (1998); see more detailed Steiger 2005.

against their bank deposits into circulation, but also banknotes which constitute a claim against the issuing bank. It is this misconception, which allows Keynes (1930a, 14; and see 1930b, 235) to maintain that "the evolution of bank money in the shape of bank notes [shows] the way towards representative money".

Keynes's concept that State liabilities – unlike private ones – could be transformed into money without any problems, stems from his experience as civil servant at the Treasury during World War I. To finance Britain's war expenditures, so-called "government-issued treasury notes" were declared legal tender. The Treasury could deliver them to the Bank of England up to the amount of a book loan granted by the Bank. The treasury notes sooner or later ended up in the hands of the commercial banks which received the notes by discounting (not rediscounting) bills of exchange approved by the Bank of England for this purpose. The resulting growth in the supply of money, in combination with government spending, created cash surpluses at the commercial banks which they used to purchase treasury bills, thereby filling again the cash accounts of the Treasury. Until all treasury notes were replaced by bills of exchange, approved by and in the possession of the Bank of England, the Bank owned a reserve of treasury notes and, accordingly, the Treasury cash at the Bank (Cunliffe Report 1918, §§ 9–14).

Keynes (1930a, 9) explicitly calls the State notes a "reserve" of the Bank of England for its central bank money. "The State money held by the central bank constitutes its 'reserve' against its deposits. These deposits we may term *central bank money*." This detour *via* the Bank of England, the exchange of State notes against central bank money, Keynes regards as superfluous. However, foregoing central bank money, Keynes (1930b, 201) considers unfeasible for reasons of practicality. He assumes that the Treasury, unlike the central bank, would have no way of controlling the demand deposits of the commercial banks. This would lead to a creation of bank money, like State money without restrictions, if the commercial banks expanded their deposits in step. Under such circumstances, even the smallest incident would show the inherent instability of the entire system, as individual commercial banks, competing with each other, could oppose neither to an increase nor a decrease in the quantity of bank money. An individual commercial bank would only be able to do this if its competitors had to equal out their balances with money they could not create themselves, central bank money.[7] Only these banknotes would threaten those banks with a withdrawal of cash, which created deposits faster. The existence of a "bank of banks" issuing this money would, furthermore, offer the facility to even out an insufficient cash balance by the delivery of assets when needed. The central bank also offers to act as a clearinghouse facilitating the easy netting off of balances between banks (Keynes 1930a, 24 f.).

---

[7] An idea of this kind pre-supposes the, however insufficient, assumption that commercial banks would offer demand deposits or banknotes in loan agreements to the public, not against goods securities but by purchasing unsecured debt titles. But if the 'monetary authority' issued banknotes against good securities, this is impossible. Good securities cannot be provided by commercial banks but by purchase in loan agreements, just as much as they cannot provide banknotes if they do not sell good securities temporarily to the central bank.

After the end of the war, the opportunity to continue the issue of State notes no longer existed. However, they remained in circulation until 1928. This allowed Keynes to transfer his idea of money proper, derived from the debt title treasury note, to interest-bearing loans of public authorities. The fact that the acquisition of money by the Treasury was done within the same institutional framework, even after the issue of treasury notes had ended, may have contributed to this view. According to the Banking Act of 1948, the Chancellor of the Exchequer is even until today not obliged to go directly to the open market, but will, in a first step, receive an advance in central bank money from the Bank of England and, in return, hand over treasury bills. The Bank then decides whether to keep the quantity of central bank money constant by selling the bills to the public or to increase it by keeping them in their reserves. This has remained the *modus operandi* of the Bank of England until our times. The Government, therefore, still has the option to *print money*.[8]

It used to be the practice that the Chancellor of the Exchequer would even determine the rate of interest for this transaction. Only in connection with the demands for independence of central banks in the European Monetary Union, this practice has been modified in so far as the *Monetary Policy Committee* of the Bank of England now determines the rate of interest. This at least provides the option of financing under market conditions, even though the Bank still has the right to determine the rate of interest in outright transactions.

After all, Keynes's ideas of the creation of money lack solid underpinning. He confuses debt titles, which *creditors* bring into circulation out of their funds of claims, with titles offered directly on the market by *debtors*. Although all these titles represent liabilities, only the creditor, not the debtor may use them as substitution for payment in money proper. Contrary to Keynes's opinion, a mere recognition of a debt is not a substitute for money, but the opportunity to *borrow* money within a credit contract for a specified period of time.

---

[8] See Begg et al., *Economics* (1984), pp. 385 f.; emphasis added): "There are two ways in which the PSBR [Public Sector Borrowing Requirement] can be financed. First, the Government can borrow from domestic residents. To do so, it sells financial securities, government bills and bonds, to domestic residents. How does this happen?

"The government sells securities to the Bank [of England] in exchange for the cash it needs to meet its deficit. In turn, the Bank undertakes an open market operation selling these securities on the open market in exchange for cash. At the end of the process, domestic residents are holding interest-bearing government securities but the money supply is unchanged. Through its deficit spending, the government has put back into the economy exactly the cash it withdrew from the economy in selling securities in exchange for cash. And the Bank, through its sale of securities, has replenished the cash it initially lent the government.

"Second, the government can finance the deficit by *printing money*. Actually, it sells securities to the Bank in exchange for cash, which is then used to meet the excess of spending over tax revenue. The stock of government securities held by commercial banks or private citizens is unaltered but the monetary base has increased. The money supply will increase by a larger amount because of the money multiplier".

Theory of Central Banking

The weaknesses of Keynes's monetary theory become apparent in his theory of central banking, which he develops in book VII of the *Treatise* (1930b, 187–347). There, he develops the idea that the central bank could control the reserves of commercial banks to the extent to which it has control over its own assets. The aim of controlling the reserves is to stabilise the economy's net investments by regulating the rate of interest. The central bank has the following assets at its disposal: (1) gold and foreign currency, (2) investments in securities and (3) loans to commercial banks. To Keynes, gold and foreign currencies only are of interest in connection with safeguarding the parity of the domestic currency. Therefore, he alone focuses on the two latter items. By buying and selling securities, i.e. transactions on the open market, or, alternatively, variations in granting loans by discounting bills of exchange at varying discount rates, the central bank has the opportunity to regulate the quantity of central bank money in a way that would counterbalance disequilibria within the economy as a whole. Such situations always occur if investment, I, differs from savings, S, or, in other words, the market rate of interest, i, and Wicksell's natural rate of interest, n, are unequal.

If I is lower than S, or i is greater than n, this means that speculators anticipate a slump, which is characterised by a preference to hold "bank money" rather than corporate bonds,[9] as it is expected that the bonds may later be purchased at a lower price. The opposite situation, i.e. if I is greater than S or i lower than n, indicates a boom in speculation. Holding corporate bonds is preferred to holding "bank money", as it is expected that bonds can later be sold at a higher price.

Out of the two scenarios, the following recommendation for the central bank's operations to bring the economy back to equilibrium can be derived: (1) by buying securities and, consequently, lowering the rate of interest, it can counterbalance a slump in speculation and (2), conversely, by selling securities or increasing the discount rate, it can slow down a boom in speculation.

Furthermore, debt titles issued by public authorities can be used by the central bank to regulate the quantity of money. Keynes does not make a distinction between titles the Bank purchased under market conditions and the Treasury notes it received from the Chancellor of the Exchequer and then has to sell on the open market to forestall an expansion of the quantity of central bank money.

At first sight, the difference between the two ways of creating money seems to be only a technical one. Equal results in monetary policy are imaginable under both methods. However, institutional circumstances will lead to opposite results.

---

[9] Keynes's emphasis on the difference between holding bank money and holding corporate bonds only becomes understandable when considering the British financial system. Direct loans of banks to private companies, so-called *industrial loans*, are only granted for investment in working capital, i.e. wages, raw material, *etc.* Loans for investment in fixed assets are not granted directly by the banks, but are financed by the asset owners on the markets for bonds and equities. That is why they are called *financial loans*. If they cannot debit their deposits at the banks, the proprietors of these assets ask for bank loans, and will then purchase the titles from brokers.

The British system requires a strong government and a central bank policy consequently focussing on the stability of its currency to achieve an equilibrium rate of interest on the money market, which will encourage investors to risk their assets at this rate as security for generating money. This will always be the case if (1) assets are purchased that can be sold as readily as those assets which have to be collateralized for the acquisition of money and (2) the nominal rate of interest, which has to be paid for the acquisition of money, is sufficiently compensated for by the expected rate of return of the assets acquired. This means that whenever assets are demanded as securities for refinancing at the central bank, the problem can arise that the supply of suitable securities to maintain the current circulation of money will be insufficient. This will in any case occur if the asset proprietors expect to only see, with the money they get for their good securities, investments in nominal assets generating too small a return, because the assets and the capital invested will be devalued dramatically by inflation. In this case, the central bank would, according to Keynes, still issue money, namely against titles which it needs to keep in its portfolio because it bought them at its own risk and which it hopes to sell at a later date on the market.

However, the sale of securities on the market is, in a non-interventionistic central banking system, ensured by market forces, i.e. the interplay of rate of interest and price of securities. Debt titles, carrying a rate of interest estimated to be too low by the market, will receive a higher equilibrium return by a decline of the price at which they are traded. Consequently, a sufficient supply of money at the market is not only ensured if the government is particularly stringent in its budgetary practices and the central bank is particularly concerned with stability. It is mainly ensured, as the creation of money is only based – besides the rate of interest – on good securities. This rationale is unknown to Keynes, because he never focuses on good securities in the relationship between commercial banks and the central bank as he definitely does with respect to that between banks and non-banks. Obviously, he realises that commercial banks always have to pay attention, not only to credible promises to pay interest for their loans but also to sufficient delivery of good securities. Thereby, Keynes distinguishes between (direct) industrial loans for investment in working capital and (indirect) financial loans for investments in fixed assets. Generally, the securities provided for direct loans consist of the own capital of loan seeking corporations, usually their machinery. For indirect loans, the securities provided are the good securities of asset proprietors who buy corporate bonds with bank loans. Keynes's discussion of securities, however, only aims to invalidate the prejudice that financial loans are more insecure for banks than industrial loans. The former contain a speculative element and are not self-liquidating. Self-liquidation happens when industrial loans are used as working capital for the production of commodities (Keynes 1930b, 310–312).[10]

---

[10] Keynes (1931, 150–158) gives an in-depth discussion of the meaning of securities in credit contracts and the dangers that are linked with their devaluation.

Pursuant to Keynes's (1930b, 243) opinion, the central bank is not led by the profit motive, but a public or monetary authority, guided by the interests of society. "What the law – or, failing the law, the force of a binding conventions – should attend to is the regulation of the reserves of the member banks, so as to ensure that the decision as to the total volume of bank money outstanding shall be centralised in the hands of a body whose duty it is to be guided by considerations of the general social and economic advantage and not of pecuniary profit." Good securities, therefore, are of no interest to the central bank, as opposed to commercial banks. Basically, its task is to purchase potentially high-risk debt titles of the government to correct the outcome of the market caused by the profit motive, in order to stabilise the general price level or to reflate output after a contraction (Keynes 1930a, 227). Such ideas have always been met with enthusiastic applause from the audience who hardly worried that intervention of this kind could, to paraphrase a parable by Keynes, be one of those remedies that would cure the disease of unemployment by killing the patient (Keynes 1936, 323), the monetary economy. Keynes's ideas seem even stranger when it is considered that German monetary theory already at the beginning of the twentieth century had developed convincing distinctions between "paper money", issued as State notes, and money proper, issued by credit banks. Wilhelm Lexis (1901, 15), for instance, had clearly concluded that "paper notes" issued by the state "exclusively serve the issuer ... as a means of *borrowing*". Therefore, they have to be distinguished from private securities, such as bills of exchange, and are dramatically different from banknotes.

In his enthusiasm for the alleged victory of "bank money" over money proper and the transformability of state debt titles into money proper, Keynes only insufficiently looks for an analysis of the conditions and operations of the central bank within a monetary economy. His judgement about this institution, therefore, remains contradictory. On the one hand, he assumes that commercial banks could infinitely increase the quantity of demand and time deposits, if they act in step and are not bound by the restriction of adjusting balances with a kind of money they cannot create themselves. On the other hand, he emphasises that the central bank can, without restrictions, create money for the Chancellor of the Exchequer, because it is not the central bank but he who decides in the end what has to be accepted as money proper in loan contracts and economic transactions.

Keynes reaches the first conclusion, because he does not ask the crucial question: against what are those demand and time deposits generated? Had he noticed that such deposits are generally only to be granted against good securities, he would have also recognised that nobody in the banking system would pledge good securities for deposits if he could not realise them by investment or consumption activities, which would compensate for the loss of unrestricted disposal of his property. Consequently, an infinite expansion in the volume of demand and time deposits certainly would not occur.

Keynes reaches his second verdict, because he overlooks that the restriction to the expansion of private loans does not apply to the Chancellor of the Exchequer, if he can always trigger the creation of new means of payment (representative money) against his treasury bills. The loss of stability, which Keynes expects from a system in which commercial banks are not controlled by the central bank, would arise from the public sector which can finance itself at will with the help of the central bank. Consequently, the central bank will decide either not to increase the monetary basis as far as the public sector's demand for money is expanded or it will do just that. In the first case, it would have to sell the treasury bills of the Chancellor of the Exchequer as liquidity papers to the non-banks. By doing this, savings each time will be withdrawn from private investments, and they will increase the stock of State-issued bills. This would result in what Keynes (1936, 220 f. and 376 f.) describes as nationalisation of investments in Chaps. 16 and 24 of his *General Theory*: constantly increasing the inducement to invest by "State action... as a balancing factor" to compensate for the decline of the private investor, i.e. "the euthanasia of the rentier, of the functionless investor". This would be a situation in which the State would abolish exactly those market forces, which Keynes in his supposedly revolutionary theory believed would be able to explain better than the Classical School. In the second case, the central bank would have to accept a collapse of the value of money. Inflationary expectations would be on the rise, but the rate of interest would at the same time decline due to the over-supply of money. Instead of being channelled into public projects, investment would gravitate towards securities in foreign currencies. This would be the case until, by rising exchange rates and prices, demand and supply on the money market would allow for a rising rate of interest which in the end, in accordance to the conditions created by financial and monetary policy, would be again at an equilibrium level and, thereby, counter-balance the initially intended effects (see more detailed Stadermann 1996, 141–148).

Theory of Interest and Employment

The weaknesses in Keynes's theories of money and central banking continue to reappear in his theory of employment in the *General Theory*. His analysis of the links between employment, interest and money differs from that in the *Treatise* in two aspects, the second being the result of the first. While in his *Treatise* aggregate output is regarded as constant, in the *General Theory* it is considered to be a variable. Therefore, investment and savings are always equilibrated by a variation in output, and they are not a result of changes in the rate of interest. This, in turn, downgrades the (neoclassical) theory of the rate of interest to a "bootstrap" theory. The rate of interest needs a new explanation.

In Chap. 13 of the *General Theory*, Keynes argues that the decision to accumu-late savings out of a given income merely means a reduction of consumption. If this is true, savings are not, as in the Classical School, brought into equilibrium with investment by the rate of interest. Interest only matters when it comes to deciding on how to hold the income saved. Savings could be held as "bank money", as fixed-interest-bearing securities, or as direct investment in real capital assets. Only when choosing between "bank money" and bonds, which Keynes considers as a case of retaining vs. giving up money and, therefore, money's *liquidity premium*, the rate of interest could emerge. This assumption seems to be strange in two ways. On the one hand, the existence of money is taken for granted (and therefore ignored) when it comes to choosing between "bank money" and bonds, and also ignored is the fact that the rate of interest already stems from the credit creation of money by the central bank. Keynes confuses the opportunity to gain interest by giving up money with an explanation of the rate of interest itself (see more detailed Heinsohn und Steiger 1996, 194–206; and see 2000a, 496).[11] On the other hand, it needs to be considered that "bank money" *per se* already carries a rate of interest, even if simply a lower one than that in the credit market. In actual fact, it would only be necessary to consider a choice between hoarding of central bank money and interest-bearing titles in general. The fact that Keynes uses the term "hoarding" seems to be evidence for this. However, this contradicts his linking of holding money to speculation funds. The latter consists of "bank money", which is held by those who consider the level of the current rate of interest on bonds as insufficient with respect to the uncertainty of their future rate (Keynes 1936, 208 f.). Whenever expectations are certain, this explanation of the rate of interest is redundant, as demonstrated already by Marshall (1908, 73; see more detailed Stadermann and Steiger 2001, 278–280).

Keynes's new theory of the rate of interest becomes a significant part of his principle of "*the effective demand*", which, as the decisive determinant of output and employment, he regards as the core of the *General Theory* (Keynes 1936, 25). He develops the principle in Chap. 3 as a counterpart to the law, which he like others falsely accredits to Say and according to which any supply will create its own demand, thereby insuring "that crises *do not occur*" (Keynes 1933b, 125).[12] Keynes gives the example of an individual producer who generates returns on the goods market to cover his costs of production. He does this by increasing the employment of his resources until marginal costs equal marginal returns, i.e. until he maximises his profits. Keynes realises that the producer thereby generates income for the factors of production, other producers and for himself.

He then transforms the individual producer's choice-theoretical constellation to one applicable for producers in the aggregate. For that purpose, Keynes develops an aggregate supply function in which increasing employment, N, leads to a rise of the

---

[11] Hajo Riese (2000, § 39, 493) has tried to defend the liquidity premium theory of the rate of interest by formulating the idea that in creating money the central bank produces "money as an asset" and at the same time "foregoes the free disposal of its asset 'money'". However, he overlooks that the central bank does not have the option at all, other than a proprietor of money, to hold the money it created. Therefore, the central bank cannot forego its holding either. The notes that are returned to the central bank are no longer money and, therefore, deleted from its books. Furthermore, Riese does not recognise that in the process of creating money, assets are valued in money when purchased by the central bank, but this valuation does not turn money into an asset. Look at comments on Riese by Heinsohn and Steiger 2000b, § 10, 518, and Stadermann 2000, § 8, 535.

[12] Stadermann and Steiger (2001, 134–140) have shown that a closer look at Say's famous Chap. 15, "Of the demand or the market for products", in his *Treatise* (1803, 132–140) reveals that "Say's law" does not contain remarks about crises, but in fact is a theory of stagnation or growth. Its formulation as a theory of the impossibility of crises is due to David Ricardo in 1817 and James Mill in 1821.

Fig. 26.1 Aggregate demand
function and aggregate
supply function modified
by Say's law

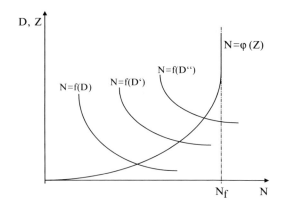

"aggregate supply price", Z. This in turn leads to the equation $Z = \varphi(N)$, where Z is the price per output unit multiplied by the aggregate quantity of output. The prerequisites necessary for this function are given by the assumption of fixed nominal wages and production techniques.

This assumption could, with some modification, be made to conform to Say's law as formulated by Ricardo and James Mill. An increase in aggregate demand, stemming from increased employment and income, which Keynes calls "aggregate demand price", D – meaning price per unit demanded multiplied by the aggregate quantity of demand –, would lead to a softening or outward shift of the budget restriction of consumers.[13] This, in turn, would trigger a right and upward move of the position of the traditional aggregate demand function, $N = f(D)$, in proportion to the increase of employment on the traditional aggregate supply function, $N = \varphi(Z)$. This will continue until full employment, N_f, is achieved (see Fig. 26.1).

---

[13] It has to be noticed that an individual demand curve, other than an individual supply curve, is derived from a *given* income. Changes in income, therefore, lead to a *move* on the supply curve and to a *shift* of the demand curve. For the meaning of this difference for the specification of Keynes's aggregated demand and supply functions see Hagemann and Steiger 1988, 27–32.

The same applies to the aggregate demand curve, moving from top left to bottom right, $N = f(D)$, as seen in *graph 1*, which pre-supposes that aggregate income has to remain constant. Only under this condition, the statement of the aggregate demand curve, which may at first sight seem surprising, holds true that with increasing employment, N, the aggregate demand price, D, has to fall or that N can only rise together with a declining D. If N, however, is rising, this can only mean that in this particular D, made up by price level and quantity of demand, the price level has to fall – admittedly by more than the quantity of demand is rising.

Basically, $N = f(D)$ does not say anything else than the aggregate demand curve, AD, in macroeconomic textbooks, namely, that when the price level, P, is falling, aggregate real income, Y, will rise: $Y = f(P)$. The only difference is that, instead of income, the nominal volume of money, M, has to be held constant, as can be seen by the derivation of an AD-curve from an IS/LM-model with variable P.

However, Keynes rejects any such possibility, as he believes that an automatic adjustment of D to Z would lead to employment being indeterminate. Accordingly, the economy would continue to remain in an instable equilibrium until full employment of resources is reached. As distinct from the accepted view of neoclassical theory, Keynes considers full employment not to be the point of intersection between the demand and supply curve in the traditional wage-labour diagram of the labour market, but a condition under which aggregate supply of labour ceases to be elastic. A constellation of this kind, however, ignores the true law of the relationship between aggregate supply and aggregate demand, which is determined by effective demand. The latter Keynes (1936, 25) defines as follows: "The value of D at the point of the aggregate demand function, where it is intersected by the aggregate supply function, will be called *the effective demand*."

Effective demand, therefore, is the aggregate demand for consumption and investment goods, $D = f(N)$, expected by producers at a special level of employment. This expectation at the same time will limit the aggregate supply, $Z = \varphi(N)$, this being the reverse of the explanation of employment in the traditional school. Keynes, therefore, rejects the idea of a demand curve varying its position with and being itself independent of income. Instead he defines an aggregate demand curve on its own right, which appreciates the fact that an increased income, generated by an increase in employment, will not automatically and totally be spent for consumption or investment goods. Expenditure for consumption will rise with income, but according to a "psychological law" only by an amount lower than the increase in income meaning that the marginal propensity to consume, dC/dY, is smaller than 1 (one). This propensity will trigger the expected aggregate demand for consumption goods, $D_1 = \chi(N)$, which in turn determines the shape of the total demand curve: $D = f(N) = D_1(N) + D_2$ (see Fig. 26.2 below).

The term D_2, defined as $D_2 = \varphi(N) - \chi(N)$, is the aggregate demand for investment goods expected by the producers. Here Keynes does not further elaborate on investment, which he instead regards as exogenous. This allows him to determine the shape of the aggregate demand curve by the aggregate demand function for consumer goods. This, in turn, leads to the possibility to specify a clear point of intersection between the aggregate demand and supply curves. This point determines a quantity of employment, N_u, which can be lower than that of full employment, N_f (see Fig. 26.2 below, upper section).

Keynes's way of determining employment by effective demand has an inherent weakness, which becomes apparent when looking at the shape of the aggregate supply curve. This function shows over-proportional growth of aggregate supply when employment increases. This means that the marginal productivity of labour and, consequently, real wages, w/p, will decline with increasing employment (see Fig. 26.2, lower section). In Chap. 2 of the *General Theory*, Keynes (1936, 17) does not reject this apparent correlation between real wages and employment, which is at the heart of neoclassical theory, but reverses the functional relationship of the two terms: not the level of real wages determines the level of employment, but the level of the latter is the determinant of the level of real wages.

Fig. 26.2 Aggregate demand and supply curves according to Keynes's principle of effective demand

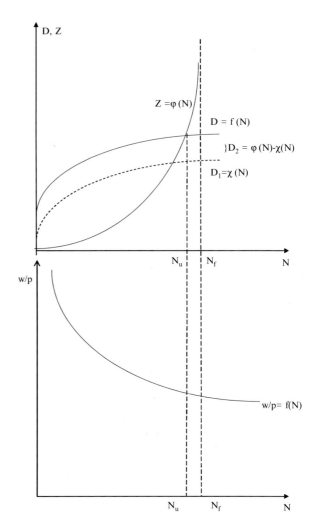

However, pursuant to Keynes's assumption of constant nominal wages, w, falling real wages have to be the result of a rising price level, p. A rise in effective demand by increasing employment can, therefore, only be achieved by selling money illusion to labourers, and this will, in every case, lead to a decline in labour productivity.

The success of recommendations based on this theory is also bound to further conditions that Keynes does not elaborate on. In order to achieve an increase in the price level and a decrease in labour productivity under the condition of constant nominal wages, an increase in output needs to be lower than an increase in labour. In his discussion of the financing of public work programmes, Keynes assumes, not surprisingly, as will be shown in Section "Employment Policy and the Financing of the Central Bank" below, that a decrease in real wages by an increase in the price level can be achieved without any problems by simply creating "new money".

The problem – with respect to the employment level – of an insufficient effective demand could not arise in Keynes's model, if the marginal propensity to consume is equal to one or if the income not consumed, i.e. savings, is spent in total for investment purposes. In both cases, Say's law (according to Ricardo's und James Mill's interpretation) would be applicable. Keynes rejects the first scenario because of a propensity to consume smaller than one according to his "psychological law". The second scenario he rejects because he assumes that there are no market forces at work which could automatically raise the level of investment required for full employment. To Keynes, the problem of controlling the economy as a whole is, therefore, one of controlling that part of effective demand, which will close the – with rising income – widening gap between expected demand for consumption goods and expected aggregate demand in a way that full employment can be achieved.

Keynes's discussion of the relationship between aggregate supply and aggregate demand shows three options to increase effective demand (see Fig. 26.2 above, upper section): (1) moving the total supply curve, Z, to the right by lowering nominal wages; (2) moving the consumption curve, D_1, upwards by a redistribution of income which will lead to a higher propensity to consume; and (3) shifting the demand for investment function, D_2, upwards. Keynes provides an in-depth discussion about lowering money wages in Chap. 19.[14] He arrives at the conclusion that this would be successful only if expected aggregate demand, D, would not be influenced by such a policy. Assuming this, however, would not be realistic, as a fall in wages will trigger a fall in the price of goods which, as a consequence, would mean deflation. This, in turn, would have an adverse effect on the *marginal efficiency of capital*, which measures the prospective yield of an investment by discounting it to the present. An increase in the marginal propensity to consume by redistribution of income would take up too much time. The main issue, therefore, lies in determining the expected aggregate demand for investment goods, complementary to consumption. However, this will be difficult to master due to uncertainty of prospective returns of capital assets, and as consumption is increasing at an under-proportional level, investment would have to increase constantly in order to support full employment of resources.

The calculation for investment demand, as discussed in book IV of his *General Theory*, is based on comparing the marginal efficiency of capital with the current rate of interest. The optimistic thought, therefore, that investment during slumps or booms could be counterbalanced by central bank policy, i.e. by interest rate policy as discussed in his *Treatise* no longer convince Keynes in the case of a slump, which according to his *General Theory* would mean unemployment. A policy of easy money does not lead to unlimited investment in corporate bonds. Consequently,

---

[14] Keynes obviously does not propose the idea, which has often been formulated by left-wing Keynesians to strengthen effective demand by an increase in money wages, as in his model this would lead to a leftward shift of the Z-curve, with the result of a decrease in effective demand. The only alternative would be an increase in wages, which would trigger an increase in *D1* or *D2*, thereby over-compensating the increase in Z. This, however, is just what is not feasible in his model.

there is no influx of money to producers for investment into fixed capital assets. This case in Chap. 15 is called a *liquidity trap*. Even those entrepreneurs whose marginal efficiency of capital is sufficiently high in relation to the current rate of interest, will not receive cash, as all additional money created by the central bank will be held as "bank money" because of an expectation of rising rates of interest.

Another one of Keynes's arguments against an optimistic view of the possibilities of the central bank refers to his insight that the rate of interest would fall more slowly than the marginal efficiency of capital, as output increases. The reasons for this argument, as developed in Chap. 17 of the *General Theory*, are the particular characteristics of money. Money differs from goods insofar as its elasticities of production and substitution are nearly equal to zero. The first characteristic means that an increased demand for money – as opposed to goods which are not money – does not lead to its increased supply, because "labour cannot be turned on at will by entrepreneurs to produce money in increasing quantities as its price rises in terms of wage unit" (1936, 230). The second characteristic means that an increase in the value of money in the case of deflation does not trigger – as opposed to non-money goods – a substitution of money by goods, which are now less expensive. This means that an increase in the value of money will not stimulate a demand for an alternative to money.

Keynes's discussion of money as a good with peculiar characteristics completely fails to recognise the importance of money as a means of guiding the production of goods. To reach this goal, it is necessary that money is only brought into circulation at the market rate of interest and against good securities, and not by arbitrary issue. Furthermore, money cannot be substituted by another good, as it is the basis of contracts in a monetary economy. Contracts, therefore, can only be satisfied by money. But first of all, the supposition of elasticity near zero fails practice in money market. Indeed, "money production" seems to be inelastic for producers of commodities. But it is not inelastic at all for proprietors of assets which are refinanciable at the central bank. These owners are able to pledge their property as long as it is free of liabilities. The proportion of property converted to money by creating temporary liabilities against the banking sector depends on the rate of interest and the marginal efficiency of capital. A difference between both rates has to equal the *property premium* at least.[15] If the property premium will not be realised in credit market, owners of suitable assets are not inclined to use their property as collateral. Keynes imagines that if commodity producing entrepreneurs are unable to "produce" money instead of goods (in case of deflation), then the market as a whole will be unable to do it. As a result of this, he argues that it is a task of fiscal policy to create increasing demand in the commodity market by printing money, as will be shown in the following section.

---

[15] The term "property premium" has been coined by Heinsohn and Steiger and is fundamental to their property theory of interest and money. It means the immaterial yield arising from the potential of property titles to be burdened and encumbered in a money loan; see Heinsohn and Steiger 1996, 15, 20–22, 91, 122 f, and 181 f.; and see 2000a, 484 and 499–501.

Employment Policy and the Financing of the Central Bank

In his discussion of the links between employment, the rate of interest and money, Keynes moves away from the conditions that determine a monetary economy. His economic-political recommendations, therefore, are inappropriate in this context. According to his argumentation, a slump cannot be met by central bank policy alone. Consequently, autonomous investments by the State should stabilise employment. In his economic-political publications prior to the publication of his *General Theory*, in which he vehemently favours State investment programmes, he simply remarks that they should be financed by loans (Henderson and Keynes 1929, 110; Keynes 1933a, 341 f.).[16]

In the *General Theory* itself, such programmes are not the central topic, although the necessity of fighting unemployment keeps cropping up. In his notes on mercantilism in Chap. 23, Keynes criticises the Classical School's idea that the rate of interest could, by market forces, be brought to a level that would give rise to the investment necessary for full employment. "In truth the opposite holds good. It is the policy of an autonomous rate of interest … and of a national investment programme directed to an optimal level of employment which is twice blessed in the sense that it helps ourselves and our neighbours at the same time." (1936, 349).

There are practically no statements in literature on how Keynes in his *General Theory* thought to finance his national employment programmes. This may have had something to do with the fact that his followers were not convinced that their master had thought of financing it by a central bank. However, this was exactly what Keynes had in mind. He openly talks about the government's printing money (1936, 200). As far as it is known to us, only Victoria Chick (1983, 318 f. and 335, fn. 1) has clearly revealed that Keynes indeed had in mind financing State investment programmes exclusively by central bank credit. However, she is also embarrassed to call it "printing money" because this could be "misleading" and prefers, therefore, the more harmless phrase "creating new money": "Keynes … was very specific about the source of finance for his 'public works': new money. … or newly-created money." However, as an adherent to the Post Keynesian State theory of money Chick is convinced that "the essence of the matter is well captured enough by …the phrase 'printing money'."

A quarter of a century before Keynes, in 1911, the opportunity to create new money was the prerequisite for Joseph Schumpeter's dynamic entrepreneur, who creates new combinations of goods. Schumpeter, however, did not consider the banking system as interplay of government, central bank and commercial banks; he only focused on commercial banks that grant loans. Just like Keynes, he intends to

---

[16] In Chap. 10 of the *General Theory*, in the famous Sect. 6 on burying and digging up banknotes as means against unemployment, "the term [public]'loan expenditure' … financed by borrowing from individuals" is mentioned in a footnote (Keynes 1936, 128 f., fn. 1). Although Keynes recognises that public loan expenditure "operates by increasing investment … and the propensity to consume", no analysis of its operation is given in the book; see further this section below.

prove that investments can be undertaken independently from prior savings. The money required for purchasing the means of production necessary for the new combinations does not come from savings, but from a creation of new money that is different from the money required for financing re-investments. "This [different] method of obtaining money is the *creation* of purchasing power by banks. The form it takes is immaterial. ... It is always a question, not of transforming purchasing power which already exists in someone's possession, but of the creation of *new* purchasing power *out of nothing* – out of nothing even if the credit contract by which the new purchasing power is created is supported by securities which are not themselves circulating media – which is added to the existing circulation. And *this* is the source from which new combinations *are* often financed, and from which they would have to be financed *always*, if results of previous development did not actually exist at any moment" (Schumpeter 1926b, 72 f.; the first three emphases added by the authors, following the German original, Schumpeter 1926a, 108 f).[17]

Contrary to Keynes's theory, Schumpeter's new money does not consist of central banknotes, which commercial banks could not possibly create, but of so-called "credit means of payment" like bank deposits and bank acceptances, i.e. claims on money which – not unlike Keynes's "bank money" – can also be used just like cash in transactions with non-banks. However, Schumpeter only reaches this conclusion because he – again not so unlike Keynes – makes a false distinction between money proper and "book money" used in the banking system. Schumpeter considers cash to be only coins, whereas he falsely regards banknotes to be credit means of payments. Although a banknote is usually issued in a loan contract, it must, however, not be confused with the loan itself, which is a claim on banknotes.

At first sight, there would not seem to be a problem with good securities, if money is created this way. If a bank can create something that can be used just as cash without any restriction, then it does not require securities; any claim against the bank can be fulfilled without difficulties. A consequence of this would be that if banks are not restricted by stocks of goods and ready cash when granting a loan, they could indeed lend money infinitely. Each improper use of loans for investment and each consumption of loans could be "corrected" *ex post* by the banks. Schumpeter sees that this is not really going to be possible and seeks reasons for the limitation of credit expansion. He finds his explanation in the potential failure of entrepreneurs as debtors to fulfil their obligations to pay interest and to redeem their liabilities if their innovations do not succeed. In this case, "the banker intervenes with purchasing

---

[17] In the first edition of his treatise, Schumpeter (1911, 197) formulates this idea less fiercely. Instead of letting the new money to be created "out of nothing", he assumes that "one could easily say that the banker creates money". Already in his first book, Schumpeter (1908, 417 f.) reveals a *"first-rate"* interest in the figure of the banker, who *"creates money himself*, e.g. *by issuing banknotes"*, without using his own property (or even that of his debtors). On Schumpeter's verdict that collateral, although of some advantage for a borrower, has nothing to do with the essentials of a money loan see Heinsohn and Steiger 1996, 241–257.

power drawn from the circular flow, for example with money saved by other people …
Hence the necessity of maintaining a reserve, which acts as a brake" (Schumpeter
1926b, 113).[18]

In saying this, Schumpeter reveals a fundamental lack of understanding of the
accounting principles of banking. Obviously, value adjustments on bad loans of
the bank have to be made at the cost of the bank's own capital. The bank would
immediately have to file for bankruptcy if its assets were already used up and if the
proprietors of the bank were unable to replace them. This also reveals that his
assumptions are incorrect about the necessity of a cash reserve as a substitute for
securities to be delivered by the entrepreneur as debtor or to be provided by the bank
as creditor in the form of own capital.

This problem cannot arise in Keynes's theory. The government cannot come into
a situation of over-indebtedness, as it uses the central bank like a gold mine for
printing money, meaning that it can substitute the money proper it lacks by "representative money" at any time.

Obviously, in the wake of Richard Kahn's discussion of the multiplier, Keynes
(1936, 128 f., fn. 1) notices that public works could be financed also by "borrowing
from individuals" where, however, a crowding-out of private investors by the rising
rate of interest would be impossible to prevent. This could not be counterbalanced
by a policy of easy money by the central bank alone, as Keynes concludes in Chap.
12 of *General Theory*. Instead he emphasises: "I expect the State … taking an even
greater responsibility for directly organising investment" (1936, 164). This method
of financing for such activities does not bother, as he develops, in Chap. 10 of the
General Theory, the idea that in fighting unemployment any kind of State-sponsored
activity is better than doing nothing at all. This will be especially true, however,
because the State is not concerned with profitability. Keynes illustrates this thought
with his well-known example of filling old bottles with banknotes and burying them
in disused coalmines with the intention of digging them up later on as a way to fight
unemployment, which "would be better than nothing" (1936, 129).

In Chap. 15, Keynes, then, only deals with what he feels is most important when
discussing "fiscal policy",[19] the financing of employment programmes. He considers this to be an alternative to what he calls monetary policy – the lowering of the
rate of interest by the central bank. His train of thought can be sketched as follows:
financing of public expenditure means an increase in the quantity of money, M,
which in turn will trigger an increase in national income, Y. In order for income to
increase more than only temporarily, the greater quantity of money must not only
increase the cash amounts hold for transactions, M_1, but also those hold for speculation, M_2. This will be the case because the recipients of the increased incomes will
not simply demand consumer goods, C, but will also invest in corporate securities
and, thereby, allowing entrepreneurs to demand capital goods, I. The purchase of

---

[18] The German original is even less precise; see Schumpeter 1926a, 162.

[19] As pointed out by Chick (1983, 318), "Keynes spoke of 'public works'; 'Keynesians' speak of
'fiscal policy'".

these assets will trigger a rise in their price, i.e. a decline in the market rate of interest, r, which in turn will further increase I and Y. At the same time, the increase in I will result in absorption of that part of the quantity of money not required for transaction purposes, i.e. the speculation funds. A policy of more money, implying lower rates of interest which lead to increased income, amounts to the same as a policy of easy money, meaning lower rates of interest which lead to more money and, thereby, to increased income.

The fact that Keynes approves of the nowadays frowned upon direct borrowing by the government from the central bank,[20] which ultimately means financing by the printing press, seems so incredible that we feel it is necessary to quote Keynes (1936, 200 f.; emphasis added) here in detail:

"The relations of changes of M to Y and r depend, in the first instance, on the way in which changes in M come about. Suppose that M consists of gold coins and that changes in M can only result from increased returns to the activities of gold-miners who belong to the economic system under examination. In this case changes in M are, in the first instance, directly associated with changes in Y, since the new gold accrues as someone's income. Exactly the same conditions hold if changes in M are due to *the Government printing money wherewith to meet its current [sic] expenditure*; – in this case also the new money accrues as someone's income. The new level of income, however, will not continue sufficiently high for the requirements of M_1 to absorb the whole of the increase in M; and some proportion of the money will seek an outlet in buying securities or other assets until r is fallen so as to bring about an increase in the magnitude of M_2 and at the same time to stimulate a rise in Y to such an extent that the new money is absorbed either in M_2 or in the M_1 which corresponds to the rise in Y caused by the fall in r. Thus at one remove this case comes to the same thing as the alternative case, where the new money can only be issued in the first instance by a relaxation of the conditions of credit by the banking system, so as to induce someone to sell the banks a debt or a bond in exchange for the new cash."

"It will, therefore, be safe for us to take the letter case as typical. A change in M can be assumed to operate by changing r, and a change in r will lead to a new equilibrium partly by changing M_2 and partly by changing Y and therefore M_1.

---

[20] Most astonishingly, still today even leading central bank theorists like Willem H. Buiter, chief economist of the European Bank for Reconstruction and Development and former member of the *Monetary Policy Committee* of the Bank of England, do not understand that such a financing leads to a debtor's money. In a recent paper, Buiter (2004, 45 f.; emphasis added) sees no difference in the effects between direct borrowing by the government from the central bank and in the open market:

"Can the Central Bank implement a helicopter drop of money on its own? ... In practise, Central Banks do not act as fiscal agents of the state in this way. This means that Governor Mervin King cannot send a £1,000 check, drawn on the Bank of England, to every household in the nation. He needs Chancellor Gordon Brown's help. Gordon Brown can implement the tax cut and borrow from the Bank of England to finance it. In the Eurozone, direct borrowing by national Treasuries from the ECB and the central banks of the ESCB [the European System of Central Banks] is not permitted, but *the same effect* can be achieved by the Treasury borrowing in the market and the Central Bank purchasing the same amount of Treasury debt in the secondary market."

The division of the increment of cash between M_1 and M_2 in the new position of equilibrium will depend on the responses of investment to a reduction in the rate of interest and of income to an increase of investment. Since Y partly depends on r, it follows that a given change in M has to cause a sufficient change in r for the resultant changes in M_1 and M_2 respectively to add up to the given change in M."

What is noticeable about this passage is that Keynes seems to know the correct way of creating money, namely, selling assets and delivering collateral by commercial banks to the central bank. However, his emphasis is not on the term *assets*, but *debts* or *bonds*, i.e. liabilities. Clearly, an asset, nominal asset, is always a liability. In creating money, however, the central bank is not interested in undertaking a transaction with the debtor of a title, but only with its creditor.[21] Obviously, Keynes does not understand the distinction between a *creditor's* and a *debtor's money*. Therefore, in his theory, the creation of central bank money through the purchase of assets from commercial banks does not differ from the purchase of liabilities from the government. The first scenario seems to be nothing but the more widespread method of creating money, which could easily be replaced by another, as "new money" in both cases and, therefore, new income would be created. It is apparent how Keynes focuses on technical processes but does not understand their meaning. Good securities as the basis of the creation of money by a central bank never occurred to him.

After all, in view of what we know from Keynes's discussion of State debts and money proper in general and from the practices of the Bank of England since 1948 in financing State expenditures in particular, this statement is hardly surprising. Furthermore, it is not surprising that nobody reproached Keynes for this, because James Steuart's principles of the creation of banknotes were buried in oblivion. Apart from some interesting insights on the subject by Jean-Baptiste Say and Henry Thornton (1802; see more detailed Stadermann and Steiger 2001, 179–184), no one has discussed the meaning of good securities in the process of creation of creditor's money for ages.

As shown in Section "Theory of Money" of this paper, Keynes blurs the difference between State debt titles and money proper. He claims that public liabilities could be converted without interference by the open market, just like private "bank money", into money proper by the Bank of England in the form of "representative money". In the same section, it was demonstrated how this is put into practice. It is always the Chancellor of the Exchequer who approaches the Bank of England first, which then has the *opportunity* to sell – by agreement with the Treasury – the State debt titles on the open market.

Keynes consequently defended such behaviour even after the publication of his *General Theory*. In a memorandum of May 29, 1939 to the Chancellor of the Exchequer, with a copy to the Governor of the Bank of England, Norman Montagu,

---

[21] Therefore, in the credit issue of banknotes in modern central banking systems like the Eurosystem, national central banks are forbidden to accept "as underlying assets debt instruments issued or guaranteed by the counterparty [commercial bank], or by any other entity with which the counterparty has close links" (ECB 2004, 41 and 43).

he develops the idea that the State, like a private debtor, could undertake expenditures *prior* to their financing. This difference had not existed in times when coins were the only currency. "But with modern representative money and a modern banking system, we know that the necessary 'finance' can be created by a series of 'book' or 'paper' transactions. The Treasury can 'pay' in effect by 'book' entries and the book entry can be transformed into a regular loan at a much later date" (Keynes 1939, 540).

However, only half a year later – in his recommendations of November 1939 on *How to Pay for the War* – these ideas no longer appear. Keynes (1940, 367–439) now recognises the danger of inflation resulting from such financing of government activities, as was experienced during World War I. That is why he recommends, instead of this financing Britain's war expenditures by compulsory savings, meaning that all recipients of income would have to invest a certain amount in the State-owned Post Bank.

Keynes as the Karl Marx of Neoclassical Economics

Keynes sees a policy of public employment programmes only as a relatively short-term intermediate solution. As a long-term perspective, which he discusses in Chaps. 16 and 24 of his *General Theory*, he imagines a quasi stationary economy, in which the marginal efficiency of capital and the rate of interest are brought down to almost zero. In such a state, no accumulation takes place, i.e. net investments are equal to zero and, maintenance of the capital stock apart, the entire surplus is consumed. Not unlike John Stuart Mill's famous discussion of stagnation, an increase in welfare could then only be achieved by non-economic processes. "Progress would result only from changes in technique, taste, population and institutions." (Keynes 1936, 220 f). But it is just these types of *stimuli* that neoclassical theory regards as crucial for change, too; the only difference being that they are thought to be caused by economic mechanisms.

However, more interesting than to compare Keynes with Mill is to confront him with Karl Marx, who just like Keynes tried to overcome the orthodoxy of his time. As we know, Marx's critique of classical economics did not succeed. Instead, he went so far as to insult "financial" capitalists as "parasites", which meant a fierce rejection of the rate of interest. In the end, Marx's proposal to nationalise property, which ultimately meant its abolishment, laid the foundation for the destruction of the monetary economy (Stadermann and Steiger 2001, 214 f.). Of course, Marx never understood the connection between property, i.e. good securities, and money. Instead, he developed the vision of an economy free from crises in which totally unleashed productive forces would arise from the abolishment of private property.

Also Keynes could not significantly weaken neoclassical economics with his criticism, as he substituted an insufficient analysis of the monetary economy with a theory that does not just omit the prerequisites of a monetary economy but also endangers them, not very unlike Marx's ideas. Just like Marx, Keynes furthermore believed that technical progress would resolve all the economic problems of mankind. Already prior to the Great Depression and, consequently, prior to his *General Theory*, in his article on "Economic Possibilities for Our Grandchildren" (Keynes 1928) he had wanted to prove that a farewell to economic problems is possible. The supply of goods that is already available in abundance he, therefore, reduces to a problem of administration. Marx probably did not have significantly different ideas when thinking about socialism. Keynes, therefore, can be called with due right the Karl Marx of neoclassical economics.

References

Begg D, Fischer S, Dornbusch R (1984) Economics. McGraw-Hill, London, 1997

Buiter WH (2004) A small corner of intertemporal public finance – new developments in monetary economics: two ghosts, two eccentricities, a fallacy, a mirage and a mythos. In: NBER Working Paper Series, No. 10524, May

Chick V (1983) Macroeconomics after Keynes: a reconsideration of the general theory. Ph. Allen, London

Cunliffe Report (Committee on Currency and Foreign Exchange after the War) (1918), *First Interim Report*, London: HMSO (British Parliamentary Papers), Cd. 9182

ECB (2004) The implementation of monetary policy in the euro area: general documentation on eurosystem monetary policy instruments and procedures, Frankfurt am Main. European Central Bank (ECB), February

Hagemann H, Steiger O (1988) Keynes's 'general theory' nach fünfzig Jahren. Duncker & Humblot, Berlin, pp 9–57

Hawtrey RG (1919) Currency and credit. Longmans, London, 1923

Hawtrey RG (1930) Credit. In: Encyclopaedia of the social sciences, vol III. Macmillan, New York, pp 545–550

Heinsohn G, Steiger O (1996) Eigentum, Zins und Geld: Ungelöste Rätsel der Wirtschaftswissenschaft; 3 rd, reset and additional corrected edition, Marburg: Metropolis, 2004; English version: property, interest and money: foundations of economic theory. Routledge, London, 2005, forthcoming

Heinsohn G, Steiger O (2000a) The property theory of interest and money; reprinted, with corrections and additions. In: Hodgson GM (ed) Recent developments in institutional economics. Edward Elgar, Cheltenham, 2003, pp 484–517

Heinsohn G, Steiger O (2000b) Warum eine Zentralbank nicht über ihr Geld verfügen kann. Ethik und Sozialwissenschaften: Streitforum für Erwägungskultur 11(4):516–519

Henderson H, Keynes JM (1929) Can Lloyd George do it? In: The collected writings of John Maynard Keynes, vol IX. Essays in persuasion (1931). Macmillan, London, 1972, pp 86–125

Keynes JM (1928) Economic possibilities for our grandchildren (1930). In: The collected writings of John Maynard Keynes – vol IX: Essays in persuasion (1931). Macmillan, London, 1972, pp 321–332

Keynes JM (1930a) A treatise on money – vol 1: The pure theory of money. In: The collected writings of John Maynard Keynes vol V. Macmillan, London, 1971

Keynes JM (1930b) A treatise on money – vol 2: the applied theory of money. In: The collected writings of John Maynard Keynes, vol VI. Macmillan, London, 1971

Keynes JM (1931) The consequences to the banks of the collapse of money values. In: The collected writings of John Maynard Keynes – vol IX: Essays in persuasion. Macmillan, London, 1972, pp 150–158

Keynes JM (1933a) The means to prosperity. In: The collected writings of John Maynard Keynes – vol IX: Essays in persuasion (1931). Macmillan, London, 1972, Part VI, Later Essays, pp 335–336

Keynes JM (1933b) ["A Monetary Theory of Production"]. In: Der Stand und die nächste Zukunft der Konjunkturforschung: Festschrift für Arthur Spiethoff, edited by Clausing G. Duncker & Humblot, Munich, pp 123–125

Keynes JM (1936) The general theory of employment, interest and money, corrected edition in: The collected writings of John Maynard Keynes – vol VII. Macmillan, London, 1973, pp xxi–xxii, 1–384, and 413–428

Keynes JM (1939) Government loan policy and the rate of interest – memorandum of 29 May. In: The collected writings of John Maynard Keynes – vol XXI: Activities 1931–1939: World crises and policies in Britain and America. Macmillan, London, 1982, pp 534–546

Keynes JM (1940) How to pay for the war. In: The collected writings of John Maynard Keynes – vol IX: Essays in persuasion. Macmillan, London, 1972, pp 367–439

Knapp GF (1905) Staatliche Theorie des Geldes. Duncker & Humblot, Munich and Leipzig, 1923; abridged translation as The State Theory of Money. Macmillan, London, 1924

Lexis W (1901) Papiergeld. In: Handwörterbuch der Staatswissenschaften, 2nd edn, vol. 6. G. Fischer, Jena, pp 15–38

Riese H (2000) Geld – die unverstandene Kategorie der Nationalökonomie. Ethik und Sozialwissenschaften: Streitforum für Erwägungskultur 11(4):487–498

Say J-B (1803) A treatise on political economy; translated from the 4th French edition (1819) by Prinsep CR, corrected by Biddle CC. Claxton, Remesen & Haffelinger, Philadelphia (1834), 1880; reprint A.M. Kelley, New York, 1964

Schumpeter JA (1908) Das Wesen und der Hauptinhalt der theoretischen Nationalökonomie. Duncker & Humblot, Leipzig

Schumpeter JA (1911) Theorie der wirtschaftlichen Entwicklung. Duncker & Humblot, Leipzig

Schumpeter JA (1926a) Theorie der wirtschaftlichen Entwicklung: Eine Untersuchung über den Unternehmergewinn, Kapital, Kredit, Zins und den Konjunkturzyklus; 2nd edition of Schumpeter (1911). Duncker & Humblot, Munich

Schumpeter JA (1926b) The theory of economic development: an inquiry into profits, capital, credit, interest, and the business cycle; slightly abridged translation of the 2nd edition of Schumpeter (1911) by Opie R. Harvard University Press, Cambridge, 1934

Stadermann H-J (1996) Monetäre Theorie der Weltwirtschaft. J.C.B. Mohr (P. Siebeck), Tübingen

Stadermann H-J (2000) Aus Nichts wird Nichts. Ethik und Sozialwissenschaften: Streitforum für Erwägungskultur 11(4):534–537

Stadermann H-J, Steiger O (2001) Allgemeine Theorie der Wirtschaft – Volume I: Schulökonomik. Mohr Siebeck, Tübingen

Stadermann H-J and Steiger O (2011) James Steuart and the theory of the monetary economy, in this volume, Chapter 27, pp xxx–xxx

Steiger O (2005) Schuldnergeld: Der wunde Punkt in der keynesianischen Staatstheorie des Geldes. In: Huber G, Krämer H, Kurz HD (eds) Verteilung, Technischer Fortschritt und Strukturwandel: Festschrift für Peter Kalmbach. Metropolis, Marburg, pp 169–188

Steuart J (1767) An inquiry into the principles of political oeconomy: being an essay on the science of domestic policy in free nations. A. Millar & T. Cadell, London; reprint Verlag Wirtschaft und Finanzen, Düsseldorf, 1993, vols I and II

Thornton H (1802) An enquiry into the nature and effects of the paper credit of Great Britain, edited with an introduction by von Hayek FA. G. Allen & Unwin, London, 1939; reprint A.M. Kelley, Fairfield, 1978

Wray LR (1998) Understanding Modern Money: The Key to Full Employment and Price Stability. Edward Elgar, Cheltenham

Chapter 27
James Steuart and the Theory of the Monetary Economy*

Hans-Joachim Stadermann and Otto Steiger

A Short Outline of the Life of Sir James Steuart

James Steuart (1713–1780) was born in Edinburgh as the only son of Sir James Steuart, Solicitor General of Scotland. After a 6-year journey to the Continent, between 1735 and 1740, he became an advocate of the Jacobite Restoration, and after the Stuart army lost the battle of Culloden in 1745 he had to leave the United Kingdom. Shortly after returning to Scotland in 1763, he published his magnum opus, *An Inquiry into the Principles of Political Œconomy* (Steuart 1767). It is the most comprehensive work on mercantilistic thought and one of the most important books in economic literature. In more than 1,300 pages, it deals with topics of the most various natures – from population, agriculture, trade and industry, to banking and money, exchange rates and taxes.

In 1771, Steuart was finally pardoned for his role in the 1745 Jacobite Rebellion. This allowed him to become an adviser to the East India Company. In 1773, he inherited several estates on the condition that he added Denham to his name. This explains why his entry in several dictionaries is as Denham, Sir James Steuart.

*Slightly revised and abridged version of Stadermann and Steiger 1999; and see 2001, 45–86
Translation by Ariane Stadermann

H.-J. Stadermann (✉)
Berlin School of Economics and Law, Hochschule für Wirtschaft und Recht Berlin,
Badensche Straße 50–51, 10825 Berlin, Germany
e-mail: stadermann@aol.com

The Place of Steuart in the History of Economic Thought

The monetary economy is a system of production of goods governed by a controlled scarcity of money. As opposed to the picture drawn by the classical and neoclassical theorists, monetary economy is not just the barter of goods or real exchange in which the use of a special good called money is just a way of simplifying the exchange. The central factor in budget restraint in the monetary economy is a scarcity of money and not a scarcity of resources or goods. However, the restraints are not – as will be demonstrated below – made up of a currency, which is created out of the blue by means of debts by the central bank and kept scarce by the interest rate, as Post Keynesian – for example, Wray 1998 – or Monetary Keynesian's[1] assert. A more convincing view is brought forward by the perfector of mercantilism, James Steuart, who presents a surprisingly accurate analysis of monetary economy.

James Steuart's *Inquiry* was published 9 years prior to Adam Smith's *Wealth of Nation*. It is he who first uses the term *Political Economy* in the title of an economic publication, within the English-speaking world – a term which had been introduced 150 years previously by Antoyne de Montchrétien (1616). It can be argued that Steuart, by using the term, wanted to dissociate himself from the mercantilist project makers who had suggested one adventurous plan after the other to their sovereigns.

Steuart, after all, is regarded to be the most significant theorist of mercantilism (Lippert 1901, 1104). However, as his work was published at a time when mercantilism was being confronted with physiocracy, it did not get much attention from the beginning, as it seemed to be a theory of the *ancien regime*. The victory of Adam Smith contributed to the fact that most of Steuart's work remained unknown.[2] This undoubtedly includes his original ideas about banknotes. Whenever Steuart is referred to, he is at best known as a population theorist, who anticipated the theory of Thomas R. Malthus, or as a price theorist and discoverer of the *numéraire*.

In Eli F. Heckscher's (1931) classical study on mercantilism, Steuart is not mentioned at all. The same applies to the significant study of Thomas Guggenheim (1978). In Valentin Fritz Wagner's (1937, 162, 169 and 273) famous treatise on the history of the theories of credit, Steuart plays only a minor role. The same holds true of Charles Rist's (1938) classical work about the history of monetary and credit theory, a profound work that deals with the authorities of the eighteenth and

---

[1] A modern German school of Keynesianism founded by Hajo Riese, Freie Universität Berlin; see Riese (2000).

[2] Not only the victory of Smith's theory but also his method not to refer to Steuart's treatise at all. Smith knew Steuart's treatise very well and was eager to reject the latter's theory, as has been revealed in a letter of 2 September 1772 by Smith to a member of the British parliament published first in 1972: "I have the same opinion of Sir James Steuart's Book that you have. Without once mentioning it I flatter myself, that every false principle in it, will meet with a clear and distinct confutation of mine" (Smith 1972, 163).

nineteenth centuries, and in which Steuart is only mentioned briefly and, in addition, interpreted incorrectly. His suggestion of a monetary system of banknotes based on solid collateral is inappropriately introduced as an idea of a "currency without a specific basis" (1938, 336). More recently, he is regarded as the anticipator of the Keynes's theory of effective demand (Vickers 1959, 268; and Eltis 1987, IV, 496). Even in the extensive comments on the occasion of publication of the facsimile edition of his work of 1767, the following perplexing statement can be found: "Steuart's interesting points of view about banknotes, credit and banking can unfortunately not be discussed in detail here" (Schefold 1993, 11).

In the following sections, these "interesting points" shall, as far as to our knowledge for the first time, be analysed in detail. In the third section, we will examine how Steuart views the transition from the feudal system to the monetary economy. The fourth section discusses the core of Steuart's theory of the monetary economy, the connection between money of account, money proper and good securities. The fifth section examines Steuart's conditions for keeping banknotes in circulation. In the sixth section, we look at the question of why, whenever Steuart was examined so far, his revolutionary views of monetary theory were not recognised. In the last section, Steuart is discussed as a precursor of Walter Bagehot.

The Change from Scarcity and Lack of Freedom to Wealth and Liberty

For his thoughts on monetary theory, Steuart starts to focus on the analysis of population and agriculture as basis of a *free* nation's economy. By so doing, he intends to show how the break-up of feudal governments leads to the freedom of citizens, which in turn leads to the development of trade and industries, and ultimately to credit and wealth, the counterparts of which are debts and taxes. It is important to note that this development leads Steuart to establish a whole new system of economics. Unlike all his contemporaries, he understands how the feudal system was based on imposing force on unfree workers while the new one gives incentives for workers to show entrepreneurship and creates demand based on needs for new goods. In former times, people were "forced to labour because they were slaves of others, men are now forced to labour because of their own wants" (Steuart 1767, I, 40).

Labour is performed in all systems of production; it can be forcibly done, but real industriousness develops only under the conditions of freedom. Ingenuity and a lack of freedom cannot be reconciled. "INDUSTRY *is the application to ingenious labour in a free man, in order to procure, by the means of trade, an equivalent, fit for the supplying every want*" (Steuart 1767, I, 166). Steuart uses his population theory to explain the transition from the feudal system to an economy of free citizens.

He regards the possessors of land in a feudal system as heavily restricted in their actions. "Formerly a gentleman who enjoyed a bit of land knew not what it was to have any demand made upon him, but in virtue of obligations by himself contracted. He disposed of the fruits of the earth, and of the labour of his servants or vassals, as he thought fit. … The only impositions commonly known to affect landed men were made in consequence of a contract of subordination, feudal or other, which had certain limitations; and the impositions were appropriated for certain purposes" (Steuart 1767, I, 13). In these societies, production supplied the goods for self-consumption and for barter, which Steuart describes as "trade in its simplest form." In the original state of feudal society, the amount of agricultural produce would put a limit on the population. This limitation can be lifted by labour, which consciously aims to increase the agricultural produce. However, this surplus does not increase wealth *per capita*, as the increased production leads to a rise in population. An increase in wealth is only possible if the labour of the rural population, which is aimed at increasing crops, produces a surplus, which in turn could feed free workers who would devote their time to fostering crafts and manufactories in villages and towns. Industry is the mean which rids the countryside of unnecessary consumers of foodstuffs and creates goods that satisfy new needs and also lay a foundation for trade between countryside and town. While in its original state, barter only means the exchange of simple goods and does not necessitate money, the industrial production, achieved through trade, is dependent on money and credit from its very beginning.

The model developed by Steuart on the transition from barter to trade is essentially different from the one that is proposed by the classical and neoclassical theorists even up to modern times. His model deals not about an inherent inclination in human beings towards advantageous exchanges of goods. There is no problem if the number of exchange partners increases, only the barter model runs into difficulties (transaction costs), since it ultimately makes the partners use a means of exchange, a special *good* called money. Steuart does not introduce credit as a loan of saved consumption goods. "The most simple of all trade, is that which is carried on by bartering the necessary articles of subsistence. If we suppose the earth free to the first possessor this person who cultivates it will first draw from it his food, and the surplus will be the object of barter: he will give this in exchange to any one who will supply his other wants" (Steuart 1767, I, 175). That barter develops as a means of combating shortages and overcoming scarcity is to Steuart equivalent to the "conveniences of a simple life". He distinguishes it from the consumer's demand, which develops according to the products created by the industries, which Steuart calls "luxuries". He makes a clear distinction between consumption of simple material reproduction and consumption, which goes beyond this, namely of goods, which were created by the ingenious work of craftsmen. As long as scarcity can be averted by mutual barter, there is no need at all for money, and money will, should it exist, be stashed away in a chest. Although he does not explicitly say so, he does think that the clinking coin, stashed away, is something quite different to the money in trade and industry. While the former is only a leftover of past times, he cannot imagine the latter without credit.

A consequence of this credit-based money is "that the free hands of the state, who before stopped working, because all their wants were provided for, having this new object of ambition before their eyes, endeavour, by refinements upon their labour, to remove the smaller inconveniences which result from a simplicity of manners. People, I shall suppose, who formerly knew but one sort of cloathing for all seasons, willingly part with a little money to procure for themselves different sorts of apparel properly adapted to summer and winter, which the ingenuity of manufacturers in their desire of getting money may have suggested to their invention" (Steuart 1767, I, 178).

In this transition process from production of basic needs to trade and industry, Steuart sees the merchant as playing a central role. He is primarily the one who, in place of those coins uselessly lying around, supplies the money through credit for those who wish to trade and produce. He is a representative of the producers to the consumers and of the consumers to the producers. He combines in one person all those functions, which, in modern economic theory, are attributed to the market as the location for the exchange of goods. Therefore, his role is not limited to mediating between acting producers and reacting consumers – as in classical theory – or between acting consumers and reacting producers – as in neoclassical economics. The merchant as the central person in the mercantile system has consequently vanished from barter-oriented classical and neoclassical theory. The loss of this agent has a greater meaning than may be apparent at first sight. It cannot simply be replaced by Adam Smith's invisible hand or Leon Walras' auctioneer. Both these auxiliary constructions exclude a meaningful use of money, let alone give it a foundation. However, Steuart's merchant has the function of spreading the wealth of the well-off by creating money for the industrious.

The merchant as mediator between producers and consumers is also the one who determines the value of goods. Steuart makes a distinction here between two components in the price of goods, the so-called real value of the good and the profit at the time of sale. The real value is determined by the merchant who estimates the value of the following three components: first, the productivity of work, secondly the necessary maintenance of the producer, and thirdly the value of the raw materials used in producing this good. In general, the price cannot fall below this real value. If the price is above this value, it indicates a profit. While the consumers limit the profit by their demand, the producers avoid a loss by not selling their products to the merchants below their production costs. The latter are interested in a "moderate" profit, as this leads to the greatest demand[3] possible, which in turn has the advantage of enabling a large supply of goods, with the ability to cover the costs. What at first sight looks exactly like Adam Smith's price theory – determination of price by adding a profit rate to the costs – turns out to be something quite different. While in Smith's theory, the potential demand is *limited* by production, Steuart shows that demand is *independent* of production.

---

[3] Steuart (1767, I, 172–175 and 181–183) distinguishes between a "large" demand in terms of quantities, which enables a large supply, and a "high" demand in terms of prices, which indicates a demand greater than the supply. In modern theory, the first constellation is a buyer's and the second a seller's market.

This view stems from his discussion of the "demand and supply equilibrium" (Steuart 1767, I, 205 f. and 216–225),[4] where he makes the distinction between a "complete" and an "incomplete" equilibrium. A complete equilibrium is defined as competition on the demand side being almost equalled by competition on the supply side. Based on "double-sided competition", this equilibrium can fluctuate only within certain limits. It can be disturbed in two ways: (1) demand increases in relation to supply and (2) supply increases in relation to demand. Both cases lead to an incomplete equilibrium.

Steuart calls these disturbances of the equilibrium one-sided competition, that means, competition that only exists amongst the suppliers or the demanders. In case of surplus supply, the suppliers cannot sell their entire production at the planned profit. The production will either be reduced or they will try to get rid of their excess production by lowering prices. Even in this case, the incomplete equilibrium will continue to exist because on the one hand the consumers will benefit from the lower prices, while on the other the producers will incur a loss. The decline in prices will lead to the sale of all goods produced. However, it will ultimately trigger a decrease in production, without which covering the costs and gaining a moderate profit margin will not be feasible. What we have here is an *equilibrium with unemployment*. Steuart calls this equilibrium incomplete because not all offers can effectively be realised. Nowadays, we would call this state a stable equilibrium, as the rate of interest – unlike neoclassical theory – will not harmonise the constellation.

The case of surplus demand will trigger competition amongst those who demand, with no competition at the same time amongst the suppliers. Now profits are generated through increases in prices, the profits will be temporary only as they lead to an increase in the real value, that means, the costs. To put it in Steuart's words, "these profits become … virtually *consolidated* with the real value of this merchandize" (1767, I, 221 f.). This is an incomplete equilibrium, because increasing profits are consolidated with increasing costs. Steuart's analysis clearly shows how sceptical he would have been towards Keynes's suggestion that an increase in demand would stimulate an increase in output and employment. The great demand he talks about can only be achieved by stimulating trade, in order to improve the conditions for credit against good security.

Money of Account, Money Proper and Good Security

What does Steuart mean by fostering trade? He discusses the opportunity to achieve the following two aims:

"1. To promote the ease and happiness of higher classes, in making their wealth subservient to their wants and inclinations.

---

[4] It is an equilibrium of demand and supply and not of supply and demand, because of the independency of demand. Steuart uses the term work synonymously to supply. In his model of the supplier, the producer is a workman. The workman is an independent producer of goods and not – like in classical theory – a wage labourer.

"2. To promote the ease and happiness of the lower classes by turning their natural faculties to an infallible means of relieving their necessities.

"This communicates the idea of a free society; because it implies the circulation of a real equivalent for every service; to aquire which mankind submit with pleasure to the hardest labour" (Steuart 1767, I, 302).

The "real equivalent" in this process is money. At first, Steuart considers money to be what still in today's theory is described as *numéraire* and for the recognition of which Joseph Schumpeter (1954, 296 f.) has praised him. "By MONEY, I understand *any commodity, which purely in itself is of no material use to man ..., but which acquires such as an estimation from his opinion of it as to become the universal measure of what is called value, and an adequate equivalent for any thing alienable*"(Steuart 1767, I, 32). However, Steuart does not further pursue this definition of association of the term "money" to a standard good in his later discussion, a point for which Schumpeter (1954, 296 f.) has criticised him. Quite to the contrary to that and the opinions of his fellow scholars, Steuart mainly understands money to be a *money of account*. He generally sees a distinction there between the coins, the intrinsic value of which is supposed to be caused by the value of the precious metal of which they are made, and money of account. "Money, which I call of account, is no more than *any arbitrary scale of equal parts, invented for measuring the respective value of things vendible* (Steuart 1767, I, 526)."[5] Steuart associates the use of money of account with commodities, not as Keynes (1930, 3) later would, as primarily measure for credit and sales contracts. However, Steuart introduces money of account as an abstract measure, and *not* as a *unit* of account like Keynes's (1936, 41–45) *wage unit* linked to a real phenomenon, the price of which acts as the norm for all goods. This is particularly true in the case of precious metals, the value of which measured in money of account can be subject to daily fluctuations.

Which *money proper* corresponds, in Steuart's theory, to the money of account? It is both coins and banknotes; however, he makes a clear distinction between the monetary characters of the two. Coins made of metal are the means of payment for people who are not creditworthy, as had already been emphasised by the French mercantilist Pierre Boisguilbert (1704, 235).[6] They are an anachronism from feudal society. Money proper, which Steuart actually is interested in, exists as banknotes that facilitate payments between creditworthy proprietors. "A bank note is an obligation. When I pay with a bank note, I do no more than to substitute the credit of the Bank in the place of my own, in favour of the man to whom I give it." Here Steuart (1772, 7) makes the distinction between payments in coin and payments in

---

[5] For the first time, Steuart uses the expression *money of accompt* in a treatise on the principles of money published six years earlier (Steuart 1761, 175). Money of account here refers to coins only and not to paper money.

[6] "Only the poor are in need of the security of bullion money [coins]. As the other people get wealthier by their industry, they use bills of exchange instead of coined money" (our translation of the German translation). The quotation reveals that Boisguilbert still had no idea that coins can be substituted by another money: banknotes. "Bills of exchange" are not money but a claim on money.

banknotes very clear: "When I pay in coin, I put the person in possession of the real value of what I owe him. After this payment, he has no claim on me, or on any other person whatever." However, from this distinction one must not conclude that Steuart makes the mistake which was common until the end of the gold standard where coins were regarded as the actual money that is only substituted by banknotes. He emphasises that the credit arrangements, which arise from the banknote, do not cease to exist by using this note for further payments. So the only addition that might be made is that he never explicitly mentions that money, if it circulates in the form of precious metal coins, was never introduced into the economy by means of a credit arrangement.

Here Steuart follows up on the ideas on the origins of money of earlier mercantilists, which can be described as pawn or pledge theory of money. Arthur Monroe (1923, 82 f.) states it in the following terms: " 'The first use of money', says [Rice] Vaughan, 'was as a pledge; for, since one of the parties to an exchange was often unable to repay the other exactly, the corruption of man's nature soon gave rise of the use of pledges, in order to put exchanges on a more secure basis'. The same idea appears later in [John] Locke and [John] Asgill. The latter goes on to say that at first, man used as pledges 'particular tokens between one man and another', till by degree silver and gold, having acquired a value for other uses, became the common pledge of the world". This thought about the origin of coins can be found with many mercantilists, especially Richard Cantillon. The latter explains why the use of money stems from the previous use of precious metals, especially gold and silver: "As this metal was esteemed at its cost value, at least, if few people who possessed some of it, finding themselves in need, could pawn it to borrow the things they wanted, and even to sell it later outright. Thence arose a custom of fixing its value in proportion to its quantity or weight as against all products and merchandise" (Cantillon 1755, 103).

For these mercantilists, a relation existed between the credit agreements, the security needed for it and money in the form of precious metal coins. Any different view of money seemed strange to them. The fact that Steuart makes a distinction between creditworthy and non-creditworthy people allows him to overcome the fixation on the origin of money from precious metals and instead to elaborate on money's *credit* origins. Neither gold nor silver is money, but the note issued by the merchant for good security. The merchant has a fund from his own wealth and later, as a banker, he also has access rights to the assets of non-banks which seek credit from him. Therefore, it is to be the first and fundamental rule that notes have to be issued against the best assets. For this process, Steuart creates the metaphor of *converting land into paper money*.

The thought behind this metaphor is also a central one in Gunnar Heinsohn and Otto Steiger's (1996, 221–307; and see 2000 [2003]) property theory of interest and money. Steuart anticipates their theory in the example of a proprietor, *A*, who would like to consume the goods of a producer, *B*, but lacks the coins to pay for them. *A* solves this problem by issuing a promissory note in the amount of the goods he would like to purchase, secured by his property and gives it to *B*. *B*, for his part, receives rights for *a parcel of A's property*. The advantage of this operation is that

B is given the opportunity to produce, while *A* still has use of his property. This means that to Steuart investing is possible without previous saving – as against to the opposite conviction in the later classical and neoclassical theories.

"Which operation being over, the land and the industry remained as before, ready to produce anew. Here, then is the effect of credit or symbolic money; and here I ask, whether or not the notes of hand given by (A) to (B), do not contain as real a value, as if he had given gold or silver?" (Steuart 1767, I, 365) We will see that to Steuart's mind, this operation is not achievable without a promise by the borrower, *A*, to pay interest to a further lender, *C*, the bank, who gives banknotes to *A* (which the bank issued itself) so *A* can pay *B*.

Banknotes presume the existence of a bank, which is not primarily, as to a classical theorist's mind, a savings bank. The latter issues receipts after coins have been deposited, which are believed to have circulated as actual banknotes. The example that is always quoted in the literature for this case is the goldsmiths who did not just issue these receipts for coins deposited but also for gold bars. This option is not unknown to Steuart, but his focus is on credit banks that create or issue new money and which make the existing money circulate more efficiently. Steuart sees this bank – in accordance with economic reality – as a union of proprietors (at his time these were usually merchants) in an association. On the basis of a banking contract, which under certain circumstances may require governmental approval, the bank proprietors have to establish confidence with the public. To get this, they form a stock which may consist of various species of property. Then "they grant credits, or cash accompts upon good security; concerning which they make the proper regulations. In proportion to the notes issued in consequence of those credits, they provide a sum of coins, such as they judge to be sufficient to answer such notes as shall return upon them for payment" (Steuart 1767, II, 150).

The bank will only issue banknotes to debtors if it is able to gain the trust of the public in three ways. It has to win the trust of investors who are willing to deposit precious metals at the bank against demand deposits or its banknotes. Furthermore, the bank has to win the trust of those who, by selling goods and services, become proprietors of its notes, so that redemption of banknotes does not erode its own capital or equity, its stock of bullion coins. However, most of all it needs to find proprietors who are willing to mortgage their good security for banknotes issued by the bank in a credit contract and to pay interest on them.[7] It is that security and not the deposits of the proprietors of the bank that are crucial for the issue of banknotes. "When paper is issued for no value received, the security of such paper stands alone upon the original capital of the bank, whereas when it is issued for value received, that value is the security on which it immediately stands, and the bank stock is properly speaking, only subsidiary" (Steuart 1767, II, 151).

---

[7] A bank which does not enjoy the confidence of the debtors does not get any good securities transferred. The debtor must fear a withdrawal of the pledges – which are the assets of the bank – in case of bankruptcy. Enforcement threatens him even in the case he has fulfilled his duties as debtor *vis-à-vis* the bank.

Steuart understands that the consumers of luxury goods first of all are coming from the class of landed proprietors and, therefore, he recommends the banks to issue bank notes secured by property of land.

"When a proprietor of lands gives his bond to a bank, it should be understood, that as long as he regularly pays the interest of the money borrowed, the bank is not to demand the capital."

"For this bond they give notes, which are considered as ready money, and therefore carry no interest. So the profit of the bank is to receive interest for what they lend, and to pay none for what they owe."

"What they owe is the paper they issue. They owe this to the public; and the security which the public has, is the security which the bank received from the person who borrowed from them."

"Hence the solidity of banks upon mortgage. Their notes become money, and the whole property engaged to them."

"But as the stock of the bank is of determinate value, and as the notes they issue may very far exceed it, the credit of a bank will be precarious, unless the value of the securities upon which they lend, be equal to all the notes in circulation. It will also be precarious in proportion as the securities themselves are so. Hence the interest the public has to take care that banks give credit upon nothing but the best security" (Steuart 1767, II, 603).

But what happens if the banks forgo to ask for good securities from their debtors or pay their own bills with their own notes? In this case, they would actually be liable with their own capital. Steuart points out that the bank's own capital is only a subsidiary form of security. What makes banknotes safe is the trustworthy pawns of the debtors. Steuart claims that most people do not understand that banks can be short of money, because they own some form of a money-generating mechanism that requires no more than some "paper and ink to create millions". However, if one follows the principles of banking, one will see that an issue of banknotes that is not backed by securities results in a decrease of its own capital or its profits as it puts a debenture into circulation. "I have dwelt the longer upon this circumstance, because many, who are unacquainted with the nature of banks, have a difficulty to comprehend how they should ever be at a loss for money, as they have a mint of their own, which requires nothing but paper and ink to create millions. But if they consider the principles of banking, they will find that every note issued for value consumed, in place of value received and preserved, is neither more or less, than a partial spending either of their capital, or profits on the bank" (Steuart 1767, II, 151 f.).

Steuart states a principle which should also be applied to modern central banks. However, it is often the case that the notes issuing banks neglect this very rule and issue money backed by the purchase of worthless materials or collaterals. The result is easy to be seen: not only do they incur a loss of own capital and profit, they also weaken their currencies in relation to others. In history, the user of those currencies always paid for such behaviour in a decline in welfare.

Therefore, own capital is an important factor for banks. However, if the principle of good security is taken into consideration, own capital becomes secondary. Generally, banknotes that are issued on the basis of good security from the bank's debtors can be kept in circulation without causing the bank any problems – as long as there is sufficient belief in the quality of these securities. As soon as the bank cannot rely on this unconditionally, it needs to keep sufficient own capital in liquid form in order to comply with any wishes to redeem the notes at any time. It is obvious that gold and silver coins, and not parcels of property of land, are the best suited assets to be held as own capital of the bank to secure its granting of credit.

The same principle that applies to individual buyers also applies to banks: only a bank that has a questionable ability to redeem its notes into adequate assets actually has to keep bullion coins, and therefore, to redeem with the money of those who are not creditworthy. A bank that is undoubtedly going to have good security will, in turn, always be able to settle all of its liabilities with its own notes. Steuart considers this also to be true for transactions with foreign banks. A negative balance of payments is not corrected by specie flow but by drawing exchange bills on corresponding banks at the foreign place, if credit is beyond doubt (1767, II, 346 f.). However, a nation whose banks have made doubtful security the basis of their notes–issue will never realise this. It will be forced to transfer precious metals, that means, the money of those who have no credit.

Preconditions for the Ability for a Banknote to Circulate

Steuart (1767, I, 131 f.), furthermore, discusses the obvious question why bank debtors who own the best securities do not, as suggested above, issue notes themselves, backed by their own security, and then bring them into circulation. Could they not avoid the payment of interest considering that they give the same amount to the bank with their liabilities that they received in banknotes?

This question refers to John Law's famous suggestion to the Scottish Parliament to turn land into paper money in order to overcome the scarcity of silver currency and to get rid of its instability. A committee of the parliament was supposed to be authorised to issue notes at market value for land. Law considered three possibilities for this: (1) The issue of notes shall be done by the committee backed by the land as security. This should happen without actually transferring the legal rights to the land and shall be limited to one half or two thirds of its value. However, the value of the land itself is not further determined. (2) The notes shall be issued on a basis of a transfer of property of land at its full value to the committee. The value being calculated on the basis of twenty annual instalments computed in silver currency. In this scenario, the seller keeps the option of buying back his property. (3) There shall be the opportunity to issue notes at the price of the property as determined in case (2), but without the option to buy it back (Law 1705, especially 82 f.).

All three scenarios aim at providing money backed by security to an extent that corresponds to the aggregate demand in the economy. However, Law does not consider that – as the bank's own capital is made up of land and not of gold and silver – the bank can only redeem land, which conflicts with the guaranteed buy-back option the initial proprietors are granted. Furthermore, he does not consider that *both* the sellers of property and the creditors receive *banknotes*. This contradicts the rules of banking, as the proprietors of the bank's own capital do not receive money from or credit in the bank but a tradable claim against the bank which, however, is non-redeemable. What kind of security would that be if the providers of the bank's own capital can have their shares paid out if needed? Although the volume of the issue is limited by the parliament, the demand for money as a matter of principle is still to be fulfilled by the bank because otherwise – as Law fears – the nation would incur a loss of profitable employment opportunities.

Law's suggestion actually only simulates a refinancing of securities, as it is common practice in banking. Instead of linking a sum of money to property, which could be regulated by the market, he just aims at fixing the maximum issuance. For this purpose, however, he would not need property at all. Every randomly made limitation would have the same effect. Law also fails to notice that not the finite nature of the money supply is the essence of the monetary economy but rather the regulation of this supply by the market.

Obviously, Law does not only focus on a political committee as monetary authority that, by purchase and mortgaging of land which becomes its capital, issues paper money at the going market rate of interest. He rather wants to provide a seemingly serious justification for the possibility to enlarge credit in principle. But why take this complicated and dangerous detour of doubling the note issuance through a bank called committee? Would it not be simpler for the landed proprietor to issue paper money himself and, thereby, avoid the doubling that might endanger his property? This takes us back to the question put forward by Steuart.

In contrast to Law, Steuart shows that the self-issuing of notes is dangerous for another reason. He points out that the notes issued by the bank, but not the property owner's liabilities, can be kept in circulation. Here Steuart develops an explanation of the rate of interest, which in parts anticipates Heinsohn's and Steiger's property theory of the rate of interest. According to this theory, debtors are willing to pay interest on money they borrowed although they already mortgaged good securities. The debtor, however, wants to continue making use of his securities and, therefore, he needs to avoid that someone makes claims on them although he fulfils his contractual obligations. Steuart expresses this as follows: "And for what does he [the debtor] pay that interest? Not that he has gratuitously received any value from the bank; because in his obligation he has given a full equivalent for the notes, but the obligation carries interest and the notes carry none. Why? Because the one circulates like money the other does not. For this *advantage*, therefore, *of circulation*, not for any additional value, does the landed man pay interest" (Steuart 1767, II, 131 f.; emphases added).

This should be examined in more depth, as it not only gives an explanation of the rate of interest but also avoids a weakness in Heinsohn's and Steiger's original formulation of the property theory of the rate of interest.[8] In fact, the owner of

---

[8] The weakness has been corrected, in accordance with our interpretation of Steuart's analysis, in Heinsohn and Steiger 2000, especially 505 f.

property finds himself in a wholly different position if he uses the bank's credit facilities and acquires its notes backed by his liabilities than if he issued his own banknotes backed on his property. If he fulfils the duties imposed on him by the loan agreement, the bank cannot interfere with his property rights. Banknotes that are issued by the bank always have to be redeemable by its own capital, which has to be available in the form of precious metals and not in the form of securities the bank received by its debtors. Notes which a debtor would issue at sight against his own assets admittedly would not carry interest; however, every possessor of such a note would be able to claim redemption into its issuer's property at any time. This would mean that the crucial point of mortgaged property still being of use to the dutiful debtor is no longer realisable. Every increase in the value of land would trigger such claims for redemption. Obviously, a credit system of this kind would be of little appeal to a landed proprietor, because every borrowing would be equal to a sale of his property which would only include a guaranteed buy-back option if during the period of the loan the price of land would decline. Furthermore, it is apparent that those things that give the lender security pose a threat to the borrower. The landed proprietors are only willing to go into debt if they expect the quality of their securities to depreciate. The creditor can avoid this only by claiming more collateral – in relation to the current value of the security – and, thereby, re-establishing the state in which the proprietors are unwilling to get indebted. This dilemma can only be resolved by the bank and its promise to redeem the notes in another form of assets, namely precious metals.

Taking this into account, Steuart is sure that in every country the "current [quantity of] money" always adapts to economic transactions. Wherever the supply of money is insufficient, a part of the landed property will be, as he calls it, *melted down and made to circulate in paper*, which in turn reduces the shortage.

After all, it is hardly surprising that Steuart also gives a market-based explanation of the rate of interest. He distinguishes between two kinds of proprietors. One kind mortgages his property in order to receive a loan to finance investments in trade and industry projects. Such proprietors generate profits by the loans and would never grant higher rates of interest than they are able to pay with their profits. The other kind borrows for consumption. Such a proprietor is characterised as a person "who can give good security, to pay to perpetuity, a regular interest for money" and who "will obtain credit for any sum, although it should appear evident, that he never can be in capacity to refund the capital" (Steuart 1767, II, 109 and 117–119). The spendthrift incurs, in Steuart's theory, no limiting criteria for his premature consumption. That is why, at first sight, he poses a threat for the development of trade and industry. By raising the market rate of interest through his intense demand for credit, he prevents those proprietors from borrowing who aim to generate profits by investments. Instead of turning immobile assets into labour opportunities for the poor, the spendthrift only serves the purpose of satisfying the demand for foreign luxury goods and to turn the balance of trade into deficit. The rise in the rate of interest due to this behaviour would, therefore, hinder trade and industry; it would make money vanish and everything prone to collapse.

Things would, though, rarely get this far, says Steuart, because the increase in the rate of interest would immediately trigger a decline of the price of any kind of immobile property. The spendthrift, therefore, would get rid of his property very quickly by "that cancer worm" of high rates of interest. Countries with flourishing trade would have more cautious proprietors, and the bad example that the spendthrift sets would lead to a more vigilant lifestyle of the proprietors, which eventually could bring the interest rate down to a level that will allow sufficiently profit-orientated lending (Steuart 1767, II, 118 f.).

These two groups of borrowers are faced on the market with the merchants-proprietors acting as bankers. The bank aims to generate profits by lending money. However, it also has to safeguard its own capital, which will be subject to redemption whenever doubts arise about the quality of the securities used for the loans. As the bank is restricted by competition, its pressing need to generate profit forces it to offer low rates of interest. If it subjects to the temptation of raising the rate of interest to a level that even the biggest spendthrifts are just willing to pay, then it would deprive trade and industry of the opportunity to take up loans. Such a decrease in the demand for loans would soon lead to a decline in the rate of interest.

Steuart's discussion makes apparent the degree to which Adam Smith's theory is insufficient. The classical harmony, due to the illusion that a loan offer is created by individual savings of a creditor, is not even remotely taken into consideration here. The current profit from investments is, in Steuart's theory, not brought into equilibrium by a rate of interest that evens consumption forgone today by a sufficiently high expected level of improvement of living conditions tomorrow.[9] It was this condition that allowed fluctuations in the economy to be "assumed away" in classical and neoclassical theory (Keynes 1933, 125). The willingness to renew loans, to enlarge or to decrease them has nothing to do whatsoever with a willingness to forgo consumption. This, in turn, also does not influence producer's willingness to enter into debt. A transfer of the use of savings from the creditor to the debtor is not part of the loan agreement. It is, rather, that the debtor competes with the money he borrowed with other consumers on the goods market for the current supply. Consequently, those who have an unchanged income will, assuming that production initially remains at the same level, have to decrease their consumption because of increased prices. This means that savings will be forced amongst the agents in the economy. Equilibrium on the loan market is ensured on the one hand by the debtors' expectation of profit and on the other by the creditors' assessments of the quality of their debtors' securities. These estimations are prone to change in the economic process.

Steuart clearly shows the conditions required for genuine money which is always a *creditor's money*. He brings into the open why notes like the *assignats* of the French Revolution, in spite of looking quite similarly, lack the quality of

---

[9] Smith develops his theory of interest in two different parts of the *Wealth of Nations* (1776, 96 and 325).

the notes created by credit. Such notes, therefore, should only be called State or arbitrary means of payment, that means a *debtor's money*. Steuart lays the foundation for the way modern central banks should, according to the principles he elaborates, bring their notes into circulation, which is simply for the provision of good securities. These do not necessarily have to be mortgages on land property. Many assets show the characteristics that are prerequisite for qualifying as good securities. Consequently, today's central bank practice does not show a coherent picture.

In the case of the *assignats* that were issued after 1789 against royal domains, expropriated church and emigrant's possessions, the required securities were not available. These assignats lacked the property element of guaranteed execution. It was lacking because they could only be transferred into private property from the *possession* of the State by means of competition amongst the holders of the assignats. At the same time, it was predetermined that, as soon as there was a desire to redeem these titles, the competition would not stop until the price of landed property had risen to infinity and the value of the *assignats* had decreased to zero.[10] The opposite is true with regard to the circulation of the notes of today's central banks, which is regulated in accordance with an amount of secured assets of equal value, owned by the central banks.

The Later Misjudgement of James Steuart's Achievements

So why is it that Steuart's insights into the monetary theory have not achieved the recognition they deserve? The best known analysis of his monetary theory, by the Keynesian Douglas Vickers in 1959, contains many quotes that are also used in this paper. However, Vickers' main interest is not to show what money is, how it is created and why it is needed. He is interested rather in interpreting Steuart as a

---

[10] As we have shown in our contribution on Keynes in this volume (Stadermann and Steiger 2011), this great economist failed to detect the missing monetary properties of the *assignats*. On the contrary, Keynes praised them as a revolution in the development of the monetary economy.

The original *assignats* issued at sight at the *Caisse de l'Extraordinaire* were never paid at all. They were received in payment for the national domains bought by competing individuals. However, as has been admirably demonstrated by Jean-Baptiste Say, their nominal value could never give any determinate value to the *assignats*, because the value of the former increased exactly in proportion as that of the latter declined. The Treasury did not bother about this, because the rise in the price of its domains enabled it to cash a greater amount of *assignats* and re-issue new ones for its expenditures, without enlarging the quantity of the *assignats*. The Treasury was not aware that, notwithstanding these advantages, the rise in the price of the domains meant a rapid devaluation of the *assignats*. "The error was discovered in the end, when it was impossible any longer to purchase the most trifling article with any sum of *assignats*, whatever might be its amount. The next measure was to issue *mandats*, that is to say, papers purporting to be an order for the absolute transfer of the specific portion of the national domains expressed in the *mandat*: but, besides that it was then too late, the operation was infamously executed" (Say 1803, 283).

precursor of Keynes's theory of effective demand.[11] On the other side, Vickers understands that Steuart's association between money and good securities is quite different from Law's fanciful foundations of paper money. Furthermore, Vickers concedes that Steuart had recognised the insufficiency of linking money to precious metals that change in value by attempting to bind paper money to more stable securities. But it is just this discussion Vickers considers to be irrelevant, as he believes good securities to be somewhat anachronistic in the age of irredeemable paper money. He, therefore, accuses Steuart of never intending to analyse the introduction of a non-redeemable fiat money (Vickers 1959, 276).

Vickers (1959, 287) also reprimands that Steuart did not integrate Keynes's idea of interest as the price of giving up liquidity into his explanation of the rate of interest. However, he overlooks that Steuart – just like Heinsohn and Steiger (1996, 141–219, especially 193–214) – does not believe for a good reason in the idea of holding money in a free economy: "The intention of permitting loans upon interest, is not to provide a revenue to those who have ready money locked up, but to obtain the use of a circulating equivalent to those who have a sufficient security to pledge for it". (Steuart, 1767, I, 379).

According to Vickers (1959, 280), Steuart got on the wrong track, because he had overlooked that even the best securities can be subject to fluctuations in their market price. Instead, he should have replaced the precious metals simply by "trust" in banks to be able to redeem their notes on demand at any time. By saying this, Vickers gives an account of just what is still a widespread view in mainstream monetary theory, namely that, with the rise of the central bank, banks of issue only replaced precious metal currencies by unredeemable paper money, which is kept scarce without any specific security. In order for fiat money to be accepted as genuine money, no specific security is needed anymore, especially since the final establishment of central banks. This view, however, is confirmed neither by today's central banks' constitution nor by their re-financing policies.

A more detailed account of Steuart's principles, especially his monetary theory, can be found in the works of Sama Ranjan Sen (1947 and 1957). This author emphasises even more of Steuart's work that is of interest to us than Vickers does. As opposed to the latter, Sen does not provide us with a unique analysis, and those parts he does analyse, he unfortunately interprets incorrectly. For instance, he claims that "by paper money Steuart always understands credit and never irredeemable fiat money" (Sen 1957, 81). This is a double mistake. Steuart never makes this confusion: he only insists that money has to be issued in a credit contract, backed by good securities and against interest. Like Vickers, Sen does not understand that the non-redeemability of central banknotes in no way means they are issued without good security.

---

[11] Similar to Vickers, M.A. Akhtar (1778, 64–66; and see 1979, 289–293) also detects that for Steuart, money is not a veil laying over real economic transactions. He stresses, nevertheless, only the role of Steuart's paper money as a dynamic element and as a means to determinate the level of economic activities, without considering that creating money affords an interest-bearing credit contract and good securities.

Sen (1957, 97) further reprimands Steuart for "confusing money with capital" by attributing to money effects that only capital can achieve: the improvement of welfare in general through higher productivity. Sen proves that even having a good knowledge of an important work of mercantilism does not protect one from the prejudices against mercantilism common until today.

Sen's criticism is similar to Adam Smith's, the creator of the term "mercantile system", who accused the mercantilists of abusing the popular equation of money with wealth and coming up with a wrong explanation for the promotion of export. An active balance of trade, they are assumed to have maintained, would be the best way of increasing the wealth of a nation, as this brings money into the country (Smith 1776, 398–419, especially 400–403).

From the time of Eli F. Heckscher, still today the leading authority on mercantilism, this judgement was reinforced even more. Since that time, the word is that Mercantilists identified money with wealth. Heckscher (1931, II, 169–174, especially 169) quotes mercantilists who seem to justify this judgement, but Thomas Mun, whom Smith mentions as his only source, had already pointed out that his theory is about the acquisition of money by means of the highest possible refinement of industrial goods. Export for Mun (1664, 5–19, especially 11–13) means only an extremely lucrative form of the acquisition of money.

It only seems as if the critics of mercantilism find their critique reinforced in Steuart's work. For instance, he states that "by wealth, I understand this circulating ... equivalent in money" (Steuart 1767, I, 359). Heckscher takes this short statement out of context. Steuart, however, continues to develop the line of argumentation as follows: "The desires of the rich and the means of gratifying them make them call for the services of the poor: the necessities of the poor, and the desire of becoming rich, makes them cheerfully answer the summons; they submit to the hardest labour, and comply with the inclinations of the wealthy, for the sake of an equivalent in money" (Steuart 1767, I, 359 f.). Goods and services on the one hand *and* money on the other constitute the circulation as reciprocal equivalents and lead to the question "which products can be bought by money". Money is crucial in this, as goods and land by themselves cannot circulate. Regarding money and wealth as equals, therefore, does not mean anything else but the acquisition of money by producing goods and services.

Consequently, "the acquisition of money, by the sale of industry to strangers ... was a way of augmenting the general worth of a nation" (Steuart 1767, I, 464). Therefore, it is not surprising that Steuart (1767, I, 516) does not just measure the wealth of a nation by the amount of silver it possesses: "In short, the riches of a trading nation may resemble those of a trading man; who may be immensely rich, with very little specie in his possession".[12] Rather, he concludes that it does not make any

---

[12] The same statement can be found already in Boisguilbert 1695, 67: "Money can only be regarded as a means or way ... to a comfortable life. ... This means that a certain country, in which the quantity of money in circulation is small, can be regarded as rich, while the reverse is true for a country with a large quantity of money, which can be in a state of misery, especially when it is difficult to exchange its money for commodities" (our translation of the German translation).

sense to get as much precious metal as possible into the country by means of a surplus in the balance of trade. If a nation has generated a surplus by trading with foreigners, the result will be "that all nations will endeavour to throw their ready money … into that country where the interest of money is high with respect to their own and where in consequence the value of property in land is low" (Steuart 1767, I, 464). In opposition to the prevailing views of the subject, Steuart reveals a correct understanding of the relations within the balance of payments. Surpluses in trade do not lead to a useless accumulation of precious metal but to an export of capital, meaning capital investments in foreign countries. Thereby, Steuart distinguishes between buying bonds (with a fixed rate of interest) in foreign currency and making real investments in a foreign country, in his case buying land in that country.

This also applies to the opposite situation. If a nation incurred a deficit, it had the opportunity to even it out by a transfer of precious metals. If this was to be avoided, it could not be achieved by export of domestic banknotes that only circulated within the country, because it was impossible to export the assets against which they were issued: the land. In order to obtain the bills of exchange or the precious metal which would be needed to even out the balance, the bank should sell annuity debts to its foreign creditors. This can be achieved by issuing these titles at a sufficiently high rate of interest, payable by the domestic debtors and backed by good security. Steuart forcefully suggests the supply of credit not to be rationed. In such a case, the bank would transfer a part of its annual income to foreign creditors, as it in turn will transfer a part of its earned interest abroad.

Steuart also has no doubt as to why the bank would undertake these transactions. If it did not offer such titles, the balance could only be evened out by transfers of precious metals. This would mean that the notes of the bank would be presented to that bank for redemption in a corresponding amount of precious metal. The import of capital triggered by a bank, therefore, is a way of keeping its own notes in circulation. Steuart clearly sees that a bank will not behave in a manner that would be congruent with the prevailing opinions since the florid of the classical school. Equilibrium will not be achieved by a domestic rationing of credit. Steuart reminds us that the domestic rationing of credit will *not* lead to equilibrium in the balance of payments, but may trigger severe problems for the country. If a bank does not lend to those who offer good security, then the result will lead the nation into a crisis, which ultimately also will affect the bank because of the contraction of its business activity (Steuart 1767, II, 161–195; and see II, 605–610 where the idea is resumed).

Steuart as a Precursor of Walter Bagehot

To advance loans to all those who wish to borrow against good security and at the market rate of interest, Steuart (1767, II, 611) states as follows: "The melting down of property, and keeping circulation full at all times. This is the business of banks." With this statement, he anticipates an idea, which first in 1873 was brought back into the discussion by Walter Bagehot under the name of *open discount window*, the unlimited refinancing of good security at market conditions by the central bank, especially at times of liquidity crises.

"There are two rules: – First. That these loans should only be made at a very high rate of interest. ... Secondly. That at this rate these advances should be made at all good banking securities, and as largely as the public ask for them" (Bagheot 1873, 187–189). For Bagehot (1873, 188,) even in times of crisis, it is not necessary that the central bank grants loans against securities which bears the risk of causing it a loss. Equally, it should not grant advances at preferential rates of interest. In order to prove this, he uses the following two arguments: First, if "bad" securities were accepted from the "unsound" people, the central bank would run the risk of incurring a loss in its "banking reserve" (Bagehot 1873, 187 f.).[13] Secondly, if preferential rates of interest *were* paid, the danger might arise that the "sound" people will no longer offer their securities to the bank for refinancing. "The great majority, the majority to be protected, are the 'sound' people, the people who have good securities to offer" (Bagehot 1873, 188).

Bagehot, however, only briefly mentions this danger but does not explore its ramification any further. The protection for the "sound" people is needed because competition for money needs to be safeguarded. If this competition for money is weakened or eliminated, money no longer has the ability to control the economy, as the "sound" people (with their properly calculated investment plans) will not be able to compete with "unsound" people offering less valuable titles. This alarms them as they can predict that a central bank with bad titles in its portfolio will have more trouble reducing the quantity of money than expanding it. Therefore, they fear a depreciation of the value of their nominal assets (see more detailed Stadermann 1994, 97-240).

References

Akhtar MA (1978) Sir James Steuart on economic growth. Scott J Polit Econ 25:57–74
Akhtar MA (1979) An analytical outline of Sir James Steuart's macroeconomic model. Oxf Econ Pap 31:283–302
Bagheot W (1873) Lombard Street: a description of the money market; new edition by Withers H. J. Murray, London

---

[13] The possible loss of the central bank does not mean a loss of its own capital, which Bagehot – as opposed to Steuart for his notes issuing credit bank – does not recognise, but a loss of its "banking reserves" or reserve of banknotes. The holding of a reserve of banknotes is a characteristic of the Bank of England due to its partition into an Issue and a Banking Department. An "ordinary" central bank does not hold its banknotes as reserves, of course, but deletes them from its balance, when they return to it after the assets, which triggered their issue, have been sold or given back. At the Bank of England, this deletion is made by the Issue Department when it returns gold to the redeemers of its notes. The Banking Department, however, has to hold a reserve of banknotes in accordance with the deposits at the Bank of England by the commercial banks; see Bagehot 1873, 248. For a merger of the separate balances of the both of its departments to a consolidated balance of the Bank of England of 16 September 1903, in which the "banking reserves" are deleted, see Andréades 1904, 296.

Boisguilbert P (1695) "Detail von Frankreich" (*Le détail de la France*). In: Denkschriften zur wirtschaftlichen Lage im Königreich Frankreich, edited and translated by Toepel A, Akademie, Berlin 1986, pp 9–159

Boisguilbert P (1704) Die Gründe für die Geldknappheit (Summary of *Traité de la nature des richesses, de l'argent et des tributs*) In: Denkschriften zur wirtschaftlichen Lage im Königreich Frankreich, edited and translated by Toepel A. Akademie, Berlin, 1986, pp 233–246

Cantillon R (1755 [1730–1734]), Essai sur la Nature du Commerce en Général: Traduit de l'anglois, edited and retranslated by Higgs H. Macmillan, London, 1931

Eltis W (1989) Steuart, Sir James. In: The new palgrave: a dictionary of economics, vol. IV. Macmillan, London, 1987, pp 494–497

Guggenheim Th (1978) Preclassical monetary theories; translated from the French. Pinter, London, 1989

Heckscher EF (1931) Mercantilism, translated from the Swedish by Shapiro MG Allen & Unwin, London, 1935; revised edition 1955; quoted from the German translation by Mackenroth G, Der Merkantilismus (1931). G. Fischer, Jena, 1932, vols I and II

Heinsohn G, Steiger O (1996) Eigentum, Zins und Geld: Ungelöste Rätsel der Wirtschaftswissenschaft; 3rd· reset and additional corrected edition, Marburg: Metropolis, 2004; English edition: Property, interest and money: foundations of economic theory. Routledge, London, 2006, forthcoming

Heinsohn G, Steiger O (2000) "The Property Theory of Interest and Money"; reprinted, with corrections and additions, In: Hodgson GM (ed), Recent developments in institutional economics, Edward Elgar, Cheltenham, UK, 2003, pp 484–517

Keynes JM (1930) A treatise on money – volume 1: The pure theory of money. In: The collected writings of John Maynard Keynes volume V. Macmillan, London, 1971

Keynes JM (1933) ['A Monetary Theory of Production"]. In: Clausing G (ed) Der Stand und die nächste Zukunft der Konjunkturforschung: Festschrift für Arthur Spiethoff. Duncker & Humblot, Munich, pp 123–125

Keynes JM (1936) The general theory of employment, interest and money, corrected edition in: The collected writings of John Maynard Keynes – volume VII. Macmillan, London, 1973, pp. xxi–xxii, 1–384, and 413–428

Law J (1705) Money and trade considered with a proposal for supplying the nation with money. A. Anderson, Edinburgh; reprint A.M. Kelley, New York, 1966

Lippert P (1901) Steuart, James Stanham. In: Handwörterbuch der Staatswissenschaften, 2nd edn, vol. VI. G. Fischer, Jena, pp 1104–1106

Monroe AE (1923) Monetary theory before Adam Smith; reprint A.M. Kelley, New York, 1966

Montchrétien, A. de, Sieur de Watteville (1616) Traicté de l'Œconomie Politique; nouveau édition avec introduction et notes par Th. Funck-Brentano. Plon, Paris, 1889

Mun Th (1664) England's treasure by forraign trade: or, the balance of forraign trade is the rule of our treasure; reprint B. Blackwell, Oxford, 1928, 1967

Riese H (2000) Geld – die unverstandene Kategorie der Nationalökonomie. Ethik und Sozialwissenschaften: Streitforum für Erwägungskultur 11(4):487–498

Rist, Ch., Geschichte der Geld- und Kredittheorien von John Law bis heute (1938) Translated from the French and taking account of the English edition by K. Büscher. A. Francke, Bern, 1947

Say J-B (1803) A treatise on political economy; translated from the 4th French edition by Prinsep CR, corrected by Biddle CC. Claxton, Remsen & Haffelinger, Philadelphia (1834), 1880; reprint A.M. Kelley, New York, 1964

Schefold B (1993) Die Verbindung von Theorie, Geschichte und Politik bei James Steuart. In: Schefold B (ed) *Vademecum zu einer klassischen Synthese von Theorie, Geschichte und Politik* (A volume of comments to the reprint of the original edition of Steuart [1767] in two volumes). Verlag Wirtschaft und Finanzen, Düsseldorf

Schumpeter J (1954) History of economic analysis, edited from the manuscript by E Boody Schumpeter. Oxford University Press, Oxford

Sen SR (1947) Sir James Steuart's General theory of employment interest and money. Economica, NS 14:19–36

Sen SR (1957) The economics of Sir James Steuart. The London School of Economics and Political Science/G. Bell & Sons, London

Smith A (1772) Letter [no. 132] to William Pulteny, Kirkcaldy, 3 September. In: Mossner EC, Ross IS (eds) The correspondence of Adam Smith (1977). Oxford University Press, Oxford, 1987, pp 163 f

Smith A (1776) An inquiry into the nature and causes of the wealth of nations; edited from the 6th edition of 1791 by Cannan E. Modern Library, New York, 1937

Stadermann H-J (1994) Die Fesselung des Midas: Eine Untersuchung über den Aufstieg und Fall der Zentralbankkunst. J.C.B. Mohr, Tübingen (Paul Siebeck)

Stadermann H-J, Steiger O (1999) James Steuart und die Theorie der Geldwirtschaft. In: Stadermann HJ, Steiger O (eds) Herausforderung der Geldwirtschaft: Theorie und Praxis währungspolitischer Ereignisse. Metropolis, Marburg, pp 19–39

Stadermann H-J, Steiger O (2001) Allgemeine Theorie der Wirtschaft – Erster Band: Schulökonomik. Mohr Siebeck, Tübingen

Stadermann H-J, Steiger O (2011) John Maynard Keynes and the theory of the monetary economy, *in this volume*, Chapter 26

Steuart J (ed) (1761) A dissertation upon the doctrine and principles of money, applied to the German coin. In: The works, political, metaphysical, and chronological by the late Sir James Steuart, edited by (his nephew) Steuart J. D. T. Cadell & W. Davies, London, 1805; reprint A. M. Kelley, New York, 1967, vol. V, pp 171–265

Steuart J (1767) An inquiry into the principles of political oeconomy: being an essay on the science of domestic policy in free nations. A. Millar & T. Cadell, London; reprint Wirtschaft und Finanzen, Düsseldorf, 1993

Steuart J (ed) (1772) The principles of money applied to the present state of the coin of Bengal. In: The works, political, metaphysical and chronological, of the late Sir James Steuart, edited by (his nephew) Steuart J. D.T. Cadell & W. Davies, London, 1805; reprint A.M. Kelley, New York, 1967, vol. V, pp 1–170

Vickers D (1959) Studies in the theory of money 1690–1776. Chilton, Philadelphia

Wagner FR (1937) Geschichte der Kredittheorien: Eine dogmenkritische Darstellung. Springer, Vienna; reprint Scientia, Aalen, 1966

Wray LR (1998) Understanding modern money: the key to full employment and price stability. Edward Elgar, Cheltenham

Chapter 28
Friedrich August Hayek (1899–1992)

Gerrit Meijer

Introduction

This essay concentrates on the contribution to economics and economic policy of Hayek. This can be conceived as an extension and correction of the general economic equilibrium theory of Walras, Pareto and Barone. In the next sections, the following themes will be treated, in order to show this, and to evaluate the significance of the contribution:

1. Biographical sketch
2. Market economy and the centrally administered economy: the use of knowledge in society
3. Theory of money and business cycle theory: the monetary over-investment theory
4. Developments in the theory of market structures: the meaning of competition
5. Legal and political philosophy: economic and political systems
6. Economic policy and market economy
7. The history of ideas, psychology and methodology
8. Theory of evolution of institutions
9. Evaluation

G. Meijer (✉)
Department of Economics, Maastricht University, Larixlaan 3,
1231 BL Loosdrecht, The Netherlands
e-mail: g.meijer@hetnet.nl

J.G. Backhaus (ed.), *Handbook of the History of Economic Thought*,
The European Heritage in Economics and the Social Sciences,
DOI 10.1007/978-1-4419-8336-7_28, © Springer Science+Business Media, LLC 2012

Biographical Sketch

The life of Hayek (Raybould 1999; Machlup 1977; Kresge and Wenar 1994) can be divided into four phases and the catchwords can be Vienna, London, Chicago and Freiburg i.Br. (Germany). He was born on May 8th, 1899 in Vienna. His father August von Hayek (1871–1928) was a medical doctor. He later combined this with a Honorary Professorship (*Privatdozent*) of Botany. His mother was Felicitas von Juraschek (1874–1967). He had two younger brothers, Heinz and Erich (later to become Professor of Chemistry and Anatomy, respectively). He characterizes his youth as a happy time and his family (also in the wider sense of the word) as a happy family.

Very influential upon his life was the First World War during – and shortly afterwards – which the Austrian-Hungarian Empire was destroyed. In the later years of this war, he served in the army as an officer. As we will see later experiences during and just after the war (years of hyper-inflation, poverty and political and social upheavals and experiments) have influenced his life and work.

He studied at the University of Vienna. He got a doctorate in Law and in Economics. After this, he worked from 1921 to 1926 at the *Abrechnungsamt* in Vienna as a legal advisor of Ludwig von Mises. This office took care of the financial consequences of the Peace of St Germain. In 1926, he became the Director of *Das Osterreichische Konjunkturinstitut* that was founded at the initiative of Ludwig von Mises. Also he became a *Privatdozent* at the University of Vienna.

In 1926, he married Hella von Fritsch. They got two children: a daughter Christine (1929), and a son Laurence (1934–2004). They did not go in the footsteps of their father. Christine became an entomologist; Lawrence a medical microbiologist.

In 1923/1924, Hayek visited the United States (by boat of the Holland – Amerikalijn: De Amsterdam and in the possession of a letter of introduction and recommendation written by J.A. Schumpeter).

In 1931, he left Vienna for London. He got a professorship in Economics in the London School of Economics (the Tooke Chair). At that time, Lionel Robbins was the Director. In this way, Hayek moved to the financial centre of the world and to the capital of the most powerful empire of the world in that time. In 1938, he became a citizen of the United Kingdom, and in 1943 (just before he destroyed his reputation as an economist by publishing The Road to Serfdom), apparently at the proposal of his friend J.M. Keynes, a Member of the British Academy. He was to stay in the United Kingdom until about 1950. The decline of the British Empire under the Labour Party of Attlee and Bevan both nationally and internationally, dissatisfaction with the intellectual climate in the United Kingdom (especially in economics and political science) belong to the reasons for this change. The most decisive factors are after my opinion personal reasons. He had a divorce and a second marriage with Helene Bitterlich, which brought him in conflict for instance with Robbins. Moreover, he became more and more interested in research in fields outside theoretical economics since about 1940 until he left at the end of the forties.

From 1950 to 1962, he was a Professor of Social and Moral Sciences at Chicago. He was appointed to the Committee on Social Thought. He was not appointed as a Professor of Economics (the majority of the economists were of the opinion that the writer of the Road to Serfdom had disqualified himself as an economist). This professorship (financed by the Volcker Foundation) gave him freedom of teaching and research in whatever subject he wanted.

From there he left in 1962 for Freiburg i.Br. (Germany) to become again a Professor of Economics. In 1968, he became emeritus. He was active and taught and published until the end of his life, for example, at the University of Salzburg (Austria). In 1974, he got to his complete surprise the Nobel Prize in Economics (together with G. Myrdal). On March 23rd, 1992, he died in Freiburg. He was buried in Vienna.

Market Economy and Centrally Administered Economy: The Use of Knowledge in Society

Between both world wars the centrally administered economy was put in practice in several countries. In the non-communist countries, direct controls were used on a large scale (New Deal, etc.). The free exchange economy was at that time heavily criticized, because of monopolizing, unemployment, etc. The centrally administered economy on the other hand was posed opposite the free exchange economy as a shining example. It is therefore understandable that Hayek was especially occupied with the analysis of both the centrally administered economy and the free exchange economy in order to study the economic process in and the performance of both ideal types.

Hayek prefers the free exchange economy over the centrally administered economy for non-economic and economic reasons. He is of the opinion that the abolishment of economic freedom will destroy other freedoms. It is for that reason that he rejects the centrally administered economy and prefers a free exchange economy.

With regard to the economic aspects, he argues that economic calculation in the centrally administered economy is not or not as well possible as in the free exchange economy, where economic calculation takes place through the pricing process.

In an article published in 1920, Mises argued that in a free exchange economy with money, the economic subjects value consumption and production goods, of which they are the possessors, through exchange. The objective exchange value, brought about in that way, is measured in money prices. The calculation in money prices is restricted. In the first place, the value of money is subject to fluctuations, but mainly not to such an extent that it impedes the calculations. Of more importance is that the calculation in money is based on exchange value and for that reason is only possible for goods that are exchanged.

Two conditions have to be satisfied in order to make economic calculation possible. All consumption and production goods have to participate in the exchange. Moreover, there has to be a commonly used medium of exchange (money). Otherwise, there will not be a common denominator. These conditions are fulfilled by calculation in money prices within the above-mentioned constraints.

In the centrally administered economy, these conditions are not satisfied. Von Mises thinks in this connection of a centrally administered economy with collective property, completely central administration of production and free exchange of consumption goods. Because the means of production are collective property, they are not exchanged and priced. This means that exact economic calculation is impossible. The decisions of the central administration are arbitrary. The argument that there is no exchange and no pricing does not apply of course to consumption goods. Mises also indicates the bureaucratic character of this society. The associated drawbacks are in the area of initiative and responsibility (accountability).

The article of Mises (1920) initiated a fierce exchange of views, about the question of pricing and consequently the possibility of economic calculation in the centrally administered economy. Three reactions ought to be mentioned here (Hayek 1935, pp. 207–214; 217–220; 1952c, pp. 197–204; 207–210).

The first reaction is connected with the general equilibrium theory of Walras, Pareto, and Barone. It implies that a solution is possible by using the system of equations of general equilibrium theory. It would only be necessary to collect all relevant data in a statistical fashion and to fill in and compute the equations.

The second reaction is an extension of Barone's theory (1908; Hayek 1935, pp. 245–290). The central administration would be able to come to a solution by trial and error. In some way, prices have to be taken as a starting point. The economic subjects react on these prices. These prices have to be changed and are changed in such a way that excesses and shortages do not occur any more.

The third reaction especially elaborated by Lange and Taylor (1938) and Lerner (1944), implies that pricing can be used. Then prices become again indicators for economic calculation. Two variants are suggested. The first variant will order competition between individual firms, the second between industries. The managers are appointed by and are responsible to the central administration of which they obtain their instructions. In this case, there exists pseudo-competition. The managers of the firms have to behave as if there is perfect competition.

Some of these authors admit that no pricing exists in the centrally administered economy. The third reaction is a denial of the thesis of Mises that exchange and pricing are absent when private property (de jure or de facto) is abolished. The above-mentioned ideas are extensively discussed and criticized by Hayek (1935, Chaps. 1 and 5; 1952c, Chaps. 7–9).

According to him (Hayek 1952c, Chaps. 2 and 4), the central question is how to use the existing knowledge in society in the best possible way. In every society, there is planning. The planning always has to be based on knowledge, that is in first instance not available to, but has to be acquired by whoever does the planning. In principle, there are only two possibilities: the free exchange economy and the centrally administered economy.

Which of the two possibilities is the best depends on the question whether it is easier to supply the planning authority with the knowledge, regarding the data, that is originally in possession of the economic subjects or to provide the economic subjects with the knowledge that makes it possible to co-ordinate their plans.

To answer this question, Hayek distinguishes between the knowledge at the disposal of the economic subjects and the knowledge that is available to the planning authority. The choice depends on the relative significance of both kinds of knowledge. The knowledge possessed by the economic subjects does not have a scientific or general character, but concerns several details regarding the data. The knowledge of the planning authority, however, has a scientific character and concerns general laws. In relation to the many changes in economic life, the knowledge possessed by the economic subjects is the most important. This knowledge cannot be provided to the planning authority in a statistical fashion. The statistics that should be used by such an institution can only be arranged in such a way that has to be abstracted from exactly these details. The planning authority is for that reason not able to take into account all those details. This is the fundamental problem of the centrally administered economy.

In the free exchange economy, the knowledge available to the economic subjects is dispersed over the economic subjects. Moreover, the knowledge of the individual subjects is incomplete and often contradictory. For that reason, further information has to be provided to the economic subjects in order to bring about the co-ordination of all plans. It is not necessary for the economic subjects to know why the price of goods has changed, but that the price is changed and how much. This knowledge is provided by the pricing process that registers and transmits changes of data in economic life and can be considered as a process of information and discovery (Hayek 1968).

In view of this background, it is not surprising that Hayek (1935, pp. 207–214; 1952c, pp. 197–204) is of the opinion that the first conception (calculation with the aid of the system of equations of the theory of general equilibrium) is logically correct, but impracticable.

He asks two questions, namely about the nature and the extent of the data that are needed and the extent of the calculations that have to be done to solve the equations. In this connection, the point is not how detailed the data and how exact the calculations have to be in order to obtain an exact solution. It is only necessary to ask how far one must go to get a result that is comparable with that of the pricing process. It concerns the knowledge of the data which in the exchange economy is dispersed over the economic subjects.

In the first place, the central authority needs data about the goods that are available. These goods differ not only physically but also by the location, the age, the packing, etc. Also all goods have their own individuality. Almost all goods have to be included separately into the equations. The collection of all these data in a statistical fashion is not well possible. In that case, attention would have to be paid to too many details.

In the second place, the central authority must have the disposal of all technical data regarding the production of goods. These data are also dispersed over the economic subjects and change continuously. The same is the case with the wants of the consumers. Also these data cannot be made available to the central authority in a statistical fashion. The results, however, would be far more worse than in the case of pricing, because the pricing process includes all details in its operation. If one assumes for a moment that the central authority does have all the mentioned data at its disposal, then the calculations involved in the hundreds of thousands of equations, that at every decision have to be solved would have such an extent, that this solution is impracticable.

Hayek remarks that already Pareto (1927 (2), pp. 233–234) has pointed to the practical impossibility of this solution with similar arguments. Only the market would be able to provide a solution.

Hayek (1935, pp. 213–214; 1952c, pp. 213–214) also points out that this solution is not meant as a practical one but only as one possible in principle. As a matter of fact, these authors were of the opinion that a socialist society could simple use the existing capitalist pricing system and by means of trial and error adjust these prices to changes. With this, the first opinion merges into the second one.

Hayek argues against this point of view that through the transition of capitalism to socialism, the valuations will strongly change and completely new prices will be necessary. With the system of trial and error, the government would have to set prices and would have to change these as often as this would happen in a capitalist society, in order to reach a result comparable to the competitive system.

The change of one price causes the change of many other prices. Most prices do not change proportionally but vary according to elasticity of demand, possibilities of substitution and methods of production. It is absurd to think that the government would be able to fix all these prices and to change them until an equilibrium is reached. The changes cannot take place as often, as fast and as accurate as necessary. Moreover, a differentiation in time, place and quality will fail to appear. For that reason, in this way, a worse result will be achieved than with pricing.

With the variants of the third conception, according to Hayek (1935, pp. 217–220; 232–237; 1952c, pp. 207–210; 222–227, Chap. 9), the problem arises whether the combination of competition, central direction and public property is possible. The decisions about the factors of production and the responsibility for them would rest with the managers, who, however, are neither owners nor responsible to private owners.

Both variants, competition between firms as well as between industries, evoke many problems. Who has to become manager? What has to be the industry or firm? Which factors of production will be entrusted to the managers? How will their success or failure be determined? The means of production are public property. An authority to administer all these factors is needed. Which criteria will have to be applied in the decision making process?

The authority cannot act like a kind of bank who assigns the means to the highest bidder. The managers have no private property and are therefore not at risk. The whole risk is for the central authority. This authority will therefore have to decide who will get the means of production. Moreover, it will have to be decided who is allowed to expand or contract production, to stop the firm, to change over to the production of a new product or to reinvest.

This means therefore that all important decisions who have to be made in our dynamic society as a consequence of many often unforeseen changes cannot be made by the manager. In this respect, he depends on the central authority. This authority has almost as much power as it would have in the case of central administration of the economic process without competition.

The central authority in her decisions can only rely on the results of the managers in the past and on their expectations for the future. The expectations of the individual managers will be different. The central authority will be inclined to judge the managers by their previous performances, but even the best managers will sometimes take losses because of technological changes and changes in demand.

Under these circumstances, the managers would give rise to risk-avoiding behaviour. This system is a house divided in itself. The managers as well as the central authority take decisions with regard to the means of production. The responsibility for decisions is for that reason difficult to determine. This society will therefore develop a bureaucratic character in which freedom of initiative has little chance and conservatism (careful management to avoid risk) becomes dominant.

The above-mentioned criticism holds for both variants of the third view. On the top of that, there are still some special arguments that apply to the second variant (1935, pp. 220–222; 1952c, pp. 210–212). This variant leads to a world of competing monopolies. Assuming profit maximizing, the following objections can be raised against this arrangement: a general equilibrium and optimum allocation of production factors does not occur; the production will be smaller and the price will be higher than in the case of more competition.

These objections do not hold any more if the government dictates to these firms the marginal cost rule. However, according to Hayek (1935, pp. 226–231; 1952c, pp. 216–221), the government is groping in the dark when it wants to fix marginal cost. These costs can only be determined through competition. Through the process of competition, the price becomes equal to marginal cost. In the absence of competition, the government may fix marginal cost and dictate corresponding prices, but these prices will always be arbitrary.

The Theory of Money and Business Cycle Theory: The Monetary Over-Investment Theory

The monetary over-investment theory (or perhaps better the theory of wrong investment (*Kapitalfehlleitung*)) is an attempt to explain the business cycle in the framework of the general equilibrium theory. The monetary over-investment theory studies the influence of money on the economic process in a free exchange economy. At present, money creation is for a large part in the hands of the primary banks. According to the monetary over-investment theory, this can disturb the economic process.

The monetary over-investment theory refers to a contradiction in the course of business in the capital goods industry and the consumption goods industry. In the boom, the former develops stronger than the latter. In the depression, the fall in the former is stronger than that in the latter. For that reason, disproportions originate in the production structure: the capital goods industry and the consumption goods industry are maladjusted.

The depression is caused by the disproportions that originate during the boom and have to be corrected during the depression. The monetary over-investment theory regards the depression as a consequence of the over-investment in the capital goods industry which originates in the boom. This over-investment is possible under the existing monetary system, in which banking has the power to create money. Banking is therefore important for the origin of periodical disproportions in the production structure. However, the business cycle is not in essence a monetary phenomenon.

The interpretation of the role of banking goes back to certain theories of Wicksell (1898) about the connections between the money supply, interest and prices.

Wicksell distinguished between the monetary or market interest rate and the natural interest rate. The natural interest rate is the interest rate at which savings equal investments. The monetary interest rate, also called bank interest rate, may deviate from the natural interest rate through the action of banking and other factors. If banks set the market interest at a lower rate than the natural interest rate, investments will exceed savings. The investments are then partially financed by money creation. This leads to inflation; the price level rises.

In the case of a natural interest rate, which is lower than the monetary interest rate, savings will exceed investments. This leads to deflation; the price level falls. If the natural interest rate equals the monetary interest rate, savings are equal to investments. There will be a stable price level.

The monetary over-investment theory of Mises (1912, 1924, 2; 1928), Hayek (1929b, 1931a, 1939b, 1941a) and other German and Austrian authors, in the twenties and thirties, builds upon this theory. This development is accompanied by important contributions to the theory of money (Hayek 1929b, 1931b), the theory of capital formation and the theory of interest (Hayek 1939b, 1941a). Of course, also other authors, especially the students of Wicksell, who formed the so-called Swedish School (e.g. G. Myrdal), and in the Netherlands M.W. Holtrop (1972), J.G. Koopmans and other Dutch authors, have contributed to these developments (de Jong 1973). In 1933, Hayek edited the book *Beiträge zur Geldtheorie*, with contributions of M. Fanno, M.W. Holtrop, J.G. Koopmans, G. Myrdal and K. Wicksell.

The theories mentioned culminate in the synthetic theory of interest and the theory of monetary equilibrium and/or neutral money (Lutz 1938, 1969). We confine ourselves to the exposition of the main lines of the above-mentioned business cycle theory.

If the banks lower the bank interest rate in a situation of equilibrium with full employment, then the bank interest rate becomes lower than the natural interest rate. Investments will rise. This is especially the case with investments in durable means of production, because they are the most sensitive to changes in the rate of interest.

The increase of investments is not matched by savings. The firms are nevertheless capable to finance their investments by borrowing from the banks. In a situation of full employment, producers of investment and consumption goods will compete for the means of production.

In this competitive struggle, the capital goods industry has an advantage. For that reason, they are able to snatch away the means of production from the consumption goods industry. This means that the consumption goods industry has to contract and that the capital goods industry will expand.

The consumers consequently are able to buy fewer goods. The prices of the consumption goods will rise in consequence of the rise in prices of the means of production but also because of the fall in the quantity supplied of consumption goods. To maintain their consumption level, the consumers are willing to pay higher prices. Nevertheless, real consumption will fall. This is the phenomenon of so-called forced savings.

It is true that income received by the consumers will rise. This will, however, not happen immediately but with a delay. Moreover, a redistribution of income and wealth occurs. While other incomes (profits e.g.) rise, those with fixed incomes stay behind. As a consequence, real consumption falls further.

The rise of prices means a fall in the value of money. This is to the disadvantage of creditors and to the advantage of debtors. For that reason, the distribution of wealth changes. If the income of households has increased because they earn more in the capital goods industry than the consumers get more purchasing power. They will try to re-establish their consumption level. The prices of the consumption goods will rise again. The producers of these goods will have better profit prospects. They are able to pay more for means of production. But as long as the producers of capital goods are able to borrow money from banks, they are able to outbid producers of consumption goods.

For their credit policy, banks focus on the ratio between their reserves and the amount of credit outstanding. If this ratio becomes too low, the banks will slow down their credit supply or even curtail outstanding credits. If this ratio is higher than minimal, it is profitable to expand the granting of credit.

A bank will take this decision sooner if the risks are small and the prospects of the investors are good. Also of importance is how easy it is to obtain reserves, for example by rediscounting. Only if it is strictly necessary, the interest rate will be raised. The banks do not like to loose clients to their competitors. Only if the individual banks or the banking system approach this limit, they will restrain their credits or even reduce their outstanding credits. This leads to a rise in the interest rate, tightening up of other conditions and cancellation of credits. This will slow down investments especially in durable means of production. The source of which the investors draw their additional purchasing power dries up.

These circumstances cause that these firms are not able to realize their investment plans anymore (this is the phenomenon of *Kapitalfehlleitung*). Even in some circumstances, they have to be stopped or interrupted. The production becomes less profitable. Under these circumstances, producers of consumption goods grow stronger and are now better able to compete for the means of production. They have the advantage of getting higher prices for their products. Expansion of production is then profitable. The prices of the means of production are rising now because of the higher bids of the consumer goods industry. The investments of the capital goods industry will fall sharply. There exists a situation of capital scarcity. Banks do not want to grant credits and households do not want to save. The producers in the capital goods industry are not able to realize their investment plans. This causes a sharp decline in the demand for investment goods. This fall leads to a cut in production in the capital goods industry and unemployment develops. The means of production that come available cannot all be employed in the consumption goods industry. National income falls. Hoarding and destruction of money occur. The banks and the firms strive for liquidity. Pessimism spreads. The investment level falls even further. This situation can change again when the liquidity of the banks improves, so that they can lower the interest rate and the entrepreneurs gain so much confidence that investment will rise again.

These views conflict with the Keynesian business cycle theory. The deeper origins behind the clash between Hayek and Keynes (Hayek 1995) appear to be theoretically the following:

(a) Hayek prefers micro-analysis that starts with the plans of the economic subjects. His central problem is the co-ordination of the plans through the pricing process under different market structures and money systems. In the analysis of Keynes, relationships between macro-quantities are used. For that reason, the pricing process recedes in the background. This explains why Hayek theoretically does not follow the Keynesian approach. He is not adverse to macro-analysis. Both approaches have always co-existed in the history of economics. He acknowledges, however, the primacy of micro-analysis and joins the methodological individualism of Menger (1883).

(b) Within the framework of the general equilibrium model with perfect competition, the economic process tends to equilibrium by prices that adjust demand and supply. Originally, theory has not paid much attention to processes of adjustment, which are continuously necessary to bring about equilibrium after changes in the data. There is, however, an exception with regard to the monetary adjustment process. By and after Wicksell and Mises, it was realized that the disturbances in the monetary sphere are not neutralized by an equilibrating adjustment process. In contrast, the adjustment process is characterized by an oscillating movement around equilibrium: the business cycle. Business cycle theory concentrates on the dynamic problems, which arise when the question is asked how the equilibriums, which according to statics can exist, are brought about. The possibility of an equilibrium with full employment is the starting point of the monetary over-investment theory. The business cycle is an oscillation around this equilibrium.

According to Keynes, the business cycle is a fluctuation of effective demand and connected quantities, especially the price level and employment. The depression is characterized by a deficiency of demand. A full employment policy has for that reason to be directed to the stimulation of effective demand.

According to the Keynesians, equilibrium is not automatically restored in the direction of full employment. The economy can be in equilibrium at every level of employment. The Keynesians have lost confidence in the equilibrating character of the economy, at least at the point of employment. The monetary over-investment theory has not lost that confidence.

The so-called stagnation thesis advocates that effective demand will be continuously deficient. This is strongly rejected by Hayek. The theory is also proven to be contrary to the facts.

Here, it is necessary to point to the fact that Hayek's aversion to the Keynesian theory and Keynesian policy also results from the fact that the strive for full employment at any price according to his judgement will lead to non-conform government interference that spreads like an oil-slick (Hayek 1951a, 1951b, 1972, 1975, 1980).

The task of economic policy in this respect is to try to prevent or restore this situation by monetary reform (this amounts to the removal of the money creation power from the commercial banks) or by a monetary policy while maintaining the existing organization of the banking system, with the instruments of monetary policy.

Hayek (1937, 1943b, 1960, 1965) made important contributions on problems related to the national and international monetary system during the whole period in which he was publishing. In these publications, he discussed almost all proposals that are to be found in the economic literature during this period and made also himself original proposals. In his last proposal, he argues in favour of competition among private issuers of fiat money (Hayek 1976a).

In the light of the recent monetary problems at the national and the international level, these questions are still relevant and will gain even more importance in this century.

Developments in the Theory of Market Structures: The Meaning of Competition

In the free exchange economy, decisions are made by the economic subjects themselves. The individual plans are co-ordinated through pricing. That is why Hayek is interested in the functioning of the pricing process. The co-ordination of the plans and the course of the economic process are different according to the market structure and the monetary system.

How prices are formed in the different market structures and how money influences pricing and in general the economic process are important topics for Hayek. The central problem is to analyse the consequences of economic freedom in a free exchange economy under different market structures and monetary systems. The influence of money on the economic process has been discussed in the former section. This section will focus on the developments in the theory of market structures and the meaning of competition.

Hayek (1952c, Chap. 5) pointed out, against the theorists of monopolistic competition (Sraffa, Robinson, Chamberlin, and Stackelberg) as well as against the Chicago-School (Knight and Stigler) that the theory of perfect competition does not explain the process of competition, because this theory assumes the condition produced by the competition process as existing. If this condition exists, competition is no longer possible. The process of competition is a dynamic social process, in which the individual plans are co-ordinated under changing data. Theory has to explain how this happens. The theory of perfect competition, however, does not do this. The current assumptions: constant data, homogeneity, the absence of personal relationships, a large number of consumers and suppliers of whom nobody expects to have influence on the price, free entry and the lack of other restrictions on the movement of goods and prices, complete knowledge of the relevant facts possessed by all parties are unrealistic. This is especially the case with complete transparency. The economic subjects do not possess complete knowledge. On the contrary, their knowledge is incomplete and contradictory. But always competition especially between substitutes causes lower costs and better products. Competition and the pricing process are conceived by him as a process of information and discovery (see "Market Economy and Centrally Administered Economy: The Use of Knowledge in Society").

With these opinions, Hayek moves in the direction of the so-called workable competition. This concept has been introduced and elaborated in economic theory by Clark (1940, 1982). J.M. Clark points out that even if the conditions of perfect competition are absent, there may exist effective competition, because imperfections may neutralize each other. For example, oligopolies can form a price cartel, in which the price is fixed somewhat higher than the average cost of the efficient firms. Then less efficient firms will be closed. This is according to Clark a case of workable competition. Similar situations may be found in industries with rather transparent markets, large firms and a small degree of product differentiation.

But in the case of oligopolies, there may exist ineffective competitive relations, because they get involved in a price war. The price in a price cartel may be much higher than the average cost and is caused by a lack of competition. For the existence of workable competition, he requires that the average price during a business cycle is covered by the average total cost.

In the literature, it was tried very hard to specify the concept. De Jong (1958) formulates following in the footsteps of Bain (1950), six criteria for workable competition. The most important are:

(a) The efficiency of the firms must approach, to reasonable extent, the best attainable efficiency. There has to be a stimulus to attain this condition. Therefore, an open market is necessary.
(b) The possibilities in the area of technological advancements must not be grossly neglected. For that reason, the existence of potential competition is also necessary.

These conditions are satisfied if artificial barriers of free entry are absent. That is why we state that Hayek's ideas move in this direction. Under these conditions, there exists a continuous struggle for the patronage of the consumer. This brings about quality improvements, cost reductions and technological innovations in which one or the other alternately gains the lead. Only if the lead is lasting there exists in this view a monopoly.

Economic and Political Systems

Marx and his direct followers have hardly paid attention to the question how socialism works economically. The same can be said in relation to other aspects. The question whether the liberal ideals with regard to the constitutional state etc.

are consistent with a society based on collective property of the means of production, was hardly paid attention to. Socialism saw itself placed before all these problems later on. The socialists could especially in East and West Europe not longer avoid these questions after the First World War. Since that time, a discussion took place about the political and economic aspects of the centrally administered economy. This discussion reached its height in the thirties and forties.

Hayek (1939a, 1944) argued for political and economic reasons for the free exchange economy and against the centrally administered economy. He considered the centrally administered economy incompatible with democracy, the constitutional state, fundamental human rights, social security, social justice, the rule of law, and the federal state. The free exchange economy is considered by him to be consistent with all this.

In the centrally administered economy, a union of power with the government comes about. There exists a strong interdependence of economic and non-economic aspects of reality. According to authors like Lange and Taylor (1938), Lerner (1944), and Schumpeter (1942), it is possible to separate political and economic liberalism. Political liberalism would be consistent with the centrally administered economy.

The second important point at issue is related to the economic aspects of the centrally administered economy. In the centrally administered economy, the leadership of economic life rests with the government. According to Hayek, the government meets in this way problems in the field of economic calculation which are very difficult to solve. The centrally administered economy will stay behind in productivity compared with the free exchange economy, where economic subjects through the formation of prices can accomplish the problem of economic calculation. He holds this opinion not only on the basis of the analysis of theoretical models but also on the basis of the analysis of historical experiences with the centrally administered economy especially in Russia and Hitler-Germany. His above-mentioned colleagues are of the opinion that the problem of economic calculation in the centrally administered economy is solvable, by using price formation. The discussion on this has been summarized in the third section.

The above-mentioned objections concern an international centrally administered economy. When the world economy is divided in national centrally administered economies, there is still another point that can be made. Then there exists internationally seen no freedom of movement (mobility) of goods, services, capital and labour. In the international economic positions quota, bilateral trade agreements, state trade, clearing of foreign exchange (currency), immigration and emigration restrictions are rule. Through that an optimal allocation of the means of production is not achieved. Of greater importance is that the international relations are drawn in the political sphere, through which political frictions arise, which can even be dangerous for world peace. On the other hand, the free exchange economy, in which optimal allocation of the means of production arise, can also be united with a peaceful society of people. On all these questions, he continued to publish since the publication of his *Road to Serfdom* (Hayek 1955, 1960, 1967, 1968, 1973a, b, 1976b, 1978, 1979, 1997).

Economic Policy and the Market Economy

Hayek (1944, Chap. III) distinguishes measures which foster competition vs. measures which weaken competition (planning for competition and planning against competition). The second group contains the measures which hamper or even eliminate the working of price formation. To this, he counts the planning of the economic process and the price and quantity controls which eliminate the market. But also such interference in the economic order that hampers competition belongs to it.

To the first group belong measures which are focused on an economic order in which competition functions as well as possible. For that first of all a free market is necessary. Activities to destroy the free market by restricting free entry have to be forbidden. Concerning direct interference, he makes an exception for restrictions with regard to methods of production that hold equally for producers. He mentions as such the prohibitions of the use of poisonous substances, safety prescriptions, the restriction of labour time and prescriptions with regard to the health of labourers. It is true that this causes an increase in production costs, but the economic and non-economic advantages preponderate. In general, it is about not taking measures, which eliminate or replace the market, but which are directed to provide such a framework for the market, that price formation functions as well as possible. Besides the government has to supplement the market with a system of provisions, namely on those areas on which the market does not function or not as well.

This relationship is the central problem in *The Road to Serfdom*, especially in Chap. III (1944) and his article on Free Enterprise and the Competitive Order (1952c, Chap. 6; 1948). In the Chicago period, it was followed by the Constitution of Liberty. A Liberal Utopia (1960). Later on, it was the subject of the three volumes on Law, Legislation and Liberty. This trilogy is on (1) Rules and Order (The Idea of Spontaneous Order); (2) The Mirage of Social Justice; and (3) The Political Order of a Free Society (Hayek 1973a, 1976b, 1979).

The leading principle is clearly formulated in the third volume of Law, Legislation and Liberty, on p. 65. There Hayek cites Mises as follows:

> The pure market economy assumes that government, the social apparatus of compulsion and coercion, is intent upon preserving the operation of the market system, abstains from hindering its functioning, and protects it against encroachment on the part of other people. (Mises in Human Action, 1949, p. 239)

The History of Ideas, Psychology, Methodology

The history of ideas has a prominent place in the work of Hayek. This forms an important part of his publications as stepping stones on the way to his main publications (see the volumes 3 and 4 of The Collected Works, 1991 and 1992). They allowed him to take roots in economic and political theory.

To this kind of work belong his preface to the (re-)edition of Gossen (original 1854) in 1927; Wieser, Gesammelte Abhandlungen, 1929; and the Collected Works of Menger (four volumes 1934–1936): the founders of subjectivism and method-ological individualism and the Austrian School; the prefaces to Cantillon 1931 (orig. 1755), Thornton, 1939c) (orig. 1802), and his work on Rae and Mill 1943a, 1945; Hayek 1942, 1943a, 1945, 1951c, 1963b, have to be mentioned. Further on his studies on three other English Classical Political Economists: Hume (1963), Mandeville (1966), and Smith (1976), have to be mentioned (see Hayek 1991). It brings him to insights on which he elaborates in his theory of institutions.

Capitalism and the Historians (Hayek 1954) was one of the books that Hayek edited. Its purpose was similar to his work in the field of the history of ideas: to rectify the historical analysis of capitalism, in other words to clear decks.

Strange in the whole of his publications is his book The Sensory Order (Hayek 1952a). It was published in the same time as his study John Stuart Mill and Harriet Taylor (1951c). Nevertheless, the manuscript of The Sensory Order originates from about 1920, the beginning of his career. This work may be another key to Hayek's work. It may explain why he chose the field of human action as his subject of study and not one of the natural sciences. He himself writes on this book:

My colleagues in the social sciences find my study on The Sensory Order. An Inquiry into the Foundations of Theoretical Psychology uninteresting or indigestible. But the work on it has helped me greatly to clear up my mind on much that is very relevant to social theory. My conception of evolution, of a spontaneous order and of the methods and limits of our endeavours to explain complex phenomena have been formed largely in the course of the work on that book. As I was using the work I had done in my student days on theoretical psychology in forming my views on the methodology of the social science, so the working out of my earlier ideas on psychology with the help of what I had learnt in the social science helped me greatly in all my later scientific development. It involved the sort of radical departure from received thinking of which one is more capable at the age of 21 than later, but which, even, though years later, when I published them they received a respectful but not very comprehending welcome by the psychologists (Law, Legislation and Liberty, Vol. III, pp. 199, 200).

On methodology, he published more extensive. At first, in the thirties (Hayek 1933a, b, included in Hayek 1991; 1937, included in 1952c), on the methodology of economic science. Later on the methodology of the social sciences in relation to the natural sciences became the main subject. He published articles in Economica, titled The Counter-Revolution of Science (Hayek 1941b) and Scientism and Society (Hayek 1942–1944). These were republished in 1952 under the title The Counter Revolution of Science and Other Essays. In the same time as an editor of Economica, he accepted a series of articles of Karl Raimond Popper on The Poverty of Historicism (1944, 1945). They were republished in 1957 under the same title. Still later on, he discussed these problems with Popper in several publications (Hayek 1967, 1978; Bunge 1964).

In his speech in which he accepted the Nobel Prize in 1974 he said:

If man is not to do more harm than good in his efforts to improve the social order, he will have to learn that in this, as in all other fields were essential complexity of an organized kind prevails, he cannot acquire the full mastery of the events possible. He will therefore have to use what knowledge he can achieve, not to shape the results as the craftsman shapes his handiwork, but rather to cultivate a growth by providing the appropriate environment, in the manner in which the gardener does this for his plants. There is a danger in the exuberant feeling of ever growing power of which the advance of the physical sciences has engendered and which tempts man to try, "dizzy with success", to use a characteristic phrase of early communism, to subject not only our natural but also our human environment to the control of a human will. The recognition of the insuperable limits to his knowledge ought indeed to teach the student of society a lesson in humility which should guard him against becoming an accomplice in men's fatal striving to control society – a striving which makes him not only a tyrant over his fellows, but which may well make him the destroyer of a civilization which no brain has designed but which has grown from the free efforts of millions of individuals (1978, p. 34).

The Theory of Evolution of Institutions

From all this, he got the insight necessary for the theory of evolution of institutions. Here the idea of the "invisible hand" (Smith), the idea of institutions as "being the unintentional consequences of human action, and not of human design (Hume), use of knowledge, methodological individualism and subjectivism (Menger), Popper and Mises come together. This is the idea of 'spontaneous order', or better, self-generating order (order without command but through rules)" or "kosmos".

Some authors think that there is here a contradiction in the work of Hayek. They even speak of Hayek I and Hayek II. They like Hayek II, because he can be used as the basis of their theory of evolution of economic and political systems. However, after the opinion of the present writer, there is continuity in Hayek's thinking, and not taking him as one Hayek leads to misinterpretations of his position. In a sense, Hayek's work itself is a result of spontaneous order. In this particular case, the ideas of subjectivism and methodological individualism are consequently used for the interpretation of the formation of institutions.

His ideas in this field are not in conflict with his ideas on the (extensive) role of government with regard to the market order, because the political and economic, and in a broad sense all institutions, have to be conducive to this spontaneous order. The concept of planning for competition and his concern for a political order that makes it very difficult for government, but also for private powers (e.g. the entrepreneurs, the trade unions, and other pressure groups) to hamper the market order as elaborated in his Constitution of Liberty (1960) and his trilogy on Law, Legislation and Liberty (1973a, 1976b, 1979).

Hayek (1988) has tried to figure out the necessary and sufficient conditions for the creation and preservation of what he called the great society or extended order. He distinguishes three kinds of rules: genetically inherited rules, designed rules and spontaneous rules. The gist of inherited rules is instincts. Designed rules are created or designed by reason. Spontaneous rules are the result of human action but not of human design. Also he distinguishes between biological and cultural evolution. The first class of rules is the result of biological evolution, the third of cultural evolution. With these distinctions, there arises a difficulty: Where do we find the rules of reason (the second class of rules) and what is their relation to biological and cultural evolution? In his first chapter of The Fatal Conceit, Hayek's thinking in this respect is confused and speculative and consequently it has to be seriously doubted whether this chapter gives a good impression of his work.

Hayek does not see cultural and moral evolution and the evolution of the extended order as one and the same thing. Hayek is concerned with the interplay of two kinds of order. The first kind of order is formed by the set of rules of conduct. The second is the order of actions formed within the set of rules of conduct. For an extended order, we have to rely on spontaneous rules of conduct. But what about the possibility of misdirected spontaneous order?

To answer this question, a short digression will be made. Ever since the beginning of the industrial revolution, there have been discussions on the development of society, often called capitalism. We can mention Saint-Simon, Marx, Mill, Schmoller, Schumpeter, Sombart, Eucken, Röpke and Rüstow. Hayek shared their concern with the development of society. There were optimists and pessimists among them.There were those who thought society ought to be wholly restructured and that this could be done with a combination of state power and reason (science). Hayek's position was that, by studying the evolution of human society, it would be possible to find out where the existing order had developed in ways that had to be corrected (e.g. money). He also believed this kind of analysis would enable to foresee where society would go wrong in the future (e.g. his critique of Lange). But he warned against the hubris of reason and the possibility of the destruction of freedom by the omnipotent totalitarian state. Therefore, he prefers selective intervention by the state, in the form of planning for competition.

In his Road to Serfdom (Chap. III), Hayek makes the distinction between planning for and planning against competition. In 1960, he presented a paper to the Mont Pèlerin Society on the principles of a liberal social order in which he first gives the reasons why he rejects the criteria of welfare economics (and efficiency), and then provides his own criterion: equal opportunity (Hayek 1969, p. 121). This is the yardstick for reform, not efficiency.

In Law, Legislation and Liberty, Volume II, p. 128 f., Hayek also gives criteria for interference. In this connection, he writes (p. 188):

> The distinction introduced by Wilhelm Röpke, Die Gesellschaftskrise der Gegenwart (fifth ed., Erlenbach-Zürich, 1948) between acts of interference which conform and those which do not conform to the market order (or, as other German authors have expressed it, are or are not systemgerecht) aims at the same distinction, but I should prefer (in the footsteps of Mises, G.M., see also p. 188) not to describe conform measures as interference.

Hayek was in this respect an optimist. He thought that a just mixture of spontaneous order and reason would make it possible to avoid dreadful developments. He fought against the ideas of pessimists like Sombart and Schumpeter. Looking at the possibility of misdirection and totalitarianism, he thought it more likely that we can create a good society relying on spontaneous order than by relying on reason and state power, which tends to destroy spontaneous order. He calls the latter planning against competition.

In this respect, Hayek has a close affinity to the School of Freiburg and especially to Eucken. Eucken (1990, 6) attacked Schmoller for his overly optimistic view that ad hoc and unsystematic interference is enough to create a good society. He attacked other writers (e.g. Marx and to a degree Schumpeter) for their view that societal developments could not be influenced (1990, 6, pp. 200–212), and were inevitable. According to him (1990, 6), it was possible to create a competitive order. He referred to the churches, science and the state as the institutions that are the constitutive forces for society. He defends the competitive order and clearly points out, that spontaneous orders have to conform to this system (Eucken 1990, 6, p. 179).

In 1962, Hayek gave an inaugural lecture at the University of Freiburg, in which he acknowledged this affinity. He said in this lecture called Wirtschaft, Wissenschaft und Politik (Economy, Science and Politics):

> Besonders musz ich aber der persönlichen Beziehungen zu Freiburger Kollegen gedenken, die mich schon seit Jahrzehnten mit dieser Universität verbinden. … Weitaus am wichtigsten für mich war aber meine langjährige Freundschaft, gegründet auf völlige Ubereinstimmung in theoretischen und politischen Fragen, mit dem unvergeszlichen Walter Eucken (Hayek 1963a, b, p. 1, 2).

Why did Hayek raise this conception of spontaneous order more and more in the centre of his work? The reason is that among the economists – even within the Mont Pèlerin Society – there was growing prominence of mechanistic views and policies. There was disagreement on methodology between Hayek and Friedman and Buchanan. There were differences on monetary and business cycle theory and policy, leading him to formulate his proposal of Denationalization of Money in 1976a. There was also an important difference on the concept of perfect competition (Knight and Stigler) and on welfare economics (critique on Buchanan).

Hayek was in the end an Austrian economist. This is the background of his life-long quarrels with economists working in the train of thought of Pareto and the political proposals coming from this source, whether they were proposals for a policy of the market order or a policy of the centrally administered order.

There are many questions left in Hayek's expositions on spontaneous order. In this respect, Hayek was already following Karl Popper (1944, 1945; 1976; Hayek 1948, 1952c, 1967) in the thirties (Hayek 1933a, b, 1937; see Hayek 1991). His ideas on the role of knowledge are heavily influenced by Popper. This influence is also strong in the first chapter of The Fatal Conceit.

Hayek (1973a, Chaps. I and II and 1979) makes a distinction between constructivist and evolutionary rationalism. This distinction has affinity to Popper's distinction between naive and critical rationalism. The choice for the latter has consequences for the nature of (economic) policy to be followed. Liberalism constrains conscious regulation of the order of society to the enforcement of rules that are necessary for the formation of a spontaneous order. Hayek distinguishes spontaneous order or "nomos" and organization or "taxis". Although a spontaneous order is thinkable without force, as a rule (en)force(ment) is necessary. The nomos originates spontaneously and is improved by law, morals and customs. The government (as organization) has as its first tasks the enforcement and improvement of law. As a rule, government also has to provide services which this spontaneous order needs but cannot adequately produce. This implies the management of factors of production. As a rule, these two functions are not clearly recognized. The first task is an essential condition for the maintenance of the whole order. In the second function, government is an organization among many in a free society. There are two kinds of rules: law and legislation. The government has two tasks. First, government has to make and to enforce rules (legislation) and in the second place to provide services, which otherwise would not be adequate (management of production factors).

In this connection, Hayek propagates the installation of two representative bodies: the Legislative Assembly (with the task of legislation) and the Governing Assembly. If there is a difference of opinion on competence, the last body decides. The Legislative Body can then protest with the High Civil Court. This Court watches the constitution. In this constitution, social justice is ruled out as a policy objective, because it ultimately destroys the market economy, in case of democratic majority rule. Furthermore, the government is not allowed to have the monopoly of money supply. There has to be free choice of currency (denationalization of money).

In the light of this short summary and exposition, it may be wholly clear that according to Hayek:

1. There is an enforcement problem in the spontaneous order.
2. The spontaneous order may be improved by rules of reason.
3. It is government that has the task to do this.

For that reason, the necessary and sufficient conditions for the creation and pre-reservation of the spontaneous order has always been at the centre of Hayek's research agenda. Therefore, he wrote extensively on problems of economic policy, to find out which policy ought to be conducted in order not to destroy but if possible to improve the spontaneous order (See e.g. Hayek 1960).

Evaluation

The evaluation of Hayek's contributions is not easy. He is not only one of the founders but also one of the representatives of modern economic thought. I think the best way is to judge him according to his own expressed views. Kresge and Wenar (1994, pp. 143–144) think he has made two main mistakes in his career: First, not to go into discussion with Keynes on his General Theory. Second, not to discuss with Friedman (1953) on his (in the eyes of Hayek) mistaken views on methodology.

In 1976, he published his study on Denationalization of Money (a better title would have been Demonopolisation of Money). He gave as his opinion that this was a better proposal for national and international monetary systems than all the previous ones, inclusive monetarism. It has all the advantages of previous proposals (partly by himself) and even more. He was opposed to the theory of the monetarists à la Friedman and the theory of rational expectations. These theories had mistakes, partly because they were based on wrong methodological views.

His influence has been fostered by several events. The most important are his international orientation and career, the Mont Pélerin Society (founded in 1947) and the Nobel Memorial Prize in 1974. When he received the Nobel Memorial Prize in Economic Science, this was a complete surprise to him. He wrote:

> I didn't approve of Nobel Prizes for economists – until they gave it to me of course! Of course there is a very big advantage to fame: people suddenly listen to you.

He received the prize for his distinguished contributions in monetary theory and business cycle theory, and the theory of economic systems in the interbellum. Further on for his interdisciplinary work in the field of the functioning and evolution of economic and political (legal) systems. The core of this work are his ideas on spontaneous order, and market competition as a system of information and discovery.

An earlier important source of influence in this respect comes from the Mont Pélerin Society. The MPS was founded in April 1947 (Hartwell 1995). Hayek was the first president during the period 1947–1960 and from that time until his death in 1992 the honorary president. In this way, he contributed much to its vitality and existence.

The Statement of Aims of 1947 declares:

> Its object is solely, by facilitating the exchange of views among minds inspired by certain ideals and broad conceptions held in common, to contribute to the preservation and improvement of the free society (Hartwell 1995, p. 2).

In science, there seems to be an irremediable inclination to label. Also especially in politics there, exists the tendency of politicians to refer to renown economists as there source of inspiration. Hayek was no exception to this rule. This is especially the case with regard to the United Kingdom during the Thatcher period. He was not a political activist. He wanted to convince by scientific discussion, and in this way to strengthen the moral and intellectual support for a free society.

The work of Hayek covers a wider field than even political economy, and it is still too early to evaluate its significance. He contributed to the discussion on the main controversies in all important fields on which economists can shed their light: economic history, history of ideas and methodology (inclusive the relation of economics and ethics), economic theory, theory of economic philosophy, in a balanced, eclectic and non-doctrinarian way. In this way, he elaborated also a philosophy of freedom: How to combine freedom and order in a changing human society.

During his life, totalitarianism in several forms especially national socialism, fascism and communism was an danger for freedom. He, however, did not only criticize these movements but also tried to find solutions for an as good as possible functioning free society.

In this way, he made important contributions to law and economics, economic and political theory, the theory of economic and political systems, gave impulses to (neo-)Austrian economics (Kirzner), and last but not least the theory of economic policy for a free society.

References

Bain JS (1950) Workable competition in oligopoly: theoretical considerations and some empirical evidence. Am Econ Rev XL:53–77

Barone E (1908; 1935) The Ministry of Production in the Collectivist State. In: Hayek FA (ed) The collectivist economic planning. Routledge, London. Originally in Italian in 1908

Bunge M (1964) (ed) The critical approach to science and philosophy, The Free Press, Glencoe

Cantillon R (1931) Abhandlung über die Natur des Handels im Allgemeinen, translated by Hella von Hayek, Jena, Introduction and annotations by Hayek. Originally published in French in 1755

Clark JM (1940) Toward a concept of workable competition. Am Econ Rev XXX:241–256

Clark JM (1982) Competition as a dynamic process. Brookings Institution, Washington. First published in 1961

de Jong FJ (1958) Concurrentieregime en prijsvorming, Preadvies voor de Vereniging voor Staathuishoudkunde. M. Nijhoff, 's-Gravenhage

de Jong FJ (1973) Developments in monetary theory in The Netherlands. Rotterdam University Press, Rotterdam

Eucken W (1990(6)) Grundsätze der Wirtschaftspolitik, Mohr/Siebeck, Tübingen, First published in 1952

Friedman M (1953) The methodology of positive economics. In: Essays in positive economics. The University of Chicago Press, Chicago

Gossen HH (1927) Entwicklung der Gesetze des menschlichen Verkehrs, 3rd edn. Springer, Berlin. Introduction by Hayek. Orig. 1854

Hartwell RM (1995) A history of the Mont Pèlerin Society: Liberty Fund, Indianapolis

Hayek FA (ed) (1929a) Gesammelte Abhandlungen von Friedrich Wieser. J.C.B. Mohr, Tübingen

Hayek FA (1929b) Geldtheorie und Konjunkturtheorie. Hölder-Pichler-Tempsky, Wenen

Hayek FA (1931a) Preise und Produktion. J. Springer, Wien

Hayek FA (1931b) Prices and production. George Routledge & Sons, London

Hayek FA (1933a) Monetary theory and the trade cycle. Jonathan Cape, London

Hayek FA (ed) (1933b) Beiträge zur Geldtheorie. J. Springer, Wien

Hayek FA (ed) (1934–1936) The Collected Works of Carl Menger, vols 1–4. London School of Economics & Politics, London

Hayek FA (ed) (1935) Collectivist economic planning. Critical studies on the possibilities of socialism. Routledge & Sons, London

Hayek FA (1937) Monetary nationalism and international stability. Longmans, Green & Co., London

Hayek FA (1939a) Freedom and the economic system. U. of Chicago Press, Chicago

Hayek FA (1939b) Profits, interest and investments. Roudledge and Sons Ltd., London

Hayek FA (ed) (1939c) An enquiry into the nature and effects of the Paper Credit of Great Britain, by Henry Thornton. Allen & Unwin, London

Hayek FA (1941a) The pure theory of capital. U. of Chicago Press, Chicago

Hayek FA (1941b) The counter-revolution of science, parts I-III, Economica, N.S. 8

Hayek FA (1942) Introduction to J. Stuart Mill, The spirit of the Age. University of Chicago Press, Chicago

Hayek FA (1942–1944) Scientism and society, in Economica, 1942, N.S. 9; 1943, N.S. 10; 1944, N.S. 11

Hayek FA (ed) (1943a) John Rae and John Stuart Mill: a Correspondence, Economica, N.S. 10

Hayek FA (1943b) A commodity reserve standard. Economic Journal LIII:176–184

Hayek FA (1944) The road to serfdom. University of Chicago Press, Chicago, 1961 (with new preface)

Hayek FA (ed) (1945) Notes on N.W. senior's political economy, by John Stuart Mill, Economica, N.S. 12

Hayek FA (1948) Individualism and economic order. Routledge & Kegan Paul, London
Hayek FA (1951a) Vollbeschäftigung, Planwirtschaft und Inflation. In: Hunold A (ed)
    Vollbeschäftigung, Inflation und Planwirtschaft. Erlenbach, Eugen Rentsch, pp 184–197
Hayek FA (1951b) Volledige werkgelegenheid, geleide economie en inflatie, in Verslag van de
    buitengewone vergadering gehouden te Amsterdam op maandag 11 september. M. Nijhoff,
    's-Gravenhage
Hayek FA (1951c) John Stuart Mill and Harriet Taylor. Routledge, London
Hayek FA (1952a) The sensory order: an inquiry into the foundations of theoretical psychology.
    University of Chicago Press, Chicago
Hayek FA (1952b) The counter-revolution of science. Studies in the abuse of reason. The Free
    Press, Glencoe
Hayek FA (1952c) Individualismus und Wirtschaftliche Ordnung. E. Rentsch, Erlenbach-Zürich
Hayek FA (ed) (1954) Capitalism and the Historians. University of Chicago Press, Chicago
Hayek FA (1955) The political ideal of the rule of law. National Bank of Egypt, Cairo
Hayek FA (1960) The constitution of liberty. University of Chicago Press, Chicago
Hayek FA (1963a) Wirtschaft, Wissenschaft, und Politik, Freiburger Universitätsreden, N.F., Heft
    34, Freiburg
Hayek FA (1963b) Introduction to "The Earlier Letters of John Stuart Mill," Collected works of
    John Stuart Mill, vol XII. Toronto and London
Hayek FA (1964) The Theory of complex phenomena. In: Bunge M (ed)
Hayek FA (1965) Was der Goldwährung geschehen ist. Ein Bericht aus dem Jahre 1932 mit zwei
    Ergänzungen. J.C.B. Mohr, Tübingen
Hayek FA (1967) Studies in philosophy, politics and economics. Routledge and Kegan Paul,
    London
Hayek FA (1968) Der Wettbewerb als Entdeckungsverfahren, Kieler Vorträge, Neue Folge 56,
    Hrsg. E.Schneider. Institut für Weltwirtschaft, Kiel
Hayek FA (1969) Freiburger studien. J.C.B. Mohr, Tübingen
Hayek FA (1972, 1978) A tiger by the tail: the Keynesian legacy of inflation. Institute of Economic
    Affairs, London
Hayek FA (1973a) Law, legislation and liberty, vol. I: rules and order. University of Chicago Press,
    Chicago
Hayek FA (1973b) Economic freedom and representative government. Institute of Economic
    Affairs, London
Hayek FA (1975) Full employment at any price. Institute of Economic Affairs, London
Hayek FA (1976a) Denationalisation of money. The argument refined: an analysis of the theory
    and practice of concurrent currencies. Institute of Economic Affairs, London
Hayek FA (1976b) Law, legislation and liberty, vol. II: the mirage of social justice. University of
    Chicago Press, Chicago
Hayek FA (1978) New studies in philosophy, politics and economics. Routledge and Kegan Paul,
    London
Hayek FA (1979) Law, legislation and liberty, vol. III: the political order of a free people. University
    of Chicago Press, Chicago
Hayek FA (1980) 1980's unemployment and the unions: the distortion of relative prices by
    Monopoly in the Labour Market. Institute of Economic Affairs, London
Hayek FA (1988) The fatal conceit: the errors of socialism. The Collected Works of F.A. Hayek,
    vol 1. Ed. by W.W. Bartley. Routledge, London
Hayek FA (1991) The trend of economic thinking: essays on political economists and economic
    history. The Collected Works of F.A. Hayek, vol 3. Ed. by W.W. Bartley III and S. Kresge.
    Routledge, London
Hayek FA (1992) The fortunes of liberalism: essays on Austrian economics and the ideal of free-
    dom. The Collected Works of F.A. Hayek, vol 4. Ed. Peter G. Klein. Routledge, London
Hayek FA (1995) Contra Keynes and Cambridge. Essays, Correspondence. The Collected Works
    of F.A. Hayek, vol. 9, Ed. Bruce Caldwell. Routledge, London

Hayek FA (1997) Socialism and war. Essays, Documents, Reviews. The Collected Works of
    F.A. Hayek, vol. 10, Ed. by Bruce Caldwell. Routledge, London
Holtrop MW (1972) Money in an open economy. Stenfert Kroese, Leiden
Kresge S and Leif W (1994) (eds) Hayek on Hayek. An autobiographical dialogue. Chicago
    University Press, Chicago
Lange O, FM Taylor (1938) On the economic theory of socialism, University of Minnesota Press,
    Minneapolis. BJ Lippincott (ed). MacGraw Hill Books, London, 1965
Lerner AP (1944) The economics of control. MacMillan, New York
Lutz FA (1938) The outcome of the saving-investment discussion. Q J Econ XII:588–614
Lutz FA (1969) On neutral money. In: Streissler EW (ed) Roads to freedom. Essays in Honour of
    F.A. Hayek. Routledge and Kegan Paul, London
Machlup F (1977) Essays on Hayek. Hillsdale College Press, Hillsdale
Menger C (1883) Untersuchungen über die Methode der Sozialwissenschaften und der Politischen
    Okonomie. Duncker und Humblot, Leipzig
Mises L (1920) Die Wirtschaftsrechnung im Sozialistischen Gemeinwesen, Archiv für
    Sozialwissenschaft und Sozialpolitik, Bd. 47. Also included in English in F.A. Hayek (1935)
Mises L (1928) Geldwertstabilisierung und Konjunkturpolitik. G. Fischer, Jena
Mises L (1949) Human action. Yale University Press, New Haven
Mises L ([1912], 1924(2)) Theorie des Geldes und der Umlaufsmittel, München/Leipzig: Duncker
    und Humblot. In English: The Theory of Money and Credit, London: J. Cape 1953. Liberty
    Press, Indianapolis, 1981
Pareto V (1927(2)) Manuel d'Economie Politique. M. Giard, Paris
Popper KR (1944, 1945) The Poverty of Historicism, Economica, 11, May 1944, pp. 86–103,
    August, pp. 119–137; 12, May 1945, pp. 69–87
Popper KR (1957) The poverty of historicism. Routledge and Kegan Paul, London
Popper KR (1976) Unended quest. An intellectual biography. Fontana Collins, Glasgow
Raybould J (1999) Hayek, a commemorative album. Adam Smith Institute, London
Schumpeter JA (1942) Capitalism, socialism and democracy. Allen and Unwin, London
Wicksell K (1898) Geldzins und Güterpreise. G. Fischer, Jena

Index

J.G. Backhaus (ed.), *Handbook of the History of Economic Thought*,   713
The European Heritage in Economics and the Social Sciences,
DOI 10.1007/978-1-4419-8336-7, © Springer Science+Business Media, LLC 2012